Frommer's

30th Edition

FRUGAL TRAVELER'S GUIDES

Hawaii
FROM $60 A DAY

by Faye Hammel and Sylvan Levey
assisted by Alexandra Horn

with Nature, Sports and Recreation
coverage by Jeanette Foster

Macmillan • USA

ABOUT THE AUTHORS

Faye Hammel and **Sylvan Levey**, a husband-and-wife writing team, have been reporting on Hawaii for the last 30 years. When not in the islands, they live in New York City. In addition to authoring *Frommer's Hawaii from $60 a Day* and *Frommer's Honolulu, Waikiki & Oahu* and co-authoring *Frommer's New York City,* Faye has also published *The Dream Theater* and *The New York Lunch.*

Jeanette Foster, a resident of Hawaii, has skied the slopes of Mauna Kea—during a Fourth of July ski meet, no less—and scuba dived with manta rays off the Big Island's Kona coast. A prolific writer widely published in travel, sports, and adventure magazines, Jeanette is also a contributing writer to numerous travel guides, including *Frommer's Honolulu, Waikiki & Oahu.*

MACMILLAN TRAVEL

A Simon & Schuster Macmillan Company
1633 Broadway
New York, NY 10019

ISBN 0-02-860643-4
ISSN 1059-7603

Editor: Cheryl Farr
Map Editor: Doug Stallings
Design by Michele Laseau
Digital Cartography by Jim Moore & Ortelius Design

Contents

List of Maps

AN INVITATION TO THE READER

When researching this book, we discovered many wonderful places—hotels, restaurants, shops, and more. We're sure you'll find others. Please tell us about them so we can share the information with your fellow travelers in upcoming editions. If you were disappointed with a recommendation, we'd love to know that, too. Please write to:

Faye Hammel, Sylvan Levey & Jeanette Foster
Frommer's Hawaii from $60 a Day, 30th Edition
Macmillan Travel
1633 Broadway
New York, NY 10019

AN ADDITIONAL NOTE

Please be advised that travel information is subject to change at any time—and this is especially true of prices. We therefore suggest that you write or call ahead for confirmation when making your travel plans. The authors, editors, and publisher cannot be held responsible for the experiences of readers while traveling. Your safety is important to us, however, so we encourage you to stay alert and be aware of your surroundings. Keep a close eye on cameras, purses, and wallets—all favorite targets of thieves and pickpockets.

WHAT THE SYMBOLS MEAN

✪ Frommer's Favorites

Hotels, restaurants, attractions, and entertainment you should not miss.

⑤ Super-Special Values

Hotels and restaurants that offer great value for your money.

The following abbreviations are used for credit cards:

AE	American Express	EU	Eurocard
BC	Bankcard	JCB	Japan Credit Bank
DC	Diners Club	MC	MasterCard
DISC	Discover	V	Visa
ER	en Route		

Saving Money in Hawaii

There's a long-standing myth that we aim to dispel: It's the belief that a fabulous island getaway is beyond the means of the frugal traveler. Well, we're here to tell you it just isn't so. Less than 5 jet hours from the west Coast lie the islands of Hawaii, a name to conjure dreams— and a great place to explore on a shoestring budget.

People will tell you, of course, that the 50th American state is one of the most expensive vacation spots in the world. It is—and it isn't—depending on which Hawaii you care to see. If you choose prepackaged Hawaii, you'll undoubtedly stay at plush hotels, dine at expensive restaurants, be herded around in sightseeing limousines with people just like the folks you left back home—and you'll pay a pretty penny for it. But if you believe that travel is a do-it-yourself activity, if you'd rather leave the preconceived nonsense to others and strike out on your own to discover the real Hawaii, you'll find that a Hawaiian vacation is one of the best travel bargains anywhere. Contrary to popular belief, Hawaii has dozens of comfortable, clean, and reasonable places to stay; scores of exotic, inexpensive restaurants; and an almost endless list of free and low-cost entertainment, from sunbathing to snorkeling, from museum browsing to mountain climbing, from hiking to hula dancing, and much more. Add to all that low airfare and a spectacular setting, and you've got the makings for an idyllic budget vacation—even in these costly times.

We've given up counting how many times we've been to Hawaii; in the course of over 30 years of reporting on the islands, it's become almost a second home. We like to think that we're almost *kamaainas*. We've explored countless hotels, restaurants, sightseeing establishments, shops, and attractions; we've approved enthusiastically of many, discarded more than a few. We extensively revise each edition each and every year. We check and recheck, query local people, gather insider information, and pass all that we've learned on to you. Your task, then, is simply to consider your own traveling budget, tastes, and timetable, and make your own choices from our carefully researched and chosen bests.

1 The "From $60-a-Day" Premise

Can you really "do" Hawaii on $60 a day? Absolutely! Depending on how much you want to pinch pennies, it can even be less; depending on how much you want to splurge, it can be much more.

Our aim is simply to show you how to keep your basic living costs—a comfortable room and three good meals—down to as little as $60 a day. The costs of transportation, shopping, sightseeing, and entertainment are all in addition to that figure. But don't worry—we'll provide tips on saving money in those areas as well.

Here's how the budget breaks down: We assume that two of you are traveling together and that, between the two of you, you have at least $120 a day to spend. (The solo tourist, unfortunately, does not do so well in Hawaii, since almost all accommodations rates are the same, single or double; on the other hand, since Hawaii has lots of apartment- and cottage-style accommodations, larger groups and families can beat our minimum budget substantially.) Let's say you spend between $50 and $90 for a hotel, condo, or bed-and-breakfast; that leaves at least $30 to $70 to spend on meals. You can get your breakfast for free if you stay at a B&B, cook it yourself at a condo, or pick up breakfast at any market and eat in your hotel room. Lunch can cost anywhere from a couple of dollars to $10 each, and dinner anywhere from $12 to $20 or more, if you want to splurge. By applying a variety of strategies—staying in a better hotel but eating in more often; staying in a hostel or a national or state park cabin and splurging on gourmet cuisine; camping on one island, staying in a condo on the next—it's easy enough to work out a regime that stays well within this minimum budget. If you're a frugal traveler who wants to know where to find the best for the money but doesn't necessarily want to stick to a penny-pinching budget, this book will meet your needs as well.

There's one thing about Hawaii that we want to make perfectly clear: Even on the most stringent of budgets, you're still going to have a wonderful time. In Hawaii, more than anyplace else we know, the best things in life—the beach, the sun, the near-perfect climate, the fresh, fragrant air, the glories of nature all around you, and the smiling faces of people who are sure that they're living in paradise—are free. Aloha!

2 Forty-five Money-Saving Tips

AIR TRAVEL TO HAWAII

1. Try to travel off-season, if possible, avoiding the period from mid-December to April 1. Airfares are most inflated during the high season.
2. Schedule your flights for midweek; prices go up on weekends.
3. Shop, shop, shop for the lowest airfares; they differ from airline to airline and within the same airline on different days. Ask about any special promotional fares and take advantage of them if your schedule is flexible.
4. Be willing to pay in advance—usually either 14 or 21 days—for the lowest fare.
5. Inquire about fly/drive packages; some of them are very good.

INTERISLAND AIR TRAVEL

6. Take advantage of Hawaiian Airlines' Island Pass if you have a limited stay.
7. Fly Mahalo Air's propeller aircrafts for savings of about $20 per flight.
8. Ask the airlines about neighbor-island fly/drive packages and about senior, military, and other discounts.

ACCOMMODATIONS

9. Try to travel off-season; most room rates increase $10 to $20 from mid-December to April 1. The cheapest times to visit Hawaii are the months of May and June and from Labor Day to December 15.

10. Forget about Christmas in Hawaii—the highest rates of the year are over the Christmas–New Year's period.

11. Invest in a copy of the *Hawaii Entertainment Book* ($38 from Entertainment Publications, 4211 Waialae Ave., Honolulu, HI 96816, ☎ 808/737-3252). You can save 50% on regular hotel rack rates at scores of quality hotels on all the major islands—many of them described in this book—or 10% on any special promotions a hotel may be offering (whichever gives you the greater discount). There are some restrictions, of course, but, all in all, the discount book is quite a deal.

12. Consult HALE (Hawaiian Apartment Leasing Enterprises), 479 Ocean Ave., Suite B, Laguna Beach, CA 92675 (☎ 714/497-4253 or 800/854-8843), which offers savings of up to 50% on condo and vacation rentals on all the major islands.

13. Try a home exchange. Your midtown Manhattan apartment or L.A. condo might be the perfect swap for a romantic bungalow on Maui. (See Home Exchange listings, Chapter 3).

14. Singles and couples can do well at bed-and-breakfasts. Though most B&Bs in Hawaii are no longer cheap (they've become Laura Ashley–ized), they are lovely and do cost less than most hotels. And they do provide breakfasts—a great money-saver—and have friendly hosts who can fill you in on all kinds of money-saving tips.

15. Families do best in condominium or hotel apartments with kitchenettes; not only does everyone have a chance to get out of each other's hair, but you can save a good deal of money by cooking at least one meal per day; dishes and utensils are always provided.

16. Lacking a kitchenette, at least get a room with a refrigerator; that way you can store fruit, milk, and snacks.

17. If you stay in a hotel that has a minibar, ask housekeeping to remove the contents, they are invariably overpriced. Use the mini-refrigerator space for your own perishables.

18. Avoid room service, hotel telephones, and dry-cleaning and laundry services. Try the nearest coffee shop, make your phone calls in the lobby, and find a laundromat. (Some smaller hotels and B&Bs do allow free local calls; inquire.)

19. Travel with a friend—better yet, with two. Hotel room rates in Hawaii are almost never less for single occupancy. Three in a room adds a surcharge of about $10. If you're dividing the total cost by three, a $90 hotel room becomes just $30 a night.

20. Investigate private rooms in youth hostels; there are a few.

21. Consider taking a summer course at the University of Hawaii. Dormitory rooms are inexpensive, and your student ID entitles you to all kinds of discounts and privileges.

DINING

22. Eat at food courts. There are many of them on all the islands, except Molokai and Lanai. They offer a variety of local and ethnic dishes as well as standard American fare, and you can easily put together a meal for $6 or less. Some of our favorites are the food courts at Aloha Tower Marketplace and Ala Moana Shopping Center on Oahu and at Kaahumanu Shopping Center on Maui.

23. Have breakfast in your hotel room. Pick up fruit and baked goods at a supermarket or convenience store. Take along a handy immersion heater and make your own instant coffee or tea. Look for a room with a small refrigerator.

24. If you have a kitchenette, cook at least one meal a day (in addition to breakfast) at home. Order takeout and eat at home or have a picnic on the beach.

25. Have your major meal of the day at lunchtime rather than dinner.

26. Have an early dinner. Early Bird Specials offer significant savings.

27. Use the coupons in the *Hawaii Entertainment Book* ($38; ☎ 808/737-3252) for discounts of up to 50% at hundreds of restaurants on all the major islands. These include top dining establishments as well as casual family eateries and takeout places, many of which are covered in this book. Both two-for-one dining discounts and 50% off menu items for solo diners are available.

28. Check the two-for-one and discount offers in free tourist publications such as *This Week on Oahu, Maui Gold,* and *This Week on the Big Island.* Discounts offered there are not nearly as extensive as those in the *Hawaii Entertainment Book,* but are worth looking into.

29. Go for the pupus. Don't depend on it, but you can sometimes almost fill up on the free appetizers at local bars during Happy Hours. Studebaker's at Restaurant Row in Honolulu even offers a free buffet meal along with the booze. (See "Honolulu After Dark" in Chapter 7).

30. Go local. It won't be a sophisticated culinary experience, but eating local food and Hawaiian-style plate lunches is a great way to have a tasty meal for little money. What's more, dining localstyle is one of the most genuine—and interesting—Hawaiian experiences you can have.

LOCAL TRANSPORTATION

31. On Oahu, ride TheBUS. Hawaii's public bus system has won awards as the best in the country. Buses go everywhere—even all the way around the island—maintain good schedules, and charge only 85¢ (less for seniors).

32. Renting a car is essential on the neighbor islands, so shop around for special rates and inter-island deals. Be sure to check all one-way rental contracts for drop-off charges.

33. Check your home auto insurance policy carefully before you leave; it may insure you in Hawaii and you will be able to avoid the cost of collision-damage waivers (anywhere from $10 to $12 per day) that the car rental companies are eager to sell you.

RECREATION AND ENTERTAINMENT

34. Swim and snorkel for free at beaches around the state, even those in front of fancy hotels; they're all open to the public up to the high-water mark.
35. Golf at municipal courses; greens fees are tiny compared to those at fancy golf clubs. You'll find the most reasonable fees in Hilo, on the Big Island.
36. Play tennis for free at dozens of public courts.
37. Go hiking with groups like the Hawaiian Trail and Mountain Club. Check the "Today" section of the *Honolulu Star-Bulletin* for listings. Cost: $2.
38. Catch the free entertainment at the Royal Hawaiian Shopping Center, the Aloha Tower Marketplace, Kings' Village, Ala Moana Shopping Center, and many more. You'll see everything from name entertainers to local hula schools to wandering musicians.
39. Go local. Check the local papers for upcoming dance recitals, carnivals, crafts fairs, concerts, even luaus presented by churches and other groups. These downhome events are always fun, and you get to meet and socialize with islanders in their own setting.

SHOPPING

40. Catch the open markets. Every island has its own flea markets, farmer's markets, and the like. The biggest is the Aloha Swap Meet at Aloha Stadium in Honolulu (☎ 808/486-1529); the one we like best is the Wednesday and Saturday morning Farmer's Market in downtown Hilo on the Big Island.
41. Shop for souvenirs at the ABC Discount stores and Woolworth's—the prices are right. Also check the Japanese department stores for unique, inexpensive items.
42. Check the Liberty House Penthouse stores on Maui, the Big Island, and Oahu; automatic discounts make for huge savings on unsold merchandise from the prestigious Liberty House stores around the islands. You'll find clothing, accessories, pots and pans, towels, linens, and gift items, too.
43. If you're going to the Big Island, get your Kona coffee there; it's grown locally and the prices are the best.
44. Bargain for goods at the International Market Place and Kuhio Mall in Honolulu; it's part of the game (this is not so elsewhere, however).
45. Patronize local thrift shops; you can often find astonishing bargains, like gently used muumuus for a couple of dollars.

3 Best Bets on a Budget

HAWAII'S TOP ATTRACTIONS FOR FREE—OR ALMOST

1. A visit to the USS *Arizona* is a stirring memorial to December 7, 1941, Pearl Harbor's "day of infamy." (See "The Top Attractions," Chapter 7.)
2. The view from Nuuanu Pali, a glorious panorama from the top of a jagged cliff, is one of the great sights of Oahu. Thousands of defeated warriors fell to their deaths on the rocks below in the fierce battle of 1795, when Kamehameha the Great vanquished the Oahuans. (See "From Waikiki to the Windward Coast," Chapter 8.)

3. Snorkeling is near-perfect at Hanauma Bay, an idyllic Oahu beach and marine preserve where placid turquoise waters cover the coral reef and fish are so gentle they eat right out of your hand. (See "Beaches," Chapter 6.)
4. The Byodo-In Temple on Windward Oahu, an exact replica of the venerable Byodo-In in Japan, has a magnificent carving of Amida, the Buddha of the Western Paradise. This is a must for lovers of Asian art and culture. (See "From Waikiki to the Windward Coast," Chapter 8.)
5. On the Big Island, step into Hawaii's primitive past at Puu'uhonua O Honaunau, an ancient "city of refuge" with a restored *heaiu* and statuary at water's edge. This is one of Hawaii's most mystical spots. (See "Exploring the Kona Coast," Chapter 14.)
6. Madame Pele, the goddess of the volcanoes, is still alive and well on the Big Island, and putting on spectacular fire shows as Kilauea continues to erupt. You can pay your respects to Madame Pele and see the oozing lava up close. (See "Hawaii Volcanoes National Park," Chapter 14.)
7. Drive up a 10,000-foot volcano in the dark to see the sun rise from the summit of Maui's Mt. Haleakala. This is one of the great island experiences. (See "Haleakala National Park & Upcountry Maui," Chapter 10.)
8. We could swim and snorkel forever at Kapalua Beach in West Maui. Protected from wind and waves by an ancient lava flow that extends well out into the water, this white-sand crescent beach is one of the world's best. (See "Beaches," Chapter 10.)
9. Waimea Canyon on Kauai is known as the "Grand Canyon of the Pacific." Don't miss the spectacular view of Kalalaua Lookout, where thick tropical rain forest suddenly drops 4,000 feet down to the breathtaking blue sea (See "Hiking" and "Touring the Southern & Western Shores," Chapter 16.)
10. The view from the lookout above Hanalei Valley on Kauai is pure magic. You might think you're somewhere in Asia when you look down to the valley floor, with neatly terraced taro patches and the silvery Hanalei River snaking through the verdant mountains. Try it at sunset. (See "Touring the Eastern & Northern Shores," Chapter 16.)

BEST BUDGET ACCOMMODATIONS
OAHU

1. Does a studio apartment with its own kitchen at a close-to-the-beach location in Waikiki for $47 to $57 sound good to you? That's what Aloha Punawai offers. The building is very well maintained and the proprietor goes out of her way to take care of her guests.
2. Hale Pua Nui in Waikiki is a half-block from the good swimming beach in front of the Outrigger Reef Hotel. Large studio apartments (which accommodate up to four) with kitchenettes run from $45 to $55 single or double.

MAUI

3. Popular with backpackers, active travelers, and windsurfers (it's about a 10-minute drive to Maui's best windsurfing beaches), Banana Bungalow Too in Wailuku offers beds or bunks in a community room for $15. Private singles are $31.95 and private doubles are $38.95; all have shared bathrooms. Guests have use of the kitchen, garden, and sand volleyball court; lots of communal activities are offered.

4. Considering the scarcity and high prices of accommodations in popular Lahaina, a $40 to $60 double at Aloha Tony's simple guest house is one sweet deal. Lahaina Beach is just across the yard and the center of town is a short walk away.

5. There's no better bargain in upcountry Maui than Elaine's Upcountry Guest Rooms. Elaine and Murray Gildersleeve charge only $55 double for a guest room in their elegant Hawaiian pole house; three rooms share a separate kitchen and living room. A delightful cottage is $95 for four people (the cottage can accommodate up to six).

BIG ISLAND

6. Arnott's Lodge and Hiking Adventures in Hilo offers everything from $15 hostel bunks to rooms with private baths ($26 single, $36 double) to two-bedroom kitchen suites that can accommodate up to five people ($80). With a lovely tropical setting not far from ocean beaches and parks and a short drive to the center of Hilo, it's a terrific buy.

7. Oceanfront rooms are always pricey, except at petite Kona Tiki in Kailua-Kona, where every room has its own private lanai close to the pounding blue-green surf. The tab at this modest hotel is only $54 single or double, $59 with kitchenette.

8. The H. Manago Hotel, in Captain Cook on the Kona Coast, has been a Big Island favorite since 1917. Rooms in the newer wing are just $25 to $38 single, $38 to $41 double, $41–$44 triple with private bath. $52 single, $55 double gets you a Japanese room with futons and furo. Vegetables from the Hotel's garden are served in its restaurant, a big favorite with local residents.

KAUAI

9. Some of the best bed-and-breakfast rates—$35 to $50 single, $45 to $70 double—can be found at Kay Barker's Bed & Breakfast, a very casual and most relaxing establishment.

10. Rustic facilities in a beautiful setting make Kokee State Park's cabins easier than camping, cheaper than a hotel. Cabinettes and cabins run from $30 to $45 per night.

BEST BUDGET RESTAURANTS
OAHU

1. Gargantuan buffet tables, attractive settings, and surprisingly good food for the price (breakfast buffets under $6, lunch buffets under $7, dinner buffets under $10) have made the Perry's Smorgy restaurants, 2380 Kuhio Ave. and 240 Lewers St., Waikiki institutions ever since the last ice age.

2. Artists from nearby galleries and downtown business folk keep A Little Bit of Saigon, 1160 Maunakea St. in Honolulu's Chinatown, hopping. Most of the delicious Vietnamese dishes can be had either as pupus, as meals in a bowl, or as rice-paper rollups (ask the waiter for instructions). Main courses run $5.95 to $15.

3. In our humble opinion, Kua'aina Sandwich, 66-214 Kam Hwy. in Haleiwa on the North Shore, has the best and best-priced sandwiches in Oahu (cases in point: mahimahi with melted cheese and Ortega peppers at $5.40.) Surfers and local people coming in from the beach heartily agree.

MAUI

4. Nothing on the menu is more than $5.95 at Pupule Pub & Cafe, 318 N. Market St. in Wailuku, which describes itself as "Part Nouveau-Vegetarian Cuisine and Part Truck Stop Diner." The food is all good, be it a barbecue beef sandwich, a spinach-and-brown-rice casserole, or Hoisin marinated baked chicken with rice pilaf.

5. Not only does Lahaina's Cheeseburger in Paradise have just about the biggest, gooeyest burgers around, both their upstairs and downstairs dining rooms have wonderful ocean views. Great onion rings, ice cold beer, and tropical rock, too, at modest prices from $5 to $10.

6. On a recent visit to Lahaina Coolers Restaurant & Bar, 180 Dickensen St. in Lahaina, we shared an Evil Jungle Pizza—Thai-style chicken in a peanut sauce—for $10.75, and it was a full meal. Everything else on the constantly changing menu in this summery place is good, too—Mexican dishes, pastas, fresh fish, gourmet burgers—with many dishes under $10.

THE BIG ISLAND

7. At Broke the Mouth, 93 Mamo St., a counter-takeout restaurant in downtown Hilo, the best sauces we've ever tasted grace vegetarian gourmet meals served on paper plates. The organic greens and herbs are grown a few miles away on the Hamakua Coast. Full meals are $5 to $6, and you can buy the sauces to take home with you for about $4 each.

8. You never know from one day to the next what could be on the menu at Ann Sutherland's Mean Cuisine, Opelo Plaza, in cowboy-town Waimea. Sutherland, once a private chef to the Ethel Kennedy clan, offers about 30 main dishes a day, from downhome turkey with mashed potatoes to gourmet treats like taro goat cheese eggplant roulade or Hunan lamb. Prices are a mere $4 to $7.

9. For over 50 years, local folks have been patronizing family-run Lihue Barbecue Inn at 2982 Kress St. The reason: good Japanese and American food, with more than 20 complete dinners for under $14.

10. If you don't mind doing a little work—like broiling your own steak, burgers, mahimahi, barbecued chicken—you can have a good meal at the lively Koloa Broiler, Koloa Rd. for $7 to $11.95—and that includes salad bar and sides.

4 How This Guide Can Save You Money

Everything you need to know about traveling to and around Hawaii and how to have an affordable and enjoyable time there is packed between the pages of this book. Of course, you'll decide on your own itinerary and choose for yourself the places where you want to stay and dine. What follows is merely an idea of what your vacation could look like and how much it would cost. We've plotted out hotels and meals for you for a 10-day trip to the islands, assuming you'll spend 4 days in Oahu, 3 in Maui, and 3 on the Big Island. We're not counting the traveling days to and from Hawaii, and we haven't included taxes and tips. Our selections go from budget to mid-range to an occasional splurge or two. Per-person accommodations and meal rates are given. Remember, rates are averages only; accommodations prices vary, and you're on your own for menu choices.

Day 1 in Honolulu and Waikiki

Accommodations Patrick Winston's Hawaiian King Rentals—
$37.50 each
Breakfast In room. Fixings from market—fruit, muffins, coffee, etc.—
$2.50 each
Lunch Jamaican Cuisine—$7 each
Dinner Perry's Smorgy—$10 each
Per-Person Total for Day 1 $57

Day 2 in Honolulu and Waikiki

Accommodations Same as for Day 1
Breakfast In room—$2.50 each
Lunch Food Court at Aloha Tower Marketplace—$6 each
Dinner Duke's Canoe Club—$25 each
Per-Person Total for Day 2 $71

Day 3 in Honolulu and Waikiki

Accommodations Same as Day 1
Breakfast In room—$2.50 each
Lunch Tsuruya Noodle Shop—$7 each
Dinner Chiu Chau Bistro—$14 each
Per-person Total for Day 3 $61

Day 4 Traveling around Oahu

Accommodations Same as for Day 1
Breakfast In room—2.50 each.
Lunch Kua'Aina—$7 each.
Dinner Sunset Grill—$25 each.
Per-Person Total for Day 4 $72

Day 5 Flying to Maui in morning

Accommodations Ann & Bob Babson's Bed-and-Breakfast—$40 each
Breakfast In Waikiki apartment—$2.50 each
Lunch Sir Wilfred's Espresso Café at Maui Mall (close to airport)—$6 each
Dinner Margarita's Beach Cantina—$16 each.
Per-Person Total for Day 5 $64.50

Day 6 in Maui, visiting Lahaina/Kaanapali area

Accommodations Same as Day 5
Breakfast At bed-and-breakfast
Lunch Avalon—$15 each
Dinner Aloha Cantina—$13 each
Per-Person Total for Day 6 $68

Day 7 in Maui, visiting Haleakala National Park

Accommodations Same as for Day 6
Breakfast At bed-and-breakfast
Lunch Casanova—$6 each
Dinner Hailimaile General Store—$25 each
Per-person Total for Day 7 $71

Day 8 Flying to Hilo on the Big Island in morning

Accommodations   Dolphin Bay Hotel—$32.50
Breakfast   At bed-and-breakfast in Maui
Lunch   Bears Cafe—$6 each
Dinner   Cafe Pesto—$18 each
Per-Person Total for Day 8 $56.50

Day 9 On the Big Island, driving cross-island to Kona via the Hamakua Coast

Accommodations   Kona Riviera Village—$40
Breakfast   In room in Hilo ($2.50 each for breakfast fixings from market)
Lunch   Merriman's in Waimea—$12 each
Dinner   Kuakini Terrace Chinese Buffet—$13 each
Per-person Total for Day 9 $67.50

Day 10 in Kona

Accommodations   Same as for Day 9
Breakfast   In room—$2.50 each
Lunch   Island Lava Java—$6 each
Dinner   Under the Palms—$12 each
Per-person Total for Day 10 $60.50

Total Estimated Cost Per Person $649
Total Estimated Cost For Two $1298

Getting to Know Hawaii

2

"Why go all the way to Hawaii," asks a friend of ours, a sophisticated woman who travels regularly to Europe, "just to find yourself at a beach?" Now no one in his or her right mind would dispute the glory of Hawaii's beaches, some of the best in the world. But anyone who looks on Hawaii as merely a seaside resort is missing some of the most profound, exciting, and exotic travel experiences available anywhere.

Most people think of Hawaii as synonymous with Honolulu and Waikiki Beach (and probably know that both are on the island of Oahu), but they're a bit vague about the names of the other islands. Actually, there are 122 islands in the Hawaii chain, a great volcanic mountain range spreading 1,500 miles across the floor of the Pacific, from Hawaii on the southeast to Midway and Kure islands in the northwest. Many of these are just jagged rocks or sand shoals, however, and the term "Hawaiian Islands" usually refers only to eight: Oahu, Hawaii or the Big Island, Maui, Kauai, Molokai, Lanai, Kahoolawe, and Niihau.

The essence of Hawaii, its special mystery, lies in its startling and subtle paradoxes. Take its people, as fascinating a mixture of humanity as you'll find on this planet. The children and grand children of Polynesian settlers, New England missionaries, and Asian plantation workers mingled and intermarried to create nothing less than a new race. Scratch an islander and you'll find a Hawaiian-Chinese-Portuguese, a Japanese-American-Tahitian, or perhaps an English-Filipino-Korean. The typical islander—if such a creature exists—long ago gave up counting the racial strains in his or her background; it got too complicated. Hawaii's people, American in ideals, optimism, and drive, still retain the serenity of Polynesia and Asia. They avidly follow the scores of baseball games played by fellow citizens 6,000 miles away in Boston or Philadelphia, yet many of them dream of going to visit the "old country"—Japan, China, the Philippines.

But the paradoxes don't stop here. The islands are even more astonishing on a sheer topographical level; Hawaii has the kind of scenery that all but overwhelms the senses. Steep cliffs tumbling down to coral beaches, tropical rain forests that run a hundred shades of green, black-sand beaches and pounding blue surf, scores of tropical blossoms vying for attention at every turn—this is the landscape. Even more awe-inspiring, the volcanoes that created these islands from the vast nothingness of ocean are still alive; the land is still being born. Drive mile after mile on the Big Island of Hawaii and see where the lava flows have scalded their way to the sea and how slowly life renews itself over the years. Then go to Kauai and see what the centuries and the forces of erosion have done to a much older extinct volcano. You'll have a sense of the youth—and the age—of the earth that you can get nowhere else.

The paradox of Hawaii continues on a third level as well. In less than 200 years it has gone from Stone Age to Space Age, from an ancient island kingdom ruled by stern gods of nature to one of the fastest growing states in the country, ruled by equally stern laws of economics. For the past number of years, industry has thrived, hotel and apartment construction has grown astronomically, and population and tourism have increased to record levels. There is some pulling back: Hawaii is rethinking its dependency on tourism now that plantation agriculture and military spending have decreased. The state is concerned about its fragile ecosystem and the siphoning off of profits to foreign investors. A movement for Hawaiian sovereignty, small but vocal, is growing. And yet Hawaii still remains one of the most popular visitor destinations on earth: almost seven million travelers per year. For despite the complications of changing times, the spirit of aloha remains untouched, the tranquil eye of the hurricane of progress. Perhaps this is why so many people who have been everywhere and back can't seem to get enough of Hawaii.

1 A Look at the Past

The Hawaiian Islands were settled between 1,200 and 1,500 years ago by Polynesians who most likely came from the Marquesas and Tahitian islands. They crossed thousands of miles of ocean in double-hulled sailing vessels, connected by long bamboo poles that supported a tiny hut between the canoes. They brought with them their animals and plants, introducing such new foods as the sweet potato.

They settled primarily on the largest islands of the Hawaiian archipelago—Hawaii, Kauai, Maui, Molokai, and Oahu. The islands were fragmented into little kingdoms, each ruled by its own chief, with its own *kapus* (taboos) and particular customs. Power belonged to the strongest, and the bloody overthrow of leaders was quite common. But life was stable, and very probably even comfortable. None of the settlers ever made any attempt to return to the tribes from which they had come. These people remained undisturbed and untouched by outsiders until the 18th century.

COOK ARRIVES In 1777 Capt. James Cook, looking for the Northwest Passage, stumbled onto the island of Kauai. The islanders, who had long believed that their great god Lono would one day return to them, mistook Cook and his crew for the god and a full entourage of lesser deities. At first Cook received a god's reception, but soon fighting broke out between the natives and the sailors; eight

Impressions

The loveliest fleet of islands that lies anchored in any ocean.
—Mark Twain, 1872

"See Naples and die"—They spell it differently here: See Hawaii and live.
—Jack London, 1916

months later, on another voyage, Cook was clubbed to death by islanders and drowned off the Kona shore of the island of Hawaii. But from that time on, the Sandwich Islands, as Cook had named them in honor of the Earl of Sandwich when he claimed them for Great Britain, became part of the modern world.

By 1790, King Kamehameha the Great, based on the island of Hawaii, conquered the other islands in the chain in a series of bloody forays (except for Kauai, which surrendered) and united them under his rule. Hawaii was already one nation when the first emissaries from the Western world—merchants, fur traders, whaling men—started their invasion of the islands.

19TH CENTURY   In 1820 a band of New England missionaries arrived in Hawaii, determined to save the heathen islanders from the devil. They brought piety, industry, and Congregationalism to the natives; their arrival speeded the end of the old Hawaiian life. (Their story is eloquently told in James Michener's *Hawaii*.) They smashed the idols and continued the destruction of the rigid *kapus* (already weakened by the king prior to their arrival), taught the people to read and write, and "civilized" the natives. Many of the islanders here have never forgiven them, as the island saying goes, for doing so well. Some of the missionaries' children turned into business people, bought up the land, and started industries; it is their descendants who are still among the ruling forces of Hawaii's great corporate empires.

The native Hawaiians never really adjusted to the *haole's* (white man's) world; they refused to work the plantations and died from diseases in horrendous epidemics. Today, just a few thousand pure-blooded Hawaiians remain. The rest have disappeared or have blended with the other races—mostly Japanese and Chinese—who came to work the plantations.

The Asians began to arrive around 1852, when the whaling trade was dropping off and the sugar plantations were becoming big business. The Chinese came first to work the plantations, then the Japanese, last the Filipinos. The Hawaiian melting pot began to simmer.

Meanwhile, the reign of the second Kamehameha had been short; he and his queen died of measles in London in 1824. Kamehameha III reigned for 30 years, during which time the independence of the island kingdom was recognized by France, Great Britain, and the United States. An English-language newspaper was started and a public school opened, both in the islands' capital, Lahaina, on Maui. But the capital remained there only until 1845, when the king and his court moved to Honolulu. Commerce was picking up in the harbors, and in 1850 that city was declared the capital of the 19th-century kingdom.

The line of the Kamehameha descent ended by 1872, after Kamehameha IV and V. The legislature elected William Lunalilo as successor, but he died within a year; David Kalakaua succeeded him. Queen Emma, the widow of Kamehameha IV, appeared to have a rightful claim to the throne, and it was to this end that many riots were staged; American and British marines were called in.

In the latter part of the 19th century, industry continued to boom, with sugar the leading crop and coffee a close second. Finally, in 1875, the Hawaiian sugar planters worked out a reciprocal agreement with the U.S. government by which Hawaiian sugar companies were assured an American market; when it was renewed in 1887 the Americans were given the freedom to use Pearl Harbor as a coaling station for American ships. The American Age was beginning in Hawaii; the annexation of the Republic of Hawaii took place in 1898, but statehood would not be achieved until more than half a century later, in 1959.

King Kalakaua, "The Merrie Monarch," was followed by Queen Liliuokalani, the last reigning monarch of the islands. When her plans for a new constitution were violently opposed, she was removed from office in the bloodless uprising of 1893 and replaced by Sanford B. Dole, a haole representing American commercial interests. While she was under house arrest, the queen wrote the poignant "Aloha Oe," now a song of farewell to those leaving the islands. But it was also a lament, a farewell to the days when kings and queens, and even an occasional god, walked the earth.

20TH CENTURY   The 20th century saw the booming of the pineapple industry in Hawaii. Although Hawaii was not directly involved in World War I, many islanders had volunteered for the French and German armies before the United States entered the conflict. The Great Depression of the 1930s blew through the islands with the relative calm of a trade wind; big business was not yet too big, industry not yet well developed.

But Hawaii felt the impact of World War II more than any American state. Because the United States had developed the harbors and military installations on the islands, they were a prime target area for the enemy. After the dreadful bombing attack of December 7, 1941, Hawaii entered a period of martial law. Liquor consumption was regulated, curfews were imposed, and blackouts were common. Fortunately, the island's Japanese population was not herded off into concentration camps as Japanese-Americans were in California. In fact, a group of Nisei volunteers fighting in southern Europe became one of the great heroic regiments of the U.S. Army. The 442nd Regimental Combat Team has been called "probably the most decorated unit in United States military history," and one of its members, Daniel K. Inouye, is the senator of Watergate fame. This participation in the war did a great deal to break down race lines in Hawaii. Today, Japanese-Americans are the largest single ethnic group—and one of the most powerful—in the state.

After the war, increasing lines of transportation developed between the American mainland and Hawaii. Tourism became a major industry and the already-existing industries grew at phenomenal rates. Years of labor disputes in the 1940s, spearheaded by the militant ILWU, raised the standard of living for the Hawaiian worker to an all-time high. Finally, in 1959, after a 30-year struggle for statehood, Congressional delegate John A. Burns (later Hawaii's governor) affected passage of the bill that made Hawaii the 50th American state. Dancing in the streets celebrated a goal long promised and arduously won.

Since statehood, Hawaii has blossomed and boomed and burst forth into a new era. Garment industries, steel mills, and cement factories are growing. Agriculture uses the most advanced techniques, and pineapple and sugar are still big business. Technology has moved in and made Hawaii the mid-Pacific outpost of America's space efforts and oceanography research. The University of Hawaii and the East-West Center for Cultural and Technical Interchange have raised the state's academic reputation remarkably, bringing in scholars from all over the world. Population is up to 1.1 million; more than six million tourists are expected annually. Despite economic uncertainty here as everywhere, Hawaii is still going strong.

A Republican stronghold for many years, Hawaii, with the rise of labor unions and ethnic groups to positions of political and financial power, has become strongly Democratic in its politics. Both of its senators in the U.S. Congress, Daniel K. Inouye and Daniel Akaka, are Democrats, as are its representatives in Congress, Patsy Mink and Neil Abercrombie. Both Inouye and Mink are of

Japanese-American backgrounds; Akaka is pure Hawaiian; and Abercrombie is 100% haole. In the state legislature, there are 51 representatives (only 6 are Republicans), and 25 senators (2 are Republicans). Most are of mixed backgrounds; 5 are Hawaiian. The lieutenant governor, Mazie Hirono, is Japanese-American.

2 A Melting Pot of Its Own: Hawaii's Peoples & Languages

By Lisa Legarde

Lisa Legarde graduated from Wellesley College with a degree in English and worked as an assistant editor at Macmillan Travel before embarking on her career as a travel writer. She has authored a number of Frommer's travel guides, including *Frommer's Maui*.

Hawaii's population reflects a multiculturalism found virtually nowhere else in the world. Its people represent a unique ethnic mix of Hawaiian, Filipino, Portuguese, Japanese, Korean, Irish, German, Chinese, and *haole* (or Caucasian) people, most of whom immigrated to Hawaii in search of a better life. They brought with them their languages, cuisines, modes of dress, art forms, and cultural entertainments, all of which have impacted Hawaii's social structure. Cultural influences can be experienced today simply by taking a walk along the beach, where you might hear a surprising number of different languages. A walk down Lahaina's Front Street or through Honolulu's Chinatown will dazzle you with art galleries that hold the works of Asians, Hawaiians, and haoles alike. Island restaurants represent a cross-section of cultural tastes and the blending of the spices of East and West.

PEOPLES

HAWAIIANS   The story of the native Hawaiian people is one of disaster. Today, the number of full-blooded Hawaiians is a mere fraction of the 300,000 living in the islands at the time of Captain Cook's arrival. The early introduction of venereal diseases by Cook's shipmates proved devastating for the Hawaiians, whose women displayed little or no inhibition when it came to sexual contact with the European sailors. By 1820, the Hawaiian population was estimated at less than half of what it was in 1778. The influx of foreign visitors also brought other diseases, both major and minor, against which the Hawaiians had no natural resistance, and wars between ruling chiefs obliterated another portion of the Hawaiian population. It is also believed that one-quarter of all Hawaiian men simply shipped out, never to return as they pursued careers in the whaling industry and found their livelihoods elsewhere. The final blow to the Hawaiian race came, simply, with the increase in interracial marriages. Today, most of those people claiming Hawaiian heritage are not full-blooded Hawaiian; in fact, the current portion of the population that is 100% Hawaiian is probably somewhere in the neighborhood of 1,500.

CHINESE   It is believed that the first Chinese to arrive on the Hawaiian archipelago came aboard an American ship skippered by Captain John Meares. None of them stayed. The first real migration of Chinese to the Hawaiian islands began in 1852, when the first contract field laborers arrived from Hong Kong. Their passage was paid, and their five-year contracts granted them a salary of $3 a month plus room and board. They worked long, hard days on the sugar plantations and looked forward to the ends of their contracts when they would set up their own businesses, leaving plantation work to the next wave of immigrants. Some of the first interracial marriages that took place in Hawaii were among the Chinese and the native Hawaiians. Today the Chinese population remains strong, although it makes up only a small percentage of the general population.

JAPANESE   Some historians believe that the Japanese arrived in Hawaii long before Captain Cook dropped anchor; however, the first documented Japanese arrivals took place in 1868. Originally, over 300 Japanese intended to migrate to Hawaii in search of plantation work, but only about one-third of that group actually left Japan, because the Japanese government disapproved of their departure. Japanese immigration halted until 1885, when huge numbers of Japanese workers began immigrating to Hawaii. Only 15 years later, the Japanese population in Hawaii was figured to be just over 60,000. Japanese workers were as industrious as the Chinese labor force, but they found themselves the victims of cruel discrimination and were not given the same opportunities as their Chinese and Hawaiian coworkers.

Eventually, in spite of the discrimination, the Japanese were able to rise through the ranks from plantation workers to the professions. The children and grandchildren of the first large group of immigrants were educated in American schools and felt a strong alliance with the United States—so much so that many of them fought valiantly in World War II. After the war, these Japanese men who emerged as heroes were able to take advantage of the G.I. Bill, which allowed them to pursue college educations. Many of them became doctors, dentists, lawyers, teachers, and businessmen. The first Japanese-American governor, George Ariyoshi, was elected in Hawaii in 1974. Currently, the Japanese make up about 25% of Hawaii's total population.

HAOLES   Today the word *haole* refers to any person of Caucasian descent. Basically, to Hawaiians, it really doesn't matter where you're from—if your skin is white, you're a haole.

The haole history of Hawaii goes all the way back to John Young and Isaac Davis, sailors who were held prisoner by King Kamehameha during the Olowalu Massacre in 1790. More significant, though, were the numbers of haole immigrants who came as missionaries from New England. They established themselves permanently on the islands long before the Chinese and Japanese, and have been the most powerful economic force ever to settle in Hawaii, adopting a "colonist" attitude toward the natives, whom they looked down upon and whose customs and cultural activities they considered primitive and, oftentimes, disgusting. Most of the New England missionaries did not mingle with the Hawaiians, and so dilution of pure haole bloodlines among the missionaries was rare.

Between 1878 and 1887, approximately 12,000 Portuguese immigrants arrived in Hawaii, and another 6,000 came in the early 1900s. The olive-skinned Portuguese immigrants were welcomed with traditional Hawaiian aloha, mainly because they were dark enough not to be considered haole. Many Portuguese men and women worked on sugar plantations and rose into the top ranks of plantation laborers. They weren't, however, well educated, which is probably why they were often the butt of Hawaiian jokes. Here again, as with the other ethnic groups, there was some interracial marriage among the Portuguese and the Hawaiians. When any member of the white population marries a Hawaiian, their offspring is referred to as *hapa-haole,* or "half-white, half-Hawaiian."

With the development of the resort properties, more haoles arrived; this time they came primarily from the U.S. mainland, and they have upheld the haole tradition of having a controlling interest in Hawaii's economy, sometimes at the expense of Hawaii's native people. Today, haoles make up approximately 33% of Hawaii's general population.

FILIPINOS   American nationals since the Spanish-American War in 1898, Filipinos did not have as much difficulty immigrating to Hawaii as the Chinese or Japanese did, mainly because they were not restricted by the same kinds of immigration laws that stopped many Asians. Hailing from the northern Philippines, 120,000 Filipinos were imported to Hawaii as plantation laborers between 1907 and 1931. Japanese workers in Hawaii had gone on strike in 1909, and plantation owners looked elsewhere for workers. They couldn't believe their luck when they discovered that the Filipinos would take the lowest-paying jobs and work under conditions that no other group would.

Like the Chinese, most of the Filipinos who immigrated to Hawaii were men (between 1924 and 1930 the ratio of Filipino men to Filipino women in Hawaii was approximately 19 to 1) who planned to return to their families and homeland after they saved a bit of money. By 1950, the Filipino population was about one-eighth of Hawaii's general population. Today the Filipino population is 14% of Hawaii's general population.

OTHER PEOPLES   The rest of the Hawaiian population is made up of Koreans (who immigrated between 1903 and 1905), Puerto Ricans (who arrived at approximately the same time as the Koreans), African-Americans, Vietnamese, and a small but fast-growing group of Samoans.

LANGUAGE

With such a diverse population, it should come as no surprise that Hawaii is a multitongued state. Of course, English is the dominant language spoken here, so you won't have any trouble communicating. Occasionally you'll hear some Chinese, Japanese, Portuguese, and Spanish, but there are two other Hawaiian languages that are the key to understanding the Hawaiian spirit and culture:

PIDGIN   In early Hawaii, when migrant plantation workers came to the islands from all over the world, all speaking different languages, communication was difficult. Over time, they all learned to communicate with each other in a language now known as pidgin. Pidgin is a true reflection of Hawaii's ethnic mix and it is quite literally a combination of several different languages. Its base is Hawaiian, but it has English, Japanese, Filipino, Chinese, and Samoan elements. The Portuguese had their own influence—not in terms of vocabulary but intonation and musicality.

Some people consider pidgin low-class, nonsensical, and illiterate, and many have even tried to wipe it out, but to no avail. *Brah* (brother), *cockaroach* (steal), *geev um* (sock it to them), *hele on* ("right on" or "hip"), *lesgo* (let's go), and *tita* (short for sister, but used only with friendly, earthy types) are just a few of the words you might pick up during your trip. Today, pidgin is such a part of daily Hawaiian life that the Hawaiian House of Representatives has declared it one of Hawaii's official languages. If you'd like to learn more, try reading the very funny

Pidgin to Da Max and *Fax to Da Max* (Bess Press, Honolulu), both of which are humorous "studies" of the language.

HAWAIIAN The Hawaiian language has its roots in the languages of the Polynesians; however, the Hawaiian spoken today is probably very different from the Hawaiian of old. Over the years, as the oral tradition was changed to a written one, translations and transcriptions inadvertently changed the spellings and meanings of certain words and phrases. For a long while, after the introduction of English and pidgin, Hawaiian was a dying language. Fortunately, today it is experiencing a rebirth through courses of study and the Hawaiian people's general interest in their roots.

Two of the most commonly used Hawaiian words are *aloha* (hello or goodbye; an expression of love) and *mahalo* (thank you). Below is a short list of common words and phrases. If you're interested in learning more, virtually every bookstore stocks a Hawaiian dictionary or two. A good pocket version is *Instant Hawaiian,* which is available throughout the islands.

There are just 12 letters in the Hawaiian alphabet: five vowels—*a, e, i, o, u*—and seven consonants—*h, k, l, m, n, p, w*. Every syllable ends in a vowel, every vowel is pronounced, and the accent is almost always on the next-to-the-last syllable, as it is in Spanish. Consonants receive their English sounds, but vowels get the Latin pronunciation: *a* as in farm, *e* as in they, *i* as in machine, *o* as in cold, and *u* as in tutor. Note, also, that when *w* comes before the final vowel in a word, it is given the "v" sound, as in Hawaii. Purists say Ha-VYE-ee for Hawaii, but most people call it Ha-WYE-ee.

The following glossary will give you an idea of what the Hawaiian language sounds like. No one, of course, expects you to go around spouting phrases like "Holo ehia keia?" to ask what time it is, but a familiarity with the most important words is what distinguishes the kamaainas from the malihinis.

Hawaiian Words & Phrases

English	Hawaiian	Pronunciation
Rough lava	Aa	AH-ah
Eat	Ai	EYE
Friends, as in "Aloha, aikane"	Aikane	eye-KAH-nay
Road, as in Ala Moana (Ocean Road)	Ala	AL-lah
Noblemen, the old royalty of Hawaii	Alii	ah-LEE-ee
Welcome, farewell, love	Aloha	ah-LOW-hah
No	Aole	Ah-OH-lay
Alas! woe!	Auwe	OW-way
In the direction of Ewa, a town on Oahu ("Drive ewa 5 blocks.")	Ewa	EH-vah
The pandanus tree, the leaves of which are used for weaving	Hala	HAH-lah
School (as in hula halau)	Halau	HAH-lau
House	Hale	HAH-lay

Caucasian, white	**Haole**	HOW-lay
White man	**Haolekane**	how-lay-KAY-nay
White woman	**Haolewahine**	how-lay-wah-HEE-nay
Happiness	**Hauoii**	how-OH-iee
Ancient temple	**Heiau**	hey-EE-au
To sleep	**Haimoe**	hee-ah-MOW-ay
To go, to walk	**Hele**	HEY-lay
To run	**Holo**	HO-low
To have fun, to relax	**Holoholo**	ho-low-HO-low
To kiss, as in "Honikaua wikiwiki!" (Kiss me quick!)	**Honi**	HO-nee
A club, an assembly	**Hui**	HOO-ee
A dance, to dance	**Hula**	HOO-lah
Underground oven lined with hot rocks, used for cooking the luau pig	**Imu**	EE-moo
Sweetheart	**Ipo**	EE-po
Ancient (as in hula kahiko)	**Kahiko**	kah-HEE-ko
Sea	**Kai**	KYE
Money	**Kala**	KAH-lah
To bake underground	**Kalua**	kah-loo-AH
Old-timer	**Kamaaina**	kah-mah-EYE-nah
Man	**Kane**	KAH-nay
Tapa, a bark cloth	**Kapa**	KAH-pah
Forbidden, keep out	**Kapu**	kah-POO
Food	**Kaukau**	kow-KOW
Child	**Keiki**	kay-KEE
Help, cooperation	**Kokua**	ko-KOO-ah
South	**Kona**	KO-nah
Sun, light, day	**La**	LAH
Porch	**Lanai**	lah-NYE
Heaven, sky	**Lani**	lah-NEE
Leaf of the hala or pandanus tree	**Lauhala**	lau-HAH-lah
Garland	**Lei**	LAY
Stupid	**Lolo**	low-LOW
Massage	**Lomilomi**	low-mee-LOW-mee
Feast	**Luau**	LOO-au
Thank you	**Mahalo**	mah-HAH-low
Good, fine	**Ma'i ka'i**	mah-ee-KAH-ee
Toward the sea	**Makai**	mah-KEY
Stranger, newcomer	**Malihini**	mah-lee-HEE-nee
Free	**Manawahi**	mah-nah-WAH-hee
Heavenly, or heavenly powers	**Mana**	MAH-nah
Toward the mountains	**Mauka**	MAU-kah
Song, chant	**Mele**	MAY-lay

A mysterious race who inhabited the islands before the Polynesians (mythology claims they were pygmies)	Menehune	may-nay-HOO-nay
Loose dress (Hawaiian version of missionaries "Mother Hubbards")	Muumuu	moo-oo-MOO-oo
Lovely	Nani	NAN-nee
Coconut	Niu	nee-OO
Big, as in "mahalo nui" ("big thanks")	Nui	NOO-ee
Sweet taste, delicious	Ono	OH-no
Stubborn	Paakiki	pah-ah-KEE-kee
Precipice, cliff	Pali	PAH-lee
Hawaiian cowboy	Paniolo	pah-nee-OH-low
Finished, done	Pau	POW
Crushed taro root	Poi	POY
Hors d'oeuvre	Pupu	POO-poo
Crazy	Pupule	poo-POO-lay
Rain	Ua	OO-ah
Female, woman, girl	Wahine	wah-HEE-nay
Fresh water	Wai	WHY
To hurry	Wikiwiki	wee-kee-wee-kee

Phrases

English	Hawaiian	Pronunciation
Be careful	Malama pono	mah-LAH-mah PO-no
Bottoms up	Okole maluna	oh-KO-lay mah-LOO-nah
Come and eat	Hele mai ai	HEY-lay MY-EYE
Come here	Hele mai	HEY-lay MY
Come in and sit down	Komo mai e noho iho	ko-MO my ay NO-ho EE-ho
Go away	Hele aku oe	HEY-lay AH-koo OH-ay
Good evening	Aloha ahiahi	ah-LOW-hah AH-hee-AH-hee
Good morning	Aloha kakahiaka	ah-LOW-hah kah-kah-hee-AH-kah
Greatest love to you	Aloha nui oe	ah-LOW-hah NOO-ee OH-ay
Happy Birthday	Hauoli la hanau	hah-OO-oh-lee-lah hoh-NAH-oo
Happy New Year	Hauoli Makahiki Hou	hah-OO-oh-lee man-kah-HEE-kee HO-oo
Here's to your happiness	Hauoli Maoli oe	hah-OO-oh-lee mah-OH-lee OH-ay

How are you?	**Pehea oe?**	pay-HAY-ah OH-ay
I am fine	**Ma'i ka'i**	mah-EE-kah-EE
I am sorry	**Ua kaumaha au**	OO-ah cow-mah-HAH OW
I have enough	**Ua lawa au**	OO-ah LAH-wah OW
I love you	**Aloha wauia oe**	ah-LOW-hah vow-EE-ah OH-ay
Let's go	**E hele kaua**	au-HEY-lay COW-ah
Many thanks	**Mahalo nui loa**	mah-HAH-low NOO-ee LOW-ah
Merry Christmas	**Mele Kalikimaka**	may-LAY kah-lee-kee-MAH-kah
Much love	**Aloha nui loa**	ah-LOW-hah NOO-ee-LOW-ah
No trouble	**Aole pilikia**	ah-OH-lay pee-lee-KEE-ah
What is your name?	**Owai kau Inoa?**	OH-why KAH-oo ee-NO-ah

3 The Natural World: An Environmental Guide to the Hawaiian Islands

By Jeanette Foster

The Hawaii of today—with its thundering waterfalls exploding into cavernous pools, whispering palms bordering moonlit beaches, vibrant rainbows arching through the early morning mist, and fiery lava creating a blanket of destruction as it slowly pours down slopes—differs dramatically from the Hawaii that came into being at the dawn of time.

Born of violent volcanic eruptions from deep beneath the ocean's surface, the first Hawaiian islands emerged about 70 million years ago—more than 200 million years after the major continental land masses had been formed. Two thousand miles from the nearest continent, Mother Nature's fury began to carve beauty from barren rock. Untiring volcanoes spewed forth curtains of fire that cooled into stone. Severe tropical storms, some with hurricane-force winds, battered and blasted the cooling lava rock into a series of shapes. Ferocious earthquakes flattened, shattered, and reshaped the islands into precipitous valleys, jagged cliffs, and recumbent flat lands. Monstrous surf and gigantic tidal waves rearranged and polished the lands above and below the reaches of the tide.

It took millions upon millions of years to grind lava rock into the white-sand beaches of Kauai, to chisel the familiar form of Diamond Head on Oahu, to form Maui's majestic peak of Haleakala, to create the waterfalls of Molokai's northern side, to shape the reefs of Hulopoe Bay on Lanai, and to establish the lush rain forests of the Big Island. The result is an island chain like no other on the planet— a tropical dream of a landscape, rich in unique flora and fauna, surrounded by a vibrant underwater world that will haunt your memory forever.

THE ISLAND LANDSCAPES

Hawaii is more than palm trees and white sands: Nearly every type of climate and topography in the world exists in the Hawaiian islands, from sub-arctic conditions to lava-rock beaches, from verdant rain forests to arid deserts, from fertile farming areas to swamps. Each island has its own particular climate and topography.

THE BIG ISLAND   The largest island at some 4,034 square miles (and still growing), the Big Island is twice the size of all the other Hawaiian islands combined. Measuring 93 miles long by 76 miles wide, this island is home to every type of climate zone existing in Hawaii. It's not uncommon for there to be 12 feet of snow on the two largest mountain peaks, 13,796-foot Mauna Kea and 13,680-foot Mauna Loa. These mountains are the tallest in the state; what's more, when measured from their true base on the ocean floor, they reach 32,000 feet, making them the tallest mountains in the world. At 4,077 feet, Kilauea Volcano has been continuously erupting since January 3, 1983; it has added more than 600 acres of new land to the Big Island since then. Just a few miles from the barely cooled barren lava lies a pristine rain forest, and on the southern end there's an arid desert. The rest of the island contains tropical terrain; white-, black-, even green-sand beaches; windswept grasslands; and productive farming and ranching areas producing tropical fruits, macadamia nuts, coffee, and ornamental flowers.

MAUI   When two volcanoes—Mauna Kahalawai, a 5,277-foot ancient volcano in the West Maui Mountains, and Haleakala, a 10,000-foot dormant volcano—flowed together a million or so years ago, the event gave the "Valley Isle" of Maui a range of climates from arid desert to tropical rain forest. The 728-square-mile island is the only place in the world where you can drive from sea level to 10,000 feet in just 34 miles, passing through tropical beaches, sugar and pineapple plantations, rolling grassy hills, past the timber line, up to the lunar-like surface of the top of Haleakala. In addition to 33 miles of public beaches on the south and western shores, Maui is home to the arid dry lands of Kihei, the swampy bogs of the West Maui Mountains, the rain forest of Hana, and the desert of Kaupo.

KAHOOLAWE   Just seven miles southwest of Maui is Kahoolawe, the smallest of the main Hawaiian islands. This island has a very unique topography: After years of overgrazing by ranchers, then a U.S. Military bombing target from 1945 to 1994, the fairly flat island has lost most of its top soil. Kahoolawe is an arid island with some beautiful white-sand beaches. Native Hawaiians, who recently reclaimed the island from the federal government, are attempting to restore, reforest, and replant the island. Access to Kahoolawe is restricted.

LANAI   This small, kidney bean–shaped island—only 13 miles wide by 17 miles long—rises out of the ocean like the shell of a turtle, with cliffs on the west side that rise to a high point of 3,370 feet. Lanai slopes down to sea level on the east and south sides. The only town on the island, Lanai City, sits in the clouds at 1,600 feet. The high point of the island is covered with Norfolk pines and is usually shrouded in clouds. The arid beaches survive on minimal rainfall. One area in particular stands out: the Garden of the Gods, just seven miles from Lanai City. Here, oddly strewn boulders lie in the amber- and ocher-colored dirt,

---

Impressions

Midway across the North Pacific, space, time and life uniquely interlace a chain of islands named "Hawaiian." . . . These small fragments of land appear offered to the sky by water and pressed to earth by stars.

—Charles A. Lindbergh

The Hawaiian Islands

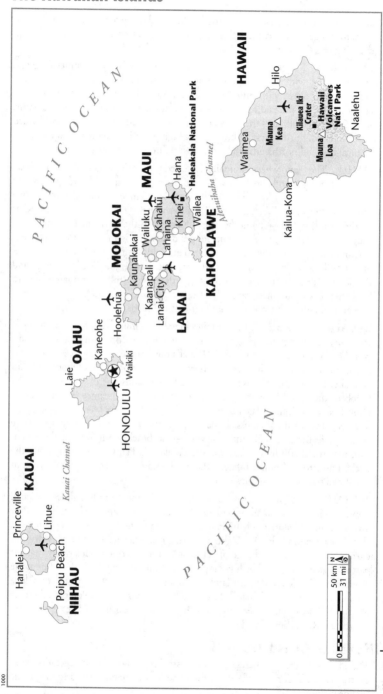

Airport ✈   Mountain △

and bizarre stone formations dot the landscape. The ancient Hawaiians formed romantic legends explaining this enigma, but modern-day scientists are still debating this mystery.

MOLOKAI   Roughly the shape of Manhattan, Molokai is 37 miles long and 10 miles wide, with a thumb protruding out of the north shore. The north shore begins on the west, with miles of white-sand beaches that fringe a desert-like landscape. At the protruding thumb—the Kalaupapa Peninsula—a fence of cliffs, some 2,000 feet tall, lines the remainder of the north side. Molokai can be divided into two areas: the dry west end, where the high point is 1,381 feet; and the rainy, tropical east and north ends where the high point is Mt. Kamakou, at 4,970 feet.

OAHU   The island where Honolulu is located is the third largest island in Hawaii (behind the Big Island and Maui). It's also the most urban, with a population of nearly 900,000. Oahu, which is 40 miles long by 26 miles wide, is defined by two mountain ranges: the Waianae Ridge (Mt. Kaala, at 4,050 feet, is the highest point on the island) in the west and the jagged Koolaus in the east, which form a backdrop for Honolulu. The mountain ranges divide the island into three different environments: The windward side of the island is lush with greenery, ferns, tropical plants, and waterfalls. On the other side, the area between the Waianae Range and the ocean is drier, with sparse vegetation, little rainfall, and an arid landscape. In between the two mountain ranges lies the central valley; it's moderate in temperature and vibrant with tropical plants, agricultural fields, and trees.

KAUAI   This compact island, 25 miles long by 33 miles wide with 137 miles of coastline, has topography ranging from the wettest spot on earth to a barren canyon. Mt. Waialeale, which stands as Kauai's high point at nearly 5,000 feet, has the distinction of being the earth's wettest spot, with more than 400 inches of rain annually. Just west of Mt. Waialeale is the barren landscape of Waimea Canyon (dubbed "the Grand Canyon of the Pacific"), the result of the once 10,000-foot-tall Olokele shield volcano, which collapsed and formed a caldera (crater) some 3,600 feet deep and 14 miles across. Peaks and craters aren't Kauai's only distinctive landscape features, though; miles of white-sand beaches rim most of the island, with majestic 2,700-foot cliffs—the spectacular Na Pali Coast—completing the circle. Lush tropical jungle inhabits the north end of the island and balmy, palm tree–lined beaches live in the south.

NIIHAU   Just 17 miles across the Kaulakahi Channel from Kauai lies the small 6-by-18-mile square island of Niihau, the "forbidden island." This is a privately owned island, inhabited only by Hawaiians living a simple life (no telephones, no electrical generating plant). It's also a working cattle ranch. Niihau is very dry and barren because it sits in the lee of Kauai; moisture-bearing clouds rarely make it past Kauai's mountains. The highest point on Niihau is only 1,281 feet, but at the center of the bleak and desolate landscape lies Lake Halalii, the largest natural lake (182 acres) in Hawaii. Niihau's white-sand beaches border emerald-colored waters offshore. You can take a day trip from Kauai to Niihau if you like; see "Water Sports and Recreation" in Chapter 16.

THE FLORA OF THE ISLANDS

The Hawaii of today radiates with sweet-smelling flowers, lush vegetation, and exotic plant life. Some of the more memorable plants and flowers found in the islands include:

AFRICAN TULIP TREES   Even at a long distance, you can see the flaming red flowers on these large trees, which can grow over 50 feet tall. Children in Hawaii love the trees because the buds hold water—they use them as water pistols.

ANGEL'S TRUMPET   This is a small tree that can grow up to 20 feet tall, with an abundance of large (up to 10 inches in diameter) pendants—white or pink flowers that resemble, well, trumpets. The Hawaiians call this *nana-honua,* which means "earth gazing." The flowers, which bloom continually from early spring to late fall, have a musky scent. However, beware: All parts of the plant are poisonous and all parts contain a strong narcotic.

ANTHURIUM   One of Hawaii's most popular cut flowers, anthuriums originally came from the tropical Americas and the Caribbean islands. There are more than 550 species, but the most popular in Hawaii are the heart-shaped flowers (red, orange, pink, white, even purple) with a tail-like spath (green, orange, pink, red, white, purple, and in combinations thereof). Look for the heart-shaped green leaves in shaded areas. Anthuriums are very prolific on the Big Island of Hawaii. These exotic plants have no scent, but will last several weeks as cut flowers.

BIRDS OF PARADISE   This native of Africa has become something of a trademark of Hawaii. They're easily recognizable by the orange and blue flowers nestled in gray-green bracts, looking somewhat like birds in flight.

BOUGAINVILLEA   Originally from Brazil and named for the French navigator Louis A. de Bougainville, these colorful, tissue-thin bracts (ranging in color from majestic purple to fiery orange) hide tiny white flowers. A good place to spot them is on the Big Island along the Queen Kaahumanu Highway stretching from the Keahole Airport to Kailua-Kona.

BROMELIADS   The pineapple plant is the best known bromeliad; native to tropical South America and the islands of the Caribbean, there are more than 1,400 species. "Bromes," as they are affectionately called, are generally spiky plants ranging in size from a few inches to several feet in diameter. They're popular not only for their unusual foliage but also for their strange and wonderful flowers, which range from colorful spikes to delicate blossoms resembling orchids. Used widely in landscaping and interior decor, especially in resort areas, bromeliads are found on every island.

COFFEE   Hawaii is the only one of the states that commercially produces coffee. Coffee is an evergreen shrub with shiny, waxy, dark-green, pointed leaves. The flower is a small, fragrant white blossom that develops into half-inch berries that turn bright red when ripe. Look for coffee at elevations above 1,500 feet on the Kona side of the Big Island (where it has been cultivated for more than 100 years), and on large coffee plantations on Kauai, Molokai, and Maui.

FRUIT TREES   Papaya   Yellow pear-shaped fruit (when ripe) found at the base of the large, scalloped-shaped leaves on a pedestal-like, non-branched tree. Papayas ripen year-round.

Breadfruit   A large tree—over 60 feet tall—with broad, sculpted, dark-green leaves. The fruit is round and about six inches or more in diameter. The ripe fruit, a staple in the Hawaiian diet, is whitish-yellow.

Banana   Edible bananas are among the oldest of the world's food crops. By the time Europeans arrived in the islands, the Hawaiians had more than 40 different types of bananas planted. Most banana plants have long green leaves hanging from the tree, with the flower giving way to fruit in clusters.

Lychee This evergreen tree, which can grow to well over 30 feet across, originated in China. Small flowers grow into panicles about a foot long in June and July. The round, red-skinned fruit appears shortly afterward.

Macadamia nut A transplant from Australia, macadamia nuts have become a commercial crop in recent decades in Hawaii; the commercially grown trees can be seen on the Big Island of Hawaii and Maui. The large trees—up to 60 feet tall—bear a hard-shelled nut encased in a leathery husk, which splits open and dries when ripe.

Mango From the Indo-Mala area comes the delicious mango, a fruit with peach-like flesh. Mango season usually begins in the spring and lasts through the summer, depending on the variety. The trees can grow to more than 100 feet tall. The tiny reddish-flowers give way to a green fruit that turns red-yellow when ripe. Some people enjoy unripe mangoes, sliced thin or in chutney as a traditional Indian preparation. The mango sap can cause a skin rash on some.

GINGERS Some of the most fragrant flowers in Hawaii are white and yellow gingers (which the Hawaiians called *'awapuhi-ke'oke'o* and *'awapuhi-melemele*). Usually found in clumps, growing four to seven feet tall, in the areas blessed by rain, these sweet-smelling, three-inch wide flowers are composed of three dainty petal-like stamen and three long, thin petals. White and yellow gingers are so prolific that many people assume they are native to Hawaii; actually, they were introduced in the 19th century from the Indo-Malaysia area. Look for yellow and white ginger from late spring to fall. If you see them on the side of the road, stop and pick a few blossoms—your car will be filled with a divine fragrance for the rest of the day. The only downside is that, once picked, they live only briefly.

Other members of the ginger family frequently seen in Hawaii (there are some 700 species) include red, shell, and torch gingers. Red ginger consists of tall, green stalks with foot-long red "flower heads." The red "petals" are actually bracts; inch-long white flowers are protected by the bracts and can be seen if you look down into the red head. Red ginger (*'awapuhi-'ula'ula* in Hawaiian), which does not share the heavenly smell of white ginger, will last a week or longer when cut. Look for red ginger from spring through late fall. Cool, wet mountain forests are ideal conditions for shell ginger; Hawaiians called them *'awapuhi-luheluhe,* which means "drooping" ginger. Natives of India and Burma, these plants, with their pearly white, clam shell–like blossoms, bloom from spring to fall.

Perhaps the most exotic gingers are the red or pink torch gingers. Cultivated in Malaysia as seasoning (the young flower shoots are used in curries), torch ginger rises directly out of the ground; the flower stalks (which are about five to eight inches in length) resemble the fire of a lighted torch. One of the few gingers that can bloom year-round, the Hawaiians called this plant *'awapuhi-ko'oko'o,* or "walking-stick" ginger.

HELICONIAS Some 80 species of the colorful heliconia family came to Hawaii from the Caribbean and Central and South America. The brightly colored bract (yellow, red, green, orange, etc.) overlap and appear to unfold like origami birds. The most obvious heliconia to spot is the lobster claw, which resembles a string of boiled crustacean pincers—the brilliant crimson bracts alternate on the stem.

Another prolific heliconia is the parrot's beak. Growing to about hip height, the parrot's beak is composed of bright-orange flower bracts with black tips, not unlike the beak of a parrot. Look for parrot's beak in the spring and summer, when they bloom in profusion.

HIBISCUS   One variety of this year-round blossom, the yellow hibiscus, is the official state flower. The four- to six-inch hibiscus flowers come in a range of colors, from lily white to lipstick red. The flowers resemble crepe paper, with stamens and pistils protruding spire-like from the center. Hibiscus hedges can grow up to 15 feet tall. Once plucked, the flowers wither quickly.

JACARANDA   Beginning about March and sometimes lasting until early May, these huge, lacy-leaved trees metamorphose into large clusters of spectacular lavender-blue sprays. The bell-shaped flowers drop quickly, leaving a majestic purple carpet beneath the tree.

NIGHT-BLOOMING CEREUS   Look along rock walls for this spectacular night-blooming cactus flower. Originally from Central America, this vine-like member of the cactus family has green scalloped edges and produces foot-long white flowers that open as darkness falls and wither as the sun rises. The plant also bears a red fruit that is edible.

ORCHIDS   In many minds, nothing says Hawaii more than orchids. The orchid family is the largest in the entire plant kingdom; orchids are found in most parts of the world. There are some species that are native to Hawaii, but they're inconspicuous in most places, so most people overlook them. The most widely grown orchid—and the major source of flowers for leis and garnish for tropical libations—are the vanda orchids. The vandas used in the commercial flower industry in Hawaii are generally lavender or white, but they grow in a rainbow of colors, shapes, and sizes. The orchids used for corsages are the large, delicate cattleya; the ones used in floral arrangements—you'll probably see them in your hotel lobby—are usually dendrobiums. When you're on the Big Island, don't pass up a chance to wander through the numerous orchid farms around Hilo.

PLUMERIA   Also known as frangipani, this sweet-smelling, five-petal flower, found in clusters on trees, is the most popular choice of lei makers. The Singapore plumeria has five creamy-white petals, with a touch of yellow in the center. Another popular variety, ruba—with flowers from soft pink to flaming red—is also used in making leis. When picking plumeria, be careful of the sap from the flower, as it is poisonous and can stain clothes.

PROTEA   Originally from South Africa, this unusual plant comes in more than 40 different varieties. Proteas are shrubs that bloom into a range of flower types. Different species of proteas range from those resembling pincushions to a species that looks just like a bouquet of feathers. Proteas are long-lasting cut flowers; once dried, they will last for years.

TARO   Around pools, streams, and in neatly planted fields, you'll see the green heart-shaped leaves of taro. Taro was a staple to ancient Hawaiians, who pounded the root into poi. Originally from Sri Lanka, taro is not only a food crop, but is also grown as an ornamental.

OTHER TREES & PLANTS   **Banyans**—among the world's largest trees—have branches that grow out and away from the trunk, forming descending roots that grow down to the ground to feed and form additional trunks, making the tree very stable during tropical storms. The banyan in the courtyard next to the old Court House in Lahaina, on Maui, is an excellent example of a spreading banyan—it covers two-thirds of an acre.

Monkey-pod trees are among Hawaii's most majestic trees; they grow more than 80 feet tall and 100 feet across. Seen near older homes and in parks, the leaves of the monkey pod drop in February and March. The wood from the tree is a favorite of wood-working artisans.

One very uncommon and unusual plant—in fact seen only on the Big Island and in the Haleakala Crater on Maui—is the **silversword.** Once a year, this rare relative of the sunflower family blooms between July and September. Resembling more of a pine cone than a sunflower, the silversword in bloom is a fountain of red-petaled, daisy-like flowers that turn silver soon after blooming.

One not so rare-and-unusual plant is **marijuana,** or *pakalolo*—"crazy weed" as the Hawaiians call it—which is grown (usually illegally cultivated) throughout the islands. You probably won't see it as you drive along the roads, but if you go hiking you may glimpse the feathery green leaves with tight clusters of buds. Despite years of police effort to eradicate the plant, the illegal industry continues. Don't be tempted to pick a few buds, as the purveyors of this nefarious industry don't take kindly to poaching.

THE FAUNA OF THE ISLANDS

When the first Marquesans arrived in Hawaii between 500 and 800 A.D., scientists say they found some 67 varieties of endemic Hawaiian birds, a third of which are now believed to be extinct, including the **koloa** (the Hawaiian duck). What's even more astonishing is what they didn't find—there were no reptiles, amphibians, mosquitoes, lice, fleas, not even a cockroach.

When the Polynesians from the Society Islands arrived in Hawaii, around 1000 A.D., they found only two endemic mammals: the **hoary bat** and the **monk seal.** The small bat, called *ope'ape'a,* must have accidentally blown to Hawaii earlier from either North or South America. It still can be seen during its early evening forays, especially around the Kilauea Crater on the Big Island of Hawaii. The Hawaiian monk seal, a relative of warm water seals previously found in the Caribbean and Mediterranean, was nearly slaughtered into extinction for its skin and oil during the 19th century. Recently these seals have experienced a minor population explosion, forcing relocation of some males from their protected homes in the inlets north of the main Hawaiian Islands. Periodically, these endangered marine mammals turn up at various beaches throughout the state. They are protected under federal law by the Marine Mammals Protection Act. If you're fortunate enough to see a monk seal, just look; don't disturb one of Hawaii's living treasures.

The first Polynesians brought a few animals from home: dogs, pigs, and chickens (all were for eating). A stowaway on board the Polynesian sailing canoes was the rat. All four animals are still found in the Hawaiian wild today.

BIRDS

Nene   Endemic to the islands, the nene is Hawaii's state bird. It is being brought back from the brink of extinction through captive breeding and by strenuous protection laws. A relative of the Canadian goose, the nene stands about two feet high and has a black head and yellow cheek, a buff neck with deep furrows, a grayish-brown body, and clawed feet. It gets its name from its two syllable, high nasal call "nay-nay." The approximately 500 nenes in existence can be seen in only three locations: at Haleakala National Park on Maui, at Mauna Kea State Park bird sanctuary, and on the slopes of Mauna Kea on the Big Island.

Pueo   The Hawaiian short-eared owl, which grows to about 12 to 17 inches in size, can be seen at dawn and dusk on Kauai, Maui, and the Big Island when the black-billed, brown-and-white bird goes hunting for rodents. Pueos were highly regarded by Hawaiians; according to legend, spotting a Pueo is a good omen.

Other birds   More species of native birds have become extinct in Hawaii in the last 200 years than anywhere else on the planet. Of the 67 native species of birds in Hawaii, 23 are extinct, 29 are endangered, and one is threatened. Even the Hawaiian crow, **'alala,** is threatened.

The **a'eo,** or Hawaiian stilt, a 16-inch-long bird with a black head, black coat, white underside, and long pink legs, can be found in protected wetlands like the Kanaha Wild Life Sanctuary on Maui (where it shares its natural habitat with the Hawaiian coot), the Kealia Pond on Maui, and the Hanalei National Wildlife Refuge on Kauai, which is also home to the Hawaiian duck. Other areas to see protected birds are the Kipuku Puaulu (Bird Park) and the Ola'a Rainforest, both in Hawaii Volcanoes National Park on the Big Island, and at Goat Island bird refuge off Oahu, where you can see wedge-tailed shearwaters nesting.

Another great birding venue is the 4,345-acre Kokee Wilderness Forest on Kauai. Various native birds that have been spotted include some of the 22 species of the native honey creepers whose songs fill the forest. Frequently seen are the **'apapane** (a red bird with black wings and a curved black bill), the **'i'iwi** (another red bird with black wings but with orange legs and salmon-colored bill), the **'amakihi** (a plain olive-green bird with a long straight bill), and the **'anianiau** (a tiny yellow bird with a thin, curved bill). Also seen in the forest is the **'elepaio,** a small, gray flycatcher with an orange breast and an erect tail. A curious fellow, the 'elepaio comes out to investigate any unusual whistles. The most common native bird at Kokee—and the most easily seen—is the **moa,** or red jungle fowl, a chicken that was brought to Hawaii by the Polynesians.

To get a good glimpse of the seabirds that frequent Hawaii, drive to Kilauea Point on Kauai's north shore. Here, you can easily spot **red- and white-footed boobies, wedge-tailed shearwaters, frigate birds, red-tailed tropic birds,** and the **Laysan albatross.**

OTHER FAUNA

Geckos   These harmless, soft-skinned, insect-eating lizards come equipped with suction pads on their feet that enable them to climb walls and windows, so that they can reach tasty insects like mosquitoes and cockroaches. You'll see them on windows outside a lighted room at night, or hear their cheerful chirp.

Mongooses   The mongoose is a mistake. It was brought here in the 19th century to counteract the ever-growing rat problem. But rats are nocturnal creatures, sleeping during the day and wandering out at night. Mongooses, however, are day creatures. Instead of getting rid of the rat problem, the mongooses eat bird eggs, enhancing the deterioration of the native bird population in Hawaii.

Snakes   Hawaii has but one tiny earthworm-like snake. Strict measures are taken to keep other snakes out of Hawaii. On the island of Guam, the brown-tree snake has obliterated most of the bird population. Officials in Hawaii are well aware of this danger, and are committed to preventing snakes from entering the state.

SEALIFE

Hawaii has an extraordinarily unique underwater world. Approximately 680 species of fish are known to inhabit the waters around the Hawaiian islands. Of those, approximately 450 species stay close to the reef and inshore areas.

CORAL The reefs surrounding Hawaii are made up of various coral and algae. The living coral grow through sunlight that feeds a specialized algae, called zooxanthellae, which in turn allows the development of the coral's calcareous skeleton. It takes thousands of years for reefs to develop. The reef attracts and supports fish and crustaceans, which use the reef for food, habitat, mating, and raising their young. Mother Nature can cause the destruction of the reef with a strong storm or large waves, but humans—through a seemingly unimportant act such as touching the coral—has proven even more destructive to the fragile reefs.

The coral most frequently seen in Hawaii are hard, rock-like formations named for their familiar shapes: antler, cauliflower, finger, plate, and razor coral. Wire coral looks just like its name—a randomly bent wire growing straight out of the reef. Some coral appear soft, such as tube coral; it can be found in the ceilings of caves. Black coral, which resemble winter-bare trees or shrubs, are found at depths of over 100 feet.

REEF FISH Of the approximately 450 reef fish, about 27% are native to Hawaii and found no where else on the planet. This may seem surprising for a string of isolated islands, 2,000 miles from the nearest land mass. But over the millions of years of gestation of the Hawaiian islands, as they were born from the erupting volcanoes, ocean currents—mainly from the Indo-Malay Pacific region—carried the larvae of thousands of marine animals and plants to Hawaii's reef. Of those, approximately 100 species not only adapted, but thrived. Some species are much bigger and more plentiful than their Pacific cousins; many developed unique characteristics. Some, like the lemon or milletseed butterfly fish, are not only particular to Hawaii but also unique within their larger, worldwide family in their specialized schooling and feeding behaviors. Another surprising thing about Hawaii endemics is how common some of the native fish are: You can see the saddleback wrasse, for instance, on virtually any snorkeling excursion or dive in Hawaiian waters.

Some of the reef fish you might spot while you're underwater are:

Angel Fish Often mistaken for butterfly fish, angel fish can be distinguished by the spine, located low on the gill plate. Angel fish are very shy; several species live in colonies close to coral for protection.

Blennys Small, elongated fish, blennys range from 2 to 10 inches long, with the majority in the 3-to-4-inch range. Blennys are so small that they can live in tide pools; you might have a hard time spotting one.

Butterfly Fish Some of the most colorful of the reef fish, butterfly fish are usually seen in pairs (scientists believe they mate for life) and appear to spend most of their day feeding. There are 22 species of butterfly fish, of which three (blue-stripe, lemon or milletseed, and multiband or pebbled butterfly fish) are endemic. Most butterfly fish have a dark band through the eye and a spot near the tail resembling an eye, meant to confuse their predators (the moray eel loves to lunch on butterfly fish).

Eels Moray and conger eels are the common eels seen in Hawaii. Morays are usually docile unless provoked, or if there is food or an injured fish around.

Unfortunately, some morays have been fed by divers and—being intelligent creatures—associate divers with food; thus, they can become aggressive. But most morays like to keep to themselves, hidden in their hole or crevice. While morays may look menacing, conger eels look downright happy, with big lips and pectoral fins (situated so that they look like big ears) which give them the appearance of a perpetual smiling face. Conger eels have crushing teeth so they can feed on crustaceans; in fact, since they're sloppy eaters, they usually live with shrimp and crabs who feed off the crumbs they leave.

Parrot Fish   One of the largest and most colorful of the reef fish, parrot fish can grow as large as 40 inches long. Parrot fish are easy to spot—their front teeth are fused together, protruding like buck teeth and resembling a parrot's beak. These unique teeth allow the parrot fish to feed by scraping algae from rocks and coral. The rocks and coral pass through the parrot fish's system, resulting in fine sand. In fact, most of the sand found in Hawaii is parrot fish waste; one large parrot fish can produce a ton of sand a year. Hawaiian native parrot fish species include yellowbar, regal, and spectacled.

Scorpion Fish   This is a family of what scientists call "ambush predators." These fish hide under camouflaged exteriors and ambush their prey when they come along. Several sport a venomous dorsal spine. These fish don't have a gas bladder, so when they stop swimming, they sink—that's why you usually find them "resting" on ledges and on the bottom. Although they're not aggressive, an inattentive snorkeler or diver could feel the effects of those venomous spines—so be very careful where you put your hands and feet in the water.

Surgeon Fish   Sometimes called tang, the surgeon fish get their name from the scalpel-like spines located on each side of their bodies near the base of their tails. Some surgeon fish have a rigid spine; others have the ability to fold their spine against their body until it's needed for defense purposes. Some surgeon fish, like the brightly colored yellow tang, are boldly colored. Others are adorned in more conservative shades of gray, brown, or black. The only endemic surgeon fish—and the most abundant in Hawaiian waters—is the convict tang, (*manini* in Hawaiian), a pale white fish with vertical black stripes (like a convict's uniform).

Wrasses   This is a very diverse family of fish, ranging in size from 2 to 15 inches. Several wrasses are brilliantly colored and change their colors through aging and sexual dimorphism (sex changing). Wrasses have the unique ability to change gender from female (when young) to male with maturation. There are several wrasses that are endemic to Hawaii: the Hawaiian cleaner, shortnose, belted, and gray (or old woman).

GAME FISH   Fishing lovers have a huge variety to choose from in Hawaii, from pan-sized snapper to nearly 1-ton marlin. Hawaii is known around the globe as *the* place for big game fish—marlin, swordfish, and tuna–but its waters are also great for catching other offshore fish (like mahimahi, rainbow runner, and wahoo), coastal fish (barracuda, scad), bottom fish (snappers, sea bass, and amberjack), and inshore fish (trevally, bonefish, and others), as well as freshwater fish (bass, catfish, trout, bluegill, and oscar).

Billfish are caught year-round. There are six different kinds of billfish found in the offshore waters around the islands: Pacific blue marlin, black marlin, sailfish, broadbill swordfish, striped marlin, and shortbill spearfish. Hawaii billfish range in size from the 20-pound shortbill spearfish and striped marlin to an 1,805-pound

Pacific blue marlin, the largest marlin ever caught on rod and reel anywhere in the world. **Tuna** ranges in size from small (a pound or less) mackerel tuna used as bait (Hawaiians call them *oioi*), to 250-pound yellowfin ahi tuna. Other species of tuna found in Hawaii are bigeye, albacore, kawakawa, and skipjack.

Some of the best eating fish are also found in offshore waters: **mahimahi** (also known as dolphin fish or dorado) in the 20- to 70-pound range, **rainbow runner** (*kamanu*) from 15 to 30 pounds, and **wahoo** (*ono*) from 15 to 80 pounds. Shoreline fishermen are always on the lookout for **trevally** (the state record for giant trevally is 191 pounds), **bonefish, ladyfish, threadfin, leatherfish, and goatfish.** Bottom fishermen pursue a range of **snappers**—red, pink, gray, and others—as well as **sea bass** (the state record is a whopping 563 pounds) and **amberjack,** which weigh up to 100 pounds.

Reservoirs on Oahu and Kauai are home to Hawaii's many freshwater fish: **bass** (large, smallmouth, and peacock), **catfish** (channel and Chinese), **rainbow trout, bluegill sunfish, pungee,** and **oscar.** The state record for freshwater fish is the 43-pound, 13-ounce channel catfish caught in Lake Wilson on Oahu.

WHALES   Humpback Whales   The most popular visitors to Hawaii come every year in the winter, around November, and stay until the springtime (April or so) when they return to their summer home in Alaska. Humpback whales—some as big as a city bus and weighing many tons—migrate to the warm, protected Hawaiian waters in the winter to mate and calve. You can take whale-watching cruises on every island that will let you observe these magnificent leviathans close up, or you can spot their signature spouts of water from shore as they expel water in the distance. Humpbacks grow to up to 45 feet long, so when they breach (propel their entire body out of the water) or even wave a fluke, you can see it for miles.

Other whales   Humpbacks are among the biggest whales found in Hawaiian waters, but other whales—like pilot, sperm, false killer, melon-headed, pygmy killer, and beaked whales—can be seen year-round, especially in the calm waters off the Big Island's Kona Coast. These whales usually travel in pods of 20 to 40 animals and are very social, interacting with each other on the surface.

SHARKS   Yes, Virginia there are sharks in Hawaii, but more than likely you won't see a shark unless you specifically go looking for one. About 40 different species of sharks inhabit the waters surrounding Hawaii; they range from the totally harmless whale shark—at 60 feet, the world's largest fish—which has no teeth and is so docile that it frequently lets divers ride on its back, to the not-so-docile, infamous—and extremely uncommon—great white shark. The ancient Hawaiians had great respect for sharks and believed that some sharks were reincarnated relatives who had returned to assist them. The most common sharks seen in Hawaii are white-tip reef sharks, gray reef sharks (about five feet long), and blacktip reef sharks (about six feet long). Since records have been kept, starting in 1779, there have been only about 100 shark attacks in Hawaii, of which 40% have been fatal. The biggest number of attacks occurred after someone fell into the ocean from the shore or from a boat. In these cases, the sharks probably attacked after the person was dead.

General rules for avoiding sharks are: Don't swim at sunrise, sunset, or where the water is murky due to stream runoff—sharks may mistake you for one of their usual meals. And don't swim where there are bloody fish in the water (sharks become aggressive around blood).

HAWAII'S ECOSYSTEM PROBLEMS

Officials at Hawaii Volcanoes National Park on the Big Island saw a potential problem a few decades ago with people taking a few rocks home with them as "souvenirs." To prevent this problem from escalating, the park rangers "created" a legend that the fiery volcano goddess, Pele, did not like people taking anything (rocks, chunks of lava) from her home, and bad luck would befall anyone disobeying her wishes. There used to be a display case in the park's visitor center filled with letters from people who had taken rocks from the volcano, relating stories of all the bad luck that followed. Most of the letters begged Pele's forgiveness and instructed the rangers to please return the rock to the exact location that was its original home.

Unfortunately, Hawaii's other ecosystem problems can't be handled as easily.

MARINE LIFE Hawaii's beautiful and abundant marine life has attracted so many visitors that they threaten to overwhelm it. A great example of this over-enthusiasm is Oahu's Hanauma Bay. A marine preserve, thousands of people flock to this beautiful bay, which features calm, protected swimming and snorkeling areas loaded with tropical reef fish. It was such a perfect spot that too many people flocked here, forcing government officials to limit the number of people which can enter the bay at any one time. Commercial tour operators have been restricted entirely in an effort to balance the people-to-fish ratio.

Another marine life conservation area that suffers from overuse is Molokini, a small crater off the coast of Maui. In the 1970s, residents made the area a conservation district in order to protect the unique aquarium-like atmosphere of the waters inside the arms of the crater. Unfortunately, once it was protected, everyone wanted to go there just to see what was worth special protection. Twenty years ago, one or two small, six-passenger boats made the trip once a day to Molokini; today, it is not uncommon to sight 20 or more boats, each carrying 20 to 49 passengers, moored inside the tiny crater. One tour operator has claimed that, on some days, it's so crowded that you can actually see a slick of suntan oil floating on the surface of the water.

People who fall in love with the colorful tropical fish and want to see them all the time back home are also thought to be impacting the health of Hawaii's reefs. The growth in home, office, and decor aquariums has risen dramatically in the last 20 years. As a result, more and more reef fish collectors are taking a growing number of reef fish from Hawaiian waters.

The reefs themselves have faced increasing impacts over the years. Runoff of soil and chemicals from construction, agriculture, erosion, and even heavy storms can blanket and choke a reef, which needs sunlight to survive. In addition, the intrusion of foreign elements—like breaks in sewage lines—can cause problems to Hawaii's reef. Human contact with the reef can also upset the ecosystem. Coral, the basis of the reef system, is very fragile; snorkelers and divers grabbing on to coral can break off pieces which took decades to form. Feeding fish can also upset the balance of the ecosystem (not to mention upsetting the digestive systems of the fish). One glass-bottom boat operator reported that they fed an eel for years, considering it their "pet" eel. One day the eel decided that he wanted more than just the food being offered and bit the diver's fingers. Divers and snorkelers report that in areas where the fish are fed, the fish have become more aggressive; clouds of certain reef fish—normally shy—surround divers, demanding food.

FLORA One of Hawaii's most fragile environments is the rain forest. Any intrusion—from a hiker carrying seeds in on their shoes to the rooting of wild boars—can upset the delicate balance in these complete ecosystems. In recent years, development has moved closer and closer to the rain forest. On the Big Island of Hawaii, people have protested the invasion of bulldozers and the drilling of geothermal wells in the Wao Kele O Puna rain forest for years, claiming that the damage done is irreparable.

FAUNA The biggest impact on the fauna in Hawaii is the decimation of native birds by feral animals, which have destroyed the bird's habitats, and by mongooses that have eaten the birds' eggs and young. Government officials are vigilant about snakes because of the potential damage tree snakes can do to the remaining birdlife.

VOG The volcanic haze—caused by gases released by the continuous eruption of the volcano on the flank of Kilauea, on the Big Island, and the smoke from the fires set by the lava—has been dubbed "vog." The hazy air, which looks like smog from urban pollution, limits viewing from scenic vistas and plays havoc with photographers trying to get clear panoramic photographs. Some people claim that the vog has even caused bronchial ailments.

CULTURE Virtually since the arrival of the first Europeans, there has been a controversy over balancing the preservation of history and indigenous cultures and lifestyles with economic development. The question of what should be preserved—and in what fashion—is continually debated in Hawaii's rapidly growing economy. Some factions argue that the continuously developing tourism economy will one day destroy the very thing that visitors come to Hawaii to see; another sector argues that Hawaii's cost of living is so high that new development and industries are needed so the residents can earn a living.

4 The Arts & Crafts of the Islands

By Lisa Legarde

Art has always been integral to Hawaiian life. The art of early Hawaii often took forms that were useful in everyday life. Kapa cloth was used as bedding and clothing. Beautiful featherwork capes, cloaks, helmets, and leis were worn by the Hawaiian ali'i to indicate rank; and beautifully carved wood bowls were designed specifically to hold poi, a staple of daily life. Ancient Hawaiians took great pride in their work and elevated its execution to an art form. Unfortunately, some of the traditional arts and crafts of Hawaii have died out. This is due, in part, to the commercialization of the islands, but also because the natural supply of craft materials has diminished.

Today, native Hawaiian art is highly prized, and every effort is being made to revitalize traditional arts and crafts. Many hotels sponsor lei-making classes, and some even hold quilt-making lectures and demonstrations. There are also arts-and-crafts shows celebrating local artisans.

Below you will find descriptions of a variety of traditional Hawaiian arts and crafts that will, I hope, lead you to a greater understanding of Hawaiian culture.

KAPA (TAPA) CLOTH Before woven fabrics made their way from Europe and the U.S. mainland to Hawaii, the women of Hawaii made cloth from the bark of a variety of trees and plants. The kapa-making process was long and somewhat tedious and it was so much a part of daily life that many households reserved a separate hut in which to work. Each day, village men would go out searching for wauke, mamake, ma'aloa, or poulu plants, the branches of which they would cut and take back to their wives. The women would peel the bark from the branches (not in strips, but whole), and then set the inner bark in a stream to soak until it reached the desired softness. After the bark had soaked long enough, the women would beat it on a log (*kua*) with a round club (*hohoa*) until it was flat and paper thin. The soaking and flattening process might take up to four days. The last step was to set the kapa in the sun to dry. Mamake bark was preferred above all others because its cloth was the most durable, but rather than being soaked first, mamake was steamed in an oven with a *pala'a* (a fern that gave out a dark red dye in the cooking process). After the steaming process was finished, mamake was soaked and beaten just like the other types of bark.

Most Hawaiian women dyed their kapa using a variety of different plants. The mao plant would stain the cloth green, while the hoolei gave it a yellow tint. It was also customary for women to print patterns on the cloth. Almost every design was different and as individual as the artists who created it.

HAWAIIAN QUILTS   Not so ancient as the art of kapa, but equally as beautiful, the art of quilting has been in existence in Hawaii since the mid-19th century. In fact, the first quilting bee held in the Hawaiian islands took place on April 3, 1820. The basic techniques were introduced to the women of the islands by missionary women from New England; however, the appliqués and stitch patterns you'll see on original Hawaiian quilts are authentically Hawaiian. Early quilt patterns were similar to designs found on kapa cloth, and very often women were inspired to create original designs by dreams or major events in their lives.

Usually the quilt consisted of a single-colored appliqué on a white background. The material to be used for the appliqué could be cut freehand, or with a paper pattern. The paper pattern was often made of kapa. Usually the appliqué material would be folded four or eight times before it was cut so the pattern would be uniform in all sections of the quilt. Most often the designs were inspired by the leaves of various trees and plants, like the fig or breadfruit trees and ferns. Outlines of pineapples, the octopus, and the sea turtle were also popular design elements.

Many of the patterns were unique to a particular artist, and most women knew the designs of their fellow quilters. If a woman invented a particular design, it would forever be associated with her; other women were not allowed to copy her design without crediting her. However, if a pattern was not carefully guarded before a quilt was completed, it could be (and was often) stolen by someone else who might try to claim it as her own.

While the patterns and design elements of the appliqué were important, so were the stitches around the appliqué, because the stitching is actually what makes a quilt a quilt. Traditional New England–style stitch patterns used parallel lines and diagonals; Hawaiian women incorporated these patterns into their work, but later they began inventing their own freehand stitch patterns that are much more elaborate and, in many ways, more beautiful than what we recognize as traditional stitching. This technique is referred to as "quilting following the pattern." The stitches flowed in free-form lines around the appliqué, in most cases following the pattern of the appliqué, but I've seen quilts with free-form stitching around the appliqué and cross-hatching superimposed on the appliqué. You can view antique quilts like the ones described above at some of the island's hotels.

FEATHERWORK Unfortunately, little is known about the origins of Hawaiian featherwork because its history has been lost over the years, but David Malo recorded that "the feathers of birds were the most valued possessions of the ancient Hawaiians," and Captain Cook, along with members of his crew, reported and marveled at Hawaiian featherwork in their writings. Some of the ali'i of Kauai who greeted Cook and his shipmates went aboard the ship wearing feather cloaks, leis, and helmets, and presented Cook with half a dozen feather cloaks. He was awed by the brilliant colors and the intricacies of the work.

Because feathers were so sacred, a guild of professional bird catchers was established. They caught the birds by enticing them onto a branch or stick covered with a sticky substance, trapping them, or throwing stones at them until they fell to the ground. The most valued feathers were yellow, particularly those found under the tail and wings of the mamo. Red feathers, especially those of the i'iwi, were next in order of importance, and black feathers were the least well liked. Many of the birds with the most prized plumage have fallen into extinction.

Lei Hulu Adornments known as lei hulu were worn on the heads of Hawaiian women, as well as around the neck, and were constructed in several ways. Some are completely cylindrical (or *pauku*), like the more common flower leis you'll see today. Some pauku might have been made from the light yellow feathers of the o'o while others were made of green, red, black, and yellow feathers (some in a spiral pattern, others in blocks of color). Another style lei was known as *kamoe*. The feathers on these leis were laid flat and attached directly to the lei backing. Leis made solely of yellow feathers were the most highly prized, and any other leis made only of one color were more valuable than those made of two or more. The lei hulu *manu* was worn by women of the ali'i class to distinguish them from the Hawaiian commoners, and later, men wore the leis as hatbands.

Kahili These plumed staffs of state resemble giant bottle brushes. Everywhere the king went the kahili (and kahili bearer) followed. In the evenings when the king slept the kahili were used to keep flies from settling on his highness's face. One report insists that rather than flies, the kahili were used to chase off bad *mana* (the Hawaiian equivalent of karma). No Hawaiians other than the ali'i could carry kahili. Because of their association with Hawaiian royalty, kahili were made with great care and came in an endless variety of shapes and sizes. The feathers from which they were formed were usually the tail and wing feathers of larger birds, such as the nene, the frigate bird, or even ducks and chickens. Handles were frequently made of tortoise shell or whale bone and the staffs might reach 10 to 25 feet in height.

Head Gear *Manihole,* or feathered head gear, were also mentioned in the journals of Captain Cook, who described these ornate head coverings as ". . . caps . . . made so as to fit very close to the head with a semicircular protuberance on the crown exactly like the helmets of old." He also comments that "the Groundwork of the Cap is Basket Work, made in a form to fit the Head, to which the

You'll never know Hawaii 'til you've felt the foaming surf about your knees; 'til you've plunged into the breakers with a cry of pagan glee.
                                                                                    —Don Blanding, 1928

Feathers are secured." Hawaiians believed the head to be the most important part of the body, and feathers were thought to have the power to ward off evil.

There were several different types of manihole, including the crescent-crested, low-crested, wide-crested, hair helmets, and ornamented helmets. No one really knows the significance of each style, but it is safe to assume that all who wore them had some connection to Hawaiian royalty. Most of the helmets that survive today have lost the majority of their feathers and what you'll see is the basket work described by Captain Cook. There are a few, however, that have been well preserved over the years—for example, the helmet of Kaumuali'i, the last king of Kauai, covered with red feathers and trimmed (on the crest) with feathers of an exquisite gold, which can be seen at the Bishop Museum on Oahu.

Capes Perhaps the most spectacular and beautiful pieces of Hawaiian featherwork are the capes and cloaks once worn by Hawaiian royalty. They are said to have been worn as a means of identification in battle. Each high chief or king had his own design. We do know from Cook's writings, however, that wartime was not the only time these capes were worn.

The majority of the capes (which reached to the feet of the wearer) were made with a background coloring of red or yellow, and design elements, like circles, triangles, or crescent shapes were most frequently made of the opposite color (if the background were red, the design elements would be yellow, and vice versa). Sometimes black feathers were introduced into the pattern as well. Some people believe that the geometrical designs were representational of gods or birds, but in truth, not much is known about the patterns. Unless you visit the Bishop Museum, you probably won't get a look at a feather cape, but many bookstores carry books about Hawaiian featherwork.

LEIS Of all ancient Hawaiian art forms, traditional lei making is the only one that has survived intact throughout the ages and is still being practiced island-wide today. Leis of all shapes and sorts have special significance. They are presented at comings and goings of all varieties—births, deaths, weddings, graduations, departures to another land, as well as homecomings, and they represent and encompass the true spirit of aloha. During your trip you'll have no trouble finding flower and ti leaf leis, and if you're lucky you'll come across an even rarer one.

Perishable Leis There are all sorts of perishable leis being made in the islands today, the most common of which is the flower lei. The manner in which the flowers are strung depends entirely on the shape and size of the flowers being used. Leis made with fragrant plumeria blossoms are particularly popular with tourists. Easily strung, these flowers can be found almost everywhere on the island. My personal favorite flower lei is made with white ginger, which has a light but distinctive fragrance. If someone presents you with a white ginger lei you should be deeply flattered, for it is one of Hawaii's most special leis. Gardenia leis are also very fragrant, but are less common. Experienced Hawaiian lei makers can construct a lei with virtually any flower of any shape or size.

Leis can also be made of ferns and garlands of almost any variety. Ti leaf leis can be extraordinarily beautiful because the ti leaf is pliable and easily manipulated. Ancient Hawaiians believed that the ti plant had special healing powers, and the kahunas of Hawaii often used it to ward off evil spirits. If you buy a ti leaf lei to wear home, don't throw it out or hang it to dry when you get there—put it in the freezer, where it will keep its shape and color until you feel like wearing it again.

Nonperishable Leis   While flower and ti leaf leis are most often purchased by visitors, there are several types of nonperishable leis that you can buy and keep forever. Some of the most popular are *lei pupu* (shell leis) and *lei hua* (seed leis).

Shell leis can be both simple and extremely intricate. Early Hawaiians gathered shells from the beaches of Kauai and Niihau, and either filed them down to make holes for stringing or strung them using the shells' natural holes. The first lei pupu were typically made up of several separate strands, each holding up to 200 shells. Other lei pupu were fashioned out of shells that are flat, like buttons, after having been worn down by the constant wave action of the ocean. Ancient Hawaiians collected the shell fragments that had washed ashore, punched holes in them, and strung them together. Many of today's shell leis are made much the same way as they were in ancient Hawaii. Lei pupu might be sold for a few dollars or a few thousand dollars, depending on the quality and rarity of the shells.

The most common seed lei is the kukui nut lei. I say common, but even as I write, these leis are becoming less and less easy to find. This is largely because the process of polishing the kukui nuts is so difficult and time-consuming that it is simply not cost-effective. The fruit of the candlenut tree, the kukui nut might be "blond," brown, or black. In old Hawaii, the leis made of black kukui nuts were the most coveted. The nuts would be gathered by lei makers after they'd fallen from the tree, and then sorted according to shape and size. In old Hawaii, all the polishing was done by hand. The outer layer of the shells in their raw form has a cloudy, whitish layer that must be removed. Then the grooves, which give the nut a walnut-like quality, have to be filed down, and finally, the shell is polished to a high shine. Ancient Hawaiians used natural files, such as sea urchin spines, and natural sandpapers like shark skin. The final polish was done with a pumice stone. Old-time kukui nut lei makers had an interesting way of extracting the nutmeat from the shell—they would make a hole in the top and bottom of the nut and then they would bury it until the nutmeat was eaten out by insects. Today there are polishing machines available, but most kukui nut lei makers believe it's best to polish the shells by hand. Kukui leis are moderately expensive, depending on where you buy them, but they are uniquely Hawaiian, and they're quite beautiful.

WOOD CARVING   For ancient Hawaiians, wood carving was a way of life. Primitive wood sculptures have been found all over the islands, and it seems that they were used for religious as well as practical purposes. Many religious figures were sculpted for the dedication of a heiau, or for a religious ceremony, and are thought to have been representational of particular Hawaiian gods. Ancient Hawaiians also carved food vessels (such as poi bowls), canoes, and furnishings out of wood. Some of the woods used by ancient woodcraftsmen included koa and ohi'a, both of which can be found in the islands today.

Koa wood is especially favored by current-day artists, but it is becoming more and more difficult to find. As a result, koa pieces you find in gift shops, from bracelets to bowls, are fairly costly. You'll probably end up buying a koa piece anyway—the wood is so rich and light that you'll have a difficult time passing it by. A word of advice: Be wary of carved figurines. Though they might appear to be Hawaiian, chances are they weren't even made in Hawaii.

5 The Cuisine of the Islands

The food of Hawaii, like its people, reflects a cultural diversity—a lot of American, quite a bit of Japanese, some Chinese, a smattering of Hawaiian, Korean, Filipino, and you-name-it thrown in for good measure. You quickly get used to the facts that a delicatessen can be Japanese and that saimin (a noodle soup with a seaweed base) is just as popular as a hamburger and is often served at the same counter.

You soon learn that *mahimahi* is Hawaiian for dolphin, a pleasant-tasting fish—not the intelligent mammal of the same name. You'll be introduced to poi (crushed taro root), the staff of life of the early Hawaiians, at your very first luau—you may develop a liking for this purple-gray goo that's one of the most nutritious foods known, so high in vitamin B and calcium that it's fed to babies and invalids. Just ignore the old joke that it tastes like library paste; the Hawaiians, and quite a few malihinis, think it's delicious.

Hawaii's fruits are among the islands special glories. Pineapple, while not exactly invented here, might just as well have been. It's well priced in the markets, served everywhere, and as good as you'd imagine. If you hit the mango season in summer, when the local trees are bursting with this succulent fruit, you're in for a great treat. Guavas, coconuts, and papayas (one of the most common breakfast foods) are all superb, as are guava juice and passion-fruit juice, which you'll often see listed under its Hawaiian name, *lilikoi*. In the supermarkets, you'll see a very popular drink called POG—that's short for passion-fruit orange, and guava juice—very popular and very good. Macadamia-nut pancakes, as well as coconut ice cream and syrup, are special treats that taste better in Hawaii than anywhere else. We should warn you coffee addicts right here and now—the kind of coffee you'll get everywhere is Kona coffee, grown on the Big Island, and it's so good that you may find yourself drinking innumerable cups a day.

Don't miss the chance to try Hawaii's game fish, caught fresh in local waters. You'll see ahi (a kind of tuna and a personal favorite), aku (another tuna), marlin, ulua, opakapaka, rock cod, and a special island delicacy, ono, on island menus. That word has, slipped into local parlance as meaning "delicious"—or even "great"—as in "ono ono."

LUAUS You'll probably first experience Hawaiian food at a luau, and then you'll find the same dishes in Hawaiian restaurants. You're already on speaking terms with poi. Other basic dishes are kalua pig (pig steamed in an underground oven, or *imu*), laulau (ti leaves stuffed with pork, salt fish, bananas, sweet potatoes, and taro shoots, and steamed), chicken luau (chicken cooked with coconut milk and taro or spinach leaves), sweet potatoes, pipikaula (jerked beef), and lomilomi salmon. The last is a triumph of linguistics: Lomilomi means massage; this is salmon massaged with tomatoes and chopped onions, then marinated. Haupia (coconut pudding) and coconut cake are the usual desserts, along with fresh pineapple.

Most luaus are serve-yourself buffet affairs; food is usually eaten from paper plates, with plastic cutlery. The correct way to eat poi, by the way, is to dip one or two fingers in it (in the old days, you could actually order "one-" or "two-finger" poi), scoop it up quickly, and attack. But nobody expects that of a malihini.

LOCAL FOOD   Local food does not really have deep roots in Hawaiian culture. What most people refer to as local food—and it's eaten in "plate lunches" popular everywhere in Hawaii—consists of dishes such as beef stew, teriyaki pork, breaded mahimahi, and the like; much of it is deep-fried. This is invariably accompanied by *two* carbohydrates, usually rice and a macaroni, or potato-macaroni salad. A very popular local dish is called the loco moco—that's a hamburger patty over rice topped with a fried egg and brown gravy. Don't go local if you're counting calories or looking for "heart-healthy" food!

HAWAII REGIONAL CUISINE   A style called Hawaii Regional, or sometimes Pacific Rim, cuisine is served more and more in better restaurants. This cuisine marries the remarkable fresh local produce of the islands, the freshly caught fish, the locally grown beef, and the like, with the best of European and Asian cooking traditions. Prime examples: Avalon Restaurant on Maui, A Pacific Café on Kauai, and Roy's in Honolulu, Maui, and Kauai.

KOREAN CUISINE   The islands contain quite a few Korean restaurants, and they're good to know about for the budget traveler because of their modest prices and delicious food. Although Koreans make up a small part of the population, their culinary tradition has left its mark, especially in the ubiquitous kimchee—pickled cabbage seasoned with red-hot peppers. Korean cuisine has much more to offer, including barbecued meat and chicken, hearty noodle soups, tasty meat dumplings, fish filets sautéed in spicy sauces, and daintily shredded vegetables. Some dishes are served with fiery hot sauces.

SHAVE ICE   A unique treat that's loved by just about all islanders is a phenomenon called shave ice. That's not "shaved" ice, or a snow cone, or a slush. You can have a "plain" shave ice—that's just the incredibly fine ice particles bathed in syrup—and there are all kinds of syrups. Strawberry is the most popular, but there's also vanilla, guava, lemon, cherry, orange, root beer, coconut, and combinations of the above. Or you can have ice cream, azuki beans (a sweet Japanese bean), or both on the bottom. Shave ice is served in a cone-shaped paper cup, with both a straw and a spoon.

BEVERAGES   Generally, you need not worry about drinking tap water, except in some areas on Maui and upcountry on the Big Island. Because of acid rain pollution, it's best to drink bottled spring water here. Soft drinks and mineral waters are the same as you find back home. There's a potent local liquor called okolehao, distilled from the ti root. Wine is now produced on Maui: Tedeschi Vineyards offers a pineapple wine, a champagne, a blush, and a red table wine in the Beaujolais Nouveau tradition. Wine and liquor are sold in supermarkets.

A GLOSSARY OF ISLAND FOODS

Here are some helpful definitions:

Adobo   Filipino dish made with pork or chicken.

Bento   Japanese box lunch.

Chicken luau   Chicken cooked with coconut milk and taro or spinach leaves.

Crackseed   Chinese confection that's a cross between preserved fruit and candy.

Guava   Slightly tart tree fruit made into jams and juice. They grow wild on the mountainsides, and are under cultivation on Kauai, at Guava Kai Plantation.

Haupia Coconut pudding, the traditional luau dessert.

Kimchee Korea's contribution, pickled cabbage and red-hot peppers.

Kona coffee Grown on the Big Island on many small family plantations.

Laulau Ti leaves stuffed with pork, salt fish, bananas, sweet potatoes, and taro shoots, then steamed.

Lilikoi Passion fruit (named after the passion of Christ). A tart fruit that's turned into wonderful juice or sherbet.

Macadamia nuts Delicious nuts grown on Big Island plantations. Chocolate-covered macadamias are one of the most delicious gifts you can bring home.

Malasadas Deep-fried Portuguese doughnuts, served hot and sugared. They have no holes.

Manapua Steamed dumplings filled with pork, meat, or bean paste. The Chinese call them dim sum.

Maui onions Mild, sweet onions, sometimes known as Kula onions.

Papayas Grown on the Big Island, available everywhere: one of the favorite breakfast fruits in the islands. Highly nutritious and rich in vitamin C.

Pipikaula Jerked beef.

Poha Wild berry, used in jams.

Poi The pasty, purple-gray staple starch of the Hawaiian diet, made from cooked and mashed taro root. Very digestible and nutritious.

Portuguese bean soup Savory soup made from Portuguese sausages, beans, and vegetables; a veritable meal in a bowl.

Portuguese sweet bread Very soft bread made with eggs, wonderful as french toast.

Saimin Most popular soup in the islands, a thin noodle broth topped with bits of fish, shrimp, chicken, or pork, and vegetables.

Sashimi Raw fish, a favorite Japanese delicacy.

Sushi Vinegared rice topped with either raw fish or other toppings, and then rolled in seaweed, another great Japanese delicacy.

3

Planning a Trip to the Islands

In this chapter, the where, when, and how of your trip to Hawaii is discussed—the advance planning that gets your trip together and takes it on the road.

After deciding where to go, most people have two fundamental questions: What will it cost? and How do I get there? This chapter not only helps answer those questions, but addresses such important issues as when to travel, whether to take a tour, what kind of health precautions to take, what kind of insurance to carry, where to obtain additional information, and much more.

WHICH ISLANDS TO VISIT

Too many tourists start and end their Hawaiian holidays in Honolulu on Oahu—and think they've seen Hawaii. Yes—and no. They've seen the largest city and the principal resort area, but far more awaits: a Hawaii at once more gentle and more savage, where the old gods still have powers. To see the desolate moonscapes of the volcanoes and Hawaiian cowboys riding the range, to see beaches so remote and pristine as to make Waikiki seem like Times Square, and to visit South Seas villages just coming into the modern age, plan to venture beyond the obvious.

Following is an overview of the individual Hawaiian islands. Much more information on each appears later in this guide.

OAHU Known as the Gathering Place, the island of Oahu contains Honolulu, Hawaii's capital and main cultural center, in the southeast, and great ocean surfing locations in the northwest and west. Among Oahu's many other attractions are the USS *Arizona* Memorial at Pearl Harbor, Waimea Falls Park, and Nuuanu Pali, scene of a bloody battle in 1795.

KAUAI Kauai, the Garden Isle, is gaining in popularity. It's refreshingly rural, small and beautiful. Waimea Canyon, a smaller version of the Grand Canyon, is its principal natural attraction. It also has a string of unforgettable beaches, some of the most beautiful in the world (you've seen them as Bali H'ai in the movie version of *South Pacific* and as Matlock Island in the television production of *The Thorn Birds*). Most of the devastation wrought by Hurricane Iniki in 1992 is now history.

THE BIG ISLAND   The Big Island of Hawaii encompasses the most varied geography of the islands; with 21 separate climate zones and landscapes ranging from lava desert to rain forest to snow-capped mountains, it's like a continent in miniature. It has few beaches, but the ones there are like nothing you've ever seen: black sands, salt-and-pepper, even emerald green. It contains the islands' second-biggest city (Hilo), the volcanic wonderlands of Mauna Kea, Mauna Loa, and the currently erupting Kilauea (Volcanoes National Park is a must on any itinerary), and a cattle ranch big enough for Texas.

MAUI   Maui has become the most popular of the neighbor islands and appeals especially to an affluent condo crowd; it has some of the best golf courses in the state of Hawaii. Maui's great natural wonder is Haleakala, the largest dormant volcano in the world, with a moonlike crater that you can explore on foot or horseback. Also alluring are the popular, picturesque old whaling town of Lahaina, remote and lovely Hana, and a succession of golden beaches.

MOLOKAI   Next to largely inaccessible Niihau, Molokai is the most Hawaiian of the Hawaiian Islands, with the largest number of native Hawaiians. A festival celebrating the birth of the hula takes place there every year.

LANAI   The island of Lanai, once nothing more than a gigantic pineapple plantation, is now known as the "Private Island." It has entered the world of modern tourism with two posh Rockresorts—Manele Bay and Koele Lodge. A more modestly priced hotel and a bed-and-breakfast here and there are the only accommodations for the budget-minded. You may want to splurge on one of the sailing-ship cruises out of Lahaina, Maui, and spend a day on Lanai.

1 Information, Entry Requirements & Money

SOURCES OF INFORMATION

For further information on traveling and living in Hawaii, you can contact the **Hawaii Visitors Bureau (HVB),** which has offices in the following cities:

On the Mainland   Suite 2210, 180 N. Michigan Ave., **Chicago,** IL 60601 (☎ 312/236-0632); Room 610, Central Plaza, 3440 Wilshire Blvd., **Los Angeles,** CA 90010 (☎ 213/385-5301); Suite 808, 350 Fifth Ave., **New York,** NY 10018 (☎ 212/947-0717); and Suite 450, 50 California St., **San Francisco,** CA 94111 (☎ 415/392-8173).

In Hawaii   *On Oahu:* Suite 801, Waikiki Business Plaza, 2270 Kalakaua Ave., Honolulu, HI 96815 (☎ 808/923-1811). *On the Big Island:* 75-5719 W. Alii Dr., Kailua-Kona, HI 96740 (☎ 808/329-7787); 250 Keawe St., Hilo, HI 96720 (☎ 808/961-5797). *On Maui:* Maui Visitors Bureau, 1727 Wili Pa Loop (Wailuku Millyard), P.O. Box 580, Wailuku, HI 96793 (☎ 808/244-3530). *On Kauai:* Suite 207, Lihue Plaza Building, 3016 Umi St., Lihue, Kauai, HI 96766 (☎ 808/245-3971).

ENTRY REQUIREMENTS/MONEY

If you're a U.S. citizen or permanent resident, one of the nicest things about going to Hawaii is that you don't have to fiddle with passports or visas. Nor do you have to worry about currency exchange. Despite its exotic flavor, Hawaii is still part of the U.S.A. Entry requirements for foreigners are discussed in Chapter 4.

What Things Cost in Hawaii	U.S.$
Taxi from Honolulu International Airport to Waikiki	$20–$25
Van from Honolulu International Airport to Waikiki	$7.00
Local telephone call	.25
Double room at the Westin Maui (deluxe)	$210–$345
Double room at the Maui Islander (moderate)	$69.00
Double room at the Royal Grove, Honolulu (budget)	$36.00–$55
Lunch for one at Lahaina Coolers, Maui (moderate)	$7.00
Lunch for one at Broke The Mouth Inn, Big Island (budget)	$6.00
Dinner for one, without wine, at Cascada, Honolulu (expensive)	$25.00–$30
Dinner for one, without wine, at Café Pesto, Big Island (moderate)	$12.00
Dinner for one, without wine, at the Old Spaghetti Factory, Honolulu (budget)	$9
Bottle of beer	$2.50
Cup of coffee	$1.00–$2.50
Coca-Cola	$1.15
Roll of ASA 100 Kodacolor film, 36 exposures	$4.69
Admission to Bishop Museum, Honolulu	$7.95
Movie ticket	$5.50–$6
Theater ticket to Manoa Valley Theater, Honolulu	$19–$27
Don Ho, Waikiki Beachcomber Hotel	
show	$46
cocktail show	$26

2 When to Go

CLIMATE

The Hawaiian "season" has little to do with the weather in the islands. Rather, it's tied to the weather back home. In the islands, the weather is usually good year-round. Hawaii's climate is tropical, with springlike temperatures averaging about 75°F and seldom ranging more than 6° or 7° above or below this point. In midwinter, you can occasionally get some "raw" days in the low- to mid-60s, and in mid-summer, you can experience some humid ones in the 80s. (August is probably the most humid month of the year; if your room does not have cross-ventilation to allow the trade winds to come through, air conditioning is essential at that time.) Cool waters drifting down from the Bering Sea make the islands 10° cooler than other places in the same latitude—and the trade winds provide balmy breezes. As for rain, we have experienced some dreary, rainy days here, especially in winter—anytime from November to March. But most of the time, showers are brief and seldom heavy enough to spoil the pleasures of a vacation.

HAWAII CALENDAR OF EVENTS

For a list of spectator sporting events on each island in addition to the calendar below, see "Other Outdoor Activities" in each island's "What to See & Do" section.

January

- **50th Annual Hula Bowl Game.** Celebrating "50 Years of Glory," the annual college all-star football classic will be the center of a week-long series of festivities, which will include former Hula Bowl participants. Many concerts and other events. At Aloha Stadium, Honolulu, January 21. For ticket information, ☎ 808/947-4141. Prices range from $5 to $15.

- **Cherry Blossom Festival.** An ethnic festival that champions Japanese culture in Hawaii, complete with a Queen Pageant, a Coronation Ball at which the Governor crowns the new cherry blossom queen, culture and crafts fairs at Kapiolani Park, and the Red and White Song Festival at Blaisdell Concert Hall, Honolulu. From mid-January through April. Information: ☎ 808/955-2778.

- **Seventh Annual Senior Skins Golf Tournament.** This popular event draws big crowds to the fabulous Mauna Lani Resort on the Big Island. Raymond Floyd will return to defend his 1995 Senior Skins title. January 27 and 28. Information: ☎ 808/885-6655.

- **Molokai Makahiki.** The annual Hawaiian "time of peace" celebration takes place on the island of Molokai, usually on the last Saturday of January. In addition to a skin-diving tournament and competitions in Hawaiian games, several of Hawaii's most popular music groups perform. For information, phone Walter Ritte at 808/553-3688.

February

- **NFL Pro Bowl.** The annual all-star football game involving the National and American Conferences of the National Football League will be played at Honolulu's Aloha Stadium on February 4. Information: ☎ 808/486-9300.

- **Narcissus Festival.** February 19 marks the beginning of the Chinese New Year—this year, the Year of the Rat. The weekend before, Chinatown celebrates with lion dances, live entertainment, arts and crafts demonstrations, and fireworks at the Chinese Cultural Plaza in Honolulu. Information: ☎ 808/533-3181.

- **Chinese New Year on Maui.** The New Year is ushered in with lion dances, firecrackers, and an Asian food festival at the Wo Hing Temple on Front Street in Lahaina. Information: ☎ 808/667-9175.

- ✪ **Punahou School Carnival.** One of the most popular family events in Honolulu, this yearly carnival features 23 rides, including a Ferris wheel and a merry-go-round, and 60 booths offering plants, foods, arts and crafts, and so forth. Best of all is the White Elephant tent at the end of the carnival, when leftovers—often clothing in good condition—sell for ridiculously low prices.

    Where: Punahou School, 1601 Punahou St., Honolulu. **When:** First week in February. **How:** Free admission. Call 808/944-5753 for information.

- **$50,000 Makaha World Surfing Championships.** This international traditional and cultural longboard competition is one of the major surfing events of the year. Team members from Australia, Brazil, Costa Rica, Europe, Japan, Mexico, New Zealand, Puerto Rico, South Africa, California and Hawaii will share their country's culture and traditions with spectators and other competitors. Activities include pageants, parades, hula and musical entertainments, and a recreation of traditional Hawaiian Makahiki celebrations. The Buffalo Big Board Surfing Classic, in which old-timers compete on the kind of huge wooden surfboards used in early Hawaii, is part of the event. The action takes place at world-famous Makaha Beach on Oahu's leeward coast. February 3 to 18. Information: ☎ 808/951-7877.

March

- **Second Annual Honolulu Festival.** This two-day U.S./Japanese Cultural Exchanges Festival includes kite workshops, U.S./Japan High School Sumo Championships at Bishop Museum, and a finale festival at Aloha Tower Marketplace, Honolulu. March 8 to 10. Information: ☎ 808/922-0200.

- **Prince Kuhio Day.** Hawaii's beloved "people's prince" and first delegate to the U.S. Congress is honored with impressive ceremonies at Prince Kuhio Federal Building. At Kuhio Beach in Waikiki, the site of his home, a memorial tablet is decorated with leis, and Hawaiian societies hold special programs and events. On Kauai, where Kuhio was born in 1871, there will be a week-long series of festivities, including the 27th Annual Prince Kuhio Iron-woman Canoe Race, an elegant Holoku Ball, a commemorative service at Prince Kuhio Park, arts and crafts exhibits and entertainments at various sites around the island. March 26. Information for Kauai events: ☎ 808/245-3971.

- **Outrigger Hotels Hawaiian Mountain Tour.** Four days of fast, furious downhill bike riding by daredevils from near and far. March 28–31. Information: ☎ 808/521-4322.

April

- **Easter Sunrise Service** at the National Memorial Cemetery of the Pacific (Punchbowl) is a moving Honolulu tradition. The gates open at 4:30am; the service begins at 6am. For further information, phone the Hawaii Council of Churches, 808/263-9788.

- **4th Annual Ritz-Carlton Kapalua Celebration of the Arts.** Maui's only hands-on arts, music, and cultural festival takes place at the posh resort on Easter weekend. More than 30 island artists participate. The festival is free, but on Saturday night, April 7, there will be a concert for which admission is charged, featuring renowned Hawaiian musician Henry Kapono. April 4 to 7. Information: ☎ 808/669-6200.

- ✪ **Merrie Monarch Festival Competitions.** The statewide olympics of hula and one of the most popular events in the islands. Workshops, performances and more hula than you can shake a hip at. Nightly television broadcasts are watched by just about everyone.
  Where: Edith Kanakaole Multi-Purpose Center, Hilo, HI. **When:** April 16-22. **How:** On January 1 send ticket order to Merrie Monarch Festival, Dorothy Thompson, Executive Director, Hawaii Naniloa Hotel, 93 Banyan Dr., Hilo, HI 96720 (☎ 808/935-9168). Send cashier's check or money order only. **Prices:** $15 to $20 for three nights.

May

- ✪ **Lei Day.** May Day is Lei Day in Hawaii. Lei competitions are held throughout the state. Everybody wears a lei, a Lei Queen is crowned, and there's a Lei Day concert at the Waikiki Shell, usually with the beloved Brothers Cazimero in the evening.

Where: Oahu events are held in Kapiolani Park. **When:** May 1. **How:** Tickets are on sale at Waikiki Shell after 5pm (before that at Blaisdell Center and Sears outlets). The price is around $15 for general admission. Come early, bring a picnic supper and a blanket, and join Hawaii's people for a joyous event. Some visitors plan their entire trip around this event.

- **Buddha Day.** Flower festival pageants at island temples throughout the state celebrate the birth of Buddha. May 7.
- **Fourth Annual Pineapple Festival.** What better place for a pineapple festival than Lanai, the "Pineapple Island." On the first weekend in May, there will be arts and crafts, demonstrations, a cooking contest, an on-shore fishing tournament, tennis tournament, and local and ethnic music and dancing. Information: ☎ 808/565-7600.
- **The 8th Annual Hula Pakahi and 17th Annual Lei Festival.** Early in May, the Maui Inter-Continental Resort presents an annual competition for solo hula dancers from leading hula halaus throughout the state. Tickets are $12 in advance, $14 at the door. The Lei Festival features Hawaiian artists demonstrating their skills. The festival is free. Information: ☎ 808/879-1922.
- **The 22nd Annual Seabury Hall Crafts Fair.** Here's a chance to see the work of some of Maui's finest artisans, on sale at the annual fund-raiser for Maui's top prep school. Entertainment, booths, a Silent Auction, and more. At the Seabury Hall campus in Makawao. Free admission. May 11. Information: ☎ 808/572-7235.
- **Molokai Ka Huia Piko.** A celebration of the birth of the hula takes place on Molokai and features performances by Molokai hula halau, musicians, and singers, along with demonstrations of traditional Hawaiian crafts. Crafts, Hawaiian foods, and Molokai specialties can be purchased throughout the day-long celebration. Third weekend in May. For information, telephone Molokai Visitors Association at 808/553-3876, or toll free 800/800-6367.

June

- **Kamehameha Day.** A state holiday (many offices closed) honoring Kamehameha the Great, Hawaii's first monarch. It's one of the biggest celebrations of all; there are parades and festivities all over the islands. In Honolulu, the annual King Kamehameha Celebrations Floral Parade includes floral floats, pageantry, Pa'u mounted riders, bands, and more, concluding with a cultural and arts festival at Kapiolani Park. June 11, with festivities starting a few days earlier. (The parade may be cancelled because of budget cuts; call Keahl Allen at 808/586-0333 to see if it's on this year.)
- ✪ **Waiki'i Music Festival.** One of the most popular music events in the islands, this two-day celebration of Hawaiian music and culture draws up to 10,000 fans a year from all over the state. Top Hawaiian groups, including Hoku-winning artists (the Hoku Awards are the local equivalent of the Grammys) of the calibre of Ho'okena, Kapena, Olomana, Tropical Knights, and Israel Kamakawiwo'ole (all performers in last year's concert) are on stage from 10am to 6pm, eight groups a day. (To see any one of these artists at a nightclub show in Honolulu would be at least $25.) There are also food booths and arts and crafts. This is a great way to celebrate Father's Day.

   Where: The Polo Field at Waikii Ranch, 5,000 feet up, on the Big Island. **When:** June 16 and 17. **How:** Call 808/329-8037 for information on ticket outlets. The Festival is a benefit for local groups; tickets are $15 in advance, $20 at the gate.

- **Taste of Honolulu.** Here's a way to sample the culinary creations of Hawaii's top restaurants and support a good cause at the same time. Hawaii's largest food event, Taste of Honolulu, draws some 100,000 residents and visitors to the grounds of Honolulu Hale (City Hall) each June for a festive three-day event. Scrip is sold for the tastings and all proceeds go to benefit the Easter Seal Society of Hawaii. In addition, there's continuous entertainment, cooking demonstrations, wine tasting, a gourmet marketplace, and children's festivities. What a blast! Information: ☎ 808/536-1015.
- **23rd Annual King Kamehameha Hula Competition.** This international competition features groups coming from as far away as California and Japan. Both modern and ancient (kahiko) hulas are presented. Programs are held on June 22 at Blaisdell Center in Honolulu. Admission is $7.25 to $15.25.
- **Annual Duke Kahanamoku Longboard Surfing Classic.** The Hawaii Longboard Surfing Association presents this event in the months of June and July at Kuhio Beach in Waikiki. Similar events are held at Sunset Beach on Oahu's North Shore in April and at Makaha Beach, on the leeward coast, in December. In May they present the Ohana Surf Festival at Poipu Beach in Kauai, and in January, the Tiger Espere Longboard Classic at Kawaihae Breakwater on the Big Island. Information: ☎ 808/949-4572.
- **Art Night Celebration.** Front Street in Lahaina, Maui, turns into an outdoor art festival—with gallery displays, art-in-action projects, music, food booths, and lots more—as artists from Front Street's many galleries take to the streets. June 29. Information: ☎ 808/667-9175.

July

- **Fourth of July.** Statewide celebrations include the 41st Annual Makawao Rodeo—Hawaii's largest—in Makawao, Maui (information: ☎ 572-9928) and the Parker Ranch Rodeo and Horse Races, with top entertainment by Hawaiian cowboys from Parker Ranch, at Paniolo Park, Waimes, on the Big Island. Information: ☎ 808/885-7311.
- **Hale'iwa Bon Odori Festival.** This is one of the happiest and most colorful events in the islands, and includes traditional dances to welcome the arrival of departed souls in paradise. The dances are sponsored by Japanese Buddhist temples whose members practice their steps for months. Usually mid-July.
- **Prince Lot Hula Festival.** Local hula halaus perform ancient and modern hulas in a festival that honors King Kamehameha V. At Moanalua Gardens in Honolulu. Usually the third week in July.
- **6th Hawaii All-Collectors Show.** True collectors of Hawaiana never miss this show, the largest selection of Hawaiiana available for sale under one roof, from early historical artifacts to Boat Day memorabilia. Held at Blaisdell Exhibition Hall, Honolulu, July 26, 27, and 28. Admission: Adults $3, Children ages 7 to 11, $2.

August

- ✪ **36th Annual Hawaiian International Billfish Tournament.** This is the leading international merlin fishing tournament in the world, drawing fishers and fans from everywhere.

  Where: Kailua-Kona, Big Island. **When:** August 17–23, with a parade on August 17. **How:** Book rooms in Kailua-Kona well in advance; the place is mobbed. Information: ☎ 808/326-7826.

- **21st Annual Queen Liliuokalani Keiki Hula Competition.** The first week in August, children from the ages of 6 to 12, representing 25 hula halaus (schools) from around the state, compete in a delightful program at Blaisdell Center in Honolulu. Information: ☎ 808/521-6905.
- **14th Annual Ka Himeni'ana.** Over $2,000 in cash prizes are awarded at this old-style Hawaiian singing contest and concert. All songs are in the Hawaiian language and date before World War II. The event takes place August 9 and 10 at the University of Hawaii's Orvis Auditorium in Honolulu. Tickets are $6, $8 and, $10. For tickets, call Marge Hansen at 808/742-0421.
- **14th Annual Bankoh Ki'Hoalu Hawaiian Slack Key Guitar Festival.** About 20 of Hawaii's best slack-key artists get together for a five-hour free concert at Makoi Pavilion in Ala Moana Park on Sunday, August 18. There will be solo instrumentalists as well as singers accompanied by slack-key guitar. BANKOH (Bank of Hawaii) also sponsors Slack-Key Guitar Festivals on the Big Island in Kona in mid-April, on Maui in early June, and on Kauai in early November. Information: ☎ 808/537-8610.
- **Toro Nagashi-Floating Lantern Ceremony.** Each year on August 15, the anniversary of the end of World War II, local Buddhist groups float 2,000 colorful paper lanterns bearing the names of departed souls from the Waikiki-Kapahulu Public Library to McCully Bridge. The ceremony begins with a Bon Dance at Ala Wai Park, followed by an Obon ceremony, all part of the annual Bon season.
- **Puukohola Heiau 24th Annual Cultural Festival.** This Establishment Day cultural festival takes place in Kawaihae, on the Big Island, August 17 and 18. Ancient Hawaiian heritage is celebrated with cultural demonstrations featuring the Royal Court, Hawaiian food tasting, arts and crafts workshops, and hula kahiko. Free. For information, Daniel Kawaiaea at ☎ 808/882-7218.

September

- **Aloha Festivals.** Take the celebrations of all the ethnic groups, roll them into one, and you'll get some idea of Aloha Festivals, which are held on the different islands in a more-or-less progressive order. The Asian, Polynesian, and Western groups all get together for this *hoolaulea* (gathering for a celebration), each vying to demonstrate the warmth and beauty of the wonderful Hawaiian aloha. Music and dance events, demonstrations of ancient arts and crafts, a beautiful orchid show, water sports, an enormous flower parade, pageants, the crowning of both a king and a queen, are featured. Check with the Hawaii Visitors Bureau for the exact dates of the Aloha Festivals. They usually begin on Oahu at the end of August, then move to Hawaii, Molokai, and Lanai, before ending in late October on Kauai and Maui. Call 808/944-8857 for information.
- **A Taste of Lahaina.** Here's a good reason to be in Lahaina in mid-September. The largest food festival on Maui features over 30 different restaurant booths, continuous entertainment, a beer garden, and a separate area for kids. Free. Information: ☎ 808/667-9175.
- **7th Annual Outrigger Hotels Hawaiian Oceanfest.** A 10-day celebration of sports and entertainment, much of it nationally televised. The Waimea Open Ocean Challenge on the 4th, the Outrigger's Waikiki King's Race on the 8th, and the Diamond Head Biathlon on the 14th are all open to the public. The Hawaiian International Ocean Challenge on the 6th and 7th are for professional

international lifeguard teams only. The Diamond Head Wahine Windsurfing Classic on the 8th is for professional women boardsailors only. Information: ☎ 808/521-4322.

- **Parade of Homes.** Here's a chance to see what's behind the closed doors of Hawaii's homes, town houses, and high-rise apartments. The major annual event of Hawaii's building and real estate industries, the Parade of Homes showcases the latest trends in homebuilding, remodeling, interior design, and landscaping, with entrants competing for a variety of awards. Realtors host open houses from 10am to 5pm on the third and fourth weekends in September. Information: ☎ 808/847-4666.

October

○ **Waimea Falls Park Makahiki Festival.**   Hawaiian games, music, and food are featured in this festival whose highlight is the Hula Kahiko Competition, in which ancient dances of Hawaii are performed.

    Where: Waimea Falls Park, Oahu. **When:** Usually the first week in October. **How:** Events are included in general admission to the park. Information: ☎ 808/638-8511.

○ **Gatorade Ironman World Triathlon Championships.**   Only world-class athletes need apply for this Big Island event. This internationally acclaimed event, which will take place on October 26 this year, includes a 2.4 mile swim, a 112-mile bicycle ride, and a 26.2 mile run, with no resting between events.

    Where: Kailua Kona, Big Island. **When:** October 26. **How:** Make hotel reservations at least 3 months in advance. You're welcome to join the 20,000 spectators, or—better yet—the 5,000 volunteers, whose assistance is greatly appreciated. And, it's a lot of fun. Information: ☎ 808/329-0063.

- **Compadres South Pacific Chili Cookoff.** A hundred teams—from community organizations, restaurants, hotels, businesses, and the military—compete to create Hawaii's best chili. The gigantic block party, held out on the street at Ward Centre, features chili tasting and continuous entertainment. It's usually held in October, with admission charges of about $10 (all proceeds go to local charities). Information: ☎ 808/591-8300.

- **Tour O' Hawaii.** This world-class bicycle competition brings top amateur cyclists from around the world to Oahu from October 31 to November 3. The Oahu Cycle Classic, a preliminary competition open to the public, is October 26–27. Information: ☎ 808/521-4322.

November

- **Kamahameha Schools Ho'olaule'.** This old-time—taking place this year on November 9—Hawaiian festival features continuous hula, Hawaiian and contemporary entertainment, arts and crafts, Hawaiian children's games, and food. Alumni groups from five islands participate in these Oahu events. Information: ☎ 808/842-8412.

- **World Invitational Hula Festival.** Moanalua Gardens Foundation sponsors an annual international hula festival called "E Ho'i Mai I Piko Hula," which usually takes place at Blaisdell Arena the second week in November. Competing hula halua have come from many mainland states, Europe, and Japan to compete. Information: ☎ 808/839-5334.

- **Mission Houses Museum Christmas Fair.** This popular Honolulu event features many specialty gift items for Christmas and food. Craftspeople from all over the islands show their wares. Free admission. Thanksgiving weekend. Information: ☎ 808/531-0481.

- **26th Annual Kona Coffee Cultural Festival.** Celebrating the harvest of the local Kona coffee crop and the multi-cultural traditions surrounding the harvest, this annual event features coffee picking contests, coffee tasting, parades, brunch at the Farmer's Market, farm and mill tours, song fests, art exhibits, and more. The event takes place this year November 1–8 in Kailua-Kona on the Big Island. With the exception of a few separate admission charges, the $2 Festival booster button admits wearers to all official Festival events. Information: ☎ 808/326-7820.

December

- **Bodhi Day.** The enlightenment of Buddha is commemorated with religious observances in the Buddhist temples and with Japanese dance programs and ceremonies elsewhere. Nearest Sunday to December 7.

- ✪ **Honolulu Marathon.**   This is one of the most popular—and scenic—U.S. marathons. It draws some 39,000 entrants, about 20,000 from Japan, but many from the U.S. mainland, Europe, Canada, Mexico, and Australia.

  Where: Starts at the Ala Moana Beach Park and ends at Kapiolani Park. **When:** December 10 **How:** Spectators line the route; there is no admission fee. For runners: To obtain entry forms, send a stamped, self-addressed business-size envelope to Honolulu Marathon Association, 3435 Waialae Ave., Room 200, Honolulu, HI 96816.

- **Na Mele d Maui Song Contest and Hula Festival.** This is one of the most delightful events on the Maui calendar. It's dedicated to preserving Hawaii's heritage of song, dance, and art through its young people. It is held early in December of each year, under the auspices of the Kaanapali Beach Resort Association, at various hotels within the Resort. The weekend event includes a Friday morning song concert (free admission) and a Saturday evening Hula Festival (tickets $15 to $20). Proceeds go to a scholarship fund supporting students continuing their higher education in Hawaiian Studies. Information: ☎ 808/661-3271.

- **Princess Bernice Pauahi Bishop's Birthday.** Throughout the islands, societies and schools remember the beloved princess on December 19.

- **Christmas.** What could be nicer than a Polynesian Christmas? There aren't any chimneys, so Santa might arrive in an outrigger canoe or on a surfboard. He might—it's not as bad as it sounds—be wearing a hula skirt. Carols are sung to ukulele accompaniment. Christmas lights are hung on everything from evergreens to bamboo; the decorations in downtown Honolulu are enchanting. There are special programs for children at the Honolulu Academy of Arts. The stores are jammed, just as they are on the mainland—a view of the bustling crowds (thronging the mall at Ala Moana Center, for example) is one of the prettiest of holiday pictures. The Christmas greeting: "Mele Kalikimaka!"

- **Jeep Eagle Aloha Bowl Football Classic.** The 15th annual NCAA-sanctioned post-season football game features two top-ranked college football teams competing at Aloha Stadium on Christmas Day. The event will benefit local Hawaiian charities. For ticket information, ☎ 808/947-4141. Ticket prices range from $10 to $25.

3 Planning a Hawaiian Wedding

What could be nicer than marrying in Hawaii? You can marry and honeymoon in the same place, and the cost need not be exorbitant. The idea has become so appealing that thousands of visitors are now seeking out Hawaiian weddings in offbeat settings: on the beach, on top of a mountain, aboard a catamaran, in a helicopter—even in a church. For help in planning a Hawaiian wedding, you can contact several private organizations suggested by the Hawaii Visitors Bureau:

Aloha Wedding Planners offers a variety of picturesque locations and takes care of every detail, from the ministers to the photographers. Susan and Sheryl, the wedding coordinators in charge, are both incurably romantic and decidedly practical; they promise that their service is always first class, even if your budget is strictly economy. Contact them at 1860 Ala Moana Blvd. No. 115, Honolulu, HI 96815 (☎ 808/943-2711; fax 808/949-1128).

Waimea Falls Park is one of Hawaii's most popular locations for weddings. The experienced staff can make all the necessary arrangements for the perfect ceremony and reception, including minister, flowers, music, limousine, champagne, and more. Custom wedding packages are available with a wide range of prices suitable for any budget. Contact the Wedding Department, Waimea Falls Park, 59-864 Kamehameha Hwy., Haleiwa, HI 96712 (☎ 808/638-8511; fax 808/638-7900).

Planning to marry in Maui? We can't think of a more romantic or lovely spot than **The Westin Maui** at Kaanapali Beach, where couples can exchange vows in a variety of idyllic natural settings and even have their ceremony blessed with Hawaiian prayers. A Director of Romance arranges everything from minister to musicians, flowers and photographers—the works. A variety of honeymoon packages is available at the same hotel. It's also an ideal spot for renewing vows or celebrating anniversaries. Contact The Westin Maui, 2365 Kaanapali Pkwy., Lahaina, HI 96761 (☎ 800/228-3000).

The **Hyatt Regency Maui,** also on Kaanapali Beach in West Maui, offers several dream wedding packages for ceremonies on its lovely grounds, all including clergy, leis for the bride and groom, musicians, cake, and champagne. Packages range from the relatively simple "Maui Enchantment" to a land-and-sea nuptial adventure called "Mele Makai (seaward wedding). Phone 808/661-1234 for details. In East Maui, the spectacular **Grand Wailea Resort** has it's own wedding chapel, surrounded by flower-filled gardens and overlooking the ocean. The hotel's wedding specialist handles all the details, including ordering flowers and cake, planning the reception, and even coordinating wedding attire. Wedding packages include the Plumeria Package, which adds a couples' lomi-lomi massage and other beauty treatments at it's Spa Grande. Phone 808/875-1234 for information.

Remote Hana is one of the most scenic and romantic areas of Maui, and **Heavenly Hana Weddings,** P.O. Box 2609, Wailuku, HI 96793 takes full advantage of its lush natural beauty—tropical flowers, waterfalls, ocean cliffs, and beaches—in arranging weddings. They even offer a "classic horseback wedding" in spectacular Kipahulu Valley. Horses are dressed with lush flowers and fern leis, and mane and tail braids and satin saddle covers are used. Call for a quote.

A Hawaiian Wedding Experience began by specializing in West Maui weddings, but it became so popular that it has expanded its services to the other major islands as well. They've been pioneers in planning romantic weddings for islanders as well as visitors for many years, offering everything from sunrise ceremonies on the slopes of Haleakala to sunset weddings at the beach or on a private sailing catamaran, weddings at a breathtaking waterfall in Hana as you fly there by a private sightseeing helicopter, or lavish Royal Hawaiian Wedding Luaus. Contact Kalani Kinimaka, who runs this family operation, at Aloha! Hawaiian Weddings!, Central Reservations, P.O. Box 8670, Honolulu, HI 96830-8670 (☎ 808/926-6688 or 926-6689, fax 808/926-6677), for wedding information on Maui, Kona, Kauai, and Waikiki.

On the Big Island, **Paradise Weddings Hawaii** is an all-inclusive wedding coordination service specializing in sunset ceremonies. Their motto, "Intimate to Outrageous," sums up the broad range of offerings, from simple, barefoot beach ceremonies to weddings on horseback. Owner Debbie Cravatta has a reputation for creating exactly the kind of wedding the couple envisions to match their budget. Prices start at $295. Contact Debbie at **Paradise Weddings Hawaii,** P.O. Box 383433, Waikoloa, HI 96738 (☎ 808/883-9067, or 800/428-5844; fax 808/883-8479).

Also on the Big Island, a sunset wedding at the lush **Kona Village Resort** would be pure heaven: P.O. Box 1299, Kaupulehua-Kona, HI 96745 (☎ 800/367-5290). Guests of the **Kona Surf Resort** on the Big Island can be married at the hotel's Kona Royal Chapel. For information on wedding and honeymoon packages, contact Kona Surf Resort & Country Club, 78-128 Ehukai St., Kailua-Kona, HI 96740 (☎ 800/367-8011).

If you'd like to be married in Kauai, the people at **Weddings on the Beach** can help you. Not only do they arrange weddings on beautiful beach locations, but they can also arrange mountain-top and oceanfront settings, as well as adventure weddings aboard sailing ships and cabin cruises, even helicopters. They claim Kauai is a spiritual island, and there's plenty of *mana* (power) here to get a marriage off to a good start. Contact them at P.O. Box 1377, Koloa, Kauai, HI 96756 (☎ and fax 808/742-7099 or 800/62KAUAI).

Traditional weddings are the order of the day at the **Hyatt Regency Kauai.** The bride can arrange for a replica of an authentic Hawaiian wedding gown, featuring a Hawaiian quilt pattern on the train of the satin and lace gown. A variety of wedding packages are available, including the "Maile and Mokihana Wedding Package," complete with a Hawaiian conch-shell blower getting things off to an auspicious start. Call 808/742-1234 for information.

Kauai's restored plantation estate of the 1930s, **Kilohana,** is also the site of numerous weddings; they can be held indoors in an elegant living room overlooking the gardens, in the gardens themselves, or even in a turn-of-the-century carriage riding through the plantations grounds. Write to Wedding Coordinator Kilohana, P.O. Box 3121, Lihue, Kauai, HI 96766.

Wedding Tips: If you're planning the details yourself, you should contact the State Health Department, 1250 Punchbowl St., Honolulu, HI 96813 (☎ 808/548-5862), for rules and regulations. You will need a permit to be married in a state park. Contact State Parks Division, P.O. Box 621, Honolulu, HI 96809 (☎ 808/548-7455). If you plan to be married in one of Hawaii's national parks, contact the Superintendent, Haleakala National Park, P.O. Box 369, Makawao, HI 96768 (☎ 808/572-9306); or the Superintendent, Hawaii Volcanoes National Park, HI 96718 (☎ 808/967-7311). Of course, if you use the services of a wedding planner, these details will be handled for you.

4 Getting There

THE AIRLINES

The largest carrier with the most frequent service to Hawaii is United Airlines, closely followed by Continental. To get into the mood of your Hawaiian vacation the minute you leave the West Coast, you might consider flying Hawaiian Airlines, the largest airline based in the Hawaiian Islands, and the only one offering service to the mainland. Hawaiian offers two flights a day from Los Angeles, one from San Francisco and Seattle, and four flights a week from Portland and Las Vegas, all on widebodied DC10s. Fares are very competitive and they often offer special promotional fares. You can also save a bundle by booking one of their package deals. Hawaiian works with Fly AAway Vacations, the tour operations unit of American Airlines. For information, phone Hawaiian Airlines Vacations at 800/353-5393, or ask your travel agent.

Airlines that fly into Honolulu include **Air New Zealand** (☎ 808/836-4988 or 800/262-1234), **American Airlines** (☎ 808/526-0044 or 800/433-7300), **Canadian Airlines International** (☎ 800/426-7000), **China Airlines** (☎ 808/955-0088 or 800/227-5118), **Continental Airlines** (☎ 808/523-0000 or 800/231-0856), **Delta Air Lines** (☎ 800/221-1212), **Garuda Indonesian** (☎ 808/945-3791 or 800/826-2829), **Hawaiian Airlines** (☎ 808/537-5100 or 800/367-5320), **Japan Airlines** (☎ 808/521-1441 or 800/525-3663), **Korean Air** (☎ 808/923-7302 or 800/223-1155 on the East Coast, 800/421-8200 on the West Coast), **Northwest Airlines** (☎ 808/955-2255 or 800/225-2525), **Philipine Airlines** (☎ 808/536-1928 or 800/435-9725), **Qantas** (☎ 808/836-2461 or 800/227-4500), **Trans World Airlines** (☎ 800/221-2000), and **United Airlines** (☎ 808/547-2211 or 800/225-5825).

BEST-FOR-THE-BUDGET FARES

APEX/Economy   Although it carries restrictions and cancellation penalties, this fare is decidedly the best for the budget, APEX stands for Advance Purchase Excursion and typically you are required to reserve and pay for the ticket 14 or 21 days in advance, stay for a minimum and maximum number of days, and possibly fulfill some other requirements like flying before a specific date.

Hawaiian's Apex/Economy fares for Los Angeles to Honolulu range from $300 to $350 round-trip, depending on which days of the week you travel and how far in advance you purchase your ticket. They are invariably the cheapest way to fly. These fares are known interchangeably as economy or APEX fares.

Regular Airfares   Here's a price breakdown on how economy-class tickets compare with first class. Hawaiian's fares for a first class ticket from Los Angeles to Honolulu in the winter of 1995 were $799 roundtrip as compared to $300 to $350 for economy round trip. Hawaiian has a popular offer: on the day of travel, it may be possible to upgrade an economy class fare to first class by paying an additional $125. This offer is available only on a standby basis. (Hawaiian's First Class fares, incidentally, are 20% to 30% lower than those of other airlines.)

Special Promotional Fares   You never know when an airline is going to offer promotional fares. Sometimes there's a price war, and then the consumer really benefits. Keep watching the newspapers for announcements of special deals. A few years ago, one airline was flying from Los Angeles to Honolulu for $99 for a very short period of time. Always ask your travel agent to inquire about promotional fares, too.

Bucket Shops Discount travel agencies purchase blocks of tickets directly from the airlines at wholesale prices, which they then discount. **Community Travel Service,** 5299 College Ave., Oakland, CA 94618 (☎ 510/653-0990) may be able to get you a discount ranging anywhere from 20% to 40%—depending on the season in which you fly and availability. You may do as well on your own or with your regular travel agent, but it wouldn't hurt to give these people a call and see what they have for you. Remember that it's very difficult to return these tickets, and many restrictions apply: So once you've bought them, they're all yours.

5 Getting Around

INTERISLAND TRAVEL
BY PLANE

Hawaii's two major interisland carriers are Hawaiian Airlines and Aloha Airlines; both have been around for many years and offer similar fares, give or take a few dollars. Because fares change often, and because both offer periodic promotional fares and tie-ins with hotel and car-rental packages, it pays to do some personal shopping either by calling the airlines directly or by consulting your travel agent. Expect fares to be highest during peak winter and summer travel periods. Standby tickets are no longer offered. Ask about special rates for children.

Hawaiian Airlines (☎ 800/367-5320) operates one of the most exciting concepts in interisland travel in many years. Similar to a Eurail train pass, Hawaiian's Island Pass allows visitors to take an unlimited number of interisland flights for a flat fee. Considering that a regular flight costs $74, the bargains are substantial: A 5-day Airpass costs $169; an 8-day pass $189; a 10-day pass $229; and a 2-week pass $269. With prices like these, you can island-hop at will, or use one island as your base and make day trips to see the others. For those with limited vacation time, it's ideal. In addition, users of the Hawaiian Island Pass receive special prices on car rentals with Alamo Rent A Car. A phone call to the airline or to your travel agent can give you the details.

Hawaiian now also offers passengers the option to earn miles in AAdvantage, the frequent travel program of American Airlines. AAdvantage members may also redeem their miles for award travel on Hawaiian.

Aloha Airlines (☎ 800/367-5250; TFD 800/554-4833) provides scheduled interisland service between all major airports in Hawaii with a fleet of modern Boeing 737 jet aircraft. Aloha mileage counts toward United Airlines Mileage Plus or Canadian International Airlines Canadian Plus programs. Aloha's sister company, Island Air, provides daily service to all of Hawaii's smaller resort airports. Aloha is highly regarded by frequent business travelers, and rates very favorably in the area of low passenger complaints, according to U.S. Department of Transportation surveys.

Mahalo Air (☎ 800/277-8333), the latest upstart airline to challenge the Big Two with budget fares, is continuing to hold its own. Their rock-bottom fares are available to *kamaainas* (local residents) only, but nonresidents can still make substantial savings. On occasion, they offer special rates—check with them. They fly only from Honolulu to Lihue, Kahului, Kona, Molokai, and Lanai and back on propeller aircraft that seat 48 people; there are about five flights a day to each destination. The seat configuration is two abreast, so every seat offers an excellent view because of the unique placement of the wings above the aircraft.

ON THE NEIGHBOR ISLANDS

Your major expense on the outer islands will be transportation. Only one city on one island—Hilo, on the island of Hawaii—has anything resembling a public transportation system, and even that is not very extensive. (Buses do cross the island of Hawaii east to west and back.) There is also bus service in the Lahaina-Kaanapali area of Maui, but none of the buses run for any great distance. So unless you want to stay put, you have only two choices: taking expensive sightseeing tours or renting your own car.

BY RENTAL CAR

The quoted price for a car rental is not always what it appears to be. There have, in fact, been a great many complaints from consumer groups who are hoping to force the industry to include all mandatory charges in their basic advertised fees; many car-rental companies oppose the plan. Thus, the budget-wise car renter must be on the alert for hidden charges (delivery, drop-off, extra charges for drivers under 25, for example, and most especially for insurance coverage).

If you're under 21, you're out of luck here when it comes to renting a car. Hawaii state law prohibits anyone under 18 from driving with an out-of-state license (even though islanders can get licenses at 15!). There used to be one or two agencies that would rent to drivers 18 to 20, but at press time, there are none that we know of. There may be special stipulations for 21-to-24-year-olds, like paying a surcharge. When you reach 25, you can just show your license, fill out the papers, and drive away.

A further tip: In general, it's cheaper to pick up a car at the airport than to have it delivered to your hotel and picked up when you're finished with it. And airport pickup, of course, avoids the costs of cabs or bus coming into town.

If you're going to visit several of the major islands, the easiest way to rent your cars is to make one telephone call to a company that provides service on all of them. We've had excellent cars and service from **Alamo Rent A Car.** Give them a call and find out if they're offering one of their specials if you're traveling in the winter. Regular rates depending on the season, go from about $30 to $40 per day, $145 to $187 per week for an air-conditioned, automatic, economy car, all with unlimited free mileage, and often less. Alamo is in Honolulu, Waikiki, Maui, Hilo, Kona, and Lihue (cars at airport terminals on neighbor islands, courtesy bus in Honolulu). Call Alamo at 800/327-9633, 24 hours a day. Certain restrictions apply, including age and credit-card requirements. Rates do not include gas, tax, or a nominal under-25 surcharge.

With a fleet of over 7,000 cars, **Budget Rent A Car of Hawaii,** the well-known mainland and international car-rental agency, offers a vehicle for every taste and pocketbook. Since rates fluctuate so much, Budget does not care to quote them, but they're always competitive. Their exclusive gift program—given to all renters— includes many free admissions, meals, and gifts. There are 5 offices in Waikiki (☎ 808/537-3600) and 13 others throughout the state, with airport locations on Oahu, Maui, Molokai, Kauai, and the Big Island. For reservations, call 800/527-0700, or write Budget Rent-A-Car of Hawaii, Central Reservations, P.O. Box 15188, Honolulu, HI 96830-0188.

National Interrent has nine convenient airport and downtown locations on Oahu, Hawaii, Kauai, and Maui and offers competitive unlimited-mileage rates on it's fleet of GM cars. Inquire about special daily and weekly rates, during the summer; for the rest of the year, subcompacts begin at $40 daily. They're known for excellent service. The number is 800/CAR-RENT.

Thrifty Car Rental has locations on Oahu, Maui, and Kauai (not on Hawaii). They have direct-line courtesy phones at all baggage-claim areas. Usually, standard compacts rent for $25.95 daily, $165 weekly. There's no mileage charge. Call 808/833-0046 in Honolulu or 800/367-2277 for reservations, or write to them at 3039 Ualena St., Honolulu, HI 96819.

Avis Rent A Car, Honolulu International Airport (☎ 808/834-5536, or toll free 800/331-1221) serves all five major islands, and offers a special for seven days of driving an automatic Dodge or similar car on a combination of two or more islands—about $149 a week. For reservations, call 800/831-8000.

Hertz Rent A Car, 233 Keawe St., Room 625, features an All-Island touring rate that covers seven days or more on any combination of the four major islands. Days do not have to be consecutive and there is no mileage charge. The seven-day rate starts at $209 for a compact car, or $46 for one day. Daily rates offer free unlimited mileage. For reservations and information, call 800/654-3131. Hertz has offices at airports and hotels on all the major islands. You are advised to reserve at least a day in advance. A major credit card is required.

Dollar Rent A Car has locations on the six major islands—including Molokai and Lanai. Rates average $34 a day, $185 a week. They will rent to drivers under 25 at an extra charge of $5 per day, with a major credit card. For reservations from the U.S. call 800/367-7006.

AUTO INSURANCE   Since Hawaii is a no-fault state, if you don't have insurance you are required to handle any damages before you leave the state. However, you may be able to avoid the cost of collision-damage waivers (anywhere from $10 to $12 per day), which the car-rental companies are eager to sell you, if your car insurance back home provides rental-car coverage. Your policy should include personal liability, property damage, fire, theft, and collision. Your insurance company should also be able to provide fast claim service in the islands. It would be a good idea to obtain the name of your company's local claim representative in Hawaii before you leave home; bring along your policy or identification card if you plan to do that. And check with your credit card company to see if it provides rental-car coverage.

DRIVING TIPS   In general, Hawaiian drivers seem more courteous than those in big cities on the mainland—and they often drive more slowly. You should be aware of some special rules:

• The state has a mandatory seat-belt law. Be sure to buckle up.
• You may make a right turn in the right lane at a stoplight after coming to a full stop, unless noted otherwise.
• You may make a left turn at the stoplight from the left lane on a one-way street onto another one-way street after coming to a full stop.
• The pedestrian is usually right.
• Remember that driving distances on the neighbor islands can be great, particularly on the Big Island, and you may have trouble finding gas stations open, especially on Sunday. Keep the tank full.

- Should you have a breakdown, call your car-rental agency for emergency service.
- Current mainland driving licenses may be used until their expiration date. After that, you'll need a Hawaiian license, obtainable from the Department of Motor Vehicles, for those 15 and older.

ROAD MAPS   For most driving, the road maps printed in the various "Drive Guides" to the neighbor islands, and given free with your car rental, are excellent. Should you wish to have topographic maps, they can be ordered by mail from the Hawaii Geographic Society, P.O. Box 1698, Honolulu, HI 96808 (☎ 808/ 538-3952, fax 808/536-5999), or the Map Information Center, Federal Center, Denver, CO 80225.

6 Alternative Accommodations Networks

BED-AND-BREAKFAST & HOUSE/CONDO RENTAL SERVICES

If the B&B alternative appeals to you, check out the reservations services listed below. Remember that B&B accommodations are no longer necessarily the cheapest; that they are best for couples, since there is usually only one double (or queen-size) bed; and that they usually do not provide cooking facilities. For a family or several people traveling together, an apartment with kitchenette usually works out more economically. Also, most B&Bs are in residential areas rather than tourist areas, so a car is essential.

BED & BREAKFAST RESERVATIONS SERVICES   Evelyn Warner and Al Davis started **Bed & Breakfast Hawaii,** P.O. Box 449, Kapaa, HI 96746 (☎ 808/ 822-7771, or 800/733-1632; fax 808/822-2723) years ago, "not as a big business operation, but as a low-key, intimate way for people to visit Hawaii." They offer accommodations in private homes and apartments on all the islands, for rates ranging from $35 to $125 single, $40 to $180 double, including continental breakfast. They can often pass on substantial savings on car rentals to their guests. Write or phone for a free brochure. For $12.95 you receive a directory of homes and apartments with rooms for rent called *Bed & Breakfast Goes Hawaiian.*

Mary Lee, the woman who runs **Bed & Breakfast Honolulu** (Statewide), 3242 Kaohinani Dr., Honolulu, HI 96817 (☎ 808/595-7533, or 800/288-4666; from U.S. and Canada fax 808/595-2030), doesn't believe directories do the trick; in almost 12 years of operating her business she's found that almost any place a guest picks from a directory will probably be unavailable at the time the request comes in. So Mrs. Lee installed an 800 number and she, or one of her family, will engage you in a personal conversation and help you find accommodations— either a room in a home or a studio in an apartment building. She charges a $10 reservation fee for each unit she reserves. She currently offers more than 400 "homestays" and studios on all the major islands, plus Molokai and Lanai. Prices range from about $45 to $175 single or double. Mrs. Lee also handles car rentals and inter-island flights, and she can get you good discounts on each.

Readers Recommend

"Some hotels will give a 25% to 50% discount off published room rates for military personnel and their families. We stayed at three- and four-star hotels at half the normal rate. I believe that many of your readers are in the U.S. military and would be happy to know about this benefit."—Joe and Robin Gruender, Wright-Patterson AFB, Ohio

Doris Epp of **Pacific-Hawaii Bed & Breakfast,** 99-442 Kekoa Place, Aiea, Oahu, HI 96701 (☎ 808/487-1228 or 800/999-6026; fax 808/487-1228 or 808/261-6573), has many rentals in the lovely suburb of Kailua, not far from Waikiki. It's one of our favorite areas, since both Kailua and Lanikai beaches are superb—and it's also one of the new meccas for windsurfers. She also has about 200 listings on all the Hawaiian Islands, ranging from $45 a day for two guests. She requests 20% of the cost of the stay for confirmation, but she promises a complete refund if the room does not meet your expectations or you do not take occupancy because of a serious emergency; she's serious when she says "satisfaction guaranteed."

Upscale B&B lodgings throughout the state are the province of **Hawaii's Bed & Breakfasts,** hand-picked by Barbara Campbell from her headquarters on the Big Island. Each home, private cottage, or country inn is selected for its distinctive personality, attention to details, and the warm hospitality of its hosts. Daily rates go from $75 to $175. For a brochure describing these hidden gems, contact Barbara Campbell, P.O. Box 563, Kamuela, HI 96743 (☎ 808/855-4550; fax 808/885-0559 or 800/262-9912 for reservations).

Go Native . . . Hawaii, 65 Halaulani Place (P.O. Box 11418), Hilo, HI 96721 (☎ 808/935-4178 or 800/662-8483), has been matching guests with Hawaiian hosts for more than a decade. Coordinator Fred Diamond has 250 locations on all islands except Lanai, ranging from oceanfront to mountain sites, from traditional B&B rooms in private homes to unhosted studios and cottages. Rates begin around $40 single, around $65 double.

My Island, P.O. Box 100, Volcano, HI 96785 (☎ 808/967-7110; fax 808/967-7719) is a Hawaii-island-only reservation service run by Gordon and Joann Morse; they have rentals all over the Big Island, and encourage people to move around to explore the different atmospheres and climates of the various districts. Prices run about $40 to $70 single, $60 to $125 double, and go up.

Three Bears Hawaii Reservations, 72-1001 Puukale, Kailua-Kona, HI 96740 (tel/fax 808/325-7563 or 800/765-0140 from the mainland) is a family-run business specializing in reasonable accommodations on all the islands. Some of their rates start as low as $65 per night; most average between $65 and $85 double. Special attention is given to European guests. Their own B&B, The Three Bears, is on the Big Island.

Ann and Bob Babson, 3371 Keha Dr. in Maui Meadows, Kihei, Maui, HI 96753 (☎ 808/874-1166 or 800/824-6409), who rent four oceanview hideaways just above the posh Wailea Resort on Maui, can also make reservations on all islands for B&Bs, cottages, condominiums, and car rentals at the best rates available.

Focusing on Maui, but with accommodations on the Big Island and Kauai as well, **Affordable Accommodations,** P.O. Box 98, Puunene, HI 96784 (☎ 808/879-7865 or 800/848-5567) has lodgings all over Maui, from oceanside to mountain slopes. They handle rooms in private houses from $45 to $60 double, and vacation rentals in condos, cottages, studios, and homes, which go for $65 to $100. They're happy to offer advice on out-of-the-way places and activities.

A CONDO & HOUSE-RENTAL SERVICE Savings of up to 50% on condo rentals can be realized by working through **HALE** (Hawaiian Apartment Leasing Enterprises), 479 Ocean Ave., Suite B, Laguna Beach, CA 92651 (☎ 714/497-4253 or 800/854-8843, from the U.S. mainland and Canada), which handles rentals on all the major islands (including Molokai) with a wide range of prices, sizes, and locations. Most of the condos are custom-decorated and of high quality. Rates run roughly between $60 and $95 per night double. HALE also has some 200 private homes available, beginning with a two-bedroom house in Kauai for $445 a week. Cleaning services, cooks, chauffeurs, day care, and additional custom services can be arranged.

HOME EXCHANGES

If you'd like to exchange your own home or apartment for a place to stay in Honolulu, contact the **Vacation Exchange Club,** P.O. Box 650, Key West, FL 33041 (☎ toll free 800/638-3841), a worldwide home-swapping group. You can be listed in their directory for $65 a year and find out what's available in Hawaii. (A recent listing, for example, offered a three-bedroom/two-bath house, along with two cars and two bikes, in the posh Kahala region, for a three-month exchange.) Rentals are also available. Vacation Exchange Club provides information only (it is not a travel agency); the actual arrangements are all up to you.

Another organization that provides a similar service is Intervac U.S. International Home Exchange, P.O. Box 590504, San Francisco, CA 94159 (☎ 415/435-3497 or 800/756-HOME; fax 415/386-6853). It publishes four catalogs a year, containing over 9,400 homes in more than 36 countries, with about 100 in the Hawaiian Islands. Members contact each other directly. The $65 cost includes your own listing in one catalog and receiving all four catalogs. Seniors over 62 pay $60. Photos cost $11. Postage is extra. Hospitality and youth exchanges, as well as rentals, are also offered. This is the largest worldwide home-exchange network. **Trading Homes International,** P.O. Box 787, Hermosa Beach, CA 90254 (☎ toll free 800/877-TRADE; fax 310/798-3865), provides worldwide home-exchange listings and a goodly number in Hawaii. Membership, which includes your home listing (including photograph) and receipt of three directories per year, is $65. They also distribute *Trading Places,* a useful handbook of home trading for $12, and are the headquarters of the International Home Exchange Association, with member agencies throughout the world.

Teachers have more time for vacations than most of us, so it was inevitable that a service like **Teacher Swap Directory of Homes** would come about. They have an excellent list of international locations, as well as quite a few in Hawaii. The price is $42 for both a listing and the directory, $50 for the directory only. Contact Teacher Swap, P.O. Box 454, Oakdale, NY 11769-0454 (☎/fax 516/244-2845).

The first computer bulletin board service for home exchanges is **Home Exchange Network,** Box 915253, Longwood, FL 32791 (☎ 407/862-7211). This new company is building national and international listings, with a growing number in Hawaii. There is no charge for membership as of this writing: a computer user with a modem can dial 407/869-5956 and sign on for a free six-month membership, or request an application form.

Readers Recommend

"We spent five weeks in Oahu, having previously arranged to exchange homes with a couple who lived in a delightful home in Manoa Valley. Surprisingly, many island people do like to have excursions to the mainland, and home exchange is an ideal way of providing the basis for a really inexpensive vacation.—David Brokenshaw, Santa Barbara, Calif.

FAST FACTS: Hawaii

Area Code   All the Hawaiian Islands share one area code: 808.

Business Hours   Most office workers in Hawaii are at their desks by 8am, sometimes even earlier, and it's *pau hana* (finish work) at 4 or 5pm, the better to get in an afternoon swim or a round of golf. Normal bank hours Monday through Thursday are 8:30am to 3 or 3:30pm, until 6pm on Friday. Most shopping malls are open Monday through Friday from 9 or 10am to 9pm, on Saturday until 5:30pm, and for a shorter period on Sunday, usually until 4pm.

Cigarettes   Noncitizens over 21 are allowed to bring in 200 cigarettes or 50 cigars or two kilograms of tobacco.

Driving Rules   See "Getting Around," in this chapter.

Electricity   Hawaii uses standard North American current, 110 volts AC, 60 cycles.

Emergencies   Dial 911 for an ambulance, a fire, or the police.

Legal Aid   The main office of the Legal Aid Society of Hawaii is at 1108 Nuuanu Ave. (☎ 808/536-4302).

Liquor Laws   The legal drinking age in Hawaii is 21.

Newspapers   In Honolulu, it's the *Honolulu Advertiser* and the *Honolulu Star-Bulletin;* in Maui, it's the *Maui News;* in Kauai, the *Garden Island News.*

Radio and TV   See "Fast Facts: Honolulu," in Chapter 4, for a comprehensive listing of Honolulu radio and TV stations. All the major islands are equipped with cable TV and get all major mainland television channels.

Safety   There's crime and violence in Hawaii, just as there is everywhere else in the world. And because Hawaii was indeed a trouble-free paradise for so many years, people tend to ignore basic safety precautions. Our advice is: Don't! Never carry large sums of cash; traveler's checks are much safer. Don't go hiking on deserted trails except in a group; don't go wandering on isolated beaches alone; and don't go jogging in the cane fields alone at the crack of dawn. Stay in well-lighted areas at night, travel with a friend if possible, lock your car and remove valuables from your trunk, and use your common sense—just as you would at home.

It's always advisable to put your valuables into your hotel's safe or an in-room safe. If you don't want to use a safe, then at least take your valuables with you. Never leave them unprotected in a hotel room, to which any number of people—staff, service personnel, guests past or present, and others—could have access.

Taxes   The hotel occupancy tax is 9.17%. Sales tax is 4%.

Telephone   The cost of a local call (from any one part of an island to another) at a pay phone is 25¢. Interisland calls cost more. Be aware that most hotels impose a surcharge on all calls.

Time   There are five time zones between the East Coast of the United States and Hawaii. That means that when it's noon Hawaiian standard time, it's 5pm eastern standard time, 4pm central, 3pm mountain, and 2pm Pacific. Hawaii does not do daylight saving time as the rest of the nation does, so from May through October, noon in Hawaii would mean 6pm eastern, 5pm central, and so on.

4 For Foreign Visitors

Although American fads and fashions have spread across Europe and other parts of the world, and America may seem like familiar territory before your arrival, there are still many peculiarities and uniquely American situations that any foreign visitor will encounter.

1 Preparing for Your Trip

ENTRY REQUIREMENTS

DOCUMENT REGULATIONS   Canadian citizens may enter the U.S. without visas; they need only proof of residence.

Citizens of the U.K., New Zealand, Japan, and most Western European countries traveling on valid passports may not need a visa for fewer than 90 days of holiday or business travel to the U.S., providing that they hold a round-trip or return ticket and enter the U.S. on an airline or cruise line participating in the visa waiver program.

(Note that citizens of these visa-exempt countries who first enter the U.S. may then visit Mexico, Canada, Bermuda, and/or the Caribbean islands and then reenter the U.S., by any mode of transportation, without needing a visa. Further information is available from any U.S. embassy or consulate.)

Citizens of countries other than those stipulated above, including citizens of Australia, must have two documents:

- a valid **passport,** with an expiration date of at least 6 months later than the scheduled end of the visit to the U.S.; and
- **a tourist visa,** available without charge from the nearest U.S. consulate. To obtain a visa, the traveler must submit a completed application form (either in person or by mail) 1 1/2-inch square photo and demonstrate binding ties to a residence abroad.

Usually you can obtain a visa at once or within 24 hours, but it may take longer during the summer rush from June to August. If you cannot go in person, contact the nearest U.S. embassy or consulate for directions on applying by mail. Your travel agent or airline office may also be able to provide you with visa applications and instructions. The U.S. consulate or embassy that issues your visa will determine whether you will be issued a multiple- or single-entry visa and any restrictions regarding the length of your stay.

MEDICAL REQUIREMENTS   No inoculations are needed to enter the United States unless you are coming from, or have stopped over in, areas known to be suffering from epidemics, particularly cholera or yellow fever.

If you have a disease requiring treatment with medications containing narcotics or drugs requiring a syringe, carry a valid signed prescription from your physician to allay any suspicions that you are smuggling drugs.

CUSTOMS REQUIREMENTS   Every adult visitor may bring in free of duty: one liter of wine or hard liquor; 200 cigarettes or 100 cigars (but no cigars from Cuba) or 3 pounds of smoking tobacco; $100 worth of gifts. These exemptions are offered to travelers who spend at least 72 hours in the United States and who have not claimed them within the preceding six months. It is altogether forbidden to bring into the country foodstuffs (particularly cheese, fruit, cooked meats, and canned goods) and plants (vegetables, seeds, tropical plants, and so on). Foreign tourists may bring in or take out up to $10,000 in U.S. or foreign currency with no formalities; larger sums must be declared to Customs on entering or leaving.

INSURANCE

There is no national health system in the United States. Because the cost of medical care is extremely high, we strongly advise every traveler to secure health coverage before setting out.

You may want to take out a comprehensive travel policy that covers (for a relatively low premium) sickness or injury costs (medical, surgical, and hospital); loss or theft of your baggage; trip-cancellation costs; guarantee of bail in case you are arrested; costs of accident, repatriation, or death. Such packages (for example, "Europe Assistance" in Europe) are sold by automobile clubs at attractive rates, as well as by insurance companies and travel agencies.

MONEY

CURRENCY & EXCHANGE   The U.S. monetary system has a decimal base: one American **dollar ($1) = 100 cents (100¢).**

Dollar bills commonly come in $1 (a "buck"), $5, $10, $20, $50, and $100 denominations (the last two are not welcome when paying for small purchases and are not accepted in taxis or at subway ticket booths). There are also $2 bills (seldom encountered).

There are six denominations of coins: 1¢ (one cent or "penny"), 5¢ (five cents or a "nickel"), 10¢ (ten cents or a "dime"), 25¢ (twenty-five cents or a "quarter"), 50¢ (fifty cents or a "half dollar"), and the rare $1 piece.

TRAVELER'S CHECKS   Traveler's checks denominated in U.S. dollars are readily accepted at most hotels, motels, restaurants, and large stores. But the best place to change traveler's checks is at a bank. Do not bring traveler's checks denominated in other currencies.

CREDIT CARDS   The method payment most widely used is the credit card: VISA (BarclayCard in Britain), MasterCard (EuroCard in Europe, Access in Britain, Chargex in Canada), American Express, Diners Club, Discover, and Carte Blanche. You can save yourself trouble by using "plastic money" rather than cash or traveler's checks in most hotels, motels, restaurants, and retail stores (a growing number of food and liquor stores now accept credit cards). You must have a credit card to rent a car. It can also be used as proof of identity (often carrying more weight than a passport), or as a "cash card," enabling you to draw money from banks that accept them.

Note: The "foreign-exchange bureaus" so common in Europe are rare even at airports in the United States, and nonexistent outside major cities. Try to avoid having to change foreign money, or traveler's checks denominated other than in U.S. dollars, at a small-town bank, or even a branch in a big city; in fact, leave any currency other than U.S. dollars at home—it may prove more of a nuisance to you than it's worth.

SAFETY

GENERAL   While tourist areas are generally safe, crime is on the increase everywhere, and U.S. urban areas tend to be less safe than those in Europe or Japan. Visitors should always stay alert. This is particularly true of large U.S. cities. It is wise to ask the city's or area's tourist office if you're in doubt about which neighborhoods are safe. Avoid deserted areas, especially at night. Don't go into any city park at night unless there is an event that attracts crowds—for example, the Waikiki Shell concerts in Kapiolani Park. Generally speaking, you can feel safe in areas where there are many people, and many open establishments.

Avoid carrying valuables with you on the street, and don't display expensive cameras or electronic equipment. Hold on to your pocketbook, and place your billfold in an inside pocket. In theaters, restaurants, and other public places, keep your possessions in sight.

Remember also that hotels are open to the public, and in a large hotel, security may not be able to screen everyone entering. Always lock your room door—don't assume that once inside your hotel you are automatically safe and no longer need be aware of your surroundings.

DRIVING   Safety while driving is particularly important. Question your rental agency about personal safety, or ask for a brochure of traveler safety tips when you pick up your car. Obtain written directions, or a map with the route marked in red, from the agency showing how to get to your destination. And, if possible, arrive and depart during daylight hours.

Recently more and more crime has involved cars and drivers. If you drive off a highway into a doubtful neighborhood, leave the area as quickly as possible. If you have an accident, even on the highway, stay in your car with the doors locked until you assess the situation or until the police arrive. If you are bumped from behind on the street or are involved in a minor accident with no injuries and the situation appears to be suspicious, motion to the other driver to follow you. *Never* get out of your car in such situations. You can also keep a pre-made sign in your car which reads: PLEASE FOLLOW THIS VEHICLE TO REPORT THE ACCIDENT. Show the sign to the other driver and go directly to the nearest police precinct, well-lighted service station, or all-night store.

If you see someone on the road who indicates a need for help, do *not* stop. Take note of the location, drive on to a well-lighted area, and telephone the police by dialing 911.

Park in well-lighted, well-traveled areas if possible. Always keep your car doors locked, whether attended or unattended. Look around you before you get out of your car, and never leave any packages or valuables in sight. If someone attempts to rob you or steal your car, do *not* try to resist the thief/carjacker—report the incident to the police department immediately.

2 Getting To & Around the U.S.

Travelers from overseas can take advantage of the **APEX (Advance Purchase Excursion) fares** offered by all the major U.S. and European carriers. Aside from these, attractive values are offered by **Icelander** on flights from Luxembourg to New York and by **Virgin Atlantic Airways** from London to New York/Newark. Advance purchase fares are available to travelers from Australia via **Qantas Airways,** which runs daily flights from Sydney to Honolulu (plus additional flights four days a week); they are also available for travelers from New Zealand via **Air New Zealand,** which runs 40 flights per week from Auckland.

Some large American airlines (for example, TWA, American Airlines, Northwest, United, and Delta) offer travelers on their transatlantic or transpacific flights special discount tickets under the name **Visit USA,** allowing travel between any U.S. destinations at minimum rates. They are not on sale in the United States, and must, therefore, be purchased before you leave your foreign point of departure. This system is the best, easiest, and fastest way to see the United States at low cost. You should obtain information well in advance from your travel agent or the office of the airline concerned, since the conditions attached to these discount tickets can be changed without advance notice.

The visitor arriving by air, no matter what the port of entry, should cultivate patience and resignation before setting foot on U.S. soil. Getting through Immigration control may take as long as two hours on some days, especially summer weekends. Add the time it takes to clear Customs and you'll see that you should make very generous allowance for delay in planning connections between international and domestic flights—an average of two to three hours at least.

For further information about travel to Hawaii, see "Getting There" in Chapter 3.

FAST FACTS: For the Foreign Traveler

Automobile Organizations   Auto clubs will supply maps, suggested routes, guidebooks, accident and bail-bond insurance, and emergency road service. The major auto club in the United States, with 955 offices nationwide, is the **American Automobile Association (AAA).** Members of some foreign auto clubs have reciprocal arrangements with the AAA and enjoy its services at no charge. If you belong to an auto club, inquire about AAA reciprocity before you leave. The AAA can provide you with an **International Driving Permit** validating your foreign license. You may be able to join the AAA even if you are not a member of a reciprocal club. To inquire, call 800/336-4357. In addition, some automobile rental agencies now provide these services, so you should inquire about their availability when you rent your car.

Automobile Rentals   To rent a car you need a major credit card. A valid driver's license is required, and you usually need to be at least 25. Some companies do rent to younger people but add a daily surcharge.

Business Hours   **Banks** are open weekdays from 9am to 3 or 3:30, until 6pm on Friday; 24-hour access to the automatic tellers (ATMs) at most banks and other outlets. Generally, **offices** are open weekdays from 8am to 4 or 5pm. **Stores** are open six days week, with many open on Sunday, too; department stores usually stay open until 9pm at least one day a week.

Climate   See "When to Go" in Chapter 3.

Currency   See "Money" in "Preparing for Your Trip" above.

Currency Exchange   You will find currency services in major airports with international service. Most major banks on the four largest islands of Hawaii provide currency exchange. In addition, in Honolulu, the capital city, you can get reliable currency service at **Thomas Cook Currency,** 830 Fort Street Mall (☎ 808/523-1321); **A1 Foreign Exchange,** Royal Hawaiian Shopping Center (☎ 808/922-3327); and **Monyx International,** 307 Royal Hawaiian Ave. (☎ 808/923-6626).

Drinking Laws   See "Liquor Laws" in "Fast Facts: Hawaii" in Chapter 3.

Electricity   The United States uses 110–120 volts, 60 cycles, compared to 220–240 volts, 50 cycles, as in most of Europe. In addition to a 100-volt converter, small appliances of non-American manufacture, such as hairdryers or shavers, will require a plug adapter, with two flat, parallel pins.

Embassies & Consulates   All embassies are located in the national capital, Washington, D.C.; some consulates are located in major cities, and most nations have a mission to the United Nations in New York City. Foreign visitors can obtain telephone numbers for their embassies and consulates by calling "Information" in Washington, D.C. (☎ 202/555-1212).

   The consulate general of **Australia** is located at 1000 Bishop St. in Honolulu, HI 96813 (☎ 808/524-5050): the consulate general of **Japan** is located at 1742 Nuuanu Ave. in Honolulu, HI 96817 (☎ 808/536-2226).

Emergencies   Call **911** to report a fire, call the police, or get an ambulance. If you encounter traveler's problems, check the local directory to find an office of the **Traveler's Aid Society,** a nationwide, nonprofit, social-service organization geared to helping travelers in difficult straits. Their services might include reuniting families separated while traveling, providing food, and/or shelter to people stranded without cash, or even emotional counseling. If you're in trouble, seek them out.

Gasoline   One U.S. gallon equals 3.75 liters, while 1.2 U.S. gallons equals one Imperial gallon. You'll notice there are several grades (and price levels) of gasoline available at most gas stations. And you'll also notice that their names change from company to company. The unleaded ones with the highest octane are the most expensive (most rental cars take the least expensive "regular" unleaded) and leaded gas is the least expensive, but only older cars can take this, so check if you're not sure.

Holidays   On the following legal national holidays, banks, government offices, post offices, and many stores, restaurants, and museums are closed:

   New Year's Day   January 1
   Martin Luther King Day   Third Monday in January
   Presidents Day   Third Monday in February
   Memorial Day   Last Monday in May
   Independence Day   July 4
   Labor Day   First Monday in September
   Columbus Day   Second Monday in October
   Veterans (Armistice) Day   November 11
   Thanksgiving Day   Last Thursday in November

Christmas Day   December 25

Election Day, which falls on the Tuesday following the first Monday in November, is a national holiday during presidential-election years.

Languages   Major hotels may have multilingual employees. Unless your language is very obscure, they can usually supply a translator on request.

Legal Aid   The foreign tourist, unless positively identified as a member of the Mafia or of a drug ring, will probably never become involved with the American legal system. If you are pulled over for a minor infraction (for example, of the highway code, such as speeding), never attempt to pay the fine directly to a police officer; you may wind up arrested on the much more serious charge of attempted bribery. Pay fines by mail, or directly into the hands of the clerk of the court. If accused of a more serious offense, it's wise to say and do nothing before consulting a lawyer. Under U.S. law, an arrested person is allowed one telephone call to a party of his or her choice. Call your embassy or consulate.

Mail   If you want your mail to follow you on your vacation and you aren't sure of your address, your mail can be sent to you, in your name, **c/o General Delivery** at the main post office of the city or region where you expect to be. The addressee must pick it up in person and produce proof of identity (driver's license, credit card, passport, etc.).

Generally to be found at intersections, mailboxes are blue with a red-and-white stripe and carry the inscription U.S. MAIL. If your mail is addressed to a U.S. destination, don't forget to add the five-figure postal code, or ZIP (Zone Improvement Plan) Code, after the two-letter abbreviation of the state to which the mail is addressed (HI for Hawaii, FL for Florida, NY for New York, and so on).

Newspapers/Magazines   National newspapers include the *New York Times, USA Today,* and the *Wall Street Journal.* National news weeklies include *Newsweek,Time,* and *U.S. News & World Report.* The *Honolulu Advertiser* and the *Honolulu Star-Bulletin* are the major local newspapers.

Radio and Television   Audiovisual media, with four major coast-to-coast networks—on ABC, CBS, NBC, and Fox—joined by the Public Broadcasting System (PBS) and the cable network CNN, play a major part in American life. In big cities, televiewers have a choice of about a dozen channels (including the UHF channels), most of them transmitting 24 hours a day, without counting the pay-TV channels showing recent movies or sports events. All options are usually indicated on your hotel TV set. You'll find a wide choice of local radio stations, each broadcasting particular kinds of talk shows and/or music—classical, country, jazz, pop, gospel—punctuated by news broadcasts and frequent commercials.

Taxes   In the United States there is no VAT (Value-Added Tax) or other indirect tax at a national level. Every state, and each city in it, has the right to levy its own local tax on all purchases, including hotel and restaurant checks, airline tickets, and so on. In Hawaii, sales tax is 4%.

Petrol   See "Gasoline," above.

Telephone, Telegraph, Telex   The telephone system in the U.S. is run by private corporations, so rates, especially for long distance service, can vary widely—even on calls made from public telephones. Local calls in the U.S. usually cost 25¢.

Generally, hotel surcharges on long-distance and local calls are astronomical. You are usually better off using a **public pay telephone,** which you will find clearly marked in most public buildings and private establishments as well as on the street. Outside metropolitan areas, public telephones are more difficult to find. Stores and gas stations are your best bet.

Most **long-distance** and **International** calls can be dialed directly from any phone. For calls to Canada and other parts of the U.S., dial 1 followed by the area code and the seven-digit number. For international calls, dial 011 followed by the country code, city code, and the telephone number of the person you wish to call.

For **reversed-charge or collect calls,** and for **person-to-person** calls, dial 0 (zero, not the letter "O") followed by the area code and number you want; an operator will then come on the line, and you should specify that you are calling collect, or person-to-person, or both. If your operator-assisted call is international, ask for the overseas operator.

For local **directory assistance** ("information"), dial 411; for **long-distance information,** dial 1, then the appropriate area code and 555-1212.

Like the telephone system, **telegraph** and **telex** services are provided by private corporations like ITT, MCI, and above all, Western Union, the most important. You can bring your telegram in to the nearest Western Union office (there are hundreds across the country), or dictate it over the phone (a toll-free call, 800/325-6000). You can also telegraph money, or have it telegraphed to you, very quickly over the Western Union system.

Telephone Directory   There are two kinds of telephone directories available to you. The general directory is the so-called **White Pages,** in which private and business subscribers are listed in alphabetical order. The inside front cover lists the emergency number for police, fire, and ambulance, and other vital numbers (like the Coast Guard, poison-control center, crime-victims hotline, and so on). The first few pages are devoted to community-service numbers, including a guide to long-distance and international calling, complete with country codes, and area codes.

The second directory, printed on yellow paper (hence its name, *Yellow Pages*), lists all local services, businesses, and industries by type of activity, with an index either in the front or in the back. The listings cover not only such obvious items as automobile repairs by make of car, or drugstores (pharmacies), often by geographical location, but also restaurants by type of cuisine and geographical location, bookstores by special subject and/or language, places of worship by religious denomination, and other information that the tourist might otherwise not readily find. The *Yellow Pages* also include city plans or detailed area maps, often showing postal ZIP Codes and public transportation routes.

Time   The United States is divided into four **time zones** (six, if Alaska and Hawaii are included). From east to west, these are: eastern standard time (EST), central standard time (CST), mountain standard time (MST), Pacific standard time (PST), Alaska standard time (AST), and Hawaii standard time (HST). Always keep changing time zones in mind if you are traveling (or even tele-phoning) long distances in the United States. For example, noon in New York City (EST) is 11am in Chicago (CST), 10am in Denver (MST), 9am in Los Angeles (PST), 8am in Anchorage (AST), and 7am in Honolulu (HST).

Daylight saving time is in effect from the last Sunday in March through the last Saturday in October (actually, the change is made at 2am on Sunday) except in Arizona, Hawaii, part of Indiana, and Puerto Rico. Daylight saving time moves the clock one hour ahead of standard time.

Tipping   This is part of the American way of life, on the principle that you must expect to pay for any service you get. Here are some rules of thumb:

Bartenders: 10%–15%.
Bellhops: at least 50¢ per piece; $2–$3 for a lot of baggage.
Cab drivers: 15% of the fare.
Cafeterias, fast-food restaurants: no tip.
Chambermaids: $1 a day.
Checkroom attendants (restaurants, theaters): $1 per garment.
Cinema, movies, theaters: no tip.
Doormen (hotels or restaurants): not obligatory.
Gas-station attendants: no tip.
Hairdressers: 15%–20%.
Redcaps (airport and railroad station): at least 50¢ per piece, $2–$3 for a lot of baggage.
Restaurants, nightclubs: 15%–20% of the check.
Sleeping-car porters: $2–$3 per night to your attendant.
Valet parking attendants: $1.

Toilets   Foreign visitors often complain that public toilets are hard to find in most U.S. cities. True, there are none on the streets, but the visitor can usually find one in a bar, restaurant, hotel, museum, department store, or service station—and it will probably be clean (although the last-mentioned sometimes leaves much to be desired). Note, however, a growing practice in some restaurants and bars of displaying a notice that "toilets are for the use of patrons only." You can ignore this sign, or better yet, avoid arguments by paying for a cup of coffee or soft drink, which will qualify you as a patron. The cleanliness of toilets at railroad stations and bus depots may be more open to question, and some public places are equipped with pay toilets, which require you to insert one or more coins into a slot on the door before it will open.

5

Settling Into Honolulu & Oahu

Oahu means "the gathering place" in Hawaiian, and no other name could be so apt. Although it's merely the third largest of the islands in size (40 miles long, 26 miles wide), it is the most populous (850,000, and more arriving all the time). It also has the most sky-scrapers, schools, hospitals, radio and television stations—and the most tourists.

Honolulu, the bustling capital city plunked in the middle of the Pacific, is the center of island life, the metropolis youngsters from the other islands dream of. It is also a tremendous military stronghold—approximately one-tenth of the island is owned by the military; defense is a major industry.

Just 10 minutes away from Honolulu is **Waikiki Beach,** a favorite resort of Hawaiian royalty long before the word "tourist" was invented. For the visitor, this is an ideal situation; it's as if Mexico City were just 10 minutes away from Acapulco, Paris a short bus ride from the Riviera. You can, with such geography, have the best of both worlds—as much beach or city, relaxation or excitement, as you choose.

The island is dominated by two mountain ranges: the Waianae, along the west coast, and the Koolaus, which form the spectacular backdrop to the city of Honolulu. On the other side of the Koolaus is **Windward Oahu,** which is what islanders are referring to when they talk of going to the "country." Commuters tunnel through the mountains to pretty little suburbs there. For the visitor, it's the closest thing you'll see—if you don't visit the neighbor islands—to rural Hawaii: tiny plantation villages, miles of red earth planted with pineapple and sugarcane, a breathtaking succession of emerald beaches, and gorgeous trails for riding and hiking.

1 Orientation

ARRIVING

BY PLANE   Honolulu International Airport, about 5 miles out of town, is one of the world's largest and busiest airports. If you're traveling light you can hop right on TheBUS no. 19 (Hickam-Waikiki) or no. 20 (Pearlridge-Waikiki). Both lines go from the terminal to the beach area for 85¢. (The bus has no special section for luggage—your bag must not take up any extra space.)

What's Special About Honolulu & Oahu

Natural Wonders
- Diamond Head Crater, the sleeping volcano that has become the symbol of Honolulu.
- Hanauma Bay, a marine reserve excellent for snorkeling. This idyllic beach cove was created centuries ago when one side of Koko Head Crater washed into the sea.
- The Blow Hole, a natural geyser where water surges up through an underwater vent in the lava rock, sometimes as high as 60 feet.

Beaches
- World-famous Waikiki Beach, great for swimming, surfing, people-watching.
- Lanikai Beach on Windward Oahu—gentle surf, no crowds—like Waikiki before the world discovered it.
- Superb sandy swimming beaches all over the island of Oahu, especially Sunset Beach and Waimea Bay in the mild summer months.

Outdoor Activities
- Great snorkeling, notably at Hanauma Bay.
- Surfing, all over Oahu. The mightiest winter waves are at Sunset Beach and Waimea Bay on the North Shore.
- Hiking the mountains and valleys, with many opportunities to go out with local groups.
- Sailing, day and night. Recreational and dinner cruises leave from Honolulu Harbor.
- Golf and tennis at many public and private facilities.

Museums and Historic Houses
- Bishop Museum, a prime resource center and a lively showcase for Pacific culture.
- Hawaii Maritime Center, tracing Hawaiian maritime history from ancient times to the present.
- Mission Houses Museum, for a look back at the days of the New England missionaries in Hawaii.

Major Historical Attractions
- Pearl Harbor, where history was made on December 7, 1941.
- National Memorial Cemetery of the Pacific at Punchbowl Crater, final resting place for thousands of American war dead.
- Iolani Palace, the only royal palace on U.S. soil, where Hawaii's embattled monarchy made its last stand.

Botanical Gardens
- Foster Botanical Gardens, 15 splendid acres of rare trees, flowers, and plants.
- Lyon Arboretum, a research and educational center prized as a beautiful nature spot.

Shopping
- Ala Moana Center, one of the world's best malls, with products ranging from downhome to upscale.
- International Market Place and Kuhio Mall, giant outdoor bazaars.

Honolulu at a Glance

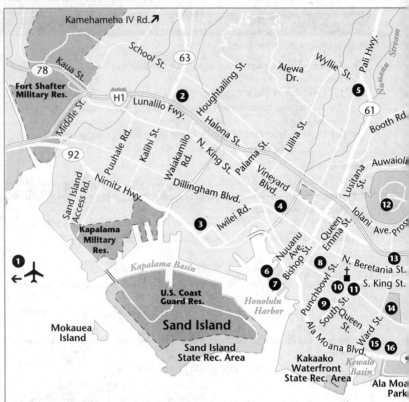

Ala Moana Park ⑱
Ala Moana Shopping
  Center ⑰
Aloha Tower Marketplace ⑥
Bishop Museum ②
Diamond Head State
  Monument ㉓
Dole Cannery Square ③

Foster Botanic Garden
Hawaii Maritime Center
Hawaii Visitor's Bureau ⑧
Honolulu Academy of
  Arts ⑬
Honolulu International
  Airport ①
Ilikai Marina ⑲

Makiki Valley ... Top Dr
Round ...
Tantalus Dr.
Puu Ualakaa
State Wayside
△
Round Top
Waahila Ridge
State Rec. Area
E. Manoa Rd.
Manoa Rd.
Manoa Rd.
Pukele Stream
Waiomao Stream
Manoa Stream
Neho a St.
Wilder Ave.
Makiki St.
Punahou St.
20
**University
of Hawaii**
University
Dole St.
St. Louis Dr.
Bertram St.
Palolo Ave.
Palolo Stream
Piikoi St.
Keeaumoku St.
S. Beretania St.
McCully St.
S. King St.
University
Ave.
Kikeke Ave.
Waialae Ave.
10th Ave.
Sierra Dr.
Wilhelmina Rise
Koko
Head
Ave.
H1
Lunalilo Fwy.
Kapiolani Blvd.
Atkinson Dr.
Kapahulu Ave.
Date St.
Lunalilo Fwy.
H1
16th Ave.
18th Ave.
17
18
**Ala Moana
State Rec.
Area**
19
**Fort
DeRussy
Military Res.**
ⓘ
Kalakaua Ave.
Ala Wai Canal
Ala Wai Blvd.
Campbell Ave.
Kilauea Ave.
Alohea Ave.
21
Waikiki Beach
**Kapiolani
Park**
Sans Souci
State Rec.
Area
22
**Military
Res.**
**Diamond Head
State Monument**
23
Trail
△ Diamond Head
Beach Park
Leahi
Diamond Head Rd.
U.S. Coast
Guard Res.

Iolani Palace **8**
Kapiolani Park **22**
Kawaiaihao Church **10**
Mission Houses Museum **11**
Neal S. Blaisdell Center **14**
Punchbowl Crater **12**
Restaurant Row **9**

Royal Mausoleum State
  Monument **5**
University of Hawaii **20**
Ward Centre **16**
Ward Warehouse **15**

Mountain △ Church ✝■ Information ⓘ Airport ✈

If you are traveling with luggage, you can take the **Airport Waikiki Express shuttle bus** (☎ 808/735-7797), which operates 24 hours a day and makes pick-ups outside the airline baggage-claim areas every 20 to 30 minutes (depending on the time of day). The fare is $7 each way (or $12 round-trip) for adults, $4 for children (2 and under free).

A taxi into Waikiki should cost between $20 and $22. Taxi stands are located adjacent to the shuttle-bus stops.

If you've rented a car in advance, you can pick it up right at the airport.

TOURIST INFORMATION

The **Hawaii Visitors Bureau,** 2270 Kalakaua Ave., 7th floor (☎ 808/923-1811), in the heart of Waikiki, has a helpful staff. Stop in to pick up leaflets and brochures on all kinds of activities and on neighbor-island hotels.

For daily news of what's going on, consult the *Guide to Oahu, This Week on Oahu, Spotlight Oahu, Paradise News,* or *Key,* **free publications** found in most hotel lobbies, on Kalakaua Avenue, and elsewhere. (These papers also carry many bargain discount coupons, which can add up to considerable savings on shopping, restaurants, car rentals, and the like.) The "Aloha" section of the *Sunday Star-Bulletin & Advertiser* lists events for the coming week. *Oahu Drive Guide,* available at the offices of rental-car companies, has plenty of information, plus driving maps.

CITY LAYOUT
GETTING YOUR DIRECTIONAL SIGNALS

In order to get your bearings, you should know that one seldom refers to directions in the standard north–south, east–west layout here. Since the islands sit in a kind of slanted direction on the map, those terms wouldn't make much sense.

This is how it's done in Hawaii. Everything toward the sea is **makai,** (MAH-kye); everything toward the mountains is **mauka** (MOW-kah). The other directions are **Diamond Head** (roughly eastward) and **Ewa** (roughly westward), named after two of the major landmarks of the city. Once you move out beyond Diamond Head, roughly eastward directions are referred to as **Koko Head** (Aina Haina is Koko Head of Kalani Valley, for example). Once you learn to use these simple terms, you'll be well on the way to becoming a kamaaina yourself.

NEIGHBORHOODS IN BRIEF

The Honolulu neighborhoods most tourists will be concerned with are:

Waikiki　The Waikiki area runs from Ala Moana Boulevard in an Ewa direction, up to Kapahulu Avenue in a Diamond Head direction, and from the Ala Wai Canal on the mountain side to the ocean. Within Waikiki, Kalakaua Avenue is the main thoroughfare, bordering the ocean; parallel to it is Kuhio Avenue; and parallel to that is the Ala Wai Boulevard. Along these avenues and their side streets are the main hotels, restaurants, shops, and sights of the tourist area.

Kapahulu　This is the area centered around Kapahulu Avenue, going one or two blocks on either side of the H-1 Highway, otherwise known as the Expressway. Many stores, businesses, and restaurants are located here.

University　This district runs from McCully to South King Street, until South King becomes Waialae Avenue, then mauka (toward the mountains) up into Manoa Valley. It includes the University of Hawaii.

McCully-Moiliili   The area of McCully-Moiliili runs from Kapiolani Boulevard to South King Street. There are stores, businesses, and Asian restaurants.

Ala Moana   The Ala Moana area extends mauka of Ala Moana Boulevard, between Waikiki and Restaurant Row. The Ala Moana Shopping Center is here.

Downtown Honolulu   This includes everything from Restaurant Row to the Historical Chinatown District. The latter is bordered by Beretania Street on the mountain side, Nuuanu Avenue on the Diamond Head side, Nimitz Highway on the harbor side, and River Street on the Ewa/airport side. Downtown contains the city's major business and financial district.

MAIN STREETS & HIGHWAYS

Your first introduction to the thoroughfares of Honolulu will probably be **Nimitz Highway/Ala Moana Boulevard,** a two-way divided highway that runs between the airport and Waikiki. **King Street** goes one way from downtown Honolulu to the University of Hawaii, passing Iolani Palace and the downtown historical sights. **Beretania Street** is one way going in the opposite direction; it starts at University Avenue and runs through Chinatown. The **H-1 Freeway** runs from Pearl Harbor Airport to Kahala Mall, then continues as a divided express highway, **Kalanianaole,** which goes around the island.

STREET MAPS

Locals consider the best Oahu maps to be Bryan's *Sectional Maps of Oahu* and the *Oahu Reference Maps,* by James A. Bier, Cartographer. Both can be obtained in many bookstores, or from Hawaii Geographic Maps and Books, 49 S. Hotel St., Suite 218 (P.O. Box 1698), Honolulu, HI 96808 (☎ 808/532-3952). Maps in free tourist publications are acceptable for most ordinary touring.

2 Getting Around

Many people think it's difficult to get around and succumb to package deals that wrap up the vacation in advance: transportation, hotels, sightseeing from the limousine window, all for one flat—and unnecessarily high—fee. And even if they've already discovered the do-it-yourself trick of staying at budget hotels and eating at low-cost restaurants, panic strikes when it comes to sightseeing—and how else to "do" Honolulu unless someone takes you by the hand on a guided tour?

Tours are pleasant and useful, of course, if you have only a day or two and want to pack in as many sights as you can. And you may want to take one (or else rent a car) when you circle the island of Oahu. But for sightseeing in Honolulu, at your own pace, there are options that are much cheaper, and much more fun.

BY BUS/TROLLEY

TheBUS   TheBUS is owned by the city and county of Honolulu and has routes all over the island. It operates daily from 5am to 12:30am on main routes. Adults pay 85¢ for a ride on TheBUS; children pay 25¢ (children under 6 free). Exact fare in coins is preferred. Free transfers, which can extend your ride considerably in one direction, must be requested when you board and pay your fare. Senior citizens can use the buses at a savings by showing a bus pass. A $15 pass is good for four years. (☎ 808/848-4444 for information on the Senior Bus Pass program.)

Bus schedules are not, unfortunately, available on the buses themselves, but if you have any questions about how to get where, simply call **TheBUS**

TheBUS

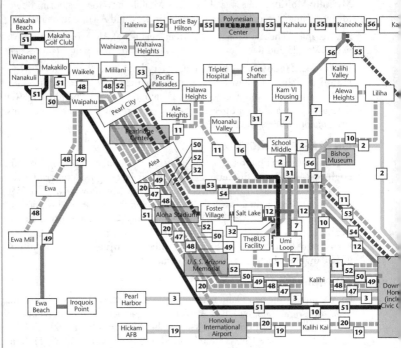

Common Bus Routes:

Ala Moana Shopping Center: Take bus #8 & #58 ALA MOANA CENTER, #19 & #20 AIRPORT or #47 WAIPAHU. Return #8 WAIKIKI or #19 WAIKIKI, or across Ala Moana Blvd. #20 & #47.

Bishop Museum: Take #2 SCHOOL STREET get off at Kapalama St., cross School St., walk down Bernice St. Return to School St. and take #2 WAIKIKI.

Byodo-In Temple: Take bus #2 to Hotel-Alakea St. (TRF) to #55 KANEOHE-KAHALUU. Get off at Valley of the Temple cemetery. Also #19 & #20 AIRPORT to King-Alakea St., (TRF) on Alakea St. to #55 KANEOHE-KAHALUU.

Circle Island: Take a Bus to ALA MOANA CENTER (TRF) to #52 WAHIAWA CIRCLE ISLAND or #55 KENEOHE CIRCLE ISLAND. This is a four-hour bus ride.

Chinatown or Downtown: Take any #2 bus going out of Waikiki, to Hotel St. Return take #2 WAIKIKI on Hotel St., or #19, #20, #47 WAIKIKI on King St.

Contemporary Museum & Punchbowl (National Cemetery of the Pacific): Take #2 bus (TRF) at Alapai St. to #15 MAKIKI-PACIFIC HGTS. Return, take #15 and get off at King St., area (TRF) #2 WAIKIKI.

Diamond Head Crater: #22 or #58 HAWAII KAI-SEA LIFE PARK to the crater. Take a flashlight. Return to the same area and take #22 WAIKIKI or #58 ALA MOANA.

Dole Plantation: Take bus to ALA MOANA CENTER (TRF) to #52 WAHIAWA CIRCLE ISLAND.

Foster Botanic Gardens: Take #2 bus to Hotel-Riviera St. Walk to Vineyard Blvd. Return to Hotel St. Take #2 WAIKIKI, or take #4 NUUANU and get off at Nuuanu-Vineyard. Cross Nuuanu Ave. and walk one block to the gardens.

Hawaii Maritime Center: Take #19-#20 AIRPORT, #47 WAIPAHU and get off at Alakea–Ala Moana. Cross the Street to the Aloha Tower.

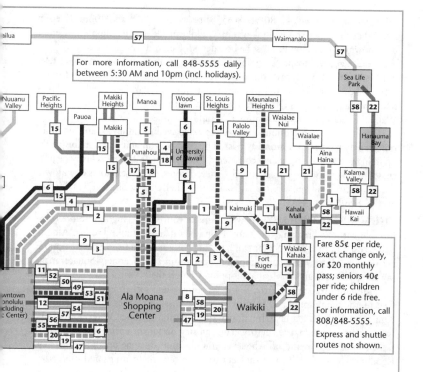

For more information, call 848-5555 daily between 5:30 AM and 10pm (incl. holidays).

Fare 85¢ per ride, exact change only, or $20 monthly pass; seniors 40¢ per ride; children under 6 ride free.

For information, call 808/848-5555.

Express and shuttle routes not shown.

Honolulu Zoo: Take any bus on Kuhio Ave. going DIAMOND HEAD direction to Kapahulu Ave.

Iolani Palace: also State Capitol, Honolulu Hale, Kawaihao Church, Mission Houses, Queen's Hospital, King Kamehameha Statue, State Judiciary Bldg., take any #2 bus and get off at Punchbowl and Beretania St. Walk to King St. Return #2 WAIKIKI on King St.

Kahala Mall: #22 or #58 HAWAII KAI–SEA LIFE PARK to Kilauea Ave. Return #22 WAIKIKI or #58 ALA MOANA CENTER.

Kodak Hula Show: (Tues-Thurs 10AM.) Free. Take #8, #19, #20, #47 WAIKIKI or #2 KAPIOLANI PARK to Kapiolani Park. Walk to the Waikiki Shell.

Pearl Harbor (Arizona Memorial): Open Daily 8AM to 3PM. Free. Take #20 AIRPORT or #47 WAIPAHU. Get off across from Memorial, or take a bus to Ala Moana Center (TRF) to #49, #50 or #52.

Polynesian Cultural Center: Take a bus to ALA MOANA CENTER (TRF) to #55 KANEOHE CIRCLE ISLAND. Bus ride takes two hours one way. PCC opens at 12:30PM. Closed on Sundays.

Queen Emma's Summer Home: Take #4 NUUANU and it will take you there, or board a bus to ALA MOANA CENTER (TRF) to #55 KANEOHE, #56-#57 KAILUA.

Sea Life Park: #22-#58 HAWAII KAI-SEA LIFE PARK. #22 will stop at Hanauma Bay enroute to the park.

University of Hawaii: Take #4 NUUANU. The bus will go to the University enroute to Nuuanu.

Waimea Falls Park: Take a bus to ALA MOANA CENTER (TRF) to #52 WAHIAWA CIRCLE ISLAND or #55 KANEOHE CIRCLE ISLAND.

information number (☎ 808/848-5555) between 5:30am and 10pm. Keep in mind that the buses you will take from Waikiki to Ala Moana Shopping Center or to downtown Honolulu must be boarded on Kuhio Avenue.

If you're at Ala Moana Shopping Center, you can use the no-cost direct telephones to TheBUS information, located at the bus stops on the north and south sides of the center. You should also note that traffic on Kalakaua Avenue, Waikiki's main thoroughfare, goes Diamond Head most of the way. All buses running from Waikiki either uptown or downtown should be boarded on Kuhio Avenue.

If you're staying in Honolulu and doing extensive bus riding for any length of time, it may pay to buy a **monthly pass.** They cost $20 for adults, $7.50 for youths up to high-school age (generally considered 19 or younger). Bus passes may be purchased at Food land Supermarkets, all 7-Eleven stores, all Russell stores downtown, the main City Hall and satellite city halls, and TheBUSPass office at 811 Middle St. (☎ 808/848-4444).

THE WAIKIKI TROLLEY   A way to make your sightseeing a bit more comfortable without breaking the bank: Hop aboard the Waikiki Trolley. All-day passes cost $15 for adults, $5 for children, and you can travel from 8am to 4:30pm between the Royal Hawaiian Shopping Center and Dole Cannery Square, making stops en route at Ala Moana Shopping Center, the Hilton Hawaiian Village, the Honolulu Academy of Arts, Ward Warehouse and Fishermans Wharf, Ward Centre, the state capitol and Iolani Palace, the Mission Houses Museum and the King Kamehameha Statue, Chinatown, the Hawaii Maritime Center, Restaurant Row, and the Hilo Hattie Factory. You can stay on for the entire two-hour, narrated trip or hop on and off whenever you like and continue on another trolley. Recalling Honolulu's turn-of-the-century streetcars, these jaunty red motorized trolleys with an old-fashioned look (etched-glass windows, polished brass rails, hand-carved oak interiors) stop each hour at the locations listed above. As you study the trips outlined below, you'll be able to see when and where the trolley can take you to some destinations. Call 808/591-2561 or check local papers for exact routes and schedules. Tours operate daily between 8am and 4pm.

BY TAXI

It's easy to get a cab in Waikiki. Simply step to the edge of any major thoroughfare, lift your hand to signal, and within five minutes you'll undoubtedly be on your way. Although not cheap (the first flip of the meter is usually $1.50), taxis are useful for emergencies and for short trips, and can be practical if you are traveling in a group. If you want to call a cab in advance, your hotel desk can usually get one for you, or you can call any of the numerous companies listed in the telephone book. Here are a few: **Charley's Taxi** (☎ 808/531-1333), **City Taxi** (☎ 808/524-2121), **Aloha State Cab** (☎ 808/847-3566), and **Sida of Hawaii** (☎ 808/836-0011).

BY BICYCLE

Honolulu, like big cities everywhere, has become very bicycle conscious. Bicycles used to be available for rental at a number of locations, but lately most hotels and car-rental agencies (like Hertz) have stopped renting them because of the high equipment-mortality rate. "We kept finding them in the ocean," said one supplier. But we did find *one* place where they can still be rented: **Blue Sky Rentals,** 1920 Ala Moana Blvd. (☎ 808/947-0101), at a rate of $15 for 24 hours.

BY RENTAL CAR

If you're going to stay mostly in Waikiki and only venture forth to downtown Honolulu, the convenience of renting a car will not justify the expense. On top of that, street parking is very difficult to find, and most lots are very expensive. Most hotels charge parking fees. If, however, you want to spend time on the wind-ward side of Oahu, or tour the entire island, then a car is a must.

See "Getting Around," in Chapter 3, for details on the car-rental agencies that operate throughout Hawaii and for some general tips on renting a car.

PARKING   Parking for the night can be a problem in the Waikiki area. *Tip:* Ala Wai Boulevard, along the canal, is less crowded than other main thoroughfares. In the downtown area, there are both municipal and private parking lots. Most street meters charge 1¢ per minute; in some busy locations the meters allow no more than 12 to 24 minutes. Read each meter carefully.

DRIVING RULES   A few words about driving in Honolulu. Many major thor-oughfares are now one-way streets, which helps the flow of traffic, but often makes it seem that you are driving miles out of your way to reach a specific destination. Downtown Honolulu is an especially confusing place to get around. You may want to keep in mind that in this area Beretania Street is Ewa, King Street is Diamond Head, Pensacola traffic now heads makai (to the sea), and Piikoi cars go in a mauka (to the mountains) direction. In Waikiki, Kalakaua traffic is Diamond Head most of the way, with a short stretch downtown running in both directions; Kuhio Avenue is two-way and the Ala Wai Boulevard is Ewa.

Those painted white arrows on the various lanes are not to be ignored. They indicate in which directions you are permitted to drive from each lane: right only, left only, left and straight ahead, or right and straight ahead. It's legal to make right turns when the light is red at most—but not all—intersections, so read the signs first. And if you come across a sign reading WE APPRECIATE YOUR KOKUA it's not an invitation to pay a toll. *Kokua* means cooperation in Hawaiian.

FAST FACTS: Oahu

AAA Hawaii   The local office of the American Automobile Association is at 590 Queen St. (☎ 808/528-2600, or 537-5544 for road service).

Area Code   The entire state of Hawaii has one telephone area code: 808.

Babysitters   Check first at your hotel desk. You can also try Aloha Babysitting Service (☎ 808/732-2029), Available Sitters (☎ 808/951-6118), and Sitters Unlimited (☎ 808/262-5728).

Car Rentals   Major car-rental companies, which rent automobiles on all four major islands, include Alamo, 2055 N. Nimitz Hwy. (☎ 808/833-4585 or 924-4444, or 800/327-9633); Avis at Honolulu International Airport (☎ 808/834-5536 or 800/831-8000); Budget, with many locations in Honolulu (☎ 808/922-3600 or 800/527-0700); Dollar of Hawaii, 1600 Kapiolani Blvd. (☎ 808/944-1544 or 800/367-7006); Hertz (☎ 800/654-3131); and Tropi-cal Rent-A-Car Systems, 765 Amana St. (☎ 808/957-0800 or 800/678-6000). See "Getting Around," in this chapter and in Chapter 3, for details.

Dentists   Dental Care Centers of Hawaii offers 24-hour emergency ser-vice. There are many locations around the island; addresses can be found in the telephone book. The after-hours number is 808/488-5200. Hawaii Family Dental Center (☎ 808/944-0011) is conveniently located at Sears at the Ala Moana Shopping Center, 1450 Ala Moana Blvd., and has a number of dentists on hand who can provide speedy treatment at reasonable cost.

Doctors   We hope it won't happen, but should you need medical assistance while youre in Honolulu, it is readily at hand. Prominent Queens Medical Center has a Waikiki affiliate: Queens Health Care Center, 1860 Ala Moana Blvd. (☎ 808/943-1111). The clinic is open Monday through Friday from 8am to 8pm, Saturday and Sunday from 8am to 4pm, and no appointment is needed.

Kuhio Walk-In Medical Clinics has a very convenient location at 2310 Kuhio Ave., #223 (second floor), across from the International Market Place (☎ 808/924-6688). They are open Monday through Saturday from 9am to 5pm; no appointment is required; they also make house/hotel calls.

Doctors on Call (DOC) has several clinics at Waikiki hotels; phone their central number, 808/971-8000, and you will be directed to the one closest to you. Should you require a house call, or hotel call, call DOC at 808/926-4777 and a physician will arrive at your hotel room promptly. The charge is a hefty $170!

Of course, in a medical emergency, you can always call **911** and ask for an ambulance, or go to the emergency department of the Queens Medical Center, 1301 Punchbowl St. (☎ 808/547-4311).

Emergencies   Dial **911** for fire, ambulance, or police; if you cannot reach 911, dial 0 (zero, not the letter "O") and the operator will assist you. For **poisoning** emergencies, call the Poison Center (☎ 808/941-4411).

Hospitals   For emergency medical service, Queens Medical Center, 1301 Punchbowl (☎ 808/547-4311), has 24-hour emergency-room service and offers outstanding trauma care. On the windward side, it's Castle Medical Center, 640 Ulukahiki in Kailua (☎ 808/263-5500).

Networks and Resources   Students: The University of Hawaii at Manoa sponsors a number of low-cost activities for the benefit of its students; non-students may also join in the fun and savings simply by paying an activity fee that covers a six-week summer session. Inquire at the Campus Center, Room 212, on the Manoa Campus of the University of Hawaii. **For Gay Men & Lesbians:** Call the gay-and-lesbian information line at 808/536-6000. **For Seniors:** Contact the Department of Parks and Recreation at 808/973-7262, or 808/973-7258 for news of senior-citizen activities. **For the Disabled:** Handicabs of the Pacific, P.O. Box 22428, Honolulu, HI 96823 (☎ 808/524-3866), provides special transportation for the disabled: wheelchair taxi service and a variety of tours, including luaus, cruises, and sightseeing journeys.

Newspapers and Magazines   There are two daily newspapers, both published by the Hawaii Newspaper Agency. The *Honolulu Advertiser* is the morning paper; the *Honolulu Star-Bulletin* is the evening paper with the bigger circulation. The Sunday paper is produced exclusively by the *Advertiser*.

Aloha magazine, published bi-monthly, and *Honolulu* magazine, published monthly, make for interesting reading.

Police   Dial **911;** if that doesn't work, dial 0 for the operator.

Post Office   In Waikiki, it's at 330 Saratoga Rd., next to Fort DeRussy (☎ 808/423-3990), open Monday, Tuesday, Thursday, and Friday from 8am to 4:30pm and on Saturday from 9am to noon.

Radio and TV   For all-Hawaiian music, tune in KCNN (1420 AM); for island music, contemporary Hawaiian to reggae, it's KCCN (1003 FM). KHPR (88.1 FM) is Hawaii Public Radio for classical music and news; KIPO (1380 AM and 89.3 FM) is Hawaii Public Radio for news and jazz, classical, and folk music. Station KTUH (90.3 FM) presents jazz, classical, rock, and Hawaiian music. Try KHVH (990 AM) for news, sports, and talk.

Most hotels have cable TV, as cable is necessary virtually everywhere on Oahu; 95% of the island is served by Oceanic Cablevision, whose major channels are: Channel 3, KHON (NBC); Channel 6, KITV (ABC); Channel 7, KGMB (CBS); Channel 10, PBS; Channel 14, CNN; Channel 24, HBO; Channel 25, Cinemax; Channel 26, AMC; Channel 28, A&E; Channel 29, TNT; Channel 31, MTV; Channel 32, Nickelodeon; Channel 33, Showtime; Channel 34, Disney; Channel 44, TMC. Channel 12 is the Oceanic Cable listing channel; it runs continual lists of what is running on the 32 free channels.

Telephone Calls   Five dollars doesn't buy a great deal in Hawaii, but it can buy you an eight-minute phone call back to the mainland, or a series of phone calls for up to eight minutes. Here's how it works: You go to one of Phone Line Hawaii's Waikiki telecom centers at either the International Market Place, 2330 Kalakaua Ave., or the Discovery Bay Center, 1778 Ala Moana Blvd., where the cards are on sale, every day from 8:30am to 11pm. Then you use your card from any telephone, either in a phone booth or your hotel room, and you eliminate the charges that hotels levy on operator-assisted calls. Cards for calling Canada cost $15 and cards for other countries are also available at $10 and $20.

Transit Information   For information on TheBUS, call 808/848-5555 or see "Getting Around," above.

Useful Telephone Numbers   For time, call 808/983-3211. For a surf report, call **808/836-1952**.

Visitors Bureau   The Hawaii Visitors Bureau (☎ 808/923-1811) is at 2270 Kalakaua Ave., 7th floor.

Weather   In the Honolulu area, call 808/833-2849; for the rest of Oahu, call 808/836-0121; for the Hawaiian waters, call 808/836-3921.

3   Where to Stay in Town & Around the Island

For those on a budget, Oahu is a good choice; it's the cheapest of all the Hawaiian Islands—and one of the most fascinating to boot. However, inflation—as it is elsewhere—has been rampant. Many of the cozy little guesthouses that used to enable budget tourists to live comfortably and very cheaply some years ago have been torn down and new, more expensive structures have been built. Because of the tremendous number of accommodations in Waikiki, though, it's still possible to find plenty of good rooms that are reasonably priced.

PRICES   Remember that prices fluctuate, so they may vary slightly from the figures quoted below. Even so, these establishments will be your best hotel buys on the island. Almost all hotels up their rates—by as much as $10 to $20 per unit—during the busy winter season, roughly December 20 to April 15. In slow seasons, however, rates are often discounted, and you can do especially well on weekly rentals. The hotel may eliminate cleaning service (which is costly), but you may be able to book a decent apartment for a low price.

Unless otherwise stated by us, all rooms listed below have private bath.

Note that you must add 4.17% Hawaii state tax plus 6% hotel room tax to all rates. Tax rates are subject to change.

HOW THE LISTINGS ARE ORGANIZED   The hotels are listed by price and then by geographic location. The Waikiki hotels are split into the following areas: **Diamond Head Waikiki,** that part of town closest to Kuhio Beach and Kapiolani Park; **Central Waikiki,** the area centering, roughly, around the International Market Place; **Ewa Waikiki,** the section near the Hilton Hawaiian Village Hotel and Ilikai Hotel and the closest area to downtown Honolulu; **Near the Ala Wai,** that area closest to the Ali Wai Boulevard; and **Near Ala Moana,** the area close to the Ala Moana Canal. Remember that all these areas are close to each other and all are comparable in terms of comfort and convenience. And they're all near the beach. The other geographic areas we've used are **Downtown Honolulu** and **Windward Oahu.**

HOTELS IN WAIKIKI   Most tourists stay in Waikiki, mecca of the malihinis. This is a relatively small area of Honolulu, but within it are concentrated most of the town's best beaches, and therefore most of the hotels and entertainment facilities. Downtown Honolulu is only a short bus ride away.

Whether you choose to spend $50 or $100 a night, you'll be living sensibly and pleasantly—and far more inexpensively than most tourists, who are led to believe that a hotel in Waikiki under $100 a day doesn't exist. It certainly does exist, particularly at the Hawaiian wonder of wonders: the **apartment-hotel with kitchenette.** Many of them are individually owned condominium units, and they're almost always cheaper than the rooms in large seaside hotels.

As a point of orientation, remember that most fancy hotels are located right on the beach and on Kalakaua Avenue, the main drag. Between Kalakaua and Ala Wai Boulevard (which marks most of the makai and mauka boundaries of Waikiki) are dozens of tree-lined pretty streets containing the bulk of the smaller and less expensive hotels. Waikiki itself is small enough that you can easily walk from any of these hotels to the beach; they are also near each other, so you should have no trouble in getting from one to another if you have to do some hotel hunting.

SAVING MONEY ON HOTELS   A new publication called the *Hawaii Entertainment Book* could save you a bundle. Its coupons offer 50% discounts off regular hotel rates (with some restrictions) at scores of quality hotels on all the major Hawaiian islands, including many described in this book. In addition, there are hefty discounts on restaurants, travel, shopping, sightseeing, and sports activities. We usually don't get excited about publications of this sort, which often promise more than they deliver. But this one is for real. Good friends came back from a recent trip and calculated they'd saved over $1,000 using the coupons from the book. Books can be ordered directly from the publisher, and, at a cost of $38, make a very worthwhile investment. Write *Hawaii Entertainment Book,* Entertainment Publications, 4211 Waialae Ave., Honolulu, HI 96816 (☎ 808/737-3252; fax 808/734-2051).

You can also save money on hotels through **Hotel Exchange,** 1946 Ala Moana Blvd., Honolulu, HI 96815 (☎ 808/942-8544; fax 808/955-2627), an organization that makes deals with hotels at substantial discounts and passes on some of the savings to guests. They will take advance reservations with an approved credit card, or you can simply walk in if you're already in town and not happy where you're staying. Savings could be as little as $5 or as much as $100 a day at many leading hotels.

Note: A number of hotels listed in this chapter bear the name "Outrigger." While all are now under the Outrigger Hotels Hawaii umbrella, they are not standardized chain hotels; each offers the traveler something a little different.

A CONDO- & HOUSE-RENTAL SPECIALIST   If you're thinking of staying in a condo or a house on any of the Hawaiian islands, you should know about **HALE** (Hawaiian Apartment Leasing Enterprises), 479 Ocean Ave., Suite B, Laguna Beach, CA 92651 (☎ 714/497-4253 or 800/854-8843). Hale means "home" in Hawaiian, and this outfit aims to provide visitors with a "home away from home" either in a privately managed condominium or a private house.

Daily rates in condominiums can be up to 50% less than the regular rate, and weekly and monthly rates are even lower. Most condos are custom decorated, and high quality. And they're often available when a property seems sold out, since this is a separate inventory within the property. HALE's condos offer a wide range of price, size, and location. For example, a studio at the Island Colony on Oahu starts at $60 a night for two in the low season, while Foster Towers studios are $75 a night for two in the high season. On Maui, rates range from $350 a week for two in Kihei at Kihei Bay Surf in low season and $455 a week for two in high season. Just north of Kaanapali, an oceanfront studio for two at Papakea is $65 a night in low season and $95 a night in high season. Condos are also available on Kauai, the Big Island, and Molokai.

As for private houses, there are some 200 of them available on all the islands; cleaning staff, cooks, chauffeurs, day care, and additional custom services can be arranged. Possibilities include a two-bedroom/two-bath, oceanfront house on the Kona Coast of the Big Island at $930 a week for six, and a three-bedroom/two-bath house in Poipu on Kauai for $775 a week in low season.

For information write HALE, requesting their brochure, which describes the properties and also shows proximity to golf, tennis, restaurants, and shopping.

DOUBLES FOR ABOUT $40 TO $70
DIAMOND HEAD WAIKIKI

Hale Waikiki Apartment Hotel
2410 Koa Ave., Honolulu, HI 96815. ☎ **808/923-9012.** 15 apts. TV. Summer, $38.50–$45 apt. Winter, $49–$54 apt. No credit cards.

This is an old-but-livable building. Outside, an iron gate is kept locked most of the time. Inside, a long walkway lined with greenery fronts the low-rise building that is very well secured. Each unit accommodates two people comfortably, with a kitchenette and a bath with shower. New ceiling fans have been installed. There is no phone, but you can install your own (the room is appropriately wired). There is cleaning service twice a week on request and laundry facilities on the premises. You might have to scurry to find parking, but the central location, just one block from the beach and big hotels, makes up for it.

Honolulu Prince
415 Nahua St., Honolulu HI 96815. ☎ **808/922-1616,** or toll free 800/922-7866 on the mainland U.S., 800/445-6633 in Canada. Fax 808/922-6223. 103 rms, 22 apts. A/C TV TEL. Apr–Dec 22, $66–$78 double; $105 one-bedroom apt; $130 two-bedroom apt. Dec 23–Mar, $77–$87 double; $120 one-bedroom apt; $140 two-bedroom apt for four. CB, DC, DISC, JCB, MC, V. Parking $9 per day.

One of Waikiki's older apartment hotels, this place has seen many years of comfortable, casual living. Our favorite units here are the spacious, nicely furnished one-bedroom apartments that have full kitchens and separate bedrooms and can accommodate four. Four to six people can be accommodated in the two-bedroom kitchen apartments, which have two double beds, a sofa bed, and plenty of room for puttering around. The studios are furnished with either two doubles or a king-size bed plus a sofa bed. Most units have lanais. Cleaning service is provided every day. On the premises is Legends, a popular sports bar with satellite TV, darts, and video games. The hotel is managed by Aston Hotels & Resorts.

Lealea Hale Apartment Hotel

2423 Cleghorn St., Honolulu, HI 96815. ☎ **808/922-1726.** 20 rms. A/C TV. Apr–Dec 20, $45–$65 twin or double. Dec 21–Mar, $60–$95 twin or double. Discounted weekly rates available. DISC, JCB, MC, V. Parking $7 per day.

On a quiet narrow, one-way road in the center of Waikiki, this three-story hotel is in well-preserved condition and boasts bedrooms with double or twin beds, full kitchen, lanai, and bath with shower. Weekly rates offer good bargains. There is no pool and few amenities. Parking is limited. One of the better budget bets in Waikiki during the summer months.

✪ Royal Grove Hotel

151 Uluniu Ave., Honolulu, HI 96815. ☎ **808/923-7691.** 87 rms. A/C TV TEL. $36–$55 single or double; $75 one-bedroom suite; $75–$95 condo. Each additional person $10. Discounted weekly rates available. AE, DC, MC, V. Parking $4–$6.50 per day.

An old standby in this part of town, this is one of the prettiest of Waikiki's small hotels. The six-story pink concrete building is about three minutes from Kuhio Beach, but if you're really lazy you can dunk in the tiny pool right on the grounds. Some studios have kitchenettes, and efficiencies have private lanais. The accommodations become fancier as prices go up; all are nicely furnished and comfortable and have tub/shower facilities; the kitchens are all electric. It's best to ask for an air-conditioned room to drown out street noises. Amenities and dining facilities include round-the-clock desk service; twice-weekly or weekly cleaning service; Ruffage Natural Foods and Sushi Bar for health-food supplies, sand-wiches, and sushi; and Na's B-B-Que offering Korean plate-lunch specials. Both restaurants are open daily.

Over the years, readers have continued to write to comment on the friendliness of the owners, the Fong family, who frequently have potluck dinners and parties so that everyone can get acquainted. Lots of aloha for a small price at this one.

The Fongs also rent a number of units at the lovely **Pacific Monarch Hotel and Condominium,** just across the street. These are comfortable, spacious quarters wonderfully set up for family living. Inquire about these when you call.

Waikiki Hana

2424 Koa Ave., Honolulu, HI 96815. ☎ **808/926-8841,** or toll free 800/367-5004 in the continental U.S. and Canada. Fax toll free 800/477-2329. 73 rms. A/C TV TEL. Apr–Dec 17, $65–$97 double; $160 one-bedroom suite. Dec 18–Mar,$75–$110 double; $170 one-bedroom suite. AE, DC, MC, V. Parking $10 per day.

Tucked away behind the posh Hyatt Regency Hotel and just a short block from Kuhio Beach is the Waikiki Hana. A new management took over several years ago and totally renovated and refurbished this older hotel. The sparkling lobby is filled

Waikiki Accommodations

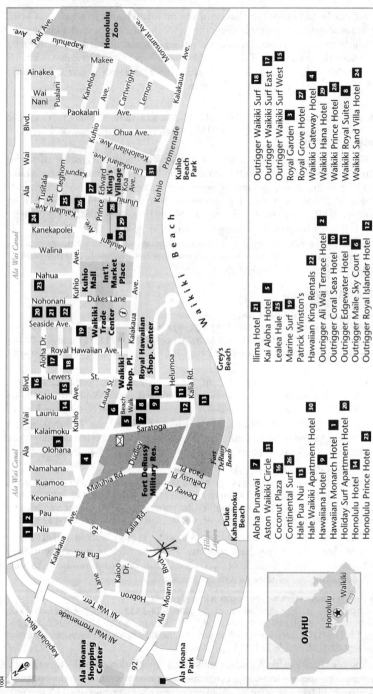

Outrigger Waikiki Surf **18**
Outrigger Waikiki Surf East **17**
Outrigger Waikiki Surf West **25**
Royal Garden **3**
Royal Grove Hotel **27**
Waikiki Gateway Hotel **4**
Waikiki Hana Hotel **29**
Waikiki Prince Hotel **28**
Waikiki Royal Suites **8**
Waikiki Sand Villa Hotel **24**

Ilima Hotel **21**
Kai Aloha Hotel **5**
Lealea Hale **25**
Marine Surf **19**
Patrick Winston's
Hawaiian King Rentals **22**
Outrigger Ali Wai Terrace Hotel **2**
Outrigger Coral Seas Hotel **10**
Outrigger Edgewater Hotel **11**
Outrigger Maile Sky Court **6**
Outrigger Royal Islander Hotel **12**

Aloha Punawai **7**
Aston Waikiki Circle **31**
Coconut Plaza **16**
Continental Surf **26**
Hale Pua Nui **13**
Hale Waikiki Apartment Hotel **30**
Hawaiiana Hotel **9**
Hawaiian Monarch Hotel **1**
Holiday Surf Apartment Hotel **20**
Honolulu Hotel **14**
Honolulu Prince Hotel **23**

Post Office ⊠   Information ⓘ

with wicker chairs, while the smartly decorated rooms have light woods, rose walls, and blue quilted bedspreads. Only the top-of-the-line rooms have a kitchenette, which consists of a combination sink, refrigerator, and electric hotplate. All rates include the use of a car. The reasonably priced Super Chef Restaurant is located in the lobby. Considering that this is a full-service hotel with an excellent location, it's one of the better values on the beach.

Ⓢ Waikiki Prince Hotel

2431 Prince Edward St., Honolulu, HI 96815. ☎ **808/922-1544.** 30 rms. A/C TV. Apr–Dec 19, $40–$50 per day. Dec 20–Mar, $43–$53 per day. Weekly rates on request. DC, MC, V. Parking $3 per day.

Some of the most reasonable prices in this close-to-the-beach area are offered by this modest little hotel, which is mostly for undemanding types. But there is cable TV in all the rooms, and the 20 rooms with kitchenettes have new drapes, bedspreads, and pots and pans. The location needs no improvement: It's right behind the Hyatt Regency Hotel, just two short blocks from Kuhio Beach. The Waikiki Prince is very popular with foreign travelers (they make up about 75% of the clientele), and many students stay here when school is out. There are no phones, but a buzzer system alerts you to your messages. Rooms are cleaned every three or four days, and towels are changed every day.

CENTRAL WAIKIKI

Outrigger Waikiki Surf Hotel

2200 Kuhio Ave., Honolulu, HI 96815. ☎ **808/923-7671,** or toll free 800/688-7444 in the U.S. and Canada, 1/800/124-171 from Australia. Fax 800/622-4852. 303 rms. A/C TV TEL. $70–$85 single or double; $115–$200 suite. AE, CB, DC, DISC, JCB, MC, V. Parking $7 per day.

Like all the Outrigger properties, this hotel is set up well for comfortable living. The spacious rooms usually have twin beds (a few double and queen-size beds are available) and a long, narrow lanai that is shared with the next room. Doubles with complete kitchenettes are available, and suites have kitchens. No-smoking and handicapped rooms are also available. The bustle of Kalakaua is just one long block away; the Pacific, two. There's a pleasant pool for at-home swimming.

Outrigger Waikiki Surf West

412 Lewers St., Honolulu, HI 96815. ☎ **808/923-7671,** or toll free 800/688-7444 in the U.S. and Canada, 1/800/124-171 from Australia. Fax toll free 800/622-4852. 38 rms, 77 suites. A/C TV TEL. $70–$80 double/kitchenette; $90–$100 one-bedroom suite/kitchenette. Each additional person $15. AE, CB, DC, DISC, JCB, MC, V. Parking $7 per day.

This hotel shares the lobby and front desk with the main Waikiki Surf across the street, but it has its own large pool area. All the recently renovated rooms have kitchenettes, a bath with shower, and lanais. Suites can accommodate up to four. No-smoking and handicapped rooms available.

✪ Patrick Winston's Hawaiian King Rentals

417 Nohonani St., Honolulu, HI 96815. ☎ **808/924-3332,** or toll free 800/545-1948. 11 units in 66-unit hotel/condominium. A/C TV TEL. Apr 15–Dec 15, $59–$89. Dec 16–Apr 14, $75–$109. Each additional person $10. Airline employees' discounts. Minimum stay four days. AE, MC, V. Parking $7 per day.

You could call Patrick Winston's units here a hotel-within-a-hotel—they're really something special. Winston, a delightful young man who takes a caring, personal interest in his guests, many of whom return year after year, purchased his first unit

Readers Recommend

Patrick Winston's Hawaiian King Rentals. *"Never in some 30 years of traveling have I experienced such personal attention as I did from Patrick Winston himself when my son and I arrived at midnight not knowing where we would stay. We ran into Pat quite by accident. He is a most accommodating and helpful individual, and a genuine gentleman. We would both highly recommend his spacious, immaculate, and completely furnished condos to anyone and sincerely believe you could not find a better bargain anywhere."* —Katherine A. Nash, Arlington, Il.

in the Hawaiian King when it became a condominium hotel back in 1981. He was the interior designer–contractor who furnished the entire project. All his units have gone through complete $20,000-and-more renovations. Two large units (788 sq. ft.) are called the Corporate Suites; they contain a separate room with a complete work station including a typewriter, calculator, and other business supplies, along with a large living room with VCR, electronic safe, and a conference area. The Mount Fuji Suite has white and black accents along with Oriental furniture, futons, and shoji screens. His other one-bedroom units have new carpeting and furniture, ceramic tiles, floor-to-ceiling mirrors, stereos and cable remote TVs, kitchens with microwave and convection ovens, and washer/dryers. A rowing machine and bicycle are available in certain units. Winston states: "I am dedicated to concepts that ring out time and again in your literature; that is quality lodging at a reasonable price, with the aloha spirit ringing in loudly."

The Hawaiian King is a five-story building built around a lovely pool and garden area, about two blocks from the beach. There's a laundry on the premises, a cocktail lounge, a minimart, and 24-hour front-desk and telephone switchboard service.

White Sands Waikiki Resort

431 Nohonani St., Honolulu, HI 96815. ☎ **808/923-7336.** 80 rms. A/C TV TEL. $62–$88 single; $69–$95 double. AE, DC, DISC, MC, V. Free parking, but very limited, in the hotel; public lot across the street.

On pleasant Nohonani Street, about halfway between Kuhio Avenue and Ala Wai Boulevard, this low-rise garden hotel is a longtime favorite. It's a time-sharing establishment, so it's not always easy to get an opening here, and reservations cannot be confirmed until two weeks before your arrival date. However, when you consider that rooms are nicely furnished and that you get a kitchenette and a private lanai with even a standard room, it's worth a try. Each apartment is furnished differently, but nicely, in a Polynesian decor, and the beds are large and comfortable. Rooms have every-other-day cleaning service. The deluxe swimming pool, in an inner court, is surrounded by gardens, shady nooks, and pathways for exploring this tranquil acre in the heart of Waikiki. Coffee is served free in the lobby in the morning.

EWA WAIKIKI

Aloha Punawai

305 Saratoga Rd., Honolulu, HI 96815. ☎ **808/923-5211.** 19 apts. A/C TV. $47–$52 studio for one without air conditioning; $52–$57 studio for one with air conditioning; $57–$62 bedroom for one with air conditioning; $62–$67 large bedroom for one with air conditioning. Each additional person $8. Children under 12 free. Minimum stay three days; weekly and monthly discounts available. No credit cards. Parking $5 per day.

The owners of this place try hard to keep a low profile, but we are revealing their secret: There are not many places in Waikiki that are this reasonable. Here you get a clean, comfortable apartment with a furnished kitchen and a lanai. There are no telephones, although phones can be installed for those on long stays. Stay a month and the rates go down to $32 and $52 a day. There are also both small and large one-bedroom apartments available. Towels and linens are provided and there is cleaning service twice a week. Aloha Punawai has been family-owned and -operated since 1959. Saratoga Road is near Fort DeRussy, and the hotel is only a block from the beach.

✪ Hale Pua Nui

228 Beach Walk, Honolulu, HI 96815. ☎ **808/923-9693.** 22 studio apts. TV TEL. Apr 1–Jun 30 and Oct 1–Nov 30, $44 single or double, $267 weekly. Jul 1–Sept 30 and Dec 1–Mar 31, $55 single or double, $325 weekly. Each additional person $10.43. Parking $5 per day, $27 per week.

One of our favorite streets in Honolulu is Beach Walk, a tiny street running from Kalakaua smack into the ocean, and relatively—for Waikiki—quiet. Here you'll find this lovely little complex of large studio apartments, many of whose guests come back year after year. The location is tops—just half a block to the beach at the Outrigger Reef Hotel and just around the bend from Fort DeRussy, where the swimming is excellent. The studio apartments have either twin or double beds and are tastefully outfitted with new carpets, drapes, bedspreads, and artistic touches. They all have cross-ventilation, soundproofing, and ceilings. Kitchenettes are thoroughly equipped (even to ironing boards). A maximum of four people can stay in a room. Rollaways are available. Hugh and Gloria Cave are the resident managers. An excellent value!

Kai Aloha Hotel

235 Saratoga Rd., Honolulu, HI 96815. ☎ **808/923-6723.** Fax 808/922-7592. 18 apts. A/C TV TEL. $60–$65 studio apt with lanai; $68–$73 one-bedroom apt for two people. $80–$85 for three, $90–$95 for four. Each additional person $10. AE, DC, DISC, JCB, MC, V. Parking $7 per day.

Faithful fans return year after year to this simple little hotel. They prefer the homey atmosphere, the friendliness of the management, and the feeling of intimacy, which is rare at the more impersonal high-rise hotels. The location, very close to the beach and shopping area, is convenient, and the lush tropical plantings add an island flavor. Every unit has either a modern kitchen or kitchenette. Apartments have

---

Readers Recommend

Aloha Punawai. *"We thought we had died and gone to heaven at this place. Everything was clean, well-lighted, and airy. The furnishings all look like new. The kitchen has plenty of spotless counter space and is very well stocked with dishes and cookware. The bathroom is full sized and immaculate. The air conditioner is quiet yet keeps the apartment deliciously cool. The neighborhood is attractive; the hotel is well placed for whatever a tourist desires to do; and the street noise is minimal. In addition to all of the above-mentioned wonders, the Aloha Punawai comes complete with Florence Barientos. I have stayed in a lot of hotels, with a lot of wonderful proprietors, but nobody can compete with Florence. She treated us like guests in her own home. She was concerned with our every need and showered us with many kindnesses which made our stay a delight."* —Taffy Curtis, Healdsburg, Calif.

full-size refrigerators; the studios, half-size ones. All units have a garbage disposal, toaster, and ironing board. There are coin-operated laundry facilities available on the premises. One-bedroom apartments can accommodate families of four or five; children are welcome. (Please note that rates may be changing soon.)

Outrigger Maile Sky Court Hotel

2058 Kuhlo Ave., Honolulu, HI 96815. ☎ **808/947-2828,** or toll free 800/688-7444 in the U.S. and Canada, 1/800/124-171 from Australia. Fax toll free 800/622-4852. 554 rms. 42 studios and suites. A/C TV TEL. $70–$85 double; $80–$150 double/kitchenette; $180–$200 suite/kitchenette. Maximum two in doubles, three people in studios. Each additional person $15. AE, CB, DC, DISC, JCB, MC, V. Parking $7 per day.

Designed for the easy life, this hotel is located across the road from the well-known Nick's Fishmarket Restaurant, at the "Gateway to Waikiki," within easy walking distance of the beach and all the attractions of Kalakaua Avenue. There's a very pleasant ambience here, evident as soon as you walk into the pretty open-air lobby. This 44-story resort offers a variety of accommodations. Rooms are of modest size, but most have views (some, from the higher floors, are spectacular) and all have attractive furnishings and cable TV. Sorry—there are no lanais. Even the hotel rooms boast small refrigerators; studios and suites add a two-burner electric range for light cooking. There's a pool and a Jacuzzi on the large, 360° sun deck and a poolside snack bar. No-smoking and handicapped rooms are available.

Waikiki Gateway Hotel

2070 Kalakaua Ave., Honolulu, HI 96815. ☎ **808/955-3741,** or toll free 800/633-8799 in the mainland U.S. and Canada, 1/800/125-921 from Australia. Fax 808/955-1313. 190 rms. A/C TV TEL. Apr–Dec 22, $55–$100 double; $110 penthouse suite. Dec 21–Mar, $77–$112 double. AE, DC, JCB, MC, V. Parking $7 per day.

This hotel is well-known as the home of Nick's Fishmarket, one of Honolulu's favorite restaurants. It's also well-known as a good-value hotel. It offers rooms with a private lanai, cable TV, an under-the-counter refrigerator, an in-room safe, and a luxurious bath. There's daily cleaning service and a guest laundry. The beach is less than a 10-minute walk, but if you'd rather swim at home, try the beautiful pool backed by a volcanic rock wall and a spacious sun deck.

NEAR THE ALA WAI

Holiday Surf Apartment Hotel

2303 Ala Wai Blvd., Honolulu, HI 96815. ☎ **808/923-8488.** 34 rms. TV. April–Jun and Sept–Nov, $39 studio; $48 one-bedroom. July and Mar, $48 studio; $54 one-bedroom. Aug and Dec–Feb, $54 studio; $60 one-bedroom. Each additional person $3. AE, CB, DC, DISC, JCB, MC, V. Free parking.

This clean, white six-story building stands at the corner of Ala Wai Boulevard and Nohonani Street. It's anything but imposing, but well worth considering because it offers delightfully appointed accommodations at low rates. Most of the units have small lanais that accommodate two chairs. Most of the bathrooms have stall showers, but some have tub/shower combinations. There are no telephones in the rooms, but guests may make free local calls at the lobby office phone. Kitchens are fully equipped with full-size refrigerators and stoves. The one-bedroom apartments can accomodate up to five people. From here to the beach it's two long blocks, about a seven-minute walk.

Outrigger Ala Wai Terrace Hotel

1547 Ala Wai Blvd., Honolulu HI 96815. ☎ **808/949-7384,** or toll free 800/462-6262 in the U.S. and Canada, 1/800/124-171 from Australia. Fax toll free 800/622-4852. 196 rms,

43 apts. A/C TV TEL. $55 studio; $60–$110 one-bedroom. Each additional person $15. AE, CB, DC, DISC, JCB, MC, V. Parking $3.50 per day.

Some of the lowest rates in Waikiki are being offered at this hotel, which is located at the very beginning of Ala Wai Boulevard, not far from Ala Moana. This 47-year-old apartment building was converted into a hotel a few years ago, and while there's nothing at all fancy about it (don't expect tourist amenities like a pool or restaurant), it does offer clean and comfortable units all with full kitchens and all the necessities.

Waikiki Sand Villa Hotel

2375 Ala Wai Blvd., Honolulu, HI 96815. ☎ **808/922-4744,** or toll free 800/247-1903 in the U.S. Fax 808/923-2541. 211 rms. A/C TV TEL. Off season, $69–$91 double; $130 one-bedroom suite. Winter, $77–$120 double; $160 one-bedroom suite. Each additional person $10. Children under 12 stay free in parents' room using existing bedding. AE, DC, DISC, JCB, MC, V. Parking $4 per day.

The Waikiki Sand Villa Hotel is looking better than ever these days, thanks to a $3-million top-to-bottom renovation. The lobby now has a Hawaiian plantation-style ambience. The best views are of the Ala Wai Canal, the golf course across it, and the Koolau Mountains, but even the opposite views are not obscured by neighboring buildings. Rooms are adequate in size, and the decor is handsome; two tables—one inside and one out on the cozy lanai—afford a choice of breakfast spots. The rooms include a refrigerator and an in-room safe for valuables. Opening off the lobby is the Lobster Hut Restaurant, serving lunch and dinner and featuring $1^{1}/_{2}$-pound stuffed lobsters.

NEAR ALA MOANA

Big Surf Hotel

1690 Ala Moana Blvd., Honolulu, HI 96815. ☎ **808/946-6525.** 10 small rms. 18 mountain-view studios, 20 ocean-view one-bedroom suites. TV. $25–$37 single small rooms; $35–$45 single or double mountain-view studios; $50–$75 one-bedroom ocean-view suites. MC, V. Parking $4 per day.

Located $1^{1}/_{2}$ blocks from Ala Moana Beach and a block from the Ala Moana Shopping Center, this hotel has some of the lowest rates in Waikiki. There is no pool, no restaurant, and the only telephone is one for local calls in the small lobby. The small single rooms have one bed and a private bath with shower. A couple would require one of the larger studios, which come with twin beds and lanais. For parties of up to five people, there are one-bedroom suites with full kitchens. Color TV is available in the larger studios and some of the singles.

Most of the accommodations have been renovated and, though simple, are adequately furnished. Don't expect spaciousness at this price. The hotel is a few minutes stroll around the Ilikai lagoon to the beach, and just a few minutes in the other direction to the Ala Moana Shopping Center.

Colony's Hawaii Polo Inn

1696 Ala Moana Blvd., Honolulu, HI 96815. ☎ **808/949-0061,** or toll free 800/777-1700. Fax 808/949-4906. 65 rms. TV TEL. $55–$85 single or double; $95–$115 minisuite with kitchenette. Each additional person $10. AE, CB, DC, DISC, MC, V. Parking $5 per day.

This small boutique hotel is across the road from the luxury Hawaii Prince Hotel; it's also at the other end of the price spectrum. All rooms have been attractively renovated, and offer refrigerators, in-room coffee service, and daily cleaning service. There is a swimming pool, launderette, and parking on the premises. The hotel is less than two blocks from the Ala Moana Shopping Center and Ala Moana Beach Park, an excellent swimming beach and a local family favorite.

A stay at the Hawaii Polo Inn also entitles you to two tickets to the Hawaii Polo Club's Sunday polo matches from March through August; off-season, you can get a 10% discount on a polo lesson or beach ride.

DOWNTOWN HONOLULU

Tourists who prefer to stay in downtown Honolulu (an easy bus ride from Waikiki) rather than in the beach area will have somewhat tougher sledding. There are so few hotels outside Waikiki that most tourists never hear about them at all. They are primarily occupied by businesspeople. But there are a few in our budget category, and because this area is ideal for serious sightseeing, you may want to consider them.

Nakamura Hotel

1140 S. King St., Honolulu, HI 96814. ☎ **808/593-9951.** 41 rms. TEL. $40 single; $45 double; $47 twin. Each additional person $5. No credit cards. Free parking.

Though this isn't a large hotel, you may be lucky enough to find a room on the spur of the moment since this small, family-run establishment is out of the tourist mainstream. Just off Piikoi Street, this clean and quite comfortably appointed building offers rooms with wall-to-wall carpeting, a large tiled bathroom, good drawer and closet space, and even a telephone. We prefer the rooms facing the mountains; even though they do not have air conditioning, they do catch those refreshing trade winds. In the air-conditioned rooms, the machine also drowns out the traffic on King Street. Some of the rooms are too small for a third person. TVs can be rented. Mrs. Winifred Hakoda, the personable desk clerk and day manager, advises that no late arrivals (after 9pm Monday through Saturday, after 8pm Sunday and holidays) are accepted.

Town Inn

250 N. Beretania St., Honolulu, HI 96817. ☎ **808/536-2377.** 26 rms. TEL. $36–$49 single or double; $49 one-bedroom air-conditioned suite. MC, V. Free parking.

This tastefully modern Japanese establishment is where you'll mingle, so the management promises, "with important personages and travelers of every race." And all this cosmopolitanism is very reasonable, too! Lower-priced singles and doubles do not have air conditioning; the higher-priced do. Don't expect to sleep on the floor Japanese style; the bedrooms are as Western as the air conditioning. There's a Japanese restaurant, Miyajima, on the premises.

WINDWARD OAHU & THE NORTH SHORE

Windward Oahu is on the other side of the mighty Koolau mountain range, which serves as a backdrop to Honolulu. The scenery is comparable to what you'll find on the neighboring islands. This is "the country," where many local people spend their vacations, and it's off the usual tourist track. Although this is a good jumping-off spot from which to visit many of the attractions of the windward side and North Shore, it's essentially a place where you sit on the gorgeous beach surrounded by sea, sky, and fragrant blossoms and do absolutely nothing at all.

Dreaming of a cottage right on the beach? Pat O'Malley of **Pat's Kailua Beach Properties,** 204 S. Kalaheo Ave., Kailua, HI 96734 (☎ 808/261-1653 or 808/262-4128; fax 808/262-8275 or 808/261-0893), may be able to help you out. Pat offers more than 25 fully furnished houses and cottages along Kailua Beach, from a million-dollar beachfront estate to "beachy" cottages on or close to the water. About half of these fall within our budget, costing $65 to $95 a day. Each is different, but all are fully furnished and provide cooking and dining utensils, bedding and towels, tele-phone, and TV. Some are duplexes. The interiors of the cottages we saw were well maintained; some have been recently renovated. The exteriors of some are weather-beaten, which gives them a rustic look. Settings and views are lovely, and many have delightful yards and gardens. Call Pat O'Malley for information and reservations, and ask about the deposit requirements.

Marilyn and Lucky Cole, who run **North Shore Vacation Homes,** 59-229 C Ke Nui Rd., Haleiwa, HI 96712 (☎ 808/638-7289, or 800/678-5263; fax 808/638-8736), have four lovely vacation homes for rent on the North Shore, just 1 ¹/₂ miles west of the Turtle Bay Hilton Resort. All oceanfront, these are two- and three-bedroom beachfront cottages and homes with large, covered redwood decks, plentiful indoor space, and a sleeping capacity of from 4 to 10 persons. During the off-season, after Labor Day to Thanksgiving and after Easter to the first of June, the rates are $105, $150, and $160 per day; from Thanksgiving through Easter and from June 1 through Labor Day weekend, rates are $125, $165, and $175 per day; during the week before and after Christmas, rates are $150, $185, and $200. A minimum stay of one week is required, except during Christmas, when the minimum stay is two weeks.

⊗ Backpackers, Vacation Inn/Plantation Village

59-788 Kamehameha Hwy., Haleiwa, HI 96712. ☎ **808/638-7838.** Hostel bunks, rms, apts, cabins. At Vacation Inn, $14 hostel bunk across from the beach, $16 hostel bunk oceanfront. $40–$45 room across from the beach; $70–$85 oceanfront studio apt. At Plantation Village, $16 hostel bunk; $100–$120 cabin for four to six, $105–$120 large cabin for six, $110–$120 deluxe ocean-view cabin for six; $120 large ocean-view cabin for eight. Weekly rates available. MC, V. Free parking.

This place is definitely not for the perfectionist, as buildings and furniture have seen wear and tear, but management is always fixing and upgrading as much as possible. It caters to young and young-at-heart travelers from around the world. There are several possibilities here for casual country living. At Vacation Inn, one can find basic accommodations overlooking Waimea Bay. Backpackers like the inexpensive hostel facilities, which consist of several rooms furnished with four bunks each. There's a common living room with TV, a bathroom, and a kitchen. The quarters are cleaned each morning. Moving one step up, you can rent a single or double room with a common bath, kitchen, and TV room. Studio apartments can sleep four to six and are comfortably furnished, with TV and kitchenette; all have good views of surf and beach. Some of these units are right on Three Tables Beach, which is next to Waimea Bay; others are higher up in a building on the mountain side of the road and command great ocean vistas.

Plantation Village consists of nine restored plantation cabins located across from Three Tables Beach Park, on an acre of gardens. Each cabin has its own kitchen and bath, cable TV, linens and dishes; a common area offers pay telephone, picnic and barbecue areas, and laundry facilities. The Circle Island bus no. 52 stops out front every half hour; it's a short walk to Waimea Bay, Waimea Falls Park, and a good supermarket, so one could conceivably get by without a car here. A protected area is safe for children's swimming. Boogie boards and snorkels are part of the North Shore lifestyle, so they are supplied free to guests, as are tennis racquets and balls. Chaz Wagner and Sharlyn Foo are warm hosts, who provide inexpensive sailboat and hiking trips and island tours. Scuba-diving instruction is available in summer. Remember that Waimea Bay is perfect for summer swimming and snorkeling, but the water is extremely rough in winter.

✪ Schrader's Windward Marine Resort

47-039 Lihikai Dr., Kaneohe, HI 96744. ☎ **808/239-5711,** or toll free 800/735-5711. Fax 808/239-6658. 53 units. A/C TV TEL. $49–$146 one-bedroom; $110–$190 two-bedroom, $170–$320 two-bedroom with den (for up to six persons). Each additional person $7.50. AE, CB, DC, DISC, JCB, MC, V. Free parking.

On the shores of Kaneohe Bay, this older, rural hotel, about a half-hour drive from both Waikiki and downtown Honolulu, is something special for those who like a country setting. It's a world unto itself, dedicated to introducing marine recreation to its guests. Its own pier services the North Bay Boat Club and Sailing School; daily boat trips are available and a variety of sailboats, Windsurfers, kayaks, and jet boats are on hand; beginners can learn how, and experts can just take off.

Five buildings here share a compound bordered by a stream on one side and Kaneohe Bay on the other. There's a swimming pool and a therapy pool (a Jacuzzi with unheated water). Picnic tables and barbecues abound.

Each unit has a living room, bathroom, lanais, and full-size refrigerator; some have kitchen facilities as well. Furnishings are modest but comfortable; you might have an old-fashioned tub instead of a shower. Rooms with waterfront views are more expensive. Daily cleaning service is provided. Three-bedroom suites are also available.

DOUBLES FOR ABOUT $70 TO $100
DIAMOND HEAD WAIKIKI

Aston Waikiki Circle Hotel

2464 Kalakaua Ave., Honolulu, HI 96815. ☎ **808/923-1571,** or toll free 800/922-7866 in the mainland U.S. and Canada. Fax 808/926-8024. 104 rms. A/C TV TEL. $79 city view single or double; $99 partial ocean-view single or double; $109 ocean-view single or double. $20 additional Dec 22–Apr 1. Each additional person $12. Children under 18 stay free in parents' room. No rollaways or cribs. AE, CB, DC, DISC, JCB, MC, V.

Some of the best views available in Waikiki can be found in this cylindrical-shaped budget hotel directly across the street from the beach. Built in 1962 and inspired by the design of the traditional Japanese lantern, the aging hotel was recently treated to a first-class interior and exterior renovation. The mood is beachy, casual, and fun, from the open-air lobby with its sky-blue ceiling painted with fluffy white clouds and its underwater seascape mural, to the whimsical, attractive guest rooms, each of which is pie-shaped and exactly the same, except for the view. Of the eight rooms on each floor, five have an ocean view that is picture-postcard perfect; the others have views of the city or the Koolau Mountains. Many rooms have desks; all have private lanais and personal safes. Bathrooms have showers only.

Ewa (East-West Adventure) Hotel Waikiki

2555 Cartwright St., Honolulu, HI 96815. ☎ **808/922-1677,** toll free 800/359-8639. Fax 808/923-8538. 90 studios, 12 suites. A/C TV TEL. $90 studio, $135 one-bedroom suite; $175 two-bedroom suite. AE, MC, V. Parking $4 per day.

Up near the Honolulu Zoo, this old hotel has a new name and look thanks to a $3-million renovation. Italian-marble floors and counters, grass cloth on the walls, sand-colored carpets, and pastel color schemes make this hotel very attractive. The higher-priced studios have kitchenettes; all units have in-room safes. Most have twin beds; some have queen-size beds. Studios are for one to three people, and suites, one to four people. There is no swimming pool or dining facility, but with the ocean and restaurants two short blocks away, this is no problem.

Kaulana Kai

2425 Kuhio Ave., Honolulu, HI 96815. ☎ **808/922-7777**, or toll free 800/367-5666 in the U.S. and Canada, 1/800-125-434 from Australia. Fax 808/946-8777. 69 rms, 21 suites. A/C TV TEL. $91–$110 studio; $140–$150 one-bedroom suite; $180–$190 suite for four with kitchen. (Rates include continental breakfast.) AE, DC, JCB, MC, V. Parking $7 (limited).

Located in a great spot three minutes from Kuhio Beach, this tall, pyramid-like building has been taken over and transformed by a new Japanese management. The hotel is a little jewel. Rooms are not large but they are attractive, with twin beds, small lanais, and a tidy two-burner kitchenette with a refrigerator underneath the range. Bathrooms are marble, and the kitchen and bathroom floors are tiled, as are the lanais. It's fun to relax in the pool, whirlpool, and sauna. Continental breakfast is served poolside each morning. The lobby is beautiful, with its marble floors, indented Japanese-style ceiling, and gorgeous flower arrangements.

Kuhio Village Resort

2463 Kuhio Ave., Honolulu, HI 96815. ☎ **808/926-0641**, or toll free 800/367-5004 in the U.S. and Canada. Fax 808/533-0472, or toll free 800/477-2329. 138 rms, 12 suites. A/C TV TEL. Apr–Dec 24, $80–$90 double; $120 family suite with kitchenette; $130 one-bedroom suite with kitchenette. Dec 24–Mar 31, $90–$115 double; $135 family suite with kitchenette; $150 one-bedroom suite with kitchenette. (Rates include free rent-a-car or sixth night free.) AE, DC, JCB, MC, V. Parking $4 per day.

Just 1¹/₂ blocks from the beach, this renovated Hawaiian Pacific Resorts hotel enjoys a convenient central location. The 21-story two-tower structure has its own restaurant, a round-the-clock minimart, a launderette, and lots of big-hotel amenities. The rooms are furnished in soft pastels, with white furniture, in-room safes, and a refrigerator in every room. The rooms and suites with kitchenettes have microwaves and dining areas, and cooking and dining utensils. The junior suites have a sitting room with a sofa bed, and all bedrooms have queen-size beds. The handsomely renovated lobby is paneled in natural koa wood and has sections that are open to the sky, with planter boxes filled with palms and ferns.

Ocean Resort Hotel Waikiki

175 Paoakalani Ave., Honolulu, HI 96815. ☎ **808/922-3861**, or toll free 800/367-2317, 800/999-6640 in Canada. Fax 808/924-1982. 450 rms, 7 suites. A/C TV TEL. Diamond Head Tower, Apr–Dec 22, $69–$137 single or double; Dec 23–Mar, $86–$104 single or double. Pali Tower, Apr–Dec 22, $76–$91 single or double; Dec 23–Mar, $116–$140 single or double. Year-round $150–$280 suite. Each additional person $12. AE, DC, DISC, ER, JCB, MC, V. Parking $4 per day.

A very welcome find close to Kapiolani Park, this is a cheerful, sparkling hotel with a waterfall at the entrance, a golden lobby, and friendly people behind the desk. It has every hotel amenity, including two small swimming pools on the third floor, a tour desk, laundry room, and daily maid service. Prices are lowest in the Diamond Head Tower; rooms here do not have kitchenettes, but there are compact refrigerators, and you'll enjoy your lanai and the view. All rooms in the Pali Tower have kitchenettes. Rooms in both buildings are of standard size, and have dressing areas, and stall showers large enough and deep enough for a bath. The Mala Restaurant, adjacent to the lobby, serves three Japanese/American meals a day.

Royal Kuhio

2240 Kuhio Ave., Honolulu, HI 96815. ☎ **808/538-7145** or 808/538-7145, or toll free 800/ 367-5205. Fax 808/533-4621. 385 apts. A/C TV TEL. Apr 16–Jun 30, $80 one-bedroom apt. Jul 1–Aug 31, $90 one-bedroom apt. Sept 1–Dec 15, $80 one-bedroom apt. Dec 16–Apr 15, $110 one-bedroom apt. AE, DC, DISC, MC, V. Free parking.

Apartments at this towering condominium building are quite attractive and nicely decorated, with a bedroom with twin beds that can be closed off from the sitting room or opened to make one big area. The sitting room has sofa beds, and rollaways are available for additional people. The kitchens are all electric (with dishwashers), the closet space is ample, and every apartment has its own lanai. A pool and sun-deck area, billiard room, Ping-Pong, a shuffleboard court, and a huge laundry room and recreation area all make for easy living—not to mention that the Royal Kuhio is close to the beach. There is weekly chamber service.

Waikiki Grand

134 Kapahulu Ave., Honolulu, HI 96815. ☎ **808/923-1511,** or toll free 800/535-0085. Fax 808/922-2421. 105 rms. A/C TV TEL. $99–$109 double; $109 studio with kitchenette. Each additional person $15. Children under 18 stay free in parents' room (using existing bedding). AE, MC, V. Parking $5 per day.

Now a member of the MarcResorts Hawaii group, this older hotel has recently been upgraded and remodeled. And what a pleasant location this one has, just across the street from Kapiolani Park and all its activities, and just around the bend from Kuhio Beach. From the lower-priced rooms, views are of the center of Waikiki, but go a little higher and you'll be rewarded with breathtaking views of Diamond Head. The rooms are pleasant if small (there's very little closet space). All rooms have refrigerators and coffee/tea makers. There's a pleasant swimming pool on the 10th floor sun deck.

CENTRAL WAIKIKI

Coral Reef

2299 Kuhio Ave., Honolulu, HI 96815. ☎ **808/922-1262,** or toll free 800/922-7866 in the mainland U.S. and in Canada, 800/321-2558 in Hawaii. Fax 808/922-8785. 247 rms, 45 suites. A/C TV TEL. Apr–Dec 20, $70–$80 double; $85–$95 junior suite; $95–$105 one-bedroom suite. Dec 21–Mar, $99–$110 double; $105–$115 junior suite; $115–$125 one-bedroom suite. Each additional person $12. AE, DC, MC, V. Parking $10.

You get a really large room at this modern high-rise hotel directly behind the International Market Place and a short walk from Waikiki Beach. The hotel boasts every facility—swimming pool, garage, restaurants, shops—and nicely furnished rooms that have either one or two double beds (or a double and a single) and private lanai. A $1-million renovation has upgraded all the rooms and the lobby. The hotel is managed by Aston Hotels & Resorts.

Hotel Honolulu

376 Kaiolu St., Honolulu, HI 96815. ☎ **808/926-2766,** or toll free 800/426-2766. Fax 808/ 922-3326. 15 studios, 9 one-bedroom suites. A/C TV TEL. $66–$85 studio; $103 one-bedroom suite. Each additional person $9. AE, DISC, JCB, MC, V. Free parking, covered off-street.

A beautiful orchid collection, tropical birds, and hundreds of potted plants give a garden atmosphere to Hawaii's only gay hotel. They call it "deco–post modern," but we call it a reminder of the plantation days. Whatever you call it, the Hotel Honolulu is an oasis in time and space. Located two blocks from the beach, the hotel's two buildings are isolated from traffic. There's a rooftop garden sun deck, very popular for evening barbecues and drinks, and a variety of clubs, restaurants, and shops just around the corner. A welcome amenity package on arrival offers free cocktails, discounts at restaurants and clothing stores, and more.

The best choice for budgeteers here is the smaller, two-story building called the Bamboo Lanai, where small, nicely furnished studios go for $70. They have a small, fully equipped kitchenette and a bathroom with a tile shower. Larger studios and one-bedroom suites in the three-story main building, which is air-conditioned, are more elaborate and more expensive, with sitting areas, lanais, and complete kitchens. There's free coffee all day in the lobby and a laundry room.

Ilima Hotel

445 Nohonani St., Honolulu, HI 96815. ☎ **808/923-1877,** or toll free 800/367-5172 in the mainland U.S. and Canada. Fax 808/924-8371. 74 studios, 18 one-bedroom suites. 6 two-bedroom suites. A/C TV TEL. Apr–Dec 14, $72–$88 single; $77–$99 double; $105–$125 executive suite; $129–$139 large one-bedroom suite; $149–$159 two-bedroom suite; $179–$220 two- or three-bedroom penthouse. Dec 15–Mar 31, add $12 to all rates. Each additional person $8. AE, DC, DISC, JCB, MC, V.

Still going strong after 26 years, the Ilima is eminently comfortable and offers many facilities and services, and a $1.2-million renovation has not upped the rates unreasonably. You can really kick off your shoes and feel at home here; floors are carpeted, rooms are condominium-size spacious, and the studios include two double beds, a fully equipped kitchen with microwave, plenty of storage space, and a private lanai. There's a swimming pool at ground level and two sun decks on the 10th floor, as well as an exercise room and sauna. Generosities not usually found in most Waikiki hotels include free parking and free local phone calls. And it's a 10-minute walk to the beach. Sergio's Italian Restaurant is right at hand.

✪ Marine Surf

364 Seaside Ave., Honolulu, HI 96815. ☎ **808/923-0277,** or toll free 800/367-5176 in the mainland U.S., 800/663-1118 in Canada. Fax 808/926-5915. 115 studios, 1 one-bedroom suite. A/C TV TEL. Apr–Dec 20, $74–$85 studio single or double; $135 one-bedroom penthouse suite. Dec 21–Mar, $85–$98 studio single or double; $150 one-bedroom penthouse suite. Each additional person $10. Children under 18 stay free in parents' room. Cribs $10 a day. CB, DC, DISC, MC, V. Parking $4 a day.

The Marine Surf has just about everything going for it: Located about 1 1/2 blocks from the beach, this 23-story condominium hotel features smartly decorated studio apartments, each one with two extra-length double beds, lots of drawer space, a dressing room, and a safe. Best of all, each studio has a full electric kitchen, just in case you choose not to eat every night at Matteos Italian Restaurant, one of the finest in town, right in the lobby. Rooms, which have been completely renovated, are serviced daily. You can swim and sun at the lovely outdoor pool on the fourth floor. Studios accommodate up to four, and penthouse suites, six.

Outrigger Coral Seas Hotel

250 Lewers St.,Honolulu, HI 96815. ☎ **808/923-3881,** or toll free 800/688-7444 in the U.S. and Canada, 1/800/124-171 from Australia. Fax toll free 800/622-4852. 109 rms, 7 suites. A/C TV TEL. $75–$95 single or double; $125 suite. Each additional person $15. Children under 18 stay free in parents' room. AE, CB, DC, DISC, JCB, MC, V. Parking $7 per day.

Conveniently located a block from the beach and a block from the main drag in Waikiki, the Outrigger Coral Seas is one of the original hotels in the empire of Outrigger Hotels Hawaii. The rooms and lobby were recently renovated and are more comfortable than ever. Spacious rooms have either two queen-size or three twin beds, in-room safes, and colorful decor; all have private lanais. Most rooms have small kitchenettes (with microwave oven, utensils, and refrigerator). No-smoking rooms are available, and the suites for four are a real family find. The beach is down the street, and right in the hotel are three restaurants: Pieces of Eight, House of Hong, and Perry's Smorgy, which offers good buffet bargains.

Outrigger East Hotel

150 Kaiulani Ave., Honolulu, HI 96815. ☎ **808/922-5353,** or toll free 800/688-7444 in the U.S. and Canada, 1/800/124-171 from Australia. Fax toll free 800/456-4329. 407 rms, 38 suites. A/C TV TEL. $95–$120 double; $175–$250 suite. Each additional person $15. AE, CB, DC, DISC, JCB, MC, V. Parking $7 per day.

This renovated hotel is the top of the line in Outrigger's mid-priced category. The 18-floor building is a short block from Waikiki Beach and has just about everything a visitor needs, from four restaurants (Pepper's, Islander Coffee Shop, Chuck's Cellar, and Jolly Roger) to a beauty shop, travel and tour desks, and laundry facilities. Rooms have been smartly furnished, each with either two double beds, a king, or a queen; all have in-room safes and refrigerators; studios have kitchenettes. Studios can accommodate up to three guests and suites can accommodate up to four. No-smoking rooms and handicap facilities are available.

Outrigger Edgewater Hotel

2168 Kalia Rd., Honolulu, HI 96815. ☎ **808/922-6424,** or toll free 800/688-7444 in the U.S. and Canada, 1/800/124-171 from Australia. Fax toll free 800/622-4852. 176 rms, 8 suites. A/C TV TEL. $75–$95 double; $140 suite. Each additional person $15. AE, CB, DC, DISC, JCB, MC, V. Parking $7 per day.

Situated right on the corner of Lewers, this hotel has long enjoyed one of the best locations in Waikiki. Halfway between the ocean and Kalakaua Avenue, it's a two-minute walk to either the beach or the bustle of restaurants, shops, and nightspots. Rooms are pleasantly furnished. Your lanai will be furnished, but nothing will separate you from your neighbor's porch. This is a homey place, with lots of space to stroll. The Trattoria Restaurant, right on the grounds, is a Waikiki favorite for northern Italian food, Chuck's Original Steakhouse is another popular old-timer, and the Pâtisserie is a favorite French bakery.

Outrigger Malia Hotel

2211 Kuhio Ave., Honolulu, HI 96815. ☎ **808/923-7621,** or toll free 800/688-7444 in the U.S. and Canada. 1/800/124-171 from Australia. Fax toll free 800/622-4852. 280 rms, 47 suites. A/C TV TEL. $90–$115 single or double. Each additional person $15. AE, CB, DC, DISC, JCB, MC, V. Parking $7 per day.

This bright and beautiful place has two wings. The rooms in the Malia wing, the taller of the hotel's two sections, have two double beds with Polynesian-print bedspreads and wall-to-wall carpeting. All rooms have a lanai, a small refrigerator, and an ironing board. There are 16 handicapped-accessible rooms in this wing, with wider doorways, grab bars in the bathrooms, and twin-size rather than double beds for greater wheelchair mobility.

The Luana wing has junior suites that can accommodate four guests comfortably; all contain a sitting room with two couches and a bedroom with two beds. The lanais in the suites are much larger than those in the bedrooms of the Malia wing. Pluses for guests at both wings include a Jacuzzi whirlpool, a rooftop tennis court, and the excellent Wailana Coffeeshop, open 24 hours a day. And, of course, the beach is just three blocks away.

Outrigger Surf Hotel

2280 Kuhio Ave., Honolulu, HI 96815. ☎ **808/922-5777,** or toll free 800/688-7444 in the U.S. and Canada, 1/800/124-171 from Australia. Fax toll free 800/622-4852. 251 rms. A/C TV TEL. $75–$120 double. Each additional person $15. AE, CB, DC, DISC, JCB, MC, V. Parking $7 per day.

For those watching their dollars, this hotel on the corner of Nohonani Street and a short walk from the beach is one of the most suitable. It has the greatest number of standard units, with kitchenettes throughout. No-smoking rooms are available.

The tall, modern building has 16 floors of comfortable studios, each with a lanai, carpeting, in-room safe, and beds in a studio arrangement providing a living-room look. There's a stall shower in the bathroom, two closets for storage, a two-burner range, and small refrigerator. The lobby is small but comfortable, and there's a pool on the lobby level. The Waikiki Pasta Company is right at hand.

Outrigger Village Hotel

240 Lewers St., Honolulu, HI 96815. ☎ **808/923-3881,** or toll free 800/688-7444 in the U.S. and Canada, 1/800/124-171 from Australia. Fax toll free 800/622-4852. 399 rms, 41 kitchenettes. A/C TV TEL. $85–$110 single or double; $125–$135 suite. Each additional person $15. AE, CB, DC, DISC, JCB, MC, V. Parking $7 per day.

The lobby of this hotel is a quadrangle built around the pool, so you can swim and sunbathe while checking out the new arrivals. The hotel is decorated in a bright blend of contemporary and Polynesian styles. Each of the units has an in-room safe, and most have lanais. No-smoking rooms are available. Steens Villager, a family-style restaurant, is at hand, as is the Red Lion Dance Palace. The location is superb, right in the middle of everything and close to the beach.

Outrigger Waikiki Surf East Hotel

422 Royal Hawaiian Ave., Honolulu, HI 96815. ☎ **808/923-7671,** or toll free 800/688-7444 in the U.S. and Canada, 1/800/124-171 from Australia. Fax toll free 800/622-4852. 102 rms. A/C TV TEL. $80–$90 single or double/kitchenette; $110 one-bedroom suite/kitchenette. Each additional person $15. AE, CB, DC, DISC, JCB, MC, V. Parking $7 per day.

This is one of the lower priced of the Outrigger hotels, but there's no obvious reason why. It's quiet, rooms are tastefully and newly appointed, and there are many amenities. Perhaps it's the size; there's no wasted space here—when you register at the desk, be careful not to fall into the pool! All rooms have a refrigerator, cooking top or microwave, toaster and dining ware, stall shower in the bathroom, and a sliding glass door leading to a lanai large enough for dining or sunbathing. The corner rooms have two lanais. It's a five-minute walk to the beach, the International Market Place, and the heart of the Waikiki action.

Outrigger Waikiki Tower Hotel (A Best Western)

200 Lewers St., Honolulu, HI 96815. ☎ **808/922-6424,** or toll free 800/688-7444 in the U.S. and Canada, 1/800/124-171 from Australia. Fax toll free 800/622-4852. 439 rms. A/C TV TEL. $85–$110 single or double; $125–$140 suite. Each additional person $15. AE, CB, DC, DISC, JCB, MC, V. Parking $7 per day.

This renovated hotel is next to the Outrigger Edgewater Hotel, which means that it shares a prime, close-to-the-beach location. Access to restaurants is just as easy as to the beach: The Waikiki Broiler is downstairs, Trattoria Restaurant and Chuck's Original Steakhouse at the Edgewater, and Denny's across Lewers Street. The open-air lobby is chock full of convenience desks and shops. The pleasantly decorated rooms have a lanai, an in-room safe, and a king-size or queen-size bed or two twin beds. Studios have kitchenettes; all units have a refrigerator. Kitchenette units include a microwave oven, refrigerator, and utensils. No-smoking rooms are available.

EWA WAIKIKI

Ambassador Hotel of Waikiki

2040 Kuhio Ave., Honolulu, HI 96815. ☎ **808/941-7777.** Fax 808/922-4579. 315 rms. A/C TV TEL. $72–$96 single; $80–$104 double; $140–$170 one-bedroom suite. AE, CB, DC, JCB, MC, V. Parking $4 per day.

An old-timer in Waikiki, the Ambassador still gives good value for the dollar. It's a comfortable hotel with all the conveniences. No wonder you always find airline personnel staying here! All the rooms in this high-rise building are approached from outside walkways. Even the lower-priced studios, from the second through seventh floors, boast private lanais, contemporary furniture, and deep furo-type shower tubs. You can relax at the big pool and sun deck on the second floor and eat at the Café Ambassador; you're also fairly close to all the attractions of Waikiki. The deluxe one-bedroom suites are equipped with full electric kitchens. Studios with kitchens are available on request.

Hawaiiana Hotel

260 Beach Walk, Honolulu, HI 96815. ☎ **808/923-3811,** or toll free 800/367-5122 in the mainland U.S. and Canada. Fax 808/926-5728. 95 studios, 7 one-bedroom suites. A/C TV TEL. $80–$90 single; $85–$95 double; $135–$143 one-bedroom suite; $165–$190 Alii Studio. Each additional person $8. Packages available. AE, MC, V. Parking $7 per day (limited).

A favorite old-timer in Hawaii, this place gets more mellow every year. One of the few low-rise garden hotels left in Waikiki, the Hawaiiana is wonderfully located just half a block from a good swimming beach. Rooms are situated around a tropical garden and two swimming pools, so you can step out your door for a swim in the pool or a complimentary breakfast of juice and coffee out on the patio. Comfortable chairs at poolside are occupied most of the day by guests too content to move. All rooms have an electronic safe and an electric kitchen; most have a lanai. One-bedroom suites can accommodate up to four guests. Niceties include free newspapers in the morning or afternoon, Hawaiian shows twice a week, and free use of washers and dryers.

Outrigger Reef Lanais

225 Saratoga Rd., Honolulu, HI 96815. ☎ **808/923-3881,** or toll free 800/688-7444 in the U.S. and Canada, 1/800/124-171 from Australia. Fax toll free 800/622-4852. 62 rms. A/C TV TEL. $95–$115 double, $100–$140 double with kitchenette; $140–$175 suite. AE, CB, DC, DISC, JCB, MC, V. Parking $7 per day.

This recently renovated hotel is yet another member of the popular Outrigger chain. It's tops in location, with the beach just a hop-skip-and-a-jump away; there's a public right-of-way to the ocean just across Kalia Road. Although it lacks some of the frills of the other Outrigger hotels, this spot still offers good value. Guest rooms are nicely decorated and have either double or queen-size beds, an in-room safe, and a shower (no tub); some rooms have kitchenettes, which include a microwave oven, refrigerator, and utensils. No-smoking rooms are available. There is no pool on the premises, but guests may use the one at the nearby Outrigger Village. The ever-popular Buzz's Steak & Lobster is on the premises.

Outrigger Royal Islander Hotel

2164 Kalia Rd., Honolulu, HI 96815. ☎ **808/922-1961,** or toll free 800/688-7444 in the U.S. and Canada, 1/800/124-171 from Australia. Fax toll free 800/622-4852. 94 rms, 7 apts. TV TEL. $75–$100 double; $155–$160 suite. Each additional person $15. AE, CB, DC, DISC, JCB, MC, V. Parking $7 per day.

Rooms here are not large, but they are tastefully decorated. Each room has a private lanai, refrigerator, and a modern bathroom. Families will do well in the one-bedroom apartments and suites. This hotel has a superb location, right near the Halekulani and Outrigger Reef hotels, across the road from a very good beach. Complimentary coffee is available in the mornings. There's a McDonald's right in the hotel. No-smoking rooms are available.

✪ The Royal Garden at Waikiki

440 Olohana St., Honolulu, HI 96815. ☎ **808/943-0202** or toll free 800/367-5666 from U.S. and Canada. Fax 808/946-8777. 230 rms, 17 deluxe suites, 2 royal suites. A/C TV TEL MINIBAR. $95–$180 double; $295–$500 suite. Each additional person $15. Children 17 and under stay free in parents' room. Family rates, second room at 50% savings. (Rates include continental breakfast.) AE, CB, DC, JCB, MC, V. Parking $7 per day valet parking.

While many of the rooms in this stunning new $45-million luxury hotel are beyond our budget, there are still some 75 standard rooms for just $95. Considering the charm of this place, they're well worth the tab. The lobby is right out of a movie set: marble in every imaginable color, crystal chandeliers, ornate gilded mirrors—smashing! There are two swimming pools in the huge garden; the larger one is a vision in marble with a huge Romanesque bathhouse in the middle and a cascading waterfall. The guest accommodations are also very special. Every room has a lanai, attractive rattan furniture, a coffee maker, in-room safe, and a refrigerator. Many of the rooms are wheelchair accessible. The only difference between the standard rooms at $95 and the moderate rooms at $120 is the height of the floor; they all are 365 square feet in size and have either a queen-size bed or twins. The beach is about a 10-minute walk away, but guests can use the two swimming pools, two whirlpools, sauna, and fitness center with state-of-the-art equipment. There's a business center, and concierge service is available. Also at hand are two splendid and very popular restaurants: Cascada for Euro-Island cuisine and Shizu for classic Japanese cookery. Complimentary continental breakfast daily and complimentary scheduled shuttle service to Ala Moana Shopping Center, Royal Hawaiian Shopping Center, and Kapiolani Park add even greater value.

✪ Waikiki Royal Suites

255 Beach Walk, Honolulu, HI 96815. ☎ **808/926-5641,** or toll free 800/535-0085. Fax 808/922-2421. 47 suites. TV TEL. $159–$179 one-bedroom suite for up to four; $259–$299 two-bedroom suite for up to six; cheaper on a weekly basis. Crib $5, rollaway $15. (Rates include continental breakfast.) AE, DISC, JCB, MC, V. Parking $6 per day.

Enjoying a superb location half a block from the ocean, this is Waikiki's first all-suite hotel. You'll be able to stretch out and relax here, since the suites are all of good size, and the lanais, many of which have ocean views, are extra large. There's a queen-size sofa bed in the living room, large mirrored closets, and in-room safes, and each suite has its own fully equipped kitchen, with microwave oven, coffee makers, and fresh ground coffee. There is no pool. There's a warm feeling of hospitality here, and there's a sunset evening cocktail party daily. Rates include daily maid service. Laundry facilities are available.

✪ Waikiki Terrace Hotel

2045 Kalakaua Ave., Honolulu, HI 96815. ☎ **808/955-6000,** or toll free 800/445-8811 in the mainland U.S. and Canada. Fax 808/943-8555. 250 rms and 3 suites. A/C TV TEL. Apr–Dec 19, $115–$145 double; $295 suite. Dec 20–Mar, $125–$155 double; $295 suite. Each additional person $18. Children 17 and under stay free in parents' room when using existing bedding. AE, CB, DC, DISC, JCB, MC, V. Parking $7 per day.

"Affordably elegant" is the operative term here. A $10.5-million renovation has transformed an older hotel into a sparkling new property, with four-star service and amenities not usually found in hotels in this price category. Completely refurbished guest rooms are handsome, with splendid marble and granite bathrooms and Berber carpeting. Each room has its own safe, a refrigerator, and a dry bar with an instant hot-water dispenser and a complimentary basket of coffees and teas. Views from your private lanais—of the ocean or mountains—are special. Rooms for the disabled and non-smokers are available on request. A great stretch of Waikiki Beach is about a seven-minute walk away (through Fort DeRussy Park), but there's also a sun deck with pool and spa at home, as well as a fitness center. And there's room service too, from the hotel's outstanding restaurant, the Mezzanine.

NEAR THE ALA WAI

Coconut Plaza

450 Lewers St., Honolulu, HI 96815. ☎ **808/923-8828,** or toll free 800/367-7040 in the mainland U.S. Fax 808/537-3701. 80 rms, 10 suites. A/C TV TEL. Apr–Dec 19, $85–$110 single or double. Dec 20–Mar, $95–$120 single or double. $150 suite for up to four persons. Inquire about special senior rates. (Rates include continental breakfast.) AE, DISC, JCB, MC, V. Parking $7 per day.

A smashing $2.3-million renovation has made this charming boutique hotel lovelier than ever, from its open-air plantation-style lobby to the lobby bar where guests gather for breakfast and the tropical guest rooms with whitewashed rattan furniture and Mexican floor tiles. As comfortable as they are beautiful, all rooms have either a wet bar or a kitchenette with microwave oven and a private lanai. Pluses for this intimate hotel are a sun deck with pool, exercise equipment, a concierge desk, on-site Laundromat, and indoor parking. Coconut Plaza is across from the Ala Wai Golf Course, and $3^1/_2$ blocks from Waikiki Beach.

Hawaiian Monarch

444 Niu St., Honolulu, HI 96815. ☎ **808/949-3911,** or toll free 800/535-0085 in the mainland U.S. Fax 808/922-2421. 293 rms, 73 suites. A/C TV TEL. $89–$94 double; $109–$119 suite. Each additional person $15. Children under 18 stay free in parents' room. AE, MC, V. Parking $6 per day.

This skyscraper hotel is very close to the Ala Wai Canal and halfway between Ala Moana Shopping Center and the beaches of Waikiki. It's a well-run establishment with a mixed international clientele, and complete with all the amenities of tourist life: a huge sun deck and regular pool, plus plenty of shops in the arcade. There's also the excellent Tandoor Restaurant.

The Hawaiian Monarch is part hotel, part condo, and the hotel rooms, which occupy the 7th through 24th floors, all have refrigerators, coffee bars, and in-room safes. They are done in modern tropical decor. The nicest views are those overlooking the Ala Wai Canal. Studio suites are available with kitchenette or kitchen.

NEAR ALA MOANA

Aston Inn on the Park

1920 Ala Moana Blvd., Honolulu, HI 96815. ☎ **808/946-8355,** or toll free 800/922-7866 in the mainland U.S., 800/445-6633 in Canada. Fax 808/922-8785. 134 units. A/C TV TEL. Apr–Dec 21, $70–$100 double; $89–$104 studio. Dec 22–Mar, $83–$100 double; $104 studio. Each additional person $12. AE, CB, DC, DISC, JCB, MC, V. Parking limited, $6 per day.

Not far from the Hilton Hawaiian Village and a block from the popular Fort DeRussy Beach, this is a completely renovated hotel/condominium. The smallish but pretty rooms have modern furnishings and decor. Refrigerators and wet bars are in most of the units; kitchenette units are also available. This place would be most suitable for two, or perhaps three, people in a room, but families might find it a bit tight. There's a modern lobby with a convenience store, and a nice pool and sun deck on the fifth floor. Castagnola's Restaurant, a favorite, is right on the premises.

Accommodations here are in three classes: standard (city or mountain view); superior (ocean view); and deluxe kitchenette (city view or ocean view), the latter on request only. In standard or superior accommodations, refrigerators and lanais are available on request only.

Outrigger Hobron

343 Hobron Lane, Honolulu, HI 96815. ☎ **808/942-7777,** or toll free 800/688-7444 in the U.S. and Canada, 1/800/124-171 from Australia. Fax toll free 800/622-4852. 550 rms, 46 suites. A/C TV TEL. $70–$130 single or double; $180–$210 suite. Each additional person $15. AE, CB, DC, DISC, JCB, MC, V. Parking $7 per day.

A skyscraper for this area, this 44-story condominium has attractive accommodations; it's very popular with tour groups. All rooms have attractive blond-wood furniture (desk, vanity, chair) and in-room safes; they are small but well appointed, and many offer very good views of ocean, city, mountains, and the nearby Ala Wai Yacht Harbor. Most rooms have twin beds; only four on each floor have queen-size beds, which must be requested in advance. The rooms have refrigerators only; the studios have mini-kitchenettes. There's a pool on the mezzanine level, a sun deck plus Jacuzzi whirlpool and sauna on the fifth floor. Steens Bar & Grill offers continental breakfast and sandwiches, big-screen TV, and karaoke. No-smoking and handicapped rooms are available. All the excitement of the Ilikai and Hilton Hawaiian Village complexes is about five minutes away. Cars from Dollar Rent A Car are available for $5 a day.

Pagoda Hotel

1525 Rycroft St., Honolulu, HI 96814. ☎ **808/941-6611,** or toll free 800/367-6060 in the mainland U.S. and Canada. Fax 808/922-8061. 361 rms. A/C TV TEL. Pagoda Hotel, $82–$92 single or double. Pagoda Terrace, $76 studio apt; $97 one-bedroom apt; $115 two-bedroom apt. Each additional person $15. AE, CB, DC, DISC, JCB, MC, V. Parking $4 per day.

Although this hotel is about a 10-minute drive from Waikiki, you won't be isolated here: Not only are you near the Ala Moana Shopping Center, but right on the grounds is one of Honolulu's most spectacular restaurants, the Pagoda, with its colorful displays of flashing carp. Two buildings flank Rycroft Street—Pagoda Terrace and the Pagoda Hotel. All rooms at the Pagoda Hotel have been refurbished and are cheery and bright. Rooms at the Pagoda Terrace offer studio apartments nicely set up for housekeeping, with a full-size refrigerator, four-burner range, and all the necessary equipment. One- and two-bedroom apartments also offer plenty of comfort. Two swimming pools are here for dunking.

Waikiki Parkside

1850 Ala Moana Blvd., Honolulu, HI 96815. ☎ **808/955-1567,** or toll free 800/237-9666. Fax 808/955-1564. 250 rms, 5 suites. A/C TV TEL. $100–$136 single or double; $175–$375 suite. Children 17 and under stay free in parents' room when using existing bedding. Each additional person $15. Inquire about "Value Special" rates. AE, CB, DC, DISC, JCB, MC, V. Parking $5 per day.

Located close to the Ala Moana Shopping Center and Ala Moana Beach Park, this older hotel offers cozy, comfortable lodgings at fair prices. Newly refurbished guest rooms have rattan furniture, double or queen-size beds, mini-refrigerators, private safes, and tile bathrooms. Guests enjoy the fitness room, the outdoor pool with its snack bar, and the convenience of having a Denny's for meals or snacks 24 hours a day (room service from 7am to 9pm). Senior-friendly rooms are available on request, as are rooms for the disabled and non-smokers.

WINDWARD OAHU & THE NORTH SHORE

Ke Iki Hale

59-579 Ke Iki Rd., Haleiwa, HI 96712. ☎ **808/638-8229.** 12 units. $85–$125 one-bedroom unit; $145 one-bedroom cottage; $150–$165 two-bedroom cottage. AE, MC, V. Free parking.

Here's a place for those who long to be right on the beach, or just a few steps away from it. Alice Tracy's rental cottages on the North Shore are on 1 1/2 acres of palm-fringed land near Waimea Bay. They are nicely furnished, with full kitchens; some have large picture windows overlooking the ocean. Guests can enjoy the barbecue facilities, the picnic tables at water's edge, and a small volleyball court. There's a public telephone on the premises, but not a TV in sight. Remember that Waimea Bay is ideal for swimming in the summer months, but during the winter its sky-high waves are for experienced surfers only.

Rodeway Inn Hukilau Resort

55-109 Laniloa St., Laie, HI 96762. ☎ **808/293-9282,** or toll free 800/LANILOA (526-4562). 48 rms. A/C TV TEL. $79 single or double; $89 triple or quad. Children under 8 stay free in parents' room. AE, DC, DISC, MC, V. Parking $7 per day.

Next door to the Polynesian Cultural Center, this modern, motel-like building offers lots of comfort and a good location. Right at your feet is a sandy ocean beach and pool; a short drive away is swimming, surfing, windsurfing, diving, horseback riding, and championship golfing, in the Sunset Beach and Haleiwa area. Waimea Bay offers some of the world's best swimming (in summer) and best surfing (in winter). Waimea Falls Park is delightful, and Haleiwa has many shops and restaurants and an artsy-craftsy atmosphere. Rooms overlook the pool and courtyard and boast refrigerators, microwave ovens (on request), and private lanais. The inn is within walking distance of the Brigham Young University Hawaii Campus and the Mormon Temple. Temple-patron rates are available upon request.

AT THE AIRPORT

✪ Honolulu Airport Mini Hotel

Main Terminal Central Lobby, Honolulu International Airport. ☎ **808/836-3044.** Fax 808/834-8985. 17 rms. $30 sleep and shower (8 hr.), $17.50 nap and shower (2 hr.), $7.50 for shower only, including towels and toiletries. (Rates per person, single occupancy only.) MC, V.

Here's something every airline traveler should know about—just in case. If your plane departure is delayed, in case you have to wait several hours to make a connecting flight, if you arrive late at night and there's no interisland plane service until the next morning—or in case you simply need a place to go if you've checked out of your hotel early and have a late-night flight. That's where the Honolulu Airport Mini Hotel comes in. This clean and pleasant facility offers private rooms and resting facilities and the opportunity to take a shower. Each guest receives personal attention and a real feeling of aloha. There's a coffee pot perpetually brewing, plus a kitchen where flowers or medication can be refrigerated. The Honolulu Airport Mini Hotel is open 24 hours a day. Reservations are advised for sleeping space; they are usually booked after 10pm.

BED & BREAKFASTS

Hawaii Kai, Kailua, and Kaneohe are suburban, easygoing, and just a few miles but seemingly worlds away from the hustle-bustle of Waikiki. We've picked a handful of B&Bs in this area, where you can enjoy rural charm, but be in town in a half hour or less when you crave excitement.

In addition to the following, see "Alternative Accommodations Networks" in Chapter 3 for information on several organizations that will hook you up with the perfect bed & breakfast.

HAWAII KAI

Joan Webb and Barbara Abe

P.O. Box 25907, Honolulu, HI 96825. ☎ **808/396-9462.** 2 rms (1 with bath), TV. $55–$65 double. (Rates include breakfast.) No credit cards. Free parking.

If you'd like a bed-and-breakfast accommodation close to Hanauma Bay and Sea Life Park (and about a 25-minute drive from Waikiki), contact Mrs. Joan Webb, or her daughter, Barbara Abe—two Englishwomen who have a beautiful home, with garden and swimming pool, in Hawaii Kai. The larger room, with access to the pool area, has a queen-size bed, a small refrigerator, and a private bath. The smaller room, also cozy, has a double bed and shares a bath with the hosts. Joan and Barbara prepare full island breakfasts for their guests, who join them at the dining table for fresh fruits, juices, homemade breads, English muffins, cereals, and beverages. They are generous with sightseeing advice and tips and also provide beach mats and towels.

KAILUA

Akamai Bed & Breakfast

172 Kuumele Place, Kailua, HI 96734. ☎ **808/261-2227,** or toll free 800/642-5366. 2 studios (with bath). TV. $65 double. Each additional person $10, to a maximum of four. Minimum stay three nights. No credit cards. Free parking.

Three blocks and an eight-minute walk from the beautiful white-sand beaches of Kailua is this charming home. A separate wing from the main house has two spacious studios, each with its own kitchen, including a refrigerator and microwave oven. The refrigerator is stocked with some breakfast foods, and guests are free to do light cooking. Guests enjoy the convenience of the pool and lanai in a lovely tropical setting. Diane Van Ryzin and her husband, Joe, are cordial hosts.

Fairway View Bed & Breakfast

515 Paumamua Place, Kailua, HI 96734. ☎ **808/263-6439** or 808/262-0485. 2 rms, shared bath. $40–$50 single or double, depending on length of stay. (Rates include breakfast.) No credit cards.

Louise (Weezie) and Neal Wooden's charming home is located at the end of a quiet cul-de-sac and has the Mid Pacific Golf Course—perhaps the most beautifully landscaped course on the island—right in its backyard. Weezie, a Lanikai girl from 'way back, is a delightful hostess and a veritable treasure trove of resource material and ideas about intriguing and fun things to do and places to go. There are two guest rooms: One has a queen bed and carries out the dusty-rose and seafoam-green color scheme of the living room and family room, where breakfast is served by the big picture window overlooking the golf course and the Koolau Mountains. The other room has twin beds with cream-and-black bedspreads and, like the queen room, Pegge Hopper prints framed in koa and beautiful etched-glass mirrors. The two guest accommodations share a big bath, which is across the hall. The queen room has its own TV (and there's a big TV in the family room). Two of the most glorious beaches on the island are just down the hill. The Wooden family includes Krista, champion West Highland Terrier.

✪ Lanikai Bed & Breakfast

1277 Mokulua Dr., Kailua, HI 96734. ☎ **808/261-1059.** 1 studio, 1 apt (with bath). TV TEL. $60 garden studio, $85 one-bedroom apt, single or double. MC, V. Free parking.

If you love being right on the beach, you can't beat this one. Mahina and Homer Maxey's large, comfortable home is just across the street from idyllic Lanikai Beach with its soft white sand and inviting, always-calm water. There's a large covered lanai in front, with banana trees, lawa'e ferns, and plenty of tables and chairs. The studio, which has a private entrance, is at the back of the house overlooking the garden, and has a stunning view of the Windward Koolaus. There's a queen-size bed, a sitting room/TV area, and a kitchen/dining area, complete with microwave, refrigerator, and coffee maker. Upstairs is a spacious apartment with a living room/dining area, a den, one bedroom with a king-size bed, another with a queen-size bed, refrigerator, coffee maker, toaster, and small appliances for light meal preparation. Every few days Mahina will bring homemade bread, muffins, juice, and coffee for your continental breakfast. There are ceiling fans, lots of beautiful plants, and, of course, that heavenly beach just across the street. By the way, both Maxeys are from old kamaaina families; ask Mahina about the family photos.

Papaya Paradise

195 Auwinala Rd., Kailua, HI 96734. ☎ and fax 808/261-0316. 2 rms. $70 single or double. Each additional person $15. Three-day minimum. (Rates include breakfast.) No credit cards.

Very popular with a number of German-speaking guests who return year after year, Jeanette and Bob Martz's cozy home is located on a residential street in the Enchanted Lake section of Kailua, a short walk from Kailua Beach. There's a separate entrance to the bed-and-breakfast units through the garage, which leads to the lanai and pool with Jacuzzi and an enormous backyard. Papayas were just taking hold at this writing (a previous crop had succumbed to disease), but there are plenty of shade trees and flowers and a delightful rock garden. The two units, each with private bath, air conditioning, and ceiling fans, are decorated Polynesian style in rattan and wicker. There's a well-stocked library of books in both English and German. Breakfast is served on the lanai by the pool overlooking that yard; it's a great place for birdwatching.

✪ Sharon's Serenity

127 Kakahiaka St., Kailua, HI 96734. ☎ **808/263-3634** or 808/262-5621. 2 rms with private baths. TV TEL. $50–$55 single; $55–$60 double. No credit cards.

Sharon and Bob Price's lovely home is located on a quiet residential street a short walk from Kailua Beach. The house is decorated in an elegant Asian and contemporary style enhanced by Sharon's striking floral arrangements. The two-room suite has a sitting room with a comfortable daybed, ceiling fans, small refrigerator, a queen-size bed, a full bath, and a door opening to the pool area. The Blue Room also has a queen-size bed, ceiling fans, and a small refrigerator. The Yellow Room, with a twin bed, is used only with the suite and shares the same bath. Each room has its own color TV, but guests are welcome to join the Prices in their spacious living room, with its huge comfy couches, big TV, and plenty of books. The setting is gorgeous, with beautiful flowers, Kaelepulu Stream running by, and views of a golf course and mountains. A cuddly Bichon Frise named Trouble (a misnomer if we've ever heard one) completes the Price ménage. A good breakfast is served; a washer/dryer is available for a small fee.

Sheffield House Bed & Breakfast

131 Kuulei Rd., Kailua, HI 96734. ☎ **808/262-0721.** 1 rm, 1 one-bedroom suite (both with bath). $40 double; $60 one-bedroom suite; $95 two-bedroom suite. Minimum stay three days; monthly rates on request. No credit cards. Free parking.

Architects Paul and Rachel Sheffield and three bouncy little Sheffield children plus cat Hillary comprise the household here. Their house is in an ongoing process of renovation, but the cozy guest accommodations are all finished. Each has a private entrance, Mexican tile floors, bright tropical-print bedspread and accessories, and a kitchen area with a refrigerator, microwave, toaster oven, and coffee maker. The suite has its own sitting room, a small dining area, a queen-size bed in the bedroom, and a view of its own private garden. The room, which is wheelchair-accessible, has a queen-size bed. The two units may be combined as a two-bedroom/two-bath suite. There's no pool, but who needs one when you're just a hop, skip, and a jump from beautiful Kailua Beach. *Note:* Complimentary continental breakfast is provided on the first day only.

KANEOHE

A 5-Star Bed & Breakfast—BJG's

44-491 Kaneohe Bay Dr., Kaneohe, HI 96744. ☎ **808/235-8235** or toll free 800/235-5214. 3 rms (1 with private bath). $75 and $85 single or double. No credit cards. Free parking.

Next door to the posh Kaneohe Bay Yacht Club is the movie set–style home of Bonnie and Richard Green. We were entranced by the magnificent Italian tile pool nestled in a tropical garden and guarded by two stone lions; at night the area is illuminated by tiki torches. The house is decorated in an Asian motif with some extraordinary antiques and pictures. The living room has a great collection of books and magazines, which guests are invited to peruse. Two rooms share a bathroom; one has twin beds and the other has a queen-size bed. The master bedroom, which has a king-size bed, overlooks the pool area. Both bathrooms are gracefully appointed. The entire home, which comfortably sleeps six adults and four children, can be rented for $300 daily, with a seven-day minimum. There's a 20% discount for one month or more.

✪ Ali'i Bluffs Bed & Breakfast

46-251 Ikiiki St., Kaneohe, HI 96744. ☎ **808/235-1124.** 2 rms (with bath). $50 Circus Room; $55 Victorian Room. No credit cards. Free parking.

Set in a lush tropical garden with a pool, this charming home is filled to the brim with Victorian antiques—toys, posters, teddy bears, ornaments—and fine paintings, reminders of the days when hosts L. De Chambs and Donald Munro ran an art gallery in New York. Now they're here in Hawaii, in a gracious home overlooking Kaneohe Bay and very close to wonderful swimming beaches. Their guest wing consists of the Victorian Room, with a wonderful old china doll on its double bed, and an attached private bath. The Circus Room has antique teddy bears on each of the twin beds, circus posters from all over the world on the walls, and a private bath across the corridor. The hosts are delightfully warm people who enjoy having their guests in for late-afternoon tea. And they serve breakfast—fruits, cereal, juices, toast, and coffee—out on the pool lanai whenever guests wish.

✪ Hula Kai Hale

44-002 Hulakai Place, Kaneohe, HI 96744. ☎ 808/236-6754. 2 rms (with bath). King Room $65; with den for extra person, $25; Queen Room $50 single, $55 double. Discounted weekly rates available. No credit cards.

Take an idyllic location right on Kaneohe Bay, a wonderful house with a swimming pool fronting the bay, and a pair of gracious hosts, and you have Hula Kai Hale, the House of the Dancing Water. Tom and Ditty Pico, long-time Hawaii residents, thoroughly enjoy having guests. They provide an ample breakfast, served poolside or on the huge waterfront dock. There are two nicely furnished guest rooms, each with color TV, bar-refrigerator, coffee maker, microwave, and toaster oven. The King Room has an adjacent den with twin daybed, ideal for a teen family member. Each room has its own spacious bathroom and an exit to the outdoors. Kailua and Lanikai, about a 10-minute drive away, are two of the best beaches in Hawaii.

OTHER ALTERNATIVE ACCOMMODATIONS
HOSTELS

Hostels are for "the young at heart, regardless of age," although students—Australian, European, Canadian, Japanese, as well as American—do predominate. Simple chores are expected of all guests.

Waikiki

Hostelling International-Waikiki

2417 Prince Edward St., Honolulu, HI 96815. ☎ 808/926-8313. Fax 808/946-5904. 50 beds, 4 studios. $15 bed; $35 studio. MC, V. Parking $2 per day.

This hostel is just the ticket for beach buffs, since it's two short blocks from Waikiki Beach. It's for AYH or IYHF members only (you can purchase a $25 membership at the hostel in Manoa Valley—see below), and offers dormitory accommodations for 20 women and 30 men. Two common rooms provide kitchens, patios, TV, and the relaxed camaraderie for which youth hostels are famous. Dorms are closed and locked from noon to 2pm daily in accordance with the hostel tradition of promoting outdoor life. Couples might consider renting one of the four studios here that feature private bath and shower, mini-refrigerators, private entrance, and 24-hour access to the rooms; some have TV. The staff is helpful with information on low-cost vacationing and travel. Stays are guaranteed for three days; they'll let you stay longer if they're not busy.

⑤ Interclub Hostel Waikiki

2413 Kuhio Ave., Honolulu, HI 96815. ☎ 808-924-2636. 140 beds in shared rms (three-night minimum stay), 11 private rms. $15 bed; $45 private rm. Each additional person $10. JCB, MC, V. Free parking but limited, mostly on street.

This hostel, just two blocks from the beach at Waikiki, is for international travelers only: You must show a passport and a ticket. (Foreigners need only show tickets to the United States; Americans must be going beyond Hawaii.) According to one guest, "it's the looser of the hostels" in Waikiki, since it's open 24 hours and has no curfew, and there are no chores to be done. Each dorm room, with four or seven bunks, has its own private bath and shower. Private rooms are nicely set up with a couch, a bed, and private bath. There are common rooms, a game room with pool and Ping-Pong tables, a bar with TV lounge, laundry facilities, and a friendly atmosphere. Movies on Wednesday and barbecues on Saturday are among the many special events.

Near the University of Hawaii

Hostelling International–Honolulu
2323A Seaview Ave., Honolulu, HI 96822. ☎ **808/946-0591.** Fax 808/946-5904. 38 beds. $12 members; $15 nonmembers. JCB, MC, V. Free parking.

In lovely Manoa Valley, this hostel facility has developed a reputation over the past 24 years as a safe, clean, friendly environment for world travelers. Nonmembers are accepted. There are beds for 18 women and 20 men. Common rooms, a kitchen, a Ping-Pong table, games, and a patio under the stars create a relaxed mood. House parents Thelma and Susan Akau are helpful sources of information. Waikiki is a 10-minute bus ride away. Walking, hiking, and restaurant tours are available. Facilities are locked between noon and 4pm daily.

THREE Y'S

Waikiki

⑤ Central Branch YMCA
401 Atkinson Dr., Honolulu, HI 96814. ☎ **808/941-3344.** Fax 808/941-8821. 114 rms. TEL. $30 single without bath, $36.50 single with bath; $43 double without bath, $51.50 double with bath. Weekly rates available. AE, MC, V. Free parking 6pm–6am.

Located across the street from Ala Moana Beach Park and the Ala Moana Shopping Center, just a five-minute bus ride to the heart of Waikiki, this is a good choice for the single male tourist as well as couples (women are allowed only in those rooms with a private bath). It's a beautiful place, complete with an outdoor swimming pool and lovely grounds. The "Y-style" rooms are small but adequate, and you can add a rollaway bed to create a double. The Y has a reasonably priced coffee shop, a large-screen TV in the residents' lounge, and no end of recreational activities; guests are welcome to use all athletic facilities, including the weight-training center and racquetball courts. Reservations are accepted and welcomed.

Readers Recommend

University of Hawaii at Manoa. "*Might I suggest to your readers that they visit Hawaii as I did? I spent 6 weeks as a student at the University of Hawaii at Manoa. The cost of dorm room and board was very economical. Many tours, at special prices, were provided through the university. Our summer-student IDs even got us 'kamaaina' rates at various clubs and attractions. We were roomed with local students and were thus able to share our different cultures. There were also some dorm facilities for couples. The course selection is wide, ranging from golf and tennis to more academic studies. By the end of 6 weeks, I was referring to the dorm as 'home.'*"—Susan McEwin, Stratford, Ontario, Canada.

Downtown Honolulu

⊕ Fernhurst YWCA

1566 Wilder Ave., Honolulu, HI 96822. ☎ **808/941-2231**. 60 rms (all with adjoining bath). TEL. $30 single, $25 per person double for nonmembers; $28 single, $20 per person double for members. (Rates include two meals Mon–Fri.) No credit cards. Limited parking at daily, weekly, and monthly rates. After a stay of 3 nights, you must join the YMCA ($30 per year).

Women can stay for up to six months at this pleasant tropical residence about halfway between downtown Honolulu and Waikiki. The residence accepts both short- and long-term visitors, many of the latter from afar, so staying here is a good way to get to know people from many countries and backgrounds. The accommodations consist of nicely furnished double rooms, each joined to another room by a common bath. Sometimes single rooms are available. Rates include two meals a day on weekdays—surely one of the best buys in town! Linens may be rented for a nominal fee. Pluses include a swimming pool, garden, laundry room, and a lounge area. Also available for use: typewriters, piano, TV, sewing machine. Advance reservations are accepted with a one-night deposit. Fernhurst recommends that you write to inquire about future accommodations.

⊕ Nuuanu YMCA

1441 Pali Hwy., Honolulu, HI 96813. ☎ **808/536-3556**. 70 rms. $28–$30 single. Weekly rates available. AE, MC, V.

This modern, $1.3-million men's facility downtown, convenient to bus lines, is a good bet. Advance reservations are accepted. There's a cafeteria, excellent athletic facilities, and local phone calls are free.

A MILITARY HOTEL

Hale Koa Hotel

Armed Forces Recreation Center, Fort DeRussy, 2055 Kalia Rd., Honolulu, HI 96815-1998. ☎ **808/955-0555**, or toll free 800/367-6027. Fax 800/833-6060. 419 rms. A/C TV TEL. $47–$75 standard, $56–$87 superior, $62–$89 park view, $70–$106 ocean view, $82–$114 oceanfront. Single occupancy deduct $2; more than two persons, add $10 per person. Children under 12 stay free in parents' room using existing bedding. Cribs $4. (Rates depend on rank.) AE, CB, DC, MC, V. Parking $3 per day.

This hotel has a select guest list: It's available only to active-duty and retired military of all services, including Reserve and National Guard members and their families. But what a deal! Fronting a superb stretch of Waikiki Beach, it's comparable to many first-class hotels in Waikiki, and prices, depending on one's rank, are far less than what one pays in regular hotels. Reservations can be hard to come by; they can be made up to a year in advance, and are often honored within a much shorter time period. Rooms are of good size and nicely furnished, and most have two double beds. There's a pool, fitness center with sauna, volleyball and racquetball courts, and many services on the premises, including a Post Exchange, a military discount travel office, laundry facilities, and car-rental desk.

4 Camping on Oahu

By Jeanette Foster

Camping is a year-round experience in Hawaii thanks to the balmy weather. However, there is a wet (winter) and dry (summer) season, and you should be prepared for rain year-round. You also need to be ready for insects (a good repellent for mosquitoes), water purification (boiling, filtration, or iodine crystals) and sun protection (sunscreen, hat, and long sleeve shirt).

A few notes on personal safety—don't hike or swim alone and never turn your back on the ocean. Remember that you are a guest in Hawaii and treat the land you visit, as well as the people you meet, with respect and dignity.

If you do not plan to bring your own camping equipment, you can rent equipment at **Omar the Tent Man,** 650A Kakoi St. (☎ 808/836-8785); or **The Bike Shop** at 1149 S. King St. (☎ 808/595-0588) or Windward City Shopping Center (☎ 808/235-8722). Both also have equipment for sale.

Oahu is the only island with a public transportation system that serves the entire island. To get information on TheBUS, call 808/848-5555. However, one problem with getting to a camping site on the TheBUS is that luggage larger than you can hold on your lap or place under your seat is forbidden. Metal-frame packs are not permitted. Drivers do use discretion, but be forewarned.

The best places to camp on Oahu are:

HOOMALUHIA BOTANICAL GARDENS   This relatively unknown camping area outside of Kaneohe on the windward side is a find. Hoomaluhia means "peace and tranquility," an apt description of this 400-acre botanical garden. It's hard to believe that you are just a half-hour from crowded downtown Honolulu in this lush garden setting with rare plants and craggy cliffs in the background. The facilities at this tent-camp area include restrooms, cold showers, dishwashing stations, picnic tables, grills, and water. A public phone is available at the visitor center, and shopping and gas can be obtained in Kaneohe, one mile away.

A perfect spot from which to explore the windward coast, the botanical gardens also offer numerous hikes. The gardens are laid out in areas devoted to the plants specific to tropical America, native Hawaii, Polynesia, India-Sri Lanka, and Africa. A 32-acre lake sits in the middle of the scenic park (no swimming or boating allowed). The visitor center can also suggest a host of activities ranging from guided walks to demonstrations of ancient Hawaiian plant use.

Permits are free, but camping stays are limited to five nights (the park is closed on Tuesday and Wednesday). For information contact **Hoomaluhia Botanical Gardens,** 45-680 Luluku Road, Kaneohe, HI 96744 (☎ 808/233-7323). The closest bus service is TheBUS no. 55 (Circle Island), which stops four miles from the park entrance. The gate to the gardens is locked from 4pm to 9am; you are locked in for the night from 4pm on.

KUALOA REGIONAL PARK   Located on a peninsula on Kaneohe Bay is a spectacular site, with the quiet waters of the bay on three sides and a view of Mokolii Island (Chinaman's Hat) offshore. The white-sand beach is excellent for swimming and snorkeling, and the fishing can be productive. There are two campgrounds, one in a wooded area with palm trees, ironwoods, *kamani,* monkeypods, and a sandy beach, which is mainly reserved for groups but does have a few sites for families. The other campground is situated on the main beach with fewer shade trees but a great view of Chinaman's Hat. Facilities at both sites are nearly the same: restrooms, showers, picnic tables, drinking fountains, and a public telephone. The group campground also has dish-washing sinks, a volleyball court, and a kitchen building. Gas and groceries are available in Kaawa, 2¹/₂ miles away.

In the summer, the group campground is nearly always filled (frequently by groups with young children) so you might want to consider this when requesting a campsite. Permits, which are free but limited to five days (no camping on Wednesday and Thursday), can be obtained from **Honolulu Department of Parks and Recreation,** 650 South King St., Honolulu, HI 96713 (☎ 808/523-4525), or at any satellite city hall. The two closest satellite city halls to the campgrounds are in Hauula, 54-316 Kamehameha Hwy. (☎ 808/293-8551), or in Kaneohe, 46-018 Kamehameha Hwy. (☎ 808/235-4571). To get to the park, take TheBUS no. 55 (Circle Island).

MALAEKAHANA STATE RECREATION AREA   One of the most beautiful beach-camping areas in the state, Malaekahana is located north of Laie, along the windward side of the island. Here a gorgeous sandy beach backs up into a wooded grove of ironwoods, kamani, and hao trees. Offshore lie several small islands; the largest one is Moku'auia (Goat Island), which is a bird sanctuary. Most of the long white-sand beach is excellent for swimming—on calm days, at low tide, you can wade in the waist-high water to Moku'auia. Snorkeling, surfing, and fishing are also available when conditions are right. Beachcombing, walks, and hikes on the grounds of the state park are just a few of the activities here.

There are two areas for tent camping at this state campground. Facilities include a picnic table and small table to hold a portable stove at each campsite, restrooms, showers, dishwashing sinks, drinking water, and phone. Groceries and gas are available in Laie and Kahuku, less than a mile away. To get to the park, take TheBUS no. 55 (Circle Island). Permits, which are free but limited to five nights (no camping on Wednesday and Thursday), can be obtained at any state park office. On Oahu you can get a permit at The **State Parks Division,** P.O. Box 621, Honolulu, HI 96809 (☎ 808/548-7455). The park gate is closed between 6:45pm and 7am; vehicles cannot enter or exit during that time.

5 Where to Eat in Town & Around the Island

Can the average tourist still find romance, happiness, and a good, inexpensive meal in Hawaii? Well, we won't make any promises on the first two counts (that's up to you), but on the third we are quite positive. Although the price for dinner at one of the really elegant restaurants can easily zoom into the stratosphere, there are still plenty of places where you can get a terrific meal for under $20, and there are also lots of places where you can eat well for under $12.

DIAMOND HEAD WAIKIKI
MEALS FOR LESS THAN $12

Na's Bar-B-Que
In the Royal Grove Hotel, 151 Uluniu Ave. ☎ **808/926-9717** for take-out orders. Reservations not accepted. Main courses $6.69–$7.50. No credit cards. Daily 7am–9pm. KOREAN.

If you like tasty Korean barbecue dishes, you'll be thrilled to discover Na's, where it's no trick at all to have a hearty meal for around $7. Each of the dishes—like our favorite, the barbecued chicken—comes with a choice of vegetables, plus two scoops of rice. The hot noodle and soup dishes are also delicious. This is a tiny place, with a counter inside (always seemingly jammed) and just a few tables outside. Lots of condo dwellers nearby come here for take-out.

Ruffage Natural Foods
In the Royal Grove Hotel, 2443 Kuhio Ave. ☎ **808/922-2042.** Reservations not accepted. Main vegetarian courses $3.50–$5.25. MC, V. Mon–Sat 8:30am–7pm, Sun 10am–6pm; sushi bar, Mon–Sun 6pm–midnight. VEGETARIAN/SUSHI BAR.

Ruffage specializes in organic foods and those that are as free as possible of processing, all modestly priced. They serve freshly squeezed juices; good fruit and vegetable salads; lunch and dinner dishes on the order of whole-wheat spaghetti with chili-and-cheese or veggie burritos; sandwiches like zucchini-cheese or tofu-tuna, or multigrain bread, stuffed with tomatoes and sprouts and practically a meal in themselves ($3.50 to $5.85), and yummy shakes and smoothies. At the front of the store is an authentic Japanese sushi bar, where you can order by the piece (yes, they have vegetable sushi). Take it out and go to the beach, or dine here at one of the several open-to-the-street tables. While you're here, pick up a few organically grown papayas to take back to your hotel for breakfast.

CENTRAL WAIKIKI
MEALS FOR LESS THAN $18

✪ Duke's Canoe Club

At the Outrigger Waikiki Hotel, 2335 Kalakaua Ave. ☎ **808/922-2268.** Reservations recommended. Main courses $7.95–$19.95. AE, CB, DC, DISC, JCB, MC, V. Breakfast daily 7–10:30am; Barefoot Bar Menu daily 11am–midnight; dinner daily 5–10pm; cocktails daily 11:30am–1am. AMERICAN.

Duke's is exactly the kind of restaurant you hoped you would find in Hawaii. It's right out there on the beach, romantic in the old Hawaiian style, with thatched umbrellas, teak chairs, and photographs and other memorabilia recalling the legend of Duke Kahanamoku, the great surfer and Olympic swimming champion— long known as Hawaii's "Ambassador of Aloha"—to whom the restaurant is dedicated. Duke would have loved it; so do we—especially since you can enjoy all this atmosphere and still dine well for very little money.

If you're really watching the budget, order from the Barefoot Bar Menu, which is served from 11am to midnight. Hawaiian local plates—stir-fry chicken cashew, fresh fish, and the like—go from $8.95 to $9.95. Sandwiches, burgers, pizza, and pastas all range from $6.45 to $6.95. Ordering from the regular menu is still reasonable: Fresh fish of the day, Pacific seafood fettuccine, and Koloa pork ribs are all well priced, and all include a trip to the fabulous salad bar, which includes fresh papayas and pineapple, handmade Caesar salad, freshly baked muffins, sourdough rolls, and steamed rice. In fact, you can make your entire meal off the salad bar alone for just $7.95. Keiki dinners are priced from $4.50 to $5.95, so bring the whole family. Now for desserts: Of course you'll have to have Kimo's original hula pie ("this is what the sailors swam to shore for"), and some fabulous tropical drinks from the bar. And if you hang around for the local Hawaiian entertainment, which takes place from 4 to 6pm and again from 10pm to midnight, you could easily while away the better part of your vacation here.

Islander Coffee House

In the Outrigger Reef Towers Hotel, 247 Lewers St. ☎ **808/923-3233.** Reservations not accepted. Main courses $7.25–$9.95. No credit cards. Daily 6am–11pm. AMERICAN.

Both locations of this coffeehouse are always dependable for excellent food at very reasonable prices, and both are impeccably clean and attractive. The original Islander is oceanfront in the Outrigger Reef Tower Hotel; the newer, and much bigger one, at 150 Kaiulani Ave., is in the Outrigger East Hotel. You won't go wrong at either one. At both you can get their famous fresh-baked orange bread. Those who love breakfast food should note that the Islanders serve breakfast all

Waikiki Dining

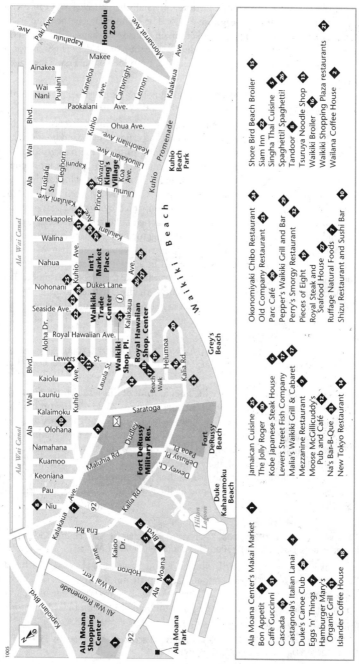

Ala Moana Center's Makai Market
Bon Appetit
Caffé Guccinni
Cascada
Castagnola's Italian Lanai
Duke's Canoe Club
Eggs 'n' Things
Hamburger Mary's Organic Grill
Islander Coffee House

Jamaican Cuisine
The Jolly Roger
Kobe Japanese Steak House
Lewers Street Fish Company
Malia's Waikiki Grill & Cabaret
Mezzanine Restaurant
Moose McGillicuddy's Pub and Café
Na's Bar-B-Que
New Tokyo Restaurant

Okonomiyaki Chibo Restaurant
Old Company Restaurant
Parc Café
Pepper's Waikiki Grill and Bar
Perry's Smorgy Restaurant
Pieces of Eight
Royal Steak and Seafood House
Ruffage Natural Foods
Shizu Restaurant and Sushi Bar

Shore Bird Beach Broiler
Siam Inn
Singha Thai Cuisine
Spaghetti! Spaghetti!
Tandoor
Tsuruya Noodle Shop
Waikiki Broiler
Waikiki Shopping Plaza restaurants
Wailana Coffee House

Post Office ☒   Information ⓘ

day: the Jamboree Breakfast, a favorite, offers all the pancakes you can eat, plus bacon or sausage and two eggs, for $4.95. The menu is largely the same at lunch and dinner. At dinner, along with your main course—perhaps mahimahi, teriyaki steak, or shrimp-fry platter—you get home-style soup or salad, potatoes or rice, plus hot bread. Don't miss one of their great pies from their Yum Yum Tree Bakery.

⑤ Jamaican Cuisine

2310 Kuhio Ave. ☎ **808/924-JERK.** Reservations not required. Main courses $5.95–$9.50. No credit cards. Lunch Mon–Sat 11am–4pm; dinner daily 4–11pm. JAMAICAN.

There's a real bit of Jamaica right here in Waikiki. Owner Clarence Allen, originally from Jamaica, has created the colorful ambience of his island homeland in Jamaican art on the walls, and reggae playing softly in the background (some of the recordings are by Brother Walter, one of the Big Island's most popular "Jawaiian" artists). The menu is simple and basically the same for lunch and dinner, except that dinner comes with soup or salad and is priced about $2 to $4 more. At both meals, main courses are accompanied by rice and peas or steamed rice, mixed vegetables, and a festival (that's a fried mixture of cornmeal, flour, and seasonings). Don't worry about the food being too hot: The jerk chicken and pork are served with both mild and fiery condiments—you choose what you like. The escoveitch fish—fried snapper steak served in vinegar with spicy garnishes—can be cooked as hot as you like. For those of us who like their food a bit milder, thank you, consider the shrimp or chicken curry, or my personal favorite, the plum chicken: tender cuts of chicken sautéed in Asian spices, simmered in a tangy plum sauce. They'll pack anything for takeout.

Lewers Street Fish Company

In the Outrigger Reef Towers Hotel, 247 Lewers St. ☎ **808/971-1000.** Reservations not required. Main courses $6.95–$16.95. AE, MC, JCB, V. Dinner only, daily 5–10pm. SEAFOOD/PASTA.

It doesn't surprise us a bit to see the lines in front of this restaurant at dinnertime. This place has just about everything a hungry tourist could want: great tasty food, a piano bar, an attractive '40s deco, and prices that are downright appetizing. There are several main dishes under $10. Fresh fish from their own fishing boat is featured ("subject to season and condition of the weather and our captain") and handsomely presented. All dinners come with a choice of rice, french fries, or fresh pasta (our favorite) and freshly baked bread. Start your meal with an excellent seafood chowder and end with one of their homemade cheesecakes, each only $2.95.

Malia's Grill & Cabaret

311 Lewers St. ☎ **808/922-7808.** Reservations not accepted. Main courses $5.95–$13.95. No credit cards. Daily 11am–10:30pm; full bar til 4am. AMERICAN.

This is a tasty American grill with an island flair, great prices, and a fun and friendly atmosphere. Pastas, seafood, salads, plate lunch specials, steaks, Mexican favorites, and more, bring in the crowds. A large bar covers one side of the wood-paneled restaurant, which has a large photomural of Diamond Head, circa 1910.

Moose McGillycuddys Pub and Cafe

310 Lewers St. ☎ **808/923-0751.** Reservations not accepted. Main courses $5.95–$10.95. AE, DC, MC, V. Daily 8am–2am. AMERICAN.

Although it's primarily a night spot, the Moose is well worth knowing about when the daytime hungries hit. It's very popular among the local folks, since portions are large and prices very reasonable. It opens for breakfast at 8am, when you can catch the Early Bird Breakfast Special—two eggs, bacon, toast or rice or potatoes, and orange juice—a great buy for $3.50. Lunch and dinner feature such fare as gourmet hamburgers, several Mexican dishes, hot soups, sandwiches, good salads, and hot specials, like teriyaki chicken and mahimahi. The Moose serves up great margaritas and daiquiris for $4—and to go with them, fried potato skins or nachos.

Eating as the Locals Eat: Where to Find Honolulu's Best Plate Lunches

The food of Hawaii—like its people—reflects the islands' cultural diversity: Japanese, Chinese, Hawaiian, Korean, Filipino, and other cuisines abound, as does a good deal of American-style eating. The unique down-home cuisine that is an amalgam of these various ethnic styles is known as "local food," and sampling some of it might possibly be the most interesting eating you do in the islands. Probably the best—and most authentic—way to try the real eats of the islanders is by ordering yourself a genuine "plate lunch," a Hawaiian-style sampler unto itself.

Some of the foods you'll find as part of your average carbohydrate-filled plate lunch are *lomi-lomi salmon* (well-seasoned, hand-kneaded salmon), *laulau* (ti leaves stuffed with pork, salt fish, bananas, sweet potatoes, and taro shoots, then steamed), *loco moco* (a hamburger patty topped with a fried egg and gravy), and rice, potato salad, and/or macaroni salad—two scoops of one or more of these starchy sides are almost always included. You may want to supplement your plate with the islands' most popular soup, *saimin* (a thin noodle broth topped with bits of fish, shrimp, chicken, pork, and/or vegetables), or a *manapua* (steamed dumplings filled with pork, meat, or bean paste) or two. Enjoy!

- Even before it was immortalized in song by Hawaii's favorite funny man, Frank DeLima, **Grace's Inn** 1296 S. Beretania St. *(see p. 124)*, and the plate lunch were all but synonymous. Specialties at this modest but immensely popular eatery include chicken and beef katsu, teriyaki beef, and sweet-and-sour pork—all served with two scoops of rice, of course.
- Restaurant Row's **I Love Country Cafe,** 500 Ala Moana Blvd. *(see p. 132)*, may be the most stylish setting in which you can enjoy a local-style lunch. Here, the traditional island favorites, such as pork adobo, are accompanied by both rice *and* macaroni.
- If you're near the University, stop in at the unassuming **Aloha Poi Bowl,** 2671 S. King St., in University Square *(see p. 143)*, for an authentic plate lunch. In addition to the regularly featured Hawaiian staples such as kalua pig and tripe stew, there's always a daily special—and the *haupia* (traditional Hawaiian coconut pudding) is great.
- What **Ono Hawaiian Foods,** 726 Kapahulu Ave. *(see p. 123)*, lacks in size, it makes up for with aloha. This friendly place, easily accessible to Waikiki, includes *pipikaula* (Hawaiian beef jerky), lomi-lomi salmon, poi or rice, and haupia with all of their plates.

—Faye Hammel

There's another Moose at 1035 University Ave. (☎ 808/944-5525), where the UH kids hang out, and it's a lot of fun, too.

Pepper's Waikiki Grill and Bar

150 Kaiulani Ave. ☎ **808/926-4374.** Reservations not accepted. Main courses $4.95–$15.25. AE, CB, DC, JCB, MC, V. Daily 11:30am–2am. TEX-MEX.

Here you are in the tropics, but you love the desert, too. What to do? Ride that lonesome trail to Pepper's, a hybrid of the islands and the Southwest, sprouting both cacti and palm trees, and serving some of the best Tex-Mex food in town. It's a casual yet sophisticated spot, dominated by a lively bar but with well-spaced booths and tables conducive to good conversation. The Kiawe woodsmoke oven gives a true barbecue taste to the chicken and ribs, and the lava rock grill turns out super burgers and steaks. In addition to the Mexican dishes, you can order smoke-oven baby back ribs and excellent salads. Nachos, sandwiches, quesadillas, and yummy potato skins offer inexpensive and tempting possibilities for grazing. For dessert, try hula pie, a specialty of Hawaii, or fried ice cream, a specialty of Mexico (no, it's not really fried, but in such a *simpatico* spot, it's hard to quibble).

Shore Bird Beach Broiler

In the Outrigger Reef Hotel, 2169 Kalia Rd. ☎ **808/922-2887.** Reservations not accepted. Main courses $6.95–$16.95. AE, JCB, MC, V. Daily 7:30am–10pm. SEAFOOD/STEAK.

It's not hard to figure out why this spot quickly became one of the most popular restaurants in Waikiki. First of all, you can't beat the location: The large, attractively decorated open dining room is right on Waikiki Beach. Second, the food is good; and third, the price is right, because you're the chef, broiling your own portion of teriyaki chicken, ribs, fresh fish, seafood, New York steak, ground steak, or top sirloin. While the fire is doing its work, you can have a few drinks, then fill up on salad bar, chili, rice, and fresh pastas, all included in the price of your main course (salad bar alone is $6.95). Dessert (including their homemade cheesecake) is extra. This is the perfect place for sunset drinks and dinner. Early-bird specials are from 5 to 6:30pm. They also have an all-you-can-eat breakfast buffet ($6.95) served until 11am. Lunch, 11am to 2:30pm, features chicken; veggie, turkey, and beef burgers; fish sandwiches; and an all-you-can-eat salad bar at $4.95.

Siam Inn

407 Seaside Ave. ☎ **808/926-8802.** Reservations recommended at dinner. Main courses $7.95–$18.45. AE, MC, V. Lunch Mon–Sat 11am–3pm; dinner daily 5–10:30pm. THAI.

This pretty second-floor restaurant is the place to make, or renew, acquaintance with the subtle (and not-so-subtle) spices of Thai cuisine. When last we lunched here, the daily specials, $6.95, were Bangkok chicken, served with rice and the chef's special soup, and the chicken masaman curry—slices of tender chicken on a bed of avocado, peanuts, and coconut milk, served with curried rice and cucumber sauce (mild or hot). Other luncheon possibilities are also very reasonable (there are 16 dishes at $7.50) and include a variety of noodle dishes featuring chicken, beef, pork, or shrimp. Your waiter will ask if you wish your meal mild, hot, or very hot. Main dishes are also reasonably priced.

Spaghetti! Spaghetti

In the Royal Hawaiian Shopping Center, 2201 Kalakaua Ave. ☎ **808/922-7724.** Reservations not required. Spaghetti buffet and salad bar $6.99 lunch, $7.99 dinner. AE, DC, JCB, MC, V. Daily 11am–10pm. ITALIAN.

Everybody seems to like spaghetti, so it's good to know that you can eat your fill for little money. This is a large multilevel restaurant with stylish furnishings, a huge and busy bar, and, on the buffet table, a choice of four different pastas, four freshly made sauces, and a variety of salad ingredients. A slice of garlic bread rounds out the meal nicely. Also available are soups, sandwiches, and burgers. Top off a not-exactly-slimming meal here with cheesecake or a super Baskin-Robbins mud pie.

Tsuruya Noodle Shop

315 Lewers St. ☎ **808/922-3434.** Reservations not accepted. Main courses $4.75–$6.75. MC, JCB, V. Mon–Sat 11am–10pm, Sun 11am–9pm. JAPANESE.

We're great fans of Japanese noodle houses; they're just the ticket for those times you want a simple, tasty, nutritious, and extremely low-cost meal. So we were delighted to find this sparkling, clean little place with a horseshoe-shaped-counter in the middle and four tables with comfortable leather chairs. Try the hot soba broth called sansai, with vegetables and garnishes, or the teriyaki chicken teishoku—grilled marinated chicken and salad, which comes with miso soup and pickled vegetables. Cold soba (buckwheat) noodles are available, as are side orders of shrimp tempura, cooked in 100% vegetable oil. Your food is served promptly, in a beautiful bowl on a lacquered tray. Take-out is available.

Waikiki Broiler

In the Outrigger Waikiki Tower, 200 Lewers St. ☎ **808/923-8836.** Reservations not accepted. Main courses $9.75–$19.50. AE, CB, DC, JCB, MC, V. Daily 6am–2am. AMERICAN.

The budget crowd is kept well in mind at this cozy place. The dining room overlooks the pool area of the Outrigger Edgewater Hotel. The Broiler offers low-priced dinner main courses, like fried scallops, teriyaki chicken breasts, and mahimahi, in addition to such higher-priced offerings as steak, scampi, and prime rib, the specialty of the house. At lunch, there are special sandwiches served with soup or salad (around $6), plus daily specials like teriyaki chicken for $4.50. Breakfast is served all the way from 6am to 2pm, with a $2.49 special of pancakes, bacon, and egg. And there's always a "two for $15.95" dinner special—two teriyaki steak dinners served with soup or salad, rice or fries, and a croissant. Children have their own menu ($2.75 to $4.25).

Waikiki Seafood and Pasta Company

In the Outrigger Surf Hotel, 2280 Kuhio Ave. ☎ **808/923-5949.** Reservations not accepted. Main courses $6.95–$14.95. AE, MC, JCB, V. Dinner daily 5–10pm. SEAFOOD/PASTA.

The same management responsible for Lewers Street Fish Company runs this place, and it's an equally good bet. And it's so pretty, with its dining room ceiling covered with plants, and a smart New York–style deli and bar up front. The food is inexpensive and delicious; gourmet pastas are made on the premises, so you know they're fresh. The pasta comes with house specialties, such as garlic basil chicken and chicken parmesan. Other popular menu items are calamari steak, teriyaki beef kebab, and baby back ribs. Good food, good value, and a fun atmosphere.

MEALS FOR LESS THAN $20

Caffè Guccinni

2139 Kuhio Ave. ☎ **808/922-5287.** Reservations recommended for more than four. Main courses $10.95–$15.95. AE, MC, V. Dinner only, daily 4–10:30pm. ITALIAN.

Everyone likes Caffè Guccinni. This is a modest place, with a counter inside, tables outside, and the menu posted beside the counter. Everything is homemade in owner Jocelyn Battista's kitchen. Dinner specials include various pasta dishes (we're partial to the manicotti stuffed with five kinds of cheese) and two or three daily specials. Homemade ravioli is a specialty as is spaghetti marinara, which is just $5.95. Main courses are accompanied by soup or salad and homemade bread. As for desserts, we're always hard put to decide among a heavenly crème brûlée or chocolate torte, a Sicilian cannoli, or the amaretto cheesecake. The best solution is to bring a group of friends and share. Desserts are all $3.50. (If you've eaten elsewhere, come here just for dessert.) Mango daiquiris are also special.

The Jolly Roger

150 Kaiulani Ave. ☎ **808/923-2172.** Reservations not accepted. Main courses $8.25–$14.45. AE, DC, JCB, MC, V. Daily 7am–midnight. AMERICAN.

While the venerable Jolly Roger on Kalakaua Avenue recently shut its doors, its newer, sister restaurant, at the corner of Kuhio and Kalakaua, is still going strong. It's a big and bright space with its own cocktail lounge. As for the food, it's American coffeehouse style, quite tasty and well priced. Complete dinners are served with soup or salad, potatoes or rice, and dinner roll; burgers, salads, and sandwiches are also available. Breakfast is a special treat, since that's when you can get the MacWaple, a waffle covered in sliced, spiced hot apples topped with macadamia nuts. The cocktail lounge is open until 2am.

Okonomiyaki Chibo Restaurant

In the Royal Hawaiian Shopping Center, 2201 Kalakaua Ave. ☎ **808/922-9722.** Reservations recommended. Main courses $9–$29. AE, DC, MC, JCB, V. Lunch Mon–Sat 11:30am–2pm; dinner daily 5–10:30pm. JAPANESE.

There's a quiet elegance about this attractive place, an altogether new dining experience for Hawaii. The Chibo restaurants were founded in 1973 in Osaka, the city referred to as the "gourmet kitchen of Japan." Okonomiyaki originated in the Edo period as a snack made of baked flour flavored with miso. Okonomiyaki itself hasn't changed radically since the Edo period, but the Chibo restaurants have made it into something unique—a sort of Japanese pancake—by heaping it with all sorts of wonderful things. The Okonomiyaki "Chibo," the house specialty ($27 at dinner), is smothered in sirloin, prawns, squid, and scallops. On a smaller scale, you can build your own Okonomiyaki for $14.50, choosing any two of the following: bacon, sirloin, pork, octopus, chicken, prawns, scallops, or Japanese mushrooms. Then there's Yoshokuyaki, which looks almost like a tortilla with lots of green onions, vegetables, and an egg on top—definitely something different. At lunch, prices go down $3 to $4 for pretty much the same specialties: We like the special Okonomiyaki lunch served with chef's salad, at $19.

Old Company Restaurant

2256 Kuhio Ave. ☎ **808/923-3373.** Reservations not accepted. Main courses $11.45–$15.95. AE, CB, DC, JCB, MC, V. Breakfast daily 6am–4pm; lunch daily 11am–4pm; dinner daily 4pm–midnight. AMERICAN.

When you step off Kuhio into this spot, it's almost like entering someone's living room. Art, comfortable captain's chairs, polished wood tables, low rafters, and plants contribute to the homey feel. Lunch is fun here, since it features an all-you-can-eat fruit and salad bar for $7.95. Sandwiches run the gamut from grilled cheese at $3.65 to chicken and avocado at $6.45. And dinner prices are modest, too: Barbecued ribs, for example, are $12.95; the seafood combination plate is $13.95. All regular dinners include a trip to the salad bar, plus vegetables and rice or potatoes. There's a bar with three TVs for viewing sports events, and live entertainment nightly, from 9pm. Arrive before noon and you can take advantage of the Sunrise Special: pancakes, egg, and bacon, for only $2.49.

Pieces of Eight

In the Outrigger Coral Seas Hotel, 250 Lewers St. ☎ **808/923-6646.** Reservations not required. Main courses $6.95–$18.95. AE, MC, V. Dinner only, daily 5–11pm. SEAFOOD/ STEAK.

Waikiki's oldest steak and seafood house, Pieces of Eight has won many dining awards since it opened in 1967. The cannon located on the piano bar goes all the way back to the time of King Kamehameha II, and was presented to him by a Russian sea captain in 1822; that's only one of their many authentic nautical antiques. This is the place for fresh fish, Pacific oysters, beer-battered shrimp, top sirloin, and steak-and-seafood combos. Add $3.50 to your check if you take a turn at the salad bar; the salad bar alone is $7.95. In typical steakhouse fashion, there's one major dessert: homemade cheesecake, $2.95. The bar is open from 4pm to midnight, and there's a daily happy hour from 4:30 to 6pm, offering free pupus. The piano bar is alive nightly except Monday.

Royal Steak and Seafood House

2201 Kalakaua Ave., in the Royal Hawaiian Shopping Center. ☎ **808/922-6688.** Reservations recommended Sat–Sun. Main courses $12.95–$24.95. AE, MC, V. Lunch daily 11:30am– 2:30pm; dinner daily 5:30–10pm. STEAK/SEAFOOD.

This is an attractive place, decorated in ocean colors, with a huge marine aquarium. The specialty here is seafood and meat combos; main courses include rice or potatoes and vegetables. Some of our favorites are the steak and shrimp, the steak and salmon, and steak and fresh oysters. Luncheon main dishes are similar fare.

EWA WAIKIKI
MEALS FOR LESS THAN $12

Egg's 'n' Things

1911B Kalakaua Ave. ☎ **808/949-0820.** Reservations not accepted. Main courses $4.25– $10. No credit cards. Daily 11pm–2pm. AMERICAN.

This longtime Waikiki favorite is near Ala Moana Boulevard. It's a spick-and-span white tile dining room with decorative wall plaques containing amusing sayings. Various early- and late-riser specials are available, like the early-riser breakfast, served from 5 to 9am, and the late riser, served from both 1 to 2am and pm; that's when pancakes and two eggs are $2.75. The house specialty is the three buttermilk pancakes with eggs any style and a choice of meat (from $6 for Vienna sausage to $8 for steak). Also special are the nine kinds of crêpes suzette ($6 to $7.25), even more varieties of omelets ($7 to $10), 10 ways to enjoy pancakes ($4.25 to $7.25), and 9 different approaches to waffles ($4.50 to $7.25). Lots of side orders and fruit juices, too. Great for those who are truly devoted to breakfast.

Hamburger Mary's Organic Grill

2100 Kuhio Ave. ☎ **808/922-6722.** Reservations not accepted. Burgers and sandwiches $4.25–$7. No credit cards. Daily 7am–11pm. AMERICAN.

Hamburger Mary's is known as one of Honolulu's most popular gay gathering places, but everyone is welcome here. The food is very good, the price is right, and the place itself looks like a bit of old Hawaii. Booths are upholstered with imitation leopard-skin fabric, and the lamps on each table sport shades made of aloha fabric decorated with fur and fringe (you really have to see this to believe it!). In the little front garden, there are umbrella tables and ice-cream chairs, and the bar's ceiling is decorated with photographs of Marilyn Monroe, Jean Harlow, and other departed luminaries. Breakfast is served all day and designed for the hearty eater. Hamburger is king here, served in many varieties, on either multigrain or Hawaiian sweetbread, but you can also have good turkey and chicken sandwiches, and Mary's Mahi, a charbroiled fish sandwich served either teriyaki style or with mustard sauce. Several vegetarian items, including a garden burger, are popular. Charbroiled steak, mahimahi, and chicken are also offered, from $9.25 to $11.75. Desserts are fresh and different every day.

Wailana Coffee House

1860 Ala Moana Blvd. ☎ **808/955-3735.** Reservations not required. Main courses $7.25–$11.25. AE, DC, MC, V. Daily 24 hours. AMERICAN.

Although this place looks imposing and expensive, its prices will surprise you. The nicest thing about the Wailana is that lunches and dinners are the same price—the tab does not go up after 5pm, as it does in so many other places. So any time of the day you can have the homemade soup and sandwich lunch for $5.25, or the delicious "broasted" chicken, juicy and tender, served with a generous helping of french fries, coleslaw or salad, roll and honey, for $7.95. Other good buys are the old-fashioned beef stew at $7.75 and the New York steak at $11.25. All these are served with soup, salad bar, or fresh-fruit cup, as well as a choice of potato or rice. The salad bar is available from 11am to 11pm. Breakfast is served around the clock, so you can come by anytime to try their delicious classic french toast or all the pancakes you can eat, plus bacon and eggs at just $4.50.

There's another Wailana Coffee House in mid-Waikiki, with the same menu; it's called the **Wailana Malia** and it's located in the Outrigger Malia Hotel, 2211 Kuhio Ave. (☎ 808/922-4769). It's also open 24 hours a day.

MEALS FOR LESS THAN $20

✪ Castagnola's Italian Lanai

In the Inn on the Park, 1920 Ala Moana Blvd. ☎ **808/949-6277.** Reservations recommended. Main courses $8.40–$17.90. AE, CB, DC, DISC, MC, JCB, V. Lunch Tues–Fri 11:30am–2pm; dinner Tues–Sun 5–10pm. ITALIAN.

This old favorite is a beauty, located on an open-air lanai, typical of trattorias found throughout Italy. The floor is flagstone, and the decor, reminiscent of the Italian flag, is all green and white with touches of red. Castagnola's food is superb: Everything is fresh, and sausages, meatballs, desserts, and breads are all homemade. Complete meals, offered all day, can be ordered in regular-size portions or in smaller ones for the light eater: For instance, rigatoni ricotta, linguine marinara, and eggplant parmigiana are all $11.90 regular, or $8.40 for the light eater. There are lunch sandwiches under $7. Castagnola's is one of the few places in Honolulu where you can find cannoli. Try it, or chocolate gelato, spumoni, or zabaglione for dessert. Top wines, usually sold by the bottle elsewhere, are available here by the glass.

Kobe Japanese Steak House

1841 Ala Moana Blvd. ☎ **808/941-4444.** Reservations recommended. Main courses $13.90–$23.90. AE, DC, JCB, MC, V. Dinner only, daily 5:30–10:30pm. JAPANESE.

A meal here is a show in itself. First, there's the beautiful Japanese country-inn surroundings and artifacts everywhere; second, the splendid sushi bar; and third, and most important, the communal tables where you and fellow diners can chat and watch your meal being prepared teppanyaki-hibachi style, by a master chef who stands at the grill in the center of it all. Order yourself teriyaki chicken, sukiyaki sirloin, teppan shrimp, or a steak-and-teriyaki combo, and you have a complete meal. First, the chef sautés some teppan shrimp and serves you a delicate soup; then he stir-fries your order with mushrooms, onions, peppers, and bean sprouts. Vegetables, rice, and tea come with the meal, and you top it all off with delicate green-tea ice cream.

✪ Mezzanine Restaurant

In the Waikiki Terrace Hotel, 2045 Kalakaua Ave. ☎ **808/955-6000.** Reservations recommended. Main courses $7.95–$21; breakfast buffet $8.95. AE, CB, DC, DISC, JCB, MC, V. Breakfast daily 6–10:30am; dinner Mon–Sat 5:30–10pm, Sun/holidays 6–10pm. CONTEMPORARY AMERICAN.

The raves keep coming in for this one: It was recently acclaimed for "Best Pizza" and "Best Seafood" at the annual "Taste of Honolulu" competition, and we're not a bit surprised. Mezzanine is on the mezzanine level of the sparkling Waikiki Terrace Hotel; like the hotel, it's handsome, with a sleek, contemporary look. Casual elegance is the keynote here. The indoor-outdoor setting showcases a kiawe-wood-burning oven and grill, from which come some extraordinary breads and pizzas, with the chef concocting new and exciting combinations every evening ($10.75 to $15.25). From the kiawe-wood broiler come rack of lamb and skinless breast of chicken, and there are wonderful pasta platters, fresh salads big enough to share, and such tantalizing appetizers as black-and-blue ahi, stuffed mushroom caps, and smoked salmon wontons (their prize "Best Seafood" dish). The chef dreams up extraordinary specials every day, including heavenly desserts. There's entertainment nightly.

New Tokyo Restaurant

286 Beach Walk. ☎ **808/923-5411.** Reservations recommended. Main courses $10.95–$36.95. AE, DC, JCB, MC, V. Lunch Mon–Sat 11:30am–2pm; dinner daily 5:30–9:30pm. JAPANESE.

This restaurant is getting to be an institution in Waikiki, attracting tourists and locals alike. For lunch, you might have the grilled fish marinated in soy sauce for $4.95 or the assorted tempura vegetables with tempura fish at $6.25. Combination lunches run $5.50 to $9.50. At dinner, main courses range from noodle dishes to old favorites, such as sukiyaki and shabu-shabu.

Shizu Restaurant and Sushi Bar

Fourth floor, Royal Garden Hotel, 440 Olohana St. ☎ **808/943-0202.** Reservations recommended. Main courses $8–$14; 10-course dinner $32. AE, CB, DC, JCB, MC, V. Lunch daily 11:30am–2pm; dinner daily 5:30–10pm. JAPANESE.

Classic Japanese cuisine in an elegant modern setting awaits at Shizu, named in honor of the wife of the owner of the exquisite new Royal Garden Hotel. A marble-and-brass entryway leads to the fourth floor dining room, with its green-and-black marble floors and walls, blond-wood furniture, and Japanese rock garden. The terrace, overlooking the hotel's gardens, is popular for alfresco dining. Waitresses wear elaborate kimonos and obi sashes. Master Chef Hideaki Moribe (formerly chef at Honolulu's Japanese consulate and most recently with the Westin Kauai) was trained in Osaka and is dedicated to classic Japanese cuisine of the Kyoto–Osaka areas—among the most subtle and refined cooking in Japan. The best way to experience Shizu is to order the 10-course Kaiseki dinner at $32, but you can also enjoy such appetizers as assorted sashimi, and main courses not likely to be found outside of Japan. For dessert, try the tempura ice cream—it's fried! Lunch has a variety of entrées priced under $10.

✪ Singha Thai Cuisine

1910 Ala Moana Blvd., corner of Ena Rd. (diagonally across from Hilton Hawaiian Village). ☎ **808/941-2898.** Reservations recommended. Main courses $7.95–$22.95. DC, JCB, MC, V. Lunch Mon–Sat 11am–4pm; dinner daily 4–10pm. THAI.

Singha is the only sister restaurant of the original in Bangkok, a four-time winner as best restaurant in that city. The interior is filled with soft lights and orchids; there are handsome Thai artifacts everywhere, soft classical music in the background, dining room windows open to the courtyard and the balmy trade winds, and a delightful terrace for alfresco dining. And the food is wonderful, including all the classics—spring rolls, coconut chicken soup, pad thai, grilled beef salad, and the like—plus some only-in-Hawaii specialties featuring fresh Hawaiian seafood. Try the scallops with Thai chili black-bean sauce, or the fresh local fish with curry sauce. The Royal Thai Dancers entertain at dinner every evening (from 7 to 9pm) except Wednesday.

✪ Tandoor

In the Hawaiian Monarch Hotel, 444 Niu St. ☎ **808/940-3112.** Reservations recommended on weekends. Main courses $9.50–$22.95. AE, DC, MC, V. Lunch daily 11am–2pm; dinner daily 5–10pm. INDIAN.

Indian food is relatively rare in Honolulu, so fans of this subtly spiced cuisine will be delighted to find Tandoor. It's a lovely place; lighting is soft, the ambience quiet and romantic. A discreet sign over the dark wood bar proclaims Tandoor the home of the Honolulu Cricket Club (shades of the Raj!). Tandoor specialties—baked in a traditional clay oven, which is charcoal-heated 24 hours a day—are featured. We like both the tandoor chicken and the shish kebab, and, as a side dish, the tasty masala kulcha, baked nan bread stuffed with minced vegetables and spices. Dal mutton, a savory dish of lamb and lentils, is a specialty.

KAPAHULU

Hee Hing

449 Kapahulu Ave. ☎ **808/734-8474.** Reservations not accetped. Main courses $6.45–$18.95. MC, V. Daily 10:30am–9:30pm. CHINESE

One of the most popular Chinese restaurants in Honolulu since 1963, Hee Hing is still going strong. There's good reason for its popularity: It's a handsome, spacious restaurant with superb Cantonese cuisine. And the prices are always reasonable. The menu is voluminous, so take a little time to study it, or ask the waiter for advice. Don't miss the dim sum; they serve over 75 Hong Kong–style dim sum every day. The house specialty is drunken prawns—live prawns, marinated in white wine, cooked tableside. There's a vast variety of other live seafood dishes too, as well as fresh fish. Or you might decide to feast on one of the sizzling specialties, such as chicken with black-bean sauce. Earthen-pot casserole dishes ($7.25 to $15.75) are another way to go. Then there are taro-nest specialties and at least 16 vegetarian offerings. Everything we've tried here has been excellent. For dessert, forego the fortune cookies in favor of a seasonal fruit pudding or fried apple fritters. A great find!

Irifune

563 Kapahulu Ave. ☎ **808/737-1141.** Reservations not accepted. Main courses $6.50–$9.50. MC, V. Lunch Tues–Fri 11:30am–1:30pm; dinner Tues–Sun 5–9:30pm. JAPANESE.

For Japanese food with a local flavor, try Irifune. Short on decor, this place is long on good food, large portions, and low prices. It's only $7.50 for the kushiyaki stick meal, which consists of miso soup, pickled vegetables, three skewers of barbecued chicken and veggies, a salad, rice, and green tea. With seafood it's $8; with mixed seafood and chicken, $9. Irifune specialties include their barbecued chicken and beef teriyaki, and a variety of garlic creations, such as garlic tofu with veggies. Be sure to try their breaded tofu among the appetizers. Best of all, go with their fresh spicy garlic ahi. Unlike most Japanese restaurants, Irifune does serve dessert, and a delicious one at that: ice-cream crêpes, filled with seasonal fruit, for just $3. No liquor, but B.Y.O.B.

Jo-ni of Hawaii

1017A Kapahulu Ave. ☎ **808/735-8575.** Reservations not accepted. Main courses $4.50–$10.50. MC, V. Lunch Tues–Sun 11am–2pm; dinner Tues–Sun 5–9pm. FILIPINO.

Filipino food, it is said, originated with Malay settlers, was spread by Chinese traders, stewed for 300 years of Spanish rule, and was finally hamburgerized by the Americans. What has arrived in Honolulu is delicious, especially so at this bright place. Your first decision is whether to select a festive main dish or a regional specialty: You needn't worry about prices, since both are inexpensive. Festive items include langua—tender slices of ox tongue simmered in mushroom sauce (delicious!)—and beef flank rolled and stuffed with boiled eggs and sausage. Among the regional specialties, you might try adobo Manila, a stew with pork and/ or chicken in a vinegar, garlic, and soy sauce; or the more delicate hipon sa gatong bicol, shrimp simmered in coconut milk, along with squash and long beans. There's a smaller version of Jo-ni at Makai Food Court at Ala Moana Center.

La Bamba

847 Kapahulu Ave. ☎ **808/737-1956.** Reservations not necessary. Main courses $6.50–$12.95. No credit cards. Lunch Sun–Fri 11am–2pm; dinner Sun–Fri 5–9:30pm. Closed Sat. MEXICAN.

There's nothing very unusual about the decor here—tile floors, ceiling fans, white tablecloths, and scenes of old Mexico. But the food is very good for the price, and you'll always get an enthusiastic welcome. The taco salad appetizer is a favorite; for something unusual, try the butaquito—that's a large flour tortilla filled with chicken, lamb, beef or fresh mixed vegetables, deep-fried, then cut into small pieces and served with guacamole and sour cream. There are various Mexican plates for $6.50, a range of burritos from $6.95 to $8.95, and several Mexican-style dinners from $11.95 to $12.95. Bring your own bottle and enjoy.

Ono Hawaiian Foods

726 Kapahulu Ave. ☎ **808/737-2275.** Reservations not accepted. Main courses $6.50–$8.75. No credit cards. Mon–Sat 11am–7:30pm. HAWAIIAN.

Close to Waikiki, this very popular spot offers great Hawaiian food. It's a friendly little place; the walls are covered with photos of popular local entertainers who are patrons. Try the kalua pig at $6.50, the laulau plate at $6.75, or go mad and have the combination kalua pig *and* laulau at $8.75. These and other plates come with pipikaula (Hawaiian beef jerky), lomilomi salmon, poi or rice, and haupia.

MCCULLY/MOILIILI
MEALS FOR LESS THAN $12

Chiang-Mai Thai Restaurant

2239 S. King St. ☎ **808/941-1151** or 808/941-3777. Reservations recommended. Main courses $6.50–$10.95. AE, DISC, MC, V. Lunch Mon–Fri 11am–2pm; dinner daily 5:30–10pm. THAI.

Here's a small restaurant that the locals favor. With perhaps a dozen tables, and simple decor, it specializes in the food of northern Thailand, and calls itself the "home of sticky rice and exotic food." You can order anything from golden-fried calamari with fresh lemongrass and spices and creamy tofu soup to a shrimp pineapple curry, hot-and-spicy clams, or ginger beef. Vegetarians have almost two dozen dishes from which to choose.

✪ Diêm Vietnamese Restaurant & Coffee Shop

In University Square, 2633 S. King St. ☎ **808/941-8657.** Reservations recommended. Main courses $5.55–$12.55. CB, MC, V. Daily 10am–10pm. VIETNAMESE.

To sample the exotic cuisine of Vietnam, you need only go to this little place, just a block Diamond Head of University Avenue. The small, family-run eatery is kept sparkling clean; there's nothing fancy here but the food. Spring rolls and beef grilled with lemongrass make good appetizers. There's a wide range of noodle dishes—curry chicken vermicelli, seafood saimin, barbecued shrimp cake, chicken noodle soup—and none will set you back more than $6.50 for a filling meal. The Vietnamese shrimp crêpe, the coco-steamed chicken, and the seafood and vegetables are especially good. Desserts are cool and soothing—yellow mung-bean pudding, black-eye bean pudding, banana pudding—and just $1.95. The friendly management invites you to call ahead "for even faster service," and take-out orders are welcome.

Vegetarians are especially welcome at Diêm, and for them, the best time to come is on a Monday or Wednesday night, when they are invited to meet others of like mind and partake of five different (and delicious) vegetarian entrées for $8.95.

Down to Earth Deli

2525 S. King St. ☎ **808/949-8188.** Reservations not accepted. Main courses $3.75–$6.95. No credit cards. Daily 10am–9pm. VEGETARIAN.

Enter Down to Earth Natural Foods, just west of University Avenue, go to the rear, and there you'll find this delightful spot where you can dine on "healthy, home-style vegetarian cooking at its best." Only natural ingredients are used (no sugar, white flour, eggs, lard, rennet, caffeine, MSG, or preservatives); there are many nondairy alternatives for vegans and those watching their cholesterol—and the food is delicious. There's a changing parade of hot specials every day that might include almond-vegetable tofu, chickpeas à la king, nondairy lasagne, or shepherd's pie. Always on hand are tofu or tempeh burgers, a variety of veggie sandwiches, hearty homemade soups, and a plentiful salad or pita-pocket sandwich bar that goes for $3.75 a pound. There are plenty of cold deli items, like tabbouleh, pesto pasta, burritos, and basmati salad to take out. Healthful desserts await your guilt-free enjoyment, none more than $2. There's a counter, a few tables right there, and more seating upstairs.

Grace's Inn

1296 S. Beretania St. ☎ **808/537-3302.** Reservations not accepted. Main courses $4.60–$5.65. No credit cards. Mon–Sat 6am–10:30pm, Sun 7am–10pm. LOCAL.

Grace's Inn and the staple food of Hawaii—the plate lunch—are inseparable in the minds of Oahuans. Her food isn't fancy or unique, but its popularity is mind-boggling. Chicken or beef katsu, teriyaki beef or pork, sweet-and-sour pork, mixed beef curry, ribs, and teri pork plates, with the traditional two scoops of rice and salad, are the staples. Specialties include fried noodles, fish tempura, and big bowls of curry stew. There are a few tables inside, but the bulk of Grace's trade is take-out. The lady is definitely doing something right. Consult the telephone book for other locations around town.

✪ Jenny's

2671D S. King St. ☎ **808/949-2679.** Reservations not accepted. Main courses $4.95–$7.25. No credit cards. Mon–Sat 10am–9pm, Sun 11am–8pm. KOREAN.

Honolulu has only a handful of Korean restaurants, and this one in Moiliili, on the way to the university, is the oldest and best. This is the kind of family-style place that gives you a genuine dining experience. Small and tidy, it caters to local Korean and other Asian families—lots of cute keikis mill about—and a smattering of university students. There are a few booths and tables up front from which you can see the big open kitchen in the back. We love the combination of mon doo and kuk soo—hot noodle soup with Korean dumplings stuffed with beef, pork, and vegetables. The waitress once explained to us that this is "New Year's soup, but so popular we make it every day." The house specialty is kalbi—barbecued short ribs—and it's excellent. The plate lunch—barbecued meat, na mul (Korean-style vegetables and fish fried in an egg batter), and rice—is a buy at $4.40. Kimchee and hot sauce come with all orders. While you're here, try the famed Korean ginseng tea.

King Tsin

1110 McCully St. ☎ **808/946-3273.** Reservations recommended. Main courses $4.75–$8.95. MC, V. Lunch daily 11am–2pm; dinner daily 5–9:30pm. CHINESE.

There are precious few northern Chinese restaurants in the islands, so praise be for this attractive, pleasantly decorated place, popular with both visitors and local folk. The food is reasonably priced, subtly flavored, and most fun to eat with a group. Our party of four began with potstickers, small dumplings stuffed with pork, and two orders of sizzling rice soup. For our main courses, we had moo shu pork; dry-fried beef—super hot; King Tsin chicken, a delicate combination of tender white meat of chicken and pea pods; braised bean curd; and sweet-and-sour fish—an entire rock cod, complete with tail and head—smothered in sauce. We all ate until we couldn't manage another bite—and still had a huge doggie bag to take home. Lunch prices are about 10% lower than dinner. With the exception of the aforementioned beef—about which the menu warns you—the food here is not overly spicy, as it can be at other northern Chinese restaurants.

Kozo Sushi Hawaii

In Old Stadium Square, 2334 S. King St. ☎ **808/973-5666.** Sushi rolls 98¢–$5.50. Most locations daily 9am–7pm; Sun 9am–6pm. SUSHI.

These little sushi-counter take-out places are insanely popular in Hawaii; everybody seems to love them. Sushi is fresh and delicious, the platters are artfully presented, and prices are remarkably low. The $4.90 lunch box is generous. California maki (a blend of avocado, crab, and cucumber), at $3.50, is one of their biggest sellers. Would you believe the BLT maki—red lettuce, bacon, tomato, and rice! Almost all the Kozo Sushi Hawaii shops are strictly take-out, but the main one does have a few tables.

Kozo Sushi Hawaii has shops at the Aiea Shopping Center (☎ 808/483-6800), Pearl Ridge Shopping Center, Phase II (☎ 808/483-6805), Kahala Mall (☎ 808/733-5733), and 1150 Bishop St. (☎ 808/522-9515). For other locations around the island, consult the telephone book.

✪ Maple Garden
909 Isenberg St. ☎ **808/941-6641**. Reservations recommended. Main courses $6.75–$25. AE, MC, V. Lunch daily 11am–2pm; dinner daily 5:30–10pm. CHINESE.

Rating high with the local Chinese community is this small, attractive dining room. The Szechuan dishes are so tasty and authentic that a doctor friend of ours from Taiwan brings all his visiting friends and relatives here. Mr. Robert Hsu, the owner, is constantly adding new delights to the menu. The house specialty is Szechuan smoky duck, crispy on the outside and tender on the inside, served with steamed buns—you tuck the meat into the buns. A very generous order (you'll probably need a doggie bag) is $7.75. If you really like the super-hot Szechuan-style cooking, you'll love the eggplant with hot garlic sauce or the pork with hot garlic sauce; they're real eye-openers. (The eggplant recipe has received an award from the *Los Angeles Times*). There are more than 60 main dishes on the menu priced at $7.50 or less, including hard-to-find singing rice—actually it's more of a whistle—served either with pork and vegetables or with shrimp.

✪ Mekong Restaurant
1295 S. Beretania St. ☎ **808/521-2025** or 808/523-0014. Reservations not required. Main courses $6.95–$8.95. AE, DC, MC, V. Lunch Mon–Fri 11am–2pm; dinner daily 5:30–9:15pm. THAI.

Every now and then one discovers a place where the food is exotic and delicious, the staff cordial and attentive, the atmosphere warm and cozy, and the prices painless. Such a find is Mekong. The voluminous menu will explain the basics of Thai cooking, but you'll do just as well to tell your waiter what you like and follow his or her suggestions. While Thai cooking can be highly spicy, almost every dish can be ordered either mild, medium, or hot. The hottest—and most popular—dishes are Thai green curry (beef, pork, or chicken sautéed in green chile and curry fresh coconut milk) and Evil Jungle Prince (beef, pork, or chicken sautéed with hot spices with either hot or sweet basil leaves). Mild dishes include not-to-be-missed spring rolls, a memorable chicken-ginger soup in a fresh coconut-milk base, and shrimp curry. Bring your own bottle if you want wine. (Mekong II, listed below, serves both beer and wine.) Dessert is another unforgettable treat: tapioca pudding unlike any you've ever tasted, in a warm coconut milk; and half-ripe Thai apple-bananas, again cooked in coconut milk. Thai teas are just a little bit different, brewed with vanilla beans and served with condensed milk to make them quite sweet.

A branch called **Mekong II** is located at 1726 S. King St. (☎ 808/941-6184).

✪ Salerno
In the McCully Shopping Center, 1960 Kapiolani Blvd. ☎ **808/942-5273**, or 808/946-3229. Reservations recommended. Main courses $7.90–$12.90 small, $9.90–$16.90 regular. AE, DC, MC, V. Lunch Mon–Sat 11am–2:30pm; dinner daily 5–10pm. ITALIAN.

Everybody raves about the authentic Italian food at Salerno, and no wonder. Only the freshest pastas, vegetables, and seafood are used in preparing the dishes; all the wonderful breads and pastries are baked right in their own kitchens; and they are happy to satisfy special dietary needs. And the price is right! You have your choice of excellent antipasti, soups, salads, pizzas, and a variety of pastas in small or regular portions. Among the notable main courses are veal marsala, shrimp scampi, chicken oregano, and such house specialties as calamari vegetable and stuffed eggplant. Beer, wine, drinks, and espressos are modestly priced, as are some filling Italian pastries. The setting is pretty, with soft lighting, plants, and partitions affording a feeling of privacy. On the way out, check out Salerno's Italian Grocery and maybe take home some homemade bread, pastas, sauces, or deli items for your hotel kitchenette.

Suehiro

1914 King St. ☎ **808/949-4584.** Reservations recommended. Main courses $7.25–$26. MC, V. Lunch daily 11am–2pm; dinner Mon–Fri 5–9pm, Sat–Sun 5–9:30pm. JAPANESE.

We've always liked Suehiro. Try to get one of their ozashiki or tatami rooms, where you sit on the floor and dine at a low lacquered table (take off your shoes before you enter); the setting will immediately put you in a tranquil mood. You usually need a party of eight and a reservation for these rooms, but if one happens to be open you may double up with other waiting guests. On one visit we teamed up with a big, charming family of Japanese-Americans and had a family-style dinner at $15.50 per person that included a tasty miso soup, namasu (pickled cucumber), sashimi, shrimp tempura, tenderloin filet, and mixed sushi, served with several side vegetables, sauces, rice, and plenty of tea. At the regular restaurant tables, you may order a similar dinner special à la carte. There is an extensive sushi menu, and a half-dozen special lunches for $7.95 to $8.50. You can also get a tasty Japanese box lunch or bento for picnics and trips.

Woodlands Potsticker Restaurant

1289 S. King St. ☎ **808/526-2239.** Reservations not required. Main courses $6.25–$26. MC, V. Lunch Wed–Mon 11am–2:30pm; dinner Wed–Mon 4:30–9pm. CHINESE.

Do you like potstickers? All the food here is especially good, and this attractive place is a local favorite. We like the pan-fried dumplings, the chicken with chives, and the onion cake ($5.95 to $6.25). Bird's-nest soup—the real thing—with chicken is another impressive starter, or try the crabmeat tofu soup. Prawns, scallops, and steamed catch-of-the-day dominate the dozen seafood dishes. Best bargains are some 30 specialty chicken and duck choices (most $5.95 to $7.25), but watch out—some of these may be highly spiced.

Yuen's Garden Seafood Restaurant

2140 S. Beretania St. ☎ **808/944-9699.** Reservations not required. Main courses $5.50–$7.95. MC, V. Daily 10:30am–10pm. CHINESE.

Of the many items on the menu, which includes Cantonese, Szechuan, and Mandarin dishes, it is the seafood that inspires most of the raves here. Prawns can be bought by the pound at $18; a half-pound is usually five large prawns. We like the fried prawns, served with radish and cilantro. Other good seafood choices are scallops, clams with black-bean sauce, sweet-and-sour shrimp, and sea bass filet. Also great are the hot-pot courses served in casseroles; we vote for the seafood combo and the roast duck hot pot made with eggplant and plum sauce.

NEAR WAIKIKI
MEALS FOR LESS THAN $12

Hard Rock Café

1837 Kapiolani Blvd. ☎ **808/955-7383.** Reservations not accepted. Main courses $7.50–$13.95. AE, DISC, MC, V. Sun–Thurs 11:30am–12:30am. Fri–Sat 11:30am–1am. AMERICAN.

Honolulu is home to the world's ninth Hard Rock Café, which, like its sibling restaurants in Europe and on the mainland, is a restaurant-cum-museum of rock-music memorabilia. Nonstop rock blares forth. Gold records and musical instruments—either donated by their famous owners or purchased at auctions—adorn the walls. A real '50s Cadillac Wagon is suspended from the ceiling over the bar! Larger-than-life busts of Mick Jagger and Keith Richards dominate the foyer, where souvenirs such as T-shirts, lapel pins, baseball caps, and cigarette lighters bearing the HRC logo are for sale. Like all the other Hard Rocks, this one will not accept dinner reservations; lines are common but seem to be part of the fun. The menu features house specials, such as watermelon barbecued ribs; burgers served with home-cut fries, green salad, and your choice of made-from-scratch dressing; sandwiches; and fruit smoothies. Absolutely no preservatives or additives are used.

ALA MOANA AREA
MEALS FOR LESS THAN $12

Auntie Pasto's

1099 S. Beretania St., at Pensacola. ☎ **808/523-8855.** Reservations not accepted. Main courses $6.25–$11.95. MC, V. Mon–Thurs 11am–10:30pm, Fri 11am–11pm, Sat 4–11pm, Sun 4–10:30pm. ITALIAN.

With its brick interior, cafe curtains, and checkered cloths, this place resembles a little trattoria in Florence or Rome. The food here is marvelous, and at lunchtime Auntie Pasto's attracts a lively work crowd. Special lunches, $3.95–$8.95, include cheese ravioli, spinach soufflé and salad, baked cavatelli, and a club sandwich served with pasta salad. Also very popular are Auntie's big sandwiches (meatball, salami subs) for $3.50 to $4.50, and her super pastas for $5.25 to $8.95. At dinnertime, there are also some flavorful specialties like stuffed calamari, chicken marsala, and osso buco.

Chicken Alice's

1470 Kapiolani Blvd., at the corner of Keeaumoku. ☎ **808/946-6117.** Reservations not accepted. Plate lunches $3.95–$5.95. No credit cards. Daily 9am–10:30pm. FRIED CHICKEN.

One of our favorite places to pick up wonderful, portable food is this spot. The stellar attraction here is Alice Gahinhin's flavorful fried chicken: It's ever-so-delicately spiced and definitely habit-forming. And you can't beat the price—$5.25 for a small box containing 12 pieces, $10.50 for the large box of 25 pieces, $25 for some 60 pieces (in case you're throwing a party or have a very large family to feed.) Chicken is also available by the piece. And plate lunches are king-size, to say the least. Our favorite is the combination Korean plate: kalbi (tender barbecued ribs), chicken, rice, and kimchee, for $5.75.

Emilio's Pizza

1423 Kalakaua, near the corner of King St. ☎ **808/946-4972.** Reservations accepted only for parties of six or more Fri–Sat. Main courses $6.95–$13.50. MC, CB, DC, V. Dinner only, Mon–Thurs 5–10pm, Fri–Sat 5–11pm. ITALIAN.

One of Honolulu's favorite pizza parlors, Emilio's is a cozy spot with a homey atmosphere. *Honolulu* magazine recently gave them four stars among independent Italian pizza/pasta restaurants. This is Sicilian-style pizza with a professional touch. Prices run from about $8.50 for the 10-inch cheese pie up to $20 for the mind-blowing combo with six toppings. Emilio's makes their own tasty dough every day, and their own sausages and sauces. They also make an excellent soup of the day—it might be seafood bisque or black bean—in addition to the regular homemade minestrone. There are also pasta specials every day, unusual appetizers like fresh pesto and cream cheese, and many vegetarian and low-fat specialties, all gourmet quality. Customers are welcome to bring their own beer or wine; there is no corkage charge. And yes, they will deliver to most hotels and condos in Waikiki.

Quintero's Cuisine

1102 Piikoi St. ☎ **808/593-1561.** Reservations not accepted. Main courses $10.75–$14.50. MC, V. Mon–Sat 11am–3pm and 4:30–10pm. Closed Wed. MEXICAN.

Authentic Mexican dishes, cooked in the Aztec tradition, would be baked in underground ovens; that's not quite feasible in a city like Honolulu, but Mary and Louis Quintero do the next best thing in their restaurant, which is next to the Old Stadium Square shopping area. Tasty dishes include carne al arriero, steak cooked with garlic, onions, and peppers. Pollo a la mexicana, chicken fried with ranchero sauce, is also good. Among the appetizers and soups, we like the nachos and the fideo, a tomato-based broth with sautéed noodles and Mexican spices ($3.75). This is a small and plain little restaurant, but the service is personal and homey.

Siam Orchid

1514 Kona St. ☎ **808/955-6161.** Reservations not required. Main courses $6.50–$10.95. AE, DC, MC, V. Lunch Mon–Sat 11am–2pm; dinner daily 5:30–9:30pm. THAI.

Just across Kona Street from the Ala Moana Shopping Center is the charming Siam Orchid. The menu is authentic, and prices are modest at both lunch and dinner. There's a huge array of dishes, some hotter than others (ask your waiter), but you can't go wrong with such appetizers as stuffed chicken wings or papaya salad. Choose from such main dishes as fresh chile chicken, beef on a sizzling platter, pork with ginger-curry sauce, or Thai garlic shrimp. As in most Thai restaurants, there's a healthy list of vegetarian specialties. Lunch is always a good buy, with half a dozen noodle specials around $6. Everything is prepared to order, and no MSG is used.

Vim and Vigor Foods

1450 Ala Moana Blvd., at Ala Moana Shopping Center. ☎ **808/955-3600.** Reservations not accepted. Sandwiches $4.25 and $4.95; hot main courses $3.50 and $3.95. AE, DC, JCB, MC, V. Mon–Sat 9am–9pm, Sun 9am–5pm. VEGETARIAN/AMERICAN.

Need a healthful snack while you're shopping Ala Moana? Vim and Vigor, the big health-food store on the lower level, mountain side, has a tidy little take-out bar up front, which keeps huge lunch crowds happy with luscious sandwiches like avocado, tuna, or egg combinations on whole grain breads with sprouts. Hot dishes, such as veggie burgers, chicken adobo, and teriyaki chicken, are also available. Fruit smoothies made with fresh Hawaiian fruits are especially good. There are a few tables where you can picnic in front of the store.

The Wisteria

1206 S. King St. ☎ **808/531-5276.** Reservations not required. Main courses $7.25–$12.50. MC, V. Sun–Thurs 6am–10:30pm, Fri–Sat 6am–11:15pm. JAPANESE/AMERICAN.

When a restaurant has been going strong for over 40 years, it must be doing something right. Such a place is The Wisteria, a family restaurant very popular with the local crowd. The dining room is bright and airy, the service swift and professional, and the deep booths comfortable. The menu is mostly Japanese, but there's a little bit of everything here: Daily specials often include Hawaiian plates, and such dishes as boiled corned-beef brisket with cabbage and Hungarian beef goulash with egg noodles. For a real local experience, try the chef's famous bowl of oxtail soup, served steaming hot with rice and grated ginger ($8.35). For dessert, go with the Portuguese doughnut—deep-fried and filled with ice cream—or have the peach

Melba or strawberry sundae. The cocktail lounge, which always features daily bar specials, is open from 11am to 1am. A Saturday and Sunday brunch buffet is $5.25.

Zippy's
1450 Ala Moana Blvd., at Ala Moana Shopping Center. ☎ **808/942-7766.** Main courses $3–$6. No credit cards. Daily 6:30am–9:30pm. LOCAL.

The kamaainas are mad about Zippy's and it's no wonder. The food is plentiful and the prices are as reasonable as you'll find anywhere in Hawaii. There are 17 Zippys restaurants on Oahu (they're all listed in the phone book), including this convenient one at Ala Moana Shopping Center. Two of their most popular specialties are chili and fried chicken. In fact, many local clubs and children's athletic teams sell tickets for the chili to raise funds, and they sell like . . . Zippy's chili! A "barrel" of this taste treat is $16.35; a take-out for four people is $5. Fried chicken is $14.65 for a 12-piece bucket. And everyone seems to love Zippy's plate lunches: big platters of beef or pork, teriyaki, breaded beef cutlet, fried chicken, and the like. There's good news for the diet-conscious, too: Zippy's huge salads—we especially like the Italian chicken and chef's salads—are all $5.80 or less. Zippy's are self-service restaurants where you place your order at one window, pay, and collect it in very short order at the next windows.

MEALS FOR LESS THAN $20

Hackfeld's
Ground level of Liberty House, 1450 Ala Moana Blvd., at Ala Moana Shopping Center. ☎ **808/945-5243.** Reservations not accepted. Main courses $8.25–$13.50. AE, CB, DC, JCB, MC, V. Mon–Sat 11am–8:30pm. FRENCH/CONTINENTAL.

Call Hackfeld's an elegant bistro: The food has a French accent, and the artful presentations make continental dishes as pleasing to the eye as to the palate. Such dishes as New England crab cakes, seared ahi, medallions of turkey, osso buco, and Kashmir curry are all nicely done. Try the escargots maison or the fettucine Alfredo among the appetizers, and the wonderful Burnt Creme (or any of the French pastries and Viennese tortes) for dessert.

Le Guignol
1614 Kalakaua Ave. between King Street and Kapiolani Boulevard.. ☎ **808/947-5525.** Reservations recommended. Main courses $14.95–$19.95. AE, MC, V. Dinner only. Tues–Sun 5:30–10pm. FRENCH.

At last, a moderately priced French restaurant par excellence in Honolulu! This pleasant, tiny place, reminiscent of a small dining room in a French boîte, is owned by French chef Marcel Trigue and his wife, Madeleine. Appetizers are typically Gallic: pâté, escargots, crevettes provençal; some are a bit different, like scampi flambé in Pernod with cream and garlic. The French onion soup is flavorful. Main courses include Cornish game hen in a mustard sauce; rack of lamb béarnaise; sliced veal in a light, creamy mushroom sauce; and shrimp with fresh basil sauce. These are served with bread and butter, vegetable, and potato. Finish your dinner with a light sherbet, caramel flan, or blueberries jubilee.

Pagoda Floating Restaurant
1525 Rycroft St. ☎ **808/941-6611.** Reservations recommended. Main courses $11.95–$15.95. AE, DISC, MC, V. Lunch daily 11am–2pm; dinner daily 4:30–9:30pm. SEAFOOD.

The Pagoda Floating Restaurant is one of those rare places where the scenery alone is worth a visit. The glass-enclosed Koi Room on the first floor, which specializes in seafood, and the more elegant La Salle above, overlook a lotus-blossom pond stocked with almost 3,000 brilliantly colored Japanese carp. Walkways lead to individual pagodas seemingly afloat in the pond. The pagodas are reserved for groups of eight or more, but don't despair—the view from the main dining rooms is also quite beautiful. Mahimahi is a favorite at $11.95. At lunch, you can order from the menu, or choose the local-style Kamaaina Lunch Buffet ($9.95 adults, $6.95 children 10 and under). There are also a variety of evening buffets: Monday and Tuesday it's a Family Night Buffet ($15.95 adults, $7.95 children); Wednesday and Thursday it's a gala Island Dinner Buffet ($17.95 adults, $9.95 children); and Friday, Saturday, and Sunday, it's the Prime Rib Weekend Buffet ($17.95 adults, $9.95 children). Plan your visit to catch the grand show at carp-feeding time— 8am, noon, or 6pm. Bring the kids and the cameras.

✪ Tahitian Lanai Restaurant

In the Walkikian Hotel, 1811 Ala Moana Blvd. ☎ **808/946-6541.** Reservations recommended. Main courses $14.95–$28.95. AE, CB, DC, JCB, MC, V. Breakfast daily 7am–11am; lunch daily 11am–2:30pm; dinner daily 5–10pm. AMERICAN/SEAFOOD.

To have breakfast at one of the most glamorous tropical settings in town—at coffeehouse prices—try this favorite old-timer, nestled beside a tranquil lagoon and surrounded by tikis, native carvings, Polynesian-style huts, and tapa designs. You can dine outdoors under striped umbrellas or in the casual, open-air dining room. Recommended for breakfast: their renowned eggs Benedict or Florentine ($7 for half order, $9.75 whole), served with hash browns and a banana muffin or popover (weekends only). Coconut waffles or fresh banana pancakes ($4.75 each) are other winners.

   Lunch and dinner are also good bets. You can still get those eggs Benedict or Florentine at lunch, plus specialties like chicken and shrimp curries ($8.50 to $10.25) and some very good salads—spinach, niçoise, and the Green Goddess Surprise: chicken or shrimp tossed with romaine lettuce ($7.25 to $8.50). There are complete dinners, with choice of soup or greens, potatoes or rice, garlic roll, and beverage accompanying such main courses as teriyaki steak, chicken curry, and seafood fettuccine, for $16.95 to $19.50. Don't miss the lively singing around the piano in the Papeete Bar nightly.

RESTAURANT ROW

Restaurant Row, one of Honolulu's prime dining-shopping addresses, is alive and well and flourishing mightily at 500 Ala Moana Blvd., not far from downtown Honolulu. It's a high-tech, strikingly modern neon environment—an enjoyable contemporary urban playground.

   From Waikiki, take any no. 19 or 20 bus from the Kuhio Avenue bus stop; it will take you directly to Restaurant Row.

MEALS FOR LESS THAN $12

✪ Cafe Athena

One Waterfront Plaza, in Restaurant Row. ☎ **808/526-0071.** Reservations not required. Main courses $8.95–$11.55. AE, CB, DC, MC, V. Mon–Sat 11am–11pm. Sun 5–10pm. GREEK.

Authentic Mediterranean cuisine, low prices, and a cozy setting make this place a winner. Only one menu is served all day, and everything on it is delicious. All dishes and sauces are made from "mom's authentic recipes." We like to start with the tasty taramosalata among the appetizers, then move on to one of the platters served with Greek salad and either rice or pita bread: perhaps the lamb kebab, the delicately spiced and marinated chicken Athena, or a beef-and-lamb gyro, right off the grill. Terrific sandwiches ($3.95 to $4.55) and salads ($4.50 to $5.85) are also good possibilities. Don't skip dessert—the Martinica, a blend of ice-cream cake and brandied rum chocolate, is nifty and just $2.95.

Chiu Chau Bistro

500 Ala Moana Blvd., in Restaurant Row. ☎ **808/524-8188.** Reservations not required. Soups $2.50–$5.50; main courses $5–$10. AE, DC, DISC, JCB. Lunch daily 11am–2:30pm; dinner Sun–Thurs 5:30–10:30pm, Fri–Sat 5:30pm–midnight. CHINESE SEAFOOD.

Besides being one of the most striking establishments in Restaurant Row, a study in red and black from the dramatic facade to the black lacquer tables and red walls, Chiu Chau also offers some of the best values in the complex. The menu concentrates on Chinese seafood dishes; the most expensive item—the chef's special fresh Maine lobster—is all of $10! Most of the other delicious seafood preparations— baked clams, steamed fresh oysters with spicy garlic sauce, Dungeness crab with black-bean sauce, and the like—are a comfortable $8.50 or $9.50. The hot pot shabu-shabu of assorted seafood is another favorite.

I Love Country Cafe

500 Ala Moana Blvd., in Restaurant Row. ☎ **808/537-1112.** Reservations not required. Plate lunches $5.45–$7.25; main courses $5.25–$7.50. No credit cards. Mon–Fri 6am–9pm, Sat 9am–3pm. AMERICAN.

The best bet for stylish budget dining here is this cute little cafe. Miniature jukeboxes at each table play popular oldies, and the food is homemade, country style—lots of vegetarian and local favorites, many dishes with low salt and no preservatives. For those reducing their intake of fat, cholesterol, and sodium, there are house specialties like grilled chicken breast with fresh papaya salsa, fresh roast turkey, a vegetarian stir-fry, and a tofu-burger plate. For those who want to eat local style, there are the traditional plate lunches (with both rice and macaroni), including such island favorites as chicken katsu and beef lasagne. The menu also offers deli sandwiches, salads, burgers, and more—there's a bit of something for everybody here.

⑤ Pizza Bob's Restaurant, Game Room & Bar

500 Ala Moana Blvd., in Restaurant Row. ☎ **808/532-4600.** Reservations only for parties of six or more. Pizzas $10.45–$15.95; pastas $6.95–$9.95. AE, DC, MC, V. Mon–Thurs 11am–11pm, Fri–Sat 11am–2am, Sun 5–11pm. ITALIAN.

This longtime favorite continues to pack in the crowds. It's a big, bustling place with a game room in back where you can try your hand at pinball or miniature basketball, and a lanai in front where you can eat, sip an espresso, and ogle the passing parade. In between is a large, rather high-tech–looking room done in black and gray, with a big and very popular bar. Despite its name, Pizza Bob's has lots more than just pies. There are beautiful salads and hot sandwiches like grilled mahimahi and cold ones like the garden burger. But to get back to those pizzas: They are super-fresh and delicious, and range from traditional to innovative. We like the grilled chicken Milano, with mushrooms, artichoke hearts, fresh tomatoes, and sweet onions. You can get individual slices, too, of spicy pepperoni or their five-cheese blend, for $2.95. A good place to pop into anytime—especially on Friday and Saturday nights, when local entertainers jam.

Salsa Rita's

500 Ala Moana Blvd., in Restaurant Row. ☎ **808/536-4826.** Reservations not required. Main courses $5.55–$14.99. AE, CB, DC, MC, V. Daily 11am–11pm. MEXICAN.

There's good food and fun here. The bar, outside on the mall, is always filled with a noisy, friendly crowd. The tiny dining room, done in brilliant yellow and hung with pictures of chili peppers and Mexican scenes, is the place for flavorful quesadillas, enchiladas, tacos, and the like. The light eater's and children's dishes— charbroiled chicken with tortillas ($5.99), quesadillas ($7.99), and vegetarian burrito ($4.99)—are good values. The huevos rancheros are a special treat.

MEALS FOR LESS THAN $20

✪ Sunset Grill

500 Ala Moana Blvd., in Restaurant Row. ☎ **808/521-4409.** Reservations recommended. Main courses $12.95–$23.95. AE, DC, MC, V. Mon–Thurs 11am–11pm, Fri–Sat 11am– midnight, Sun 10:30am–10pm. CONTEMPORARY AMERICAN.

One of our favorites in all Honolulu is this handsome 200-seat restaurant featuring grilled, rôtisserie, wood-fire, and oven-roasted foods in a sophisticated indoor-outdoor setting. Blond woods, glass walls, and a large grill in the center of the restaurant set the mood for dining that's casual in style but elegant where it counts, in every detail of food preparation and service. Have a drink—they're known for terrific martinis—and doodle on the placemats (crayons are provided) while you're waiting for your meal; the best placemat art is displayed on the walls up front, along with autographs of famous visitors.

If you're watching the budget, come for just a sandwich. Their grilled marinated chicken breast, with honey Dijon glaze, cheddar, and grilled red peppers on a cracked whole wheat roll, is a wonder at $9.95. Or splurge a bit and try some of the appetizers, like the oven-roasted garlic and herbed goat cheese or the Dungeness crab cakes with smoked papaya sauce and tamarind citrus vinaigrette. If you're having a full meal, make your main course the smoke-infused marinated salmon with shiitake mushroom salsa, or perhaps the fettuccine with Florida rock shrimp; or choose one of the excellent rôtisserie dishes, which come with fresh vegetables. Desserts are always splendid here, especially the vanilla bean cheesecake with macadamia-nut crust and warm caramel sauce.

Sunset Grill is also a great spot for Sunday brunch (10:30am to 2pm); brunchgoers get complimentary copies of the major weekend papers. Remember it, too, on a Friday or Saturday night for a late-night bite or just dessert.

Trattoria Manzo

500 Ala Moana Blvd., in Restaurant Row. ☎ **808/522-1711.** Reservations not required. Main courses $8.25–$15.95. AE, DC, DISC, MC, V. Mon–Fri 11am–11pm, Sat–Sun 5–11pm. ITALIAN.

Open to the court at Restaurant Row, with a beautiful fountain right outside the main entrance and ornate black iron gates to enclose it at night, this little trattoria might well be in Florence or Rome. Personable owner Signor Manzo greets passersby with a cheery "buono sera" and directs traffic within. Signor Manzo points out that, since they have six kinds of pasta and a huge variety of sauces to choose from, they offer 201 ways to eat pasta. Whichever one you choose—maybe fruitti di mare (seafood), pollo (sliced chicken and vegetables), vongole (clams with white or red sauce), or just a simple aglio olio (oil and garlic), it's going to be very good. And the antipasti, soups, salads, open-face sandwiches, the chicken parmigiana, and the veal milanese are also fine choices. Stylish and fun.

WARD WAREHOUSE

Just opposite Kewalo Basin is the delightful Ward Warehouse shopping complex, where there are several charming restaurants that match the appeal of the shops. Siam Orchid (see "Ala Moana Area," above) also has an attractive outpost here.

MEALS FOR LESS THAN $12

Chowder House

1050 Ala Moana Blvd., in Ward Warehouse, ☎ **808/521-5681.** Reservations not accepted. Main courses $4.05–$12.95. AE, DISC, JCB, MC, V. Mon–Sat 11am–9pm. SEAFOOD.

The Chowder House is a bright, bustling, and inexpensive seafood house, where you can watch the boats of Fisherman's Wharf through the glass wall behind the bar and have a light seafood lunch or dinner for under $10. At a recent meal, we enjoyed a good-size fresh salad, French bread, and a filet of red snapper with french fries for $9.95. Prices are the same all day. Fish sandwiches, also served with fries, are also inexpensive: $4.05 for mahimahi, $4.40 for calamari. There are also salads, seafood, cocktails, and three kinds of chowder, all reasonably priced.

Old Spaghetti Factory

1050 Ala Moana Blvd., in Ward Warehouse. ☎ **808/531-1513.** Reservations not accepted. Main courses $3.95–$8.95. DC, MC, V. Lunch Mon–Sat 11:30am–2pm; dinner Mon–Thurs 5–10pm, Fri–Sat 5–11pm, Sun 4–10pm. ITALIAN.

This is perhaps the most stunning budget restaurant in town. It's worth a visit just to see the setting, which might be described as "fabulous Victorian," the rooms brimming with authentic European antiques and Oriental rugs, ornamental lamp shades, overstuffed chairs, and huge chandeliers. You may dine in an authentic trolley car, or more likely, at large, comfortable tables on plush velvet seats. So popular is this place that you can always anticipate a wait for lunch and dinner.

The menu is modest, concentrating mostly on spaghetti; the food is not as dazzling as the surroundings, but you'll eat heartily and well. Main courses include a good green salad with choice of dressing, and fresh-baked bread with marvelous garlic butter (a whole loaf is brought to your table with a knife, and seconds are available). Our favorite sauces are the clam and the browned butter with mizithra (a Greek cheese). Baked chicken Mediterranean style is tasty, and so is the homemade lasagne and spinach tortellini. Lunch offers smaller portions and slightly lower prices. Beer, wine, and cocktails are available.

Orson's Restaurant

1050 Ala Moana Blvd., in Ward Warehouse. ☎ **808/591-5681.** Reservations recommended. Main courses $9.25–$24.95. AE, DISC, JCB, MC, V. Daily 11am–10pm. SEAFOOD.

The people who run the Chowder House at Ward Warehouse also operate this much fancier restaurant upstairs. It's a lovely dining room with ocean and mountain views and a delightfully open and breezy feeling. You can get a good variety of fish and seafood sandwiches, served with salad and fries, for under $13; the smoked-salmon Reuben on sourdough bread is one of our favorites.

WARD CENTRE

The elegant Ward Centre shopping/dining complex at 1200 Ala Moana Blvd. and Auahi Street, a block from Ward Warehouse, boasts a number of first-rate restaurants. We could happily spend weeks eating here and nowhere else.

MEALS FOR LESS THAN $12

⑤ Crêpe Fever

1200 Ala Moana Blvd., in Ward Centre. ☎ **808/521-9023.** Reservations not accepted. Main courses $5.50–$8.75. MC, V. Mon–Sat 8am–9pm, Sun 8am–4pm. GOURMET VEGETARIAN.

The quality of food and the charm of the surroundings make this casual restaurant, on the street level of Ward Centre, quite special. Red-tile floors, oak tables, plus tables in the pretty garden outdoors, set a sparkling background for a menu that is appealingly diverse and not limited to just crêpes. Breakfast is served all day, with entrées ranging from a variety of omelets (made with Egg beaters® if requested) to whole-wheat pancakes, waffles, and fresh-fruit crêpes. Our favorite lunch item is the homemade vegetarian soup served in a whole-grain bread bowl with salad for $5.50; also excellent are sandwiches, stuffed croissants, many fresh salads, and a host of main course crêpes—Mexican chicken, lemon spinach, tuna melt, and the like—all served with steamed brown rice or green salad. A special vegetarian menu and daily specials are offered evenings. Beer, wine, or specialty drinks can accompany your meal.

Keo's

1200 Ala Moana Blvd., in Ward Centre. ☎ **808/596-0020.** Reservations recommended. Main courses $8.95–$11.95. AE, DC, MC, V. Lunch Mon–Sat 11am–5pm; dinner daily 5–10pm. THAI.

The most picturesque restaurant at Ward Centre must surely be Keo's, one of the many creations of Thai restaurateur Keo Sananikone. Keo runs six restaurants in town (See review of Mekong, under "McCully/Moiliili," above). This one is exquisite, with lovely plantings, flowers, a fountain splashing into a languid pool, pink tablecloths, black bentwood chairs, and seating indoors and out—just beautiful! Enjoy the European-Asian café ambience at either lunch or dinner. While you're here, pick up a copy of *Keo's Thai Cuisine,* so you can try your hand at creating delicate wonders back home.

✪ ScooZee's

1200 Ala Moana Blvd. ☎ **808/597-1777.** Reservations not required. Main courses $5.50–$10. AE, DC, MC, V. Mon–Thurs 11am–10pm, Fri–Sat 11am–11pm. ITALIAN.

If the prospect of great food served in generous portions—at reasonable prices—in a fun and friendly atmosphere excites you as much as it does us, make tracks to ScooZee's. Everything is made from scratch, and the preparation and style belie the tiny prices; nothing on the menu is over $10. "Pizza, Pasta and Pizzaz" is the house motto. Standouts on the menu include the Italian pea soup with smoked ham and Italian sausage, the grilled chicken Caesar salad, the ahi with rigatoni, the eggplant parmigiana, and the mussels broiled in marsala wine and garlic. Watching your budget? For a mere $6.50, you can feast on a Peasant's Dinner, imported cheese, fresh fruit, Italian prosciutto, a chunk of fresh-baked peasant bread, and a glass of Chianti. And desserts are the best: the "Tita I Miss Su" (an original rendition—and spelling—of tiramisù), the ricotta cheesecake, and the Grand Marnier chocolate fudge cake are too good to pass up. Ice-cream and liquor smoothies and a nice selection of beers and wines, are the beverages of choice. ScooZee's is an altogether pleasant place to be, and service is fast and friendly.

✪ Yum Yum Tree

1200 Ala Moana Blvd., in Ward Centre. ☎ **808/523-9333.** Reservations not required. Main courses $7.95–$14.20. AE, CB, DC, JCB, MC, V. Daily 7am–midnight. AMERICAN.

Fans of the delightful pie shop and restaurant at Kahala Mall (see "Waialae-Kahala," below) are thrilled to find another branch at Ward Centre. Stop in whenever the urge for pie—maybe macadamia-nut, lemon-crunch, or English-toffee—becomes overwhelming; take home a whole pie or have a delicious slice here. In addition, all three meals are served, all at low prices. The setting is charming, both inside and out, with the feel of a big country house with a large porch, shady and cool, thanks to the big blue umbrellas. Cocktails are served from 7am to 2am. As you travel around the island, you'll find Yum Yum Trees at Pali Palms, Mililani, and Pearlridge.

MEALS FOR LESS THAN $20

Andrew's

1200 Ala Moana Blvd., in Ward Centre. ☎ **808/523-8677.** Reservations recommended. Main courses $10.75–$25.95. AE, CB, DC, JCB, MC, V. Lunch Mon–Fri 11am–4pm. Sun 10am–4pm; dinner Sun–Tues 4–10pm, Wed–Fri 4–11pm, Sat 5–11pm. ITALIAN.

Another star at Ward Centre is this gourmet Italian restaurant. Muted rose and brown tones from floor to ceiling produce a sedate effect, reinforced by the upholstered banquettes with dropped lamps, fabric-covered walls, and flowers on the tables. You could have a complete dinner, including antipasto, mixed green salad, minestrone, ice cream, plus a beverage along with your main courses for $17.25 to $24.95. Or choose à la carte; pastas begin around $10.75, and include a tasty and filling cannelloni di mare (stuffed with seafood). There are also a few seafood and chicken dishes for under $14. Lunch is à la carte, with a dozen pastas for $10.25 to $15.95. There are choices galore of fish and fowl in the same price range; beef and veal run a little higher. Daily specials, such as spaghetti putanesca, are $10.75. Skilled service contributes to a memorable experience.

✪ Compadres Mexican Bar & Grill

1200 Ala Moana Blvd., in Ward Centre. ☎ **808/523-1307.** Reservations not required. Main courses $7.45–$16.95. AE, DC, MC, V. Mon–Thurs 11am–11pm, Fri–Sat 11am–midnight, Sun 9am–10pm. MEXICAN.

Mexico is represented at Ward Centre by Compadres, which gets a resounding *olé!* from us. We're not at all surprised that it has been voted "Best Mexican Restaurant" in Hawaii by the *Honolulu* magazine poll for several years in a row. It's a big, very attractive place with comfortable rattan basket chairs, soft lights, and a young and energetic staff. It's fun to sit on the lanai outdoors. The food is *muy bueno* and the prices won't damage your budget. The sandwiches, like the chicken and avocado at $8.95, are all good, but you'll probably want to sample such Mexican specialties as the various combinaciones, which include refried beans, fiesta rice, and Mexican salad, $10.95 to $13.95. Arroz con pollo and mahimahi ala Vera Cruz are both good, and everybody loves the fajitas—grilled, marinated beef or chicken, sliced thin and stuffed into warm tortillas with a great salsa. The new Quesadillas Internacionales menu offers such creative options as Baja, Thai, and Japanese quesadillas. Vegetarians have a number of good choices. As for the desserts, we can't resist the banana chingalinga—a whole banana wrapped in a flour tortilla, rolled in cinnamon, and topped with ice cream. And the "Compadres 400" Menu features dishes of 400 or fewer calories, including the grilled chicken breast and turkey enchiladas. On weekends only, Compadres serves breakfast, offering a wide assortment of omelets, plus chile rellenos, huevos dos Ricardos, and much more. A reasonably priced children's menu is always available.

Monterey Bay Canners

1200 Ala Moana Blvd., in Ward Centre. ☎ **808/536-6197.** Reservations not required. Main courses $9.95–$26.95. AE, DC, JCB, MC, V. Lunch Mon–Fri 11am–4pm; dinner Sun–Thurs 4–11pm, Fri–Sat 4pm–midnight. SEAFOOD.

This is one of Honolulu's most popular restaurants, a big, bustling, nautical-type place which serves a tremendous variety of seafood specialties. If you're lucky enough to get a table by the window, you can overlook Kewalo Basin, where the commercial fishing charter boats are berthed. Fresh fish is the specialty of the house; in fact, several of the local radio stations carry MBC's "Fresh Catch" report several times a day. Fish is broiled over kiawe-wood charcoal; choose from mahimahi, Hawaiian ono, Alaskan halibut, catfish, salmon steak, and seafood combination ($16.95 to $20.95). San Francisco–style sourdough bread, fresh steamed vegetables, and a choice of starch are included; add another $1 to $1.50 and you get chowder or salad as well. For dessert, try the watermelon sherbet. A similar lunch menu offers smaller portions ($7 to $16). There's music and live entertainment Tuesday through Saturday nights from 9pm to 1:30am.

Ryan's at Ward Centre

1200 Ala Moana Blvd., in Ward Centre. ☎ **808/523-9132.** Reservations recommended at dinner. Main courses $8.95–$17.95. AE, MC, V. Lunch Mon–Fri 11am–5pm; dinner daily 5–11pm. AMERICAN.

Ryan's is a big, rambling stunner of a room with highly polished wood floors, gleaming brass, lazily rotating ceiling fans, windows all around, greenery, and a shiny kitchen open to view. Ryan's is seriously committed to "foods for all moods"—and that means quality in everything from simple fare to gourmet dishes, from "heart-healthy" recipes to sinfully rich creations. The menu includes meat and chicken broiled with Hawaiian mesquite-wood charcoal; fish fresh from Hawaiian, mainland, and Alaskan waters; pasta made fresh daily; and desserts that range from frozen yogurt to key lime pie. Special dietary needs will be met. Prices, considering the high quality, are quite reasonable. A good selection of California wines is available by the bottle or glass. There are also temperature-controlled beers and a moderately priced bar list. Ryan's prides itself on having the largest draught beer and Scotch collection on Oahu. The bar serves light meals—scaled-down portions of the regular fare—from $5.95 to $9.95, and stays open until 1:15am.

ALOHA TOWER MARKETPLACE

The hottest, most "happening" scene at the moment in Honolulu is Aloha Tower Marketplace, a dining-shopping-festival complex right smack out on Honolulu's waterfront. Each of its half-dozen or so major restaurants offers a spectacular view. The local business crowd jams the marketplace at lunchtime (reservations are not taken), and tourists and residents alike keep it hopping until the wee hours. You can reach the marketplace from Waikiki via the Aloha Tower Express Trolley, which makes pickups at many hotels (phone 808/528-5700 for details).

MEALS FOR LESS THAN $7

Happily for the budget crowd (and for those who don't feel like braving the lines at the other restaurants), there's the **Fabulous Food Lanai,** big enough to seat 700 hungry souls at tables overlooking the water. The food stalls offer everything from Cajun and Japanese to pizza and pasta and natural foods. Our favorite here, the Cajun Big Easy, has wonderful combination plates for $6.25; choose among entrées like shrimp étouffé, bourbon chicken, and blackened fish.

MEALS FOR LESS THAN $20

✪ Gordon Biersch Brewery Restaurant

At Aloha Tower Marketplace, 101 Ala Moana Blvd. ☎ **808/599-4877.** Reservations not accepted. Main courses $12.95–$18.95. AE, DC, MC, V. Lunch daily 11am–5pm; dinner Tues–Sat 5–11pm, Sat–Sun 5–10pm. PACIFIC RIM.

The world's largest microbrewery restaurant-cum-beergarden, Gordon Biersch's has plenty going for it: a fantastic waterfront setting, an open-air dining lanai with an adjoining beergarden, two bars, and its own German-style lagers. The place is big—it seats almost 400—but the kitchen does an amazing job of getting food to the table quickly. Best of all, the San Francisco–based chain has hired one of the best local chefs around, Kelly Degala (we've been fans of his for years at other restaurants). Degala's menu does not disappoint; the combinations are imaginative, the flavors intense. The pupu menu in the beergarden is an expansion of the appetizer menu; you must try the Gordon Biersch Garlic Fries (if you love garlic). The grilled chicken skewers in a spicy peanut sauce and the garlic lamb and red-pepper flatbread are other worthy starters. Salads are lovely, especially the Asian pear with spiced walnuts and blue cheese on baby greens. Main courses offer such possibilities as seafood curry with steamed banana leaf and sticky rice, red curry braised lamb shank, and seared scallops with grilled leeks and red peppers over pasta. The lunch menu is similar but shorter; that's when we usually opt for one of the pizzas, like the rock shrimp with goat cheese, basil, and oven-dried tomatoes. Combine that with a glass of beer and you have a good meal for about $12. As for desserts, they're good whenever, although they do tend to lean toward the chocolate decadence syndrome, with a double chocolate brownie sundae and an especially good chocolate espresso crème brûlée. Live entertainment prevails Wednesday through Saturday after 7pm (no cover).

DOWNTOWN HONOLULU & ENVIRONS
MEALS FOR LESS THAN $6

✪ Broke the Mouth

1148 Bishop St., at Union Mall. ☎ 808/524-0355. Reservations not necessary. Plate lunches $4–$6. No credit cards. Mon–Fri 9am–2pm. ORGANIC VEGETARIAN.

If you've heard about Hawaii Regional cuisine but aren't ready to spring for a high-priced meal, here's the perfect solution: A little takeout restaurant serving gourmet meals on paper plates that taste as good as anything you'll find in the celebrated restaurants. Broke the Mouth is the second venture of a farm cooperative on the Hamakua Coast of the Big Island, which first set-up shop in Hilo in 1992 (see Chapter 12) to rave reviews; now they're in downtown Honolulu and—with some luck—they may even be in Waikiki by the end of the year. The concept is simple: Everything they serve is organic, vegetarian, and fresh; makes use of such traditional Hawaiian staples as taro and sweet potato; and is brilliantly seasoned with their own homemade sauces and dressings. Order the Bamboola plate for $6 and savor the fresh greens, the OnoPesto pasta, a Hawaiian salad, summer roll, and manapua. Everything is exceptional: the Hawaiian salad, for example, uses no lettuce; instead, it's comprised of basil, mizuna, kale, collards, red chard, sorrel, and edible flowers. Their potato salad ($1.50 a side order) is like no potato salad you've had before: It's made with taro, sweet potatoes, steamed green papaya, green onions, and MacGado sauce. The staff will gladly let you sample some of the fabulous sauces that you may buy to take home with you, or purchase later by mail order: MacGado is a sweet-and-sour sauce made with macadamia nuts, fresh ginger, and lemongrass (it's a takeoff on Indonesia's gado-gado sauce); Guava Lava is a spicy ketchup made with guava, taro, and ginger; OnoPesto is done in the Hawaiian style, with macadamia nuts, basil, and taro (mix it with some rice at home for a great dish). With food like this, the old image of the greasy, calorie-laden Hawaiian plate lunch may be forever changed.

Union Mall is a pleasant place with public seating (much nicer than Fort Street Mall a few blocks away), so take your lunch outside and enjoy. Or, phone ahead for a picnic lunch and it will be waiting for you. In case you were wondering, "broke the mouth" is pidgin; it means "delicious"—and this food is.

MEALS FOR LESS THAN $12

ⓢ A Little Bit of Saigon

1160 Maunakea St. ☎ **808/528-3663.** Reservations not required. Main courses $5.95–$15. MC, V. Daily 10am–10pm. VIETNAMESE.

Because it's just around the corner from many of the Chinatown art galleries, you'll always find artists—as well as savvy businessfolk—frequenting this place. Changing art exhibits are the main decor. The food is artistic too, simple but sophisticated, and appealing to a wide variety of tastes. There's plenty for vege-tarians. Only vegetable oils and coconut water (not the fat-rich coconut milk used in many Asian restaurants) are used in the food preparations, so cholesterol-watchers can rest easy. Many of the dishes can be ordered as pupus, as meals in a bowl, or as rice-paper rollups. That last preparation is especially intriguing: You're presented with a large tray containing rice-paper wrappers, vegetables, sprouts, condiments, and your main course. You dip the wrappers in a finger bowl, stuff them like a burrito, then dip it all in a peanut or pineapple/anchovy sauce. Also recommended are the curries, the hearty noodle soups, and the sweet and tender coconut chicken. Try the desserts—you may never again get a chance to taste azuki beans and tapioca strips in coconut milk. A treat!

The Buddhist Vegetarian Restaurant

100 N. Beretania St. ☎ **808/532-1868.** Reservations not required. Main courses $6.50–$15.95. MC, V. Lunch daily 10:30am–2pm; dinner daily 5:30–9pm. CHINESE VEGETARIAN.

Devout vegetarians will have the best time ever here, because the entire menu is devoted to Chinese vegetarian cuisine, the kind favored by Buddhist monks. Mr. Anthony Tsui, the proprietor of this pretty little place—nicely decorated, brightly lit, and very modern—opened it in honor of his 83-year old mother, who has always been very fond of Chinese vegetarian cooking. And you will be, too, once you try some of these unique dishes—many using wheat gluten or bean curd to make them appear meat- or fish-like. You could start your meal with a soup of bamboo pith with vegetarian slices or an appetizer like deep-fried gluten in mashed taro. Then go on to a tofu dish or one of the entrées like braised elm fungus with bamboo shoots and mushrooms, satay kabobs on a sizzling platter, an edible basket of taro filled with vegetables, or even sweet-and-sour vegetarian "pork." There's a good selection of congee, noodles, and rice, too. It's hard to find meatless dim sum, but it's served here at lunchtime every day. For dessert, try something new: maybe steamed bamboo pith with coconut or green bean soup—sure beats fortune cookies and canned pineapple!

Columbia Inn

645 Kapiolani Blvd. ☎ **808/531-3747.** Reservations not accepted. Main courses $5.75–$12.95. MC, V. Sun–Thurs 6am–11pm; Fri–Sat 6am–midnight. AMERICAN.

The news about food is good at this large, wood-paneled spot with leather booths, an old-timer favorite with the staffs of Honolulu's two daily newspapers headquartered just a few doors away. At lunch you can choose from 26 complete lunches between $6.05 and $9.95; choices include corned beef and cabbage, rib-eye steak, and "award-winning" beef stew, all accompanied by fish chowder or fruit salad, dessert, and beverage. Order à la carte and the range is $5.50 to $9.95. At dinner there are some two dozen choices for $9.95 and under. This is also a great spot for old-fashioned hearty breakfasts.

Donna's Diner

1148 Bishop St. ☎ **808/531-8660.** Reservations not accepted. Soups $2.75–$5.95; plate lunches $3–$5.25. No credit cards. Mon–Fri 5:30am–2:45pm. AMERICAN.

For a quick, inexpensive, and very good breakfast or lunch while shopping or sightseeing downtown, pop in at this tiny-but-popular place. Breakfast begins at $1.75 and includes coffee. Soups are a specialty and a meal in themselves: Portuguese bean soup is $4.50; pig's feet or oxtail soup is $4.25; wonton min, $3.75; and saimin, $3.25. Generous plate lunches start at $4.75, burgers at $1.85.

Donna has another diner at 2227 S. Beretania St., in the McCully-Moiliili area.

Double Eight

1113 Maunakea St. ☎ **808/526-3887.** Reservations not accepted. Main courses $3.50–$6.95. No credit cards. Mon–Sat 10:30am–10:30pm; Sun 11am–3pm and 5–10pm. CHINESE.

Before we first went to the Double Eight, we wondered what so many of our Honolulu friends were making such a fuss about. After a meal at this tiny "hole-in-the-wall" restaurant, though, we knew. The family who runs the place will be delighted to see you and treat you as an honored guest in their home. The food is delicious, and the prices rock-bottom. You could have Singapore mai funn or oyster-sauce chicken chow mein for $4.75; maybe splurge on stir-fried shrimp with black-bean sauce or sautéed mixed seafood for $6.95. This one's very, very popular with the downtown crowd at lunchtime, and they do a booming takeout business; it's quieter in the evening.

Flamingo Kapiolani

871 Kapiolani Blvd. ☎ **808/538-6931.** Reservations not required. Main courses $7.55–$11.95. AE, MC, V. Daily 6am–2am. AMERICAN.

For years the Flamingo restaurants have been offering terrific quality for little money. Pink booths and paneled walls at this remodeled Flamingo provide a good background for the excellent food. They're well known for their oxtail soup ($7.90), roasts, and specials (brisket of beef, pot roast with noodles, and the like). Lunch offers half a dozen sandwich platters, including soup and fries for $6.15 to

$6.95, as well as some 20 lunch plates for $6.80 to $11.20. At dinner, you get a complete meal, with a choice of soup or salad, vegetable, starch, buns, and beverage. After 10pm, the crowd gathers at the bar for karaoke.

Forum

100 N. Beretania St. ☎ **808/599-5022.** Reservations not required. Main courses $6.95–$21.50. DC, MC, V. Lunch daily 11am–2pm; dinner daily 5–9pm; snacks, drinks, and karaoke daily 9pm–2am. CHINESE.

Despite its elegant appearance, this spacious, attractive place in the Chinese Cultural Plaza offers its luscious Cantonese food—with an emphasis on unusual seafood dishes—for very reasonable prices. Should you desire live Dungeness crab, scalded filet of king clam, or sautéed oysters, they're all available. So, too, are cold jelly fish and spiced cold chicken feet among the appetizers, as well as hard-to-find bird's-nest and shark's-fin soups. But even if you go with the more ordinary dishes, as we did at a recent meal, you'll be well satisfied. Deep-fried spring rolls ($5.95) are ample for two as starters. Both the fiery Szechuan-style shrimp and the stir-fried diced chicken are excellent. For dessert, the preserved, salty lemon cool drink is for exotic tastes, but the French iced coffee is easy to take.

Hawaiian Bagel

753B Halekauwila St. ☎ **808/596-0638.** Reservations not accepted. Main courses $2–$5.80. No credit cards. Mon–Thurs and Sat 6am–3:30pm, Fri 6am–5:30pm. BAGELS/DELI.

Hawaiian Bagel—how's that for a marriage of concepts? This wholesale-retail delicatessen with a few tables for those who can't make it out the door is in a new, contemporary-style building located in the run-down but picturesque Kakaako section of Honolulu. The sights and scents are surpassed only by the tastes. Needless to say, proprietor Stephen Gelson is not a full-blooded Hawaiian; nor are the bagels, blueberry muffins, and homemade rye bread. But the little restaurant and take-out bakery-deli is a hit with the local folk. And our readers love it, too.

They carry 16 varieties of bagels at 40¢ each. Muffins, bearclaws, and cinnamon rolls are 95¢. The sandwiches are typical deli variety: roast beef, lox or whitefish and cream cheese, corned beef, liverwurst, turkey, pastrami, and the like, for $4.65 to $5.80. In true deli tradition, they even serve celery tonic. You may want to take home a fragrant, round loaf of fresh-from-the-oven rye bread.

Heidi's Downtown Bistro and Deli

Grosvenor Center on Queen St. at Alakea. ☎ **808/536-5344.** Reservations not required. Main courses $8.95–$12.95. AE, DISC, DC, MC, V. Mon–Fri 6:30am–8pm. PIZZA/PASTA/VEGETARIAN/SEAFOOD/SOUTHWESTERN.

A great place to break a sightseeing tour of downtown Honolulu, Heidi's Downtown Bistro is just half a block from Aloha Tower and the Fort Street Mall. It's always busy and there's good reason why: It's an intimate, attractive spot, and everything is fresh, cooked from scratch, keeping in mind health-and-budget-conscious folk who want to enjoy something special. The full menu is served from 11am to 8pm, so anytime you're hungry you can feast on gourmet pizzas (we like the Thai chicken and the shrimp pesto best), pasta dishes (Angelina—black tiger shrimp sautéed with garlic and broccoli—is a favorite), southwestern dishes like spinach and potato enchiladas, or house specialties like chicken piccata, eggplant parmesan, or fresh catch of the day. Heidi's also offers sandwiches, burgers, and generous salads. It's all done with a gourmet flair, and everything on the menu can be prepared for takeout.

The cozy lounge with full bar is a popular downtown hangout for Honolulu businesspeople. There's a free pupu buffet between 5 and 6pm Tuesday through Friday nights. Non-drinkers can sip on smoothies, juices, and coffee drinks. The Thursday night happening with "Rolando Sanchez—Salsa Night" may be downtown Honolulu's hottest "pau hana" party.

Legend Seafood Restaurant

108 N. Beretania St., in the Chinese Cultural Plaza. ☎ **808/532-1868.** Reservations not required. Main courses $7.50–$15.95. AE, CB, DC, DISC, JCB, MC, V. Lunch daily 10:30am–2pm; dinner Mon–Sat 5:30–10pm. CHINESE.

This place has become something of a legend in these parts—for one of the best dim sum lunches in town and for some of the best Chinese seafood around. It's all served in a large, attractive space that looks expensive but isn't. It seems to be a favorite among residents for birthday and anniversary parties, showers, and any other excuse to get the whole family together. The biggest crowds, though, are at lunchtime, because that's when the staff comes around with rolling carts, taking orders and offering sweet creambuns, egg tartletts, steamed shrimp dumplings, braised chicken feet with black peppers, barbecued pork pastry, and more—all in small, delicious portions, most priced from $1.95 to $3.05. If you want a regular meal, you can have that, too: wonderful seafood specialties include baked live crab with ginger and green onion, skewered live prawns with spicy salt (both seasonal), and sautéed scallops Szechuan style. The friendly staff bustles about, making sure everyone is happy—and they are.

Rosarina Pizza

1111 Maunakea St. ☎ **808/533-6334.** Reservations not necessary. Pizzas $8–$16; pastas $4.75–$6.50. MC, V. Mon–Sat 11am–10pm. PIZZA/PASTA.

Where's the best pizza in town? It really depends on whom you're talking to, but Rosarina's name keeps coming up. They call their pizzas New York style; we're not sure what that means—we just know they're terrific. Ditto for their pastas (the old-fashioned kind, with meatballs, sausages, meat sauce—nary a designer ingredient anywhere). Takeout and free delivery are available.

There's another popular Rosarina's at 1425 S. King St. (at Keeaumoku; ☎ 808/941-6634), closer to Waikiki.

Yong Sing

1055 Alakea St. ☎ **808/531-1366.** Reservations not required. Main courses $5.75–$17.25. MC, V. Daily 9am–9pm. CHINESE.

One of the most popular Chinese restaurants in town, Yong Sing is a huge place that occupies an entire downtown building. Its vast dining room is nicely, if not elaborately, decorated in red and gold. There's a huge menu from which to choose, with many well-priced goodies. The last time we were here we had succulent almond duck and chicken with oyster sauce, the house specialty. An excellent $23 dinner for two includes egg-flower soup, almond chicken, sweet-and-sour pork, beef broccoli, and fried rice. For something unusual, ask the waiter for a dim sum lunch. This consists of many different varieties of Chinese dumplings: either steamed, baked, or fried, some filled with sweetmeats and served as main dishes; others, dainty pastries for dessert. Have five or six of these and plenty of the free-flowing tea, and you've had a lovely, inexpensive treat. But be sure to get there between the hours of 9am and 2pm for the dumplings; they sell out fast. Take out is available anytime.

MEALS FOR LESS THAN $20

Kabuki Restaurant at Kapiolani

600 Kapiolani Blvd. ☎ **808/545-5995.** Reservations recommended. Dinners $5.95–$17.45. AE, DC, MC, V. Lunch Mon–Sat 11am–2pm; dinner Mon–Sat 5–9:30pm (sushi bar until midnight), Sun 5–9pm (sushi bar until 10pm). JAPANESE.

Here's a very pretty restaurant—light-wood paneling, an attractive little sushi bar—that offers a chance to sample many Japanese dishes at reasonable prices. Live Maine lobsters and live Dungeness crabs are available and prepared to your liking; also popular is the lobster sashimi. Hibachi dinners, cooked at your table for two or more people, include soup, rice, tsukemono, special sauces, and tea, along with main courses, such as beef or chicken yakiniku, and are mostly $10.75 to $15.95. Tasty teishoki dinners might include a main course of salmon, sashimi, and assorted vegetables for $12.75. For lunch, the combination teishoki meal is $10.75.

UNIVERSITY AREA
MEALS FOR LESS THAN $12

Aloha Poi Bowl

2671 S. King St., in University Sq. ☎ **808/944-0798.** Reservations not accepted. Main courses $5.75–$8. No credit cards. Sat 11am–8:30pm, Sun 3–8pm. HAWAIIAN.

This is a good spot for Hawaiian food close to Waikiki. There are only six booths and a few big, white plastic-topped tables in a plain, storelike room, but the food is the star here. In addition to those luau staples like laulau, lomi-lomi salmon, kalua pork, tripe or beef stew, and chicken long rice (all run $3 to $5.25), there's always a daily special; the day we were there it was fried akule fish at $7. Be sure to top off your meal with that coconut dessert, haupia.

Campus Center

University of Hawaii. ☎ **808/956-7327.** Snacks $1–$3.50; main courses $3–$5. No credit cards. Mon–Fri 7am–2pm. AMERICAN/LOCAL.

The best place to eat at the University of Hawaii is this spot close to University Avenue in the middle of campus. It's huge, upstairs cafeteria serves both breakfast and lunch. Depending on the day, you may get lemon chicken, tasty seafood items, veal cutlets, or barbecued ribs. They also have fresh saimin, pasta, grilled items, and a variety of salads and desserts. Bakery items and gourmet Lion's coffee can be purchased in the convenience store, Kampus Korner (open 9am to 6:30pm). A variety of snacks are offered from 7am to 1:30pm.

✪ Chan's Chinese Restaurant

2600 S. King St. ☎ **808/949-1188.** Reservations not accepted. Main courses $5.25–$16.95. AE, MC, V. Daily 10:30am–10:25pm. CHINESE.

We like everything about this restaurant, from the sparkling clean, modern decor to the cheerful service and that delicious food—at very reasonable prices. Owner Jennifer Chan blends an array of Mandarin, Szechuan, Shanghai, Cantonese, and Peking dishes; Chef Kenneth travels widely each year and always brings back exciting new recipes. His Szechuan chicken with deep-fried spinach leaves is a treat; so is the sea bass with black-bean sauce. The Mandarin menu offers slightly spicier fare, such as the spicy stir-fried shrimp. If it's in season, go for the lusty crab with black-bean sauce. Or feast on a meal of tasty dim sum; wagon service is offered from 10:30am to 2pm. If you'd like to try a Chinese breakfast, then join the locals who come here for their *jook*—that's rice soup, with a choice of chicken, seafood, meat, or fish; most jooks are $3.25 to $6. For lunch or dinner, there are dozens of dishes at $6.50 or under—like a chicken with black-mushroom casserole, moo shu pork, or roast duck. Parking in Pucks Alley is validated.

Mama Mia

1015 University Ave., in Pucks Alley. ☎ **808/947-5233.** Reservations not accepted. Pizzas $7.80–$22.50; subs $4.65–$6.50; main courses $7.95–$9.95 AE, DC, MC, V. Daily 11am–2am. ITALIAN.

The longtime mecca for pizza-lovers in this area is Mama Mia's, and real "New York pizza" it is—the owner is a transplanted New Yorker. There's a pie for every taste (even a vegetarian pizza with whole-wheat crust), terrific spaghetti and lasagne dinners for under $10, and some really lusty and crusty hero sandwiches. The place stays open late, so it's fun to come here after the movies or a show. They have a full liquor license. Occasionally there's entertainment here, too—perhaps a grown-up puppet show, or just music.

Manoa Garden

Hemenway Hall, University of Hawaii. ☎ **808/956-6468.** Reservations not accepted. Main courses $3.45–$5. No credit cards. Daily 8am–8pm. DELI/STIR-FRY.

Quite pleasant at UH is Manoa Garden, which features deli sandwiches to order, "Grab 'N' Go" sandwiches, and delicious stir-fry concoctions made before your eyes. The bar opens at 2:30pm daily. On most Fridays, a Manoa Garden Jam Session features live outdoor entertainment.

O-Bok

2756 Woodlawn Dr., in Manoa Marketplace. ☎ **808/988-7702.** Reservations not accepted. Main courses $4–$7.25. MC, V. Tues–Sun 10am–8pm. KOREAN.

Small, sparkly clean, and friendly sums up this little Korean place, serving wonderful food at very moderate prices. The menu is the same all day. All main dishes are served with na mul (vegetables), kimchee (a fiery coleslaw), and rice. The most popular Korean specialty in Hawaii seems to be kalbi, tender barbecued short ribs. They are particularly good here, and priced at $7.25. Other very good dishes are the barbecued chicken, the fish or meat jun (breaded with an egg batter), and the bi bim bap (mixed vegetables, beef, and fried egg on rice). Very tasty, too, are the mon doo (a kind of Korean wonton); try them in soup or fried. To explore several taste sensations, order one of the mixed plates. The special plate at $5.50 includes kalbi, barbecued chicken, mon doo, tae-ku (dried codfish), and na mul.

✪ Shark's Cafe

2535 Coyne St. ☎ **808/94-SHARK.** Reservations recommended on weekends. Main courses $10.50–$15.95. DISC, MC, V. Lunch Mon–Fri 11am–2pm; dinner Sun–Thurs 5–10pm, Fri–Sat 5–11pm. Cocktail lounge open between lunch and dinner for drinks and pupus. AMERICAN.

They don't come any cuter than Shark's Cafe; it's an altogether delightful place to have dinner. The building itself is beautiful; the first-floor bar and lounge, with turquoise walls and white tables and chairs, is more casual than the handsome upstairs dining room with its starched pink linen, and beautiful furniture. There is also dining on the lanai. Plants abound, and the restaurant's signature decor—great big sharks (no, not real ones, but quite convincing imitations) "swim" overhead, grinning evilly. UH students are much in evidence in the lounge, but they're an orderly bunch—perhaps intimidated by the fisheye from on high.

The menu changes every six weeks, but depend on innovative appetizers (like a hot spinach with artichoke hearts dip or blackened fresh ahi), several pastas (we like the garlic and basil shrimp pasta), crusty pizzas (maybe Cajun seafood, vegetarian, or chicken), and several main-course salads (like the chicken avocado). Tempting choices from the kiawe broiler usually include fresh mahimahi, barbecued baby back ribs, steak, jerk chicken, and, on Friday and Saturday only, prime rib, done in the old Hawaiian manner, covered with Hawaiian salt and herbs and slowly roasted, a bargain at $12.95 (10ozs) and $14.95 (14ozs).

Waioli Tea Room

2950 Manoa Rd. ☎ **808/988-9488.** Reservations recommended. Sat lunch buffet $11.95; Sun lunch buffet $15.50; Thurs Hawaiian lunch $11.95; Fri dinner buffet $13.95. MC, V. Lunch Thurs and Sat–Sun 11am–1:30pm; dinner Fri 5:30–7:30pm. AMERICAN.

Great news! The famous Waioli Tea Room, a Honolulu tradition for many years and shuttered for the past few, is open once again. The charming restaurant, done in historic "plantation style," is operated by Tad & Pat, Hawaii's premier caterers, and their skill is apparent here. Many private banquets and special theme events take place here, so the restaurant is only open to the public several times a week; it would be wise to check in advance to make sure the schedule has not changed. Friday night's Italian buffet is festive, with a salad bar, pasta and vegetable soup, a good selection of hot dishes and pastas, and island banana cake for dessert. The Saturday lunch buffet consists of salads, sandwiches, and soups. Our favorite, the Sunday lunch buffet, is more elaborate, with a full salad bar, entrées on the order of chicken curry with basil, Caribbean barbecue pork, mahimahi with lemon caper sauce, coq au vin, and vegetable lasagne (plus a glorious dessert table). And on Thursday, there's a traditional Hawaiian luau lunch in addition to the regular à la carte menu, with strolling island musicians.

The Waioli Tea Room is on the Historical Register; it is rumored that Robert Louis Stevenson courted the muse in the little grass shack now rebuilt as the Robert Louis Stevenson Memorial Grass House. The beautiful tropical grounds are yours for the strolling, and unless there's a wedding going on, you can visit the Little Chapel on the grounds, designed for the children of Waioli.

MEALS FOR LESS THAN $20

✪ Café Brio

2756 Woodlawn Dr., in Manoa Marketplace. ☎ **808/988-5555.** Reservations recommended. Main courses $11–$17. AE, DC, DISC, JCB, MC, V. Lunch Mon–Fri 11:30am–2pm; dinner Mon–Sat 5:30–10pm. CONTEMPORARY AMERICAN.

An island friend of ours says that the only thing wrong with Café Brio is that you never want to leave. It's a veritable indoor garden, and there are whimsical murals on the natural-wood plank walls and fresh flowers on the tables.

Chef Richard Shimizu's menu is creative with a contemporary touch: Witness the julienne of zucchini, smoked salmon with lemon-zest crème fraîche, and tomato among the appetizers; grilled boneless chicken breast with tomatillo-corn salsa and grilled zucchini, squash, and creamy polenta is among the main courses. Lunch is similar, with dishes $1 or $2 lower, plus tostadas, crêpes, and sophisticated sandwiches. Desserts are spirited, too—there are different homemade ones, plus gelatos and sorbets every day. And, of course, the music is sprightly—the last time we had dinner there, Offenbach provided the background. Outside there's Brio Garden, a "light-food" wine bar where a three-item snack costs $6 to $8.

India House

2632 S. King St. ☎ **808/955-7552.** Reservations recommended. Main courses $7.95–$15.50. MC, V. Lunch Mon–Fri 11am–2pm; dinner daily 5–9:30pm. INDIAN.

Ram Arora, formerly the specialty chef at the elegant (and super-expensive) Third Floor Restaurant at the Hawaiian Regent Hotel, owns this restaurant near Puck's Alley. His own place, besides being much more in line with our budget, is attractive, cool, and relaxing. Brass lamps and lush plants abound in the small dining room that accommodates perhaps a dozen tables. A sari-clad hostess will greet you, make you welcome, and assist you in ordering. Should you wish to try tandoori (clay oven cooking), have the boti kebab, the fish tikka, or tandoori chicken, served with pullao (rice pilaf) and a wonderful naan bread. Combination dinners are a good buy, and there are plentiful à la carte choices. A particularly good dessert choice is the gulab jaman, a "dairy delicacy served in rosewater syrup." This is one thoroughly delightful dining experience.

Paesano

2752 Woodlawn Dr., In Manoa Marketplace. ☎ **808/988-5293.** Reservations recommended on weekends. Main courses $8.90–$17.95. AE, MC, V. Lunch Mon–Sat 11am–2:30pm; dinner daily 5–10pm. ITALIAN.

At Paesano, you can watch the pastry chefs at work turning out lovely, chewy Italian bread and *bellissimo* pastries through the glass picture windows or from the dining room. Partitioned with wood panels for a feeling of privacy, the inviting dining room has white walls adorned with Hawaiian flower paintings; the round tables all have spiffy white cloths and crimson napkins. And, yes, there are portions of the room where you won't see the immense TV screen at the bar, usually tuned to some sports event. Start perhaps with a hearty bowl of pasta fagiolo or the delicate vichyssoise, then move on to one of the pastas, which come in both small ($7.90–$9.90) and large ($10.90 to $11.90) portions. Veal saltimbocco, chicken marsala, fish-of-the-day alla piccata and fish arregenata—with oregano, garlic, and oil—all are good. Homemade desserts are super, especially the zabaglione with imported marsala and the New York cheesecake.

DESSERTS ONLY

Bubbies

1010 University Ave. ☎ **808/949-8984.** Reservations not accepted. Desserts 96¢–$12.95. No credit cards. Mon–Thurs noon–midnight. Fri–Sat noon–1am, Sun noon–11:30pm. ICE CREAM/DESSERTS.

A popular destination in the Varsity Center is Bubbies, a favorite after-theater spot. Keith Robbins, who hails from the East Coast and named the shop after his grandmother, serves wonderful homemade ice cream and desserts. In addition to delectable ice cream ($2.40 for a single dip), you can have rich ice cream cakes, pies, and confections to go along with your gourmet coffees—espresso, cappuccino, latte, etc. Curtains at the window, fans overhead, plants, and an old-fashioned pendulum time clock—plus a photograph of "Bubbie"—complete the scene. Bubbies' ice cream is also served at many of Honolulu's finest restaurants.

WAIALAE-KAHALA
MEALS FOR LESS THAN $12

Bernard's New York Deli

In Kahala Mall Shopping Center. ☎ **808/732-DELI** (3354). Reservations not accepted. Main courses $6.95–$9.99. AE, DC, MC, V. Mon–Sat 7am–9pm, Sun 7am–8pm. DELI.

Manhattan-style delicatessens may be catching on in Hawaii—this one is certainly getting kudos. Bernard's is kosher style, from chicken soup to apple strudel. New Yorkers will get homesick just reading the menu. You might want to start your meal with a bowl of homemade chicken soup or borscht with sour cream. Then perhaps on to a deli sandwich of corned beef or chopped liver, hot pastrami or kosher salami. Fancy a side dish, such as potato latkes, potato knishes, stuffed derma? They're all available. So are blueberry or cheese blintzes with sour cream, delicious old-fashioned creamy rice pudding, and cheesecake. Deli breakfasts are served all day.

The Pâtisserie

In the Kahala Mall Shopping Center. ☎ **808/735-4402.** Reservations not required. Sandwiches $3.60–$4.75. MC, V. Mon–Fri 7am–9pm, Sat 7am–7pm, Sun 7am–5pm. SANDWICHES/DESSERTS.

For a bit of Mittel Europa in Kahala Mall, stop in at the Pâtisserie, a bakery that also serves sandwiches and pastries at its sparkling counter and several little booths. Sandwiches, served on home-baked breads (we like the country Swiss) with sprouts or lettuce, include Black Forest ham, head cheese, roast beef, bratwurst, and pastrami. There's hot German potato salad, quiche Lorraine, and carrot salad, too. If you don't want anything quite so heavy, Black Forest cake, dobosh, and freshly baked pies should be just right.

Look for Pâtisserie shops at the Edgewater and Outrigger Westin hotels in Waikiki, and downtown at 33 S. King St. and 700 Bishop St.

Verbano

3571 Waialae Ave. ☎ **808/735-1777.** Reservations recommended on weekends. Main courses $7.90–$15.90. AE, DC, MC, V. Lunch Mon–Sat 11am–2:30pm; dinner daily 5–10pm. ITALIAN.

The minimalist decor of this stunning restaurant makes for a warm, quiet elegance: the lights are low, the ceiling fans turn lazily, the wood partitions give a feeling of privacy. And the food is terrific and not at all overpriced, especially if you choose to go for one of the lighter portions offered on many dishes; we've always found them ample enough. All the traditional Italian meat, chicken, and seafood dishes come with a choice of vegetable, potato, or pasta. The pastas are delicious—we like the unusual rigatoni with sautéed bacon, ham, and fresh garlic tomato sauce, just $7.90 or $9.90. There are plenty of vegetarian pastas, too: pesto, Alfredo, and primavera. If you have room for dessert, don't pass up the light, lovely zabaglione. Our local friends like this place so much they go back time and again.

Yen King Restaurant

In the Kahala Mall Shopping Center. ☎ **808/732-5505.** Reservations recommended. Main courses $7.95–$10.95. AE, MC, V. Sun–Thurs 11am–9:30pm, Fri–Sat 11am–midnight. NORTHERN CHINESE/VEGETARIAN.

Vegetarians who love Chinese food swear by this place near the Kahala Hilton. So do a lot of other folks who've discovered this attractive restaurant that specializes in the cuisines of Peking and Szechuan. There's a lot to choose from here—including at least 30 meatless dishes—but two dishes that we never miss are the famous Sizzling Rice Soup (it sizzles when the crispy rice is added to the hot broth), and Chinaman's Hat, which consists of very light "pancakes" that you stuff and wrap at the table with a luscious filling of pork and vegetables. From then on, choose what you like: crackling chicken, lemon beef, sautéed clams—they're all good. As for vegetarian dishes, we found the lo hon chai vegetable dish delectable. MSG is never used. Desserts at many Chinese restaurants are unimaginative, but not here. If they're not too busy, they might make you their unforgettable fried apple with honey: flaming apple cubes covered with a honey-maple syrup sauce and dipped in ice water right at your table. Everything on the regular menu is available for take-out, and take-outs during the dinner hours are charged lunchtime prices. Yen King has full bar service. There's karaoke music Wednesday through Sunday nights from 9:30pm to 2am.

Yum Yum Tree Restaurant and Pie Shop

In the Kahala Mall Shopping Center. ☎ **808/737-7938.** Reservations not required. Main courses $7.95–$14.25. AE, CB, DC, JCB, MC, V. Daily 7am–midnight. AMERICAN.

Long a favorite in the lovely Kahala residential area, this pretty place has seating both on the lanai and indoors. Service is fast and friendly, and the food is always good. We like their delectable chicken pot pie, a meal in itself for $8.95. Salads such as papaya stuffed with shrimp and chicken salad Oriental, and sandwiches, burgers, and pasta dishes are good, too. Dinners are served with soup or green salad, rice or potato, plus vegetables and fresh-baked cornbread and honey butter. Best of all are the yummy pies for dessert, baked in their own kitchens; the pie display at centerstage makes it difficult to resist taking a whole one back to your hotel.

KAIMUKI
MEALS FOR LESS THAN $20

Hale Vietnam

1140 12th Ave., Kaimuki. ☎ **808/735-7581.** Reservations recommended. Main courses $7.25–$11.25. MC, V. Daily 11am–10pm. VIETNAMESE.

Chef Mark Fu, who is well known for his catering work, specializes in the cuisine of the Mekong Delta region, served in a casual setting of Southeast Asia art and tropical plants. Your main course is accompanied by an appetizer of imperial rolls, fried or nonfried Southeast Asian delights wrapped in rice paper and filled with seafood, pork, and fresh herbs. The complete dinner also includes a hearty Vietnamese beef-noodle soup. You may also order à la carte. Favorites include the chicken with ginger, the catfish in black-pepper sauce, the sautéed tofu and vegetables in a peanut-curry sauce, and the Vietnamese fondue, cooked at your table.

KEEHI LAGOON
MEALS FOR LESS THAN $20

La Mariana Restaurant & Bar

50 Sand Island Rd. ☎ **808/841-2173.** Reservations not required. Main courses $7.75–$19.95. AE, DC, MC, V. Lunch Mon–Fri 11am–2pm; dinner Mon–Fri 6–9pm, Sat–Sun 5–9pm. SEAFOOD/STEAK.

This restaurant is a well-kept secret, a hideaway for the boat owners of the La Mariana Sailing Club at Keehi Lagoon. The restaurant and the marina itself are owned by a feisty lady named Annette La Mariana Nahinu, who has been fighting to keep the area alive for over 40 years. The restaurant is ramshackle romantic, its furnishings—wooden tables, rattan chairs, glass balls, and fishing nets—reputedly salvaged from the old Don the Beachcomber restaurant. Dine either indoors or on the shaded lanai, in full view of the boats. Nothing formal, nothing fancy here—just the way Hawaii used to be before the big money took over. The restaurant's chef is excellent, specializing mostly in steak, seafood, and freshly caught fish. Prices are reasonable, and island favorites, including ahi, marlin, ulua, and red snapper, are all available. The price of a main course includes french fries, mashed potatoes, or rice; salad; hot rolls; and coffee or tea. Lunch is reasonable too, with the emphasis on meaty sandwiches (burgers from $4.50, a steak sizzler on a bun at $7.50). You'll need to drive here (it's not far from the airport); it's best to call for precise directions.

NEAR CANNERY SQUARE

✪ Angelica's Cafe
At Gentry Pacific Center, 560 N. Nimitz Hwy. ☎ **808/537-6619.** Reservations recommended. Main courses $8.75–$18.95. AE, DC, DISC, JCB, MC, V. Breakfast Mon–Fri 8–10:30am; lunch Mon–Fri 11am–3pm; dinner Mon–Sat 5:30–10pm. CONTEMPORARY AMERICAN.

Scarcely known to tourists but very much "in" with the local cognoscenti, Angelica's is a find. You'll find it just a few blocks from the outlet stores at Cannery Square, so it can easily be tied in with a drive there; it's also an easy stop if you're going to or from the airport. It's an uncommonly pretty place, feeling a bit like an English garden, with soft peach umbrellas covering the tables out in the mall. And the food is marvelous—fresh, wonderfully imaginative, beautifully prepared. Only a few items are on each week's dinner menu, but they are distinctly different, and most appealing. For example, among the appetizers might be seared scallops with a roasted three-pepper sauce, or chopped lamb in radicchio cups with fresh plum sauce; among the main courses, osso buco with twice-roasted potatoes, or a roasted half-chicken stuffed with goat cheese and shiitake mushrooms, served with garlic mashed potatoes. Lunch provides a variety of gourmet treats at refreshingly low prices. Among our favorites on the sandwich menu ($7.95 to $9.25) are the scallops on homemade focaccia bread with herb-caper mayonnaise, and the Szechuan shrimp with oven-dried tomatoes and won bok on a French roll. People rave about their salads, too ($7.95 to $13.95), especially the Oriental spicy chicken salad and the pasta salad with chicken, tarragon, apples, and capers. Their scones, made fresh daily, are just not to be missed.

PEARL HARBOR

The Marina
Naval Station, Pearl Harbor. ☎ **808/471-0593.** Reservations recommended. Main courses $9.95–$15.95. DC, JCB, MC, V. Lunch daily 11am–1:30pm; dinner Tues–Sat 5:30–9pm. SEAFOOD/STEAK.

If you're driving out to Pearl Harbor, here's a good place for lunch. The Marina really is situated on a small boat harbor not far from the Pearl Harbor museum. Enter the Pearl Harbor *Arizona* Memorial complex and follow the simple directions. The restaurant is situated on the second floor of a building that overlooks the harbor and the *Arizona* Memorial in one direction and the Waianae Mountains in the other. Ships' lanterns provide pleasant, soft lighting in the big wood-paneled room. Lunch focuses on hearty meat and fish sandwiches ($3.50 to $6.95) and a daily hot plate, like the top sirloin at $6.25. Best time for an evening meal is Thursday, when there's a terrific prime rib and crab-leg buffet at $17.95 adults, $8.95 kids. On the regular dinner menu, such specialties as lobster tail, seafood platter, pepper steak, and deep-fried chicken all come with salad bar, soup, vegetables, hot rolls with butter, and a starch. "Smart Heart" selections include broiled or poached salmon, broiled mahimahi, oven-baked skinless chicken, and broiled Pacific prawns ($8.95 to $13.95). And there's a neat little menu for kids, too ($3.75 to $6.95). A nice choice off our usual beaten path.

IN NEARBY KAILUA & KANEOHE
MEALS FOR LESS THAN $12

Gee . . . A Deli!
418-F Kuulei Rd. ☎ **808/261-4412.** Reservations not accepted. Daily sandwich special $3.95. No credit cards. Mon–Fri 10am–7pm, Sat 10am–6pm, Sun 11am–5pm. DELI.

You'll know this is a New York–style deli right away: Sandwiches can be served on onion roll or rye and are inches thick. There are all the usuals—hot pastrami, corned beef, Hebrew National salami—plus a terrific Italian sub at $4.95, a dozen or more clubs and subs, and bagels with cream cheese and lox. This is an extremely popular place, but service is fast and efficient. There are a few tables, so you don't have to eat in the car. Located directly behind McDonald's.

☉ Kin Wah
45-588 Kamehameha Hwy. ☎ **808/247-4812** or 808/247-5024. Reservations not accepted. Main courses $3.75–$12.50. MC, V. Daily 10am–9pm. CHINESE.

A friendly and bustling family-owned and -operated place off the tourist track in peaceful Kaneohe, Kin Wah is always full of local families gobbling up the terrific food. It's a spotless, attractive place. You really can't go wrong with anything on the extensive menu, but the sizzling platters—such as chicken with black-bean sauce, combination seafood with vegetables, and scallops with vegetables ($5.50 to $7.50)—are definite winners. There are dozens of main courses priced at $5.50 or less.

MEALS FOR LESS THAN $20

Assaggio Italian Restaurant
354 Uluniu St. ☎ **808/261-2772.** Reservations recommended, especially on weekends. Main courses $8.80–$17.90. AE, CB, DC, MC, V. Lunch Mon–Fri 11:30am–2:30pm; dinner daily 5–10pm. ITALIAN.

A place that's won a big following for its wonderful food at oh-so-reasonable prices, Assaggio is something special. The whole staff takes care of everyone; there's always someone watching to see if you're happy. At dinner the hot antipasto—which has *everything*—is exceptional. At dinner only, one may order a small or regular portion of pasta or any other main course. Our favorite pasta here—and one you don't see everywhere—is the baked ziti alla siciliano. Chicken, veal, seafood dishes—they're all good, especially the sauces. Lunch courses are pretty much the same, and go down $1 or $2 in prices. Even if you have to get a take-out bag, don't leave Assaggio without sampling their liqueur-infused cheesecakes ($4). The restaurant is pleasant enough, with changing art work on the walls—but it's the food that shines here. Our one complaint: Sometimes the baked pastas are overcooked and too soft, not al dente, as we prefer.

Cinnamon's
315 Uluniu St. ☎ **808/261-8724.** Reservations recommended for parties of more than four. Main courses $7.50–$17.95. DISC, MC, V. Breakfast daily 7am–2pm; lunch daily 11am–2pm; dinner Thurs–Sat 5–9pm. AMERICAN.

Cinnamon's is an immensely popular restaurant on the ground floor of a neighborhood shopping plaza. Its aim is to provide wholesome, natural, nutritious foods with no preservatives in a smoke-free atmosphere, and this it does—with style. The restaurant is small and cozy; four of the tables are under a pretty white gazebo. And the tab will be very reasonable. For lunch, we like the chicken-cashew salad ($6.50) and the grilled three-cheese deluxe sandwich ($3.95). Country quiches with salad, the garden vegetable platter, and burgers are all very popular, too. At dinnertime, pick one of the house specials, such as chicken fantasy, with "made from scratch" hollandaise; kebabs of chicken, beef, or mahimahi; or barbecued ribs. Meals come with soup or salad; rice, fries, or baked beans; vegetables; and hot dinner rolls. On the à la carte dinner menu, the fiesta taco grande salad and the chef's super salad ("a veritable salad bar brought to your table") are inexpensive and fun, as are the roast pork or roast turkey with apple dressing, chicken cutlet with country gravy and vegetables, and seafood crêpes Florentine. Breakfast has its own delights, including eggs Benedict, carrot pancakes, three-egg omelets, and freshly baked cinnamon rolls.

✪ El Charro Avitia

14 Oneawa St. ☎ **808/263-3943.** Reservations recommended. Main courses $7.75–$14.50. AE, DISC, MC, V. Daily 11am–9pm. MEXICAN.

It's best to come here on a weekday if you can, because this place is insanely popular and on weekends, even with a reservation, you'll probably still have to wait a little. But it will be worth it. This is some of the best Mexican food you'll find anywhere, prepared with love and care by the Avitia family (they have several successful restaurants in California and Nevada as well), and served in astounding portions; we always leave with doggie bags. The decor is beautiful indoors and out; you can dine outdoors surrounded by ficus trees in mammoth clay pots, or indoors in a room laden with Mexican artifacts, colorful Mexican pottery, and clay lanterns decorating your table. The chairs are carved in ornate Mexican style, and the music is pure south-of-the-border; you'll soon forget that you're in beautiful downtown Kailua. Anything you choose on the all-day menu will be good. Huevos Mexicanos—rancheros, colorados, revueltos—are served all day long. House specialties include shrimp enchiladas, ceviche tacos, sizzling shrimp fajitas, and a few specialties of Veracruz, like sautéed fresh fish smothered in a traditional Veracruz sauce. Start with a fresh fruit margarita; end with a simple flan or even fried ice cream. A treat.

✪ Harry's Cafe & Deli

629 Kailua Rd. ☎ **808/261-2120.** Reservations not required. Main courses $6.95–$11.95. CB, DC, MC, V. Lunch Mon–Sat 11am–3pm; dinner daily 5:30–9pm. MEDITERRANEAN.

Back in the 1930s and '40s, Harry Owens was one of the foremost composers of popular Hawaiian music: "Sweet Leilani" (which won him an Academy Award in 1939), "To You, Sweetheart, Aloha," and "Hawaii Calls" are standards of the hapa-haole repertoire. Now his son, Tim, has opened a charming restaurant that recalls the man and the era. Originals of his sheet music adorn the walls, as do superb Hawaiian quilts and changing art exhibits. The young staff is impeccably trained: Servers are able to tell you exactly how each dish is prepared. And they know a good deal about wines, too (only wine and beer are served). The food lives up to the setting: We like to start with the pane formaggi (French bread stuffed with provolone cheese and baked with garlic-and-basil butter) or the rare carpaccio. Then we move on to such main courses as shrimp Provençale and pasta primavera. As for desserts, it's a hard choice: There are usually four kinds of cheesecakes made on the premises (strawberry, rum, amaretto, and chocolate are among the most popular), and there's always a sour-cream fudge cake with cream-cheese frosting, carrot or banana cake, and chocolate mousse. Lunch is reasonable, especially the Beggar's Banquet—a bowl of soup with salad for $7.25. The Mediterranean shrimp salad, the Cobb salad, and the Reuben sandwich are all good bets, from $5.50 to $7.95. Relax over your meal as long as you like; no one is going to rush you. Harry's is a hit!

Pepper's Place

301-A Hahani St. ☎ **808/261-5331.** Reservations not accepted. Sandwiches $4.79–$5.99. No credit cards. Mon–Thurs 7am–9pm; Fri 7am–10pm; Sat 8am–10pm; Sun 11am–8pm. AMERICAN.

This is just a tiny place, but it has really caught on with the local folk and the B&B guests in the area. It has a '50s look about it; there are old Coke posters, and behind the counter is none other than . . . Elvis! The specialty is cheesesteaks (their slogan is "6,000 miles to Philly—better eat here!"), but everything is good, especially their baked and french-fried potatoes, both served three different ways, and their sandwich rolls. They also have chicken and vegetarian sandwiches. The menu is over the counter; you order and pay and they'll give you a holler when your order is ready. We like the bottomless sodas—unlimited refills. This is a favorite spot to pick-up lunch to take to the beach.

BUFFETS

Dynasty II

1050 Ala Moana Blvd., In Ward Warehouse. ☎ **808/531-0208.** Reservations not required. Weekday buffet lunch $8.45; weekend brunch buffet $11.45; main courses $7.75–$15.75. AE, CB, DC, DISC, JCB, MC, V. Lunch daily 11am–2pm; dinner daily 5:30–10pm. CHINESE.

This elegant Chinese restaurant offers two popular lunch buffets: during the week, you can eat all you want for $8.45; on Saturday and Sunday, when there's an expanded menu, the price goes up to $11.45. For a splurge, you might want to come back here for an à la carte dinner. Appetizers such as stuffed crab claw, and main courses like whole Peking duck and king prawns sautéed with honey-glazed walnuts, have earned this restaurant many awards.

Kengo's Royal Buffet

1529 Kapiolani Blvd. ☎ **808/941-2241.** Reservations accepted only for groups of six or more. Buffet lunch $10.95 Mon–Fri, $11.95 Sat–Sun; buffet dinner $20.95 (all including beverage, tax, and tip). MC, V. Breakfast Sat–Sun 6–10am; lunch daily 11am–2pm; dinner daily 5–9:30pm. JAPANESE/AMERICAN.

This spot is immensely popular with local people, who keep it packed day and night. Although the atmosphere is plain, the combination of hearty food and low prices makes it a winner. The dinner buffet is especially good, with many luscious seafood dishes, such as shrimp tempura and lobster in black-bean sauce, as well as roast beef carved to order. There are two buffet tables, one laden with Japanese specialties such as sushi and salads; the other, haole favorites such as fried fish and lamb chops. Lunch offers a continental buffet. There's a modest dessert bar. Soup (we sampled a tasty Portuguese bean soup) is served at your table, as is your beverage. There's karaoke singing in the bar and lounge from 6pm to 2am, and in the main dining room from 9:30pm to 1am, every night.

✪ Parc Café

In the Waikiki Parc Hotel, 2233 Helumoa Rd. ☎ **808/921-7272.** Reservations recommended. Breakfast buffet $11.50; regular lunch buffet $13.50; Wed Hawaiian lunch buffet $15.50; dinner buffet $18.50; Sun brunch $19.50. AE, CB, DC, JCB, MC, V. Breakfast daily 7–10am; lunch daily 11:30am–2pm; dinner daily 5:30–9pm; brunch Sun 11am–2pm. AMERICAN/JAPANESE/HAWAIIAN.

For a buffet meal that's also a fine dining experience, the Parc Café, across from the Halekulani Hotel, is just the ticket. The garden-terrace atmosphere is charming, the service attentive, and the food of a gourmet quality not usually found on buffet tables. The dinner buffet features the likes of Peking duck salad, celery rémoulade, fresh fish of the day, pastas, and Asian favorites. The carving station offers grilled prime rib, leg of lamb, and rotisseried duck. For dessert, you can have freshly baked pies and cakes or chocolate mousse, or make your own frozen yogurt sundaes with a lavish choice of toppings. Sunday brunch is another feast. One of our favorite things to do is to stop by on Wednesday for a spectacular Hawaiian lunch buffet (the food is better than at many a luau). Lomi-lomi salmon, kalua pig, chicken long rice, laulau, and the traditional haupia pudding are all featured, along with such treats as seafood chowder, wild-bamboo-shoot salad, and mashed Molokai sweet potatoes. The rest of the week, the luncheon buffet features a create-your-own sandwich bar, a Cobb salad station, a fresh taco-salad station, pastas, chicken from the rôtisserie, a do-it-yourself frozen-yogurt bar, and more. The breakfast buffet has a table full of goodies, including exotic fresh fruits, pastries, eggs, meats, cereals, pancakes, and delicious french toast. A great place to conduct quiet business or a morning tête-à-tête. A la carte service is also available.

Peacock Room and Garden Lanai

In the Queen Kapiolani Hotel, 150 Kapahulu Ave. ☎ **808/922-1941.** Breakfast buffets $8.95; lunch buffets $11.95; dinner buffets $15.95. AE, CB, DC, JCB, MC. Breakfast daily 6:30–11am (plus menu service); lunch daily 11am–2pm (plus menu service); dinner daily 5:30–9pm. AMERICAN/JAPANESE/HAWAIIAN.

This restaurant provides a variety of intriguing buffets at all three meals. The most popular is the crab leg and Hawaiian dinner buffet, with many traditional Hawaiian dishes, held every Friday, Saturday, and Sunday night. On Thursday, there's a Japanese buffet at lunch and dinner. A Hawaiian luncheon buffet is held every Friday, Saturday, and Sunday. Prices, schedules, and types of buffets are subject to change, so be sure to check in advance.

⑤ Perry's Smorgy Restaurant

2380 Kuhio Ave., at the corner of Kanekapolei. ☎ **808/926-0184.** Reservations not accepted. Breakfast buffet $5.20; lunch buffet $6.24; dinner buffet and Sun brunch $9.36 (prices subject to change). AE, MC, V. Breakfast daily 7–11am; lunch Mon–Sat 11:30am–2:30pm; dinner daily 5–9pm; brunch Sun 11:30am–3pm. AMERICAN.

Just about the best buffet values are offered at the two Perry's restaurants, which have been serving hearty American-style buffet meals for as long as we can remember. The food is really good, there's no limit to how much you can eat, and the prices are certainly right. Both restaurants are attractive, especially the one on Kuhio, with its lush indoor-outdoor garden setting. At both, lunch and dinner feature a huge fruit and salad bar; hot vegetables; rice or potatoes; homemade corn muffins and dinner rolls; and lots of hot main dishes, including mahimahi, beef and vegetable stew, southern-style chicken, Italian spaghetti and garlic bread, and baked macaroni and cheese. Dinner adds a hand-carved round of roast beef, golden fried shrimp, and sliced turkey. In addition to the generous dessert table, there's also a create-your-own sundae and dessert bar. Fresh island pineapple and local Kona coffee are served. Breakfast features carved smoked ham, french toast, pancakes, blueberry muffins, fresh pastries, an attractive fruit bar, and more. You can have as many refills as you like, but no doggie bags, please.

The second Perry's is at the Coral Seas Hotel, 240 Lewers St., oceanside of Kalakaua Avenue (☎ 808/922-8814).

Pikake Terrace Buffet & Broiler

In the Princess Kaiulani Hotel, 120 Kaiulani Ave. ☎ **808/922-5811**. Reservations recommended for dinner. Breakfast buffet $15.75; lunch buffet $16.75; dinner $24.10, $26.25 Fri. AE, CB, DC, JCB, MC, V. Breakfast daily 6–11am; lunch daily 11:30am–2pm; dinner daily 5:30–10pm. AMERICAN.

It all began with a few tables around the pool at the newly expanded Princess Kaiulani Hotel; now this restaurant, with sumptuous buffets served morning, noon, and night, is a dominant feature of the hotel's poolside and public areas. All-you-can-eat breakfast buffets offer juices, fruits, cereals, a made-to-order omelet station with a variety of luscious fillings, waffles, meats, eggs, and more. At lunch, choose from a huge salad table, a hot table with half-a-dozen choices, broiled-to-order hamburgers, a pasta bar, a taco bar, and a dessert table that tempts you to take one of each. There's a theme buffet dinner every night: Sunday, it's a Hot Tropical Barbecue featuring steak and steamed Dungeness crab; Monday, it's a Blue Hawaii Beach Bonanza featuring barbecue steak and shrimp; on Tuesday, it's the Hukilau Clambake, when the specialty is hibachi steak and steamed clams. The Paniolo Barbecue is home on the range Wednesday, and the specialty is steak and Texas-style barbecue baby back ribs. The Lurline Cruise buffet on Thursday tempts with flame-broiled steak and Alaskan snow crab legs, and on Friday it's the Hawaiian Pau Hana Lobster Barbecue. Saturday is South Pacific Night, featuring barbecue steak and shrimp tempura. Prime rib is served at all dinner buffets. And there's wonderful entertainment every night from 5:45 to 9:45pm. If you're not coming here for a meal, you can have a drink and watch the show, or just enjoy the music and dancing from the sidelines.

Plantation Cafe

In the Ala Moana Hotel, 410 Atkinson. ☎ **808/955-4811**. Reservations not required. Breakfast buffet $10.95; lunch soup-and-sandwich bar $8.50; weekend dinner buffet $14.95. AE, DC, JCB, MC, V. Breakfast daily 6–11am; lunch daily 11am–5pm; dinner daily 5pm–midnight. INTERNATIONAL.

Although this place serves more than just buffets, it's hard to resist the luscious treats at the smörgåsbord. The restaurant looks opulent, but prices are not out of line. The sumptuous breakfast buffet includes fruits, juices, eggs, meats, and pastries galore. Lunch features a soup-and-sandwich bar. The regular menu includes nasi goreng, Indonesian fried rice with chicken, shrimp, veggies, and eggs, and there are also Chinese, Indian, and other exotic dishes. Come dinnertime, the chef's talents are displayed with out-of-the-ordinary soups and tantalizing appetizers, such as the shrimp and vegetable tempura.

At this writing, buffet dinners were being held on weekends only; Friday, a seafood one, Saturday, prime rib, and Sunday, Hawaiian buffets. Call to make sure of the schedule.

✪ Rainbow Lanai

At Hilton Hawaiian Village, 2005 Kalia Rd. ☎ **808/949-4321**. Reservations not required. Adults $10.95; children $5.95; salad bar only $7.95. Lunch buffet daily 11:30am–2pm (à la carte service also available). CONTINENTAL.

Now here's a neat way to combine a good meal and a swim at one of the best stretches of Waikiki Beach. The Rainbow Lanai offers a plentiful buffet lunch in a lovely setting near the water. Enjoy the salads, soups, make-your-own deli sandwiches, and hot main dishes of fish and meats. Eat as much as you like. For dessert—plunge right into the Pacific. The Rainbow Lanai serves a nice à la carte menu at breakfast, lunch, and dinner, too, but the buffet is by far the best buy.

COFFEEHOUSES

Coffeehouses have made a comeback all over the country, and Honolulu is no exception. In most, you'll find local people relaxing, catching up with their friends, and enjoying some wonderful brews.

WAIKIKI

Cappuccino's Cafe
320 Lewers St. ☎ **808/936-1530.**

Located in the elegant Waikiki Joy Hotel, Cappuccino's was once one of our favorite restaurants. Recently, it has re-invented itself as a coffee bôite. It's a pretty room with its sea-green banquettes in the little galleries; tiny, round pedestal tables with upholstered chairs on the main level; arched Romanesque windows; and coffee bar at the back. Plants and lovely flowers complete the striking decor; contemporary music plays softly. (Perfect for a tête-à-tête!) There's a nice variety of coffees with or without liqueurs, and lovely things to nibble on. Last time we visited, the special of the day was espresso with cheesecake, $4.95. Open daily from 10am to 10pm.

MANOA MARKETPLACE, NEAR THE UNIVERSITY

Coffee Manoa
Manoa Marketplace. ☎ **808/988-5113.**

This little place, popular with the UH crowd, is open to the sidewalk and has several outdoor tables. The walls are decorated with menus and Coffee Manoa T-shirts. They serve cappuccino and latte, cafe mocha and cafe au lait, Thai coffee and cafe cacao—not to mention plain espressos and all sorts of tea (iced and hot)—for 85¢ to $2.45. They carry an astounding array of coffee by the pound, from such exotic places as Ethiopia, Kenya, Sumatra, Mexico, plus Hawaiian tea bags. The coconut shortbread, mint chocolate brownies, and lilikoi lemon and guava-raspberry tarts are *ono*—as is the Hawaiian biscotti. The daily papers and various erudite magazines are there for perusal. This is a lovely place to unwind—for hours. Open daily from 7am to 9pm.

KAHALA MALL

Bravissimo
Kahala Mall. ☎ **808/735-6574.**

Shades of Seattle right out on the mall at Kahala. This little round espresso cart has all kinds of coffees and teas, cakes and cookies. Try a granita float (a slush float with gelato ice cream), or an espresso milkshake (espresso mellowed by creamy vanilla gelato, milk, and a dash of chocolate, blended and frosted) for the ultimate coffee experience. In addition to lattes, mochas, Thai coffees, and the like (most drinks are $2.15 to $3.65), there are cakes, cookies, fruit tarts, plus gelatos and sorbets in exotic flavors. Open mall hours.

KAPAHULU

Java Java Café
760 Kapahulu Ave. ☎ **808/732-2670.**

Very popular with the college crowd, Java Java Café is also fun for people of all ages. The space is small, with little marble-topped tables and café chairs; there's always music playing in the background, either classical or jazz, depending upon who's on duty. There's a limited menu (salads, sandwiches), plus a variety of coffee and espresso drinks and an "eggnog smoothie" for $2.95. Entertainment is a sometime thing (call to find out if anything's happening), but you could catch a poetry reading, a "work-in-progress," or a jazz and folk combo. (Sometimes there's a cover charge—inquire.) Open Monday through Friday from 8am to midnight, Saturday from 8am to 1am, and Sunday from 10am to 10pm.

KAIMUKI

Coffee Talk
1152 Koko Head Ave., in Kaimuki. ☎ **808/737-7444.**

A popular and fun place to go to after the movies or theater, Coffee Talk is full of charming eccentricities: chairs that don't match (one is "upholstered" in painted-on leopard skin), a mobile that looks like a bunch of petrified bagels, immense coffee cups that are more like soup bowls with handles, window lamps with bases made of brightly colored plastic toys. There are plenty of newspapers and magazines to peruse while you're drinking your giant cup of coffee. Any time of day, there will be happy people talking, reading, dining on light food, and generally having fun. There's the usual line-up of coffees, including espresso, all priced from $1 to $2.50, plus hot chocolate and a wonderful vanilla iced tea!

EXOTIC SNACK FOOD

Honolulu has myriad snack bars where you can sample exotic cuisines at penny-pinching prices. Right in Waikiki, for example, is the **Hung Yun Chinese Kitchen** in Kuhio Mall, where the luscious aromas wafting from the restaurant will lead you to Chinese dishes that start at $1 for pieces of chicken, beef, and pork. Top prices on other main courses: $3.60 to $4.25.

Ala Moana Center has an extraordinary source for sampling Japanese food: the gourmet food department on the second floor of **Shirokiya,** the large Japanese department store. Booths offer freshly roasted chestnuts, tasty manapuas, and, of course, a vast array of wonderful sushi and other traditional Japanese fare. Incidentally, two cone sushis—cold, marinated rice cakes—tucked in your bag make a tasty lunch-on-the-run. (Many of the ubiquitous **ABC Discount Stores** also carry cone sushi to go.) You can assemble a meal for yourself out of these offerings, and then take them home or to a little dining lanai to savor on the spot. Most days, from 3:30 to 8pm, there's an evening buffet and sushi bar, priced according to what you eat.

Rada's Piroscki, 1144–1146 Fort Street Mall (☎ 808/533-2388), is practically a Honolulu institution. This Russian snack bar specializes in piroscki—delicate, flaky buns stuffed with beef, cheese, cabbage, mushrooms, or whatever combination suits your fancy. We simply can't resist the chicken, mushrooms, and cheese piroshki, but the other combinations are also delicious. One big pirog is $1.50.

The Russian fried squid at $1.25 a bag are . . . different. Rada's is a family opera-
tion, and the people in charge make you feel welcome.

What, you've never had a Vietnamese sandwich? A stop at one of the numerous **Ba-Le Sandwich** shops will quickly take care of that. There's one in Waikiki
at 2330 Kuhio Ave. (☎ 808/926-4707), and another downtown at 1154 Fort St.
Mall (☎ 808/521-4117); more shops are listed in the phone book. In case you
didn't know, a Vietnamese sandwich mingles both French and Asian influences.
They use French bread or croissants, stuff them with ingredients like steamed pork
or chicken or Chinese meatballs, then add Asian condiments like daikon, pickled
carrots, onions, and soy sauce. Prices range from $1.75 for the vegetarian sandwich
to $3.75 for the roast beef. Take-out is the thing here. Closed Sundays.

For take-out barbecue—barbecued chicken, barbecued short ribs, deep-fried
shrimp, and the like—the local people favor the chain of **L&L Drive-Inns;** the
closest one for us is downtown at 100 N. Beretania St. (☎ 808/524-3313).
Everything is grilled rather than fried. Plate lunches, including two scoops of rice
and two scoops of potato or macaroni salad, are priced from $3 to $4.95.

DINING COMPLEXES

INTERNATIONAL MARKET PLACE & KUHIO MALL

Few tourists who set foot in Waikiki leave without at least one visit to the **International Market Place,** in the heart of the beach area at 2330 Kalakaua Ave.
Immediately adjoining it, and fronting on Kuhio Avenue, is **Kuhio Mall,** another
lively bazaar. Just about in the middle of the two of them is the attractive **International Food Court** (follow the yellow-brick line), where some 30 fast-food
stands offer a variety of tempting foods that you eat at central tables. You can certainly make a meal here, lunch or dinner, for $5 or under: Some of our favorites
include Peking Garden, Beef & Burger, The Mad Greek, Aloha Yakitori, Beaches
and Cream, Choi's Kitchen, Bautista's Filipino Kitchen, Yummy Korean BBQ,
and Mario's Pizza and Pasta. Cinn-a-Yums dispenses enormous, fattening, delicious cinnamon buns with various toppings. Open daily from 8:30am to 11pm.

WAIKIKI SHOPPING PLAZA

Shopping here (2250 Kalakaua Ave., at the corner of Seaside) can be expensive,
but the below-street level is a veritable bonanza for the budget-conscious diner who
wants something a little bit different. Start in the Japanese sector at **Ramen** for
freshly made Japanese noodles. You can have them seated at the open tables or at
the Japanese counter flanked by Japanese lanterns. Prices start at $6.25 for shoyu
ramen and go to $7.50 for gyoza—Japanese dumplings—and shrimp tempura.
This is one of the few plaza spots that opens early, at 10am. There are no tables
at the Japanese fast-food outlet **Okazu-Ya Bento** (*bento* means take-out). Here
they custom-design your take-out lunch or dinner, filling the large plate with Japanese favorites: yaki soba, meatballs, chicken cutlet, and cone sushi, for 65¢ to
$5.25. All items are in view in a glass showcase, Japanese style, so you can just
point, or take their daily special at $5. To round off this Japanese trio, there's **Plaza
Sushi,** a tidy little restaurant that serves a mostly Japanese crowd (prices run $6.50
to $12.25 during the day, $8.90 to $26.95 at night).

Want more variety? At the **Chinese Kitchen,** you get your choice of main
dishes, plus noodles, chow fun, or steamed rice at the price of $5.30 for two main

dishes, $6.30 for three, $7.30 for four. Your best all-around choice here, though, is the huge **Plaza Coffee Shop,** where changing lunch specials go for $4.45 to $6.75 and include the likes of boneless barbecued chicken, corned beef and cabbage, and filets of mahimahi. Similar specials at dinner are mostly in the 8.95 to $12.95 range.

ALA MOANA SHOPPING CENTER'S MAKAI MARKET

Makai Market, has a score of self-service specialty kitchens. Name your desire— Hawaiian, Italian, New York deli, seafood, Japanese, Chinese, health food—the food is here and you can put together a meal for around $4 to $5 at lunch, $6 to $7 at dinner. You serve yourself, then take your food to the pretty tables under the bright buntings overhead. You can start with a drink from the center bar with its LET'S MAKE A DAIQUIRI neon sign; daiquiris, piña coladas, and other favorites are about $3 to $4, and there are smoothies, espressos, and nonalcoholic cocktails as well. **Thirst Aid Station** has "Remedies and Prescriptions" that include sodas, smoothies, yogurt, and soup (72¢ to $2.50). **Tsuruya Noodle Shop** dishes up bowls of hot soba or udon, at $3.75 to $5.29.

Panda Express has both Mandarin and Szechuan dishes. Try the Mandarin spicy chicken with peanuts at $3.59, or go Szechuan with roast duck at $5.99. There's no way you can miss **Hawaiian Poi Bowl,** which dishes out food from a bright-red lunchwagon. There's a teri-chicken plate and a poi-bowl combo, for $5.20 to $6.90.

Yummy Korean BBQ has full-meal combo plates at $4.75 to $6.25, lunch or dinner. The **Aloha Grill** is a '50s theme eatery, with '50s music on the jukeboxes; it has its own bar seats on which to enjoy the super burgers, at $1.99 to $5.99. They also have good hot dogs and old-fashioned milk shakes.

Looking for light food? Try the **Kitchen Garden,** which offers croissant sandwiches and salads, plus baked potatoes, plain and fancy; both quiche and chili go for $3.59. For a cholesterol feast, however, **La Rôtisserie** offers a fried-food buffet including seafood, beef burgundy, and mahimahi in ginger butter for $3.75 to $5.50—as well as a delicious shrimp and crab salad for $7.50.

For years before Makai Market opened, **Patti's Chinese Kitchen** and **Lyn's Delicatessen** were bywords among visitors and locals alike. Now they've moved into the market and are still mighty crowd pleasers. Patti's is famous for its plate lunches; for a choice of any two items, the price is $4.50, $5.50 for three items, $6.50 for four. As for Lyn's, it has long been one of the best kosher-style delis in town, known for thick corned beef and pastrami sandwiches ($4.88), lox and bagels, fragrant and garlicky hotdogs, plus plate lunches, and very special buys on steak dinners.

Want more? **Orson's Chowderette** is a small version of the popular Orson's in Ward Warehouse. Finger foods like fish nuggets and clam strips, salads, and burgers of mahimahi, shrimp, or oysters, are all low-priced, $3.50 to $6.40. You can sample Thai food—plate lunches for $4.95 to $6.29, spring rolls at $2.99— at **Little Café Siam.** No MSG here! **Wingo** is fine when you crave fried chicken; it's served on a jumbo plate for $4.55 and up. **Mama's Italian Pastas** is another good choice: they offer pastas from $4.75 to $6.50, and main courses such as shrimp marinara, garlic steak, and the like, from $5.95 to $7.50.

WORTH A SPLURGE

✪ Roy's

6600 Kalanianaole Hwy., Hawaii Kai. ☎ **808/396-7697.** Reservations recommended; call several days in advance to reserve for weekends. Main courses $14–$28. AE, CB, DC, DISC, JCB, MC, V. Dinner Mon–Thurs 5:30–9:30pm, Fri 5:30–10:30pm, Sat 5–10:30pm, Sun 5–9:30pm. HAWAII REGIONAL.

Roy's is the place where everyone wants to go and it's no wonder why: The 39-year-old wunderkind chef/owner is still hailed, after 10 years, as the master for his innovative marriage of Asian and Western cooking styles and ingredients. Both *Honolulu* magazine and *Zagat* have named Roy's as "Hawaii's Most Popular Restaurant," and Roy has received The James Beard Award for "Best Chef" in the Pacific and Northwest. If you've got wheels, hop in your car and drive the eight miles out to Hawaii Kai to see for yourself—you won't be disappointed.

Roy's is a two-level restaurant; downstairs there's a piano bar and lounge. But the main action—and the open display kitchen from which the wondrous dishes emerge—is upstairs. The huge room, with striking flower arrangements accenting its minimalist decor, has a wraparound window affording uninterrupted views of Maunalua Bay, Diamond Head, and Koko Head. The lighting is indirect, the decor elegant and subdued, and the service meticulous.

The food is exquisite. Since Roy is constantly coming up with new inspirations, there are perhaps 30 specials on the menu every night—and they always include original appetizers, pastas, salads, wood-fired individual pizzas, and many fresh fish dishes, including local spiny lobster. And on the regular menu you'll get a chance to try many of his signature dishes. Our favorites among the appetizers are potstickers in a lobster miso sauce and lemongrass-crusted fish sah-teh with Thai peanut sauce. As for main courses, you can choose among the likes of a Northern Chinese–style roast duck with Oriental stir-fry vegetables; a smoked lime chicken with rosemary and sausage black-bean-bellpepper stuffing in achiote chile sauce; or an Asian pesto mahimahi with shiitake mushrooms, tomatoes, and cranberries in a Thai curry, ginger, basil, and coconut sauce. Desserts are special, too, and change every night. The wine list is well chosen, and not overpriced. There's entertainment—contemporary music and vocals on Thursdays and Fridays from 8 to 10pm, and Hawaiian slack-key guitar and vocals every Saturday from 8:30 to 10pm.

6

Beaches & Outdoor Activities in Honolulu & Around Oahu

By Jeanette Foster

When people usually think of Oahu, the Waikiki skyline, with its rows of hotels, or downtown Honolulu, with its concrete canyons, are the images that immediately come to mind. Oahu, however, is much more than an urban jungle or a tropical Disneyland blighted by overdevelopment—it's also a haven for the nature lover and outdoor enthusiast. With year-round air temperatures in the upper 70s, ocean temperatures in the mid- to high 70s, and miles of verdant, unspoiled landscape, Oahu is perfect for activities of all kinds: hiking, golf, tennis, biking, horseback riding—Oahu has it all and much more. The island's waters, though, is where the majority of residents and visitors head for relaxation, rejuvenation, and recreation.

1 Beaches

Oahu has more than 100 beaches of every shape, kind, and size, from legendary white-sand stretches to wild, rocky bays. Waikiki, of course, is the best known of Oahu's beaches, but many others are just as beautiful, and generally less crowded. What follows is a selection of the finest beaches, carefully chosen to suit every taste and interest, from the sunbather in repose to the most ardent diver.

Keep in mind—wherever you are on Oahu—that you're in an urban area; don't leave valuables in your car. Most of the beaches are reachable by TheBUS, as I've indicated; it's always a great way to get around, particularly for the budget traveler who wants to save their car-rental money for outdoor adventuring.

WAIKIKI BEACH

The name of the world-famous two-mile stretch means "spouting water," probably referring to the duck ponds that once occupied this former swamp land. A crescent-shaped beach of imported sand on Oahu's south shore, Waikiki extends—interrupted periodically by sea walls, rock groins, and a yacht harbor—from the Ala Wai Canal to the foot of Mt. Leahi (better known as Diamond Head). Hawaii's most popular beach, Waikiki is nearly always crowded with tourists. You can experience nearly every imaginable type of ocean activity here: One of the best places on Oahu for swimming, Waikiki also offers both board surfing and bodysurfing, outrigger canoeing, diving, sailing, snorkeling, and pole fishing. Every imaginable type of marine equipment and toy is available for rent. The many hotels that line the beach offer every conceivable type of food and drink. The best place to park is at Kapiolani Park. Facilities include showers, lifeguards, restrooms, and pavilions at the Queen's Surf end of the beach.

HANAUMA BAY

Formerly a playground for Hawaiian royalty, this beautiful bay is now a Marine Life Conservation District and the most popular snorkeling spot on Oahu. The small (2,000-foot) beach just east of Koko Head fronts a pristine bay, which is actually a volcanic crater open to the ocean on one side. Hanauma's shallow shoreline waters and bountiful marine life are both a blessing and a curse; the number of people who come to the bay is so overwhelming that the ecology of the marine preserve is in danger. Because of the existing threat, the government has restricted both parking and access by commercial operators. Since this is a conservation district, taking anything from the ocean here is prohibited. Facilities include parking, restrooms, a pavilion, grass volleyball court, lifeguard, barbecue, picnic tables, and food concession. To avoid the crowds and to ensure yourself a parking space, go early on a weekday morning; take Kalanianaole Highway to Koko Head Regional Park. Or, take TheBUS to escape the parking problem. The Hanauma Bay Shuttle runs from Waikiki to Hanauma Bay every half hour from 8:45am to 1pm; you can catch it at the Ala Moana Hotel, the Ilikai Hotel, or at any city bus stop. It returns every hour on the hour from noon to 4:30pm. At this writing, the city regularly closes the bay on Wednesdays for maintenance.

SANDY BEACH

Also part of the Koko Head Regional Park, Sandy Beach is one of the best bodysurfing beaches on Oahu. Unless you're experienced, though, you might be restricted to watching the expert bodysurfers and boogie boarders ride the waves and the chiseled bodies strut up and down the shore. This 1,200-foot long beach is pounded by waves nearly all year long. The steep, quick drop-off underwater adds to the intensity of the waves and produces a strong, forceful backwash. The backwash is especially dangerous for children and weak swimmers. Sandy Beach's lifeguards make more rescues in a year than those stationed at any other beach except nearby Makapuu. Visitors unfamiliar with the beach and its dangers—and fooled by the experienced bodysurfers making wave-riding look so easy—all too often find themselves overwhelmed by the waves. As a result, the lifeguards have developed a flag system warning of the dangers of the day's surf. Green means safe, yellow caution, and red indicates very dangerous water conditions. Be sure to check the flags before you dive in. Facilities include restrooms and parking. The best times to avoid the crowds are weekdays; the best times to watch the bodysurfers are weekends. TheBUS no. 22 (Kuhio) will get you there from Waikiki.

MAKAPUU BEACH PARK

At the base of the Koolau Mountains on Oahu's easternmost point is Makapuu Beach Park, the most famous bodysurfing beach in Hawaii. Movie fans will recognize this classically beautiful, 1,000-foot-long white-sand beach, bordered by the stark black cliff of Makapuu Point, as a location for the famous Burt Lancaster–Deborah Kerr love scene in *From Here to Eternity*. Rabbit Island lies just off the coast. During the summer months the ocean can be as gentle as a backyard pool, making swimming and diving a breeze. But extremely dangerous current and surf can be present from September through April, when the pounding waves erode the beach and expose rocks and boulders in the shorebreak area. Because these conditions are ideal for expert bodysurfers, board surfing is prohibited by state law. Small boards, three-feet or less with no skeg (bottom fin), are permitted. Facilities include restrooms, lifeguard, barbecue grills, picnic tables, and parking. To get to Makapuu, follow Kalanianaole Highway toward Waimanalo. TheBUS no. 57 or 58 (Sea Life Park) will get you there from Waikiki.

LANIKAI BEACH

Hidden by the residential area of Mokulua Drive on the windward side of the island, Lanikai is a beautiful mile-long beach that's safe for swimming and—with the prevailing trade winds—excellent for sailing and windsurfing. The fine, hard-packed sand along the shoreline is perfect for jogging. Offshore, the two tiny islands called the Mokuluas (which are sea-bird sanctuaries) are easily reachable by kayak. Because Lanikai is off the main roads, undeveloped, without facilities, and surrounded by residential homes, it's less crowded than other beaches on the windward side. It's the perfect place to claim a remote, isolated spot for a morning of swimming and relaxation. Sun worshipers should arrive in the morning, as the Koolaus' shadow will block your access to the rays in the afternoon. From Waikiki, take TheBUS no. 56 or 57 (Kailua), then transfer to the shuttle bus.

KAILUA BEACH PARK

A 30-acre public park located on the east end of Kailua Bay, Kailua Beach Park is a broad, grassy area with picnic tables, a public boat ramp, restrooms, a pavilion, a volleyball court, and food stands. The wide, sandy beach area is popular for diving, swimming, sailing, snorkeling, and board and windsurfing. In fact, the dependable winds make this one of the more popular windsurfing areas on Oahu. The water conditions are generally safe. But parents should keep an eye on young children, who are often attracted to the brackish water pond in the middle of the park; the seemingly shallow pond has deep holes and has been the scene of several drownings. It gets extremely crowded on weekends, when local families come here; the best time to come is weekdays. To get to Kailua Beach Park, take the Kalanianaole Highway to Kailua Road, which loops around to Kawailoa Road. Parking is available. From Waikiki, take TheBUS no. 56 or 57 (Kailua) into Kailua, then take the no. 70 shuttle.

MALAEKAHANA STATE RECREATION AREA

This beautiful, long (over a mile), curving, sandy beach was once hidden from public access as the domain of wealthy families, who used the area for private beach homes. The state has since reclaimed the area and made it into a state park with public access, picnicking areas, and camping. TheBUS no. 55 (Circle Island) takes you right to the park. As you enter through the main gate off Kamehameha Highway, two miles north of the Polynesian Cultural Center, you'll come upon the wooded beach park area; it's excellent for swimming, picnicking, and shore activities. There's no lifeguard here, but the beach is protected most of the year. Mokuauia (Goat) Island, just offshore, is a state bird refuge. You can wade out to the island at low tide to visit secluded Mokuauia Beach, on the island's leeward shore. Surprisingly, very few visitors come here, one of the best beaches on Oahu—it's a true find.

Beaches & Outdoor Activities On Oahu

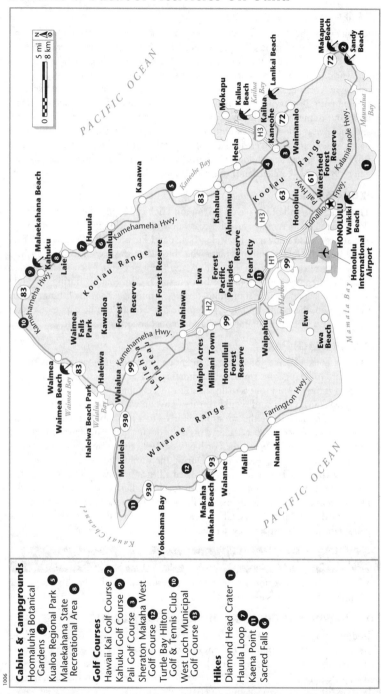

Cabins & Campgrounds
Hoomaluhia Botanical Gardens **4**
Kualoa Regional Park **5**
Malaekahana State Recreational Area **8**

Golf Courses
Hawaii Kai Golf Course **2**
Kahuku Golf Course **9**
Pali Golf Course **3**
Sheraton Makaha West Golf Course **12**
Turtle Bay Hilton Golf & Tennis Club **10**
West Loch Municipal Golf Course **13**

Hikes
Diamond Head Crater **1**
Hauula Loop **7**
Kaena Point **11**
Sacred Falls **6**

Airport ✈

1006

WAIMEA BEACH PARK

Despite what the Beach Boys' croon in their hit song (why-a-MEE-ah), the name of this famous surfing beach is pronounced why-MAY-ah. Waimea Bay is known in the surfing circuit as the home of some of the biggest ridable surfing waves in the world. During the winter—October to April—huge, pounding waves come rolling in, creating strong rip-currents. Even expert surfers think twice when confronted with 30-foot waves. When the surfs up, it seems like everyone on Oahu drives out Kamehameha Highway to Waimea to get a look at the monstrous waves and those who ride them. It's hard to believe, but during the summer this same bay is glassy and calm, a great place for swimming, snorkeling, and diving. Since this beach is popular with local residents, weekdays are best. From Waikiki, take TheBUS no. 52 (Circle Island) to get to Waimea Beach Park.

YOKOHAMA BAY

The area at the end of the paved Farrington Highway begins the 853-acre Kaena Point State Park, a remote and wild coastline with picnicking, hiking, swimming, and surfing. Also known as Keawalua Beach and Puau Beach, Yokohama got its name from the Japanese immigrants who traveled to this bay to fish. This is the last sandy stretch of shore on the northwestern coast of Oahu. There's a fairly wide beach between two rocky points. When the surf is calm (mainly during the summer) this is a good area for snorkeling, diving, swimming, and shore fishing. When the surf's up, the board- and bodysurfers are out. Surfing can be dangerous here. There are no lifeguards, no facilities, and no bus service to this beach.

MAKAHA BEACH PARK

Makaha means "fierce" or "savage;" many people think the name refers to the giant surf and dangerous rip currents, shorebreak, and backwash that occur from October through April. But actually it alludes to a community of robbers who lived in the Makaha Valley and would threaten anyone who walked through. Today Makaha still may not be the safest place for visitors to roam, but when the surfs up at Makaha Beach it's spectacular. This is the original home of Hawaii's big-wave surfing championship: When the north or west swells run during the winter, monstrous waves pound the beach here. During the summer months, the waters are perfectly safe for swimming. To get to Makaha Beach from Waikiki, take TheBUS no. 51 (Makaha). You'll not find many visitors here; there's some sentiment in the local community that there are plenty of beaches for visitors and this beach should be reserved for local residents. Chances are good that no one will bother you, but you might want to respect these feelings and stop at another beach for swimming.

2 Water Sports & Recreation

Whatever water recreation you might be interested in, whether you're a beginner or an expert, you can find it on Oahu.

BODYBOARDING (BOOGIE BOARDING) & BODYSURFING

Bodysurfing—riding waves without a board, becoming one with the rolling water—is immensely popular in Hawaii. Some bodysurfers just rely on their outstretched hands (or hands at their sides) to ride the waves. Others use handboards (flat, paddlelike gloves). An excellent beach to learn bodysurfing is Kailua. The best beaches for experts are Makapuu and Sandy Beach.

For additional maneuverability, try a boogie- or bodyboard (also known as belly boards or paipo boards). These three-foot-long vehicles, which support the upper part of your body, are easy to carry and very maneuverable in the water. The same open-heel fins that are used in bodysurfing are used in bodyboarding.

Boogie boards can be rented for as little at $13 a day from **Surf & Sea,** 62-595 Kamehameha Hwy., Haleiwa (☎ 808/637-9887); **Aloha Beach Service,** Sheraton Moana Surfrider Hotel, 2365 Kalakaua Ave., Waikiki (☎ 808/922-3111); and at all **Local Motion** locations: 1714 Kapiolani Blvd., Honolulu (☎ 808/955-7873); Koko Marina Shopping Center, Honolulu (☎ 808/396-7873); Windward Mall, Kaneohe (☎ 808/263-7873); and Pearl Kai Center, Aiea (☎ 808/486-7873). These outfitters will rent you the fins you need as well.

OCEAN KAYAKING

Gliding along the ocean, with only the sound of your paddle dipping into the water to disturb your peace, is what kayaking is all about. There are several kayak clubs that have regularly scheduled outings and can provide visitors with useful information. The three I recommend are **Hui Waa Kaukahi,** P.O. Box 88143, Honolulu, 96744; **Kanaka Ikaika,** P.O. Box 438, Kaneohe, 96744; and **Women's Kayak Club of Hawaii,** P.O. Box 438, Kaneohe, 96744.

Neophytes who want to try this sport should go to **Waimea Valley,** Waimea Falls Park, 59-864 Kamehameha Hwy., on the North Shore. (☎ 808/638-8511), for kayak lessons and equipment, at a cost of $15 per person. To get there, take TheBUS no. 52 (Circle Island). The kayaking takes place along the Waimea River; you paddle out to the white sands of Waimea Bay, where kayakers can rest or swim.

Kayak equipment rental starts at $10 an hour or $37 for a day; try **Prime Time Sports,** Fort DeRussy Beach, Waikiki (☎ 808/949-8952), or **Kailua Sailboard,** 130 Kailua Rd., Kailua (☎ 808/262-2555). A wonderful adventure is to rent a kayak, arrive at Lanikai Beach just as the sun is appearing, and paddle across the emerald lagoon to the pyramid-shaped islands off the beach called Mokulua— it's an experience you won't forget.

PARASAILING

This relatively new ocean adventure sport is something of a cross between skydiving and water skiing. You'll sail through the air, suspended under a large parachute attached by a tow line to a speedboat. Ten-minute rides are $36 to $49 (book directly with the parasail company and save money; activities centers charge commissions). Hawaii's original parasail company, **Aloha Parasail** (☎ 808/521-2446) takes you over the Waikiki and Ala Moana coastlines. They also provide free pick-up service. Or, try **Sea Breeze Parasailing** (☎ 808/396-0100), the largest parasail business on the island.

SAILING

From a two-hour sunset sail to a day-long adventure on the waves, Oahu offers a variety of sailing activities, including sailing lessons—picture yourself at the helm! **Honolulu Sailing Co.,** 47-335 Lulani, Kaneohe (☎ 808/239-3900), has been in the business for nearly two decades, providing everything from weddings at sea to honeymoon cruises, sailing-snorkeling sails, private lessons, and exclusive charters. The fleet ranges from 36- to 70-foot yachts. Charters start at $50 per person and lessons start at $125 per person per day.

SCUBA DIVING

Scuba (which is the abbreviation for Self Contained Underwater Breathing Apparatus) involves using a source of air to allow lengthy exploration underwater. Oahu is a wonderful place to scuba dive, especially for those interested in wreck diving. One of the more famous wrecks in Hawaii is the *Mahi,* a 185-foot former mine sweeper easily accessible just south of Waianae. Abundant marine life makes this a great place to shoot photos—schools of lemon butterfly fish and *ta'ape* are so comfortable with divers and photographers that they practically pose. Eagle rays, green sea turtles, manta rays, and white-tip sharks occasionally cruise by, and eels peer balefully from the wreck.

For non-wreck diving, one of the best dive spots in the summer is Kahuna Canyon. In Hawaiian, Kahuna translates as priest, wise man, or sorcerer; this massive amphitheater, located near Mokuleia, is a perfect example of something a sorcerer might conjure up: Walls rising from the ocean floor create the illusion of an underwater Grand Canyon. Inside the amphitheater, crabs, octopus, slipper, and spiny lobsters abound (be aware that taking them in the summer is illegal). Giant trevally, parrotfish, and unicorn fish congregate here. Outside the amphitheater, an occasional shark can be seen in the distance.

But before you can experience all of this you have to become a certified diver. Since vacation time is precious, take a dive class at home so when you arrive in Hawaii you're prepared to dive. If you are unsure if scuba diving is for you, most dive operators offer what is known as an introductory dive. No experience is necessary (the cost ranges from $40 to $95), and you'll learn if this glimpse into Neptune's world makes you hunger for more.

Since the best dives on Oahu are offshore, we suggest that you book with a dive operator for a dive from their dive boat. **Atlantis Reef Divers,** 1085 Ala Moana

---

Whale Watching from the *Navatek I,*
Honolulu's High-Tech Cruiser

If you're in Honolulu in the winter months; especially if you're there in February, be sure to go whale watching! Although the best whale spotting is usually from the coasts of Maui, Oahu does get its share of visiting whales, too. The easiest way to sight them is to board the *Navatek I,* a boat whose revolutionary SWATH (small waterplane area twin hull) design gives it high speed and remarkable stability in the rough waters where whales are usually found. The morning cruise, from 8:30 to 11am, departs from Pier 6, next to Aloha Tower, and includes a light breakfast and commentary by an expert naturalist from the University of Hawaii. Cost is $39 adults, $24 children. The Deluxe Luncheon whale-watching cruise, from noon to 2pm, features a two-hour cruise along the Kahala Gold Coast where whales often gather, a buffet lunch, two cocktails, and live Hawaiian music, at a cost of $47 for adults, $28.50 for children.

What's more, you're given a foolproof guarantee: On any cruise that the naturalist does not sight a whale, each passenger receives a coupon good for one free return passage on a morning cruise, Tuesday through Friday.

—Faye Hammel

Blvd. (☎ 808/592-5801), offers two-tank dive trips at $74. One dive is in the *YO-257* wreck and the other is in a shallower reef canyon famous for its green sea turtles. Free hotel pick-up is available in the Waikiki area. Atlantis also offers to videotape your dive—a great way to take Hawaii home with you. On the other side of the island, try **Ocean Concepts Scuba,** 94-547 Ukee St., Waipahu (☎ 808/677-7975); they'll take you into local lava caves, volcanic ledges, and the *Mahi* wreck. Prices range from $45 to $220, depending on the number of dives you do.

If you prefer to dive on your own, write for a copy of the *Dive Hawaii Guide* by Dive Hawaii, a nonprofit association, and the University of Hawaii Sea Grant Extension Service. Mapped and described are 44 locations. Send $2 to UH/SGES, 100 Pope Rd., MSB 226, Honolulu, HI 96844, Attention: Ray Tabata.

SNORKELING

You don't need to take courses to enjoy snorkeling—all you need is a mask, fins, and a snorkel. A word of advice on snorkeling equipment: Many tour operators provide equipment for free, but if your equipment doesn't fit you, it's all but worthless; there's nothing worse than having a snorkeling trip ruined by a leaky mask. You might want to make the investment (about $15 a week) and rent snorkel gear that fits. If you wear eyeglasses, you should be able to rent a suitable prescription mask for an extra charge. The equipment that must fit well is your mask: It should stick to your face without the strap when you inhale (make sure all hair is away from the mask—men with moustaches often have leakages in that area). Fins should fit comfortably and float (you are snorkeling, not swimming great distances, so monstrous fins are not necessarily better).

Snorkel rentals are available at most dive shops and beach activity centers, including **Aloha Dive Shop,** Koko Marina Shopping Center, Honolulu (☎ 808/395-5922), the closest dive shop to the underwater park at Hanauma Bay; **Snorkel Bob's,** also on the way to Hanauma Bay at 700 Kapahulu Ave., Honolulu (☎ 808/735-7944); and **Haleiwa Surf Center,** 66-167 Haleiwa Rd., Haleiwa (☎ 808/637-5051). Haleiwa Surf Center also teaches snorkeling and offers guided snorkeling tours.

Some of the best snorkeling in Oahu is at the underwater park at Hanauma Bay. Sometimes it seems there are more people than fish, but Hanauma has clear, warm waters, an abundance of friendly reef fish, scenic beauty, and protection from the waves. It's easy to get there; go early (by 10am it's packed) and take TheBUS to avoid the crowded parking conditions. For full transit and shuttle information—or directions, if you choose to drive—see "Beaches," above. Hanauma Bay has two reefs, an inner and an outer—the first for novices, the other for experts. The inner reef is calm and shallow (less than 10 feet; in some places you can wade and put your face in the water). Here you'll experience clouds of reef fish, including Moorish idols, scores of butterfly fish, damsel fish, and wrasses.

Serious snorkelers should send for a copy of the book *Dive Hawaii Guide*; for full details, see "Scuba Diving," above.

SNUBA

This new underwater activity is a cross between snorkeling and scuba diving—it allows to stay underwater without the required certification and equipment needed for scuba; an air tank floats on a raft on the surface. A 20- to 25-foot hose is attached to the air tank and provides air for the diver, so that he or she can stay down without the hassle or responsibility of a bulky air tank on their back. **SNUBA Tours of Oahu,** 172 Nawiliwili (☎ 808/922-7762), offers tours from $65 to $95, which includes hotel pick-up, equipment, and instruction.

SUBMARINE DIVING

Here's your chance to play Jules Verne and experience the beauty of the underwater world, all in the comfort (air-conditioned, comfortable seating) of a 65-foot submarine. **Atlantis Submarines Hawaii,** 1600 Kapiolani Blvd. (☎ 808/973-9811), will be happy to take you below the surface. A catamaran picks you up at the Hilton Hawaiian Village hotel dock in Waikiki and takes you to the sub, moored offshore. The submarine (equipped with large portholes) dives to 100 feet for a view of the underwater world. The entire trip is narrated, with professional divers outside the sub feeding the tropical fish so you can get a close look at the critters of the deep. The tour is $79 for adults, $38 for children.

SURFING

In the summertime, when the water is warm and there's a soft breeze in the air, the south swell comes up; it's surf season in Waikiki, the best place to learn how to surf on Oahu. At last count, Oahu had more than 100 surf sites—this is the place to be when the waves are happening.

To learn to surf, go early to **Aloha Beach Service,** next to the Sheraton Moana Surfrider Hotel in Waikiki (☎ 808/922-3111). The beach boys offer surfing lessons for $25 an hour; board rentals are $8 for one hour and $12 for two hours. The only requirement is that you know how to swim.

More experienced surfers should check with the myriad surf shops around Oahu, or call **808/596-SURF** (Surf News Network Surfline) or 808/836-1952 to get the latest information on the surfing conditions. A good surfing spot for advanced surfers is The Cliffs, at the base of Diamond Head. The four- to six-foot waves allow for high-performance surfing. And the view of Diamond Head is great, which helps to make this place paradise for surfers.

WINDSURFING

This is another ocean activity that combines two sports: sailing and surfing. Windsurfers stand on a surfboard that has a sail attached to it, thus bringing the wind and the waves together in a ride that enthusiasts claim is a real adrenalin rush. On Oahu, Kailua Beach Park on the windward side is the home of champion and pioneer windsurfer Robbie Naish. It's also the best place to learn. The oldest and most established windsurfing business in Hawaii is **Windsurf Hawaii,** 156-C Hamakua Dr., Kailua (☎ 808/261-3539). The company offers everything: sales, rentals, instruction, repair, and free advice on where to go when the wind and waves are happening. Lessons start at $37.50 and equipment rental is $25 for a half day and $30 for a full day. Or, you can just venture out to the North Shore to watch the windsurfers dance over the waves from shore.

3 Hiking

Oahu has more forest hiking trails than the Big Island of Hawaii (which is six times Oahu's size). The remote beauty of many of the island's forests, waterfalls, and scenic overlooks can only be reached on foot.

For complete information on Oahu's hiking trails and to obtain free trail maps, contact the **Honolulu Department of Parks and Recreation,** 650 S. King Street, Honolulu, HI 96813 (☎ 808/527-6343) and the **State Division of Forestry and Wildlife,** 1151 Punchbowl, Room 325, Honolulu, HI 96813 (☎ 808/587-0166). For information on trails, hikes, camping, and permits in all state parks, contact the **Hawaii State Department of Land and Natural Resources,** State Parks Division, P.O. Box 621, Honolulu, HI 96825 (☎ 808/587-0300). Another good source of information is the *Hiking/Camping Information Packet* from **Hawaii Geographic Maps and Books,** 49 S. Hotel St., Suite 218, Honolulu, HI 96813 (☎ 808/538-3952), for a cost of $7 (postage included).

The **Hawaiian Trail and Mountain Club,** P.O. Box 2238, Honolulu, HI 96804, offers regularly scheduled hikes on Oahu. You bring your own lunch and drinking water; you'll meet up with the club at the Iolani Palace to join them on a hike. They also have an information packet on hiking and camping in Hawaii, as well as a schedule of all upcoming hikes; send $1.25, plus a legal-sized, self-addressed, stamped envelope to the address above. The **Sierra Club,** 1111 Bishop St., Honolulu, HI 96813 (☎ 808/538-6616), also offers regularly scheduled hikes. The **Hawaii Nature Center** (☎ 808/955-0100) is another organization that offers organized hikes, as well as "Sunday Adventures" for children. Some of their activities require a small fee, but some are free.

Some of Oahu's best hikes are:

KAENA POINT

At the very western tip of Oahu lie the dry, barren lands of Kaena Point. The 853 undeveloped acres of Kaena Point State Park consist of a remote, wild coastline of jagged sea cliffs, deep gulches, sand dunes, endangered plantlife, and a wind- and surf-battered coastline. Kaena means "red hot" or "glowing" in Hawaiian; the name refers to the brilliant sunsets visible from the point.

Kaena is steeped in numerous legends. A popular one concerns the demigod Maui: Maui had a famous hook that he used to raise islands from the sea. He decided that he wanted to bring the islands of Oahu and Kauai closer together, so one day he threw his hook across the Kauai Channel and snagged the island of Kauai (which actually is visible from Kaena Point on clear days). Pulling with all his might, Maui was only able to pull loose a huge boulder, which fell into the waters very close to the present lighthouse at Kaena. The rock is still called Pohaku o Kauai (the rock from Kauai). Like Black Rock in Kaanapali on Maui, Kaena is thought of as the point on Oahu from which souls depart.

To hike out to the departing place, take the clearly marked trailhead from the parking lot of the Makua-Kaena Point State Park. The moderate, five-mile round-trip hike to the point will take a couple of hours. The trail along the cliff passes tide pools abundant in marine life and rugged protrusions of lava reaching out to the turbulent sea; sea birds circle overhead. There are no sandy beaches and the water is nearly always turbulent. During the winter months, when a big north swell is running, the waves at Kaena are the biggest in the state, averaging heights of 30 to 40 feet. Even when seemingly calm, the offshore currents are incredibly powerful, so don't plan to swim. Go early in the morning to see the school of porpoises that frequent the area just offshore.

To get to the trailhead from Honolulu or Waikiki, take the H-1 Freeway west to its end; continue on Hi. 93 past Makaha and follow Hi. 930 to the end of the road. There is no bus service to Kaena Point.

SACRED FALLS

It's easy to see why this place was given the name "Sacred." Clear, cold water, originating from the top of the Koolau Mountains, descends down the Kaluanui Stream and cascades over Sacred Falls into a deep, boulder-strewn pool. The hike to this awe-inspiring waterfall passes under guava and mountain apple trees and through a fern-filled narrow canyon that parallels the stream bed.

A few words of warning before you grab your walking shoes: Do not attempt this hike in wet weather. In fact, the State Parks Division closes the falls if there is a danger of flash floods. This is no idle warning—in 1987, five hikers attempting to reach the falls died in three separate incidents when the normally babbling stream flooded. In October 1993, a Boy Scout troop had to be rescued by helicopter during a flash flood. Another warning of a more human kind: Go in a group—there have recently been a few muggings along the 2.2-mile trail.

The best time to take this hike is in the morning, when the light is good. Be prepared with rain gear and insect repellent. The easy 4.4-mile round-trip will take about two to three hours. To get to the trail, drive north on the Kamehameha Hwy. (Hwy. 83) to the turn-off for Sacred Falls State Park, or take TheBUS no. 20 (Circle Island). The trail begins at the parking lot and heads for the mountains, paralleling the Kaluanui Stream. About a mile into the trail is a grassy area with emergency warning equipment inside a cyclone fence; the trailhead is to the left of the fence. The beginning is a bit rough—the trail is muddy and passes under tangled branches and through a tunnel of Christmas berry. About a half-mile beyond the trailhead, you'll cross the Kaluanui Stream; if the water is high or muddy, don't cross—you could become trapped in the canyon during a flash flood. As you continue up the trail, the canyon becomes increasingly narrow, with steep walls on either side. Be on the lookout for falling rocks. At the end of the trail are the majestic falls and deep pool. The extremely cold pool is home to spidery Malaysian prawns and other species.

HAUULA LOOP

For one of the best views of the coast and the ocean, follow the Hauula Loop Trail on the windward side of the island. It's an easy 2¹/₂-mile loop on a well-maintained path that passes through a whispering ironwood forest and a grove of tall Norfolk pines. The trip takes about three hours and gains some 600 feet in elevation.

To get to the trail, take TheBUS no. 55 (Circle Island) or take Hwy. 83 to Hauula Beach Park. Turn toward the mountains on Hauula Homestead Road; when the road forks to the left at Maakua Road, park on the road. Walk along Maakua Road to the wide, grassy trail that begins the hike into the mountains. The climb is fairly steep for about 300 yards, but continues on to easier-on-the-calves switchbacks as you go up the ridge. Look down as you climb, you'll spot wildflowers and mushrooms among the matted needles. The trail continues up, crossing Waipilopilo Gulch, where you'll see several forms of native plantlife. Eventually you reach the top of the ridge, where the views are spectacular.

The Division of Forestry allows permit camping along the trail, but it's difficult to find a place to pitch a tent on the steep slopes and in the dense forest growth. There are a few places along the ridge wide enough for a tent. Contact the **Division of Forestry and Wildlife,** 1151 Punchbowl St., Honolulu, HI 96813 (☎ 808/587-0166), for information on camping permits.

DIAMOND HEAD CRATER

The entire family can handle this easy walk to the summit of Hawaii's most famous landmark. Children will especially love reaching the top of the 760-foot volcanic cone, where they'll have 360-degree views of Oahu up the leéward coast from Waikiki. The 1.4-mile round-trip will take about an hour.

Diamond-Head was created by a volcanic explosion about half a million years ago. The Hawaiians called the crater Leahi (meaning the brow of the *ahi*, or tuna, referring to the shape of the crater). Diamond Head was considered a sacred spot; King Kamehameha offered human sacrifices at a *heiau* (temple) on the western slope. It wasn't until the 19th century that Mt. Leahi got its current name. A group of sailors found what they thought were diamonds in the crater. It turned out they really only found worthless calcite crystals, but the Diamond Head moniker stuck.

Before you begin your adventure, gather a flashlight (you walk through several dark tunnels), binoculars (for better viewing at the top), water, and your camera (the panoramic view definitely should be captured on film). Go early in the day. To get to the trail, take TheBUS no. 58 from the Ala Moana Shopping Center or drive to Diamond Head Road and 18th Avenue. Follow the road through the tunnel (closed from 6pm to 6am) and park in the lot. The trailhead starts in the parking lot and proceeds along a paved walkway (with handrails) as it climbs up the slope. You'll pass old World War I and II pillboxes, gun emplacements, and tunnels built as part of the Pacific defense network. Several steps take you up to the top observation post on Point Leahi. The views are indescribable.

4 Golf

There are numerous golf courses located all over the island, from reasonably priced public golf courses (with very long waiting lists for tee times, of course) to spectacularly beautiful resort courses.

WEST LOCH MUNICIPAL GOLF COURSE

This municipal course is located about 30 minutes from Waikiki in Ewa Beach. This 6,615-yard, par-72 course is a very challenging course. The big factors here are water—there are lots of water hazards—and constant trade winds, combined with narrow fairways. In fact, the entire layout of the Robin Nelson and Rodney Wright–designed course is a bit unusual. The first hole plays right in front of the clubhouse, the next 10 holes are located on the other side of the freeway, and holes 12 to 18 are back on the starting side. You'll have some help on the water hazards; the course features a "water" driving range, complete with a lake to practice your drives. This is a popular course (greens fees are only $36, including cart) so be sure to call **808/676-2210** at least one week in advance to get a tee time. Facilities include practice greens, pro shop, and restaurant.

HAWAII KAI GOLF COURSE

This par-72, 6,350-yard public course is located between Sandy Beach and Makapuu Point. To get there, take TheBUS no. 58 (Circle Island). This is a moderately challenging course with scenic vistas, and the greens fees are easy on the pocketbook—$80; rates for the par-3 course are a mere $37. Lockers are available. Call **808/395-2358** for tee times.

PALI GOLF COURSE

This beautiful municipal course sits on the windward side of the island near Kaneohe, just below the historical spot where King Kamehameha the Great won the battle to unite the islands of Hawaii. Built in 1953, this par-72, 6,494-yard course has no man-made traps, but it does have a small stream that meanders through the course. If you're off line on the ninth, you'll get to know the stream quite well. The course, designed by Willard G. Wilkinson, makes use of the natural terrain (hills and valleys that make up the majority of the 250 acres). The challenge of the course is the weather—whipping winds and frequent rain squalls. The views include Kaneohe Bay, the towns of Kailua and Kaneohe, and the verdant cliffs of the Koolau Mountains. Due to the frequent rains, you might want to pay for just nine holes and then check out the weather before signing up for the next nine. Greens fees are $30, plus another $12 for an optional cart. Call **808/296-7254** for tee times. Facilities include practice greens, club rental, locker rooms and a restaurant.

TURTLE BAY HILTON GOLF & TENNIS CLUB

Choose either the George Fazio–designed 9-hole course—this is the only course he designed in Hawaii—or the 18-hole Links at Kuilima, designed by Arnold Palmer and Ed Seay; *Golf Digest* rated the latter the fourth best new resort course in 1994. Turtle Bay used to be labeled a "wind tunnel;" it still is one, but the iron-wood trees-have matured and abated the winds somewhat. But Palmer and Seay never meant for golfers to get off too easy—this is a challenging course. The front 9 holes, with rolling terrain, only a few trees, and lots of wind, play like a British Isles course. The back 9 holes have narrower, tree-lined fairways and water. The course circles Punahoolapa Marsh, a protected wetland for endangered Hawaiian waterfowl. To get to Turtle Bay, take TheBUS no. 52 or 55 (Circle Island). Facilities include a pro shop, driving range, putting and chipping green, and snack bar. Greens fees are $99 for the Links at Kuilima and $55 for 18 holes on the 9-hole course. Twilight rates are available. Weekdays are best for tee times; call **808/293-8574**.

KAHUKU GOLF COURSE

Okay, so this is only a 9-hole municipal course and there are no facilities, except a few pull carts that go out with the first few golfers. But this oceanside course is located in the country and has beautiful views, and it's all available at 1950s prices. This is strictly recreational golf, but you'll get plenty of exercise, since you'll most likely have to carry your clubs and walk. Holes 3,4,7, and 8 are right on the shoreline, offering gorgeous views of the North Shore coast. The par-3 holes are not as easy as they look. The greens are small—you better be accurate right from the tee or you'll be in trouble. No reservations are taken; it's all on a first-come, first-served basis (and there are a lot of retired residents who don't mind getting there early). Greens fees are $19 for 9 holes; a pull cart (if there's one available) is another dollar. No club rental is available, so bring your own. *Hint:* if you are staying in Waikiki, call **808/293-5842** to check on the weather, as it can be sunny and clear in Waikiki and rainy and windy in Kahuku.

SHERATON MAKAHA RESORT WEST COURSE

Some 45 miles west of Honolulu is this challenging course, surrounded with tropical beauty—swaying palm trees, brilliant bougainvillea, even strutting peacocks.

Designed by William Bell, the par-72, 7,091-yard course meanders toward the ocean before turning and heading into the Makaha Valley. With the Waianae Mountains rising in the background, the beauty of the course might make it difficult to keep your mind on the game if it weren't for the challenges of it: eight water hazards, 107 bunkers, and constant wind. Facilities include a pro shop, bag storage, and a snack shop. This course is packed on weekends, so it's best to try weekdays. To get there, take TheBUS no. 51-A (Makaha). Greens fees are $80 for Sheraton Makaha Resort guests and $150 for non-guests. Twilight rates are available. Call **808/695-9544**.

5 Other Outdoor Activities

Oahu can fulfill all of your outdoor needs—and even a dream or two—from galloping on horseback over a white-sand beach at sunset to watching top cowboys from across the country compete in a rodeo competition that draws people from all over the globe, and much more.

BICYCLING

Island Triathlon and Bike, 569 Kapahulu Ave. (☎ 808/732-7227), has mountain-bike rentals complete with lock, pump, repair kit, and helmet for $25 the first day and $10 for each additional day. They are also in the know about upcoming bicycle events or interesting bike rides you can enjoy on your own. If you would like some company while you bike, contact the **Hawaii Bicycle League,** P.O. Box 4403, Honolulu, HI 96812 (☎ 808/735-5756). Not only will they fix you up with someone to ride with, but they can also provide you with a schedule of upcoming rides, races, and outings.

GLIDING

Silently soaring through the air on gossamer-like wings, with a bird's-eye view of northern Oahu and the multi-hued reefs below, is an experience you won't want to miss. You can take a glider ride from Dillingham Air Field, in Mokuleia, on Oahu's north shore. A 1- or 2-passenger glider is towed behind a plane; at the right altitude, the tow is dropped and you're left to soar in the thermals—it's the ride of a lifetime. The gliders are grounded only 30 days out of the year, when the normal northerly trade winds shift to southerly winds. To book glider rides, call **Glider Rides** (☎ 808/677-3404 or 808/637-4551); Mr. Bill at Glider Rides has been offering piloted rides longer than anyone else on the island (since 1970). The cost is $60 for one person (plus pilot) for a 20-minute ride, and $90 for two passengers. If you get bit by the gliding bug, Glider Rides also gives instruction at $45 to $70 per session. **Soar Hawaii** (☎ 808/637-3147) also offers rides, starting at $70 for one passenger and $75 for two. Be sure not to leave the ground without your camera!

HORSEBACK RIDING

Kualoa Ranch, 49-560 Kamehameha Hwy., Kaneohe (☎ 808/237-8515), has a number of different tours through their 4,000-acre ranch, starting at $45. They require that you wear long pants and closed-toe shoes. Or you can gallop on the beach at the **Turtle Bay Hilton Golf and Tennis Resort,** 57-091 Kamehameha Hwy., Kahuku (☎ 808/293-8811), where one-hour tours start at $32. If you've dreamed of learning how to ride, the **Hilltop Equestrian Center,** 41-430 Waikupanaha St., Waimanalo (☎ 808/259-8463), will be happy to teach you.

They offer lessons in either British or Western riding style from British Horse Society–accredited instructors for $35.

SPECTATOR SPORTS

Even though Hawaii isn't home to professional football, baseball, or basketball teams, islanders love these sports. The 50,000-seat **Aloha Stadium,** located near Pearl Harbor (☎ 808/486-9300), is host to high school and University of Hawaii football games. It's also the home of three televised football games a year: the Aloha Bowl (top collegiate teams) during Christmas week, the Hula Bowl in January (an all-star game of the top college senior players), and the Pro Bowl (the National Football League's all-star game) played right after the Super Bowl at the beginning of February. There are usually express buses that will take you to the stadium on game nights; they depart from the Ala Moana Shopping Center (TheBUS nos. 47-50 and 52) or from Monsarrat Avenue near Kapiolani Park (TheBUS no. 20). Call TheBUS at 808/848-5555 for times and fares.

The **Neal Blaisdell Center,** at Kapiolani Boulevard and Ward Avenue (☎ 808/521-2911), features the University of Hawaii basketball games—in December you can see the Annual Rainbow Classic, a collegiate basketball invitation tournament—plus professional boxing, Japanese sumo wrestling, and other sporting events. For bus information, call TheBUS at **808/848-5555**.

Another popular spectator sport is polo, played every Sunday from March through August in Mokuleia or Waimanalo. Bring a picnic lunch and enjoy the game. Call **808/637-7656** for details on times and admission charges.

Hawaiian outrigger canoe racing is an extremely popular local sport that takes place every weekend from Memorial Day through Labor Day at various beach parks around Oahu. The races are free and draw huge crowds. Check the local papers for information on the race schedule.

Motor-racing fans can enjoy their sport at **Hawaii Raceway Park,** in Campbell Industrial Park (☎ 808/682-7139), on Friday and Saturday nights.

Some of the other sports events that are scheduled during the year are:

Morey Boogie World Bodyboard Championships. In January at the Bonzai Pipeline, depending on the surf conditions. For information call **808/396-2326**.

Hawaiian Open Golf Tournament. Top professional golfers participate in this nationally televised PGA tournament at the Waialae Country Club in January. For information call **808/526-1232**.

Hawaiian Ladies Open. Top women golfers from the United States and Japan compete at Ko Olina Golf Course in February for a $500,000 purse. For information call **808/676-9957**.

Hawaii Challenge International Sport Kite Championship. Kite fliers from around the world gather in Kapiolani Park in March to compete. For information call **808/922-5483**.

Hawaiian Professional Rodeo. Cowboys compete in rodeo events, which are rounded out with barbecue, country music, and dancing in the dirt for a true Hawaiian *paniolo* experience, in April in Waimanalo. For information call **808/235-3691**.

Bankoh Kayak Challenge. This open-ocean kayak race from Molokai to Oahu takes place in May. For information call **808/254-5055**.

America's Favorite Pastime, Hawaiian Style: Winter Baseball

The winter of 1996 will mark the fourth season for the Hawaii Winter Baseball League. This is professional baseball, played each year from mid-October to mid-December. There are four teams: the Honolulu Sharks, who play at Rainbow Stadium at the University of Hawaii; the West Oahu Cane Fires, who play on the leeward side of Oahu at Hans L'Orange Park in Waipahu; the Hilo Stars, whose home base is Wong Stadium in Hilo on the Big Island; and the Maui Stingrays, whose games are held at the War Memorial Stadium in Wailuku. These are all top-notch players and prospects from the United States, Japan, and Korea. Each team plays some 54 games in 60 days, with the championship game at the end of the season, on December 15. While going to a baseball game anywhere is a uniquely—and universally—American experience, we think it's just a multicultural blast in the islands. Ticket prices are extremely reasonable—from $4 to $6—for an entire evening of fun. Even if you don't like baseball, go for the food; we hear the chili dogs at Maui's War Memorial Stadium are the best anywhere! And we know there are no other ball parks where you can also get a Japanese Bento or a teriyaki plate.

For schedules, consult the local papers or call the team offices: Honolulu Sharks, 808/973-1935; West Oahu Cane Fires, 808/973-7247; Maui Stingrays 808/242-2950; Hilo Stars 808/969-9033.

—Faye Hammel

Kenwood Cup. This international yacht race is held during July in odd-numbered years only, so you won't be able to catch this one until 1997. Sailors from the United States, Japan, Australia, New Zealand, Europe, and Hawaii participate in a series of races around the state. For information call **808/946-9061**.

Na Wahine O Ke Kai. This 41-mile, open-ocean Hawaii outrigger-canoe race from Molokai to Waikiki, which happens in September, attracts international teams. For information call **808/262-7567**.

Waikiki Rough-Water Swim. This popular two-mile, open-ocean swim from Sans Souci Beach to Duke Kahanamoku Beach in Waikiki takes place in September. For information call **808/522-7045**.

Bankoh Molokai Hoe. Top outrigger-canoe teams from around the world compete in a 41-mile, open-ocean race from Molokai to Waikiki in October. For information call **808/261-6615**.

Outrigger Top Gun Hydrofest. From the flying Blue Angels performing acrobatics to hydroplane racing, this is a fun week of aerial activities at Pearl Harbor in October. For information call **808/254-6788**.

Triple Crown of Surfing. The top surfing events held in Hawaii, these November to December competitions include the Pipeline Masters, the Hawaiian Pro, and the World Cup of Surfing. For information call **808/623-8409**.

Honolulu Marathon. More than 20,000 runners descend on Honolulu for the world's second-largest 26.2-mile race in December. For information call **808/734-7200**.

TENNIS

Oahu has 181 free public tennis courts. To get a complete list of all facilities, as well as upcoming tournaments, contact the **Department of Parks and Recreation,** 650 S. King St., Honolulu, HI 96813 (☎ 808/523-4182). The courts are available on a first-come, first-served basis; playing time is limited to 45 minutes.

If you're staying in Waikiki, the **Ilikai Sports Center** at the Ilikai Hotel, 1777 Ala Moana Blvd. (☎ 808/949-3811), has six courts, equipment rental, lessons, and repair service. Courts are $7.50 per person per hour. If you're on the other side of the island, the **Turtle Bay Hilton Golf and Tennis Resort,** 57-091 Kamehameha Hwy., Kahuku (☎ 808/293-8811, ext. 24), has 10 courts, 4 of which are lighted for night play. You must make reservations for the night courts in advance, as they are very popular. Court rates are $12 for the entire day. Equipment rental and lessons are available. The "Thursday Night Mixer" is a very popular activity where both resort guests and non-guests, including local residents, participate in a clinic from 5 to 7pm for $9 per person.

What to See & Do in Honolulu

The fantastic bargain of Honolulu is the enormous number of things to see and do that are inexpensive or free. Part of the reason for this, of course, is Hawaii's need to attract tourists—for tourism is one of its largest industries. But commercial motivations aside, there's enough genuine aloha to go a long way—and to give you so much to do that it becomes hard to decide what to sample and what to pass up!

There are three vital areas where all of the Oahu action takes place; they surround each other like concentric circles. First, there's Waikiki, the heart of the tourist scene. Some people never leave it and feel they've had a marvelous vacation. Just beyond that is the big, exciting world of Honolulu, one of the great cities (the 12th-largest in the United States, in fact). And beyond that, Windward Oahu and the joys of country life and rural beauty. (For details on exploring the island beyond Honolulu and Waikiki, see Chapter 8.) We think you ought to try some of the doings in all three areas.

1 The Top Attractions

DOWNTOWN HONOLULU

✪ Honolulu Academy of Arts

900 S. Beretania St. ☎ **808/531-8865.** Suggested donation $4, $2 students, seniors, and military. Tues–Sat 10am–4:30pm, Sun 1–5pm. Closed major holidays. Bus 1 or 2; get off at the corner of Ward and Beretania, about a 15-minute ride from Waikiki.

Don't leave Hawaii without a visit to the academy, one of the most beautiful small art museums in the world; it offers a look at the best of both Eastern and Western art. Divided into a series of small galleries that open into tranquil courtyards, this is an ideal setting. The Asian courtyard, in particular, is exquisite. There's a superb collection of Asian art—a magnificent sculpture of Kwan Yin, the Chinese goddess of mercy; Chinese scrolls and carvings; Korean ceramics; Japanese screens—as well as a good representation of Western masters, including Picasso, Braque, Monet, and van Gogh. Note also the Kress Collection of Italian Renaissance painting. Stop in the bookshop for prints and other distinctive gift items, and perhaps have a meal at the lovely Garden Café.

> ⭐ **Frommer's Favorite Oahu Experiences**
>
> **Snorkeling at Hanauma Bay.** This idyllic beach cove is the island's best snorkeling area. This marine preserve is home to so many different species, you'll feel like you're in an aquarium, and the fish are generally so tame they'll eat right out of your hand.
>
> **A Stroll Through Historic Chinatown.** Browse the open-air fish and vegetable stalls at the Oahu Market, peek in at herbalists' shops and noodle factories, choose a fresh-baked snack from a Chinese bakery, and visit some of Honolulu's most sophisticated art galleries
>
> **Swimming at Waikiki's Sans Souci Beach.** Just across from Kapiolani Park the turquoise ocean is gentle, the water temperature perfect, and the crowds far away.
>
> **A Visit to Byodo-In Temple on the Windward Coast.** Surrounded by a fragrant and beautiful classical Japanese garden, this exact replica of the venerable Byodo-In in Uji, Japan, is home to a magnificent carving of Amida, the Buddha of the Western Paradise.
>
> **Sunset Cocktails at the Open-Air House Without a Key.** A great way to experience one of Waikiki's premier (and original) resorts, the Halekulani Hotel. As a beautiful hula dancer sways to a traditional Hawaiian melody and the sun sinks slowly into the placid Pacific, you'll know that picture-postcard paradise still exists.

✪ Mission Houses Museum

553 S. King St. ☎ **808/531-0481.** Admission (including 45-minute tour) $5 adults, $4 seniors and military, $1 youths 6–15, free for children under 6. Tues–Sat 9am–4pm, Sun noon–4pm. Bus 2 to the State Capitol; then walk one block down Punchbowl to King St., turn left, and walk half a block to the Mission Houses. The Waikiki Trolley also passes within a block.

Three 19th-century buildings offer tremendous insight into the lives of the missionaries in Hawaii—and the unlikely intermingling of New England and Polynesia. One of the houses, the home of missionary families, was built of ready-cut lumber that was shipped around Cape Horn from New England; a second, made of coral, houses a replica of the first printing press in the islands, which produced a Hawaiian spelling book in 1822; the third, also of coral, was the warehouse and home of the mission's first business agent.

An orientation exhibit and video introduces the Mission, its work with Hawaiians, and the controversy that still surrounds the role it played in Hawaii's history. Monthly "Living History" programs feature historical role-playing, hearth cooking, storytelling, work demonstrations, and candlelit evenings. Contact the museum for a current schedule of monthly events.

Be sure to visit the Museum Shop, with an outstanding collection of Hawaiian and Pacific handcrafts, Hawaiian quilt patterns and kits, children's games and clothing, and many books. And try to take one of their morning walking tours of historic Honolulu, held on select weekdays; call for days offered. Reservations are required. The cost of $7 includes museum admission.

✪ Kawaiahao Church

957 Punchbowl. ☎ **808/522-1333**. Admission free. Mon–Fri 9am–3pm, Sat 9am–noon, Sun services at 8 and 10:30am. Group tours Mon–Fri by appointment. Bus 2 to Punchbowl and Beretania Sts.; then walk one block to King St.

The tall, feathered kahilis signify at once that this is royal ground. You're standing in the Westminster Abbey of Hawaii, the scene of pomp and ceremony, coronations, and celebrations since its dedication in 1841. On March 12, 1959, the day Hawaii achieved statehood, the old coral church was filled with ecstatic islanders ringing its bell noisily, giving thanks for the fulfillment of a dream long denied. The next day, the Rev. Abraham Akaka linked the spirit of aloha with the spirit of Christianity in a sermon that has since become a classic in the writings of Hawaii. Note the vestibule memorial plaques to Hawaiian royalty and to the Rev. Hiram Bingham, the missionary who designed the church. Note, too, the outstanding collection of portraits of the Hawaiian monarchy by artist Patric. If you have time, come back on Sunday morning at 8 or 10:30am to hear a Hawaiian-English service and some beautiful Hawaiian singing.

✪ Iolani Palace

S. King and Richards Sts. ☎ **808/522-0832**. Tours, $4 adults, $1 children 5–12; children under 5 not admitted. Tours, Wed–Sat every 15 minutes 9am–2:15pm. Bus 2 to Punchbowl and Beretania Sts.

Take a good look at the only state residence of royalty on American soil. The state capitol until 1969, it was built during the glittering golden era of Hawaii by King Kalakaua and his queen, Kapiolani. But it housed its royal tenants for only 11 years, from 1882 until the monarchy was overthrown in 1893 by a group of haoles linked to American sugar interests. Kalakaua's successor, his sister, Queen Liliuokalani, spent nine months in the royal bedroom under house arrest after the abortive coup to restore the monarchy. (She is known for her song of farewell, "Aloha Oe.")

Now, after nine years of work and at a total cost of $7 million, a massive restoration has been completed by the Friends of Iolani Palace, and the Hawaiian flag flies over it once again. Some of the furnishings are still being restored, but several rooms are ready for the public, and the American-Florentine building is eminently worth seeing. The crowns of King Kalakaua and Queen Kapiolani, as well as the royal scepter and sword of state, are on display in the throne room.

Tours are conducted by extremely knowledgeable docents who will fill you in on plenty of Hawaiian history as they show you the throne room with the king's tabu stick (made of narwhal tusk and topped by a gold sphere), the king's quarters, the entry hall, and the dining room with its royal portraits of European monarchs. Reservations are requested, and tickets not claimed 15 minutes before the start of a tour will be sold to anyone who happens to be waiting for a cancellation. You'll have to don enormous khaki "airplane slippers" over your shoes to protect the delicate wooden floors.

Also on the grounds are the Archives of Hawaii (open Monday through Friday from 8am to 4:30pm), the largest collection of Hawaiiana in existence.

✪ Hawaii Maritime Center

Pier 7. ☎ **808/536-6373**. Admission (including boarding *Falls of Clyde*) $7 adults, $4 children 6–17, free for children under 6. Daily 9am–5pm. Closed Christmas. Bus 19 or 20 (Airport) to the Federal Building. There's a free shuttle to and from Waikiki via Hilo Hattie buses; the Waikiki Trolley also stops here.

Honolulu Attractions

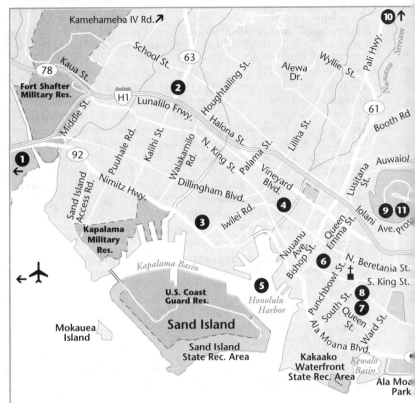

Kamehameha IV Rd.

School St. — 63

78 — Kaua St.

Fort Shafter Military Res.

H1 — Lunalilo Frwy.

Middle St.

92 — Nimitz Hwy.

Sand Island Access Rd.

Puuhale Rd.

Kalihi St.

Waiakamilo Rd.

Dillingham Blvd.

N. King St.

Iwilei Rd.

Houghtailing St.

Halona St.

Palama St.

2

Alewa Dr.

Wyllie St.

Pali Hwy.

Nuuanu Stream

10

Liliha St.

Vineyard Blvd.

4

61

Booth Rd.

Auwaiol

Lusitana St.

Iolani Ave.

Pros

9 11

Kapalama Military Res.

3

Kapalama Basin

U.S. Coast Guard Res.

Sand Island

Sand Island State Rec. Area

Mokauea Island

5

Honolulu Harbor

Nuuanu Ave.

Bishop St.

Queen Emma St.

6

N. Beretania St.

Punchbowl St.

S. King St.

South St.

8

Queen St.

7

Ward St.

Ala Moana Blvd.

Kakaako Waterfront State Rec. Area

Kewalo Basin

Ala Moa Park

M a m a l a   B a y

OAHU

Honolulu

Bishop Museum & Planetarium **2**
The Contemporary Museum **12**
Damien Museum **16**
Dole Pineapple Cannery **3**
Foster Botanical Garden **4**
Gandhi Statue **18**
Hawaii Maritime Center **5**

Honolulu Academy of Arts **9**
Honolulu Zoo **17**
Iolani Palace **6**
Kapiolani Park **19**
Kawaiahao Church **8**
Lyon Arboretum **13**
Mission Houses Museum **7**

1007

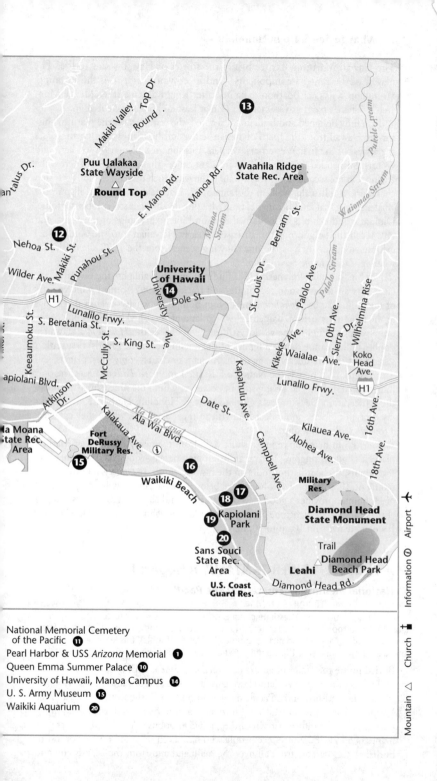

National Memorial Cemetery
  of the Pacific ⓫
Pearl Harbor & USS *Arizona* Memorial ❶
Queen Emma Summer Palace ⓾
University of Hawaii, Manoa Campus ⓮
U. S. Army Museum ⓯
Waikiki Aquarium ⓴

Mountain △   Church ✝︎■   Information ⓘ   Airport ✈

The Hawaii Maritime Center brings the stories of Hawaii's seas to life. The newest of the center's components—and its crowning glory—is the stunning, $6-million Kalakaua Boathouse, named after King Kalakaua (the "Merrie Monarch"). There's plenty to see here, so plan at least an hour to take it all in.

Tastefully designed and brilliantly executed, the center traces the maritime history of Hawaii from the first Polynesian settlers of the islands, and encompasses the arrival of the first Westerners, whalers, missionaries, plantation workers, and visitors. Suspended from the ceiling are giant canoes that once voyaged across the Pacific. On the second floor, you'll want to linger at such displays as the 1850s ship chandlery, a full-scale, walk-in diorama of H. Hackfeld & Co., the all-purpose whaler's store that later became Hawaii's leading department store, Liberty House. Dioramas and exhibits of the famed Matson Line luxury ships of the 1930s and '40s recall the languorous romanticism of early Hawaiian tourism. Audiovisual exhibits abound, such as the one showing scenes from the 1922 silent film on whaling, *Down to the Sea in Ships.*

Exhibits include "Polynesian Wayfinding," which highlights the revival of ancient Hawaiian navigation techniques and tracks the 1992 South Pacific voyages of the sailing canoe *Hokule'a,* The 45-foot humpback whale skeleton that hangs in the museum's atrium, named Leiiwi (garland of cherished bones), is one of the only two of its kind in the world. At Pier 7 you can see the *Hokule'a,* a Hawaiian double-hulled canoe that is a replica of the one in which the islands' first settlers sailed from the Marquesas, using no instruments or charts—only stars, planets, and ocean signs. Also here is the National Historic Landmark *Falls of Clyde,* the only four-masted, full-rigged sailing ship in existence. Climb the nine (short) flights to the Observation Deck to see a glorious view of Honolulu Harbor. Kids will enjoy everything here, and especially a visit to the *Cory Sause,* where they can steer a tot-size replica of a ship.

Note: From here you're just a short walk from the new Aloha Tower Marketplace, a fabulous ongoing festival and shopping bazaar, with over 200 shops and restaurants, fireboat harbor tours on the historic *Abner T. Longley,* and free entertainment. (For details, see "Shopping," below.) Aloha Tower itself, long a symbol of Honolulu, provides a good view of the harbor and city in all directions, and it's also a fine spot for nighttime photography of harbor lights and the downtown area. It's open daily from 10am to 10pm.

PUNCHBOWL, LOWER TANTALUS & NUUANU

✪ National Memorial Cemetery of the Pacific

Punchbowl Crater. ☎ **808/541-1434.** Admission free. Daily 8am–5:30pm. *Note:* Possible federal budget cuts may necessitate closings on some days; call before coming out. Directions: Take bus no. 2 from Waikiki toward town (request a transfer). Get off at Alapai Street and walk half a block left and pick up bus no. 15 (Pacific Heights); this leaves every hour on the half hour, so time your trip carefully. Get off at Puowaina Drive and walk 10 minutes.

Buried inside the crater of an extinct volcano (named, with prophetic irony, the Hill of Sacrifice by the ancient Hawaiians) are some 37,000 American service personnel who perished in the Pacific during World War II, the Korean War, and the Vietnam War. Astronaut Ellison Onizuka is also buried here (visit the administration office for information regarding grave locations). Also listed here are the names of all Pacific war service people who have been recorded missing or lost or buried at sea. Parents from all over the mainland and from the islands come to

Punchbowl on pilgrimages. The endless rows of gravestones of young people form a sobering sight. Walk for another 10 minutes to the lookout at the crater's rim for a sweeping panorama of Honolulu just below.

Note: There's an easier way to get to Punchbowl and to also be guided on a walking tour of the cemetery, thanks to the American Legion, which began last year to offer $15 one-hour tours which include round-trip transportation from Waikiki hotels. Inquire at your hotel travel desk, or phone the American Legion at **808/946-6383.**

Queen Emma Summer Palace

2913 Pall Hwy. ☎ **808/595-3167.** Admission $4 adults, $1 children 12–18, 50¢ children under 12. Daily 9am–4pm. Directions: From Waikiki take bus no. 4 (Nuuanu/Dowsett from the mountain side of Kuhio Ave.); ask the driver to let you off near the palace.

Emma and her husband, King Kamehameha IV, called their Victorian country retreat Hanaiakamalama, and it is faithfully maintained as a museum by the Daughters of Hawaii. Hawaiiana mingles comfortably with the 19th-century European furnishings of which Hawaiian royalty was so fond. Note the superb collection of feather capes and kahili. There are conducted tours through the rooms for all visitors.

Royal Mausoleum

2261 Nuuanu Ave. Admission free. Mon–Fri 8am–4:30pm. Closed Holidays, except Kuhio Day (March 26) and Kamehameha Day (June 11). Directions: See Queen Emma Summer Palace, above.

Here's where the last of the Kamehameha and Kalakau dynasties and others of royal blood are buried. The curator gives a short orientation in the chapel; then you're free to pay your respects.

Foster Botanical Garden

50 N. Vineyard Blvd. ☎ **808/522-7060.** Admission (to Foster Garden) $1, free for children under 13 with an adult; guided tours free with admission. Daily 9am–4pm. Guided tours, Mon–Fri at 1pm (reservations recommended; call 808/522-7066). Closed New Year's Day, Christmas Day. Directions: From Waikiki take bus no. 2, 19, or 20 (Airport or Airport-Hickam) toward downtown (request a transfer); get off at the corner of Hotel and Bethel Sts. and change to bus no. 4 (Nuuanu/Dowsett); ask the driver to let you off at the garden, located at the corner of Nuuanu Ave. and Vineyard Blvd. The Waikiki Trolley also stops here.

This is a marvelously cool oasis on a hot day, and an impressive botanical collection can be found here. There are 14 acres of rare trees, flowers, plants, and unusual species of vegetation, collected from the tropics and subtropics of the world. Orchids bloom throughout the year. Here you can measure your minuteness against a tree 20 times taller than you are, and ogle such rare specimens as the cannonball tree, the bombax, and the gold tree. On the grounds is a C-shaped granite monument, presented in 1960 to Honolulu by its cousin city of Hiroshima, from which most of the first Japanese immigrants came to work the island plantations. A free, self-guided-tour brochure is available at the reception area.

Note: Foster Botanical Garden is one component of the Honolulu Botanical Gardens, which also has four other splendid gardens to visit: the **Liliuokalani Botanical Garden** on N. Kuakini Street, a $7^1/_2$-acre site, once part of Foster Botanical Garden but now separated from it by the HI Freeway, with native plants, a stream, and waterfalls; the **Wahiawa Botanical Garden** in Wahiawa, a 27-acre rain forest in central Oahu; **Hoomaluhia Botanical Gardens** in Kaneohe, 400 lush acres at the base of the Koolau Mountains in Windward Oahu, and **Koko**

Crater Botanical Garden, near Sandy Beach, still in the early stages of development. Free admission to these four gardens. For information on all of these gardens, phone 808/522-7060.

UNIVERSITY OF HAWAII

Although many of Hawaii's socially prominent families still send their children off to mainland colleges (in the old days it was the Punahou-Yale route), the island's own university is the goal of thousands of others. Established in 1907 as a small agricultural and mechanical arts college, the Manoa campus (☎ 808/965-8855) has grown into an important center for the study of tropical agriculture, marine biology, geophysics, astronomy, linguistics, and other fields.

The **East-West Center** at the Manoa campus is particularly noteworthy. A meeting place of Eastern and Occidental cultures, it brings together students, professionals, and research scholars from Asia, the Pacific islands, and the United States for an exciting exchange of ideas.

The starkly simple East-West Center buildings are a masterful blend of Eastern and Western styles. Free tours leave Wednesday at 1:30pm from the Friends Lounge on the garden level of Thomas Jefferson Hall, but it's easy enough to walk around by yourself. The lounge area of Jefferson must certainly be one of the most interesting student centers in the world. Where else might you pick up copies of *Thailand Illustrated,* the *Wall Street Journal,* and *Social Casework,* all from one rack? Asian and other art exhibitions are frequently held in the lounge art gallery.

Walk now to the rear of Jefferson for a peaceful moment at the lyrical Japanese garden, with its waterfalls, stone ornaments, lanterns, and flashing carp. And be sure to see the **John Fitzgerald Kennedy Theater,** one of the best equipped in the world for staging both Western and Eastern dramas. It's the official home of the university's dance and drama department, and a technological center that draws theater people from both sides of the Pacific to study, teach, and produce plays. A typical season includes productions of a Japanese Kabuki classic, Shakespeare, and a contemporary Broadway comedy. An authentic Beijing opera was recently staged here—in English.

You'll want to tour the rest of the University of Hawaii campus, too. Stop in at the University Relations office in Bachman Annex 6 to obtain maps and directions for a self-guided tour. You'll find plenty to see, especially if you're interested in art: There are two art galleries, and frescoes, sculptures, and works in other media are everywhere. If your visit falls on a Monday, Wednesday, or Friday, you can be taken on a one-hour walking tour that focuses on history, art, and architecture. It leaves at 2pm from the forum area of the Manoa Campus Center. For information, call **808/956-7235.** Nature-lovers can have a treat here, too, trying to identify the 560 or so varieties of tropical plants and trees that bloom all over campus. The university's map shows names and locations.

GREATER HONOLULU

✪ Bishop Museum
The State Museum of Natural and Cultural History, 1525 Bernice St. ☎ **808/847-3511.** Admission (including a 1pm daily music-and-dance presentation and entrance to the Bishop Museum Planetarium, see below) $7.95 adults; $6.95 children 6–17, active military, and seniors; children under 6 free. Daily 9am–5pm. Closed Christmas. Directions: Bus no. 2 to School and Kapalama Sts.; walk one block makai on Kapalama and then turn right on Bernice St.; the entrance is midblock.

Inside the museum's stone walls (which look more like those of a fortress) is a world center for the study of the Pacific—its peoples, culture, history, artifacts. Most fascinating for visitors is the Hawaiian Hall, where special exhibits illustrate particular aspects of early Hawaiian culture. Note the collection of priceless feather cloaks; one uses half a million feathers from the rare mamo bird (each bird produced only a few feathers, so the kings built up feather treasuries—which were among the prime spoils of war). Other exhibits re-create the way of life of the Hawaiians, showing the outrigger canoes, a model heiau, weapons, or wooden calabashes; tracing the history of the Hawaiian monarchy; or exploring the marine and plant life of the Pacific. A "please touch" gallery for children in the Hall of Discovery ties in with exhibits throughout the museum. All this, plus the fascinating exhibits of ethnographic art, makes for a rewarding visit. Stop in at Shop Pacifica for Hawaiian gifts, a cut above the usual, with books on Hawaiian and other Pacific cultures, handcrafted feather leis and native koa-wood boxes and bowls, reproductions of Polynesian artifacts, and rare and unique jewelry of the Pacific.

Note: If you're interested in studying **Hawaiian crafts,** you've come to the right place. Classes are held Monday through Saturday from 9am to 3pm, at a nominal charge (usually $5, plus a materials cost). It's quilting on Monday and Friday, fresh-flower lei-making on Tuesday, lauhala weaving and hula-implement making on Wednesday. Classes are held in the Atherton Halau (call **808/847-3511** for schedules), also the site of special events, which are usually held on weekends. Inquire, too, about field trips and special programs.

Bishop Museum Planetarium

☎ **808/848-4136** for recorded program information. Admission $3.50; or included with museum admission. Directions: See Bishop Museum, above.

Here's a great spot for anyone interested in space exploration and astronomy. Sky shows are held every day at 11am and 2pm, and also on Friday and Saturday at 7pm. After the evening shows, there's free observatory telescope viewing, weather permitting.

PEARL HARBOR

✪ USS *Arizona* Memorial

☎ **808/422-0561.** Admission free. Tours daily 8am–3pm. Directions: From Waikiki, bus no. 20 and 47 go to Pearl City; from the Ala Moana Center, take bus no. 51 or 52. The trip should take about an hour. Ask the driver to let you off at the USS *Arizona* Memorial. Private bus service is $6 round-trip (☎ 808/926-4747).

Anyone who remembers—or has heard about—December 7, 1941, should not leave the Hawaiian Islands without seeing Pearl Harbor. As many as 5,000 visitors—many from Japan—come here every day. The handsome $4.2-million visitor center provides the starting point for your boat trip to the USS *Arizona* Memorial. Its museum contains exhibits related to the events surrounding the attack on Pearl Harbor by Japan. Step up to the information desk, where you will be given a tour number, and find out exactly when your shuttle boat will leave. While you're waiting, you can study a detailed mural of the *Arizona* or check out the bookshop. When your number is called, you enter the theater to see a short film, and are then ferried on a navy boat to the memorial.

Dedicated in 1962, the memorial is a white-concrete bridgelike structure rising starkly above the hull of the battleship USS *Arizona,* victim of several direct hits on the day that bombs fell on Hawaii, and the tomb of over 1,100 American service personnel (some 2,395 in all were killed that day). The outlines of the ship shimmer just below the water, and oil slicks still rise from the rusting hulk.

Note: If the weather is stormy, call the *Arizona* Memorial at 808/422-2771, ext. 119 to find out if the boats will be operating. Bathing suits and bare feet are taboo.

USS Bowfin Submarine Museum & Park

☎ **808/423-1341.** Admission $8 adults, $5 military, $3 children. Children under 4 admitted to the museum free, but are not allowed on the submarine for safety reasons. Daily 8am–5pm. Directions: For shuttle service from Waikiki, $3 each way, call 808/732-4436. For public transportation, see the USS *Arizona* Memorial, above. Closed Thanksgiving, Christmas, and New Year's Day.

Adjacent to the USS *Arizona* Memorial visitor center, this is the home of the USS *Bowfin,* a World War II submarine launched a year after the attack on Pearl Harbor. Children in particular will enjoy going below to explore the decks of the submarine where the 80-man crew served. *Bowfin* completed nine successful war patrols and earned the Presidential Unit Citation and Navy Unit Commendation. There are fewer than 20 U.S. World War II submarines in existence today, and USS *Bowfin,* nicknamed the "Pearl Harbor Avenger," was named a National Historic Landmark in 1986. You can also explore the Bowfin Museum, with its impressive collection of submarine-related artifacts, see a 1960s TV film featuring the *Bowfin,* and tour the park grounds to view rare artifacts such as a *kaiten,* a Japanese suicide torpedo. The Waterfront Memorial honors submariners lost during World II.

VISITING PEARL HARBOR BY SEA

Another way to get to Pearl Harbor—and a moving and dramatic one—is by sea, aboard Paradise Cruise's sleek luxury vessel, *Star of Honolulu.* During the roughly 45-minute cruise to Pearl, '40s music plays on the loudspeaker, and a thoughtful narration, in both English and Japanese, sets the scene for the momentous events of December 7, 1941. At the *Arizona* Memorial, the ship stops for a few moments as the captain tosses a lei upon the waters in tribute to those still entombed there. The trip takes the better part of the morning (from about an 8am pickup at Waikiki hotels to a return around noon). Cost is $26.50 adults, $13.25 for children. Highly recommended. For reservations, call **808/593-2493** or **800/ 334-6191** from the continental U.S.

2 More Attractions

✪ The Contemporary Museum at the Spalding Estate

2411 Makiki Heights Dr. ☎ **808/526-1322.** Admission $5 ages 13 and over; free for children 12 and under; free for everyone the third Thurs of every month. Tues–Sat 10am–4pm. Bus 15 to Makiki Heights Dr.

With the opening of this museum, Honolulu has become the art center of the Pacific. The lovely old 1920s mansion in a magnificent garden setting overlooking the city and the sea has been transformed into a series of state-of-the-art galleries, housing temporary exhibits of works by artists of local, national, and international reputation. A permanent pavilion houses David Hockney's installation based on his stage set from the Metropolitan Opera production of *L'Enfant et les Sortilèges,* complete with a stereo sound system playing the Ravel opera that inspired this major work. Galleries, art, gardens—all vie for attention. The gardens alone, a series of exquisite terraces meandering down a hillside to a stream bed, falls, and pools, are worth the trip. They were designed by a Japanese landscape artist as a place to experience harmony, so each vista has its stone seat for contemplation.

Damien Museum

130 Ohua St. ☎ **808/923-2690.** Admission free, donations accepted. Mon–Fri 9am–3pm, Sat 9am–noon. Closed Holidays. Directions: Within walking distance of most major hotels, or take TheBUS no. 8, 19, or 20 running in a Diamond Head direction.

In the Diamond Head area, behind St. Augustine's Catholic Church, this small museum presents a moving account of the work that Father Damien did with the victims of leprosy on the island of Molokai. The museum contains prayer books used by Father Damien in his ministry, as well as his personal items. A continuously running video recounts Damien's story.

Dole Pineapple Cannery

At Cannery Square.

Although the Dole Pineapple Cannery is no longer in operation, you can still take a free bus out to Cannery Square to see a multi-media show on the role of Dole in Hawaiian history and to shop and browse at Cannery Courtyard. By the time you read this, there will be a huge (44 acres eventually) outlet shopping complex— to be constructed in five phases—here. Unfortunately, as we go to press, the names of the shops (up to 100 of them) are not for publication, but we can tell you this: The Horizon Group, the developers, are committed to preserving the history of this important Hawaiian landmark. A self-guided tour of the area is planned, and much of the actual cannery equipment will be on view as sculpture—a tribute to this major era of the economic history of Hawaii.

Especially for Kids

Many of the attractions described above are perfect for kids. At Pearl Harbor, U.S. history comes to life with a visit to the **USS *Arizona* Memorial** and **USS *Bowfin* Park.** At the **Hawaii Maritime Center,** kids can steer a child-size ship's replica. Youngsters will love a ride on the historic fireboat **Abner T. Longley** at the Aloha Tower Marketplace. The **Bishop Museum** hosts regularly changing exhibitions for families on a wide range of topics, such as ecology and archeology. Older children will be enthralled with the exhibits at the **Bishop Museum Planetarium.** By the end of 1996, the **Kahala Hilton Hotel** should have finished its renovation, and then kids can get close to porpoises at the daily feedings. **Sea Life Park Hawaii** (see Chapter 8, "Exploring Oahu") is a big favorite with kids of all ages, as is the **Polynesian Cultural Center** (also in Chapter 8). The excellent Hawaii Children's Museum was "on vacation" as of this writing, but will reopen in mid-1996 as the Children's Discovery Center in the as-of-yet unbuilt Kakaako Waterfront Park. Check local papers for information, or phone 808/592-5437. Kids also love the **Honolulu Zoo** and the **Waikiki Aquarium.** And the best place to take the kids to let off some steam and have some real Hawaiian fun is . . . Waikiki Beach, of course!

For bus information (pickups are made every hour at 10 Waikiki hotels), see local tourist papers or call **808/548-6601.** You can also take TheBUS no. 19 (Airport Hickam) to Cannery Square.

Gandhi Statue

In front of the Honolulu Zoo. Directions: See Honolulu Zoo, below.

An impressive statue of Mahatma Gandhi was created by New York artist Zlatko Paunov as a gift to the people of Hawaii from the Jhamanadas Watumull Fund. The statue is accompanied by a plaque quoting from Gandhi's philosophy: "It is possible to live in peace."

✪ Honolulu Zoo

151 Kapahulu Ave. ☎ **971-7171.** Admission $3 adults, free for ages 12 and under. Daily 9am–4:30pm (June–Aug, also Wed to 7:30pm). Closed New Year's Day and Christmas Day. Directions: You can walk from most major hotels or take TheBUS no. 8, 19, 20, 58, or 2 (Kapiolani Park), running in a Diamond Head direction.

The big news at the Honolulu Zoo is the opening of their multimillion-dollar African Savanna, which allows the visitor to see wild animals in settings approximating their native habitats. The Asiatic elephants are great favorites with the crowd; call for times of their public demonstrations. With Diamond Head providing the background, plenty of trees and flowers (including orchids, a giant banyan, and date palms), it's one of the most charming small zoos anywhere.

During the summer there's free entertainment on Wednesday starting at 6pm at the stage under the earpod tree, just behind the flamingos. Take a picnic supper and join the fun. Local artists hang their work on the fence outside on Tuesday, Saturday, and Sunday.

Kapiolani Park

Kalakaua and Monsarrat Aves. Admission free. Directions: Take TheBUS no. 2 (Waikiki-Kapiolani Park) from Kuhio Ave. in a Diamond Head direction.

This 99¹/₂-acre park has facilities for just about every recreation, from tennis, soccer, and rugby to archery and picnicking. The Royal Hawaiian Band plays on Sundays in the bandstand, and major musical events take place in the Waikiki Shell. For a particularly beautiful view, note Diamond Head framed in the cascading waters of the splendid Louise C. Dillingham Fountain.

Bordering the ocean on the right is a stretch of wide, palm-dotted grass lawn with a fringe of sand to let you know you're still at the beach. Swimming here is excellent, since the surf is quite mild; it's a big favorite with local families. Kapiolani Beach Park, with restrooms, picnic tables, and snack bar, is just ahead.

Lyon Arboretum

3860 Manoa Rd. ☎ **808/988-7378.** Donation requested. Mon–Sat 9am–3pm. Tours given first Fri and third Wed at 1pm, third Sat at 10am; group tours by prior arrangement. Closed public holidays. Directions: Take TheBUS no. 8 from Waikiki to Ala Moana; transfer to no. 5 (Manoa Valley); from the end of the line, it's a 30-minute walk. (Phone for driving directions.)

Few tourists know about the arboretum, but Honolulu residents certainly do. It's prized as one of the most beautiful nature spots in Honolulu, an important research facility for the University of Hawaii, and an educational center where you can take short courses in such subjects as flower arrangement, bonsai, island cookery, orchid growing, and much more. You're welcome to visit on your own, admiring the beautiful gardens lush with orchids, camellias, gardenias, ginger, coffee, and many native plants; if you can manage to take a tour (see Section 3 below), even better. Visit the gift and bookstore, which has high-quality items.

U.S. Army Museum

Fort DeRussy Park. ☎ **808/438-2821.** Admission free. Tues–Sun 10am–4:30pm. Bus 8 (Ala Moana Shopping Center) from Kuhio Avenue, in an Ewa direction.

Housed in Battery Randolph, built in 1909 as a key installation in defense of Honolulu and Pearl Harbor, this museum contains military memorabilia dating from ancient Hawaiian warfare to the present. On the upper deck, the Corps of Engineers Pacific Regional Visitors Center graphically shows how the corps works with the civilian community in managing water resources in an island environment.

Waikiki Aquarium

2777 Kalakaua Ave. ☎ **808/923-9741.** Admission $6 adults, $4 seniors, $2.50 juniors 13–17; children 12 and under free. Daily 9am–4:30pm. Closed Thanksgiving and Christmas. Directions: Take TheBUS no. 2 (Waikiki-Kapiolani Park) from Kuhio Ave. in a Diamond Head direction.

A 19-month, $3.1-million renovation has made the always entertaining Waikiki Aquarium more enthralling than ever. New exhibits include the Sea Visions Theater and accompanying jellyfish display, the outdoor Northwest Hawaiian Islands habitat with endangered Hawaiian monk seals, the Mahimahi Hatchery, and an expanded Hunters on the Reef shark exhibit. You can also see, among other sea creatures, the *lauwiliwilinuknukuoioi;* if you can't pronounce it, just ask for the long-nosed butterfly fish. An outdoor display, Edge of the Reef, is a simulated living-reef environment that includes hundreds of colorful fish, live coral, and a tidal surge.

A Historic Chinatown District Walking Tour

Take this two- to three-hour tour during the day—the area is not considered safe at night. From Waikiki, take TheBUS no. 2 or 19 (Airport or Airport-Hickam) or no. 20 (Airport) toward downtown Honolulu. Get off at Maunakea Street and you'll find yourself in the midst of the **Historic Chinatown District.** With its jumble of shops laden with crafts, herbs, and Chinese groceries, and with many new merchants from Vietnam, Thailand, and other parts of Southeast Asia here, the area is more fascinating and exotic than ever. There are several Chinese acupuncturists and Hong Kong herb doctors here (many locals swear by them).

Begin with a look at an old Chinatown fixture, the **Oahu Market,** on King Street near the waterfront. The open-air stalls contain all variety of fish, poultry, and vegetables, in a dizzying array. A look at pre-supermarket Hawaii!

Next, walk over to one of the area's newer landmarks, the **Chinese Cultural Plaza,** in the block bounded by Beretania, Maunakea, Kukui, and River streets. This is not one of our favorite shopping centers, since many of the goods seem overpriced. We do, however, like the Dragon Gate Bookstore, with dragon puppets, books, and calendars (in Chinese, of course), as well as Excellent Gems and Bin Ching, both of which carry pearls and jade and do jewelry repairing.

The biggest new development in Chinatown, however, is the **Maunakea Marketplace,** in the block bounded by Hotel, Puahi, and Maunakea streets. There's a statue of Confucius, a clock tower, and thousands of bricks engraved with personal messages. The office of the Historical Hawaii Foundation is here, as is the Chinese Visitor Center, where you can pick up self-guided tour maps and tapes of Chinatown, and see a historical presentation on old Chinatown.

The Maunakea Marketplace Food Court has a truly international array of fastfood stands, with a central courtyard for dining. You can sample the foods of

Historic Chinatown District

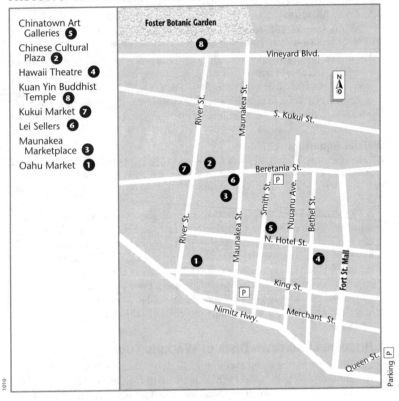

Chinatown Art Galleries **5**
Chinese Cultural Plaza **2**
Hawaii Theatre **4**
Kuan Yin Buddhist Temple **8**
Kukui Market **7**
Lei Sellers **6**
Maunakea Marketplace **3**
Oahu Market **1**

Foster Botanic Garden

Vineyard Blvd.

River St.

Maunakea St.

S. Kukui St.

Beretania St.

Smith St.

Nuuanu Ave.

Bethel St.

N. Hotel St.

Fort St. Mall

King St.

Nimitz Hwy.

Merchant St.

Queen St.

Parking

Thailand, Korea, the Philippines—even Puerto Rico—as well as China, of course. Directly behind the food court is a fresh seafood market, wholesale and retail; many restaurants shop here.

As you wander through Chinatown's little streets, you'll notice that Old Chinatown is giving way to several new buildings, a park, and continued upgrading of historic older buildings such as the **Hawaii Theatre,** 1130 Bethel St., which is in the process of being restored to its original '20s art deco architecture. It has hosted everything from beauty pageants and band concerts to the Hawaii International Film Festival and even political functions.

There are now about a dozen art galleries in the neighborhood, including **Pegge Hopper,** at 1164 Nuuanu St. (her works are seen all over the islands); and **Ramsay,** 1128 Smith St., the renowned pen-and-ink artist, who has the charming Gallery Café adjacent, for light, sophisticated meals.

Before you leave Chinatown, be sure to check out the **lei sellers** on Maunakea Street, near Beretania. There are at least a dozen of them, and they offer the best prices and finest work in Honolulu.

You could end your tour here, or you may choose to walk another few blocks to climax your trip with an exotic sight: the Kuan Yin Buddhist Temple. Walk three blocks mauka from King Street to Beretania. Turn left and walk Ewa a block or two to the Nuuanu Stream, where the ambience is slightly Southeast Asian. Much of the old Japanese neighborhood that used to be here—scrubby little saimin stands and pool halls, fish and grocery stores under quaint Asian roofs—has been torn down to make way for new construction. You'll see the **Kukui Market,** with its distinctive blue roof. Now follow River Street toward the mountains—you're likely to see local people fishing for tilapia, a nutritious fish that breeds rapidly in such brackish water—then cross Vineyard Boulevard and you'll be at the **Kuan Yin Buddhist Temple,** 170 N. Vineyard St. Slip off your shoes and walk inside. Joss sticks and incense burn at the altar, food offerings calm the ancestral spirits, and the USA seems far, far away. (There is another statue of Kuan Yin—far more splendid, we think—in the Honolulu Academy of Arts.)

3 Organized Tours & Activities

WALKING TOURS   The people at **Honolulu Time Walks,** 2634 S. King St., Suite 3 (☎ 808/943-0371), would like to take you for a walk. In the course of their popular 2¹/₂-hour walking tours, which leave from various points on Oahu, you can meet with the ghosts of Hawaii, relive the events of December 7, 1941, or follow in the footsteps of Mark Twain. Many of these tours are led by master storyteller Glen Grant, who has been collecting tales of the supernatural in Hawaii for over 25 years. In addition to the walking tours, there are trolley tours, and special showings at the Waikiki Heritage Theater in the International Marketplace on such subjects as "Obake . . . Japanese Tales of the Dead" and "Ghosts of Hawaii." Special tours are available for children. Most tours cost between $7 and $10; trolley tours can go up to $50. Call the number above for timely information and reservations. Local friends rave about these tours!

Kapiolani Community College presents a unique series of walking tours into Hawaii's past, including visits to Honolulu's famous cemeteries, to the almost-vanished "Little Tokyo" neighborhood, to the old plantation community of Waialua, and much more. Tours cost $5; for information and reservations, call **808/734-9245.**

The **Mission Houses Museum** presents a walking tour of "Historic Downtown Honolulu" on selected weekdays at 9:30am. The cost of $7 also includes admission to the museum. Call **808/531-0481** for tour days and reservations.

The **Hawaii Geographic Society** (☎ 808/538-3952) offers several unusual and highly worthwhile tours from April through September. One is "A Temple Tour," including Chinese, Japanese, Christian, and Jewish temples, cathedrals, and houses of worship; another is an archeology tour in and near downtown Honolulu. Each is guided by an expert from the Hawaii Geographic Society. A brochure is available on request. Cost is $10 per person, a minimum of three persons required. Call for details and reservations.

The society's brochure, "Historic Downtown Honolulu Walking Tour," is a good self-guiding look at a fascinating part of Hawaii—the part that is 200 years old! It's $3, including postage, from Hawaii Geographic Maps and Books, 49 S. Hotel St., Suite 218 (P.O. Box 1698), Honolulu, HI 96808.

The **Moanalua Gardens Foundation** (☎ 808/839-5334) offers walking tours of Kamananui Valley on the second Saturday and fourth Sunday of every month. Tours begin at 9am and last until 1pm. A donation is requested.

Two different organizations offer walking tours of Chinatown. The three-hour "Walk-A-Tour," run by the Chinese Chamber of Commerce only on Tuesday mornings at 9:30am, is an old favorite. It includes visits to shops, markets, and historic sites. The price is $5, and lunch can be arranged. The tour leaves from the

Chinese Chamber of Commerce headquarters at 42 N. King St. (☎ 808/ 533-3181 for reservations).

The **Hawaii Heritage Center** at 1168 Smith St. (☎ 808/521-2749), conducts walking tours which focus on the history and cultural uniqueness of the Chinatown area. Tours assemble at 1128 Smith St. (outside the Ramsay Gallery) on Fridays at 9:30am. The donation is $4 per person. Reservations are required only for groups of 15 or more, and may be arranged on other weekdays.

TOURS FOR THE DISABLED   **Handicabs of the Pacific** offers special tours for handicapped passengers, including luaus, cruises, and sightseeing tours in specially equipped vans that can handle six wheelchairs. Typical city tours cost $45 per person per hour. For information, call **808/524-3866**.

HARBOR CRUISES   A former municipal fireboat has turned into a jaunty passenger ship, offering one of the best bargains in town. For a mere $7.50, visitors can take a very enjoyable 45-minute historic tour of Honolulu Harbor aboard the *Abner T. Longley,* berthed at Pier 7 at the Hawaii Maritime Center. The tour consists of a full narration of Honolulu Harbor, including stories, legends, and historical sites. Tours depart daily at 10:15am, 11:30am, 1pm, 2pm, 3pm, and 4pm. Children under 5 (one per adult) ride free.

Even more fun are the evening and nighttime cruises. The Early Evening Sunset Cruise, from 5:30 to 6:30pm, costs $15 for adults and $11.50 for children ages 5 to 12, and offers a free cocktail and pupus to complement the historic tour of the harbor. Nightly water show extravaganas are held at 7pm and 8:30pm. On these cruises, passengers are allowed to operate the water cannons, which are maintained to original fire-fighting standards. The cruises conclude with a computer-controlled water show featuring lighted water cannons synchronized with sound effects. The cost of $15 for adults, $11.50 for children ages 5 to 12, includes a complimentary cocktail. For tour information, call **808/526-FIRE**.

CHANOYU: THE JAPANESE TEA CEREMONY   As refreshing as a quick trip to Japan, the twice-weekly demonstrations of the Japanese tea ceremony held at 245 Saratoga Rd. (near Fort DeRussy) offers a fascinating look at the ancient "Way of Tea." Sponsored by the **Uresenke Foundation of Hawaii,** a nonprofit group whose goal is "to find peacefulness through a bowl of tea," the demonstrations are held every Wednesday and Friday (excluding holidays) from 10am to noon: Donations of $2 are welcomed. Seated in a formal Japanese tatami room in a garden setting, guests are introduced to the proper customs for the preparation and partaking of tea, and are served a sweet and powdered green tea from exquisite "tea bowls." You may ask questions and take pictures if you wish. A must for lovers of Asian culture. For information, call **808/923-3059**.

HULA DANCING   You, too, can do the hula! Hula-dancing lessons are given everywhere—at the Ys, at the university, and at any number of private dance studios. Free classes are sometimes given at hotels and shopping centers, but since the times of these lessons change with the seasons, it's best to consult the local tourist papers. The **Waikiki Community Center** (☎ 808/955-0100) has a wide variety of classes, including hula. And free hula classes are usually given Monday, Wednesday, and Friday at the **Royal Hawaiian Shopping Center,** Building C, third floor, at 10:30am. Call **808/922-0588** for further details.

4 Shopping

WAIKIKI

SHOPPING CENTERS

International Market Place
2330 Kalakaua Ave. ☎ **808/923-9871.**

The oldest and most colorful shopping area in Waikiki, this touristy place is still fun, despite the fact that there are now so many booths and shoppers that it sometimes reminds us of rush hour in the New York subway. And prices are apt to be a mite higher than they are in the department stores or at Ala Moana Shopping Center, although they might come down considerably if you do a bit of bargaining. And do note that comparison shopping pays off here; one booth might be selling T-shirts for $12 that one around the corner sells for $8 or $9. It seems that the farther you go from the main street, the better the prices become. Informal, semi-open shops set around a giant banyan tree and interspersed among tropical plantings allow for alfresco browsing.

Unfortunately, few of the shops here now carry genuine Hawaiian and Polynesian craft items. What you will find are scads of places selling jewelry (everything from plastic to shell, ivory, coral, and lapis), candles, T-shirts, beach cover-ups, and resort wear. Many stands called **The Pearl Factory** sell pearls in the oyster. Shops and kiosks turn over with great rapidity, so our best advice is simply to roam. If you like lovely Balinese clothing, check out a well-stocked shop called **Bali Designs,** which imports clothing for men and women direct from Indonesia. The **All Elvis Gift Shop** speaks for itself. Art lovers should pay a visit to **Arts of Paradise,** an attractive gallery featuring original art by artists residing in Hawaii. Frequent lecture and slide shows are presented.

The International Market Place is open daily from 9am to 11pm.

King's Village
131 Kaiulani Ave. ☎ **808/944-6855.**

It's supposed to look like a 19th-century European town, with its cobblestone streets and old-fashioned architecture, but King's Village is very much a part of modern Honolulu. Behind the gates at the corner of Koa and Kaiulani avenues, across the street from the Hyatt Regency Waikiki, is a cozy bazaar that contains a variety of shops, several restaurants, and an open market—all done up in a style that recalls the 19th-century monarchy period of Hawaiian history, when royal palaces were built in Honolulu, and Hawaiian kings and queens journeyed to London to be presented at the court of Queen Victoria.

The shops, however, are not so much European as the typical Honolulu-international mix, with lots of Asian and Polynesian crafts, plus plenty of Hawaiian resort wear and souvenirs. All are small and in good taste; King's Village is a commercial venture, certainly, but there's no commercial ugliness about it. We think you'll enjoy browsing here. Prices range from just a little to quite a lot. For about $45, you can take home a good wooden tiki, courtesy of **Hime,** an intriguing wood-carving shop, which has many lower-priced items as well, like a collection of whaling figurines.

Kuhio Mall

2301 Kuhio Ave. ☎ **808/922-2724.**

Kuhio Mall is directly behind the International Market Place, and looks exactly like it. Here you'll find **Tribal Connection** (look for the cigar-store wooden Indian out front), which has some interesting Native American work, including silver belt buckles and jewelry. **Pictures Plus** features a display of posters and pictures by local artists at very affordable prices—and they can be shipped anywhere. Visitors can watch candle-making at **Sheila's Art Candle** and **Young's Candles** on the ground level.

Free Polynesian shows are held nightly at 7 and 8pm, featuring Faye "Aloha" Dalire, a noted hula artist, whose halau (hula troupe) features many talented keikis. It's a charming show. Kuhio Mall is open daily from 9am to 11pm.

Royal Hawaiian Shopping Center

2201 Kalakaua Ave. ☎ **808/922-0588.**

Across Kalakaua from the International Market Place is one of Waikiki's newer shopping centers, and in many respects its most sophisticated. "An oasis of green in Waikiki" is what the builders promised when ground was broken, and despite the outcry against the lavish use of concrete, it's pretty much what they've delivered. Occupying three city blocks along Kalakaua Avenue and fronting the entrance to the Royal Hawaiian and Sheraton Waikiki hotels, this stunning 6½-acre, 150-store complex is indeed graced with flowers and trees, ferns and shrubbery, and hundreds of trailing vines and Hawaiian plants. High style is evident in the shops, restaurants, and a huge variety of daily programs—Polynesian minishows, classes in coconut-frond weaving, ukulele playing, hula dancing, lei stringing, and Hawaiian quilting, as well as special events—enough to keep the visitor busy and happy for a long time. Unfortunately for us budgeteers, the trend here is toward more and more upscale marketing. On the first level, wealthy visitors sometimes wait in line to get into the designer shops. However, the budget shopper can still do pretty well here at several discount stores, such as the **Sale Studio at Andrade's** or **McInerny's Sale Studio,** where sportswear can be found for up to 75% off the original prices. Other lower-priced apparel shops include **Swim Suit Warehouse** on the third level.

Be sure to visit the ✪ **Little Hawaiian Craft Shop,** on the third level, where a fantastic assortment of unusual finished jewelry sits alongside buckets and barrels of raw materials, the same kinds that were used by the ancient Hawaiians. This is a workshop for craftspeople using natural island materials in both traditional and contemporary styles. Replicas of museum pieces sit among handcarved tikis and buckets of inexpensive shells. They have some wonderful hard-to-find sandalwood necklaces—fragrant, lovely, and well priced, from about $22. The hand-painted floral tote bags done by watercolor artist Terrie Marie are a special find at $27. This is also a good source for Hawaiian quilting and cross-stitch—patterns, books, kits, and some finished pieces. Almost everything here is handmade in Hawaii. Great ideas for presents include kukui-nut rings at $6, coconut soap at $3, and coconut-shell necklaces at $10.

The shop also includes an outstanding wood gallery that shows local woodworkers, such as Pai Pai, known for his wood-carved replicas of Hawaiian and Pacific images, and Pat Coito, for traditional Hawaiian calabash bowls. Only island woods—among them koa, mango, Norfolk pine, milo, macadamia, ohia lehus, and kiawe—are used. Prices range from $3.50 to $3,000. Collectors will want to see the traditional and contemporary handcrafts from the islands of the Pacific with an ever-changing kaleidoscope of spirit figures, tapas, weavings, war clubs, drums, masks, and spears. The owners make frequent trips to these areas to find these treasures. Well worth a look.

The ✪ **Hawaiian Heirloom Jewelry Factory,** located on the third level, deserves a stop. It conducts free factory tours every hour on the hour, from 10am to 4pm Monday through Friday. You'll learn something of the history of Hawaiian heirloom jewelry and see how these heavy gold handcrafted pieces are made today, each inscribed with the owner's name and accompanying floral designs. Check out their new Museum of Hawaiian Heirloom Jewelry. Worth a stop for those who like Chinese crafts is the **China Marketplace,** which has an excellent selection of cloisonné vases and handmade cloisonné animals, at very good prices. They also have tongue scrapers with a Chinese saying on an accompanying card, an amusing present for all of $1.45.

Ready to treat yourself to something special? Stop in and visit Marlo Shima who runs ✪ **Boutique Marlo,** on the third level of Building C. Using only silk, cotton, and other natural fabrics, and dying them in the subtlest and softest of colors, Marlo creates women's clothing of great beauty. Although dresses go for about $80 to $200, you can find many modestly priced scarves, necklaces, fabric bags, and the like. **Van Brugge House** has a huge two-level store; the lower level sells pricey Australian opal jewelry and watches, plus pink and champagne diamonds, but the upper level is more in our price range. It's got a smashing selection of Australian-designed sportswear, and is truly a surfer's paradise—you could even get yourself a Surfarang (a surfer's boomerang) here.

If you've bought a lot, and are wondering how to get it all home, visit **GBS Boxes & Packaging,** on the third floor. They'll do professional packing, wrapping, and shipping, or else sell you the materials—corrugated boxes, mailing tubes, sealing tapes, etc.—that you'll need to do it yourself. United Parcel Service is available here, and there's a U.S. post office inside the store.

Free entertainment, lectures, and demonstrations go on all the time; check the local papers for details. The Royal Hawaiian Shopping Center is open from 9am to 10pm Monday through Saturday, until 9pm on Sunday.

Waikiki Shopping Plaza
2250 Kalakaua Ave. ☎ **808/923-1191.**

The traffic-stopper here is the five-story fountain by island designer Bruce Hopper, a wondrous, half-million-dollar creation. The fountain has a different point of interest at each level, creating new surprises as you ride the escalators.

If your Japanese isn't up to snuff, fully half the stores, their names, and merchandise descriptions will be unintelligible to you. Sticking to English, however, you can still browse around and find a few shops of interest. **Hawaii Cloisonné Factory,** for one, makes some nice jewelry, fashion artifacts not available elsewhere in the U.S. and not expensive. It also has a colorful collection of wall hangings from Peru and appliquéd murals handmade in Pamplona; they begin at just $25. Art lovers will enjoy the **Art Forum Gallery. Island Casuals** is known for wide selections and good bargains. There's a nice array of swimsuits at **Beach Avenue,** and **Treasure Island** is the place to find Hawaiian Heirloom Jewelry Factory items. **Wood Creations** has lots of knick-knacks to browse through.

While most of the shops at the Waikiki Shopping Plaza are not budget-oriented, the basement restaurants certainly are, with a bevy of fast-food counters offering varied ethnic foods (See "Where to Eat," in Chapter 5). Open daily from 9:30am to 9:30pm.

CLOTHING & GIFT SHOPS

Prices for Hawaiian clothes are pretty standard everywhere: Better muumuus average $60 to $70 (short), $80 to $90 or more (long). To realize substantial savings on aloha wear, your best bet is a place outside Waikiki that we'll tell you about later: Hilo Hattie Fashion Center. For antique Hawaiian shirts, see "Vintage Aloha Shirts," below.

Casa D'Bella
2352 Kalakaua Ave. ☎ **808/923-6426.**

We like this store a lot. They carry some stylish designs from New York and California as well as local resort wear, and they have a good collection of fashion jewelry, too.

✪ Liberty House
2314 Kalakaua Ave. ☎ **808/941-2345.**

The Waikiki branch of Hawaii's premier department store has an extremely attractive selection of clothing for men, women, and children, with a good collection of shoes and accessories for men, women, and juniors and an extensive selection of cosmetics and fragrances. Liberty House is not inexpensive, but it gives you an idea of the best of mainland and Hawaiian fashions.

Period Clothing

✪ Reminisce
2139-A Kuhio Ave. ☎ **808/921-9056.**

This pretty little shop, one block from the Kuhio Theater, specializes in period clothing in mint condition for men and women, dating from the turn of the century through the 1950s. Evening and bridal fashions are the specialty here. We coveted the wonderfully outrageous beaded and sequined flapper dresses, the beaded cocktail gowns from the 1930s and 1940s, the Victorian and Edwardian ballgowns and bridal dresses, and the divine hats from all periods. We almost succumbed to a very Myrna Loy black taffeta dinner dress. There's a super collection of costume jewelry, plus shoes, hats, and handbags. For gentlemen, there are authentic 1950s Aloha shirts, amazing cravats, and fascinating, one-of-a-kind cufflinks from more gracious days. Prices here are not, of course, of the bargain- basement variety—some of the Victorian bridals are priced well up into the thousands—but there were great retro earrings and brooches for as little as $5: something for everyone. Don't miss it if you love elegant things from days gone by.

Vintage Aloha Shirts

You know, of course, that "antique" aloha shirts—those from the 1930s, '40s, and '50s have become high fashion on the mainland. Why show-biz celebrities and socialites are willing to pay $100 to $1,000 for rayon shirts that have been hanging in somebody's closet for 30 or 40 years is a mystery to us, but the demand is there. In addition to the shops listed below, see Reminisce above. For a history of the aloha shirt, read the book called *The Hawaiian Shirt,* by H. Thomas Steel (Abbeville Press), available at many local bookstores.

✪ Bailey's Antique Clothes & Aloha Shirts

517 Kapahulu Ave. ☎ **808/734-7628.**

The shirts that make their way into places like this are snatched up quickly by folks like Robin Williams, Tom Selleck, and Steven Spielberg, to drop just a few names. Bailey's is a fascinating store (it also stocks other early island wear from various cultures), and it's well worth a look; if you can't afford one of the pricey items, choose one of their more than 1,000 shirts in the $5-to-$10 range, 1,500 shirts for $10 to $20, or something like 500 shirts from the 1950s, which range from $20 to $125. Approximately 300 "silky" rayon shirts from the 1940s command prices of $100 to $1,000. They have the world's largest inventory of aloha shirts. Have a look, too, at their nifty (albeit expensive) art deco and retro jewelry.

Kula Bay

In the Royal Hawaiian Hotel, 2259 Kalakaua Ave. ☎ **808/923-0042.**

This store, which also has a branch at the Hilton Hawaiian Village (☎ 808/ 943- 0771), has done some clever work taking authentic prints from shirts of the 1930s, 1940s, and early 1950s, having them painted on long-staple cotton in more muted colors, and turning out handsome, very well-tailored aloha shirts for about $50.

POLYNESIAN ARTS & CRAFTS

South Seas Mercantile & Trading Co.

2310 Kuhio Ave. ☎ **808/923-5509.**

Strangely enough, authentic Hawaiian and Polynesian crafts are a rarity in Hawaii, so it's nice to find this attractive new store in a central location in Waikiki. Everything in this exemplary shop is handmade by Hawaiian and Polynesian craftspeople, replicating whenever possible the same techniques that were used in ancient times. Although owners Joseph and Susie Berardy focus mainly on Hawaiian crafts, they also journey regularly to the villages of Polynesia and Micronesia in search of treasures. The results of their labors are evident here: There are museum-replica handcarved tiki figures, tapa cloths, Tahitian dance skirts, authentic hula instruments, kukui-nut leis, and much more. Of special interest to collectors are the ceremonial masks and handcarved Polynesian weapons, for which crafters used the same woods and ancient methods as were used in the past. They range in price from $65 to $350. Be sure to check out Joseph's own beautiful tie-dyed pastel pareus, which he creates in his North Shore home using a sun-sensitive heliographic process. At just $22.50, they are affordable works of art. Prices begin around $2 for a coconut bracelet and could go up to $2,700 for a nine-foot totem.

There's another South Seas Mercantile at Dole Cannery Square at 650 Iliwei Rd. And the pareus can be bought at Pakipika Trading Company in the Aloha Tower Marketplace (see below). For a free, 32-page catalog, write or phone the shop at the address above.

ALA MOANA CENTER

Honolulu's fabulous modern shopping center (the largest open-air mall in the world), the Ala Moana Center, 1450 Ala Moana Blvd. (☎ 808/946-2811), just across Ala Moana Beach Park, is an example of island architecture at its best. Landscaped with trees, flowers, fountains, and a meandering stream down its Central Mall, which is graced with large works of sculpture, the Ala Moana Center is always packed with enough island families to make it worth seeing for that reason alone. But the stores are, of course, the main attraction—more than 200 of them, an international bazaar full of intriguing wares. We'll mention just a few, but shopping buffs will come back here many, many times.

We always enjoy browsing around in the large Japanese-owned department store ✪ **Shirokiya,** which has everything from state-of-the-art stereos to kids' T-shirts that glow in the dark. This is a great place to find unusual and inexpensive gift items. Check out the first-floor section on shiatsu foot massagers, chairs, etc. Shirokiya's gourmet-food department, on the second floor, is worth a trip in itself. A vast array of wonderful sushi and other traditional Japanese fare is offered at dozens of booths and counters. There's plenty of food to take home. Or you can create a meal for yourself and devour it on the spot in the dining lanai. Most days from 3 to 8pm there's an evening buffet and sushi bar.

There are also dozens of small shops in the center, reflecting just about every interest and taste. One of our favorites is ✪ **Artlines,** with a highly tasteful collection of jewelry, animal masks, carving, statuary, crystals, bells, Tiffany-type lamps, and the like, collected from all over the world—especially from Egypt, Morocco, India, Indonesia, Greece, and Africa. There's an exotic collection of sterling-silver earrings. Prices begin at $1 for unpolished stones and could go as high as $3,500 for a superb Buddha.

No need to travel all the way to the Big Island to get some of that wild and wonderful tropical clothing for which **Noa Noa** is so well known, now that owner Joan Simon has opened a store right here at the center. In addition to original batik designs for women and men, she has exotic gift items as well—wall hangings, masks, ceramics, chests, and basketry from China.

Stop in at **Musashiya** for wonderful fabrics. They have Japanese kimono fabrics in polyester crepe, as well as Yukata prints, batiks from Holland (Dutch Java wax prints), silks from Paris, and calico prints for quilters—not to mention custom-made Japanese futons. **Tahiti Imports** takes Tahitian prints of their own design and makes them into muumuus, aloha shirts, bikinis, and pareus. They also sell their exquisite hand-printed fabrics by the yard.

We often pick up gifts from **The Compleat Kitchen and More.** Spicy Hawaiian Quilt trivets, potpourri-filled and made in Maui, are silk-screened and handsewn with traditional Hawaiian quilt patterns. **Island Shells** has lots of stunning jewelry, shell and wood chimes, shell roses, and the like, and prices are always fair. And their shell flower arrangements are beautiful. It's fun to go fly a kite in Honolulu, and the place to get your equipment is **High Performance Kites,** right near Centerstage. Many of their kites come from one of our favorite places on Molokai, the Big Wind Kite Factory. Also near Centerstage, and in a sense the "heart" of the shopping center, is the ✪ **Honolulu Book Shop,** with superb selections in every category, especially Hawaiiana.

For over 30 years, **Irene's Hawaiian Gifts** has been a favorite with residents and visitors alike for unique island gifts. Their specialty is bird and sealife carvings from native woods and collector's items like porcelain dolls, handcrafted Christmas ornaments, quilt kits, lauhala purses, and koa-wood outrigger canoes with tapa sails, made locally and sold at good prices.

Feet getting to you? The **Slipper House** is a good place to replace whatever worn-out sandals you're trudging around in. They claim to have the widest selection of casual footwear in the state, with over 400 styles of made-in-Hawaii sandals, plus popular Tevas, Birkenstock, Reefs, and Flojos. Stop in, too, at the **Crackseed Center,** if you want to know what Hawaiian youngsters clamor for (crackseed, originally a Chinese confection, are a cross between seed and candies—very sticky, very tasty).

One of the most intriguing stores at Ala Moana is the **Foodland Supermarket.** It's like an international food fair, reflecting the cultures that make up Hawaii—and the rest of the world. You walk along seemingly endless aisles of exotic foods: fresh-frozen coconut milk, packages of Japanese dried fish, health foods, tortillas, English biscuits, French cheese, you name it—if it's edible, this place has got it. You can, in addition, pick up some okolehao, Hawaii's potent ti-root drink, in the large liquor department.

The best bargins at Ala Moana are available when the stores take to the sidewalks—the ground-floor level, that is—displaying racks and racks of clothing for very low prices.

Remember the center, too, for free shows. Centerstage, on the main floor, features a variety of entertainment by some of the best island talent and international performing groups. Over 500 performances—from Hawaiian hula shows and ballet to martial-arts demonstrations and fashion shows—are scheduled throughout the year. Check tourist publications for exact times.

Most Ala Moana Center establishments stay open seven days a week: Monday through Saturday from 9:30am to 9pm, and on Sunday from 10am to 5pm.

From Kuhio Avenue in Waikiki, you can take TheBUS no. 8 and you'll be at Ala Moana (barring heavy traffic) in about 10 minutes. Parking areas are numerous—and they even have coconut palms coming through the concrete!

AROUND TOWN
SHOPPING CENTERS

✪ Ward Warehouse
1050 Ala Moana Blvd. ☎ **808/591-8411.**

One of the most eye-catching of Honolulu's shopping centers is Ward Warehouse, located on Ward Avenue between Auahi Street and Ala Moana, across from Fisherman's Wharf. More than 65 shops and restaurants occupy the handsome two-story structures fashioned out of great rough-hewn planks, and there seems to be a higher-than-usual level of taste and selectivity here. It's a favorite shopping destination for local people and visitors alike.

A dazzling showplace for handcrafts is **Nohea Gallery,** a gallery and outlet for many local craftspeople: You'll see beautiful ceramics, leaded glass, fine furniture made of local hardwoods, flower pillows, jewelry, modern and traditional metal sculpture, and soft sculpture. Note the Old Hawaiian prints (from $12) and lovely notepapers, too. For American folk art, most of it collected on the mainland and all of it handcrafted, visit **Crescent Gallery.** Wood carvings, arks, building signs, weather vanes, checkerboard quilts, Steiff bears, boxes, glassware, and more are all impressive. So, too, is the collection of Oriental and European treasures—carvings, jade, Chinese vases, boxes, ceramics, hand-screened T-shirts, hand-painted bead necklaces, and more—to be found at **Heavenly Lotus.** There are many small, surprisingly affordable items here, too.

The most striking women's clothing at Ward Warehouse might well be found at ✪ **Mamo Howell.** Mamo Howell was a well-known island hula dancer and later became a Christian Dior model in Paris. She's turned her artistic flair to designing, and the results are stunning muumuus long and short; their inspiration comes mostly from Hawaiian-quilt motifs. Her designs are unmistakable once you've seen

Oahu's Vibrant Art Scene

Many young artists are busy cultivating their talents on Oahu and throughout the Hawaiian Islands. Perhaps because of the natural beauty that surrounds them, their works tend to be more representational than those currently coming out of other international art centers. But this is no lagging group—the Hawaiian artists' perspectives are as modern as those of their counterparts in Paris or New York. What's more, as yet another example of the fortuitous cross-fertilization that goes on in every arena of Hawaiian life, not a few of these up-and-coming young artists and craftspeople have intriguingly—and successfully—married Eastern atmosphere with Western techniques.

Galleries in Town

To view some excellent works (and perhaps to pick up some distinctive small presents), pop into some of our favorite places. **Following Sea,** at Kahala Mall, is a visual experience. It's home to works in ceramics, glass, jewelry, fiber, and woodwork. Each piece is more glorious than the next. Many island artists are represented. Superior taste and artistry is evident in the works found at **Nohea Gallery** at Ward Warehouse. With the work of more than 450 island artists and craftspeople in handcrafted jewelry, paintings, Koa boxes, chests and furniture, basketry, feather-work, quilts, pottery, glass, and sculpture, Nohea offers just about the widest selection of fine arts and crafts in the island. **From Ed and Friends,** 2563 S. King St. (☎ 808/943-8680), is a mesmerizing hodgepodge of the work of 60 to 70 artists and artisans from Hawaii and the mainland. Owner Ed Higa is a master potter and his ceramic pieces are treasures. Also represented are a glassblower, several jewelry artisans, and woodworkers. Take note of the line of tie-dyed T-shirt animals—the shirts are tied and manipulated to resemble dragons, alligators, caterpillars, dinosaurs, and other fanciful critters. They are then dyed and allowed to remain in their tied state. Take your choice: untie it and wear it as a shirt, or keep the charming creature intact.

A great lady of the arts in Hawaii was Madge Tennent, who came to the islands at the turn of the century via South Africa and Paris and broke away from the academy and its conventions to record on canvas her massive portraits of the Hawaiian people. You can visit her gallery, the **Tennent Art Foundation,** on the slopes of Punchbowl at 203 Prospect St. (☎ 808/531-1987), from 10am to noon Tuesday through Saturday, 2 to 4pm on Sunday, or by special appointment.

Other fine galleries are all over town. You'll want to visit **Arts of Paradise** on the second floor of the International Market Place. Artist-owned, it features work in all mediums of Hawaii's top professional artists. Call about free demonstrations and talks by participating artists (☎ 808/924-2787). Then there's **Images International of Hawaii** at Ala Moana Shopping Center (☎ 808/926-5081), featuring internationally acclaimed artists Hisashi Otsuka, Caroline Young, Tatsuo Ito, Zen har Zang, Gary Hostallero, Robert Lyn Nelson, and the unique leather sculptor Liu Miao Chan. Worth your attention at Ward Centre is **Art A La Carte** (☎ 808/597-8034), an artists' co-op featuring ceramics as well as paintings.

Downtown, the impressive **Honolulu Advertiser Gallery** on the first floor of the News Building at 605 Kapiolani Blvd, (☎ 808/526-1322) continues to be a showcase for local and mainland artists despite its newer galleries at the Contemporary Museum (see above). The **Gallery at Pauahi Tower** in Bishop Square always has an outstanding show. The **AMFAC Plaza Exhibition Room** at AMFAC Center, Fort Street Mall and Queen Street, has interesting group exhibitions of contemporary paintings, crafts, sculpture, and photography, as well as cultural and historical presentations. Exhibitions change monthly. It's open 9am to 5pm Monday through Friday. On Saturday and Sunday, local artists exhibit and sell their work on the zoo fence near Kapiolani Park.

In Chinatown, something of an artistic renaissance is going on these days. Old buildings have been refurbished, there is new construction, and a small artistic colony continues to grow—at last count, there were a dozen galleries here. Pen-and-ink artist **Ramsay,** who has achieved national and international fame (an exhibition of her masterful architectural drawings appeared at the Senate Rotunda in Washington, D.C., in 1988), has her own gallery at 1128 Smith St. (☎ 808/537-2787), where she also shows works by prominent artists in other media. Next door is her café, with a sophisticated, medium-priced menu. **Pegge Hopper,** whose images of Polynesian women are seen everywhere in the islands, also has her own gallery here, at 1164 Nuuanu Ave. (☎ 808/524-1160). It features Hopper's original paintings, drawings, and collages, in addition to her posters, limited-edition prints, calendars, and gift items. At the corner, at 1050 Nuuanu, is an upbeat gallery, the **Gateway Gallery** (☎ 808/599-1559), featuring fine arts and unique gift items. They specialize in floral and tropical theme paintings and sculpture. Accessories start at $20.

Galleries Around The Island

As you drive around the island, you'll have a chance to visit several worthwhile galleries, The ✪ **Ko'olau Gallery,** located on the second level of the Windward Mall Shopping Center in Kaneohe, is a co-op gallery, staffed by the artists themselves, showing a variety of locally produced artworks in many media. More than 40 artists from around the island are represented. You can say hello to the gallery artists daily from 9:30am to 9pm. Also in Kaneohe, serious lovers of art and beauty must not miss a visit to **Hart, Tagami & Powell Gallery and Gardens,** 45-754 Lamaula Rd., where painters Hiroshi Tagami and Michael Powell open their gallery and tranquil botanical garden to visitors on Saturday, Sunday, and Monday from around 10am to 3:30pm. An appointment is necessary: Call 808/239-8146. The **Fettig Art Studios,** 61-427A Kamehameha Hwy. in Haleiwa, shows work by artist Beverly Fettig, by appointment only (☎ 808/637-5340).

The **Waimanu Street Gallery,** at 66-521 Kamehameha Hwy. in Haleiwa (☎ 808/293-5000), features the works of Jerry Kermode, whose bowls, made of Hawaiian woods, are examples of the woodmaster's art par excellence. Each creation is different; sometimes two woods are combined into one piece. Potter Bob McWilliams is also represented by his functional, Oriental-influenced pieces, as is Janet Holaday, with her wonderful screen-printed shirts, cards, and bags. Open Monday through Friday from 10am to 6pm, Sunday from 10am to 5pm.

them—and you'll see them on the best-dressed women in town. Dresses are out of our price range (they go upward of $135), but quite affordable and also lovely are an array of small items using similar patterns, especially the quilted tote bags, lined with nylon, $35. Mamo creates charming children's clothing too.

In the few years that it's been here, ✪ **Pomegranates in the Sun** has established a loyal following of fashion-conscious women. It features clothing by local artists and designers inspired by the Hawaiian atmosphere. There are many one-of-a-kind items. Prices are not generally low, but there are some affordable items: We saw delightful cotton sundresses at $55, long T-shirts for around $25, designer umbrellas from Australia at $30. Look for the smashing Pomegranates in the Sun in Haleiwa when you journey around the island.

There are tons of good buys—clothing, Balinese masks and carvings, paintings by Chinese artists, and more—at **Imports International.** Men can find good aloha shirts at $19; women can find many attractive items from Bali at delightfully low prices. (A good portion of our summer wardrobe comes from here!) For discounts on the popular Bebe line of women's sportswear, check the **Bebe Discount Outlet,** where savings can be as much as 40% to 75%.

You may want to pick up some gorgeous fans among the Chinese arts and crafts at **Heavenly Lotus.** They have charming inexpensive items—cinnabar necklaces at $10, Chinese cutout notepapers at $2.50, hand-painted T-shirts at $29—in addition to more costly treasures.

Searching for antiques of the '20s, '30s and '40s? Nostalgia buffs seek out **Claire de Lune,** where they snap up everything from rattan furniture to outrigger-canoe models to framed prints, old sheet music and books, antique aloha shirts, dishes, boxes, candlesticks, even Hawaiian quilt-design earrings by Leighton Lane for $15 and under. Hand-carved chess sets, wind chimes, bells, furniture, textiles, quilts, and some lovely clothing, all from Indonesia, are shown in the handsome, **Indo Pacific Trading Company Store.**

Ward Warehouse's **Amphitheatre** hosts a variety of events and entertainment, from hula shows to jazz concerts to fashion shows and then some. Shopping hours are 10am to 9pm Monday through Friday, until 5pm on Saturday and Sunday. Restaurants stay open until late in the evening. From Waikiki, take TheBUS no. 8, marked WARD AVENUE, from Kuhio Avenue or Kalia Road. It's about a 15-minute ride from Waikiki. It's also located on the Waikiki Trolley route.

Ward Centre
1200 Ala Moana Blvd. ☎ **808/591-8411.**

Down the road a block from Ward Warehouse is Ward Centre, another sophisticated collection of boutiques and restaurants, all with a high level of charm and taste. The emphasis is on small, somewhat expensive boutiques, so we usually find ourselves coming here to eat at some of our favorite restaurants (see "Where to Eat" in Chapter 5, for details) and browsing in some of the more affordable shops.

Owner Valerie Tanabe set out to combine the uniqueness and variety of a local crafts fair with the convenience and service of a retail store. The result: **Craft Flair,** whose name says it all. Over 150 artists, both local and mainland, are featured in a delightful collection of one-of-a-kind handcrafted clothing, accessories, and gift items. Prices go from just a little to a lot: there are pin cards for $5, porcelain earrings for $26, baby blankets for $24, marbled silk ties for $44, and vintage kimono vests for $147. Great fun.

When we strike it rich, we're planning to furnish our home with all the beautiful handcrafted Koa furniture at **Hawaiian Heritage** (koa is a native Hawaiian hardwood). Until then, it's fun to look; one could pick up a koa bracelet for as little as $15. Art lovers will want to spend time at **Art A La Carte,** a cooperative venture featuring the work of a dozen local artists who take turns "sitting" the gallery and often work right here. Unframed works begin at $25, matted cards at $10.

To reach Ward Centre, again take TheBUS no. 8 marked Ward Avenue or 19 or 20 from Waikiki, a 15-minute ride.

✪ Aloha Tower Marketplace

1 Aloha Tower Dr. ☎ **808/528-5700**.

It's a festival, a celebration, a cultural experience, a shopping bazaar, a place to browse and mingle and dine by the waterside and watch the world go by. The Aloha Tower Marketplace, finally a reality after years of planning and an outlay of over $100 million, has transformed the once shabby Honolulu waterfront area. Developed by James Rouse, who also revitalized the waterfronts in Baltimore and Boston, this is definitely one of the great gathering places of Honolulu.

To call this a shopping mall would scarcely do it justice. Adjacent to the newly revitalized Aloha Tower (long the symbol of Honolulu), it recalls the time when local residents gathered here on Boat Days to greet the great passenger ships of the '30s and '40s with dancing, singing, entertainment, and celebration. The architecture is Mediterranean in style with Hawaiian accents that evoke those days. Distinguished artworks, more than 14,000 blooming plants and 300 trees (including a coconut grove), an ongoing program of free entertainment and wandering street musicians, a bevy of restaurants and bars, and an oldtime fireboat that offers $7.50 harbor cruises, all combine to make a visit here an extraordinary experience.

As for the shops, they live up to the overall high artistic standards of the marketplace, and are noticeably lacking in "tourist junk." Scores of retail establishments and some 70 colorful kiosks and pushcarts in the Boat Days Bazaar showcase art, Hawaiian crafts, jewelry, clothing, unique furniture, and more.

The shops at Aloha Tower Marketplace are open daily from 10am to 10pm. Restaurants and bars from 11am to midnight, often until 2am.

The easiest way to get here is via the Aloha Tower Express Trolley, which operates daily from 8:45am to 2am; the cost is $1 each way. From Waikiki, one can hop on the trolley on either the Kuhio Avenue route which stops at the Ilikai Hotel, Waikiki Gateway Hotel, Outrigger Malia Hotel, Outrigger East Hotel, Pacific Beach Hotel, Outrigger West Hotel, and Outrigger Surf Hotel; or on the Kalakaua Avenue route, which stops at the Hilton Hawaiian Village, Buzz's Steak House, Holiday Isle Hotel, Waikiki Police Substation, Hawaiian Waikiki Beach Hotel, and Prince Kuhio Hotel. Trolleys run every 30 minutes; after 9:45pm, once an hour.

Kahala Mall

Waialae Kahala Shopping Complex. ☎ **808/732-7736**.

Kahala Mall is an enclosed shopping center, with a bevy of interesting stores. At some of the boutiques, it will be "just looking, thanks," but there are still many places of interest to the dollar-wise shopper.

Worth a special trip is ✪ **Following Sea,** a shop-gallery that represents the work of some 350 professional craftspeople from 40 states, and sponsors outstanding monthly exhibitions. Everything is unique, and the inventory changes constantly. Prices range from a little to a lot, but there is a fine selection of ceramics, woodwork, and jewelry in the $30-to-$60 range. Their most popular items are hand-blown oil lamps, from $20. On a recent visit we saw koa beautifully crafted into notebook covers, chimes, jewel chests, and unique boxes, for $25 to $300; plus exquisite leaded-glass boxes each with a beautiful seashell set into the top, for $53 to $75. Following Sea is working with local craftspeople to develop new and unique items.

To reach Kahala Mall, take TheBUS no. 58; or by car, take Kapahulu to the Lunalillo Freeway East to the Waialae exit. Open Monday through Saturday from 10am to 9pm, Sunday from 10am to 5pm.

Pearlridge Shopping Center
Aiea ☎ **808/488-0981.**

Out in Aiea, about a half-hour drive from Waikiki, is the Pearlridge Shopping Center, a multimillion-dollar complex that's a big favorite with the local people. Pearlridge boasts 170 stores, 16 theaters, two food courts, and three "phases." It's built on opposite sides of an 11-acre watercress farm. Shoppers travel between Phase I and Phase II in Hawaii's only monorail train. From your perch in the monorail, you'll enjoy a panoramic view of Pearl Harbor. Across the street, Pearlridge Phase II houses several more shops, theaters, and an office complex. This is a good place to keep in mind for a rainy-day family excursion.

As at most of the shopping centers catering to the local trade, familiar names such as **Liberty House** and **Ross Dress for Less** dominate the scene. **Shirokiya** shows the Japanese influence, with many captivating art objects from Asia. **Fernandez Fun Factory's Flagship** in Pearlridge Phase II must surely be one of the world's fanciest "penny arcades," featuring the newest and most elaborate electronic games.

Official store hours at Pearlridge are Monday through Saturday from 10am to 9pm, Sunday from 10am to 5pm. You can easily squeeze your visit to Pearlridge into your trip to Pearl Harbor. If you're driving to Pearl Harbor on Kamehameha Highway, you see it on your right just after you reach the entrance to the USS *Arizona* Memorial. If you're driving out the H1 Freeway, take the Aiea exit. When driving out the Lunalilo Freeway from downtown, you'll see Pearlridge on the freeway directory signs. TheBUS no. 20 from Waikiki goes to Pearlridge. *Note:* You can combine your visit to Pearlridge with one to the **Kam Super Swap Meet,** which is held at the Kam Drive-In, across from the shopping center, Wednesday and on weekends, beginning at 6am.

SHOPPING A TO Z
Discount Shops & Factory Outlets
ⓢ Crazy Shirts Factory Outlet
At Costeo Commercial Center, 4400 Lawehana St., In Aiea. ☎ **808/422-4522.**

You'll see Crazy Shirt stores all over the Hawaiian Islands—everybody loves their clever designs and sayings. They make great presents too, so if you want to buy a lot of them, you can save a bundle by going to their factory outlet store, which offers factory seconds and display merchandise for 40% to 60% off retail prices.

✪ Daiei

801 Kaheka St. ☎ **808/973-4800.**

A mecca for penny-pinchers, this huge discount store is in a residential neighborhood two blocks mauka of the Ala Moana Shopping Center. It's jammed with local people busy buying everything from groceries to books to toys to toasters, all at fat discounts. Buys are especially good if you watch for specials in Hawaiian wear for men, women, and keikis. While you're here, stock up on groceries and booze—the prices are excellent, much better than in the smaller stores at the beach. If it's time for lunch, you can join the crowd at the outside Chinese cafeteria deli, which has a good take-out department, as well as some 20 items on the steam table. Open Monday through Saturday from 8am to midnight, until 10pm on Sunday.

✪ Hilo Hattie Fashion Center

700 Nimitz Hwy. ☎ **808/537-2926.**

If garment factories appeal to you, here's one you can bused to at no charge with extras thrown in. (They'll also take you to the Dole Pineapple Cannery.) This place offers something like 40,000 Hawaiian fashions to browse through, all for sale at factory prices, plus free refreshments, free hemming, and a lei greeting.

✪ Komil

96-1185 Waihona St. (Pearl City Industrial Park, Bldg.) ☎ **808/456-4272.**

Advertised as "Hawaii's best kept secret," Komil is situated in a warehouse. There are no frills; the unique and lovely clothing (all made in India) hangs from iron-pipe racks, and there are small curtained fitting rooms. A well-dressed Honolulu friend of ours buys more than half of her clothes there and has never paid more than $40 for a dress. Their clothes retail around the islands for up to $175. For women, there are dresses, jumpsuits, blouses, and skirts; for preteen girls, there are all four of the above plus playsuits; for men, there are often some great-looking aloha shirts for $10! The stock changes constantly, but the warehouse is a season behind the retail shops; yet at these prices, who can complain? *A word of caution:* Be sure to try everything on; the sizing leaves something to be desired.

⑤ Liberty House's Penthouse

1 N. King St. ☎ **808/941-2345.**

Downtown is where the local people do a lot of their shopping, and we'll let you in on a kamaaina secret known to very few tourists: Discounted merchandise from all Liberty House stores around town is brought here, and the initial reduction is a whopping 50%. On top of that, the price is automatically dropped another 30% on the first Monday of each succeeding month. Most of the items consist of women's, children's, and men's clothing and accessories. There are also terrific values on special-purchase items. On a recent shopping foray we found $100 handbags at $50, $150 dresses at $75, and $30 aloha shirts at $15. Enough said? At their clearing house, you can also get towels, sheets, pots and pans, and gift items at 50% off. This is one of those places where on some days you'll find nothing suitable, on other days you'll strike it rich!

Outlet Shops at Dole Cannery

Cannery Square. ☎ **808/548-6601.**

Honolulu will have as many as 100 new outlet stores by the time the new outlet center at the Dole Cannery is completed. The developers, The Horizon Group, are committed to preserving the history of this important Hawaii landmark. A self-guided tour of the area is planned and much of the actual cannery equipment will be on view as sculpture—a tribute to this major era of the economic history of Hawaii. There are free bus pickups from 10 Waikiki hotels every hour. For information, call **808/548-6601.**

Princess Kaiulani
1222 Kaumaulii St. ☎ **808/847-4806.**

Their dresses are ultra-feminine, with eyelet or lace or ruffles; the fabrics are top-quality. This attractive factory showroom offers its own products and others at about 30% savings on most retail stores. Long muumuus, selling here in the $75-to-$80 range, would be well over $100 at most stores. Open to the public Monday through Saturday from 8am to 5pm.

ⓢ The Ultimate You
851 Pohukaina St., Bldg. C Bay 4 ☎ **808/591-8388.**

Just a few blocks opposite Ward Centre is a shop known to few tourists; but the "Bergdorf Goodman of the consignment shops," as it might be called, is very well known indeed to Hawaii's most fashion-conscious women. This is where they come for new and next-to-new high fashion at surprisingly low prices. Owner Kelsey Sears has contacts with socialites and celebrities in the islands, on the mainland, and in Europe; when they get slightly bored with their designer duds after a wearing or two (or when they've compulsively bought five-of-a-kind sweaters and never worn them), they send them to Sears, who resells them for anywhere from 50% to 90% off retail price. She insists that everything be in pristine condition. Half the store consists of brand-new merchandise, much of it from European designers, that is also heavily discounted. Obviously, the stock here changes daily, so you never can tell what you'll find, but it's worth a look-see. A $100 dress could go for as little as $49, a $75 silk blouse for as little as $25. We've picked up designer muumuus for under $25. The Ultimate You is open Monday through Friday from 10am to 6pm, Saturday from 9am to 5pm.

Waikele Factory Stores
About 20 minutes from downtown and about 40 minutes from Waikiki, on the leeward side of the island, Waikele Center is like a little country shopping village. It boasts its own free trolley to take you around from store to store. The center recently won an award for environmental awareness for its commitment to recycling.

The outlet is open Monday through Saturday from 9am to 9pm, Sunday from 10am to 6pm. Some of the stores represented here are **Borders Books & Music, Saks Fifth Avenue Clearinghouse, Local Motion, The Sports Authority,** and **Discovery Zone.** As for whether or not you'll get major bargains here, you must consider that anything manufactured on the mainland or in Europe could cost approximately as much in an "outlet" store in Hawaii as it would in a non-outlet store on the mainland because of the enormous charges for shipping and handling to get it here. Be that as it may, prices are always attractive and a visit here is a great deal of fun. If you're driving, take the H-I Freeway to the Waikele Interchange at Exit 7, then enter the center via Kamehameha Highway and Lumiaina Street or via Paiwa Street and Lumiaina. If you're going by public transportation, take TheBus no. 2 from Waikiki to downtown, then no. 48 from downtown.

Fashions

✪ Nake'u Awai

1613 Houghtailing St. ☎ 808/841-1221.

This store is a bit out of the way—unless you combine it with a visit to the Bishop Museum—but it's worth a trip if you like unusual fabrics and designs. Joel Nake'u Awai is a young Hawaiian designer whose beautiful silk-screened fabrics are a blend of the traditional and the contemporary in Hawaiian art. After he designs and produces the textiles, he has them whipped up into long skirts, shirts, muumuus, bags, and sundresses. They're not cheap, but the prices are certainly competitive with those of the better department stores and specialty shops, and the designs are exclusive. We also saw some very good-looking T-shirts with Hawaiian designs and an interesting array of locally crafted items—lauhala fans, koa-bound books, gift cards, woven bags—for $16 and up. Inquire about his fashion shows; if you can catch one of them you're in for a treat. They're as imaginative as the clothes and include appearances by guest luminaries. Open until 3:30pm Monday through Friday, until 2pm on Saturday. TheBUS no. 2 will take you there.

Nui-Mono

2645 S. King St. ☎ 808/946-7404.

Elaine Costello and her daughter, Lue Zimmelam, have been at their tiny shop in the University area for 25 years. Their specialty is clothing made of Kasuri and Shiori cotton. Kimonos in beautiful colors and prints, some of them tie-dyed, are designed by Elaine and made right there in the shop. For clothing of this quality, prices are not unreasonable. You could pick up a jacket for $75; others are higher. Other clothing, dresses, and pants outfits, fashioned of silk, are made elsewhere. Whimsical gifts and collectibles are available, too. The front door is always locked, but you are very welcome; just ring the bell.

Flea Markets

⑤ Aloha Swap Meet

Aloha Stadium. ☎ 808/486-1529.

Dauntless shoppers swear by this flea market, the biggest and best in Honolulu, with some 1,000 booths to browse through. This is definitely the place to get T-shirts: Hanes Beefy-Ts can usually be found here at a fraction of what they cost at Ala Moana or in Waikiki. University of Hawaii sweatshirts cost less here than at the university bookstore. Men can often get shorts at three pairs for $6 or $7. Seems the vendors here vie to undersell each other, and the shoppers get the benefit. Aloha Swap Meet is every Wednesday, Saturday, and Sunday (and daily for the three weeks before Christmas) from 6am to 3pm, and the really serious folks get there early. Take TheBUS no. 20 from Waikiki right to Aloha Stadium. Admission is 35¢ per person.

Food

If you're going to do any cooking in your kitchenette, you're going to be shocked when you do your first shopping for groceries. Food costs in Honolulu are substantially higher than in big cities on the mainland (almost one-third more, in some cases) and they are especially high in hotel shops. Hotel shops are a nice convenience, but if you're going to do any serious shopping, you're far better off taking your rented car and heading for the **supermarkets.**

The big Honolulu chains are Star, Times, Safeway, and Foodland (and Emjay's, a subsidiary of Foodland). There are several of each of these, with addresses in the phonebook. Gem on Ward Avenue and Holiday Mart (801 Kaheka St., two blocks mauka of the Ala Moana Shopping Center), also offer low prices. In Waikiki, the best prices are found at Food Pantry, 2370 Kuhio Ave., an enormous super-market located in central Waikiki, behind the International Market Place. Liquor prices are especially good here. There's another Food Pantry at 444 Hobron Lane, not far from the Ilikai Hotel. Prices are also good, although selection is limited, at the ABC Discount stores.

Natural foods are generally not inexpensive, so we were delighted to find "healthy food at prices that don't make you sick" at ✪ **Down to Earth Natural Foods,** 2525 S. King St. (☎ 808/947-7678), near University Avenue. *Honolulu* magazine has rated this friendly place as the best overall natural-food store in Honolulu. As big as a supermarket, Down to Earth has dozens of bins of grains and beans, a large refrigerator of organically grown fruits and vegetables, and a Natural Medicine Center that features, among other items, Chinese herbs, including ginseng and "dragon eggs." All products, including vitamin and mineral supplements, are totally vegetarian. Also on the premises is the Down to Earth Deli for excellent vegetarian meals (see "Where to Eat," in Chapter 5). Open daily from 8am to 10pm.

Just down the block, **Kokua Market, Natural Foods Co-Op,** 2649 S. Beretania St. (☎ 808/941-1922), offers a full line of natural foods and organic produce. They have fresh sandwiches, cold drinks, and a wide variety of snacks and gourmet vegetarian deli items. Open daily.

Terrific baked goods—freshly baked whole-grain breads (oatmeal, raisin, cinnamon, sprouted wheat), pies, and cakes—are the main reason for tracking down the popular **Vim and Vigor** store at Ala Moana Center. They also have good prices on an extensive selection of dried fruits, nut butters, fresh produce, and many other natural and organic items. Their snack bar is great, too.

If you'd like to shop for produce, fish, and meat with the locals, visit the **Ala Moana Farmer's Market** (a block from the Ala Moana–Ward intersection at Auahi Street), where the atmosphere is pungent and the prices low. It's a great place to get acquainted with local Hawaiian foods and taste sensations. The long, low building is lined with a number of stalls, some with ready-to-eat items. Here you can sample poi, raw fish, and other delicacies such as ogo, palu, and tako. In case you're not feeling all that adventurous, you can settle for a 12-ounce can of New Zealand corned beef or imu kalua pig, both cooked and ready for your own private luau. At **Haili's Hawaiian Foods,** in business since 1867, we saw one-day and two-day poi and even sour poi, all quite difficult to find.

It's also good fun—and good value—to attend one of the **People's Open Markets,** sponsored by the city of Honolulu. Farmers bring their produce to various spots on different days. The market closest to Waikiki takes place on

Readers Recommend

Dole Pineapple Cannery, Cannery Sq. (☎ 808/523-3653). *"We ordered our pine-apples to bring home at the Dole Pineapple Cannery. They delivered them to a fruit stand at the airport. These were the best pineapples we have ever had. Plus, they made wonderful gifts to bring back for office coworkers."* —Julie Clark, Olean, N.Y.

Wednesday, from 9:45am to 10:45am, at Paki Playground; you'll find it on an outdoor basketball court behind the fire station on Kapahulu Avenue.

Gifts/Novelties

✪ The Zootique

At the Honolulu Zoo, 151 Kapahulu Ave. ☎ **808/923-7472.**

This nonprofit museum store operated by the Honolulu Zoological Society features educational and fun merchandise such as toys, books, posters, jewelry, apparel, and gift items with an animal theme. You'll find T-shirts designed exclusively for the Zootique, and an array of exotic plush animals and souvenir items such as bumper stickers, pennants, and coffee mugs. The Zootique is open daily from 9am to 5:30pm (closed Christmas and New Year's).

Leis

When local people need to buy leis, they usually head for Chinatown—and so should you. Although leis are sold all over town, especially at the airport and on the ocean side of Kalakaua Avenue, the best prices and finest quality can usually be found among the Chinatown lei sellers. There are several stores on Maunakea Street; some of our favorites are **Cindy's Lei Shoppe** at no. 1034, **Violet's** at no. 1165, **Jenny's Lei Stand** at no. 1151, and **Lin's** at no. 1107. **Lita's Leis** is around the corner at 59 N. Beretania St., and **Aloha** is at the corner of Puuahi. Cindy and Lita both make beautiful haki-head leis that dry splendidly and can be worn for a long time. Cindy's carries the largest selection of flower leis in the state, and all six make up orchid, plumeria, double carnation, and other leis, at prices ranging from $5 to $10 and up, depending on the season and the availability of flowers. Should you want to send leis to your friends back home—a lovely but no longer inexpensive gift—expect to pay $27 and up by Express Mail. (And they may not be very chipper when they arrive. Near the University of Hawaii, good places to know about are **Rudy's** at 2122 S. King St. (☎ 808/944-8844), and **Flowers by Jr., Lou and T.** at 2652 S. King St. (☎ 808/947-5527). We also like the flowers—and the low prices—at **Chiyo's,** located inside and at the front of the Thrifty Drugstore at 3610 Waialae Ave. in the Waialae-Kahala area. You can shop by phone (☎ 808/734-6337 or 808/737-5055), and be assured that your order will be well and speedily taken care of. They'll bill you later.

Buyers beware: The most expensive times to buy leis are May Day, the graduation season (end of May), and New Year's; that's when $5 vanda orchid leis can suddenly become $15 to $18!

Surf Stuff

Local Motion

1714 Kapiolani Blvd., near Ala Moana Shopping Center. ☎ **808/955-SURF.**

If you're really serious about surfing, or learning to surf, you should know about this place. Any surfer will tell you that in order to learn to surf safely and joyously you need good instruction and a well-constructed board. Many of those for rent at beach stands are outdated, hence the need for a source like Local Motion. Here you can rent a board for $20 for the first day and $15 for every day thereafter. By the week, it's $75. And they also sell snappy sports and leisure clothes. Local Motion is also at the Windward Mall in Kaneohe, at Koko Marina in Hawaii Kai, and at the Walkele Shopping Center in the Pearl City area, as well as on Maui.

Thrift Shops

An excellent thrift shop is **St. Andrew's Economy Shop** at St. Andrew's Cathedral, downtown at Beretania and Queen Emma streets (☎ **808/536-5939**), open Monday, Wednesday, and Friday from 9:30am to 4pm, Saturday until 1pm. The **Punahou Thrift Shop,** run by the famed Punahou School, also offers good values, and is open Monday, Wednesday, and Friday from 9am to 2pm. Should you happen to be in town for the Punahou Carnival (usually held in mid- or late January) be sure to check their flea market, especially at the close of the event, for sometimes extraordinary savings. The **Iolani School Thrift Shop,** 563 Kamoku St. (enter through the Laau Street entrance off Date Street), has great bargains, new and used. Located only five minutes from Waikiki across the Ala Wai, its open on Wednesday from 10am to 3pm and on Monday and Saturday from 9am to noon. **La Pietra Thrift Shop,** 2993 Poni Moi Rd. (☎ **808/922-2744**), has some designer clothing plus very good housewares. The shop is open Monday, Wednesday, and Saturday from 9am to noon. Hours can change at these shops, so be sure to call before you go.

5 Honolulu After Dark

Honolulu has a rich cultural life: Classical music, opera, theater, and dance are abundant, and of excellent quality. And ticket prices are often lower than in most other artistic centers. Check the local papers when you arrive, and also call the **Mayor's Performance Hotline** (☎ 808/527-5666) for a recording that describes activities planned for the current month at Honolulu Hale (City Hall), Iolani Palace, Kapiolani Park Bandstand, and Tamarind Park on Bishop Street. The service also announces any last-minute cancellations.

UNIQUELY HAWAIIAN ENTERTAINMENT

LUAUS   Luaus are fun affairs—everyone arrives dressed in aloha shirts and muumuus, a great ceremony is made of taking the pig out of the imu (camera buffs have been known to go wild with joy at this part), there's lively Polynesian entertainment, and the mai tais flow freely.

Honolulu offers a number of luaus, but one that's most consistently praised is the **Paradise Cove Luau** (☎ 808/973-LUAU, or toll free 800/775-2683 in the mainland U.S.), held in a Hawaiian theme park 27 miles from Waikiki, on a 12-acre beachfront site in the town of Ewa. (Nearby is Oahu's newest resort development, Ko Olina, home to the exquisite Ihilani Resort & Spa.) Guests can wander through a village of thatched huts, learn ancient Hawaiian games and crafts, enjoy the spectacular sunset over the ocean, help pull in the fish in the nets during the hukilau, and watch a program of ancient and modern hula at the imu ceremony. Then it's a buffet meal and a Polynesian show: The fire dancer alone is worth the price of admission. Bus fare from Waikiki is included in the admission prices of $47.50 or $55 (upgrade-seating) adults, $27.50 or $32.50 adults, $25 children 6 to 12. The luau is held every night of the week.

HERITAGE SHOWS   There are quite a few opportunities to catch free Hawaiian entertainment. If you're in town on a Friday, don't miss the King's Jubilee, a tribute to King Kalakaua at the **Hilton Hawaiian Village;** it's an imaginative re-creation of the period of Hawaiian monarchy in the late 19th century. Things get underway at 6:30pm with a march to the hotel's porte cochère, where the Hawaiian anthem is sung; from then on it's a torchlight ceremony, Hawaiian music, and hula dancing at 7, fireworks at 8, plus more entertainment until 10pm (☎ 808/949-4321 for details). There's a one-drink minimum ($3.50) for table seating; standing room is free.

The same Hilton Hawaiian Village is also the place to catch dancers and musicians from the Polynesian Cultural Center who perform on the **Village Green** every Tuesday from 3 to 6pm. A different Polynesian culture is highlighted each month; phone 808/847-8200 for information. Every evening between 5:30 and 9:45pm, the lovely poolside terrace at the **Sheraton Princess Kaiulani Hotel** is the scene of a free show featuring songs and dances of Polynesia. Have a drink or not, as you like (☎ 808/922-5811).

HULA DANCING   Just as you expected, virtually everyone in Hawaii does the hula. Island youngsters learn it just as mainland children take ballet or tap lessons. Social directors and hotel instructors patiently instruct the malihinis, and wherever you look there's a hula show underway. All of this is fun, and some of it is good dancing, but much of it is a bastardization of a noble and beautiful dance, Hawaii's most visible contribution to the arts.

Happily, there has been a great revival of interest in serious hula lately, and if you're lucky you may get to see outstanding dancing at some of the better nightclub shows or at concert presentations. True devotees of hula should visit the islands during the month of April. That's when the ✪ **Merrie Monarch Festival** is held in Hilo, on the Big Island of Hawaii, a week-long virtual Olympics of hula, with dancers from all the various hula halaus (schools) of the islands competing in both ancient and modern hulas. You probably won't be able to get tickets to the events themselves (they're usually sold out by the preceding January), but they are fully covered on television and are a true joy to watch. On a recent trip, we sat enthralled viewing the competition and the judging—as did just about everyone else on the islands.

Not only hula shows but also ballet performances, choral and band concerts, martial-arts demonstrations, and fashion shows are held frequently at **Centerstage** at Ala Moana Shopping Center. More than 500 free programs a year are presented, by island talent and international performing groups. Check tourist publications for exact times. The new **Aloha Tower Marketplace,** on the waterfront downtown, is the scene of constant entertainment and cultural events, including hula shows—and they're all free.

The **Kodak Hula Show** is actually a daytime event. It's a venerable Waikiki institution that showcases authentic music and dance by talented artists. Naturally, it's nirvana for photographers. There is special seating for the disabled. The show is held at the Waikiki Shell in Kapiolani Park, Tuesday through Thursday at 10am. Get here early for a good seat, because even with bleachers that seat 4,000 people, it's always crowded. (For free Hilo Hattie bus transportation, call 808/537-2926.)

Kuhio Mall presents a free hula show every night at 7 and 8pm. Usually, there's a free show at the beach in front of the **Reef Hotel** every Sunday from 8pm to 9:30 or 10pm. Lots of bright amateurs get into the act. Free concerts and cultural shows are given in the Great Hall of the **Hyatt Regency Waikiki,** often at noon or 5pm, but since the schedule varies greatly, you should check with the Hyatt Hostess Desk (☎ 808/922-9292) for exact times. The Pau Hana show, Friday at 5pm, featuring Aunty Malia Solomon, is a perennial favorite. Hawaiian music and dance performances are presented at the **Bishop Museum,** Monday through Friday at 1pm. There's free entertainment galore at the **Royal Hawaiian Shopping Center.** You can usually count on a minishow presented by the Polynesian Cultural Center, on Friday and Saturday between 6:30 and 8pm and on Saturday between 10:30am and noon, in the Fountain Courtyard. For exact times, and news of special programs check the local papers.

Look for notices in the papers of concerts presented by **Dances We Dance,** an educational and performing organization that sponsors both ethnic and modern dance concerts throughout the state. On one trip we were lucky enough to catch a concert by the Ladies of Na Pualei O Likolehua, as part of a special season of Hawaiian dance. Performances are usually held in the state-of-the-art Mamiya Theatre at the St. Louis Center for the Arts, on the St. Louis–Chaminade campus, 3140 Waialae Ave. To see a noncommercial dance presentation by a respected hula halau like this one is a very special experience.

Probably the best ethnic dancing of the Pacific Islands is done by the dance group at the **Polynesian Cultural Center.** They often do free minishows at the Royal Hawaiian Shopping Center. Watch for outstanding programs of Japanese, Korean, and other Asian dances at the University of Hawaii.

CONCERTS   Free concerts are generally held on Sunday at 2pm at the **Kapiolani Park Bandstand.** Entertainment includes Polynesian revues, ukulele clubs, visiting mainland troupes, jazz and rock musicians, and usually the famed Royal Hawaiian Band; call **808/926-4030** for more information. You can nearly always be sure to catch the Royal Hawaiian Band at its Friday noontime concerts at the **Iolani Palace bandstand.** These lunchtime concerts are very popular with the local people who work nearby; bring a lunch and have a listen. Also popular is the free concert at **Wilcox Park** (King Street next to Fort Street Mall) on the second and fourth Mondays of each month from noon to 1pm. On the fourth Thursday of each month, there's a free concert at 7pm in City Hall Courtyard. Or join the local crowd on Friday at noon for the **Mayor's Aloha Friday Music Break,** held at Tamarind Park, at the corner of Bishop and King streets (☎ 808/527-5666). Tuesdays at noon it's the **Mayor's Chinatown Music Break,** at Gateway Park at the corner of Bethel and Hotel streets (☎ 808/527-5666). Local bands play Hawaiian music at the free **Pau Hana concerts** at the Mainstage at Aloha Tower Marketplace Fridays from 5 to 7pm (☎ 808/528-5700).

LOCAL JAZZ   There are frequent free jazz events at Ward Warehouse (check newspapers or call Victoria Ward, Limited at 808/531-6411). For jazz on the radio, tune in to Station KIPO (1380 AM and 89.3), Hawaii Public Radio for news and jazz, classical, and folk music. You can also phone Seth Markow at the station (☎ 808/955-8821) for information on jazz events throughout the state. Seth has a nightly show on KIPO at 6pm Monday through Friday.

THE CLUB & MUSIC SCENE
NIGHTCLUBS, CABARET & COMEDY

Let's be perfectly honest: To see the top nightclub shows in Hawaii, you're going to break your budget—and then some. When a big name is entertaining, the local clubs usually impose a cover charge plus a minimum of two drinks, which can swiftly add up to more than you'd think. On top of that, many of them prefer to accommodate their dinner guests only—and dinner at these places is usually in the

$50 or $60 bracket. Luckily, many of the clubs also have cocktail shows at about half the price, which usually include one drink and tax.

Here's the information on the top names and places. Check the local tourist papers when you're in town for exact details; a top star might just happen to be on the mainland when you're in the islands, but somebody new and unknown might be making a smashing debut.

○ The Brothers Cazimero

At the Bishop Museum, 1525 Bernice St. ☎ **808/847-3511.** Admission $37.50 with dinner; $22.50 without. Includes admission to the Bishop Museum.

We'd give up almost anything to catch a show by The Caz. They are beloved champions of authentic Hawaiian music and dance, and many of their songs—and the dances of their company, featuring the incredible Lein'ala—are truly from the heart of Hawaii. After many years at the Royal Hawaiian Hotel, The Caz have relocated to what, at first, seems an unlikely venue; actually, it works perfectly. Surrounded by the ancient artifacts of the islands, the Brothers delve even more deeply into their love for Hawaiiana. Seating is theatre style. Since the museum does not close before the show (7pm, Wednesday, Saturday, and Sunday), you might want to come early, tour the museum, have a picnic supper out on the lawn, and then spend an evening with The Caz. The picnic supper, included in the higher-priced admission ticket, comes in a lauhala basket that you may keep, and consists of barbecued chicken, salad, and dessert. Wine and beer are available for purchase at carts: fruit punch is free.

Frank DeLima

At Polynesian Palace Showroom, Outrigger Reef Towers Hotel, 227 Lewers St. ☎ **808/923-SHOW.** Cover charge, cocktail show $27.50, plus two-drink minimum.

Although a lot of his material is local—he loves poking fun at the various ethnic groups of Hawaii—Frank DeLima seems to be adored by both islanders and tourists alike. He's a musical comedian rather than a standup comic, and he uses the guys in his back-up group (who are also very funny) in his song parodies and skits. Frank is not smutty, so you can feel perfectly comfortable bringing older children. Readers of *Honolulu* magazine have voted him "Best Local Celebrity/Entertainer." His show here is on Tuesday through Saturday at 9pm.

Loyal Garner and Glenn Medeiros—and Charo!

At the Polynesian Palace Showroom, 227 Lewers St. ☎ **808/922-SHOW.** Cover charge, cocktail show $29.50 18 and over, $23.50 students 12–18, $18.50 12 and under; dinner show $47.50 12 and over, $38.50 under 12.

The early show at the Polynesian Palace alternates every three months. You might get to see Loyal Garner and Glen Medeiros, two of the best voices in the islands, making mellow music, or then again, you might catch Charo. The show is on Tuesday through Saturday at 7pm.

John Hirokawa

In the "Magic of Polynesia" at the Hilton Hawaiian Village Dome Showroom, 2005 Kalia Rd. ☎ **808/949-4321,** ext. 25. Cover charge, cocktail show $29.50 adults, $20.50 children; dinner show $49.50 adults, $34.50 children.

Hawaii-born illusionist John Hirokawa is a kind of modern-day Harry Houdini. How he performs his daring feats of illusion nobody knows, but he's a great showman. The show is fine for older children, but it might be a bit scary for really tiny tots.

Don Ho
At the Waikiki Beachcomber Hotel, 2300 Kalakaua Ave. ☎ **808/931-3034.** Cover charge, cocktail show $28 adults, $14 5–20 year olds; dinner show $46 adults, $23 5–11 years olds.

Don Ho has been called "the Frank Sinatra of Hawaii." In one respect, at least, the comparison is apt: Like Ol' Blue Eyes, Don just keeps getting mellower all the time. An international star for over 30 years, Don still sits center stage at his organ, telling stories, singing island music, calling up local talent to perform. It's great campy fun.

Honolulu Comedy Club
In the Ilikai Hotel, 1777 Ala Moana Blvd. ☎ **808/922-5998.** Cover $12.

Local and mainland comedians are featured in 90-minute performances held on Tuesday, Wednesday, and Thursday at 8:30pm, on Friday at 8 and 10pm, and on Saturday at 8 and 10:15pm.

Pau Hana Show
At the Hyatt Regency Waikiki, 2424 Kalakaua Ave. ☎ **808/923-1234.** No cover.

On Friday at 5pm, when local people finish work, they like to head for this spot. So should you. Traditional Hawaiian music, dances, and songs are presented for the cost of a few drinks. You can also stand by the giant waterfall and just watch.

Polynesian Revue
At the Hyatt Regency Waikiki, 2424 Kalakaua Ave. ☎ **808/923-1234.** No cover.

Every Monday, Tuesday, and Thursday, you can listen to the drums of the South Pacific. Te Vai Ura Nui performs from 5 to 5:30pm.

Sheraton's Spectacular Polynesian Revue
Ainahau Showroom, in the Princess Kaiulani Hotel, 120 Kaiulani Ave. ☎ **808/922-5811.** Cover charge, dinner show 5:15pm seating $56, 8pm $49; cocktail show 5:45 and 8:30pm, $27.50.

There are several good Polynesian shows on the beach, but if you're going to see just one, make it this stunning 1^1/$_2$-hour-long authentic Polynesian revue that pulls out all the stops (Fiji war chants, Samoan fire-knife dancers, Tahitian aparimas, and much more). You have a choice of a dinner show (consisting of an excellent prime rib buffet and one drink) or cocktail show.

Society of Seven
Main Showroom, in the Outrigger Waikiki, 2335 Kalakaua Ave. ☎ **808/922-6408** or 923-0711. Cover charge, cocktail show $29.50 adults, $24 students 12–20, $23.50 children; dinner show $50.50 adults, $39.50 children under 12.

For more than 20 years, the show put on by the seven talented entertainers who call themselves the Society of Seven has been an island favorite. These young men sing, act, play a variety of musical instruments, and even reprise Broadway musicals (we caught them once in their miniversion of *Phantom of the Opera*), and they know how to keep an audience cheering. Music, imitations, comedy routines, rock music, oldies, and island favorites are all part of the act. It's held at 7 and 9pm Monday through Saturday (on Wednesday at 9pm only). The cocktail show includes tax, tip, and either one soft drink or one cocktail.

DANCE CLUBS
The dance club and rock scenes are bigger, better, and noisier than ever in Honolulu. A recent look around revealed something like a dozen clubs packing them

in, and more on the way (there's also a fairly high rate of turnover).The local clubs are mostly inexpensive; usually, they have a modest cover charge or none at all, and just a few insist on a two-drink minimum and/or a fee. Live bands usually alternate with disco, and the action gets under way between 9 and 10pm in most clubs and only ends when everyone drops from exhaustion—anywhere between 2 and 4am.

In addition to the listings that follow, **Studebaker's,** in Restaurant Row (☎ 808/526-9888), is the best dancing spot outside Waikiki. Not only can you "bop till you drop," but you are given sustenance while doing so. See the listing under "Happy Hours," below, for more details.

Irish Rose Saloon

In the Outrigger Towers Hotel, 227 Lewers St. ☎ **808/924-7711.** No cover.

There's dancing every night from 9pm to 2am to a live band. There's also a free jukebox that plays old-time music, a giant TV for sports fans, and 20 kinds of beer.

Kento's

In the Hyatt Regency Waikiki, 2424 Kalakaua Ave. ☎ **808/923-7400.** Cover $10.

The Copycats are usually the featured artists and they draw the crowds for a lively evening of '50s to '70s "Oldies but Goodies." The rocking and rolling goes on from 7pm to 2am nightly.

Maharaja Restaurant and Disco

At the Waikiki Trade Center, 2255 Kuhio Ave. ☎ **808/922-3030.** Cover $5.

The first Maharaja Club outside Japan (which has 100), this $5-million extravaganza has the best sound-and-light system in the islands. The theme is East Indian, the mood is opulent (mirrored ceilings, Italian marble), and the crowd is an international mix, which perhaps accounts for the stiff dress code—no jeans, T-shirts, or sneakers (no formal wear, either). They play all types of music, including Top-40 hits. A restaurant serves a wide range of both Japanese and Western dishes at moderate prices. Open daily from 9pm to 4am.

Rumours

At the Ala Moana Hotel, 410 Atkinson Dr. ☎ **808/955-4811.** Cover $5 after 9pm.

There's an upscale feeling and dress code to match at this completely redone spot, which has first-of-its-kind-in-Hawaii audio, video, and lighting gear. It features music videos, a light show complete with special effects, laser karaoke on Tuesdays, and four of the islands' best DJs. During the Friday happy hour, they play music from the early '60s through the late '70s, which they call "The Big Chill."

Scruples

In the Waikiki Marketplace, 2310 Kuhio Ave. ☎ **808/923-9530.** Cover $5 after 9pm.

One of the town's hottest nightspots, Scruples has DJs spinning Top-40 hits every night from 8pm to 4am.

Wave Waikiki

1877 Kalakaua Ave. ☎ **808/941-0424.** Cover (beginning at 10pm) $5.

Hawaii's biggest, brassiest, rock-and-roll nightclub features a live band and light show every night, cocktails and dancing from 9pm to 4am. You must be 21 or over. No dress code.

KARAOKE

Karaoke GS Studio

At the Waikiki Joy Hotel, 320 Lewers St. ☎ **808/921-3534.**

The Japanese karaoke craze is also very big in the islands—karaoke machines can be found in a number of clubs. In case you didn't know, karaoke means "empty orchestra"—an orchestra minus the singer. That's where you come in. A laser-disc video machine provides the words, and guests—which could mean you—take turns providing the singing. Prices begin at $10 per hour for two people, and there's a 50% discount if you check in before 7pm. There are even "happy singing hours" from 5 to 9pm, two hours for the price of one. To reserve a studio, call the number above.

BAR SCENE
BARS WITH LIVE MUSIC

Beach Bar

In the Sheraton Moana Surfrider, 2365 Kalakaua Ave. ☎ **808/922-3111.** No cover.

The music at this bar begins at 2:30pm and continues—with some interruptions—until 11pm at night. Hawaiian style entertainers and various steel-guitar groups can be heard daily to 11pm. A neat place for a drink near the water's edge, the bar is tucked into one of Waikiki's classic oceanfront hotels, which has undergone a magnificent period restoration.

Gordon Biersch Brewery Restaurant

At Aloha Tower Marketplace, 101 A La Moana Blvd. ☎ **808/599-4877.** No cover.

Hawaii's first microbrewery is the best place in town for beer. The hugely successful combination restaurant and open-air beer garden (see "Where to Eat," Chapter 5) is also the place to catch live entertainment every Wednesday through Saturday, from 7pm on; Strange Brew, an engaging group, will be playing contemporary music. The brewing vats are fully visible; from them emerge three German-style lagers: Dunkles, the house specialty, dark, malty, and yeasty; Export, a light brew for American tastes; and Marzen, an Octoberfest style beer. All are $2.75 for 10 ozs., $3.50 a half-litre.

Mai Tai Bar

In the Royal Hawaiian Hotel, 2259 Kalakaua Ave. ☎ **808/923-7311.** No cover.

Right on the sands of Waikiki, this is a glorious spot to hear Hawaiian music as the sun goes down. And who better to deliver it than Keith and Carmen Haugen, a highly admired local couple. They make their music from 5:30 to 8:30pm Tuesday and Wednesday evenings; the rest of the week, it's The Brothers. There's no drink minimum.

Sloppy Joe's

At Aloha Tower Marketplace, 101 Ala Moana Blvd. ☎ **808/528-0007.** No cover, except for special events such as Mardi Gras.

Modeled after the original in Key West, Florida, and bedecked with Hemingway memorabilia, Sloppy Joe's offers a variety of live entertainment, every day from noon to closing.

COCKTAILS WITH A VIEW

Hanohano Room of the Sheraton-Waikiki
2255 Kalakaua Ave. ☎ **808/922-4422.** No cover.

For one of the most majestic views in town, try this glorious spot where the panorama stretches all the way from Diamond Head to Pearl Harbor. There's entertainment and piano music nightly, from 6:30pm on. Beers will cost you around $4; gin and tonic, $5. Cocktails served from 4 to 11:30pm. No drink minimum. There's dinner dancing nightly from 8:30pm.

✪ House Without a Key
In the Halekulani Hotel, 2199 Kalia Rd. ☎ **808/923-2311.** No cover.

If ever you've dreamed of picture-perfect Hawaii, treat yourself to sunset cocktails in the oceanside lounge of this classic Honolulu resort. Here, under a century-old kiawe tree, you can watch the waves splash up on the breakfront, see the sun sink into the ocean, and hear the music of a top island group, The Islanders (Sunday, Monday, Tuesday, and Thursday from 5 to 8:30pm) and the Hiram Olsen Trio (Wednesday, Friday, and Saturday from 5 to 8:30pm). Kanoe Miller, a former Miss Hawaii, does some beautiful dancing. Don't miss this one. A sunset cocktail pupu (appetizers) and light dinner menu are served from 5 to 9pm daily. Bottled draft beers are $5; exotic drinks are $7.

Papeete Bar
In the Tahitian Lanai Restaurant at the Waikikian on the Beach Hotel, 1811 Ala Moana Blvd. ☎ **808/946-6541.**

At some of the Waikiki hotels, the cocktail lounges overlook the lagoon—and one of our favorites of these is the Tahitian Lanai. In this delightfully "old Hawaii" hotel, a lively local crowd hangs out at the bar, known for its sing-alongs, from 5pm to 1am. During the afternoon happy hour, 2 to 6pm, beer and standard drinks are $2.25, exotic drinks $6.50.

Top of Waikiki
Waikiki Business Plaza Building, 2270 Kalakaua Ave. ☎ **808/923-3877.** No cover.

At the center of Waikiki is a revolving restaurant that resembles a gigantic wedding cake. The top tier is the cocktail lounge, very glamorous by candlelight and starlight. Views of all of Waikiki are yours for the price of a drink. Beer begins at $3.50; a gin and tonic, $4.

HAPPY HOURS

Now we come to the more practical side of pub-crawling; how to drink at half the price and sometimes get enough free food for almost a meal at the same time. The trick here is to hit the bars during their happy hours (usually from 4 to 6pm, but sometimes greatly extended), when they serve free pupus or lower their prices, or both. Note that these hours and prices are apt to change often, but these places always offer a good deal of one sort or another.

Heidi's Lounge
At the Downtown Bistro and Deli, Grosvenor Center on Queen St. at Alakea. ☎ **808/536-5344.**

This is a popular hangout for the downtown after-work crowd who know a good deal when they see it. There's a daily happy hour from 4:30 to 6:30pm, and on Tuesday through Friday there's a free pupu buffet from 5 to 6pm. Thursday night it's "Rolando Sanchez-Salsa Night."

Monterey Bay Canners Lounge
In the Outrigger Hotel, 2335 Kalakaua Ave. ☎ **808/922-5761.**

There's nothing skimpy about the happy hour here. It runs from 7am to 7pm, and during all that time, mai tais are $2.50. As if that weren't enough, there's a second happy hour between 4 and 7pm, when well drinks are $2.50 and beer is $2.75. Oysters and clams on the half-shell are 85¢ each.

Rigger
In the Outrigger Hotel, 2325 Kalakaua Ave. ☎ **808/922-5544.**

Here there's a big-screen TV for sports events and entertainment nightly beginning at 9pm. Snackmix is served free all day. The ever-popular mai tais are just $2.50 during the 11am to 6pm happy hour.

Rose and Crown
At King's Village, 131 Kaiulani Ave. ☎ **808/923-5833.**

This jolly Old English pub offers brews from the mother country, of course, plus an assortment of beers and cocktails, sing-along piano (from 8pm to 1am Thursday), darts, and all sorts of special nights. Happy hours run from 11am to 7:30pm; during that time, draught beer is $1.50 and a gin and tonic costs $2.25—other times, they're twice as much. On Sunday, mai tais are $3.75 ($4.25 at other times).

Scott's Seafood Grill & Bar
At Aloha Tower Marketplace, 1 Ala Moana Blvd. ☎ **808/537-6800.**

During the daily happy hour at this popular spot overlooking the waterfront, domestic beers, house wines, and specialty tropical drinks are all $2.50.

Ⓢ Studebaker's
In Restaurant Row, 500 Ala Moana Blvd. ☎ **808/526-9888.** Cover charge, $1 to $4, plus one drink.

The all-out winner for free food has to be this lively, deafeningly noisy, 1950s time warp complete with a bright-red Studebaker, lots of neon, and a DJ spinning platters. A free buffet is served along with your drinks weekdays from 5:30 to 7:30pm. There are always four hot main dishes—perhaps pepper steak, teriyaki chicken, or shrimp fettuccine, to name a few—plus four or five salads, brown breads, and raw veggies with dip. "Happy Hour" simply refers to the patrons' delight in the free buffet. (*Note:* No one under the age of 21 is allowed; IDs are checked.) Beer is $3.25 and $3.75; standard drinks, $3.50.

Waikiki Broiler
In the Waikiki Tower Hotel, 200 Lewers St. ☎ **808/923-8836.**

Their inside bar serves mai tais for 95¢ between 6 and 9pm. Billy Champion and the Edge perform nightly from 9pm to 1:30am.

Exploring Oahu

Y ou haven't really seen Hawaii until you've left the urban sprawl of Waikiki and Honolulu and traveled to the other side of the mountains for a look at Windward Oahu and the North Shore. And what a look that is! There are jagged cliffs and coral beaches; Stone-age ruins and tropical suburbs; backwoods country towns sleeping in the sun; endless stretches of breadfruit, banana, papaya, hibiscus, lauhala, coconut palms—the glorious vegetation of the tropics so ubiquitous as to be completely taken for granted. And best of all, some of the most intriguing sightseeing attractions in the 50th state are here: Sea Life Park Hawaii, the Byodo-In Temple, and the Polynesian Cultural Center. What's more, not one billboard defaces the landscape; they're kapu in Hawaii. The only signs you will see are those of the Hawaii Visitors Bureau's red-and-yellow warrior pointing to the places of interest. There are dozens of spots for beaching and picnicking, so be sure to have your bathing suit at hand.

TRANSPORTATION You can see a good part of the island by sticking to public transportation. TheBUS no. 55, "Circle Island," which leaves Ala Moana Shopping Center daily at 5 and 35 minutes after the hour from 6:05am on, will enable you to see many island points of interest: the big surf at Haleiwa, Sunset Beach, and the North Shore, and the Polynesian Cultural Center, to name some. (The cost is $1.70, with no transfers; you'll have to pay 85¢ every time you reboard the bus.)

Many of our readers travel the island via public transportation and praise it highly, but we prefer to rent a car, since it's much more efficient time-wise and quite reasonable, especially for more than one person. *Note:* If you do drive, remember to lock your car doors and take your valuables with you when you get out to look at the sights. If you must lock things in your car trunk, do so before you arrive at your destination: You never know who may be watching.

Alternatively, take one of the around-the-island sightseeing tours, such as those offered by **E Noa Tours** (☎ 808/599-2561).

MAPS The maps in this book are for the purpose of general orientation. When doing any extensive driving, we suggest you follow a more detailed road map. We have personally found the maps in *Drive Guide to Oahu,* free from any car-rental company, to be excellent.

1 The Top Attractions

Later on in this chapter, we'll take you on a driving tour around Oahu's Waianae coast. But even if you can't visit the rest of the island at your leisure, there are still some major sites that you shouldn't miss. We've highlighted below the best of the island's attractions beyond the Honolulu and Waikiki limits (and directed you to where they are oriented in the subsequent island drives) in order to help you decide where to spend your vacation time and energies.

Please keep in mind that, in addition to the sights below, the North Shore and windward and leeward coasts are rife with great beaches, hiking trails, and more. For complete details on the island's beaches, water sports, hiking, golf, and other outdoor activities beyond the confines of Honolulu and Waikiki, see Chapter 6, "Beaches and Outdoor Activities in Honolulu and Around Oahu."

Byodo-In Temple Just outside of He'eia, set on beautifully landscaped grounds in the midst of a fragrant Japanese garden, is one of Hawaii's treasures. This $2.6-million replica of the beautiful 900-year-old original Byodo-In in Uji, Japan, was dedicated on June 7, 1968–100 years after the arrival of the first Japanese immigrants to Hawaii. Before you enter the imposing temple itself, ring the bell outside for good luck and the blessing of Amida, the sacred golden Buddha of Western Paradise within. (To get to the temple, see "From Waikiki to the Windward Coast," below.)

Hawaii's Plantation Village This outdoor, nonprofit museum, not far from Pearl Harbor along the leeward coast in Waipahu, is a collection of 30 restored and replica buildings dating from 1840 to 1903. This is a living history experience re-creating the lives of Hawaii's immigrants—the Chinese, Japanese, Portuguese, Filipinos, Puerto Ricans, Okinawans, and Koreans—who came to work on the great sugar plantations alongside Hawaiians. Created and maintained by members of each ethnic community, the homes come alive with the reenactment of traditional ceremonies and the events of daily life. You'll see everything from a Japanese *tofuya* (a building where tofu is made) and a Shinto shrine to an authentic Hawaiian *hale* and a large taro patch, to a restored Chinese cookhouse and a Puerto Rican celebration of Christmas. Plan on spending an hour or two here.

A $5 donation is suggested, $3 for seniors and children. It is open Monday through Saturday from 9am to 3pm and Sunday from 10am to 3pm; reservations are requested. Guided tours are given on the hour.

Makaha Valley and Kane'aki Heiau Makaha Valley is spectacular, with white pheasants strutting about (the best time to see them is in the months of March, April, and May) and glorious views. It's no wonder that the famed Makaha Inn was built here over 25 years ago as a golf resort. Now it's the Sheraton Makaha Golf Club, and it's very pleasant, indeed. Stop in and ask for precise directions to the heiau.

Throughout Hawaii, ancient heiaus are mostly ruins—piles of rocks where one has to use a good deal of imagination to recall the past. Not so with the Kane'aki Heiau: It has been splendidly restored by the Bishop Museum, the National Park Service, and the Makaha Historical Society. Because it is tucked away deep in a valley an hour's drive from Waikiki, and because it is on private property, it does not get a great deal of attention. That's a pity, because for those who have a serious interest in ancient Hawaii, this is one sight not to miss.

Especially for Kids

- **Hanauma Bay.** Most everybody snorkels at this wonderful beach and marine preserve, but even if kids just stand in the water, fish will come up to them and eat right out of their hands.
- **Hawaii's Plantation Village.** Older children in particular will enjoy this trip back to the birth of Hawaii as we know it at this indoor-outdoor living history museum.
- **Hawaii Railway Society Train Rides.** Kids of all ages who remember "the little engine that could" will identify with this beautifully restored oldtime train that also does its utmost; they'll love the way it chugs along on its original narrow-guage track at a maximum speed of 17 m.p.h.—downhill.
- **Jungle River Mini Golf Village.** Kids get a thrill and a chill—and a chance to play miniature golf here; it's landscaped to look like a real jungle village, complete with banana trees, hibiscus, bamboo, even shrunken heads, skeletons, and a huge dinosaur (all bogus, of course). Recorded bird calls fill the air. Open from 10am to 10pm Sunday through Thursday and 10am til midnight on weekends. "Greens fees" are $6 for adults, $5 for kids. You can combine this with a shopping excursion, as it's in Phase III of Pearlridge Center. For information call **808/488-8404.**
- **Polynesian Cultural Center.** Kids are made to feel very welcome at this family-oriented attraction re-creating the cultural heritage of Hawaii. They love the guided canoe tours and the chance to see their own friends perform in the "Keiki Polynesian Show."
- **Sea Life Park Hawaii.** This is perhaps the top children's attraction in Hawaii. It's hard to tear kids away from this marine park (also a marine mammal research center); they especially adore the shows where the dolphins and penguins—and even a killer whale—are put through their paces.

The *heiau* was originally constructed between 1450 and 1640 A.D. and was modified and enlarged three times; each modification reflects the efforts of the alii and kahuas, the chiefs and priests, to strengthen the relationship between the people and the gods. Originally, it was used for agricultural worship; but the third, and final modification, is believed to have transformed it into a *luakini heiau,* or a place of human sacrifice. It was probably used by Kamehameha the Great to honor the war god, Kukailimoku, when he was attempting to consolidate his kingdom in the years between 1795 and 1812. The heiau is open Tuesday through Sunday from 10am to 2pm.

Polynesian Cultural Center   Seven authentic Polynesian villages—Hawaiian, Tongan, Fijian, Samoan, Maori, Marquesan, and Tahitian—have been re-created at this popular site, built more than 30 years ago as a center for the rediscovery and study of ancient Polynesian cultures. Polynesian scholars and staff offer living history presentations, craft demonstrations, ancient music and dance performances, children's programs, and luaus. All in all, though their evening show is glitzier than it should be, they do a terrific job. (See "Along the Windward Coast," below.)

Sea Life Park Hawaii   This marine park and center for marine mammal research is one of Hawaii's biggest sightseeing attractions. In addition to performances by penguins, sea lions, seals, dolphins—even a killer whale—you can visit sanctuaries for endangered marine birds, green sea turtles, Humboldt penguins, and Hawaiian monk seals. There's also a 300,000-gallon Hawaiian Reef Tank filled with 3,000 species of fish, a touch pool for hands-on experiences with sea creatures, and the largest collection of whaling artifacts. (See "From Waikiki to the Windward Coast," below.)

Senator Fong's Plantation and Gardens—The Adventure Center   Former U.S. Senator Hiram Fong has opened his magnificent 725-acre estate to the public; visitors are taken on guided tours in open-air trams through five delightful gardens named for the presidents under whom Fong served during his 17 years in Congress. (See "From Waikiki to the Windward Coast" below.)

Waimea Valley and Waimea Falls Park   Just across the road from Waimea Bay, Waimea Falls Park is situated in the lush 1,800-acre Waimea Valley, an area rich in the history of old Hawaii. The park is home to one of the world's finest arboretums and botanical gardens, a wildlife preserve and bird sanctuary, magnificent endemic flora, miles of hiking trails, a site for trying your hand at a variety of ancient Hawaiian games—and the spectacular falls themselves, of course. (See "The North Shore," below.)

2 From Waikiki to the Windward Coast

From Waikiki, drive Diamond Head on Kalakaua Avenue past Kapiolani Park to Diamond Head Road, which runs into Kahala Avenue past the sumptuous residential area of Black Point. Sculptor Kate Kelly's monument to aviatrix Amelia Earhart is just past the Diamond Head Lighthouse. On your right, a paved trail leads to the cliffs, where you can watch some fancy surfing. At the end of Kahala Avenue, where it hits the Waialae Golf Course, turn left onto Kealaolu Avenue; follow this road to Kalanianaole Highway (Hi. 72); the entrance will be on the right. Before you turn, you come to **Waialae Beach Park,** with modern facilities, covered pavilions, and wide, wide beaches, right next door to the prestigious Waialae Country Club. The rocks in the water make the swimming here not very good. Next door is the splendid Kahala Hilton Hotel; you might want to have a look at the lovely grounds.

Just before you reach Koko Head, you'll pass the entrance to Henry Kaiser's once-controversial **Hawaii Kai**—a 6,000-acre, $350-million housing development that's a small city in itself. You can drive in for your own tour of inspection. (A resident advises us that there's a beautiful view at the top of the hill past the Hawaii Kai Golf Course overlooking the ocean and the south end of Windward Oahu.) While you're in this area, you may want to stop in at **Waterfront Village,** a charming small shopping complex perched right out on the waters of Koko Marina, and tied in by walks and a shared parking lot with the much larger Hawaii Kai shopping center.

Koko Head and **Koko Crater,** now coming into view ahead, are reminders that Oahu, like all the Hawaiian Islands, is a volcanic mountain spewed out of the Pacific. During Oahu's last eruption (volcanologists say it was at least 10,000 years ago), these craters and the one that houses **Hanauma Bay** were born. One side of Koko Head has been washed away into the sea and the result is an idyllic beach, one of the most popular in the islands. Since the placid turquoise waters cover a cove in the purple coral reef, it's a perfect place for beginning and advanced

Eastern Oahu & The Windward Coast

Bellows Field Beach Park **10**

Blow Hole **5**

Brigham Young
University—Hawaii **26**

Byodo-In Temple **16**

Crouching Lion **21**

Diamond Head Crater **1**

Haiku Gardens **15**

Hanauma Bay State Underwater
Park **4**

Hawaiian Temple **28**

Hoomaluhia Botanical Gardens **14**

Kaawa Beach Park **20**

Kailua Beach Park **12**

Koko Head **3**

Laie-Maloo Beach **24**

Laie Point **27**

Kualoa Sugar Mill Ruins **19**

Lanikai Beach **11**

Makapuu Beach Park **7**

Pali Lookout **13**

Polynesian Cultural Center **25**

Sacred Falls State Park **23**

Sandy Beach Park **6**

Sea Life Park **8**

Senator Fong's Plantation
& Gardens **18**

Swanzy Beach State Park **22**

Valley of the Temples **17**

Waimanalo Beach Park **9**

Waterfront Village **2**

Waialae Beach Park

Mokuauia
(Goat Is.)

*Laie
Bay*

Laie

Laie Point

Laniloa
Beach

Oahu

Hauula

Punaluu

Kahana Bay

Kaaawa

Mokolii Island
(Chinaman's Hat)

Kamehameha
Hwy.

Heeia

*Heeia Kea
Harbor*

Kahekili
Hwy.

Moko O Loe
(Coconut Is.)

(under construction)

Kaheohe

Mokapu

Kailua

*Kailua
Bay*

Pali Tunnels

Makiki
Heights

Kailua Rd.

Lanikai

Waimanalo

Mokulua
Islands

Diamond Head

Kahala

Manana
(Rabbit Is.)

Hawaii Kai

*Hanauma
Bay*

Kalanianaole Hwy.

snorkelers. (Rent snorkels in Waikiki or bring your own; none are available here.) Hanauma Bay is now a marine reserve, and so gentle have the fish become that parrot fish, bird wrasses, and others will eat bread from a swimmer's hand. There are dressing facilities, and camping, barbecue, and picnic areas. The beach is a very long walk from the parking area, but you can take a little bus for a small fee. *Be sure to lock your car and remove any valuables!* Needless to say, the islanders love this place, and the only problem is that you've almost always got to share it with quite a lot of them. The beach regularly closes on Wednesdays for maintenance.

For the next few miles along Hi. 72, you drive along one of the islands' most impressive stretches of rocky coastline. Black lava cliffs hurtle down to the sea to meet a surging purple Pacific, all set against a brilliant blue-green background of sky, trees, and flowers. Park the car at any of the designated areas or at the popular **Blow Hole,** where the water geysers up through an underwater vent. (The areas before the Blow Hole are just as pretty and much less crowded.) With the wind in your hair and the surf crashing below, you'll feel light-years away from civilization. Just beyond the Blow Hole is **Sandy Beach Park;** beyond that is **Makapuu Beach Park,** where people are actually surfing on those horrendous waves. These beaches are strictly for experts; beginners had better watch from the sand.

More important, this is the site of one of Hawaii's biggest sightseeing attractions—✪ **Sea Life Park Hawaii,** where there's plenty of entertainment, education, and fun for the whole family. Descend 3 fathoms and see the thousands of colorful fish that inhabit Hawaiian waters at the 300,000 gallon Hawaiian Reef Tank; see whales and dancing dolphins at the Whaler's Cove Show; attend a training session at the Hawaii Ocean Theater Show, where dolphins, penguins, and sea lions show off their agility, strength, and intelligence. And you won't want to miss their newest show, Kolohe Kai, which features some of the fun-loving antics of seals and sea lions.

In addition, you'll want to visit the Bird Sanctuary, and see endangered marine birds such as the booby or iwa; the Penguin Habitat, with a colony of endangered Humboldt penguins; and the 1,500-gallon Touch Pool, where you can touch a sea cucumber or a sea urchin. Observe endangered Hawaiian monk seals at the Hawaiian Monk Seal Care Center or endangered green sea turtles at the Turtle Lagoon. Visit the Pacific Whaling Museum, which houses the largest collection of whaling artifacts—scrimshaw, harpoons, rope work—in the Pacific.

Admission to the park is $19.95 for adults, $10.95 for seniors (over 65), $8.95 for juniors (6 to 12), $3.95 for children (4 to 5), free for those under 4. (Prices are subject to change and include tax.) The park is open daily from 9:30am to 5pm, to 10pm on Friday. On Friday nights, Hawaiian entertainment is included in the regular price of admission. For more information, call the park at **808/ 259-7933.** Sea Life Park Hawaii provides free round-trip shuttle transportation from Waikiki. Call 808/955-FISH for more information. Public buses make hourly runs to the park (☎ 808/848-5555 for information).

A new way to get to Sea Life Park, and also to Waimea Valley (see"The North Shore," below) is now available: The Oahu Nature Bound Circle Island Express costs $29.95 (price subject to change), and includes admission to both parks as well as a coastal trip along the windward side of Oahu. It leaves Waikiki daily at 8am and returns by 5:30pm. For information on pick-up times and locations, call **808/947-OAHU.**

Continuing north on Hi. 72, you soon see **Rabbit Island,** where the water is turquoise. The inland view along this coast is also spectacular, thanks to the towering **Koolau Range;** its corrugated slopes (examples of erosion at work on volcanoes) provide a nice balance to the restless sea on your right.

Just past Sea Life Park, you'll find **Waimanalo Beach Park,** which many island families consider the best beach on Oahu: pleasant surf, grassy knolls, picnic tables, the works. You may want to come back here for a long stay. For now, drive on for a few more miles and, east off Hi. 72, you'll come upon what was long considered one of Oahu's most magnificent beaches by the few people lucky enough to enjoy it—the military. This is **Bellows Field Beach Park,** nestled against the mountains, a 46-acre strip of fine sand, lively but not dangerous surf, and wooded picnic groves of palm and pine. After long years, Bellows has been opened to the public, but on weekends only, from Friday noon to midnight Sunday; and on federal and state holidays. There are public bathhouses. (It's a favorite spot for tent and trailer camping; permits are available from the Recreation Department, City and County of Honolulu.) Bellows is a perfect place for a picnic lunch (bring your own, as there's nothing to buy), or a swim. The only danger (aside from an occasional Portuguese man-of-war) is that you may be tempted to spend the whole day and forget about your exploring. Keep going, for the best is yet to come.

At this point in the journey, make a brief side trip to **Kailua,** one of Honolulu's most pleasant suburbs. Stay on Hi. 72 until it intersects with Hi. 61, turn right (east) and continue until you reach **Kailua,** a few miles down the road. The reason for this trip is the beach: **Kailua Beach Park,** and especially **Lanikai,** are absolutely beautiful, with gentle waves, white sand, and much smaller crowds than you see at Waikiki. We feel this is what Waikiki must have been like in the old, pretourist days.

If you have time for a bit of shopping after your swim, check out some distinctive Kailua shops. **Elizabeth's Fancy,** 767B Kailua Rd. (☎ 808/262-7513), is a delightful little place, set back from the road and filled with beautiful fancies. A nationally known designer of Hawaiian quilts, Elizabeth offers superb quality at very respectable prices—pillows from $60, full-size quilts from $995. Many of the over 400 products bearing Elizabeth's designs can be seen in shops throughout the state, but you find *all* of them here: Hawaiian quilt-design bookmarks, ornaments, beverage napkins, jewelry, embossed cards, stationery, wrapping papers, T-shirts, jellies and sauces, mugs and teas–and, of course, a full selection of ready-made pillows, wall hangings, appliqué tops, kits, and pattern books.

Another wonderful place is **The Garden Art Shop,** 404 Uluniu St. (☎ 808/261-1463). It features hand-painted furniture, rare plants, fresh flowers, and unique artifacts. Also displayed are striking stained-glass pieces by Kelene Blaine and magical, mystical paintings by fine artist Lola Stone. In its tiny quarters you'll find wood carvings, Hawaiian dolls of the collector's variety, and the shop's owner, Cindi Tomei, at work decorating one of the popular garden benches.

Art lovers may also want to stop in at **Oceanic Gallery** in Kailua Town Center, 108 Hekili St. (☎ 808/262-3267). It features the work of artist Richard Pettit, known internationally for his realistic watercolors of marine animals.

If it's the weekend and you're in the mood for a hike, you should know about **Ho'omaluhia Botanical Garden** in Kaneohe, at 45-680 Luluku Rd. Here, at the foot of the Koolau Mountains, are pleasant hiking trails, a Hawaiian garden, a lake, and much more. (See "Hiking," Chapter 6.) At the center, you'll find a small art gallery and exhibit hall. Free guided nature walks are offered on Saturdays at 10am and Sundays at 1pm. Individuals and groups should call in advance to make reservations for these hikes (☎ 808/233-7323). Wear proper footwear and take an umbrella, since showers are common in any season. The garden is open daily from 9am to 4pm.

From Kaneohe, drive inland on Hi. 65 to Hi. 83, and go north. You might want to stop and stretch a bit at a lovely area called **Haiku Gardens,** just west of the Kahekili Highway. For years, Haiku Gardens Restaurant occupied this lovely kamaaina estate. Now it's a handsome Chart House Restaurant. The gardens are open to the public free, during daylight hours. From the lily pond—which dominates everything—trails lead off to, among other things, a lovely grove of golden bamboo from Java, Hawaiian grass huts, a palm grove, bird sanctuary, fragrant plantings of ginger and anthurium, and exotic fish ponds. To reach the gardens, turn left off the highway at Haiku Road and proceed mauka about a mile. It's open Tuesday through Sunday.

For devotees of Eastern culture, we know of no more rewarding spot in the islands than the **Byodo-In Temple** in the Valley of the Temples, which should be your next destination. It's about two miles from Haiku Road, and you can reach it by driving back to Kahekili Highway from Haiku Gardens and proceeding north. (If you haven't stopped at Haiku Gardens, continue on Kamehameha Highway to the intersection on Pineapple Hill, then turn left the way you came onto Kahekili Highway; you'll come to the Valley of the Temples in about half a mile.) An exact replica of the venerable Byodo-In, reputed to be the most beautiful temple in Uji, Japan, this temple was constructed at a cost of $2.6 million and dedicated on June 7, 1968, almost 100 years to the day after the first Japanese immigrants arrived in Hawaii. The temple sits in a magnificently landscaped classical Japanese garden fragrant with pine, plum, and bamboo. Inside, you can gaze at the intricately carved screens and panels, and pay obeisance to the magnificent gold carving of Amida, the Buddha of the Western Paradise. Many of the Buddhist faithful in the islands come here, of course, but a visit is as much an aesthetic as a spiritual experience. While you're meditating turn the kids loose in the gardens, supply them with a package of fish food (thoughtfully sold in a tiny teahouse gift store), and let them feed the flashing carp in the two-acre reflecting lake. The shop also imports religious items and other Japanese gifts from Kyoto. Admission is $2 for adults, $1 for children under 12.

On Saturday, Sunday, and Monday from 10am to 3:30pm, art lovers who have made an appointment in advance by calling **808/239-8146** can stop to see the exquisite **Hart, Tagami & Powell Gallery and Gardens,** just a few miles from the Valley of the Temples. This combination art gallery and botanical garden is the home and studio of two of Hawaii's leading painters, Hiroshi Tagami and Michael Powell. A visit here is a rare privilege, an extraordinary entry into a world of beauty. When you call for an appointment, ask for directions.

Just two miles past the Valley of the Temples, you'll come to one of Oahu's newer visitor's attractions: **Senator Fong's Plantation and Gardens—The Adventure Center.** Former U.S. Senator Hiram Fong has opened his magnificent 725-acre estate to the public; visitors are taken on guided tours in open-air trams through five gardens named for the various presidents under whom Fong served in his 17 years in Congress. After the tour stop at the visitors center, perhaps have lunch or take a class in lei making ($5 fee). Check out the Banana Patch gift shop, too. Plan on an hour or so for this delightful excursion. Admission is $8.50 for adults, $5 for children 5 to 12. Open daily from 10am to 4pm; the last tram tour departs at 3pm (☎ 808/239-6775).

For a change of pace, get back on Hi. 83 and head south to **Heeia,** on Kaneohe Bay. This is a good place to stop, stretch your legs, and switch to another mode of transportation. Glass-bottom boats at **Heeia Kea Pier** take you on a narrated excursion at a charge of $7.50 for adults, $3.50 for children under 12. Cruises depart at approximately 10 and 11am, and 12:30, 1:30, and 2:30pm daily. Make advance reservations by calling **808/235-2888.** Also, check to see if the water is clear that day; if not, there's not much point in going out. The Deli Snack and Gift Shop, right on the pier, offers local-style plate lunches (around $4), as well as the usual snacks.

ALTERNATE ROUTE TO HEEIA   You can begin your around-the-island trip via the **Pali and Makiki Heights** and pick up the route at Kaneohe on Hi. 83. This route takes you to a major attraction that our recommended route omits— the view from the **Nuuanu Pali,** a glorious panorama from the top of a jagged cliff. It's a historic spot, too, because it was here that Kamehameha the Great vanquished the Oahuans in a fierce battle in 1795. Thousands of the defeated fell to their deaths on the rocks below. The only drawback to this route is that you miss the scenery in the Koko Head area, which we find more appealing.

To see the Pali, turn left off Nimitz Highway (Hi. 92) in downtown Honolulu onto Nuuanu Avenue or Bishop Street. Follow it to Pali Highway (Hi. 61), which leads there. Just before you reach the Pali, however, you might want to drive about a mile up the Pali Highway and turn left at Jack Lane to reach the beautiful **Tendai Mission of Hawaii** and its enormously impressive 25-foot statue of Senju Kannon, the Thousand-Armed Goddess of Mercy. The Tendai sect of Mahayana Buddhism ended 1,200 years of confining its worship halls to Japan when it opened the Hawaii mission in 1973. You're welcome to inspect the grounds and building any day during regular activity hours. (There are no specific times of opening or closing.) Occasionally, you'll see local groups using the facilities for flower-arranging, tea ceremonies, and handcraft exhibits.

Another spectacular view that we think you shouldn't miss is the one from **Makiki Heights,** which you can see on your way to Nuuanu Pali. In a way, we like it better than the Pali, since this is a top-of-the-world view, completely unobstructed. Here's how to get there: From Waikiki, take Kalakaua Avenue until it ends at South Beretania Street. Go past Makiki to Keeaumoku Street, turn right, cross Interstate H1, and turn right onto Wilder. After one block, turn left onto Makiki, which runs into Round Top Drive, then Tantalus Drive, and continues up, up, and up. The road, which is excellent all the way, goes through the Round Top Forest Reserve. Stop at **Puu Ualakaa State Park** (open daily from 7am to 6:45pm) for the glorious view from Round Top. Back in the car, continue in the same direction you were going. When you reach H1 turn left and take it to Hi. 61 (the Pali Highway), which leads to the Pali.

WHERE TO EAT
KANEOHE

Several shopping malls in Kaneohe offer a bonanza of inexpensive eateries. At the enclosed **Windward Mall,** for example, the standout restaurant is **Kin Wah,** a cozy family-style Chinese place (see "Where to Eat," in Chapter 5). There is also a large food court, where you'll find many more places to choose from.

Pizza fans have **Harpo's,** and brag of their fresh veggies on hand-rolled dough, secret-recipe sausage, and hand-rolled homemade pastas. Two slices of their gourmet deep-dish–style pizzas, plus green salad and soda, will set you back $5.75

for pepperoni, $6.35 for vegetarian. If you've been to Ala Moana Center, you know that **Patti's Chinese Kitchen** is great. Now there's a Patti's here too, and it's inexpensive and filling.

Still hungry? The **Taco Shop** features tacos at $1.75 and enchiladas at $3.59; **Yunnie's Korean BBQ** offers barbecue chicken at $5.20, veggies and rice included. **Island Mixed Plate** creates a variety of sandwiches from $3.75 to $4.75, all with lettuce, tomatoes, and alfalfa sprouts. If you haven't tasted "luau food" yet, this is a good place at which to do so; get the Hawaiian plate of laulau, lomi-lomi salmon, kalua pig, chicken long rice, and poi. **Little Tokyo** displays a score of items in plastic replicas to help you decide, such as the teriyaki chicken or beef at $4.79 and $4.99. And don't forget the coffee shop on the second floor of **Liberty House,** where you can eat vegetarian sandwiches for $3.75 and roast beef for $4.95, as well as hot plates, such as a health plate or honey-dipped chicken, each at $4.95. Dinners, including soup and salad, run $7.50 to $10.95. Windward Mall's opening and closing times vary with holidays, seasons, and days of the week.

If you'd like an excellent Thai meal, drive to the intersection of Likelike and Kamehameha highways where you'll find **Thao Phya Thai** (☎ 808/253-3555). Here, in a garden atmosphere enlivened by Thai art, the staff radiates the Thai brand of warm aloha. We like to order their luscious vegetarian spring rolls as soon as we're seated, wrap them in lettuce, and dip them into a delicious sauce while we're making our menu decisions. Curries excel because they are made with fresh coconut milk. The same menu is in effect all day.

3 Along the Windward Coast

Outside Heeia, it's one awesome view after another as you drive north on Hi. 83 along the coast, weaving along past acres of tropical flowers and trees whose branches frequently arch across the whole width of the road. You can't miss spotting **Pineapple Hut** on the right, which has a good selection of carved wood, shells, macrame planters, and the like at reasonable prices.

You're now coming to the end of Kaneohe Bay, and the next HVB marker you'll see will point to an island that looks like its name, **Mokoli'l** (little lizard), also called Chinaman's Hat. On the other side of the road, covered by weeds, are the ruins of a century-old sugar mill. Cane grown here was once shipped by boat to "distant" Honolulu.

Just over two miles past the large garment factory building on your left, look for a fruit stand on the right. The only indication is a sign reading COLD COCONUT JUICE. Here you can purchase local fruits grown right in this area, at Waikane. In our opinion, they're the best.

In a short while you'll come to a rocky cliff that seems to resemble a crouching lion, hence its official name: **Crouching Lion.** The scenic **Crouching Lion Inn** is just in front. This area is fine for a picnic; **Kanawa Beach Park** has good swimming, as does **Swanzy Beach State Park,** just south of Punaluu, and both are fully equipped with amenities. The next beach, at **Kahama Bay,** is safe for swimming inshore, but there are no dressing facilities, and the bottom is muddy.

There's a stop that art lovers should make in Punaluu, the town coming up next: that's **Punaluu Gallery,** at 53-352 Kamehhameha Hwy. (☎ 808/237-8009), a longtime showplace for island artists.

As you approach Hauula, you'll see the HVB marker pointing to a side road leading to the 87-foot **Sacred Falls (Kaliuwaa)**. Even though the trail is lined with impressive trees and flowers, our advice is to pass this one up; in order to see the falls and the mountain pool below, you have to hike for about an hour on a rather rough path. Over the past few years there have been a number of drownings, robberies, and accidents here; locals definitely consider this place bad news. During the rainy season, killer flash floods can occur suddenly. Coming up now, the beach park at Hauula is well equipped with the usual bathing facilities, and the swimming is safe inshore. But keep going; you're about to reach the picturesque village of Laie, one of the high points of your Windward Oahu sojourn.

Laie is Salt Lake City with palm trees. No slouches at missionary work, the Mormons arrived in Hawaii not long after the first Protestants; more than 100 years ago they founded a large colony of Hawaiian and Samoan members of the Church of Jesus Christ of Latter-day Saints, whose descendants still live here.

In 1919 the Mormons established a Hawaiian Temple, the first Mormon house of worship outside the mainland; in 1955 the Brigham Young University–Hawaii Campus, a fully accredited liberal arts institution; and in 1963, the ✪ **Polynesian Cultural Center,** a loving re-creation of Polynesia. Built more than 30 years ago to provide work and scholarships for Polynesian students and to revitalize the ancient Polynesian cultures, it is the most popular paid-admission visitor attraction in Hawaii. Seven authentic Polynesian islands have been re-created: Hawaii, Tonga, Fiji, Samoa, Maori, Marquesas, and Tahiti, all staffed by Polynesians who came here just for this purpose.

The center offers families a full day of fun with a variety of activities for all ages. You could start with a guided canoe tour or a leisurely walking tour. Friendly villagers in each island greet and involve visitors in demonstrations: making *ngatu* or *tapa* cloth from the inner bark of the mulberry plant in Tonga; watching a villager climb a coconut tree with amazing agility and speed in Fiji; or pounding boiled taro roots into poi in Hawaii. In addition to the villages, demonstrations, and hands-on activities, the center also stages a variety of vibrant shows: "Mana! The Spirit of Our People," a 90-minute evening extravaganza with a cast of more than 100 islanders; the "Ancient Legends of Polynesia," a colorful water-borne introduction to island myths; a brass band concert; an island farewell festival; even a "Keiki Polynesian Show" in which visiting keikis can see their own friends perform.

Since a visit here could take up to eight hours to enjoy it all, you may want to plan accordingly by arriving no later than 1pm. Admission to the "islands" and the afternoon highlights is $25 for adults, $13 for children. Add to this the buffet and admission to the evening production, "Mana!" and costs will be $42 adults, $25 children. Many of our readers consider this preferable to the luau package (see below). For $54 adults and $35 children, you get a luau package, which also includes the IMAX presentation "Polynesian Odyssey." Reservations can be made at the center's ticket office on the ground floor of the Royal Hawaiian Shopping Center in Waikiki: call **808/293-3333,** or toll free from the mainland 800/367-7060.

The Polynesian Cultural Center is open Monday through Saturday; closed Thanksgiving and Christmas. If you're driving directly to Laie from Honolulu, take the Pali Highway (Hi. 61) and turn north on Kamehameha Highway (Hi. 83). Plan on at least an hour's drive.

While you're here, you'll also want to see the **Hawaiian Temple;** it stands back from the road on high ground, above a pond, an illuminated fountain, and at the head of a long avenue of royal palms. The best approach for a Taj

Mahal–like vista is to leave the highway at Halelaa Boulevard. A complimentary Historical Laie Tour is available. You'll tour the Mormon Temple, Brigham Young University–Hawaii, and the Laie community on a re-created 1903 Hawaiian streetcar. By the way, not all the students here are Mormons; the school is open to others, provided they take the pledge not to smoke or drink, and "to live good Christian lives."

Laie-Maloo Beach used to be the scene of the Mormon hukilaus, once considered one of the island's top visitor attractions. The ocean at Laie-Maloo is safe for inshore swimming, although the beach is not a public park and has no dressing facilities.

You won't want to leave Laie without a drive out to **Laie Point** (the turnoff is just past the entrance to the cultural center), where you get a dramatic view of the rugged coastline. Walk out over the porous lava rock as far as you can go safely for the best view of all. Some old Hawaii hands swear it's the best view in the islands. Sunset devotees shouldn't miss this one.

4 The North Shore

Highway 83 starts to run inland through sugar country at the village of Kahuku, the halfway point of your trip and the home of the **Kahuku Sugar Mill.** Alas, the color-coded walk-through tour that was so appealing to children is no longer available, but it's worthwhile to take a peek at the mill from the outside (sugar mills, a major part of Hawaii's agricultural history, are scarce these days), and perhaps stop nearby for lunch at **Ahi's** (see "Where to Eat" below). A number of local vendors also offer souvenir items.

Now look for the Old Tanaka Plantation Store, newly restored, and now home to **The Only Show in Town** (☎ 808/293-1295), Paul Wroblewski's engaging antiques emporium, one of our favorites from Kauai in the pre–Hurricane Iniki days. Collectors and browsers can have a field day here: The selection of Hawaiiana, from stone artifacts to just about everything through the 1950s, is incredible. So, too, is the collection of old bottles (about which Paul is very knowledgeable) and multicolored insulators. Then there's a wonderful array of antique jewelry and ivory netsukes, as well as vintage political buttons and American trade memorabilia, particularly Coca-Cola items. We could get lost here for hours.

Sharing the Tanaka Plantation Store with The Only Show in Town is **Patagonia Forest.** The shop is filled with exotic things from Indonesia, South America, and points between. We loved the gorgeously colored caftans, beaded bustiers, leather purses, and custom swimwear, the latter designed by the shop's owner in stunning batik fabrics. Open every day.

The road reaches the shore again at Kuilima, where you might want to have a look at the sumptuous Turtle Bay Hilton and Country Club, one of the most beautiful resorts in the islands. The scenery is spectacular here, especially the view from the swimming pool, perched atop a cliff overlooking the ocean on two sides as the waves pound in. (If it's time for lunch, you might want to try the 11am-to-2:30pm "minideli" buffet in the scenic Bay View Lounge. There's a charge for parking here, but your parking ticket can be validated at lunch.)

Back to the car again for a drive down the coast a bit to **Sunset Beach,** with its huge breakers crashing in at your right. It's safe for summer swimming, but in winter it's a wild, windy stretch, exciting to walk along; better still, you may be lucky enough to see some spectacular surfing, for this is Oahu's North Shore,

The North Shore

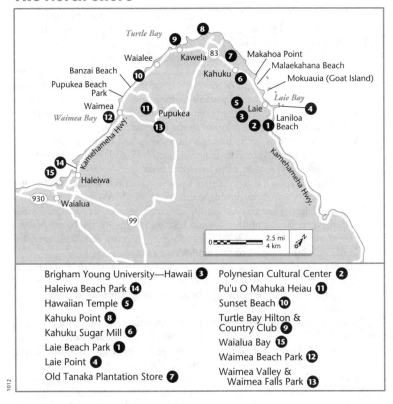

Brigham Young University—Hawaii **3** Polynesian Cultural Center **2**
Haleiwa Beach Park **14** Pu'u O Mahuka Heiau **11**
Hawaiian Temple **5** Sunset Beach **10**
Kahuku Point **8** Turtle Bay Hilton &
Kahuku Sugar Mill **6** Country Club **9**
Laie Beach Park **1** Waialua Bay **15**
Laie Point **4** Waimea Beach Park **12**
Old Tanaka Plantation Store **7** Waimea Valley &
 Waimea Falls Park **13**

currently *the* place for the surfing set. Traffic may be jammed for miles from here south to Haleiwa if there's an important surfing contest going on. If you're wondering whether you should try it yourself, be advised that the surfing areas range from pretty dangerous to very dangerous to one that's called "Banzai Pipeline." (Remember the wartime suicide cry?) **Waimea Bay,** just below Sunset, has the distinction of having Hawaii's biggest waves, sometimes crashing in as high as 30 feet. However, in the summer months Waimea Bay is tranquil, the waves are gentle, and swimming here is close to perfection. **Pupukea Beach Park,** for instance, has good swimming and outstanding snorkeling in the summer months.

While the surfers on Waimea Bay are tempting fate, you can survey a more primitive form of human sacrifice (and this time we're serious) by turning left onto Pupukea Road, one of the few paved roads here, opposite a fire station and next to a marker. As soon as the road begins its ascent up the hill, take your first right and continue up to **Puu O Mahuka Heiau.** Here, on a bluff overlooking Waimea Bay (another view-collector's spot), are the ruins of a temple where human sacrifice was practiced. When Captain Vancouver put in at Waimea Bay in 1792, three of his men were captured and offered to the bloodthirsty gods. Today all is tranquil here, and the faithful still come, offering bundles of leaves in homage. Sadly, the road leading up to this National Historic Landmark is littered with trash and abandoned automobiles.

For a refreshing change of pace, head back to nature now at **Waimea Valley, home of Waimea Falls Park,** off Hi. 83 a little south of Pupukea Road, opposite Waimea Bay Beach Park. There's a lot to do at this botanical Eden nestled in a lush, 1,800-acre historic Hawaiian valley. You can watch world-class cliff divers plunge 60 feet into the waterfall pool, or see the park's resident hula troupe, dressed in authentic costumes, perform beautiful ancient (*kahiko*) hula. At the Hawaiian Games Site, you can play the sports of old Hawaii, such as *ulu maika* (lawn bowling), *o'o ihe* (spear throwing), or *konane* (Hawaiian checkers). You can wander through more than 30 botanical gardens that showcase some of the world's most exotic and rare plants, or explore numerous trails that wind their way through the park. Hop onto the narrated minibus to the waterfall, then join knowledgeable park guides for walking tours through the gardens and historical sites. At the *kauhale kahiko* (ancient Hawaiian living site), step into old Hawaii and experience the way Hawaiians were thought to have once lived.

Adventure seekers will enjoy the park's newest attraction, **Waimea Adventure Tours,** a series of activities allowing guests to explore "never before seen" areas of Waimea Valley. They include guided all-terrain vehicle rides along 10 miles of wilderness trails; downhill mountain bike tours through the North Valley; and kayak rides along Waimea River and out to Waimea Bay. Fees vary; for information, phone the park at **808/638-8511.**

You can also enjoy a relaxed picnic in the grassy meadow or a sumptuous lunch at the **Pikake Pavilion,** a spacious open-air dining center overlooking the mouth of the valley. Browse through **Waimea Valley Store** for island gifts and mementos.

Twice each month the park offers romantic evening strolls to the waterfall and back by the light of the full moon. A donation of $5 per family directly benefits the Waimea Arboretum Foundation, a nonprofit scientific and educational organization dedicated to protecting Hawaii's rare and endangered plants.

Waimea Valley is also one of Hawaii's most popular wedding locations; couples can exchange vows in a lush, secluded garden or next to a gorgeous waterfall. For more information on planning such a special event, contact the park's **Wedding Department** at 59-864 Kamehameha Hwy., Haleiwa, HI 96712.

Admission is $19.95 for adults, $10.95 for seniors (over 65), $8.95 for juniors ages 6 to 12, $3.95 for children 4 to 5, and free for children 3 and under. Waimea is open-daily, including holidays, from 10am to 5:30pm. For more information, call **808/638-8511** or **808/942-5700.** Free round-trip transportation on air-conditioned buses is available twice daily from five Waikiki hotels. Call **808/955-TARO** for more information.

Another way to get to Waimea Valley and also to Sea Life Park Hawaii (see "From Waikiki to the Windward Coast," above), is to take the Oahu Nature Bound Circle Island Express, which costs $29.95 (prices subject to change) and includes admission to both parks. It leaves Waikiki daily at 8am and returns by 5:30pm. For information on pick-up times and locations, call **808/947-OAHU.**

A few miles farther along Hi. 83, at **Haleiwa Beach Park** on Waialua Bay, you'll find the last swimming spot before you strike into the heart of Oahu. It's a fine family-type place—lawns, play areas, pergolas, dressing rooms, showers, fishing, camping, and a picnicking area.

YOUTH SCENE AT SUNSET BEACH AND HALEIWA   If you're seriously interested—or even slightly—in the youth culture, you'll be welcome among the inhabitants of Sunset Beach and Haleiwa, an area that attracts a number of young people who want to live close to nature and the big surf. They're not putting on a show for sightseers or tourists, just quietly doing their thing—and an attractive thing it is. Haleiwa is like a very tiny version of Cape Cod's Provincetown, with its distinctively artsy atmosphere, small gift shops, art galleries, and boutiques. **Outrigger Trading Company,** 62-540 Kamehamena Hwy., in Jameson's By the Sea, has an outstanding collection of works by local artists: hand-thrown pottery, leaded glass and seashell boxes, Hawaiian quilt pattern pillows, unique pillows and toys—starfish and sea horses and mermaids—and much more. They share their space with **Jameson's Fudge Works,** where fudge is creamed on marble tables. **Silver Moon Emporium** is tucked away behind a garden with picnic tables at 66-037 Kamehameha Hwy. This is the place for knockout, very feminine clothes and for jewelry and accessories that you won't see elsewhere. Much of it is hand-made and one-of-a-kind; we saw beaded Mexican circular skirts, clingy Uru Uru dresses, earrings starting at $10, and lots more.

Hand-painted dresses and original designs, most of them made in the area, are offered by Inge Jausel at **Oogenesis Boutique** at 66-249 Kamehameha Hwy. Japanese-inspired designs grace tops, pants ensembles, and simple dresses that can be worn belted or unbelted. Prices are reasonable. Under the "Inge Hawaii" label, these garments are now being sold in mainland stores. Inge's other store, **Deeni's Boutique,** at 66-079 Kamehameha Hwy. in Haleiwa, specializes in swimwear, T-shirts, and sportswear, with some of the lowest prices and best selections in town.

We always like to make at stop at the **North Shore Marketplace,** 66-250 Kamehameha Hwy., especially to visit **Pomegranates in the Sun,** with a smashing collection of clothing by Hawaiian artists and designers, inspired by the sun-drenched colors of Hawaii. Be sure to shop the consignment rack where they "recycle" Pomegranate clothes; we've made some terrific buys here! Then there's **Jungle Gems,** where you can shop for jewelry, crystals, and a variety of arts and crafts at very good prices. The owners make frequent trips to Australia and elsewhere collecting rough opal, which they polish and set at the store. Also in the same North Shore Marketplace complex is **Kau'ala Tropical Farms,** which offers free samples and fair prices on macadamia nuts. **Coffee Gallery** is a must for coffee fanatics, since they offer an enormous selection of Hawaiian and other coffees, roast their own beans, and sell them at very good prices. Organic coffee is available. You can also have a meal here on their outdoor terrace (see "Where to Eat," below).

Art galleries abound in Haleiwa. At **Galerie Lassen,** 62-540 Kamehameha Hwy. (☎ 808/637-8866), there's an exquisite collection of artwork, much of which can be found nowhere else. We were especially drawn to the work of Maui artist Andrea Smith, who creates fascinating prints using ancient Egyptian symbols. Christian Riese Lassen's paintings of the sea and its creatures are reproduced by a process called Artagraph; each picture is three-dimensional and looks like an original. California artist Douglas Wylie spends three months each year as a boat driver for a whale research team which gives him the opportunity to study the magnificent creatures he sculpts firsthand. The gallery is open every day.

Then there's **Wyland Gallery** (there are many branches throughout the islands), 66-150 Kamehameha Hwy., which specializes in the work of noted marine artist Wyland (everything from originals to posters) and also shows photographs, wood sculptures, and much more. Have a look, too, at the **Fettig Art Studio,** which exhibits local paintings by Beverly Fettig. Several prints are available at $20 each. Call **808/637-4933** for an appointment.

Hungry? You've come to the right town. Some of our favorite North Shore restaurants are here (see "Where to Eat," below). Wherever you eat, skip dessert and drive over to **Matsumoto's Grocery** at 66-087 Kamehameha Hwy. in Haleiwa (across from the intersection of Emerson Street) for the ultimate shave-ice experience. Local people drive out from all over the island to line up here, while no fewer than four workers form an "assembly line" to shave and season the ice. We won't swear that you'll really love shave ice with ice cream and azuki beans on the bottom, but can you say you really know Hawaii unless you've tried it? **Aoki's,** just down the road, is an alternative if the lines are just too long.

Since Sunset Beach is a spiritually attuned community, it abounds in centers for yoga, Zen, and other such disciplines; the people at any of the shops can give you information on any groups that may interest you. This area is a world apart from the urban crush of Honolulu, the tourist scene at Waikiki, and the rat race everywhere. Try to schedule your visit in time for the fantastic sunset, which turns the horizon to a brilliant blazing red.

WHERE TO EAT
KAHUKU

Ahi's
☎ **808/293-5650.** Reservations not accepted. Main courses $8.25–$9.50. No credit cards. Mon–Sat 11am–9pm. SEAFOOD.

If you love seafood—shrimp in particular—don't pass up a chance for a meal at Ahi's; residents drive from all over the island to partake. Ahi offers a variety of shrimp specials: scampi, shrimp cocktail, lightly fried shrimp tempura, deep-fried shrimp, or a sampler of all, served with hot vegetables, grilled buttered bread, and either rice or mashed potatoes. The rest of the food is okay, too, but everybody comes for the shrimp. Ahi's looks like a gracefully aging Hawaiian *hale* (house) halfway down a country road in Kahuku (if you're coming via Kaneohe and you reach the sugar mill, you've gone a little too far). Look for the weathered old blue building with a green roof, decorated with fishing nets and glass floats. Ahi and his family (sons, nephews, nieces) are friendly and delightful, and treat you like a guest in their own home. This is a real taste of old Hawaii.

HALEIWA

Coffee Gallery
In North Shore Marketplace, 66-250 Kamehameha Hwy., Haleiwa. ☎ **808/637-5571.** Reservations not accepted. Sandwiches $3.75–$6.95; main courses $3.95–$8.95. AE, MC, V. Mon–Fri 6am–9pm, Sat–Sun 7am–9pm. ETHNIC/VEGETARIAN.

It's so pleasant to sit at the outdoor cafe here in the screened lanai and have a very special cup of freshly roasted gourmet coffee or a light lunch or dinner. The emphasis is on healthy, fresh foods; the pastries, baked right in the back, are made without eggs or sugar. Lunch features quiches, waffles, veggie burgers, salads, and chili and rice; dinner always offers a vegetarian specialty like tortillas, pesto, pastas, crêpes, a Thai specialty, or lentil burgers, along with a house salad. There's a nice little menu for children. The espresso bar has some delightful combinations, like vanilla ice cream topped with espresso. To go along with the coffee, try a "death by chocolate brownie"—if you dare.

Jameson's by the Sea
62-540 Kamehameha Hwy., Haleiwa. ☎ **808/637-4336.** Reservations recommended. Main courses $15.95–$18.95. AE, DC, MC, V. Daily 11am–9pm. SEAFOOD.

While the food isn't what it used to be, this is still a wonderfully picturesque spot for lunch or dinner. Savor the ocean view and the sunset while you dine. Lunch is served downstairs in the Pub, and features hearty fish, seafood, and meat sandwiches; some good shrimp, crab, and seafood Louie salads; and a variety of interesting pupus (prices range between $5.50 and $11.95). There are many well-priced daily lunch specials. Dinner features seafood caught daily in local waters.

✪ Kua'Aina Sandwich

66-214 Kamehameha Hwy., Haleiwa. ☎ **808/637-6067.** Sandwiches $3.50–$5.40. No credit cards. Daily 11am–8pm. SANDWICHES.

Where can you get the best sandwich on the North Shore, maybe on all of Oahu? We cast our vote for Kua'Aina, a sparkling sandwichery across the street from the courthouse in Haleiwa. It's tiny, neat as a pin, with wooden tables, framed pictures of local scenes, a few tables on the porch. And the atmosphere is casual, with people coming in off the beach. We haven't stopped raving yet about the sandwiches we had on our last visit: mahimahi with melted cheese, Ortega pepper, lettuce, and tomato at $5.40; tuna and avocado ("the tastiest combo in the Pacific") at $4.50; and a great baconburger at $5.40. Sandwiches are hearty enough to be a whole meal and are served on either a kaiser roll, honey wheat-berry bread, or earthy rye. Two years in a row, the Zagat survey voted them as no. 10 in the state for food and no. 2 for "Bang for the Buck."

Rosie's Cantina

In the Haleiwa Shopping Plaza, 66-165 Kamehameha Hwy., Heleiwa. ☎ **808/637-3538.** Reservations not required. Main courses $4.95–$12.70. MC, V. Daily 7am–10pm. MEXICAN.

This attractive, high-tech–looking spot is a favorite for tasty Mexican food. Rosie's serves all three meals, features delicious tortas (hamburger or chicken with fries or beans on thick bread) as well as generous servings of the traditional Tex-Mex favorites. Since it opened 10 years ago, it's been famous for its frosty fruit margaritas. A good stop before or after the beach.

5 Central Oahu: From Haleiwa to Waikiki

Follow Hi. 82 from Haleiwa and turn left onto Hi. 99 (Kamehameha Highway) as it climbs to **Leilehua Plateau.** Here the tall sugarcane gives way to seemingly endless miles of pineapple—dark green and golden against the red earth. It's the largest pineapple area in the world. Just as you're beginning to feel like the Ancient Mariner (you can't pick any), you'll find the **Dole Pineapple Pavilion,** just north of Wahiawa, where you can buy a whole "pine" or get half a dozen delicious spears, fresher than any you've ever tasted. The custom here is to sprinkle a little unrefined Hawaiian salt on the pineapple; it helps cut the acidity. A fountain spouts juice that you can drink, free. You can also shop for Hawaiian souvenirs here and order fresh pineapple packs delivered to the airport for your flight back home. Dole does not conduct tours through the fields, but many operations are visible from the highway. In case you're curious, the variety of pineapple grown here is called sweet cayenne.

In the midst of these Wahiawa pineapple fields, one mile past the pineapple hut, is the Del Monte Corporation's **Pineapple Variety Garden,** near where the Kamehameha Highway becomes Hi. 80 for a short time. It's small, but it's well worth a brief stop to see a huge variety of species and pineapple plants from all over the world—Asia, Africa, South America, and various small islands. Just ignore the tremendous spiders that build their webs among the plants; they're nonaggressive and totally harmless—to people and pineapples.

Next stop is for the history-anthropology buffs: a Stone Age spot where the royal chieftains of Hawaii were born. Just before Wahiawa on Hi. 80, watch on the right for an HVB warrior marker pointing to a dirt road leading off to the right to a clump of eucalyptus trees in a pineapple field—the Sacred Birthstones-Kukaniloko. These large stones and the village that once surrounded the spot afforded prenatal care and birthing support to high chiefly women in childbirth—thus ensuring healthy mothers and children to continue the lineages of the high chiefs, the alii.

Just before you reach Wahiawa, still in the pineapple fields, you may want to stop and stretch your legs at a five-acre, working vegetable and flower farm called **Helemano Plantation,** which serves a tasty and inexpensive buffet lunch at $8.25 between 11am and 2:30pm. If it's past lunchtime, you can still browse at the gift shop, get some fresh produce at the country store, visit the bakery, or even join a lei-making class.

Now take Kamehameha Highway to Wahiawa, a town that serves as a center for personnel stationed at **Schofield Barracks** (where James Jones met his muse) and **Wheeler's Field.** It's also a huge pineapple depot. The bright spot here is **Kemoo Farms,** a famous name in these parts since 1921. The old restaurant building overlooking Lake Wilson now houses a good Mexican restaurant. Next door is the Kemoo Farms Visitor Center, where owner Dick Rodby has lined the walls and shelves with antiques, old photos, and historic memorabilia of the area, some of it for sale. Also for sale are Kemoo Farms' Happy Cakes (a very rich holiday fruitcake made with pineapple, coconut, and macadamia nuts, a big favorite of Ronald Reagan's), homemade chocolates, and other goodies.

You may also want to visit the **Tropic Lightning Museum,** depicting the history of the 25th Infantry Division and Schofield Barracks. Open Tuesday through Saturday from 10am to 4pm; admission is free. Garden lovers will want to make a stop at the **Wahiawa Botanical Garden,** at 1396 California Ave. (three-quarters

---

Take the Train: Historic Hawaii Railway Society Tours

Attention railroad buffs: Between the years of 1890 and 1947, the narrow-gauge tracks of the Oahu Railway and Land Company were busy transporting passengers and freight for the sugar mills from Honolulu to as far away as Kahuku. The stalwart members of the Hawaii Railway Society (who come from all over the world) have worked for more than 30 years, restoring engines and maintaining the existing railway track so that the beautifully restored little train is once more back in business. Every Sunday at 1 and 3pm, the train leaves from Ewa Beach, west of Pearl Harbor, for a 13-mile round trip across the Ewa plain to the Ka Olina resort and back. The rail trip takes 1^1/2 hours, since the train can only go 17 m.p.h. (downhill) and it has to stop for *everything*—including golf carts. The most recent addition is Ben Dillingham's private parlor car, which, in its heyday, carried such VIPs as Queen Liliuokalani, Prince Kuhio, and President William Howard Taft. Passengers can sit either in an open gondola or in a covered car, where they will hear a narration about the history of trains on Oahu.

The fare is $7 for adults, $4 for children; seating is on a first-come, first-served basis. Directions: Take H-1 West, Exit 5A, drive south 2^1/2 miles, turn right onto Renton Road drive 1^1/2 miles to the end. For information, phone **808/681-5461.**

Central Oahu & the Waianae Coast

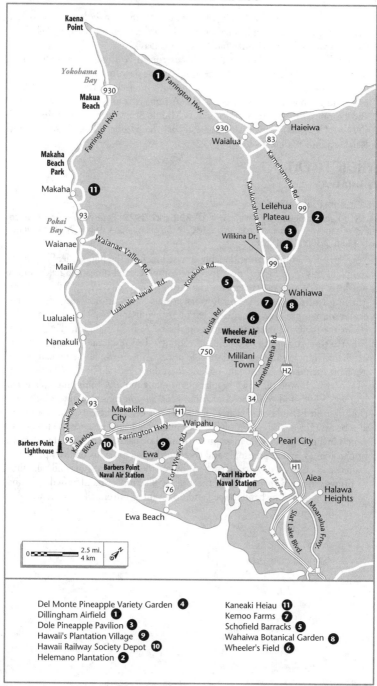

Kaena
Point

Yokohama
Bay

Makua
Beach

1

Farrington Hwy.

930

Waialua

930

83

Haieiwa

Kamehameha Rd.

Makaha
Beach
Park

Makaha

11

93

Pokai
Bay

Waianae

Maili

Waianae Valley Rd.

Lualualei Naval Rd.

Kaukonahua Rd.

Leilehua
Plateau

99

2

3

Wilikina Dr.

4

99

Kolekole Rd.

5

Wahiawa

7

8

6

Kunia Rd.

Wheeler Air
Force Base

Lualualei

Nanakuli

750

Mililani
Town

Kamehameha Rd.

H2

34

Makakole Rd.

93

Makakilo
City

H1

Waipahu

Barbers Point
Lighthouse

95

Kalaeloa
Blvd.

10

Farrington Hwy.

9

Ewa

Fort Weaver Rd.

Pearl City

H1

Aiea

Barbers Point
Naval Air Station

76

Pearl Harbor
Naval Station

Pearl Harbor

Slat Lake Blvd.

Moanalua Frwy.

Halawa
Heights

Ewa Beach

0   2.5 mi.
         4 km

Del Monte Pineapple Variety Garden **4**
Dillingham Airfield **1**
Dole Pineapple Pavilion **3**
Hawaii's Plantation Village **9**
Hawaii Railway Society Depot **10**
Helemano Plantation **2**

Kaneaki Heiau **11**
Kemoo Farms **7**
Schofield Barracks **5**
Wahaiwa Botanical Garden **8**
Wheeler's Field **6**

1013

of a mile east of Kamehameha Highway), to wander through 27 lovely acres of rare trees, ferns, and shrubs, and a Hawaiian garden. Admission is free (open daily from 9am to 4pm except Christmas and New Year's Day).

You'll pass through more sugar fields as you drive along the now-four-lane Kamehameha Highway (Hi. 99 once again) or the new Interstate H2. From here on, it's fast sailing home. At the intersection with Interstate H1, turn left and drive past Pearl Harbor (you might visit the USS Arizona Memorial if you have the time) and Honolulu International Airport. At Middle Street, turn right onto Hi. 92 (Nimitz Highway), which will take you past the harbor. Take Ala Moana and Kalakaua into Waikiki.

WHERE TO EAT
WAHIAWA

Helemano Plantation

64-1510 Kamehameha Hwy., Wahiawa. ☎ **808/622-3929.** Reservations not required. Buffet or sandwich and salad bar $8.25. MC. V. Breakfast open daily 7:30–11am; lunch daily 11am–2:30pm. CHINESE.

You can get a substantial, reasonably priced lunch in the big, gardenlike dining rooms of this spot, located on a five-acre complex amid pineapple fields on the outskirts of Wahiawa. Helemano Plantation is not only an agricultural farm, growing fruits, vegetables, and flowers; it's also a vocational and educational center for many of Hawaii's citizens with learning disabilities. They work as trainees in the many areas of Helemano: on the farm, the restaurant, the gift shop, country store, or in the bakeshop. Its Country Inn restaurant is known for its excellent Chinese cuisine and reasonable prices. At least five hot main courses are available each day, which might include roast duck, teriyaki beef, Chinese spareribs, beef with broccoli, spicy eggplant, and many more. A mini-lunch plate will cost you $3.95, and your choice of either a full all-you-can-eat Chinese buffet including fruit bar or a sandwich with all-you-can-eat salad bar is $8.25. You can also browse through the tempting display of freshly baked treats at the bakeshop, which includes island-style manapuas (steamed or baked buns stuffed with pork or chicken) as well as pineapple and coconut danish, and chocolate chip, peanut butter, and coconut-drop cookies. Stop by for the free hula show and take time to browse through their "Best of the Best" collection of handcrafted gifts and souvenirs made by the handicapped and disadvantaged from all over the world.

Settling in on Maui 9

In addition to possessing some of the world's most marvelous beaches, this second-largest island in the Hawaiian archipelago—nicknamed the Valley Isle—boasts one of the great natural wonders of the planet: Haleakala, the world's largest dormant volcano. Add to this a string of gorgeous little jungle valleys where the modern world seems incredibly remote, a picturesque whaling town kicking its heels after a long sleep in the South Seas sun, and a wonderfully hospitable local citizenry intent on convincing you that Maui *no ka oi*—Maui is the best! You just might end up agreeing.

Maui is about 70 miles southeast of Oahu, and can be reached via plane in about 20 minutes. Geologically, the island is the result of the work of two volcanoes, Puu Kukui in the west and Haleakala in the east, which formed separate land masses as they grew and eventually created the valley in between that is now central Maui (hence its nickname). But according to the legends of the ancient Hawaiians, their own special demigod, Maui, pulled up both ends of the island from the sea bottom with his fishhook. (There's an imposing statue of Maui doing just that on the grounds of the Stouffer Wailea Beach Resort.) The island is 729 square miles, 25 miles from north to south and 38.4 miles from east to west. Roads are excellent and it's very easy to explore.

Maui has been going through the throes of expansion. But while new hotels and condominium apartments continue to spring up, the island still manages to retain a graceful, unhurried feeling. The building codes here are stricter, so nowhere on Maui has there been such wanton destruction of natural beauty as in Waikiki.

Maui is "hot" right now; Maui is "in." Next to Honolulu, it's the place most travelers want to visit (many are bypassing Honolulu altogether and heading straight for Maui). A bevy of exciting new restaurants have opened here in the past year, making Maui a first-class dining destination in addition to everything else. Maui is generally more expensive than Oahu and the other neighbor islands, but you will find accommodations and restaurants in all price ranges. Again, a major expense will be car rentals or guided tours (your only alternatives on an island with no public transportation).

1 Orientation & Getting Around

ORIENTATION

ARRIVING BY PLANE Your plane will probably land at the very modern and airy **Kahului Airport.** The terminal is located in the 7-mile-wide valley that binds together the West Maui Mountains and Haleakala, just a few miles from modern Kahului and graceful old Wailuku, neighboring towns competing peacefully for the title of largest city. There is shuttle service to Kihei and Kaanapali. If you need assistance, stop by the information kiosk at the airport.

If you're going to be staying in West Maui, you can save some driving time by flying directly to the newer **Kapalua-West Maui Airport** via either Hawaiian or Island Air (☎ 808/669-0255) on limited schedules.

CHOOSING A BASE Maui is small enough so that you can logically make your headquarters at one hotel and take off each day for various sightseeing and beach excursions. The **Wailuku-Kahului** area, closest to the main airport, is centrally located for sightseeing excursions but lacks a really good beach. The best beach area close to Kahului is **Kihei** (about a 15-minute drive), which is also centrally located. The liveliest and most beautiful area, to our taste, is the **Lahaina-Kaanapali-Napili** region, about 40 miles from Kahului, but it's generally more expensive than the Kihei area, which has a far greater number of condo accommodations. All of these places work as a base; the only place on the island that is inconvenient if you want to move around is **Hana** in East Maui, a 3-hour drive from the airport; you might want to plan an overnight stay there, as the drive each way is a long one, although most people do it on a 1-day trip.

TOURIST INFORMATION The **Maui Visitors Bureau** is at 1727 Wili Pa Loop (Wailuku Millyard), P.O. Box 580, Wailuku, HI 96793 (☎ 808/244-3530; fax 808/244-1337).

GETTING AROUND

BY RENTAL CAR The major low-cost, all-island car-rental companies—like **Alamo, National, Budget, Dollar**—are all represented on Maui.

Word of Mouth Rent-A-Used Car, 150A Hana Hwy., Maui, HI 96732 (☎ 808/877-2436 or 800/533-5929; fax 808/877-2439) has significantly upgraded its fleet. They offer clean, well-maintained newer cars at very good rates. A compact four-door without air conditioning is $115 per week; with air conditioning, $130 per week. Daily rates are $18.95 and $23.95. There is a three-day minimum. They are close to Kahului Airport, and offer free pickup and drop-off.

Atlas Rent A Car, P.O. Box 126, Puunene, Maui, HI 96784 (☎ 808/871-2860 or 800/367-5238), offers late-model compacts from $21.95 per day or $139 per week with "absolutely no hidden charges." All sizes of cars are available. They rent Suzuki Samurai four-wheel-drives and Jeep Wranglers starting from $29.95 per day. They provide prompt and courteous airport service.

TRAVEL ARRANGEMENTS FOR THE DISABLED Maui definitely need not be off-limits to the physically handicapped—even those who want to partake of the island's exhilarating outdoor activities. Jan and David McKown, the young couple who run **Over the Rainbow Disabled Travel Services,** 186 Mehani Circle, Kihei, Maui, HI 96753 (☎ 808/879-5521 or 800/303-3750), can help out in a number of areas, from airline flights, airport arrangements, wheelchair-accessible

What's Special About Maui

Natural Wonders

- Haleakala Crater, 10,023 feet high, the world's largest dormant volcano with a crater big enough to swallow the island of Manhattan.
- Hana, one of the most unspoiled places in all Hawaii, reached by a 52-mile road around the base of Haleakala, with 617 hairpin turns, 56 one-lane bridges, dozens of sparkling waterfalls, plus bamboo groves and gardens.

Outdoor Activities

- Superb sandy swimming beaches, from Kapalua Beach in the west to Kamaole Beach Park in the south to Hana Beach Park in the east.
- Snorkeling spots in West Maui, Kapalua and Kaanapali Beaches; in East Maui, Wailea Beach; the offshore island of Molokini, reachable by boat only.
- Hookipa County Beach Park in Paia, Windsurfing Capital of the World, scene of many a competition; winter waves can be as high as 15 feet.
- A chance to ride 10,000 feet down Haleakala Volcano on a guided bike tour; all you need is a cool head—and good brakes.
- Alaskan humpback whales, wintering in Maui to mate and bear their young, visible from many coastal locations and on whale-watching cruises.
- Fourth of July Rodeo in Makawao, erstwhile cowboy town.

Museums

- Alexander & Baldwin Sugar Museum in Puunene, especially for its working model of sugar-factory machinery.
- Bailey House Museum in Wailuku, with fascinating exhibits from ancient Hawaii to missionary days.
- Whalers Village Museum at Kaanapali Beach, with photos, artifacts, and an absorbing collection of whaling memorabilia.

Historic Lahaina

- Baldwin Home, a missionary house museum, one of the projects of the Lahaina Restoration Foundation.
- The *Carthaginian,* an authentic replica of a 19th-century sailing vessel, also run by the Lahaina Restoration Foundation.

Antiques

- Good antique hunting on North Market Street in Wailuku.

Local Foods and Wines

- Maui onions, the sweetest in the world (sometimes called Kula onions).
- Maui potato chips, available in local stores—the best.
- Maui wines, made from local pineapples and grapes grown on the slopes of Haleakala by Tedeschi Vineyards.

Mountain Flowers

- Proteas, grown on farms along the lower slopes of Haleakala.
- Silverswords, rare botanical specimens which blossom only once, and only on lava rocks at the highest altitudes; found on the higher slopes of Haleakala.

Shopping

- Lahaina, with hundreds of exciting shops.
- Whaler's Shopping Village at Kaanapali Beach.
- Artistic boutiques and galleries in Paia and Makawao.

vans, accommodations in hotels or condos equipped with roll-in showers, and personal care service to arranging helicopter or kayak trips, luaus, whale watching, snorkeling, or even scuba diving. After entertaining David's brother, a quadriplegic, they realized that they had a great deal of information and many resources they could share with others—which they do, with a great deal of care and aloha. They can act as a full-service travel, tour, and activity agency for the disabled. Write or call for information.

FAST FACTS: Maui

Area Code   The telephone area code is 808.

Dentists   Emergency dental care is available from Maui Dental Center, 162 Alamaha St., Kahului (☎ 808/871-6283).

Doctors   Doctors on Call will make hotel visits (☎ 808/667-7676). You can also call West Maui Healthcare Center, Whalers Village, Suite H-7 (☎ 808/667-9721), until 10pm nightly.

Emergencies   Call 911 for police, fire, and ambulance.

Hospitals   Major hospitals are Maui Memorial Hospital, 221 Mahalani, Wailuku (☎ 808/244-9056); Hana Medical Center, Hana Highway, Hana (☎ 808/248-8924); and Kula Hospital, 204 Kula Hwy., Kula (☎ 808/878-1221).

Newspapers   The *Maui News* is the most important daily paper.

Other Useful Numbers   Help is available from the State Commission on Persons with Disabilities (☎ 808/244-4441; voice/TDD); Sexual Assault Crisis Center (☎ 808/242-4357); and Suicide and Crisis Center (☎ 808/244-7404). On Call (☎ 808/246-1441), a 24-hour free service available from any pushbutton phone, offers the latest news, local and worldwide weather, community services, sports, horoscopes, soap opera updates, and more. See also the Aloha Pages of the Maui telephone book.

Poison Control Center   Call toll free 800/362-3585.

Post Office   In Kihei, it's at 1254 S. Kihei Rd. (☎ 808/879-2403); in Kahului, 138 S. Puunene Ave. (☎ 808/871-4710); in Lahaina, 1870 Honoapiilani Hwy. in the Lahaina Civic Center (☎ 808/667-6611) and at Lahaina Shopping Center (☎ 808/661-0550)

Taxis   Alii Taxi offers islandwide 24-hour service (☎ 808/661-3688, or 808/667-2605). Or try Kihei Taxi (☎ 808/879-3000), Wailea Taxi (☎ 808/874-5000), and Yellow Cab of Maui (☎ 808/877-7000).

Weather Reports   For current weather, call 808/877-5111 from 4:30 to 8:30pm; for Haleakala weather, 808/572-7749; for surf and wave conditions, 808/877-3477.

2 Where to Stay

Although most condominium apartments are in the luxury category, some are fine for us. But even with these additions to the hotel scene, a room on Maui is probably going to be more expensive than one in Waikiki.

BED & BREAKFASTS Those of you looking for bed-and-breakfast homes should know about **Affordable Accommodations Maui,** P.O. Box 98, Puunene, HI 96784 (☎ 808/879-7865 or 800/848-5567). Although headquartered in the Kihei area, where many of its accommodations are located, Affordable Accommodations Maui has discoveries all over the island: in Lahaina, Iao Valley, and upcountry in Kula, Haiku, and Olinda. They delight in being "matchmakers," finding just the right accommodation, the right host, and the right price for their clients. On their roster are rooms in private houses, which run from $45 to $60 for a single or double, and vacation rentals in condos, cottages, studios, and homes, which go for $75 to $125. A very popular car-and-condo package starts at $84. They also have secluded, romantic hideaways at higher prices, and even magnificent properties suitable for retreats or executive conferences. They can even arrange car rentals. The staff is available for advice and assistance once you're on Maui.

Ann and Bob Babson, 3371 Keha Dr. in Maui Meadows, Kihei, Maui, HI 96753 (☎ 808/874-1166 or 800/824-6409), the young couple whose vacation rentals are described below, also have an all-island reservation service. If their own place is full, they can recommend others in Maui. They can also get you car rentals at a good price, recommend wedding planning services, and provide plenty of inside information on Maui.

The people at **Maui Windsurfari,** P.O. Box 330254, Kahului, Maui, HI 96733 (☎ 808/871-7766 or 800/736-MAUI), who specialize in complete windsurfing vacation packages, also service nonwindsurfers, with a good selection of North Shore and Kihei accommodations, ranging from simple studios and condos with full kitchens from $60 a night to luxurious oceanfront homes at $120 to $500 a night. Bed & breakfast accommodations are also available. There are good rates for car-and-accommodations packages as well.

KAHULUI

Kahului has a string of four hotels within minutes of the main airport and across the road from three very attractive shopping centers dotted with inexpensive restaurants. The ocean, here, however, is rocky and can be fairly rough. With a very good beach area in Kihei, just 15 minutes away, these hotels have become largely the place for business travelers and very large tour groups, since Kahului does offer a central location for touring all of Maui.

Edy and Ray Roberts Bed & Breakfast
433 Nihoa St., Kahului, Maui, HI 96732. ☎ **808/244-4667.** 2 rms (with shared bath). $50 for one person, $60 for two. (Rates include breakfast.) No credit cards. Minimum stay 2 nights. Free parking.

Mr. and Mrs. Roberts' home is centrally located, just a few minutes away from Kahului airport. One of the two rooms has twin beds, the other a queen-size bed; they share a common bath. Guests can relax in the quiet surroundings of the pool, ureka palms, and coconut trees. Continental breakfast is served on the patio each morning. Adults only, no alcohol, and no smokers. Reservations should be made at least a month in advance.

Maui Seaside Hotel
100 W. Kaahumanu Ave., Kahului, Maui, HI 96732. ☎ **808/877-3311** or toll free 800/367-7000 from the mainland U.S., 800/451-6754 interisland. Fax 808/922-0052. 190 rms, 10 kitchenette units, 6 suites. A/C TV TEL. Apr–Dec 14, $54–$78 single or double; $83 kitchenette unit; $88 junior suite. Dec 15–Mar, add $10 per room per night. Each additional

person $12 extra. Children 17 and under stay free with parent using existing beds. Add $19 per night for rental car. AE, MC, V. Free parking.

This is your best bet in Kahului. The entire complex has recently been renovated and is very attractive; there is also a new sand beach. Rooms are large, light, and tastefully furnished, with two double beds. The standard rooms face the garden, while the deluxe rooms are beside the pool. The superior tower rooms are the most expensive and include a refrigerator by request. There's a coin-operated laundry. You can save money by dining at Vi's, which offers a long menu of seafood, American, Mexican, Italian, and Asian dishes—most for $8.50 to $12.50.

WAILUKU
DOUBLES FOR ABOUT $35 TO $50

⑤ Banana Bungalow Too
310 N. Market St., Wailuku, Maui, HI 96783. ☎ **808/244-5090** or toll free 800/ 8-HOSTEL. 27 rms (none with bath). $31.95 single; $38.95 double; $15 per person in shared community rooms. MC, V. Free parking on side street.

This international budget hotel and hostel has a casual atmosphere and is well suited to backpackers, active travelers, and windsurfers. It's virtual heaven for the last, since it's just 10 minutes from Kanaha and Spreckelsville and 15 from Hookipa, three of Maui's best windsurfing beaches. A dozen or more windsurfing shops carrying all the latest equipment are within a 10-minute drive. Single rooms have a double bed, double rooms have either a queen-size bed or twins, and community rooms house two or three people in either twin beds or cedar bunks. Bathrooms are shared. There's a large-screen cable TV lounge; free coffee and tea; a kitchen with refrigerators, microwaves, and a gas cooker; an activity center; a guest pay phone; laundry facilities; a picnic area with tropical fruit trees; and a sand volleyball court. There are beach parties and daily activities, plus a free airport and beach shuttle with a free phone at the airport. Managers Mark and Janna Folger can help guests find the cheapest car rental companies (some of which give special discounts) and will book local activities, too.

⑤ Northshore Inn
2080 Vineyard St., Wailuku, Maui, HI 96793. ☎ **808/242-8999.** Fax 808/244-5004. 60 beds (no rms with bath). $33 single; $43 double or twin; $16.50 per person in community rooms. MC, V. Free parking.

Here's more good news for the active budget crowd. This hotel right in the heart of historic Wailuku town offers some of the most reasonable rates on Maui. After traveling around the world, owner Katie Moore looked for a way to settle on Maui and create an inexpensive, comfortable, friendly lodging. She discovered the old Wailuku Grand Hotel and has completely renovated and remodeled the old building, so that it's now quite pleasant. There's a common room with TV and VCR; a full kitchen (with free coffee all day) where guests may cook; and a storage room for surfboards and other equipment.

The six double rooms are small but cozy, with white stucco walls, roll-up blinds, a small refrigerator, and either double or twin beds. There are 12 dormitory-style rooms, with two double-decker beds each, and a refrigerator. There are no private bathrooms, but there are six shared bathrooms, all with showers. The Northshore Inn attracts a lively international crowd. It's convenient to many inexpensive restaurants, and good beaches are about a 15-minute drive away.

KIHEI-WAILEA

The best beach area closest to Kahului (about 15 minutes away) is the Kihei-Wailea section of Maui—a windswept stretch of sea and sand, with miles and miles of unspoiled beach, the waves lapping at your feet, air warm and dry, and the mighty volcano of Haleakala and its changing cloud colors to gaze at from the shore. It's blessed with the least rain and best weather on all of Maui. Full-scale tourist development began here not so long ago, and the area has blossomed mightily since then, with scores of condominiums, plus new restaurants and small shopping centers opening to keep pace. There are splendid luxury resorts in Wailea and Makena. Beaches here can be rather windy in the afternoon; swim in the morning and save sightseeing for later. Despite its beauty, the Kihei-Wailea region remains less glamorous and exciting, at least for us, than the Lahaina-Kaanapali region (see below), but if you like a quiet vacation, you'll do well at any of the places described below.

Doubles for About $50 to $75

Hale Kamaole

2737 S. Kihei Rd., Kihei, Maui, HI 96753. ☎ **806/879-1221** or toll free 800/367-2970 in the U.S. and Canada. Fax 808/879-5576. 188 apts. TV TEL. Apr 1–Dec 15, $67 one-bedroom apt for two, extra person $5; $87 two-bedroom/two-bath apt for four, extra person $5. Dec 16–Mar 31, $99 one-bedroom apt for two, extra person $8; $129 two-bedroom/two-bath apt for four, extra person $8 per day. Minimum stay 3 nights. No credit cards. Free parking.

This low-rise apartment complex is across the street from a fine swimming beach. No studios, only lovely one-bedroom units and split-level two-bedroom/two-bath apartments. All units are nicely furnished and have complete kitchens. Facilities include a tennis court, two pools, and barbecue grills.

Kamaole Beach Royale Resort

2385 S. Kihei Rd., Kihei, Maui, HI 96753. ☎ **808/879-3131** or toll free 800/421-3661. Fax 808/879-9163. 63 condo units (44 for rental). TV TEL. Apr–Dec 14, $65 one-bedroom apt for two; $75–$80 two-bedroom/two-bath apt for two; $85 three-bedroom/two-bath apt with double lanai for two. Dec 15–Mar 31, $90 one-bedroom apt for two; $100–$105 two-bedroom/two-bath apt for two; $110 three-bedroom/two-bath apt with double lanai for two. Each additional person $10 extra. Minimum stay 5 days. No credit cards. Free parking.

This attractive condominium complex boasts tastefully furnished apartments, each with its own private lanai, ceiling fans, and all-electric kitchen with dishwasher and washer-dryer. There's a roof garden for sunbathing and a swimming pool in the tropical garden. The complex is across the road and just a short walk from one of the lovely Kamaole beaches, excellent for swimming. Reserve well in advance, as this is a popular place.

✹ Kauhale Makai Resort

938 S. Kihei Rd., Kihei, Maui, HI 96753. ☎ **808/879-8888** or toll free 800/822-4409. Fax 808/874-6881. 164 condo units. A/C TV TEL. Apr 15–Dec 15, $60 studio ($350 per week); $70 one-bedroom apt ($450 per week); $85 two-bedroom apt ($550 per week). Dec 16–Apr 14, $75 studio ($475 per week); $95 one-bedroom apt ($600 per week); $120 two-bedroom apt ($800 per week). No credit cards. Free parking.

We've always shied away from high-rise condominiums, but after we visited Kauhale Makai (Village by the Sea) we were convinced that—in this case at least—bigger also means better. Accommodations are in two six-story buildings, and some have been superbly decorated by their owners. All have a full kitchen, central air conditioning, and color TV. The two buildings, right on the ocean, are separated by a well-tended lawn with a pool, putting green, Jacuzzi, and barbecues. Also available: sauna, shuffleboard, public tennis courts, and a public golf course nearby. An in-house convenience shop makes housekeeping easy in case you've forgotten something at the supermarket.

Kealia Condominium Resort

191 N. Kihei Rd., Kihei, Maui, HI 96753. ☎ **808/879-0952** or toll free 800/367-5222. 30 condo units. A/C TV TEL. May–Nov $55 studio; $75 one-bedroom apt for two. Dec–Apr $70 studio; $90 one-bedroom apt. Each additional person $10 extra. Minimum stay 4 nights. No credit cards. Free parking.

Its beachfront location and sensible prices are pluses for this high-rise condominium with nicely furnished studios and apartments. All have cable TVs, full kitchens, washer-dryers, and lanais with ocean views. There's an attractive swimming pool and sunning area on the grounds, as well as the glorious beach.

Kihei Akahi

2531 S. Kihei Rd., c/o Condominium Rentals Hawaii, 2439 S. Kihei Rd., Suite 205A, Kihei, Maui, HI 96753. ☎ **808/879-2778** or toll free 800/367-5242 on the U.S. mainland. Fax 808/879-7825. 70 studios and condos. TV TEL. Apr–Dec 14, $55 studio; $70 one-bedroom apt; $95 two-bedroom/two-bath apt. Dec 15–Mar, $85 studio; $100 one-bedroom apt; $135 two-bedroom/two-bath apt. Rates apply to stays of 4 (minimum) to 6 nights; less on longer stays. Inquire about possible car-rental packages with Alamo Rent A Car. No credit cards. Free parking.

Located across from a beautiful swimming beach, Kihei Akahi has the lowest rates of any of the many properties managed by Condominium Rentals Hawaii. Facilities include two swimming pools, barbecue grills, and a tennis court. Nicely furnished units have fully equipped kitchens, washer-dryers, and private lanais.

Kihei Alii Kai

2387 S. Kihei Rd., c/o Leisure Properties, P.O. Box 965, Kihei, Maui, HI 96753. ☎ **808/879-6221** or toll free 800/888-MAUI on the U.S. mainland, Fax 808/888-6284. 127 condo units (46 for rental). TV TEL. Apr 15–Dec 14, $65 one-bedroom apt for two; $80 two-bedroom apt for four; $90 two-bedroom/two-bath apt for four; $110 three-bedroom/two-bath apt for six. Dec 15–Apr 14, $90 one-bedroom apt for two; $105 two-bedroom apt for four; $115 two-bedroom/two-bath apt for four; $130 three-bedroom/two-bath apt for six. Each additional person $7 extra. Minimum stay 3 nights. MC, V. Free parking.

Although you'll have to walk a few steps and cross the road to get to beautiful Kamaole Beach, that effort will save you considerable dollars. It's much cheaper to stay here than at most beachfront condos. This is a well-kept and nicely run property. Each individually decorated apartment has its own private lanai and a full kitchen and washer-dryer. There are two tennis courts, a pool with spa, sauna, barbecue, and eating area.

✪ Kihei Kai

61 N. Kihei Rd., Kihei, Maui, HI 96753. ☎ **808/879-2357** or toll free 800/735-2357. 24 one-bedroom apts. A/C TV TEL. Apr 16–Dec 15, $70–$95 apt for two. Dec 16–Apr 15, $80–$105 apt for two. Minimum stay 4 days in summer, 7 days in winter. Each additional person $5 extra (maximum of four per apt). No credit cards. Free parking.

This one is a surprise: From the road, all one sees is a parking lot. But this complex fronts a sandy beach! These are very pleasant, breezy units, well suited for families. And the low price for on-the-beach accommodations with fully equipped all-electric kitchens has to make this one of the best bargains in Maui.

All units are nicely furnished, and most have a view of the ocean from their private 16-foot lanais; rates depend on view and location. There's a self-service laundry facility, swimming pool, cable TV, and barbecue area, too.

Leinaala Oceanfront Condominiums

998 S. Kihei Rd., Kihei, Maui, HI 96753. ☎ **808/879-2235** or toll free 800/334-3305. Fax 808/879-8366. 24 apts. A/C TV Apr 15–Dec 14, $65 studio for two; $75 one-bedroom apt for two; $100 two-bedroom apt for four. Dec 15–Apr 14, $85 one-bedroom apt for two; $110 two-bedroom apt for four. Each additional person $10 extra. Minimum stay 4 nights. 10% discount for 7 nights or more Apr 15–Dec 14. Monthly rates available. MC, V. Free parking.

Tennis buffs will be in heaven here, because this cozy little complex of apartments is sandwiched between public courts. After your game, you can cool off in the freshwater swimming pool, or snorkel or windsurf in the ocean right out front. The best swimming beaches in Kihei are about a mile away. The one- and two-bedroom apartments are nicely furnished, with fully equipped kitchens. Each of them is oceanfront, with glorious views, and the place is very quiet.

Nani Kai Hale

73 N. Kihei Rd., Kihei, Maui, HI 96753. ☎ /fax **808/875-0630** or toll free 800/367-6032. 46 condo units. TV TEL. Apr 16–Dec 14. $50 studio; $60–$90 one-bedroom apt for two; $95-$130 two-bedroom apt for four. Minimum stay 4 nights; 7-night stays discounted. Dec 15-Apr 15. $65 studio; $80–$125 one-bedroom apt for two; $120–$150 two-bedroom apt for four. Each additional person $10 extra; children under 5 stay free in parents' unit. AE, MC, V. Free parking.

Sitting on 6½-mile walking and swimming beach at the entrance to the Kihei area, this old-timer is blessed with an ideal location. There's a barbecue and picnic area, and a congenial group around the heated, oceanfront pool or out on the sandy beach. Swimming is excellent, but snorkeling is limited. All units have an ocean view; some are oceanfront. These are condominium apartments, so decor varies with the individual owners, but all are attractively furnished and have either queen- or king-size beds, sofa beds in the living rooms, well-equipped modern kitchens with microwave ovens, and private lanais. And all apartments have two baths.

Nonalani

455 S. Kihei Rd., Kihei, Maui, HI 96753. ☎ **808/879-2497** or toll free 800/733-2688. 8 cottages. Apr 16–Nov. $65 cottage for two. Dec–Apr 15, $78 cottage for two. Minimum stay 4 nights in summer, 7 nights in winter. Weekly and monthly rates available. No credit cards. Free parking.

Each of the eight cottages that comprise Nonalani stands alone in a grassy tree-filled area, within sight of the ocean. There is a swimming beach 20 yards away. Each cottage has a living room, full bedroom (with a queen-size bed), kitchen, and an open lanai with dining table. Since there are two beds in the living room, a family of four could be comfortable here.

Punahoa Beach Apartments

2142 Iliili Rd., Kihei, Maui, HI 96753. ☎ **808/879-2720.** 15 units. TV TEL. Apr 15–Dec 14, $62 studio; $82–$84 one-bedroom apt; $87–$110 two-bedroom apt. Dec 15–Apr 14, $81 studio; $109–$111 one-bedroom apt; $120–$140 two-bedroom apt. Additional person $12 extra. Minimum stay 5 days. No credit cards. Free parking.

You'll be in good hands if you choose to stay at this little place. Each of the units has a private lanai, ocean views, a fully equipped kitchen, and smart, modern furnishings. It's surrounded by gardens, and it's right on the ocean. Sandy beaches, with good swimming and surfing, are adjacent; children love it around the rocks because of the fish. Punahoa gets booked way ahead with repeat visitors in winter, but accommodations are easier to come by in summer.

Shores of Maui

2075 S. Kihei Rd., Maui, HI 96753-8799. ☎ **808/879-9140** or toll free 800/367-8002. Fax 808/879-6221. 50 condo units. A/C TV TEL. Apr 15–Dec 19, $65 one-bedroom apt for two; $90 two-bedroom apt for four. Dec 20–Apr 14, $90 one-bedroom apt for two; $115 two-bedroom apt for four. Each additional person $8 extra. Minimum stay 3 days. MC, V. Free parking.

All units are oceanfront at this attractive, two-level condo complex across the street from the beach. Snorkeling is good, and there's a sandy swimming beach just a block away. You can relax in the good-size swimming pool, soak in the spa, play a little tennis, enjoy a barbecue. Apartments are nicely decorated; all have a dishwasher and washer-dryer. The two-bedroom units also have two baths.

Sunseeker Resort

551 S. Kihei Rd. (P.O. Box 276), Kihei, Maui, HI 96753. ☎ **808/879-1261** or toll free 800/532-MAUI, Fax 808/874-3877. 8 units. TV TEL. $50–$55 studio with kitchen; $60–$65 one-bedroom apt; $80–$90 two-bedroom apt. Each additional person $6 extra. Minimum stay 3 days for studios and one-bedroom apts, 7 days for two-bedroom apts. No credit cards. Free parking.

Two former readers of this book, Milt and Eileen Preston, decided to settle islands. They've had their own place across from Kihei Beach for quite a while now, and will give you a warm welcome. All units have king-size beds, cheerful color schemes, original artwork, furnished lanais, cross-ventilation, and a full kitchen with microwave oven. Picture windows face the ocean. Hawaiian pitched roofs add a Polynesian touch. The two-bedroom apartments have two baths and a huge, private Polynesian garden in back. The Prestons will provide you with free barbecue equipment. The resort is near the beach where the 1792 arrival of Capt. George Vancouver is commemorated by an HVB marker and a Thunderbird totem carved by the Nootka people on Vancouver Island.

DOUBLES FOR ABOUT $75 TO $100

Aston Maui Lu Resort

575 S. Kihei Rd., Kihei, Maui, HI 96753. ☎ **808/879-5881** or toll free 800/922-7866 on the U.S. mainland and Canada, 800/321-2558 interisland. Fax 808/922-8785. 170 rms. A/C TV TEL. Apr–Dec 21, $79–$150 double. Dec. 22–Mar, $89–$150 double. Each additional person $12 extra. AE, DC, MC, V. Free parking.

The traditional big hotel in this area, this is a collection of low-rise, Polynesian-style buildings on 28 acres of tropical grounds, complete with a large Maui-shaped swimming pool, sandy beach, tennis courts, and a spirit of *ohana*, or "family," reminiscent of a more gracious Hawaii. The rates here are much lower than at the fancier new resorts in Wailea, and offer good value, especially when you consider the many handy conveniences, including refrigerator and coffee maker. Furnishings are attractive. The Long House Restaurant serves excellent dinners.

Kamaole Nalu Resort

2450 S. Kihei Rd., Kihei, Maui, HI 96753-8694. ☎ **808/879-1006** or toll free 800/767-1497. Fax 808/879-8693. 36 two-bedroom apts. TV TEL. Apr 2–Dec 15, $95 oceanview apt for two, $115 oceanfront. Dec 15–Apr 2, $130 oceanview apt for two, $150 oceanfront. Each additional person $12 extra. Special rates of $100 oceanfront, $80 oceanview, are offered June–Sept. Rates subject to change. Minimum stay 3 nights. No credit cards. Free parking.

Nestled between two lovely beach parks, Kamaole 1 and Kamaole 2, this one is for those who love the water. There's also a swimming pool and a barbecue grill. Apartments are all individually and nicely furnished, and good buys; each has a living room, a fully equipped kitchen with dishwasher and laundry facilities, two baths, and a private lanai. A nice place for a family to spread out in.

Kihei Beach Resort

26 S. Kihei Rd., Kihei, HI 96753. ☎ **808/879-2744** or toll free reservations 800/367-6034. Fax 808/875-0306. 54 apts. A/C TV TEL. Apr 16–Dec 15, $100 one-bedroom apartment for two; $130 two-bedroom apartment for four; Dec 16–Apr 15, $115 one-bedroom apartment, $150 two-bedroom apartment; rates based on 7-night occupancy, higher on shorter stays. Extra person $10; children under 5 free. 3-day minimum stay. DISC, MC, V. Free parking.

Each apartment at this handsomely modern high rise is oceanfront, since the building is right on the beach, parallel with the water. All are spacious and comfortable, with carpeted living-dining area and an electric kitchen with every convenience. There's free coffee in the morning, a freshwater solar-heated pool that can be enjoyed even after dark, and 6 miles of sandy Kihei beach.

Koa Resort

811 S. Kihei Rd., Kihei, Maui, HI 96753. ☎ **808/879-1161** or toll free 800/877-1314 on the U.S. mainland and Canada. 54 rms. TV TEL. Apr–Nov 30, $85 one-bedroom apt for two (maximum four); $100 two-bedroom apt for four (maximum four); $110 two-bedroom/two-bath apt for four (maximum six); $135 three-bedroom/two-bath apt for six (maximum eight), $160 three-bedroom/three-bath apt for six (maximum eight). Each additional person over minimum pays $10. Dec 1–Mar 31, add $20 to all rates. Minimum stay 5 nights; 15% discount for monthly stays. No credit cards. Free parking.

It's so cozy and comfortable, you could easily spend a long time living here—and many people do. The five two-story wooden buildings are across the road from the ocean and surrounded by over 5½ acres of green gardens and lawns. There are two tennis courts, an 18-hole putting green, an oversize pool spanned by a bridge, a Jacuzzi, barbecues, and shuffleboard courts. Apartments are spacious and comfortable, with nice furnishings, cable TV, fully equipped kitchens, and large lanais. Rates are decent for Maui. The best buy is the two-bedroom unit at $100.

Luana Kai Resort

940 S. Kihei Rd., Kihei, Maui, HI 96753. ☎ **808/879-1268** or toll free 800/669-1127. Fax 808/879-1455. 113 condo units. TV TEL. Apr–Dec 19, $105–$120 one-bedroom apt; $125–$150 two-bedroom apt; $200 three-bedroom apt. Dec 20–Mar. $130–$145 one-bedroom apt; $150–$175 two-bedroom apt; $225 three-bedroom apt. (Rates include car rental.) AE, DC, MC, V. Free parking.

Gracefully situated on 8 acres of beautifully landscaped grounds, this is one of the nicest condos in the Kihei area. There's a peaceful feeling here. Step from your room—well, almost—to the ocean or swimming pool, heated whirlpool, saunas, tennis courts, putting green, or barbecue area; everything is close at hand. Inside, carved wooden doors lead to one-, two-, and three-bedroom apartments luxuriously furnished, all with full electric kitchens, lanais, and every comfort.

✪ Mana Kai Maui Condominium Hotel

2960 S. Kihei Rd., Kihei, Maui, HI 96753. ☎ **808/879-1561** or toll free 800/525-2025 on the mainland U.S. and in Canada. Fax 808/874-5042. 66 hotel rms, 66 condo apts. TV TEL. Apr 17–Dec 16, $90 double (including breakfast); $155 one-bedroom apt; $175 two-bedroom apt for four. Dec 17–Apr 16, $95 double (including breakfast); $175 one-bedroom apt; $195 two-bedroom apt for four. Each additional person $10 extra. (Rates include car with unlimited mileage.) AE, CB, DC, MC, V. Free parking.

A unique resort in this area—or any other, for that matter—Mana Kai Maui offers a combination of condo apartments and regular hotel rooms in a lively, upbeat setting. It's situated on a mile-long, beautiful crescent of beach (it's one of the best snorkeling beaches around), with a pool, an open-air restaurant, and all sorts of activities. The hotel rooms are small bedrooms with either a king-size bed or twins, and an attractive bathroom with a large vanity. Beautifully furnished apartments include full kitchen with refrigerator, range, dishwasher, and dishes.

Menehune Shores

760 S. Kihei Rd. (P.O. Box 556), Kihei, Maui, HI 96753. ☎ **808/879-5828** or toll free 800/558-9117 in the U.S. and Canada. Fax 808/879-5218. 70 condo units. Apr 16–Dec 14, $75 one-bedroom apt for two; $88.50 one-bedroom/two-bath apt for two; $100 two-bedroom/two-bath apt for four; $120 three-bedroom/two-bath apt for four, $140 for six. Dec 15–Apr 15, $90 one-bedroom for two; $110 one-bedroom/two-bath apt for two; $120 two-bedroom/two-bath apt for four; $130 three-bedroom/two-bath apt for four, $150 for six. Each additional person $7.50 extra. Minimum stay 5 days. No credit cards. Free parking.

For family accommodations, try this big, beautiful condominium complex on the beach at Kihei. You might not want to leave the grounds—there's the ocean, a heated pool, and the "Royal Fishpond," a swimming pond protected by a stone-and-reef formation built by the ancient Hawaiians. Akina's on the Beach offers steak, seafood, and moderately priced lunches. There's even a whale-watching platform in the roof garden. All apartments face the ocean, are individually decorated, and have a full electric kitchen, with refrigerator/freezer and washer-dryer. The two- and three-bedroom apartments have two bathrooms.

Wailea Oceanfront Hotel

2980 S. Kihei Rd., Kihei, Maui, HI 96753. ☎ **808/879-7744** or toll free 800/367-5004 in the U.S. and Canada, 800/272-5275 interisland. Fax 808/596-0158. Telex 723-8582. 88 rms. A/C TV TEL. $85–$100 double; $160 one-bedroom family unit. (Rates include car rental.) AE, MC, V. Free parking.

An on-the-beach location and some of the more moderate prices in the Wailea area are pluses for this hotel, located at the entrance to the Wailea Beach Resort. Two championship golf courses and 14 tennis courts are within walking distance, and right out front is a beautiful crescent of sandy beach, perfect for swimming and snorkeling. No need for a pool here. Carelli's on the Beach, a sophisticated spot for gourmet Italian dining, is on the premises. Rooms are comfortable, nicely furnished, each with its own refrigerator. Complimentary coffee and doughnuts are available in the mornings. Most of the rooms have either double or twin beds and a garden view.

BED & BREAKFASTS

✪ Ann and Bob Babson's Vacation Rentals

3371 Keha Dr. in Maui Meadows. Kihei, Maui, HI 96753. ☎ **808/874-1166** or toll free 800/824-6409. 2 rms., 1 apt, 1 cottage (all with bath). TV TEL. $65–$80 single or double guest rm. in main house (including breakfast); $80 double one-bedroom apt; $95 two-bedroom/two-bath cottage. Additional person $10 extra. Breakfast $5 extra outside of main house. No credit cards. Free parking.

Not only are Ann and Bob Babson just about the nicest hosts around, they also have one of the prettiest homes on the southwest side of Maui, 500 feet up the mountainside, just above the grand resort hotels of Wailea and within a 5-minute drive of sparkling swimming and snorkeling beaches. One-hundred-and-eighty- degree ocean views, spectacular sunsets, gorgeously landscaped grounds (bougainvillea, plumeria, papaya trees, rose bushes, night-blooming jasmine), and tastefully decorated interiors make this the kind of place you'd like to stay at for a long, long time. An entire family could settle into the cozy Sunset Cottage, completely separate from the main house, with living room, outside deck, cathedral ceilings, two bedrooms, and two baths; it can sleep up to six. The Hibiscus Hideaway, on the ground floor of the main house, has its own private entrance and garden, living room, kitchen, separate bedroom, and bath. There are also two bed & breakfast units in the main house: the Bougainvillea Suite, a one-bedroom, one-bath with queen-size bed and a small refrigerator; and the sunny Molokini Suite, a spacious master bedroom with spectacular views of the Pacific, a king-size bed, and a glamorous bathroom with whirlpool tub. The Babson's breakfast table is a favorite place for guests to gather, since the hosts are not only generous with the food—tropical fruits, organic granola, waffles, french toast, fruit smoothies, homemade muffins, and bagels are all possibilities—but also with insider tips on favorite restaurants, hidden beaches and hiking trails, and quality attractions. And they even provide free laundry service. Plenty of that old-time aloha spirit here.

Anuhea

P.O. Box 1919, Kihei, Maui, HI 96753. ☎ **808/874-1490** or toll free 800/206-4441. 4 rms. $50–85 single, $110 double. (Rates include breakfast.) MC, V. Free parking.

Psychologist and nutritionist Dr. Elaine Willis makes this tropical hideaway, on a hill overlooking the ocean and the resort hotels of Wailea, available to guests as a private health retreat; it's perfect for those seeking personal transformation and rejuvenation. Three elegant ocean-view rooms with bath overlook tranquil gardens; a fourth single room downstairs also has its own bath and garden view. A beautiful breakfast of "fresh-living" food is served on the deck each morning; sunsets are special. For an extra fee, Dr. Willis will assist guests in creating individual Wellness Lifestyle programs. Sessions with bodyworkers and healers can be arranged.

Bed, Breakfast, Books & Beach

3270 Kehala Dr., Kihei, Maui, HI 96753. ☎ **808/879-0097.** 2 rms. TEL. $75 one rm; $125 two rooms; $5 less per rm for stays of 3–6 nights, $10 less per rm for a week or more. (Rates include breakfast.) MC, V. Free parking.

A mile from the ocean in Maui Meadows, the home of spirited psychotherapists Natalie and John Tyler is filled with classical music, fine art, and books. Guests can enjoy breakfast ("natural high-energy gourmet") on a screened lanai with mountain views, plus sunsets over the ocean with cool drinks and pupus on the deck. A variety of options range from champagne breakfasts in bed to daily meditations to gourmet dinners and individual trips. No smoking. Private bath.

MAALAEA BAY

Down by the small-boat harbor at Maalaea Bay, a few miles from Kihei, is a wonderful beach area, and at Maalaea Village, a small group of condominiums.

Hono Kai Resort

280 Hauoli St., Maalaea Village, Maui, HI 96793. ☎ **808/244-7012** or toll free 800/ 367-6084. 40 condo units. TV TEL. Summer, $60, one-bedroom apt with garden view. $75 oceanfront. Winter, $85 one-bedroom apt with garden view, $100 oceanfront. Minimum stay 5 days. Inquire about summer specials. DISC, MC, V. Free parking.

Hono Kai is one of the most reasonably priced condominiums in the area, and would make an ideal place for a family vacation. You can swim at the public beach 50 yards away—or try your luck with surf at the harbor, which, according to some of the locals, is "the fastest surf in the world." All units are on the ocean side of the street, and all are pleasantly furnished. Shoji doors separate the living room and bedroom. There are full kitchens with microwave ovens and dishwashers. There's a swimming pool, washers and dryers on every floor, and two good restaurants—Buzz's Steak House and The Waterfront—nearby. We've had several good reports from our readers about this place and about rental agent Jeanne McJannet, who also represents two adjoining properties, Makani A Kai and Kanai A Nalu.

LAHAINA

The area surrounding the historic old whaling town of Lahaina, on Maui's west coast about 30 miles from Kahului, might be a good place to go after a day or two in Kahului or Kihei; or it could serve as a base for your entire Maui stay.

DOUBLES FOR ABOUT $40 TO $70

⑤ Aloha Tony's

13 Kauaula Rd., Lahaina, HI 96761. ☎ 808/661-8040 or toll free 800/57-ALOHA. 3 rms. $40–$60 single/double. Continental breakfast $5. (Rates include morning coffee.) MC, V. Free parking.

After 17 years of adventuresome living in Alaska, journeyman electrician Tony Mamo decided to settle down on Maui, "to warm up" and run a small tourist home. Considering the high price—and relative scarcity—of accommodations in Lahaina, Aloha Tony's is a great find for budgeteers. There's nothing fancy here—it's just a clean, casual, comfortable home with three nice bedrooms (two share a bath with each other, one shares a bath with Tony) and a communal kitchen/living/dining area, where guests can stock food in the refrigerator (they have kitchen privileges), make a phone call, watch TV, or socialize in the book-filled living room. What is special is the location: Access to Lahaina Beach is just across Tony's yard, and a short walk away is the center of Lahaina, with all its myriad attractions. Tony himself sets the mood for easy, island-style living—which is, after all, what Hawaii should be all about.

Garden Gate Bed & Breakfast

67 Kaniau Rd., P.O. Box 12321, Lahaina, Maui, HI 96761. ☎ 808/661-8800. Fax 808/667-7999. 1 garden studio, 1 room. A/C. $50 double; $85–$95 garden studio for two ($10 per extra person). (Rates include breakfast.) No credit cards. Free parking.

Ron and Welmoet Glover, a friendly couple, have a lovely garden home halfway between Lahaina and Kaanapali, and 1½ blocks from a good snorkeling beach. For those on a limited budget who just need a place to "hang their hat," their Molokai room, right in their house, works fine—it's nicely decorated, has a double bed, and a private bath. Breakfast is served outdoors. For couples and families wanting more space and privacy, the garden studio (almost 500 square feet), with its own private deck, is perfect: It can sleep up to four with a queen bed and a queen sleeper/sofa; has its own sitting area with TV, plus its own bathroom and stocked kitchen. The garden itself is lush and tropical, with bananas, papayas, and guavas growing all about, and a waterfall and windchimes. Ron and Welmoet are helpful hosts who can make all sorts of suggestions about what to see and do on Maui.

❸ Old Lahaina House

P.O. Box 10355, Lahaina, Maui, HI 96761. ☎ 808/667-4663 or toll free 808/847-0761. Fax 800/667-5615. 5 rms. A/C TV. $45–$95. (Rates include continental breakfast.) AE, MC, V. Free parking.

John and Sherry Barbier, the hosts at Old Lahaina House, claim they're not aiming to run a "fantasy hotel"; what they're offering is a place where travelers can feel at home in a real Hawaiian setting. And the location couldn't be better. Their lovely home is directly across the street from a beach perfect for swimming, snorkeling, and whale watching, and just a stone's throw from the heart of Lahaina; you could conceivably get around here without a car. There are two rooms on the main floor: One is a small single in the owners' part of the house, which shares their bath; another is in a separate wing and has a private bath, a small refrigerator and microwave, and a lanai. There are three rooms upstairs in this wing: One with a private bath and small refrigerator, one with twin beds and a great view of the West Maui Mountains, and one small twin. All rooms have air conditioning, ceiling fans, and TV. Breakfast (yummy pastries from a local French bakery, fruit, juices, beverages) is served each morning on the lanai, and there's a beautiful pool that guests are encouraged to use. John and Sherry are happy to help with activity, restaurant, and shopping recommendations. A couple of interesting notes: Sherry and her mother are the proprietors of a wonderful clothing boutique called Arabesque—*and* she's a former Mrs. Hawaii USA.

Doubles from $70

✪ Lahaina Inn

127 Lahainaluna Rd., Lahaina, Maui, HI 96791. ☎ **808/661-0577** or toll free 800/669-3444. Fax 808/667-9480. 12 rms. A/C. $89–$99 standard single or double; $129 large single or double (with queen- or king-size bed). (Rates include breakfast.) AE, MC, V. Parking $5 per day.

Anyone who remembers the shabby old Lahainaluna Hotel will be stunned to see the magical transformation it has undergone, emerging as the Lahaina Inn, an intimate inn with all the grace and charm of turn-of-the-century Lahaina. The hotel was re-created from the ground up at a cost of $3 million, by Rick Ralston, of Crazy Shirts fame. Ralston, one of Hawaii's most avid preservationists, saw to every detail of the period restoration, from the turn-of-the-century wood, brass, and iron beds, Oriental rugs, and wood wardrobe closets to the marble mantel clocks, leaded-glass lampshades, and even the lace runners on the dressers. All the antiques are from his personal collection. Modern conveniences include new private baths, ceiling fans, and luxurious decorator fabrics and wall coverings. Guests are served a continental breakfast to enjoy either in bed or in the wicker rocking chairs on their balconies, which overlook busy Lahainaluna Street. All rooms are on the second floor; downstairs is a small, graceful lobby and, adjoining it, David Paul's Lahaina Grill, an upscale restaurant serving New American cuisine. If you can afford the tab, a stay here is clearly a special experience. Inquire about their special wedding and honeymoon packages.

Lahaina Roads Condominiums

1403 Front St., Lahaina, Maui, HI 96761. ☎ **808/661-3166** or toll free 800/624-8203. 17 condo units. TV $95 one-bedroom apt for up to four; $130 two-bedroom apt for four to six; $150 penthouse apt for four. Minimum stay 3 nights. AE, MC, V. Free parking.

If you'd like to settle into your own little apartment right in Lahaina, this could be the place. The five-story elevator building at the Kaanapali end of Front Street sits in a cool and breezy spot right on a good snorkeling beach; you can gaze at the ocean—and watch some spectacular sunsets—from your own lanai. A swimming beach is a half-mile away, but there's a freshwater pool right at home.

The attractively, fully furnished apartments are soundproof, with fully equipped kitchens, washer and dryer, and large living rooms with convertible couches. Local calls are free. Penthouse apartments have two baths. Cleaning service on request. A free shuttle to downtown Lahaina and Kaanapali is within 3 blocks.

✪ Lahaina Shores Beach Resort

475 Front St., Lahaina, Maui, HI 96761. ☎ **808/661-4835** or toll free 800/628-6699. Fax 808/661-4696. 199 condo units. A/C TV TEL. Apr–Dec 15, $95–$117 studio for two; $122–$172 one-bedroom apt for three; $162–$182 penthouse apt for four. Dec 16–Mar 31, $105–$137 studio for two; $147–$172 one-bedroom apt for three; $192–$227 penthouse apt for four. Cribs and rollaways $10 extra. Car/condo and special seasonal packages available. AE, MC, V. Free parking.

This beachfront resort might be worth stretching your budget for a bit. All the units have complete electric kitchens and lanais. The cheaper units face the mountains, while the more expensive ones have ocean views or are oceanfront. The seven-story building, a charming example of Victorian architecture, is very much in keeping with the rest of old Lahaina—a welcome contrast to the concrete high-rises flourishing all over the rest of the island. A swimming pool with adjacent heated therapeutic Jacuzzi sits on the ocean side, just off the huge, airy lobby. You can swim in Lahaina Harbor, right in front of the hotel, and play tennis across the street.

✪ Maui Islander

660 Wainee St., Lahaina, Maui, HI 96761. ☎ **808/667-9766** or toll free 800/367-5226 from mainland U.S. and Canada. Fax 808/661-3733. 148 hotel rms. 90 studios with full kitchen, 134 suites. TV TEL. $72 hotel rm with refrigerator; $87 studio with full kitchen; $99 one-bedroom suite with full kitchen; $150 two-bedroom suite with full kitchen. Dec 20–Apr 1, add $8 to all rates. Room-and-car packages available. AE, DC, DISC, JCB, MC, V. Free parking.

Lack of a car will not be a hindrance to anyone who chooses to stay at this hotel, which affords peace and privacy (its units are spread out over 9 acres of tropical grounds) while providing proximity to everything you could want in the area; it's a 3-block walk to a sandy beach, a 2-block stroll to the activities of Lahaina Harbor, a block away from the shops and restaurants of Front Street, 2 blocks to the supermarket, and a short free bus ride to Kaanapali Beach. You can be picked up at the airport at nominal cost. And the hotel-condo itself is lovely, its units simply but nicely decorated in island style with light woods, tile bathroom, and tidy kitchen (hotel rooms have refrigerators only). There's a swimming pool, three

---

Readers Recommend

Old Lahaina House. *"We loved Old Lahaina House. The room we stayed in was the second-floor master suite. The most outstanding feature of our room was the balcony, which had an amazing view of the Pacific Ocean to the right and the mountains of Maui to the left. In the morning we awoke to the smell of freshly brewed Kona coffee, which was served with a delicious breakfast of fresh fruit, guava juice, and pastries. But even better than the food was the conversation with the other guests as well as our hosts. John and Sherry were gracious hosts who made us feel more as if we were visiting old friends. They truly made our stay in Lahaina special."*

—Julie Schott and Chris Johnson, Boca Raton, FL.

barbecue and picnic areas, and a tennis court lit for night play. Free continental breakfast is available at the daily briefing at the Activities Center. Good value in this pricey area.

Pioneer Inn

658 Wharf St., Lahaina, Maui, HI 96761-1295. ☎ **808/661-3636** or toll free 800/457-5457. Fax 808/667-5708. 34 rms. A/C TV TEL. $80–$120 estimated. AE, JCB, MC, V. Parking $4.

At this writing, this landmark property was in the midst of an ambitious total renovation. The public areas, restaurant, and lounge were the first to be completed; all the rooms are expected to be ready by the time you read this. They're simple yet very tasteful, and still harbor their colorful histories. And you certainly won't find a location that's more in the middle of things in Lahaina town. Lots of special events like dinner dances are held in the courtyard; you'll want to check to see what's going on during your stay.

Plantation Inn

174 Lahainaluna Rd., Lahaina, Maui, HI 96761. ☎ **808/667-9225** or toll free 800/433-6815. Fax 808/667-9293. 14 rms, 4 suites. A/C TV TEL. $104 standard; $129 deluxe; $145–$157 superior; $185–$195 suite. Honeymoon drive and airfare packages available. (Rates include breakfast.) AE, DISC, MC, V. Free parking.

Just a block from the bustling waterfront and main street of Lahaina is this small, quiet, European-style country inn, whose owners have come up with some terrific innovations in the art of making guests happy. Each of the soundproof rooms is exquisitely decorated with antiques, stained glass, hardwood floors, brass and poster beds, ceiling fans, and florals. The TV (VCR on request) is tucked away in a graceful armoire. All rooms have refrigerators; some suites have cooking facilities. Guests have the use of a 12-foot-deep tiled pool with spa and sun deck out back, plus a club house for private meetings or dining. Guests receive a discount on dinner at Gerard's, one of Maui's best French restaurants, which occupies the front parlor and veranda.

Puamana

Front St., P.O. Box 11108, Lahaina, Maui, HI 96761. ☎ **808/667-2551** or toll free 800/628-6731 in the U.S. and Canada. 40 condo units. TV TEL. Apr 16–Dec 15, $95 one-bedroom gardenview apt for up to four, $120 center garden, $140 loft, $150 oceanfront; $135, $175, $200 two-bedroom house for up to six; $300 three-bedroom oceanfront house for up to six. Dec 16–Apr 15, $120 one-bedroom gardenview apt for up to four, $130 center garden, $160 loft, $175 oceanfront; $155, $225, $250 two-bedroom house for up to six; $350 three-bedroom oceanfront house for up to six. 10% discount for 7 nights; 20% discount for 28 nights. Minimum stay 3 nights (one week Xmas). AE, MC, V. Free parking.

Puamana is the first planned residential development on Maui, a colony of privately owned town houses set on 28 acres of tropical gardens right on the beach. The place is secluded, private, and very peaceful, yet it's a short drive from all the shopping and restaurant excitement of downtown Lahaina. Puamana was a private estate in the 1920s, part of a large sugar plantation; the plantation manager's home is now the clubhouse, with a patio overlooking the ocean (the ideal place for sunset watching), a library, card rooms, sauna, and office. There are three swimming pools (one, for adults only, right on the beach), a Laykold tennis court, and table tennis, too. The town houses, built back in the 1960s, are all individually furnished, all comfortable, with complete kitchens, sofa beds in the living rooms; they can sleep four to six.

KAANAPALI TO KAPALUA

A few miles outside Lahaina, on Maui's exquisite west coast, is the Kaanapali-Napili-Kapalua region, one of Hawaii's most desirable vacation areas, blessed with miles of gorgeous beach and stunningly blue skies, with several world-famous championship golf courses thrown in for good measure. The road curves around a series of graceful bays, the most beautiful of which is Napili Bay, a gorgeous little stretch of sea and sand where not very long ago the breadfruit, papaya, and lichee trees ran helter-skelter to the sea. For us, this area is the end of the rainbow. The road reaches its end at the magnificent Kapalua Resort, one of Hawaii's most naturally beautiful playgrounds.

DOUBLES FOR $65 TO $95

Hale Kai

3691 Lower Honoapiilani Rd., Lahaina, Maui, HI 96761. ☎ **808/669-6333** or toll free 800/446-7307. Fax 808/669-4747. 40 condo units. TV TEL. $90 one-bedroom apt for two; $120–$145 two-bedroom apt for four, $140–$160 three–bedroom apt for six. Additional person $10 extra. Discounts available in summer. Minimum stay 3 nights. MC, V. Free parking.

These graceful apartments look out on flowering gardens, a park, and a good-size pool that fronts the beach. Each apartment is decorated differently and each has a different view: Some guests come back year after year for the ocean view, others for the quiet parkside units. Rooms on the upper levels have handsome cathedral ceilings. All are furnished nicely with electric kitchens and private lanais. All have VCRs, microwave ovens, and ceiling fans.

Hale Maui Apartment Hotel

3711 Lower Honoapiilani Rd. (P.O. Box 516), Lahaina, Maui, HI 96767. ☎ **808/669-6312.** Fax 808/669-1302. 12 suites. TV. Apr 15–Dec 15, $60–$85 one-bedroom suite for two. Dec 16–Apr 14, $75–$85 one-bedroom suite for two. Each additional person $10 extra. MC, V. Free parking.

Hans and Eva Zimmerman have been in charge at this small hotel right on the ocean for over 25 years now. The suites—each holding up to five guests—have been refurbished, and all have private lanais, and good kitchens. There's a nice barbecue area out back. There's no pool, but steps lead from the lawn right into the water.

ⓢ Honokawai Palms

3666 Lower Honoapiilani Rd., Lahaina, Maui, HI 96761. ☎ **808/667-2712** or toll free 800/669-MAUI. Fax 808/661-5875. 4 apts available for vacation rental. TV TEL. $65 daily, one-bedroom apt for up to four; $75 daily, two-bedroom apt for up to six. AE, MC, V. Free parking.

This is one of the older apartment complexes in this area, not as luxuriously furnished as some of the new condos, but it's a good value and just across the road from a small beach park. Apartments are spacious and comfortably furnished, with ample electric kitchens. The more desirable one-bedroom apartments have ocean views and lanais. There's a large pool and a barbecue area. The management is friendly and helpful. Laundry facilities are on premises.

Hoyochi Nikko

3901 Lower Honoapiilani, Rd., Lahaina, Maui, HI 96761. ☎ **808/669-8343** or toll free 800/487-6002 from U.S. and Canada. 18 one-bedroom units, some with lofts. TV.

May 1–Dec 14, $75, one-bedroom apt for two; Dec 15–Apr 30, $95, one-bedroom apt for two. Each additional person $10 extra. Minimum stay 7 days. No credit cards. Free parking.

The "Resort of the Sunbeam" is a gracious retreat, from the Asian architecture to the spacious oceanfront lawn and garden where you could easily laze away peaceful days. You can walk down the lawn stairs to the ocean and swim and snorkel inside the reef area, or swim in a freshwater pool in the garden. The units range from standard to large to "special." All have private lanais with full ocean views, some with "long boy" twin beds, others with queen or king-size beds, and fully equipped kitchens with washer-dryers. There's a grill for barbecues, and sometimes pupu parties are held out in the garden.

Kaleialoha

3785 Lower Honoapiilani Rd., Lahaina, Maui, HI 96761. ☎ **808/669-8197** or toll free 800/ 222-8688. Fax 808/669-2502. 67 apts. TV TEL. $75 mountain-view studio for two; $90–$100 one-bedroom oceanfront apt for two. Each additional person (over age 2) $7.50 extra. MC, V. Free parking.

This lovely condo resort offers large, pleasantly furnished one-bedroom apartments, each with a queen-size bed and a double sofa bed in the living room. The well-equipped kitchens boast dishwashers and washer-dryers. The cheaper rooms have a mountain view, while the more expensive rooms face the ocean. As for swimming, you can relax around the pool in the interior courtyard, or try the ocean out back; swimming is good within the protective outer reef.

Mahina Surf

4057 Lower Honoapiilani Rd., Lahaina, Maui, HI 96761. ☎ **808/669-6068** or toll free 800/ 367-6086. 56 units. TV TEL. Apr 15–Dec 14, $85–$105 one-bedroom apt; $105–$125 two-bedroom/two-bath apt for up to four. Dec 15–Apr 14, $110 one-bedroom apt; $130 two-bedroom/two-bath apt for up to four. Each additional person (including children) $8 extra. Minimum stay 3 nights. Discounts on weekly and monthly rates. Inquire about excellent deals on car rentals. MC, V. Free parking.

This is a fine place to settle in for real at-home living. The units are not only charming and attractively furnished, but well priced for the area. Sizes of the apartments vary, but all are little "homes"; the cutest are those two-bedroom apartments with a loft area upstairs that serves as a second bedroom—these are big enough to sleep six. The one-bedroom apartment can accommodate up to four people. There are ocean views from every unit. Mahina Surf is situated on a rocky strip of oceanfront, and snorkeling is fine, but there is no sandy beach. There is, however, a big pool as compensation. Barbecue grills are out on the lawn.

Mauian Hotel

5441 Honoapiilani Rd., Lahaina, Maui, HI 96761. ☎ **808/669-6205** or toll free 800/ 367-5034. Fax 808/669-0129. 44 apts. Apr 15–Dec 14, $79–$129 studio apt for two. Dec 15–Apr 14, $116–$142 studio apt for two. Rates flexible based on occupancy (call for details). Third person $9 extra; fourth person $6. Children under 12 free, special family rates. MC, V. Free parking.

The swimming here at Napili Bay, from a gentle, reef-protected beach, is among the best in the islands. These attractive studio apartments, big enough for four, each have private lanai, electric kitchen (including microwave oven), one queen-size and one trundle bed (that opens into two), and all the conveniences of home.

There's shuffleboard, a TV room, and a freshwater swimming pool. Facilities include a big laundry and ironing area. There's a weekly "Breakfast with the Manager," featuring a fresh-baked Hawaiian treat.

Maui Kailani

4435 Lower Honoapiilani Rd., Lahaina, Maui, HI 96761. ☎ **808/669-6994.** Fax 808/669-4046. Reservations: Maui Kailani, 119N. Commercial St., Suite 1400, Bellingham, WA 98225 (☎ 206/676-1434). 114 condo apts. $65 studio with ocean view or two-bedroom apt with garden view. Minimum stay 3 nights. MC, V. Free parking.

This complex offers some of the most reasonable rates in West Maui. It's a time-share operation, very busy in the winter season, but in the slower summer months units are often available to the general public. Twenty-seven of the units are available from April to September, 11 of these oceanside studios, the others two-bedroom duplex apartments on the mountainside. Two tennis courts, two pools, and other facilities are spread out over 8 acres, and there's a stretch of sandy beach, perfect for gentle ocean swimming. Each of the seaside units is spacious, attractively furnished (with such touches as big, old-fashioned ceiling fans), and boasts a large kitchenette and an enormous lanai. TVs can be rented.

Maui Park

3626 Lower Honoapiilani Rd., Lahaina, Maui, HI 96761. ☎ **808/669-6622** or toll free 800/922-7866 on the U.S. mainland. 800/445-6633 in Canada, 800/342-1551 interisland. Fax 808/922-8785. 208 units. A/C TV TEL. Apr–Dec 21, $85–$95 studio for two; $105–$115 one-bedroom apt for four; $149 two-bedroom apt for six. Dec 22–Mar 31, $99–$109 studio for two; $119–$129 one-bedroom apt for four, $159 two-bedroom apt for six. AE, CB, DC, JCB, MC, V. Free parking.

This economy hotel, just across the road from Honokawai Beach Park, is proving very popular. The Maui Park, under the management of Aston Hotels & Resorts, consists of six separate buildings surrounding a nearly Olympic-size swimming pool and sunning area. It features apartment-size studios and larger units attractively furnished, with full kitchens, cable TVs, clock radios, large closets, and daily cleaning service. The three-story buildings do not have elevators, but three rooms are accessible to the disabled. There's 24-hour service at the desk, and a grocery and sundry store right at hand, which makes cooking at home very easy.

✪ Maui Sands

3600 Honoapiilani Rd. (c/o Maui Resort Management, Suite C) Lahaina, Maui, HI 96761. ☎ **808/669-1902** or toll free 800/367-5037 on the U.S. mainland and Canada. Fax 808/669-8790. 76 condo apts. A/C TV TEL. $80 standard one-bedroom apartment for up to three, $105 garden, $135 oceanfront; $100 standard two-bedroom apt for up to five, $130 garden, $160 oceanfront. Each additional person $9 extra. Minimum stay varies from 2 to 10 nights (Dec 15–Jan 1). Ask about weekly rates and discounts on long stays and special "Off-Season" rates. MC, V. Free parking.

These apartments are ideal for families with lots of kids or for two couples traveling together. Imagine an enormous living room (about the size of two average hotel rooms put together), beautifully decorated, with two small but comfortable bedrooms, twin beds in one, a queen-size in the other; a full electric kitchen; tropical ceiling fans; a view of gardens or ocean from your private lanai; and enough space for six people to stretch out. You can get it all here at this attractive spot just past the Kaanapali gold-coast area, for about half the price of the luxury resorts. The apartments close to the road are for heavy sleepers.

Since the Maui Sands was built when it was feasible to buy large lots of land, there is plenty of it to spare; the grounds are abloom with lovely trees and plants.

Facilities include a big laundry, a comfortable swimming pool and sunning area, and a narrow sliver of beach. At sunset, you can watch the sun sink right between the islands of Molokai and Lanai off in the distance. The condo complex is completely refurbished, including new furniture. Kay and Adel Kunisawa are cordial hosts. Readers continue to praise this one.

○ Napili Surf Beach Resort

50 Napili Place, Lahaina, Maui, HI 96761. ☎ **808/669-8002** or toll free 800/541-0638 on the U.S. mainland and Canada. Fax 808/669-8004. 53 units. A/C TV TEL. May 1–Dec 19, $79 gardenview studio; $120–$125 oceanview studio; $145–$170 oceanview one-bedroom, all for two people. Dec 20–Apr 30, $90 gardenview studio; $130–$140 oceanview studio; $155–$185 oceanview one-bedroom. Car packages available. Each additional adult $15 extra. Children 12 and under free. No credit cards. Free parking.

This complex, with its soundproof luxury units perched on the tip of Napili Bay on a particularly lovely curve of beach, is one of the nicest places to stay in the area. Each of the units is well equipped for easy housekeeping, handsomely furnished, and has a private lanai that overlooks the garden or ocean. Even the lowest-priced accommodations, in the Puamala building, are superneat and functionally designed, with full kitchens and dishwashers. There may be discounts on these units in the summer months. Every Friday morning, guests get together to have coffee, socialize, and "talk story" with Uncle Buddy, who's been part of the Napili Surf family for more than 20 years. In such a gracious setting, the coconut palms swaying in the evening wind and the sea lapping gently at your feet, it's hard to remember what you were planning to worry about.

Noelani Condominium Resort

4095 Lower Honoapiilani Rd., Lahaina, Maui, HI 96761. ☎ **808/669-8374** or toll free 800/367-6030 in the U.S. and Canada. Fax 808/669-7904. 40 condo apts. TV TEL. $87 studio, $110 one-bedroom apt; $140 two-bedroom apt; $170 three-bedroom apt. Each additional person $7.50 extra. Minimum stay 3 days. Weekly and monthly rates available, as well as car/condo packages. AE, MC, V. Free parking.

Located in the Kahana area, these oceanfront condominiums are beautifully furnished, and the view from your oceanfront lanai—of Molokai and Lanai, blue seas, and tropical gardens—is even more beautiful. There are two freshwater swimming pools at seaside (heated for evening swimming), good snorkeling is right in front, and a wide sandy beach is adjacent to the property. Managers John and Donna Lorenz host mai tai parties in an oceanfront cabaña several times a month so that guests can get to know one another. And there's a concierge service, with orientation continental breakfasts at poolside. Readers have praised the warm, homey atmosphere here, and the resort has recently received a Deluxe AAA rating. Rooms are furnished in tropical decor, and have microwave ovens and in-room VCRs. Studios have a dressing room, bath, and kitchen. One-, two-, and three-bedroom units have their own washer-dryer and dishwasher. There is also a launderette.

Polynesian Shores

3975 Lower Honoapiilani Rd., Lahaina, Maui, HI 96761. ☎ **808/669-6065** or toll free 800/433-6284 on the U.S. mainland, 800/488-2179 in Canada. Fax 808/669-0909. 52 apts. TV TEL. $80–$100 one-bedroom apt for two; $90–$110 two-bedroom/two-bath loft apt for two, $155–$165 three-bedroom/three-bath apt for four. Minimum stay 3 nights. Each additional person $10. MC, V. Free parking.

This is the kind of small, relaxed place where everybody feels right at home—so much so that many come back year after year. Every apartment has an ocean view from its own private lanai; there's a deck on the oceanfront with barbecue facilities (it's a great place to watch for whales). Snorkeling is good right out front; swimming is better at a nearby sandy beach, about a 5-minute walk away. A heated swimming pool overlooks the ocean and grounds, which are so lush that guests can pick bananas right off the trees. Once a week there's a pupu party on the Tiki Deck. Apartments are nicely furnished, with separate living rooms and private baths.

DOUBLES FOR $95 TO ABOUT $120

Honokeana Cove Resort Condominiums

5255 Lower Honoapiilani Rd., Lahaina, Maui, HI 96761. ☎ **808/669-6441** or toll free 800/237-4948 (call collect from Canada). 38 condo units. TV TEL. $100–$110 one-bedroom apt for two; $140 two-bedroom apt for four; $160 three-bedroom apt for six. $155 two-bedroom town house for four. Each additional person $10–$15 extra. MC, V. Free parking.

If snorkeling is your passion, you're going to be very happy at this lovely resort condominium directly on a private, rocky cove where the snorkeling is tops. Swimmers need walk only about 5 minutes to a gentle sandy beach. Each apartment is close to the water and the oceanside pool; the location is ideal for whale-spotting. We were told that a whale once gave birth at the entrance to the cove! When you're not busy watching whales, snorkeling, or admiring the grounds with their beautiful trees—we spotted a 160-year-old kamani nut (or false almond) tree—you can enjoy the view from your lanai and the comforts of your apartment, each individually owned and decorated. All have fully equipped kitchens with dish-washers. Outdoor barbecues are provided. The management is cordial, arranging a pupu party every Thursday to bring the guests together.

The Kahili Maui

5500 Honoapiilani Rd., Lahaina, Maui, HI 96761. ☎ **808/669-5635** or toll free 800/786-7867 or 800/SUNSETS. Fax 808/669-2561. 30 condo units. TV. $109 ($425 for 5 days) studio for two; $149 ($525 for 5 days) one-bedroom/two-bath apt for up to four. Children under 18 stay free with parents using existing beds. Rollaway bed $16 extra; crib, $5. AE, DC, MC, V. Free parking.

Kapalua is one of Hawaii's poshest resort areas; at its gateway, adjacent to the world-famous Kapalua Bay Golf Course, is this moderately priced complex. The attractively furnished guest rooms have complete kitchens and in-room washer-dryers. Napili Bay and Kapalua Bay are just a short walk away, making this one cozy for serious swimmers and snorkelers as well as golfers. It's just across the road from the ocean, heading up toward the mountains. On the premises are a pool, Jacuzzi, and barbecue, and there are 10 tennis courts nearby.

Paki Maui

3615 Lower Honoapiilani Hwy., Lahaina, Maui, HI 96761. ☎ **808/669-8235** or toll free 800/535-0085 on the U.S. mainland and Canada. Fax 808/669-7987. 75 units. TV TEL. $119–$139 studio for two; $119–$159 one-bedroom for up to four, $188–$249 two-bedroom for up to six. AE, DISC, DC, MC, V. Free parking.

This lovely condominium suite resort is right on the oceanfront. The grounds are lush, with a waterfall, a swimming pool, and a pond with koi fish. Rooms are individually furnished with a great deal of charm, and all boast fully equipped kitchens and private lanais with splendid views of Molokai and Lanai. Free continental breakfasts and a sunset cocktail reception once a week.

MOUNTAINSIDE BED & BREAKFASTS

If you like mountains better than beach, charming private homes better than impersonal hotels or condos, and refreshingly old-fashioned prices best of all, we've got some good news for you. We've discovered 17 delightful "upcountry" guesthouses and vacation rentals. Each has a slightly different style and personality, but you can't go wrong at any of them.

IN KULA

Bloom Cottage

229 Kula Hwy. (R.R.2, Box 229), Kula, Maui, HI 96790. ☎ **808/878-1425.** 1 cottage. TV TEL. $95 per night. Minimum stay 2 nights. Each additional person $15 extra. (Rates include breakfast.) No credit cards. Free parking.

Wonderfully private and romantic, with sweeping views of pasturelands extending to the sea, Bloom Cottage stands by itself behind a pretty house owned by Lynne and Herb Horner. The charming 700-square-foot cottage is tastefully decorated in country style, and has a four-poster queen-size bed in the sleeping area and a single bed in the second bedroom, plus a double foldout futon and a living-room fireplace (yes, they have them up here in the mountains). There's a VCR and a slew of old classic movies. The fully equipped kitchen includes a microwave, and Lynne and Herb stock the refrigerator with coffees, teas, yogurt, fruit juices, and muffins. Guests can pick a wide variety of culinary herbs from the garden. No smoking in the cottage; no pets; not suitable for small children.

✪ Elaine's Upcountry Guest Rooms

2112 Naalae Rd., Kula, Maui, HI 96790. ☎ **808/878-6623.** 3 rms, 1 cottage. $55 double (third person $10), 3-night minimum stay; $95 cottage for four (fifth and sixth adults $10 each), 3-night minimum stay. No credit cards. Free parking.

We'd call Elaine and Murray Gildersleeve's splendid home in Kula the best value for the money. The Gildersleeves are a retired couple from Alaska: Murray devotes a lot of attention to his pineapple farm right on the premises and Elaine looks after the guests. Their Hawaiian pole house is designer-elegant, with three guest bedrooms on the ground floor sharing a separate kitchen and living room. Guests are welcome to use the refrigerator and to cook breakfast or whatever meals they like—a rare privilege in a guesthouse. Coffee, tea, and fruit from the garden are provided. The three bedrooms are beautifully furnished, and have private baths and either two twin beds or a king- or queen-size bed (a third person can sleep on a futon). Rooms have a splendid view of the West Maui mountains and Haleakala.

Next to the main house is a delightful cottage made to order for a family. With a queen-size bed in the bedroom, twin beds in the loft, and two window seats in the living room that can also be used as extra beds, six people can sleep comfortably. There's a complete kitchen and windows on three sides. The Gildersleeves ask that guests do not smoke or drink.

✪ Halemanu

221 Kawehi Place, Kula, Maui, HI 96720. ☎ **808/878-2729.** 1 rm. $75 single or double. Minimum stay 2 nights. (Rates include breakfast.) No credit cards. Free parking.

Halemanu ("Bird House" or "Perch") is a spectacular country home filled with fine arts and ethnic artifacts 2,500 feet up on the slopes of Haleakala, seemingly light-years away from the rest of civilization. Maui-raised owner Carol Austin, who delights in sharing her home and her intimate knowledge of the area with visitors, provides a charming guest room with a queen-size bed and private bath, entered from a large deck with a nonpareil 180° view of the countryside below. Staying with Carol is like staying with a friend, although guests have as much privacy as they wish. They have the use of the entire house, including the kitchen and the loft area with its TV, VCR, movie collection, and typewriter. Carol, now a columnist for the *Maui News,* is a former caterer and gourmet cook, so there's no telling what she may be inspired to serve for breakfast. Since she's single, she often takes people snorkeling or hiking, or sometimes asks them to join her for a pasta dinner.

✪ Kula Cottage

206 Puakea Place, Kula, Maui, HI 96790. ☎ **808/871-6230.** Fax 808/871-9187. 1 cottage. TV TEL. $85. Minimum stay 2 nights. No credit cards. Free parking.

Three thousand feet up on the slopes of Haleakala, in a lush, half-acre mountain setting, is this exquisite little hideaway. Cecilia and Larry Gilbert, whose own lovely home is just up the hill from the cottage, have equipped it with just about everything one needs, from a wood-burning fireplace to a full kitchen, laundry, private driveway, gas barbecue, furniture out on the lanai, and much more. A black-and-white shoji screen leads to the bedroom, also tastefully done in black and white, with a queen-size bed; an additional futon is also available. Cecilia delivers fresh flowers and freshly baked bread every morning and is helpful with hints and tips on enjoying the best of Maui.

Kula View Bed & Breakfast

140 Holopuni Rd. (P.O. Box 322), Kula, Maui, HI 96790. ☎ **808/878-6736.** 1 suite. TV TEL. $85 single or double. (Rates include breakfast.) No credit cards. Two-night minimum stay. Free parking.

Susan Kauai, who comes from an old-time kamaaina family and knows Maui better than most, is in charge here. Her luxuriously furnished suite is located on the upper level of her home; it has a private entrance and its own deck. There's a queen-size bed, a reading area, a wicker breakfast nook, a mini-refrigerator, and a private shower. Telephone and TV are available on request. Susan is a gracious host who helps guests plan their holidays, fills their room with fresh flowers from her garden, and serves breakfast in their room—Kona coffee or tea, lush island fruits, and home-baked breads and muffins. She has blankets and warm clothing on hand for those sunrise trips to Haleakala, whose summit is not far away.

Nohona Laule'a

763-2 Kamehameiki Rd., Kula, Maui, HI 96790. ☎ **808/878-6646.** 1 cottage. TV TEL. $75 for one or two; $85 for three; $95 for four. Minimum stay of three nights preferred. No credit cards. Free parking.

It's no wonder Sue and Brian Kanegai named their wonderful cottage "Nohona Laule'a"—it's Hawaiian for "Peaceful Dwelling;" and that's a perfect description of their comfy two-bedroom place. Situated on 4 acres of land extensively planted with bananas, proteas, citrus, lychee, avocado, and flowers, the cottage is about 150 yards away from their own home, at an elevation of 2,500 feet on Mt. Haleakala. The 700 square-foot cottage is private and quiet, complete with all the comforts of home—a fully equipped kitchen, VCR, washer-dryer, well-stocked bookshelves, even a furnished deck and barbecue. The place is beautifully furnished in a tropical motif. One of the two bedrooms has twin beds, the other a double bed. The views are magnificent—the West Maui Mountains, Central Valley, and Haleakala out back. Windsurfers can even check out the north shore conditions right from the living room. The Kanegais are gracious hosts, happy to help with suggestions for things to do. Sue is an excellent baker; cottage guests always find a loaf of her delicious mango or banana bread waiting for them.

Rusty and Frank Kunz

513 Lower Kimo Dr., Kula, Maui, HI 96790. ☎ **808/263-4546.** 1 apt, 1 house. TV. $65 two-bedroom apt; $95 owner's home for up to four people. Each additional person $10 extra. Minimum stay 3 nights. No credit cards. Free parking.

This lovely home is at an elevation of 3,000 feet, set on 3 acres of lawns and pastures, 20 miles from the summit of Haleakala. The views are of the West Maui mountains and Kihei Beach, way below in the distance. Rusty and Frank divide their time between this home and one on Oahu. On Maui, they always have a two-bedroom vacation apartment available for rent—it's an excellent bargain with its own private entrance, a deck, a kitchenette (refrigerator, toaster-oven, hot plate, sink), and a private bath.

From November to June, when they're not on Maui, the Kunzes will, on occasion, rent their own quarters: living room, master bedroom, full kitchen, and private bath. It's big enough for either one or two couples.

Silver Cloud Upcountry Ranch

Old Thompson Rd., R.R. 2, Box 201, Kula, Maui, HI 96790. ☎ **806/878-6101.** 8 rms and studios, 3 suites, 1 cottage. $75–$95 rooms and studios for two; $125 suite; $135 cottage. (Rates include breakfast.) No credit cards.

Bordered by a fragrant eucalyptus forest at an elevation of 2,800 feet in the historic Ulupalakua area, Silver Cloud Ranch is a 9-acre plantation (once part of Thompson Ranch, a working cattle ranch founded in 1902), born again as a bed & breakfast establishment with a turn-of-the-century charm and elegance. Each beautifully furnished accommodation has its own private bathroom; most have private lanais and entrances; and the Paniolo Bunkhouse's roomy studios all offer kitchenettes and lanais with views of either the Pacific or Haleakala Crater. The Haleakala Suite in the Paniolo Bunkhouse has both these views, its own bedroom and living room with fireplace, and a complete kitchen. For total privacy, there's the Lanai Cottage, with a complete kitchen, spacious bathroom with a clawfooted red bathtub, a main room with a wood-burning stove, and a private lanai surrounded by flower gardens. All guests have use of the main house and kitchen. Lovely. The entire property can be rented for groups and seminars.

OFF HANA ROAD

✪ Bamboo Mountain Sanctuary

1111 Kaupakalua Rd., Haiku, Maui, HI 96708. ☎ **808/572-5106.** 5 rms (3 with bath); 1 apt. $55 single; $75 double; seventh day free. Extra adult in apt. $20. (Rates include breakfast.) No credit cards. Free parking.

Once it was the old Maui Zendo, a Japanese monastery; now this mountainside plantation house is a bed & breakfast, but it still has an air of a retreat. It's on the same grounds as Mana Le'a Gardens, one of the islands' primary New Age conference centers. If you're attending a workshop at Mana Le'a Gardens, you may want to stay here for a few days before or after. Or just come to the place itself, enjoy the peace and quiet, the wonderful grounds, with hiking trails, a natural swimming hole in the gulch, and waterfalls. Built over 50 years ago, with huge octagonal windows that overlook the ocean, the house has five bedrooms, each with a queen-size or double futon on a frame, and Japanese artwork. Some have private baths; all share the shower. The large studio apartment with its own kitchen can comfortably sleep three adults or, with the aid of futons, a family with several children. There's a hot tub, a very large communal area, and a deck where breakfast—including their own papayas and bananas—is served.

Haikuleana

555 Haiku Rd., Haiku, Maui, HI 96708-9607. ☎ **808/575-2890.** 4 rms. $65–$70 single; $80–$90 double. Discounts on stays of 5 days or more. (Rates include breakfast.) No credit cards. Free parking.

This charming old house is set amid 1¹/₂ acres of garden filled with fruit trees and flowers. Built around 1870, it has been refurbished and tastefully decorated in country style with antiques, tropical period pieces, and comforters on the beds. The house still has its original 12-foot, open-beam ceilings. Owner Dr. Frederick Fox, Jr., has four nicely decorated guest rooms, three with queen-size beds, one with twin beds, each with its own private bath. Television is available. A full breakfast is served, with Hawaiian seasonal fruits and freshly baked breads. Not suitable for children under 6 or pets; smoking is not allowed indoors. Haikuleana is 15 minutes from the airport and shopping centers, centrally located en route to Hana and Haleakala, and just 2 miles from Hookipa Beach, famous for windsurfing, as well as close to secluded coves for snorkeling and scuba diving.

Halfway to Hana House

100 Waipio Rd. (P.O. Box 675). Haiku, Maui, HI 96708. ☎ **808/572-1176.** Fax 808/572-3609. 1 studio. $55 single; $65 double. Minimum stay 2 nights. (Rates include breakfast.) No credit cards. Free parking.

A 20-minute drive from Paia town on the Hana road, Gail Pickholz's cozy private studio is spectacularly located; with a 180° wraparound ocean view. The studio has a double bed, a mini-kitchen, a private bath and entrance, and a breakfast patio with ocean views. There are bamboo groves, palm trees, citrus and papaya orchids, a pineapple field, tropical flowers, herb gardens, and a lily pond. Freshwater pools and waterfalls are a half-mile away. Gail, who has lived on Maui for 26 years, delights in graceful touches, like chocolate-covered macadamia nuts on your pillow. She's helpful with restaurant and adventure tips, and may even invite you to go snorkeling with her on a Sunday morning.

Huelo Point Flower Farm Bed & Breakfast

P.O. Box 1195, Paia, Maui, HI 96779. ☎ **808/572-1850.** 1 cottage. $95 single; $105 double. No credit cards. Free parking.

This is surely one of the most spectacular—and romantic—B&Bs in Hawaii, a great favorite with honeymooners. The glass-walled gazebo sits atop a 300-foot cliff overlooking Waipio Bay; from the patio where you have breakfast, you can often watch whales and dolphins at play. Close by are waterfalls and natural pools for swimming; right on the property is a dramatic natural swimming pool with a waterfall, plus an oceanfront hot tub. The gazebo has a queen-size koa-wood captain's bed, two wicker chairs, a dining table and chairs, a CD player, and a private half-bath with a sheltered outside shower; there's also a hot plate, small refrigerator, microwave, toaster oven, and basic dishes. Guy and Doug, the hosts, live in a spectacular executive house on the property (also available for rental by the week at $2,000) and grow tropical flowers and organic fruits and vegetables on their 2-acre retreat (guests are welcome to pick whatever they like). (In case you happened to see NBC's Hawaii feature on *The Other Side* last year, Guy and Doug were the two who received inner guidance in finding their dream home.) Although this is an isolated jungle valley, you can drive to restaurants and shops in Paia or Makawao in 20 minutes.

Maluhia Hale

P.O. Box 687, Haiku, Maui, HI 96798. ☎ **808/572-2959.** 1 cottage. $60 single; $70 double; $80 triple. No credit cards. Free parking.

The peaceful home of Diana Garrett and Robert Luyken sits on the crest of a sloping meadow looking up at the peaks of Haleakala and down to a sweeping view of the ocean; from it, one can walk to freshwater pools and waterfalls, or drive to Hookipa Beach and Paia town in 15 to 20 minutes. Diana and Robert have built a cottage on their grounds, which are planted with flowers, tropical plants, banana and papaya trees. The cottage, which has ocean views on all sides, has a king-size bed in the main room and a double bed on the glassed-in lanai, which is adjacent to the screened lanai. The place is done in creams and whites, with many antiques giving it a Hawaiian feeling. There's a kitchenette, and a separate bathroom with a shower and clawfoot tub; hung with lovely plants and with an ocean view, it feels like a garden room. The cottage can comfortably accommodate two or three. Diana provides coffee, tea, fruit, and muffins to start guests off.

Pilialoha

2512 Kaupakalua Rd., Haiku, Maui, HI 96708. ☎ **808/572-1440.** Fax 808/572-4612. 1 cottage. TV TEL. $95 for two. Each additional person $10 extra. Minimum stay 2 nights. Weekly rates available. (Rates include breakfast.) No credit cards. Free parking.

A dollhouse of a B&B cottage sits in these cool upcountry lands, next door to the home of Bill and Machiko Heyde, a young couple who aim to treat their guests as friends (*pilialoha* means "friendship"). Lovingly decorated and with a little garden out front, it's a cozy retreat, ideal for two, but able to sleep up to five, what with its queen-size bed in the bedroom, a twin bed in an adjoining room, a queen-size sofa bed in the living room, and futons in the closet. There's a full kitchen, and Machiko puts out teas and coffees, fresh tropical fruits, home-baked pastries, breads, and muffins every morning. There's a VCR, washer-dryer, ironing board and iron, plus beach chairs, mats, snorkeling equipment to borrow—everything you need for easy vacation living.

Tea House Cottage Bed & Breakfast

P.O. Box 335, Haiku, Maui, HI 96708. ☎ **808-572-5610.** 1 cottage. $65 single; $75 double. (Rates include breakfast the first morning.) No credit cards. Free parking.

The cottage sits in the midst of a tropical garden filled with flowering plants, bananas, and palm trees. You park your car and follow a tree-lined path to the front door. The picturesque screened lanai leads to a charming living room and bedroom filled with antiques and Oriental rugs; there's a small kitchen area, adequate for light cooking, in the living room. A deck leads to a private bathhouse. No electrical poles mar the landscape; an alternative energy system provides the utilities and phone. You can take long scenic walks by day, stroll along moonlit paths by night, and listen to the sounds of the surf pounding the cliffs. Does this sound like the ultimate retreat from civilization? It is, and it's located in Haiku, a mile off Hana Highway (18 miles east of Kahului), going toward the ocean. Ann DeWeese, an artist whose studio is on the premises, is the proprietor, and she makes the cottage available to guests who can appreciate the simple life. She provides fresh fruits, home-baked breads, and very good coffee and teas for breakfast the first morning. Smoking is permitted outdoors only.

Waipio Bay Lookout Lodging

P.O. Box 1095, Haiku, Maui, HI 96708. ☎ **808/572-4530.** 2 rms. $85 double. (Rates include continental breakfast.) No credit cards. Free parking.

The location's the thing at Waipio Bay Lookout. It's hard to believe that this secluded, 2-acre estate is just 30 minutes from Kahului Airport on the way to Hana. The setting—at the end of the road in Huelo—is truly spectacular. Set high on a 300-foot cliff on Maui's ruggedly magnificent north shore, the house often affords views of spinner dolphins "performing" right in Waipio Bay. The rooms in the main residence are on either end of the very large house, ensuring maximum privacy. The rooms are pleasantly furnished with white wicker, have private entries and lanais, oversize glass doors, private baths, big closets, microwaves, toaster ovens, coffee makers, and small refrigerators. The landscaping is densely tropical. There's a wonderful swimming pool and Jacuzzi on a patio leading to the cliff's edge. Nonsmokers only.

MAKAWAO & OLINDA

Makawao is Maui's cowboy town, fast turning into a mecca for city dwellers in search of the rural life. Beyond it, Olinda is even more peaceful, a true end-of-the-road retreat.

✪ McKay Country Cottage

536 Olinda Rd., Makawao, Maui, HI 96768. ☎ **808/572-1453.** Fax 808/572-1453. 1 cottage. TV TEL. $95 cottage for two. Each additional person $15 extra. Minimum stay 2 days. (Rates include breakfast.) No credit cards. Free parking.

Up the hill from Makawao, on two country roads that wind through a forest of 150-foot-tall blue-gum eucalyptus trees, lies Olinda; and it's here, at the top of Olinda Road, at a 4,000-foot elevation, that lucky travelers will find one of the nicest B&Bs on Maui. The cottage sits amid a 12-acre protea farm, a short distance from the home of Shaun and Stewart McKay. Shaun, a member of the noted Baldwin family (among Maui's missionary founders) and Stewart, a painter and decorator from Scotland, are very special hosts, indeed. They've furnished the cottage handsomely with original art by Maui artists, protea from their garden, lace curtains, a king-size bed in the bedroom, a queen-size pullout sofa in the living room (the beds sleep four adults, and futons are available for the kids), a full kitchen, and a working fireplace with enough wood for cool mountain nights. What fun to sit on the cushioned window seats, or out on the deck, and gaze at central Maui and Hookipa Beach far below! First-day breakfast supplies are left in the refrigerator for you.

HANA

Since Hana is one of the more remote areas on all Maui (in all Hawaii, in fact), you might well want to spend a few days here, far away from civilization. Happily, the number of reasonably priced accommodations is growing.

RENTAL AGENCIES

Manager Stan Collins of **Hana AAA Bay Vacation Rentals,** P.O. Box 318, Hana, Maui, HI 96713 (☎ 808/248-7727 or 800/959-7727), rents a dozen properties scattered throughout the Hana area, with a wide variety of locations, including on the beach, in and out of town, plus some in very secluded and private places. He offers apartments, cabins, and homes, with either one, two, or three bedrooms, with ocean and mountain views. All are fully equipped with the essentials for comfortable vacation living. They can accommodate as few as 1, as many as 15 in a group, at prices ranging from $65 to $200 per night for two people, plus $10 to $25 for each additional person. Each cabin and home is private, and all have full kitchens, telephones, and cable TVs.

Sina Fournier is the rental agent for **Hana Alii Holidays,** P.O. Box 536, Hana, Maui, HI 96713 (☎ 808/248-7742 or 800/548-0478), and she has a number of options for Hana vacationers, starting at $75 a night for a studio with private bath, to oceanfront and other cottages ranging in price from $90 a night all the way up to $400 for a hillside estate on eight acres. Accommodations also include condominium apartments at the Hana Kai-Maui Resort (see below), which begin at $75 per night. Contact Sina or her son, Duke Walls, and they will try to find the right setup for you. Many accommodations are within walking distance of the beach: Some of the houses are directly on Hana Bay.

DOUBLES FOR ABOUT $60

Aloha Cottages

73 Keawa Place (P.O. Box 205), Hana, Maui, HI 96713. ☎ **808/248-8420.** 5 cottages. $60–$85 cottage for two. Each additional person $10–$20 extra. No credit cards. Free parking.

Located conveniently close to Hana Bay and the stores are these pleasant redwood cottages managed by Mrs. F. Nakamura. Each cottage has either two or three bedrooms (queen-size or twin beds), a living room, complete kitchen, and one or two bathrooms. And each has a view of Hana Bay or Kauiki Head. These older, plain cottages are clean, well ventilated, and comfortably furnished. All necessities are provided, including daily cleaning service. Three cottages have TVs.

DOUBLES FROM ABOUT $80

Ekena

P.O. Box 728, Hana, Maui, HI 96713. ☎ **808/248-7047.** 2 self-contained units: downstairs rents as either a one- or two-bedroom/two-bath unit; upstairs rents as a two-bedroom/two and a half-bath unit. Downstairs: $120 for two, $130 for three, one bedroom. $165 for up to four, $15 extra per person to a maximum of six, two bedrooms. Upstairs: $275 for up to four, $300 for five or six for two bedrooms. Both units: $400 for four bedrooms, four and one half baths, maximum of 10 people. Minimum stay three days (Dec 21–Dec 31, five days). No children under 14. No credit cards. Free parking.

If you're traveling as a couple or group and looking for total relaxation, Ekena could be the place for you. This spacious, expansive home (more than 5,000 square feet) is beautifully decorated and completely furnished and equipped right down to VCR, washer and dryer, place settings for 10, beach mats, and coolers. The bedrooms are huge, and so are the closets. The house and the grounds, with lots of fruit trees and tropical flowers, are impeccably maintained. It sits on nine acres, high on a hill, and it offers a 360° view of the ocean, coastline, and the verdant Hana district from wraparound decks. Little extras make Ekena a special place: lots of fresh flowers, a chilled bottle of champagne for honeymooners. Hostess Robin Gaffney was born and raised in Hawaii and has lived in Hana for many years; she is as knowledgeable as she is helpful.

Hana Kai-Maui Resort Condominiums

1533 Uakea Rd. (P.O. Box 38), Hana, Maui, HI 96713. ☎ **808/248-8426** or toll free 800/346-2772. Fax 808/248-7482. 12 apts. $125 studio for two; $125–$145 one-bedroom apt for two (third and fourth persons $10 each). 20% off on stay of 5 or more nights. Children under 8 stay free with parents; senior citizen discount 10%. AE, MC, V. Free parking.

For first-class studio and one-bedroom apartments where you can prepare your own meals (almost a necessity in Hana, where there are very few eating places), this resort, right on Hana Bay, is a fine choice. The two low-rise condo units are located by the ocean on lush, tropical grounds. Studios include a full bath, dressing vanity, well-equipped kitchen, and a spacious private lanai with ocean views. Pluses include a large patio area a few steps from the beach, gas barbecues, Ping-Pong, daily maid service. The beach is better for surfers than swimmers, but good swimming beaches are within an easy drive. From December to May, you can watch humpback whales from your private lanai.

Hamoa Bay Bungalow

P.O. Box 773, Hana, Maui, HI 96713. ☎ **808/248-7884.** Fax 808/248-8642. 1 cottage. TV TEL. $125–$150. Two-night minimum stay. Weekly and monthly rates available. No credit cards. Free parking.

With its quaint Balinese architecture and art, this could be a bungalow in Bali; instead, it's right here in Hana. Inspired by her travels in Bali, lifelong Maui resident Jody Baldwin has created an extraordinary retreat, an elegant nest for honeymooners or other romantically inclined souls. Set amidst four acres of jungle on a small hill overlooking Hamoa Bay, the cottage is quiet and secluded, yet close to waterfalls, beaches, archaeological sites, mountain pools, and private mountain jogging trails. The 600-square-foot cottage has a giant bed draped with mosquito netting, VCR, a full kitchen, a private bath with Jacuzzi for two, and a large screened lanai with an ocean view. The kitchen is stocked with fresh coffee beans and a grinder, teas, and cereals. Every morning, baked goods and fruits fresh from the jungle-garden—pineapple, papayas, oranges, bananas, and more—are left at the door. Jody, who lives in the main house nearby, is available for inside tips and information, and can arrange personal sketching and photo tours, massage sessions, horseback riding, picnic lunches, and trips to heiaus and waterfalls. Picture-postcard Hamoa Beach, ideal for swimming, is about a 10-minute walk away. No smoking.

✪ Original Hana Plantation Houses

P.O. Box 240, Hana, Maui, HI 96713. ☎ **808/248-7049,** or 808/248-7365, or toll free 800/228-HANA. Fax 808/248-8240. 11 studios and houses. From $80 for a small studio to $160 for a two-bedroom/two-bath black-sand beach house. AE, CB, DC, MC. V. Free parking.

Blair Shurtleff and Tom Nunn aim to provide their guests with "a vacation that will leave you feeling rejuvenated and thoroughly relaxed." We're sure they succeed, for just contemplating the lovely custom homes they've created for visitors is relaxing in itself. The main compound, on five superbly landscaped acres abloom with ginger, heliconia, banana, and papaya (which guests are welcome to pick), includes a Japanese-style studio for two at $80, and a Japanese/Balinese-style two-bedroom cottage for four at $110.

A few miles away, near Hana Bay and picturesque beaches, is a two-story plantation house with two accommodations (upstairs, for four people, $140; downstairs, for two people, $100), and a superb solar-powered beach house for four, for $160 (with annex for two, $195). Amenities are plentiful. There are Jacuzzis indoors and out. Each house has its own kitchen and even its own coffee grinder. Hosts Blair and Tom are always on hand to advise guests on activities and to help them meet the people of Hana. They can set you up with anything from a hot tub spa to air tours to professional massage therapy. A 3-minute walk from the main compound is a secluded, natural spring- and ocean-fed pool, surrounded by lush, tropical plants. The ocean is a few steps away, and beautiful Hamoa Beach is less than a mile away. Waterfalls and jungle trails abound.

3 Camping & Wilderness Cabins

By Jeanette Foster

Camping is a year-round experience on Maui due to the balmy weather. However, there is a wet (winter) and dry (summer) season, and visitors should be prepared for rain year round. Campers also should be ready for insects (a good repellent for mosquitoes), water purification (boiling, filtration or iodine tablets), and sun protection (sun screen, hat, and long-sleeve shirt). A note on personal safety: Don't hike or swim alone and never turn your back on the ocean; the waves might be closer and more powerful than you think.

Plan to bring your own camping equipment, or rent it on another island, as there are no rentals available on Maui. If you would like to purchase equipment, you can do so at **Gaspro,** 365 Hanakai, Kahului (☎ 808/877-0056). **Maui Expedition,** Kihei Commercial Center, (☎ 808/878-7470), or **Maui Sporting Goods,** 92 N. Market, Wailuku (☎ 808/244-0011).

For information on trails, sites, and permits, contact **Hawaii State Department of Land and Natural Resources,** State Parks Division, P.O. Box 1049, Wailuku, HI 96793 (☎ 808/243-5354). The **Hawaiian Trail and Mountain Club,** P.O. Box 2238, Honolulu, HI 96804, offers an information packet on hiking and camping in Hawaii. Send $1.25, plus a legal-sized, self-addressed, stamped envelope for information. Another good source of information is the *Hiking/ Camping Information Packet* from **Hawaii Geographic Maps and Books,** 49 S. Hotel Street, Suite 218, Honolulu, HI 96813 (☎ 808/538-3952), for $7, which includes postage.

You'll find the best camping on Maui at the following two parks:

HALEAKALA NATIONAL PARK

Haleakala, which translates as "House of the Sun," is one of the largest volcanic craters in the world—$7\frac{1}{2}$ miles long and $2\frac{1}{2}$ miles wide, 21 miles in circumference, with 36 miles of trails. There are three tent campgrounds available and three cabins. This is one of only two places in the world where you can find a silversword plant (the other place is on the Big Island of Hawaii). If you walk from the crater rim down the Kaupo Gap to the ocean in Kipahulu, more than 20 miles away, you'll pass through climate zones ranging from arctic to tropical. On a clear day, you can see every island except Kauai from Haleakala's summit.

Be prepared for a wide range of temperatures, from 77 down to 26 degrees (and lower with the wind chill factor). High winds at the top are frequent. Rain can vary from 20 inches a year on the west end of the crater to more than 200 inches on the eastern side.

The most comfortable way to stay here is in the cabins. They're warm, protected from the elements, and reasonably priced. Each cabin has bunks with mattresses (no bedding), table, chairs, utensils, and a wood-burning stove (firewood provided). The sliding scale rate starts at $19 a night for one person, $23 a night per person for two, and $9 per person per night for 3 to 12 people. The cabins are spaced throughout the crater so each one is an easy walk to the other: **Holua** cabin is on the Halemauu Trail, **Kapalaoa** cabin on Sliding Sands Trail, and **Paliku** cabin on the western end by the Kaupo Gap (see "Hiking" in Chapter 10).

The cabins are very, very popular—so popular that the National Parks Service has a lottery system for reservations. Requests for cabin reservations must be made three months in advance (be sure to request alternate dates). You can request all three cabins at once (you are limited to no more than two nights in one cabin and no more than three nights within the crater per month). For information contact: **Haleakala National Park,** P.O. Box 369, Makawao, HI 96768 (☎ 808/572-9306).

If you don't win the cabin lottery, all is not lost, as there are three tent camping sites: two inside the crater and one outside at Hosmer Grove. Actually, **Hosmer Grove** is the best camping area, inside or outside the crater. Located at 6,800 feet, it's a small but open grassy area surrounded by a forest of trees. The trees protect the campers from the high winds, but the nights are still cold. Facilities include a covered pavilion with picnic tables and grills, chemical toilets, and drinking water. Food and gas is a long way down the mountain. There are no permits needed at Hosmer Grove; staying there is free, and you do so three nights a month.

The two tent camping areas inside the crater are: **Holua,** just off sliding Sands Trail at 7,250 feet, and **Paliku,** just before the Kaupo Gap at the western end of the crater at 6,380 feet. Facilities at both camp grounds are limited to pit toilets and catchment water from the cabin roof. The water supply at Holua is limited, especially during the summer. No open fires are allowed inside the crater, so bring a stove if you want to cook. Tent camping is restricted to the rocky campsite or the horse stable near the cabin; it's not allowed on the more inviting grassy lawn in front of the cabin. Camping at these sites is free, but limited to two consecutive nights and no more than three nights a month inside the crater. Permits are issued at Park Headquarters on a first-come-first-served basis on day of use. Occupancy at each camping area is limited to 25 people. For more information, contact the Haleakala National Parks at the address and phone number above.

WAIANAPANAPA STATE PARK

Just outside of the rural town of Hana, tucked in the tropical jungle is Waianapanapa State Park, bordered by a black-sand beach and trimmed with tropical trees. This may be as close to Eden as you will ever get. Hiking (described in Chapter 10), beach activities (see Chapter 10) and just lazing are the main activities here. The rural town of Hana is just 4 miles away, and the beauty of the Seven Sacred Pools at Ohia Gulch is about a half-hour drive.

Waianapanapa has 12 cabins and a tent campground available. No question—go for the cabins. It rains a lot here and there is no covered pavilion, which means not only will you and your tent be in the puddled camping area, but cooking and eating in the inevitable rain without shelter is no fun. The cabins, on the other hand, come complete with kitchen, living room, bedroom, and bathroom (with hot shower!), and are furnished with bedding, linen, towels, dishes, and cooking and eating utensils. They're extremely popular and are reserved far in advance (especially for summers, holidays, and weekends). The fees for using the cabins are on a sliding-scale, ranging from $7 per person per night for two down to $5 per person per night for six. Contact the **State Parks Division,** P.O. Box 1049 Wailuku, HI 96793 (☎ 808/243-5354).

If you do opt to rough it and tent-camp here, it's free. Permits can be obtained at the above address and are limited to five nights in a 30-day period. Facilities include restrooms, outdoor showers, drinking water, and picnic tables.

4 Where to Eat

KAHULUI

Near the airport and around the big shopping centers across the way from the hotels—Kahului Shopping Center, Maui Mall, and Kaahumanu Shopping Center—are almost a dozen places that are fine for a modest meal.

⑤ Class Act

Maui Community College, 310 Kaahumanu Ave. ☎ 808/242-1210. Reservations recommended, and accepted up to 2 weeks in advance. 4-course lunch $9.50. No credit cards. Lunch only, Wed and Fri 11am–12:30pm. Closed Mid-May to mid-Sept. AMERICAN.

The benefits of higher education can definitely be enjoyed at Class Act. Students in the college's food-service program get a chance to practice their skills; you get a chance to have a four-course gourmet meal for under $10. What a deal! The decor is pleasant enough, and the food can be excellent. Each week, the cuisine of a different country or region is featured: you may be treated to "A Taste of New Orleans," "A Taste of France," "A Taste of Vietnam," or "A Taste of New England," to mention a few possibilities. Each menu includes a "heart-healthy" selection low in sodium and cholesterol. Yes, there's a catch—lunch is the only meal served, except at the end of each semester, when a $35 gourmet dinner is presented. On Wednesday, half of the students cook and the other half serve; on Friday, they switch. High marks for this one.

Marco's Grill & Deli

444 Hana Hwy., corner of Dairy Rd. ☎ 808/877-4446. Reservations not required. Main courses $10.95–$19.95, MC, V. Breakfast Mon–Fri 7am–10:45am, Sat–Sun 7am–1pm; lunch/dinner 10:45am–10pm. ITALIAN.

Whether you're shopping in Kahului, on your way to or from Hana, even going to or from the airport, Marco's is a convenient and tasty choice. Marco's became popular fast, especially with the local folks who work in town, which is always an endorsement of both food and service. Marco DeFanis, who owns and operates the restaurant with his wife, Debbie, learned to cook at the elbow of an Italian grandmother in his native Philadelphia. He is also an experienced butcher, so if you enjoy meat, you won't go wrong here.

The authentic Italian flavors of this place are present even at breakfast, in the form of specialties like the shrimp and eggplant omelet ($8.95). The salads are particularly excellent and many are available in half-orders (which are as large as full orders in many other places). The Italian antipasto is a favorite and a half-order is just $7.95. Other salads and cold sandwiches range in price from $6.95 to $9.95. Hot sandwiches (the meatball is delicious) are priced from $5.95 to $10.95. We like the hot and tangy deep-fried mozzarella marinara among the appetizers and the pasta penne in spicy tomato sauce with ricotta cheese among the pastas—there are many to choose from, with a variety of sauces.

Maui Bagel

201 Dairy Rd. ☎ 808/871-4825. Bagels 50¢; main courses $3–$5.50. No credit cards. Mon–Sat 6:30am–5:30pm. BAGELS/DELI/SANDWICHES.

Maui Bagel is an idea whose time has come. It's the only bagel bakery on Maui, and it's been doing a thriving business ever since it opened 7 years ago. Since Maui Bagel is near the airport and on your route to Hana or Haleakala, it's a good first—or last—stop on the island, as well as a good spot to get a picnic lunch for your sightseeing trips. It's a cute little place, with blue-and-white cafe curtains and a warm, friendly atmosphere. In addition to 11 varieties of bagels, warm from the oven, as well as delicious French, rye, and wheat bread baked daily, and challah on Friday, they also have yummy bakery items (brownies, macaroons, strudel, etc.), plus very good deli selections. There's also an excellent selection of salads, meats, and cheese. Call ahead for take-out.

Maui Beach Hotel

170 Kaahumanu Ave. ☎ **808/877-0051.** Reservations requested. Buffet lunch $9.75 for all you can eat. AE, DC, MC, V. Lunch only, daily 11am–2pm. ASIAN BUFFET.

If you like buffet meals as much as we do, then you should know about the Rainbow buffet lunch served in the pretty **Rainbow Dining Room** and on the pool terrace. Locals like it because it includes many Asian dishes not usually seen on buffet meals; we too are partial to the tsukemono (pickled-vegetable salad) and kamaboku (fish cakes). Also there for the taking—and still more taking—are those delicious Kula onions, Maui potato chips, lots of greens, rice, two hot main courses daily (fish, chicken, or beef, plus a noodle dish), soup, and cakes baked daily.

If you're in this area in the evening, visit the **Red Dragon Room,** which serves an all-you-can-eat Chinese buffet, 10 courses that include such favorites as shrimp Canton, ginger chicken, sweet and sour pork, priced very reasonably at $12.95. It is on Wednesday through Sunday, from 5:30 to 8pm. On Friday night only, from 5:30 to 8:30pm, the Rainbow Dining Room offers an all-you-can-eat prime rib, sautéed fish, and pasta buffet for $16.95. **The Maui Palms Hotel** next door (same management) serves the Imperial Teppanyaki Dinner Buffet every night from 5:30 to 8pm, for $16.95. This is our favorite of the three: it's an incredible assortment of such delights as sweet potato tempura, yakitori chicken, teriyaki steak, local fish, salads, and much more.

Maui Coffee Roasters

444 Hana Hwy. ☎ **808/877-2877.** Reservations not required. Fresh coffee menu 50¢–$3.90, bakery items $1–$1.95; breakfast $1.70–$7.25; sandwiches/salads $4.50–$7.95. AE, DISC, MC, V. Mon–Fri 7:30am to 6pm; Sat. 8am to 6pm. Sun 9am to 3pm. HEALTHFUL AMERICAN.

You may hear it referred to as "Bean's World" or "Nicky Beans," or even just "Nicky's." It's all the same charming, fun place, serving some of the best coffee drinks you've ever tasted (the coffee is roasted on the premises), along with fresh and delicious fare. "Nicky," by the way, is Nick Matichyn, the proprietor, who's been roasting and selling coffee around these parts for years. If you have the time and the inclination, this is a good place to stop, sit a spell, read the newspaper, and people-watch. There are lots of interesting regulars.

They're big on bagels here—the variety of stuffings include veggie, turkey, and, of course, lox ($1.75 to $7.25). There are turkey ($5.95), "Basmoto" (basil, mozzarella, tomato), and chicken salad ($4.50) sandwiches; Caesar ($5.95) and garden ($4.50) salads for lunch; as well as daily specials and soup of the day. Cake stands filled with goodies line the counter: scones, croissants, muffins, cookies, biscotti, cakes, and more. Three different coffees, five espressos, nine steamed espresso drinks, hot chocolate, iced specialty drinks, and all kinds of teas are served at the counter or at the funky, old tables—all with mismatched chairs that only add to the charm. Many of the beverages are served in whimsical, oversized vessels. We think the Caramel Cappuccino is incredible.

ⓢ Ming Yuen

In the Kahului Light Industrial Park, 162 Alamaha St. ☎ **808/871-7787.** Reservations recommended. Main courses $5.95–$10.25. DISC, MC, V. Lunch Mon–Sat 11am–5pm; dinner daily 5–9pm. CHINESE.

Attractive, moderately priced Chinese restaurants are hard to find on Maui, so praise be for Ming Yuen, recently chosen by readers of the *Maui News* as the best Chinese restaurant of the year. The food here just gets better all the time, and the service, by many longtime employees, provides a "family feeling." The specials here are authentic Cantonese and the spicier Szechuan cuisine. We always like to start off with crispy wonton and Chinese spring rolls. Vegetarians can have a field day here; there are at least 15 vegetarian specialties, including silken tofu with black bean sauce, mock sweet and sour pork with seitan, and minced mock squab with high fiber tofu. Desserts here are a little different; we like the Mandarin or chocolate mousse. Should you happen to be on Maui during Chinese New Year in February, don't miss their 10-course banquet, complete with firecrackers. Fabulous! Even if it's not New Year's, all you need is a party of eight people and you can enjoy a splendid banquet anytime, starting at about $13 a person.

MAUI MALL

Sir Wilfred's Espresso Caffè serves breakfasts and light lunches, soups, home-baked croissants, and a variety of hot and cold coffee drinks; it also boasts a full bar. Prices are low, and the quality of the food, atmosphere, and service is high. **Restaurant Matsu** serves fast and delicious Japanese-local-style food at very inexpensive prices. Sushi starts at $1.20, and there's a plate-lunch special each day for just $5. They're famous for their California rolls ($4.50). Right next door is **Siu's Chinese Kitchen.** Go through the cafeteria-style line for Chinese combination plates. Rice or noodles and one dish is just $4.10; two items are $4.49; three are $5.49. If your taste leans in a more Western direction, try **SW Barbecue** for local-style barbecue plate lunches, hamburgers, and sandwiches. And if you're a real adventurer, you'll want to try **Tasaka Guri Guri.** There's no way to adequately describe the frozen dessert; the best way we've come up with is as a cross between sherbet and tapioca. It comes in pineapple and strawberry, it's made fresh daily, and sells out every day. Henry Tasaka now operates this business, which was started by his great-grandfather more than 70 years ago.

KAAHUMANU SHOPPING CENTER

Kaahumanu's new Food Court offers a handful of fast-food outlets, including **Edo Japan, Esplendido Mexican Food, Mama Brava, Yummy Korean B-B-Q,** and our favorite, **Aloha Mixed Plate,** which serves local style plate lunches, manapua, and "real" shave ice; if you've not yet tried it, this is the place. And here's a special tip for lovers of sushi: Visit the bento (take-out) section at **Shirokiya's,** the Japanese department store at Kaahumanu Center. Order an assortment of sushi for about $4.50 to $6.75 and have yourself a picnic. The food is scrumptious (other Japanese dishes are also available), and the price is about half of what it would cost to have sushi in a restaurant.

Koho Grill and Bar

At Kaahumanu Shopping Center. ☎ **808/877-5588.** Reservations not required. Main courses $8.65–$14.95. AE, MC, V. Daily 8am–11pm. AMERICAN.

This one's a big local favorite, especially at lunch and before and after the movies. We like it anytime. It's attractively decorated in island style, with paintings by local artists on the walls. The menu is varied, the service excellent, the atmosphere friendly, and the prices certainly right. Burgers are great at lunchtime, and so are the sandwiches, the plate lunches ($4.95 to $5.65), and such offerings as fajitas, tacos, and a blackened chicken. Dinner offers pastas, stir-fries, and steak and seafood dishes. Most main courses are served with salad or soup and a side dish. Come before 11am and treat yourself to one of their omelets. Happy hour, 3 to 6pm, is very popular.

WAILUKU

If you'd like to sample "local" food, there's no better place than Wailuku, which is a bit off the tourist track (it's the commercial and professional center of the island and the seat of Maui County). Prices are geared for the locals, which means that they're refreshingly low. Visit **Takamiya Market** on North Market Street. This old-time grocery store has a huge selection of terrific prepared foods to go, like sushi or smoked salmon belly or mahi tempura or whatever, all at small prices. While you're there, throw in a piece or two of their equally outrageous "lemon booze cake" or "pistachio booze cake" for very good measure.

MEALS FOR LESS THAN $12

Chums

1900 Main St. ☎ **808/244-1000.** Reservations not accepted. Main courses $4.50–$6.99. MC, V. Breakfast Mon–Sat 6:30–10:30am, Sun 7–10am; lunch and dinner Mon–Sat 11am–10:30pm. LOCAL.

Local-style food served in hearty portions at old-fashioned prices, and in gracious surroundings—that's the combination that made Chums a favorite right from the start. The pretty dining room, with its koa-wood booths, is a great place for "chums" to hang out. And the food is delicious, from the homemade oxtail soup with grated ginger, two scoops of rice and Chinese parsley, practically a meal in itself; to the burgers and sandwiches; to the island-style plate—mahimahi, hamburger steak, roast pork, and the like—all served with vegetables and macaroni salad plus a choice of rice or potatoes. Breakfast favorites include more island favorites, like fried rice with an egg or Loco Moco—that's a hamburger patty, an egg, rice, and gravy, at $3.50.

Maui Bake Shop & Deli

2092 Vineyard St. ☎ **808/242-0064.** Reservations not accepted. Sandwiches and light lunches $1.75–$5.25. No credit cards. Mon–Fri 6am–6:30pm, Sat 7am–5pm, Sun 7am–1am. BAKERY/DELI/SANDWICHES.

This is a sophisticated little spot just fine for a lunch or a break while shopping the Wailuku antique stores. It's nice just for coffee and some of their yummy pastries, but if you want more, try their salads, stuffed chicken, or one of the three soups made fresh every day. There's always a dish for vegetarians. A soup and sandwich lunch is a good deal at $5.50. As for sandwiches, choose turkey, pastrami, ham, or, our favorite, lox and bagel ($4.95).

✪ Maui Boy Restaurant

2102 Vineyard St. ☎ **808/244-7243.** Reservations not required. Main courses $3.75–$8.95. MC, V. Breakfast daily 7–11am; lunch and dinner daily. LOCAL.

Ramshackle outside but coffeehouse cute inside, Maui Boy is a find. At lunchtime it's mobbed with local professionals and with county office workers. Breakfast is popular too, and filling: three-egg omelets ($3.50 to $5.25) come with a choice of rice or hash browns, plus two dollar-size hotcakes. And we love their French toast, made from Portuguese sweet bread with strawberry or blueberry filling, $3.50. A savvy local friend considers Maui Boy to have the best teriyaki on Maui; we tried their teri ono, potatoes, and macaroni salad, all for $6.95—delicious! They also have the best Hawaiian plate in town: poi, laulau, lomi-lomi salmon, and kalua pig, all for $7.95 (get it early; they always sell out!). Plate lunches all come with rice or whipped potatoes, vegetables, *and* potato macaroni salad, guaranteeing your carbohydrate fix for the day.

Pupule Pub & Cafe

318 N. Market St. ☎ **808/42-8449.** Reservations not accepted. $2.95–$5.95. No credit cards. Breakfast Mon–Sat 8–11am; lunch Mon–Fri 11am–2:30pm; dinner Mon–Sat 5–10pm. AMERICAN.

Mark and Janna Folger, who manage Banana Bungalow Too (see "Where to Stay," above), have opened a neat little breakfast, lunch, and dinner place just across the street from their hostel. We think they describe it best right on the menu: "A Funky Little Hard-To-Describe Place that's Part Nouveau-Vegetarian-Cuisine and Part Truck Stop Diner! Come in and try us for yourself!" Homemade soft palm-tree pretzels are just 75¢, and you get two of them with feta and walnut pâté with veggies for $2.95. Sandwiches—from a veggie melt for $4.50 to a barbecue beef or chicken at $5.95—are served on whole wheat bread with tossed salad or cole slaw. Three varieties of "Super Spuds" are just $3.95; combined with the tossed salad or cole slaw that accompanies them, they make a fine meal. House specialties range from spinach and brown rice casserole ($4.95) to Hoisin marinated baked chicken with rice pilaf ($5.95); all are served with tossed salad or cole slaw and a roll.

ⓢ Saeng's Thai Cuisine

2119 Vineyard St. ☎ **808/244-1568.** Reservations not required. Main courses $7.50–$9.95. AE, MC, V. Lunch Mon–Sat 11am–2:30pm; dinner daily 5–9:30pm. THAI.

This gardenlike restaurant, with tiled floors and lush greenery, is a very popular local spot. Aromatic Hawaiian herbs are used to advantage in the cooking here. Specialties of the house include kai yang (grilled Cornish hen, marinated with lemongrass and kaffir lime leaves), shrimp asparagus, and cashew-nut chicken delight, each $7.25. Vegetarians are well taken care of, with a choice of 16 dishes, including a fairly mild garlic mixed vegetables and a sweet-basil tofu (*Warning:* This dish can be very hot). A typical Thai tapioca pudding as well as an untypical coffee or macadamia-nut mud pie tops off a refreshing meal.

ⓢ Sam Sato's

The Mill Yard, 1750 Wili Pa Loop. ☎ **808/244-7124.** Reservations not accepted. Plate lunches $4.90–$5.75. No credit cards. Mon–Sat 7am–2pm. LOCAL.

Now ensconced in a brand-new building with a dining room seating 50, this old favorite is still a down-home Wailuku restaurant. It's always filled with local families and office workers happily gobbling up chow tun, wonton soup, plate lunches, or sandwiches. Try their wonton special—it's hearty, delicious, and a complete meal at $4.30. This is the place where you should sample those filled pastries called manju, as Sam Sato's is reputed to have the best on Maui.

Siam Thai

123 N. Market St. ☎ **808/244-3817.** Reservations not required. Main courses $5.95–$14.95. AE, MC, V. Lunch Mon–Fri 11am–2:30pm; dinner daily 5–9:30pm. THAI.

A big favorite among the residents of East Maui, this restaurant serves inexpensive, delicious Thai food. It's a pretty place too, typically Asian in decor, with a reclining Buddha near a small aquarium. You won't go wrong with the Evil Prince dishes (take your choice of beef, chicken, pork, or vegetables); the meat is sautéed in hot spices with fresh sweet basil and served on a bed of chopped cabbage. Even those who hate eggplant are converted by the eggplant tofu dish; it's sautéed with fresh basil and hot sauce, and available either hot, medium, or mild. Then there's Tofu Delight—tofu and other vegetables sautéed in a special sauce and served over steamed bean sprouts. Thai ginger shrimp sautéed with string beans and ginger, served on cabbage, is another winner.

Tokyo Tei

1063 E. Lower Main St. ☎ **808/242-9630.** Reservations recommended. Main courses $5.50–$12. MC, V. Lunch Mon–Sat 11am–1:30pm; dinner Mon–Sat 5–8:30pm, Sun 5–8pm. JAPANESE.

A local favorite: The atmosphere is simple and pleasant, the quality of the food high, and the prices easy to take. Lunch and dinner include rice, miso soup, and pickled vegetables along with such main courses as teriyaki pork, beef sukiyaki, and sashimi. You'll know why the restaurant is famous for its tempura dishes once you bite into the shrimp tempura. And their teishoku combination plates, $8.75 to $9.75, are very popular. This is a nice place for families, as children are treated graciously here.

MEALS FOR LESS THAN $20

✪ A Saigon Cafe

1792 Main St. ☎ **808/243-9560.** Reservations recommended for dinner. Main courses $6.25–$16.95. DISC, MC, V. 10am–9pm daily; karaoke Mon–Sat 9pm–1am. VIETNAMESE.

Jennifer Nguyen is one hard-working, smart business lady who serves up some of the best Vietnamese food we've ever tasted. Local residents are all raving about this place. The interior is light and bright, with booth seating and Vietnamese artifacts on the walls. Because the restaurant is housed in the old Naokee's Steak House, which had been destroyed by fire and was beautifully rebuilt, there's a small menu section called "Maui's famous Naokee's Steaks."

The rest of the very extensive menu is authentic Vietnamese—fresh, flavorful, and extremely well prepared. Should you be unfamiliar with the subtleties of this cuisine, the menu explanations will be of help. Banh Hoi are specialties of the house and they're great. Items like grilled pork meat balls, boneless chicken breast with garlic, and shrimp pops are garnished with freshly picked island basil, mint leaves, cucumber, romaine lettuce, bean sprouts, vermicelli cake noodle, pickled carrots, and daikon: You simply wrap up all the ingredients in rice paper and dip in the sweet-and-sour garlic sauce. Voila! Vietnamese burritos! The Pho (Vietnamese beef noodle soups with different toppings) are also famous ($6.25). And the choices go on and on. This is a place you'll want to visit more than once if time permits.

IN & AROUND PAIA

Paia is one of our favorite little towns—full of seekers from everywhere who've found the natural lifestyle they were looking for in these Hawaiian uplands. Since the area is only a 15 minute drive from Kahului, at the beginning of the road to Hana and just past the cutoff to Hi. 37 (the Haleakala Highway), a visit to the restaurants here can be worked into almost any itinerary.

Bangkok Cuisine

120 Hana Hwy. ☎ **808/579-8979.** Reservations recommended. Main courses $5.95–$13.95. AE, DISC, MC, V. Lunch daily 11am–2:30pm; dinner daily 5–9:30pm. THAI.

Mike Kachornsrichol, the former owner of Siam Thai in Wailuku, has brought his authentic and delicious Thai recipes to a great little indoor/outdoor spot in Paia. The food is fresh with clean, distinctive Thai flavors. You'll definitely want to try the Mee Krob (crispy Thai noodles), the Pad Thai (rice noodles stir-fried with chicken, bean sprouts, and tofu), the Evil Prince (beef, pork, or chicken sautéed in hot spices with fresh sweet basil, served on a bed of chopped cabbage), and our personal favorite, Award Winning Bangkok Cuisine Fried Chicken (Cornish game hen deep-fried with a special sauce of garlic and black pepper). Yum! Most dishes can be prepared mild, medium, or hot.

VEGETARIAN

⊙ The Vegan Restaurant

115 Baldwin Ave. ☎ **808/579-9144.** Reservations not accepted. Main courses $5.95–$8.95. MC, V. Lunch and dinner Tues–Sun 11am–8:30pm. GOURMET VEGETARIAN.

This little place never advertises—its popularity keeps growing by word of mouth. It's heaven for vegetarians since the cooks turn out some delicious dishes, like vegan burgers, organic carrot salads, avocado delights, and organic hummus. There's a fresh selection daily of $8.95 main courses that might include a Thai vegetarian special like pad Thai noodle or Thai curry vegetables, as well as lemon-broiled tempeh, vegetable kugel, enchilada pie, or seitan peppersteak. We like their desserts, too, especially the vanilla cake with cashew frosting and fruit topping and the strawberry shortcake.

The Wunderbar

89 Hana Hwy. ☎ **808/579-8808.** Reservations recommended. Main courses $12–$25. AE, MC, V. Breakfast daily 7:30–11:30am; lunch daily 11:30am–2:30pm; pupus and salads daily 2:30–5pm; dinner daily 5–10pm (bar open till 1am). EUROPEAN.

There's a lively feeling about the Wunderbar Restaurant and Bar. The place has a handsome, huge wooden bar, tables made of monkeypod, and a little garden patio out back. The chef, who has cooked in seven different European countries, brings an island flair to his food: Andalusian paella, fresh fish, and lots of specials nightly, plus pastas and vegetarian specialties. The Ono Avocado Salad ($10.50) is an award winner. Plan your meal with dessert in mind—it would be a shame to miss the likes of strawberry and chocolate crêpes, chocolate mousse, or one of the special nightly desserts. There's live music and dancing on Thursday, Friday, and Saturday after 10pm and on Sundays from 4:30 to 7:30pm.

PICNIC FARE

⊙ Pic-Nics

30 Baldwin Ave. ☎ **808/579-8021.** Reservations not accepted. Sandwiches $4.50–$5.15; box lunches $7.95–$42.50. No credit cards. Daily 7:30am–3pm. SANDWICHES/BOX LUNCHES.

If you need a picnic lunch for your trip to Haleakala or Hana, this is the place to stock up in Paia. Pic-nics, a cheerful, clean Formica-tables-and-benches place, is known all over the area for its sandwiches: especially the spinach-nut burgers, served on whole-wheat sesame buns, and piled high with lettuce, tomato, sprouts, and dressing; they're $5.50 and terrific. They also serve a filet of mahimahi for the same price. Everything is delicious, since they use, as much as possible, freshly grown local produce and organically raised island beef. The very popular excursion lunches include sandwiches, Maui potato chips, salads, seasonal fruits, beverages, great muffins, and homemade cookies and desserts, plus many other basket stuffers, and begin at $7.95. No need to call ahead—your order will be prepared quickly. Picnics also features cappuccino, freshly baked breakfast pastries, scrambled eggs, and muffins for breakfast while you're waiting for your order.

HAIKU

Pauwela Cafe

375 W. Kuiaha Rd. (Old Pauwela Cannery), ☎ **808/575-9242.** Reservations not accepted. Full meals $5–$7; coffee and scone $2.50. No credit cards. Mon–Sat 7am–4:30pm; Sun 9am–2pm. INTERNATIONAL.

The lovely little Pauwela Cafe is owned and operated by a culinary couple well known to Maui foodies: Chris Speere, formerly a sous chef at the Maui Prince Hotel, is a respected Chef/Instructor at Maui Community College's outstanding Food Service Program. Too humble to admit it, he had a major role in making the college's Class Act Restaurant one of the best eateries in Central Maui. Becky Speere is a fine cook in her own right, trained in the European style. Baking is her strongest suit. Before she opened the cafe, her creations used to show up on numerous island restaurant dessert trays. For breakfast, steaming hot coffee is accompanied by blueberry scones or fresh fruit strudels and tarts. For lunch, try the spicy Hawaiian ceviche ($6 including bread) or the outrageous kalua turkey sandwich for just $4.95, including pasta salad. Lots of good Mexican specialties are available, too. Pauwela Cafe can be a bit difficult to find—it's beyond "off-the-beaten track," but we promise it will be worth it. (Phone for driving directions.)

PUKALANI, KULA & MAKAWAO

Since there is no food to be had in Haleakala National Park, you might want to eat on your way to or from the crater. We've often found that being at the 10,000-foot altitude of Haleakala can build up quite an appetite.

Casanova Italian Restaurant and Deli

1188 Makawao Ave., Makawao. ☎ **808/572-0220.** Reservations recommended at dinner. Restaurant, main courses $8–$22; pizzas $8.95–$14.50. Deli, most dishes around $5–$6. MC, V. Deli, daily 8am–6:30pm. Restaurant, lunch Mon–Sat 11:30am–2:30pm; dinner Mon–Sat 5:30–9:30pm. Pizza available til 11pm. Bar open to 1am. ITALIAN.

An enjoyable place to eat is in nearby Makawao, a few miles off your route to Haleakala, but worth making a little detour for; turn right at Pukalani. Casanova looks as if it belongs more in Rome or Milan, Bologna or Naples, than it does in cowboy-town Makawao. These cities are, in fact, the homes of the four young partners, all professionals in other fields, whose restaurant has created quite a stir: People come from all over Maui for their fresh pastas and divine pastries; Casanova supplies them to some of the best hotels and restaurants on the island. Casanova has been voted "Best Italian restaurant in Maui" for several years by readers of the *Maui News.* There are two parts to the operation. One is the original deli, which serves breakfast, lunch, snacks, and classic Italian dishes in the $5 to $6 range. They have sandwiches with an international flair, such as Paris (Brie with artichoke hearts) and Parma (prosciutto and tomatoes), plus sensational pastries in the $2 to $3 range: lemon-brandy cheesecake and chocolate cheesecake are worthy of bravos, and people drive miles for their tiramisù.

For more relaxed dining, try the restaurant itself. It's divided into a cafe and bar on one side and a huge dance floor and stage area on the other, the scene for nightly entertainment and dancing. From the huge, wood-fired Italian oven emerge delicious crispy-crusted pizzas with a decidedly imaginative flair, like the Genova (pesto sauce, prawns, and fresh tomato) at $15.50 and the Romana (goat cheese, roasted peppers, thyme, and garlic), $13.95. The organic salads are wondrous. There are a variety of antipasti (try the carpaccio di salmone—natural smoked salmon topped with sweet onions and Italian capers) and pastas, from $7.50 to $19. One of the best items on the menu is the Pesce Intero al Forno, a whole fresh opakapaka (red snapper) baked with fresh herbs and white wine, served on a large tray and enough for two or three. Save some room for the wonderful desserts.

Grandma's Coffee House

End of Hi. 37, Keokea. ☎ 808/878-2140. Reservations not accepted. Main dishes $2–$5.65. No credit cards. Mon–Sat 7am–5pm, Sun 7am–3pm. AMERICAN.

This makes a nice stop if you're driving to Tedeschi Vineyards after you come down from the volcano (see Chapter 10). It's a green building right next to the gas station in the tiny town of Keokea. Alfred Franco, a young man whose family has been growing and roasting coffee on Maui since 1918 (you can buy a pound to take home), opened this cozy little mom-and-pop café about 7 years ago. It's always busy, filled with neighborhood people who come for his wife's freshly baked breads, coffee cakes, cinnamon rolls, and such. Sit down, have a sandwich, a bowl of chili or saimin, a salad or a bread pudding or a pineapple coconut square, and some fragrant coffee—perhaps cappuccino or café au lait. Or try one of the changing daily hot plate lunch specials at $5.78.

Kula Lodge

Haleakala Highway, ☎ **808/878-2517** or 800/233-1535. Reservations recommended at dinner. Main courses $14–$20. MC, V. Breakfast daily 6:30–11:30am; lunch daily 11:45am–4:30pm; dinner daily 4:30–8:30pm. HAWAII REGIONAL.

The most scenic spot for a meal in this area is on the slopes of Haleakala, in the delightful town of Kula. This country inn has a fireplace and a nonpareil view of the West Maui mountains from its 3,200-foot elevation. Feast at breakfast on their eggs benedict, served with cottage fries and a rich hollandaise; it's $7.75 and delicious. The chef uses fresh produce grown upcountry, plus homegrown herbs and spices. Start with a steamed, baked, and stuffed Kula artichoke or maybe the Kula onion soup, perhaps choose a hot or cold spinach salad or papaya and shrimp salad for a main luncheon course. You could go with sandwiches like the vegetarian macadamia-nut garden burger, the mahimahi, or even a hot pastrami sandwich. Main courses, which include soup or salad, freshly baked bread, rice or potatoes, and a vegetable, always feature a boneless breast of chicken stuffed with ricotta cheese and broccoli, and a unique Thai soba noodle dish, with roasted eggplant and snow peas.

Polli's Cantina

1202 Makawao Ave., at the corner of Olinda Rd., Makawao. ☎ **808/572-7808.** Reservations not accepted. Main courses $6.50–$15. MC, V. Daily 11:30am–10pm; brunch Sun 10:30am–2:30pm. MEXICAN.

This old standby is a cute little place that specializes in "cold beer and hot food." The decor is Mexican, the clientele is local, the music is lively, and the food is very tasty. Many vegetarian dishes are available. We love their desserts, especially the buñuelos: Mexican pastries topped with vanilla ice cream, hot pure maple syrup, and cinnamon, $3.25. *¡Muy bueno!* Happy hour is from 3 to 5pm.

✪ Upcountry Cafe

7-2 Aewa Place (just off Haleakala Hwy, in the Andrade Building in Pukalani). ☎ **808/572-2395.** Reservations not taken. Full breakfast $3.75–$6.25; lunch $4.95–$7.50. No credit cards. Mon, Wed–Sat 6:30am–3pm; Sun 6:30am–12 noon. Dinner Thurs–Fri 6–9pm Closed Tues. LOCAL STYLE/AMERICAN.

Food like mom made (especially if you grew up in Hawaii), friendly service, and a decor so cute you'll smile your way through your meal—all make the Upcountry Café a very popular little spot. Muffins fresh from the oven, steaming bowls of saimin, and plates piled high with another local favorite—loco moco—are just a sampling of the breakfast items available. Lunchtime brings simple, hearty home-made food: Cobb salad served with homebaked bread, sandwiches, a plate lunch special, and fresh soup of the day are all available at very reasonable prices. If you're in the neighborhood on a Thursday or Friday night, stop by for dinner: main courses such as fresh fish ($10.95), hibachi baby back ribs ($9.25), and bouilla-baisse ($12.95) all come with soup or salad, rice and vegetable. And some luscious desserts, like a chocolate basket with fresh fruit mousse, are offered then. The place literally teems with black-and-white cows—on aprons, menus, walls, and even salt and pepper shakers. So, it's no surprise that the signature dessert is cowpie—chocolate cream cheese with macadamia nuts in a chocolate cookie crust.

KIHEI

This area has a number of good eating spots for budget-watchers. There's also A Pacific Café Maui, a local counterpart of Chef Jean-Marie Josselin's famed restaurant on Kauai, known for extraordinary Hawaii Regional cuisine.

Alexander's Fish & Chicken & Chips

1913 S. Kihei Rd. ☎ **808/874-0788.** Reservations not required. $4.95–$10.95. No credit cards. Daily 11am–9pm. AMERICAN.

One long-time Kihei resident we know says he eats here at least *five* times a week because he couldn't even prepare fish at home for the price he pays here. For $5.95 you get mahimahi, ono, or ahi—broiled or fried—plus french fries or rice and cole slaw. Or, you can choose smoked ribs or chicken instead. "Baskets to go," a 13-piece fish basket, is just $14.95; and oodles of side orders, such as green salad, onion rings, deep-fried mixed veggies or mushrooms, corn bread, french fries and chicken wings, are the perfect answer for condo-dwellers, especially those traveling with their family or in a group. There's indoor and outdoor seating here.

Margarita's Beach Cantina

In Kealia Beach Plaza, 101 N. Kihei Rd. ☎ **808/879-5275.** Reservations recommended. Main courses $6.95–$14.95. AE, DC, MC, V. Daily 11:30am–midnight. MEXICAN.

Here's one restaurant that really lives up to its name: It's practically *on* the beach, with a huge dining lanai with umbrellaed tables overlooking the water. The inside is pleasant too, with tall, beamed ceilings, wooden tables, straw chairs, tile floors, plants, and piñatas. The lanai is quite a spot for sunset watching, whale watching, people watching, or just sitting in perfect contentment as you sip your margaritas and munch on delicious Mexican food with an island flair: Everything is made from scratch each day. Margarita's Munchies (appetizers) are first-rate, including buffalo wings and nachos. Ask if they have their Fajita Special. For entertainment, there's satellite TV, electronic darts, and—on occasion—live music. The daily Happy Hour, (2:30 to 5:30) offers margaritas at 96¢ a glass, $4 a liter.

The New York Deli

In Dolphin Plaza, 2395 S. Kihei Rd. ☎ **808/879-1115.** Sandwiches $4.95–$5.95. MC, V. Daily 8am–8pm. DELI.

Just across the courtyard from Pizza Fresh (see below) is the New York Deli, a must for any homesick New Yorker—they even have a picture of Ed Koch on the wall. The wonderful bagels air-expressed from the homeland, the hot pastrami and corned-beef-on-rye sandwiches ($4.95), the pasta and potato salads (sold by the pound) will all soothe the pangs of Manhattan separation anxiety. This is a tiny but sparkly place, with red-checkered cloths on all three tables. Have a slice of their New York cheesecake, or pick up your lunch and take off for the beach—you won't miss New York a bit.

Pikake Bakery

300 Ohukai Rd., in the Kihei Commercial Center (mountainside of Piilani Hwy.). ☎ **808/879-7295.** Reservations not accepted. 65¢–$4.25. No credit cards. Mon–Fri 7:30am–6pm; Sat 7:30am–5pm. EUROPEAN-STYLE PASTRIES AND UNIQUE BREADS.

Although it's a great place to stop for pastry and coffee or a cappuccino, it's the bread that has made Pikake Bakery famous. Peter Teimorabadi makes really special breads: provolone and fresh garlic, red potato and rosemary, sun-dried tomato, kalamata olive, red onion and walnut, jalapeño, and cheddar cheese and corn are truly memorable. Breads average $4. Peter was corporate pastry chef for Ritz Carlton before he moved to Maui, so you can be sure his assortment of pastries is wonderful, too.

Pizza Fresh

In Dolphin Plaza, 2395 S. Kihei Rd. ☎ **808/879-1525.** Pizzas $6.95–$26.95. No credit cards. Daily 3–9pm. PIZZA.

Doug Malone of Pizza Fresh came to Maui with a reputation to live up to: His pies had been voted "Best Pizza in Dallas." They may also be the best pizza on Maui. His motto "We make it, you bake it" means that this is something to take back to your condo rather than eat there. We sampled the Garden Lite pizza—a whole-wheat vegetarian special with a variety of veggies light on the cheeses, and with a thin crust—quite delicious. On Tuesday all pizzas are 40% off (pickup only). They also have very good salads—veggie, Greek, and Caesar. Free delivery in the Kihei, Wailea, and Makena areas. Call-in orders for pickup or delivery are appreciated.

There's another Pizza Fresh in Makawao, 1043 Makawao Ave. (☎ 808/572-2000).

Sand Witch

At Sugar Beach, 145 N. Kihei Rd. ☎ **808/879-3262.** Main courses $2.95–$6.95. AE, MC, V. Daily 11am–11pm. SANDWICHES/SNACKS/SALADS.

In addition to turning out great tropical drinks, this cozy beach bar cooks up a variety of hot dogs, pupus, burritos, burgers, and sandwiches to go with them. Piled high with meats, cheeses, onions, Maui tomatoes, sprouts, and romaine lettuce, they are a meal in themselves. Eat indoors or take out.

Shaka Sandwich & Pizza

1295 S. Kihei Rd. (behind Jack in the Box). ☎ **808/874-0331.** Reservations not taken. Pizza $1.50 & up/slice; $12.95 & up/pie. Sandwiches $3.50 & up/small; $7 & up/large. No credit cards. Mon–Sat 10:30am–9pm. PIZZA AND SUBS.

We have a well-traveled friend who moved to Maui from New York more than a decade ago, who swears that this is the closest she's ever found to the real thing. This is the kind that droops and drips lots of olive oil onto the wax paper sheet on which it's served. You can add anything you like to your slice for just 25¢ per topping. An 18" cheese pie is $12.95 and you can add any topping to that for $1.75 each. Our friend also delights in the fact that this is the only pizza place on Maui that sets out *big* shakers of oregano, garlic salt, parmesan, and dried chile peppers—just like back home! Visitors from the South Jersey–Philly area will want to try the Philly cheesesteak sandwich, served on homemade Italian bread. We think it'll bring tears to your eyes—and not just because you've topped it with sweet, luscious fried onions! And yes, Shaka does deliver—on minimum orders of $10, for just $1 to anywhere in Kihei; $2 Wailea.

Stella Blues Cafe & Deli

In Long's Center, 1215 S. Kihei Rd. ☎ **808/874-3779.** Reservations not required. Complete dinners, $10.95–$16.95. MC, V. Breakfast Mon–Sat 8–11am. Sun 8am–2pm; lunch daily anytime after 11am; pupus, beer and wine from 3pm on; dinner daily 5–9pm. AMERICAN.

On a hot Kihei day, this crisply air-conditioned place hits the spot. It's spacious, with cool white walls, plants aplenty, vibrant tablecloths, white chairs, and several umbrellaed tables outside. The former owners of the Maui Bagel have created a flavorful menu here, and they make everything from scratch. Crab cakes served over rice pilaf with lemon-chive butter sauce, several chicken dishes (Cajun chicken, chicken parmigiana, and sweet Thai chili chicken), prime rib, baby back ribs, and fish specials are featured every night. And there are lots of imaginative vegetarian specialties on the order of Vegetarian Delight: tomato Provençal, grilled leeks, roasted eggplant, red peppers and garlic, steamed broccoli and snow peas, asparagus and shiitake mushrooms, served hot with sun-dried tomato dressing over a wild rice blend. Dinners come with salad, vegetable, French bread, and a choice of starch. The daytime menu features similarly sophisticated sandwiches, plus hearty deli sandwiches. Homemade soups, generous salads, and fresh bagels and toppings are also popular. This is a good place to drop in for just coffee or espresso or cappuccino and some homemade pastries and desserts. The East Coast Scramble—two eggs scrambled with Nova Scotia lox and Maui onions, home fries, and a toasted bagel—is a breakfast treat at $7.75. There's live music Wednesdays through Sundays, 7 to 9pm.

KAI NANI VILLAGE

The Greek Bistro

2511 S. Kihei Rd. ☎ **808/879-9330.** Reservations not accepted. Main courses $11.95–$18.95. AE, JCB, MC, V. dinner daily 4–9:30pm. CONTINENTAL GRECIAN/MEDITERRANEAN.

In the rear courtyard of Kai Nani Village, this cute little place has about 18 tables, some of them outside under the blue-and-white striped umbrellas. A new cocktail lounge offers ouzo, Metaxa, cocktails, and tropical drinks. Dinner features homemade dishes on the order of moussaka, lamb shish kebab, spanakopita, and pastitsio (Greek lasagne); it also offers such "bistro specialties" as a chicken-and-mushroom pasta, Mediterranean chicken, and the house specialty, fresh fish Greek style. Everything is nicely done. A lamb gyro sandwich served in pita bread makes a tasty dish at either meal for $7.95. For dessert, go with the homemade baklava or the white-chocolate raspberry cheesecake. Lots of readers praise this one.

Kihei Prime Rib House

2511 S. Kihei Rd. ☎ **808/879-1954.** Reservations recommended after 6:30pm. Main courses $19.95 and up; Early Bird specials $11.95–$13.95. CB, DC, MC, V. Dinner only, daily 5–10pm. AMERICAN.

This has long been an island favorite. It's a bit high for our budget, but arrive early—between 5 and 6pm—and enjoy their Early Bird specials: prime rib, Polynesian chicken, or fresh island fish—ahi is the best—for $11.95. Their salad bar, included with all dinners, uses only locally grown fruits and vegetables, and can be enjoyed alone at $11.95. Oceanview dining and the work of internationally known artists on the walls add to the warmth and charm.

WORTH A SPLURGE

✪ A Pacific Cafe Maui

1279 S. Kihei Rd. (in Azeka Place II). ☎ **808/879-0069.** Reservations recommended. Main courses $15.50–$22.95. AE, DC, MC, V. Dinner nightly 5:30–10pm. HAWAII REGIONAL.

Yes, folks: Yet another of the Distinguished Dozen—the 12-member Hawaii Regional Cuisine chefs' organization—has opened a long-awaited Maui location. Jean-Marie Josselin, who also owns and operates A Pacific Cafe on Kauai, has brought his particular interpretation of Hawaii Regional Cuisine to Kihei. This is a large, interestingly designed restaurant—warm, honey-orange colored walls, lots of copper accents, the whole room in a kind of "S" shape—in an unlikely spot (straddling the rear of Azeka Place II and Long's Center). A Pacific Cafe has been playing to standing-room-only crowds since it opened in July of 1994. It's not a surprise when you consider that the food is fabulous, the service excellent, and the atmosphere, on most nights, electric. Like their HRC brothers and sisters, Josselin and talented chef George Gomes have seemingly limitless imaginations and change their menu often. Flavors are bright, clear, sometimes assertive. Some examples: red curry Thai coconut soup with squid and Hawaiian fish; warm local potato salad with clams, calamari, and green beans; rack of lamb with sweet potato hash and spicy greens, prepared in the restaurant's Tandoori oven; wood-grilled Hawaiian swordfish with spicy peanut crust, smoked shrimp, green papaya vinaigrette, and asparagus tempura. Desserts could be anything from a trio of creme brûlées to a rich tropical fruit tart. Go hungry, and share, share, share to best experience one of Maui's brightest new restaurants. Be sure to make reservations.

WAILEA-MAKENA

Wailea-Makena, just beyond the Kihei area, is Maui's newest resort area and perhaps its most spectacular. The restaurants in the grand hotels here are all top of the line and very pricey, but there are a couple of surprisingly good buys.

Cafe Kiowai

At the Maui Prince Hotel, 5400 Makena Alanui. ☎ **808/874-111.** Reservations recommended. Main courses $6.50–$12.50. Continental breakfast buffet $11; complete hot breakfast buffet $16.95. Breakfast daily 6:30–11am; lunch daily 11am–5pm. HAWAII REGIONAL.

Everything is delicious at this pleasant café. The food is created by Roger Dikon, the same brilliant chef known for his culinary magic at the Prince Court (see below); it's a great alternative for those who prefer a much more casual atmosphere and a much smaller check. You could start your lunch with freshly made Maui onion rings or the hearty Maui onion soup glazed with mozzarella cheese. Then, move on to a filling sandwich like the house smoked pastrami on herb and rye bread—with passion fruit mustard and baby island greens—or try one of the house specialties, like steamed clams in sake and soy butter. Go ahead, treat yourself to dessert, too: lilikoi creme brûlée and macadamia nut brittle flan are both terrific. The menu changes frequently, but trust us, everything will be good.

Maui Onion

In the Stouffer Wailea Beach Resort, 3550 Wailea Alanui. ☎ **808/879-4900.** $8–$12.50. AE, DC, DISC, JCB, MC, V. Lunch daily 10am–6pm. AMERICAN.

A delightful place to enjoy lunch or a snack, the Maui Onion sits both pool-and oceanside at this lush Wailea resort. The menu is small but varied, with salads, sandwiches, and light lunches from which to choose. We have a friend who drives from way upcountry just for the onion rings ($5.75) and for the incredible ice-cream smoothies, made with or without alcohol.

✪ Prince Court

In the Maui Prince Hotel, 5400 Makena Alanui. ☎ **808/875-5888.** Reservations recommended. Main courses $13.50–$25.95. Sunday Brunch $29.95, including champagne. AE, CB, DISC, JCB, MC, V. Dinner daily 6–8:30pm; Sun Brunch 9:30am–1pm. HAWAII REGIONAL.

Thanks to the considerable talents of Executive Chef Roger Dikon, the Maui Prince Hotel justifiably boasts some of the very best restaurants in Hawaii under one roof. And the brightest jewel in the crown is surely Prince Court. Everything, right down to the smallest detail, is first class. The atmosphere is comfortably elegant. The service is impeccable. But great food is what fine dining is all about, and great food is what you get at Prince Court. Prices have recently come down here, which makes things even more delightful.

The innovative menu, which stresses locally grown produce and locally caught seafood, changes often. Tiger-eye sashimi—fresh ahi infused with wasabi, rolled in a light tempura batter and quickly fried—gives you just a hint of the magnificent creations here. Even a simple steak is lifted to great heights—here served with home-fried poatoes mixed with lobster meat. Two of you should share the Taste of Hawaii Regional Cuisine appetizer plate: sampler portions of volcano sashimi, oysters, ceviche, summer roll, puna chevre won ton, and manapua ($11.95). You could enjoy the Hawaii Regional cuisine salad bar as an inexpensive ($8.95) main course, or also dine reasonably on, say, kiawe grilled shrimp on angel hair pasta ($15.95). Whatever you have, though, save room for one of pastry chef Steve Holton's masterpieces, like chocolate macadamia nut flan garnished with caramel brittle, or guava and lilikoi mousse served in a chocolate basket.

If you don't manage to get here for dinner, by all means, come on Sunday morning for the fantastic brunch. Chef Dikon is proudest of his 80-foot-square antipasto table, piled high with fresh salads and veggies of every description artfully prepared. Hot breakfast and lunch dishes change weekly and might include Hawaiian macadamia-nut and banana pancakes; baby lobster tail and caviar omelets; sashimi; crispy smoked duck on couscous with roasted pepper and olives, roasted fig sauce, and Ulupalaku oranges; and much more. And, with an entire table of hot and cold desserts, what more can we say? Make reservations. One local friend swears this has always been—and still is—the best brunch on Maui.

LAHAINA

Lahaina is undoubtedly Maui's most enjoyable dining area. It's got everything, from French country bistros to barbecue houses to glamorous oceanside watering spots.

MEALS FOR LESS THAN $15

B.J.'s Chicago Pizzeria

730 Front St. ☎ **808/661-0700.** Reservations only for 10 or more. Pizzas $4.95–$21.95. AE, MC, V. Mon–Thurs 11am–11pm; Fri–Sat 11am–midnight. PIZZA/PASTA.

Here's the most glamorous setting for a pizza parlor we know. BJ's is serving up Chicago-style pizza, pasta, sandwiches, and salads as patrons enjoy fabulous ocean/harbor views from the open-air dining room. This is the place for thick, buttery pizza crust smothered with all the traditional toppings and then some. Individual 6-inch mini-pizzas are available from 11am to 4pm, and make a neat lunch along with a salad. And the appetizers are pretty special for a pizza joint: Brie and papaya quesadilla, toasted ravioli, and Charleston crab cakes are all delicious. Local delivery is available. There's live contemporary Hawaiian music every night.

⑤ Cheeseburger in Paradise

811 Front St. ☎ **808/661-4855.** Reservations not accepted. $6–$10. AE, MC, V. Daily 11am–11pm. AMERICAN.

If it's a great big juicy, gooey burger you crave, this is the place to order it. And at Cheeseburger in Paradise it comes with a side order of ocean in both the downstairs and the upstairs dining rooms. No pretense here. We're talkin' all-American, five-napkin burgers, great onion rings ($4), and ice cold beer. There's also live tropical rock from 4:30 to 11pm, seven days a week.

Juicy's Tropical Fruit Bar

In the shopping arcade at 505 Front St. ☎ **808/667-5727.** Reservations not accepted. Sandwiches $4–$5; main courses $2.95–$5.95. No credit cards. Mon–Sat 7:30am–9pm, Sun 10am–6pm. NATURAL FOODS.

Juicy's is hardly big in size but it is very big in popularity among Maui's natural-foods set. Every day there is a fresh vegetarian or vegan specialty: It could be shepherd's pie, chile rellenos, Mexican fiesta veggies, or coconut-curry soup. In addition, there are sandwiches, smoothies, baked potatoes, and freshly squeezed juices.

Pacific'o

505 Front St. ☎ **808/667-4341.** Reservations recommended. Main courses $15–$22. AE, DC, DISC, JCB, MC, V. Lunch daily 11am–3pm; dinner daily 5:30–10:30pm; pupus all day 'til midnight. CONTEMPORARY PACIFIC.

This pretty little restaurant serves tasty, creative dishes in a fantastic setting right on the beach. If dinner is the meal you choose at Pacific'O, we recommend timing your reservations with the sunset. House specialties at dinner include shrimp wontons filled with prawns and basil and served with spicy sweet-and-sour sauce and Hawaiian salsa ($10); and banana "imu" style fish—fresh fish grilled in banana leaf, lemon grass pesto, and vanilla bean sauce ($21). At lunch, the fare is simpler and less expensive, but just as good. A Caesar salad with marinated roasted bell pepper, macadamia nuts, and anchovies is $7.50; pasta with smoked spicy shrimp is $9.50. Live music fills the tropical air on Thursday, Friday, and Saturday nights.

Planet Hollywood

744 Front St. ☎ **808/667-7877.** Reservations not accepted. Main courses $6.95–$19.95. AE, DC, MC, V. Daily 11am–midnight (merchandise booth opens at 10am). CALIFORNIA.

The Planet Hollywood opening in the summer of 1994—probably the glitziest evening ever in Lahaina—brought stars like Arnold Schwarzenegger and Sylvester Stallone to this once-sleepy little town. Many of the locals, including ALL of the media, were unimpressed: too much "attitude" and not nearly enough "aloha". You may find that still prevails (we did), but if you crave lots of neon and Hollywood memorabilia with your burger, hey, go for it. The life-sized, bloodied Arnold/ Terminator model at the door didn't do anything for our appetites, but . . . . In addition to burgers and pizzas, menu choices include fajitas, pastas, and grilled rib, chicken, pork chop, sirloin, and fish platters. There's a long list of desserts, from apple strudel to Hollywood mousse pie.

⑤ Sunrise Cafe

693A Front St., at the corner of Market St. ☎ **808/666-8558.** Reservations not accepted. Sandwiches $3.95; main courses $5–$6. AE, DISC, MC, V. Daily 6am–10pm. AMERICAN.

Home cooking, low prices, and a very casual atmosphere have made this little indoor-outdoor place, just across the road from the library (and next door to Lappert's), very popular very quickly. There are specials every day, including good vegetarian choices. If you're not feeling too hungry, you could have just a bowl of homemade soup with French bread for $2.95, or a croissant sandwich for $3.90; or quiches, or some luscious pastries from the Bakery, Lahaina's best. Gourmet coffees are featured at the full Espresso bar. Smoothies, freshly squeezed carrot juice, and healthy drinks like spirulina protein are also available for disciplined souls.

Thai Chef

In the Lahaina Shopping Center. ☎ **808/667-2814.** Reservations recommended. Main courses $5.95–$13.95. DC, DISC, JCB, MC, V. Lunch Mon–Fri 11am–2:30pm; dinner daily 5–closing. THAI.

The local people praise this cute little restaurant offering Thai specialties in a pleasant setting. Tell the waiter if you want your food mild, medium, or hot, so he can help you choose from among salads, soups (we like the chicken soup simmered in coconut milk with ginger at $8.50), a variety of curries, noodles, and such specialty dishes as stuffed chicken wings or sautéed seafood with bean sauce. Vegetarians have a complete menu of their own: appetizers, soups, noodles, and main dishes. Prices are reasonable. No liquor is served, so BYOB.

There's now another Thai Chef in Rainbow Mall, 2439 S. Kihei Rd., in Kihei (☎ 808/874-5605). The menu is the same, although prices are slightly lower, and they do serve liquor.

Westside Natural Foods

193 Lahainaluna Rd. ☎ **808/667-2855.** $1.50–$4.95. MC, V. Mon–Sat 7:30am–9pm, Sun 8am–8pm. VEGETARIAN.

This local health-food store has salads, sandwiches, soup of the day, smoothies, and hot food to eat informally at outdoor tables or to go. Main courses include lasagne, chili, and enchiladas. Help yourself to goodies from the organic salad bar, $4.95 a pound. The shopping is good here too: You can get strawberry-papayas, unsprayed pineapples, and organic Maui mangoes.

World Cafe

At Lahaina Center, 900 Front St. ☎ **808/661-1515.** Reservations only for 8 or more. Main courses $7.75–$14.50. AE, DC, DISC, MC, V. Daily 11am–1:30am. ISLAND/CALIFORNIA.

Soon after the first World Cafe opened in Honolulu's Restaurant Row, Maui got its very own. It's a contemporary, high-tech kind of sports bar, definitely a cut above what you might think of when you hear those words. It's home to twelve pool tables, darts, air hockey, "foosball," big screen TV, and an ocean view—what more could a sports fan ask for? Good food, you say. Well, World Cafe's got that, too. There's a long list of appetizers, from fried mozzarella and potato skins to oysters on the half shell and ahi sashimi. Pizzas, pasta, burgers, fajitas, and a few soup and salad selections round out the menu. A fun place, especially for the college set.

MEALS FOR LESS THAN $20

Aloha Cantina

839 Front St. ☎ **808/661-8788.** Reservations not accepted. $7–$20. AE, MC, V. Daily 11am–1am. SOUTHERN CALIFORNIA/MEXICAN.

The owners of Cheeseburger in Paradise (see above) have another big winner to their credit here. Like the other restaurant, this one has both lower- and upper-deck dining; both locations jut out over the water. It's worth a margarita stop just to check out the incredible interior: brightly painted oil drums for bar stools, a great tropical mural on one wall, even a simulated hurricane that blows through every hour or so. The most popular dish is the Maui fish tacos, made with fresh local fish. You get two tacos, rice, and yummy refried beans for $10.95. Or, splurge on the lobster tacos for just $2 more. Fruit margaritas are the bartenders' calling cards; all margaritas are hand-shaken. "Tropical Rock," featuring various musical groups, is on from 8:30 to 11:30pm Sunday through Thursday; there is dancing to live bands from 10pm to 1am on Fridays and Saturdays.

Compadres Mexican Bar & Grill

At the Lahaina Cannery, 1221 Honoapiilani Hwy. ☎ **808/661-7189.** Reservations not required. Main courses $10–$17. AE, MC, V. Daily 11:30am–10pm (bar open to 1am). MEXICAN.

The first neighbor island location of Honolulu's popular Compadres Restaurant is a smash hit in Lahaina. And rightfully so—there's terrific food, respectable prices, a wonderful setting, and an upbeat, fun atmosphere. The indoor-outdoor setting is both casual and exotic, with a fountain, an aviary, a garden of greenery, pastel-colored terra-cotta pots, and an array of Mexican artifacts. The chefs take their inspiration from the cooking of northern Mexico, Arizona, and California, and strive for food that is wholesome as well as flavorful. They use only the freshest of ingredients, make everything from scratch, and never use lard. For the calorie-conscious, they've come up with a number of "Compadres 400" selections, dishes of 400 or fewer calories. We love the nachos and the queso fundido among the appetizers, the taco split and mud pie among the desserts—not to mention those super margaritas! On Sundays, there's a champagne Buffet brunch from 10am to 2pm for $12.95.

Hard Rock Cafe

At Lahaina Center, 900 Front St. ☎ **808/667-7400.** Reservations not accepted. Main courses $7.95–$13.95. AE, MC, V. Daily 11am–midnight. AMERICAN.

If ever a restaurant was suited to the Lahaina night scene, this is certainly it. Like Lahaina itself, it's big, noisy, brash—and very endearing. Like its companion restaurants around the world, this Hard Rock is decorated with rock music memorabilia and 1950s artifacts; here they mingle with surfboards and ukuleles. Nonstop rock makes it unlikely that you can indulge in much conversation with the waiter, but the choices are easy. Everything is made from scratch, using the freshest ingredients, and absolutely no preservatives or additives. We'll have to agree with the menu that "If you've been to the Hard Rock and haven't had our lime chicken or watermelon ribs, then you haven't been to the Hard Rock!" Other good choices include a variety of burgers and sandwiches, including grilled ahi; a top-notch grilled tostada salad; and, of course, Maui onion rings. Desserts are out of the 50s; root-beer float, hot fudge sundaes, and our favorite, the fresh strawberries on homemade angelfood cake, topped with whipped cream. You're likely to see lines at the door of Hard Rock, but don't be put off; they are usually for the HRC logo shop, which dispenses insanely popular T-shirts, baseball caps, and the like; the restaurant is so large that you're usually seated in a very short time.

Kimo's

845 Front St. ☎ **808/661-4811.** Reservations recommended. Main courses $9.95–$19.95. AE, MC, V. Lunch (downstairs bar) daily 11:30am–2:30pm; dinner (upstairs restaurant) daily 5–10:30pm. Bar open 11:30am–midnight. STEAK/SEAFOOD.

Call Kimo's your quintessential Lahaina-style restaurant. It's been there forever—right out on the waterfront—serves good fresh fish and steaks, and is a perfect place to nurse a drink, discuss the meaning of life, and/or watch a sunset. Fresh fish of the day, prepared in a variety of styles, is available from $17.95 to $19.95, but there are many tasty favorites priced much lower: veggie brochettes and a luscious upcountry vegetarian pasta are each $9.95; kushiyaki (marinated chicken breast and sirloin brochette) and Koloa pork ribs and Polynesian chicken are $15.95, a cheeseburger (available on the regular dinner menu) is $7.95. All main dishes come with tossed green salad and house dressing, a basket of freshly baked carrot muffins and sourdough rolls, and steamed herb rice. Don't forget to save room for the original hula pie.

Kobe Japanese Steak House

136 Dickenson St. ☎ **808/667-5555.** Reservations recommended. Sushi $4–$16.50; main courses $13.90–$39. AE, DC, DISC, JCB, MC, V. Dinner only, daily 5:30–10pm. Sushi Bar 5:30–midnight. JAPANESE.

What a surprise this place is! Just one block behind traditional Baldwin House is what could pass for an authentic Japanese country inn, magnificently decorated with Japanese artifacts, serving delicious food. You can eat at the enormous sushi bar, but we prefer to take our seats at one of the communal tables and watch, along with other diners, the master chef on as he whips up our meal at the center grill, teppanyaki-hibachi style. Every meal begins with grilled teppan shrimp pupus, followed by shabu-shabu soup. Then the chef takes whatever you've chosen—steak, chicken, shrimp—and sautées it with fresh vegetables and flavorful sauces. For dessert, wonderful green-tea ice cream and green tea itself, hearty because it's roasted with rice. Teriyaki chicken is $13.90; hibachi steak, $19.90, teppan shrimp, $19.90 and a steak-and-shrimp teriyaki combo is $22.90. Other steak, fish, and lobster choices go higher. If you don't mind eating early, from 5:30 to 6:30 pm, you can save a few bucks on the Early Bird Specials: teriyaki chicken $9.90, sukiyaki steak, $10.90; teriyaki combo, $12.90. Special menus are offered for childeren. Cocktail service begins at 5pm and continues to 2am. There's a Late Night Happy Hour from 10pm until closing.

✪ Lahaina Coolers Restaurant & Bar

180 Dickenson St. ☎ **808/661-7082.** Reservations not required. Main courses $7.50–$14.50. AE, DC, MC, V. Breakfast daily 7–11am; lunch daily noon–5pm; dinner daily 5pm–midnight. Bar open to 2am. NEW AMERICAN.

Located two blocks from busy Front Street, this is exactly the kind of place Lahaina needed—a place where you can get creative, upbeat food in a relaxing setting and at a reasonable price. No wonder it became so popular so quickly! The restaurant looks like somebody's summer porch, with open windows on three sides (windsurfing sails provide shade), blue-and-white tiled floor, whirling fans overhead, and lots of potted plants. For a snack or a starter, the spinach and feta cheese quesadilla and the tempura calamari rings are both great. Pastas are a specialty: The fettucine Diane—chicken and mushrooms in a brandy Dijon sauce—is a favorite. There are also burgers from the grill, creative pizzas, fresh fish right off the boat, and a garden burrito with garbanzo bean spread and rice salad. Don't miss dessert—the chocolate taco filled with tropical fruit and berry "salsa" is worth a postcard home. Try the Norwegian Benedict with smoked salmon and dill for breakfast. The bar is popular, especially during the 4 to 6pm and 10pm to closing happy hours, when drinks and pupus are less. And don't miss their mango daiquiri!.

Lahaina Fish Co.

831 Front St. ☎ **661-3472.** Reservations recommended. Main courses $8.95–$21.95. AE, MC, JCB, V. Dinner daily 5–10pm. SEAFOOD.

With an oceanfront dining room jutting right out over the water, good fresh fish, and moderate prices, Lahaina Fish Co. is always packed. Start with the chef's fresh fish chowder, thick and hearty and served with a cruet of sherry. Then proceed to one of the main courses—many of which are under $10—like the mahimahi fish-and-chips, the calamari, sautéed oysters, prime rib, grilled chicken, and vegetarian pasta. The sautéed scallops and the fresh fisherman's pasta are a treat. All main courses come with a choice of garlic-pesto pasta, french fries, or steamed rice. Keiki dinners are available for $7.95. For desserts, take a pick of cheesecakes ($3.95).

Longhi's

888 Front St. ☎ **808/667-2288.** Reservations not required. Main courses $12–$25. AE, DISC, MC, V. Daily 7:30am–10:30pm. ITALIAN.

Everybody seems to like this across-from-the-ocean cafe, where Italian-accented specialties are fresh and hearty, the mood convivial, and the desserts—and sunsets—spectacular. Owner Bob Longhi goes to great lengths (to New York and Italy) to bring in the finest and freshest cheeses, produce, and Italian cold cuts. He makes his own pastas, bakes his own breads and pastries, and maintains a high standard throughout. Our main problem here is that the menu is always verbal, and so long that you feel you need to take notes; it's also difficult to figure out just how much your meal is going to cost. It's easy for the bill to escalate, since main courses are served alone, and side dishes can add up (salads from $5, fresh vegetables for $5.50 to $8, etc.), so our recommendation is either go all out and consider this a big splurge, or tell the servers how much you want to spend and let them plan the menu for you. (You can also ask for a menu with prices before being seated.)

It's wise to eat lightly and save your strength, because Longhi's other-worldly desserts have become something of a legend around town. You never know what they'll come up with; an incredible strawberry shortcake, a superb macadamia-nut pie (better than any pecan pie we had ever tasted), a mouth-watering mango-topped cheesecake, and a cooling strawberry mousse. All desserts are priced at $6, and they are huge, so be sure to bring a friend to help you. There's an extensive wine list; Longhi's has won many awards from wine societies. The breakfast menu includes frittatas, omelets, homemade coffee cake, and strudel. On Friday and Saturday nights various bands provide music for dancing, from 10:30pm until 1:30am.

Moose McGillycuddy's Pub/Cafe

844 Front St. ☎ **808/667-7758.** Reservations not accepted. Main courses $5.75–$17.95. AE, MC, V. Breakfast daily 8–11am; lunch daily 11am–4:30pm; dinner daily 4:30–10pm. AMERICAN.

Like the Moose in Waikiki, this pub/café offers the same brand of good food, good drinks, and good fun here in Lahaina. It's one flight up, with a big bar, a lively atmosphere, and some tables set out on the lanai overlooking busy Front Street. The Moose is known as a "bargain" in pricey Lahaina; main courses include fresh fish tacos, baby back ribs, chicken and steak fajitas, and all come with soup or salad, baked potato or rice or fries, and hot garlic bread. Early Bird dinners, served from 4:30 to 5:30pm, feature prime rib, mahimahi, and barbecued chicken for only $8.95 to $9.95. Then there are other favorites like the giant chicken taco salad, giant burritos, a variety of burgers like the University Burger ("highly ranked bacon and intelligent Cheddar"). Margaritas and daiquiris are the big drink selections here, along with coffee drinks, and Hawaiian exotics. And the Moose's breakfast specials are considered the best deals in Lahaina.

✪ Old Lahaina Cafe

505 Front St. ☎ **808/661-3303.** Reservations recommended for dinner. Main courses $5.95–$19.95. AE, MC, V. Breakfast daily 7:30–11:30am; lunch daily noon–3:30pm; dinner daily 6–10pm; brunch Sun 7:30am–3pm. SEAFOOD/AMERICAN.

What could be nicer than a beachside breakfast or lunch or a sunset dinner in this charming café overlooking the grounds of the Old Lahaina Luau? This is sophisticated cuisine, using fresh local ingredients and featuring just-caught fish with a variety of preparations—maybe kiawe broiled with shoyu lime chile, or poached with passionfruit cream—dreamed up by veteran chef Michael Ducheneau. There are also vegetarian selections, broiled chicken and steak, and a luau dinner as well. The lunch menu—which can also be ordered in the evening—features hot and cold sandwiches (including kalua pig!) and some hearty salads. Breakfast offers many bargains, including $3.95 for a generous continental breakfast. Sunday brunch features their entire breakfast and lunch menu as well as brunch specials. What with the view and the sounds of the luau below, this is just the place to sit and linger over a fabulous tropical drink. Most Hawaiian!

Pioneer Inn

658 Wharf St. ☎ **808/661-3636.** Reservations recommended. Main courses $11.75–$24.50. AE, DC, MC, V. Breakfast daily 6:30–11am; lunch daily 11am–3pm; dinner daily 5:30–10pm. Café menu served in the lounge daily 11am–10pm. HAWAII REGIONAL.

With the renovation of the Pioneer Inn, there's a new, improved look to its dining room. Local art and harborside artifacts grace the walls. Executive Chef Randall A. Pouck's menus are imaginative and tasty. Breakfast specials include banana fritters with cinnamon and lemon curd, eggs Benedict, even grilled fresh fish. For lunch, try the grilled rare ahi niçoise salad, or the duck confit white-bean cassoulet (also available at dinner), first-prize winner in a recent "Taste of Lahaina" competition. Start dinner with pan-fried Dungeness crab cakes, the lovely Tuscan bread salad, or the tart apple and chicken sausage salad. Then, proceed on to such main courses as herb roasted ranch chicken, coriander crusted rack of lamb, or a simple burger for just $7.95. Desserts are superb, especially the stout pound cake with caramel ice cream and the fudge cake with raspberry sauce.

The cafe menu, served in the lounge all day long, has a large pupu menu, and a good selection of main courses, including a regular or vegetarian burger, penne pasta, chicken breast sandwich, and grilled sausages, from $7.95 to $14.50. There's live entertainment nightly, and you can hang out in the lounge and listen to the oldtimers' stories until 4am, Tuesday to Saturday.

Scaroles Village Pizzeria

505 Front St. ☎ **808/661-8112.** Reservations not required. Pizzas $2.25–$24; pastas $6.50–$11.95; sandwiches $5.95–6.95. AE, DISC, MC, V. Sun–Thurs 11am–11pm, Fri–Sat 11am–midnight. ITALIAN.

Scaroles has so many great pizzas that you may just have to eat here more than once. Pizza by the slice and by the pie is offered in either Neapolitan (thin crust) or Sicilian (thick crust) versions. There are 12 toppings to choose from, among them house-made meatball and sausage. The clam-and-garlic house special is fantastic. But there's more than just great pizza here. Choose from a full selection of appetizers like fried calamari and baked stuffed clams; have a sandwich like sausage and peppers or Italian cold cuts and cheese on homemade Italian bread; or go for pastas like spaghetti marinara or sausage lasagne. They have rich Italian desserts, too, like tiramisù and ricotta cheesecake with chocolate chips.

Yum Yum Tree

At the Lahaina Cannery, 1221 Honoapiilani Hwy. ☎ **808/667-7437.** Reservations only for 10 or more. Main courses $5.25–$11.95. AE, DC, DISC, JCB, MC, V. 7am–10pm daily. AMERICAN.

If you know and love the Yum Yum Tree restaurants in Honolulu as we do, you'll be happy to find another big, comfy one here. Like its Honolulu sister, Maui's Yum Yum Tree serves home-style cooking for breakfast, lunch, and dinner. Prices are very affordable and menus are kept in tune with the times, offering healthful choices as well as traditional favorites. They're all served with french fries or cole slaw, and you can add soup or salad for just 95¢. Pot pies are a house specialty and are made fresh daily; you can even choose to bypass the crust and have the steamy beef, chicken, or turkey stew served over fettucine instead. The Yum Yum Tree is also known for its pies—more than a dozen different flavors are baked daily.

WORTH A SPLURGE

✪ Avalon

844 Front St. ☎ **808/667-5559.** Reservations recommended. Main courses $14.95–$27.95. AE, MC, V. Daily 11:30am–midnight. HAWAII REGIONAL.

Mark Ellman, a highly respected innovator of Hawaii Regional cuisine, continues to provide exuberant and imaginative cuisine at his restaurant in the courtyard of Mariner's Alley. The dining room is decorated with antique Hawaiian shirts and oversize Fiestaware. Using fresh local ingredients, Chef Mark is always trying something new, so you can never tell what delights may be in store. Among the appetizers are such treats as summer rolls, Maui onion rings with a homemade tamarind catsup, and seared sashimi. The signature main course is chill-seared salmon tiki style, a layered salad of mashed potatoes, eggplant, salmon, greens, and salsa with a plum vinaigrette—fabulous! The whole fresh opakapaka in garlic black bean sauce, the Indonesian stir fry, and the mixed seafood grill are also favorites. Vegetarians have about five choices, including the Gado Gado salad, a Balinese dish of raw vegetables on brown rice with peanut sauce and condiments.

Still with us? How can we describe the caramel Miranda, the only dessert offered? Imagine a plate of fresh raspberries and strawberries, framed on one side by an incredibly delicious, thick, warm caramel sauce and on the other side by a giant scoop of Haägen-Dazs macadamia-nut-brittle ice cream. Unforgettable! Depending on the season and the availability of exotic fruit, it might include, instead, coquitos (full-grown minicoconuts from Chile), or Kula blackberries and huckleberries. If you don't get to have dinner here, at least come by afterward for coffee and desserts (about $5). Lunch is well priced, under $15.

✪ David Paul's Lahaina Grill

187 Lahainaluna Rd. ☎ **808/667-5117.** Reservations required. Main courses $13.95–$24.95. AE, MC, V. Dinner daily 6pm–closing; wine tastings and complimentary cheese Mon–Fri 5pm. NEW AMERICAN.

David Paul Johnson is considered one of the rising young stars of Hawaii's culinary firmament; his charming restaurant, newly expanded and prettier than ever, is a must for those who seek out truly imaginative fare. Readers of *Honolulu Magazine* have voted it "Best Restaurant on Maui" two years in a row. The menu is eclectic and ever changing, but you're likely to find such signature items as spicy crab cakes and pan-fried Pacific oysters among the appetizers; tequila shrimp and firecracker rice (marinated tiger prawns with a blend of vanilla bean and chili rice), kalua duck, or an unusual Kona coffee–roasted lamb among the main courses. For dessert, it could be sweet red-chili carrot cake or triple berry pie with créme fraîche and berry sauce.

There's an excellent wine list, and every evening at 5pm David Paul's offers complimentary cheese and specially priced wines by the glass; these tastings give customers the chance to "judge" wines that are being considered for their list. There's nightly entertainment. Children are welcome.

PICNIC FARE

The Bakery

991 Limahana Place. ☎ **808/667-6062.** Pastries from 95¢; breads from $1.25; sandwiches $2.50–$4.50. No credit cards. Mon–Sat 5:30am–3pm, Sun 5:30am–noon. BREADS/PASTRIES/SANDWICHES.

Next to the train depot is a "Maui secret;" many of the fine restaurants in town get their bread and pastries here. The Bakery is a popular spot, crowded with locals who come early in the morning for the best croissants around, and brioches and pain au lait hot from the oven. Chocolate–cream cheese croissants and coconut macaroons are memorable. They've been known for years for their fabulous French bread in many shapes and sizes, but now they're doing a fantastic assortment of natural and whole-grain breads as well; these stay fresh much longer than conventional loaves, so you can buy one and have great sandwiches and morning toast for days. They also offer gourmet-quality deli items and sandwiches to go. It's worth stopping by just to inhale the aromas!

Mr. Sub

129 Lahainaluna Rd., near Front St. ☎ **808/667-5683.** Sandwiches $2.50–$6.50. No credit cards. Mon–Fri 7am–5pm, Sat 7am–4pm. SANDWICHES/SALADS.

Long one of Honolulu's most popular submarine shops, Mr. Sub is repeating its quality act in Lahaina, with wonderfully fresh ingredients, seven varieties of breads and rolls, huge sandwiches, great salads, quick service, and low prices. You can eat right in their air-conditioned shop, but the best bet is to choose from the 31 combination sandwiches (or create your own combination) and head for your picnic. Special picnic packages, with coolers for the beach, include a sandwich, chips, fruit, and a drink, and run about $5 to $7. Call them the day before, and everything will be ready for pickup by 7am.

KAANAPALI BEACH

The strip of luxury hotels along Kaanapali Beach boasts but very few restaurants, where the budget diner can relax. Some worthy exceptions:

MEALS FOR LESS THAN $15

⑤ Kaanapali Beach Hotel Koffee Shop

2525 Kaanapali Pkwy. ☎ **808/661-0011.** Reservations not required. Breakfast buffet $6.95; lunch buffet $6.95; afternoon deli buffet $5.95; dinner buffet $11.95. Early Bird buffet 4–6pm $9.95. Breakfast daily 6–10:45am; lunch daily 11am–2pm; afternoon deli buffet daily 2–4pm; dinner buffet daily 4–9pm. BUFFETS.

Quality food is served buffet style here all day long, and at very low prices. Plan to catch the dinner buffet and work it in with the free Sunset Hula Show, held nightly at 6:30pm. Authentic Hawaiian live entertain-ment continues until 9pm at the Tiki Terrace. Both lunch and dinner buffets feature a choice of six main courses (including fish, chicken, beef, pork), a salad-soup-and-fruit bar, rice, vegetables, desserts, and beverages; in addition, the dinner buffet offers prime rib. During the afternoon deli buffet, you can help yourself to soup, salad, and desserts, and fix your own sandwiches. Breakfast features fresh pineapple and papaya, eggs, pancakes, french toast, sausage, ham, muffins, and more.

MEALS FOR LESS THAN $25

Cook's at the Beach

In The Westin Maui Resort, 2365 Kaanapali Pkwy. ☎ **808/667-2525.** Reservations not accepted. Main courses $7.75–$29; breakfast buffet $14.95; prime rib buffet $23.95. AE, CB, DC, DISC, MC, V. Breakfast daily 6:30–11am; lunch daily 11:30am–2pm; dinner buffet daily 6–9pm; brunch Sun 9am–2pm. AMERICAN.

It's worth the price of admission just to see the spectacular grounds of this hotel, with its waterfalls and islands and tropical lagoons, but it's also reasonable for the whole family to eat poolside at Cook's at the Beach, which even has a kid's menu, for $3.50 to $4.75. But the real knockout here is the prime rib buffet, a fabulous spread featuring unlimited roast beef carved to order, plus fresh local seafood, salads, and desserts. While you're feasting, enjoy a free hula show every night (except Sunday) at 7pm. True seafood lovers should opt for the seafood buffet at the Villa in the same hotel. The $24.95 meal features freshly cut sashimi, lomi-lomi salmon, steamed Alaskan snow crab legs, and catch of the day.

Tiki Terrace

In the Kaanapali Beach Hotel, 2525 Kaanapali Pkwy. ☎ **808/661-0011.** Reservtions suggested for brunch and dinner. Main courses $15.95–$22.95. Breakfast buffet $11.95; Sunday champagne brunch $18.95. AE, CB, DC, DISC, MC, V. Breakfast Mon–Sat 7–11am; dinner daily 6–9pm; Sunday champagne brunch 9am–2pm. HAWAIIAN/LOCAL.

Because the Kaanapali Beach Hotel is the most Hawaiian of Maui hotels—both the hotel and its restaurant have won recognition for their contribution to the preservation of traditional Hawaiian culture—it's no surprise to find the Native Hawaiian Diet on the menu at the attractive indoor-outdoor Tiki Terrace. Nutritionists now realize that the ancient Hawaiians had very healthy eating habits. Basically, their diet consisted of lots of poi, taro in other forms, sweet potatoes, bananas, and fish; its updated version includes some chicken and plenty of raw fruits and vegetables. (A local friend reports she went on the diet for 1½ years, lost 25 pounds, and felt great!) You can sample their Native Hawaiian Diet (complete dinner $17.95), or dine on more familiar favorites. Two award-winning chefs (grand prize winners Hawaii Seafood Festival) turn out succulent seafood and fish preparations every night (all fresh fish dinners are $19.95), as well as meat, poultry, and vegetarian specialties in both traditional and Hawaiian interpretations. Salad bar is included with all main courses; and is generous enough to stand on its own as a very moderately priced meal ($9.95). For appetizers, we like to go with the Maui-onion lumpia or the trio of raw Hawaiian seafood. The festive Sunday champagne brunch (with music by Polihale from 10am to 2pm) includes a whole rotisseried pig and other Hawaiian favorites; you'll see plenty of local people partaking. There's a hula show at 6:30 each evening, and an authentic Hawaiian trio plays from 6 to 9:30pm.

WHALER'S VILLAGE

There's a salty but slick flavor to this handsome complex of shops and museums; you can be sure that old-time seamen never had food as good as you'll find here.

MEALS FOR LESS THAN $15

Chico's Cantina & Cafe

In Whaler's Village. ☎ **808/667-2777.** Reservations recommended. Main courses $8.95–$11.95. AE, MC, V. Lunch daily 11:30am–2:30pm; dinner daily 5–10:30pm. Taco Bar 11:30am–11pm. AMERICAN/MEXICAN.

The atmosphere is tropical and the menu is half-Mexican, half-American. On the Mexican side, there are fajitas, enchiladas, burritos, and all the rest; and such specialties as carnitas, carne asada, pollo asada, and mahimahi done in the style of Veracruz. American favorites feature mango fettuccine and smoked chicken, London broil, Cajun shrimp, plus chicken and ribs barbecues, sandwiches, salads, burgers—a menu to please many tastes. If you come by during happy hour from 3 to 7pm, you can enjoy $2.50 margaritas, draft beer for $1.50, and a generous portion of nachos for only $2.90! There's Mexican music during lunch and dinner; rock 'n' roll late night and during the 3 to 7pm happy hour. A fun spot.

MEALS FOR LESS THAN $20

✪ Hula Grill

At Whaler's Village. ☎ **808/667-6636.** Reservations recommended. Main courses $11.95–$22.95 AE, MC, V. Dinner nightly 5:30pm to closing. Barefoot Bar menu 11:30am to closing: cocktails from 11am to closing. HAWAII REGIONAL SEAFOOD.

Question: What do you get when you combine one of Hawaii's best chefs and one of Hawaii's most successful restaurant chains? Answer: Hula Grill. Peter Merriman, the "Pied Piper" of Hawaii Regional cuisine (his original restaurant is in Waimea, on the Big Island) joined forces with TS Restaurants (Grill & Bar at Kapalua, Kimo's, Leilani's, etc., etc.) to create a beautiful, casual, fun restaurant in yet another spectacular spot—beachfront at Whaler's Village. What you will get here—in addition to glorious sunsets and sand between your toes— is good, fresh, unfussy food (and plenty of it). Tahitian poisson cru, shrimp and ginger wontons, lobster and chipotle chile pepper pizza, grilled opakapaka with Asian black bean and ginger sauce, Peter's wok-charred ahi—the Merriman-signature seafood preparations are all simple, fresh, outstanding. The restaurant itself is a tribute to Hawaii's history, from the 120-year-old outrigger canoe to the kitschy, wiggly hula dancer dolls of the 50s. Something wonderful fills every nook and cranny—you'll feel as if you are dining in the beach home of a friend.

The Rusty Harpoon

In Whaler's Village. ☎ **808/961-3123.** Reservations recommended for parties of six or more. Main courses $14.75–$22.95. AE, DC, DISC, JCB, MC, V. Breakfast daily 8–11am; lunch daily 11am–5pm; dinner daily 5–10pm. CONTEMPORARY AMERICAN.

This old Whaler's Village standby boasts a handsome interior (green colors, beautiful woods, a view of the ocean as well as the kitchen from every table), and a neat menu concept: "nouvelle California–Maui cuisine." And it's still known for excellent value for the dollar. Come for the Early Bird specials, nightly between 5 and 6pm, and for $10.95 you can have dishes like pasta primavera, salsa chicken, prime rib, or fresh fish of the day, including fresh vegetables and rice pilaf or baked potato. Regular dinner main courses include pineapple teriyaki chicken, stir-fry beef, shrimp scampi, and prime rib. Rusty's still has its famous half-pound burgers at $7.50 to $8.25, and there are some super salads for $8.75 to $9.25. Appetizers have an international flavor, from fried mozzarella to kalbi ribs to nachos. Rusty's uses only fresh local produce and makes its own pastas and wonderful desserts. Of course those famous fresh-fruit daiquiris (how about banana or pineapple?) are still there and still make Rusty's the "Daiquiri Capital of the World." There's a full bar, a lively crowd, lots of fun.

KAHANA

MEALS FOR LESS THAN $20

Kahana Keyes Restaurant

4327 Lower Honoapiilani Rd., at the Valley Isle Resort. ☎ **808/669-8071.** Reservations recommended. Main courses $8.95–$19.95. AE, DC, JCB, MC, V. Dinner only, daily 5–10pm. AMERICAN.

Located 3 miles north of the Kaanapali Beach Resort, this has long been a favorite in the Kahana area. People like it because it has one of the best salad bars in the area (reputed to be Maui's largest), plus a variety of Early Bird dinners (from 5 to 7:30pm) including prime rib at $10.95, as well as all-night specials, which include steak and lobster at $16.95. The regular menu features steak and seafood and broiler items; salad bar alone is just $8.50. Every night local bands play contemporary Hawaiian music, plus Top 40 hits and oldies, with dancing until 1:30am. Children's menus are also available.

WORTH A SPLURGE

✪ Roy's Kahana Bar and Grill

4405 Honoapiilani Hwy., at Kahana Gateway. ☎ **808/669-6999.** Reservations recommended. Main courses $15.95–$24.95. AE, DC, JCB, MC, V. Dinner only, daily from 5:30pm. HAWAII REGIONAL.

Honolulu's most highly praised restaurant is also on Maui, and the mood and food are every bit as good—which means wonderful. *Wunderkind* Roy Yamaguchi's executive chef Tod Michael Kawachi blends the best of European and Asian cooking styles and techniques and uses the freshest of local ingredients to produce a new and exciting Hawaiian cuisine. And the setting is upbeat and exciting too—a large room with an open kitchen, wraparound picture windows with views of rolling meadows, paintings by local artists, and gorgeous flowers. Kawachi's innovations are apparent in such main courses as the mesquite-smoked Peking duck and the grilled chicken linguine with feta cheese and Mediterranean-style vegetables. Every night there's a long list of specials, including four or five imaginative fish presentations. And prices are surprisingly modest for food of this caliber; there are always individual pizzas on the menu, at an average price of $6.95. The restaurant is also known for its extremely creative and well-priced wine list, with many offered by the glass. Desserts change every night and are always memorable. No wonder this is one of Maui's hottest dineries.

✪ Roy's Nicolina Restaurant

4405 Honoapiilani Hwy., at Kahana Gateway. ☎ **808/669-5000.** Reservations recommended. Main courses $15.95–$26.50. AE, DC, JCB, MC, V. Dinner only, daily from 5:30pm. HAWAII REGIONAL.

Next door to Roy's Kahana Restaurant is this slightly newer place, showing off the talents of Executive Chef Jacqueline Lau. California-born Lau brings her own natural feel for California-Southwest flavors to Roy's Euro-Asian style, with some delectable results. If you get a chance, try to dine at both Roy's restaurants. Lau's nightly specials might include smoked cheddar chili rellenos and rosemary shrimp bruschetta among the appetizers; basil-kiawe–grilled rack of lamb with blue cheese red potatoes, grilled southwestern chicken with Anaheim chili tortilla hash and smoked tomato sauce, and lemongrass crusted mahimahi with toasted peanut sticky rice, sesame chips, and a roasted banana curry sauce are among the main courses. In addition, there are always a number of vegetarian specialties. Roy's Nicolina does not offer the individual pizzas that Roy's Kahana does, but both oblige with Roy's most famous dessert: the Original Dark Chocolate Soufflé with its liquid chocolate center.

NAPILI

Ⓢ Maui Tacos

Napili Plaza. ☎ **808/665-0222.** Reservations not required. $1–$6.50. No credit cards. Mon–Sat 10am–9pm; Sun 11am–7pm. MEXICAN.

This is the first of what owner Mark Ellman says will be several high-quality Mexican fast-food locations he'll open around the island. (Mark's other restaurant is the immensely popular Avalon in Lahaina.) He has pledged to keep every menu item under $7. The menu is extensive, with all kinds of burritos, enchiladas, tostadas, tacos, chimichangas, and quesadillas. His special hand-held burritos are stuffed with different combinations of rice, black beans, cheese, meats, and veggies. Top your selection with any one of the unusual and freshly made salsas at the salsa bar.

You may bring your own beer or wine. There are a dozen or so seats at the restaurant—or you can grab a taco to go.

By the time you read this, the second Maui Tacos should be open in Lahaina Square, (☎ 808/661-8883) with the same menu and hours of operation (see above).

KAPALUA

⑤ The Market Café

At Kapalua Shops, 115 Bay Dr. ☎ **808/669-4888.** Reservations recommended for dinner. Main courses $5–$15. AE, DC, MC, V. Daily 8am–9pm. AMERICAN.

You'd hardly expect to find any moderately priced eating places in the posh pastures of Kapalua Bay Resort, but here's one: The Market Café, a fun place for all-day dining. Breakfast offers such sophisticated choices as eggs Benedict or béarnaise, lox and bagel with cream cheese, and pancakes cooked with fresh fruit. The "All-Day Dining" menu, available from 11am to 9pm, features a variety of deli sandwiches ($4.95 to $8.95), homemade soups, salads, burgers, and pastas. The "After Five" menu adds various Italian-style main selections, including chicken marsala and several pastas. On Wednesday nights, you can get two pastas for the price of one. Stop by anytime for a fruit smoothie, a variety of wines and beers, tropical drinks, and flavorful coffees from the espresso bar.

✪ Plantation House Restaurant

In the Plantation Golf Course Clubhouse, 2000 Plantation Club Dr. ☎ **808/669-6299.** Reservations recommended. Main courses $16–$23. Breakfast and lunch daily 8am–3pm; dinner daily 5:30–10pm. ISLAND REGIONAL.

There's a traditional, "old Hawaii" feeling about this handsome restaurant; it's reminiscent of the way things were back in the '40s—simple, comfortable, elegant. It sits high on a hill, affording extraordinary 360° views—of the mountains, the ocean, the golf course, and the most spectacular sunsets on Maui. Whitewashed mahogany, tables made of teak, upholstered chairs, original artwork, and a double-sided fireplace dominating the room create the feeling of a warm and cozy lodge. Dinnertime appetizers are great fun, especially the crab cakes with a green-peppercorn-lime mayonnaise and Hawaiian-style sashimi. House specialties among the main courses include fresh local fish in a variety of presentations (we like it charbroiled and served with a shiitake-soy sauce) and double-cut lamb chops. The chef creates new specials every night. Lunch is very reasonable, with such dishes as chicken breast, steak, and wok-fried vegetables going for $6.25 to $9.95, most accompanied by a choice of soup or salad, french fries, or sticky rice. Good sandwiches, salads, and burgers, too. As for desserts, fudge brownies with ice cream and chocolate sauce and the pot de crème au chocolate are decadence personified.

HANA

Outside of the famed—and very expensive—Hotel Hana-Maui, there are very few public restaurants in Hana. The hotel restaurant is wonderful, but very pricey.

✪ Hana Gardenland Cafe

Corner of Kalo Rd. and Hana Hwy., before entering Hana town. ☎ **808/248-7340.** $2.25–$6.75. Reservations not taken. Daily 9am–5pm, same menu all day.

There's such a paucity of restaurants in Hana that almost any new one would be welcome. But when the restaurant happens to be delightful and inexpensive to boot, cheers are in order. The cafe is dripping with baskets of flowering plants and herbs and even Miró puzzles to solve on every table. After you've wandered around, meditated by the lily pond stocked with koi, and visited the tasteful art gallery and gift shop, stop in for something delicious (Hillary Rodham and Chelsea Clinton did).

The cafe serves delicious fresh food, much of it grown on the property. From avocados to starfruit and from herbs to eggplant, whatever is in season is featured on the menu. Breakfasts range from homemade banana bread, served warm with cream cheese and honey, to steamed eggs and salsa served with Maui Crunch toast. Lunch is luscious: huge sandwiches of ahi tuna salad, veggies, and smoked turkey are served with sweet cherry peppers and a pickle spear. Or choose lasagne, salads, quiche, or a house specialty, hanamole and chips. Fresh-picked avocados are made into the cafe's own-style guacamole and served with taro chips—there's more than enough to satisfy at least two people. Yummy! Espresso Bar beverages are $2 to $3. A basketful of brightly colored cloth napkins invites patrons to "Help yourself and place in laundry basket when *pau* (done);" it's just one small indication of the environmental consciousness of the folks here.

There's a special feel and fragrance to the Hana air; Hana Gardenland is an excellent way to experience it, especially for those unable to hike to more remote parts of this magical district.

Hana Ranch Restaurant

☎ **808/248-8255.** Reservations recommended. Main courses $18.95–$37 Lunch buffet $13.95. AE, DC, MC, V. Buffet lunch 11am–3pm; take-out counter 6:30am–6:30pm. Dinner Fri–Sat 6–8:30pm. AMERICAN.

The Hana Ranch Restaurant is the same Hana Ranch complex as the Hotel Hana-Maui. It's a good choice, with an indoor dining room that features a nice buffet lunch for $13.95 (salad bar only, $7.95). Wednesday night is "Pizza Night": choose your own topping for a thick-crust pie; prices range from $7.50 to $19.50. A take-out counter serves up burgers, sandwiches, and hot dogs.

Tutu's

At Hana Bay. ☎ **808/248-8224.** Reservations not accepted. Plate lunches $5.25–$5.50. No credit cards. Daily 8:30am–4pm. LOCAL.

This longtime favorite is the best place for a reasonable lunch (or breakfast). Tutu's specializes in local-style plate lunches, plus very good fresh-fruit salads, green salads, sandwiches (mahimahi is a favorite), and ice cream (try the haupia flavor).

What to See & Do on Maui

It would be nice to have a week or more to spend on Maui. But even if you have only a few days, you can still get to see and experience much of Maui's magic. *Note:* Excellent maps are in the *Maui Drive Guide,* free from your car-rental company.

1 Beaches

By Jeanette Foster

Maui has a plethora of sandy beaches—white, black, salt-and-pepper, even red—including some 33 miles of nearly continuous beaches on the south and west shores. Maui's beaches offer a range of activities for all interests, from riding the surf to lazily floating in warm salt water. The beaches listed below are just some of the more attractive beaches on Maui's shoreline:

HONOLUA BAY/MOKULEIA BEACH

These twin bays are located off Highway 30, just past D.T. Fleming Park (look for the Mokuleia-Honolua Marine Reserve signs). They make up one of the three Marine Life Conservation Districts in Maui County, which means that nothing can be taken (fish, coral, etc.) from the water. Honolua is well known for its world-class surfing in the winter and for excellent snorkeling in the summer. Mokuleia, also part of the protected area, has great bodysurfing (for experts only) in the winter and swimming and snorkeling (for all levels) in the summer. Mokuleia Bay is known as "slaughterhouse beach" by local residents—a slaughterhouse once occupied the cliff above the bay. Few tourists venture down to these beaches in the winter, most preferring to watch the surfing action from the cliffs above. In the summer, the steep access down to the beaches weeds out some beach goers, but the beach is rarely without sunbathers and swimmers on bright sunny days.

D.T. FLEMING BEACH PARK

Want to get away from the crowds? Here's the place to go. This is not always a swimming beach—conditions can be treacherous—but it's great for surfing and bodysurfing in the winter. Fleming Beach is an exquisite white-sand beach bordered with ironwood trees, with a shaded grassy area for picnicking and a view of Molokai just across the channel. This is a place for quiet contemplation, resting, or just listening to the wind singing through the ironwoods. It's located just past Kapalua on Highway 30 (look for the sign). Restrooms, showers, picnic tables, barbecue grills and parking (on the road) are available.

KAPALUA BEACH

At the entrance to Kapalua, off Lower Honoapiilani Road just past the Napili Kai Beach Club, look for a public beach right-of-way sign—this will lead you directly to Kapalua Beach. Formerly known as the Fleming Beach (which is now the name of another nearby beach), this one comes straight out of central casting call for the perfect Hawaiian beach. It's a crescent of white sand bordered by two black rocky points with palm trees providing the shade. Because it's a sheltered bay, swimming and snorkeling are excellent and safe for children. Above the beach is the Kapalua Bay Hotel, so the sand is always packed with hotel guests and local residents. To get a parking space at this popular place, you must arrive early in the day; the beachfront parking lot holds only 30 to 40 cars. Facilities include showers, restrooms, and plenty of shade.

KAANAPALI BEACH

Not surprisingly, one of Maui's best beaches—with granular white sand as far as the eye can see—fronts the elaborate line of hotels and condominiums in Kaanapali. This beach is excellent for summertime swimming. The Kaanapali resort area was built before the public raised a hue and cry over public access, so parking is a problem for non-resort guests. There are two entrances: At the south end, turn off the Honoapiilani Highway into the Kaanapali Resort and pay for parking there; or, continue on the Honoapiilani Highway and turn off at the last Kaanapali exit, at the stop light near the Maui Kaanapali Villas, and park next to the public access beach signs.

⭐ Frommer's Favorite Maui Experiences

Sunrise at Haleakala Crater. Drive up the volcano to catch the spectacular first light of the day from the summit, 10,000 feet above the sea. On your way back down, stop at Sunrise Market and Protea Farm for a hot cup of Kona coffee and a fresh mango muffin.

Snorkeling at Black Rock. There's an underwater world you'll never forget waiting for you just off the white sands of Kaanapali Beach.

Inter-Island Sailing. Sail one of Trilogy Excursions' sleek, multi-hulled yachts from historic Lahaina's harbor to the island of Lanai, where you can explore with local guides and snorkel at the remote Hulupo'e Bay Marine Preserve.

Antique Hunting and Gallery Browsing. Wander through the intriguing array of antique stores in historic Waikulu town, or browse Paia's arts-and-crafts galleries after a relaxing lunch at Halilimaile General Store.

Watching World-Class Windsurfing. Colorful windsurfers and wave jumpers swirl in the wind and pirouette over the waves, high into the air, at Hookipa Beach, one of the most famous windsurfing sites in the world. When the waves are calm, get out your snorkel gear and explore the reef.

Facilities include outdoor rinse-off showers; you can use the restrooms at the hotel pools. Various beach activity vendors line the beach in front of the hotels, offering nearly every conceivable type of ocean recreation activity and equipment. Because the Kaanapali Beach is so long and because most hotels have swimming pools adjacent, the beach is crowded only in pockets—there's plenty of room to find seclusion. A paved beach path offers a comfortable way to stroll along the beach, people watching.

The best place to snorkel is around **Black Rock,** which sits in front of the Sheraton Hotel. The water is nearly always clear, calm, and populated with clouds of tropical fish. Black Rock (or *Puu Kekaa,* as the Hawaiians call it) is known as the place where souls leap into the afterlife. According to Hawaiian tradition, when someone is near death, their soul leaves the body and wanders around, making sure that all their earthly obligations have been fulfilled. If all is right, then the soul proceeds to Puu Kekaa to leap from this world into the next.

KAMAOLE III BEACH PARK

Along South Kihei Road, in Kihei, are three county parks: Kamaole I, II, and III. All are popular with local residents and visitors because they are easily accessible and have good parking. On weekends, all three are jam-packed with fishermen, picnickers, swimmers, and snorkelers, but the most popular of the three seems to be Kamaole III. It is the biggest of the three beaches, with wide pockets of white sand, and it's the only one with a playground for children; it also has the most parking. Other facilities include restrooms, showers, picnic tables, and barbecue grills. Swimming is safe here, but parents should watch to make sure that their children don't venture too far out, as the bottom slopes quickly offshore. The winter waves attract bodysurfers. This beach is also a wonderful place to watch the sunset.

ULUA BEACH

This is the most popular beach in Wailea for a variety of reasons: It's a long, wide, crescent-shaped, white sand beach between two rocky points, and it offers the best snorkeling in Wailea when the ocean is calm.

When it's rough, the waves are excellent for bodysurfers. It's located close to the Wailea Ocean Activity Center, where a variety of rental equipment is available. The ocean bottom is shallow and gently slopes down to deeper waters, making swimming generally safe. Facilities include showers and restrooms. The beach is usually occupied by guests of the nearby Wailea resorts; during the high season (Christmas to March and June to August), the beach is carpeted with beach towels and the ocean is standing room only. To find Ulua Beach, look for the public access sign (Ulua/Mokapu Beaches) on the South Kihei Road in Wailea, near the Stouffer Wailea Beach Resort. A very small parking lot—get there early in the day if you want to get a space—is located nearby.

ONELOA BEACH (BIG BEACH) AT MAKENA

Oneloa means "long sand" in Hawaiian; that's a perfect description of this extraordinary beach, also called "Big Beach" by local residents or "Makena Beach" by visitors. Oneloa is 3,300 feet long and more than 100 feet wide, and it's one of the most popular undeveloped beaches on Maui. To get there, take the Old Makena Highway to the second dirt road, which leads all the way down to the beach. When the ocean is calm, there is good snorkeling around the north end of the beach at the foot of Puu Olai, a large cinder cone that rises 360 feet above sea level. During a storm—there is no protective reef offshore—the waves roll onto the beach with a dangerous rip current. Occasionally, the surf is appropriate for board and bodysurfing, but only by those who are experienced. Under the waves the ocean bottom has a quick, sharp drop-off, that, combined with a strong rip current, spells disaster for inexperienced surfers and swimmers. There are no public facilities, but this is a great place for a picnic and the view of Molokini and Kahoolawe.

On the other side of the cinder cone Puu Olai is a smaller white sand beach, known locally as "Little Beach." Various visitor publications have labeled this beach as a clothing-optional area, but skinny dipping is illegal in Hawaii and occasionally the police conduct "raids" at Little Beach (the charge for nude sunbathing is lewd conduct).

HAMOA BEACH

A couple of miles past Hana, on the way to Kipahulu, is Hamoa Beach (look for the Hamoa Beach turn-off from the Hana Highway). The gorgeous beach is 1,000 feet long, 100 feet wide, and surrounded by 30-foot high lava cliffs. The left side of the beach is the calmest, offering the best snorkeling in the summer. Hamoa is known as a popular surfing and bodysurfing area. This is an unprotected beach, however, vulnerable to the open-ocean, and surf rolls right onto the beach, creating powerful rip currents at times. The upscale Hotel Hana Maui maintains the beach and has numerous facilities for its guests. There is an outdoor shower and restrooms for non-guests. Entrance is via steps. Parking is limited.

WAIANAPANAPA STATE PARK

Four miles before the town of Hana, off the Hana Highway, is Waianapanapa State Park. The park takes its name from the legend of the Waianapanapa Cave, where Chief Kaakea, a jealous and cruel man, suspected his wife, Popoalaea, of having an affair. Popoalaea left her husband and hid herself in a chamber of the Waianapanapa Cave. She and her attendant ventured out only at night, for food. Nevertheless, a few days later, Kaakea was passing by the area and saw the shadow of the servant. Knowing he had found his wife's hiding place, Kaakea entered the cave and killed her. During certain times of the year, the water in the tidepool turns red as a tribute to Popoalaea, commemorating her death. Scientists claim, however, that the water turns red because of the presence of small, red shrimp.

Waianapanapa State Park's 120 acres have 12 cabins, a caretaker's residence, a beach park, picnic tables, barbecue grills, restrooms, showers, a parking lot, a shoreline hiking trail, and a black sand beach (the sand is actually small black pebbles). This is a wonderful area for shoreline hikes—bring insect repellent as the mosquitoes are plentiful—and picnicking. Ocean activities are generally unsafe, though, due to strong waves breaking offshore, which roll into the beach unchecked, and strong rip currents. Because Waianapanapa is crowded on weekends with local residents and their families as well as tourists, weekdays are generally a better bet.

HOOKIPA BEACH PARK

Two miles past Paia, on the Hana Highway, is one of the most famous windsurfing sites in the world. Due to the constant winds and steady supply of waves (especially in the winter), Hookipa attracts the top windsurfers and wave

Beaches & Outdoor Activities On Maui

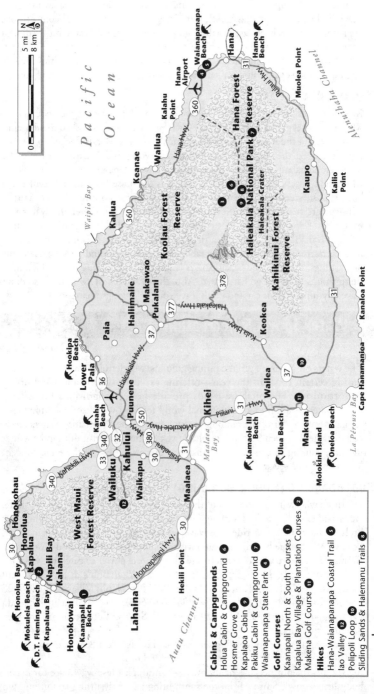

Cabins & Campgrounds
Holua Cabin & Campground ⑥
Hosmer Grove ③
Kapalaoa Cabin ⑨
Pakiku Cabin & Campground ⑦
Waianapanapa State Park ④

Golf Courses
Kaanapali North & South Courses ①
Kapalua Bay Village & Plantation Courses ②
Makena Golf Course ⑪

Hikes
Hana–Waianapanapa Coastal Trail ⑤
Iao Valley ⑫
Polipoli Loop ⑩
Sliding Sands & Halemanu Trails ⑧

Airport ✈

1014

jumpers from around the world. Surfers and fishermen enjoy this small, white-sand beach and surrounding grassy cliff, too. Except when international competitions are being held, weekdays are usually a good time to come and watch the colorful windsurfers swirl in the wind and pirouette over the waves, high into the air. When the waves are absent, snorkelers and divers explore the reef. Facilities include restrooms, showers, pavilions, picnic tables, barbecue grills, and a parking lot.

KANAHA BEACH PARK

Kanaha means "shattered thing," stemming from a Hawaiian legend about a man who stole the eggs of a Hawaiian *Pueo* (owl), and senselessly smashed them against a stone wall in the Kanaha area. Owls from all over the islands flocked to Kanaha and destroyed the man, his family, and everyone living in the area. Today, however, Kanaha is a peaceful place: Shaded lawns slope down to the mile-long, white-sand beach; the only distraction here is the noise from the adjacent Maui airport. On weekends, the park is filled with local families. In the winter, windsurfers from all over the world come here to skim over the water like butterflies. Kanaha Beach is located just before the Kahului Airport—turn left at the sign Kanaha Beach Park, then right on Ahahao Street. Its numerous facilities include restrooms, showers, picnic tables, barbecue grills, and parking. A couple of warnings, though: The beach park is landscaped with *kiawe* trees, which drop sharp thorns, so don't go barefooted. Also, this is an area rife with theft, so don't leave anything in your car and don't leave your belongings unattended.

2 Water Sports & Recreation

By Jeanette Foster

The waters off Maui are prolific fishing grounds, wonderful for swimming, and—during certain times of the year—offering excellent surfing and windsurfing opportunities. The offshore winds provide perfect conditions for sailing. Underwater, you'll find a phenomenal world teeming with exotic marine life—virtually every color of the rainbow is represented. The aquamarine waters are so comfortable that even 30-ton humpback whales choose to visit during the winter months, coming so close to shore that you can often observe these magnificent leviathans "up close and personal."

BODYBOARDING (BOOGIE BOARDING) & BODYSURFING

For those who want to be a part of the waves as they ride the surf into the shore, either bodyboarding or bodysurfing is the sport of choice. When bodysurfing, your body is the vehicle that rides the wave; in bodyboarding, a small, foam board (known as a boogie board) that supports the upper part of your body is utilized. Both sports require a set of swim fins to give you the power to catch the wave.

You can rent boogie boards and fins from **Snorkel Bob's** at three different locations: 34 Keala Pl., Kihei (☎ 808/879-7449); Napili Village Hotel, 5425 Lower Honoapiilani Rd., Napili (☎ 808/669-9603); and 161 Lahainaluna Rd., Lahaina (☎ 808/661-4421) for $29 a week. All Snorkel Bob's locations are open 8am to 5pm daily.

In winter, the best bodysurfing spot on Maui is Mokuleia Beach (known locally as slaughterhouse beach because of the slaughterhouse that once stood overlooking the beach, not because of the waves—although these waves are for expert bodysurfers only). Storms from the south bring fair bodysurfing conditions and great boogie boarding on the lee side of Maui: Oneloa (or Big Beach) at Makena, Ulua Beach in Wailea, Kamaole III Beach in Kihei, Maalaea Beach, Kapalua Beach and D.T. Fleming Beach in Honokahua.

DEEP-SEA FISHING

The waters around Maui are home to many game fish: marlin, tuna, ono (wahoo), mahimahi, and bottom fish. No license is required; all you have to do is book one of the dozens of sport fishing vessels out of Lahaina or Maalaea harbors. Most charter boats troll for big game fish and carry no more than six passengers.

There are a couple of ways to book a charter. You can actually walk the docks at either of the two harbors, inspecting the boats and talking to the captains and crew; or, you can book through an activities desk. For those unfamiliar with fishing in Hawaii, many boats tag and release marlin; other fish caught (tuna, mahimahi, or ono) do not belong to the angler catching the fish, but remain with the captain and crew. If these terms are unacceptable—if you want to keep your fish or a portion of it or you want to take a marlin and have it mounted—you should discuss your desires with the captain in advance (not after the fish has been caught or is struggling at the end of your fishing line).

If you plan to fish out of Maalaea, I recommend **Rhythm & Blues Sportfishing** (☎ 808/879-7098) with Captain Mike Crawford, an experienced fisherman with top-flight fishing gear and a comfortably equipped 36-foot Pacifica sportfishing boat. Or try the activities desk at the harbor, **Maalaea Activities** (☎ 808/ 242-6982), to book any other fishing boat.

In Lahaina, I recommend **Hinatea Sportfishing,** slip 27, Lahaina Harbor (☎ 808/667-7548); **Ace Sportfishing,** Lahaina Harbor (☎ 808/667-7548), which represents 11 sportfishing boats offering both trolling and bottom fishing; or check with **West Maui Charter** (☎ 808/669-6193) for boats that offer everything from light tackle to heavy tackle fishing.

The budget-conscious deep-sea angler should definitely shop around. Prices vary according to the type of boat and the type of fishing, whether you share the boat, and how hungry the charter captain is on any particular day. A shared boat for a half day of fishing starts at $75; this is probably the way to go, as a full-day exclusive boat (you decide who gets to join you on board) can range from $450 to $900.

OCEAN KAYAKING

Glide silently over the water, propelled by just a paddle and your imagination— that's what ocean kayaking is all about. For the uninitiated, Michael and Melissa McCoy of **South Pacific Kayaks,** 2439 S. Kihei Rd., Kihei (☎ 808/875-4848) or 505 Front St., Lahaina (☎ 808/661-8400) offer kayak tours (with snorkeling), which include lessons and a guided tour. Tours run from $2^{1}/_{2}$ to 5 hours, and range in price from $39 to $125. The McCoys also offer kayak rentals starting at $20 a day.

One of the best kayaking spots (when there are no storms) is along the Kihei coast, where there's plenty of easy access to the calm water. Mornings are best, as the wind comes up around 11 a.m., making paddling more difficult.

PARASAILING

Basically, parasailing entails being hooked to a parachute and attached to a tow line behind a boat; when the boat goes, you'll sail hundreds of feet into the air.

But the basics don't describe the spectacular reality of what that entails: panoramic views from high in the sky, the sense of floating, and the free, omniscient feeling of being alone up there. On Maui, parasailing "season" is limited to mid-May through mid-December due to the restrictions placed on boats during the humpback whale season. Hopefully, if you're on Maui during the right time of year and feel a thrillseeker's urge to splurge, you'll have a chance to try this aqua-aerial activity. Rides are 10 to 15 minutes and cost around $40 to $50. Several companies can pick you right up off the beach. Call **UFO Parasail** (☎ 808/661-7UFO); they have a self-contained "winch" boat, which allows you to stand on a platform at the back of the boat. As your parasail fills, you are reeled out some 200 to 400 feet. After 10 to 15 minutes, they reel you back in—you never touch water.

SAILING

The blustery winds that funnel through the isthmus between Haleakala and the West Maui Mountains past Maalaea, as well as the constant trade winds off the Lahaina coast, make sailing from Maui a pleasurable and often exhilarating opportunity. Every type of boat you can dream of—from a three-masted schooner to spacious trimarans, from boats that take on only 6 passengers to those carrying 146 passengers—is available. Many types of sailing adventures are available: Sail for the sheer pleasure of feeling the wind filling the sails, to a destination (like Lanai), or just to see the sun set or enjoy a special dinner.

My favorite (and, in my mind, the best) Hawaii sailing trip is offered by **Trilogy Excursions,** 180 Lahainaluna Rd., Lahaina, (☎ 808/661-4743). Operated by the Coon family, with their fleet of custom-built, comfortable, multi-hull sailboats. Trilogy offers day-long trips to Lanai and memories for a lifetime. Your trip begins with homemade cinnamon rolls as the stable vessel makes its way to Lanai. The crew takes time to provide personalized instruction on how to snorkel in Hulopoe Bay, a Marine Conservation District. After a little snorkeling, they prepare an island-style barbecue lunch, then offer a van tour of the island. The price of $139 for adults and $69.50 for children is worth every penny.

Or, you can sail out of Maalaea Harbor to Molokini on a classic 60-foot topsail pilot schooner with **Maui Classic Charters** (☎ 808/879-8188). This restored vessel (built in 1926) offers whale watching and sunset trips as well. Sail/snorkel Molokini trips cost in the $56 to $66 range.

For shorter trips, try **Kamehameha Catamaran Sails,** Lahaina Harbor, slip number 67 (☎ 808/661-4522). This 40-foot Hawaiian beach catamaran offers regularly scheduled sailing and snorkeling trips with snacks, soft drinks, free snorkeling equipment, and free use of an underwater camera—just bring your own film. Cost, depending on the length of the trip, runs from $24 to $34.

SCUBA DIVING

Diving on Maui means not only accessing the Maui coast line, but nearby Molokini, Kahoolawe, Lanai, and Molokai, as well. Unforgettable dive opportunities are found at Molokini, a 160-foot wide, crescent-shaped crater with three tiers of diving: a 35-foot plateau inside the crater basin (used by beginning divers and snorkelers), a wall sloping to 70 feet just beyond the inside plateau, and a sheer wall on the outside and backside of the crater that plunges to 350 feet. This is the most popular dive site in the state due to calm, clear, protected water—it's an underwater park—and an abundance of marine life (from manta rays to clouds of butterfly fish).

The second most popular dive site in the state is known as Cathedrals, off the south coast of Lanai. Just a 45-minute boat ride from Lahaina, this dive site is known the world over for its majestic topography. The Cathedrals earned its name from the way the light shines through a lattice of coral, looking much like the stained glass windows in a magnificent church. The parishioners here are a multitude of tropical fish. In the choir loft are crustaceans and invertebrates, and occasionally the confessional houses a white-mouth moray eel.

Since most visitors have limited time on their Maui vacation to enjoy these underwater wonders, I suggest taking a dive class at home, so that you are prepared to dive when you get to the islands. If you don't have an opportunity to prepare before you arrive, most dive operators offer what they call an introductory dive. No experience is necessary, and the cost ranges from $40 to $95; you can learn from this glimpse into the Neptunian world if diving is for you.

For personalized diving, I recommend **Ed Robinson's Diving Adventures,** Kihei (☎ 808/879-3584). This widely published underwater photographer offers specialized charters for small groups. The majority of his business is repeat customers, for good reason. Ed offers two-tank dives for $85. In Lahaina, call **Lahaina Divers,** 143 Dickenson St., (☎ 808/667-7496), one of Maui's few Five-Star PADI-IDC facilities, offering every sort of diving service and instruction you could possibly need.

Maui's largest diving retailer, with everything from rentals to scuba diving instruction to dive boat charters, is **Maui Dive Shop.** Maui Dive can be found all over the island: in Kihei at Azeka Place II Shopping Center (☎ 808/879-3388), Kamaole Shopping Center (☎ 808/879-1533), and Kihei Town Center (☎ 808/879-1919); in Lahaina at Lahaina Cannery Mall (☎ 808/661-5388) and 626 Front St. (☎ 808/667-0722). Other locations include: Wailea Shopping Village (☎ 808/879-3166), Whalers Shopping Village, Kaanapali (☎ 808/661-5117), Kahana Gateway, Kahana (☎ 808/669-3800), and 444 Hana Hwy., Kahului (☎ 808/871-2111).

SNORKELING

You don't have to strap on scuba tanks and swim down to 60 feet in order to enjoy the underwater world on Maui. A mask, snorkel, and fins are all you need to paddle around with the colorful clouds of tropical fish like convict tang (which the Hawaiians called *manini*), light green fish with black (convict-like) vertical stripes running the width of their bodies. Or, you might see one of Hawaii's unique native fish, the saddle wrasse (*hinalea lauwili*), with its purple head and wide orange stripe intersecting a dark green body.

If you have never snorkeled before, most resorts and excursion boats offer snorkeling equipment and lessons. If you are unsure of yourself in the water, you can use flotation devices to buoy up your courage. A word of caution, though: many people become so fascinated with the underwater world that they forget that the sun is slowly simmering them through the cool ocean water. Be sure to use water-resistant sunscreen, or better yet, wear a T-shirt.

Mask, fins, and snorkel can be rented from dozens of dive shops and activity booths. The best deals, though, are at **Snorkel Bob's**—not only do you get mask, fins, and snorkel for $15 a week, but ol' Bob will throw in a bag, a snorkeling map, fish food (not recommended—feeding fish in the wild can have deleterious effects), no-fog goop for your mask (although spitting in it works just as well), and a fish identification card. Prices go up for prescription masks and higher-end gear, but they're still a deal. Snorkel Bob's can be found at three different locations: 34 Keala Pl., Kihei (☎ 808/879-7449); Napili Village Hotel, 5425 Lower Honoapiilani Rd., Napili (☎ 808/669-9603); and 161 Lahainaluna Rd., Lahaina (☎ 808/661-4421).

Generally, you can snorkel in front of the hotel or condo where you are staying. Summer, when the water is calm, is generally the best time for snorkeling. Mornings are also best, because local winds don't generally increase until around noon. A few words of advice: Always snorkel with a buddy, and look up from the underwater world every once in a while to see where you are, how far off shore you are, and if there is any boat traffic. Do not touch anything; not only can you damage coral, but there are a few camouflaged fish and shells with poisonous spines that you wouldn't want to contact. And lastly, ask before you go—check with your hotel or a dive shop about the area you want to snorkel in (what you should look for, if there are any dangerous conditions you should know about) and the predicted weather and surf conditions.

If you want to take a snorkel excursion to Molokini or Lanai, check with the **Ocean Activities Center,** 1847 S. Kihei Rd., Kihei (☎ 808/879-4485), which also operates out of a number of hotels and condominiums. They can book you on the most appropriate boat for the type of snorkeling experience you want. Snorkeling cruises usually run about $50. For the ultimate snorkeling trip, see **Trilogy Excursions** (☎ 808/661-4743) under "Sailing" (above).

Or, you can just rent your own gear and go exploring. Maui's best snorkeling beaches include Kapalua Bay (adjacent to the Kapalua Bay Hotel); Black Rock (in front of the Sheraton-Maui Hotel in Kaanapali); along the Kihei coast line, especially Kamaole Beach Park III; and along the Wailea coast line, particularly at Ulua Beach.

SNUBA

Snuba is a new water sport that sort of combines snorkeling and scuba diving. You can explore the underwater world without the experience and bulky equipment required by scuba; you have a mask and an air hose connected to the tank, which rides in a floating sled on the surface. The disadvantage of Snuba is that you are limited to 20 to 25 feet (as far as the air hose will reach). Since Snuba is a relatively new sport, there are few operators. **Maui Classic Charters** (☎ 808/879-8188) offers Snuba for an extra $50 on their charters to Molokini.

SUBMARINE DIVING

For those who would like to explore the underwater world without getting wet, **Atlantis Submarines** (☎ 808/667-2224), out of Lahaina Harbor, offers a once-in-a-lifetime journey into Neptune's world. A shuttle boat takes passengers out to the submarine. Once you're on board, the comfortable, U.S. Coast Guard–licensed sub, 65 feet long and weighing 80 tons, gently enters the marine world. It levels off at 150 feet below the waves in the Auau Channel between Maui and Lanai. Rides on this futuristic vessel are $79 for adults and $39 for children.

If 150 feet below raises your blood pressure or if you are on a tight budget, try the **Nautilus Semi-Sub,** also out of Lahaina Harbor (☎ 808/667-2133). Sort of a cross between a submarine and a glass-bottom vessel, the Nautilus is a surface boat with an underwater viewing cabin. Hour-long trips cost $45.

SURFING

Even if you have never seen a surfboard before, surf instructor Andrea Thomas says she can teach you. Her classes at **Maui Surfing School** (☎ 808/875-0625) have instructed thousands in the art of riding the waves. She backs her classes with a guarantee that you'll be surfing or you'll get 110% of your money back. Two-hour lessons are $55 and available by appointment only.

For surf experts, visit Maui in the winter when the surf's up. The best surfing beaches include: Honolua Bay; Lahaina Harbor (in the summer, there'll be waves just off the channel entrance with a south swell); Maalaea (a clean, world-class left); and Hookipa (watch out for the sailboards when the wind is up). Surfboards can be rented from **Hunt Hawaii Surf and Sail** in Paia (☎ 808/575-2300) starting at $20 a day.

WHALE WATCHING

From December to April, Hawaii's most impressive visitors—45-foot humpback whales—come to spend the winter. They make the journey from Alaska to calf and mate in Hawaii's calm, warm waters. Once nearly hunted to extinction, humpback whales are now protected by federal law. Individuals or watercraft are not allowed to approach the animals within 100 yards.

Whales can frequently be seen off the leeward side of the island (and, on calm days, sometimes off the windward side). If you spot the recognizable spout of water—a sign the whale is exhaling—there's a good chance you will see the animal come to the surface. If you are in a car, please pull over, as numerous accidents have occurred when visitors try to spot whales and drive at the same time.

For a closer glimpse of whales, contact the **Pacific Whale Foundation,** 101 N. Kihei Rd., Kihei (☎ 808/879-8811). This is a non-profit organization that not only studies the animals, but also offers whale-watching tours; all proceeds go to whale research. Cost for the cruise is $27.50 and $15 for children.

If all their tours are booked, try **Windjammer Cruises** (☎ 808/661-8600), **UFO Whale Express** (☎ 808/661-7836), and **Island Marine Activities, Inc.** (☎ 808/661-8397). Prices average $30 for adults and $16 for children.

WINDSURFING

Maui has the best windsurfing beaches in the state. Hookipa, known all over the globe for its brisk winds and excellent waves, is the site of several world championship contests. Kanaha also has dependable winds, and—when conditions are right—it's packed with colorful butterfly-like sails. During the winter, the town of Paia becomes windsurfing central, with windsurfers from around the world flocking there to check out the wind, the waves, and those who ride them.

Complete equipment rental (board, sail, rig harness, and roof racks) are available from $35 to $45 a day to $200 to $250 a week. Lessons, from beginning to advanced, range in price from $60 to $75 for a 2- or 3-hour lesson. **Hawaiian Island Windsurfing,** 415 Dairy Rd., Kahului (☎ 808/871-4981), offers everything from lessons and rentals to full-service repairs. Other shops featuring rentals and lessons are **Hawaiian Sailboarding Techniques,** 444 Hana Hwy., Kahului, (☎ 808/871-5423); **The Maui Windsurf Co.** (520 Keolani Pl., Kahului, (☎ 808/877-4696); and **Second Wind Windsurfing,** 111 Hana Hwy., Kahului, (☎ 808/877-7467).

For daily reports on the wind and surf conditions call the **Wind and Surf Report,** 808/877-3611.

3 Hiking, Golf & Other Outdoor Activities

By Jeanette Foster

HIKING

Maui is nothing if not majestic, from the top of its 10,000-foot dormant volcano, Haleakala, to the whispering waves sweeping its shorelines. In the past couple of decades, Maui has grown from a rural island to a fast-paced resort destination, but there are still many places of breathtaking beauty that can be explored only on foot.

For more information on Maui hiking trails and to obtain free hiking maps, contact **Haleakala National Park,** P.O. Box 369, Makawao, HI 96768 (☎ 808/ 572-9306), and the **State Division of Forestry and Wildlife,** 52 S. High Street, Wailuku, HI 96793 (☎ 808/243-5352). For information on trails, hikes, camping, and permits for state parks, contact: **Hawaii State Department of Land and Natural Resources,** State Parks Division, P.O. Box 1049, Wailuku, HI 96793 (☎ 808/243-5354).

The **Hawaiian Trail and Mountain Club,** P.O. Box 2238, Honolulu, HI 96804, offers an information packet on hiking and camping in Hawaii. Send $1.25, plus a legal-sized, self-addressed, stamped envelope for information. Another good source for hiking information is the *Hiking/Camping Information Packet* from **Hawaii Geographic Maps and Books,** 49 S. Hotel Street, Suite 218, Honolulu, HI 96813 (☎ 808/538-3952); it's available at a cost of $7, which includes postage.

Those interested in seeing the backcountry—complete with virgin waterfalls, remote wilderness trails, and quiet meditative settings—should contact Ken Schmidt at **Hike Maui,** P.O. Box 330969, Kahului, HI 96733 (☎ 808/ 879-5270). Ken not only has lived on Maui for 17 years (three years living on the land, sleeping under the stars, and existing on wild fruits, vegetables, and roots), but he knows Maui's backcountry like some people know their living room. He's an excellent guide, historian, botanist, geologist, and storyteller of ancient legends. A few days with Ken can teach you how to locate a safe place to camp, how and what to eat in the wilderness, and what to watch out for. He has more than 50 different kinds of trips for small groups, ranging in price from $75 per person for a half-day tropical valley hike to $110 for the trip of a lifetime into Haleakala.

Some of Maui's best hikes are:

POLIPOLI LOOP

One of the most unusual hiking experiences in the state can be found in Polipoli State Park, which is part of the 21,000 acres of the Kula and Kahikinui Forest Reserve on the slope of Haleakala. First of all, at 5,300 to 6,200 feet, where the hiking takes place, it's cold (even in the summer). Second, this former forest of native *koa, ohia,* and *mamane* trees (which was overlogged in the 1800s) was reforested in the 1930s with introduced species: pine, Monterey cypress, ash, sugi, red alder, redwood, and several varieties of eucalyptus. The result is a cool area, with muted sunlight filtered by towering trees. At Polipoli, it's hard to believe that you're in Hawaii.

The Polipoli Loop is an easy, 5-mile hike that takes a little over 3 hours; dress warmly for it. To get there, take the Haleakala Highway (Hwy. 37) to Keokea and turn right on to Hwy. 337. After less than a half-mile on Hwy. 337, turn on Waipoli Road. The road climbs swiftly. After 10 miles, Waipoli Road ends at the Polipoli State Park campgrounds. The well-marked trail head is next to the parking lot, near a stand of Monterey cypress; the tree-lined trail offers the best view of the island.

Polipoli Loop is really a network of three trails: Haleakala Ridge, Plum Trail, and Redwood Trail. After a half-mile of meandering through groves of eucalyptus, blackwood, swamp mahogany, and hybrid cypress, you'll join the Haleakala Ridge Trail. About a mile into the trail, Polipoli Loop joins with Plum Trail (named for the plums that ripen in June and July); this trail passes through massive redwoods and by an old Conservation Corps bunkhouse and a rundown cabin. Just after the cabin, the Polipoli Loop continues on Redwood Trail, which climbs through Mexican pine, tropical ash, Port Orford cedar, and—of course—redwood.

Camping is allowed in the Polipoli State Park with a permit from the **Division of State Parks,** P.O. Box 1049, Wailuku, HI 96793 (☎ 808/243-5354). There is one cabin that is available by reservation.

SLIDING SANDS & HALEMAUU TRAILS, HALEAKALA NATIONAL PARK

The view into the Haleakala Crater looks like a cross between a barren lunarscape and the backdrop to the 1950s B-movie *The Angry Red Planet.* The view from the top, however, is nothing compared with the experience of hiking into the throat of the dormant volcano. The crater has some 32 miles of marked hiking trails, two camping sites, and three cabins. The terrain ranges from burnt-red cinder cones to ebony-black lava tubes.

The best hikes here are Sliding Sands Trail, which begins on the rim at 9,800 feet and descends into the belly of the beast—to the crater floor at 6,600 feet; and the hike back out, Halemauu Trail. This is a difficult hike and should be done in two days. Only the hardiest hikers should consider making the 11.3-mile one-way descent, which takes 9 hours, and the equally long returning ascent, in one day.

The descending and ascending trails are not loops. In fact, the trail heads are miles apart. Arrangements need to be made in advance to provide transports between the two. The best thing to do is to arrange to stay at least one night in the park (two or three nights would allow more time to actually explore the fascinating interior of the volcano). There are cabins in the National Park which must be booked at least three months in advance. Contact **Haleakala National Park,** P.O. Box 369, Makawao, HI 96768 (☎ 808/572-9306). Camping permits are available on a first-come, first-served basis at the park headquarters.

A word of warning before you head up the mountain: The weather at nearly 10,000 feet can change suddenly and without warning. Come prepared (no matter how beautiful it is at the time) for cold, high winds, rain, even snow in the winter, by bringing boots, waterproof wear, warm clothes, extra clothing layers, and lots of sunscreen—at 10,000 feet the sun shines very brightly.

Stop at the park headquarters on your way up to get information regarding camping and hiking. Day hikers must register for the hike down Sliding Sands Trail at the box near the Haleakala Visitor Center. The trailhead to Sliding Sands is well marked and the switchback trail over ash and cinder rocks is easy to follow. As you descend, look around—the view of the entire crater is breathtaking. In the afternoon, waves of clouds flow into the Kaupo and Koolau gaps. Vegetation is spare to nonexistent at the top, but the closer you get to the crater floor the more vegetation you see: bracken ferns, pili grass, shrubs, and even flowers appear. On the crater floor the trail travels through flat, ash-covered flows of basalt and cinder-covered cones, passing by rare silversword plants, volcanic vents, and multi-colored cinder cones. Leading out, the Halemauu Trail goes over red and black lava, past vegetation like evening primrose, as it begins its ascent up the crater wall. Occasionally, riders on horseback use this trail as an entry and exit from the park. The proper etiquette is to step aside and stand quietly next to the trail and let the horses pass.

HANA-WAIANAPANAPA COASTAL TRAIL

This is an easy 6-mile trail that takes you hiking back in time. Allow 4 hours to walk along this relatively flat trail, which parallels the sea, along lava cliffs and by a forest of hala tress. The best time to take the trail is either in the early morning or late evening, when the light on the lava and surf makes for great photos. Midday is the worst time for the hike; not only is it hot (lava intensifies the heat) but there is no shade and no potable water.

There is no formal trailhead; the trail can be joined at any point along the Waianapanapa Campground and traversed in either direction. Along the trail, you'll see remains of an ancient *heiau* (temple), stands of lauhala trees, caves, a blowhole, and a remarkable plant, *naupaka,* that flourishes along the beach. Upon close inspection, you'll see that the naupaka have half-blossoms only. According to Hawaiian legend, a similar plant living in the mountains has the other half of the blossoms. One ancient explanation for this is that the two plants represent never-to-be-reunited lovers: As the story goes, the two lovers bickered so much that the gods, fed up with their incessant quarreling, banished one lover to the mountain and the other to the sea.

IAO VALLEY

This is the easiest hike on Maui—you can take your grandmother on this half-hour long, ¹/₂-mile loop on a paved trail. Iao Valley—with its famous landmark, the Iao Needle (actually a volcanic ridge) rising to 2,250 feet—is a massive green amphitheater ringed by chiseled cliffs and topped by seemingly perpetual clouds. At the back of this amphitheater is the 5,788-foot high rain-drenched Puu Kukui, the West Maui Mountains' highest point. Iao is a historic valley, where Kamehameha the Great defeated Kalaikupule, chief of Maui, in 1790. The Maui warriors, prepared to fight with spears and clubs, were mowed down by Kamehameha's cannons (supplied by the English). The result was a bloody massacre that was said to have clogged the Iao Stream with bodies.

The easily accessible paved trail wanders through the park and over a footbridge crossing the Iao Stream. This leisurely walk will allow you to enjoy lovely views of the needle and the lush vegetation. Go early in the morning or after 4pm to avoid the hoards of tour buses, which deposit hundreds at the park during the day.

GOLF

The golf courses on Maui are so popular that Maui has been acclaimed as "the gold coast of golf." Challenging and breathtakingly beautiful courses offer a range of golfing opportunities for everyone, from duffer to professional; even for budget-conscious travelers, a day at one of these dream courses might be worth the splurge if golf is your thing. Make your tee time reservations early so you won't be disappointed. All the courses listed below include the required cart rental fee in the greens fee; most offer twilight fees.

KAPALUA BAY, VILLAGE AND PLANTATION GOLF COURSES

Even if you don't play golf, the views from these three championship courses are worth the drive to the Kapalua Resort. The first of the 54 holes to open was the Bay Course, a par-72, 6,761-yard course inaugurated in 1975. Designed by Arnold Palmer and Ed Seay, this course is a bit forgiving with its wide fairways. The greens, however, are difficult to read. The well-photographed 5th overlooks a small ocean cove; even the pros have trouble with this rocky par-3, 205-yard hole.

The Village Course, another Palmer/Seay design, is a par-71, 6,632-yard course that opened in 1980. The most scenic of the three courses, the hole with the best vista definitely is the 6th, which overlooks a lake with the ocean in the distance. But don't get distracted by the view—the tee is between two rows of Cook pines.

The Plantation course, scene of the Lincoln/Mercury Kapalua International and the Kirin Cup World Championship of Golf, is Ben Crenshaw–Bill Coore designed. A 6,547-yard, par-73 course on a rolling hillside of the West Maui Mountains, this one is excellent for developing your low shots and precise chipping.

Facilities for the three courses include locker rooms, driving range, and an excellent restaurant. Greens fees at the Village Course and the Bay Course are $110 and fees at the Plantation are $120; twilight rates are available for budget-conscious travelers. Fifty-four holes gives you a better chance at getting a tee time; weekdays are best. Call 808/669-8044.

KAANAPALI NORTH AND SOUTH GOLF COURSES

From high handicappers to near-pros, both Kaanapali courses offer a challenge. The North Course (originally called the Royal Lahaina Golf Course) is a true Robert Trent Jones Sr. design: an abundance of wide bunkers, several long, stretched-out tees, and the largest, most contoured greens on Maui. The par-72, 6,305-yard course has a tricky 18th hole (par-4, 435 yards) with a water hazard on the approach to the green. The South Course, a par-72, 6,250-yard, is an Arthur Jack Snyder design; although shorter than the North Course, it does require more accuracy on the narrow, hilly fairways. Just like its sister course, the South Course also has a water hazard on its final hole—don't tally up your score card until the final putt is sunk. Options include driving range, putting course, lunch at the clubhouse, and 9-hole twilight rate. Greens fees are $120; weekday tee times are best. For information call 808/661-3691.

MAKENA GOLF COURSE

Here you'll find 36 holes of "Mr. Hawaii Golf" (Robert Trent Jones Jr.) at its best. Add to that spectacular views: Molokini Crater looming in the background, humpback whales cavorting offshore in the winter, muted tropical sunsets, and sailboats lazily cruising in the nearshore waters. This is a golf course not to be missed. The par-72, 6,876-yard South Course has a couple of holes you'll never forget. The view from the par 4 15th hole, which shoots from an elevated tee 183 yards downhill to the Pacific, is magnificent. The 16th hole has a two-tiered green that is blind from the tee 383 yards away (that is, if you make it past the gully off the fairway). The par-72, 6,823-yard North Course is more difficult and more spectacular. The 13th hole is located partway up the mountain with a view that makes most golfers stop and stare. The next hole is even more memorable: a 200-foot drop between tee and green. Facilities include clubhouse, driving range, two putting greens, pro shop, lockers, and lessons. Beware of crowded conditions on weekends. Greens fees are $80 for Makena Resort guests and $110 for non-guests; twilight rates are available. Call 808/879-3344.

OTHER OUTDOOR ACTIVITIES

BICYCLING

Bicycling on Maui means cruising down the 10,000-foot volcano Haleakala from the lunar-like landscape at the top, past flower farms, pineapple fields, and eucalyptus groves. **Cruiser Bob's Downhill Bicycle Tour,** 99 Hana Hwy., Paia (☎ 808/579-8444 or 800/654-7717), was the original operator busing people up to the top of the volcano and letting them "cruise" back down. This is a safe, comfortable, no-strain bicycle trip for everyone, from the kids to grandma. The $120 trip includes hotel pick up, transportation to the top, the bicycle and safety equipment, and meals. If Cruiser Bob is booked, call **Maui Downhill,** 199 Dairy Rd., Kahului (☎ 808/871-2155).

HORSEBACK RIDING

Maui offers spectacular adventure rides through rugged ranch lands, into tropical forests, and to remote swimming holes. For a day-long tour on horseback—complete with swimming and lunch—call **Adventure on Horseback,** Makawao (☎ 808/242-7445 or 572-6211); the cost is $130 per person. Or, ride from sea level to the cool pastures of upcountry Maui for a personal tour of Tedeschi Winery with **Makena Stables,** 7299 S. Makena Rd. (☎ 808/879-0244), for $145 per person. If you are out in Hana, **Oheo Stables,** Hana Hwy., Kipahulu (☎ 808/667-2222), has relaxed, casual rides through the mountains above Oheo Gulch (Seven Pools) for $95.

If you'd like to ride down into Haleakala's crater, contact **Pony Express Tours** in Kula (☎ 808/667-2200). Pony Express offers half-day rides down to the crater floor and back up, lunch included, for $120 per person. A full-day ride, at $140 per person, explores the crater floor extensively. Gentler one- and two-hour rides are also offered at Haleakala Ranch, located on the beautiful lower slopes of the volcano, for $35 and $60. All levels of riding experience are accommodated; Pony Express provides well-trained horses and experienced guides. In order to ride, you must be at least 10 years old, weigh no more than 230 pounds, and be wearing long pants and closed-toe shoes.

If you enjoy your ride, kiss your horse and tip your guide.

SPECTATOR SPORTS

Maui's two most popular spectator sports are outrigger canoe racing and polo. Every weekend from Memorial Day to Labor Day, canoe races are held on Maui. Hundreds of residents, from children to grandparents, participate in the island-wide canoe races held at different harbors and bays every week. For information on the canoe race schedule, check the local papers.

Every weekend from September through November, spirited polo is played on Maui. Spend a pleasant afternoon picnicking on a grassy lawn as the polo players from nearby ranches compete. For information on times and places of polo matches, call 808/244-3530. The grand event of the year is the Michelob Polo Cup and Barbecue, an exhibition match of the highest-rated players, which takes place at the Olinda Outdoor Polo Field in Makawao (☎ 808/877-3987 or 808/661-4685).

Other spectator sporting events include:

BASKETBALL In December, top college teams participate in the Maui Invitational Basketball Tournament at the Lahaina Civic Center (☎ 312/755-3577).

GOLF Several golf tournaments take place on Maui, including the Asahi Beer Kyosan Golf Tournament at the Wailea Golf Course in February (☎ 808/879-4465), the Kaanapali Classic Senior PGA Golf Tournament in October (☎ 808/661-3271), and the Kapalua International Golf Championship in November (☎ 808/669-0244).

RODEO Makawao Statewide Rodeo on the Fourth of July and the Maui County Rodeo Finals in November, both at the Oskie Rice Arena in Makawao (☎ 808/572-9928).

RUNNING Maui Marathon in March (☎ 808/661-3271), Haleakala Run to the Sun—a 36-mile race up a 10,000-foot volcano in August (☎ 808/871-6441) and the Hana Relay, a 54-mile team relay run from Kahului to Hana (☎ 808/871-6441).

Beholding Paradise from the Air:
Helicopter Tours of the Valley Isle

Although these tours may be beyond your budget, you might want to indulge yourself and splurge on a helicopter trip from Kahului Airport—it could prove to be your most memorable Maui experience. Many residents don't love the helicopters because of their noise and their impact on the fragile environment, but in 1994 the Federal Aeronautics Administration (FAA) instituted more stringent minimum-altitude regulations in order to address these concerns.

The three most reliable helicopter tour operators are:

Sunshine Helicopter, Kahului Airport (☎ 808/871-0772, or toll free from the mainland and other islands 800/544-2520), may well be the best budget choice, since they offer standby rates of 50%. They also offer a budget $59, 20-minute tour of the West Maui Mountains, including a look at the incredible "Wall of Tears," a spot where 17 waterfalls converge. Their deluxe tour, which circles the island, is certainly value-priced at $159. A 40-minute Hana–Haleakala tour is only $99. Tours are provided in Japanese, German, and Spanish as well as English. Fares include a videotape of your adventure, and Sunshine boasts Maui's only four-camera video system; thanks to their in-cabin camera, you can actually see yourself flying!

Papillon Helicopters, Kahului Airport (☎ 808/877-0022, or toll free from the mainland 800/367-7095, toll free from other islands 800/272-3403), has been operating for more than 16 years on Maui and is well recommended. Prices range from a low $69 for a 30 minute tour of the West Maui Mountains to $149 for a 65-minute tour of West Maui and the stunning shores of Molokai. All flights include a videotape of your trip.

At **Hawaii Helicopters,** Kahului Airport (☎ 808/877-3900, or toll free from the mainland 800/346-2403, or toll free from other islands 800/994-9099), prices range from $89 for a half-hour tour of either the West Maui Mountains or Mt. Haleakala to $250 for a 2¹/₂-hour detailed tour of the island *and* a champagne picnic in Hana. If you can afford the splurge, you'll have an adventure to remember. Once again, a complimentary video is part of the deal.

TENNIS   Kapalua Junior Vet/Senior Championships in May (☎ 808/669-5677), Lahaina Junior Summer Tournament in August (☎ 808/661-8173), Kapalua Open Tennis Championship in September (☎ 808/669-5677), and the Kapalua Betsy Nagelson Pro-Am Tennis Invitational in November (☎ 808/669-5677).

WINDSURFING   Marui/O'Neil Invitational in April at Hookipa (☎ 808/572-4883) and the Aloha Classic (☎ 808/579-9765), also at Hookipa, in October and November are spectacular spectator events, even if you know nothing about windsurfing.

YACHT RACING   In even-numbered years, the Victoria-to-Maui Yacht Race arrives at Lahaina Harbor in June (☎ 808/661-3557).

TENNIS

Maui County has excellent tennis courts located all over the island. All are free and available from daylight to sunset; a few even have night lights, allowing play to continue until 10pm. The courts are available on a first-come, first-served basis. When someone is waiting for a court, please limit your play to no more than 45 minutes. For a complete list of all public tennis courts, contact: **Maui County of Parks and Recreation,** 200 S. High St., Wailuku, 96793 (☎ 808/243-7232).

Private tennis courts are available at most resorts and hotels on the island. The **Kapalua Tennis Garden and Village Tennis Center,** Kapalua Resort (☎ 808/669-5677), is home of the Kapalua Open, featuring the largest purse in the state, on Labor Day weekend and the Kapalua Betsy N. Aglesen Tennis Invitational Pro-Am in November. Court rentals are $10 an hour for resort guests and $12 an hour for non-resort guests. In Wailea, the **Wailea Tennis Club,** 131 Wailea Iki Pl. (☎ 808/879-1958), has both grass and plexi-pave courts. Court rentals are $10 a day for paved courts and $20 a day for grass courts for resort guests, and $15 a day for paved courts and $25 a day for grass courts for non-resort guests.

4 Exploring Central Maui: Kahului & Wailuku

KAHULUI AREA

Kahului is too new to have any historic sights, but it's considered a good example by city planners of what a model city should be. Kahului boasts the only deep-water harbor on Maui, a bulk-sugar-loading plant, the cannery of the Maui Pineapple Company, and the Hawaiian Commercial and Sugar Company, the driving force behind the town's development (most of the homes belong to plantation workers). If you want to get a head start on seeing Maui's windsurfers do their stuff, drive to **Kanaha Beach Park,** next to the airport (go down the road from the Alamo Car Rental building heading toward the beach and turn right). Surfboard rentals and lessons are also available (see "Beaches" and "Water Sports and Recreation" earlier in this chapter).

SHOPPING

KAAHUMANU SHOPPING CENTER   A better name for Maui's biggest shopping complex, located at 275 Kaahumanu Ave., might be Ala Moana No. 2. Like its Honolulu counterpart, it has Sears at one end, Liberty House at the other, and J.C. Penney and that fascinating Japanese department store, Shirokiya, in between. Some of the delightful locally owned stores here include **Tiger Lily,** with

Central Maui

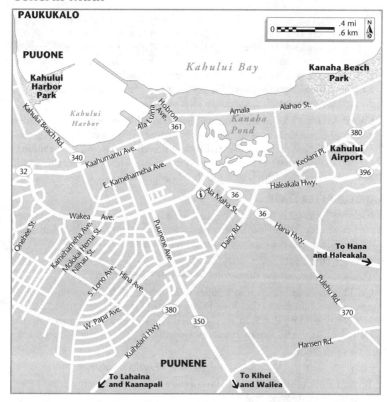

PAUKUKALO

women's clothing in exotic natural fabrics; **Shapers,** a surf shop that features the cutting edge in surf fashion as well as the leading names in surfboard craftsmanship; and **Maui Hands,** which shows an in-depth array of handcrafted works by local artisans.

Penthouse at Liberty House, like its Honolulu namesake, features closeout merchandise—designer clothing, shoes, linens, towels, and the like—from various Liberty House stores. You never know what great bargains you might find here.

You can get island prints by the yard, well priced, at **Sew Special,** which also has some wall hangings that would make neat gifts. You might find some saké cups to take home with you, or charming Hakata dolls, at **Shirokiya,** which also has those wonderful sushi take-out lunches we told you about in the preceding chapter. In case you haven't sampled crackseeds yet, **Camellia Imports** is the place.

Kaahumanu Center is open Monday through Friday from 9:30am to 9pm, Saturday from 9:30am to 5:30pm, and Sunday from 10am to 5pm.

MAUI MALL   It's also fun to visit the Maui Mall, located at 52 Kaahumanu Ave., a community-style shopping center, more value oriented and with more local flavor than its large competitor just up Kaahumanu Avenue. There are frequent sidewalk sales and free entertainment; check the local papers for details. Lovely umbrellaed tables and chairs are placed throughout the area.

Look for the kiosk called **Crystal Dreams,** which has lots more than crystals. We spotted some chimes made of crystal, brass, and copper that start at about

$8.75 and go up to about $50, and lots of lovely jewelry, including beige shell nerite leis, very rare, mostly from the South China Seas, for about $30.

You can stock up on groceries at **Star Super Market,** where the locals shop; if you're going to be cooking in your kitchenette apartment, it pays to stop here after getting off the plane before driving on to the more expensive resort areas. Stop in at **Maui Natural Foods** for anything and everything in the health-food line; it's the most complete store of its kind in the area.

SWAP MEET   Flea-market fans will have a good time here. Every Saturday morning from 6:30am to noon, vendors gather next to the post office on Puunene Street to sell everything from vegetables and flowers to new and used clothing, jewelry, beautiful baskets and sculptures, exotic items from all over the world. Always worth a stop. Check with your hotel desk to make sure it's on.

KAHULUI AFTER DARK

Nightlife is limited in this area; your best bet is in the big hotels. Check the shopping centers for free Polynesian shows, presented several times a week. Maui Mall, for one, sometimes presents top revues from Honolulu clubs—free.

East West Dining Room

170 Kaahumanu Ave., in Maui Palms Hotel. ☎ **808/877-0071.** No cover.

On Thursday and Friday from 8:30pm to midnight, it's karaoke. (This is video taped for public access cable TV on Friday nights.) On Saturday from 9:30pm to 1:30am, it's The Sakuras, a very popular musical group, playing Top 40, Hawaiiana, Japanese, country music, and more.

Red Dragon Room

170 Kaahumanu Ave., in Maui Beach Hotel. ☎ **808/877-0051.** No cover.

The mood is more mod than Hawaiian; a DJ keeps the crowd happy on Saturday from 10:30pm to 2:30am.

Luigi's Pasta and Pizzeria

At Maui Mall, 52 Kaahumanu Ave. ☎ **808/877-3761.**

This busy family eatery is always a popular place at night. There's disco Wednesday (Ladies Night) and Thursday from 10pm to 1:30am. Karaoke is on Friday and Saturday.

WAILUKU AREA

Historic old Wailuku, the commercial and professional center and the seat of Maui County (which also includes Molokai and Lanai), is quite different from Kahului—even though it's right next door. It's a bit ramshackle, strictly local. It's great fun for browsing and antiques shopping (see below), and for inexpensive dining at local greasy spoons (see Chapter 9).

WAILUKU

Maui Historical Museum

2375-A Main St. ☎ **808/244-3326.** $3 adults, $2.50 seniors and students, $1 children. Mon–Fri 10am–4pm. Directions: Drive westward along Kaahumanu Avenue out of Kahului about 3 miles; you'll pass the Maui Professional Building at High Street on the right, and then, about a block farther, to the left on Iao Road, you'll reach the museum.

These buildings, on beautiful shaded grounds, once housed the Wailuku Female Seminary (where young females could be kept safely "away from the contaminating influences of heathen society") and the home of Edward Bailey, the seminary instructor. Today they are full of fascinating bits of Hawaiiana, from ancient petroglyphs and necklaces of human hair worn by the alii of Maui to missionary patchwork quilts and furnishings. Dating back to 1833–50, the building itself was completely restored in 1974–75, and is an excellent example of Hawaiian quality work and Yankee ingenuity. The smaller building, once the dining room of the school and later Bailey's studio, has been restored as a gift shop.

WAIKAPU

Maui Tropical Plantation
Hi. 30, Waikapu. ☎ **808/244-7643.** Admission to the Plantation is free; Tropical Express tour, $8 adults, $3 children. Daily 9am–5pm. The Tropical Express tour leaves every 45 minutes, 10am–4pm.

Not far from Wailuku, in the sugar-plantation village of Waikapu, you can sightsee, shop, eat, and have an educational experience—all under one roof (or better yet, one sky)—at Maui Tropical Plantation. This showplace and marketplace for the tropical agriculture of the islands offers free admission to its agricultural pavilions and exhibits, but charges $8 for a 45-minute tour aboard the Tropical Tram, which traverses some 50 acres planted in bananas, papayas, coffee, pineapple, macadamia nuts, sugarcane, and other crops. What we like best about this place is the Tropical Market, where a huge variety of made-on-Maui products, plantation-grown fresh fruit, and gift items are available. And a mailing service makes it easy to send gifts back home. Mailing service is also available at their Tropical Nursery, where you can get orchids, hibiscus, or anthuriums.

There are dining and entertainment possibilities here as well. The Tropical Restaurant offers a buffet luncheon and à la carte service for light meals. A Hawaiian Country Barbecue, including a quick tram ride through the fields, takes place every Tuesday, Wednesday, and Thursday at 5pm, featuring Buddy Fo and his Hawaiian Country Band. Dinner is an all-you-can-eat Hawaiian tropical feast. Cost is $48.90 for adults, $20.80 for children. Inquire about transportation available from Lahaina/Kaanapali and Kihei/Wailea for the Hawaiian Country Barbecue.

IAO VALLEY

Drive down Hi. 30 in the direction of Iao Valley, and about 2 miles from Wailuku, on the right, you'll note a sign reading BLACK GORGE PRESIDENT KENNEDY PROFILE. The jagged mountain cliff ahead of you, which does bear a resemblance to JFK's profile, has been there for centuries, but not until relatively recently, of course, did people begin to notice its timely significance.

In another mile you'll come to Iao Valley, a wildly beautiful gorge dominated by the **Iao Needle,** 2,250 feet of green-covered lava rock reaching straight up into the sky. In this dramatic setting, Kamehameha won the battle that was to give him the island of Maui; the local warriors, accustomed to spears and javelins, were no match for Kamehameha's forces supplied with a cannon by two English sailors. The carnage was so intense that the waters of Iao Stream were dammed up by the bodies of the conquered, giving the stream is present name: Kepaniwai, "damming of the waters." Now all is tranquil here, save for the shouts of happy keikis wading through the pools at **Kepaniwai Park,** where present-day Mauians love to go for a picnic or a swim. Beautifully landscaped gardens with Asian pagodas, swimming, and wading pools provide a palatial playground in this crisp mountain valley. For an easy hike here, see "Hiking" earlier in this chapter.

PUUNENE

The Alexander & Baldwin Sugar Museum

3957 Hansen Rd., Puunene. ☎ **808/871-8058.** $3 adults, $1.50 students 6–17, free for children under 6. Mon–Sat 9:30am–4:30pm. Directions: From Kahului, take Hi. 350 to Hi 311 toward Kihei. The museum is at the Hansen Road intersection.

This former residence of superintendents of the mill (still in operation next door) has been transformed into an award-winning museum with artifacts dating back to 1878, absorbing photo murals, and authentic scale models, which include a working model of sugar-factory machinery. Educational for the kids, entertaining for grown-ups too. Be sure to visit the museum shop, with unique items relating to the sugar industry and plantation life, including contributions of the various ethnic groups who came to the islands to work the plantations.

SHOPS & GALLERIES

Shopping in Wailuku is offbeat. Shops are unpretentious, not a bit touristy. Antique lovers will be in heaven at **Antique Row,** a cluster of shops and galleries on North Market Street offering one-of-a-kind items from around the globe as well as from times gone by. **The Iao Theater,** the oldest theater in the state of Hawaii, currently undergoing major renovation to become the focal point of the town, is right here. Next to the theater, at 62 N. Market, is **Traders of the Lost Art,** where you might find owner Tye Hartall, unless he happens to be on one of his yearly journeys to New Guinea to collect ancestral carvings and primitive ritual art. His shop is reminiscent of a New Guinea spirit house, complete with split drums, crocodile tables, and a host of spirit masks and figures. Up front is more contemporary stuff: exotic silk shirts from Asia, tropical oil paintings and vintage Hawaiian prints, antique furniture and jewelry.

Memory Lane, at 158 N. Market St., is where Joe Ransberger shows the unusual and one-of-a-kind items he's collected from all over the world. Joe specializes in American artists—originals, lithos, stone engravings, woodblock prints—and also has a good collection of Hawaiiana. He has those "silky" aloha shirts, starting at about $15 and going as high as $350. **Alii Antiques,** 139 N. Market St., is known for its fine collection of Asian art from the Ming and Ch'ing dynasties, as well as items from Europe and the mainland. A recent browse turned up antique guns from the Civil War, Persian rugs, paintings by local artists.

More antique and offbeat emporiums are in store for this neighborhood, so if antiques are your thing, be sure to save some time for exploring this area.

Gima Boutique

21 Market St. ☎ **808/242-1839.**

Elaine Gima is undoubtedly Maui's—perhaps Hawaii's—foremost silk artist, and her extraordinary hand-painted garments have won major crafts awards. Now she's opened her own shop in Wailuku, and while her pricier creations may not be within reach, there are, surprisingly, many affordable things here, like cotton T-shirts with hand-painted silk appliqués for $34. Any of her men's silk ties with Hawaiian motifs or her fanciful scarves would make fine presents, from $28 to $48.

Jovian Gallery

7 Market St. ☎ **808/244-3660.**

Gallery owner Marcia Godinez not only shows some of Maui's best contemporary artists here, she also has a line of unusual jewelry, writing papers, art notecards, contemporary greeting cards, koa boxes, and much more, in every price range.

Shell's Bag's Hats

In the Wailuku Industrial Park. ☎ **808/669-8349** (call first).

Have you always wanted a genuine Panama hat—not the imitation that passes for the real thing? Shell Hansson, who has been making hats in Maui for over 20 years, recently gave up his Lahaina retail store location and now invites customers to his warehouse, where they can see how genuine Panama straw handcrafts are made in the time-honored fashion. Hansson also has scads of other chapeaux—every known type of hat weave, including Maui lauhala, for men, women, and children. Most hats run $3 to $40 and up; prices are very competitive and the value is excellent. He asks you to phone first, as he is not in the warehouse at all times.

5 The Kihei-Wailea Coast

Just past the end of Kihei, the road takes you into one of the most beautiful planned destination resorts in the islands. Should you like to see how the other half lives, by all means, visit some of the splendid, multimillion-dollar resorts here; they are examples of island indoor-outdoor architecture at its best. You definitely must make a stop at the **Grand Wailea Resort Hotel & Spa,** opened a few years ago to the tune of $800 million. Explore the spectacular grounds, note the Ferdinand Botero sculpture garden, stop in for a reasonably priced meal at Café Kula (spa cuisine with a special menu for children) or at the charming Bistro Molokini. Spa Grande is equal to the best in Europe, and, surprisingly, many of their treatments are quite affordable. Should you happen to be in the area on a Tuesday or Friday at 10am, treat yourself to a complimentary tour of the resort's art collection. Led by a Maui artist schooled in art history, the tour highlights the collections of Picasso, Leger, Botero, and Warhol, while explaining the lore behind the many works depicting Hawaiian legend and history. Then you'll want to visit the **Maui Inter-Continental Wailea Resort,** newly redone to make it more Hawaiian in feeling and more gracious than ever: Its Hula Moon Restaurant, decorated with artwork and poetry of Don Blanding, is a delight. **Stouffer Wailea Beach Resort,** a AAA Five-Diamond winner for more than 10 years, has beautiful grounds, splendid artworks, the cute little Maui Onion for an inexpensive meal, Raffles and the Palm Court for superb breakfasts and dinners. **Four Seasons Resort Wailea** is exquisite, like a never-ending flower garden indoors and out. Stop by, have a drink or a meal at any of these places, stroll the beach (all beaches are public in Hawaii), and enjoy a taste of *la dolce vita,* Hawaii style.

Drive a little farther and you can explore the **Makena Resort Maui Prince Hotel,** very modern and elegantly understated. Two waterfalls run down into the central courtyard and lead to the Japanese rock garden. You may want to stop in at the Café Kiowai on the garden level for an exotic dessert and a cup of coffee. Better yet, come back on a Sunday morning for one of the most elaborate and exquisite Sunday brunches in Maui ($29.95 including champagne).

Shopping

While there's nothing remarkable about shopping in the Kihei-Wailea area, shopping malls are going up at a great rate, so you could easily spend an hour or two browsing, before—or after—the beach.

AZEKA PLACE & AZEKA PLACE II   You'll find these twin malls, owned by an old Maui family, located in the heart of Kihei. **Azeka Place,** 1280 S. Kihei Rd. (oceanside), is where you'll find the gift boutique **Rainbow Connection.** Admire the handmade, hand-painted porcelain jewelry, the volcanic glass jewelry, and the unique craft items created by Maui residents. Right next door is **Island Memories,** which specializes in quality Hawaiian-made products and collectibles. You can pick up swimwear and casual aloha wear at **Leilani's** and original resort wear at Tropical Tantrum.

Azeka Place II, 1279 S. Kihei Rd. (mountainside), is where you'll find **Maui's Best,** which features locally made crafts: handmade jewelry, potpourri oils and creams, koa-wood boxes, Christmas-tree ornaments, great hand-painted T-shirts—all reasonably priced. And Texas customers swear the macadamia-nut popcorn and macadamia-nut brittle is even better than the kind at Neiman-Marcus! **Maui Dive Shop** offers scuba and snorkeling gear, beachwear, and even charter-boat dive trips. Discover rare and exotic shells, shell jewelry, and gift items right next door at **La Pre Shells and Gifts.**

MARKETS   If you're in Kihei on a Wednesday, Friday, or Saturday morning, visit the **Kihei Open Air Marketplace,** an enjoyable flea market held at 1945 S. Kihei Rd., next to McDonalds, from 8am to 3pm. Or stop in at the **Kihei International Marketplace,** located between the Foodland Supermarket and the 76 Gas Station. Open daily from 9am to 6pm, it's worth a visit anytime you're driving by. At both of these markets you can find everything from T-shirts to works by local artisans, all at great prices.

Pick up some Molokai watermelon, Hana sweet corn, or other locally grown produce at the **Maui Farmers Market,** on Tuesday and Friday from 2 to 5:30pm on the grounds of the Suda store. Cheeses, juices, and freshly baked breads are also available. (The farmer's market moves to Honokawai, in West Maui, on Monday and Thursday from 7:30am to 1:30pm.)

THE KIHEI-WAILEA COAST AFTER DARK

There are several luaus to choose from in this area. Check local listings when you arrive; prices, days, and entertainers change frequently.

Wailea's Finest Luau (☎ 808/879-1922 for reservations) takes place on Tuesday, Thursday, and Friday evenings at 5pm at the oceanfront Luau Gardens at the Maui Inter-Continental Wailea Resort. A lavish buffet meal precedes the colorful Polynesian Revue featuring Paradyse and Ka Poe O Hawaii. Adults pay $52; children 6 to 12, $26.

If it's a Thursday, it must be the luau at the **Stouffer Wailea Beach Resort** (☎ 808/879-4900 for reservations). A traditional Hawaiian party held in a beachfront garden setting at 6pm. Adults pay $52, children under 12, $28.

Grand Wailea Resort
3850 Wailea Alaniu Dr. ☎ **808/875-1234.**

The scenery here is so spectacular that you really don't need any other entertainment, but watching the sun go down in the Pacific from the lounge of Humuhumunukunukukuapua's restaurant, which "floats" on its own saltwater lagoon, is one of the greatest shows on the islands. The price of one of Humuhumu's 32 custom-made tropical drinks is the only cost.

Maui Prince Hotel
5400 Makena Alanui. ☎ **808/874-1111.** Admission free.

A "Mini-Hula" show is performed poolside Monday, Wednesday, and Friday, 6 to 8pm.

The Kihei-Wailea Coast

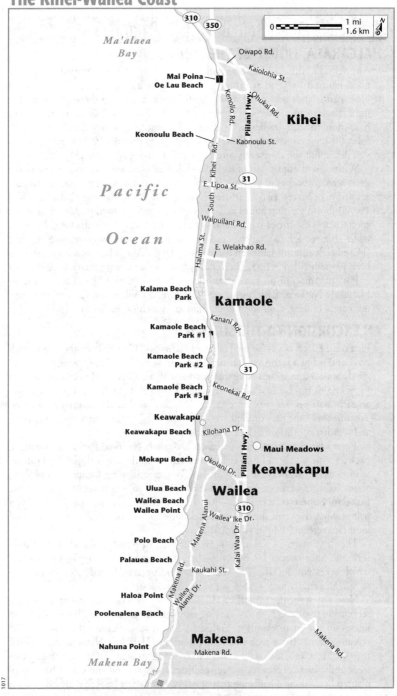

Ma'alaea Bay

310 350

Owapo Rd.

Kaiolohia St.

Mai Poina
Oe Lau Beach

Ohukai Rd.

Piilani Hwy.

Kenolio Rd.

Kihei

Keonoulu Beach

Kaonoulu St.

Pacific

Kihei Rd.

South

E. Lipoa St.

31

Ocean

Halama St.

Waipuilani Rd.

E. Welakhao Rd.

Kalama Beach
Park

Kamaole

Kanani Rd.

Kamaole Beach
Park #1

Kamaole Beach
Park #2

31

Kamaole Beach
Park #3

Keonekai Rd.

Keawakapu

Keawakapu Beach

Kilohana Dr.

Piilani Hwy.

Maui Meadows

Mokapu Beach

Okolani Dr.

Keawakapu

Ulua Beach

Wailea

Wailea Beach
Wailea Point

Makena Alanui

Wailea' Ike Dr.

310

Kalai Waa Dr.

Polo Beach

Palauea Beach

Kaukahi St.

Haloa Point

Makena Rd.

Poolenalena Beach

Wailea
Alanui Dr.

Nahuna Point

Makena

Makena Rd.

Makena Bay

Makena Rd.

0   1 mi
1.6 km

N

1017

6 Haleakala National Park & Upcountry Maui

HALEAKALA, HOUSE OF THE SUN

Any schoolchild on Maui can tell you the story of the demigod Maui, the good-natured Polynesian Prometheus who gave human beings fire, lifted the Hawaiian Islands out of the sea on his fishhook, and trapped the sun in his lair until it agreed to move more slowly around the earth—so that his mother could have more time to dry her tapa before night came. And where did this last, most splendid achievement take place? Why, right at Haleakala, 10,023 feet up in the sky, just about the closest any Stone Age person—or god—ever got to the sun.

With or without benefit of legends, Haleakala is an awesome place, one of the great scenic wonders of Hawaii. It's the world's largest dormant volcano (its last eruption occurred two centuries ago), whose 33-mile-long, 24-mile-wide, 10,000-foot-high dimensions make Vesuvius seem like a mud puddle. Even more spectacular is the size of the volcano's great cinder desert, 7$^{1}/_{2}$ miles long, 2$^{1}/_{2}$ miles wide—big enough to swallow a modern metropolis within its moonlike expanse. (Haleakala's summit has been carved away by erosion. The summit valleys have been partially filled in by later eruptions and are dotted with many small craters.)

For information on camping, hiking, bicycling, and horseback riding in Haleakala National Park, please see "Camping & Wilderness Cabins" in Chapter 9 and "Hiking, Golf and Other Outdoor Activities" earlier in this chapter.

AN EXCURSION TO THE SUMMIT

Plan on at least 3 hours for the Haleakala excursion (37 miles from the airport each way) and bring a warm sweater or jacket with you—it gets surprisingly cold and windy almost 2 miles up. Note that anyone with a cardiac condition is advised not to make this trip because of the stress of the high altitude. We feel it's best to get an early start on this trip, since there's less likelihood of clouds early in the day. You might call the park headquarters (☎ 808/572-7749) to check on cloud, road, and weather conditions before you start out.

There's no place to eat once you enter **Haleakala National Park,** but you might pack a picnic lunch and stop at **Hosmer Grove** on the lower slopes. You can get sandwiches at **Subway,** in the Pukalani Terrace Shopping Center, in Pukalani, about halfway between Kahului and the park. You might also stop off at the **Pukalani Superette,** a real upcountry store, where you can get mangoes for about half of what they cost in town, plus delicious homemade sushi and lumpia, and local Japanese and Filipino delicacies.

The drive starts in Kahului on Hi. 32; head eastward to the Hana Highway (Hi. 36). Shortly after Hi. 36 swings left, it's intersected on the right by Hi. 37, which takes you to Hi. 377, where you head up into a cool forest of flowers, cactus, and eucalyptus.

Now watch for the turnoff to Hi. 378 to the left, Haleakala Summit Road, a serpentine two-lane highway curving through the clouds. You'll see cattle and horses on the pasturelands of Haleakala Ranch as you climb the slopes of the volcano. At 6,700 feet, you reach the entrance to Haleakala National Park. You'll then see Hosmer Grove on the left, a scenic place to picnic (or camp) among rare trees and plants. Temperate tree seedlings from around the world have been planted here, along a half-mile trail of native shrubs and trees that are home for a variety of birds; you may see a pueo (short-eared owl) or a ring-necked pheasant.

Haleakala National Park

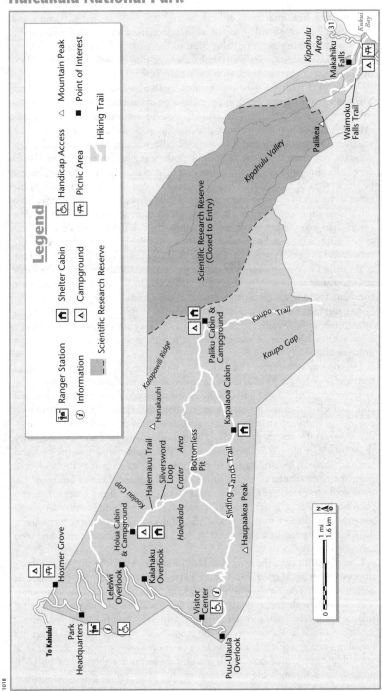

Stop at **park headquarters** a mile ahead at 7,030 feet, where the friendly and knowledgeable rangers will give you maps, instructions, directions for hiking the trails, and camping permits. Admission to the park is $4 per car and $2 per bicycle. The choicest way to see Haleakala is to go into the volcanic desert on foot or horseback; it's best to check with the rangers before you do.

Now you're ready for the ascent on this South Seas Everest, to the **Haleakala Visitors Center,** almost 2 miles up, on the edge of the crater. Inside the observatory, you learn that the early Hawaiians used the volcano as a highway across eastern Maui, camping in its caves and building rock shelters. The last eruption was just 200 years ago, and it's very likely the volcano will erupt again; it is *dormant,* not extinct. But the most thrilling show is what lies beyond the glass: a dark kaleidoscope of clouds and colors and light played against what might well be the deserts of the moon. On a clear day you can see over 100 miles to the horizon, your field of vision encompassing 30,000 square miles of the Pacific; from this altitude, the volcano's vast cones look like so many sand dunes. Their rustlike colors change as the day grows old. At sunrise the volcano is in shadow; it seems to give birth to the sun. From midday to sunset the play of sun and shadow is more subtle, and sunset, according to some, is the most muted and lovely of all. One of the easiest ways to get a spirited debate going among Mauians is to ask whether sunset or sunrise is more superlative at Haleakala; suffice it to say that both are considered among the great natural sights of the world.

The summit of Haleakala is half a mile beyond, at **Red Hill,** atop a cinder cone 10,023 feet high. Nearby, there's a satellite-tracking station and the Haleakala Observatories (the clear air here in mid-Pacific permits research that could be done nowhere else).

On the way down from Haleakala, you should stop for some different—and spectacular—views at Kalahaku and Leleiwi lookouts. At **Kalahaku Lookout,** you view the vast cinder desert on one side; on the other you'll spot western Maui and your first silverswords. The silversword is a botanical rarity, a plant that grows at the highest altitudes. These curious, oversize cousins of the sunflower have sword-like leaves, and when they're ready to blossom (between June and October) they shoot up a stalk up to 6 feet high. The whole thing turns into a tower of pink and lavender flowers, blooms once, and dies, scattering its seeds into the cinders to begin the phenomenon all over again. At the next lookout, **Leleiwi Lookout,** you may, with great luck, get to see the rather spooky specter of the Brocken; the sun must be strong at your back with misty clouds in front of you in order for you to see your own shadow in the rainbow mist. It doesn't happen often, but when it does, it's unforgettable; a ranger told us that he has seen it many times, and with several rainbows!

Coming down from the heights of Haleakala, it's pleasant to stop on the lower slopes at **Sunrise Market and Protea Farm,** near the beginning of Haleakala Summit Road. You can have a free sample of Maui pineapple, buy some sandwiches, homemade fudge, or local fruits, and get a cup of coffee and a muffin (maybe mango or banana or walnut) to go with it. If you like, take your picnic lunch out to the tables surrounding the protea fields outside. Sunrise Market has just about the best prices around on the operation; this is a good chance to walk around and see protea growing (several protea farms dot these Maui uplands; protea are becoming a big commercial crop). Their protea gift shop displays fresh protea bouquets, as well as dried arrangements, and crafts, which can be shipped home.

MAKAWAO

On your way back down from Haleakala, it's easy to visit Makawao, Maui's very own cowboy town, the scene of the Famed Makawao Rodeo every Fourth of July. Turn right at Pukalani and continue for just a few miles and you'll find yourself on the main street, whose clapboard storefronts make it look like something out of the Old West.

WHERE TO EAT

This is a good stop off for a snack: Local people swear by the fried doughnuts on a stick at **Komoda's General Store,** as well as by their great macadamia nut cookies and cream puffs. **Kitada's Kau Kau Korner** is known for the best saimin upcountry; many of the local people come here for home-cooked meals. **Casanova Italian Restaurant and Deli** and **Polli's Cantina** (see "Where to Eat," in Chapter 9) are both right here on Makawao Avenue. **Courtyard Deli** is a charming indoor-outdoor spot, at 3620 Baldwin Ave., where you might enjoy an imaginative sandwich or salad (several vegetarian choices) or a coffee from the espresso bar, accompanied by wonderful, ever-changing desserts, like maple bread pudding with vanilla sauce. **Crossroads Caffè,** at the Crossroads Center, is a popular lunch spot with both residents and visitors. It has great salads and sandwiches, all fresh and homemade, as well as lunch specials each day and various regional cuisines (French country, Indian, Chinese, Japanese) every night. We've found the breakfasts and lunches absolutely delicious. You could pick up some sandwiches or California sushi at the **Rodeo General Store,** or have dinner at the **Makawao SteakHouse** at 3612 Baldwin Ave., which has long been popular in these parts.

SHOPS & GALLERIES

As a sophisticated, upscale group moves into Makawao and other upcountry towns, the local shops are changing too, with blacksmiths, barbershops, and pool halls giving way to trendy boutiques, art galleries, and New Age shops. Baldwin Avenue offers many enjoyable examples of this transformation.

The restored **Makawao Theater Building** is worth a stop for several reasons. The first is **Viewpoints Gallery,** in the rear, Maui's only fine arts cooperative, showing the works of 30 of Maui's most respected artists, in a variety of media. The space invites serious looking. Across from that is **Hot Island Glass,** an actual glassblowing studio and gallery where you are invited to watch award-winning glassblowers Bill and Sally Worcester and their son Mike at work as they transform molten glass into exquisite pieces of art. The furnace is in operation from 10am to 5pm. Prices for these treasures can go up to about $1,000, but check out the unsigned seconds; some lovely things go for under $35, like their knobby "pickle glasses" at just $10. Also in the same building, **Upcountry Legends** has clothing, jewelry, and the like, as well as locally made quilts, pillows, and other fine handcrafts; and **Upcountry Kids,** with wonderfully unique children's clothing. **Maui Hands** shows the work of 66 artisans in basketry, prints, watercolors, jewelry, quilting, and more. The **Courtyard Deli** (see above) is just one more reason for a visit here.

Up and down Baldwin Avenue, the browsing and shopping continues. Art lovers should be sure to make a stop at **Hui No'eau Visual Arts Center** at 2841 Baldwin Ave. The historic Baldwin home, Kaluanui, now houses an exhibition gallery, art studios, and a gift shop on a superb 9-acre landscaped estate, worth a visit in its own right. Open Tuesday to Sunday, from 10am to 4pm (☎ 808/572-6560).

Makawao After Dark

⊙ **Casanova Italian Restaurant**

1188 Makawao Ave. ☎ **808/572-0220.** Usually $12–$20 for name entertainment, $5 on disco nights. The cover charge is waived for diners on weekdays and when local bands are featured.

Maui's cowboy town, Makawao, suddenly became an entertainment venue when Casanova opened a few years ago. Now they consistently bring in big talents—performers like jazz greats Mose Allison and Jon Hendricks, and zydeco legend C. J. Chenier and his Red Hot Louisiana Band, to name just a few. Willie Nelson, Kris Kristofferson, Thomas Mapfumo, Los Lobos, and Richie Havens have performed here in recent years. There's disco dancing Wednesday (ladies' night) and Thursday nights; country dancing Tuesdays; live music Fridays and Saturdays.

A STOP IN PAIA

Unless you're planning to stop at Paia on the way to Hana (see "The Road to Hana," below), we recommend that you do so now. Instead of taking the road back to Pukalani, just take Baldwin Avenue a few miles into Paia, where you can shop for gifts and antiques and hobnob with the local people before heading back home.

TEDESCHI VINEYARDS

An unusual side trip you might want to take on your way back from an early trip to Haleakala is to the **Tedeschi Vineyards,** on Hi. 37 in beautiful upcountry Maui at the Ulupalakua Ranch. It's about 10 miles from Kula. Hawaii's only winery, Tedeschi cultivates 22 acres of grapes on the slopes of Haleakala to produce a champagne, a blush, and a red table wine in the Beaujolais nouveau tradition. The winery also produces a pleasant light, dry pineapple wine. You're welcome to take a free guided tour daily, from 9:30am to 2:30pm, to observe various phases of the bottling operation. After the tour, stop in at the tasting room in one of the early 18th-century buildings, sample the wines, perhaps purchase some. If you've brought your picnic lunch, there are tables outside the tasting room, amid beautiful scenery (including a splendid, huge camphor tree planted in the late 1800s) and spectacular views.

7 The Road to Hana

Some 10,000 feet down from the moon canyons of Haleakala, curving around the base of the old volcano, is a world light-years away, a place of such tropical lushness and splendor that it conjures up the word "primeval." This is remote Hana and the curving road leading to it—a road carved under the fringe of the lava cliffs, plunging down on one side to the sea, emerging on the other from overhanging jungle watered by the thousand streams of Haleakala.

In all of Hana, there are just a few dozen modestly priced accommodations. (The town's chief industry is the exquisite Hana Kai–Maui Resort, which caters to wealthy travelers only.) If you can reserve one of these (see "Where to Stay," in Chapter 9), it would be worth your while to stay overnight (See "A Reader's Warning," below) otherwise, you'll have to do Hana in a 1-day trip. Count on 2 to 3 hours each way from Central Maui, more if you want to savor the magnificent scenery. *A word of caution:* Be sure to check with the Highway Department about road conditions before you take off. If the weather has been wet, you could get stuck in landslides or mud. If it's raining heavily before you begin; forget the

Hana trip altogether. If it begins to rain before you get halfway to Hana; you should probably turn back, experienced readers advise. Parts of the road are easily washed away, and it may take hours for you to be rescued (which happened one year to friends of ours). There's always tomorrow, or the next visit to Maui.

Even though extensive highway repaving has made it much easier to drive the Hana road, it is still rugged and winding. There are plenty who love it, but some think that—despite the glory of the scenery—it's just not worth the effort. A picnic lunch is essential, unless you want to eat at the expensive Hana Kai–Maui or one of the little snack shops on the road or in Hana. Besides, you'll be traveling through the kind of country for which picnics surely were invented.

Hana glories in its remoteness. Rumor has it that a road is not being built because the local people like to keep Hana the way it is—difficult to get to. The current road was not completed until 1927, and by that time the Hasegawa General Store had already been in business 15 years and a hotel was already operating there. Hana's lush isolation attracted the late aviator and environmentalist Charles Lindbergh, who spent his vacations in Hana and is now buried there (the Lindbergh family has requested that his gravesite be kept private). Because of its remoteness, Hana has been slow in accepting change. Throughout its history it has assimilated new cultures, new religions, and new institutions, but Hana has not become part of them; rather, they have become a part of Hana.

One thing we strongly recommend you do before you set out on your trip to Hana is to rent a cassette tour; it's like having your own guide in the back seat. Try either of the following; they're both terrific.

Best of Maui Cassette Tours, 333 Dairy Rd., Kahului (☎ 808/871-1555 for reservations, 808/871-6339 for information). Scott Golladay's entertaining tours have been widely praised. Included in the $25 cost is a $10 discount on the second tour, plus a 30-minute video called "Visions of Maui" (a tour of Maui by helicopter). You also get a guidebook, a huge full-color map, flower and bird ID cards, a picnic lunch discount coupon, a "Survivor's Certificate," and Scott's Tip Sheet. If you have a tape player in your car, they will sell you the tape for $15, and all the extras are still included. Tapes are also available at locations in Lahaina, Kahului, and Paia, as well as at the main office. Ask at the concierge desk of your hotel or at an activities desk for the 10%-Off VIP Card.

Hana Cassette Guide, on Dairy Road at the Shell service station (☎ 808/572-0550 for reservations). This tour is the creation of Craig Henderson, a local photographer who narrates the trip himself and is well versed in the lore and legends of the Hana Road. Craig no longer rents tapes; he *sells* them. Included in the $20 fee is a Hana Coast map and flower guide; a video of the Hana Coast drive is available for only $5 at the time of the tape/map purchase. Craig also narrates an excellent tour of Haleakala—$10 when you buy the "Hana Package." Readers continue to praise this one.

FIRST STOP: PAIA

Start eastward on Hi. 32 in Kahului or Wailuku and switch (right) to Hi. 36. You may want to stop at **Pic-Nics** on Baldwin Avenue in Paia to pick up a picnic lunch (see "Where to Eat," Chapter 9).

SHOPS & GALLERIES

Take some time now, or on the return trip, to browse in some of the antique, decorator, and gift shops that have sprung up in this unspoiled upcountry community. The nice thing about shopping in Paia is that it's a local, not a tourist, area. Rents are not as high as in Lahaina or Kihei, so shopkeepers can afford to sell lovely things at good prices.

Be sure to visit the ✪ **Maui Crafts Guild,** at 43 Hana Hwy., a cooperative gallery showing outstanding work by local craftspeople. The two-story gallery carries a variety of crafts, ranging from bamboo (directly from the bamboo groves of Maui) to wooden bowls and boxes made of exotic local woods, baskets woven from native plants, jewelry, ceramics, hand-painted silk and cotton clothing, Hawaiian fish prints (gyotaku), and stone carvings. Prices are comparable to "direct from the artist" prices, and can go way up for some of the prints, collages, and sculptures. There are many items at low prices too: We recently spotted black bamboo calligraphy brushes at $14, raku lava eggs at $20, and banana bark paintings at $17.50. Most prices range from $10 to $70.

Just You & Me Kid, has children's clothes designed by owner Carol Ann and manufactured on Maui. The newly enlarged store now has a large outlet section. (There's another Just You and Me, Kid at the Maui Marriott Resort in Kaanapali.) Original artwork by Maui arists is featured at **Hana Hou Gallery,** which also has an impressive collection of Hawaiiana. **Summerhouse** is an old favorite here: Their specialties are casual island wear in natural fibers, Asian imports, and a swimsuit collection extraordinaire.

Around the corner from these shops at 12 Baldwin Ave. is **Maui Girl Co.,** a spot that has been sought out by such customers as Billy Joel, Cindy Lauper, and Ringo Starr for its collection of vintage rayon and silk aloha shirts. The collection, from the 30s, 40s, and 50s, comes from Canada, the mainland, and Japan. If you can't afford the prices ($50 to $500), just browse and have a look at some of their other fashionable sportswear; they do their own line of bikinis and clothing under the "Maui Girl" label and sell many suits at wholesale prices of $28.

HOOKIPA COUNTY BEACH PARK

Before you get back on the road to Hana, you might want to make a short detour in Paia to **Hookipa County Beach Park,** otherwise known as the "Windsurfing Capital of the World." Windsurfing, or sailboarding, as it is also known, is an enormously popular sport, and nowhere are conditions better for it than right here on the northern shore of Maui. It's fun to watch the windsurfers anytime, and if there happens to be a competition going on (make local inquiries), you're in for a special treat. The park is right on the road. Get out your cameras—the views are incredible. See "Beaches," above, for more information.

BACK ON THE ROAD TO HANA

The highway here runs straight and easy, through cane fields, until you get to Pauwela. That's where the road becomes an Amalfi Drive of the Pacific; the view is spectacular, but keep your eye on the curves. The variety of vegetation is enough to drive a botanist—or photographer—wild. Waterfalls, pools, green gulches beckon at every turn. You'll be tempted to stop and explore a hundred times, but keep going, at least until you get to **Kaumahina Park,** where you might consider picnicking high on the cliff looking down at the black sand beach of Honomanu Bay below, watching the local folk fish and swim.

Believe it or not, from here on the scenery gets even better. From the road, you can look down on the wet taro patches and the peaceful villages of **Keanae** and **Wailua,** to which a short side trip, to see the old Catholic church built of lava rock and cemented with coral, is eminently worthwhile. It seems that this coral was strewn ashore after an unusual storm in the 1860s, providing the villagers with the

Hana

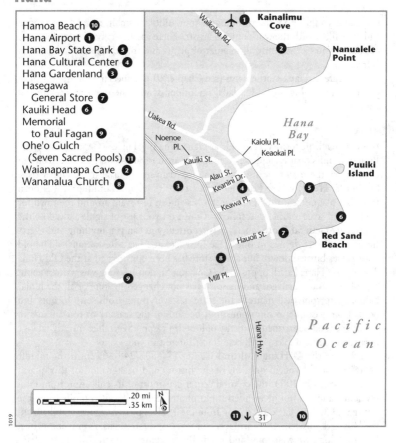

Hamoa Beach ⑩
Hana Airport ①
Hana Bay State Park ⑤
Hana Cultural Center ④
Hana Gardenland ③
Hasegawa
  General Store ⑦
Kauiki Head ⑥
Memorial
  to Paul Fagan ⑨
Ohe'o Gulch
  (Seven Sacred Pools) ⑪
Waianapanapa Cave ②
Wananalua Church ⑧

Kainalimu
Cove

Waikoloa Rd.

Nanualele
Point

Hana
Bay

Uakea Rd.

Noenoe
Pl.

Kaiolu Pl.
Keaokai Pl.

Kauiki St.

Puuiki
Island

Alau St.
Keanini Dr.

Keawa Pl.

Red Sand
Beach

Hauoli St.

Mill Pl.

Hana Hwy.

Pacific
Ocean

0   .20 mi
       .35 km

31

necessary material to construct their church. To commemorate this miracle, they constructed the **Miracle of Fatima Shrine,** which you will see on the Wailua Bay Road, at the 18-mile marker (turn left at the road sign).

In a little while, you get another vista of Keanae from **Koolau Lookout.** In the other direction you look through a gap in the cliff over into Haleakala. A little farther on is **Puaa Kaa Park,** another made-in-heaven picnic spot. The flowers are gorgeous here, and so are the two natural pools, each with its own waterfall.

On you go, past grazing lands and tiny villages, to **Waianapanapa Cave,** another possible side excursion. This lava tube filled with water is the place where a jealous Stone Age Othello was said to have slain his Desdemona. Every April the water is supposed to turn blood-red in remembrance. Near the cave is a black sand beach (not always safe for swimming), another great place for a picnic.

A wonderful garden awaits you when you enter Hana. ✪ **Hana Gardenland,** at the corner of Kalo and Hana Roads, has 5 acres of splendid botanical gardens, plus a gallery, plants, gifts, and Hawaiian crafts for sale. Blair Shurtleff and Tom Nunn (the people who own and operate Hana Plantation Houses—see preceding chapter) have transformed this 5 1/2-acre property from a place where one would quickly stop and buy an orchid plant into an experience so delightful you'll want to spend an hour or more if you can afford the time. Stroll through the botanical gardens and jungle trails or just sit beside the lily pond stocked with koi (Japanese carp) and you'll know the meaning of tranquility. A small, tastefully arranged gallery is filled with the work of local artists. There are also Hawaiian crafts. And, of course, you can still buy all manner of plants and tropical flowers. Admission is free.

The **Café** at Hana Gardenland (see Chapter 9) is a special delight; you sit at picnic tables dining on fresh salads, smoothies, sandwiches, and many kinds of coffees.

HANA

More than a little history was made at Hana. The Big Three—Captain Cook, the Protestant missionaries, and vacationing Hawaiian royalty—were all here. You can even follow the road to a historic Stone Age delivery room near the cinder cone of **Kauiki Head,** where Kamehameha's favorite wife, Kaahumanu, was born (there's a plaque near the lighthouse). Or you can just walk around the town for a while and soak up the atmosphere. A must on your list of sights should be the **Hasegawa General Store** where, it is reported, you can get anything and everything your heart desires in one place (just like at Alice's Restaurant). (The old Hasegawa's burned down, but a new store has been constructed at the Old Hana Theater, on Hana Road, opposite the Chevron Station.) A song was written about this place some years ago, and its spirit has not changed in spite of all the hullabaloo. As for practical matters, the store has everything from soup to nuts and bolts, from gasoline to muumuus, but because of the scarcity of rest-aurants in Hana, the food department—plenty of local fruit, some vegetables, mostly sausage meats, and some staples—will be of most interest to you.

A visit to the ✪ **Hana Cultural Center** (☎ 808/248-8622), in the middle of town, will fill you in on a bit of the history and background of this quaint town. Opened in 1983, the cultural center gets most of its collection from local residents, and it's full of wonderful old photographs, Hawaiian quilts (note the unusual Hawaiian-flag quilt dating from the 1920s), plenty of memorabilia from the '30s and '40s, as well as artifacts and tools, and rare shells. Admission is free, but donations are welcome (and needed); the center is open daily from 10am to 4pm.

Hana's best beach, **Hamoa,** is at the Hana Kai–Maui Resort, but you can also swim at the public beach on Hana Bay, at the black sand beach at Waianapanapa State Park,and at the red sand beach (ask locals how to get there).

Most visitors drive about 10 miles past Hana on to Kipahulu, an unspoiled extension of Haleakala National Park and **Ohe'o Gulch** (formerly known as the Seven Sacred Pools; that appelation is now considered politically incorrect), a gorgeous little spot for a swim. Here waterfalls drop into one another and then into the sea. But it's a roller-coaster ride on a rough, narrow road filled with potholes, and again, unless you enjoy this kind of driving, it may not be worth your nerves; it could take you 45 minutes to an hour to drive it.

En route to Ohe'o Gulch, you'll pass **Wailua Gulch** and a splendid double fall cascading down the slopes of Haleakala. Nearby is a memorial to Helio, one of the island's first Catholics, a formidable proselytizer and converter. A tribute to his work stands nearby—the *Virgin of the Roadside,* a marble statue made in Italy and draped every day with the fragrant flower leis of the Hawaiians.

The good road runs out a little farther on at Kipahulu, so it's back along the northern route, retracing your way past jungle and sea to home base.

8 The Western Maui Coast: Lahaina, Kaanapali & Kapalua

If Haleakala and Hana are nature's showplaces on Maui, Lahaina is humanity's. It was there that some of the most dramatic and colorful history of Hawaii was made: Over a century ago, Lahaina was the whaling capital of the Pacific, the cultural center of the Hawaiian Islands (and for a time its capital), and the scene of an often violent power struggle between missionaries and sailors for—quite literally—the bodies and souls of the Hawaiians.

Your trip to Lahaina and the western Maui coast happily combines history with some of the most beautiful scenery in the islands. Take your bathing suit and skip the picnic lunch, since there are plenty of places en route where you can eat. Since there's no paved road completely circling the western tip of Maui, we'll take the road as far as Honokahua, and return by driving back along the same road to Kahului—a route that is more interesting and comfortable than the drive on the unpaved portion between Honokahua and Waihee on the northern shore.

The trip begins on Hi. 32, which you follow through Wailuku to Hi. 30 (High Street), where you turn left. At Maalaea the road swings right at the sea and continues along the base of the West Maui Mountains, along a stretch of cliffs pounded by strong seas, until it reaches Lahaina, 22 miles from Kahului. During the winter, whale sightings are frequent along this stretch of ocean.

LAHAINA

Lahaina today is a comfortable plantation town, with pretty little cottages, a cannery, a sugar mill, and acres of cane and pineapple stretching to the base of the misty western Maui hills. Thanks to its having been declared a National Historic Landmark property, it still retains its late 19th- and early 20th-century architectural charm. New buildings must fit in with this architectural scheme, so there's no danger that it will ever look like Waikiki.

STROLLING AROUND TOWN   For some years, Lahaina has been in the process of a restoration covering the 150 or so years from the reign of King Kamehameha I to the annexation of Hawaii by the United States. Re-created will be the days when Lahaina was the capital of the Hawaiian monarchy (before the king, in the mid-1840s, moved the palace to Honolulu, where there was a better harbor); the coming of the missionaries; the whaling period; and the beginning of the sugar industry.

The restoration is being lovingly and authentically carried out by the **Lahaina Restoration Foundation,** a devoted group of local citizens and county and state interests. You may visit their office in the Master's Reading Room at the corner of Front Street and Dickenson Street (☎ 808/661-3262), open Monday through Friday from 10am to 4:30pm, for further information.

As you tour Lahaina, you'll notice various signs reading LAHAINA HISTORIC SITE: Those with a square at the bottom indicate buildings that are either original or restored; those with a circle indicate structures that no longer exist. A booklet called *Lahaina Historical Guide,* free at many Lahaina locations, provides useful maps and descriptions.

Begin your exploration out on the old pier in the center of town, where you can gaze at the famed **Lahaina Roads;** from the 1820s to the 1860s this was the favorite Pacific anchorage of the American whaling fleet. Over on your left are the soft greens of Lanai, to the north the peaks of Molokai, on the south the gentle slopes of Kahoolawe. During the winter and early spring, you may get to see some non-paying tourists sporting about in the water; these are the sperm whales that migrate from their Aleutian homes to spawn in the warmer waters off Lahaina.

For the whalers, this place was practical as well as beautiful: They were safe here in a protected harbor, they could come or go on any wind, and there was plenty of fresh water at the local spring, plenty of island fruits, fowl, and potatoes. And there were also Hawaiian women, who, in the old hospitable way of the South Seas, made the sailors feel welcome by swimming out to the ships and staying a while. To the missionaries, this was the abomination of abominations, and it was on this score that violent battles were fought. More than once, sailors ran through the streets setting houses on fire, rioting, beating up anyone who got in their way, even cannonading the mission house. You can see the evidence of those days at **Hale Paaho,** the old stone prison (on Prison Street, off Main), where sailors were frequent guests while the forays lasted.

Across the street from the waterfront you'll see the **Pioneer Inn,** which may look oddly familiar—it has been the set for many a South Seas movie saga. Back in 1901 (it has since been tastefully renovated and enlarged) it was quite the place, the scene of arrival and departure parties for the elegant passengers of the Inter-Island Steamship Company, whose vessels sailed out of Lahaina. And since it was too difficult to make the hot trek to central Maui immediately, arriving passengers usually spent the night here. Walk in and have a look around: Note the lovely stained-glass window one flight up from the entrance to the Harpooner's Lanai and the grandfather clock at the foot. The lanai itself is a wonderful place to waste a few years of your life soaking up the atmosphere.

Across Wharf Street from the hotel, a little to the north of the lighthouse, is the site of a palace used by Kamehameha in 1801, when he was busy collecting taxes on Maui and the adjoining islands. And across from that, where the Lahaina Branch Library now stands, is another spot dear to the lovers of the Hawaiian monarchy, the **royal taro patch** where Kamehameha III betook his sacred person to demonstrate the dignity of labor.

The huge banyan tree just south of the Pioneer Inn covers two-thirds of an acre; it's the favorite hotel for the town's noisy mynah bird population. In the front of the tree is the **Court House,** a post office, and police station, the post office part of which has been functioning since 1859. Between the Court House and the Pioneer Inn, you'll see the first completed project of the Lahaina Restoration, the **Fort Wall.** It's built on the site of the original fort, but since rebuilding the whole fort would have destroyed the famed banyan tree, the authorities decided to reconstruct the wall instead, as a ruin—a ruin that never existed.

Now that you've seen how the whalers lived, let's see how their arch opponents, the missionaries, fared. Walk 1 block mauka of the waterfront to Front Street and the **Baldwin House**—so typical, with its upstairs and downstairs verandas, of New England in Polynesia. The old house, built in the late 1830s of coral and stone, served as a home for the Rev. Dwight Baldwin, a physician and community leader as well as a missionary (and the founder of a dynasty—the Baldwins are still an important family in Maui). Thanks to the Lahaina Restoration Foundation, the house has been faithfully restored; you can examine Dr. Baldwin's medical kit (the instruments look like something out of a Frankenstein film), kitchen utensils, china closets, old photographs and books, the family's furniture and mementos—all the

Lahaina

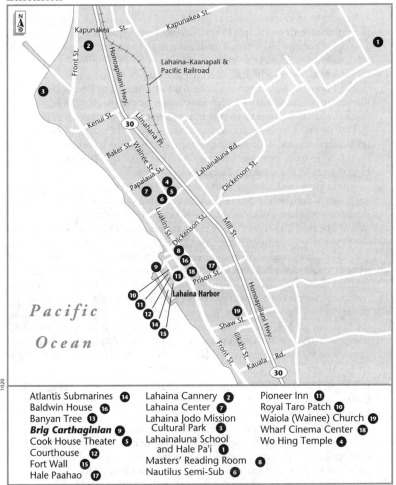

little touches of life 100 and more years ago. Open daily. Admission is $5 for families, $3 for adults, $2 for seniors, and free for children.

After you've seen Baldwin House, stop next door to visit the **Master's Reading Room,** a former seamen's library and chapel that now houses the office of the Lahaina Restoration Foundation. The unique coral-block-and-fieldstone construction has been preserved exactly as originally built in 1847.

Next stop might be the **Wo Hing Temple,** on Front Street, near Mariner's Alley. The restored 1912 fraternal hall is now a museum, with a display on the history of the Chinese in Lahaina. Stop in at the **Cook House Theater,** adjacent, which shows movies of Hawaii taken by Thomas Edison in 1898 and 1903. Open daily from 10am to 4:30pm; admission donation requested.

The Restoration Foundation also operates the floating museum ship *Carthaginian,* moored opposite the Pioneer Inn. Its "World of the Whale" exhibit features a series of colorful multimedia displays on whaling, whales, and the sea life of Hawaii. Maui's own humpback whale, which comes to these waters each winter to mate and calve, gets special treatment through videotape presentations made on the spot by the National Geographic Society, the New York Zoological Society, and others. The ship is a replica of a 19th-century brig and is open daily from 10am to 4:30pm. Admission is $5 for families, $3 for adults, $2 for seniors, free for children with their parents.

Head now for Wainee Street (to the right of Lahainaluna Road); here, where the recently built **Waiola Church** now stands, is the site of Wainee, the first mission church in Lahaina, to which the Reverend Baldwin came as pastor in 1835. The old cemetery is fascinating. Buried among the graves of the missionary families are some of the most important members of the Kamehameha dynasty, including no fewer than two wives of Old King Kam: Queen Keoupuolani, his highest-born wife, and Queen Kalakaua.

On the grounds of Lahainaluna High School stands **Hale Pai,** the original printing house of Lahainaluna Seminary, which the missionaries built in 1813. From the hand press here came the school books and religious texts that spread the Word. The coral-and-lava structure has been turned into a charming museum by the Restoration Foundation. Open Monday through Friday from 10am to 3pm.

For those interested in Asian culture, it would be unthinkable to leave Lahaina without a visit to the **Lahaina Jodo Mission Cultural Park.** In a beautiful spot perched above the water is a 3^1/$_2$-ton statue of Amitabha Buddha, erected to commemorate the centennial anniversary of Japanese immigration in Hawaii. It's the largest Buddha outside Japan. You can meditate here as long as you wish, strike the huge temple bell, and perhaps leave a small donation in the offertory (there is no admission charge). *Note:* It's easy to miss this place. As you drive along Front Street, look for the big sign that reads JESUS IS COMING SOON. Then turn makai on Ala Moana Street and you'll find the Buddha.

JUST OUTSIDE TOWN   Opposite Wahikuli State Park is the **Lahaina Civic Center,** an auditorium and gym, with a dramatic mosaic by one of Maui's most famous artists, Tadashi Sato.

Five miles east of Lahaina, on the highway headed toward Kahului, are the well-preserved **Olowalu Petroglyphs.** Two to three hundred years old, these rock carvings depicted the occupations—fishing, canoe-paddling, weaving, etc.—of the early Hawaiians. Unfortunately, they are rather difficult to get to.

On the other side of Lahaina, on the road leading toward Kaanapali, is another historical spot, the **Royal Coconut Grove of Mala.** Mala, one of the wives of Kamehameha, brought the trees from Oahu over a century ago. They are now being replaced by local citizens as part of the restoration.

ENTERTAINMENT

Check the local papers for news of frequent entertainment at the malls and shopping centers. On one visit to the **Wharf Cinema Center,** for example, we saw a full Polynesian review, including Samoan knife dances done by women on the center stage. And the **Lahaina Cannery** presents a vast amount of free entertainment, so be sure to see if anything is going on while you're there. You may be lucky enough to catch someone of the caliber of noted island funny man Frank DeLima, as we did on a recent visit. Fabulous!

SHOPPING

While the reconstruction of the historical sights is proceeding slowly, Lahaina (and Whaler's Village at Kaanapali Beach; see below) is fast emerging as one of the best shopping areas in the islands, second only to Honolulu. On each one of our visits there are new and exciting shops, boutiques, galleries to visit. Perhaps it's the influence of the young people and other newcomers moving into the area; they keep everything constantly stimulating and alive.

Finding a parking spot on the street is not easy, although it's often possible on Front Street, on the ocean side. There are 800 parking spaces at the new Lahaina Center, a good walk to the center of town. Also try the Lahaina Shopping Center, the area behind the Wharf Shopping Center, at the corner of Front and Prison Streets, and at the corner of Front and Shaw Streets. If none of that works, however, drive to one of the commercial parking lots, such as the one behind Baldwin House, at the corner of Luakini and Dickenson Streets: Charges are reasonable. Across from the parking lot is a place where you can get fresh island produce to take home, and in front of that is a stand selling ice-cold coconut juice.

Malls and Shopping Centers

Lahaina Center
900 Front St.

Everything about Lahaina Center, which is located at the Kaanapali end of town, between the ocean and Wainee Street, is big, including the biggest Hilo Hattie's Fashion Center in the neighbor islands, a large Liberty House, and—especially welcome in a town where parking spaces are scarcer than gold nuggets—a 1,000-car parking lot!

For budget buys in aloha wear and island gifts, it's hard to beat **Hilo Hattie's Fashion Center.** Selections are enormous, prices are right, and the nice people here even give you free pineapple-orange juice and a shell lei when you walk in. And, there's **Liberty House,** Hawaii's premier department store, with its usual quality selection of nationally recognized brands as well as lovely made-in-Hawaii merchandise.

There's plenty of activity in addition to shopping at Lahaina Center. **Front Street Theatre** is a state-of-the-art 4-plex cinema. **Blue Tropic** is a lively night spot. Every Wednesday and Friday at 2pm, the Center presents a free hula show, featuring musician and respected kumu hula Cliff Ahue as emcee.

Wharf Cinema Center
658 Front St.

Central to the Lahaina shopping scene, this stunning three-story arcade is built around a giant tree, with a fountain and a stage on the lower level, a glass elevator, a triplex theater complex, a number of attractive eating places, and dozens of shops. Shops stay open late, so a visit here can be a good evening's activity. (The free Lahaina Express trolley, a double-decker British bus, makes its last run to Kaanapali at 10pm; it runs daily from Kaanapali every 35 minutes, beginning at 9:30am.)

Everything at ✪ **Tropical Artware** is handmade—by 25 local artists and by craftspeople from around the world. This is one of the best sources for hard-to-find dichroic glass jewelry; metallic vapors fused into glass create a range of subtly changing colors. Dichroic glass earrings begin at $14; earcuffs and ornaments start as low as $10. Baskets, wood carvings, ceramics, and toe rings are all available. **Hawaii Memories–Maui** is a source for small shops and for individual customers as well: It has vast quantities of beads, necklaces, corals, earrings, crystals, amber, and more. **Gigi's Fashion Boutique** boasts classic design clothing from the 1920s, 30s, and 40s; there's a Gigi's leather boutique, too. And children can be nicely outfitted with island clothes at **Little Polynesians.**

We never miss a visit to **Tropic Provisions Bookstore and Coffee Shop,** where you can sit and sip on their peaceful patio. This full-service bookstore is always supporting an artistic event of some sort, and also has gift items and a variety of coffees and pastries. We often find stunning local books of art and photography and Hawaiiana here that are not readily available elsewhere.

Lahaina Cannery
1221 Honoapiilani Hwy.

Once it was a pineapple cannery; now, the heavy equipment and the factory workers are gone, and in their place are a supermarket, a drugstore, scads of boutiques and restaurants, and plenty of tourists. One of Lahaina's newer shopping centers and its first enclosed, air-conditioned one, the Cannery is a very pleasant place to shop. It's sunny but cool, with lots of light and space. It's a boon to people staying out this way, since the **Safeway Supermarket** stays open around the clock, and **Long's Drugs** fills a variety of needs. There is ample parking, as well as free shuttle service from the Honokawai and Kaanapali areas.

As for the smaller shops, there's men's and women's clothiers **Reyns,** where you must check out their Artwear collections of T-shirts; they make wonderful gifts. Other favorites include **Blue Ginger Designs,** where everything is made of hand-blocked batik fabrics.

For collectors of maps and old prints, internationally renowned **Lahaina Printsellers** is a must stop. Hawaii's largest gallery specializing in antique maps and engravings, it also holds the largest collection of Captain Cook material in the Western hemisphere. Stop by, if you can, on a Monday, Wednesday, or Friday at 2pm to see Stephen Strickland, Lahaina Printsellers' exclusive artist and one of the nation's few *intaglio* artist/engravers, give a free demonstration. We were fascinated by the process. Steve inks the engraved (reverse image) copper plate and then presses it through his traditional handpress, producing a sharp, clear print. He often offers a magnifying glass to his audience, allowing them to see his minute figures, which are invisible to the naked eye!

Maui on My Mind is one of the more tasteful shops around, with a variety of wearable crafts and handmade jewelry. They even have T-shirts with prints by some of Maui's favorite artists; we like Robert Lynn Nelson's underwater scenes.

If you admire the works of Guy Buffet, a French artist who lives on Maui, as much as we do, be sure to see **The Guy Buffet Collection.** Buffet's whimsical paintings of island life have been reproduced on a line of dinnerware and placemats, as well as calendars, dishes, cookware, lithographs, scarves, shirts, and more.

Attention chocoholics and/or potato-chip junkies: Before you leave the Cannery, stop in at **Long's Drugs** and treat yourself to a gourmet munchie craze: **Chocolate Chips of Maui.** These are Maui potato chips, dipped by hand in either rich dark or milk chocolate, packed in an elegant box, and signed by the dipper. They can be gobbled as is or, if you can wait, frozen and served with ice cream or sherbet or brandied whipped cream! It's $3.69 for a ¹/₄-pound box.

Specialty Shops

✪ South Seas Trading Post
780 Front St. ☎ **808/661-3168.**

There aren't too many places like the South Seas Trading Post left in Lahaina, places where the owners still search out and find authentic South Seas and Asian treasures. Although there are many collector's items here—primitive art from New Guinea, bronzes and Buddhas from Thailand, precious jades and porcelains from China—most of the items are surprisingly affordable: Consider, for example, one-of-a-kind jewelry designs using antique pieces ($25 to $75), freshwater pearl necklaces with precious gemstones (from $18), 100-year-old porcelain spoons from China (at $15)—and much more.

The Whaler Ltd.
866 Front St. ☎ **808/661-4592.**

Here's a unique shop with a nautical flavor. One of the oldest establishments on Front Street, it features a great variety of American crafts, especially art glass from Hawaii and the mainland, each piece with a nautical theme—fish, dolphins, and whales. There's also an intriguing collection of jewelry, perfume bottles, paper weights, vases, sculptures, scrimshaw, prints, and watercolors.

Lahaina Hat Company
705 Front St. ☎ **808/661-8230**

If you can't find a hat here, you're not really trying! The collection is enormous, and all are reasonably priced. They carry a good selection of tote bags too.

A Swap Meet
Handmade Hawaiian dresses, baskets, hand-painted clothing and T-shirts, and handcrafted jewelry are just some of the items for sale at the Sunday-afternoon **Lahaina Crafts Fair.** It's held either once, twice, or three times a month at the Lahaina Civic Center, next to the main post office in Lahaina. Check with your hotel desk to see when it's scheduled.

LAHAINA AFTER DARK

Lahaina at night is the place for the drinking set, with no shortage of swinging bars. And for families, check the local papers to see what entertainment is being presented at the malls.

Drinking, Dancing, and Listening
In addition to the places listed below, keep in mind the following: The **Pioneer Inn** on Front Street always attracts a lively crowd for moderately priced drinks. The **Hard Rock Café** at Lahaina Center, 900 Front St., has one of the biggest bars in town and one of the jolliest crowds. **Compadres Bar & Grill** at the Lahaina C annery is the spot for Mexican munchies and great margaritas. **Lahaina Coolers,** 180 Dickenson St., offers two popular happy hours, one from 4 to 6pm, the other from 10pm to closing (which could be 2am) every day.

Aloha Cantina
839 Front St. ☎ **808/661-8788.** No Cover.

Hand-shaken fruit margaritas, sunset music daily, and live bands to dance to on Friday and Saturday from 10pm to 1am make this one of the most popular stops on Front Street. All this, and Maui fish tacos, too.

Blue Tropix
At Lahaina Center. ☎ **808/667-5309.** Cover $5 after 9pm, more for special events.

You can have a medium-priced dinner here or just come for the disco dancing and entertainment. Mostly there's a DJ, but there's also plenty of live entertainment and special concerts.

Moose McGillicuddy's Pub & Cafe

844 Front St. ☎ **808/667-7758.** Cover $3 Thurs–Sat after 9pm.

A young crowd comes here to listen to rock and roll. There's a 3 to 6pm happy hour every day, special prices on Tijuana Tuesdays, Ladies' Night on Thursday, videos every night, and on Thursday, Friday, and Saturday, live bands from 9:30pm until closing.

Navatek II Sunset Cruises

☎ **808/661-8787** or toll free 800/852-4183.

Here's a unique way to enjoy the Maui night—on a cocktail or dinner cruise aboard the *Navatek II,* whose revolutionary SWATH design (Small Water Plane Twin Hull) makes sailing smooth as glass. It's $39 for a cocktail cruise and $78 for a dinner cruise, with island music setting the background for a spectacular scenic sail from Maalaea Bay to Lahaina. A snorkeling trip to Molokini ($65) and a half-day cruise around the island of Lanai ($120) are also available on this unique vessel.

Friday Evening Art Nights

Lahaina boasts numerous galleries, and the best time to visit them is on Friday night. Friday evening, from 7 to 9pm, is "Art Night" in Lahaina; galleries present special appearances by artists and offer free entertainment and refreshments. Great fun! Check the local papers for what's happening where. Among the numerous galleries involved are **South Seas Trading Post, Dolphin Galleries, Wyland Gallery, Metropolitan Galleries,** and the **Lahaina Arts Society.**

ON TO KAANAPALI

If you want to continue your sightseeing out in the Kaanapali resort area now, there are two ways to go, in addition to driving your own car. The first is free: It's the **Lahaina Express,** a fleet of two blue double-decker London buses and a quaint green trolley that provides shuttle service between Banyan Tree Square and the hotels in the Kaanapali Resort every 35 minutes from 9am on. The last trolley leaves the Wharf Cinema Center in Lahaina at 10pm (for information, phone the Wharf Shops at 808/661-8748).

It's more fun, however (and also more expensive: $12 round-trip, $8 one way, half fare for children), to hop the old-timey **Lahaina-Kaanapali & Pacific Railroad,** a reconstructed, turn-of-the-century sugarcane train, for the 12-mile round-trip between Lahaina and Kaanapali. You'll be entertained with songs and stories en route by a singing conductor, and kids will get a kick out of the hoot of the locomotive's whistle. The railroad terminal is on Honoapiilani Highway, one block north of Papalaua Street; there is free transportation via a double-decker bus from the harbor and Front Street. Before or after the trip, you might want to check out the **Depot Snack Shop,** which friendly and knowledgeable Brad Reith has been operating for years. There are goodies here you can't get anywhere else. Fresh sugarcane, sweet and juicy, is $2.25 per package. And Brad isn't called the "king of the coconuts" for nothing! You can buy coconut in different stages of development: drink the delicious "milk" or enjoy the gourmet form "spoonmeat." Spoonmeat coconuts are $3. If you're really lucky, you'll visit on a day when Brad has homemade mango muffins, huge and unbelievably delicious, for just $1.50. Don't miss **Sugar Cane Gifts** (☎ 808/661-3325) right at the railroad depot. They have some of the most handsome T-shirts and sweatshirts we've seen on Maui, as well as a variety of other gift items.

Luau, Maui Style: Where to Go for a Traditional Hawaiian Feast (or Something Like It)

If you're looking to experience an authentic Hawaiian celebratory feast, or *luau*, while you're on Maui, you'll be hard pressed to find one that's truly reminiscent of those thrown by the ancient Hawaiians. After all, by definition, the traditional luau was a relaxed, ritualized family affair commemorating a special occasion or happy event (often a baby's first birthday). A good modern-day commercial luau, however, will serve as a good introduction to traditional Hawaiian food, such as kalua pig (prepared in an *imu*, or underground lava rock oven) and poi, as well as entertainment like the ancient hula (performed by both men and women).

Your best bet on Maui—and maybe in all of the Hawaiian Islands—is the lovely and intimate **Old Lahaina Luau**, right on the beach behind the shopping arcade at 505 Front St. (☎ 808/667-1998). This old-style luau is smaller, more personal, and more authentic than the standard slick hotel presentations. *Maui Magazine* has called it the best luau on the island, and it recently won the Hawaii Visitors Bureau's "Five Kahili" award for enhancing Hawaiian culture and aloha spirit—we couldn't agree more with either of these kudos.

The setting on the grounds of Kamehameha's royal compound, is picture perfect: You dine as the sun sets over water—with Kahoolawe, Molokai, and Lanai in the distance—then watch the traditional Polynesian hulas by starlight. Everyone receives a fresh-flower lei greeting, and a duo plays ukeleles as guests are seated either on mats in the traditional fashion or at tables. Frozen tropicals like piña coladas, chi chis, mai tais, and Blue Hawaiis flow from the open bar all evening. The food, better than the usual luau fare, is served buffet style. Authentic Hawaiian dishes—including lomi-lomi salmon, laulau, poke, kalua pig, poi, and haupia—is served, as well as fare more recently introduced to the islands, such as sirloin steaks and chicken barbecued over a kiawe grill. The after-dinner dancing and music is performed by authentically attired men and women well schooled in the ancient history and arts.

The Old Lahaina Luau is held Monday through Saturday evenings at 5:30pm; the cost is $56 for adults and $28 for children under 12. Be sure to make your reservations several days in advance.

THE KAANAPALI BEACH RESORT

Now for some sightseeing, shopping, and swimming at the glamorous hotels of the Kaanapali Beach Resort (signs from the road lead you directly down to the hotels). Your first stop should be at the splendid ✪ **Hyatt Regency Maui,** where you can have a look at the $80-million, 40 acre complex, lush with waterfalls, gardens, tropical birds, a half-acre swimming pool with a 150-foot water slide and swinging rope bridge and its own bar in a lava cavern, an atrium lobby, and an elegant shopping arcade that rivals Rodeo Drive. A walk here is like touring a park and botanical garden and an indoor-outdoor museum of priceless Asian art. This aesthetic and architectural tour de force offers gorgeous vistas wherever you look. You might want to pause and have a drink at the Weeping Banyan Bar beside a lagoon—but please don't throw crumbs at the penguins! Note, too, the unusual ceilings in the shops—there's one in stained glass—and perhaps pick up a trinket at a place like Elephant Walk. If you—or your children—are interested in astronomy, make plans to come back some evening to take the Hyatt Regency Maui's **"Tour of the Stars."** Guided by the resort's director of astronomy, participants first learn to interpret the sky with the naked eye, then giant binoculars, and then view it through a revolutionary new deep-space telescope that yields brilliant images of stars, planets, galaxies, and nebulae. Sessions are held every night (except Sunday) at 8, 9 and 10pm; cost is $12 for adults, $5 for children 12 and under. Be sure to make reservations as soon as you arrive; the demand is great (information: 808/661-1234).

And while you're touring the Hyatt Regency, you can actually take a helicopter tour without leaving the lobby! Incredible Journeys is the first helicopter tour flight simulator in the world: it offers a "virtual reality" helicopter tour of Maui to those who are reluctant to fly in a real helicopter or don't want to spring for the high prices. And there's no harm done to the environment this way! Fare for the simulated journey is $39.95 for adults, $29.95 for children 12 and under. You can walk in or call ahead to reserve "flight time"; call 808/661-0092.

By all means, pay a visit to the **Maui Marriott Resort,** on Kaanapali Drive next to the Hyatt Regency. This is an example of modern hotel architecture and landscaping at its best, especially beautiful at night, when lights, flowers, and a tropical moon over the ocean create dazzling effects.

Your next stop should definitely be the **Westin Maui Resort,** a sensational $165-million remake of the old Maui Surf Hotel. It's a toss-up as to whether this or the Hyatt Regency Maui (both Christopher Hemmeter creations) is the more sumptuous—you decide. This gorgeous pleasure palace by the sea has $2.5 million worth of artwork gracing the public areas and gardens, a spectacular, multilevel swimming pool complex fed by waterfalls and bridges (twice as big as the giant pool at the Hyatt Regency), and swans gliding just a few feet from the registration desk. Art tours are held on Tuesday and Thursday at 9am, botanical tours on Friday at 10:30am, and wildlife tours on Sunday, Monday, and Wednesday at 10am—a great chance to photograph the flamingos, swans, and macaws. You'll need reservations (☎ 808/667-2525).

As you continue driving, you may want to stop at the **Sheraton Maui Hotel,** which sits atop **Black Rock,** the perch from which the souls of the dead Hawaiians were said to leap into the spirit world beyond. The majestic hotel, not in the least bit haunted, is worth having a look at, especially for the 360° view from the top, a sweeping panorama of ocean, islands, and mountains. The tasteful Polynesian formal lobby is on the top floor; you've got to take the elevators down to everything else, including Kaanapali Beach. A major renovation of the hotel should be completed by fall of 1996.

MUSEUMS, SHOPS & GALLERIES

WHALER'S VILLAGE   The main shopping attraction out here is Whaler's Village, recently done over and now bigger and better than ever. The one- and two-story buildings are of uniform design and materials, authentic reproductions of the type of buildings that the New England missionaries constructed in Lahaina between 1830 and 1890. First, pay a visit to the **Whaler's Village Museum** (on the top floor of Building G), to study its absorbing collection of whaling memorabilia, and perhaps see the whaling film shown every half hour in the museum's theater. Then visit **Hale Koholo, House of the Whale,** a newer museum

The Kaanapali Coast

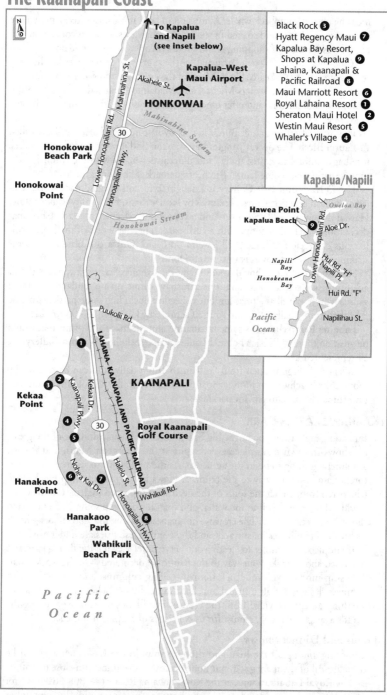

Black Rock ❸
Hyatt Regency Maui ❼
Kapalua Bay Resort,
  Shops at Kapalua ❾
Lahaina, Kaanapali &
  Pacific Railroad ❽
Maui Marriott Resort ❻
Royal Lahaina Resort ❶
Sheraton Maui Hotel ❷
Westin Maui Resort ❺
Whaler's Village ❹

N

To Kapalua
and Napili
(see inset below)

Akahele St.

Kapalua–West
Maui Airport

HONKOWAI

Mahinahina St.

Lower Honoapiilani Rd.

Honoapiilani Hwy.

Mahinahina Stream

30

Honokowai
Beach Park

Honokowai
Point

Honokowai Stream

Kapalua/Napili

Hawea Point
Kapalua Beach ❾

Oneloa Bay

Aloe Dr.

Lower Honoapiilani Rd.

Hui Rd. "H"

Napili Pt.

Napili
Bay

Honokeana
Bay

Hui Rd. "F"

Pacific
Ocean

Napilihau St.

Puukolii Rd.

❶

LAHAINA, KAANAPALI AND PACIFIC RAILROAD

Kekaa Dr.

Kaanapali Pkwy.

KAANAPALI

❸ ❷

Kekaa
Point

❹

30

❺

Royal Kaanapali
Golf Course

Nohea Kai Dr.

Halelo St.

❻ ❼

Hanakaoo
Point

Wahikuli Rd.

Honoapiilani Hwy.

❽

Hanakaoo
Park

Wahikuli
Beach Park

Pacific
Ocean

focusing on the humpback whale. Admission to both museums is free. After you've boned up on history and soaked in some gorgeous views, you can concentrate on the serious business of shopping—and there's plenty to concentrate on.

"One-of-a-kind," "rare," "unusual"—these are words to describe the very special offerings at ❂ **Sea & Shell.** Many of the employees do watercolors or create belts and hair jewelry; owners Michael and Madaline Abrams do all the beautiful mountings and mirrors, and offer unique jewelry by island artisans, like the Kroma Glass line.

The magical art of Laurel Burch has its own store at Whaler's Village, called ❂ **Laurel Birch The Secret Jungle.** In it one can find jewelry, sculpture, T-shirts, tote bags, umbrellas, coffee mugs, and notecards—many with the whimsical cat motifs that have become Laurel Birch's trademark. Enchanting.

The ❂ **Ka Honu Gift Gallery** is a delight, with lots of handmade works: collector dolls in traditional dress, ceramics by local artisans, fine quality wooden ware, Hawaii designs in gold and silver, and a year-round selection of island Christmas decorations, including Santa with a surfboard. They have one of the largest collections of precious Niihau shell jewelry on Maui. **Outta the Blue** features the striking designs done by Australian Ken Done.

Scrimshaw collectors should head straight for **Lahaina Scrimshaw,** where there's an impressive selection of quality scrimshaw (done on nonendangered fossil walrus ivory), as well as a prize antique collection, including some particularly fine Buddhas from Thailand. Do-it-yourself scrimshaw kits go for $8.95 to $21.

Lahaina Printsellers has some fascinating antique maps and prints that would be great on those walls back home. Island regulars, including **Wyland Gallery,** are all represented here.

Whaler's Village is open from 9:30am to 10pm daily, and can be reached by foot on the beachwalk or on Kaanapali Resort's free trolley. If you drive, you will, unfortunately, have to pay for parking.

KAANAPALI AFTER DARK

Fun and games await you at the big beach hotels at Kaanapali. One of the greatest shows in town takes place every night at the **Sheraton Maui,** and it costs absolutely nothing to be in the audience. As the sun begins to set over the water, torches are lit all the way to the point. A Hawaiian boy stands atop Black Rock (the perch from which the souls of the dead were supposed to depart to the other world), throws his leis into the water, and then looks down some 20 feet or so to the waiting ocean below. The crowd—on the beach, lining the lobby floors—holds its breath. He plunges in, surfaces, and the evening festivities are under way.

If you need something to steady your nerves after viewing the diving spectacle described above, make your way to the nautically decorated "On the Rocks" Bar. The ship models, volcanic rock floor-to-ceiling columns, and the tables with compass designs are all unusual and handsome, but somehow we never notice anything except the view; from the crest of this black-lava cliff overlooking the sea it's a spectacular one, a must for us collectors of Hawaiian sunsets.

Luaus and Dinner Shows

Choosing among all the luau and dinner shows in the Kaanapali area can be difficult: All of them are good, but none is inexpensive (most run close to $50).

The **Royal Lahaina Luau,** at the Royal Lahaina Resort (☎ 808/661-3611 for reservations), is considered one of the best; it's presented nightly, September through April at 5:30pm, May through August at 6pm. It costs $49.50 for adults, $24.75 for children 12 and under. Children under 5 are free. On Tuesday and Friday "Family Nights," children 12 and under are free with a paying adult.

Drums of the Pacific at the Hyatt Regency Maui (☎ 808/667-4420 for reservations) offers a spectacular production of Polynesian dancing (Samoan slap dances, Tahitian drum dances and shimmies, spear and knife dances, fire dances, etc.), along with a traditional Luau Buffet and an imu ceremony. Festivities are held in an outdoor amphitheater beneath the stars. The dinner show is $48 for adults, $15 for children 6 to 12, but you can see the same show and enjoy a cocktail for just $26.

Another top choice is the **Marriott Luau,** at the Maui Marriott on Kaanapali Beach (☎ 808/667-1200 ext. 380 for reservations), held at the hotel's beautiful oceanfront luau gardens Tuesday through Sunday at 5pm. Admission is $48 for adults, $22 for children 5 to 12, free for 4 and under.

Contemporary and Hawaiian Music

Live at Ludwig's

4405 Honoapiilani Hwy. Suite 214 of the Kahana Gateway Center, Kahana. ☎ **808/669-3785.** Sometimes no cover; other times, depending on who is playing, cover from $2 to $10.

The music's the thing that brings people to Live at Ludwig's. Owner Bill Ludwig has lined the walls of his state-of-the-art live music club with treasures and memorabilia from his family's collection. There's a big dance floor, and live groups every night—rock, jazz, reggae, you name it. Bill's great-grandfather started the Ludwig Drum Company in 1909 and they've been making drums for the industry's very biggest stars ever since. Almost every legendary drummer you can think of—including Ringo Starr—has sat behind a Ludwig drum kit. There's full bar service, a nice, short wine list and a constantly changing selection of pupus ($4.50 to $7). Always available are Ludwig's Drumstix (of course), which are seared spicy or mild Greek style with blue cheese dressing, burgers, and tossed salads. The joint jumps every single night.

Makai Bar

At the Maui Marriott. ☎ **808/667-1200.**

There's live music here every night—plus spectacular sunsets. Readers of the *Maui News* have voted this "Maui's Best Pupu Bar" for two years in a row.

A Comedy Club

Lobby Bar

At the Maui Marriott. ☎ **808/667-1200** for reservations. Cover $12. No one under 21 admitted. Tickets are available in advance at the front desk.

The Honolulu Comedy Club is one of the top nightclub attractions in Waikiki; on Monday night it moves to Maui. You never know who the talent will be, but be assured they are among the nation's hottest stand-up comedians; you've probably seen them on TV with Jay Leno or David Letterman or Arsenio Hall.

TO KAPALUA

As you drive north from Kaanapali on Honoapiilani Highway through Kahana and Napili to Kapalua, you're seeing some of the most beautiful countryside in West Maui. Some of the best beaches are here too, as well as the lovely Kapalua Bay Resort, perched on a promontory and surrounded by blue sea.

Although you could conceivably swim at Honokawai Beach Park, it's not particularly desirable, so we suggest you drive farther along until you come to some better beaches. Our favorite, still farther north on this road, is **Kapalua Beach** (also known as old Fleming Beach), a perfect crescent of white sand, gentle surf, the ideal spot for the whole family to swim, play, and snorkel. There's a public right-of-way sign past the Napili Kai Beach Club, which leads to a small parking lot for this very popular beach. If it's full, we'll let you in on a secret: The parking lot at the Shops at Kapalua, adjacent to the plush Kapalua Bay Hotel, usually has plenty of space and you can walk from it, through the hotel, and down through the lovely grounds to the ocean. The Kapalua Bay Hotel itself is exquisite, and well worth a look. For details on Kapalua and other great beaches in the area, see "Beaches" earlier in this chapter.

Note: Despite any information you may receive locally, nude sunbathing is definitely against the law in the state of Hawaii.

FREE SHOWS

Cook's at the Beach, at the Westin Maui Resort (☎ 808/667-2525), is a charming indoor-outdoor café that hosts a free hula show Monday through Saturday at 7pm.

One of Maui's best entertainments is free. It's the presentation of ✪ **Hula Kahiko O Hawaii** at the Shops at Kapalua, at the Kapalua Bay Resort, every Thursday morning at 10am. Unlike most hulas done in commercial shows, these are the authentic ancient dances of Hawaii, presented by a local hula halau (school), with Kumu Hula Cliff Ahue relating enchanting stories of Hawaii's history and ancient religion.

SHOPPING

THE SHOPS AT KAPALUA   We always stop to visit the Shops at Kapalua, at the Kapalua Bay Resort, one of the most serenely tasteful of island marketplaces. Most of the shops here are way beyond our budget, but there are many affordable items at places like **Kapalua Kids,** which can outfit teens as well as children, and at the **Kapalua Logo Shop,** where you can pick up T-shirts, bags, and many ßaccessories with the distinctive trademark logo: the Kapalua butterfly.

Like its other shop in Lahaina, the **South Seas Trading Post** showcases arts, handcrafts, and jewelry from Bali, New Guinea, and Asian and South Pacific shores, much of it of museum quality. But there are some charming low-priced items too. We especially like the jewelry created from 350- to 600-year-old shards of Ming Dynasty Chinese porcelain: These are set in sterling-silver rings, pendants, and earrings, and start at just $22. **Lahaina Printsellers,** Hawaii's largest gallery specializing in antique maps and engravings, has a handsome new shop here.

Have a sandwich and an espresso, now, at the European-style **Market Café,** which also purveys cookbooks, cheeses, wines, and deli items. Or walk through the lobby of the adjoining Kapalua Bay Hotel and have lunch at the lovely **Pool Terrace.** Best of all, wander out to the **Bay Club.** Here you can have a fancier lunch, a drink, or simply a walk outside to see the breathtaking views, with blue sea at every vista. Beautiful Kapalua Beach is right below you. Let the peace and beauty of the beaches stay in your memory as you turn around and go back the way you came—the road continuing around the island is a poor one, and usually off-limits to drivers of rented cars.

Molokai, the Most Hawaiian Isle

11

What's the most Hawaiian of the Hawaiian Islands? If you're thinking in terms of the Hawaii of 50 years ago—the Hawaii before high-rises and shopping centers, before billboards and commercialism, it might well be the little island of Molokai. The closest of the neighbor islands—only 20 minutes by plane from Oahu—261-square-mile Molokai is the least developed and most sparsely populated of the major Hawaiian Islands. Its resident population (less than 7,000) has the highest percentage of people with native Hawaiian ancestry anywhere in the islands (with the exception, of course, of privately owned Niihau). The environment is rural and the lifestyle traditional. Imagine a place with no buildings over three stories high, no elevators, no traffic lights (let alone freeways!), no movie theaters, no fast-food or supermarket chains. Instead, think of great natural beauty, vast uncrowded spaces, and ideal conditions for golfing, hunting, riding, windsurfing, big-game fishing, boating (swimming is not ideal here, since the beaches can be beautiful but the water rough), and leading the lazy life in an unspoiled setting. It's a favorite weekend spot for family holidays. And it's rapidly becoming a popular destination for those interested in eco-tourism and cultural tourism.

In the past, Molokai was known mostly as a pineapple plantation island and as a treatment center for Hansen's disease (leprosy) at Kalaupapa. It was here that Father Damien (now known as Blessed Damien since his beatification in 1994) did his magnificent work among the lepers. But somehow the tidal wave of progress that has swept the islands since statehood left Molokai behind; it appears, at first glance, like a midwestern town in the Depression 30s. Yet there's a real downhome feeling here that most people find appealing, and a genuine friendliness among the locals. Artists and craftspeople, seeking a last refuge from overpriced civilization, have settled here. In some parts of the island there is a sense of tranquility that's almost palpable. And Molokai is changing. Although the pineapple industry has been phased out and many of the local people are experiencing hard economic times, luxury facilities for visitors are on the rise. Before Molokai changes too much, come see what rural Hawaii is still like. A visit to Molokai can be a rewarding experience, especially since you won't have to break the bank to do it; prices here are still somewhat lower than elsewhere in the state.

What's Special About Molokai

Natural Wonders
- Halawa Valley, a once-populous valley decimated by the tidal wave of 1946, and its high point, spectacular Moaula Falls.
- Palaau State Park, where trails lead to Phallic Rock and to Kalaupapa Lookout, from which one can see the world's tallest (3,330 feet high) sea cliffs, at Umilehi Point.

Historic Attractions
- Kalaupapa Peninsula, where Father Damien performed his labor among the lepers; now a National Historic Park and treatment center for the few remaining Hansen's disease patients.
- R. W. Meyer Sugar Mill, an authentic restoration of an 1878 sugar mill now in operating condition; listed on the National Register of Historic Places.

Special Adventures
- Going on camera safari at Molokai Ranch Wildlife Park, where more than 1,000 Asian and African animals roam free on a 1,000-acre natural wildlife preserve.

Molokai Foods
- Molokai French bread, famed throughout the islands; Kanemitsu Bakery is the source.

Sports and Outdoor Activities
- Big-game fishing, hunting, golfing, horseback riding, windsurfing, and boating are all popular. Beaches are fine for sunbathing, but often rough for swimming.

Annual Events
- Annual August statewide rodeo at Molokai Ranch.
- The September/October Molokai-to-Oahu Canoe Race, the Olympics of outrigger canoeing. It's September for the women's race, October for the men's.
- The celebration in May of the birth of the hula on Molokai: Molokai Ka Hula Piko. A joyful event.
- January's Molokai Makahiki, a traditional Hawaiian "time of peace" celebration.

Molokai, now "The Friendly Isle," was once known as "The Lonely Isle." The power of Molokai's kahuna priests was feared throughout the other islands. Warring island kings kept a respectable distance from Molokai until, in 1790, Kamehameha the Great came to negotiate for the hand of the queen, Keoupuolani. Five years later he returned with an army to conquer Molokai on his drive for Oahu and dominion over all of Hawaii.

Today Molokai presents a tranquil scene, an island mostly given to rural pursuits. The only town really worthy of the name is Kaunakakai, on the southern shore, almost in the center of the island, and it has only one street. A thickly forested backcountry populated with axis deer, pheasant, turkey, and other wild game makes life exciting for the hunter. For those of you who just like to sightsee, there is magnificent Halawa Valley, on the southeastern coast, about 25 miles from Kaunakakai, with its healing pool at the foot of Moaula Falls; the less-rugged Palaau State Park, about 10 miles north of Kaunakakai, with its Phallic Rock and Kalaupapa Lookout; and Kalaupapa itself, an isolated peninsula, once an exile colony for the victims of leprosy, which today you can visit on a guided tour. But more about that later.

You won't have to rough it on Molokai. The few hotel facilities are excellent, the roads for the most part are quite good, and you'll be able to get whatever comforts and supplies you need—from rental cars to color movie film. The drinking water is as pure as you'll find anywhere in the world, and the restaurants, especially those in the three major hotels on the island, serve very good meals.

One word of advice: Go directly to your hotel from the airport and get comfortable and adjusted to Molokai before visiting its nearby principal town, Kaunakakai. This sleepy village, made famous by the song "Cock-eyed Mayor," is best appreciated once you're in the Molokai mood.

To get a little head start on your sightseeing, you might note that, between the airport and town, on the ocean side of the road is Kapuaiwa, one of the last surviving royal coconut groves in the Hawaiian Islands, planted in the latter part of the 19th century. It was planted in honor of Kamehameha V and given his pet name. Opposite the grove is Church Row, a lineup of tiny rustic churches.

1 Orientation & Getting Around

ARRIVING BY PLANE   Molokai is 20 air minutes from Honolulu, 15 minutes from Maui. It is easily reached via **Hawaiian Airlines,** which runs 50-seat DH-7 aircraft into Hoolehua Airport on a frequent schedule. **Mahalo Air,** Hawaii's budget airline, recently started service to Molokai and now offers four flights a day. (It also offers a flight from Molokai to Lanai.) Two commuter airlines, which run small planes (anywhere from 9- to 18-seaters), also fly to Molokai: These are **Air Molokai** and **Island Air Paragon** flies to Molokai from Maui. Flying low on these small planes can be quite thrilling, as we discovered on a recent Air Molokai flight. Molokai lies between the islands of Oahu and Maui (it can easily be seen from western Maui) and is, in fact, part of Maui County. Route it on your way to or from either Maui or Honolulu. A one-day trip is quite feasible.

ARRIVING BY SHIP   A more leisurely—and scenic—way to get to Molokai is to take the interisland ferry, *The Maui Princess,* a 118-foot luxury vessel that plies the routes between Maui and Molokai every day. It's about a 1¼-hour trip. One-way fare is $25 for adults, $12.50 for children. The tour is narrated, there are plentiful opportunities for taking pictures, and if it's between December and May, you may spot a few humpback whales taking the same trip you are. For

Readers Recommend

Flying via Kalaupapa. *"If possible, when flying from Maui to Molokai, take an Aloha Island Air Twin Otter flight via Kalaupapa. One flies on a level with the 3,000-foot-high cliffs on the northern shore of Molokai, and what a spectacular sight that is! In using this form of interisland transport, we got for free what most people would pay $75 to $100 for on a helicopter tour! This flight was the highlight of our trip."*—Mrs. Jane Beecham, Victoria, Australia.

reservations, call 808/533-6899 on Oahu, 808/661-8397 on Maui, 808/553-5736 on Molokai. From the mainland, call toll free 800/833-5800. Note that a number of attractive packages are available, including rental cars and guided tours; both one-day trips and overnights are available.

INFORMATION

The **Molokai Visitors Association** will send you a comprehensive brochure listing hotels, resort condominiums, tour companies, auto-rental companies, restaurants, visitor activities, and airlines serving the island, as well as individual brochures put out by these firms. From Canada and the continental United States as well as Alaska, Puerto Rico, and the Virgin Islands, call toll free 800/800-6367. If you're already in the islands, call 800/553-0404. The local number is 808/533-3876. Their office is at the 0 mile highway marker.

GETTING AROUND
BY RENTAL CAR

You're going to need a car if you want to explore Molokai on your own. It won't be difficult to get one, since Molokai now has local outlets of three major all-island rental companies: Budget Rent A Car, Dollar Rent A Car, and Avis. (See Chapter 3 for details on all-island rentals.) They're all located at the airport. Rates vary according to the season and business, and can vary from day to day, so it's wise to shop around.

BY TAXI & TOUR SERVICE

Kukui Tours & Limousines (☎ 808/553-5133), run by Vandale K. Dudoit Jr. and Joyce Dudoit, prides itself on its personal service and attention. Their air-conditioned limos provide half-day and full-day tours of the island, plus airport-hotel shuttle service. They can also provide wedding packages.

Molokai Style Services (☎ 808/553-9090) not only offers VIP limousine taxi services and tours, including airport and harbor pickup and hotel transfers on a 24-hour basis—they also provide a wide variety of other services: they handle cottage and car rentals; weddings; hiking, biking, camping tours; rentals of camping and fishing equipment; whale watching; spear fishing; dinner and shoreline cruises—you name it. They even deliver pizzas, beverages, and groceries.

Molokai Off-Road Tours and Taxi, aka **Friendly Isle Tours and Transportation** (☎ 808/553-9046) offers full- and half-day island tours and transfers, using 15-passenger vans or 20-passenger minibuses.

FAST FACTS

Molokai is part of Maui County. For details, see "Fast Facts: Maui," in Chapter 9. For local emergencies on Molokai, call 808/553-5355 for **police,** 808/553-5401 for **fire,** 808/553-5911 for an **ambulance,** and 808/553-5331 for **Molokai General Hospital.**

2 Where to Stay

Molokai now has a grand total of eight hotels and condos plus some vacation rentals and a few bed and breakfasts—and that's more than twice what it had a few years ago! Since there are so few, we'll give you the details on all of them; they're not all budget, but they all offer good quality for the money. In addition, **Bed and**

Breakfast Hawaii (☎ 800/733-1632), **Bed and Breakfast Honolulu** (Statewide) (☎ 800/288-4666), and **All Islands Bed and Breakfast** (☎ 800/542-0344) offer Molokai listings.

KAUNAKAKAI

Kaunakakai is Molokai's most central area, and the following hotels are just a mile or so down the road from the town's center, Ala Malama Street.

Pau Hana Inn

Kamehameha Hwy. (P.O. Box 546), Kaunakakai, Molokai, HI 96748. ☎ **808/553-5342,** or toll free 800/423-MOLO. Fax 808/531-5047. 40 units. $45–$90 single or double; $90 studio; $125 suite. Each additional person $10 extra. DC, MC, V. Free parking.

The drive from Hoolehua Airport to the town of Kaunakakai takes about 10 minutes, across what seems to be typical western grazing land. About a quarter of a mile from the town, following Hi. 45 along the beach, you'll see the Pau Hana Inn, the best choice in town for budgeteers, the most local and the most laid-back. Pau Hana is a relaxed, cottage-type hotel with some units in the garden, others facing the ocean or pool. All rooms and public areas have been refurbished recently. The lowest rates are for small, plain, but clean budget rooms, with two twin beds and a shower, in the longhouse. The more expensive rooms, by the pool or the ocean, accommodate up to four people with two double or queen-size beds. The superior rooms with kitchenettes and deluxe oceanfront suites sleep up to four people. The one-bedroom units have a kitchenette, sitting room, a queen-size bed and a couch, also for four. A swimming pool compensates for the rather poor ocean beach. The oceanfront Banyan Tree Terrace Restaurant is open for three reasonably priced meals a day. On weekends, it's the local hot spot for dancing.

Hotel Molokai

Kamehameha Hwy. (P.O. Box 546), Kaunakakai, Molokai, HI 96748. ☎ **808/553-5347,** or toll free 800/423-MOLO. Fax 808/531-5047. 51 rms. $59–$125 single or double. Each additional person $10 extra. CB, DC, MC, V. Free parking.

The Hotel Molokai is a modern Polynesian village that maintains the aura of the gracious past. The separate, three-unit cottages have rustic bedrooms with baths and all the modern-day comforts, including wall-to-wall carpeting and very comfortable basket swings out on the furnished lanais. There's a swimming pool (the waterfront here is a shallow lagoon behind the reef, popular for snorkeling but not good for swimming), a comfortable open lobby, and the Holo Kai Restaurant, where the "family" (staff) entertains their guests at dinner. Although this is an oceanfront hotel, the waves break a quarter mile out, leaving the lagoon tranquil and still, with only a lapping sound to lull you to sleep. (*Note:* Light sleepers may want to ask for a room away from the restaurant area.) The cheapest rooms are standard, superior rooms are on the garden floor, and deluxe rooms on the upper floor have a lanai or face the ocean. Only deluxe rooms can accommodate one or two extra people.

Molokai Shores Suites

Kamehameha Hwy. (P.O. Box 1037), Kaunakakai, Molokai, HI 96748. ☎ **808/553-5954,** or toll free 800/535-0085. 102 apts. TV. Apr–Dec 22, $119 one-bedroom apt; $149 two-bedroom apt. Dec 23–Mar, $95 one-bedroom apt; $125 two-bedroom apt. Discounted weekly and "no frills" rates available during low season. AE, DC, DISC, MC, V. Free parking.

Molokai Shores is located just a mile from Kaunakakai, between the Pau Hana Inn and the Hotel Molokai. The three-story, oceanfront apartment building has very pleasant units, all with ocean views, well-equipped kitchens, and private lanais overlooking tropical lawns. The one-bedroom units accommodate up to four people; the two-bedroom units, which have two baths, accommodate up to six (all at rates above). Picnic tables, barbecue units, and a putting green make outdoor life pleasant, and there's a pool for swimming (the beach is not particularly good here).

THE EAST END

The eastern shore of Molokai is a newer area for tourist development and it's quite lovely, a good base of operations for ocean swimming and excursions to Halawa Valley.

Kamalo Plantation Bed & Breakfast

HC 01, Box 300, Kaunakakai, Molokai, HI 96748. ☎ and fax **808/558-8236.** 1 cottage, 2 rms in main house. $75 cottage; $55 and $65 room. No credit cards. (Rates include breakfast.) Free parking.

On the eastside of Molokai, across from Father Damien's historic St. Joseph's Church, lies Kamalo Plantation, a 5-acre tropical garden at the foot of Mt. Kamakou. Waterfalls, rainbows, coves, and nearby beaches make this a delightful area. The island-style cottage sleeps two to four, has a king-size bed, a queen-size sofa bed, a shower, and a fully equipped kitchen. Breakfast items, including fresh home-grown fruits and breads, are provided. Lounges on the lawn and a hammock among shady lauhala trees allow for some serious relaxation. Two rooms in the guest wing of the main house share a bath; each has a small deck overlooking a garden and the remains of an ancient Hawaiian temple. Each room has a refrigerator and tea and coffee facilities. House guests enjoy breakfasts of tropical fruit and freshly baked breads in the dining room. Kamalo Plantation is a logical stopover on the way to or from Halawa Valley.

Honomuni House

HC 01, Box 700, Kaunakakai, Molokai, HI 96748. ☎ **808/558-8383.** 1 cottage. TV $85 double per night, $510 per week. Each additional adult $10 extra; each additional child, $5. No credit cards. Free parking.

Surrounded by lush green tropical forest, Honomuni House is a country cottage that can accommodate up to four adults. There's a private enclosed sleeping area, a large living/dining area with color TV and a sofa bed, a nicely equipped kitchen, a full bath plus a hot-water shower outdoors, and a covered lanai. Hosts Jan and Keaho invite guests to enjoy the papayas and other tropical fruits fresh from their garden.

Puu O Hoku Ranch

HC 1, Box 900, Kaunakakai, HI 96748. ☎ **808/558-8109.** 1 cottage, 1 hunting lodge. Cottage $80 double, $10 extra person, up to six; hunting lodge, $825, up to 20. No credit cards.

Planning a retreat? Want to get away from it all at a rustic country cottage? Puu O Hoku (Hill of Stars), a working cattle ranch that covers most of the eastern end of Molokai, may be just the place for you. The splendid lodge, with fireplace and vaulted ceiling, can accommodate 20 people in nine bedrooms. The cozy cottage, with two bedrooms and two baths, can sleep up to 6. The vistas—cattle grazing on the hillside and the ocean beyond—are magnificent. The ranch is at the 25-mile marker on the East End; it's about a 15-minute drive to Halawa Valley.

Wavecrest Resort

HC 01, Box 541, Kaunakakai, Molokai, HI 96748. ☎ **808/558-8101** or toll free 800/ 367-2980. Fax 808/558-8206. 126 units. TV. $99 garden/oceanview units; $125 oceanfront units. Minimum stay three nights. Each additional person $5 extra. MC, V. Free parking.

Nestled against the eastern Molokai mountains, Wavecrest Resort has tennis courts, a swimming pool, and all the amenities necessary for at-home resort living. There's not much of a beach, but it's good for fishing. The one-bedroom apartments, recently upgraded, are all smartly furnished with fully equipped kitchens. From your private lanai, you can see Maui and Lanai across the water. You can pick up picnic supplies, groceries, and drinks at the store here.

KALUAKOI RESORT

Molokai's loveliest resort area is on the western shore, about 15 miles from the airport, next to the glorious, 3-mile stretch of almost-deserted Kepuhi Beach.

✪ Colony's Kaluakoi Hotel & Golf Club

P.O. Box 1977, Kepuhi Beach, Molokai, HI 96770. ☎ **808/552-2555** or toll free 800/777-1700. Fax 808/552-2821. 174 rms. TV TEL. $90–$110 double; 135–$140 studio; 170 one-bedroom suite for four; $190 one-bedroom oceanview cottage for four. Each additional person $15 extra. AE, CB, DC, DISC, JCB, MC, V. Free parking.

This is the grandest of Molokai hotels. The rooms, which are in two-story buildings overlooking either ocean or golf course, are beautifully appointed with wood, rattan furnishings, and vibrant colors; some have high-beamed ceilings. All rooms have refrigerators. Besides the beautiful ocean (often not safe for swimming), there's a handsome free-form swimming pool, bar service at poolside, the championship 18-hole Kaluakoi Golf Course (a friend tells us that at night deer come out to drink at the water hazards), four lighted tennis courts, a tennis pro, and all sorts of shops and services. Ohia Lodge provides excellent meals. Inquire about golf packages.

Kaluakoi Villas

Kaluakoi Resort, P.O. Box 350 Maunaloa, Molokai, HI 96770. ☎ **808/552-2721** or toll free 800/525-1470. Fax 808/552-2201. 95 units. TV. $120–145 studio; $145 suite; $195 golf/ ocean villa. AE, MC, V. Free parking.

Kaluakoi Villas is very luxurious and very lovely. All its units have private lanais affording some degree of ocean view, and are richly decorated in island style with rattan furnishings. They boast a refrigerator, a countertop range, microwave oven, cooking utensils, china, and glassware. The golf and ocean villas have a full range and a dishwasher. All the activities and facilities of Colony's Kaluakoi Hotel & Golf Club—the restaurants, day-and-night tennis courts, and 18-hole championship golf course—are available to guests. There's a freshwater swimming pool. Special "Molokai Magic" packages are available.

Ke Nani Kai

P.O. Box 126, Maunaloa, Molokai, HI 96770. ☎ **808/552-2761** or 800/888-2791. Fax 808/ 552-0045. 120 apts. TV TEL. $95–115 one-bedroom apt for up to four; $125–$135 two-bedroom apt for up to six. Crib $8 extra. Minimum stay 2 nights. AE, DC, MC, V. Free parking.

There's an air of tranquility here that makes you feel like you could stay for weeks and simply unwind, never missing civilization a bit. Located at the entrance to the Kaluakoi Hotel (actually, between the 8th and 17th fairways of the golf course), this is a superb condominium resort, with some 55 units available to the general public. The apartments, each with a view of garden or ocean, are handsomely furnished, with very large living rooms, bedrooms with sliding doors, lanais affording splendid views, superbly equipped kitchens, VCRs, and washers and dryers. On the grounds are an enormous swimming pool, a volleyball court, two horseshoe pits, two tennis courts, and a whirlpool spa; the beach is just a short walk away. Hanging flowers cover the trellises. This is the most popular condo in the area for families because of the large pool and the dining/barbecue facilities.

Molokai Beachfront Condos

P.O. Box 249, Hana, Maui, HI 96713. ☎ **808/248-7049** or 808/248-7365 or toll free 800/228-4262, fax 808/248-8240. 2 units. TV. May 2–Dec 19, $70 for two; Dec 20–May 1, $98 for two. Each additional person $10.

Here's a little Molokai secret: two delightful second-story oceanfront units with perhaps the best views at the Kaluakoi Resort. These large studios with lanais have 20-foot-high ceilings and are custom-decorated in a modern Hawaiian motif, with Hawaiian quilts, VCR, a king-size bed in one unit and a queen-size bed in the other, both with sofa beds. One has a complete kitchen, the other a mini-kitchen. The studios can connect to house a group traveling together. Guests here have use of all the facilities of Colony's Kaluakoi Hotel & Golf Club (see above), including the free-form swimming pool, four lighted tennis courts, and the 18-hole Kaluakoi Golf Course (the units are, in fact, on the first tee).

Paniolo Hale

P.O. Box 190, Maunaloa, Molokai, HI 96770. ☎ **808/552-2731** or toll free 800/367-2984 (call collect from Canada and Hawaii). Fax 808/552-2280. 77 apts. TV TEL. $95–$135 studio for two; $115–$160 one-bedroom apt for up to four; $145 (garden view) and $195 (ocean view) two-bedroom apt for up to four. Fifth and sixth persons in two-bedroom apt $10 each. Minimum stay 3 nights. AE, MC, V. Free parking.

Next door to the Kaluakoi Hotel, on Kepuhi Beach, Paniolo Hale is adjacent to the golf course; in fact, one must cross the fairway to get to the beach. Wild deer and turkeys are frequently seen on the grounds. There is a swimming pool and a paddle-tennis court, and guests receive a reduced rate when golfing at Kaluakoi. The Kaluakoi Hotel also offers its four lighted tennis courts to Paniolo Hale guests for a nominal fee. This is a luxury condominium complex. The best buys are the one-bedroom units, which have two baths and sleep up to four; the two-bedroom units, also with two baths, sleep up to six. Hot tubs are available on the lanais of all two-bedroom units for an additional charge. There are also oceanview units. All the apartments have full kitchens, VCRs, and attractive island furnishings, and each unit has its own screened lanai (a touch of old Hawaii), which you walk right onto from your room, without going through a door. The nearest restaurant is at the Kaluakoi Hotel, about a block away along the sea wall, and the nearest grocery store is 7 miles away. We continue to receive good reports on this one. Inquire about room/car packages or golf specials.

3 Camping

By Jeanette Foster

As it is on the other islands, camping is a year-round experience on Molokai. There is a wet season (winter) and dry one (summer), but campers should be prepared for rain at any time of the year. Campers need also be ready for insects (a good repellent for mosquitoes), water purification (boiling, filtration, or iodine crystals), and sun protection (sun screen, hat, and long-sleeved shirt). Also, a note on personal safety: Don't hike or swim alone and never turn your back on the ocean; the waves might be closer and more powerful than you think.

For information on trails, hikes, camping and permits in state parks around the islands, including Molokai's Palaau State Park, contact: **Hawaii State Department of Land and Natural Resources,** State Parks Division, P.O. Box 1049, Wailuku, HI 96793 (☎ 808/243-5354). The **Hawaiian Trail and Mountain Club,** P.O. Box 2238, Honolulu, HI 96804, offers an information packet on hiking and camping in the Hawaiian Islands, including Molokai. Send $1.25, plus a legal-sized, self-addressed, stamped envelope for information. Another good source of information is the *Hiking/Camping Information Packet* from **Hawaii Geographic Maps and Books,** 49 S. Hotel Street, Suite 218, Honolulu, HI 96813 (☎ 808/538-3952), for $7, which includes postage. Be sure to bring your own gear, as there are no rentals available on Molokai.

One of the best places to camp on Molokai—a campsite reachable by car but still perfect for getting away from it all—is **Papohaku Beach Park** on the western shore. This beach, the largest on Molokai, is a great spot for rest and relaxation. Facilities include restrooms, drinking water, outdoor showers, barbecue grills, and picnic tables. Limited groceries and gas are available in Maunaloa, 6 miles away. There's a coffee shop and restaurant at the Kaluakoi Resort, 1 mile away. Camping permits can be obtained by writing **Maui County Parks Department,** P.O. Box 526, Kaunakakai, HI 96748 (☎ 808/553-3204). Camping is limited to three days, but officials sometimes wave this if no one else has applied for a permit. The cost is $3 per person per night.

4 Where to Eat

KAUNAKAKAI

On Ala Malama, the main street of Kaunakakai, you can mingle with the locals for some down-home good food at old-fashioned low prices.

MEALS FOR LESS THAN $10

Kanemitsu Bakery and Coffee Shop

Ala Malama St. ☎ **808/553-5855.** Plate lunches $4.50–$5. No credit cards. Wed–Mon 5:30am–1pm ('til 11am Sun); bakery open to 6:30pm. LOCAL.

When was the last time you had a hot dog for $1.50, a hamburger for $1.56, and club sandwiches that go up to all of $3.85? These are the kinds of prices that have made this place a local standby for years. There are reasonable breakfasts, too. Kanemitsu is primarily a bakery, and a famous one, known for its flavorful Molokai French bread (a great gift item, by the way, for friends in Honolulu). They also bake excellent cheese and onion breads and seven different kinds of yummy cookies, including sandis, a shortbread cookie. All breads and pastries are baked without preservatives. If you want, you can purchase a ready-mix to bake your own Molokai bread. This humble bakery actually turns out up to 2,500 loaves a day.

Outpost Natural Foods

70 Makaena Place. ☎ **808/553-3377.** Sandwiches $2.50–$4.50; main courses $4.25–$5.49. No credit cards. Sun–Fri 10am–3pm. VEGETARIAN.

Outpost Natural Foods, at the west end of town next to the civic center, is a natural-foods store and juice bar/restaurant with picnic tables outside that's quite pleasant for a light and healthful meal. In addition to freshly squeezed orange juice, carrot juice, and the like, they offer vegetarian sandwiches (the whole-grain bread is baked fresh in Hawaii; the organic lettuce and greens are grown on Molokai), salads, burritos, and a low-fat hot lunch every day. The hot lunch has to be one of the best buys in town, since it always includes a main course, such as a pasta or tofu dish or stir-fry veggies, plus salad, for $4.50. Everything is available for takeout. The soft-serve machine dispenses a luscious all-fruit ice cream.

Oviedo's Lunch Counter

Ala Malama St. ☎ **808/553-5014.** Lunch or dinner plates $7.50. No credit cards. Daily 10am–6:30pm. FILIPINO.

To sample Filipino food, sit down for lunch or get a take-out plate at Oviedo's, a simple, home-style restaurant on the main street in Kaunakakai. Oviedo's features such Filipino specialties as pork adobo (a kind of stew), tripe stew, pigs' feet, sweet-and-sour spareribs, and roast pork.

Rabang's Restaurant

Ala Malama St. ☎ **808/553-5841.** Main dishes $3.50–$6. No credit cards. Breakfast daily 6–10am; lunch and dinner daily 10am–9pm. FILIPINO.

Filipino food is also available at Rabang's, next door to Molokai Fish and Dive. You can get a good rice and adobo dish, a different one every weekday, served "from 10am until food *pau*," according to Mrs. Rabang. Hawaiian food is served every Friday. She also suggests that you try the Filipino dessert called *halohalo*— ask her to explain what it is. Take your food out or eat in at one of just five tables.

MEALS FOR LESS THAN $20

✪ Banyan Tree Terrace

At the Pau Hana Inn. ☎ **808/553-5342.** Reservations recommended at dinner. Main courses $10.75–$17.50. Breakfast daily 6:30–10:30pm; lunch daily 11am–2pm; dinner daily 5:30–9pm. AMERICAN.

Whether you're seated indoors in the big, rustic dining room with the tremendous fireplace or outdoors on the beach under the enormous, spreading Bengalese banyan tree (the scene of nighttime entertainment), you're going to find a meal here very pleasant. The banyan, also known as an East Indian fig tree, has been standing sentinel over the ocean here for almost 100 years. Dinner is well priced, with such main dishes as shrimp tempura, barbecued beef short ribs, seafood platter, and top sirloin. Specialty of the house is prime rib, a 10-ounce cut for $16.95. The price includes soup and salad bar, hot vegetables, a choice of starch, and Molokai French bread. Lunch features daily specials at $5.25; with soup and salad bar, $7.25. And they have homemade pizza on Mondays.

Holo Holo Kai

At the Hotel Molokai. ☎ **808/553-5347.** Reservations recommended at dinner. Main courses $8.95–$18.95. AE, DC, MC, V. Breakfast daily 7–11am; lunch daily 11:30–2pm; dinner daily 6–9pm. AMERICAN.

Hotel Molokai's dining room enjoys an excellent location, right on the edge of the ocean and open to its charms. And the food is very good, too. Dinner is well priced, since all main dishes—such as huli huli chicken, prime rib, roast pork, New York steak, and mahimahi—are accompanied by soup and salad bar, vegetables of the day, a choice of steamed rice or mashed potatoes, and Molokai French bread. People rave about their hearty beef stew, a local favorite. Lunch features salads, sandwiches, and burgers, plus hot main dishes like beef stew, fried chicken, and mahimahi, for $5.75 to $6.25. Local musicians entertain at dinner.

Here's a special tip for those of you who are going to be in Molokai for only one day: Take an early-morning flight out from Honolulu or Maui, and go directly from the airport to the Hotel Molokai. Treat yourself to one of their famous breakfast specialties—banana french toast (Molokai bread in a banana-egg batter) or, our personal favorite, papaya pancakes topped with crushed macadamia nuts; both of these treats are under $5. Now, after your coffee, you're set for a day of exploring Molokai.

MAUNALOA

Jo Jo's Cafe

Maunaloa. ☎ **808/552-2803.** Reservations not accepted. Main courses $9–$15. MC, V. Lunch Mon–Wed and Thurs–Sat noon–2pm; dinner Mon–Tues and Thurs–Sat 5–7:45pm. AMERICAN.

Maunaloa, the sleepy little plantation town near the western shore, boasts one of the island's most enjoyable budget eateries. Dine with the islanders at homey Jo Jo's Café, not far from the Kaluakoi Resort; it's in the tavern section of the old Pooh's Restaurant. All main courses are served with vegetables and a scoop of rice. Jo Jo's specialty is fish; they serve several different fish dishes every day, either frozen or fresh, whenever it's available, so you may be lucky enough to get ahi, mahimahi, ono, aku, or opakapaka. Fresh fish with curry sauce is also very popular, as are the shrimp or chicken or lamb curries (a different one each day) that the owner, who hails from India, whips up in authentic style (he suggests you call a day in advance for a curry request). Korean ribs are another specialty. Lunch is a good buy, with main dishes around $5 to $8. Hamburgers, surf-burgers (a fresh fish sandwich), and salad are available, too. For dessert, try one of their fresh island homemade toppings on an ice cream sundae, or have a piece of pie—all for $2.50. Beer and wine are available. Management suggests you come early for dinner, since they take no reservations, and sometimes it's standing room only. Funky and fun.

KUALAPUU

✪ Kualapuu Cook House

☎ **808/567-6185.** Reservations not required. Main courses $6.50–$15. No credit cards. Mon–Fri 7am–8pm, Sat 7am–4pm. AMERICAN.

Look for Kualapuu Cook House, a welcome addition to restaurant-poor Molokai, as you head up Kalae Road, and then take a left turn onto Farrington Road. It actually was a cook house back in the days of the Del Monte Plantation. Owner Nanette Yamashita has turned it into a quality eating place, with seating either indoors or on an outdoor patio. Fresh foods are featured at reasonable prices; you'll get a complete breakfast—eggs, meat, rice, and pancakes or french toast—for $4.50 to $6.50. Don't miss the three-egg omelettes especially the fish omelette, with fresh garden vegetables, fresh mahimahi, and cheese—terrific! At lunch, nothing on the regular à la carte menu is over $7.50; local favorites are served, as well as gourmet burgers, made from hamburger ground fresh every day. At dinner, chicken stir-fry ($7.50) and local-style teriyaki chicken or pork ($8.50) are huge favorites; so are the New York steak and shrimp and the fresh fish of the day (when available). If you're in Molokai on a Thursday night, drop everything and come here for the boneless prime rib; served with baked potato or rice, salad, and sautéed vegetables; at $12.50, it's everybody's favorite. Even if you don't eat a full meal here, you'll have to come by for one of Nanette's homemade pies; she bakes 8 to 10 different ones every day, using fresh local fruits when in season: Molokai lime, guava cream cheese, and passion-orange cream cheese are all delectable. Nanette's chocolate macadamia-nut pie is world-famous; she ships whole pies overnight to New York or London or wherever people demand them. (Cost is $12.50; other whole pies begin at $6.50; a single slice is $2 to $3.)

5 Beaches

By Jeanette Foster

The beaches of the Friendly Isle run the gamut, ranging from the largest white-sand beach in the state to grassy areas around former Hawaiian fish ponds. What's more, Molokai's beaches are all great places to get away from it all—by most standards, they're never crowded.

PAPOHAKU BEACH

On Molokai's western shore lies one of the largest white-sand beaches in the state, more than 2 miles long and 100 yards wide. Located in the Kaluakoi Resort, off Kaluakoi Road, this is not a safe swimming beach, as rip currents and strong along-shore currents are present year-round, and heavy surf rolls in both summer and winter. It's great for picnicking and sunbathing, though, as well as whale watching (in the winter months) and fishing. Facilities include picnic grounds, barbecues, showers, restrooms, a pavilion, and parking. Papohaku is peopled mainly with guests from Kaluakoi during the week; local residents and their families camp here on weekends.

KAWAKIU BAY

Kawakiu, which means "the spy place," is aptly named—this is one of the best places on Molokai to see the city lights of Honolulu across the channel. It's safe to swim off of the wide, chalky-white beach during the summer months, when the ocean is calm, but in the winter and spring, when the high surf rolls in, the powerful rip currents and pounding shorebreak make even walking along the shoreline dangerous. Behind the beach a kiawe tree grove provides a shady picnic area. There are no facilities. The dirt access road begins on the Maunaloa Highway; to get here, look for the public right-of-way sign $2^1/_2$ miles north of the turnoff for the Sheraton Molokai.

MOOMOMI BEACH

Molokai residents refer to the entire 3-mile length of shoreline from the Hawaiian Home Lands Recreation Center to Ilio Point as Moomomi Beach. The best place to swim along the beach is the bay in front of the Hawaiian Home Lands Commission's large community recreation center pavilion. A small pocket of white sand fronts the pavilion. The inner right corner of the bay is a good swimming area for children. Fishermen also frequent this area. Access to the beach is via Hawaiian Home Lands; permission must be obtained to get in. Contact Hawaiian Home Lands, P.O. Box 198, Hoolehua, HI (☎ 808/567-6104).

HALAWA BEACH PARK

Along the eastern shore of Molokai, at the end of Hi. 450, lies a tropical paradise called Halawa Valley, where palm trees border the beach and waterfalls cascade in the distance. The valley's two well-known waterfalls are Moaula and Hipuapua.

According to the Hawaiian legend, the freshwater pool at the base of Moaula Falls is the territory of a giant *mo'o* (lizard). Visitors must drop a ti leaf into the pool before entering; if your ti leaf floats, then you may enter the water. If the ti leaf sinks, beware—the lizard doesn't want you to disturb him. The beach at Halawa is shallow inshore and safe for swimming in the summer months. The water may look murky, as the Halawa Stream empties into the ocean here. In winter months, Halawa is one of the top surfing spots in the state. The county park area has a pavilion, restrooms, barbecue grills, and a parking area. Bring your own drinking water, as the water here is brackish and not meant for human consumption.

ONEALII BEACH PARK

Molokai's oldest public beach park is located just outside of Kaunakakai, on Hi. 450. This park, a spacious meadow dotted with a coconut grove and banyan and shower trees, is perfect for families. Because children can safely swim off the narrow sand beach, the park gets extremely crowded on weekends. Park facilities include a pavilion, restrooms, and parking.

6 Water Sports & Recreation

By Jeanette Foster

BODYBOARDING (BOOGIE BOARDING) & BODYSURFING

Molokai only has three beaches that offer ridable waves for bodyboarding and bodysurfing: Papohaku Beach, Kepuhi Beach, and Halawa Beach. Even these beaches are only for experienced body surfers due to the strength of the rip currents and undertows. Boogie boards can be rented from **Fun Hogs,** Kaluakoi Resort (☎ 808/567-9292) for $5 an hour or $20 for 24 hours (fins are included in the price).

OCEAN KAYAKING

During the summer months, when the waters on the north shore are calm, Molokai offers some of the most spectacular kayaking in Hawaii. You can paddle from remote valley to remote valley, spending a week or more exploring the exotic terrain. However, this option is for the experienced kayaker only, especially those adept in open ocean swells and guiding the kayak through rough waves, which may suddenly appear. Kayak rentals and tours are available through **Fun Hogs,** Kaluakoi Resort (☎ 808/567-9292). Rentals start at $25 for a one-person kayak for a half day and go up to $45 for a two-person kayak for a full day. Guided tours of the south shore (which include whale watching and snorkeling) are available in the winter, and tours of the west end (which include snorkeling) can be taken in the summer, each at a cost $40 for the two- to three-hour tour.

SAILING

Molokai Charters, Kaunakakai (☎ 808/553-5852), offers a variety of sailing trips on *Satan's Doll,* a 42-foot sloop, from two-hour sunset sails to full day sails to Lanai with swimming and snorkeling. Price depends on the number of people (minimum of four) and the type of tour. Call for more information.

SCUBA DIVING

Want to see turtles or manta rays up close? How about sharks? Molokai resident Bill Kapuni has been diving the waters around Molokai his entire life; he'll be happy to show you whatever you're brave enough to encounter. **Bill Kapuni's**

Snorkel and Dive, Kaunakakai (☎ 808/553-9867), can provide everything you need—gear, boat, even scuba instruction. Two tank dives are $85, and include Bill's voluminous knowledge of the legends and lore of Hawaii.

SNORKELING

When the waters are calm, Molokai offers excellent snorkeling; you'll see a wide range of butterfly fish, tangs, and angel fish. Good snorkeling can be found—when conditions are right—at Kaupoa, Kaunala, Kapukahehu, Poolau, and Moomomi Beaches, and at most of the beaches on the east end, especially Fagans, Sandy, Honouli Maloo, Honouli Wai, and Murphy. Snorkeling gear can be rented for $8 a day from **Molokai Fish & Dive Corp.** in Kaunakakai (☎ 808/553-5926), or from **Fun Hogs,** Kaluakoi Resort (☎ 808/567-9292), for $7.50 a day. Both places will point out the day's best snorkeling spots. Snorkeling tours are available for $45 from **Bill Kapuni's Snorkel & Dive** (☎ 808/553-9867) or from **Fun Hogs** (☎ 808/567-9292) for $40 (see "Kayaking," above).

SURFING

Bring your own board, as there are no surf rentals on Molokai. Watch for the waves at Kaunakakai Wharf, Hale O Lono Beach, Kanalukaha Beach, Kepuhi Beach, Kawaaloa Bay, and Halawa Beach.

WHALE WATCHING

The humpback whales that frequent the waters around Molokai from mid-December through mid-March can be seen up-close-and-personal with **Molokai Charters,** Kaunakakai (☎ 808/553-5852), which has a 42-foot sloop, *Satan's Doll;* or **Shon-a-Lee II Sport and Marine,** Kaunakakai (☎ 808/553-5242), which offers whale watching on their six-passenger sport fishing boat.

✪ Frommer's Favorite Molokai Experiences

Relaxing at Papohaku Beach. Looking for a white-sand beach to call your own? This is it. Kick back and enjoy the beauty and solitude of this pristine spot.

Riding the Molokai Wagon. Discover a 13th-century *heiau* (temple), then party on the beach with Hawaiian music, traditional Polynesian net throwing, and lots of fun, games, and relaxation.

A Drive to Maunaloa Town. Visit Jonathan Socher's Big Wind Kite Factory and his Plantation Gallery to see the work of local artists and craftspeople in one of the most laid-back shopping scenes in the islands.

Kayaking to the North Coast's Remote Valleys. For a few summertime weeks, Fun Hogs of Kaluakoi can take you to see Molokai's marvelous hidden valleys, most of which are only accessible by water. This is a heavenly opportunity, but only for the experienced kayaker.

Flying into Kalaupapa Peninsula. Tour the isolated settlement dedicated to the treatment of Hansen's disease (otherwise known as leprosy) with ex-patient Richard Marks of Damien Molokai Tours, the "mayor of Kalaupapa." This is a place of incredible beauty with a history of unfathomable sorrow—it shouldn't be missed.

7 Hiking, Golf & Other Outdoor Activities

By Jeanette Foster

HIKING

For information on trails, hikes, camping, and permits in state parks around the islands, including Molokai's Palaau State Park, contact: **Hawaii State Department of Land and Natural Resources,** State Parks Division, P.O. Box 1049, Wailuku, HI 96793 (☎ 808/243-5354). The **Hawaiian Trail and Mountain Club,** P.O. Box 2238, Honolulu, HI 96804, offers an information packet on hiking in the Hawaiian Islands, including Molokai. Send $1.25, plus a legal-sized, self-addressed, stamped envelope for information. Another good source of information is the *Hiking/Camping Information Packet* from **Hawaii Geographic Maps and Books,** 49 S. Hotel Street, Suite 218, Honolulu, HI 96813 (☎ 808/538-3952), for $7, which includes postage.

Molokai's most awe-inspiring hike is probably that along the **Pepeopae Trail.** This is your chance to experience this pristine environment that is the result of millions of years of evolution in isolation. At the Pepeopae Bog in the Kamakou Preserve, venture back millions of years and see the state of nature before the arrival of humans. The Nature Conservancy protects this extraordinary ecosystem; for more information write Nature Conservancy of Hawaii, 1116 Smith St., Suite 201, Honolulu, HI 96817 (☎ 808/553-5236). Unfortunately, you need a four-wheel drive vehicle to get to the bog. Although no permit is required for this easy hike, you might want to call ahead to the Kamakou Preserve (☎ 808/567-6680) to check on the condition of the road.

To get there, take Hi. 460 west from Kaunakakai for 3¹/₂ miles and turn right on the Molokai Forest Reserve Road. After about 5 miles, you'll reach the boundary to the Forest Reserve; keep a look out for migratory birds (some from as far as Alaska) in the forest. At the Waikolu Lookout and picnic area, just over 9 miles on the Molokai Forest Reserve Road, sign in at the box near the entrance. Continue on the road for nearly 11 miles. Be on the lookout for the turn-off sign Puu Kolekole; this fork will lead to the clearly marked trailhead.

The 1¹/₂-mile round trip will take about 1¹/₂ hours to hike. A narrow boardwalk (constructed by volunteers) leads through the bog to a lookout platform near its high point. The boardwalk protects the bog and makes it easier than hiking through the mud. Don't get off the boardwalk; you could damage this fragile environment, thought to be the oldest in Hawaii. Along the cloud-draped trail you'll see mosses, sedges, native violets, ancient knee-high *ohia* trees, and lichens. The mists that blow in and out will give you an idea of what the world was like before the dawn of humans.

GOLF

The golfing on Molokai is one of Hawaii's best-kept secrets. The courses are challenging and fun, tee times are open, and the rates are lower than your score will be. Probably the best of these is **Kaluakoi Golf Course.** Designer Ted Robinson calls this par-72, 6,564-yard course "the most spectacular and unusual course in the islands," and it may indeed be. The course meanders along the ocean (six holes are along the shoreline) and through the woods (pheasants, axis deer, and wild turkeys freely roam the fairways). The course offers hilly, wooded fairways bisected by ravines, and a grand finish beginning at the par-3, 16th hole. Called "The

Gorge," the 16th plays 190 yards over a deep ravine to a two-tiered green. When you finish that, both the 17th and 18 holes are very long par-4s, with greens blind from the tee. Facilities include driving range, putting green, pro shop, and restaurant. This course is rarely crowded; greens fees are $55 for Kaluakoi Resort guests and $75 for non-guests. Call 808/552-2739.

If you're looking for a bargain, **Ironwood Hills** is for you. This is duffers' heaven—wide, forgiving fairways and the lowest greens fees around. The drawback of this fun course is that this is only a 9-hole course. Located in the highlands— for Molokai, that is—of Kualapuu, this public golf course (3,088 yards from the back tees) has a par of 35. (*High handicappers note:* Play from the back tees; not only will this strategy offer more of a challenge, but on some holes—like the 8th— it adds nearly 70 yards to the hole.) Don't be surprised if you feel like you're driving onto a pasture when you enter the course; it is a former pasture. The old Del Monte Pineapple Plantation created the course in 1928 as a recreation spot for its Scottish plantation workers. The course was redesigned and improved by Charles Pastorino and Cliff Lawson in 1990. The fairways consist of tightly woven, thick kukuya grass, which tends to make the fairway drives easier, but the bunkers have more gravel than sand, so they tend to make you hit the ball harder than you want. The course can get windy in the afternoon, so morning tee times are best; call 808/567-6000. Greens fees for 18 holes are a ridiculous $14; cart rental is $14 for a power cart and $2.50 for a pull cart (no other facilities are available).

OTHER SPORTS AND RECREATION
BICYCLING

Fun Hogs of Kaluakoi Resort (☎ 808/567-9292) rents 21-speed mountain bikes for $6 an hour or $25 for 24 hours, or at a special couples rate of two bikes for $20 each for 24 hours. For a guided tour of trails on the 53,000-acre Molokai Ranch, call the **Molokai Ranch Outfitters Center,** (☎ 808/552-2741); they offer full-day tours for $75 including all equipment rental, a gourmet picnic lunch, and shuttle transportation.

HORSEBACK RIDING

Molokai Ranch Outfitters Center, (☎ 808/522-2741), offers a 2-hour ride to a secluded beach on the west end (with swimming, lunch, kayaking, snorkeling, and relaxing included) for $95. Also available are 1¹/₂-hour rides for $35.

TENNIS

Maui County only has two tennis courts on Molokai. Both are located at the Mitchell Pauole Center in Kaunakakai (☎ 808/553-5141). Both courts have night lights and are available on a first-come-first-served basis.

8 Exploring the Island
HALAWA VALLEY & MOAULA FALLS

For a beautiful day on Molokai, get up early, have your hotel pack you a picnic box lunch (or put one together from the supermarkets in town), hop into your car, and head for Halawa Valley.

But before you do, call the Molokai Visitors Association at 808/553-3876 to see if you can gain access to the trail. For the last few years, the private land owners who own this property have forbidden all access by anyone who is not a landowner

Beaches, Activities & Attractions on Molokai

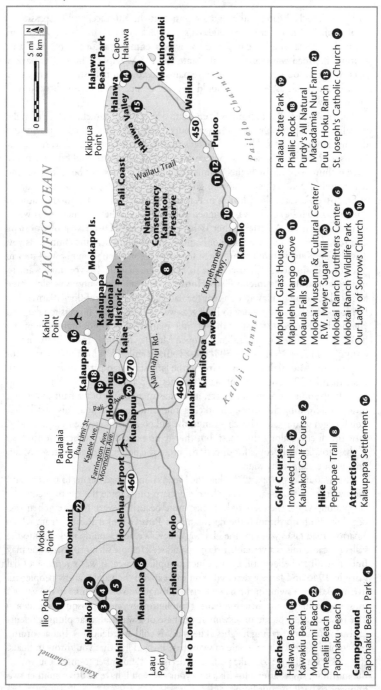

Beaches

Halawa Beach 14
Kawakiu Beach 1
Moomomi Beach 22
Onealii Beach 7
Papohaku Beach 3

Campground

Papohaku Beach Park 4

Golf Courses

Ironweed Hills 17
Kaluakoi Golf Course 2

Hike

Pepeopae Trail 8

Attractions

Kalaupapa Settlement 16

Mapulehu Glass House 12
Mapulehu Mango Grove 11
Moaula Falls 15
Molokai Museum & Cultural Center/
R.W. Meyer Sugar Mill 20
Molokai Ranch Outfitters Center 6
Molokai Ranch Wildlife Park 5
Our Lady of Sorrows Church 10

Palaau State Park 19
Phallic Rock 18
Purdy's All Natural
Macadamia Nut Farm 21
Puu O Hoku Ranch 13
St. Joseph's Catholic Church 9

in Halawa; locked gates and a sign are posted at the entrance, and trespassing is punishable by fines of up to $1,000. (It seems that someone had been injured on the trail, and a lawsuit has dampened the owners' enthusiasm for guests.) As of this writing, the road was closed, but the state and the MVA were hoping to have it opened again, soon. Even if the trail remains closed, you may still want to make the trip out as far as Waialua. Should the trail be open, follow the directions as given below.

The trip is just about 25 miles from Kaunakakai along Kamehameha IV Highway, but it will probably take you two hours to get there, since the last part of the driving is rough going. This is Molokai's southeastern coast, dotted with ancient heiaus, old fish ponds (some of which are used for scientific studies), and many coastal churches built by Father Damien and others. You won't be able to see the heiaus unless you get permission to go on private property, but you can stop in at **St. Joseph's Catholic Church** in Kamalo. The church, with a lovely statue of Father Damien beside it, was designed and built by Father Damien, who was a skilled carpenter. A little farther is Father Damien's **Our Lady of Sorrows Church,** where you'll see a statue of Damien in a pavilion near the church. As you drive by the Kamalo mountains, watch for rainbows and double rainbows—they're not uncommon here. When you get to Mapulehu at mile 15, you may want to make a stop at the **Mapulehu Glass House,** an enormous greenhouse which is the largest glass house in Hawaii (look for the flagpole). This tropical-flower farm offers free tours at 10:30am Monday to Friday, as well as bouquets of flowers to take with you or ship home. Just east of the 15-mile marker on the mountain side of the highway are a driveway and a sign. It's open Monday to Friday from 7am to noon, or by appointment (call or fax 808/558-8160). At mile 15½ look on the right for a sign to the **Mapulehu Mango Grove,** the largest mango patch in Hawaii, with more than 2,000 mango trees of many varieties, and a coconut grove. You can stop to pick up some tropical fruits here, as well as mango and other fruit juices at a little stand fronting the ocean. (Snorkeling tours and equipment are also available.) You'll begin seeing sandy beach again in the Pukoo area. There are many secluded little beach coves along this coast, but they're unmarked and difficult to find, so it's best to ask local people for directions. From the beach here, you can see Maui, only 9 miles across the water.

About 20 miles out, past Waialua, the broad country road begins to narrow, and soon you're on a one-lane road where the sharp turns force the car to practically creep along while the scenery becomes more beautiful every minute. Then you begin to climb up through the ranchlands of **Puu O Hoku Ranch,** from which a narrow road takes you into the Halawa Valley. We hope you do make it into the valley, because this is a veritable tropical paradise, a remote Shangri-la that one may find difficult to believe still exists. Once a populous area, it was swept by a tidal wave in 1946 and largely deserted. You can explore the valley (a few people still live here), have a swim in the bay, or make a roughly two-hour hike to the valley's most spectacular point, **Moaula Falls.** (You'll probably need mosquito repellent.) The rewards are a picnic or a swim at the base of a waterfall that plunges relentlessly down from dizzying heights. The water is cold and delicious, but according to Molokai legend, it's only safe to swim here if the ti leaf that you throw in floats. If it sinks, you'll have to make your own decision. Remember to make this trip in the morning, since, after a hike back to your car, you'll have to drive another two hours or so back to your hotel.

KALAUPAPA SETTLEMENT

Many people who have never been to Hawaii have heard about Father Damien of Belgium and what he did for the destitute lepers on Molokai over a century ago. Volunteering for the post, he set up a church on the isolated peninsula where victims of the dread disease were unceremoniously dumped and left to die. Damien ministered to their physical and spiritual needs and made Kalaupapa livable for them for 16 years, until he himself succumbed to the disease. In 1989, on the 100th anniversary of his death, a Damien Centennial Year was declared by both the state of Hawaii and the government of Belgium. Representatives of the Roman Catholic church, government officials, and the faithful from throughout the world gathered on Molokai to honor him. On May 15, 1994, Pope John Paul II declared him to have attained the blessedness of heaven and he has since been known as Blessed Damien; his title is "Damien of Molokai, Servant of Humanity." He performed his labors here at Kalaupapa, where a center for the treatment of leprosy—now called Hansen's disease—is still operating. Fewer than 100 patients and former patients are still at Kalaupapa, and to visit their island home is a moving experience. It is not, however, a trip we advise everyone to make. It's not for those who get nervous just thinking about diseases (although leprosy has been arrested

Discovering the Friendly Isle: Molokai's Special Events

Molokai is usually a relatively quiet place, but there are special events that draw the crowds from all over the islands. The first is the famous **Molokai-to-Oahu Canoe Race,** the most important event in the sport of outrigger canoeing. Participants paddle from Molokai to Fort DeRussy Beach in Honolulu in traditional Hawaiian canoes, going over some very rough water. The women's race takes place in September, the men's race in October.

An expression of the island's commitment to the preservation of authentic Hawaiian culture, the annual **Molokai Ka Hula Piko**—A Celebration of the Birth of Hula on Molokai—is now in its sixth season. Local hula halaus (schools) are joined by leading vocal and instrumental groups. There are also demonstrations of traditional Hawaiian crafts, and food booths selling Molokai specialties. According to legend, Molokai was the birthplace of the hula and it was here, at Ka'ana, that the goddess Laka learned to dance from her sister Kapo, and then spread the art of hula throughout the Hawaiian islands. The event is held on the third Saturday in May. For more information, call Molokai Visitors Association (☎ 808/553-3876 or toll free 800/800-6367 in the U.S. and Canada).

A third event, always held in January, is the annual **Molokai Makahiki,** a traditional Hawaiian "time of peace" celebration. In addition to a competition in Hawaiian games and a skin-diving tournament, the festivities feature several of Hawaii's most popular music groups. The event is held at Kaunakakai Park and the Manae Canoe Club; there is no admission charge.

The Molokai Ranch Rodeo, the first annual statewide rodeo on the island, takes place in August at Molokai Ranch's new rodeo area in Maunaloa. Professional cowboys vie for a $25,000 cash purse and prizes in several event competitions, from bull riding to women's barrel racing.

—Faye Hammel

by modern drugs and is presumably not contagious), and it's definitely not for the idly curious. The residents of Kalaupapa do not wish to be regarded as a tourist attraction. Getting to their beautiful but tragically isolated home takes a bit of doing, and the emotions the trip can raise have been overwhelming to more than one visitor.

There are a couple of ways to get to Kalaupapa. Unfortunately, as we went to press, the famous **Molokai Mule Ride** had been discontinued, but hopefully, it will be back by the time you read this. Check with the Molokai Visitors Association at 808/553-3876 or toll-free 800/800-6367 to find out its current status. It's an unforgettable experience, as the mule descends a spectacular, steep switchback trail 1,600 feet below the towering cliffs at Kalae into Kalaupapa. You are met at the peninsula, given a tour and a picnic lunch, and then returned to the trail for the ride to the top at 2pm. Cost should be around $120.

It's more economical, of course, to hike down the trail; it's a scenic 3^{1}/8-mile cliff walk that should take about 1^{1}/2 hours. But be advised that the hike both down and up the *pali* is arduous; many people hike down and fly back. (Make plane reservations in advance if that's what you want to do.) Be sure you call Richard Marks at Damien Molokai Tours (see below) to meet you for a ground tour of the settlement. You are not allowed in on your own.

There is, of course, an easier way to get to Kalaupapa, the one we personally favor, and that's by air both ways. Call Richard Marks's **Damien Molokai Tours** at 808/567-6171 (the only tour service operated by former patients, who know Kalaupapa from the inside out), and they will arrange for you to fly in from upper Molokai via Aloha Island Air for $50 round-trip (best time to call is between 7 and 8am and 7 and 8pm). Keep in mind that you cannot walk past the gate at the top of the cliff trail or around the peninsula without a permit, according to Health Department rules (Damien Molokai Tours will handle all permits). Minors under 16 are not allowed at Kalaupapa. Bring some lunch, as there are no stores or restaurants open to visitors at Kalaupapa. You may bring cameras and binoculars. Advance reservations for the tour are a must: Call 808/567-6171, or write Damien Molokai Tours, P.O. Box 1, Kalaupapa, Molokai, HI 96742. The full, four-hour grand tour costs $30 per person; a special eight-hour tour is $40.

What you'll see on the tour—the early settlement of Kalawo where St. Philomena Church, built by Father Damien, still stands; the cemetery where he was buried before his remains were returned to Belgium; the grave of Mother Marianne (also a candidate for canonization by the Roman Catholic church); Siloama Church; and a glorious view of Molokai's towering mountains—is just the beginning. All the tour guides are ex-patients, people who can give you a look at Kalaupapa off the record. It's a magnificent sight—a testimony to the patients who took barren lands and turned them into Eden, and a testimony to the medical pioneers and missionaries who preserved so many lives. Kalaupapa is a paradoxical place; it seems domestic, with many cozy little houses where people garden and watch TV, but it is incredibly silent, partly because there are no children. Only a small minority of the residents live with their spouses.

Under legislation passed by Congress, Kalaupapa—now known as Kalaupapa National Historic Park—will be left as it is until the last of the residents has died. The remaining residents, most in their 50s and 60s, like to joke about themselves as an endangered species. But all of them now live here by choice; what was once a veritable prison has now become a sanctuary.

The newest addition to the tour is a visit to the Kalaupapa Visitors Center, which has an excellent bookshop dealing with the history of Kalaupapa and Molokai. If you're lucky, your tour might include Richard Marks's own collection of Kalaupapa memorabilia, including antique bottles and clocks.

Note: On a recent visit to Kalaupapa, flying direct from Honolulu, we met two women who were making the exact same trip that we were; however, because they had booked the entire trip as a tour via a well-known tour operator, their cost was almost double ours. Make your own air arrangements and contact Damien Tours as we suggested: No need to waste your money.

A TRIP THROUGH PALAAU STATE PARK TO KUALAPUU

Even if you don't get to Kalaupapa itself, you should pay a visit to the Kalaupapa Overlook in Palaau State Park. It's an easy trip on very good roads, about 10 miles from Kaunakakai on Hi. 460. After you make your right on Hi. 470 and begin to climb to Upper Molokai, the air becomes fragrant with eucalyptus and pine. Park your car at **Palaau State Park,** a well-maintained and popular camping and picnicking spot for local residents. A short walk through towering cypress and pine and suddenly you're high, high up, looking down immense cliffs to the Kalaupapa Peninsula below. From the overlook, you can see the world's tallest sea cliffs, 3,300 feet high at Umilehi Point. A series of six informative plaques tell the Kalaupapa story, but official descriptions seem superfluous. Just standing here, gazing down at the peninsula below, you are caught up in some of the tremendous sorrow of those who lived their lives of exile at Kalaupapa.

There is another trail, this one a bit longer (and steeply uphill some of the way), that leads to the **Phallic Rock.** According to legend, barren women who made offerings to the rock and spent the night here would then become capable of bearing children. Supposedly, an unfaithful husband of one of the minor goddesses was transformed into this rock, and his mana still remains here.

While you're pondering this story (wrongdoers were often turned into stone in Hawaiian mythology), get back into your car and drive down the hill. Two miles below the overlook, on Hi. 470, you may want to pay a visit to the **Molokai Museum and Cultural Center/R. W. Meyer Sugar Mill** (☎ 808/567-6436), an authentic restoration of an 1878 sugar mill now in operating condition after almost a century of neglect. The only surviving 19th-century sugar mill in Hawaii, it is listed on the National Register of Historic Places. Local volunteer labor spent several years on its restoration. The original machinery, including the mule-drive cane crusher, is still in operating condition. Photos and memorabilia of the mill's original owner, and of his Hawaiian-born wife, Kalama Waha, provide a glimpse into early Molokai history. The mill is open Monday through Saturday from 10am to 2pm, for guided and self-guided tours. Admission is $2.50 for adults, $1 for children ages 5 to 18, under 5 free.

Continue down the road now to the little town of Kualapuu, where, now that the Del Monte pineapple plantation has been phased out, diversified agriculture is a growing industry (Molokai is now the state's leading producer of watermelon). Here you'll also find the pleasant little **Kualapuu Cook House Restaurant** (see "Where to Eat," above, in this chapter). Turn left on Puupeelua Avenue and you'll be back on the airport road.

If you're in the mood for traveling, continue west on Hi. 460 past the airport; you'll be on Maunaloa Road, which goes 10 miles to the old Dole pineapple village at Maunaloa, about 1,300 feet high, with its unusual little crafts shops (see "Shopping," below).

PURDY'S NUT FARM

We don't know of any other macadamia farm in Hawaii where either the owner or his mother will greet you personally and take you on a tour of the orchards. But Purdy's All Natural Macadamia Nut Farm is different. Tuddie Purdy and his mother guide you through the only working macadamia-nut grove on the island, and not only do they tell you all you ever wanted to know about macadamia nuts, but they also show you a variety of Hawaiian fruits and flowers. Most fun of all, you get to crack some macadamia nuts and try them raw. Then you'll be given some fruit and macadamia-blossom honey to taste, plus samples of their Ono Toasted Macadamia Nuts, which are remarkably light, surprisingly non-oily, and absolutely delicious. You can buy them on the spot (they'll also give you the recipe), as well as raw macadamia nuts out of the shell, and the honey. These items are also available by mail order, as is their new "Post-A-Coconut" with your message. The farm is located on 1¹/₂ acres in Hoolehua Hawaiian Homesteads and is open weekdays from 9:30am to 3:30pm, Saturday from 10am to 2pm, and Sunday by appointment only (☎ 808/567-6601 daytime, 567-6495 in the evening). It's not far from the airport, but it's best to ask them for driving directions. If you're in Molokai for a one-day trip, this could be a fun way to start the day. Admission is free.

MOLOKAI RANCH WILDLIFE PARK

Yes, you can go on a safari of sorts on Molokai; about 80 African and Asian animals live on the grounds of this 350-acre natural wildlife preserve. The dry terrain of western Molokai is similar to that of the expansive savannah lands of East Africa. The animals—including giraffe, zebra, Barbary sheep, Indian Blackbuck, eland, oryx, and wild turkey—thrive here. Tour guides lead visitors on a 90-minute photographic and educational adventure in an air-conditioned van. After the tour, visitors adjourn to the picnic area, where they can feed the friendly giraffes and other animals that gather around to see the funny people. A light refreshment is served. Cost of the tour is $35 for adults, $20 for children under 18, and $5 for children under 5; arrangements can be made at the Kaluakoi Hotel Travel Desk, or by calling 808/552-2714. Readers really like this one.

WAGON RIDES

This Molokai adventure is very popular. Your horse-drawn (or horse- and mule-drawn) wagon stops first at the Ili Ili O Pae Heiau, one of Hawaii's largest and best-preserved temples, built in the 13th century, where a guide explains the historical background; then it's back down the trail to the Mapulehu Mango Grove, the largest mango grove in the world. Then it's on to the beach for a Molokai-style barbecue and a fabulous party, complete with Hawaiian music, traditional Hawaiian net throwing, fishing, coconut husking, and many surprises. Guests are invited to try their hand at all the activities. Cost is $37 for adults, $18.50 for children 5 to 12, free for those under 5. Guided horseback rides are also available as are horses for hire. For reservations, call Larry Helm at **Molokai Wagon Ride** (☎ 808/567-6773 from 6 to 8am and after 6pm, or 808/558-8380, the wagon-ride site, from 9:30am to 12:30pm, daily).

SHOPPING

Molokai is perhaps the only place in the islands that is *not* heaven for shopping buffs. There is so little available here that many locals go off-island to do their shopping—even their grocery shopping! The local supermarkets, grocery shops,

Kaunakakai

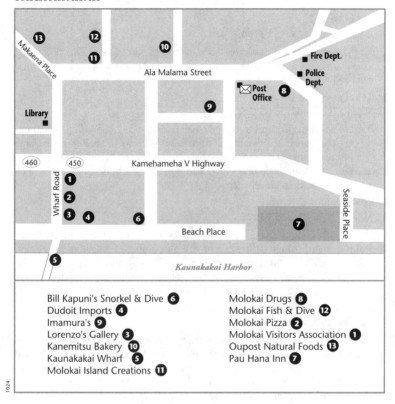

Bill Kapuni's Snorkel & Dive **6**
Dudoit Imports **4**
Imamura's **9**
Lorenzo's Gallery **3**
Kanemitsu Bakery **10**
Kaunakakai Wharf **5**
Molokai Island Creations **11**

Molokai Drugs **8**
Molokai Fish & Dive **12**
Molokai Pizza **2**
Molokai Visitors Association **1**
Oupost Natural Foods **13**
Pau Hana Inn **7**

and liquor stores on Ala Malama, the main street of Kaunakakai, a general store here and there in the country, and a handful of craft shops showing the work of local artists are just about it.

KAUNAKAKAI

Dudoit Imports

At Kahou Shopping Center on the wharf road. ☎ **808/553-3748.**

Everything—from Mexican blankets to mombasa mosquito nets, from antiques and collectibles to contemporary arts and crafts—can be found here. Many local artists and craftspeople are represented.

Lorenzo's Gallery of Fine Art and Molokai Treasures

At Kahou Shopping Center on the wharf road. ☎ **808/553-3748.**

You'll find finely crafted arts and crafts at this charming gallery. Local and state-wide artists represented here often use nature as a source of inspiration for their creations. Butch Tabano of Molokai, for example, creates his jewelry, scrimshaw, and carvings—of canoes, paddles, whales, geckos, dolphins—from the horns of the axis deer of Molokai (the deer, who run wild here, shed their horns once a year). He is known for his distinctive cribbage boards. Former sculptor-turned-basket-weaver Marguerite Pennington uses many natural materials found on Molokai—leaves, grasses, seed bracts, pods, roots, barks, and gourdes—to fashion her unique Hawaiian baskets. There's lots to look at and collect here—you'll find plenty to take home for yourself and others.

Molokai Drugs
Ala Malama St. ☎ **808/553-5790.**

For the best selection of books on the island, try Molokai Drugs. This all-purpose general store has a particularly good selection of Hawaiiana, and also sells local crafts and gift items in addition to the usual drugs and sundries.

Molokai Fish and Dive
Ala Malama St. ☎ **808/553-5926.**

To learn where the fish are biting, and to get fishing, diving, snorkeling, and camping gear, plus boogie boards and golf balls, this is the place to go. But they're more than just a sporting-goods store; they have the largest collection of Molokai souvenirs on the island, including a huge selection of T-shirts, designed and printed for them and sold exclusively here.

Molokai Island Creations
Ala Malama St. ☎ **808/553-5926.**

This friendly boutique has Hawaiian-made swimwear, muumuus, and children's clothing at surprisingly affordable prices, plus a unique collection of jewelry, including sea opal, coral, and sterling silver. They also have a good selection of books on Hawaii, cards, and much more. There's plenty to catch your eye here.

Outpost Natural Foods
70 Makaena Place. ☎ **808/553-3377.**

To stock up on organic local produce—papayas, bananas, avocados, sprouts, etc.—try Outpost Natural Foods (next door to the Civic Center), which sells the usual health-food fare plus other items at the lowest possible prices. They also have an excellent lunch bar (see "Where to Eat," above). Pick up a fruit smoothie, a sandwich, a burrito, or some Molokai Taro Chips, a local delicacy.

Imamura's
Ala Malama St. ☎ **808/553-5615.**

Like an old-fashioned general store, Imamura's has a little bit of everything, and is lots of fun to poke around in.

KUALAPUU

Coffees of Hawaii
In Kualapuu. ☎ **808/538-0800.**

Stop in for some Hawaiian coffee and see the work of about 20 Molokai artists and crafts people in the attractive Plantation Store. Marguerite Pennington's handsome Hawaiian baskets are shown here, among other works. Tie in a visit here with lunch at Kualapuu Cook House (see "Where to Eat," above).

MAUNALOA

Our favorite Molokai shopping is out in Maunaloa (not far from the Kaluakoi Resort). Once a thriving plantation town, Maunaloa has been declining since Dole closed shop in 1975; however, young artisans are seeking it out and showing their wares here. We should tell you at the start that this is the most laid-back "shopping area" we've ever come across, with only one street, and with shops staying open more or less as inspiration moves the owners, who often seem to be out fishing or surfing or visiting Honolulu.

Do-It-Yourself *Kapa Lau:* Learning the Art of Hawaiian Quilting

Until recently, kept alive only through the diligence of a few Hawaiian matrons, the unique and beautiful art of Hawaiian quilting (called *kapa lau*) is currently enjoying a rise in popularity among the younger generations. The increased interest in quilting is part of the larger Hawaiian cultural renaissance—or resurgent enthusiasm for the preservation of uniquely Hawaiian art, craft, and cultural forms—being spurred on by both the residents and tourists of modern-day Hawaii.

Each Hawaiian quilt, with its abstract forms, bright colors, bold designs, has its own name and tells its own story. Each is prized for its *mana,* or spiritual presence, as much as for its material or practical worth. The bold, geometric designs—most often cut from a single piece of solid cloth and applied to another of contrasting hue—are usually inspired by the natural beauty surrounding the quilter. Pineapples, breadfruit trees, waterfalls, volcanoes, and flowers like bird of paradise and plumeria are favorite motifs. Historically themed quilts are popular as well, particularly flag quilts (known as *kapa hae*). Fashioned from the end of the nineteenth century, when American governors declared flying the Hawaiian flag an act of treason, flag quilts were—and still are—highly prized by their Hawaiian owners.

Fine hawaiian quilts can be seen at museums and resorts around the island. In Honolulu, you can view excellent examples at the Mission Houses Museum and the Bishop Museum (where you can also observe the quilting process during twice-weekly demonstrations). Big Island collections are at the Mauna Kea Beach Hotel and the Lyman House Memorial Museum. Other collections are on display at the Hyatt Regency Maui and the Kauai Museum.

If you're interested in learning the art of *kapa lau* while you're on Molokai, get in touch with Ginger LaVoie, Fiber Artist of Molokai, HC01 Box 940, Kaunakakai, HI 96748 (☎ 808/558-8227), one of the finest quilters in the islands. She gives classes in the art of Hawaiian quilting by appointment at the Kaluakoi Resort. Complimentary lessons are offered with the purchase of one of her beginner's quilting kits. She also has for sale original quilt designs, fully basted quilts, and silk-screened T-shirts. Ginger offers lectures, slide shows, and classes in the art of quilt design, and she's happy to take commissions for custom quilts.

—Faye Hammel

✪ Big Wind Kite Factory
☎ **808/552-2364.**

Owner Jonathan Socher is always on hand and happy to greet visitors. He and his wife, Daphne, not only create beautiful, high-flying kites (which are sold in many island shops), but they even offer free flying lessons with modern 100-m.p.h. "aerobatic kites." It's also fun to take a tour of their minifactory, where they demonstrate the techniques of kite making. Their most popular items are pineapple windsox and minikites at $14.95, and rainbow-spinning windsox at $19.95 to $35. Their Hula Girl Kite—"She Dances in the Sky"—is also very popular at $35. They make their own two-string rainbow stunt kites, from $35. Their son Zachariah, 14 years old, is also designing kites, and his gecko with sunglasses and shark with sunglasses are two of their most popular designs. They now have 28-foot-long dragon-tail kites, plus butterflies, dinosaurs, and sun-moon-star kites, all with rainbow tails. The Sochers recently participated in Bali's International Kite Festival and have a spectacular collection of Indonesian and Malaysian kites on display including Daphne's 6-foot "Memories of Bali" kite.

✪ **Plantation Gallery**
☎ **808/552-2364.**

Jonathan Socher's Plantation Gallery, which shows the work of dozens of island artisans, is adjacent to the kite factory. There are handsome wood bowls and boxes by local artists Bob Moore and Rune Pederson. Woodcarver Bill Decker travels around the world, sending back tribal art such as New Guinea shields and Borneo blowguns. Unless the surf is up, you'll probably find Butch Tabanao and his deerhorn jewelry, hair combs (from $12), and cribbage boards (around $40) made from the axis deer of Molokai. There's pottery sculpture by Chuck Moore from $20, and Hawaiian pillowcase quilts by Ginger Lavoie at $25. Several local artists do hand-painted shirts at $25, long-sleeved tops at $42. On our last visit, Jonathan proudly showed us his new collection of personally chosen imports from Bali and Southeast Asia: He calls this the "Bali Hale Gift Shop." It's full of delightful surprises, such as colorful wooden bird mobiles and birds of paradise stalks, at $10 to $25; batik pillow covers; pareaus; wonderful Balinese masks called "guardians" or "crib angels"; magnificent batik quilts for $250; and colorful wooden bird and fish earrings at $9.50, and you get another pair free. Note, too, the collection of books (more than 400 titles), cards, and prints by leading island artists. The gallery/shop is decorated with orchid plants and there's a garden outside with soothing bamboo wind chimes (on sale, from $25). For lovers of the unusual, this is a must stop. Open Monday through Saturday 8:30am to 5pm, Sunday 10am to 2pm.

MOLOKAI AFTER DARK

Nightlife on Molokai, as we travelers know it, is almost all in the major hotels, and it's largely impromptu. It all depends on when local people feel like doing things (people here are not apt to let work interfere with their lives!). Every Friday and Saturday night, the **Pau Hana Inn** becomes the town's "hot spot." There's music and dancing under the 100-year-old spreading banyan tree, right at the ocean's edge. Locals turn out to kick up their heels. You'll be asked to dance. Music is provided by F.I.B.R.E., Friendly Isle Band Rhythmic Experience—and it is!

Live entertainment is also featured Thursday, Friday, and Saturday nights at the **Hotel Molokai.** The K'Kai Trio provides the entertainment, mostly Hawaiian and country-and-western music, over at the **Ohia Lodge** of the Kaluakoi Hotel. Check the local papers for news of special events, maybe even a luau at one of the hotels.

12

Lanai: Budget Living in the Playgrounds of the Rich & Famous

In the mind of the traveling public, a vacation on Lanai has become synonymous with the lifestyles of the rich and famous. Its two world-class Rockresorts—**The Lodge at Koele,** like an English manor in the hills, and the **Manele Bay Hotel,** a Mediterranean-style seaside pleasure palace—are known for their celebrity guests seeking retreat. (Lanai is advertised, in fact, as "Hawaii's private island.") So is it possible for the frugal traveler to get away from it all on pricey, private Lanai, a place where most guests are paying an average of $300 (and up) for lodgings? The answer—surprisingly—is yes. There is still one charming hotel, the **Hotel Lanai,** where rates are a comparatively moderate $95 a night for two. There are two B&Bs where doubles can be had for $60 to $75 a night. There is a decently priced restaurant in the Hotel Lanai and two humble eateries in the middle of town much favored by the local folks. The beaches are free and offer fine swimming and snorkeling. Tennis courts are free. And there are plenty of wide-open spaces, green forests, and fields in which to hike or ride horseback, and ruins to explore in a rented Jeep. Or, just come to Lanai to unwind—it's a perfect place for it. Lanai offers a real country vacation in a wonderfully peaceful setting. Some people find the island lacking in excitement and diversion; others find it a great adventure. After you've seen some of the other islands, you might want to spend a few days on Lanai.

Until 1990 and the grand opening of Koele Lodge, followed in 1991 by the opening of the Manele Bay Hotel, Lanai was not even part of the modern world of tourism. For years, the sleepy little island, the third smallest in the Hawaiian chain (13 miles wide and 18 miles long), was known as "The Pineapple Island" and little more. (The classic joke about visiting Lanai was: "After you've seen one pineapple, you've seen them all.") Jim Dole had purchased the entire island in 1921 and converted more than 16,000 of its 89,000 acres into the world's largest pineapple plantation. Dole created the plantation-owned and operated community of Lanai City. In one way or another, the livelihood of the entire population—some 2,500 people—was dependent on the company. As the pineapple industry faltered and the plantations moved to Malaysia and the Philippines, resort development replaced pineapple cultivation as Lanai's major industry. Today, all that remains of Jim Dole's 16,000 acres is a 500-acre field that provides fruit for the tables of the resorts.

What's Special About Lanai

Beaches
- Hulupo'e Bay, marine life conservation district with a crescent-shaped beach, offering some of the best swimming and snorkeling in the islands.
- Shipwreck Beach, a wild and windy strand that's great for beachcombing.

Natural Wonders
- The Garden of the Gods, a mysterious and beautiful badlands where centuries of wind erosion have sculpted ancient rocks into odd pinnacles and buttes.
- The Munro Trail, a spectacular path leading to the summit of Lanaihale, from which you have breathtaking views of the other islands in the Hawaiian chain.

Golf
- A world-class course, the Experience at Koele, that's like no other course in the world.

Privacy
- Known as "the Private Island," tiny Lanai's intimate scale and wide open spaces make it the perfect place to get away from it all.

Local Color
- The veranda and dining room of the Hotel Lanai—as well as Lanai City's other two restaurants—are great places to mix and mingle with islanders for a genuine Hawaiian experience.

Local reaction to the recent influx of tourism has been mixed. Many young people have been thrilled at the new possibilities for employment. Other groups have opposed the changes that signal the end of a lifestyle they have known and cherished for so long. Although much has changed economically, the natural beauties of the island are constant, and remain a pleasure for the visitor.

1 Orientation & Getting Around

ARRIVING BY PLANE   Getting to Lanai is easy. You can fly from either Honolulu or Maui on the jets of **Hawaiian Airlines** (☎ 800/367-5320) or on the smaller commuter planes (18 seats) of **Island Air** (☎ 800/323-3345) or **Mahalo Air** (☎ 808/833-5555, or 800/4-MAHALO from the mainland or 800/277-8333 in Hawaii.

ARRIVING BY BOAT   Expeditions (☎ 808/661-3756) runs five round-trip ferries each day from Lahaina, Maui. The cost is $50 and you can stay as many days as you like before picking up a returning ferry. (For other day trips to Lanai, see p. 383.)

GETTING AROUND

CAR RENTALS   If you're staying at Hotel Lanai, you may not need a car, as complimentary shuttle service is provided to and from the airport, the Manele Small Boat Harbor, The Lodge at Koele, and the Manele Bay Hotel. However, if you want to explore the rugged, remote areas of the island on your own, you are advised to rent a four-wheel drive vehicle, as there are only 30 miles of paved roads. **Dollar Rent-A-Car** (☎ 800/367-7006), the national company, and **Lanai City**

Service (☎ 808/565-7227), a local company, are one and the same. They rent Geotrackers for $109 a day, Jeeps for $119, and a compact for $60 per day. They'll pick you up at the airport and take you to their service station in town.

2 Where to Stay

Hotel Lanai
828 Lanai Ave., P.O. Box A-119, Lanai City, HI 96763. ☎ **808/565-7211.** 11 rms. $95 single or double. AE, MC, V.

Staying at the Hotel Lanai is like walking right back into 1923 and Lanai's plantation days. The Clubhouse became the Hotel Lanai, and for almost 70 years it was the only hotel in town. In 1992, the hotel underwent a complete renovation of its guest rooms, kitchen, bar, and public areas, although the original structure was retained. The cozy veranda, where guests and locals mingle and enjoy the views of the towering Cook Island pines that line the streets of Lanai City, is still there. So is the lovely dining room, with its wood-burning fireplace (it gets cold on Lanai at night), which serves all three meals. The rooms have been charmingly restored, with country pine furnishings, patchwork quilts, and hardwood floors; bathrooms have white tile floors, pedestal sinks, and stall showers (no tubs). In keeping with the spirit of the old plantation days, there are no TVs or radios in the rooms. Hotel Lanai is a pleasant, unpretentious place, with the cozy charm of an old-fashioned country inn.

Dreams Come True
547 12th St., P.O. Box 1525, Lanai City, HI 96763. ☎ **808/565-6961.** 3 rms. $55 single; $75 double; $10 additional child; $95 three adults (rates include tax and breakfast). Separate three-bedroom house, $195 per night (including tax) for up to 6 people. No credit cards.

Susan and Michael Hunter and their two children, 15-year-old Kahlil and 11-year-old Chahija, lived in Sri Lanka for seven years (where Michael studied gemology and made jewelry) before moving to Lanai. As a result, their lovely, rather large plantation house (six bedrooms, three baths) is furnished throughout with Asian antiques. The yard is beautifully landscaped; Susan picks mangoes, papayas, bananas, passionfruit, mountain apples, Hawaiian oranges, and more from her organic gardens. They're accompanied at the breakfast table by homemade bread, fresh island fruit jam, cappuccino, and other beverages. Two of the rooms have a private bath, one room has a shared bath. Susan knows lots about the island and will fill you in on what to see and do. The Hunters' studio is adjacent to their house; you're welcome to go in and browse (jewelry prices start at $15). Children are welcome.

Lanai Bed & Breakfast
312 Mahana Place, P.O. Box 956, Lanai City, HI 96763. ☎ **808/565-6378.** 2 rms. $50 single; $60 double.

Lucille Graham-Summer, a gracious lady of 85 years, opened Lanai's first bed-and-breakfast in 1987. Now a portrait artist, Lucille has a lovely old "rejuvenated" plantation house. One of her guest rooms has a queen-size bed and one has a single and a double bed; both rooms share a bath. She serves a full, home-cooked breakfast in her large kitchen. Her specialty is buttermilk pancakes with fruit from her own garden: papayas, bananas, and "the best pineapple in the world." The location is a plus for golfers: her house is close to the public 9-hole Cavendish Golf Course, free to residents; visitors are asked to leave a donation for upkeep (compared to the $99-a-day greens fees charged at The Experience at Koele and the Challenge at Manele, that's quite a deal).

3 Camping

By Jeanette Foster

There is really only one area in which camping is permitted on the almost completely privately owned island of Lanai: That's the **Hulopoe Beach Park,** a crescent-shaped, white-sand beach bordered by kiawe trees. The three small individual campsites are worth the effort to obtain a permit. The beach and ocean activities are wonderful. Facilities here include restrooms, showers, drinking water, picnic tables, and outdoor grills. However, since these are the only campgrounds on Lanai, the demand for the three sites (limited to six people per site) is high. Write in advance (long, long before your planned trip) to: **Koele Company,** P.O. Box L, Lanai City, HI 96763 (☎ 808/565-7233). Fees include a $5 registration fee plus $5 per person per day, with a seven-day limit.

Campers will have to bring their own equipment, as there is nowhere to rent any on Lanai. Be prepared for rain year-round, and be ready to deal with insects (you should have a good repellent for mosquitoes) and the sun (be sure to have sunscreen, a hat, and a long-sleeve shirt). A note on personal safety: Don't hike or swim alone and never turn your back on the ocean; the waves might be closer and more powerful than you think.

4 Where to Eat

Aside from those at The Lodge at Koele and the Manele Bay Hotel, there are just five restaurants in Lanai: three in Lanai City (described below), and one each at the **Golf Clubhouse** at the Experience at Koele and at **The Clubhouse** at The Challenge at Manele. All of the restaurants in Lanai City are fine for the budget diner. The Golf Clubhouse at The Experience at Koele offers a moderately priced lunch (a $6.50 burger, sandwiches from $5.25 to $8) and a very pleasant ambience. Of the restaurants at the Manele Bay Hotel, **The Pool Grille** is the least expensive, with a $6 hot dog and a $9 burger at lunch—in a glorious setting. And you should get to experience the English-country-lodge splendor of **The Lodge** at Koele, maybe with a continental breakfast at $8.50, or just by dropping in and joining the guests there for complimentary tea, accompanied by pastries and savouries, in the splendid Music Room from 2:30 to 5pm daily. (*Note:* This was open to anyone as we write this, but that could be subject to change.)

Hotel Lanai Dining Room

Hotel Lanai. ☎ **808/565-7211.** Reservations not accepted. Main courses $14–$17. AE, MC, V. Breakfast 7–9:30am; lunch 11:30am–1pm; dinner 6–8pm. AMERICAN.

In the evening, the Hotel Lanai is the social center of the island, where residents and visitors congregate for drinks out on the veranda and inside the wood-paneled dining room, with its wood-burning fireplace. The kitchen is good, the servers are pleasant, and the prices are fine. You can be sure that everything you're served will be fresh: Herbs and vegetables are homegrown, and eggs come from neighboring farms. Breakfast features pancakes, french toast, and some excellent omelettes (a build-your-own is $5.50). Burgers and sandwiches (under $7) are the mainstay at lunch (we like their charbroiled, open-face mahiburger), and dinner is pleasant, indeed. For pupus, you might try sashimi served Hawaiian style—fresh ahi on a bed of Chinese cabbage with shoyu and wasabi—or peel-and-eat tiger prawns. There are salads fresh from the garden, sandwiches, steak, chicken, and seafood main dishes as well as the fresh catch of the day from local waters and a daily pasta.

The Blue Ginger Cafe

Seventh St., Lanai City. ☎ **808/565-6863.** No reservations. Plate lunches $5.35–$7.95; main courses $7.50–$14.95. No credit cards. Breakfast and lunch 6am–2pm daily; dinner 3–9pm daily. LOCAL.

It's fun to sit at an outside table at this modest restaurant and mingle with the local people while enjoying a decent meal for a small price. Plate lunches are the big thing here—teriyaki plates, hamburger steak, mahimahi or shrimp, plus plenty of sandwiches for around $3.50 and hamburgers for $2.75. Appetizers consist of sashimi or poke (raw fish); main courses are likely to be mahimahi sautéed with capers, onions, and mushrooms; a variety of Filipino dishes (pork adobo, pork and peas, vegetables and pork); and a fresh catch (when available). All the pastries and bread are made on the premises. You'll recognize Blue Ginger by its eye-catching lavender exterior.

S&T Properties

Seventh St., Lanai City. ☎ **808/565-6363.** No reservations. Plate lunches $5. No credit cards. Breakfast and lunch 6:30am–1pm Thurs–Tues. Closed Wednesday. LOCAL.

S&T Properties has been in Lanai City for just about forever. It's your typical greasy spoon: Breakfast features local favorites like eggs with Vienna sausages; plate lunches run to Filipino favorites (pork adobo, pork and peas, etc.), and there are plenty of sandwiches and burgers from $2 to $4.75. Locals keep this place busy—your meal here will be a genuine Hawaiian experience.

5 Beaches

By Jeanette Foster

HULOPO'E BEACH

Located just 8 miles from Lanai City at the end of Hi. 441, Hulopo'e is one of the few easily accessible cream-colored sand beaches on Lanai. It's also the island's best snorkeling area. The fish here have thrived since Hulopo'e Beach was made part of the Manele-Hulopo'e Marine Life Conservation District, which prohibits the taking of marine life (except by hook and line) and anchoring inside the bay. The well-protected beach is also great for swimming. It's also good for bodysurfing, boogie boarding, and surfing. The Manele Bay Hotel overlooks the beach at one end; it has a beach shack with facilities for guests. Public facilities include picnic tables, barbecue pits, showers, and restrooms. Camping is regulated by permits from the Koele Company (see "Camping," above). Since this is the most popular picnic site on the island and the best swimming beach, there are always local residents here; yet the beach is large enough to give everybody enough room.

POLIHUA BEACH

Down Polihua Road, a long, rutted, four-wheel-drive trail on the north shore of Lanai, is a virgin beach where you're unlikely to see another soul. This is a great place to get away from it all, but people don't often come here because of the dangerous swimming conditions and the winds. During most of the year, the trade winds blow across the beach with such intensity that anyone out in the open is

Frommer's Favorite Lanai Experiences

Snorkeling at Hulopo'e Beach Park. This calm, crystal-clear bay has so much valuable marine life that the state designated it a Marine Life Conservation Area in order to protect the fish, coral, and wealth of other critters here. When the occasional surf rolls in, take advantage of the waves and do a little bodysurfing.

Exploring the Garden of the Gods. Four-wheel-drive up to these mysterious lava formations, which suddenly appear, dotting the amber and ocher-colored earth, in an otherwise remote, windy, desolate location only 7 miles from Lanai City. If you venture up at night, you might hear—as locals believe you will—ghosts whistling, as they tend to their garden of rocks.

Hiking the Munro Trail. Lanai's most spectacular trip will take you through mountain grasslands, forest, and past a variety of endemic plantlife to the island's highest point, the 3,370-foot summit of Lanaihale. Save this 7-mile hike for a clear day; if it's rainy or misty, you won't be able to enjoy the breathtaking views of Maui, Molokai, Oahu, the Big Island, and Kahoolawe from the top.

Relaxing at the Hotel Lanai. Congregating with the Pineapple Island's residents and other visitors on the veranda here, the social center of the island, for an after-dinner drink and a little conversation is the perfect—and most genuinely Hawaiian—way to end an adventurous or relaxing day on Lanai.

literally sand-blasted. However, the fishing is fabulous, and the waves—under the right conditions—are good for experienced bodysurfers, boogie boarders, and surfers. There are no facilities, so bring water.

SHIPWRECK BEACH

The 8 miles of shoreline from Polihua Beach to Kahokunui is known as Shipwreck Beach, named for the offshore wrecks that were blown into the outside reef. The primary activities here are beachcombing and shoreline fishing. Shipwreck acts as a recycling center for the sea: Glass balls, old fishing equipment, and tons of junk wash ashore year round; local residents come here to gather everything from mismatched slippers to styrofoam ice chests. Walking the sloping beach is easy, but people with allergies to insect stings should note that the 3-mile beach has occasional freshwater seeps (look for them in the rocky areas or in areas where seaweed grows) that attract bees and wasps looking for water to drink.

6 Water Sports & Recreation

By Jeanette Foster

SAILING

Contact the **Manele Bay Hotel** (☎ 808/565-7700) to arrange for a sailing/snorkeling tour of the coast of Lanai with **Trilogy Excursions**. Continental breakfast and lunch are included for $75.

SCUBA DIVING

Lanai has two of the best-known diving spots in Hawaii, Cathedrals I and II. The two sites, located just off the south shore, earn their names from the way the

Lanai

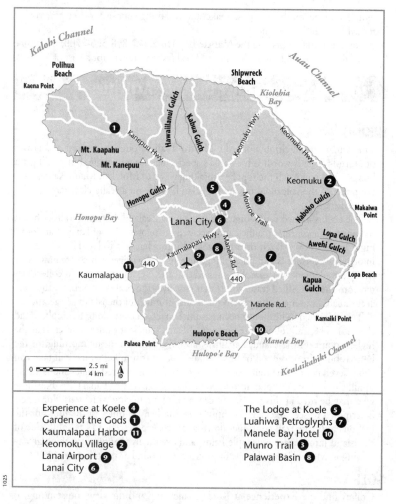

Experience at Koele	❹	The Lodge at Koele	❺
Garden of the Gods	❶	Luahiwa Petroglyphs	❼
Kaumalapau Harbor	⓫	Manele Bay Hotel	❿
Keomoku Village	❷	Munro Trail	❸
Lanai Airport	❾	Palawai Basin	❽
Lanai City	❻		

sunlight shines through the natural coral lattice, resembling stained-glass windows in a magnificent church. The parishioners here are a multitude of tropical fish. In the choir loft are crustaceans and invertebrates; occasionally making an appearance are friendly white-mouth moray eels. The **Manele Bay Hotel** (☎ 808/565-7700) at Hulopo'e Bay offers a variety of classes and dives, ranging from an introduction to scuba diving in the pool to boat dives ($125 for a two-tank dive).

SNORKELING

The best snorkeling on Lanai is from Hulopo'e Beach. The Marine Life Conservation designation not only protects the marine life but also prohibits boats from anchoring in the bay. The result is that fish are abundant and unafraid, and they let you come close to them. There's excellent snorkeling around the lava pools and near the rocks at both ends of the beach. Snorkeling equipment is complimentary to the guests of Manele Bay Hotel and the Lodge at Koele. There are no snorkel rentals available on the island, so make sure you bring your own or the gear you've rented from another island.

For sail/snorkel tours, call the **Manele Bay Hotel** (☎ 808/565-7700) to arrange a half-day cruise, including continental breakfast and lunch, for a cost of $125.

7 Hiking, Golf & Other Outdoor Activities

By Jeanette Foster

HIKING

This tough, uphill climb along the **Munro Trail** through rain forest and groves of Norfolk Pine is worth it for Lanai's spectacular scenery alone, but you'll get a bonus when you reach the top: breathtaking views of Molokai, Maui, Kahoolawe, the peaks of the volcanoes on the Big Island, and—on a really clear day—Oahu in the distance.

The trail is named for George Munro, a New Zealand–born naturalist who, at the turn of the century, planned and executed the reforestation of Lanai, transforming it from an overgrazed desert wasteland into what it is today. His genius was in planting Norfolk Island pines along the tops of the ridges, which are now practically a trademark of Lanai. He guessed that the Norfolk pine would collect water from the mist-filled trade winds that pass over the peaks. Over time, the trees accumulated water and supported the return of much of the island's vegetation.

The trail titled in his honor begins at the Lanai Cemetery along Keomoku Road (Hi. 44). The trail follows the remains of Lanai's ancient caldera and ends at the highest point on the island, Lanaihale, at 3,370 feet. Go in the morning for the best visibility from the top of this 11-mile (round trip) hike, which will take you about seven hours. The trail passes through eucalyptus-covered gullies and is a long uphill climb. About 4 miles into it, you'll get a great view of Lanai City. For those who may be tired at this point, you can return by retracing your steps. For hikers determined to see "the view," continue on another 1.3 miles to the top. For the real diehards, the trail continues down a fairly steep descent to the south side of the island into former pineapple fields, and eventually empties into the highway leading to Manele Bay. The rest of us just turn around at the top.

GOLF

Golfers find the **Experience at Koele** challenging and the views outstanding. It is indeed quite an experience in Hawaii to play golf at 2,500 feet, on a course frequently shrouded in fog and mist. An 18-hole par-72 championship course designed by Greg Norman, with Ted Robinson as the architect, this dramatic course can only be described as a series of plunges into tropical canyons. The 8th hole will remain in your memory forever: The view from the top of the tee is of a beautiful valley blanketed with mist, verdant with vegetation, and an azure lagoon in the distance. This 444-yard, par-4 is a double-tiered green with a 250-foot drop from tee to flagstick; there's the water plus some serious bunkers to your right and the jungle to your left. After that, the back 9 would seem almost easy if the trade winds would just stop. It appears as if all the wind in the world comes sweeping across the wide fairways. Facilities include a pro shop, driving range, restaurant, and putting greens. It's fairly easy to get tee times; weekdays are best. Greens fees are $99 for guests of the Lodge at Koele and Manele Bay Hotel, $140 for non-guests. Cart rental costs are included in the greens fee. Nine-hole twilight rates are available. Call 808/565-GOLF.

OTHER OUTDOOR ACTIVITIES

BICYCLING

Mountain bikes (with helmets) for the guests at the Lodge at Koele or Manele Bay Hotel are available at no charge. Bikes are not rented to non-resort guests. Call **The Lodge at Koele,** Lanai City (☎ 808/565-7300, ext. 4553), for reservations.

HORSEBACK RIDING

The Lodge at Koele (☎ 808/565-7300) offers 1- to 3-hour rides from the stables at Koele, starting at $35. Lunch rides, lessons, and private rides are also available. Long pants and shoes are required; mandatory safety helmets are provided. Carry a jacket, as the weather is chilly and it rains frequently.

HUNTING

Hunting on Lanai involves game birds, axis deer, and Mouflon sheep. All hunters must have a license; to obtain one, you must have proof of having attended a hunter's education class, and you must apply for an exemption if the course was in another state. For exemptions contact: **Enforcement, State Division of Forestry and Wildlife,** 1151 Punchbowl, Room 311, Honolulu, HI 96813 (☎ 808/587-0166). After obtaining either proof of a hunter's education class or obtaining an exemption for a class given in another state, you must apply for a hunting license. Licenses are $95 a year for non-Hawaii residents. Apply to the **State Division of Forestry and Wildlife,** 1151 Punchbowl, Room 325, Honolulu, HI 96813.

Bird season is limited to weekends and holidays, beginning with the first Saturday in November through the third Sunday in January. Axis deer hunts are limited to nine consecutive weekends, beginning with the weekend prior to the last Sunday in April. Mouflon sheep hunting season is the third and fourth Sunday in August by public lottery.

Most of the hunting areas on Lanai are private property, so in addition to a state hunting license you must also obtain a permit from the Lanai Company (most of the hunting grounds are on their property). Permits are $275 a day; the bag limit is three deer (one buck and two does) a day for hunting with a rifle. For archery hunting, the permit is $50 a day and there are no bag limits. The **Lanai Company,** P.O. Box L, Lanai, HI 95763 (☎ 808/565-8200), also offers a guide service for $750 per person, per day. The one-on-one guide service includes transportation, guide services, lunch, and processing of the deer (deboning, butchering the meat into five-pound bags and freezing, and removing the trophy horns and slating the hides). Guns and ammunition are $30 extra per day.

TENNIS

The **Maui County Department of Parks and Recreation,** Lanai City (☎ 808/565-6979), has courts available to the public at no charge. The courts are lit for night as well as daytime play. **The Lodge at Koele** (☎ 808/565-7300), and the **Manele Bay Tennis Club** (☎ 808/565-2222), offer tennis instruction, round robins, clinics, and workouts as well as court rentals.

8 Exploring the Island

Lanai's 30 miles of paved roads can take you to the airport, the freight harbor, Lanai City, the island's three hotels, its small boat harbor, and best beaches—that's about it. If you want to get off the beaten path and onto the unpaved roads through fields and over mountain ridges that lead to back-country beaches and abandoned settlements, you'll have to hike, get a four-wheel drive vehicle, or take a guided tour. Four-wheel drives are readily available; be sure to get a good map and local guidance before you take off, as this is rugged mountain driving. You may see Axis deer, Mouflon sheep, pheasant, quail, partridge, and wild turkeys as you explore the back country. We'd much prefer to shoot these creatures with a camera, but hunting is a way of life here.

THE MUNRO TRAIL

This is Lanai's most spectacular trip, 3,370 feet up to the summit of Lanaihale. Save it for a clear day; if it's rainy or misty, you won't see the breathtaking views of the other islands—Maui, Molokai, Oahu, The Big Island, even Kahoolawe— that await at the top of the mountain. The trail begins at Koele and winds for 7 fairly rugged miles on a single lane road, up through mountain grasslands and forest of ohia lehua, pine, ironwood, and eucalyptus. At the upper levels are many endemic Hawaiian plants. For details on the hike, see "Hiking," above.

George Munro, an early twentieth-century ranch manager from New Zealand, was an amateur botanist; it was he who had the foresight to plant the island with the Norfolk and Cook Island pines in order to draw the moisture from the clouds and provide Lanai with an adequate watershed.

PALAWAI BASIN AND LUAHIWA PETROGLYPHS

It was here at Palawai Basin, now given over to agriculture and grazing, that the Mormons attempted to establish their first Hawaiian colony in the mid-1850s. The colony failed and the Mormons moved on to Laie on Oahu, but Walter Murray Gibson, the founder of the colony, stayed on in Lanai. He acquired vast land holdings and—as an aside to Hawaiian history—became a friend of King Kalakaua. It was he who put up the down payment to build Iolani Palace in Honolulu and he also paid for the statue of King Kamehameha that stands across from the Palace today. There is not much to see here save for the Luahiwa Petroglyphs. Inscribed on 34 boulders on a slope overlooking the Palawai Basin, they are considered to be among the best examples of early rock art in the Hawaiian Islands.

THE GARDEN OF THE GODS (KANEPU'U)

After driving through miles of deserted pineapple fields at Palawai, you'll enter beautiful badlands where centuries of wind erosion have sculpted and carved ancient rocks into odd pinnacles and buttes. Back in the '30s, a visitor dubbed it the Garden of the Gods. The place is striking at any time, but if you can get up here at sunset, you'll see the brick-red earth washed with a spectrum of desert colors. (Visitors often leave small piles of rocks here out of respect, but locals advise that this should not be done anywhere else.)

The dirt road to the Garden of the Gods presently leads through the middle of a 462-acre forest area. This Native Hawaiian Drylands Forest at Kanepu'u is an area of rare plant life now under the stewardship of the Nature Conservancy. Some 48 native species can be found here, including the endangered Lanai sandalwood, a rare Hawaiian gardenia, and the local cousins of olive and persimmon. (The road may be rerouted in the future for the sake of the preserve.)

Lanai for the Day: Boat Excursions from Maui

Should your vacation time be limited and you still want to see Lanai—and experience snorkeling in its crystal clear waters among its pristine reefs—there are three one-day excursions from Lahaina that will get you there in the early morning and back to Maui before the sun sets:

Trilogy Excursions (☎ 808/661-4743 or toll free 800/874-2666). Trilogy's 50-foot ketch-rigged trimarans sail to Lanai in 1 1/2 hours and offer a fantastic day of sailing, snorkeling (including instruction for beginners), swimming on a perfect beach, whale watching (with luck), and a chance to tour the island with a local guide. Lunch is included. Cost: $149 adults, $75.40 children 3 to 12. You can spend a few days in Lanai and then pick up a returning boat if you wish.

Club Lanai (☎ 808/871-1144). Club Lanai has its own 8-acre beachfront property with its own pier directly across the channel from Lahaina. They provide everything: snorkeling equipment, free bicycles to ride along old sugarcane dirt roads running parallel to the beach, even free kayaks. Breakfast, lunch, juices, and iced tea are all served. Beachcombing is great here, so is the snorkeling—and the ride over on a beautiful trimaran is a lot of fun. Cost: $79 adults, $59 ages 13 to 20, $29 ages 4 to 12, 3 and under free.

Ocean Riders (☎ 808/661-3586). Here's a great trip for adventurous souls: a wild ride on a Zodiac raft to the backside of Lanai, where you can snorkel the best reefs, see the shipwrecks, and explore the Lanai coastline. The cost, including breakfast, lunch, a snack, and snorkel equipment, is $130 for adults, $95 for children 6 to 13 (not recommended for those under 6).

—Faye Hammel

SHIPWRECK BEACH

At the northern end of the main road, about 8 miles beyond Koele, is a wild and windswept strand where the rusting hull of a World War II Liberty ship has been bleaching in the sun for over 50 years. There are petroglyphs on some of the inland rocks. Glass fishing floats and driftwood often turn up on the windy shore. For more information, see "Beaches," above.

KEOMOKU VILLAGE

Southeast of Shipwreck Beach, this Hawaiian ghost town holds a fascinating bit of Lanai history. A thriving sugar plantation village back in 1898, it fell upon hard times—first a plague hit the workers, then the water supply turned brackish—after the stone platform of nearby Kahe'a Heiau was dynamited in order to build a cane railway. The Maunalei Sugar Company shut down in 1901, but the Keomoku Hotel was barged over to Lahaina in pieces, rebuilt, and still lives today—as the Pioneer Inn. All that remains of the old settlement is the picturesque Malamalama Church, which is currently being restored.

HULUPO'E BAY AND MANELE BAY

This is where you're likely to spend a good part of your vacation in Lanai. The adjacent bays flank a rocky point on the island's protected south shore. The site of an ancient Hawaiian fishing village dating back to A.D. 900, both bays are now part of a Marine Life Conservation District. Hulupo'e Bay boasts Lanai's best beach. If you're really lucky, you may get to see dolphins here—it's a preferred habitat for Hawaiian spinner dolphins. The Small Boat Harbor at Manele is the place where fishing boats, yachts, and visiting cruise boats from Maui call. It's here that you pick up boats for whale watching, snorkel and diving excursions, and sailing. For further details, see "Beaches" and "Water Sports and Recreation," above.

Settling in on the Big Island

13

Ever hear of a tropical island with black-sand beaches, snowcapped mountains, cedar forests, and one of the largest cattle ranches in the world? This is Hawaii, the orchid capital of America, about 200 miles southwest of Honolulu and twice as large as all the other Hawaiian Islands combined (about 4,030 square miles). Hawaii is also the residence of Pele, the ancient goddess of volcanoes, who stages some spectacular eruptions. Islanders invariably refer to Hawaii as the Big Island, but it's also called the Orchid Island or the Volcano Island; all the names are appropriate, and all reflect the fascination many have with this astonishing continent in miniature.

You'll immediately know why this is called the Orchid Island if you arrive in **Hilo.** Rain may be helping those orchids to grow, but don't despair—it's just a "Hawaiian blessing" and it probably won't last long. Nobody in Hilo lets a little drizzle interfere with life. (In winter, rainstorms will hit this part of the island harder than any other.) In fact, local residents feel that Hilo's sometimes soggy weather is the very thing that has kept it unspoiled and still charming.

Hilo, the only real city on the island and the second largest in the state, is the takeoff point for the imposing **Hawaii Volcanoes National Park** and the lava-scarred Puna area. Located on the east coast, Hilo has been experiencing a slump of late, but it still has its own gentle charm. Most residents of Hilo are convinced that this is the world's greatest little city and they wouldn't consider living anywhere else. The fact that they live between the devil and the deep-blue sea bothers them not a bit. Huge volcanoes dominate the skyline: Mauna Kea is extinct, but Mauna Loa is still very much alive.

If you've read James Michener's *Hawaii,* you'll remember that the Alii Nui Noelani went to Hilo in 1832 to confront Pele and implore her to halt the fiery lava that came close to destroying the town. Pele has toyed with the idea more than a few times since, as recently as 1935, 1942, and 1984, but she has always spared the city—even without the intervention of priestesses. The citizens are convinced she always will.

The citizens are just as nonchalant about tidal waves—at least they were until 1960. On the May morning when seismic waves hurtled across the Pacific headed for Hawaii, the citizens of Hilo had mere hours to evacuate; instead, some of them actually went down to the

What's Special About the Big Island

Natural Wonders
- Active volcanoes, especially Kilauea in Hawaii Volcanoes National Park, which has been spewing red-hot lava for the last 11 years.
- Mauna Kea, one of the world's great volcanoes, rising 13,796 feet above sea level.
- Rainbow Falls in Hilo, where rainbows form in the morning mist.

Sports and Outdoor Activities
- Hiking a diversity of trails, ranging from fern forests to black sand beaches, over lava fields, through desert scrubs, and along dramatic coastlines.
- Snorkeling and scuba diving off the Kona Coast, with its fascinating natural rock and coral formations.

Museums
- Lyman House Memorial Museum Complex in Hilo, for a look at how the missionaries lived.
- Puuopelu, a historic house at Parker Ranch in Waimea, home to a superb collection of impressionist works.
- Kamuela Museum in Waimea, an eclectic collection that includes an array of ancient and royal Hawaiian artifacts.
- Hulihee Palace in Kailua-Kona, once a vacation home for Hawaiian royalty, now a museum of Hawaiiana.

Beaches
- The black sands at Punalu'u and the emerald sands at Green Sand Beach, both on the southern coast.
- Hapuna Beach and Samuel Spencer Beach Park on the west coast, great for swimming and sunbathing.

Island Art
- Galleries islandwide, especially at Holualoa, an artists' colony above Kailua-Kona.
- Volcano Art Center, at Hawaii Volcanoes National Park, for superb work by Big Island artists.

Historic Sites
- Pu'uhonua o Honaunau National Historical Park, the partially restored remains of a sanctuary built more than 400 years ago.
- Petrogylphs along the Kohala coast drawn by the ancient Hawaiians.

bridge to watch the show. This time, the gods were not so kind. Sixty-one people were swept into the waves, and a big chunk of waterfront area was wiped out. For several years after, you could see the devastation along the ocean side of Kamehameha Avenue; now there's grass and palm trees there. Past Pauahi Street, to your right you'll see the surprisingly modern architecture of the county and state office buildings. Despite much opposition, they were built to inspire confidence in the devastated bayside area.

All of this knowledge impresses itself strongly on the mind of the visitor, making Hilo far more than a make-believe world for tourists. It forms a curious backdrop to the beauty and gentleness of this city arching around a crescent bay (*Hilo* means "new moon"). Once a whaling port of the Pacific, Hilo is still a seaport, from which raw sugar (note the bulk-sugar plant on the waterfront) and cattle are shipped to the other islands and the mainland. Flowers are big business, too; 132 inches of rainfall a year (most of it at night—but there are plenty of misty mornings, too) make the orchids and anthuriums grow like crabgrass on a suburban lawn. Nearly a quarter of a million tropical blossoms are sent from Hilo all over the world.

The **Kona Coast,** on the west side of Hawaii, is to the Big Island what Waikiki is to Oahu: the resort area. The little town of Kailua-Kona is the tourist center. Unlike Waikiki, though, it still has a small-town charm. Once the playground of the Hawaiian alii, Kona lures deep-sea fishermen (its marlin grounds are the best in the Pacific), families, and anyone looking for relaxation and tropical beauty. And the weather is almost always perfect there.

1 Orientation & Getting Around

GETTING THERE

ARRIVING BY PLANE   The island is large enough to have two airports, one on the east coast outside the small city of Hilo, the other at Kailua-Kona on the west coast. Which city should you choose as your first stop? We've done it both ways, and our considered opinion is that it doesn't make a particle of difference. Let your itinerary and the airline schedules—the ease with which you can make connections to the next island on your agenda—be the determining factor. Hawaiian, Aloha, and Mahalo Airlines will take you from Honolulu to Hilo on the east or to Kailua-Kona on the west in less than an hour. You can also fly directly to or from Kona from the West Coast. Pick up your car at **General Lyman Field** in Hilo or at **Keahole Airport** in Kona, or take a cab, as there is no public transportation to take you to your hotel in either area. A taxi could run about $20, plus baggage charge.

GETTING AROUND

The **Mass Transportation Agency (MTA)** provides islandwide public transportation bus service with buses operating Monday through Saturday, and fares ranging from 75¢ to $6 per ride depending on how far you ride. Bus routes connect Hilo with Kailua-Kona, Waimea, Honokaa, Pahoa, and Hawaii Volcanoes National Park, among others. Call MTA at 808/935-8241. Bus schedules are sometimes available at the **State Visitor Information booths** in the airport, at 25 Aupini St., and usually at the **Hawaii Visitors Bureau** at 250 Keawe St. (☎ 808/961-5797). Mrs. Lei Branco is the helpful woman to contact.

Hilo   For all practical purposes, you're going to need a car in Hilo, even though there is a city bus system. It's limited; however, the **Hele-On** bus does make two trips a day around town, one early in the morning, one in midafternoon. You can ask for the bus schedule at your hotel or call the MTA (☎ 808/935-8241).

BY RENTAL CAR   From either Hilo or Kailua-Kona, you can drive the 100 miles across the island and see all the sights. We prefer to visit each side of the island separately, but you can make one side your base if you don't mind long drives. Read up on the sights, hotels, restaurants, and nightlife in each area, and you'll know just where you want to stay and for how long.

Most agencies on the Big Island offer a flat rate with unlimited mileage—you buy the gas. You have your choice of the trusty and popular inter-island outfits like **Alamo, Avis, Dollar, Budget,** and **Tropical,** whose main offices are all in Honolulu (see "Getting Around," in Chapter 5 for details). Remember that reservations are a good idea at any time and a must in peak seasons; call around to see who's offering the best rates—you never know who might be offering a special rate or an inter-island deal. Other times, you may be able to get your best deal by careful on-the-spot shopping.

One of your biggest expenses if you're driving from Hilo to Kona or vice versa will be the drop-off charge; it can be as much as $65. One way to avoid it is to arrive and depart from the same airport, which means circling the entire island and putting in a lot of driving time. The other way to avoid it is to take the county bus, which crosses the island for a cost of $6 (see details on the MTA above), then rent a car in Kona if necessary. The only drawback is that you will miss the sightseeing en route.

FAST FACTS: the Big Island

Area Code   The telephone area code throughout the islands is 808.

Dentists   Contact Hilo Dental Associates, 475 Kinoole St., Hilo (☎ 808/935-1149); Dr. Frank Sayre/Dr. Daniel Walker, Frame 10 Center, Kailua-Kona (☎ 808/329-8067); or Dr. Craig Kimura, Kamuela Office Center (☎ 808/885-3300).

Doctors   Contact the Hilo Medical Group, 1292 Waianuenue Ave., Hilo (☎ 808/969-1325); Kaiser Permanente, 75-184 Hualalai Rd., Kona (☎ 808/329-3866); or Waimea Medical Associates, Kamuela (☎ 808/885-7351).

Emergencies   Ambulance, fire, and rescue 808/961-6022.

Hospitals   Major facilities are Hilo Hospital, 1190 Waianuenue Ave. (☎ 808/969-4111), and Kona Hospital, Kealekekua (☎ 808/322-9311).

Other Useful Numbers   To learn about services for the disabled, call the Commission on Persons with Disabilities (☎ 808/961-8211). Big Island Crisis & Help Line in Hilo (☎ 808/969-9111) and Kona (☎ 808/329-9111), and Sexual Assault Crisis Line (☎ 808/935-0677), can assist you. On Call (☎ 808/935-1666), a 24-hour free service available from any pushbutton phone, offers the latest news, sports, local and worldwide weather, community services, horoscopes, soap-opera updates, and more. Complete listings are given in the Aloha Pages of the Hawaii (Big Island) telephone book.

Poison Control Center   Call 800/362-3585.

Police   Call 808/935-3111 for assistance anywhere on the island.

Post Office   In Hilo, the Post Office is at 1299 Kekuanaoa Ave. (☎ 808/935-2821); in Kona, there is a branch at 74-5577 Palani Rd. (☎ 808/329-1927); in Kamuela, the Post Office is on Lindsey Rd., off Hi. 19 (☎ 808/885-4026).

Taxis   Call A-1 Bob's Taxi in Hilo (☎ 808/959-4800), or Kona Airport Taxi (☎ 808/329-7779).

Weather Information   For conditions on Hilo, call 808/935-8555; on the Big Island, 808/961-5582. For marine forecasts, call 808/935-9883.

2 Where to Stay

BED & BREAKFASTS   The Big Island is rich in **bed & breakfast** accommodations, and more are cropping up all the time. We'll tell you about many of these as we cover specific locations, but first you should know about ✪ **Hawaii's Best Bed & Breakfasts,** run by Barbara Campbell. Barbara's standards are uncompromising: She handles only upscale B&B lodgings, each home selected for its distinctive personality, attention to details, and the warm hospitality of its hosts. Selections range from the most traditional host-home rooms to splendid private country cottages, some on the grounds of fabulous estates. Her service covers all the major islands. Daily rates run $75 to $175. Call or write for a brochure describing these hidden gems. P.O. Box 563, Kamuela, HI 96743 (☎ 808/ 885-4550, fax 808/885-0559 or 800/262-9912 for reservations.

Then there's **My Island** P.O. Box 100, Volcano, HI 96785, created by Gordon Morse and his wife Joann: they offer rentals in 28 houses, all on the Big Island. Call the Morses at 808/967-7110 or 808/967-7216—any time between 7am and 9pm Hawaiian time (fax 808/967-7719). They urge people to move around the Big Island, experiencing the different climates and atmospheres of the various districts, from Hilo to Puna to Volcano, from Kailua to Waimea to Honokaa, and then some. Accommodations are mostly in "nice mom-and-pop houses," with singles $40 to $70, doubles $60 to $125.

Volcano Reservations, P.O. Box 998, Volcano Village, HI 96785 (☎ 808/ 967-7244 or 800/736-7140), is run by Brian and Lisha Crawford, whose charming Chalet Kilauea, is listed below. They have accommodations all over the state, ranging from budget to luxury including B&Bs, inns, vacation homes, cottages, and condos, in a wide price range. Car rentals are also available.

Bed & Breakfast Hawaii, P.O. Box 449, Kapaa, Kauai, HI 96746 (☎ 808/ 822-7771 or 800/733-1632; fax 808/822-2723), is an all-island reservation system. Rates start at $40 single, $45 double. Send them $12.95 for a copy of their directory of homes and apartments called *B&B Goes Hawaiian.*

Go Native . . . Hawaii, 65 Halualani Place (P.O. Box 11418), Hilo, HI 96721 (☎ 808/935-4178 or 800/662-8483), has been matching guests with Hawaiian hosts for more than a decade. Coordinator Fred Diamond has 250 locations on all islands except Lanai, ranging from oceanfront to mountain sites, from traditional B&B rooms in private homes to unhosted studios and cottages. Rates begin at around $40 for a single and around $65 for a double.

Hawaii Island Bed and Breakfast Association, P.O. Box 726, Volcano, HI 96785, offers a free pamphlet listing their members. It is available at the airports or by mail, free. (*Note:* This is not a booking service.)

Three Bears' Hawaii Reservations, 72-1001 Puukala, Kailua-Kona, HI 96740 (tel/fax 808/325-7563 or toll free 800/765-0480 from mainland U.S. is a family-run business (they also own Three Bears B&B in Kona, listed below), specializing in reasonable accommodations on all the islands. Some of their rates start as low as $55 per night; most average between $65 and $85 double.

HILO
DOUBLES FOR ABOUT $35 TO $45

⑤ **Arnott's Lodge and Hiking Adventures**

98 Apapane Rd., Hilo, HI 96720. ☎ **808/969-7097** or toll free 800/368-8752 from mainland U.S., 800/953-7773 interisland. Fax 808/961-9638. 48 bunk beds in 2 apts, 5 additional

apts, set up for singles, doubles, and suites. $15 bunk, $26 single, $36 double (per night for two). $80 two-bedroom suite for up to 5 people; each additional person $5. CB, DC, MC, V. Free parking.

Here's your best budget buy in Hilo. Popular with everyone from European student backpackers to families and small groups, Arnott's is a converted 2-story apartment building nestled in a lush tropical area, just a few minutes' walk to beaches and a short drive to the center of Hilo. Some of the rooms are hostel style with shared baths, but there are also singles, doubles, and suites. The suites are especially good for families or small groups; they have a living room with convertible sofa, two bedrooms (one with a double bed, one with two singles), a kitchen with a small refrigerator, and a private bath. All rooms have ceiling fans. Everything at Arnott's is simple, clean, casual, and very cozy. A resident manager is on hand to help plan activities. The Guest Pavilion is available 24 hours a day for "eating and drinking, partying, relaxing, gathering, late-night conversation." There's a treehouse deck in the lychee tree for communing with nature. Cooking facilities are available, and you can also have a $5 barbecue dinner here on Wednesday and Saturday nights. There's a TV lounge and laundry facilities.

Owner Doug Arnott claims there is no need to rent a car, since they offer a free shuttle to the airport and to town, as well as a series of five different hiking adventures, $20 to $25 each. Arnott advises guests to save five days to do all the excursions and to be sure to pack hiking boots, as walking on lava is rough. There's a $5 surcharge for expeditions by nonhouseguests.

Hilo Hotel

142 Kinoole St., Hilo, HI 96720. ☎ **808/961-3733.** Fax 808/935-7836. 21 rms, 6 apts. A/C TV TEL. $39–$45 single or double; $85 two-bedroom apt. Each additional person $8. AE, DC, MC, V. Free parking.

Worlds away from the pleasantly hokey tourist world of Banyan Drive is the Hilo Hotel, a businessperson's hotel in the center of town. The outside is very pleasant, with lava-rock walls, a large swimming pool, spacious gardens, and the excellent Fuji Restaurant for Japanese food and drinks, where the locals like to gather. The hotel rooms are clean and adequate, and each one has a refrigerator. The higher-priced rooms also include a TV. The hotel is very proud of its newer Niolopa Wing, which offers extraordinary value for a family; there are six very large (800 to 900 sq.ft.) two-bedroom apartments, fully furnished, equipped with TV, all the utilities, and three telephones per unit, for up to four guests.

☺ Wild Ginger Inn

100 Puueo St., Hilo, HI 96720. ☎ **808/935-5556,** or toll free 800/882-1887. 30 rms. $39 single or double; $59–$69 deluxe room. Each additional person $10. Inquire about special weekly rates. (Rates include continental breakfast.) No credit cards. Free parking.

Here's something unique—a 30-room bed-and-breakfast inn! Robert and Sandra Woodword moved to Hilo from California a few years ago, took over an aging hotel, and are gradually converting it into a charming, old-fashioned inn. The setting is very pretty, a short walk from town, and the rooms look out on a large lawn and a garden lush with wild torch ginger, bamboo, papaya, and a private stream. Rooms (all nonsmoking) are small and plain but comfortable enough, and all have a small refrigerator and a private bath with shower but no tub. There's one deluxe room with a bathtub, wicker furniture, microwave oven, and ocean view. Phones are available in the spacious lobby, which is also the scene of a plentiful serve-yourself breakfast, with their own homemade muffins, granola, tropical fruits

Hilo Accommodations & Dining

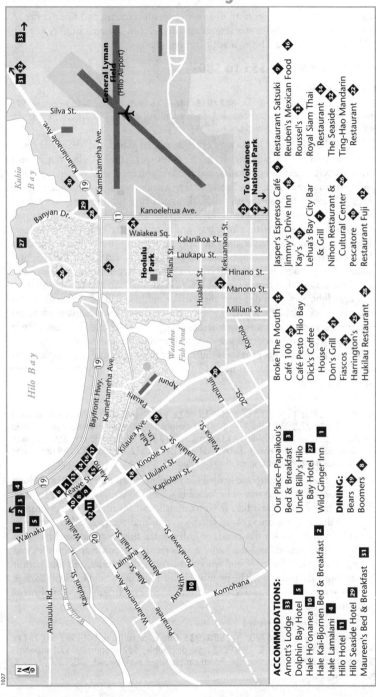

ACCOMMODATIONS:

Arnott's Lodge 33
Dolphin Bay Hotel 5
Hale Ho'onanea 10
Hale Kai-Bjornen Bed & Breakfast 2
Hale Lamalani 4
Hilo Hotel 11
Hilo Seaside Hotel 29
Maureen's Bed & Breakfast 31
Our Place–Papaikou's Bed & Breakfast 3
Uncle Billy's Hilo Bay Hotel 27
Wild Ginger Inn 1

DINING:

Bears 19
Boomers 8
Broke The Mouth 15
Café 100 20
Café Pesto Hilo Bay 47
Dick's Coffee House 25
Don's Grill 21
Fiascos 25
Harrington's 24
Hukilau Restaurant 28
Jasper's Espresso Café 7
Jimmy's Drive Inn 18
Kay's 49
Lehua's Bay City Bar & Grill 20
Nihon Restaurant & Cultural Center 26
Pescatore 10
Restaurant Fuji 12
Restaurant Satsuki 9
Reuben's Mexican Food 16
Roussel's 13
Royal Siam Thai Restaurant 14
The Seaside 32
Ting-Hao Mandarin Restaurant 22

from their own trees, eggs from their own bantam chickens, and Kona coffee. A hammock in the lobby invites serious relaxing. A coin-operated laundry is available. Improvements are being made here continually.

DOUBLES FOR ABOUT $55 TO $80

⑤ Dolphin Bay Hotel
333 Iliahi St., Hilo, HI 96720. ☎ **808/935-1466.** 18 units. TV. $55–$65 double; $75 one-bedroom apt; $85 two-bedroom apt. Each additional person $10. Discounted weekly rates available. MC, V. Free parking.

The Dolphin Bay Hote lies in a quiet residential neighborhood just a four-block walk from town. The building sits in the midst of a "small jungle," resplendent with papayas, breadfruits, bananas, and the like; you are invited to step right outside your room and pick your breakfast! The accommodations are modern, quite large, and nicely furnished with full kitchens and large tub/shower combinations in the bathrooms. The standard studios sleep one or two comfortably. The superior studios, usually with a rollaway and a queen-size bed (plus a built-in Roman-style tub!), are larger and can easily sleep three. There's also a marvelous honeymoon room with an open-beamed ceiling, and a large lanai for $65; and some really spacious one- and two-bedroom apartments, perfect for families. Since the hotel is near Hilo Bay, a cooling breeze keeps the units comfortable all year. Manager John Alexander dispenses the warmth and hospitality that have made this one of our best island finds over the years. He and his staff will map out tours, arrange trips, and advise on the best restaurants. Write or phone in advance, since the guests who come back each year—many from Canada and the Midwest—keep this place hopping. Lots of readers' hurrahs for this one continue to come in every year, even though there is no pool. Orchids are grown right on the grounds at the Iliahi Nursery.

Hilo Seaside Hotel
126 Banyan Dr., Hilo, HI 96720. ☎ **808/935-0621.** Fax 808/922-0052. (Reservations: Sand & Seaside Hotels, 2222 Kalakaua Ave., Suite 714, Honolulu, HI 96815; ☎ 800/367-7000 in the mainland U.S., fax 808/922-0052.) 135 rms. A/C TV TEL. Single or double, $80 standard; $83 deluxe; $95 with kitchenette. Each additional person $12. Children 12 and under stay free in parents' room when using existing bedding. AE, DC, MC, V. Free parking.

The Hilo Seaside Hotel (formerly the Hilo Hukilau Hotel) near Hilo Bay has long been a pleasant place to stay. The local branch of the kamaaina-owned Sand & Seaside Hotels (there are others in Kona, Kauai, and Maui) has attractive rooms (most with air conditioning) with lanais—rooms that overlook either the freshwater swimming pool, a fish pond, or lush tropical gardens. The hotel has been attractively renovated, and the lobby is decorated with contemporary tiles and Oriental hardwood floors. Wood fenceposts, Polynesian murals, and tikis permit you to forget the mainland. The popular Hukilau Restaurant and Cocktail Lounge is a longtime favorite for well-priced meals. Senior citizens get complimentary breakfasts.

Uncle Billy's Hilo Bay Hotel
87 Banyan Dr., Hilo, HI 96720. ☎ **808/935-0861,** or toll free 800/367-5102. Fax 808/935-7903. 145 rms. A/C TV TEL. Single or double, $62 moderate; $72 superior; $79 oceanfront; $74 with kitchenette. Room-car packages available. AE, DC, DISC, MC, V. Free parking.

Uncle Billy's, owned and operated by a Hawaiian family, is run on "Hawaiian time" and the pace is leisurely; you can feel that pleasant Polynesian paralysis setting in the moment you step into the South Seas lobby decorated with fish nets and tapa-covered walls. All rooms have a private lanai. The higher-priced rooms are huge: Two double beds look lost in the room. Most rooms face a tropical garden that leads to a path to the swimming pool, next to the ocean on Hilo Bay. Uncle Billy's Fish & Steak Restaurant is right in the hotel.

BED & BREAKFASTS

Hale Ho'onanea

159 Halai Hill, Hilo, HI 96720. ☎ or fax 808/934-7808. 3 rms, private baths. $75–$80 double. Minimum stay 2 nights. (Rates include breakfast.) No credit cards. Free parking.

High up in the hills above Hilo is Hale Ho'onanaea (House of Relaxation), affording wonderful views of garden, bay, and ocean from its beautifully decorated rooms. Martin Stuart, an architect, and his wife Mary, a gracious and hospitable lady, have furnished their guest rooms with the designer fabrics and accessories of Ralph Lauren, Bill Blass, and Laura Ashley. The Hono Kuhio Room has a four-poster bed and a separate dressing room; the Ehu Noe Room is done in antique wicker; the Ka Malaai Room has the ambience of a botanical garden. A combination library and snack bar with its own refrigerator is a nice gathering spot for guests; free juices and soft drinks are provided, and it's a good place to prepare a picnic lunch. All the guest rooms are downstairs. Breakfast is served upstairs in the Stuart's personal quarters at a wonderful old table with panoramic views. Mary prepares a full breakfast using fresh produce and herbs from her own garden, which abounds with grapefruit, lime, star fruit, papaya, and banana trees. Martin chats with guests over breakfast and helps them plan their day's activities. Children 10 and older are welcome. No smoking indoors.

✪ Hale Kai-Bjornen Bed & Breakfast

111 Honolii Pali, Hilo, HI 96720. ☎ **808/935-6330.** Fax 808/935-8439. 4 rms (all with private bath), 1 cottage. TV TEL. $85–$95 double; $105 one-bedroom guest cottage with kitchen. Minimum stay 2 days rooms, 4 days cottage. (Rates include breakfast.) Free parking.

You'll be warmly welcomed and made to feel right at home at Evonne Bjornen's four-star B&B. And what a home it is—a superb double-decker house with an entire wall of glass overlooking Hilo Bay and the island's best surfing spot, Honolii Surfing Beach. Guests have use of the magnificent living room looking out over the waterfront, and just beyond it, a pool with Jacuzzi and comfy lounge chairs. Downstairs are three bedrooms plus a family room, all beautifully furnished; each bedroom has either a king- or queen-size bed. All rooms face the ocean; from your cozy bed, you can watch the sea and the sky. An upstairs loft room has its own sitting room. Mrs. Bjornen likes to whip up fabulous breakfasts that include such special treats as macadamia-nut waffles and Portuguese sausages. She often puts her telescope out on the porch so guests can watch the volcano when it's in action! Staying here is like being on a lovely retreat—you may forget to go out and explore Hilo.

For those who can stay in Hilo for a week or longer, Mrs. Bjornen can offer a deluxe oceanfront penthouse condo with an incredible ocean view next to Richardson's Beach Park. Fully furnished and with all the amenities, this two-bedroom, two-and-a-half-bath penthouse can sleep up to four people. $875 per week, $2,000 per month. She also rents a beautifully furnished two-bedroom, two-bath deluxe golf course condo in the Keauhou-Kona area, right on the fairway and close to swimming and shopping. It can sleep up to four people; $875 per week, $2,000 per month November through April, $1,200 per month May through October.

Hale Lamalani
27-703 Kaieie Hmst. Rd., Papaikou, HI 96781. ☎ **808/964-5401** or toll free 800/238-8BED. 3 guest rms, 3 hostel rms. Shared bath. Guest rooms $45 single, $50 double, plus $5 per night for less than 3 nights; hostel rooms $15 single, $23 double, plus $5 per night for less than 3 nights. No credit cards. Free parking.

A thousand feet up the slopes of Mauna Kea, above the village of Papikou and 7 miles north of Hilo Bay, Walter and Elizabeth Patton have created Hale Lamalani (House of Heavenly Light), a charming retreat deep in farm country. This is really country peace and quiet: you can hear the birds singing, and from the spacious lanai you sometimes catch a glimpse of an endangered *io*—a Hawaiian hawk. There are three guest rooms upstairs, simply but nicely furnished, one with an extra long double bed, another with a king-size bed, a third with a king-size Japanese futon in a wood frame. All guest rooms share the bath, the large living room with TV and VCR and many comfy chairs, the lanai and sundecks, and the large modern kitchen, which is kept well stocked with Hawaiian breakfast fixings. Guests gather for breakfast at the tables and chairs on the covered lanai. Downstairs are two tiny "hostel" rooms, acceptable enough, and at $15 for one and $23 for two, one of the best bargains around.

A word of advice: Plan on arriving here before sunset; it might be a bit difficult to find your way up the country road for the first time in the dark.

Maureen's Bed & Breakfast
1896 Kalanianaole St., Hilo, HI 96720. ☎ **808/935-9018.** 6 rms. $40 single; $60 double. (Rates include breakfast.) No credit cards.

Owner Maureen Got has restored a classic redwood house built in 1935 and lovingly decorated it with oak, mahogany, and koa-wood antiques. The living room is out of another era: a 30-foot vaulted ceiling with double staircases leading to a wraparound balcony. Rooms have semiprivate baths. The two upstairs rooms, with views of the mountains, are very large and have California (extra-large) king-size beds. The two downstairs rooms (one large, one small) have double beds and a garden view. Two single rooms also share a bath. The grounds are manicured Japanese gardens with koi ponds. James Kealoha Beach Park is just across the street (it has a sandy bottom, brackish water, and is okay for doing laps), and Richardson Ocean Beach Park (good for snorkeling) is a mile down the road.

✪ Our Place-Papaikou's Bed & Breakfast
P.O. 469, Papaikou, HI 96781. ☎ and fax 808/964-5250 or toll free 800/245-5250. 4 rms (1 with bath). $55 double; $65 loft tree-house room; $75 master bedroom. Each additional person $10. (Rates include breakfast and tax.) No credit cards. Free parking.

Four miles north of Hilo, on Hi. 919, Our Place–Papaikou's B&B is a charming place to stay close to Hilo town. Sharon Miller, a former rolfer, and Ouida Taherne, M.D., both gave up busy lifestyles in California and Mississippi to move to Hilo and set up a guesthouse here. They've found a lovely cedar-paneled home overlooking a stream, set amid lush tropical vegetation. The "Great Room," splendid with its cathedral ceiling, has a library, fireplace, piano, and cable TV/VCR—all of which guests are invited to enjoy. Four rooms share a common lanai that

Big Island Accommodations at a Glance

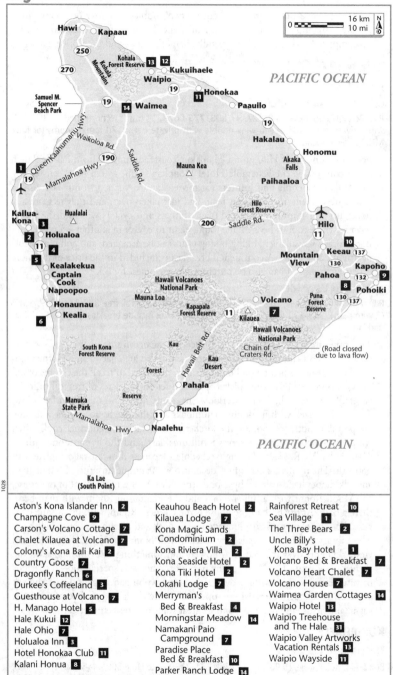

0 — 16 km / 10 mi N

PACIFIC OCEAN

Hawi Kapaau
250
270
Kohala Forest Reserve 13 12
Kohala Mountains
Kukuihaele
Waipio
19
Honokaa
11
Samuel M. Spencer Beach Park
19 Waimea 14
Paauilo
19
Hakalau
Honomu
Queenkaahumanu Hwy. Waikoloa Rd.
Mauna Kea
Akaka Falls
Paihaaloa
190
Mamalahoa Hwy.
Saddle Rd.
Hilo Forest Reserve
1
19
Kailua-Kona
Hualalai
200 Saddle Rd.
Hilo
11
3
Holualoa
10
Keeau 137
2
Mountain View 130
Kapoho
11
4
Pahoa 132 9
5
Kealakekua
Captain Cook
Napoopoo
Hawaii Volcanoes National Park
Mauna Loa
8
Puna Forest Reserve
Pohoiki
130 137
Honaunau
Kapapala Forest Reserve
11
Volcano 7
6
Kealia
Kilauea
Hawaii Volcanoes National Park
Kau
Chain of Craters Rd. (Road closed due to lava flow)
Kau Desert
South Kona Forest Reserve
Forest
Pahala
Reserve
Manuka State Park
Punaluu
Mamalahoa Hwy. 11
Naalehu

PACIFIC OCEAN

Ka Lae (South Point)

1028

Aston's Kona Islander Inn **2**	Keauhou Beach Hotel **2**	Rainforest Retreat **10**
Champagne Cove **9**	Kilauea Lodge **7**	Sea Village **1**
Carson's Volcano Cottage **7**	Kona Magic Sands Condominium **2**	The Three Bears **2**
Chalet Kilauea at Volcano **7**	Kona Riviera Villa **2**	Uncle Billy's Kona Bay Hotel **1**
Colony's Kona Bali Kai **2**	Kona Seaside Hotel **2**	Volcano Bed & Breakfast **7**
Country Goose **7**	Kona Tiki Hotel **2**	Volcano Heart Chalet **7**
Dragonfly Ranch **6**	Lokahi Lodge **7**	Volcano House **7**
Durkee's Coffeeland **3**	Merryman's Bed & Breakfast **4**	Waimea Garden Cottages **14**
Guesthouse at Volcano **7**	Morningstar Meadow **14**	Waipio Hotel **13**
H. Manago Hotel **5**	Namakani Paio Campground **7**	Waipio Treehouse and The Hale **31**
Hale Kukui **12**	Paradise Place Bed & Breakfast **10**	Waipio Valley Artworks Vacation Rentals **13**
Hale Ohio **7**	Parker Ranch Lodge **14**	Waipio Wayside **11**
Holualoa Inn **3**		
Hotel Honokaa Club **11**		
Kalani Honua **8**		

looks out over Kupuu Stream. There are two doubles, a master bedroom with a private bath, and a loft "tree house." Miller and Taherne are excellent cooks (they do complete breakfasts) and are friendly, helpful hosts—and their prices are right.

THE NORTHERN ROUTE
HONOKAA

⑤ Hotel Honokaa Club

P.O. Box 247, Honokaa, HI 96727. ☎ **808/775-0678**. 14 rms. $15 hostel beds; $50 double with private bath; $65 ocean-view double with private bath; $70 family rooms for four. MC, V. Free parking.

Forty miles north of Hilo on the Hamakua coast, and not far from Parker Ranch cattle country, is the venerable Hotel Honokaa Club, which has been serving local businesspeople and hunters for more than 50 years. On our last visit, a bright new young management team had just taken over, and they're gradually fixing up and improving the old place. Hikers and cyclers will find the hostel rooms—three to four beds in one room, eight to twelve in another—a good deal. Bike storage is available. Hiking/biking tours can be arranged, and golf is available nearby for $10 a day. A continental breakfast is included in the price of the more expensive rooms; it can also be purchased by any guest for $3.

✪ Waipio Wayside

P.O. Box 840, Honokaa, HI 96727. ☎ **808/775-0275**, or toll free 800/833-8849. 5 rms (2 with bath). $50–$90 single; $60–$100 double. (Rates include breakfast.) DC, MC, V. Free parking.

Two miles from the Honokaa Post Office, on the ocean side, is Waipio Wayside, one of the most charming new B&Bs to open in this area. Jacqueline Horne renovated a 1938 sugar plantation home. It's now decorated to recall the charms of old Hawaii. Bordered by a white picket fence and set on 1 1/2 acres of tropical fruit and vegetable gardens, the house overlooks sugarcane fields and the ocean far below. The outside deck with its double hammocks and the gazebo for sunset watching are popular spots; so, too, are the kitchen, where Jackie, a gourmet cook, often whips up special treats (she serves a full breakfast) and the living room with its 31-inch TV/VCR, where she might schedule a Japanese film festival complete with popcorn. The rooms are beautifully decorated with antique furniture, Chinese rugs, and silk drapes hand-painted by a local artist. Two rooms at the front of the house, the Moon Room with a full-size bed and the Plantation Room with twin beds, share a bath. At the back of the house is the Chinese Room, with its antique Chinese reclining barber's chairs; it overlooks the deck and gazebo, and has a half-bath. The Library Room upstairs is very special, with blond-wood paneling, an ocean view, skylights over the bed and shower, and something like 400 books on the shelves. The Bird's Eye Room at the back of the house is special, too—a spacious private bedroom suite with its own bath, blond-wood paneling, and a patchwork quilt on the bed. Double doors open onto the deck and a view of gardens, sugarcane fields, and ocean beyond. A great spot for a peaceful retreat.

KUKUIHAELE

Hale Kukui

Box 5044, Kukuihaele, HI 96726. ☎ **808/775-7130** or toll free 800/444-7130. Three units, each with private bath. $75 studio for two to four; $95 two-bedroom apt for four to six; $150 three-bedroom apt for six to ten. Additional person $10 extra. For stays of less than 3 days add $10 per night. Discounts of 5% to members of Greenpeace, Sierra Club, and other national environmental organizations. MC, V.

Kukuihaele is along the coast mid-island, about an hour from either the Hilo or Kona Coast locations. Located on over 4 acres overlooking Waipio Valley, this guest cottage is nestled on beautifully landscaped grounds, complete with a recently planted 2-acre organic orchard with 30 different species of tropical fruit (pick all you can eat!). A year-round stream sets a relaxing mood. Each modern, nicely furnished unit has its own living room, kitchenette, private full bath, and lanai; the studio unit and the two-bedroom unit can be combined to create a three-bedroom apartment. Television is available on request. Owners William and Sarah McCowatt are about 150 feet away, in the main house. Breakfast is provided the first day of your stay, but since each unit has a kitchen, you're on your own after that.

Waipio Valley Artworks Vacation Rentals

P.O. Box 5070, Kukuihaele, HI 96727. ☎ **808/492-4746.** 1 private house, 2 apts. TV TEL. $80 double two-bedroom house; $90 two-bedroom upstairs apartment; $65 one-bedroom downstairs apartment. Each additional person $15. MC, V. Free parking.

Waipio Valley Artworks, a gallery and shop known for its outstanding collection of exotic handcarved Hawaiian woodcrafts, also has three vacation rentals on the cliffs overlooking Waipio Valley, close to the public lookout. All are new and nicely furnished in an Artworks motif; views of waterfalls, ocean, and valley are superb from all three. Mahalo #1 is a private house with two bedrooms, a full bath, a very large lanai, and a complete kitchen. Aloha #1 is an upstairs apartment with two bedrooms, two full baths, a very large lanai, and a complete kitchen. Aloha #2 is the downstairs apartment of the same building; it has one bedroom, a full bath, lanai, and a complete kitchen. Smoking is allowed only outdoors on the lanais. The office is at Waipio Valley Artworks, in the town of Kukuihaele.

Waipio Ridge Vacation Rental

P.O. Box 5039, Kukuihaele, HI 96727. ☎ **808/775-0603.** 1 cottage. $75 double for only 1 night; $65 double for more than 1 night. $385 double per week. Each additional person $15 extra. No credit cards. Free parking.

A thousand feet above the floor of Waipio Valley, Roger Lasko's little cottage commands a spectacular view; from this distance, the surf breaking below gently lulls one to sleep. The modestly furnished cottage includes a large living room, a bedroom, a well-equipped kitchen, a dining area, and bath. Lasko's friendly dog, Bingo, is in residence. Lasko, a woodshop instructor in the Honokaa school system, lives next door; his phone is available for use.

WAIPIO VALLEY

⑤ Waipio Hotel

Waipio Valley, ☎ **808/775-0368** in Waipio or 808/935-7466 in Hilo; or write to Tom Araki, 25 Malama Place, Hilo, HI 96720. 5 rms (none with bath). $15 single. No credit cards.

Remote and scarcely populated Waipio Valley, which can be reached only by a four-wheel-drive vehicle or by hiking down the steep cliffs, actually has two places where you might spend a night or two. Staying in Waipio Valley is like living in the jungle, with all its lush beauty—but also with the possibility of jungle rains. Tom Araki's Waipio Hotel has all of five rooms and one bath; it has no modern amenities like hot water, telephone, restaurants, or even electricity. Linens and blankets are furnished.

WAIMEA/KAMUELA

Kamuela Inn

Kawaihae Rd. (P.O. Box 1994), Kamuela, HI 96743. ☎ **808/885-4243.** Fax 808/885-8857. 19 rms, 12 suites. $54–$67 single or double; $83–$93 kitchenette suites for three or four persons; $93 penthouse suite; $165 combination of two penthouse suites. Mauna Kea Wing $72–$79 double; $165 executive suites. (Rates include continental breakfast.) AE, DC, DISC, MC, V. Free parking.

From Honokaa, it's 15 miles on Hi. 19 to Kamuela or Waimea, the heart of the Parker Ranch cattle kingdom. A good place to stay in this deliciously cool mountain town is the Kamuela Inn, an old standby that has been attractively renovated. Rooms in the older building are all nicely furnished, and kitchenettes are well equipped with all utensils, even rice cookers. Two penthouse suites rented together are a nice arrangement for a large family or two couples traveling together: The front suite, which sleeps two on a queen-size bed, has an expansive mountain view, a full bath, and a private lanai with wet bar; the rear suite has a full kitchen and bath and generous-size bedroom, which sleeps three with a king-size and a single bed.

Continental breakfast is served in a cheery coffee lounge with broad windows admitting the morning sun. Scenic grounds (there's a bottlebrush tree with red flowers that really look like bottle brushes) and a friendly management are pluses here. There are restaurants nearby and good swimming 12 miles away at Hapuna Beach Park. For reservations, contact manager Earnest Russell.

Morningstar Meadow

P.O. Box 2396, Kamuela, HI 96743. ☎ **808/885-7674.** 3 rooms. $50–$60 single, $75–$85 double. (Rates include full gourmet breakfast.) No credit cards.

This beautiful country home is nestled at the 3,000-foot elevation in the rolling hills above Kamuela. Owner Dee Dickson is not only a gourmet cook, but also a creative interior decorator and travel-guide writer/local historian. Each of her rooms has a decor and a story to match its name. "Checkered Past" derives its name from the bricks that were taken from an old sugar mill. Inside are a pair of antique twin beds. An old koa rocker, lace curtains, Hawaiian art and artifacts, and checkered wall covering grace the room. Next is "Heavy Metal Rose," decorated with an antique iron bedstead with overhead canopy and antique metal furniture. The third room, "Sunshine Corner," is entirely different, with brightly colored walls and a queen-size bed. The rooms are beautiful, but Dee's breakfasts are unbelievable.

Hydrangea Cottage

P.O. Box 563, Kamuela, HI 96743. ☎ toll free **800/262-9921.** Fax 808/885-0559. 1 cottage, 2 suites. $110 cottage; $135 each suites. No credit cards.

Return visitors agree that Hydrangea Cottage, on a beautiful 3-acre estate is a rare jewel in Volcano Village. The cottage guest book overflows with praise from past guests. The owner, who lives on Oahu, escapes as often as possible to her Big Island retreat, a stylish home located adjacent to the cottage. When the owner/hostess is not in residence, guests are left in the capable hands of her caretaker, who lives nearby. The cottage, with views of tall hapuu ferns and ohia trees from every window, has a separate bedroom with a queen-size bed, bath with full tub, a wood stove in a cozy living room, washer/dryer, and a full kitchen that has been stocked with breakfast provisions. There are also two master suites in the main house; each has a queen-size bed and its own living room with a fireplace.

A common kitchen and dining room are in between. The hostess's spacious home is also available for executive or family retreats on request. No smoking.

The Parker Ranch Lodge

P.O. Box 458, Kamuela, HI 96743. ☎ **808/885-4100** or toll free 800/707-4111. Fax 808/885-6711. 21 units. TV TEL. $74.92 single or double; $85.93 single or double with kitchenette. Additional person $10 extra. (Rates include tax.) AE, MC, V. Free parking.

Also very pleasant in this area is the Parker Ranch Lodge, a modern motor hotel within walking distance of the Parker Ranch Center and all its sightseeing, shopping, and eating facilities. Horseback riding and golf are nearby; some excellent beaches are a reasonable drive away. Each room boasts quality furnishings, attractive decor, and beamed ceilings. From this cool, 2,500-foot elevation you have a view of rolling green meadowlands and mountains. Singles have one king-size bed and doubles have two queen-size beds.

✪ Waimea Garden Cottages

P.O. Box 563, Kamuela, HI 96743. ☎ **808/885-4550** or toll free 800/262-9912 for reservations. Fax 808/885-0559. 2 cottages. TV TEL. $110–$115 cottages per night. Additional person $15 extra. (Rates include breakfast.) Minimum stay 3 nights. No credit cards. Free parking.

This has to be one of our very favorite places on the Big Island. This is the perfect country retreat: two elegant private cottages where you can live in graceful surroundings, do your own cooking if you wish, spend your time riding or hiking in the mountains, or swimming at Hapuna Beach, just 8 miles down the road. (The hosts provide beach towels, back rests, and coolers.) Barbara and Charlie Campbell, a charming local couple, built the cottages adjacent to their own home. The newest Waimea cottage has a sitting room, gracious bedroom alcove with queen-size bed, hardwood floors, fireplace, TV, stereo, and French doors opening to a spacious brick patio. Your hosts welcome you with breakfast provisions and a tempting array of local fruits. You can even gather your own eggs from the family hens right on the grounds. The Waiaka Stream meanders right behind the property.

THE SOUTHERN ROUTE

Driving the southern route (Hi. 11) between Hilo and Kona, there are a number of delightful places to spend a night or two.

KEAAU

✪ Paradise Place Bed & Breakfast

HCR 9558, Keaau, HI 96749. ☎ **808/966-4600.** 2 rms. TV. $60 single; $65 double. 2-night minimum stay; seventh night free. (Rates include full continental breakfast.) No credit cards.

Paradise Park, six miles south of Keaau, is the home of Paradise Place, owned by Laura Richman and Steve Peyton. It's in a 1-acre rural setting, just half a mile from the ocean. The view from the two rooms takes in the steaming volcano Mauna Kea in the distance and the garden right outside the door. Each room has a private entrance, bath, kitchenette with full refrigerator, washer and dryer, patio, and hammock. Those renting a double often get the entire apartment. A hot tub/spa and a ping-pong table are pluses. Steve often travels throughout Micronesia and has decorated the B&B with artifacts from his journeys. Readers have lavished Paradise Place—as well as Steve and Laura themselves—with lot of praise for the quality of their home and the level of service they provide.

Rainforest Retreat

HCR 1, Box 5655, Keaau, HI 96749. ☎ **808/966-7712.** Fax 808/966-6898. 2 units. Studio $55 single, $65 double. Ohia House $85 double/single. Additional person $10/night. Single night stay additional $10/night. (Rates include breakfast.) No credit cards.

Tucked away in the rain forest of ohia trees and wild orchids, this is a very private, relaxing retreat. Lori Campbell, owner and operator, also has one of the largest orchid nurseries in Hawaii, specializing in cattleya and phalaenopsis. The Ohia House is on the grounds of the nursery with a second-story view of Mauna Kea and—if you're lucky—the glow from Kilauea's continuously erupting volcano. The real attraction here is the large hot tub, where you can soak away your cares and contemplate the beauties of the rain forest. The house has a complete kitchen (which Lori fills with everything you need for breakfast). Also available is the comfortable, 400-square-foot garden studio with a kitchenette, king-size bed, and full bath.

Volcano Area

The Volcano area is perfect for the guesthouse lifestyle. Country cottages are places where you can bring the kids, relax, drive off to the volcano or to the black-sand beaches farther south, or just savor the simple charms of country life. But do bear in mind that the weather is highly changeable here, and the rains come and go in the mountains; winter can be especially rainy.

Doubles for About $45 to $70

✪ Carson's Volcano Cottage

501 Sixth St., Mauna Loa Estates (P.O. Box 503), Volcano, HI 96785. ☎ **808/967-7683,** or toll free 800/845-LAVA. 3 rms., 1 private cottage, 1 suite, 2 vacation homes (all with bath). $55 single; $75 double; $140 suite; from $85 vacation home. (Rates include breakfast.) DISC, MC, V. Free parking.

Hosts Tom and Brenda Carson love meeting new people and aim to provide them with a welcome, peaceful—and romantic—environment. There is a private, cozy cottage that sleeps five, and a three-room cottage; all rooms have private baths and private entrances, and two have kitchenettes. Rooms are furnished in Victorian, Polynesian, Asian, country, and Hawaii 1940s style, with many unique pieces, homey touches, and fresh flowers indoors and out. The Carsons serve an elaborate breakfast, including Hawaiian french toast made from Portuguese sweet bread, bagels with cream cheese and lox, and cheese blintzes with strawberries. And there's a hot tub nestled among giant Hawaiian tree ferns. Vacation homes are affordable, and some sleep up to six.

The Country Goose

Ruby Ave. and 8th St., Volcano, HI 96785. ☎ **808/967-7759** or toll free 800/238-7101. 2 rms, 2 vacation houses (all with bath). $70 double (including breakfast); $85 two-bedroom/two-bath house for two; $100 three-bedroom/two-bath house. Each additional person $20. D, MC, V. Free parking.

Joan Early's house is decorated with all kinds of country geese—wood, ceramic, cloth—sent to her by guests who've enjoyed her hospitality and her delicious breakfasts. She likes nothing better than to whip up some sour cream pancakes or quiches, or Hawaiian french toast made from Portuguese sweet bread, or waffles with fresh strawberries for her guests. The full breakfast comes with the King Room with king-size bed, bath, and private entrance, and the Queen Room with queen-size bed, double futon on a frame, bath, and private entrance. Each room has a TV and VCR with tapes and books of local interest. Around the corner are

Joan's two vacation houses. The two-bedroom house can accommodate six people and the three-bedroom up to 12—so they're both very popular for small groups or family reunions. Joan has plenty of good tips on nearby attractions.

✪ The Guesthouse at Volcano

11-3733 Ala Ohia St. (P.O. Box 6), Volcano, HI 96785. ☎ **808/967-7775.** Fax 808/967-8295. 1 one-bedroom cottage. $60 for two people. Additional person $10 extra. Minimum stay 2 days; seventh day free. No credit cards. Free parking.

Bonnie Goodell is in charge at the Guesthouse at Volcano, a perfect place for a family to settle into. Nestled in a tree fern forest, it consists of a living room downstairs with a double hideaway bed, a complete kitchen, and a nice bedroom upstairs with two twins and a queen-size bed. The apartment is fully furnished, including phone, TV, books, magazines, games, electric heater, bikes for children, and even wool socks! The big outside porch has kids' toys and a big sink area for "cookouts, muddy boots, berries, etc." If Bonnie is booked, she will probably be able to help you find another similar place.

Hale Ohia Cottages

P.O. Box 758, Volcano, HI 96785. ☎ **808/967-7986.** 5 units. $65–$85 one bedroom; $75–$95 cottage. Additional person $15 extra. (Rates include continental breakfast.) No credit cards.

This was once the historic Dillingham summer estate, located on beautifully landscaped grounds just a mile from the national park. Built in 1931, Hale Ohia consists of a main house, a guest cottage, a gardener's cottage, and other structures in a botanical garden. The gardener's cottage, now known as Hale Ohia Cottage, is a charming, two-story house with three bedrooms (sleeps five), a large living room, and a complete kitchen. For smaller groups or for travelers on a budget, the Hale Lehua Cottage (once a private study in the days of the Dillinghams) is a one-bedroom house centered around a lava-rock fireplace. The limited cooking facilities include a refrigerator, microwave, and hot plate. Located in the main residence, the Dillingham suite has a living room, private bath, and private lanai.

Also available are the Iiwi and Camillia Suites, located on the first floor of the Hale Ohia Cottage. Each has private entrances and baths with gorgeous leaded-glass windows. The Camillia Suite, with parking right at the door, is easily accessible to disabled guests.

Lokahi Lodge

Kalanikoa Rd. (P.O. Box 7), Volcano, HI 96785. ☎ **808/985-8647,** or toll free 800/457-6924. 4 rms (all with bath). $65–$70 single or double. Each additional person $15. MC. V. Free parking.

There's an old-fashioned country charm about this place, even though the house is new, built specifically as a bed and breakfast. There's a player piano and organ in the living room, lots of books and games, a wood-burning stove for those crisp Volcano nights. Framed leis line the hallway, leading to four rooms, each with its own entrance to the wraparound lanai overlooking a lush ohia forest. All rooms are nicely decorated and all have two extra-long double beds. Gracious hosts Judy and Graham offer a continental breakfast with fresh tropical fruits and juice, and fresh homemade bread and jam, assorted cereal, and coffee and tea.

Volcano Bed & Breakfast

19-3950 Keonelehua St. (P.O. Box 998), Volcano Village, HI 96785, ☎ **808/967-7779** or toll free 800/736-7140. Fax 808/967-8860. 5 rms. TV. $45–$65 single; $45–$75 double. Additional person $15 extra. (Rates include full breakfast.) AC, DISC, MC, V. Free parking.

This cozy little country house is set in a pretty landscaped area in the community of Volcano Village. The house belongs to the guests: sun room, wood-burning stove, TV and VCR, CDs, and cozy country bedrooms. Saul, the engaging Resident Manager, is on hand to help guests plan their day's activities. Breakfast is simple; local fresh fruit and French toast or pancakes; it's filling, tasty, and charmingly served.

Volcano Heart Chalet

☎ **808/248-7725.** 3 rms (1 with bath). $50 single or double per night; $300 single or double per week. Minimum stay 2 nights. No credit cards. Free parking.

Although they reside in Maui most of the time, JoLoyce and John Kaia make their Volcano area home available to guests. The two-story cedar house, surrounded by trees, consists of three bedrooms (all with private locks), containing either queen-size or twin beds, warm comforters for cool nights, and either private or shared baths. All guests can use the glass-enclosed porch for cooking and eating, and there is a carpeted lounging and exercise room. It's a cute place: Each room has its own theme—hearts, cats, bears, and so on. Guests are provided with coffee, tea, cocoa, and fresh pastry. Adults only; no smoking or alcohol.

Doubles from About $75 to $90

✪ Chalet Kilauea—The Inn at Volcano

Off Hi. 11 at the corner of Wright/Lauukapu Rd. (P.O. Box 998), Volcano Village, HI 96785. ☎ **808/967-7786** or toll free 800/937-7786. Fax 808/967-8660. 3 rms, 2 suites, 5 vacation homes. TV. $75–$175 single or double; $125–$175 suites; from $75–$225 vacation homes. AE, DISC, MC, V. Free parking.

After traveling around the world for years, Brian and Lisha Crawford settled down in Volcano Village, just a mile from Hawaii Volcanoes National Park, and opened an inn. They filled it with the art and unique furniture they collected throughout their world travels. The large living room, where afternoon tea is served, boasts a fireplace and a library of books, music, and videos; it's a good place for a small business meeting. The three guest rooms in the main house include the Continental Lace suite with a private bath, featuring a double Jacuzzi tub, canopy queen-size bed, and dressing room, plus a daybed for reading; the Oriental Jade room, done in jade and gold, comes complete with queen-size bed and antique Chinese screens; and the Out of Africa room is filled with treasures from Africa—masks, baskets, artwork. All rooms have VCRs and the theme rooms feature marble Jacuzzi tubs. That's not all: Outside is a two-story "treehouse suite" with a master bedroom upstairs and a mini-kitchen and dayroom downstairs. The Jacuzzi on the lanai is available for guests' use, a fire is lit in the living room every night, and a candlelit, two-course, gourmet breakfast is served.

Chalet Kilauea's vacation homes are spacious and graced with charming decor. All offer a full kitchen, complimentary afternoon tea, and the use of the Jacuzzi. The Ohia Holiday Cottage at $75, the Hapuu Forest Cabin at $145, the Hoku Hawaiian House at $125, Pele's Pavilion at $175, and the Royal Hawaiian Haven at $225 and offer the ultimate in Volcano comfort.

✪ Kilauea Lodge

Old Volcano Rd. (P.O. Box 116), Volcano Village, HI 96785. ☎ **808/967-7366.** Fax 808/967-7367. 10 rms, 1 suite, 1 cottage (all with bath). $90–$125 single or double. Additional person $15 extra. (Rates include full breakfast.) MC, V. Free parking.

Perhaps the most beautiful rooms in this area are at Kilauea Lodge, 1 mile Hilo-side of Hawaii Volcanoes National Park, in Volcano Village. When you see the lodge—set on 10 acres of greenery, bordered by magnificent ferns and towering pine trees—you'll know why everybody on the Big Island is excited about it. This former YMCA mountain retreat has now become a restaurant offering excellent meals (sorely needed in this area) and an inn offering exquisite rooms. Lorna and Albert Jeyte (she comes from Honolulu, he hails from Germany) are in charge here: He performs the magic in the kitchen; she's created the magic in the guest rooms. You'd never believe this used to be a YMCA dorm! Architects have opened up the top of the building to create a skylight, flooding the rooms with natural light. Hawaiian quilt patterns set the mostly soft pastel color schemes for the woodwork. Furniture is made of light oak, even down to the oak tissue box. Each room is decorated differently—most are in the country style; one is strikingly Japanese—some have working fireplaces. The one-bedroom cottage has a queen-size bed in the bedroom and a queen-size sofa bed in the living room; it can sleep up to four.

Volcano House

P.O. Box 53, Hawaii Volcanoes National Park, HI 96718. ☎ **808/967-7321.** Fax 808/967-8429. 42 rms. In Ohia Wing, $79 single or double. In the main building, $105 single or double without crater view, $131 single or double with crater view. Additional person $10 extra. AE, DISC, JCB, MC, V. Free parking.

The famed and venerable Volcano House is right on the brink of Kilauea Crater, where the ancient *kahunas* (priests) once gathered to make sacrifices to Pele. This hotel has changed hands several times in recent years, but the new management has things well in hand. All the guest rooms have been renovated and refurbished with koa furniture, including koa rockers in the rooms in the main building, and cheerful Hawaiian comforters. The least-expensive rooms are in the Ohia Wing, a separate building away from the main building. Better and more expensive rooms, in the main building, vary depending on their view of the crater. Even if you don't stay at Volcano House, at least come by to soak up the atmosphere (the floor-to-ceiling lava fireplace in the cozy living room lobby has been burning steadily for 120 years!), have a drink in Uncle George's Lounge, or a meal at the Ka Ohelo dining room. Enjoying a breakfast here in the early morning mountain air, seated at a table near the window where you can gaze right into the volcano, is one of the special treats of Hawaii.

KAPOHO BEACH

Champagne Cove

Kapoho Beach. ☎ **808/965-7426.** 2 three-bedroom apts. TV. $70 for one or two readers of this book (mention when making reservations); $75 for one or two other guests. Extra charge for additional guests. Minimum stay 1 week, with some exceptions. No credit cards. Free parking.

Drs. Keith and Norma Godfrey live in Pahoa, but they rent this vacation hideaway, built on a lava bed where the ocean meets the volcanic flows at Kapoho Beach in the Puna area. It's a stark setting, but the house is warm, cozy, and beautifully decorated. Each of the two stories is a complete apartment with a superb kitchen, a living room, and three attractive bedrooms. The rates make this an extraordinary bargain. What a place for a family reunion! You can swim in a heated pool right in front of the house, or walk a short distance to a black-sand beach and a warm tide pool in the ocean (good for snorkeling). The house is a half-hour drive from Hilo.

Reservations: Drs. Keith and Norma Godfrey, R.R. 2, Box 943, Pahoa, HI 96778.

KEHENA

✪ Kalani Honua Intercultural Conference and Retreat Center

Box 4500, Pahoa, HI 96778. ☎ **808/965-7828** or toll free 800/800-6886. 30 rms, 5 cottages. $52 single without bath; $65 single with bath; $62 double without bath; $75 double with bath; $28 each triple or quad with shared bath; $85 cottage. AE, MC, V. Free parking.

Although most guests come to Kalani Honua for conferences and retreats, there's no reason why other travelers cannot enjoy its lovely facilities close to the black-sand beach at Kehena. Photographers, especially, enjoy the dawn-facing lava cliffs overlooking the sea, adjacent to the facility. Kalani Honua is situated five minutes from the former town of Kalapana, buried under a flood of molten lava in 1990.

Spacious grounds house, rustic conference facilities, a dining hall with lanai seating, cafe, gift shop, sauna, 25-meter pool, and Jacuzzi (the pool area is clothing-optional after 7pm); massage is available. Nearby are natural warm springs and steam caves, and the beach at Kehena is famed for the dolphins, which frequently play with swimmers. Winter months bring humpback whales, which also come quite close to shore.

Rooms, in four cedar lodges and private cottages, are simply decorated and comfortable. Tent space (you bring the tent and linens) costs $15 per person. Meals are mostly vegetarian and skillfully prepared by a caring staff.

THE KAILUA-KONA COAST

Aston's Kona Islander Inn

75-5776 Kuakini Hwy., Kailua-Kona, HI 96740. ☎ **808/329-3181** or toll free 800/922-7866 in the U.S. Fax 808/326-9339. 144 rms. A/C TV TEL. Apr–Dec 21, $79–$95 single or double. Dec 22–Mar $89–$105 single or double. Additional person $12 extra. AE, DC, JCB, MC, V. Free parking.

Newly refurbished and looking nicer than ever, this plantation-style complex boasts one of the most central locations in town, plus a pool set in a glorious garden and a barbecue grill out by the pool. All the rooms are identical, but the price is determined by location: garden, poolside, or with ocean view. Rooms all have either a queen-size bed or two twin beds, shower (no tub), and a private lanai furnished with a table and two director's chairs. There's a refrigerator in every unit.

The Dragonfly Ranch: Tropical Fantasy Lodging

P.O. Box 675, Honaunau, HI 96726. ☎ **808/328-2159** or toll free 800/487-2159. Fax 808/328-9570. 2 rms, 2 suites. $70–$80 double per night, $420 per week in main house; Outdoor Waterbed Honeymoon Suite $160 for one night, $400 for three nights, $800 per week; Writer's Studio, $120 for one night, $300 for three nights, $600 per week. Rates based on double occupancy; each additional person $15 per night; breakfast included. MC, V. Free parking.

Barbara Moore-Link and David Link, the lovely couple who run the Dragonfly Ranch in Honaunau, 19 miles south of Kailua-Kona, offer their place for families and small groups for weddings, reunions, workshops, and private retreats. It's a magical spot, with huge monkeypod trees and singing birds everywhere. They also have extraordinary accommodations for travelers and honeymooners—you'll be happy if you luck into one of these unusual spaces. Our favorite is the Outdoor

Waterbed Honeymoon Suite, in a jungle setting with private bathroom, outdoor shower with an old-fashioned bathtub, and a kitchenette. The king-size bed has a marvelous view of Honaunau Bay; the adjoining redwood room has a queen-size futon. This suite can accommodate four, but it's ideally suited as a romantic get-away for two. The Writer's Studio is a spacious 20-by-22 foot apartment with its own kitchen, private bathroom, outdoor shower, walk-in closet, king-size bed, and additional futons. The best bargains here are the attractively furnished two rooms in the main house, each with its own bath; one has a private deck. An outdoor shower—wonderful for bathing in the sunshine or under the stars—is also available. Room guests have full use of the main house, which is wrapped around a huge monkeypod tree. With both indoor and outdoor dining areas, a huge sun deck, and a covered lanai, the Dragonfly Ranch is a great place for relaxation. For music lovers, David has a vast selection of music as well as a piano and a professional recording studio. All units have stereo cassette players; cable TV, VCR, and videotapes are available. For breakfast, there are baked goods and fresh homegrown fruits. Guests are welcome to harvest their own organic apple-bananas and strawberry-papayas, as well as the more exotic starfruit and soursap in season. And Barbara offers the use of a massage chair, aromatherapy, and flower essences; she's an expert at the ancient Hawaiian art of lomilomi massage. An assortment of snorkeling gear is available for guests' use.

⊙ H. Manago Hotel

Hi. 11 (P.O. Box 145), Captain Cook, HI 96704. ☎ **808/323-2642.** 64 rms. Older building, $22 single without bath; $25 double without bath; $28 triple without bath. Newer wing, $35–$38 single with bath; $38–$41 double with bath; $41–$44 triple with bath. Japanese room with private furo, $52 single; $55 double. MC, V. Free parking.

Thirteen miles south of Kailua, on Hi. 11—and 1,400 feet high in coffee country—is the H. Manago Hotel, where you'll find some of the most reasonable accommodations in the Kona area. But staying here means more than getting a clean, comfortable room for rock-bottom prices. The Manago Hotel is part of the history of the Kona coast; it's been a favorite with island people since 1917. The dining room and hotel grew over the years, and now a third generation of family management has taken over. The older rooms, with community bath, are strictly for the low-maintenance guests. Rooms in the newer wing, with private baths and lanais, are modern, comfortable, and are nicely decorated. A deluxe Japanese-style room offers futons and its own furo (deep hot tub). It's delightfully quiet and cool here throughout the year. The hotel restaurant is a favorite with local people for its home-style Japanese and American cooking: breakfast starts at $4; lunch and dinner, about $6 to $10.75 (a typical meal is beef or fish with three kinds of vegetables, and beverage). They're known for their pork chops. And incidentally, the three-story frame building looks down the foot of the mountain to Kealakekua Bay, where Captain Cook met his end. Owner Dwight Manago advises reserving about three weeks ahead in season, two weeks other times.

Hale Maluhia

76-770 Hualalai Rd., Kailua-Kona, HI 96740. ☎ **808/329-1123** or toll free 800/559-6627. Fax 808/326-5487. 4 rms, 1 cottage, 2 two-bedroom suites. TEL. $55, $70, $75, $80 bedroom; $110, $125, $225 cottage and suites. Each additional person $15 extra. (Rates include full breakfast.) AE, DISC, MC, V. Free parking.

Just a 3-mile drive from the hustle and bustle of Kailua town is this peaceful country home at the cool, 900-foot elevation of Holualoa Mountain. Ken and Ann

Smith built their rambling home set on an acre of Kona-coffee land more than 22 years ago and kept adding to it as their family grew; now the family is gone, and lucky visitors find their way here instead. The interiors are comfortably appointed with open-beam ceilings, natural woods, koa cabinets, Victorian and Hawaiian furnishings—not fancy, but cozy. There are two living areas which guests may use, three decks, a kitchen, an outdoor spa and massage table, and a fully equipped business office with fax, typewriter, and computer. A full breakfast is served. The place is handicapped-accessible and wheelchair-friendly. The main house, with its two bedrooms, large lanai, and two double sofa beds, can sleep up to eight and can be rented in its entirety. The Gatehouse, the two-bedroom apartment with kitchenette and shared bath, can sleep up to seven and can also be rented in its entirety. The studio (called the Banyan Cottage) is a perfect nest for honeymooners, with its king-size bed, refrigerator, TV, Jacuzzi, and porch swing. Ken is an ordained minister and can help in making wedding arrangements.

✪ Kona Magic Sands Condominiums

77-6452 Alii Dr., Kailua-Kona, HI 96740. ☎ and fax **808/326-5662** or toll free 800/ 529-1770. 37 studio apts. TV. $65–$75 studio apt for two. Seventh night free. Additional person $5 extra. No minimum stay, but may be subject to cleaning fee. AE, MC, V. Free parking.

Each and every apartment at the Kona Magic Sands Condominium overlooks the pounding ocean and the glorious sunsets of Kona. This is one of the older condos in the area, not as luxurious as some, but it's very beachy and cozy—the kind of place where it feels good to kick off your sandals and take life easy. The good-size studio apartments, furnished for two guests, have full kitchens; instead of a separate bedroom, they have a sleeping alcove off the living room, with a double, queen, or sofa bed. There are palm trees outside your window, a freshwater pool for swimming, and the convenience of having Jameson's by the Sea, a top restaurant, right downstairs. A few of the extra-large apartments have lanais overlooking the beach.

✪ Kona Riviera Villa

75-6124 Alii Dr., Kailua-Kona, HI 96740. ☎ **808/329-1996** or toll free 800/800-6202 (Mon–Fri 9am–5pm). One-bedroom apts. TV TEL. Apr 15–Dec 14, $60 garden; $70–$80 oceanview; Dec 15–Apr 14, $70 gardenview; $80–$90 oceanview; $100 oceanfront. Additional person $10 extra. No credit cards. Minimum stay 3 nights. Free parking.

The Kona Riviera Villa is the kind of place we like best: charming, intimate, low-key, and affordable. It's an older condominium complex, set far enough back from the water to bring in the cooling breezes—and not too much ocean noise. A freshwater swimming pool and patio with barbecue grill overlook the ocean, which is too rough for swimming, but fine for snorkelers and surfers. Each apartment is comfortably furnished and nicely decorated. All units have one bedroom, and some of the living rooms have sofa beds, so that up to four people can be accommodated. Kitchens are equipped with dishwashers and garbage disposals. This is a congenial place, so much so that many of the guests come back year after year. Rates are very modest for this luxury area; make reservations early.

Kona Seaside Hotel

75-5646 Palani Rd., Kailua-Kona, HI 96740. ☎ **808/329-2455**, or toll free 800/367-7000 from U.S. mainland, 800/654-7020 from Canada. Fax 808/922-0052. 225 rms, 14 kitchenette rms. A/C TV TEL. $85 standard, $90 superior tower, $95 deluxe, $105 kitchenette. Cars available for $15 more per day. Additional person $12 extra. Children 12 and under stay free with parents when using existing bedding. AE, DC, MC, V. Free parking.

A good choice smack in the center of Kailua is the Kona Seaside Hotel and Kona Seaside Pool Wing, at the intersection of Kuakini Highway (Hi. 11) and Palani Road (Hi. 19)—just a parking lot away from the shopping and restaurant excitement of Alii Drive. Size is the byword—large rooms, spacious lanais, and an extra-large pool. Blue is the theme of the well-appointed rooms.

The rooms in the Kona Seaside Pool Wing (formerly the Hukilau Hotel), most of them overlooking another large lovely pool, are smartly furnished and have twin- or king-size beds; from many you can see the harbor across the road and a small public beach. Or you may just want to laze on the sun deck, which looks out on Alii Drive and the harbor, and watch the world go by. The pool wing leads directly into Stan's Restaurant, which serves three reasonably priced meals every day and has a popular cocktail lounge. The Calypso Restaurant specializes in seafood.

✪ Kona Tiki Hotel

75-5968 Alii Dr., Kailua-Kona, HI 96745. ☎ **808/329-1425.** 15 rms. $54 single or double. $59 single or double with kitchenette. (Rates include continental breakfast.) Additional person $7 extra (maximum of three people per room). Minimum stay 3 days. No credit cards. Free parking.

In a garden setting overlooking the ocean, away from the bustle of the center of town and very close to the Royal Kona Resort, is the petite Kona Tiki Hotel, a longtime budget stop in Kona. All the rooms have private oceanfront lanais looking out on the blue-green pounding surf (and it really does pound—noisily—against the sea wall). The ocean is great for fishing and snorkeling; there's a freshwater pool for gentler swimming. All rooms include queen-size beds, ceiling fans, and a small refrigerator. They have been redone in blue and green, with light furniture, and new kitchenette units and refrigerators. Friendliness abounds at the Kona Tiki; it's the kind of small, family-owned hotel where guests usually get to know one another. You can drive to the center of town in 3 minutes or walk in 15 minutes. Reserve a month in advance usually, two months in advance in busy seasons. Specify first and second choices on rooms with or without kitchenette (very few kitchenettes are available). The rates listed above are guaranteed to those bearing this book at check-in.

✪ Merryman's Bed & Breakfast

P.O. Box 474, Kealakekua, HI 96750. ☎ **808/323-2276,** or toll free 800/545-4390. 4 rms. TV. $65 single with shared bath, $75 single with private bath; $75 double with shared bath, $85–$95 double with private bath. (Rates include breakfast.) MC, V. Free parking.

Don and Penny Merryman's pretty home 1,500 feet up on a hill in Kealakekua, about a half-hour drive from Kailua town, has plenty of charm: rooms filled with handsome antiques (the Victorian room has a four-poster bed), views of Kealakekua Bay far below or a lovely garden, and two large lanais (one with a refrigerator and microwave), where guests can relax and have breakfast. Don and Penny are gracious hosts, and they usually put out something special for their guests: maybe quiche, or bagels and cream cheese, plus fruit, teas, and Kona coffee, of course—it's grown right on the slopes of the mountain. Each room has its own refrigerator. There's a steaming Jacuzzi outside under the palm trees.

Three Bears Bed & Breakfast

72-1001 Puukala St., Kailua-Kona, HI. ☎ and fax **808/325-7563** or toll free 800/765-0480 from U.S. mainland. 2 rms. TV. $65–$75 double per night, $410–$470 per week. Add $10 for one-night stays. (Rates include breakfast.) MC, V. Free parking.

Anne Stockel and her husband Art and daughter Nanette really take guests under their wing: Anne will even make calls for them, and see that they have the best possible time on their vacation. No wonder Three Bears has so many visitors who return for longer stays! The cozy, all-cedar house—more comfy than glamorous— is located at a 1,600-foot elevation, which means cool nighttime breezes from the trade winds, spectacular ocean views from the large lanai (you can watch the whales in winter from their telescope), and lots of wild canaries, cardinals, and parakeets flocking to the Stockels' birdfeeder. What a place to totally unwind! There are two pleasantly furnished rooms, one with a private bath; each room has its own coffeemaker, microwave oven, and small refrigerator; if you're staying for more than a few days, you can also use the kitchen. And on top of that, Anne bakes fresh bread for breakfast, and serves it along with croissants, muffins, fresh fruit, cold cuts, and 100% pure Kona coffee from her son-in-law's farm. The Stockels will loan you beach chairs, towels, mats, coolers, even boogie boards and snorkel equipment to take down the big hill to the Kona Coast Beach Park. They'll also advise you on the best things to see and do in Kailua town, about a 10-minute drive away.

If you're traveling elsewhere on the Big Island, or to the other islands, they can get you car rentals at discount prices and find you reasonable accommodations (particularly for European travelers) through their own reservation service.

Uncle Billy's Kona Bay Hotel

75-5739 Alii Dr., Kailua-Kona, HI 96740. ☎ **808/329-1398** or toll free 800/367-5102. Fax 808/935-7903. 145 rms. A/C TV TEL. $62 moderate, $72 superior, $79 oceanfront, $74 with kitchenette, single or double. Room-car packages available. From Dec 15–Mar 31 add $8 to all rates. Children under 18 stay free in parents' room. Additional person $10 extra. AE, DC, DISC, MC, V. Free parking.

Uncle Billy's Kona Bay Hotel, right in the center of town, is run by the same family that manages Uncle Billy's Hilo Bay Hotel. This newer hotel is landscaped with bridges and ponds, and a Polynesian longhouse restaurant surrounds a large circular swimming pool. The thatched roof over the registration desk and the koa-wood tables in the lobby create a warm Hawaiian feeling. The hotel's restaurant, Banana Bay, is popular for its low-priced breakfast and dinner buffets. The rooms, recently redecorated in teal, pink, and cream, are of a comfortable size. Each room has a good-size lanai and a refrigerator; many have two double beds. Some rooms have an ocean view.

Worth a Splurge

✪ Holualoa Inn

P.O. Box 222, Holualoa, HI 96725. ☎ **808/324-1121** or toll free 800/392-1812. Fax 808/322-2472. 4 rms. $125–$175 single or double. 15% discount on stays of 1 week or longer. Minimum stay 2 days. (Rates include continental breakfast.) AE, MC, V. Free parking.

Grander than most B&Bs and smaller than most hotels, the Holualoa Inn is in a class by itself: It's an exquisite small inn with spectacular ocean views, set high in the mountains in the farming community/art colony of Holualoa, about a 15-minute drive from Kailua-Kona. The three-level mansion, set on a 40-acre estate and working coffee farm, was originally built as a mountain hideaway for *Honolulu Advertiser* president Thurston Twigg-Smith. Now his nephew Desmond Twigg-Smith has taken it over and superbly decorated its guest bedrooms, which he rents out on a B&B basis to those lucky enough to find this serenely beautiful spot. The house is built of cedar wood, its floors of eucalyptus, its windows of spun glass. The handsome living room has a fireplace, reading areas, even a billiard table.

The formal dining room is the scene of morning breakfasts of fresh fruits, juices, pancakes, sausages, pastries, and homemade muffins. The Kona coffee and papayas served are grown right here. And the rooms are enchanting. In addition to the use of the living and dining rooms upstairs, guests also have a common room on the lower level, where they can store food in the refrigerator. There's a large swimming pool outside, a raised gazebo from which to watch the sunset, and singing birds everywhere.

Keauhou Beach Hotel

78-6740 Alii Dr., Kailua-Kona, HI 96740. ☎ **808/322-3441** or reservations toll free 800/367-6025. Fax 808/322-6586. 310 rms. 6 suites. A/C TV TEL. $100–$175 double; $250–$425 suite. Inquire about lower off-season rates. Extra person $15. AE, DC, MC, V. Free parking.

If you'd like to treat yourself to a stay at a lovely oceanside resort, this is the place we'd suggest. Only 6 miles away from the center of town, Keauhou Beach Hotel is relaxing enough to be a world apart. And that it is—this hotel is sprawled out on grounds that are rich in both natural beauty and Hawaiian history. This area, from which Kamehameha the Great launched his armies, was a favorite retreat of Hawaiian royalty. The hotel is almost a living Hawaiian museum, with two heiaus, a reconstructed grass shack, an ancient fishpond or "sacred pool," and petroglyphs carved out on a flat lava reef that runs straight out from the hotel. An exact replica of King Kamehameha's summer home has been reconstructed here on its original site. The hotel has its own private swimming beach (rare for Kona) adjoining Kahuluu Beach Park, and even a volcanic tidal pool facing the sunning beach, where you can watch the creatures of the deep swim. Rooms are spacious and handsome, with every facility for comfort, including a small refrigerator and a spacious bath and dressing area. All rooms have lanais; many overlook the ocean. There's a freshwater, oceanfront swimming pool, six tennis courts (two lighted), pro shop (lessons available using the most modern facilities), and a nearby championship golf course. The open-air Kuakini Terrace is popular for its Chinese and seafood buffets and its fabulous Sunday brunch. Hawaiian music is featured every night at the Makai Bar.

3 Camping & Wilderness Cabins

By Jeanette Foster

Campers get a special Big Island experience that can only be had off-road, in the peace and quiet of beautiful backcountry. Camping is a year-round experience on the Big Island due to dependable balmy weather—it's always warm and dry somewhere on the island. However, there is a wet season, winter, and a dry season, summer, and campers should be prepared for rain year-round. Also be prepared for insects (have a good mosquito repellent), water purification (boiling, filtration, or iodine tablets), and the sun (protect yourself with sunscreen, a hat, and a long-sleeve shirt). Don't hike or swim alone, and never turn your back on the ocean; you may be surprised at how close and powerful the waves are.

For information on camping on the Big Island, contact: **Hawaii Volcanoes National Park,** P.O. Box 52, Volcano, HI 96718 (☎ 808/967-7311), **Puuhonua-O-Honaunau National Historic Park,** Honaunau, HI 96726 (☎ 808/328-2326), the **State Division of Forestry and Wildlife,** P.O. Box 4849, Hilo, HI 96720 (☎ 808/933-4221), **State Division of Parks,** P.O. Box 936, Hilo, HI 96721 (☎ 808/933-4200), and the **County Department of Parks and Recreation,** 25 Aupuni Street, Hilo, HI 96720 (☎ 808/961-8311).

The **Hawaiian Trail and Mountain Club** (P.O. Box 2238, Honolulu, HI 96804) offers an information packet on hiking and camping throughout the Hawaiian Islands. Send $1.25 and a legal-size, self-addressed, stamped envelope for information. Another good source of information is the *Hiking/Camping Information Packet,* available from **Hawaii Geographic Maps and Books,** 49 S. Hotel Street, Suite 218, Honolulu, HI 96813 (☎ 808/538-3952), for $7 (postage included).

Camping equipment can be rented from **Pacific Rent-All,** 1080 Kilauea Avenue, Hilo (☎ 808/935-2974) or purchased from **C&S Cycle and Surf** in Kamuela/Waimea (☎ 808/885-5005), **Gaspro** in Hilo (☎ 808/935-3341), Kamuela (☎ 808/885-8636), or Kona (☎ 808/329-7393), and **The Surplus Store** in Hilo (☎ 808/935-6398) or Kona (☎ 808/329-1240).

For guided hiking-camping tours contact **Crane Tours:** Bill Crane, 15101 Magnolia Blvd., H10, Sherman Oaks, CA 91403 (☎ 818/742-2213 or toll free 800/653-2545), or Hilt McCauley, (☎ 818/347-6433). These are moderately strenuous week-long trips for experienced backpackers, costing about $695.

HAWAII VOLCANOES NATIONAL PARK

One of the most spectacular national parks in the country, the Hawaii Volcanoes National Park encompasses 344 lava-crusted square miles, from the summit of Mauna Loa at 13,677 feet to the ever-changing coast 20 miles away. Mauna Loa last erupted in a curtain of fire in 1984; Kilauea has been continuously flowing since 1983. You can view the fresh lava flow up close; rangers will allow you to get as near to it as safety permits—depending on conditions, that can mean as close as a few feet! This park is a wonderland for hikers and campers. Miles of trails not only traverse the lava, but also cross deserts, rainforests, beaches, and, in the winter, snow at 13,000 feet. The climate can be cool and rainy any time of the year; come prepared for hot sun as well as rain and cold.

There are three campgrounds inside the park that are accessible by car: **Kipuka Nene, Namakani Paio,** and **Kamoamoa.** Each has pavilions with picnic tables and fireplaces, but wood is not provided. Tent camping is free and no reservations are required, but stays are limited to seven days per campground per year. Cabins in the park at **Namakani Paio** are operated by the Volcano House (☎ 808/967-7321), a private concessionaire. Reservations should be made at least one month in advance, 3 to 6 months in advance for summer and holiday reservations. **Kilauea Military Camp** has a rest and recreation camp for active and retired military personnel just a mile from the park headquarters; for information, call 808/967-7315, and for reservations call 808/967-8333. Backpack camping at hiker shelters and cabins is available, but you must register at park headquarters for overnight stays. Detailed maps are sold at park headquarters and are highly recommended. Check trail conditions and water supplies before you start.

I recommend the following cabins, tent camping, and backpack camping areas as the best of what the Volcano area has to offer:

KILAUEA STATE RECREATION AREA

This state park cabin is located just outside the park in the town of Volcano, at 3,700 feet. The cabin sleeps up to six and has a kitchen, dining/living room, two bedrooms, and a bathroom with hot shower. Utensils, blankets, bedding, and towels are all provided. You can stay for up to five nights during a 30-day period at this wonderful cabin. Fees are on a sliding scale; they begin at $10 a night for one and go down to $5 per person for six. As you can imagine, lots of people want to get in on this bargain, so make your reservations well in advance—the cabin is always booked. To reserve, contact a state parks office on any island; on the Big Island, contact the **State Division of Parks,** P.O. Box 936, Hilo, HI 96720 (☎ 808/961-7200).

NAMAKANI PAIO CAMPGROUNDS

Just 5 miles west of the park entrance is a tall eucalyptus forest where you can tent camp in an open grassy field. The trail to Kilauea Crater is just a half mile away. No permit or reservations are needed for tent camping, but stays are limited to seven days. Facilities for tent camping include pavilions with barbecues and a fireplace, picnic tables, outdoor dishwashing area, restrooms, and drinking water. There are also ten cabins that accommodate up to four each. Each cabin has a covered picnic table at the entrance and a fireplace with a grill. Toilets, sinks, and hot showers are available in a separate building. Groceries and gas are available in the town of Volcano, a mile away. Reservations for the cabins are made through **Volcano House,** P.O. Box 53, Volcano, HI 96718 (☎ 808/967-7321). Cost is $32 per night for two, $38 for three, and $44 for four.

HALAPE SHELTER

This backcountry campsite is along the coast, about a 7-mile hike from the nearest road. This is the place for people who want to get away from it all and enjoy their own private white-sand beach. There is a small, three-sided stone shelter here with a roof but no floor. It will accommodate two people comfortably, and four people rather uncomfortably. You could also pitch a tent inside, but if the weather is nice, you are better off setting up near the white-sand beach (there are no ants and cockroaches by the beach). There's also a catchment water tank, but check with the rangers on the water situation before hiking in (sometimes they don't have accurate information on the water level; bring extra water just in case). Other facilities include a small grill and a pit toilet. Go on weekdays if you're looking for isolation. You'll need a permit to stay here; it's free, but you're limited to three nights. Permits are available at the Visitor's Center on a first-come-first-served basis no earlier than noon on the day before your trip. For more information, contact **Hawaii Volcanoes National Park** (☎ 808/957-7311).

WAIPIO AND WAIMANU VALLEYS

These lush valleys, described fully in the hiking section (see Chapter 14), require two different sets of camping permits. In Waipio Valley, the first valley that you can reach by road, camping is permitted on the east side of the Waipio Stream. There is a grove of ironwood trees that provides a nice shady spot. Permits, which are free but limited to seven days, must be applied for in person at **Hamakua Sugar Company** in Paauilo (north of Hilo), from 7am to 4pm Monday through Friday (☎ 808/776-1211). There are no facilities in Waipio Valley. You must dig (and cover) your own latrine. Water is available from the stream, but be sure to treat it before drinking.

Camping in Waimanu Valley, the next valley north of Waipio, is regulated by the **State Division of Forestry and Wildlife,** 1648 Kilauea Avenue, Hilo, HI 96720 (☎ 808/933-4221). Permits to the nine designated campsites are assigned by number. The permits are free, but you are limited to a seven-day stay. The facilities in Waimanu are limited to two composting pit toilets. The best water in the valley is from the stream on the western wall, about a 15-minute walk up a trail from the beach. The water from the Waimanu Stream drains from a swamp, so it's not a desirable choice. As at any other camping site in Hawaii, be sure to carry out all of your trash.

4 Where to Eat

Big Island restaurants offer a marvelous variety of foods, in every price range and to suit every taste. Hilo is especially good for the budget traveler, since its restaurants cater mostly to locals; dine with them and you'll save a bundle.

HILO
MEALS FOR LESS THAN $12

✪ Bears

106 Keawe St. ☎ **808/935-0708.** Reservations not accepted. $2.50–$7. No credit cards. Mon–Fri 6:45am–5pm, Sat 8am–4pm. GOURMET DELI/VEGETARIAN/DESSERTS.

Bears, a stylish little place (marble-topped tables indoors and out, hand-stenciled walls) next door to the Most Irresistible Shop in Hilo, is proving to be irresistible—so much so that its original menu of a variety of coffees and pastries keeps expanding: Now they start the day with breakfast items like souffled eggs (steamed light and fluffy on the espresso machine) and "egg busters" (eggs, cheese, and ham on English muffin), During the day, in addition to the original coffee and pastry menu, Bears offers deli and vegetarian sandwiches ($3.60 to $3.95), organic salads, designer bagels (create your own topping), hot and cold soups, and daily specials ($5.50 to $6.50) on the order of a chili rellenos casserole or Italian dishes such as focaccia topped mozarella and vegetables. What fun to indulge in coffee and espresso drinks like caffè latte or Mexican chocolate, and desserts like carrot cake or lilikoi cheesecake, plus their luscious chocolate brownies. You can also buy fresh-roasted coffee beans by the pound to take home. Pastries run $2.50 to $3.25. They pack neat picnic lunches to go—call two hours ahead.

Boomers

197 Keawe St. ☎ **808/935-6191.** Main courses $2.50–$4.95. No credit cards. Mon–Fri 6am–4pm, Sat–Sun 6am–1 or 2pm. AMERICAN.

This attractive, modern restaurant, with its sleek black counter and five tables, is in the front section of the Spencer Health & Fitness Center. It's the kind of place you like to have at hand when you want a quick and nutritious meal. The best choices here are the Pad Thai noodles and the cheese enchiladas. Vegetarian sandwiches run from $2.75 to $3.50. The breakfast menu includes eggs, eggs, eggs—every way you like them: in an omelet, with enchiladas, with Thai rice. Not interested in eggs? Try the tofu scramble.

✪ Broke the Mouth

93 Mamo St. ☎ **808/934-7670.** Reservations not necessary. Plate lunches $3.50–$5.50. No credit cards. Tues–Sat 9am–2pm. ORGANIC VEGETARIAN.

Gourmet meals served on paper plates keep a steady crowd of enthusiastic patrons coming to this simple takeout restaurant/lunch counter that has a few picnic tables outside. This is farm-fresh, local food: The produce, herbs, and spices are grown just a few miles away on the Hamakua Coast by a farm cooperative that sells to the island's major hotels and restaurants. Store managers Tip and Penny Davis, a former filmmaker and actress who gave up life in the fast lane to grow vegetables, create absolutely marvelous dishes—all organic, super fresh, and brilliantly seasoned with their own homemade sauces and dressings. Order the Bamboola plate for $5.50, and savor the fresh greens, the OnoPesto pasta, a Hawaiian salad, a summer roll, and manapua. Everything is exceptional: the Hawaiian salad, for example, uses no lettuce; instead it contains basil, mizuna, kale, collards, red chard, sorrel, and edible flowers. The manapua are whole wheat dumplings with fillings like eggplant Szechuan or sweet potato basil. Their potato salad ($1.50 as a side order) is like no potato salad you've had before: it's made with taro, sweet potatoes, steamed green papayas, green onions, and MacGado sauce. Treat yourself to a $1 dessert of kulolo: this blend of taro, banana, cane juice, and coconut takes six hours to make! Ask Tip or Penny to let you sample some of the fabulous sauces that you can take home or order by mail later. Call ahead if you're planning a picnic or a trip, and your meal will be waiting for you.

✪ Cafe Pesto Hilo Bay

In the S. Hata Building, 308 Kamehameha Ave. ☎ **808/969-6640.** Reservations accepted. Main courses $6.95–$16.95. AE, DISC, MC, V. Sun–Thurs 11am–9pm, Fri–Sat 11am–10pm. PACIFIC RIM/ITALIAN.

A favorite spot among Hiloans for casual meals and after-theater drop-ins, Cafe Pesto is located on the ground floor of the 1912 S. Hata Building, fully restored to its early charms under the auspices of the historic preservation society. An exhibition kitchen, the centerpiece of which is a 6-foot Italian wood-fired pizza oven highlighted with brass detail and halogen lighting, allows diners to view the goodies issuing forth. To complement the pizzas nestled in among the coals, artwork and sculpture of the Volcano and Madame Pele are scattered throughout the art deco dining room. The menu features a variety of fresh seafoods, eclectic salads, hand-tossed pizzas, and Italian and Asian pastas and risottos, all prepared with a Pacific Rim flair. We like the smoked salmon pizzette with a fresh rosemary gorgonzola sauce and the wild mushroom and chicken risotto. Fresh ahi, seared rare with Kealekekua greens, jasmine rice, and a wasabi dipping sauce, and the Pacific bistro beef salad with a Chinese mustard vinaigrette, are also popular. There's live Hawaiian music Sunday evenings.

Dick's Coffee House

At Prince Kuhio Plaza. ☎ **808/959-4401.** Reservations not required. Main courses $4.85–$7.90. MC, V. Mon–Fri 7am–9pm, Sat–Sun 7am–5pm. AMERICAN.

Dick's, a lively local place with sporting pennants on the walls, is one of the most popular coffee shops in town. On the à la carte dinner menu, you could choose chicken cutlet, grilled fish filet, teriyaki steak Oriental, or grilled pork chops; your main course comes with soup or salad, starch, rolls, and butter. Lunch features burgers from $3.20, gourmet sandwiches like pastrami on French bread or a steak sandwich for under $5—and homemade pies and cream pies for dessert for $1.30! Daily lunch specials go for $3.40 to $3.60, and there are also weekday lunch and dinner specials under $4. Breakfast is inexpensive, too: Three-egg omelets are just $3.30 to $4.15. A local friend raves about the fried chicken and the rhubarb pie, but advises that you come early, as one pie is baked each day.

✪ Don's Grill

485 Hinano St. ☎ **808/935-9099.** Reservations not required. Main courses $5.25–$11.25. AE, MC, V. Tues–Thurs 10:30am–9pm, Fri 10:30am–10pm, Sat–Sun 10am–9pm. AMERICAN.

Don's Grill has everything a good family restaurant should have: It's large, comfortable, and inexpensive, and the food is fresh and good. Owner Don Hoota

414 Settling in on the Big Island

has won a large local following for this place. Slide into a booth and treat yourself to rotisseried chicken (the house specialty), or barbecued ribs, or filet of fish; soup or salad is included. They also have good sandwiches, burgers, plus local favorites like LocoMoco, saimin, and homemade chili; it's hard to go wrong.

Dotty's Coffee Shop and Restaurant

Puainako Town Center. ☎ **808/959-6477.** Reservations not required. Main courses $6.25–$10.20. MC, V. Breakfast daily 7–10:30am; lunch daily 10:30am–2pm; dinner daily 5pm–closing. AMERICAN.

If you love fresh fish *and* modest prices, this is a place to know about. Every evening, Dotty Frasco and her family do a fish-of-the-day special for under $10—and that might be ahi, mahimahi, or ono—nicely grilled in garlic butter and white wine. What a deal! Everything else at Dotty's spiffy little coffee shop (green booths, nice photos on the wall) is a good deal too, since this is real home-cooking, with everything made from scratch ("We don't have a can opener," says Dotty). People come from all over just for her roast chicken and roast turkey, which she uses in her turkey plate. On Friday nights they come for the prime rib. Popular dishes include grilled pork chops, liver and bacon, sautéed shrimp, calamari, and shrimp scampi. Lunches, moderately priced, feature salads, sandwiches, and burgers. Dotty's pies are homemade, and at $1.75 and up, we wouldn't think of resisting.

ⓢ Jasper's Espresso Cafe

110 Kalakaua St. ☎ **808/969-6686.** Reservations not accepted. Main courses $3.75–$7.50. No credit cards. Mon–Sat 11am–8pm. VEGETARIAN/AMERICAN.

Here's a cafe that's not only charming but nutritionally, ecologically, and politically correct as well! As much a gathering place and a forum for addressing progressive political and social issues (the Green Party mayoral candidate recently spoke here) as a restaurant, it's a cute little place, with ceiling fans and a magazine rack for browsing. Owner/chef Jasper Moore uses only locally grown produce (much of it organic), even coffee beans that are chemical-free, in creating a wholesome, mostly vegetarian cuisine. Stuffed baked potato, nachos, chicken enchiladas, garden burger, and lasagne with salad are standbys on the day-long menu. Tuesday from 5:30 to 8pm is spaghetti night: all the spaghetti you can eat, plus garlic bread, $5. Breakfast features homemade granola, eggs Benedict and Florentine, omelets, home fries, and fresh island fruit salad. Coffee lovers must stop by for one of the specialty drinks, especially the Tsunami Shake—that's a double espresso frothed with two scoops of chocolate ice cream ($4). Jasper claims to sell "the strongest cup of coffee you can buy . . . without a prescription!"

Jimmy's Drive Inn

362 Kinoole St. ☎ **808/935-5571.** Reservations not required. Complete dinners $4.60–$12. MC, V. Mon–Thurs 10am–9:30pm; Fri–Sat 10am–10pm. JAPANESE/AMERICAN/KOREAN.

Jimmy's Drive Inn is a popular place with the local people, offering some of the best prices in town. The "drive inn" is misleading; you don't eat in your car, but at clean chrome tables or at the counter. The menu is divided into four sections: Korean, Japanese, Hawaiian, and seafood main courses. All are served with soup or salad, vegetable, starch, and beverage. Good bets are the Korean butterfish, Japanese shrimp tempura, the grilled island pork chops and chicken katsu, and, among the seafood options, the Captain's Platter, a combination of scallops, cod fish, shrimp, and oysters. The Hawaiian plate (laulau with pipikaula, lomi salmon, and poi or rice) is a good deal at $6.25.

○ Kay's

684 Kilauea Ave. ☎ **808/969-1776.** Reservations not required. Main courses $6–$9.25. No credit cards. Breakfast/lunch Tues–Fri 6am–2pm, Sat–Sun 5am–2pm; dinner Tues–Sun 5–8:30pm. KOREAN.

One of our favorite Hilo eateries is Kay's, which serves just about the best barbecued chicken we've ever tasted, anywhere. Local friends put us on to this large, Korean-style family restaurant, full of local color: screaming babies, people reading the newspapers, Formica tables, orange-leather booths. Never mind. The atmosphere is friendly, the staff is charming, and the food is ridiculously inexpensive, and so good that you'll want to come back more than once. The house specialty is the Korean crispy fried chicken, which we found a bit heavy; instead, go with the barbecued chicken—it's boned, flattened, marinated in a very light shoyu sauce in the Korean manner, and simply delicious. All dinners include hot rice, miso soup, vegetable of the day, and four kinds of kimchee. You can order your meal either small or large (we found small to be adequate). One choice— Korean barbecued beef, kalbi, barbecued chicken, fried fish, shoyu pork, etc.—is $6 small, $7 for a full order, two choices are $8; three choices $9. Don't be misled by the sign reading KAY'S LUNCH CENTER; Kay now serves dinner too, thank heaven.

Ken's House of Pancakes

1730 Kamehameha Ave., at the intersection of Hi. 19 and Hi. 11. ☎ **808/935-8711.** Reservations not accepted. Breakfast dishes $3.10–$8.95; dinner main courses $5.95–$9.50. AE, DC, DISC, MC, V. Daily 24 hours. AMERICAN/LOCAL.

The only place in town open 24 hours a day, Ken's is known for serving its entire menu around the clock. That means that at whatever time of day you're hungry for, say, macadamia-nut or fresh banana pancakes, eggs Benedict, or eggs with Scottish bangers or Portuguese sausage, Ken's will dish them up and at very reasonable prices. They also feature local Hawaiian specialties at lunch and dinner. Good burgers, sandwiches, salads, delicious homemade pies and cakes, and fountain specialties are also available. Dinner selections—served with soup or salad, potato or rice, vegetable, and hot roll—include grilled mahimahi, broiled steak, and southern-style fried chicken.

Restaurant Satsuki

168 Keawe St. ☎ **808/935-7880.** Reservations not required. Main courses $4.85–$9.25. MC, V. Lunch Wed–Mon 11am–1:45pm; dinner Thurs–Mon 5–8:45pm. JAPANESE.

Here's a place the locals like very much. It's small, plain, with partitions to give a little privacy; it's known for good food and large portions. The most popular meal is Satsuki's Special Teishoku ($5.85 at lunch, $6.95 at dinner), which offers a choice of two main dishes, such as shrimp tempura, yakitori, beef teriyaki, butterfish, chicken katsu, and more, served with various side vegetables, soup, rice, and tea. Donburis, noodles, and bentos are also available ($4 to $9).

Reuben's Mexican Food

336 Kamehameha Ave. ☎ 808/961-2552. Reservations not required. Main courses $7–$9. MC, V. Mon–Fri 11am–9pm, Sat noon–9pm. MEXICAN.

Reuben's Mexican Food, across from the waterfront, is a real local hangout. It's large (there's plenty of breathing room between the tables), colorful (with a shocking-pink color scheme and Mexican murals on the wall), has a big bar, and the food is good. Reuben's is run by chef Reuben and Sue Villanova (he's from Mexico, she's from Hilo). Our appetizer of nachos ($4) was hot and tasty, so was our chicken flautas (a flour tortilla with chicken, shredded lettuce, guacamole, and sour cream) combination plate. Some 34 combination plates, which include beans and rice, go for $7 to $9. There are a few interesting house specialties, like the gallina adovada (baked chicken), and a crab salad, $6 to $8. You'll find lots of local families here enjoying the food, the low prices, and the memorable margaritas.

ⓢ Royal Siam Thai Restaurant

70 Mamo St. ☎ **808/961-6100.** Reservations not required. Main courses $5.95–$9.95. AE, CB, DC, JCB, MC, V. Lunch Mon–Sat 11am–2pm; dinner Mon–Sat 5–8:30pm. THAI.

This small (16-table) unprepossessing family restaurant has won a rousing reception from the local people. Thai paintings, flowers, planters, and white tablecloths provide a pleasant setting for the superb cooking typical of the Bangkok region. The family in charge insists that everything be super fresh; in fact, they grow many of the vegetables and spices in their own gardens to ensure that. Crispy chicken and spring rolls are terrific appetizers, and among the main courses, you can't go wrong with the cashew chicken, Thai broccoli noodles with beef, or Thai garlic shrimp. They do all the traditional curries—yellow, green, red—with chicken, beef, or vegetables; if you're lucky and they have fresh salmon, order your curry made with that. Vegetarians have a full menu of their own. *Warning:* Ask that your food be prepared mild, unless you *really* like it hot! Lunch is an especially good buy, since specials begin at just $4.95.

ⓞ Ting-Hao Mandarin Restaurant

Puainako town center. ☎ **808/959-6288.** Reservations recommended. Main courses $5.50–$10.95. AE, MC, V. Lunch Mon–Sat 11am–2:30pm; dinner daily 4:30–9pm. CHINESE.

Although not many tourists know of it, the Chinese population has discovered the Ting-Hao Mandarin Restaurant, and they come to enjoy the wizardry of master chef Ting Cheng, whose repertoire includes some 200 banquet dishes. He cooks Peking, Mandarin, Szechuan, and Cantonese style, so there is quite a variety on the menu. Everything we've tried—and we've dined here many times—has been special. And they never use MSG! Corn eggdrop soup is unusual and subtly flavored; potstickers, those tasty dumplings that are both steamed and fried (on one side), are a great beginning to your meal. Outstanding main courses in the Mandarin style include shredded pork with fungus and golden egg, shredded pork with garlic sauce (watch out, it's hot), and the eggplant with garlic sauce, each $6.50. Unusual and delicious, too, are the Kung Pao ika (cuttlefish) and the Kung Pao shrimp, both with spicy paprikas. Most main dishes are inexpensive and hearty. In fact, we find the portions here so generous that we usually wind up taking containers back to our kitchenette apartment for the next day's lunch. At lunch, there are four daily specials, served with spareribs or an egg roll, for under $5. Vegetarians can enjoy a number of good dishes. Service is helpful and friendly; there's a warm, family feeling here. Puainako town center is past the airport, and not far from **Prince Kuhio Plaza;** the restaurant is near the big Sack 'n' Save store.

Note: Ting Hao recently expanded to a second location, Ting Hao Seafood Restaurant, on the lower lobby level of the Naniloa Hotel, 93 Banyan Drive, ☎ 808/969-6660. The menu is similar, slightly more expensive with more of an emphasis on seafood dishes, but equally delicious. However, it is usually jam-packed with hotel guests, so it might be easier to be seated in the original location. Open daily, except Monday, from 11am to 2pm and 5 to 10pm.

MEALS FOR LESS THAN $20

✪ Fiascos

200 Kanoelehua Ave., at Waiakea Square. ☎ **808/935-7666.** Reservations recommended on weekends. Main courses $5.95–$16.95. AE, DISC, MC, V. Sun–Thurs 11am–10pm, Fri–Sat 11am–11pm. AMERICAN.

This is one of Hilo's most popular and enjoyable restaurants. It's done up attractively, with lots of plants and wood, and the atmosphere is lively and upbeat. The food (notwithstanding the rather precious menu descriptions depicting the journeys of one mythical Hans Fiasco) is consistently good, and there are enough possibilities to appeal to a variety of tastes and budgets. Many Hilo folks swear by the salad bar; it's a bountiful table of fruits and vegetables, served with homemade dressings, and a choice of four soups, $6.25 as main course, $4.25 with any meal. There's a fresh fish sandwich every day. Hot dishes, served at both lunch and dinner, include many items for $5.95 to $10.95, like stir-fry chicken or meat loaf, liver with grilled onions and bacon, and country fried chicken. Desserts? Try the cappuccino mousse cake or the fried ice cream. There's line dancing to country music on Friday nights, blues or rock live music and dancing Saturday nights. Fiascos is good fun and good food at good prices.

✪ Lehua's Bay City Bar & Grill

90 Kamehameha Ave. ☎ **808/935-8055.** Reservations recommended for dinner only. Main courses $6.75–$20. AE, DISC, MC, V. Lunch Mon–Sat 11am–4pm; dinner daily 5–9:30pm. PACIFIC RIM.

This is the kind of sophisticated bistro that you'd expect to find in, say, San Francisco, rather than downtown in sleepy little Hilo. But there it is, attractively decorated with plants, mobiles hanging from the ceiling, a stage, a dance floor, and a big bar up front from which some of the best margaritas in town flow. Owners Mark Himmel and Larry Johnson describe their reasonably priced cuisine as "East meets West with an island flair"—and that's just what it is. Almost everything is homemade; only the freshest ingredients are used, seasonings and sauces are imaginative, and since many dishes are marinated and charbroiled, it's possible to eat food that's light as well as delicious. Homemade soups are a good bet, as are the salads and Thai coconut shrimp, and the chicken or cheese Quesadillas. The charbroiled chicken burger, a house specialty, costs $6.75. All main courses are accompanied by sourdough french bread, a garden salad (the creamy garlic dressing is very good), a hot vegetable, and a choice of fries, baked potato, or rice. Spinach lasagne and the sauté medley of fresh vegetables will keep the vegetarians in the crowd contented.

Lunch offers similar dishes at lower prices, including soup-and-sandwich specials of the day, burgers, a very popular chicken with papaya, and the hearty Bay City saimin; it's the classic noodle dish, but topped with charbroiled chicken, shrimp, and fresh vegetables, $6.25. Desserts are homemade and super: Save some room for either the White Russian mousse or the chocolate banana cake. On Wednesday and Saturday nights from 8pm on, Lehua's has country line dancing, with a DJ playing the latest country hits. Admission is free.

Nihon Restaurant & Cultural Center

123 Lihiwal St. ☎ **808/969-1133.** Reservations recommended. Sushi $2.75–$14.95; main courses $11.95–$16.95. CB, DC, JCB, MC, V. Lunch Mon–Sat 11am–1:30pm; dinner Mon–Sat 5–8pm. JAPANESE.

For a true taste of Japan, the place to go is the Nihon Cultural Center, overlooking Hilo Bay and the lovely Liliuokalani Gardens. The Nihon Restaurant houses an art gallery, a traditional tearoom, an auditorium for cultural events, and at the heart of it all, a restaurant where traditional Japanese chefs ply their art. Of course there is a sushi bar—the menu describes these dainty morsels of fish and rice as "health foods"—and a dining room for regular Japanese meals. Tempura and tonkatsu lunches are $10.95 and $9.95; sashimi is market-priced. Lunch specials, for $8.95, include a choice of two items and accompaniments, dinners include the traditional sukiyaki. Complete combination dinners feature tempura, sashimi, and beef teriyaki.

Restaurant Fuji

In the Hilo Hotel, 142 Kinoole St. ☎ **808/961-3733.** Reservations recommended. Main courses $8.25–$24. AE, DC, JCB, MC, V. Lunch Tues–Sun 11am–1:45; dinner Tues–Sun 5–8:45pm. JAPANESE.

For a traditional, authentic Japanese meal—and for an excellent bargain as well—count on Restaurant Fuji. This is one of those gracious, relaxed places where you can really enjoy a meal at the comfortably spaced tables in the dining room. The bargains are best at lunchtime, when the "teishoku" meal includes appetizers, otsukemono, rice and soup or tea along with such main courses as grilled butterfish, salmon teriyaki, or a shrimp, fish, and vegetable tempura. Prices are only a dollar or two more at dinner for the same selections. If you wish to splurge, the house specialty, the teppanyaki teishoku—a melange of beef, seafood, fish, and vegetables prepared at your own table—will run you $24 per person.

The Seaside

1790 Kalanianaole Ave. ☎ **808/935-8825.** Reservations required. Main courses $10.50–$19.95. DC, MC, V. Dinner only, Tues–Sun 5:30–8:30pm. SEAFOOD.

Want to eat the freshest fish in Hilo? Then head for the Seaside, a few miles out of Hilo town in the Kaukaha area, where the mullet or aholehole or rainbow trout on your plate will be taken out of the pond when you call to make your reservation! The Seaside, highly respected by Hilo people for years and virtually unknown to tourists, is actually a fish farm; the Japanese family in charge have been cultivating fish here for more than 50 years, in the same way that mullet was historically fattened in special fish ponds for the alii of old Hawaii. They catch fingerlings from the Waiola River, keep them in pens for six months, then release them into the pond for five years.

If you come before dinner while it's still light, somebody will show you around and explain the operation to you. (The place is a favorite stop for school groups and those interested in aquaculture). Then on to the simple dining room where you can have your fish prepared in the traditional way, steamed in ti leaves, with onion slices and lemon juice, or fried. The menu is quite simple: For dinner, there's mullet or trout at $15.95; a combination of any fish with chicken, $14.95; fried chicken only, $10.50; a combination of one steamed fish and one fried fish (perhaps the best choice for first-timers), $19.95. Bottled wine is available. And for dessert—homemade apple pie. This place is not fancy, but the fish is the freshest, and coming here is a real experience in nontourist, old-time Hawaii. Be sure to call first, as they serve only when they have fish available. A nice adventure for the kids, too.

BETWEEN HILO & KONA ON THE NORTHERN ROUTE

In Chapter 14, we'll describe the drive from Hilo to the resort center of Kona, a trip you should take. Here are some suggestions for meals as you drive the northern route, along the Hamakua Coast (Hi. 19). The first stop: Waimea.

WAIMEA

Meals for Less than $15

✪ Ann Sutherland's Mean Cuisine

In Opelo Plaza, Waimea. ☎ **808/885-6325.** Main courses $4–$7. MC, V. Mon–Sat 6am–8pm. AMERICAN ECLECTIC.

We highly recommend this delightful eatery; as a local resident put it, "This is wickedly good food at wonderfully low prices." Chef Ann Sutherland (who was once the private chef for the Ethel Kennedy clan) whips up what she calls "casual eclectic American cuisine" at unbelievable budget prices. When this warm, homey restaurant opens at 6am, wonderful smells from the bakery invite you in. Grab a cup of freshly brewed Kona coffee and wander through the bakery, a pastry and bread lover's dream come true—everything from an assortment of muffins and breads to tropical fruit turnovers and traditional pastries. Their just-made sushi (from vegetarian to classic) sell out within a few hours.

The real draw for this upcountry restaurant is Chef Ann's main courses, a complete meal from $4 to $7 featuring 30 different types of dishes a day ranging from turkey, mashed potatoes with gravy, and all the trimmings to gourmet dishes like Hunan lamb and taro goat-cheese eggplant roulades or lilikoi-cilantro fish with basmati-curry rice and fresh asparagus. There's no menu: Main courses are posted daily and can change from minute to minute. You can eat right there, with classical music playing in the background and fresh tropical flowers at each table, or you can take it out in easy-to-microwave containers. Leave room for dessert—they have everything from a heart-healthy lilikoi cream tart to a more decadent chocolate cake with a triple raspberry sauce.

✪ Café Pesto

In the Kawaihae Shopping Center, Kawaihae. ☎ **808/882-1071.** Reservations not accepted. Main courses $6.95–$16.95. AE, DISC, MC, V. Sun–Thurs 11am–9pm, Fri–Sat 11am–10pm. ITALIAN/PACIFIC RIM.

If you're driving on Hi. 19 to Kona after leaving Waimea, it's no trouble at all to stop off first at the harbor town of Kawaihae, where you'll find the highly praised Café Pesto. Ask around and you'll discover that this casual restaurant overlooking the harbor has a well-earned reputation for consistently delicious food. Like its sister restaurant in Hilo, Café Pesto features a variety of fresh seafoods, eclectic salads, hand-tossed pizzas, and Italian and Asian pastas and risottos, all prepared with a creative Pacific Rim flair. Start with the Pacific potstickers stuffed with shrimp and lobster in a mango/green peppercorn sauce, perhaps a spinach salad of sesame-crusted Puna goat cheese with broiled eggplant, or share a light pizza with basil pesto, vine-ripened tomatoes, fresh spinach, and Gorgonzola crumbles. Do save room for the tropical fruit creme brûlée and a frothy cappuccino.

✪ Waimea Coffee & Company

At Parker Square, Waimea. ☎ **808/885-4472.** Reservations not accepted. Main dishes $3.95–$5.50. MC, V. Mon–Fri 7am–5pm, Sat 8am–4pm. NATURAL FOODS.

If you're driving across the island and want to stop for some light, healthful foods, or maybe just a cup of coffee or a yummy espresso drink, and a luscious pastry, Waimea Coffee & Company is a good choice. It's a cute little place with wooden chairs and tables and some local art on the walls. Homemade soups and quiches are very popular here, as are the Caesar salad, the tabbouleh salad, and the garden burger. Quiche and a salad are $5.50. As for those pastries, some come from the noted French Bakery in Kailua-Kona and some from Beverly, the pastry chef of nearby gourmet restaurant Merriman's.

Meals for Less than $25

✪ Edelweiss

Kawaihae Rd. ☎ **808/885-6800.** Reservations not accepted. Complete dinners $15.50–$19.75. MC, V. Lunch Tues–Sat 11:30am–1:30pm; dinner Tues–Sat 5–9pm. GERMAN.

Long a favorite in Waimea, Edelweiss is a homey place with a European country feeling, seating only about 50 guests. So renowned has master chef-owner Hans Peter Hager's reputation become that there's usually a wait of an hour or so at dinnertime. But it's usually not too crowded at lunchtime; just be sure you get there before 1:30pm or you won't be seated. Hans Peter's cuisine does not disappoint. The luncheon specialty of bratwurst and sauerkraut is $5.95; also popular is the Puu Haloa ranch burger at $6.25, or in a more continental mood, the sautéed chicken breast with champignons and melted Monterey Jack cheese, $7.50. Complete dinners are served with soup of the day, salad, and beverage, and include such dishes as roast duck bigarade braised with a light orange sauce, wienerschnitzel, roast pork with sauerkraut, a wonderful roast rack of lamb for two, and the Edelweiss specialty—sautéed veal, lamb, beef, and bacon with pfifferling (European wild mushrooms)—very tasty, indeed. Since Hans Peter is also a master pastry chef, you'd be well advised to save room for dessert, especially if the incredible Grand Marnier parfait is available that day. Black Forest cake, chocolate mousse, fresh peach pie, and Edelweiss tart with raspberry sauce are also heavenly.

Island Bistro

Kawaihae Rd. ☎ **808/885-1222.** Reservations recommended. Main courses $9–$17. DISC, MC, V. Breakfast daily 7am–11pm; Lunch daily 11am–2pm; dinner daily 5–9:30pm. Pupus on the lanai in between lunch and dinner. HAWAIIAN REGIONAL.

There's a colorful, unpretentious ambience to this new place, just across the road from Edelweiss. Inside, you can watch the open kitchen; outside, you can see Mauna Kea from the tables on the lanai—they'll even loan you binoculars. Chef Michael Neff, formerly of Merriman's, is in charge of the kitchen, and he's devised a contemporary Hawaiian menu with some Mediterranean and Asian touches. We like to start with the goat cheese pesto bread or the sesame garlic eggplant, then maybe have the five-onion garlic soup or the Waimea sweet potato soup. Thai-marinated grilled natural chicken with satay and chili mint sauces and tamarind roasted leg of lamb with Indonesian pepper-papaya sauce are recommended dinner choices, as is the scampi Carib with good-and-hot spices. There are daily vegetarian and pasta specials. Most main courses are available in moderately priced half-portions. For lunch, there are soups, salads, a Szechuan sesame Caesar salad, and Thai peanut pasta as well as several bistro sandwiches; almost everything is under $6.

✪ Merriman's

In Opelo Plaza, Hi. 19. ☎ **808/885-6822.** Reservations recommended. Main courses $14.95–$24.95. AE, MC, V. Lunch Mon–Fri 11:30am–1:30pm; dinner daily 5:30–9pm. HAWAIIAN REGIONAL.

Ask local people about the best restaurants in Waimea and the first name you're likely to hear is Merriman's. In fact, ask anybody on the Big Island and you'll get the same answer. Merriman's is rated four stars by just about everybody, and Peter Merriman, the 40-year-old-owner, is rapidly gaining a reputation as one of the most innovative young chefs in the country. Stop by for a meal and see why. Merriman uses only the freshest and finest local products—10 different kinds of mangoes, for example, each with a subtly different flavor, white pineapples, or shellfish he may have gone diving for himself—to produce an imaginative, contemporary, and highly sophisticated cuisine. The setting is lovely, if a bit overdone: A dining room with Hawaiian flair done in soft peach/green colors, with comfortable upholstered chairs and plants and flowers that create a light, airy feeling in the daytime. In the evening the atmosphere is more intimate, with flickering candles on the tables highlighting the original paintings on the walls.

With such a creative chef as Merriman, the menu changes frequently—but you can be sure that whatever you eat will be outstanding. On the low side of the menu, you might go for the pan-fried Asian cake noodles, or the roast chicken at $14.95. Among the memorable signature dishes are the wok-charred ahi (seared on the outside, sashimi inside), the Kahua ranch lamb, and the locally raised filet steak with Gorgonzola and cabernet sauce. To begin your meal, try Pahoa corn-and-shrimp fritters or goat cheese baked in phyllo dough.

Lunch is very reasonable and still of the same high gourmet quality. We could happily make an entire meal of the bouillabaisse, its fresh fish and shellfish piping hot in a saffron broth, $9.95. Or try the salade niçoise, again with the distinctive Merriman difference—made with artichokes, potatoes, and grilled fish on a bed of tossed greens, $7.95. Desserts, like the fabulous lilikoi mousse, are great at both meals. And the wine list is well priced.

BETWEEN HILO & KONA ON THE SOUTHERN ROUTE

There are several interesting choices for meals on this trip listed below. One recommended stop is about halfway between Hilo and Kona, when you come upon an oasis in the lava flows. This is the beautiful town of Naalehu, the southernmost community in the United States. As you drive through town, keep your eyes peeled for the **Naalehu Fruit Stand,** next door to the library. Locals swear by this one! You get your food at the counter, then take it to eat at tables outside. Try one of their unique pizza sandwiches on homemade Italian bread, $8 to $10 for a whole sandwich. They also have the more usual kinds of pizzas, homemade pies, fruit breads, giant cookies, health foods, and deli sandwiches.

IN & AROUND HAWAII VOLCANOES NATIONAL PARK

Kilauea Lodge

Volcano. ☎ **808/967-7366.** Reservations recommended. Main courses $12.50–$26. MC, V. Dinner only, daily 5:30–9pm. AMERICAN/CONTINENTAL

One mile Hilo-side of Hawaii Volcanoes National Park is Kilauea Lodge, a current "hot" place for dining in the area. The huge room is dominated by the

"Fireplace of Friendship," its rocks donated by civic and youth organizations from 32 countries around the Pacific during the years when this was a mountain retreat of the YMCA. The place is still warm and friendly, the dining room is spacious and attractive, and chef Albert Jeyte is known for excellent continental dinners with a touch of local flavor, everything made from the freshest of ingredients. Main courses come with tiny loaves of freshly baked bread and homemade soups. There are at least four specials every day—perhaps ahi, roast duck, lamb provençale, or Hasenpfeffer (that's rabbit in wine sauce); venison and game are often on the menu. Regular dishes include seafood, beef, chicken, fresh fish of the day, plus a few vegetarian dishes, like fettuccine primavera. For dessert try the macadamia-nut or three-berry pie—quite special. *Note:* A wheelchair-lift is available.

Volcano Golf and Country Club

Volcano. ☎ **808/967-8228.** Reservations not required. Main courses $15.50–$18. AE, MC, V. Continental breakfast Mon–Fri 7–10am; full breakfast Sat–Sun and holidays 6:30–10am; lunch daily 10:30am–3pm; cocktails to 5pm. Dinner Fri–Sat 5:30–9pm. AMERICAN.

Two miles south of the Hawaii Volcanoes National Park entrance, watch for the sign that reads GOLF COURSE, directly across the Kilauea Military Camp. It will lead you to the Volcano Golf and Country Club, where many local people take visitors to avoid the Volcano House crowds. The clubhouse, open to the public, has a rustic modern dining room with glass windows, huge ceiling, and wood-burning fireplace. From the windows, you can gaze at Mauna Loa and often sight the rare Hawaiian nene goose. Lunch offers such dishes as mahimahi, honey-stung chicken, chili, and many local favorites like saimin, and Hawaiian stew. Excellent burgers, including fish burgers, run $7.25 to $7.50. Weekend dinners feature prime rib, steak, and scampi.

Volcano House

In Hawaii Volcanoes National Park. ☎ **808/967-7321.** Reservations recommended for dinner. Main courses $13.25–$22; buffet breakfast $9.90; buffet lunch $11. AE, DC, MC, V. Breakfast daily 7–10:30am; lunch daily 11am–1:30pm; dinner daily 5:30–9pm. AMERICAN.

The traditional lunch stop here has long been Volcano House, noted for its lovely buffet—a tempting array of salads, fruits, and main dishes, served with beverage and dessert, in a spectacular setting overlooking Halemaumau Crater. The dining room at Volcano House, named Ka Ohelo, in honor of the sister of Madame Pele, the fire goddess, has seating on two levels to provide views for up to 260 people. However, since lunch is a very busy time, with all the tour buses disgorging hungry passengers, we prefer to come here for a quieter breakfast served late (until 10:30am). The inviting dinner menu includes scampi, prime rib, sautéed mahimahi, and Cornish game hen; main dishes are served with a dinner salad, rice or potatoes, and vegetables, plus homemade sweet breads and rolls.

IN NAALEHU

Naalehu Coffee Shop

Naalehu. ☎ **808/929-7238.** Reservations not required. Main courses $5.95–13.95. No credit cards. Mon–Sat 7:30am–8pm. AMERICAN.

Here, in the southernmost town in the United States, the venerable Naalehu Coffee Shop has been doing business since 1941. Owners Roy and Arda Toguchi serve local dishes, fresh fish from South Point Kau, gold oranges, local bananas, and other local produce. The Hawaiian fishburger is a house specialty; other good sandwiches include the Farmer John Baked Ham and the oven-baked turkey sandwich, accompanied by relishes and salad, $4.95 to $6.95. Lunch and dinner main courses are served with salad, vegetable, bread, and rice or potatoes. After your meal, check out the art gallery and Menehune Treasure Chest and browse among the local handcrafts. If you approach from Hilo, make your third left when you pass the school; from Kona, turn right when you pass the theater.

KONA RESTAURANTS

There are three distinct areas on the Kona coast for dining: first, the Kailua-Kona area, home of the busiest tourist scene; second, Keauhou-Kona, just south of Kailua-Kona, and also a tourist area; and third, "Up Mauka" in the coffee-growing country in the mountains, where most of the local folks live.

IN KAILUA-KONA

Meals for Less than $15

Basil's Pizzeria Restaurant

75-5705 Alii Dr. ☎ **808/326-7836.** Reservations not accepted. Individual pizzas $5.95–$7.95; pasta $5.95–$7.95; main courses $7.95–$14.95. No credit cards. Sun–Thurs 10am–midnight, Fri–Sat 10am–1pm. ITALIAN.

Small and cozy, Basil's is very popular with a young 20-something and surfing set who come for the large portions and low prices. You'll probably have to wait to gain entry on a weekend, but the rest of the week should be no problem. A range of individual pizzas on fresh homemade dough can be ordered, everything from the very popular shrimp pesto pizza to the barbecued chicken pie (cilantro is the secret ingredient). For a crowd, their New York–style pizzas are design-it-yourself. Pasta dishes, served with either Caesar or house salad and wonderful garlic bread, are generous. And they also have Italian dinners (complete with salad and garlic bread), featuring eggplant parmigiana, chicken dishes, and half-a-dozen seafood specialties. There are wonderful coffees and espresso drinks and an array of daily dessert specials.

The Captain's Deck at Shipwreck Point

In the Kona Inn Shopping Village, 75-5739 Alii Dr. ☎ **808/326-2555.** Reservations not required. Sandwiches $5.99–$6.95; main courses $5.95–$11.95 AE, DC, DISC, JCB, MC, V. Breakfast 7:30–11am; lunch 11:30am–4:30pm; dinner 4:30–9:30pm daily. SEAFOOD.

Here's a nifty budget choice that shares a spectacular sunset-on-the-water location with the renowned seafood restaurant, Fisherman's Landing (see below). The lounge area of that restaurant has been turned into a restaurant of its own: Hearty fish and meat sandwiches, skewers of fish, meat, and seafood, substantial salads (crab and shrimp Louie, and pasta salad with shrimp), and fishnet baskets all make this a fine spot for a light meal. A lively bar is the centerpiece of the room. There's entertainment nightly from 6 to 10pm.

Edward's at the Terrace

78-261 Manukai St., at the Kanaloa Condominiums in Keauhou. ☎ **808/322-1434.** Reservations not necessary. Main courses $14.95–$18.50. AE, DC, JC, MC, V. Breakfast 8–11am; lunch 11am–2pm; dinner 5–9pm daily. MEDITERRANEAN.

If you're staying in the Keauhou area, or heading out to the Keauhou Shopping Village, Edward's is a good place to know about. The restaurant is on the terrace of the condominium's swimming pool, so the setting is open and casual, with a view of the ocean. Chef/owner Edward Frady specializes in Mediterranean cuisine. That could mean sardine and artichoke Napoleon, a classic Mediterranean/fish preparation, or couscous topped with baba ghanoush and served with garlic shrimp among the dinner appetizers. Fisherman's soup topped with puff pastry and flavored with Pernod, is very French, and Cornish game hen Bastya wrapped in phyllo pastry, is a Moroccan-style offering. Fresh fish is available every day. At lunch, sandwiches, burgers, pasta, and salad go from $8.50 to $10.50; the traditional salad niçoise is a favorite. Edward's menus change frequently depending on what's fresh and what's in season; trust us, it will always be good.

Call Edward's for precise driving directions; it can be a bit tricky to find.

Giuseppe's Italian Cafe

At Kailua Bay Inn, 75-5699 Alii Dr. ☎ **808/329-7888.** Reservations not accepted. Main courses $7.25–$15.25. MC, V. Lunch Mon–Fri 11:30am–9pm; dinner Mon–Sat 5–9pm. ITALIAN.

It's just a little hole-in-the-wall place, but Giuseppe's Italian Cafe turns out lusty Italian fare in generous portions and at reasonable prices—no wonder it's quickly become a Kona favorite. The place is attractive with its red-checkered tablecloths and cozy booths. This is real home cooking, with everything made from scratch. A bowl of slow-cooked minestrone, stuffed mushrooms, or fried calamari makes a good starter. There are a dozen pasta dishes to choose from, including a pleasantly light aglio e olio linguine, fettuccine al pesto, and a traditional lasagne bolognese, as well as a lighter version with spinach. Other favorites include chicken marsala, chicken parmigiana, seafood marinara, and scallops sautéed in sherry wine. All meals come with either fresh green salad or two slices of delicious garlic bread. Pastas are several dollars less at lunchtime, ranging from $4.95 to $6.95. Children's menus are available at $3.95. No liquor is served, but you are welcome to bring your own beer or wine.

The Jolly Roger

Waterfront Row, 75-5776 Alii Dr. ☎ **808/329-1344.** Reservations not accepted. Main courses $11.95–$13.95. AE, DC, DISC, MC, V. Daily 6:30am–10pm. AMERICAN.

Honolulu has its Restaurant Row, and Kailua-Kona has its Waterfront Row, a handsome on-the-ocean, multiple-level dining-shopping complex with a boardwalk and plenty of space from which to watch the pounding surf. One of the more reasonable dining establishments here is the Jolly Roger. The on-the-water location is superb and the food is the kind you remember from the popular Jolly Roger in Waikiki: good American fare with reasonable full-course meals, including teriyaki steak, barbecued beef ribs, fish-fry platter, and chicken Polynesian. (Watch the local papers for two-for-one dinner offers for about $18.) Jolly Roger also has lots of sandwiches and salads at lunch, plus hearty breakfasts, which many people consider the restaurant's best meal. Eggs Benedict, delicious Mac-Waples (waffles with cinnamon apples and macadamia nuts), and steak and eggs go for about $4.25 to $7.75. Contemporary music and rock groups playing from 9:30pm to 1:30am. Nice for a drink at sunset, too, when happy hour prices prevail.

Kona Ranch House

Hi. 11, at the corner of Kuakini and Palani. ☎ **808/329-7061.** Reservations recommended for dinner. Paniolo Room, complete meal $8.95–$14.95; Plantation Lanai, complete meal $10.95–$22.95. DISC, MC, V. Lunch 6:30am–4:30pm; dinner 4:30–9pm daily. AMERICAN.

Take your choice of food and mood at the Kona Ranch House, really two restaurants in one. For a splurge, choose the lovely Plantation Lanai, so pretty in wicker and green: Dinner features steaks and seafood ranging from $10.95 to $21.95. For a meal that's right within our budget, choose the adjoining Paniolo Room or "family style" room. Here, one can indulge in broiled or sautéed mahimahi, grilled liver and onions, paniolo stew, or vegetarian spaghetti with garlic bread, all served with soup or salad plus a choice of beans, rice, or potato. Feeling really famished? Go for the Ranch House Family Platter—these are "ranch-hand size dinners" with main courses like New York steak and deep-fried shrimp, teriyaki steak and mahimahi, and barbecued pork ribs and chicken. With them comes cornbread, soup or salad, a choice of baked beans, rice pilaf, or mashed potatoes, plus beverages, all for $14.95. Children's menus, tasty tropical drinks, luscious homemade desserts—Kona Ranch House has all of this, and reasonably priced lunches (from $5.25) and breakfasts, too, from $4.75. Japanese menus are available.

ⓢ Ocean View Inn

Alii Dr. ☎ **808/329-9998.** Reservations not required. Main courses $2.75–$13.50. No credit cards. Breakfast Tues–Sun 6:30–11am; lunch Tues–Sun 11am–2:45pm; dinner Tues–Sun 5:15–9pm. AMERICAN/CHINESE/VEGETARIAN.

Every time we dine at the Ocean View Inn, we realize why it has survived and thrived for so many years while other newer, flashier establishments come and go. This business has been owned by the same family for more than half a century. It's a big, comfy place, nothing fancy; the view across the road is ocean all the way, the tables are filled with local residents, and the waitresses are old-timers who know their trade. American and Chinese meals are inexpensive and generous. And there is a wide variety of delicious Chinese vegetarian dishes—vegetarians bored with yet another salad bar had best make tracks for this place. Dishes based on vegetarian beef (textured vegetable protein) and tofu run $3 to $5; the sweet-and-sour crisp vegetarian wontons rank with the tastiest Chinese food anywhere. Complete dinners ($7.50 to $14.50) offer good value: They include soup or fruit cup, rice or mashed potato or fries, green salad, tea, and coffee. Broiled ahi, broiled ono, breaded mahimahi, and butterfish are all good, and there are at least 24 other choices, including corned beef and cabbage, fried chicken, and roast pork with applesauce. And there are over 80 Chinese dishes beginning at $3.50. Lunch is also a good buy, with many hot plates to choose from, like shoyu chicken or teriyaki steak, for $6.50 to $9.25. These are served with rice or potato, salad, and beverage. Breakfast has everything from ham and eggs and french toast to beef stew, saimin, and poi.

Quinn's Almost by the Sea

75-5655A Palani Rd. ☎ **808/329-3822.** Reservations not accepted. Main courses $14.50–$18.50. MC, V. Lunch daily 11am–5:30pm; dinner Mon–Sat 5:30–1am, Sun 5:30–11pm. SEAFOOD/STEAK/VEGETARIAN.

There's an informal, relaxed feeling about this place. A lively young crowd hangs out in the garden dining lanai, whose walls (two open, and one lava rock) create an outdoor feeling. Blue canvas director's chairs and laminated wooden tables continue the same mood. There's food here for just about every taste, and all of it good: fresh seafood and fish, caught and delivered from the pier across the street; juicy steaks; vegetarian dishes; salads with homemade dressings. Main courses come with salad, vegetables, and potato or rice. Low-priced specialties include fish and chips, spaghetti, tenderloin tips, and shrimp and chips, from $7.95 to $8.95. At lunch, snow crab, burgers, and roast beef sandwiches run from $6.95 to $7.75. You'll find lots of cheer at the bar. Local residents call Quinn's a favorite.

✪ Sibu Café

In Banyan Court, 75-5695 Alii Dr. ☎ **808/329-1112.** Reservations not required. Main courses $8.95–$11.95. No credit cards. Lunch daily 11:30am–3pm; dinner daily 5–9pm. INDONESIAN.

The exotic Sibu Café is a semi-open place where you can sample the mood and food of Indonesia and Southeast Asia. Balinese decorations, tables topped with sarongs covered with glass, and revolving fans overhead set the scene for wonderfully flavorful food. Every year, readers write to tell us that this was their favorite place! The house specialty is satay: skewers of marinated meats or vegetables broiled over an open flame. Far Eastern dishes like Balinese chicken, spicy pork, ginger beef, Indian curries, and vegetarian stir-fries are also delicious, and everything is accompanied by either brown or fried rice plus a marinated cucumber-and-onion salad. Combination plates are excellent, as is their special peanut sauce. Prices go up a few dollars at dinnertime. Daily Indonesian and Southeast Asian specialties from Cambodia, Vietnam, Thailand, and Malaysia are also available, spiced to taste; there are always several vegetarian dishes.

⑤ Under the Palm

At the Coconut Grove Market Place, 75-5819 Alii Dr. ☎ **808/329-7366.** Reservations not accepted. Pizzas $9; salads $6.50; pasta $7; sandwiches $8. AE, DISC, MC, V. Breakfast (pastries and cappuccino) 7–11am; regular menu 11am–midnight. FRENCH/ASIAN/BISTRO FARE.

If you don't get to sample Chef Daniel Thiebaut's widely hailed French/Asian cuisine at the pricey Palm Café (see below), you can find his talents very much in evidence at his new place, Under the Palm, a sidewalk cafe in the same building. The food here is lighter, just as delicious, and—perfect for us—wonderfully inexpensive. Of the pizzas, our favorite is the Thai grilled chicken with spicy peanut sauce, and one we've seen nowhere before, the Idaho—red potatoes with rosemary, green onion, and roasted garlic, topped with dill sour cream. Salads are wonderful, too, especially the macadamia-crusted goat cheese on field greens with shallot red potatoes. You could have a light lunch of soup and a roll for $4.50, or a pasta of the day for $7. From the European Pan Bella grill comes an array of unusual sandwiches: we especially like the Leif Erickson—grilled sourdough bread with smoked turkey, smoked cheddar, basil, tomato, and field greens with a champagne mustard sauce. Because Chef Thiebaut is always coming up with something new, he does daily international specialties: the French special might feature a selection of cheeses, grapes, and sliced apples, a crusty bagette and an espresso drink or a glass of red wine. The Italian special could include a tomato, basil, and cheese salad drizzled with vinaigrette, and a sandwich on Italian fonseca bread. Desserts, too, change daily; trust us, they're all wonderful. The estate coffee, custom blended in many varieties, is also special. And as if all this weren't enough, there's live music nightly starting at 6pm.

Meals for Less than $20

Fisherman's Landing at Shipwreck Point

In the Kona Inn Shopping Village. 75-5739 Alii Dr. ☎ **808/326-2555.** Reservations recommended. Main courses $10.95–$21.95. Early Sunset Special (5:30–7:30pm) $10.95–$13.95. AE, DC, DISC, JCB, MC, V. Dinner daily 5:30pm–10pm. SEAFOOD.

A seafood restaurant in a spectacular setting. Fisherman's Landing boasts splashing fountains, pools, and nautical decorations all setting the stage for the grand show put on by the pounding surf splashing up on the beach. Fresh island fish, featured daily, is done in a variety of styles. There are also such seafood specialties as lobster tail and shrimp scampi, a few steak offerings, and a variety of Asian specialties on the order of sesame chicken and ginger teriyaki beef. All main courses come with starch, fresh vegetables, and freshly baked bread from the restaurant's own ovens. Save room for dessert, too, like the lava macadamia-nut ice cream pie. There's music every night from 6 to 10pm.

Kona Galley

75-5663 Palani Rd., across from King Kamehameha's Kona Beach Hotel. ☎ **808/329-5550.** Reservations recommended especially at dinner. Main courses $9.95–$18.95. AE, MC, V. Lunch Mon–Sat 11am–3:30pm; dinner daily 4–9:30pm. SEAFOOD.

It would be pretty hard to beat the location of Kona Galley: The one-flight up, open-air lanai dining room looks right out over Kailua Pier. The food is special, too. Only fresh, locally caught or grown ingredients are used in such ingenious dishes as the seafood baked in a Puna papaya and topped with a light curry sauce, the large shrimps sautéed in a lilikoi-basil sauce, and the skinless breast of chicken braised in coconut milk and presented on a bed of taro leaves. A baked vegetable lasagne, grilled shrimp linguine, and roast chicken served with a three-peppercorn sauce are other favorites. Start with an appetizer like the baked escargots (unusual in Hawaii) and top off your meal with a memorable dessert like the fresh apple strudel with strawberry-citrus sauce. A variety of gourmet pizzas and burgers including a meatless nut burger are available. Luncheon offers a similar menu at slightly lower prices, plus several sandwiches and meal-size salads.

Kona Inn Restaurant

In the Kona Inn Shopping Village, 75-5744 Alii Dr. ☎ **808/329-4455.** Reservations recommended at dinner. Main courses $3.95–$9.95 on the Café Grill menu, $12.95–$18.95 and up on the regular dinner menu. Café Grill menu daily 11:30am–midnight; dinner menu daily 5:30–10pm. AMERICAN/SEAFOOD.

The lovely Kona Inn Restaurant is a splurge for us at dinner, but it's such a special spot, with a spectacular view of the bay and some tables perched right at water's edge, that it's worth your while to have lunch here or choose from the Café Grill menu anytime. You can have Hawaiian chicken for $6.95, calamari for $5.95, pasta and chicken salad for $7.95, and a host of good sandwiches for $3.95 to $9.95. Having a cocktail out on the oceanfront lanai is lovely, too.

Kuakini Terrace

At the Keauhou Beach Hotel, 76-6740 Alii Dr. ☎ **808/322-3441.** Reservations recommended. Chinese buffet $12.95 adults, $6.95 children; seafood buffet, $19.95 adults, $9.95 children; Sun champagne brunch $16. 95 adults, $8.95 children. AE, MC, V. Breakfast daily 6:30–11am; lunch daily 11am–5pm; dinner daily 5–9pm. BUFFETS/CHINESE/SEAFOOD.

Keauhou is one of the loveliest areas of the Kona Coast, with its historic sites, glorious views of the bay and mountains, and grand resort hotels. It's well worth a short drive out here to enjoy the fabulous buffets for which the Kuakini Terrace has become known. Set in an open-air atmosphere, the restaurant affords views of the hotel's lush and beautifully landscaped grounds, as well as an enticing view of Kahaluu Bay. The buffet table is also enticing: Monday through Thursday evening it's a super Chinese feast, the tables laden with many unusual Far Eastern salads, greens, hot dishes like Chinese roast duck, steamed clams with black beans, sweet-and-sour shrimp, Chinese barbecued spareribs; there's a complete dim sum table, and a table of luscious desserts, as well. Considering the setting, the charm and the quality of the food, this is definitely one of the best buys in town. Also very popular is their seafood buffet, served Friday through Sunday. Sunday champagne brunch is another winner, with a wide selection of local favorites.

◯ Sam Choy's Restaurant

73-5576 Kauhola St., Koloko Industrial Area. ☎ **808/326-1545.** Reservations required for dinner. Main courses $16.95–$20.95. No credit cards. Breakfast and lunch Mon–Sat 6:00am–2pm; dinner Wed–Sat 5pm–9pm. PACIFIC RIM.

Chef Sam Choy, born and raised in Kona, has been cooking his entire life; he started by helping his father prepare traditional Hawaiian luaus on weekends and grew into a world-renowned chef. Both local residents and visitors flock to Sam's, tucked away in the Koloko Industrial Area (call to get directions). This simple, high-ceilinged restaurant with an exhibition kitchen and Formica-topped tables serves some of the best food (at hard-to-beat prices) in all of Hawaii.

The breakfast hours are packed with construction workers, attorneys, secretaries, and visitors persistent enough to find this spot. Try the french toast, made from extra-thick slices of island sweet bread for only $2.75; or, if you're very hungry, try, for $7.95, the fresh island fish (Sam has the best fishing connections and always has fresh fish), complete with eggs, choice of rice, hash-brown potatoes or home fries, and toast (you can skip lunch, you will be so full).

Lunch has everything, from traditional burgers ($4.50) to such Asian favorites as bento, spam and egg musubi, and poki musubi, as well as Koloko noodle mania (chow mein noodles cooked with fresh vegetables and meats, and served in a crisp wonton bowl) for only $6.75, including rice and salad. Nothing at lunch is more than $8.95.

Dinners are our favorite: That's when the white tablecloths come out and flowers grace the tables, transforming the restaurant. Reservations are a must—word is out on the food and the prices, so book in advance. We recommend Sam Choy's award-winning seafood lau lau, made with fresh fish and assorted vegetables in the traditional ti-leaf wrapper ($20.95), or the Chinese honey duck with Kau orange sauce ($16.95), or the nightly specials. All entrées come with soup and salad. Children's menu includes fried chicken or hamburger steak served with rice or french fries for $7.95 and hamburger sandwiches with fries, $5.95.

◯ Su's Thai Kitchen

74-5588A Pawai Place. ☎ **808/326-7808.** Reservations recommended. Main courses $6.95–$17.95. MC, V. Lunch Mon–Fri 11am–2:30pm; dinner daily 5–9pm. THAI.

Tucked away in the industrial area not far from town, this cute little indoor-outdoor restaurant with a pleasant garden draws fans from near and far: Everybody loves the authentic Thai dishes. Two people could have an exotic dinner here for under $25! Not only can you go with all the old standbys like Pad Thai or a variety of curries and coconut milk–based soups, but you can also try some rather unusual offerings: a whole fish in a sweet chili sauce, crab claws in a pot, or stir-fried chicken with macadamia nuts. Vegetarians have a dozen dishes of their own. Lunch specials are a good deal: Every dish is $5.95. Ask to be seated out on the lanai.

Note: There's another Su's Thai Kitchen at the Parker Ranch Center in Waimea (☎ 808/885-8688), but we much prefer the original one here: the one in Waimea, which also serves American, Chinese, and Japanese lunch specials, has a plain, workaday indoor setting and less interesting food.

Tom Bombadil's Food and Drink

75-5864 Walua Rd., off Alii Rd. ☎ **808/329-1292** or 808/329-2173. Reservations not required. Main courses $6.75–$13.95. MC, V. Daily 11am–10pm. AMERICAN.

There's an outpost of Middle Earth right on Alii Drive, across from the Kona Hilton Hotel, known as Tom Bombadil's Food and Drink. And while murals and decor and names on the menu are mythic (Aragorn picca, Misty Mountain sandwiches, Elven King salads), the food is downright substantial and filling. Tom Bombadil's is known for its broasted chicken (the unique taste is a result of deep-frying under pressure), about $7.25 for a two-piece dinner; for pizzas (from $11.95); and for hot or cold sandwiches starting at $5.45. There are also tasty appetizers such as fried mozzarella, calamari, and potato skins, plus soups, salads, pastas, and flame-broiled specialties, which include fish of the day, chicken teriyaki, hamburgers, and combination dinners. You can enjoy ocean-view dining from the covered lanai, relax in the cozy pub area with a drink, or view live satellite coverage of sporting events on their cocktail patio. All food is available for take-out; you can call in your order first.

Worth a Splurge

✪ Palm Café

At the Coconut Grove Market Place, 75-5819 Alii Dr. ☎ **808/329-7765.** Reservations recommended. Main courses $14.50–$23. AE, DISC, MC, V. Dinner only, daily 5–10pm. FRENCH/PACIFIC RIM.

Everything about Palm Café is special—from the great location overlooking Alii Drive and the waterfront (sunset-watchers, take note), the spacious cool interior with upholstered wicker chairs, and the arrangement of bonsai on every table, to the unique cuisine prepared by chef/owner Daniel Thiebaut, who describes his style as "French by way of Asia." Sauces are flavorful but not heavy; only the freshest natural ingredients are used; garnishes are edible. Fish preparations shine, especially the oven-baked ono, with an almond-sesame crust in a ginger-lime butter sauce, accompanied by papaya and Kona tomato relish, or the pepper Hawaiian snapper with tomato fondue and Thai salsa. Lamb chops are done Hunan style, with Puna goat cheese and eggplant-zucchini compote. Signature appetizers include the seared yellowfin tuna on a bed of spicy leek and jicama stir-fry and the ravioli stuffed with Chinese greens, with balsamic vinegar and ginger beurre blanc. There are specials and vegetarian dishes every night. Desserts are strictly for sybarites, like the chocolate croquant: two crunchy wafers filled with chocolate mousse and topped with a Tahitian vanilla ginger sauce. Once a month, visiting chefs prepare some outstanding meals here: If you catch one of these, you're in for a special treat.

CASUAL & TAKE-OUT IN KAILUA-KONA

Kona Coast Shopping Center   The lively Kona Coast Shopping Center, near the intersection of Hi. 11 and Hi. 19, offers you a chance to mingle with the local folk at some inexpensive restaurants. For great Mexican food at affordable prices, try **Poquito Mas,** a tiny take-out restaurant located right next to the umbrella-covered tables in the middle of the shopping center. You can sit and rest as you munch on tacos, burritos, or huge tostadas. We love their burrito mojada—that's a "wet burrito" with red sauce, which makes it more like an enchilada. There are also several different salsas, from mild to hot. It's a full meal for under $5. **Kim's Place** is a small take-out shop, where traditional dishes like kalbi, bulgogi, Korean chicken, and the like, are all under $5—and all very good. **Betty's Chinese Kitchen,** small but sparkling, offers Chinese food in serve-yourself cafeteria style; most dishes are $4.30 for two portions, $5.80 for three, $6.10 for four. Betty also has an interesting selection of dim sum—pork manapua, brown sugar manapua, egg rolls, and Chinese doughnuts, for 35¢ to 95¢ each. You can't go wrong with the hearty sandwiches on cracked-wheat bread sold at the health-food store, **Kona Healthways,** for around $3.95, hearty and delicious.

Lanihau Center Across the road is a newer shopping plaza, Lanihau Center, which also has several restaurants and fast-food places. **Royal Jade Garden** is a cheerful, attractive Chinese restaurant, with large round tables, fans, and paintings on the walls, and a good menu with many reasonably priced main courses. Pork and beef dishes begin at $4.50 and there are almost two dozen seafood dishes—spicy shrimp, deep-fried oysters, abalone with black mushrooms—at higher prices. A meal at **Yuni's Special Korean BBQ** is a treat: It's neat and clean, and the food is very tasty and reasonably priced.

Just below Lanihau Center, across from Hilo Hattie's, is Kopiko Plaza, home of ✪ **Kona Mix Plate,** which local friends put us on to—now it's one of our favorites. This is a bustling place with a busy counter, very popular with the local people. The homestyle local food is good and cheap, and the service is fast. Sautéed mahimahi and broiled mahimahi, each $5.80, are as good as dishes you'd pay more than twice as much for elsewhere. Also very good: the vegetable tempura and the Korean chicken. Open from 10am to 8pm; closed Sunday.

ALII DRIVE & ENVIRONS

The perfect place to relax and meditate on the beautiful Pacific Ocean is ✪ **Island Lava Java,** on Alii Drive at the Alii Sunset Plaza. Not only will you have a ringside seat on the ocean, but this informal, European-style coffee bar and sidewalk cafe is *the* coffee and bakery spot on the west side. You'll find a great assortment of coffees and espressos to complement the bakery specialties, such as biscotti (all types), scones, and—our personal favorite—macadamia-nut chocolate brownies. A new health-conscious management is introducing low- or no-fat muffins and other light dishes. Lava Java offers several good sandwiches on croissants, baguettes, and freshly made breads (smoked turkey, veggie, tuna, waldorf chicken) for $5.25, a wonderful spanakopita (spinach cheese pie) $2.99, and a daily soup and salad. The scene is especially enjoyable at night, since it's the only non-alcohol live music outlet in Kailua-Kona, featuring everything from classical acoustic guitar to country and folk music. The music is on from 6:30 nightly.

Alii Sunset Plaza is also the home of **A Piece of the Apple** for New York–style sandwiches, **King Yee Lau,** a good Chinese restaurant, **Kona Sushi,** and **Thai Rim Restaurant,** an attractive spot open to the street and the ocean (their chicken coconut soup is a winner). The Plaza is a nice spot to know about if you want to put together a meal from several establishments and sit at a sidewalk table, meet a friend, rest your feet, or just relax and watch the passing scene.

Although it's really not a restaurant, **Suzanne's Bake Shop,** at 75-5629 Kuakini Highway, in the center of Kailua town (the highway runs parallel to Alii Drive, a block up the hill), serves as a breakfast place and snack shop for many local people and visitors alike. The doors are open at 4:30 every morning, and that's when fragrant and flavorful muffins, doughnuts, danish, iron bars, iron cookies, and other goodies start coming out of the ovens. Pastries are 50¢ to $1.75 each, and the caramel-macadamia-nut danish is a special treat. Snacks, sandwiches, Kona coffee, and cold sodas are available throughout the day. A few chairs and tables outside afford a view of the passing scene. Open daily till 9:30pm.

Kona "Up Mauka"

Meals for Less than $8

ⓢ **Billy Bob's Park 'n Pork**

Keopuka Square, Captain Cook, just south of mile marker 111. ☎ **808/323-3371.**
Reservations not required. Main courses $3.95–$9.95. No credit cards. Lunch Mon–Fri 11am–
2:30pm; dinner daily 5–9pm or later. CHICKEN/RIBS/VEGETARIAN.

This little mom-'n'-pop restaurant—cute as can be, with Old West decor and
country and western music playing in the background—is a big local favorite.
Neighbors keep coming back and bringing their kids (there's a big toy box near
the window). Owners John Koch and Kathleen Markwell do everything from
cooking the food to serving it up. John, a former rodeo rider (his nickname was
"Billy Bob"), is also pretty skillful at turning out the barbecued chicken, beef, and
pork ribs, as well as creating vegetarian pastas and enchiladas, fish sandwiches,
homemade soups, and salads. His wife, Kathleen, does "Miss Kitty's Desserts,"
which could be peach cobbler or cherry crisp or cheesecake—a different one each
day. Everything is homemade from scratch and prices are ridiculously low: $7.95
buys a full "Bodacious Meal Deal"—a serving of chicken or meat, plus a choice
of two side dishes, such as campfire potatoes, chili, green salad and cornbread with
honey butter. Beverages—including soda, Kona coffee, and iced or herbal tea—
are included, and so are refills. For $9.95 you can have a complete prime-rib
dinner. Vegetarian specials are $5.95 and $6.95. It's fun to start with hot and
spicy hog fries (like nachos but with potatoes instead of corn chips). No liquor,
but bring your own beer or wine and join the local people in a fun scene. But if
western music is not to your taste, take your meal out and sit by the ocean.

Meals for Less than $14

The Aloha Café

Hi. 11, Kainaliu. ☎ **808/322-3383.** Reservations not accepted. Main courses $6.95–$14.95.
MC, V. Mon–Sat 8am–8pm; brunch Sun 9am–2pm. NATURAL FOODS.

On your way to City of Refuge at Honaunau try the Aloha Café. Located in the
lobby of the Aloha Theater in Kainaliu, it has wonderful, healthful food and an
unusual atmosphere. The artistically decorated counter-service cafe is in the lobby
of the theater, but it's even more fun to sit out on the terraced lanai that borders
the building, especially all the way down near the meadow. The menu features
homemade vegetarian burritos, tostadas, nachos, and quesadillas, generous sandwiches (veggie, tofu/avocado, fresh fish), and charbroiled burgers. These items run
about $5.25 to $6.75. Dinner adds filet mignon at $14.95, fresh fish
(market-priced), and several vegetarian specials. Wines and beers are available. If
you get here in time for breakfast, you'll be treated to three-egg omelets, pancakes,
and whole-wheat french toast. Even if you don't have a meal here, stop in for some
of the homemade fresh-baked goods.

Drysdale's Two

In the Keauhou Shopping Village ☎ **808/322-0070.** Reservations not accepted. Main
courses $7.95–$13.95. AE, MC, V. Daily 11am–midnight. AMERICAN.

Drysdale's Two, in the graceful Keauhou Shopping Village, is a popular gathering spot, especially with sports fans who will be sitting in the huge,
pennant-bedecked bar area, watching their favorite teams on TV. There are

several attractive dining areas here too, as well as very good food on a popular-priced menu that is served all day long. Possibilities include such specialties as barbecued pork back ribs, breast of chicken teriyaki, and a vegetable stir-fry, excellent hamburgers, including low-fat buffalo burgers (honest!), for $5.50 to $7.95; and hearty meat sandwiches, croissant sandwiches, homemade chili, and a good variety of salads, including a fresh Hawaiian fruit salad with sherbet at $7.95. Just about any taste can be accommodated here. Fabulous tropical drinks and ice-cream/liqueur drinks are great for sipping out on the lanai; Peggy's Peanut Butter Ice Cream Pie is a must for dessert, at $3.75.

⑤ H. Manago Hotel Dining Room

In the H. Manago Hotel, Captain Cook. ☎ **808/323-3642.** Reservations not required. Main courses $6–$10.75. DISC, MC, V. Breakfast Tues–Sun 7–9am; lunch Tues–Sun 11am–2pm; dinner Tues–Thurs 5–7:30pm. Fri–Sun 5–7pm. AMERICAN.

This old-fashioned family-style restaurant is the place to catch a slice of local life. It has enjoyed a good reputation for years among the local people, although very few tourists make their way here. Everything is served family style: big plates of rice, salad (the macaroni salad is especially good), vegetables, and whatever the cook has made that night are brought out and served to everyone at the table, along with such main dishes as pork chops, liver, ahi, opelu, ono, mahimahi, teriyaki butter-fish, chicken, hamburger, or steak. People rave about the fried pork chops; many of the other dishes are fried as well—don't come here for a low-fat meal! The menu is limited and the food is not fancy, but this a good chance to experience the real cuisine of the Kona Coast. Very pleasant.

✪ Teshima's

Hi. 11, Honalo. ☎ **808/322-9140.** Reservations not required. Main courses $6–$11. No credit cards. Breakfast and lunch daily 6:30am–1:45pm; dinner daily 5–9:45pm. JAPANESE.

For a change of ambience from the tourist world of Kailua, drive out on Hi. 11 (one block mauka from the main street of Kailua), a few miles south to Teshima's, at Honalo in coffee-growing country, a very popular place for over 46 years with the local Japanese, Hawaiians, Filipinos, and haoles. You might spot Sen. Dan Inouye there—he always comes in for a meal when he's in Kona. Say hello to Mrs. Teshima—she's a great lady. On one visit she proudly showed us the report that Teshima's had won first prize—the Gold Plate Award—for best Japanese cuisine on the Big Island, from the *Gourmet Guide of Hawaii*. You can have a complete Teishoku lunch of miso soup, sashimi, sukiyaki, plus various side dishes, served on an attractive black-lacquered tray, for $6.50 to $8. At dinner, vegetable tempura and shrimp tempura run $7.50 and $10, and there are plenty of dishes like sashimi, beef, pork, or chicken tofu, for $6.75 to $9.50, all served with miso soup, tsukemono, rice, and tea. Sashimi is market-priced.

What to See & Do on the Big Island

14

There's so much to see on the Big Island—active volcanoes, verdant tropical valleys, ancient historical sites, black-sand beaches, snowcapped mountains, lush rain forests, and funky old plantation towns where "Old Hawaii" still lives—that ideally you should spend a week or more exploring and enjoying this mini-continent. However, you'll be able to experience the best of the island—picturesque Hilo, spectacular Hawaii Volcanoes National Park, the sunny Kona Coast, and more—even if you have only a few days.

1 Beaches

By Jeanette Foster

As the youngest island in the Hawaiian archipelago, the Big Island doesn't yet have miles and miles of sandy beaches. In fact, the island is still growing from lava accumulation from the Kilauea eruption, which started in 1983 and continues to flow daily. Big Island beaches not only have older white sands, but also black, salt-and-pepper, gray, and even green sands. Some beaches have no sand at all— just dramatic lava promontories jutting out to the sea, millions of water-worn pebbles that clatter in the surf, or sometimes just huge, water-worn boulders lining the shoreline. The beaches listed below are the finest examples of the variety found on the Big Island and the range of ocean activities available there.

SPENCER BEACH PARK

Just south of the Kawaihae Harbor (where the movie *Waterworld* was filmed) is Spencer Beach Park. The beach, called Ohaiula, is well-protected from the wind and waves, making it excellent for swimming, snorkeling, and diving (there's a shallow reef right offshore). A grassy lawn with numerous shade trees, along with extensive facilities—restrooms, picnic tables, showers, tennis courts, pavilion, parking, camping area, and a lifeguard tower—makes this place very popular with families.

Above the park lies Puukohola Heiau, a giant temple that Kamehameha and his men built before setting out to unite Hawaii. The temple was built on the advice of Kapoukai, a kahuna (spiritual advisor) who predicted that if Kamehameha would build the

---

⊗ Frommer's Favorite Big Island Experiences

The Eruption of Kilauea. This is a once-in-a-lifetime opportunity: If the conditions are right, the rangers at Hawaii Volcanoes National Park will allow you to walk right up to the continuous lava flow that's oozing down the flank of the mountain and into the ocean. The residual heat and sulfur smell will send you running well before the creeping lava will.

Snorkeling at Kahaluu Beach. This lovely lagoon on the Kona Coast, bordered by salt-and-pepper sand, thanks to an ancient lava flow, just might offer the best snorkeling on the Big Island. The calm, shallow waters are particularly ideal for beginning snorkelers and children, and the tropical fish—and an occasional turtle or two—who frequent the area are friendly.

A Submarine Dive in the *Atlantis*. Dive 80 to 100 feet below the surface into the clear waters of Kona Bay to explore the spectacular world of the coral reef—without getting wet.

Big-Game Fishing in Kona, Marlin Capital of the World. Here's your opportunity to angle a giant billfish and watch it leap completely out of the water, or hook up to a 150-pound tuna and see line scream out of your reel. The thrills are endless, and no experience or license is necessary.

Hanging Out in the Picturesque Mountain Town of Waimea. Shop the boutiques and galleries, sightsee, stroll, and soak up some *paniolo* color in Hawaii's most famous cowboy town, also the headquarters of Parker Ranch.

Hiking Waipio and Waimanu Valleys. If you would like to see the Hawaii that Captain Cook found when he arrived, here's your chance. Winding along cliff-hugging trails through wild jungle and past thundering waterfalls and babbling mountain streams will give you a rare glimpse into a world that thrives without the help of humans.

---

massive temple to his war god, Kukailimoku, the god would reward him by making him the first to bring the islands together as one. Four years after the temple was complete, Kamehameha had united all the islands except Kauai; 15 years after that, in 1810, Kauai and Niihau agreed to join the other Hawaiian Islands and recognize Kamehameha as their king.

HAPUNA BEACH STATE PARK

Just off the Queen Kaahumanu Highway, south of the Hapuna Beach Prince Hotel, lies one of the most beautiful beaches in the world. In fact, *Condé Nast Traveler* consistently lists it as one of the best beaches on the planet. It is easy to see why: A half-mile of sugar-white sand arcs between two sable-colored lava flows. In the summer, when the beach grows to some 200 feet wide, it becomes the largest on the Big Island. From May to September, local island residents and visitors come to Hapuna for swimming, snorkeling, and body surfing. Facilities include A-frame cabins for camping, a parking lot, pavilions, restrooms, and showers. The beach can be very crowded by mid-day on weekends, so go early in the day. In the winter (October to April), Hapuna becomes a different beach. During winter storms the surf claims part of the beach, leaving enough for sunbathers and picnickers.

Beaches & Outdoor Activities on the Big Island

Beaches
- Anaehoomalu Bay ㉒
- Coconut Island Park ⑤
- Green Sands Beach ⑮
- Hapuna Beach ㉔
- Honaunau Beach ⑰
- Hookena Beach ⑯
- Kahaluu Beach ⑲
- Kealakekua Bay ⑱
- Kehena Beach ⑦
- Kona Coast State Park ㉑
- Punaluu Black Sand Beach ⑭
- Spencer Beach ㉗
- Waipio Valley Beach ⑤
- White Sands Beach ⑳

Cabins & Campgrounds
- Halape Campground ⑬
- Kamoamoa Campground ⑨
- Kilauea Military Camp ⑨
- Kilauea State Cabin ⑧
- Kipuka Nene Campground ⑫
- Namakani Paio Cabins & Campground ⑪
- Waimanu Campgrounds ①
- Waipio Valley Campground ③

Golf Courses
- Hapuna Golf Course ㉕
- Mauna Kea Beach Golf Course ㉖
- Waikoloa Golf Course ㉓

Hikes
- Akaka Falls ④
- Kilauea Iki Trail ⑩
- Kipuka Pualu (Bird Park) ⑥
- Waipio & Waimanu Valleys (Muliwai Trail) ②

Thunderous waves pound the shore, producing strong rip currents. There may be no lifeguard here, so be extremely cautious during the winter months.

ANAEHOOMALU BAY

The young Big Island does not have an abundance of white-sand beaches. The ones it does have, however, are some of the most beautiful in the state. A-Bay, as the local residents call Anaehoomalu, is a great example. It's nearly always filled with visitors (A-Bay fronts the Royal Waikoloan Hotel and is used by guests at all the resorts in Waikoloa) and residents who come here not only for the beach's natural beauty, but also for the diverse marine recreation options here. The beach slopes gently from shallow to deep water. The conditions are excellent for swimming, snorkeling, diving, kayaking, windsurfing, and, on some occasions, even surfing. Equipment rental and instructions in snorkeling, scuba, and windsurfing are available at the north end of the beach. At the far, northern edge of the bay is a rare turtle cleaning station where snorkelers and divers can watch endangered green sea turtles lined up, waiting their turn to have small fish clean them. Facilities include restrooms, showers, and picnic tables. Public parking is available near the hotel.

KONA COAST STATE PARK

North of the Kona Airport, down a very rough road (rent-a-car drivers be wary) lies a series of coves and inlets separated by lava inundations but tied together by the long, curving sand beach of Mahaiula. Since it's a state park, the beach is open daily from 8 a.m. to 8 p.m. (the closing is strictly enforced and there is no provision for overnight camping). Mainly local residents come here; they generally have cars and trucks that can traverse the bumpy, lava-rock road that leads to the park from Queen Kaahumanu Highway. The largest inlet is excellent for swimming, and there's great snorkeling and diving off shore. When the big winter waves roll in, this area becomes popular with surfers. Facilities include picnic tables, barbecue pits, and parking. No water is available.

WHITE SANDS (MAGIC SANDS) BEACH PARK

This tiny beach is also known as Disappearing Sands, because a winter storm can convert the sandy beach to rocks in less than 24 hours. By spring, though, the sand magically returns. Local residents primarily use this beach, especially children and teenagers learning how to body surf and boogie board, as the small waves are good for training. On calm days, the waters are placid and excellent for swimming and snorkeling. During the winter, however, the training-size waves become expert-level swells, and spectators overflow the beach and the parking lot and line up along Alii Drive to watch the action. Facilities here include restrooms, showers, a lifeguard tower, and a very small parking lot.

KAHALUU BEACH PARK

At the south end of Alii Drive, next to the Keauhou Beach Hotel, is a favorite spot for swimmers and snorkelers. The shallow water, protective breakwater, well-established reef, and schools of tropical fish make this a popular place. On weekends it's beach blanket to beach blanket, with local residents, families, and groups having picnics and parties at the large pavilion. The small parking lot fills up by mid-morning, so arrive early. This is a great place for children and beginning snorkelers to get their fins wet; the water is so shallow—3 feet or so— that you can literally stand up if you feel uncomfortable. In the winter the placid waters become turbulent and a rip current (going out to sea) can be encountered when high surf rolls in; look for the lifeguard signs informing you of conditions.

KEALAKEKUA BAY

Located next to Napoopoo Village, the 1-mile wide Kealakekua Bay is the site where Captain James Cook anchored on January 17, 1779 and where, one month later, he was killed. Today a 27-foot white obelisk stands on the spot at the north end of the bay where Cook's life ended. This is one of the state's Marine Life Conservation Districts, or underwater parks; the underwater sanctuary was created in 1969 to preserve and protect the extraordinary marine life and topography. The beach here is not much, mostly rounded pebbles, stones, and boulders with a fringe sandy beach; still, sunbathers always find an area to soak up the rays. The attraction here is not the beach but the water. Commercial boats from Kailua-Kona and Keauhou bring swimmers and snorkelers into the bay to enjoy the marine life. Throughout the day, swimmers and kayakers crisscross the bay. Early in the morning a pod of dolphins frequently comes into the bay, and occasionally approaches the swimmers and kayakers.

There is a lot of local and visitor traffic in this very small area, and the parking facilities are minimal. The adjacent small public beach park has a pavilion, restrooms, picnic tables, showers, and a basketball court. Commercial operators will frequently appear with snorkel gear and kayaks for rent.

HONAUNAU BEACH

The area alongside the Puuhonau o Honaunau National Historical Park is one of the best snorkeling and diving spots on the Big Island. The national historical park, one of the most visited attractions on the Big Island, has a visitor's center, restrooms, drinking water, a picnic area, and parking. Instead of entering the park, take the one-lane road next to the park down to the ocean. You'll find a small sandy beach, but most snorkelers and divers bypass it for the water. Clouds of tropical fish cruise the waters, turtles are frequently spotted, and tiny fish dart among the coral. During the winter beware—this placid beach becomes dangerous when high surf is present. Not only is it hazardous to be in the water during these conditions, but it is equally as risky to walk next to the water's edge. The national park posts danger signs when high surf is present; if you see one, you should take it seriously. Even if the surf is too rough in the winter months, you can stay well away from it and still have a ringside seat to view Hawaii's most popular winter visitors, the humpback whales. Frequently seen along this coast—sometimes quite close to shore—you'll best view them from the southern end of the national park.

HOOKENA BEACH PARK

Just off the main road (Hi. 11) lies the old village of Hookena, where only a handful of people now live. At the northern corner of the Kauhako Bay, which is surrounded by high cliffs on three sides, lies Hookena Beach Park. A small beach park with a black-and-white sandy beach (giving it an almost gray color), Hookena is a good place for swimming, snorkeling, and diving most of the year, except in stormy conditions. The small park has a parking area, restrooms, showers, picnic tables, and a few shade trees. Just a few minutes' walk from Hookena Beach is Kealia Beach, another excellent area for snorkeling and diving. To get there, either take the public road north of Hookena Village or walk along the shoreline north from the Hookena Beach Park. Since Hookena is quite a way off the main highway, not as many visitors venture down to this quaint beach, but the local residents use it regularly. It's wonderful in the late afternoon on weekdays, when few people are around.

GREEN SAND BEACH

Lava is composed of various minerals and mineral-like substances; one of the minerals is olivine, which is a shiny emerald-green color. The famous Green Sand Beach, in Ka'u, is located at the base of Pu'u o Mahana, a cone formed during an old eruption of Mauna Loa. It's so littered with olivine that the color of the sand is green. This beach isn't easy to get to, the unprotected bay is frequently rough, there are no facilities, no fresh water, no shade, or protection from the relentless sun, and winds frequent the South Point area of the Big Island; despite all of this, Green Sand Beach is certainly worth seeing. To get there, take the rutted road (four-wheel vehicles only) from the Kaulana Boat Ramp; after about 2¹/₂ miles, you'll come to the end of the road. Here you can climb down the cliff—go to the south end where the footing is solid—to the most unusual beach you will probably ever see. If the surf's up, you may just want to view the beach from the top of the cliff. If the water is placid, the beach is good for swimming and diving. Fishermen cast from the surrounding cliffs and nudists are occasionally seen lying on the green sands.

PUNALUU BLACK-SAND BEACH

The black sand at Punaluu resulted from a lava flow that entered the ocean here. Steam explosions occurred as the hot lava collided with the cool ocean water; the explosion formed clouds of liquid lava drops that chilled on contact with the water or air. The ocean currents then deposited this sand, and a beach was born. Located about 1¹/₂ miles off the highway, this county park has complete facilities: ample parking, showers, restrooms, pavilions, drinking water, electricity, and a camping area. This is a good spot for swimming and snorkeling; be sure to use the northeastern end of the beach—rocks offshore at the other end can be dangerous—and stay within the bay inside of the boat ramp, because a powerful rip current constantly runs off the boat channel. Most visitors bypass this unusual beach; it's generally used by local residents, especially boaters and families with children. Not usually crowded, Punaluu is also a pleasant stop for a picnic on a tour of the island.

KEHENA BEACH

Off Hi. 137 is a recently formed black-sand beach, born in 1955 from the lava flows of Mauna Kea. Mother Nature wasn't finished with the Kehena Beach then, though; in November 1975, two earthquakes that jolted the Big Island created a tsunami and sank the beach three feet. This beach is noted for the dolphins that frequent the bay, often playing with the swimmers. During the winter months, when heavy surf rolls into the unprotected bay, it's very dangerous to enter the water here, but the cliffs above the beach are an excellent vantage point for watching humpback whales. There are no facilities at this beach; there's just a small parking lot at the lookout area. The beach does have a border of ironwoods and coconuts growing out of the sand that offers some relief from the heat that the black sand generates. You're sure to spot a shoreline angler or two along the surrounding cliffs when you visit Kehena.

COCONUT ISLAND PARK

The ancient Hawaiians believed that swimming around the rock that lies offshore from Coconut Island could cure any illness. Located in the center of Hilo Bay, Coconut Island is a popular place for swimming. The grassy, tree-lined island is filled with picnickers on the weekends. This is a great place to take children swimming and a productive spot to try your hand at fishing. Facilities include a pavilion, restrooms, picnic tables, benches, and a parking lot at the adjacent Hilo Hawaiian Hotel.

WAIPIO VALLEY BEACH

Eight-miles outside of Honokaa, off Hi. 240, is spectacular Waipio Valley. The valley floor is 3 miles long and 1 mile wide, with salt-and-pepper sands extending almost the entire length of the valley's mouth. This is not a beach for swimming, because there are constantly breaking waves and strong rip currents in the summer and frequent high surf in the winter, but the valley is lush with tropical vegetation and the view is awe-inspiring. Like most remote areas, getting into Waipio Valley is not easy. The single-lane road is narrow and steep; only four-wheel drive vehicles are allowed. There are no public facilities. You might want to consider one of the commercial tour operators for a tour of the valley in order to get a glimpse of this breathtakingly beautiful area (see the section on Waipio Valley in "The Puna Coast," below).

2 Water Sports & Recreation

By Jeanette Foster

The Big Island's two 13,000-foot volcanoes block wind and inclement weather from much of the Kona-Kohala coastline, providing 340 days a year of remarkably calm seas. The forces of nature have carved the coastline with underwater formations and dramatic drop-offs that attract an abundance of marine life for snorkeling, diving, and fishing. The dependable, localized afternoon breeze is enough to make sailing and windsurfing exciting. In the winter months, the antics of humpback whales can be observed from either the shore or from a boat, and the winter waves keep the body and board surfers happy.

BOATING

For an intimate, personalized tour of the Kona Coast, try **Captain Zodiac,** out of Honokohau Harbor (☎ 808/329-3199). The 4-hour tour (available in the morning and again in the afternoon) cruises 14 miles from Honokohau Harbor to the marine life park in Kealakekua Bay, where they stop for an 1 1/2 hour of snorkeling (all snorkel gear is provided) and a snack. On the way back, the 16 passengers hear a detailed history of the Kona coast, visit sea caves, and see various marine creatures like turtles, manta rays, and schools of dolphins. The cost is $62. *A note of caution:* Pregnant women are advised not to take the trip on the very bouncy inflatable boat, and small children may not enjoy the 4-hour open-boat ride.

BODYBOARDING (BOOGIE BOARDING) & BODYSURFING

Bodyboarding (some times called boogie boarding) and bodysurfing are similar wave-riding sports. For bodysurfing, you use your body to ride the waves; in bodyboarding, you lie flat on a small foam board that supports the upper part of your body. Both sports require a pair of swim fins to help propel you through the water. Both forms of wave riding are very popular on the Big Island because the equipment involved is inexpensive and easy to carry, and both sports can be practiced in the island's year-round small, gentle waves. You can rent boogie boards and fins from **Snorkel Bob's,** located in the parking lot near Huggo's Restaurant, 75-5831 Kahakai Rd., Kailua-Kona (808/329-0770), for $29 a week. No one gives formal boogie boarding lessons, but the staff at Snorkel Bob's can suggest appropriate beaches for beginners. On the west side of the island, the best boogie boarding beaches include Hapuna, White Sands, and Kona Coast State Park. On the east side, try Leleiwi, Isaac Hale, and Punaluu.

DEEP-SEA FISHING

The ocean off Kailua-Kona is known around the globe for its superb big-game fishing—billfish, tuna, *ono* (wahoo), and mahimahi abound. In fact, Kona is the only place in the world where marlin are caught 12 months out of the year. A major advantage of fishing in Kona is that you can take game fish just minutes from the harbor, unlike in some areas, where charter fishing boats must run an hour or more just to get the fish. Many world-record fish have been taken in the Kona waters. More than 70 boats with professional captains and crew offer charters (all tackle provided, no license required) out of Keauhou, Kawaihae, and Honokohau harbors and Kailua Bay. Because Kona sits in the lee of the Big Island's two 13,000-foot volcanoes, the waters offshore are calm 340 days a year.

To book a charter boat, you can either walk the docks of Honokohau, inspecting the boats and talking to the captains to arrange the kind of fishing you are interested in (everything from battling 1,000-pound marlin to fly fishing), or you can contact a charter-boat specialty agency like **Kona Charter Skippers Association,** 75-5663 Palani Rd., Kailua-Kona (808/329-3600), **Kona Activities** (808/325-7362 or 808/329-3171), or **Charter Service Hawaii** (808/325-7076). If you're on a budget, you can share a six-passenger charter boat on an eight-hour fishing trip for about $100.

OCEAN KAYAKING

Imagine sitting right at water level, in complete quiet, up-close-and-personal with dolphins, whales, and turtles—that's kayaking. Tomi Hynes of **Kona Kai-yaks,** Gentry's Kona Marine, Honokohau Small Boat Harbor (808/326-2922), says that anyone can kayak. After a few minutes of instruction in maneuvering the boat and a little practice in a calm area (like the lagoon in front of the King Kamehameha's Kona Beach Hotel), even neophytes can venture out exploring. Beginners can practice their skills in Kailua and Kealakekua bays; intermediates by paddle from Honokohau Harbor to Kona Coast Beach Park; experienced kayakers can paddle into Waipio Valley (often through heavy surf) and travel up the river.

Kayaking can be done year-round, especially in Kona's calm waters. You can rent equipment from Kona Kai-yaks for as little as $8 an hour or $20 a day, depending on the type of equipment, which varies from one- and two-person kayaks and from wave-surfing models to larger, roomy vehicles for carrying camping and diving equipment.

PARASAILING

Maybe in your dreams you've been there: floating high above the ocean, gliding on the winds, taking in the majestic view. Well, here's your chance for your dream to come true. **Kona Water Sports,** Banyan Court Mall, 75-5695-G Alii Dr., Kailua-Kona (808/329-1593) says that 95% of the customers who sign up for the 10-minute ride at 300 to 600 feet in the air take one look at the view and forget all their fears. In fact, many of them express dismay that the ride went by so quickly. **UFO Parasail of Kailua-Kona,** P.O. Box 5438, Kailua-Kona (☎ 808/ 325-5836), also offers rides over scenic Kailua Bay. The price of making your dreams come true is about $40 for 10 minutes in the sky.

SAILING

Glide along the ocean as dolphins race to play in the wake of one of the Big Island's sailboat cruisers. Sailboats may be chartered from Honokohau Harbor, Keauhou Bay, Kawaihae Harbor, Waikoloa, and Kailua Pier. The trips range from one-hour sails to day-long adventures. Some include snorkeling, diving, and swimming, some just sightseeing (and, in the winter months, whale watching). Meals can range from snacks to sunset dinners. The boats themselves come in all sizes and makes, from racing sailboats to motorized ones with sails more for decoration than function. For an exhilarating ocean sail, with the wind in your hair as you fly along the water, try **Makani Kai Charters,** P.O. Box 3249, Kailua-Kona (☎ 808/ 329-7200). This 35-foot catamaran was used in the Elvis Presley film *Blue Hawaii.* Now owned by Ron Clark, one of Kona's friendliest skippers, Makani Kai has been completely restored. Ron takes small parties out and is happy to share his knowledge and love of the ocean.

SCUBA DIVING

If you are going to the Big Island and you love the ocean, learn to scuba dive before you arrive. No matter where you live, you can learn diving fundamentals from local dive shops or the YMCA. That way you don't "waste" your vacation learning the essential skills of scuba diving—you can just jump right in and begin to explore the kaleidoscopic underwater world awaiting you.

The lee coast of the Big Island offers some of the best diving in the world because the waters are calm, warm (75 to 81 degrees), and clear (visibility is 100-plus-feet year round). There's dive adventure here to fulfill nearly every fantasy. Want to swim with fast-moving game fish? Try Ulua Cave at the northern end of the Kohala Coast (*Ulua* is the Hawaiian name for giant trevally). How about

---

Unlimited Dives—and Swimming with Sharks, Too: The Liveaboard Kona Aggressor II

For divers who just can't get enough time underwater, we've got a solution for you: a liveaboard dive boat, the 80-foot *Kona Aggressor II,* 75-5588 Pawai Pl., Kailua-Kona (☎ 808/329-8182), which offers divers four- to seven-day diving trips—with unlimited diving opportunities—along 85 miles of Big Island coastline. The cost of a week of diving (including accommodations, meals, and beverages) is $1,795 per person—and it's worth every penny. And, if you're lucky, your liveaboard dive trip might be the stuff that dreams— or nightmares—are made of: Sometimes, these trips include close encounters with sharks from the protection of the *Kona Aggressor II*'s shark cage. Photograph to your heart's content or just watch in awe as the feared creatures of the deep come within inches of your protective cage.

—*Jeanette Foster*

a dramatic underwater encounter with large, feeding manta rays? Manta Ray Village, located outside Keauhou Bay off the Kona Surf Resort, is a proven spot.

There are a dozen dive operators on the west side of the Big Island, plus one in Hilo. They offer everything from scuba certification courses (you must be certified to dive, although some operators will offer an "intro" dive), to guided-boat dives. One of Kona's most popular dive operators is **Kona Coast Divers,** 75-5614 Palani Rd., Kailua-Kona (☎ 808/329-8802). Kona's oldest five-star PADI facility is run by Jim and Julie Robinson. You can't miss their shop, a lighthouse-shaped building located a half mile from Kailua Bay. The shop has everything: classrooms and a pool for training, gear rental, retail sales, and charter boat dives. Scuba-diving magazines have consistently rated Kona Coast Divers as one of the best outfitters in the world. A two-tank dive off one of their custom dive boats costs about $70; swimming with manta rays on a night dive—the experience of a lifetime—is $55; and certification courses run $200 to $300. Dive operators in the Kohala Coast area include **Red Sail Sports,** located at both the Hilton Waikoloa Village, Kohala Coast (☎ 808/885-2876), and at the Ritz-Carlton Mauna Lani, Kohala Coast (☎ 808/885-2000); and **Sea Adventure** at the Mauna Lani Bay Resort (☎ 808/885-7883).

SNORKELING

The close-to-shore waters around the Big Island—especially along the Kona and Kohala coasts—are home to some of the most spectacular marine life in the state. If you come to Hawaii and don't snorkel, you haven't really seen all that paradise has to offer. Snorkeling can be done year-round in the calm waters off the west side. Beach concessions at all the resorts, tour desks, and dive shops offer equipment rentals and lessons for beginning snorkelers. Some of the best snorkeling areas in the Kona-Kohala coast include Hookena, Honaunau, Keei, Kealakekua, Kahaluu, White Sands, Old Airport, Kona Coast State Park, Puako, Hapuna, and Spencer beach parks.

Gear rental is about $15 a week (including mask, fins, and snorkel); prices go up slightly for prescription masks and high-end snorkels. Dive shops and marine operators include **Kona Coast Divers,** 75-5614 Palani Rd., Kailua-Kona (☎ 808/ 329-8802); **Snorkel Bob's,** 75-5831 Kahakai Rd., Kailua-Kona (☎ 808/ 329-0770); **Red Sail Sports,** located at the Hilton Waikoloa Village, Kohala Coast (☎ 808/885-2876), and Ritz-Carlton Mauna Lani, Kohala Coast (☎ 808/ 885-2000); and **Sea Adventure,** Mauna Lani Bay Resort (☎ 808/885-7883).

Some of the most outstanding diving spots can only be reached by boat. Kona has several operators that combine sail or motorized cruises of the coast with snorkeling adventures. Kona's longest running cruise operator is **Captain Cook Cruises,** 74-5606 Pawai Pl., Kailua-Kona (☎ 808/329-6411). The four-hour round trip cruise goes from Kailua Pier to Kealakekua Bay Marine Life Conservation District. The crew of the 149-passenger boat will teach you how to snorkel and will provide all the necessary gear. In addition, a continental breakfast and lunch are served. For those not up to snorkeling, there's a large glass-bottom viewing area. The cost for the half-day cruise (including meals) is $54 for adults and $27 for children.

Another excellent snorkeling-sailing cruise is aboard the *Fair Wind* from Keauhou Bay, 78-7128 Kaleopapa Rd., Keauhou (☎ 808/322-2788). Although this large catamaran is certified for 149 passengers, the vessel only loads 100 people to make sure that everyone has plenty of space to enjoy the cruise to the marine park in Kealakekua Bay. Continental breakfast and buffet lunch are served on the 4^1/$_2$-hour morning cruise; a mid-afternoon snack is provided on the 3^1/$_2$-hour afternoon cruise. Snorkeling lessons and gear are also provided. The cruises are enjoyable for everyone, even non-snorkelers. In addition to snorkeling gear, inner tubes and underwater viewers are provided for those who are not confident in the water.

SNUBA

If you're not quite ready to make the commitment to Scuba (Self Contained Underwater Breathing Apparatus), yet are desirous of more time underwater than snorkeling allows, Snuba may be the answer for you. Lynn Ekstrom of **Big Island Snuba,** 74-5660 Palani Rd., Kailua-Kona (☎ 808/326-7446) says Snuba consists of a tank that floats on the surface; a hose connects the tank to a diver's regulator and enables a diver to stay at about 20 to 25 feet underwater. With just 15 minutes of instruction, neophytes can be in the water enjoying the marine life. Snuba can actually be easier than snorkeling on the surface because the water is calmer beneath the surface. The cost for Snuba is $50–$55 for a 45-minute dive, either from the beach or aboard a boat (the cost of the boat ride is extra). If you are in the Kohala area, you can snuba with **Mauna Kea Divers,** P.O. Box 44315, Kamuela (☎ 808/882-7730).

SUBMARINE DIVING

If taking a personal plunge doesn't thrill you but you would love to get a glimpse of Jacques Cousteau's watery world, try going under in an 80-ton submarine. Daily trips in Kailua Bay view clouds of tropical fish, fast-moving ulua, and maybe a shark, if you're lucky. **Atlantis Submarine** at the Hotel King Kamehameha, Kailua-Kona (☎ 808/329-6626) provides very professional service. A shuttle boat takes passengers out to the submarine from Kailua Pier. The sub explores the reef—going as deep as 150 feet—giving passengers a view through large windows of Neptune's world. At some point in the 45-minute dive, a scuba diver will swim alongside feeding the tropical fish, bringing the hungry critters right up next to the viewing portholes. Even experienced divers enjoy the ride. The cost of an Atlantis trip is $79 for adults and $39 for children; no children under 3 feet tall are allowed.

SURFING

Called the sport of kings, surfing includes paddling out (no mean feat itself!), matching the speed of a wave as it rolls into shore, and riding this untamed power as long as Mother Nature will allow. Most of the surfing on the Big Island is best left to surfers of some experience, but there are a few sites for novices. Surfing lessons cost about $30 an hour and surfboard rentals are $15 for the day. For lessons and rentals in Kona, check out **Hobie Sports Kona,** Kona Inn Shopping Village (☎ 808/329-1001) and **Pacific Vibrations,** 75-5702 Alii Dr., (☎ 808/329-4140). On the Kohala Coast, call **Ocean Sports,** Royal Waikoloan Hotel (☎ 808/885-5555).

Experienced surfers should check out the waves at Pine Trees (north of Kailua-Kona), Lyman's, and Kahaluu (the shoreline along Alii Drive in Kona) on the west side, and Hilo Bay Front Park and Keaukaha Beach Park on the east side.

WHALE WATCHING

From December to April, Hawaii's most impressive visitors—45-foot humpback whales—come to spend the winter. Captain Dan McSweeney has been studying different species of whales in the waters off Kona for more than 20 years. He doesn't just host whale-watching trips during the winter months; he offers **Captain Dan McSweeney's Year-Round Whale Watching,** P.O. Box 139, Holualoa (☎ 808/322-0028). Captain Dan is basically a whale researcher who has opened up his research operation to the public. He is on board every trip, conducting research and letting his passengers know what is going on with these mammoth leviathans. During the humpback season, the boat makes two 3 1/2-hour trips a day; during the remainder of the year he schedules one morning trip a day. Since Captain Dan works with the whales daily, he has no problem finding them and frequently drops a hydrophone (underwater microphone) into the water to listen to their songs. If the whales aren't singing, he may use his underwater video camera to show you what's going on via a monitor aboard the boat.

During the summer and fall, the "other" cetaceans Captain Dan concentrates on are pilot, sperm, false killer, melon-headed, pygmy killer, and beaked whales. Captain Dan said these tours are often more popular than the humpback tours because these whales are found in pods of 20 to 40 animals and are very social, interacting with each other on the surface. The cost of the whale cruise is $39.50 for adults and $29.50 for children. There are no cruises from May 1 to June 30 (Captain Dan goes to Alaska to do humpback whale research there).

WINDSURFING

On the Big Island, Anaehoomalu is one of the best beaches for windsurfing. Nailima Ahuna, a windsurfing instructor at **Ocean Sports,** Royal Waikoloan Hotel, Kohala Coast (☎ 808/885-5555), says that learning to windsurf is easy; the only requirement is that you weigh at least 75 pounds. Anaehoomalu is a particularly good spot to learn windsurfing because there are constant 5- to 25-knot winds blowing onshore (toward the beach), so if you get in trouble the wind brings you back to shore (instead of taking you out to sea). Ocean Sports has instruction ($35 an hour) and equipment rental ($20 an hour or $85 for five hours). Ahuna says that he starts beginners on a land simulator to teach them how to handle the sail and how to turn around. After about 15 minutes of instruction on land, they're ready to hit the water and sail away. Since Anaehoomalu Bay usually only has 15 to 20 windsurfers in the water at one time, beginners have plenty of room. More advanced windsurfers should try Puako and Hilo Bay.

3 Hiking, Golf & Other Outdoor Activities

By Jeanette Foster

HIKING

Hikers get to enjoy another face of the Big Island, one that strict water or coastline enthusiasts miss. Many tourists drive through Hawaii Volcanoes National Park and past the island's rain forests, and venture only to the easily accessible beaches. But hikers—both day-hikers and backpackers—get to step into the heart of a still-active volcano, experience the quiet solitude of the tropical rain forest, trek to remote, hidden beaches. They see the side of Hawaii that can only be experienced off-road, in the backcountry.

For information on hiking to these hidden treasures on the Big Island, contact **Hawaii Volcanoes National Park,** P.O. Box 52, Volcano, HI 96718 (☎ 808/ 967-7311), **Puuhonua-O-Honaunau National Historic Park,** Honaunau, HI 96726 (☎ 808/328-2326), **State Division of Forestry and Wildlife,** P.O. Box 4849, Hilo, HI 96720 (☎ 808/933-4221), **State Division of Parks,** P.O. Box 936, Hilo, HI 96721 (☎ 808/933-4200), and **County Department of Parks and Recreation,** 25 Aupuni Street, Hilo, HI 96720 (☎ 808/961-8311). In addition, the **Hawaiian Trail and Mountain Club** (P.O. Box 2238, Honolulu, HI 96804) offers an information packet on hiking and camping in Hawaii. Send $1.25 and a self-addressed, stamped legal-size envelope to them for information. Another good source of information is the *Hiking/Camping Information Packet* from **Hawaii Geographic Maps and Books,** 49 S. Hotel Street, Suite 218, Honolulu, HI 96813 (☎ 808/538-3952), available at a cost of $7 (postage included).

For guided day hikes, contact Dr. Hugh Montgomery of **Hawaiian Walkways,** P.O. Box 2193, Kamuela, HI 96743 (☎ 808/855-7759 or 800/457-7759). A life-long resident of Hawaii, Hugh offers a variety of half-day and full-day hikes ranging from shoreline trail hikes to explore ancient Hawaiian petroglyphs to hikes up 13,000-foot Mauna Kea to Lake Waiau, one of the highest lakes in the world. Half-day hikes start at $60; full-day hikes, which include lunch, are $100. For information on longer trips and alternative kinds of trips, see "Adventure Tours," below.

Some of the more interesting hikes on the Big Island include:

KILAUEA IKI TRAIL

Located in the Hawaii Volcanoes National Park, this 5-mile trail, which also takes in Byron Ledge, begins at the park headquarters. It's a fair-to-moderate walk; people with respiratory problems should be aware that fumes from the vents may cause problems. Allow four hours, because you'll want to stop and admire the work of the volcano goddess, Pele. The main reason to take this hike is to experience firsthand the result of a volcanic eruption. Kilauea Iki is famous for the "fountain of fire" eruption in 1959, when a lava fountain spurting up to 1,900 feet put on a spectacular display for 36 days. When you join the trail, you descend through a forest of tree ferns before connecting to the Byron Ledge Trail, which offers a close-up view of the Kilauea Crater. After the quick Byron Loop, the trail wanders down the wall of the Kilauea Iki Crater and actually goes onto the crater floor itself and past the 1959 vent. You'll see ohelo bushes, which have bright red berries in the summer. According to legend, you must offer some of the berries to Pele before eating any yourself, or you may suffer her wrath. Across the crater floor, past the steam vents, the trail starts up the wall via a series of switchbacks. At the top is a small loop through the Thurston Lava Tube.

KIPUKA PUAULU (BIRD PARK)

This trail offers a wonderful opportunity to see native Hawaiian flora and fauna and to experience a *kipuka,* an area that was missed—perhaps even surrounded— by a lava flow. This easy walk begins at a well-marked trailhead at Mauna Loa Road. It's 1.2 miles long; even if you dally, it shouldn't take more than an hour. You might want to stop by the park headquarters first and get a booklet by the Hawaii Natural History Association that describes all the plant life that the National Parks Service has painstakingly labeled on the trail. At the trailhead there's a display of some of the plants and birds you'll see. Go early in the morning or in the evening (or even better, just after a rain) to see some of the native birds. Two of the more common birds are the *apapane* and *iiwi*. The apapane is a small bright red bird with black wings and tail; it loves the nectar of the red-blossomed ohia lehua trees, so look for it there. The iiwi has the same colors but is much larger and has a curved bill. Some of the native trees you see on the trail are giant *ohia*, *koa*, soapberry, *kolea*, and *mamani*. Be sure to close the gate at the entrance—it's there to keep out the wild pigs that would otherwise destroy the native plants.

AKAKA FALLS

Don't pass up this easy half-mile loop into an enchanted tropical rain forest with views of two of the most impressive waterfalls in all of Hawaii. Go even if it is raining; on rainy days, the fragrance of the rain forest flowers are made stronger, and the mist makes the entire walk surreal.

The trail is maintained by the State Parks Division. To get there, take Hi. 19 about 11 miles north of Hilo; take the turn off to Akaka Falls State Park and follow the road 3.7 miles to the parking lot. The loop trail can be followed either clockwise or counterclockwise. Either way, the trail wanders through a canopy of dense tropical rain forest, passing by blood-red ginger, sweet-smelling plumeria, exotic banana plants, lush hapu ferns, and startling birds of paradise. The sound of water falling is everywhere. *Kahuna* Falls (the Hawaiian word for priest or wise man), a spectacular 100-foot thundering wonder, is really just the warm-up act. *Akaka* Falls (the Hawaiian word for clear or luminous) is the star attraction; it cascades some 420 feet into the Kolekole Stream, which is lined with fragrant white and yellow ginger. Along the trail, the Parks Department has placed benches for those who would like to rest or just take some time to soak up the beauty. At the top of the trail are restrooms, a drinking fountain, and picnic tables overhung with orchids from the trees overhead.

WAIPIO AND WAIMANU VALLEY (MULIWAI TRAIL)

This is a very difficult trail, going from sea level to 1,350 feet and back to sea level. It will take more than 9 hours to hike in and more than 10 hours to hike out, so I recommend that you allow at least two to three days for this adventure. Your reward for taking on this hike is an opportunity to experience the Hawaii of Captain Cook's day, over 200 years ago. Virgin waterfalls and pools, spectacular views, and a chance to merge with the environment are the reasons hikers return here time and time again. When you stand at the Waipio Valley Lookout and look down into the valley, you'll feel as if you've discovered Eden.

During the winter rainy season, or anytime that it's raining or even threatening a storm, you shouldn't attempt this hike. You'll have to cross 13 streams before you reach the rim of Waimanu Valley, and rain increases the likelihood of flash floods. Also, you must get permission to camp in Waimanu Valley from the Division of Forestry and Wildlife, P.O. Box 4849, Hilo, HI 96720-0849 (☎ 808/933-4221).

To get to the trailhead, take Hi. 19 to the turnoff for Honokaa. From Honokaa, drive 9¹/₂ miles to the Waipio Valley Lookout. Unless you have a four-wheel drive vehicle, this is where your hike will begin. Walk down the road and wade the Wailoa Steam, cross the beach and go to the northwest wall; the trail starts here. The trail goes up the valley floor, past a swamp, and into a forest before beginning a series of switchbacks that parallel the coastline. These switchbacks go up and down about 14 gulches before reaching Waimanu Valley. At the ninth gulch, about two-thirds of the way along the trail, is a shelter. After the shelter, the trail descends into Waimanu Valley, which looks like a smaller version of Waipio Valley but without any signs of human intrusion. Be prepared for clouds of hungry mosquitoes and be on the lookout for wild pigs—they can be dangerous.

GOLF

Because the Big Island is so young (comparatively speaking, of course), many of the golf courses are actually carved out of lava flows. Gigantic earthmoving equipment takes barren, rocky fields and turns them into spectacular fairways, manicured greens, and cunningly placed bunkers and water hazards. All the golf courses listed below require cart rental; the fee for cart rental is included in the greens fee.

MAUNA KEA BEACH GOLF COURSE

Once a wasteland of lava and scrub, this Robert Trent Jones championship course is consistently rated one of the top golf courses in the United States. Located on the grounds of the Mauna Kea Beach Resort on the Kohala Coast, this par-72, 7,114-yard challenge is breathtakingly beautiful. The signature 3rd hole is 175 yards long (and a shocking par-3), but the Pacific Ocean and shoreline cliffs stand between the tee and the green, giving every golfer, from beginner to pro, a real opportunity to improve their game. Another par-3 that confounds golfers is the 11th hole, which drops 100 feet from tee to green and plays down to the ocean, into the steady trade winds. When the trades are blowing, 181 yards might as well be 1,000 yards. Greens fees are $80 for hotel guests and $130 for non-guests. Other facilities include putting greens, a driving range, lockers and showers, a pro shop, and a restaurant serving excellent sandwiches. For tee times or more information call 808/822-7222 or 808/882-5888. Call early, as the course is popular, especially for early weekend tee times.

HAPUNA GOLF COURSE

Since its opening in 1992, this 18-hole championship course on the grounds of the Hapuna Prince Resort, next door to the Mauna Kea Beach Resort, has won numerous awards, including *Golf Magazine* awards as "most environmentally sensitive" course and one of the "top ten new courses in the nation." The U.S. Golf Association named it "The Course of the Future." Well, the future is here, and it's a 6,027-yard, links-style course that extends from the shoreline to 700 feet above sea level, with views of the pastoral green hills of the Kohala Mountains and sweeping vistas of the Kohala coastline. Designed by Arnold Palmer and Ed Seay, the elevation changes on the course may bother some golfers (not to mention the winds at the higher elevations), but it's nothing that practice won't take care of. There are few elevated tee boxes and only 40 bunkers. Facilities for this resort course include putting green, driving range, lockers and showers, pro shop, and restaurant. Greens fees are $80 for guests and $130 for non-guests. This course gets crowded on weekends, so reserve early. For reservations and tee times, call 808/882-1111.

WAIKOLOA GOLF COURSES

The Waikoloa Beach Course was designed by Robert Trent Jones, Jr., who has carried on his father's approach to design: "Hard par, easy bogey." Most golfers will remember the par-5 12th hole, at 505 yards from the back tee. An elevated tee surrounded by lava with bunkers at the corner, it plays to a sharp dogleg left.

The Waikoloa King's Course is about 500 yards longer. Designed by Tom Weiskopf and Jay Morrish, the links-style King's Course features a double green at the 3rd and 6th holes and several carefully placed bunkers that make the most of the ever-present trade winds. Greens fees are $80 for hotel guests and $95 for non-guests. Facilities include a pro shop and showers. This is a very popular course with local residents, so book early. For information and reservations, call 808/885-6060 or 808/885-4647.

OTHER OUTDOOR ACTIVITIES

The Big Island has plenty of space for pursuit of your favorite sport or recreational activity (it is, after all, the largest island in the chain). There are miles of roadways and trails to explore on bicycle, acres of wilderness to hunt in, and two 13,000-foot volcanoes to ski down. From riding a horse on remote mountain trails to cheering on paddlers in a Hawaiian outrigger canoe race, the Big Island offers all the outdoor activities you could want.

BICYCLING

For mountain-bike and cross-training bike rentals in Kona, see **Dave's Bike and Triathlon Shop,** Alii Dr., (☎ 808/329-4522). On the Kohala coast, check out the range of available bikes for rent from **Red Sail Sports,** at either the Hilton Waikoloa Village (☎ 808/885-2876) or the Ritz-Carlton Mauna Lani (☎ 808/885-2000). Bike rentals start at $5 an hour or $15 a day. Be sure to wear a protective helmet when cycling; even the famed Ironman Triathlon requires its participants to wear one not only during the race, but also during training.

HORSEBACK RIDING

From galloping along a deserted beach to carefully climbing remote forest trails, horseback riding opportunities on the Big Island offer something for everyone, from first time riders to experts. **Paniolo Riding Adventure** in Waimea (☎ 808/889-5334) has a range of different rides to suit any riding ability. They provide leather chaps, oilskin dusters, and saddles (covered with foam and fleece). They even have mules—which offer a smoother, more surefooted ride—for nervous riders. Rides begin at $70 for a 2^{1}/2-hour trip with views of the Kona and Kohala coasts. More advanced riders should call **King's Trail Rides O' Kona,** 111-mile marker, Hi. 11, Kealakekua (☎ 808/323-2388). They have been taking visitors on rides down to the Captain Cook Monument in Kealakekua Bay since 1989. The trips are limited to four people and wander down the mountain to the sea, where the riders stop to have lunch and take a quick dip in the ocean. Snorkeling gear and lunch are included in the $95 cost.

SKIING

Believe it or not, you can ski—yes, on snow—on the Big Island. The season is from Thanksgiving until the snow melts; one year it was still good enough for skiing on the Fourth of July. **Ski Guides Hawaii,** P.O. Box 1954, Kamuela, HI 96743 (☎ 808/885-4188) say that, in general, skiing can be enjoyed December through April, with February and March as the best months. They provide complete package tours: transportation from Waimea to the summit (there are no ski lifts on the mountain), guide service (there are no marked trails either), and lunch for $150 for an eight-hour day. Equipment rental and exclusive guided tours are also available. However, they do not take beginning skiers out, as Mauna Kea is not the place to learn how to ski. There actually are a couple of skiing events every year (depending on the snow, of course). In February there's the Annual Hawaii Ski Cup on Mauna Kea; in March, it's the Pele's Cup Mauna Loa Cross Country. Call 808/737-4394 for information on both events.

SPECTATOR SPORTS

Two of the most popular spectator sports on the Big Island are Hawaii outrigger canoe racing and polo. Every weekend, from Memorial Day to Labor Day, canoe races are held here. Hundreds of residents from children to grandparents participate in the island-wide canoe races, held at different harbors and bays every week. For information on the canoe race schedule, check the local papers or call 808/961-5797.

Also during the summer months, from May to August, is the Big Island polo season. Spend a pleasant afternoon picnicking on a grassy lawn as the polo players from nearby ranches compete. For information on times and places of polo matches, contact the **Waikii Ranch,** 808/885-9885.

Other spectator sports scheduled during the year include:

CANOE RACING   In addition to the regular Hawaiian Outrigger Canoe Racing season, teams from around the world come to Hawaii in September to compete in the Queen Liliuokalani World Championship Long Distance Canoe Race, the largest outrigger canoe race in the world. For information call 808/323-2565.

FISHING   Hawaii's most prestigious fishing tournament is the 38-year-old Hawaiian International Billfish Tournament, which takes places in Kailua-Kona in August with teams from around the world competing. For information call 808/329-6105.

GOLF   The Senior Skins Tournament, a televised golf tournament featuring big-name pro players, takes place in January at the Mauna Lani Resort. For information call 808/885-6655.

Exercise (and be Pampered) by the Sea at the Lotus Center

Would you like to do Yogaerobics, Chi-Kung Energetics, or Tai Chi Ch'uan in a lovely oceanside setting? You can, thanks to the Lotus Center, a spa at the Royal Kona Resort that presents $5 open classes weekday mornings in the oceanside lawn just north of Huggo's Restaurant on Alii Drive. Monday and Friday from 7:30 to 8:30am it's Yogaerobics; Tuesday, Wednesday, and Thursday it's Chi-Kung Energetics; and Tuesday, Wednesday, and Thursday from 10 to 11 am, it's Tai Chi Chu'an. Lotus Center focuses on a wholistic approach to body, mind, and spirit. And if you have time—and feel like a splurge—treat yourself to one of their splendid massage or spa treatments, including Hawaiian lomi lomi and shiatsu massage, Ayurvedic herbal facials (Ayurveda is an ancient Indian healing science and Ayurvedic services and products are much in vogue now in natural healing circles), hot herbal wraps, aromatherapy, and much more. A half-hour massage is $35, a one-hour massage $60, a half-hour hot herbal wrap $40, and a full body seaweed mask (1 hour) $80. They also have ongoing exercise classes, chiropractic service, wholistic workshops, and a New Age book and gift shop. For more information and appointments, and to check the current class schedule, call 808/334-0445.

—Faye Hammel

RODEO   In July, Hawaiian cowboys gather at the Parker Ranch Rodeo and Horse Races in Waimea. For information call 808/885-7655.

RUNNING   The Big Island hosts two "ultramarathons": one in January, the 31-mile Ultramarathon and Relay from Hilo to Volcano, during which runners race up the slopes of Mauna Loa and through Hawaii Volcanoes National Park; for information call 808/965-9191. In April, there's the Saddle Road 100km Ultramarathon and Relay, an easy 62.1-mile foot race from Hilo to Waimea; for information call 808/961-3415.

TRIATHLON   The Ironman Triathlon World Championship takes place in Kona every October. It consists of a mere 2.4-mile swim, followed by a 112-mile bike race, and winds down with a 26.2-mile marathon. For information call 808/329-0063.

TENNIS

You can play for free at any Hawaii County tennis court; for a detailed list of all the courts on the island, contact the **Hawaii County Department of Parks and Recreation,** 25 Apuni St., Hilo, 96720 (☎ 808/935-8213). The best courts are in Hilo at the Hoolulu Tennis Stadium, located next to the Civic Auditorium on Manono Street. In Kona, the best courts are at the Old Airport Park. Most of the resorts in the Kona-Kohala area do not allow non-guests to use their tennis facilities. However, two hotels in Kona that do offer court rentals are **Hotel King Kamehameha's Kona Beach Hotel,** 75-5660 Palani Rd. (☎ 808/329-2911), and **Keauhou Beach Hotel,** 78-6740 Alii Dr. (☎ 808/322-4237). Courts are $5 per person, per hour. Equipment rental and lessons are also available.

4 Adventure Tours

✪ Hawaii Forest & Trail
P.O. Box 2975, Kailua-Kona, HI 96745. ☎ or Fax **808/239-1993.**

If you'd like to discover natural Hawaii off the beaten path—but don't necessarily want to sleep under a tree to do it—here's your ticket. Naturalist and educator Rob Pacheco will take you out for day trips in his plush four-wheel drive Suburban to some of the Big Island's most remote, pristine natural areas. Rob has exclusive access into private and state land holdings that harbor some of Hawaii's best intact ecosystems, so he can show you truly native areas of the island that otherwise are inaccessible. Rob fully narrates his trips, offering extensive natural, geological, and cultural history interpretations (and not just a little humor). Since he only takes a maximum of seven people, his trips are highly personalized to meet each group's interests and abilities.

Rob offers day trips into the Pu'u o'o Ranch Rainforest, to the Hualalai Volcano (which Rob calls Hawaii's "best-kept secret"), into the Hakalau Forest National Wildlife Refuge, Hawaii Volcanoes National Park (where he'll take you hiking through a lava tube and right up to the oozing flow after dark, when the lava is most spectacular—conditions permitting, of course), and to other south Kona private access areas. He also offers customized trips (from one to several days) for birders, families, and other private groups. There are about three to four hours of easy-to-moderate walking, over terrain manageable by anyone in average physical condition, on each day trip.

Full-day trips are $119 per adult, $95 for children ages 13 to 17, and $65 for children ages 4 to 12; children under 3 are free. Rob offers a private group rate of $549 for up to six guests, with an additional charge of $50 per person for one or two more. All prices include pickup and drop-off, continental breakfast, lunch, snacks, water and other beverages, and the use of binoculars, daypacks, walking staffs, any necessary outerwear, access charges, and tax. Charges are less for half-day trips. Call for a schedule of trips offered while you're on the Big Island. This is an adventure definitely worth the splurge—it might well be the highlight of your entire trip.

Eye of the Whale, Marine/Wilderness Adventures
P.O. Box 1269, Kapaau, HI 96755. ☎ **808/889-0227,** or toll free 800/659-3544.

With a goal of promoting understanding of Hawaii's delicate ecosystem through firsthand experience, Beth and Mark Goodoni lead 6- to 10-day hiking and hiking/sailing adventures for groups of no more than 10 people. Days are spent outdoors, hiking through mountain valleys and jungles or sailing the Big Island's Kona coast. Nights are spent either on boats (for sailing trips) or in B&Bs; there's no backpacking or camping. Beth, a marine biologist and seasoned naturalist, introduces participants to the natural history of Hawaii, emphasizing the origin and identification of tropical flora, the development and exploration of coral-reef ecosystems, and the biology and observation of marine mammals. On the boat, she's the crew; husband Mark is the licensed USCG captain. Cost is about $150 per day, including meals, accommodations, transportation, and inter-island fares. A highlight of the trip is a private luau, where guests learn to dig the imu, string their own leis, and dance the old-time hulas.

5 Touring Hilo & Environs

The best way to see Hilo and the surrounding area is on a driving tour. Below are two tours. It's possible to do both in one day if you're pressed for time.

DRIVING TOUR 1

Start: Hilo Tropical Gardens.
Finish: Reed's Bay Park.
Time: 2 to 4 hours, depending on how long you spend at major stops.
Best Time: Early mornings, to see as much as possible.
Worst Time: Late afternoon.

Our first tour of Hilo begins with a visit to:

1. **Hilo Tropical Gardens.** Follow Hi. 19 to the eastern strip of town; you'll find the gardens at 1477 Kalanianaole Ave., about 2 miles from the airport. Paved walkways (accessible to the disabled) lead you through a tiny jungle of tropical flowers, shrubs and trees, splendid orchids, native Hawaiian plants and herbs, past water lily pools, waterfalls, even a Japanese pond with a footbridge and statuary. After you've seen the gardens and used up a little bit of film, stop in at their gift shop for Hawaiian handcrafts, wood products, and, of course, flowers. Anything can be shipped home. Admission is $3. Open daily from 8:30am to sunset. Call 808/935-4957 for driving directions.

Make your way back to town, now, toward Hilo Bay, where you'll soon spot the:

2. **Wailoa Center,** whose building resembles a volcano. Located just behind the state office building, it features free exhibits ranging from cultural to natural history, and a permanent exhibit on tsunamis (tidal waves). Services and admission are free. For information, phone 808/933-4360. The entrance is on Piopio Street, between the state office building and Kamehameha Avenue. Open Monday, Tuesday, Thursday, and Friday from 8am to 4:30pm, on Wednesday from noon to 8:30pm, and on Saturday from 9am to 3pm. From here it's not far to the:

3. **Suisan Fish Market,** where the freshest fish in town can be found. Weekdays at 8am the fishermen's catch is lined up and auctioned off to restaurants and grocery stores around the island. The public is invited. Don't miss the opportunity not only to experience this fast-paced auction, but also to see the magnificent bounty of Hawaii's waters: huge marlin, tunas weighing over 200 pounds, prehistoric-looking broadbill swordfish, and many other species. Coming up soon is the:

4. **Nihon Japanese Culture Center,** at 123 Lihiwai Street. In addition to serving authentic and excellent Japanese cuisine (see "Where to Eat," in Chapter 13), the center has an art gallery, a tearoom, and music, dancing, films, and other entertainment. Check to see if anything special is going on. Coming up on your right is:

5. **Liliuokalani Gardens** with its lovely Japanese bridges, ponds, plants, and stone lanterns. It's believed to be the largest such formal Japanese garden and park outside of Japan. Look for the authentic Japanese tea ceremony house. On your left is:

6. **Coconut Island,** a favorite picnic spot for the local people. If you continue around the park, you'll find yourself on Banyan Drive, which takes you past many of the resort hotels in the city. The magnificent trees are labeled in honor of the celebrities who planted them: James A. Farley was one, Amelia Earhart another; Cecil B. DeMille has a tree, as does Mrs. De Mille. Continuing in the same direction you'll come to:

7. **Reed's Bay Park,** a cool picnic spot on the bay.

DRIVING TOUR 2

Start: Nani Mau Gardens.
Finish: Lyman House Memorial Museum Complex.
Time: 2 to 4 hours, depending on stops.
Best Time: Early morning, so that you can see Rainbow Falls at its best.
Worst Time: Late afternoon.

To see one of our favorite gardens, drive $3^{1}/_{2}$ miles south on Hi. 11 (the road to the volcano) from Hilo Airport, then turn left onto Makalika Street just after Hi. 11 divides. Note the word "Aloha" landscaped by the roadside, and you'll soon find:

1. **Nani Mau Gardens,** a wonderland of 20 acres of the fruits and flowers of many lands. An orchid house, a ginger/helicona garden, an anthurium garden, a botanical museum, a tropical water-lily and carp pond, an enclosed nursery, and waterfall and stream are also featured. You can tour the gardens by foot or on

Big Island Attractions at a Glance

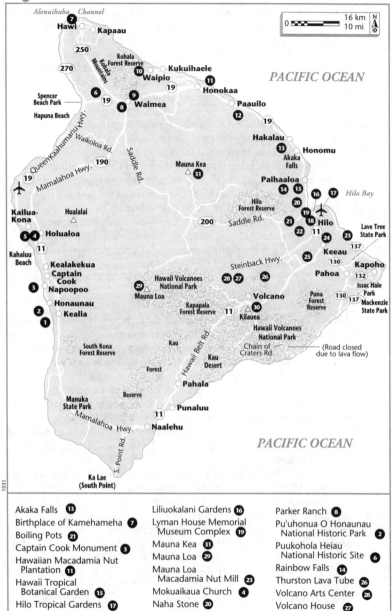

Akaka Falls **13**
Birthplace of Kamehameha **7**
Boiling Pots **21**
Captain Cook Monument **3**
Hawaiian Macadamia Nut Plantation **11**
Hawaii Tropical Botanical Garden **15**
Hilo Tropical Gardens **17**
Hulihee Palace **5**
Kalopa State Recreation Area **12**
Kamuela Museum **9**
Kaumana Cave **22**
Kilauea Iki Crater **30**

Liliuokalani Gardens **16**
Lyman House Memorial Museum Complex **19**
Mauna Kea **31**
Mauna Loa **29**
Mauna Loa Macadamia Nut Mill **23**
Mokuaikaua Church **4**
Naha Stone **20**
Nani Mau Gardens **24**
Nihon Japanese Cultural Center **18**
The Painted Church **1**
Panaewa Rain Forest Zoo **25**

Parker Ranch **8**
Pu'uhonua O Honaunau National Historic Park **2**
Puukohola Heiau National Historic Site **6**
Rainbow Falls **14**
Thurston Lava Tube **26**
Volcano Arts Center **28**
Volcano House **27**
Waipio Valley **10**

a tram ($4 per person). Lunch, available from 10:30am to 1:30pm features a buffet and made-to-order sandwiches. The gift shop is a good source for souvenir items, art posters by local artists, and USDA-certified plants and flowers to take back home. You can stay in the gardens as long as you like, to picnic or just relax. Open daily from 8am to 5pm, with an admission charge of $6.50. Call 808/959-3541 for information. Drive back up Hi. 11 and pick up Hi. 19. About 7 miles north of Hilo on the 4-mile scenic route at Onomea Bay, near Hi. 19, is the:

2. **Hawaii Tropical Botanical Garden,** a spectacular garden in a valley on the ocean—acclaimed as one of the most beautiful areas in Hawaii. Nature trails meander through a true tropical rain forest, cross streams and pass by spectacular waterfalls, and provide ocean vistas along the rugged coast. The garden's collection of tropical plants includes more than 2,000 different species collected from tropical jungles throughout the world. The garden won the coveted Kahili award for 1993 as the "Best Attraction" in the state of Hawaii. For serious students of nature and lovers of natural beauty—not to mention photographers—it's a paradise. Admission is $12 (children under 16 free), which is tax-deductible because the garden is a nonprofit foundation. It's open every day (except New Year's Day, Thanksgiving, and Christmas Day), rain or shine (they furnish umbrellas), from 8:30am to 4pm. Call 808/946-5233 for exact driving directions. No food is sold and there are no picnicking facilities.

On Hi. 11 just outside the city is the:

3. **Panaewa Rain Forest Zoo.** Turn right on the Stainback Highway and watch for signs on the right for the zoo. This is by no means the big time as zoos go; it's a small place, but with its own special Hawaiian charm. You'll see denizens of the South American rain forest, the rare Hawaiian nene (goose), the Hawaiian pueo (owl), many brightly plumaged birds, tigers wading through a jungle stream, and peacocks roaming the grounds; cutest of all are the monkeys, who seem to enjoy the funny humans walking about. (If you're short on time, skip this one.) Free admission. Open every day from 9am to 4:15pm.

Now it's time for some Kamehameha lore, since the Big Island is where that doughty old warrior was born and where he first started dreaming his dreams of glory and conquest.

Continue driving on Kamehameha Avenue, turn left onto Waianuenue Street, and drive three blocks to the modern county library on the right side. See the two stones out in front? The bigger one is the:

4. **Naha Stone,** Kamehameha's Excalibur. According to Naha legend, only a chief of the royal blood could even budge the gigantic boulder; any warrior strong enough to turn it over would have the strength to conquer and unify all the islands of Hawaii. Kamehameha did the deed, but since the stone weighs at least a ton, no one has bothered, as yet, to repeat it. Off Waianuenue Avenue at Rainbow Drive is:

5. **Rainbow Falls.** The best time to see this sight is early in the morning: Try to come between 9:15 and 10am, when the sun gets up high enough over the mango trees so that you might see rainbows forming in the mist. It's pretty at any time, however, and so are the beautiful yellow flowers growing near the parking lot. Continue along Waianuenue about 2 miles to Peepee Street to the:

6. **Boiling Pots,** deep pools that appear to be boiling as turbulent water flows over the lava bed of the river. From the parking lot you can walk over to the edge and observe the show below. Both Rainbow Falls and the Boiling Pots are part

of the Wailuku River State Park. Return to the fork at Hi. 20 and turn right onto the other branch of the fork, Kaumana Drive. About 3 miles out is:

7. Kaumana Cave, where you can see some of the work of Pele at close range. The cave is a lava tube, created in 1881, when Pele came closer to wiping out Hilo than at any other time. Lava tubes are sometimes formed when lava flows down a ravine or gully; the top and sides cool while the center keeps racing along. Millions of years of volcanic eruptions have left hollow tubes like this all over the islands; in many of them are hidden the bones of the alii, which were always buried in remote, secret places. Of the two tubes here, only the one on the right—whose entrance is an exquisite fern grotto—is safe for exploration.

The one on the left is treacherous, and who knows—perhaps the bones of Kamehameha, never discovered, are buried here.

Retrace your steps to Kamehameha Avenue, and turn onto Haili Street in a mauka direction (away from the bay and uphill); cross Keawe, Kinoole, and Ululani Streets, and on the left-hand side you'll see:

8. Haili Church. Its architecture is pure New England, but its fame stems from its great Hawaiian choir. Continuing up Haili Street from the Haili Church, cross Kapiolani Street, and on the right-hand side you'll find the:

9. Lyman House Memorial Museum Complex, at 276 Haili St. The original Lyman House is another of those old mission homes that the grandchildren and great-grandchildren turned into a museum; this one, originally built in 1839, has been fully restored and furnished as a home of the late 19th century. The white-frame building, Hilo's oldest structure, contains hand-molded New England glass windows, doors made of native koa wood, and the original wide koa floorboards. As you tour the rooms, you'll see how the missionary family lived: the clothes, old four-poster beds, and white marble-top table stands and dressers. The fascinating Hawaiian artifacts and worldwide curios that used to be displayed here have now been transferred to the recently built Lyman Museum building. In this very modern $1-million museum addition, you begin at the Island Heritage Gallery on the first floor, where a raised relief map shows routes taken by all the groups that came to Hawaii. Then you can see the artifacts of each group and study their cultures; the Hawaiian exhibit includes a full-size grass house, Stone Age implements, feather leis, etc. There are also Chinese, Japanese, Portuguese, Korean, and Filipino displays. The second floor also has fascinating exhibits, among them the Earth Heritage Gallery with its display of volcanic eruptions and worldwide gem mineral collections, one of the finest and most extensive collections in the country. The Chinese Art Gallery has pieces dating back as far as the Shang Dynasty, 13th century B.C., and the Artists of Hawaii Gallery features works by early Hawaiian artists. There's also an astronomy exhibit.

Lyman House is open Monday through Saturday from 9am to 5pm and on Sunday from 1 to 4pm. Admission is $4.50 for adults, $2.50 for children 6 to 17 and for seniors. For information, call 808/935-5021.

HILO SHOPPING

Shopping is concentrated in three areas here: at the Kaiko'o Hilo Mall (mostly of interest to locals), just behind the county and state buildings; downtown, where stores and boutiques are housed in quaint early 20th-century wooden buildings; and out on Hi. 11, at the newer Prince Kuhio Plaza Shopping Center.

DOWNTOWN

If you're in Hilo on a Wednesday or Saturday morning and you don't mind getting up early, go downtown to the bus terminal at the corner of Mamo Street and Kamehameha Highway at about 6am. This is the scene for Hilo's biggest **Farmer's Market,** where people come from all over to pick up produce, lots of flowers, some fish, and arts and crafts, all at low, low prices. Here's where you'll get the best prices on honeys, jams, unsalted macadamia nuts, T-shirts, Kona coffee, and more. Some 120 vendors show their wares. They sell out quickly—often by 8am—so it's best to arrive early.

✪ Basically Books
46 Waianuenue Ave. ☎ **808/961-0144.**

Basically Books specializes in books about Hawaii and the Pacific, with videotapes and a complete selection of maps of Hawaii, including USGS topographic maps, NOAA nautical charts, and road and street maps. They also have a good selection of travel books, posters, and attractive souvenirs, as well as a selection of maps for destinations worldwide.

Dan De Luz's Woods
760 Kilauea Ave. ☎ **808/935-5587.**

Dan De Luz is considered Hawaii's master bowl-turner, and his creations, which may range from a tiny bowl for $25 to works going up into the hundreds of dollars, are as fine as they come. De Luz works mostly with koa, but he also works in milo and sandalwood. He is known for his covered bowls and nested sets of bowls. Jewelry, bookmarks, letter openers, and the like sell for low prices. De Luz will gladly take you through his woodworking shop in the rear and show you how he produces his marvels. There's another Dan De Luz's Woods in Waimea, located at 64-1013 Hwy. 19.

Dragon Mama
266 Kamehameha Ave. ☎ **808/934-9081.**

This shop abounds with lovely wares: natural fiber futons, tatamis, kimonos, and zafus (meditation pillows), among others. Their wool sleeping pillows, at $28, are wonderfully cozy.

Hana Hou
38 Kalakaua St. ☎ **808/935-4555.**

Antique Hawaiian collectibles, old Ming jewelry, Tahitian-shell necklaces, sandalwood, and many vintage island treasures can be found in this tiny little shop. Owner Michele Zane-Faridi also has an eye for new works by local artists and crafters, and prices start low: around $15 for a vintage Hawaiian collage pin by Patti Millington, $20 for a koa and milo wood letter opener.

✪ Kaipalaoa Landing
106 Kamehameha Ave. ☎ **808/935-7077.**

Aptly named after the old landing at Hilo Bay where ships unloaded their cargoes at the turn of the century, Kaipalaoa is filled with arts and crafts by Hawaiian artists and exotic goods from around the world, all of it carefully chosen and beautifully displayed. Though prices can go up for Oriental antiques, original artwork, handpainted clothing, Japanese kimonos, and the like, there are still plenty of inexpensive finds. Consider, for example, coconut and sterling silver jewelry by Tito (earrings $12 to $15); Fimo clay earrings and necklaces by Edie Bilke ($10 to $50); woodblock prints by Avi Kiriaty ($20). Graceful pareus from Fiji, Indonesia, and Hawaii go for $20 to $30; distinctive Hawaiian T-shirts are $21. And, should you have the need, they even have Australian outback wear, including oilskin driver's coats and several Australian hats.

Moon Lilys

120 Keawe St. ☎ **808/961-4997.**

This is a charming little boutique, with graceful fashions for women by Hawaiian and mainland designers, antique Japanese kimonos, tasteful jewelry, accessories, and gift items. It's always worth a look.

Old Town Printers & Stationers

201 Kinoole St. ☎ **808/935-8927.**

This is the retail store of the Petroglyph Press, which has been publishing books on Hawaiiana since 1962. Drop in to browse through their publications, notes, and postcards, including many with Hawaiian designs. In addition, walk a few blocks to their other store, Basically Books (see above).

Sig Zane Designs

122 Kamehameha Ave. ☎ **808/935-7077.**

Sig Zane is known for his distinctive sportswear, all bearing his unique two-color Hawaiian floral designs. Although they are sold at a few places on the other islands, this is the source: muumuus, T-shirts, aloha shirts, pareus, accessories, furnishings, fabric, all bearing Sig's signature touch. Everything is 100% cotton. Prices are not low, but this is top-of-the-line stuff. Local arts and crafts by other artists are also on display. And Hawaiian music cassettes are available at the best prices in town.

✪ The Most Irresistible Shop in Hilo

110 Keawe St. ☎ **808/935-9644.**

This shop, housed with several other boutiques in the renovated and quite attractive 1922 Pacific Building, is one of our favorites. It's always worth a look-see, since owner Sally Mermel is forever coming up with something new and exciting for her flocks of loyal customers. Examples: silk pareus; silk tops, pants, and jackets made in Hawaii, lovely and reasonably priced; one-of-a-kind jewelry by local artisans, such as earrings made of Hawaiian woods; Hawaiian quilt design mugs in a variety of pastel colors; hand-batiked clothing; Hawaiian ornaments; tropical soaps; Hawaiian cookbooks; koa-wood mirrors, cutting boards, and rice paddles; island perfumes; and lots more, the best selection in Hilo. Hawaiian jams, jellies, and fruit butters make great small take-home presents. Adjoining the shop is Bears' (see "Where to Eat," in Chapter 13), with wonderful coffees, light foods, and desserts, all with a bear theme—Bear Claws, Teddy Bear Pie—and more.

PRINCE KUHIO SHOPPING PLAZA

This mall, the largest enclosed regional shopping center on the Big Island, will remind you of Kaahumanu Center on Maui or Kukui Grove on Kauai; it's vast, it cost millions to build (in this case, $47.5 million), and it boasts the traditional big department stores like Liberty House, plus 65 other specialty stores, ranging from the latest women's apparel fashion shops to charming little boutiques. **Indo-Pacific Trading Company** is an outstanding store, filled with unique clothing, jewelry, furnishings, textiles, quilts, carvings, masks, and much more from Java, Bali, New Guinea, and many points west. Always worth a stop. **The Most Irresistible Shop in Hilo** (described above) also has a shop here, this one with an emphasis on children. We always like to have a look at **Book Gallery,** especially to browse through their wide selection of island cookbooks. They carry all the local cookbooks of church groups and women's groups, and they have a good selection of Hawaiiana books and videos, books for the keikis back home, and some unique Petroglyph Press paperbacks, printed right here in Hilo. The **Hilo Hattie Fashion Center** is well worth a visit. The company is the largest manufacturer of aloha wear in the state, and it's all at less-than-usual prices. Everybody gets a complimentary shell lei and refreshments, too. (In fact, you can even get free transportation here by calling 808/961-3077). **Big Island Surf Co.** is known for their trendy fashions and accessories. For beachwear and surfing attire, **Local Style** has everything.

6 Hawaii Volcanoes National Park

You must not leave the Big Island without paying homage to the goddess Pele. Not to visit her residence at Halemaumau, the firepit crater of Kilauea (this is the smaller volcano nestled along the southeastern slope of Mauna Loa), would be unthinkable. If Pele is entertaining, you're in for one of the world's great natural spectacles; if not, just a look at a volcano and changes it has brought in the past will be quite an experience.

For information on hiking and camping in the park, see "Hiking," above, and "Camping and Wilderness Lodges" in Chapter 13.

It's more exciting than ever to visit the volcano, because for several years there has been a great deal of activity in Mauna Ulu, Pauahi Crater, and others. These new eruptions on the flanks of Kilauea have been big enough to spurt enormous fountains of fire 1,800 feet up above the crater's rim; now the lava is just bubbling along at its own leisurely pace. In 1984 both Kilauea and Mauna Loa were active at the same time, the first time this had happened since 1868. Lava flows came dangerously close to the city of Hilo. As of this writing, Pele is still acting up. Call 808/967-7977 anytime for recorded information on eruptions, or try the park rangers at 808/967-7311 before you start out, for news of the latest eruptions and viewing conditions. But whether or not anything is happening, the volcano trip is a must. If you would like to go with a knowledgeable guide, see "Adventure Tours," above. Try to plan this for a morning trip, as clouds often appear in the afternoons.

EN ROUTE TO THE PARK

Take Hi. 11 out of Hilo for about 30 miles until you reach Hawaii Volcanoes National Park. Be sure to take a warm sweater and a raincoat; the air gets refreshingly cool 4,000 feet up at Kilauea Crater. The weather can change quickly and dramatically, as sunshine gives way to mist and fog.

There are several possible stops en route for flower fanciers. The first, at the 14-mile marker in the tiny town of Mountain View, is the **Hawaiian Flower Garden Nursery,** which specializes in anthuriums at very low prices. (While you're on the main street of Mountain View, look for the Mountain View Bakery and see if they have some of their "stone cookies.") At the 22-mile marker is **Akatsuku Orchid Gardens,** a lovely botanical-type garden with many varieties of orchids; you'll receive one free as a gift. Just before you get to the park, it's fun to stop in at tiny **Volcano Village** and **Volcano Store** (on Hi. 11, make a right at Haunani Road directly to the store). Half the porch is the home of a snack bar and small

The Volcano Area

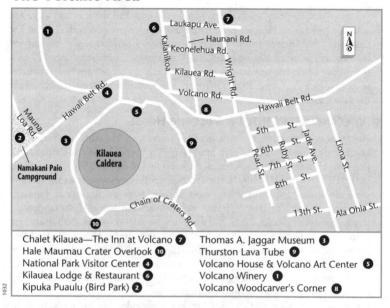

Chalet Kilauea—The Inn at Volcano ⑦
Hale Maumau Crater Overlook ⑩
National Park Visitor Center ④
Kilauea Lodge & Restaurant ⑥
Kipuka Puaulu (Bird Park) ②

Thomas A. Jaggar Museum ③
Thurston Lava Tube ⑨
Volcano House & Volcano Art Center ⑤
Volcano Winery ①
Volcano Woodcarver's Corner ⑧

restaurant called Alii Bakery and Drive-in; the other half is the place where local people go to scoop up reasonably priced flowers: Just to give you an example, we saw birds of paradise for 50¢ a blossom, 10 calla lilies for $3, king protea for $4 and less. Prices of flowers vary every day. The store will pack and ship anywhere in the United States. Poke around inside a bit—it's great for local color. The bulletin board out front often has leads on cottages to rent and news of local events.

SEEING & TOURING THE PARK

Once you reach the park (entrance $5 per car, good for seven days; free for those over 62), signs will direct you to the **Kilauea Visitor Center,** which should be your first stop. Check with the very helpful park rangers here for directions on the current eruption—if there is any. Be advised that if an eruption is going on, extreme caution must be exercised on the hiking trails, as there may be earth cracks anywhere, hundreds of feet deep, and a fall could be deadly. Those with heart and respiratory problems and pregnant women should beware of noxious fumes, children must be kept under control, and all visitors should protect themselves from the intense rays of the sun. Visitors can also simply drive to the important points on Crater Rim Drive (more about that ahead), which is safer. If you can afford it, there is, of course, nothing to compare to the spectacular helicopter flights directly over the lava flows.

First, though, explore the visitor center a bit. You can get information here on self-guided walks, the Kipuka Puaulu Walk, which is a 1-mile loop, and the Halemaumau Trail, a 6¹/₂-mile round-trip hike. Trail guides for both are available at the visitor center. And try not to miss the terrific color films of the latest eruptions, shown every hour on the hour from 9am until 4pm. There used to be a display case here consisting of letters from people who had taken rocks from the volcano—despite being warned never to do so—and had spells of bad luck, and sent the rocks back. Many of the letters ask forgiveness of Madame Pele. For example: "My friends are no longer in my life, I am divorced, I've lost my business, my property is being foreclosed. Pele is angry about something . . . I took the rock . . . Pele is a very busy woman and surely she would not miss a handful of stones from the firepit. Right? Wrong!" More letters and more rocks continue to make their way back to Hawaii.

✪ VOLCANO ARTS CENTER & VOLCANO HOUSE

Now that you know not to break any Hawaiian kapus by taking lava rocks back home, walk a few doors from park headquarters to the **Volcano Art Center,** P.O. Box 104, Hawaii Volcanoes National Park, HI 96718 (☎ 808/967-7511). Here, in the 1877 original Volcano House Hotel, a nonprofit group shows the work of some 200 artists and craftspeople, most of them from the Big Island. Fine arts reflecting the spirit of Hawaii, bowls and sculptures of native Hawaiian woods, paintings, jewelry, books, cards, and prints are for sale, as well as small distinctive items. Note the Jack Straka native wood bowls, the popular Dietrich Varez block prints, and Ira Ono's exciting paintings, sculpture, and mixed media works from recycled objects. There are concerts, theatre performances, lectures, and dance offered as well as classes and workshops for short- or long-term visitors. During the month of November and into December, the holiday season is celebrated with crafts demonstrations, a comforting fire, hot apple cider, holiday music, and the VAC aloha Santa Claus. Always a worthwhile stop.

Note: If contemporary art inspired by Hawaiian lore and local scenes excites you as it does us, plan to take part in the Volcano Artist Hui open studio tours. Call to make an appointment (☎ 808/967-7247) to personally visit some of Volcano's most talented artists in their studios and see their works in progress. If you're staying in Volcano, and it rains—well, here's a way to make the best of a rainy day.

Just across the road from the Volcano Art Center is **Volcano House** (see "Where to Stay," in Chapter 13). Situated on the rim of the crater, it's a magical spot. It's cozy just to sit here for a few minutes in front of the fireplace, where the fire, so it is said, has been burning continuously for 120 years. Burning ohia logs fill the air with a wonderful aroma. Or repair to Uncle George's Lounge, where the bartenders, volcanologists all, can whip up some unique drinks with names like Pele's Fire. Check out the two gift shops, which have a variety of souvenir items, many with the Volcano House logo. You can also inquire at the desk for information on hiking and camping tours within the park.

Some simple nature trails begin right in back of Volcano House, and we urge you to take at least one. The upland air is fragrant, the vegetation glorious, the views spectacular. The silvery trees that look something like gnarled birches are ohia, and their red-pompom blossoms are lehua, the flower of the Big Island, sacred to Pele. (It's rumored that if you pick one, it will rain before you arrive home.) That's the big bald dome of **Mauna Loa** towering 10,000 feet above you into the heavens; you're on **Kilauea,** which rises on its southeastern slopes. Pele hangs out in Halemaumau, the firepit of this enormous, 2 1/2-mile-long crater.

There is trouble in this paradise, however, according to conservationists and local people who are launching a mighty protest to stop the industrialization of the Big Island. Geothermal drilling is already getting under way on the slopes of Kilauea

Hawaii Volcanoes National Park

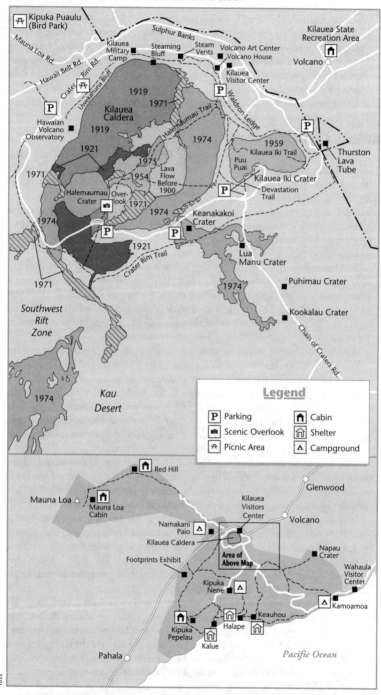

Volcano, in the midst of a Hawaiian rain forest. Planned for the near future are geothermal wells, power lines crisscrossing the island, a metals-smelting plant, a "spaceport," and an underseas cable, all of which could produce huge quantities of toxic waste and severely harm Hawaii's unique and endangered environment. Native Hawaiians also consider the drilling a desecration of their religion and their respect for the goddess Pele and her sacred places. If you'd like to get more information and perhaps help them in their cause, contact the Pele Defense Fund, P.O. Box 404, Volcano, HI 96785 (☎ 808/935-1633).

AROUND CRATER RIM DRIVE

To see the important views, take Crater Rim Drive, the 11-mile circle road, in either direction around the rim of Kilauea Crater. The rangers' map is easy to follow. Begin your trip around this wonderland of rain forests and volcanic desert at the **Sulfur Banks,** just west of park headquarters. The banks have that familiar rotten-egg odor. Farther along the road you'll see eerie wisps of steam coming out of some fissures, but don't be alarmed—they've been puffing along for centuries. You can stop to enjoy a hot blast from the steam jets, a natural underground "sauna."

Just beyond the Kilauea Military Rest Camp is a road that swings off to the right and across the highway that brought you here; if you follow this side path, you'll come upon an interesting clump of tree molds, formed in the same freakish way as the ones at Puna. The 100-acre **bird park** (Kipuka Pualu) is here too, a sweet spot for a picnic or a nature ramble through many rare trees; but you'll have to be sharp to spot the birds chirping away above your head.

Driving back to the rim of the crater road, turn right and continue the journey into the weird world ahead. You'll get your first view of Halemaumau, that awesome firepit 3,000 feet wide and 300 to 400 feet deep, from the lookout at the **Thomas A. Jaggar Museum.** Stop inside, too, to learn something about the history and development of volcanoes, and to see the murals by artist Herb Kane on the legends of Pele. The museum is named in honor of Thomas A. Jaggar, the first person to understand the necessity of having trained observers on site before and after volcanic eruptions.

Continue along the well-marked Crater Rim Drive now to **Halemaumau Overlook** itself, the home of Pele. When Pele decides to act up, everyone from there to the Philippines seems to descend on the area; whole families sit bundled in their cars all night long watching the awesome fireworks. Nobody can say when Pele will blow her top again. It is still local custom to appease her, but now that human sacrifice is out of fashion, she is reputed to accept bottles of gin! For a more intimate glimpse of Halemaumau, the 3-mile (one-way) hike through a hushed forest to the eerie heart of the volcano is recommended. The walk, a tough one, starts at Volcano House; be sure to get the descriptive pamphlet at park headquarters to guide you.

The drive now takes you to the area hit by the 1959 eruption of Kilauea Iki (Little Kilauea; all the volcanoes have little siblings here). A boardwalk has been set up over the cinder ash here; and a walk along this **Devastation Trail** will take you past the twisted ghosts of white trees felled by the lava. At the end of the trail you can look down into the **Kilauea Iki Crater.** (This walk takes about 15 minutes, so to conserve energy you might send one member of your party back to the parking lot to bring the car around to the lookout area at the end of the walk.) A favorite 4-mile hike around the crater's edge begins here.

The forest takes over at **Thurston Lava Tube,** a few miles farther, and a magnificent prehistoric fern forest it is. The lava tube shaded by this little grotto is another of those volcanic curiosities, even more spectacular than the one you saw in Hilo.

Now, if you're determined to see lava flowing into the ocean and you have more time to spend—at least two hours—continue around the **Crater Rim Drive** until you come to the Chain of Craters Road. It's a dramatic drive, the road descending 2,700 feet in 24 miles, all the way to the point where, if an eruption is going on, the lava flow enters the sea. The flow creates steam clouds that are white during the day and orange or red at night. You'll pass a jungle of ferns, an ohia forest, historic lava flows, and sea arches, as you go all the way down to the sea. But first, we repeat, you must check in with the rangers at the Mobile Visitor's Center for an update on the ever-changing conditions. They provide the latest information on where the flow is and how close you can get to it, what the weather conditions are, and everything else you'll need to know before heading out. The checklist of what to take with you includes the following: a minimum of one liter of water per person (it's unbelievably hot walking on black lava, because of the heat of the sun combined with the heat of the lava flow); good shoes (hiking boots preferred); and to protect against the sun, a hat, sunscreen, and sunglasses.

The Mobile Visitor's Center is constantly moving to keep up with the flow. Generally, it's about 20 miles down Chain of Craters Road. Park your car and walk about a quarter of a mile from where the road ends to the Mobile Visitor's Center. There's a half-mile loop trail off the paved road along the coast with good views of the flow into the ocean (be sure to carry a flashlight at night). Rangers conduct a lava exploration walk (conditions permitting) at 2:30pm (the Mobile Visitor's Center at the park entrance will know if lava-flow conditions will allow the exploration walk to take place).

Occasionally, the National History Association will be set up near the Mobile Visitor's Center, selling small bottles of water, film, and flashlights. Park rangers suggest supplying your own bottled water, as the National History Association is not present every day.

The best time to see the eruptions is at night, when the flow of lava coming down the side of the mountain is the most spectacular. Plan your trip to arrive a little before darkness falls to catch sunset at the water's edge. If you're staying at one of the guest houses in Volcano Village that has a hot tub to soak in, you'll find it the perfect way to relax after this somewhat eerie journey up and down the mountain.

Note: Since a lava flow has covered part of Chain of Craters Road, blocking the park's eastern boundary, there is no longer any way to continue on Hi. 130, which once led to Kalapana and the black-sand beach at Kaimu, destroyed by recent lava flows. You will have to return to park headquarters the same way you came, via the Chain of Craters Road. Note also that there is no food or gasoline available along this route, but both are available in Volcano Village, 1 mile Hilo-side of Hawaii Volcanoes National Park.

✪ THE VOLCANO FROM THE AIR

There's no doubt about it: The most extraordinary way to see the volcano is by air. It's not inexpensive, but a flight over the steaming volcano in a small plane could well be the high point of your trip to Hawaii. Sunset flights fly directly over active surface lava flows and over the steaming Pu'u o'o vent, where you can look down into a 2,000-degree river of molten lava flowing into the sea. The tour also takes in black- and green-sand beaches and lava deserts. If you have a little more time, the complete two-hour Circle Island Tour is recommended: It covers all 266 miles of the Big Island's spectacular coastline and includes a bird's-eye look at remote Waipio Valley and waterfalls dotting the shores. All flights leave from Keahole Airport on the Kona Coast.

Two companies offer well-recommended tours. **Hawaii Airventures** (☎ 808/329-0014) operates a high-wing, twin-engine Partenavia aircraft with large windows that seats a maximum of five adults; each seat is a window seat. An economy volcano tour is $129 per person; the Circle Island Volcano Tour is $169 per person. **Big Island Air** (☎ 808/329-4868) operates a Cessna 420 seating nine passengers, with every seat a window seat. Cost is $149 for the volcano tour, $169 for the Circle Island Volcano Tour.

7 Exploring the Puna Region

Although everybody goes to Kilauea, many tourists miss one of the most fascinating places nearby—the Puna region east of the volcano. Here you can gain an understanding of what a volcanic eruption means, not as a geologic curiosity, but rather in terms of the farms, stores, orchards, graveyards, and cucumber patches that got in its way. From Hilo, make the volcano trip your first priority; if you have a little extra time, visit the fascinating Puna region too.

FROM HILO TO KEAAU

This outing begins on Volcano Highway (Hi. 11), which branches off from Kamehameha Avenue southward past the airport. About 6 miles out of Hilo, you'll come to a possible stop, the **Mauna Loa Macadamia Nut Mill and Orchard,** the world's leading grower, processor, and marketer of macadamia nuts. Luther Burbank called macadamias "the perfect nut." This major island crop tastes better than peanuts. On the drive from the highway to the visitor center (past roads with names like Butter Candy Trail and Macadamia Road), you'll see hundreds of thousands of macadamia trees. From an observation gallery you can see the processing and packing operation, and observe colorful displays about history and horticulture. You can also take a mini-nature walk through a macadamia-nut grove with papaya, monkeypod, and banana trees. Open daily from 8:30am to 5pm.

You may want to turn left off Volcano Highway and drive through town until you find Hi. 130 and **Keaau,** an old, rather run-down plantation town that is now home to many artists and craftspeople. To the mountainside of the Keaau Police Station is **Puna Tropical Buds** (in the historic Plantation Store), a good stop if you're planning to send flowers to anybody back home. Puna is the largest grower of cymbidium orchids on the island and sells them at very reasonable prices. And once you're back home, send the nice people here $35 (or $55 for a deluxe box) and they'll ship you, pronto, a gorgeous tropical bouquet. (Write to Jonna & Scotty, P.O. Box 1593, Keaau, HI 96749; ☎ 808/966-8116.)

PAHOA

Back on Hi. 130 now, you'll find Pahoa about 10 miles farther south. Here you'll enter the area that bore the brunt of the 1955 eruption of Kilauea. This had been peaceful farm country for 100 years, dotted with papaya orchards, sugarcane fields, coffee farms, pasture lands. Then a rift in the mountain opened, and the lava fountains began to spout erratic caldrons that might turn a farm into ashes, but leave a gravestone or an old building untouched. You'll see fresh cinder cones and craters along the road, but the most spectacular—and chilling scenery comes later.

The Puna Region

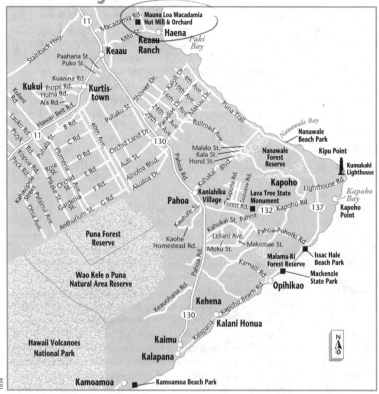

Downtown Pahoa is a funky little town you might want to explore a bit, a kind of unreconstructed hippie haven. Everything is on the main street, so wander at will along its wooden sidewalks in search of serendipity. If the ambience of the town speaks to you, make a note to come back and stay at the newly restored **Village Inn,** a remodeled 1910 hotel nicely done up with Victorian and turn-of-the-century antiques, its six rooms honoring historic figures like Mark Twain, Robert Louis Stevenson, Princess Kaiulani, and Don the Beachcomber—with decor to match their eras (P.O. Box 1987, Pahoa, HI 96778; ☎ 808/965-6444; doubles from $45 to $80, weekly rates available). The Village Inn's lobby gift shop is a favorite stop for antique collectors, especially for 1930s and 40s glassware, plus a wide variety of local, Asian, and European antiquities and collectibles. Or perhaps you'd like to stay at cozy little **Bamboo House,** an old "cane" house in a garden lane, done up into a pretty two-room apartment with one bath, queen-size sofa bed and queen-size regular bed, cable TV, small refrigerator. The rates are just $45 per night ($35 for three or more nights), and up to four can be comfortable in this no-smoking accommodation. (Contact Colleen Mandala, P.O. Box 1546, Pahoa, HI 96778, ☎ 808/965-8322, or inquire at Pahoa Natural Groceries.)

As for shopping, in general, it's cheaper to shop in this low-rent area than in Hilo. Here are some examples: $3 handpainted cards in Hilo were $2.25 here; a $15 pin was $11.50 here. We found interesting merchandise and good buys at **Pahoa Natural Emporium,** which has both clothing and antiques, and at the

Hawaiian Hemp Company, which has some interesting clothing. **Makana** is half café, half shop; they have some wonderful clothing from Bali, plus Indonesian artifacts. Blankets, bedspreads, tablecloths, quilts, caftans, and a great variety of pareus and jewelry are all well priced.

Pahoa Natural Groceries is the place to get natural deli sandwiches and fresh carrot juice. And keep your eyes open for the local vendors who can sometimes be found downtown selling anthuriums, papayas, and the like—all at very reasonable prices. Sometimes you can get six papayas for $1. Get out of your car and stock up! Nowhere can you beat these prices.

FROM PAHOA TO KAIMU

Continue along Hi. 130, and prepare yourself for a chilling sight: the lava flow that destroyed the idyllic garden community of Kalapana in May 1990. Flows from the Pu'u o'o vent of Kilauea, which began erupting in 1983, finally reached the sea seven years later, after destroying in its terrible path at least 123 houses, a church, local stores, and the idyllic Harry K. Brown Park. Also in its path was the Star of the Sea Painted Church, one of the two "painted churches" on the island, known for its colorful indoor murals painted in 1931. The church was removed before the lava flow could consume it, and has now been placed about 8 miles from Pahoa.

Go past the Painted Church to the next intersection and make a left turn toward Opihikao. The ride down to Opihikao is like going through an enchanted forest: Huge ohia trees form a canopy across the top of the road, papaya farms dot the landscape, and brilliant flowers grow wild along the roadside.

At the junction of Opihikao Road and Hi. 137, turn right; between the 17- and 18-mile markers on Hi. 137 you'll see a banner that reads KALANI HONUA. **Kalani Honua** is a unique conference and retreat center, on 20 secluded acres, hosting classes, workshops, performances, and special events year round promoting healing, the arts, and traditional Hawaiian culture. They also offer lodging, accommodations, and meals (see "Where to Stay," in Chapter 13). You may wish to stop and browse in the gift shop, which features clothing and craft items including colorful tropical pareus. Buffet-style breakfast (7 to 8am), lunch (noon to 1pm), and dinner (6 to 7pm) are served daily in the oceanview dining room. The cuisine is mostly gourmet vegetarian and it's quite delicious. Phone 808/965-7827 for daily specials and reservations.

Four miles from Kalani Honua the road has been blocked by a lava flow. The only thing to do is to retrace your steps on Hi. 137, this time bypassing Opihikao Road and continuing on Hi. 137 toward Kapoho. This fantastic 15-mile trip is one of the most exotic coastlines in Hawaii. From the red roller coaster of a road, you'll see where the tropical jungle alternates with black rivers of lava that laid waste miles of earth before they reached their violent end in the steaming Pacific. The sea pounds relentlessly on the black lava rocks, eventually grinding them into more black sand; on the land the jungle creeps back slowly, reclaiming the land for itself and breaking it down into what will once again be red earth. This is how the islands of Hawaii—and many of the earth's surfaces—were formed, and no textbook description will ever leave such a vivid picture in your mind.

Continuing toward Kapoho on Hi. 137, you'll find two good spots for picnicking, fishing, or hiking (no swimming): **MacKenzie State Park** near Opihikao and **Isaac Hale Park** at Pohoiki. Less than a mile up the road is **Pualaa.** This public park has a huge natural swimming pool—bigger than an Olympic-size pool—right on the ocean, with lava rock walls. It's possible to snorkel here at high tide when the fish come in. There's a lifeguard on duty. It may be hard to find the park; an old yellow house is a helpful marker. Not many tourists know about this place, but the locals sure do; the swimming is wonderful.

Back in the car, continue on Hi. 137 until you reach Kapoho, a Hawaiian Pompeii that was buried under spectacular lava flows in 1960. The day-by-day fight to keep the village from being overwhelmed by the lava flow and pumice cinders from the new cinder cone (which now overlooks the remains of Kapoho) was one of the most dramatic episodes in recent Hawaiian history. A cinder cone on the concrete floor is all that remains of Nakamura's Store, and nearby, a desolate lighthouse stands inland from the new coastline created by the lava flow. Come back from Kapoho on Hi. 132 and look for **Lava Tree State Park.** An old lava flow encircled the trees here, and they were eventually burned out, but the lava trunk molds remain, surrealistic witness to the whims of Pele.

You'll note that we've now described a triangle almost back to Pahoa; from here it's Hi. 130 back to Keaau, and then home to Hilo.

8   From Hilo to the Kona Coast

There are three possible routes across the Big Island from Hilo to the Kona coast:

The Southern Route   If you're continuing on from the volcano, simply follow the excellent Hi. 11 another 90 miles. You'll pass through the Ka'u Lava Desert (where an explosion of Kilauea in 1790 routed an army of Kamehameha's chief enemy, Keoua); you might stop off at Punalu'u to see the black-sand beach. You'll hit the pretty little village of Naalehu before encountering miles of lava flows, until you get to the other side of Mauna Loa and the welcoming Kona coast.

The Northern Route: The Hamakua Coast   If you're starting from Hilo, however, and have already been to the volcano, it's impractical to take the 126-mile southern route, when you can reach Kona directly in 96 miles, and sample in-between terrain so varied that Hawaii seems more like a small continent than a large island. We're referring to the drive along the majestic Hamakua coast, through the rolling pasture lands of the Parker Ranch, and then around Mauna Kea and Hualalai Volcano to Kona.

The Saddle Road   An alternative route for the first 50 miles of this trip crosses over the saddle between Mauna Loa and Mauna Kea, giving you wild, unforgettable views of both—but also a not-so-comfortable ride. Car-rental companies prohibit driving on Saddle Road—Hi. 200 out of Hilo—mostly because help is so far away. Should your car break down, the towing charge is enormous, not to mention your being stranded in the wilderness!

The drive in the opposite direction, from Kona to Hilo, is described briefly at the end of this section.

THE HAMAKUA COAST DRIVE: WAIPIO VALLEY, WAIMEA & MORE
FROM HILO TO HONOKAA

The drive we prefer—and the one that we'll explore in depth—starts from Hilo on Hi. 19, paralleling Kamehameha Avenue along the waterfront and heading for the northern shore of the island and the Hamakua coast. This is sugar-plantation country, miles of cane stretching inland to the valleys (the produce eventually goes to the bulk-sugar plant in Hilo and then to the mainland); the coastline is a jagged

Stargazing from Mauna Kea

For those interested in the heavens, there are two astronomy programs available to the public. At the 9,000-foot elevation of Mauna Kea the Ellison Onizuka Visitor's Center (named after the Hawaiian-born astronaut who died in the 1986 Challenger space shuttle tragedy) features displays and programs about Mauna Kea and the astronomical work taking place there. The center is open Friday from 1 to 5pm and Saturday and Sunday from 8am to noon, 1 to 2pm, and 4 to 5pm. Stargazing with a portable telescope takes place every Friday and Saturday at the Visitor's Center between 7 and 10pm.

The Mauna Kea Observatory at the summit has tours on Saturday and Sunday. The tours meet at the Visitor's Center at 1:30pm and proceed up to the observatory at the summit. Since the observatory is located at nearly 14,000 feet, in high-altitude, rarefied air, no one under 16 is allowed on the tour and anyone with a heart or respiratory condition, or who is pregnant, is advised not to make the trip to the summit. A four-wheel-drive vehicle is required to make the journey on the road from the Visitor's Center to the summit.

Before you venture up to either the Visitor's Center or the observatory, be advised that the weather at high altitude is changeable and can be quite dramatic. High winds and sudden drops in temperature, along with rain, hail, and snow, are common occurrences. Before you go, call the Visitor's Center for information, 808/961-2180; and call 808/969-3218 for road and weather conditions.

—Faye Hammel

edge curving around the sea, broken up by gorges and streams tumbling down from the snowcapped heights of Mauna Kea. The views from the modern and speedy Hi. 19 are good, but if you really want to soak up the scenery, get off now and then on the old road that winds through the gullies and goes to the sea.

Ten miles out of Hilo, at Honomu, the HVB marker indicates the way to **Akaka Falls.** Four miles inland on a country road, you'll find not only the falls—perhaps the most beautiful in the islands, plunging 420 feet into a mountain pool—but also a breathtakingly beautiful bit of tropical forest turned into a park that is lush and fragrant with wild ginger, ancient ferns, and glorious trees and flowers. For details on the walk to the falls, see "Hiking," above. It's a rhapsodic spot, very difficult to leave. Console yourself, then, with a bit of snacking and shopping in Honomu. At **Ishigo's General Store** you can pick up a hot cup of Kona coffee, as well as some scrumptious pastries at the bakery adjoining it. A few steps down the road is the **Akaka Falls Flea Market,** fun and inexpensive.

The little town of **Laupahoehoe**—you can drive down to it from the highway—is a "leaf of lava" jutting into the Pacific, its local park another idyllic spot for a picnic. But it's also a grim reminder of the power of nature that's always possible in Hawaii; it was in a school building here that 20 children and their teachers were swept away into the sea by the 1946 tidal wave.

If you have time for a little hiking and nature study, watch for the signs leading to **Kalopa,** a 100-acre Native Forest State Park containing trees, shrubs, and ferns indigenous to pre-Polynesian Hawaii, with trails through the ohia rain forest and many spectacular views—a nice spot for a picnic. Cabins are available for rental here through the County Department of Parks and Recreation.

Thirty miles past Akaka Falls is **Honokaa,** the Big Island's second-largest city and the site of the **Hawaiian Macadamia Nut Plantation.** You can view the plant and visit the retail store, which features a mind-boggling array of 200 macadamia-nut products. A macadamia-nut festival is held here in late August. Follow the warrior signs to the MACADAMIA NUT CAPITAL OF THE WORLD, open daily from 9am to 6pm for self-guided tours. On your way down the hill to the factory, you might want to stop in at **Kamaaina Woods** on Lehua Street, a factory and gift shop that turns out distinctive carvings in koa, milo, and other local woods. Koa bowls are their specialty. A glass panel separates the visitors from the artisans who are busy transforming raw koa logs into finished products. Handcrafted items begin under $10. Open weekdays and most Saturdays from 9am to 5pm.

Seconds to Go, on the main street in Honoka Town, is always worth a stop. You never know what antiques, collectibles, or "quality used goods" owner Elaine Carlsmith may have dug up—maybe antique kimonos ($5 to $85) or aloha shirts ($2 to $500), or even hula-girl lamps.

WAIPIO VALLEY

Honokaa is best known as the takeoff point to pastoral Waipio Valley. This side trip from your cross-island route takes you 8 miles from Honokaa, branching off to the right on Hi. 240. The best way to explore this spectacular valley (where 7,000 full-blooded Hawaiians lived less than 100 years ago; today there are fewer than 10, plus a few hippie families) is by the **Waipio Valley Shuttle,** a 1½-hour four-wheel-drive-vehicle tour starting and ending at the Waipio Valley Lookout. The tour takes you down into the valley, through taro fields, and past the $200,000 Ti House, the Lalakea fish pond, and the dramatic Hiilawe Falls (the water drops 1,200 feet here when it's running). Cost of the shuttle trip is $31 for adults, $15.60 for children under 11. Trips leave daily on the hour from 8am to 4pm. Make reservations by calling 808/775-7121 in Kukuihaele.

It costs more—$35—than the four-wheel-drive trip, but an excursion into Waipio Valley on a mule-driven wagon would surely be memorable. ♦ **Waipio Valley Wagon Tours** runs a 1½-hour tour four times a day (except Sunday) to explore the sights of the valley; mule power gets you across most of Waipio's streams and rivers, but there is one stop midpoint where passengers must walk across a stream to get to the view from the other side (appropriate footwear should be worn—passengers can borrow rubber slippers or use plastic boot covers). Reserve at least 24 hours in advance. Call 808/775-9518 or fax 808/775-9318.

Whether or not you go down into Waipio Valley, you should make a stop at the **Waipio Valley Lookout** for one of the most spectacular views in the islands. From the steep pali, the waves below look like bits of foamy lace. In winter, you can often see whales frolicking offshore. There are picnic tables and restrooms; it could be an ideal spot to break your trip. And by all means, pay a visit to ♦ **Waipio Valley Artworks,** snuggled in the sleepy town of Kukuihaele, which overlooks the valley (turn at the sign that reads KUKUIHAELE 1 MILE). Waipio Valley Artworks showcases the works of island artists exclusively, with some incredible wood products (they have the largest selection of bowls and other practical wood items on the island), as well as ceramics, basketry, hand-painted silk scarves, and original art and prints. Prices begin at $3.75 and go up, with a large selection of items to choose from under $35. (*Note:* Mail orders are now available; ☎ 800/492-4746.)

WAIMEA & PARKER RANCH

On the next leg of your trip you'll begin to see why Hawaii is so often called a continent in miniature. West of Honokaa, winding inland on Hi. 19, the sugar plantations of the tropics give way to mountain forests of cedar and eucalyptus as you climb up the slopes of Mauna Kea toward a vast prairie of rangelands and the plateau of Kamuela (also known as Waimea) and the 225,000-acre **Parker Ranch,** one of the largest cattle ranches in the United States under single ownership.

King Kamehameha started the whole thing, quite inadvertently, when he accepted a few longhorn cattle as a gift from the English explorer Capt. George Vancouver. The cattle multiplied and ran wild until John Parker, a young seaman from Newton, Massachusetts, tamed them and started his ranch. The Parker family still owns it today, and many of the current generation of paniolos are descendants of the original Hawaiian cowboys. The Parker Ranch is the biggest, but certainly not the only one—ranching is a way of life on the Big Island.

The Parker Ranch is headquartered in **Waimea,** a bright little mountain town that is one of the fastest-growing shopping areas on the Big Island, with delightful boutiques, galleries, and upscale restaurants opening all the time.

There are two visitor facilities at Parker Ranch that are well worth your time. The first is the **Parker Ranch Visitor Center,** where you'll see a historical museum and a video presentation of ranch history providing an insight into daily operations on the ranch. It's open daily from 9am to 5pm; admission is $5 for adults, $3.75 for children. The second is the **Historic Parker Ranch Homes** and their beautiful gardens. Mana, the 1847 home of the ranch founder, is built entirely of koa wood and is open for touring. Puuopelu, home of the last ranch owner, the late actor Richard Smart, houses a splendid art collection, with the works of many impressionist masters as well as objets d'art personally collected from around the world by Richard Smart. It's open daily from 10am to 5pm, and admission is $7.50 for adults, $3.75 for children. Better yet, buy a dual admission at $10 adults, $7.50 children, and see both.

Another stop in this area could well be the **Kamuela Museum** (☎ 808/885-4724), the largest private museum in Hawaii. You'll see ancient and royal Hawaiian artifacts (many of which were formerly in Iolani Palace in Honolulu) alongside European and Asian objets d'art, plus cultural objects brought to the islands by various ethnic groups in the 19th century. The museum, a charmer, is at the junction of Hi. 19 and Hi. 250; open daily, including holidays, from 8am to 5pm; $5 admission for adults, $2 for children under 12.

Waimea is also something of a cultural center for the Big Island and during your visit, you may be lucky enough to catch performances by such groups as the Peking Acrobats, the Honolulu Symphony, or even the World Famous Glenn Miller Orchestra at the 500-seat **Kahilu Theatre,** just across from the Parker Ranch Visitor Center. For ticket information, call 808/885-6017.

Shops & Galleries in Waimea

PARKER SQUARE   One of our favorite shopping complexes in town, Parker Square has a trio of tasteful boutiques. The most exciting is **Gallery of Great Things,** which shows an extraordinary collection of works by over 200 local and Pacific Islands artists; we coveted the stunning hand-sewn Hawaiian quilts and the rare Niihau shell necklaces. Prices can go way up for antique prints and primitive tribal art—(this is a veritable museum you can shop from)—but many things are surprisingly affordable: We saw handmade earrings starting at $5, koa-wood rice paddles at $8, handmade pareus at $30, and one-of-a-kind feather necklaces at $60. There's a good selection of Hawaiian music tapes, and many prints and posters by local artists. **The Waimea General Store** is a tasteful bazaar with a highly sophisticated potpourri of merchandise including distinctive handcrafts, toys and games, handmade baby quilts, pottery, and an excellent collection of Hawaiian books.

Dan De Luz's Woods
64-1013 Hwy. 19.

Look for the tikis out front and you'll find yourself at the shop of Dan De Luz, famed as Hawaii's master bowl-turner (for information on his Hilo factory, see above). While some of the superb bowls here could go up into the thousands, there are plenty of small koa-wood treasures to take home—like $15 bracelets, $10 earrings, or $1.95 bookmarkers.

PARKER RANCH SHOPPING CENTER   This mall is given over mostly to local shopping, but there are a few interesting shops for the visitor. At the **Parker Ranch Store,** adjacent to the visitor center, you can buy Parker Ranch logo items, including sweatshirts and jogging outfits. The most outstanding shop here is the **Fine Art Galleries of Hawaii,** where over 50 artists from Hawaii, the Orient, the South Pacific, and Europe are represented. Admire the collections of Hawaiian prints, pottery, handmade baskets, quilts, jewelry, and more. **Reyn's** well-known island shops for men and women has an outpost here, too. You'll find casual clothes at **Blue Sky Apparel** and **Malia Kamuela.**

WAIMEA CENTER   The newest shopping mall in town seems to be of interest mostly to local folks, but there's one place here not to be missed—**Cook's Discoveries** in the historic Spencer House in the middle of the center. For more than a century, the Spencer family's two-story home, built in 1850, served as a general store. Big Island families came to Spencer House for the necessities of life, and also for the "luxuries"—sweets, hats, fine soaps, clothing, and dozens of other treasures. The Spencer House once again offers a treasury of goods. Owners Patti and Bill Cook have filled the shop with "Made in Hawaii" products that would make superb gifts for the people back home. Choose from toys, books, Nake'u and Sig Zane clothing, koa umbrellas, jewelry, music boxes, pans, bowls, and much more. Incredible edibles—like guava-rum, lemon-macadamia, and Kona coffee chocolate truffle and triple chocolate chunk cookies—are a specialty. Prices range from $7 koa key rings, $18 feather earrings, and $25 and up koa bowls, to $92 Hawaiian quilted pillows. A note to collectors of Hawaiian quilts: quilts that we've seen in Honolulu go from $6,000 to $8,000; here, they're $4,000. You may also luck into one of Cook's Discoveries' frequent cultural demonstrations and presentations. A wonderful place, not to be missed.

Upcountry Connection is another outstanding store at Waimea Center. Paintings, pottery, prints, handsome furniture, and beautiful koa pieces by mostly Sio Island artists are shown. This place can be pricey, but we discovered koa bookmarks at $5 and delightful little "Angels from Paradise" dolls at $20. Waimea Center also boasts **Pueo Bookshop,** with books for all ages and a good selection of cards; **Princess Kailuani,** which offers great muumuus as well as long, lacy wedding dresses; and **Kamuela Hat Company,** with a great selection of men's and women's hats; should you get hungry, you can join the local folks for a Korean lunch at **Kal Si,** for Chinese food at **The Great Wall Chop Suey,** or, or for typical local dishes at **Kamuela Deli.**

A SIDE TRIP FROM WAIMEA TO NORTH KOHALA

From the cool green oasis of Waimea you can make a side excursion—its about 25 miles to the northernmost tip of the Big Island. The drive is along Hi. 250, winding uphill through the slopes of the Kohala Mountains, and the sights are unforgettable—the Pacific on your left, looking like a blue-velvet lake lost in misty horizons; the shimmering, unearthly peaks of Mauna Kea, Mauna Loa, and Hualalei, their slopes a jumble of wildflowers, twisted fences of tree branches, and giant cactus. Enroute to your destination, at Pololu Lookout, you'll view some major historical sights and experience the quaint little towns of Hawi and Kapaau. As for the historic sites, you may first want to visit the **Mookini Heiau State Monument** and the **birthplace of Kamehameha.** To reach the heiau, take Hi. 250 to Hi. 270, and turn left on Upolu Airport Road. After the airport, turn left on a dirt road and follow the signs to see the largest heiau on the island, built in the 13th century and under restoration at the time of this writing.

(*Note:* When visiting a heiau, or any sacred site in Hawaii, it is important to follow the advice of the native peoples. Show your respect by always asking permission from the spiritual forces that guard these places. Never take anything from these sites: leave your aloha, your love, and thanks. Then you will be welcomed and taken care of. Local people wrap food in a ti leaf (not a rock) and leave a lei at these places. If you are unwilling to approach a sacred place in this spirit—stay away.)

A short way further down the dirt road is the birthplace of Kamehameha. More interesting, actually, is the statue of King Kam in the little town of Kapaau. The statue of the local hero looks amazingly like the one you saw in Honolulu. Actually, this is the original; it was made in Florence, lost at sea, and then found after another just like it had been fashioned for the capitol.

The little towns of Hawi and Kapaau are undergoing a gentrification of sorts; the old wooden storefronts surviving from sugar plantation days now house art galleries, boutiques, and upcountry restaurants and coffeehouses. In downtown Hawi, for example, folks rave about **Bamboo Restaurant** for its Pacific Rim and vegetarian dishes at reasonable prices. **Kohala Coffee Mill** has the feeling of Old Hawaii and lots of good coffees, espresso drinks, and coffee accessories and gifts. A few miles further, in Kapaau, is **Tropical Dreams,** a combination ice-cream factory (free tastes!) and café. **Ackerman Galleries** has two locations in Kapaau town. Stop in to see the work of Gary Ackerman and other local artists, as well as Hawaiian artifacts, gift items, and oriental antiquities.

You'll want to continue along Hi. 270 until you reach Pololu Valley Lookout: like the similar lookout at Waipio Valley (see above), this is one of the great scenic vistas of the Big Island. (In good weather, you can hike down to the valley and be at the dark-sand beach in about a half-hour.)

The trip to this area is thrilling, but remember that you've got to come down the road again (Hi. 270) that links up to Hi. 19 and the Kona coast, adding a total of about 50 miles to your cross-island trip. (If you're based in Waimea, however, it makes a pleasant and easy excursion on its own.)

WAIMEA TO KONA VIA THE KOHALA COAST

From Waimea, you can zip right along the coastal road, Hi. 19, and be in Kailua-Kona within an hour. However, it's fun to stop off along the way to have a look at some of the fabled Kohala coast resorts that dot these shores, and maybe have a meal or a swim. Anae'hoomalu Bay, a splendid crescent-shaped white-sand

The North Kohala District & the Kohala Coast

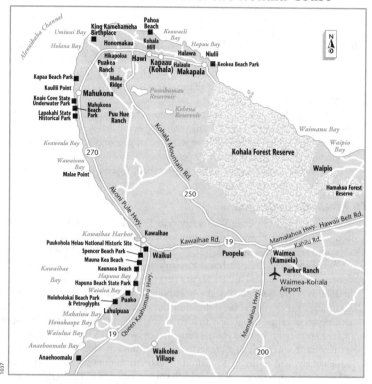

beach with public facilities and picnic tables, is actually the beach fronting the glorious Royal Waikoloan Hotel. And very close to that is the megaresort that everyone in Hawaii seems to be talking about and wants to see: the **Hilton Waikoloa Village.** You should see it and plan an hour or two to enjoy it: If you can't squeeze the time in on your cross-island trip, then come back once you've settled in Kona. Guests of the fantasy resort pay $200 a day and up for their accommodations, but you can enjoy many of the resort's facilities as a visitor. For something organized, call the Hilton (☎ 808/885-1234, ext. 2715) and reserve a space on one of their guided tours: an art tour, a garden and wildlife tour, a petroglyph tour, a facilities tour, and a back-of-the-house tour. What we like to do is simply hop one of the canal boats or tubular trams that continually circle the property, and stop where fancy leads us. There are lush tropical gardens and a wildlife collection; a multimillion-dollar, mile-long museum walkway filled with superb examples of Pacific and Asian art; a shopping arcade with upscale boutiques; enormous swimming pools with slides, waterfalls, grottoes (one even has a "riverpool," and its currents float guests from level to level); and a million-gallon saltwater lagoon, teeming with tropical fish, which is the home of six trained dolphins. Definitely get off the boat here, for here's your chance to experience or watch a dolphin encounter. (Call the hotel for details.)

If you can tear yourself away from the Hilton, and you still feel like seeing more playgrounds of the rich and famous, look for the entrance to the ✪ **Mauna Lani Bay Hotel,** 5 miles north on Hi. 19; to our way of thinking, it's one of the most purely beautiful resorts anywhere, especially in its landscaping and gardens and the massive indoor waterfall in the Grand Atrium. Golfers rave about the Francis Ii Brown golf course here, a 36-hole championship course carved out of barren lava. For details, see "Golf" above. If time permits (or if not, come back later once you're snugly ensconced in Kona), have a splurge meal at one of the most enchanting of its seven restaurants, the **Canoe House,** which features Pacific Rim cuisine by a master chef in an alfresco oceanfront setting—incomparable! (Call 808/885-6622 for reservations.)

In the same Mauna Lani Resort that houses the Mauna Lani Bay Hotel is the newer **Ritz-Carlton Mauna Lani,** another exquisite gem nestled between the ocean and the lava desert. You're welcome to take a look around and admire the glamorous setting and the lovely beach.

You can then continue along the coastal road, Queen Kaahumanu Highway (Hi. 19), until you reach Kailua-Kona.

To Kona via Kawaihae

Alternatively, you can leave Waimea on Hi. 19 and drive about 12 miles to the deep-water port of **Kawaihae,** where you descend through prairie land, grazing cows, and ocean vistas all about you, until you're suddenly in sultry tropics.

On the road above the harbor is **Puukohola Heiau National Historic Site,** a well-preserved heiau and historical park that figures prominently in the history of the islands. Here Kaahumanu, the sweetheart-queen of the great Kamehameha, began after his death the breakdown of the dread kapu (taboo) system by the startling act of eating in public with men (previously, such an act would have been punished by death). But the place is better remembered for a bloody deed. Remember Keoua, Kamehameha's biggest rival, the one who lost an army at K'au? Kamehameha had to decide to dedicate this heiau to the war god Kukailimoku, and invited Keoua to a peace parley in the new temple. Instead of offering peace, however, he had Keoua speared as he approached the land and sacrificed him to the god. Then Kamehameha was free to unify Hawaii and the other islands.

After digesting this gory bit of history, you deserve a change of pace. Return to Hi. 19 and turn right (south) for a mile to the turnoff for Spencer Beach State Park. This scenic ocean beach park has white sand and calm waters, and is very popular with local families with children. Camping is permitted here. About 3 miles farther south is the more spacious Hapuna Beach State Park, another beautiful white-sand beach; this one has strong surf (watch for signs warning about dangerous tides and rip currents). Continue on Hi. 19 through the lava desert, which on clear days will afford glorious views of all the volcanoes of Hawaii and perhaps of Haleakala on Maui, too. Lava flows from Mauna Loa and Hualalia mark the eerie landscape, punctuating the miles until you emerge at last into the verdant world of the Kona coast.

(*Note:* We're sorry to have to issue this caveat, but we've been told that rowdies sometimes hide in the bushes near these beaches, wait for tourists to dutifully put their valuables in the trunks of their cars, and then proceed to pick the locks while the tourists are out on the beach. If you're going to put anything in your trunk, do so a few miles before you reach your destination.)

THE SOUTHERN ROUTE FROM KONA TO HILO

If you've arrived at Kona first, you could drive across the island to Hilo on Hi. 11, through the K'au Desert and miles and miles of lava flows, desolate enough to be reminiscent of Doré's engravings. But before the landscape turns bleak, there's plenty of magnificent scenery. If you make the trip in November or December, you'll see unbelievably beautiful poinsettias.

Manuka State Park, with its arboretum of extraordinary plants and trees, is a good spot to stretch your legs and perhaps have a picnic lunch. The approach to the little village of **Waiohinu** is marvelously scenic, and the village itself, once a small farming center, is one of the quaintest on the Big Island. Have a look at the monkeypod tree planted by Mark Twain, and a few miles farther on you can make a side trip (about 1 1/2 miles off the highway) to the black-sand beach at **Punaluu.**

Another favorite jaunt is the 12-mile drive off the highway outside Naalehu down to **Ka Lee** (South Point). Local people fish there on this wild shore of cliffs and surf, the southernmost point in the United States.

Now you approach the desolate K'au region where Pele obligingly destroyed an army of Keoua, Kamehameha's archenemy, in 1790; the footprints of the victims can be seen under glass. The landscape is moonlike, and not only metaphorically; space scientists are studying the lava fields of the Big Island because they believe it's similar to conditions on the moon. The lava flows lead you to Kilauea, Hawaii Volcanoes National Park, and on to Hilo.

9 Exploring the Kona Coast

Kona is such a deliciously lazy spot that you may be very content to do nothing at all. Of course, looking at the surf as it smashes along the black-lava coast, noting the brilliant varieties of bougainvillea, the plumeria, and the jasmine tumbling about everywhere, and lazing on the beach can keep you pretty busy. But we suggest that you take a day off from these labors and have a look at the sights. Kona is an important historic center; within the space of a few miles, Captain Cook met his end, the New England missionaries got their start, and Kamehameha enjoyed his golden age.

KAILUA-KONA This tiny village is the resort center, modern enough to be comfortable, but still unspoiled. The people at the Hawaii Visitors Bureau office, in the Kona Plaza Shopping Arcade, can help you with all sorts of practical information.

DRIVING TOUR
Kailua-Kona to Pu'uhonua
o Honaunau National Historical Park

Start: King Kamehameha's Kona Beach Resort.
Finish: Kahaluu Beach Park.
Time: 2 to 4 hours.
Best Time: Begin early, so you can spend as long as you like.
Worst Time: Late in the day.

Your sightseeing tour begins with a stop at:

1. King Kamehameha's Kona Beach Resort. There's only one street, Alii Drive, running down the length of Kailua town, so you won't get lost. The hotel is in the northern end of town, at the site of the monarch's heiau, which has been restored. There are tasteful museum-caliber displays throughout the lobby highlighting Hawaiian history and various free activities: Ethnobotanical, historical, and "hula experience" tours are held several times a week (inquire at the hotel for a schedule). Just about 150 years ago, Kamehameha ruled the Hawaiian Islands from a grass-roofed palace on this very site. (Lahaina became the next capital; Honolulu did not become the capital until the middle of the 19th century.) The old king died here in 1819, only a year before the first missionaries arrived from Boston, bringing with them the purposeful Protestant ethic that would effectively end the Polynesian era in Hawaii. The missionaries were responsible for the:

2. **Mokuaikaua Church,** standing on the mauka (mountain) side of Alii Drive, a handsome coral-and-stone structure that's the oldest Christian church in Hawaii, built in 1838. Note the sanctuary inside; its architecture is New England, but it's made of two Hawaiian woods, koa and ohia. Across from it, on the ocean side of the street is:

3. **Hulihee Palace.** Until 1916 this was a vacation home for Hawaiian royalty. Now it's a museum, full of Hawaiian furniture and effects, as well as more primitive curiosities like Kamehameha's exercise stone (it weighs about 180 pounds, so maybe that story about the Naha Stone isn't so crazy after all). Check out the charming little gift shop; it has an especially nice selection of native wood plus books and jewelry. Profits go to the Daughters of Hawaii. The museum is open daily from 9am to 4pm; closed federal holidays. Admission is $4 for adults, $1 for students 12 to 18, 50¢ for children under 12.

The shore road extends for about 6 more miles, but we're going to leave it temporarily, taking a left at Hualalai Street and heading out of town on Hi. 11 (the mauka road) to explore:

4. **Kona "Up Mauka."** Upcountry Kona is far removed from the tourist scene at Kailua-Kona. It is, for one thing, the place where Kona coffee, that dark, rich brew you've seen all over the islands, is grown. Hawaii is the only state in the union that has a commercial coffee crop. There are no big plantations, only small farms where everybody in the family pitches in to bring in the crop. Watch the road for the shiny green leaves of the coffee bushes with the little clusters of red berries at harvest time. There are small cattle ranches here too, although they're not visible from the road.

The drive is a beautiful one, winding through the cool mountain slopes, with fruit trees and showers of blossoms all around. For those in the mood for a little offbeat shopping, continue along the road until you come to:

5. **Kainaliu Village and Kealakekua.** In Kainaliu, **Kimura's** is a favorite oldtimer. Some say Mrs. Kimura has the best collection of fabrics in the islands. Hawaiian and Japanese prints are specialties, and prices are reasonable. Look for the **Aloha Café** in Kainaliu now, and perhaps stop in for a tempting pastry or snack (see "Where to Eat," in Chapter 13). Next door is the **Aloha Store,** a tasteful gift shop with distinctive clothing, children's books, cards, jewelry, cookbooks, Hawaiiana, candles, fragrant potpourri, bath accessories, and the like. We picked up a neat Japanese parasol—great on the beach—for just $10. Across from it is **Blue Ginger Gallery,** a showcase for about 50 local artists. You'll find an enticing collection of stained glass, ceramics, jewelry, handpainted silks, and more, plus many crafts from Bali. Close to that, **The BadAss Coffee Company,** named for the hardworking donkeys that used to haul heavy loads of coffee up and down the mountains, sells fragrant, locally grown coffee. Out in back is the semi-open **Coffee Pub,** with tables, a chessboard, cards for sale—a pleasant stop. **Paradise Found Boutique** is the place for unique clothing, like raw silk

The Kona Coast

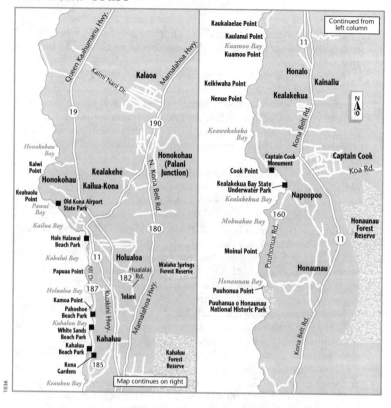

Continued from left column

Map continues on right

outfits designed here and made in China, a line of batik designer clothes, beautifully cut lacework garments from Indonesia, and men's silky aloha shirts. There are gift items by local artisans as well as Asian imports, too. They have another shop down in Kailua town and one at Lanihau Center.

A popular shop in Kealakekua is the **Grass Shack,** a real grass shack that has been here almost forever. The inside is laden with tasteful and authentic Hawaiian and South Pacific handcrafts. The nice people here will give you a native flower and some coffee beans for planting as you leave; within 3 to 4 weeks (the time it takes for the seed to germinate) you'll be on your way to having your own potted coffee plant.

About 12 miles from the beginning, the road winds gently down the slopes of the mountain (watch for the HVB marker), past Royal Kona Coffee Mill and Museum, through the lush tropical village of Napoopoo on to Kealakekua Bay. Visitors are welcome at the mill. Now, pause a bit at the:

6. Captain Cook Monument, visible across the bay, erected at a spot near where he was killed in 1779. It was here that Cook and his men pulled into the Kona coast a year after their first landing on Kauai, were again treated as gods, and then wore out their welcome. When their ship was damaged in a storm and they returned to Kealakekua a second time, the men got into a fight with the natives, and Cook was killed trying to break it up. You can't see the monument up close unless you approach it from the water or hike down a dirt trail. There's a "Captain Cook Cruise" that leaves Kailua wharf daily (☎ 808/329-6411); it gives

you a good look at the monument and lets you swim and snorkel in the bay. It's a good way to combine a suntan and a history lesson for $54 for adults, $27 for children 5 to 12. The cost includes a continental breakfast and a barbecue lunch.

There are two plaques you can see on the Napoopoo shore: One commemorates the first Christian funeral in the islands; the other is in honor of the young Hawaiian boy, Opukahaia, who swam out to a ship in 1808, got a job as a cabin boy, converted to Christianity, and convinced the missionaries that they were needed here in the Sandwich Islands. Right near the shrines are a few jewelry stands that offer good buys in clothing and necklaces of local seed and kukui-nut leis.

Continuing along the shore road now to Honaunau, you'll pass Keei Battlefield, a lava-scarred stretch where Kamehameha started winning wars. In the tiny fishing village of Keei, there's a beach with good swimming. But the best is yet to come: The high point of this little excursion is a visit to:

7. **Pu'uhonua o Honaunau National Historical Park.** This ancient, partially restored Pu'uhonua still has about it the air of sanctuary for which it was built over 400 years ago. In the days when many chieftains ruled in the islands, each district had a spot designated as a place of refuge to which kapu breakers, war refugees, and defeated warriors could escape; here they could be cleansed of their offenses and return, purified, to their villages. (There is another such place on the island of Kauai, near Lydgate Park, but this one is far better preserved.) The heiau, Hale-o-Keawe, the temple of the purifying priests, has been reconstructed (it was in such temples that the bones of the high chiefs of Kona—which had mana, or spiritual power—were kept), and so have the tall ki'i carved for the god Lono. After you've driven into the park and left your car in the parking lot (an improvement over the old days when the only way to get here was to run, or, if one came from the north, to swim, since the feet of commoners were not fit to tread on the Royal Grounds) on the north side of the place of refuge, we suggest you take in one of the orientation talks given daily at 10, 10:30, and 11am, and at 2:30, 3, and 3:30pm, in the spacious amphitheater staffed by the National Park Service, which administers this facility. Besides explaining the concept of refuge, the park ranger also talks about the plants and trees of the area. Then you're free to have a swim (but sunbathing is not allowed), a picnic, go snorkeling or fishing—or just absorb the peace on your own. Or you can tour the area by yourself with a self-guiding leaflet. "Cultural demonstrators" are usually on hand, carving woods, weaving, and performing other ancient Hawaiian tasks. Canoes, fishnets, and traps are on display, and are sometimes used outside the work sheds. Entrance fee is $2 per person, (children under 17 free).

There's one more curious sight in Honaunau, which you reach by turning north on a side road as you go back up the highway. This is:

8. **The Painted Church,** the name that everyone gives to St. Benedict's Church. The Catholic missionaries created biblical murals that gave a feeling of spaciousness to the tiny church, presumably so that the congregation would have more of a feeling of the outdoors—to which pagan nature worship had accustomed them. Between Pu'uhonua o Honaunau and the Painted Church, you might want to make a stop at:

9. **Wakefield Gardens** (☎ 808/328-9930). You can take a free, self-guided tour through this 5-acre botanical garden and macadamia-nut orchard, with some

1,000 varieties of plants and flowers. The gift shop sells those little macs very reasonably ($5 buys 2¹/₂ pounds in the shell), and also features small wood items made by local artisans. They also have a small restaurant with generally slow service—but their homemade pies are great. And they have the best macadamia-nut brittle anywhere! They're on Hi. 160, open daily from 11am to 3pm.

Now go up Hi. 160 to Hi. 11 and make a left turn north toward Kailua. Just before Middle Keei Road, on the ocean side, look for a sign that reads "Healthy Food to Go" and you're at:

10. **Bong Brothers Coffee.** This is an authentic coffee mill and store dating back to the 1920s; a roaster in back turns out a complete line of Kona coffee in medium, Vienna, and French roasts. Their country store features an espresso bar and snack bar, local fruits and vegetables, and a line of natural foods and Hawaiian food products. The gift shop sells their yummy chocolate-covered coffee beans.

Continue north on Hi. 11 headed toward Kailua. Another possible stop is Honauna, one tenth of a mile south of mile marker 105, just after the mailbox on the mountain side of the road. Here you'll find:

11. **Old Hawaiian Coffee Estate.** This historic 1879 coffee farm boasts a modern coffee pulping mill and specializes in organically grown, 100% Kona estate coffee. The people here will really take the time to show you all the steps in the production of coffee, from bean to brew. Don't be daunted by the ³/₄-mile coffee road that they are attempting to keep paved. Hungry? Stop off in Captain Cook for a visit to:

12. **The Coffee Shack.** One side of this place is a neat little deli with some good sandwiches; the other side sells Kona Coffee, roasted here. It's a good place to relax and enjoy the view of the ocean off in the distance.

Now continue for about 11 miles until you come to a turnoff to the left that brings you back to the shore at Keauhou Bay. Before you descend, though, you might want to stop off to have a look at the handsome:

13. **Keauhou Shopping Village.** Here you could have a drink or a meal with the local sports fans gathered around the large-screen TVs at **Drysdale's Two** (see "Where to Eat," in Chapter 13), or an espresso or cappuccino at **Kona Kai Coffee Café.** Just about our favorite made-in-Hawaii arts shop here is **Alapaki,** a stunning showcase of arts and crafts. You enter through a lava arch flanked by 10-foot-tall royal kahilis on either side, containing 6,000 feathers and 500 feather flowers. Inside you'll find imposing sculptures by artists like Herb Kane, paintings and posters, handcrafted native wood carvings and bowls, feather leis, baskets, and much more. The **Keahou Village Book Shop** has a vast array of books, including a strong collection of Hawaiiana, as well as some vintage postcards like the ones reading ALOHA FROM WAIKIKI, 1935. Check out **Wild Mango Fashions** for casual clothing, and **Hawaii Floral Express** for fresh flowers. At the **Showcase Gallery,** you can find works by leading island painters and craftspeople, perhaps originals by Phan Barker and Leah Neimoth, posters by Robert Lyn Nelson. A collection of beautiful jewelry ranges from about $20 to $400.

Have a look at the **Liberty House Penthouse** here. No telling what you'll find at a place like this on any particular day, but we've seen $40 jeans for $10, $50 bathing suits for as low as $7, $50 leather bags for $25. Items are from various Liberty House shops on the islands; it's worth a look.

Note that there's a U.S. Post Office substation at Keauhou Shopping Village.

Continuing down to Kailua now, the old vies with the new for attention everywhere. To your left is Keauhou Bay, a naturally occurring small boat harbor, home to a small number of charter fishing, dive, and excursion boats; to your right, faintly visible on the mountain slopes, are the remains of a rocky royal slide, down which the alii of Hawaii once scooted into the water. Coming into sight soon is:

14. Kahaluu Beach Park, and your sightseeing labors are over. Now you can concentrate on the important business of Kona, sun worshiping. Kahaluu Beach Park is a fine place for swimming, snorkeling, and picnicking. Snorkelers claim it's the best place on the Big Island. (One of our readers, Craig Kozak of Third Lake, Illinois, wrote that he came "nose-to-nose with a sea turtle that easily measured three feet in length.") There's a pretty lagoon and the swimming is safe, but note that there is no sand at low tide, and it is difficult to enter the water from the rocks.

Back in Kailua, you can swim in front of the luxurious King Kamehameha's Kona Beach Resort; the beach here is a public one, something that old King Kam would probably have approved of. The water is very gentle, safe for kids.

SHOPPING IN KAILUA-KONA

The shopping scene has blossomed just like everything else in this bubbling resort town. At last count, there were something like 100 stores and shops, some in quaint arcades, some in small centers and hotels, others just there, all on or just off Alii Drive.

KONA SQUARE A good place to begin might be the Kona Square Mall, across from King Kamehameha's Kona Beach Resort. ✪ **Island Silversmiths,** a longtime favorite (it's been here for 22 years), has a sign on the door that reads WE ONLY LOOK EXPENSIVE, and they're right. We saw coral rings here for $6 that were $15 in hotel gift shops nearby. They're known for their sterling-silver charms: The most popular is the Humuhumunukunukuapua's (oh well, just ask for Hawaii's state fish), $34. Also nice is their Cleopatra silver perfume ring at $25.

ALONG ALII DRIVE Right across the road is another neat jewelry store called **Goldfish Jewelry and Gifts.** Their specialty is 14-karat-gold charms—pineapple, marlin, reef fish, whale's tails, and the like. Prices start at $10, average $40 to $50.

Whatever else you do, don't miss the ✪ **Kona Arts & Crafts Gallery,** across from the sea wall on Alii Dr. It's one of the few places that deals solely in genuine Hawaiian crafts: Their wood carvings, for example, are made only of native woods such as milo, ohia, and koa. Prices vary for the works of fine art here, but there are many small treasures: Hawaiian sand-art petroglyphs from $9.95, banana-bark art, notecards by local artists, bookmarks made from the flowers of Hawaii, opihi and sea urchin jewelry, limu art (limu is an edible seaweed). Note their chime collection: They bear the imprints of native ferns grown on volcanic soil, pressed and fired at the temperature of red-hot lava, and they have a worldwide reputation; they're priced from $16.95. The shop also carries genuine hula instruments (made of gourds with seeds), and much more. Owners Fred and Sally Nannestad are knowledgeable about their collection and take time to explain the intricacies of these native arts. It's a very worthwhile stop.

KONA INN SHOPPING VILLAGE   Cross the street now to the ocean side where you'll find the biggest cluster of shops in town at the rambling Kona Inn Shopping Village. With more than 40 shops and restaurants and a waterfront location, it's always pleasant for browsing about. Shops come and go here, but you'll certainly find much to attract you. Women will come away with a different look from **Noa Noa.** Joan Simon's wild tropical designs on natural fabrics are stunning, and prices are not unreasonable. They also carry a selection of Indonesian artifacts which range from baskets at $39, on up to collectors' items such as masks at $100 to $350, as well as Ikat textiles, which make splendid wall hangings, starting around $175. Like to sew? Check out **Fare Tahiti,** a fabric shop with Hawaiian and Tahitian prints, mostly cottons, from $8.50 per yard. Note, too, their hand-decorated pareus, air-brushed in rainbow colors, at $21.50. They also sell men's tapa shirts, women's short and long dresses, and needlepoint and cross-stitch charts and kits.

✪ **Hula Heaven** is one of those places collectors of vintage aloha shirts seek out, and it's one of the best in the islands. Do people actually wear these shirts? We know that celebrities love them, but with prices going up to $1,000 for silk and rayon shirts of the 1940s and 1950s, our guess is that most of them wind up framed on somebody's walls. But don't despair: Hula Heaven also carries a good selection of Avanti silk reproductions of vintage aloha designs, most for about $59. You can even get yourself an exact copy of one of the aloha shirts Montgomery Cliff wore in *From Here to Eternity.* Also fun: the vintage aloha items that collectors snap up, like "nodders" (hula dolls with nodding heads) for $45 to $95, vintage ukuleles, and menu covers from the Royal Hawaiian Hotel and cruise ships of the Matson Line of the 1930s and 1940s, for about $25 to $125. They also feature reproductions of most vintage items, at more affordable prices.

Ready for a snack? **Cuzn's** offers pizzas, sandwiches, ice cream, and other snacks; chairs and tables are vintage Formica, but those breezes coming off the oceanfront are the real thing. Another way to beat the Kona heat is to pick up a beverage and some chocolate-chip cookies from the **Kona Kai Farms** coffee espresso bar and head for the oceanfront patio. It's cool out there.

KONA PLAZA SHOPPING ARCADE   Running out of things to read? Help is at hand at **Middle Earth Book Shoppe,** newly expanded in the Kona Plaza

---

Especially for Kids

While you're in the Kailua-Kona area, drive out to Keahole Airport to visit the **Astronaut Ellison S. Onizuka Space Center** (☎ 808/329-3441), a living memorial to Hawaii's first astronaut. Interactive and audiovisual exhibits provide a lively educational experience of America's manned space program: Especially exciting for kids is the "Manned Maneuvering Unit" in which the visitor sits in an MMU and manipulates the hand controls to rendezvous with an object in space. Another unique and popular exhibit allows the visitor to launch a miniature space shuttle 20 feet into the air. Open daily (except Thanksgiving, Christmas, and New Year's Day) from 8:30am to 4:30pm; admission is $2 for adults, 50¢ for children.

(across Alii Drive from the Kona Shopping Village), a shop not easy to find but well worth looking for. It's stocked with a good selection of maps as well as books.

KONA MARKETPLACE Bill Traub's little shop here called **B.T. Pottery** is worth seeking out for collectors of ceramics. Traub uses Hawaiian black sand, materialized from disintegrated lava, as part of his clay bodies: The sand melts upon firing and produces a speckled pattern unique to each piece. Cups, bowls, and vases are all well priced.

KAHAKAI MARKET No telling exactly what you'll find at this flea market held every Saturday and Sunday from 8am to 4pm in front of Huggo's Restaurant on Alii Drive, but local friends report good buys in jewelry, Balinese clothing, jams, coffee, cut flowers, koa wood products, artwork, T-shirts, baskets, hats, and lots more. Always fun for a browse.

10 Upcountry Kona: Holualoa

By Stephanie Avnet

A native of Los Angeles and an avid traveler, antique hound, and collector of Hawaiiana, Stephanie Avnet is also a contributor to *Frommer's California* and *Frommer's Los Angeles.*

Sloping gently up from the Kailua-Kona area is Hualalai, the oldest volcano of the five that comprise the Big Island. Although it has been inactive since 1801, geologists predict that a major eruption of Hualalai is inevitable within the next two centuries; until then, life on its slopes goes on. The leeward face of the volcano is a temperate and fertile area; there, you'll find a rustic retreat nestled within groves of intoxicatingly fragrant plumeria, rich Kona coffee, and irresistible sweet papaya, growing so easily in the rich volcanic soil. Perched 1,500 feet above Kailua-Kona sits the village of **Holualoa,** a quaint and thriving community of artists in the heart of upcountry Kona. This historic town was a launching point for the *holua,* Hawaiian sleds ridden down well-cleared paths on the hillside by the *alii* (royalty) and other thrill-seekers. You'll be able to see an excellent example of an ancient holua and remnants of the smooth stone slides in Kailua-Kona.

To reach Holualoa, follow Hualalai Road, which wriggles seductively throughout its $4^1/2$ mile ascent from the heart of Kailua town below. The ridge road is Mamalahoa Highway; a left turn onto it will carry you quickly into the center of town. At the junction, however, be sure to stop at **Kimura Lauhala Shop** (☎ 808/324-0053, open Monday through Saturday 9am to 5pm), renowned throughout the islands for the quality of their woven crafts. The shop was established by Mrs. Tsuruyo Kimura, legendary resident master of the vanishing art of weaving the leaves *(lau)* of the pandunus *(hala)* tree into exquisite hats, baskets, mats, handbags, and a variety of other quality pieces. Once an old plantation store selling salt, codfish, and other supplies, the shop was transformed during the Depression, when Mrs. Kimura and some other farmers' wives began selling their handicrafts to get through the tough economic times. You'll still find Mrs. Kimura and her co-workers in the shop's work area today, plaiting lauhala into salable goods. Many of the local *hala* groves are being supplanted by coffee and few of the old artisans are left, so it's worthwhile to see these fine crafts—and maybe purchase a few samples—while you still can.

Shops and art galleries are plentiful along the short stretch of Mamalahoa Highway that is the center of this tiny enclave. Don't miss **Studio 7 Gallery** (☎ 808/324-1335, open Tuesday through Saturday 10am to 4pm), established by locally born artist Hiroki Morinoue and his artist wife Setsuko. Hiroki studied in Japan and has brought an Asian aesthetic to the gallery, displaying contemporary fine arts whose simplicity and beauty blend well with the Zen-like serenity of the space. Several doors down is the **Country Frame Shop** (☎ 808/324-1590, open Monday through Friday 9:30am to 4:30pm and Saturday 9:30am to 1:30pm), whose specialty is custom framing using richly toned native koa wood. The shop also carries fine koa objects (hairbrushes and ornaments, pen sets, vases, etc.) and other decorative pieces. Across the street, the **Holualoa Gallery** (☎ 808/322-8484, open Tuesday through Saturday 10am to 5pm) exhibits the work of several area artists who work in a variety of media. Whether you prefer pottery, jewelry, sculpture, photography, or painting, there's surely something here to please. Local favorite Frances Dennis paints lovingly detailed portraits of rustic upcountry buildings, as well as warm, evocative island scenes on hand-turned pottery. Perhaps you'll be enchanted by the whimsical raku-fired ceramic fish by Randy Morehouse, a Holualoa-based artist whose pieces aren't always easy to find. If you have the time and are interested in the grass-roots creative process, stop by the **Kona Art Center** (no phone, Tuesday through Saturday 10am to 4pm), a gaily painted converted coffee mill that houses community art workshops. The students' work is displayed across the street, in a gallery installed in an old church that the Center rescued from the ravages of time and weather.

Although dining options are limited in Holualoa, the **Holuakoa Cafe** (☎ 808/322-2233, open Monday through Saturday 6:30am to 5pm) is well-known for owner Meggie Worbach's delicious home-baked sticky buns, spanikopita, and freshly brewed coffee.

The only accommodations in town are the **Kona Hotel** (worth a peek inside for its rough-hewn charm and local color) and the outstanding **Holualoa Inn** (see "Where to Stay" in Chapter 13). This 4-room bed & breakfast, on a working coffee farm and surrounded by some of the region's plentiful papaya and mango orchards, is built in the Hawaiian style, open to the warm, welcoming breezes. If you want to savor the ambiance of upcountry Kona for more than an afternoon, stay overnight at this relaxing home and enjoy a delicious breakfast (emphasizing fresh local ingredients) while gazing out over the sparkling coastline below.

11 The Big Island After Dark

HILO

Nightlife is quieter than it used to be in Hilo, what with the closing or conversion into condominium apartments of several major hotels. However, there's still enough to keep you busy making the rounds of some of the favorite places.

For an inexpensive, family-style evening in Hilo, try **Uncle Billy's Restaurant** at the Hilo Bay Hotel. The hotel and restaurant are owned and operated by Uncle Billy Kimi and his Hawaiian family, and each night from 6 to 8:30pm there's a free hula show, a totally nonslick warmhearted revue. Dinners feature fish just caught in Hilo waters, at $6.95 to $16.95; sandwiches are available for light eaters. Watch the local papers for news of entertainment at the posh **Hawaiian**

Naniloa Hotel, 93 Banyan Dr.; name performers from Honolulu sometimes play the Crown Room.

If it's just drinks and music you're after, there are several good spots around Hilo. **Harrington's,** 135 Kalanianaole St., has a scenic location overlooking the Ice Pond at Reed's Bay. You can enjoy live entertainment in the lounge Tuesday through Saturday nights, and have reasonably priced appetizers and drinks in a wonderfully romantic setting. They open at 4:30pm for the sunset cocktail hour. Sophisticated **Lehua Bay City Bar and Grill,** 90 Kamehameha Ave., has country-western line dancing every Wednesday and Thursday at 8pm, with a DJ playing the latest country hits. Admission is free. One of the town's "in" spots. There's live Hawaiian music Sunday nights at popular Café Pesto Hilo Bay.

KK Tei's Lounge, 1550 Kamehameha Ave., features karaoke sing-alongs, from 11am until closing Monday through Saturday nights. There's a vast selection of both Japanese and American songs.

The plush **Hilo Hawaiian Hotel,** 71 Banyan Dr., has the Waioli Lounge, overlooking Hilo Bay and majestic Mauna Kea volcano. Local friends rave about the authentic Hawaiian music presented Monday through Friday from 5 to 8pm by Albert and Alvin Kalima. Brothers Kili and Kalani Moki are on Thursday and Friday from 8 to 11pm and Fridays and Saturdays from 5 to 8pm. No cover, no minimum, and some of the best prices for beer and wine in town. In the historic downtown area, at 60 Keawe St., there's elegant **Roussels,** a French-Créole restaurant in a converted old bank. You can have cocktails there or after-dinner drinks nightly, perhaps treat yourself to New Orleans beignets and some dark French-roast coffee, brewed right at your table. The piano bar lounge at **Chapman's Land & Cattle Co., Ltd.** (760 Piilani St.), is a popular spot on Friday and Saturday from 9pm, when there's live entertainment. There's no entertainment and scarcely any atmosphere at the **Hilo Seaside Hotel bar** (126 Banyan Way), but always a local crowd full of fun, a big TV screen, and drinks at some of the lowest prices in town. When the bars close down, you can get some nourishment over at **Ken's House of Pancakes,** 1730 Kamehameha Ave. (see "Where to Eat," Chapter 13), where they serve not only pancakes and omelets, but everything on the menu around the clock.

KAILUA-KONA

There's plenty of nighttime entertainment in these parts, much of it centered around the big hotels. The **Keauhou Beach Hotel** is the place for fans of Hawaiian music, which can be heard Sunday mornings from 10am to 1pm and Friday evenings from 6 to 9pm at the Kuakini Terrace, during its buffet meals; and Sunday to Thursday from 6 to 10:30pm and Friday and Saturday from 5 to 11:30pm in the Makai Bar.

One of the most popular lounges in town is **Don Drysdale's Club 53** in the Kona Inn Shopping Village, on Kailua Bay, overlooking the waterfront.

The terrace overlooking the ocean at **Fisherman's Landing** is a wonderfully romantic spot, great for sunset watching or star gazing. Hawaiian and contemporary music is played every evening, from 6:30pm on. The cocktail lounges at **Jolly Roger, Kona Inn,** and **The Charthouse** are all seaside, offering super scenery along with the libations. If you're into heavy-duty rock and roll, **Jolly Roger** is the place on Friday and Saturday nights.

For jazz lovers, **Marty's Steak House,** opposite the sea wall on Alii Drive, is the place to be on Sunday afternoons from 2 to 5pm. That's when The Brothers and

The Brothers pull out all the stops. Visiting musicians often stop by to jam with them. No admission, no cover, but you're expected to buy a drink (and the sandwiches are very good). The music is live and the food and libations are also first-rate at **Under the Palms,** at Alii Sunset Plaza on Alii Drive and at Huggo's, next to the Royal Kona Resort.

If your beverage of choice is coffee rather than alcohol, you have two places to sip and listen to live music. The first, right on Alii Drive at Alii Sunset Plaza is the popular cafe–espresso bar **Lava Java,** where the sounds of classical acoustic guitar, country, folk, and more are heard every night. The other is the **Holuako Cafe,** about 6 miles up the mountain in the country town of Holualoa. There's usually a live band and sing-along on Thursday nights when a good time is had by all (be sure to call 808/322-CAFE to check as the schedule is flexible). Owner/host Meggi makes it all special.

Keep the **Kona Surf Resort** in mind, especially on Tuesday and Friday nights, when you can watch a free Polynesian Paradise Revue from 5:30 to 7pm on the Nalu Terrace, on the cliffs overlooking Keauhou Bay. Have a tropical drink and enjoy the show.

If you're in a disco mood, go to romantic **Eclipse,** 75-5711 Kuakini Hwy., across from Foodland—enjoy candles, wooden beams, mirrors, and the disco sound on Friday and Saturday nights from 10pm to 1:30am. The rest of the week, there's usually live music, call 808/329-4686 for the schedule.

The Windjammer Lounge of the **Royal Kona Resort** is one of the most scenic spots around, where you can listen to the sound of the surf smashing up against the rocks as you sit out on the patio and watch the Pacific perform. Walking around the big hotels like the Royal Kona, examining the gardens and lagoons by moonlight and floodlight, is a show in itself.

KONA COAST LUAUS

In the mood for a luau? There are two in Kona, both on the oceanfront. The luau at the **Royal Kona Resort** is held every Monday, Tuesday, Friday, and Saturday beginning at 5:30pm, at a cost of $49 adults, $18 for children 6 to 12, free for children under 5. Tihati Drums of Polynesia presents a fast-paced musical journey through the South Pacific, ending in a sensational Samoan fireknife dance. The luau at **King Kamehameha's Kona Beach Resort** is a tradition in these parts; it's held every Sunday, Tuesday, Wednesday, and Thursday at 6pm. The traditional rituals and feasting are followed by the Ports of Polynesia Revue, featuring traditional Pacific island dances. Cost is $49 for adults, $18 for children 6 to 12, free for children 5 and under. But you needn't pay anything to come and see the torchlighting ceremony. Just take yourself to the beach at 6pm and watch the beautiful ceremony, as torches are lit on land and sea in the shadow of an ancient heiau. Then you might proceed to the Billfish Bar, situated around the lovely pool, where there is a variety of musical entertainment every night from 5:30 to 10:30 pm.

15 Settling in on Kauai

About 110 miles to the west of Honolulu—yet seemingly light-years away—lies Kauai, the northernmost of the major Hawaiian islands, and one of the lushest tropical spots on earth. Kauai (pronounced correctly Kah-*wah*-ee, lazily Kah-*why*) is a small island, about 32 miles in diameter. Its central mountain receives an average of 500 inches of rainfall a year, making it one of the wettest spots on earth, which accounts for the lushness of the surrounding landscape.

Kauai is the oldest Hawaiian island both geologically and historically. In island lore, Kauai was the original home of Pele, the goddess of fire and volcanoes, before she moved southward. It was also the homeland of a race of pre-Polynesians whose origins are unknown. Some believe they were the survivors of the lost continent of Lemuria. In legend, these people, called Menehunes, were South Sea leprechauns who stood about 2 feet tall, worked only in darkness, and accomplished formidable engineering feats between dusk and dawn.

The first Polynesian settlers chose Kauai, too, and landed at the mouth of the Wailua River somewhere between A.D. 500 and 900. They crossed the Pacific in double-hulled sailing vessels in a voyage of many months, probably from the Society Islands. Other Polynesians came later, but time stood still on Kauai and the rest of the Hawaiian Islands until 1778, when Captain Cook arrived at Waimea and the modern history of Hawaii began.

You can see all the important things in Kauai in three days—but the longer you stay, the luckier you are.

AFTER INIKI

In September 1992, a devastating hurricane struck the island of Kauai, demolishing homes and buildings, sweeping roofs and even refrigerators out to sea, uprooting vegetation, and altering the very shape of the land. Since then, however, Kauai has made an amazing recovery. The mountains and fields are lush and green again, the flowers and foliage have come back, some of the beaches are wider and better than ever, the golf courses are in fine condition, and most homes, hotels, and visitor attractions have been repaired or totally rebuilt. There have been some changes in the major hotel scene: the old Westin Kauai is now the Marriott Kauai, and its formal statuary and Versailles-like atmosphere have given way to a much more Hawaiian, garden-and-waterfall ambience. Duke's

What's Special About Kauai

Natural Wonders
- Waimea Canyon, a 3,657-foot gorge dubbed the "Grand Canyon of the Pacific" by Mark Twain.
- Mount Waialeale, "the wettest spot on earth," receiving 480 inches of rain a year—best seen by helicopter.
- Spouting Horn, a saltwater geyser where water spouts up through the lava rocks to heights of 50 feet.
- The spectacularly rugged, beautiful, and isolated Na Pali Coast, accessible only by foot, boat, or air.

Beaches
- Superb swimming year-round at Kalapaki Beach in Lihue and, on the southern and western shores, at Poipu Beach Park and Salt Pond Beach Park. In summer, along the north shore, at romantic Hanalei Bay (where *South Pacific* was filmed), Haena Beach Park, and Ke'e Beach.

Snorkeling
- At many spots around the island, especially good at Poipu Beach on the southern shore and Tunnels Beach on the north shore.

Museums and Historic Homes
- Kauai Museum, with changing art, heritage, and cultural exhibits of both Asia and Hawaii, as well as a permanent showcase of Hawaiiana.
- Grove Farm Homestead, a look back into the plantation days of 19th-century Hawaii.
- Kilohana Plantation, a combination historical house, museum, restaurant, and shopping bazaar.
- Kokee Natural History Museum, a tiny museum devoted to the indigenous bird and plant life of the island.
- Wailoli Mission House in Hanalei, full of fascinating furniture, books, and mementos of 19th-century missionary days.

Botanical Gardens
- National Tropical Botanical Gardens in Lawai, Kauai's best, a 286-acre tropical garden filled with more than 5,000 varieties of tropical plants on exquisite grounds; guided tours.
- Olu Pua Gardens in Kalakeho, a botanical showplace and historic home.

Hiking
- Some of the best in the islands, with magnificent trails on the Na Pali Coast and into Waimea Canyon.

Movie and TV Locations
- Picture perfect locations that may seem familiar if you've seen *Jurassic Park, Raiders of the Lost Ark, Indiana Jones and the Temple of Doom, Blue Hawaii, Thunderball, The Thorn Birds,* or *South Pacific*—to mention just a few.

Canoe Club, its restaurant on the beach, is back, and so are the pleasures of neighboring Kauai Lagoons—golf course, wedding chapel, spa, carriage rides, and more. The famed Coco Palms Resort, however, is still involved in insurance negotiations and has not yet reopened. Kauai's economic infrastructure was dealt a blow from which it may never recover, but—to the visitor's eye, at least—the wounds have healed, the scars are fading, the pristine beauty has re-emerged. The beauty of the island and of the people of Kauai are superb testaments to the human spirit, which somehow succeeds, time and time again, in overcoming adversity.

1 Orientation & Getting Around

ARRIVING BY PLANE   Not long after your interisland plane takes off in Honolulu, it lands at the sleek $36-million Richard A. Kawakami Terminal, the third-busiest airport in the state. Rent a car or hail a cab to get to Lihue town or other destinations.

INFORMATION

The headquarters of the **Hawaii Visitors Bureau** is at 3016 Umi St., Suite 207 (☎ 808-245-3971), on the second floor of Lihue Plaza. Information is available on just about everything, including tips on where to play tennis and golf, deep-sea fishing charters, helicopter tours, boat tours, kayaking, and glider flights.

Kauai Vacation Helpers was set up after Hurricane Iniki to help visitors find their way to the best island activities. Call them at 808/246-0745 and they'll steer you right, giving you advice on which companies have the best safety and customer satisfaction records. They'll fill you in on the best places to swim, snorkel, and fish and, in general, will lend a helping hand. A phone call is all that's necessary.

GETTING AROUND

BY RENTAL CAR   For information on the major budget car-rental companies—offering excellent flat-rate packages on all the islands—see Chapter 3. If, however, you haven't done so, or prefer a time-plus-mileage deal, simply walk up to any of the car-rental agencies just across the road from the airport. We drove a car from **Sunshine of Hawaii** (☎ 808/245-9541 or 800/367-2977) on our last trip and were pleased with both the car and the courteous service. And it's especially nice that the cars are right at the airport. Rates begin at $22.95 daily for a compact two-door automatic with air conditioning, $139 weekly. For an automatic four-door with air conditioning, the price is $28.95 and $159.

BY BUS & TAXI   While a car is definitely the best way to go, there is some public transportation. The **Kauai Bus,** a new company, operates a fleet of 15 buses that serve the entire island. For scheduling and destinations, phone 808/246-4622. The bus costs $1.

Should you need a cab for a short trip, **Kauai Cab** (☎ 808/246-9554) is a reliable outfit.

FAST FACTS: Kauai

Area Code   The telephone area code is 808.

Dentists   Contact Dr. John R. Black, 4347 Rice St., Lihue (☎ 808/245-3582); or Dr. Mark Baird, 4-9768 Kuhio Hwy., Kapaa (☎ 808/822-9393).

Doctors   Kauai Medical Group has clinics in Lihue (☎ 808/245-1500), Kapaa (☎ 808/822-3431), Koloa (☎ 808/742-1621), and Princeville (☎ 808/826-6300). Physicians are on call 24 hours (☎ 808/245-1831).

Emergencies   Call 911.

Hospitals   Wilcox Memorial Hospital, 3420 Kuhio Hwy., Lihue (☎ 808/245-1100) has an emergency room open 24 hours.

Iniki Express   This free daytime bus service, set up after the 1992 hurricane, may still be in operation by the time you read this. For details, call 808/241-6410.

Other Useful Numbers   State Commission on Persons with Disabilities (☎ 808/245-4308; Voice/TDD); Helpline Kauai (☎ 808/245-3411); YWCA Sexual Assault Services (☎ 808/245-4144). On Call (☎ 808/246-1441) is a 24-hour free service offering news, sports, weather, community-service information, etc. See also the Aloha Pages of the Kauai telephone directory.

Police   Call 911 for emergencies, 808/245-9711 for all other matters.

Poison Control Center   Call 800/362-3585.

Post Office   It's at 4441 Rice St., Lihue (☎ 808/245-4994); you'll find satellite post offices all over the island.

Taxis   Call **Kauai Cab** at 808/246-9554.

Time of Day   Call 808/245-0212.

Visitors' Information Program   Call 808/246-1440.

Weather Information   For current weather, call 808/245-6001; for a marine report, 808/245-3564; for a surf report, 808/335-3611.

2 Where to Stay

Bed & Breakfast Hawaii, the largest reservation service in the islands, is headquartered right here in Kauai. Not only do they have a wide range of carefully inspected accommodations all over the state, but they also work with Avis Car Rental to provide lower prices on car rentals for their guests. For a free brochure, contact Bed & Breakfast Hawaii, P.O. Box 449, Kapaa, HI 96746 (☎ 808/822-7771 or 800/733-1632; fax 808/822-2723). For $12.95, you receive a directory of homes and apartments with rooms for rent called *B&B Goes Hawaiian.*

IN & AROUND LIHUE

The town of Lihue and its adjacent Nawiliwili Harbor are the most centrally located places to stay in Kauai. Lihue is the county seat and the center of Kauai's government, commerce, and culture.

Ⓢ Garden Island Inn

3445 Wilcox Rd., Lihue, Kauai, HI 96766. ☎ **808/245-7227** or toll free 800/648-0154. 15 rms, 6 suites. MINIBAR TV TEL. $50–$65 double; $65–$85 family room and suites. MC, V. Free parking.

One of Kauai's top budget choices is 2 miles from the center of town, at Nawiliwili Harbor. The Garden Island Inn is an older hotel that has been taken over by new owners, renovated from top to bottom. Owners Steven and Susan Layne have done a terrific job in transforming the three-story hotel, which has lovely gardens and miniature waterfalls cascading into several koi pools. You can help yourself to bananas and the fruit on the orange and papaya trees, and be at beautiful Kalapaki Beach, one of our favorites in the islands, in about a minute.

Rooms are light and sunny, with rattan furniture, ceiling fans, tropical flowers, and original watercolors. Most have ocean views, and some include private lanais. Each room features a wet bar with refrigerator, microwave oven, and coffee maker complete with complimentary Lappert's Kona coffee. Bedding is either a queen-size bed or two twin beds; bathrooms have showers but no tubs. The cheapest doubles are on the ground floor, and the more expensive doubles, with private lanais, are on the second floor. A suite with a living room, four beds, a microwave oven, and a large refrigerator could house a family of four. Another suite has a three-sided private lanai, a daybed in the living room and a queen-size bed in the bedroom, a microwave oven and a large refrigerator. Steve and Susan will lend guests beach gear, golf clubs, snorkels, coolers, etc., at no charge.

Motel Lani
4240 Rice St. (P.O. Box 1836), Lihue, Kauai, HI 96766. ☎ **808/245-2965.** 10 rms. TEL. $30–$48 double; from $48 triple. Each additional person $14 extra. Minimum stay 2 nights. No credit cards. Free parking.

This is the only budget accommodation in the center of town we think most visitors will find suitable. It's a pleasant place, patronized by both islanders and tourists. Rooms are small but modern, with a small refrigerator. Rollaway cots are provided. Owner Janet Naumu requires a 2-night deposit. Rates are subject to change without notice.

KAUAI'S EASTERN SHORE: THE COCONUT COAST

Nine miles out of Lihue, near where the Wailua River meets the ocean, begins Kauai's "Coconut Coast," stretching from here through the town of Kapaa. This area is also known as Coconut Plantation. The area has beautiful scenery, lots of good, inexpensive restaurants, and the Coconut Marketplace. The hotels here are more expensive than the ones in the Lihue area since they are situated directly on the ocean. Here, on the windward side of the island, the surf is rougher (and the weather apt to be rainier) than on the leeward side. If you have a car, it's no problem, since it's a short drive to the splendid beaches of leeward Poipu. If you don't have a car, however, and want to swim in the ocean, we recommend choosing a hotel in Poipu (see below).

DOUBLES FOR ABOUT $45 TO $75

✪ **Hotel Coral Reef**
1516 Kuhio Hwy., Kapaa, Kauai, HI 96746. ☎ **808/822-4481** or toll free 800/843-4659. TV TEL. Oceanfront Building $72–$85 double. Main Building $45–$70 double; $70–$85 suites. Each additional person $10 extra; crib or rollaway $10. Room and car packages available. (Rates include continental breakfast.) CB, DC, MC, V. Free parking.

This cute little hotel is right on the ocean and close to everything in town: a public swimming beach, freshwater swimming pool, tennis court, library, launderette, and several great little budget restaurants. The hotel has a stretch of white, sandy beach, and there's good swimming and snorkeling in the deep water between the reefs. You could even make do without a car here.

There are two wings. The Oceanfront Building, prettier than ever since its renovation after the hurricane, is a winner. Spacious rooms overlook the beach (which is just 50 yards away) and boast private lanais, new rattan furniture, small refrigerators, glass sliding doors, louvered windows (to catch the prevailing trade winds), and either double or twin beds. Bathrooms have been retiled in pastel colors and new showers have been installed. The Main Building, reopened last year, has nicely furnished rooms with both shower and tub in the private bath. Most of these rooms have ocean views; some overlook the garden. Most have private lanais. Suites, which can accommodate up to four people, have mountain views. A complimentary continental breakfast is served each morning. There's an activities center, barbecue grills, and snorkel rental.

Kapaa Sands

380 Papaloa Rd., Kapaa, Kauai, HI 96746. ☎ **808/882-4901** or toll free 800/222-4901. 21 rms. TV TEL. $75–$85 studio; $99–$109 two-bedroom apt. Minimum stay 3 days in summer, 7 days in winter. MC, V. Free parking.

One of our favorite places to stay on Kauai is the comfortable and very attractive Kapaa Sands. It's just a few minutes' walk from Coconut Plantation, yet it's secluded and right on the beach. The pretty, two-story green buildings house studios and two-bedroom apartments; choose between garden, ocean view, or oceanfront. All units have ceiling fans. Studios have lanais and separate, fully equipped kitchens. The two-bedroom units are charming duplex apartments (two bedrooms and full bath upstairs, sofa bed and half-bath downstairs), each with two lanais.

Kapaa Shore

4-0900 Kuhio Hwy., Kapaa, Kauai, HI 96746. ☎ **808/822-3055** or toll free 800/827-3922. Fax 808/822-1457. 81 condominiums (40 for rent). TV TEL. $65–$120 one-bedroom unit; $85–$140 two-bedroom unit. Weekly rates available. MC, V. Free parking.

For a touch of luxury in Kapaa, this condominium complex may be just the ticket. It's right at the beach, and each apartment has a view of the ocean, garden, or pool. All are beautifully furnished, many in avocado-and-white decorative schemes, with fully equipped kitchens, and patio furniture to make dining on your lanai a treat. The one-bedroom units can accommodate up to four people, with a queen-size bed in the bedroom and a queen-size sofa in the living room. Six people can be cozy in the two-bedroom units, which are duplexes with vaulted ceilings, a queen-size bed in one of the bedrooms, two twins in the other, and a queen-size sleeper sofa in the living room. Facilities include a tennis court, 40-foot swimming pool, sunbathing decks, and barbecue area.

Mokihana of Kauai

796 Kuhio Hwy., Kapaa, Kauai, HI 96746. ☎ **808/822-3971.** 80 studio apts. $55 single or double. MC, V. Free parking.

It's not easy to get an apartment at this attractive condominium complex in the busy winter months; that's when it's usually chock-full of owners. The best time for rentals is from late April through late September. Apartments are nicely furnished with limited kitchen facilities (refrigerators, hotplate, and electric frying pan), bath, and/or shower. The apartments are right on the ocean and 2 miles away from a championship golf course. Mokihana also boasts an 18-hole, par-36 putting green, shuffleboard, a large swimming pool, and a barbecue area. The Bull Shed Restaurant, a superb steak house, is right on the waterfront. For information, contact Hawaii Kailani, 119 N. Commercial, Suite 1400, Belingham, WA 98225 (☎ 206/676-1434).

DOUBLES FOR ABOUT $80 TO $110

Aston Kauai Beachboy Hotel

484 Kuhio Hwy., no. 100, Kapaa, Kauai, HI 96746. ☎ **808/822-3441** or toll free 800/922-7866. Fax 808/922-8785. 243 rms. A/C TV TEL. $108 standard, $128 oceanview, $130 oceanfront single or double. Each additional person $12 extra. AE, CB, DC, MC, V. Free parking.

About a mile past the famed Coco Palms Resort, on the ocean side of the road, is this very pleasant, moderately priced hotel. A branch of Honolulu's terrific Perry's Smorgy Restaurant, which serves three hearty and reasonably priced buffet meals a day, is on the premises. Rooms are nicely decorated and face either the garden or the sea; each has its own private lanai, a small refrigerator, and a large dressing room. You can swim in the ocean—the hotel is located on the white sand beach at Coconut Plantation—or in the almost Olympic-size swimming pool. Coconut Marketplace, a Hawaiian-style shopping village, is nearby.

Kauai Sands Hotel

480 Papaloa Ave., Kapaa, Kauai, HI 96746 ☎ **808/822-4951** or toll free 800/367-7000 in U.S. Fax 808/822-0052. 200 rms, 2 suites. A/C TV TEL. Apr–Jan 31, from $80 single or double, from $95 single or double with kitchenette; Feb–Mar, from $85 single or double, from $110 single or double with kitchenette. AE, MC, V. Free parking.

This attractive and informal hotel is part of the hospitable, locally owned and operated chain of Sand & Seaside Hotels. It faces green lawns and a mile of white sand beach (beautiful but often rough for swimming); there are two swimming pools as well. The good-sized rooms are decorated in ocean hues of green and blue. All have refrigerators, private lanais, and either two double beds or a king-size bed. Save money by patronizing the hotel's dining room, Al and Don's, which serves dinner main courses between $5.95 and $12.

Royal Drive Cottages

147 Royal Dr., Kapaa, Kauai, HI 96746. ☎ **808/822-2321.** 2 cottages, 1 single in the main house. $60 single; $80 double. Futon for a third person $10. 10% discount on stays of 1 week or longer. Free parking.

Up in the lush green hills of the Eden-like Wailua district, down a private road, you'll find Bob Levine's beautiful guest cottages. Bob refers to his little bit of paradise as a "cozy tropical hideaway," a most apt description. Each cottage has twin beds that make up as a king-size bed; a kitchen equipped with a small refrigerator, microwave oven, coffeemaker, blender, and everything in the way of utensils for preparing and serving a meal; a private bath; ceiling fans; and views of the garden from every window. The first cottage has a huge screened lanai facing a part of the garden planted with palm trees, heliconia, ginger, and papaya trees. The second cottage is literally *in* the garden. It has a tiny porch with one chair; down the steps is an enormous kukui-nut tree with chairs under it; nearby is a fish pond filled with water hyacinths and inhabited by sparkling fish. The temptation to settle under the tree and never move is strong. Guests are invited to pick the pomelos, papayas, and bananas in season. They are welcome to use the hot tub in the main house. There are coolers, a big beachball, and a boogie board to tote to the beach. Bob's house is between the cottages; he is available and happy to share his considerable knowledge of the islands and offer suggestions to help make your stay truly special. Bob requests that you smoke only outside.

BED & BREAKFASTS

ⓢ House of Aleva

5509 Kuamoo Rd., Kapaa, Kauai, HI 96746. ☎ **808/822-4606.** 3 rms. 1 with private bath. TV. $55 double, $40 single. (Rates include breakfast.) No credit cards.

Ernie and Anita Perry, a retired couple from Oahu (she's a former nurse, he was a Merchant Marine for many years), are the best kind of B&B hosts: They love having guests in their home and share it freely. Guests have the run of the house, which means they're more likely to be lolling out on the porch swing or in the comfortable living room, rather than in the guest rooms. There are two nicely furnished upstairs rooms—one done in pink, the other in blue—that boast their own TVs and queen-size orthopedic beds. They share a spacious bathroom. Downstairs is a small single room with its own bath and a nifty indoor/outdoor shower. Guests have use of beach towels, mats, picnic and snorkeling gear, a washer-dryer, even a full-size back massager. The Perrys will tailor breakfast to personal dietary needs. They serve papayas from their own garden. The house is situated 2 miles inland from the main highway, in the lush Wailua district, just across the road from Opaekaa Waterfall. Be sure to ask to see Anita's work; she's a talented sculptor of Hawaiiana. Many Europeans have discovered this place, so the conversation around the breakfast table is apt to be multilingual. A delightful find.

Kakalina's Bed & Breakfast

6781 Kawaihai Rd., Kapaa, HI 96747. ☎ **808/822-2328.** Fax 808/823-6833. 1 apt, 1 rm. TV. Hale Akahi $75; Hale Elua $70 single or double. (Rates include breakfast.) No credit cards. Free parking.

Kathy and Bob Offley are delightful folks who live up in the lush green pasture country above Kapaa where, in addition to running a very special bed & breakfast, they have a 3-acre working tropical flower farm. The views are glorious—not only of the ocean in the distance, but also of the lake directly below and the hillside terraces lush with flowers. Their Hale Akahi unit is a spacious two-room unit under their own house with its own entrance, screened porch, a king-size bed and a smaller one, and a kitchenette. Best of all, it has a bathroom—with bright blue tiles and an immense bathtub for soaking—that looks like something out of a Hollywood movie set; imagine sitting in that amazing tub looking out at the garden, the valley, the mountains and the ocean (that in itself would be worth the trip). Their Hale Elua unit, in a separate building from the main house, is a ground-floor studio with a queen-size bed, a futon that can serve as an extra bed or a living room couch, a private bath with shower, and a full-size kitchen. Outside the picture window are tropical flowers, the mountains, and a reservoir. Bob and his sons have built the entire place; he is a master carpenter and woodworker. Both units have a VCR, on which you can watch any of the 60-or-so movies Kathy and Bob will be happy to lend you, or you can read one of the tons of books in the bookcases. Kathy doesn't do a formal breakfast, but you have a kitchenette with microwave oven, fridge, toaster, and coffeemaker. She bakes bread and brings it—along with fresh fruit—every day, and makes sure there's plenty of coffee and tea. Rosie, a Labrador/German Shepherd (maybe) and Nicki, a Golden Retriever, are ready to be your best friends and accompany you on walks at any hour of the day or night.

Kauai Calls Bed & Breakfast

5972 Hiamo Place, Kapaa, HI 96746. ☎ **808/822-9699** or toll free 800/522-9699. 1 studio apt, 1 rm. TV. Studio apt $70 single, $75 double; rm, $55 single, $60 double. (Rates include breakfast.) No credit cards. Free parking.

Earle Schertell is fond of describing the location of his pretty pink house up above Opaeka'a Falls as "nestled in the eyebrow of the Sleeping Giant." It's way up in quiet and pristine farm and ranch country. The Sleeping Giant studio apartment has a private entrance, a king-size bed, and all the amenities—private bath, color TV, a stereo with lots of Hawaiian music to play, microwave, refrigerator, toaster, coffeemaker, and hibachi. It's decorated Polynesian style; Earle always brings in several of his blooming orchid plants. Earle prepares breakfast at night and puts it in your fridge, so it's there when you awaken. He visits the Sunshine Markets to get the freshest produce and really outdoes himself in the presentation of the meals. The Orchid Isle bedroom, also with a private entrance, is attached to the main house but can be totally closed off from it; Earle will make the beds up as two twins or one king-size one, and there's a private bath, as well as the appliances mentioned above. It is only rented with the apartment, for a family or two couples traveling together. Earle and his precious little Shih Tzu, Tang, (a wily escape artist!) greet you with a lei and their gracious aloha spirit.

Kay Barker's Bed & Breakfast

P.O. Box 740, Kapaa, Kauai, HI 96746. ☎ **808/822-3073** or toll free 800/835-2845. 5 rms. $35–$60 single; $45–$70 double. Direct booking special: 15% discount on stays over 6 days. (Rates include breakfast.) MC, V. Free parking.

This very casual bed-and-breakfast inn is on the slopes of the Sleeping Giant mountain, a 10-minute drive from Hi. 56. The back deck runs the length of the house and looks out over peaceful gardens and pastures. There is a large living room and dining room, a separate TV room, a refrigerator for storing snacks, and a washer-dryer. Guests can also use ice chests, beach mats, and boogie boards.

The Lokelani Room, next to the kitchen, has a double bed and a private bath; it rents for $35 single, $45 double. The Plumeria Room (with a king-size bed or twin beds) and the Orchid Room (king-size bed) both have private bathrooms with showers and look out over the front garden; they rent for $40 single, $50 double. The Ginger Room, "the honeymooners' favorite," has its own entrance, wicker furniture, and a private bath with tub and shower, and overlooks the back garden and pasture lands of Mount Waialeale; rates are $50 single, $60 double. Hibiscus, a two-room cottage, is private in the back garden; it has large rooms, a king-size bed, a sitting room with wet bar, refrigerator, microwave, and a private lanai from which to catch the great views; it rents for $60 single, $70 double.

Gordon Barker, who runs the place, whips up good breakfasts (they might include fresh fruits and juices, banana-nut muffins, and macadamia-nut pancakes). Families with children are welcome. Smoking is acceptable. If this place is full, he may be able to put you in touch with other B&Bs in the area.

THE NORTH SHORE: PRINCEVILLE, KILAUEA, HANALEI, HAENA

Think of luxury living, championship golf and tennis amid a green sweep of mountains and valleys, and the fabulous Princeville Hotel will immediately come to mind. You might not think of basing a budget vacation here, but there are a few needles in the haystack. *Note:* If you want ocean swimming, choose this area only in summer. In winter, high surf and treacherous currents make the north shore ocean dangerous.

KILAUEA

Hale Ho'o Maha

P.O. Box 422, Kilauea, Kauai, HI 96754. ☎ **808/828-1341** or toll free 800/851-0291 in the U.S. mainland and Canada. 4 rms (2 with bath). TV TEL. $55–$80 single or double. (Rates include breakfast.) MC, V. Free parking.

Toby and Kirby Guyer-Searles enjoy sharing their entire lovely split-level home with their guests. Nestled cliffside overlooking a freshwater stream and pond on 5 acres of landscaped grounds, the house is minutes away from fine sand beaches, rivers, waterfalls, hiking trails, and just a minute from a world-class, 45-hole golf course. A short drive leads to a natural private swimming hole enclosed by lava rocks, where waves break over one side and create a Jacuzzi-like effect. The home has four bedrooms: The Pineapple Room has a seven-foot round bed, a full private marble bath, and a private entrance off the lanai. The Guava Room has a king-size bed with a sheer canopy, a sitting area, and private bath and entrance. The Mango Room has two queen-size beds and shares a marble bath with the Papaya Room, which has a queen-size bed. Guests have full kitchen privileges and use of surf and boogie boards, beach mats, washer-dryer, and gas barbecue grill. A continental breakfast that always includes freshly baked breads and muffins is served in the dining room each morning. The handsome living room, with its wood-burning fireplace, Hawaiian and South Pacific artifacts, saltwater aquarium, and color cable TV, is a popular gathering spot. Smoking and social drinking are acceptable. Ask Kirby and Toby to show you the exquisite feather and satin leis they make. They sometimes take guests on trips to remote areas that require a four-wheel-drive vehicle, and Toby, a certified diver, often takes guests out to explore Kauai beneath the waters.

❂ Kai Mana

2840 Kauapea Rd., P.O. Box 612, Kilauea, HI 96754. ☎ **808/828-1280** or toll free 800/837-1782. Fax 808/828-6670. 4 rms, 1 cottage. $95 single, $115 double, corner room with king- or queen-size bed; $75 single, $95 double rms with queen-size bed or two double beds; two-night minimum; $125 per night, $750 per week, one-bedroom cottage, five-night minimum. (Rates include breakfast.) Free parking.

About a 15-minute drive from Princeville and in a secluded little world of its own, Kai Mana is the perfect place for rest and retreat. The lovely plantation house, high upon a cliff overlooking a secluded beach (accessible by a very steep cliffside trail) is the home of Shakti Gawain, renowned author of books on consciousness (*Creative Visualization, Living in the Light, The Path of Transformation*) and her husband, Jim Burns. Each of the four rooms has a private bath, and all are decorated differently, in island style with Hawaiian vintage or flower prints and brilliant colors. Common areas include a small lounge with TV, VCR, videos, and books; a laundry room; and a kitchenette where guests may cook their own meals. Continental breakfast foods are set out in the kitchenette; guests dine at tables out on the large lanai (with hammock and hot tub) overlooking the ocean. Each room opens onto the lanai. The octagonal cottage—everybody's favorite— is all wicker and windows from which to watch spectacular ocean and shoreline views. The lush 5-acre property is often the scene of weddings and special parties, for which arrangements can be made here. *Note:* The ocean here is for experienced swimmers only.

The Kalihiwai Jungle Home

P.O. Box 717, Kilauea, HI 96754. ☎ and fax **808/828-1626.** 1 house. $125 for up to five people; weekly rates available. No credit cards. Free parking.

The Kalihiwai Jungle Home is an unusual find, only two minutes away from Princeville Airport but in its own private world. Spectacular views of jungle, waterfalls, and lush green mountains can be seen from each of the two nicely decorated bedrooms, the spacious glassed-in living room, and the fully equipped kitchen. The house is completely surrounded by bamboo, banana, papaya, and tropical palm trees, affording complete privacy. Amenities include a washer-dryer, a private telephone, even a fax machine. It's just a 10-minute walk to Kalihiwai Beach, a 2-minute drive to windsurfing at Anini Beach, and another 2-minute drive to the nifty Princeville Spa where guests, for a mere $10 a day, can enjoy full workout facilities, spa, and an Olympic-size swimming pool. Massage, facials, and other spa services are available. In fact, a stay here could be therapeutic in more ways than one. The owner, Thomas Weinberg, Ph.D., a well-known psychotherapist and seminar leader, reports that clients often come to stay at his house (or at nearby B&Bs if the house is full) to have a series of sessions with him and enjoy the healing atmosphere of Kauai. Thomas lives upstairs in his own private quarters and is always available to help out with tips and information about Kauai. For special gatherings and occasions, it is sometimes possible to rent the entire house.

PRINCEVILLE/HANALEI

✪ Bed, Breakfast, and Beach

At Hanalei Bay, P.O. Box 746, Hanalei HI 96714. ☎ **808/826-6111.** 3 rms, 1 efficiency apt. $65–$95 single or double. Each additional person $15 extra. (Rates include breakfast.) No credit cards.

Carolyn Barnes's stylish house is in a suburban neighborhood just 100 yards from Hanalei Bay, wonderful for summer swimming. The second-floor wraparound lanai is the perfect place for viewing sunsets over the ocean and sighting rainbows and waterfalls. The house is beautifully decorated with American oak antiques and Hawaiian memorabilia. Rooms, each with a queen-size bed, fan, and private bath, are romantically furnished with calico-print wallpaper and carefully selected linens and comforters. Honeymooners love this place! Also available is a large studio apartment with a private entrance and an efficiency kitchen. A continental breakfast, island style, is served each morning on the lanai; it consists of a smoothie or juice, fresh island fruit, pancakes with homemade coconut syrup, fresh-baked muffins or bread, and coffee or tea. No smoking. Well-behaved children only; crib available.

Hale Moi Cottages

5300 Ka Huku Rd., P.O. Box 899, Princeville-Hanalei, HI 96714. ☎ **808/826-9602** or toll free 800/535-0085. Fax 808/826-4159 or toll free 800/633-5085. 40 apts. TV TEL. $99 master bedroom single or double; $129 studio with kitchen; $179 1^1/2-bedroom, two-bath, kitchen suite for up to four people. MC, V. Free parking.

Hale Moi, overlooking a Robert Trent Jones golf course, is perfect for golfers. Perched atop a cliff with wonderful mountain and garden views, the condominiums boast handsomely furnished units with either a king- or queen-size bed in the master bedroom, a refrigerator, and full bath; some have sofa beds. The studios have full kitchen and bath; the 1^1/2-bedroom suites have a full kitchen and 2 baths.

HAENA

Camp Naue, YMCA of Kauai

P.O. Box 1786, Lihue, Kauai, HI 96766. ☎ **808/246-9090** or 808/246-4411. 42 bunks. $12 bed; $10 tent space for one person, $7 each additional person. No credit cards.

Hikers, backpackers, campers, take note: If you're about to hike the Na Pali trail and need a place to relax and get a good night's sleep before or after, the YMCA of Kauai has a perfect solution for you. The camp is 1^1/2 miles from the trailhead at Kalalau, right on the beach at Haena, in an idyllic setting under the ironwood and kumani trees. Two bunkhouses situated on the crest of the beach are divided into four separate areas, each with 10 to 12 bunk beds; the facilities are coed, but there are separate baths for men and women, and hot showers. Bring your own sleeping bag, as the camp does not provide linens or towels. There's a covered beachfront pavilion, a campfire area with picnic tables, and one of the island's best beaches—in summer—for swimming, snorkeling, and surfing (in winter, the ocean is very rough here). There is no refrigeration (the kitchen is for group use only), and if you need food supplies, it's best to stock up on them in Hanalei. You can also stop in at Jungle Bob's in Ching Young Village for backpacking supplies.

Camp Naue is usually filled with large groups, but often has space for walk-in visitors. They don't take reservations, but if you call their Lihue office at 808/246-9090 not more than two weeks in advance, they'll advise you of the likelihood of getting space here. On weekends, you can call the caretaker at the camp at 808/826-6419.

✪ Hanalei Colony Resort

P.O. Box 206, Hanalei, Kauai, HI 96714-9985. ☎ **808/826-6235** or toll free 800/628-3004. Fax 808/826-9893. 52 two-bedroom apts. Jan 8–Jun 14 and Aug 16–Dec 15, $100–$175 for up to four people; Dec 16–Jan 7 and June 15–Aug 15, $120–$195 for up to four people. Seventh night free; three-day minimum. Car-and-condo packages available. AE, MC, V. Free parking.

Haena is what you always imagined Hawaii would be like—golden curving beaches, coconut palms, lush foliage, jagged cliffs tumbling down to the sea. Imagine a little cluster of condominium apartments set out right in front of the beach here and you have an idea of what Hanalei Colony Resort looks like: it's an enchanting, end-of-the-road stop where civilization can seem very far away. No noises of phones or TVs or stereos to intrude—just the sounds of the ocean and the songs of the birds to provide a backdrop for your vacation. It's a favorite spot for honeymooners, of course, but also for families, seniors, and outdoor enthusiasts who want a comfortable place to come back to after hiking the trails and exploring nature. The resort is made up of 13 two-story buildings, each with four apartments. Each unit has two nicely furnished bedrooms, a living room, dining area, a large bathroom, a fully equipped kitchen, and a private lanai. The units at the lower end of the scale, most suitable for our budget, will have garden, not ocean views. A pool, badminton, croquet, and babysitting services are available, along with lots of personal attention from the staff. The dining, shopping, and nightlife diversions of Princeville and Hanalei are not more than 20 minutes away. You'll reach Hanalei Colony only after driving a very winding country road, with dozens of one-lane bridges, past Hanalei; the drive might encourage you to stay at home, cook in, or dine at Charo's Restaurant, right at hand.

THE SOUTHERN SHORE: POIPU BEACH & ENVIRONS

In the other direction from Lihue, 12 miles south, stretches the idyllic Poipu Beach area, dry and sunny, where the Mediterranean blue-green surf crashes on palm-fringed, white-sand beaches. Of course, this area is more expensive than Lihue, but you're right at the beach (in our opinion, the best on Kauai).

DOUBLES FOR ABOUT $30

Kahili Mountain Park

P.O. Box 298, Koloa, Kauai, HI 96756. ☎ **808/742-9921.** 14 cabins, 15 cabinettes. $30 cabinettes for two people; $40 cabins with inside toilet and private outdoor shower for two people; $50 cabins with full bathroom facilities for two people. Each additional person $6 extra. Minimum stay of two days required. No credit cards. Free parking.

If you are really into the great outdoors—but not enough to backpack it and sleep under the stars—try this camp, located seven miles from Poipu Beach, off Hi. 50

west, just beyond the 7-mile marker. Mount Kahili rises majestically behind the little cabins and cabinettes nestled near a small lake where you can swim and fish for bass. The park is operated by the Seventh-Day Adventist Church, and their school is on the premises.

The cabinettes are grouped in a circle around the bathroom-and-shower buildings. Each has one room, with a small dining area where there's a small refrigerator, a two-burner hotplate, and a sink. Cookware is furnished. Cabins, consisting of either one large room or two small ones, have a bathroom with a sink and toilet; there's a private shower outside each cabin. They also have a full-size refrigerator, as well as the two-burner stove and sink. Six new cabins have private bathrooms and showers, a stove, refrigerator, and hot water. All of the accommodations have screened windows with louvers. Linens are furnished. These facilities are very rustic, in a most beautiful setting. There is a laundry room on the premises. Prepayment in full is required for all reservations.

DOUBLES FOR ABOUT $50 TO $80

Classic Vacation Cottages

2687 Onu Place (P.O. Box 901), Kalaheo, Kauai, HI 96741. ☎ **808/332-9201.** Fax 808/332-7645. 3 cottages. TV. $58 studio; $62–$68 one-bedroom cottage with breakfast. Each additional person $10 extra. No credit cards. Free parking.

A stay in the tiny country town of Kalaheo is for those who prefer to be away from the tourist scene, yet close enough to enjoy its advantages. These three self-contained cottages on a hillside are set in a garden adjacent to the custom-built home of Richard and Wynnis Grow, in a residential neighborhood. The Grows have decorated them handsomely, with stained, leaded windows, well-equipped kitchens, a living room and porch, and a queen-size bed in the bedroom. The one-bedroom units have ocean or garden views for the same price, while the studio has a garden view. Each unit has its own barbecue; daily linen service is provided. Guests are welcome to use the hot tub, Jacuzzi, and outdoor barbecue. Snorkeling equipment and boogie boards are provided free, along with beach towels. The Kukuiolono Golf Course is a five-minute drive away, and Poipu Beach about 10 minutes; tennis courts and a park for jogging are nearby.

✪ Garden Isle Cottages

2666 Puuholu Rd., Koloa, Kauai, HI 96756. ☎ **808/742-6717** or toll free 800/742-6711. 10 studios and apts. TV. $79–$93 studio; $106–$118 one-bedroom apt on ocean; $135–$145 one-bedroom deluxe; $166–$190 two-bedroom apt for four persons. No credit cards. Free parking.

An old Poipu favorite, this group of private cottages set in Hawaiian flower gardens offers true island ambience. The hospitable owners, Sharon and Robert Flynn, work hard at preserving the feeling of old Hawaii by using batiks, ethnic fabrics and furniture, and Bob's own paintings and sculpture. There are two separate locations, both picturesque. One block away from a sandy snorkeling and sunning beach are the Sea Cliff Cottages, whose unique location—perched on a cliff over Koloa Landing, where the Waikomo Stream meets the ocean—gives them an idyllic ambience; you can watch the sun come up over the water from your lanai. There are four one-bedroom apartments for two people, plus another deluxe one-bedroom to which can be added a bedroom and bath, accommodating four. There are also two Sea Cliff studio apartments. Hale Waipahu, located on the highest point in Poipu at Poipu Crater, offers a 360° view of mountains, ocean, sunrises, and sunsets. Your own private "lap pool" overlooks the coast. There's a studio and a charming one-bedroom apartment with open-beamed ceilings, latticed dining lanai, full kitchen, and bath. A smaller bedroom/bath suite is also available.

The office of Garden Isle Cottages is located in Robert Flynn's gallery and is open only from 9am to noon. Good restaurants are nearby, but remember that you'll need a car to get around here.

✪ Koloa Landing Cottages

2704B Hoonani Rd., Koloa, Kauai, HI 96756. ☎ **808/742-1470.** Fax 808/332-9584. 2 cottages. 1 studio, 11-bedroom apt, 1 house. TV TEL. $50 (plus $20 clean-out fee) studio single or double; $60 (plus $30 clean-out fee) one-bedroom apts; $85 (plus $40 clean-out fee) two-bedroom/two-bath cottage for up to four; $100 (plus $60 clean-out fee) main house (two bedrooms, two baths) for one to four people, $10 each for up to two additional guests per day. No credit cards. Free parking.

Many people dream of moving to an island, having a lovely home of their own, and renting out a handful of cottages in their garden. Hans and Sylvia Zeevat, who came to Hawaii from Holland (he's Dutch, she's Dutch-Indonesian), have realized that dream on Kauai. The result is six wonderful, reasonably priced accommodations for those lucky enough to secure them. The Zeevats are exceptional hosts, and they delight in treating their guests like family: They ply them with fresh fruit from their own trees, and give them tips on where to snorkel. Spacious and tastefully decorated, the cottages have open-beamed ceilings, ceiling fans, cross-ventilation, well-equipped kitchens (blenders, dishwashers, microwave ovens, mixers, etc.), and—hard to find in Poipu—telephones with their own private numbers! Guests can have barbecues out in the garden; restaurants and good swimming beaches are a short walk or drive away. Each cottage has two bedrooms (queen-size beds), two baths, and a lovely living room. The studio and one-bedroom apartment accommodate one or two people; one has no steps, so it's very convenient for a disabled person. Since the Zeevats have moved to a nearby town, their own main house is also now available for rent. The two-bedroom/two-bath house has a large living room, dining area, and family room, a deck, and a carport. There's a full kitchen with microwave oven. Six could settle in comfortably here.

⑤ Prince Kuhio Condominiums

5160 Lawai Rd., Koloa, Kauai, HI 96756. ☎ **808/742-1409** or toll-free 800/722-1409. 48 rms. TV. Apr 15–Dec 15, $59 studio; $69–$79 one-bedroom apt; $115 two-bedroom penthouse. Dec 16–Apr 14 $69 studio; $79–$89 one-bedroom apt; $125 two-bedroom penthouse. No credit cards. Free parking.

This is a longtime Poipu favorite. The nicely furnished apartments overlook either Prince Kuhio Park and the ocean on one side or a lovely pool and a garden on the other; there's a beach known for good snorkeling right across the road, and there are good swimming beaches nearby (the one we like best is in front of the Sheraton). The famed Beach House Restaurant is a few steps away. A variety of studios for two and one-bedroom apartments for up to four are offered, all fully equipped for housekeeping with kitchen and comfortable living space and private lanai. Two handsome two-bedroom penthouses for four are also available. The central barbecue is a popular spot, and this is the kind of place where it's easy to make friends.

Poipu Plantation

1792 Pe'e Rd., Koloa, Kauai, HI 96756. ☎ **808/742-7038** or 808/742-6757 or toll free 800/733-1632. Fax 808/822-2723. 12 units. TV TEL. $80, $85, and $90 one-bedroom unit for two; $105 two-bedroom unit for two; $80–$90 bed-and-breakfast room. Each additional person $10 extra. Free parking.

Evie Warner and Al Davis, the very nice people who run the statewide Bed & Breakfast Hawaii (see above), have built some very attractive vacation-rental units behind their house on their own tropical acre of land, just up the road from Poipu Beach Park, one of the best places to swim in this area. All the units are of good size, attractively furnished, and have tropical decor, ceiling fans, and excellent modern kitchens. Washers and dryers are outside. The units have all been rebuilt and redecorated since the hurricane. The cheaper one-bedroom units are on the garden level, and the more expensive ones have ocean views. There are also several luxury duplexes with two bedrooms, two baths, even marble floors in the bathrooms.

Evie and Al also run the Poipu Plantation Bed & Breakfast Inn right on the premises, offering three attractive rooms, each with private bath and TV; continental breakfast is included. The twin and queen rooms are $80, the king room is $90. There's a gazebo with hot tub and barbecue out in the garden, which is quite lovely, with its apple trees, blossoming plumerias, bougainvilleas, and gardenias. Evie and Al are friendly hosts and see to it that everybody is well cared for.

BED & BREAKFASTS

Gloria's Spouting Horn Bed & Breakfast

4464 Lawai Beach Rd., Koloa, Kauai, HI 96756. ☎ **808/742-6995.** 3 rms. TV TEL. $125 single or double. Each additional person $25 extra. Add $5 to rates if payment is by credit card. (Rates include breakfast.) MC, V.

If your idea of bliss is a hammock strung between two coconut palms overlooking the pounding surf, this is the place for you. Gloria's is located on an idyllic rocky coastline within sight and sound of the surf and the famed Spouting Horn saltwater geyser, and the hammock is right out there, behind the house. Good swimming beaches are a short drive away. Gloria's original house was swept out to sea by Hurricane Iniki, but her new, better-than-ever place has now reopened. It's charmingly furnished in country pine, English walnut, and American oak antiques. Each room is oceanfront—just 30 feet from the surf—and boasts panoramic views with three walls of glass. Each has a VCR, a wet bar with sink, a refrigerator, a microwave, a queen-size bed, and lovely furnishings. All three rooms have Japanese-style deep soaking tubs, plus separate showers; there's an outside (hot water) beach shower of lava rock under the mango tree. The Punana Aloha Room ("Love Nest") is a favorite for honeymooners, with a four-poster willow bed with a full canopy. Speaking of honeymoons, Gloria and her husband, Bob, who's a minister (among other things), can help arrange weddings, either right on the premises or in other island locations. Breakfast, served in the lovely dining room on fine china or out on the oceanside lanai, consists of a papaya boat filled with fresh, locally grown fruit, juice and beverages, and home-baked pastry or muffin. No children under 14, no pets, and smoking only on the lanai.

Island Home Bed & Breakfast

1707 Kalaukia St., Koloa, Kauai, HI 96756. ☎ **808/742-2839** or toll free 800/553-3881. 2 units. TV. $75 Unit One or Two, single or double. No credit cards. Free parking.

One of the first things you notice about Gail and Mike Beeson's lovely home is the collection of fine art on the walls—oils, acrylics, pointillist drawings, and more (Mike is the versatile artist). The two-story white-trimmed gray house is located in a resort complex called Poipu Kai, and the Beesons and their guests have the use of all of the facilities, which include tennis courts, pools, spa, and a lighted walking path that stretches from Shipwreck Beach all the way to Brennecke's Beach

(Poipu Beach Park). There are two units: Unit One, which is downstairs, has a sitting room with antique teak wood furniture and a queen-size bed. Unit Two is furnished with a king-size bed. Each luxuriously carpeted unit has a private entrance off the wraparound lanai, private bath, and all the amenities: microwave, refrigerator, VCR (the Bessons have on hand—at last count—100 movies), beach gear, and hairdryers. Breakfast consists of tropical fruits and Gail's scrumptious homemade bread. Gail and Mike like to invite their guests into their part of the house to watch the magnificent sunsets. If you have a thing about heights, look the other way when Paws, the family cat, does her run around the second floor lanai railing. No smoking and no children are allowed.

✪ Poipu Bed & Breakfast Inn and Vacation Rentals

2720 Hoonani Rd., Koloa, Kauai, HI 96756. ☎ **808/742-1146** or toll free 800/552-0095. 8 rms and suites; 4 apts, cottages and homes; one oceanfront condo. TV. $110–175 double. Rooms can be combined into two- or three-bedroom suites, from $200–$300; single occupancy $10 less; each additional person $20 extra; $10 more for stays of one night. (Rates include breakfast at B&B only.) AE, CB, DC, DISC, MC, V.

We'd have to call this place one of the most beautiful B&B establishments in the islands. Dottie Cichon, an artist herself as well as a collector, has lovingly restored this 1933 plantation house, and filled it with carousel horses, pine antiques, ornate Victorian wicker furniture, handcrafts, and tropical splashes of color everywhere. Each of the luxurious rooms has its own private bath (with either a whirlpool tub and separate shower or a tub-shower combination), VCR, and clock radio; some have wet bars and refrigerators. Continental breakfast is served in the morning out on the lanai or in the splendid "great room"; later on, the "great room" is the scene for afternoon tea and for evening popcorn-and-movie gatherings. (Incidentally, they'll provide breakfast *in* bed—if you ask.) Tennis and pool privileges at the nearby Kiahuna Tennis Club are included in the price of all rooms, and numerous beaches are just around the bend.

Four rooms are available in the new B&B annex, even closer to Poipu Beach. Here, the beautiful cathedral-ceilinged great room and plantation-style white lattice breakfast lanai have a lovely ocean view overlooking a lush tropical garden. One of the loveliest of the rooms is fully handicapped accessible. There are two oceanfront suites, each with giant whirlpool tubs for two.

Although some are beyond our budget, Dottie also has a number of cottages for rent nearby and in Kalaheo; these range from a $60-a-night spacious one-bedroom unit with kitchenette to a super-luxury oceanfront two-bedroom/two-bath condominium at nearby Whaler's Cove, from $250. All are furnished in exquisite taste; some could comfortably suit a family for a long stay.

Marjorie's Kauai Inn

P.O. Box 866, Lawai, HI 96765. ☎ **808/332-8838** or toll free 800/443-9180. 2 rms. TV. Vista View rm $70 single/double; Trade Wind $65 single/double. (Rates include breakfast.) No credit cards.

Marvelous Marjorie Ketcher has settled down in Paradise. Her beautiful house in the glorious pasture lands of Lawai Valley seems a million miles from nowhere, yet it's 5 minutes from Koloa town, 10 minutes from Poipu Beach, and right next door to the National Botanical Garden. Her property extends for acres and the view from anywhere in the house is spectacular. There are two units: The Vista View is brightly decorated, with a queen-size bed and a bath with tub and shower; the Trade Wind unit has a queen-size bed and a private bath with shower only. Both have private entrances; luxurious beige carpeting; blond wood furniture;

soundproofed walls and ceilings; mini-kitchens with fridge; microwave, coffeemaker, dishes and utensils; and huge closets stocked with coolers, flashlights, and all the things you need on Kauai when the power goes off! Marjorie leaves breakfast fixings each morning. There's a tennis court and a hot tub in a pretty gazebo. The big covered lanai is filled with plants and comfy furniture. Down below is a rock garden with bromeliads and beautiful flowers in riotous colors. Marjorie's part of the house, to which she frequently invites her guests, is lovely, carrying out the beige-and-blonde wood theme. There's a fireplace, and the living area is open to the lanai and those views.

✪ Victoria Place

P.O. Box 930, Lawai Kauai, HI 96765. ☎ **808/332-9300.** 4 rms with private baths. $55 Raindrop Room; $65 Calla Lily Room; $75 Shell Room; $95 Victoria's Other Secret. (Rates include breakfast.) No credit cards. Free parking.

A 10-minute drive from the beautiful beaches of Poipu, Edee Seymour's place is a gem—a gem enhanced by the gracious hospitality and wonderful cooking of the host. It's back-to-back with the National Botanical Garden, which is no more than a stone's throw from the poolside breakfast lanai. Three of the guest rooms are located in one wing of the spacious, skylit home, opening directly through glass doors to the gardenlike pool area. The Raindrop Room is for single travelers only. The Shell Room has twin beds that can be put together to form a king-size bed, and it can become barrier-free with a portable wheelchair ramp; its private bathroom has a wheelchair-accessible shower. The Calla Lily Room has a queen-size bed, a gorgeous view of the pool, and, like the others, plenty of closet and bureau space, bookcases liberally filled, and teddy bears on the bed. The fourth room, Victoria's Other Secret, has its own entrance, a kitchen, a daybed, and a California king-size bed on a loft above the main studio, a library of cookbooks, a double coffeemaker, a huge walk-in closet, laundry facilities—everything! Breakfasts are special, maybe with ginger and banana breads fresh from the oven. When you finish your breakfast feast, you can feast your eyes on Edee's glorious collection of shells and antiques. There's a library filled with almost as many books as the local library, and a TV room. Edee is happy to share her collection of restaurant menus and steer you to off-the-beaten-track fun. She can also help with car rentals, including hand-operated vehicles for the physically handicapped.

WESTERN KAUAI: KOKEE & WAIMEA

Cook's Landing Bed & Bath

9918 Waimea Rd. (P.O. Box 1113), Waimea, HI 96796. ☎ and fax **808/338-1451.** $60–$70 single or double with breakfast; $50–$60 single or double without breakfast. TV. Minimum stay three nights. No credit cards.

Those who would like to experience small-town life far from the tourist scene might enjoy this one. Just across the street from the post office in Waimea town, and at the base of Waimea Canyon, this is a tiny, private first-floor "mother-in-law's bed and bath," located in the home of Maggie and Eddie Taniguchi. A guest entrance at the back of the house leads to a bedroom and private bath, with double bed, ceiling fan, and clock radio. Guests can use the backyard covered patio with shared refrigerator/freezer and hibachi for barbecuing; they can also do light cooking in the kitchenette area, which has a toaster, coffeemaker, microwave oven, cookware, and utensils. A black-sand beach is within walking distance, and very good beaches are a short drive away. No smoking allowed.

Waimea Plantation Cottages
9600 Kaumualil Hwy., Waimea, HI 96796. ☎ **808/338-1625** or toll free 800/9-WAIMEA. Fax 808/338-1619 or 808/338-2338. 52 cottages. TV TEL. $95–$200 double. Minimum stay eight nights during holiday periods. AE, DC, DISC, MC, V.

About 45 minutes from Lihue Airport is a place where time literally seems to have stood still. The workers' cottages from the old Waimea Plantation have been restored or, in the case of the structures that were beyond restoration, rebuilt in accordance with the original 1919 blueprints. They're nestled in a grove of gigantic old coconut palms, just steps away from a black-sand beach from which you can watch the sun set over Niihau. The cottages are furnished with updated versions of the furniture that was really in the house (although the workers surely did not have the luxury of private telephones, coffeemakers, rice cookers, toasters, ceiling fans, and state-of-the-art plumbing). Several of the units have four-poster beds, faithful reproductions of the ones that used to be here. There are multiple windows in each unit from which to enjoy the views of the mountains, the sea, and the abundant banyan and fruit trees on the grounds. Each cottage has a sign identifying the former occupant. There's a large swimming pool and barbecue area, and a 1920 tennis court has been renovated. The Grove Dining Room is very pleasant with its oceanfront location.

If you're planning a family reunion, this could be a perfect spot. Because there are a number of large cottages with as many as three to five bedrooms, each room could be available for $50 to $75. The staff can assist in planning reunions that are highly structured or very informal. Call for details.

3 Camping & Wilderness Cabins

By Jeanette Foster

Camping is a year-round activity, as Kauai experiences balmy weather—at least somewhere on the island—throughout the year. There is a wet season (winter) and a dry one (summer), but campers should be prepared for rain at any time of the year. Campers also need to be ready for insects (a good repellent for mosquitoes), water purification (boiling, filtration, or iodine crystals), and sun protection (sunscreen, hat, and long-sleeved shirt). Also, a few notes on personal safety: Don't hike or swim alone and never turn your back on the ocean; the waves might be closer and more powerful than you think.

For information on trails, hikes, camping and permits in state parks—including the two discussed below—contact: **Hawaii State Department of Land and Natural Resources,** State Parks Division, P.O. Box 1049, Wailuku, HI 96793 (☎ 808/243-5354). The **Hawaiian Trail and Mountain Club,** P.O. Box 2238, Honolulu, HI 96804, offers an information packet on hiking and camping in the Hawaiian Islands, including Kauai. Send $1.25, plus a legal-sized, self-addressed, stamped envelope for information. Another good source of information is the *Hiking/Camping Information Packet* from **Hawaii Geographic Maps and Books,** 49 S. Hotel Street, Suite 218, Honolulu, HI 96813 (☎ 808 538-3952), for $7, which includes postage.

If you don't plan to bring your own camping equipment, you can rent gear at **Kayak Kauai Outfitters** in Hanalei (☎ 808/826-9844), or at **Pedal & Paddle** in Hanalei (☎ 808/826-9069). To purchase camping equipment, the best selection is at **Gaspro,** 3990-C Rice Street, Lihue (☎ 808/245-6766).

The best places to camp on Kauai are:

NA PALI COAST STATE PARK

The Kalalau Trail winds through this remote, spectacular 6,500-acre park, where 2,000-foot cliffs highlight the truly awe-inspiring scenery. You'll need a camping permit from the **State Division of Parks,** available from the State Parks Department on any island; on Kauai, the office is located at 3060 Eiwa Street, Lihue, HI 96766 (☎ 808/241-3444). Permits are free; camping is limited to five nights in any one consecutive 30-day period. The camping areas along the Kalalau Trail include **Hanakapiai Beach** (facilities are pit toilets and water is from the stream), **Hanakoa Valley** (no facilities, water from the stream), and **Kalalau Valley** (composting toilets, several pit toilets, and water from the stream). There are no roads into this area; access is only by a single hiking trail, or by boat, much as it was in ancient Hawaii. For information on hiking along the Kalalau Trail, see "Hiking" in Chapter 16, "What to See & Do on Kauai." Remember to keep your camping permit in your possession at all times.

KOKEE STATE PARK

At the end of Hi. 550 lies a 4,640-acre state park of high mountain forest wilderness (3,600 to 4,000 feet above sea level). Rain forest, pristine bogs, and breathtaking views of the Na Pali coastline and Waimea Canyon are the draw of Kokee State Park. This is the place for hiking—some 45 miles of maintained trails provide some of the best hiking in Hawaii. Camping facilities include state campgrounds (one next to the Kokee Lodge and four more primitive backcountry sites), one private tent area, and the Kokee Lodge, which has 12 cabins for rent at very reasonable rates. At 4,000 feet, the nights are cold, particularly in the winter; since no open fires are permitted at Kokee, the best deal is the cabins.

The state campground at the Kokee Lodge allows tent camping only. Permits for this site can be obtained from a state parks office on any island; on Kauai, contact: **State Division of Parks,** 3060 Eiwa Street, Lihue, HI 96766 (☎ 808/241-3444). The permits are free and the time limit is five nights in a single 30-day period. The facilities include showers, drinking water, picnic tables, a pavilion with tables, restrooms, barbecue, dishwashing sinks, and electric lights.

The more primitive back country campgrounds include **Sugi Grove** and **Kawaikoi,** located about 4 miles from the park headquarters on a four-wheel drive road. The only facilities are pit toilets, picnic tables, and water from a stream. Two-and-a-half-miles from that camping area is **Camp 10,** with a picnic area only—no restrooms. Water is available from a stream a short distance away. Camp 10 is mainly an overnight stop for hikers and hunters. Six miles past Camp 10 is the **Waialae Cabin.** Although no one can stay at the locked cabin (it's used only by forestry personnel), camping around the cabin is permitted. There are no facilities; water can be obtained from a nearby stream. Permits for Sugi Grove, Kawaikoi, Camp 10, and Waialae Cabin are available from the **State Forestry and Wildlife Division,** 3060 Eiwa Street, Lihue, HI 96766 (☎ 808/241-3433). There is no fee for the permits, but camping is limited to three nights.

Tent camping at **Camp Slogget,** owned by the Kauai YWCA, is available for $7.50 per adult per night and $5 per child. Contact: **Camp Slogget,** Kauai YWCA, 3094 Elua Street, Lihue, HI 96766 (☎ 808/245-5959).

An excellent choice are the cabins rented by the **Kokee Lodge.** There are two types of cabins: The older cabins have dormitory-style sleeping accommodations;

the new cabins have two bedrooms. Both styles sleep six and come with cooking and eating utensils, bedding, and linens. Firewood for the stove can be purchased at the Kokee Lodge. Write far in advance for reservations—holidays are booked a year in advance—to: **Kokee Lodge,** P.O. Box 819, Waimea, HI 96796 (☎ 808/335-6061). Cost is $45 per night for the new-style cabins and $35 per night for the old-style cabins, with a five-night limit.

The Kokee Lodge Restaurant is open from 9am to 3:30pm, for continental breakfast and lunch, every day. It's well known for such local specialties as Portuguese bean soup, lilikoi pie, and its own Kokee Lodge Chili (see "Where to Eat," below, for further details). Groceries and gas are not available in Kokee; stock up in advance, or you will have to make the long trip down the mountain.

Kokee plums are known all over Hawaii; in midsummer, they're ripe and ready for picking. However, the Parks Department regulates plum picking—which days, which hours, and how many. Check at park headquarters before you pick.

Kokee is one of the few places you can fish for trout in Hawaii. Trout season is 16 days in August and all weekends in September. Permits for fishing are available at the park headquarters.

4 Where to Eat

IN & AROUND LIHUE
LIHUE
Meals for Less than $12

☉ Hamura's Saimin Stand
2956 Kress St. ☎ **808/245-3271.** Main courses $3–$5.25. No credit cards. Mon–Thurs 10am–2am, Fri–Sat 10am–4am. Sun 10am–midnight. LOCAL/JAPANESE.

Locals have sung the praises of this beloved Kauai institution and gobbled up its saimin for as long as anybody can remember. It's a very simple spot, a trifle weather-beaten on the outside; inside are three rectangular counters with stools. Slide onto one, order anything on the small menu, and you're in for a great taste treat as well as one of the cheapest meals on Kauai. Our usual choice is the saimin special at $4.25—that's a large bowl of saimin topped with vegetables, eggs, and wontons—filling and delicious. Order a stick of tender barbecued chicken or beef, too (80¢), and finish up with their lilikoi chiffon pie at $1.10. All in all, quite a meal for $6.15. In the local color department: Note the sign that reads, "Please do not stick gum under counter. Thank you."

Kauai Chop Suey
In Pacific Ocean Plaza, 3051 Rice St., No. 107. ☎ **808/245-8790.** Reservations not required. Main courses $5.35–$7.95. No credit cards. Lunch Tues–Sat 11am–2pm; dinner Tues–Sun 4:30–9pm. CANTONESE.

Despite the restaurant's unimaginative name, it serves superior food, all in the Cantonese style. There area about 75 items on the menu, at least 40 of them under $6. There's something for everyone: roast duck, egg foo yong, squid with vegetables, shrimp with broccoli, lemon chicken, stuffed tofu, sweet-and-sour pork, or char sui (an island favorite). And the soups—seaweed, scallop, abalone—are quite special. The place is large and comfortable, decorated in typical Chinese style. Large parties are seated at round tables with revolving lazy Susan centerpieces, the better to sample all the delicacies. The locals rave about this place—and so do we.

⊜ Lihue Barbecue Inn

2982 Kress St. ☎ **808/245-2921.** Reservations not required. Main courses $7.95–$13.95. No credit cards. Breakfast and lunch Mon–Sat 7:30am–1:30pm; dinner Mon–Thurs 5–8pm; Fri–Sat 4:30–closing. JAPANESE/AMERICAN.

You'll know why the Barbecue Inn has been considered one of the best local restaurants in town for more than 50 years when you have a look at the low prices on the menu, which lists more than 20 complete dinners, most under $13, including soup or fresh fruit cup, tossed green salad, vegetable, beverages, and dessert. Typical main courses are shrimp tempura, baked mahimahi, broiled teriyaki pork chops, corned beef brisket with cabbage, and chow mein chicken with spareribs. Fresh fish is served when available. Complete lunches are also a good deal—there are about 20 choices, such as a seafood platter, Chinese chicken salad, a mahimahi sandwich, or teriyaki chicken, all for $6.95 to $8.95. The menu changes daily, but whatever you have here will most likely be good—especially the freshly made pies (can you believe $1?) and the homemade bread. Try their frozen chi chis—among the best on the island. One of the most appealing inexpensive restaurants in Lihue, the Barbecue is patronized mostly by local families.

Restaurant Kiibo

2991 Umi St. ☎ **808/245-2650.** Reservations recommended. Main courses $4.25–$19. No credit cards. Lunch Mon–Fri 11am–1:30pm, Sat 11am–1pm; dinner Mon–Sat 5:30–9pm. Closed Holidays. JAPANESE.

The food is outstanding at this tiny, comfortable, nicely furnished restaurant; it's just a small, spare dining room with 10 or so tables, and three tatami seating areas on a raised platform. Everything on the menu is à la carte, even the rice—that way, says the manager, you only order exactly what you wish to eat. We enjoyed our $8.95 chicken sukiyaki and $5.25 beef teriyaki to the accompaniment of soft Japanese music in the background. Other good choices include the tempura at $7.25 to $8.25, and the donburi, huge bowls of rice topped with sukiyaki or teriyaki or something equally interesting, for $5.95 to $12.50. A child's dinner is available at $6.50. This is a local favorite, off the usual tourist beat.

Tip Top Cafe

3173 Akahi St. ☎ **808/245-2343** or 808/245-2333. Reservations recommended. Main courses $4.50–$6.50. MC, V. Daily 6:30am–2pm. CHINESE/AMERICAN.

Located just north of the Lihue Shopping Center, this air-conditioned family eatery is a local favorite. The prices are modest, and while the food is not of gourmet quality, it's dependable. We often have breakfast here (pancakes are served all day—macadamia-nut ones, at $5, are delicious). Lunch features local favorites like oxtail soup, beef stew, breaded mahimahi, and loco moco with two eggs, all served with vegetables and a choice of rice or fries. Bento lunches, for take-out, are $5.75. As of this writing, Tip Top was not serving dinner; inquire when you're there. Pick up some homemade jams from the gift department or some macadamia-nut cookies from the Tip Top Bakery.

Meals for $25 or Less

Cafe Portofino

3501 Rice St., Nawiliwili ☎ **808/245-2121.** Reservations recommended. Main courses $11.50–$18.75. AE, MC, V. Lunch Mon–Fri 11am–2pm; dinner daily 5–10pm. ITALIAN.

One of the more stylish spots in town, Café Portofino is the place for an elegant and not overly priced Italian meal. Windows all around the dining room and a big lanai overlooking Kalapaki Beach and Nawiliwili Harbor also afford a splendid view of the surrounding luxuriant mountains. The ambiance is decidedly romantic: candles and flowers on the tables, opera music (Italian, of course!) on the stereo, sparkly glassware and silver, and abundant greenery hanging from the ceiling. We like the prosciutto and papaya (only in Hawaii) among the antipasti, the traditional Caesar among the salads, and, among the pastas, the linguine alla puttanesca. Rabbit in white wine, osso buco in orange sauce, and sweetbreads in a white cream sauce are some of the signature specialty items. Desserts vary daily, but always include freshly made gelati and sorbets.

✪ JJ's Broiler
3416 Rice St., in the Anchor Cove Shopping Center at Nawiliwili Harbor. ☎ **808/246-4422.** Reservations recommended for weekend dinners. Main courses $14.75–$25.95. DISC, MC, V. Lunch daily in lounge downstairs 11am–4:30pm, light food until closing; dinner daily upstairs 5–9 or 9:30pm. STEAKS AND SEAFOOD.

This is one of our perennial favorites: we've followed it around the island for more than 20 years. Mary and Jim Jasper have always set a fine table in their several locations, but we definitely like the present one best of all. It's absolutely delightful to sit out on the lanai at lunchtime, enjoying the ocean and sky and watching the swimmers and the seabirds; full-moon nights are spectacular. The restaurant is decorated in a nautical fashion, with polished wood and brass, captain's chairs, ship fittings, and the like. You can have lunch for under $10; there is a soup-and-salad duo for $7.25, a soup-and-sandwich duo for $6.95, and an array of sandwiches and burgers from $6.25 to $8.50. But you'll have to come at dinner to sample the house specialty, Slavonic Steak—a broiled, sliced tenderloin fillet dipped in a butter, wine, and garlic sauce. It comes alone at $14.95, and with various combinations of lobster tail, crab, and fish at market prices. Other good main courses include a sizzling vegetable or chicken stir fry, a combination tempura platter, and broiled chicken fettucine, all from $14.95 to $16.95. This is the kind of place just meant for lingering over drinks and ending with a sinfully rich dessert.

Fisherman's Galley
At junction of Hi. 50 and Puhi Rd., (just across from Kauai Community College). ☎ **808/246-4700.** Reservations not accepted. Main courses $5.95–$28.95 (for steak and lobster). AE, DISC, MC, V. Mon–Thurs 10am–9pm, Fri 10am–10pm, Sat–Sun 12noon–8pm. SEAFOOD.

Straightforward, super-fresh seafood dishes served in a pleasant atmosphere made this new place extremely popular from day one. People wait patiently on the front porch of the wooden building, which looks like an upscale fishing lodge. There are booths all around the cheery dining room, and deep-sea fishing photographs and mounted fish covering the walls (including a giant squid hovering from the ceiling). No wonder—the restaurateur also owns Gent-lee Sports Fishing Charters. Of course the specialty of the house is seafood, and they definitely do it justice. You can dine very inexpensively here if you stick to the fish-n-chips ($5.95–$8.95); the broiled fish sandwich ($7.95); or the lobster, shrimp, and crab seafood melt ($9.95). Most of the other main courses—like the Hawaiian fish platter or the fish and shrimp combo—are under $14.95; only the steak and lobster dishes go into the $20 range. The ono chowder is so good you'll probably want to take some home. The smoked fish salad, with homemade smoked fish and feta cheese on a bed of greens, is a fun way to start your meal. For dessert, the classic seafood house choice: Cheesecake, of course.

Tokyo Lobby

Pacific Ocean Plaza, 2501 Rice St. ☎ **808/245-8989.** Reservations recommended for weekend dinners. Main courses $9.95–$19.95. AE, DISC, MC, V. Lunch Mon–Sat 11am–2pm; dinner nightly 5–9:30pm. JAPANESE.

This one is a perfectly elegant Japanese dining room, but don't let the elegance fool you: You can still get a good meal here for a reasonable price. A number of main courses—such as sesame chicken, curry chicken, katsu, vegetable tempura, and calamari steak—run from $9.95 to $11.95; all are served with soup, tsukemono, and rice. All of the food is excellent and what you'd expect, with just a few surprises, like the smoked salmon donburi at $8.50 (which we'd have no problem eating every day), and the Tokyo Lobby Love Boats, combination meals served in large wooden boats, $19.95. The green-tea ice cream is a perfect finale.

KUKUI GROVE

Kauai's multimillion-dollar shopping center, Kukui Grove, just outside Lihue on Hi. 50 toward Poipu Beach, has several attractive budget eateries. In addition to the following, there are several good snack shops for everything from Chinese food at **Ho's Chinese Kitchen** to "local grinds" at **Joni Hana,** Filipino at **Sidewalk Café,** or **Sumo's Restaurant** for traditional Japanese food, including sushi.

Si Cisco's Mexican Cantina & Restaurant

In Kukui Grove Shopping Center. ☎ **808/246-1563.** Reservations not required. Main courses $9.95–$16.95. DISC, MC, V. Mon–Sat 11am–10pm, Sun 11:30am–9pm. MEXICAN.

Probably the most popular specialty restaurant at Kukui Grove is Si Cisco's, in an attractive, cozy indoor-outdoor setting. You can dine leisurely here on Mexican and American favorites. Combination plates run $10.95 to $13.50. Don't pass up the margaritas; a 60-ounce pitcher is $15.

Zack's

In Kukui Grove Shopping Center. ☎ **808/246-2415.** Reservations not required. Nothing more than $4.99. MC, V. Mon–Wed and Sat 9:30am–5:30pm; Thurs–Fri 9:30am–9pm; Sun 10am–4pm. AMERICAN.

This cute little place looks like an old-fashioned ice cream parlor. The menu runs from burgers to chicken and salads; everything is good, but the specialties are Mely's divine Portuguese bean soup, $2.99 a bowl (spicy!) and their "Royal Family of Spuds"—big baked potatoes with a variety of fixin's. A Prince spud (with butter, cheese, and broccoli), $3.89, and a petite Caesar salad, $3.09, make a more-than-satisfying lunch.

KILOHANA PLANTATION

Gaylord's

Hwy. 50, 1 mile southwest of Lihue. ☎ **808/245-9593.** Reservations recommended for dinner. Main courses $14.95–$23.95. Lunch daily Mon–Sat 11am–3:30pm; dinner daily 5–9pm; brunch Sat–Sun 9am–3pm. HAWAII REGIONAL.

One of the nicest restaurants to open on Kauai in many a tropical moon is Gaylord's, at Kilohana, the legendary plantation estate of the 1930s that has been lovingly restored and is open to the public. Gaylord's is a courtyard restaurant facing a manicured green lawn around which tables are arranged on three sides. The restaurant is done in whites, pinks, and greens, with soft-cushioned chairs and fresh flowers on every table. Dinner at Gaylord's *is* pricey, but at lunchtime you can have a first-class dining experience for a modest tab—and many agree that the food is better at lunchtime. We like both Gaylord's Papaya Runneth Over, island papaya stuffed with delicate bay shrimp (or salmon or chicken) salad, at $8.95. Baby back ribs with onion rings ($10.95) and the seafood quesadilla ($8.95) are signature lunch choices. At dinnertime, you can stay on the low side of the menu, with selections like angel-hair pasta with sautéed prawns, seafood linguine, and roasted chicken ($15.95 to $16.95), or come early, before 6:30pm, to enjoy the baby back ribs for $14.95 instead of $16.95. Homemade desserts, such as Kilohana mud pie, and triple tropical fruit mousse (layered coconut, guava, and passion-fruit mousse) are all treats. The brunch menu offers cheese blintzes, eggs Benedict, Belgian waffles, and the like for $9.95 to $13.95. A lovely choice.

HANAMAULU

Hanamaulu Restaurant and Tea House

Hi. 56. ☎ **808/245-2511.** Reservations recommended. Main courses $11–$17. MC, V. Lunch Tues–Fri 11am–1pm; dinner Tues– Sun 4:30–9pm. JAPANESE/CHINESE.

This old-time favorite is known for its Japanese garden, beautifully landscaped with stone pagodas, pebbled paths, and a pond filled with carp. We suggest that you call a day in advance and reserve one of the charming *ozashiki,* or teahouse rooms; you take off your shoes and sit on the floor at a long, low table, and the shoji screens are opened to face the lighted garden. (You may be able to get one of the rooms without reservations, but it's best to call ahead.) The food is excellent and inexpensive; the Chinese and Japanese plate lunches are a good value at $6.75 to $7. Special dinner platters are $12.95, and you can feast on a veritable Eastern banquet for about $15 per person. An excellent sushi bar and robatayaki are attractions here. The Miyaki family are cordial hosts.

KAUAI'S EASTERN SHORE: THE COCONUT COAST
WAILUA & KAPAA
Meals for Less than $15

Aloha Diner

In Waipouli Complex, 4-971 Kuhio Hwy. ☎ **808/822-3851.** Reservations not accepted. Main courses $5.50–$10.50. No credit cards. Breakfast and lunch Tues–Sat 10:30am–pm; dinner Tues–Sat 5:30–9pm. HAWAIIAN.

If you've developed a taste for real Hawaiian food, you can satisfy it here in plain surroundings. Best bets are the lunch specials for $5.50 to $7, including kalua pig or laulau, lomi-lomi salmon, rice or poi; and the more elaborate dinner specials for $8.50 to $10.50—including kalua pig or laulau, lomi-lomi salmon, chicken lau, poi or rice, and haupia (coconut pudding). Typical à la carte choices, at $3.75, include beef stew, squid lau, and other favorites.

Bubba's

1384 Kuhio Hwy. ☎ **808/823-0069.** Reservations not accepted. $2.50–$7. No credit cards. Mon–Sat 10:30am–6pm. SNACKS.

Bubba's calls itself an old-fashioned hamburger stand that "cheats tourists and drunks and attorneys." Don't you believe it! The burgers, hot dogs, chicken burgers, fish-and-chips that you get here are really good and really cheap. You dine right on the sidewalk at polished wooden picnic tables with benches. The friendly proprietors know everyone who passes by, the food dispensed from their kitchen counter is plentiful and tasty, and the friendly spirit is contagious.

Bull Shed

796 Kuhio Hwy. ☎ **808/822-3791**. Reservations only for parties of 6 or more. Main courses $10.95–$18.50 ($25.50 for steak and lobster). AE, MC, V. Dinner daily 5:30–10pm; cocktails from 4:30 pm. AMERICAN.

A favorite of steak and seafood lovers, the Bull Shed, just north of Coconut Plantation, behind the Mokihana of Kauai condos, is a Kauai tradition. The atmosphere is great: a large airy, wooden-frame building overlooking the ocean, so close to it that waves wash up against the sea wall. If you're watching your budget or your waistline, you can make do with visits to the superb salad bar (salad bar alone is $6.95). Or splurge on some of the specialties, including prime rib, garlic tenderloin, yakitori, shrimp, scallops, and a variety of Hawaiian fish. The price of the main courses includes steamed rice and a trip to the salad bar. The restaurant is apt to be crowded, so get there early; prime rib, the house favorite for which many people make a special trip, can run out early on.

Ginger's Grille

4-831 Kuhio Hwy., in Kauai Village, near Safeway. ☎ **808/822-5557**. Reservations not accepted. Main courses $12.95–$16.95. Senior citizen discounts available: ask server. MC, V. Soups, salads, sandwiches 11am–10pm daily; dinner 5–10pm daily. SEAFOOD/ STEAKS.

Ginger's is definitely a happening place: wildly-colored faux parrots hanging from the ceiling, a blond-wood bar filled with friendly regulars, etched glass mirrors, and visiting celebs' autographs on the wall all create an upbeat setting for food that is delicious and very reasonably priced. And the fact that you can get soups, salads, and sandwiches throughout the day make it ideal for those who may want to eat lightly around dinnertime. Burgers and sandwiches ($5.75–$9.95) include a terrific shrimp or crab melt, a mahimahi fillet, and a charbroiled chicken sandwich; a soup-and-sandwich combo is $5.95. For dinner, Ginger's whips up tasty stir-fries (with beef, chicken, shrimp, or just veggies) at $12.95; a delicious scampi dish and a mahimahi filet, both bargains at $12.95; and steak and scampi for $16.95. As if these prices weren't fair enough, they throw in a cup of homemade soup of the day or green salad, steamed white rice or spicy fries, and steamed vegetables. Dessert? Just one gooey one: Shari's Island Pie is their version of the mud pie—an Oreo cookie crust, Kona coffee ice cream topped with fudge, sliced toasted almonds, and a bit of whipped cream.

⑤ King and I

4-901 Kuhio Hwy., in Waipouli Shopping Plaza. ☎ **808/822-1642**. Reservations recommended. Main courses $6.25–$9.95. AE, DC, MC, V. Dinner Mon–Thurs 4:30–9:30pm, Fri–Sat 4:30–10pm. THAI/VEGETARIAN.

The King and I is a find. It's a small, family-run establishment with a gentle atmosphere. The family grows all their own herbs and spices. The food is exceptionally good, and the prices are easy to take. Start with one of the appetizers, like the spring rolls or stuffed chicken wings, then have a soup (we like the Siam chicken-coconut soup) and a main dish, perhaps the garlic shrimp, the Siam eggplant with chicken, or one of the curries—like yellow curry with shrimp. (Watch out, though: Those curries can be hot, unless you tell your server you'd like them mild.) Vegetarians have a choice of 13 good dishes. Now for dessert: How about banana with coconut milk, followed by Thai iced coffee with milk? Super!

Kountry Kitchen

1485 Kuhio Hwy. ☎ **808/822-3511.** Reservations not required. $4–$8.50. Breakfast daily 5:30am–11pm; lunch daily 11am–1:30pm. AMERICAN/LOCAL.

This is an old standby in Kapaa, with an atmosphere like that of an old-fashioned midwestern family restaurant. It's certainly one of the most popular places on this side of the island for breakfast; don't be surprised if you see a line at the door. However, service is fast, so you generally won't have to wait more than 5 or 10 minutes. Build-your-own omelets complemented by freshly-baked cornbread and crispy golden hash browns are favorites, along with buttermilk and banana pancakes. Lunch is fun, too, with fresh local fish when available, super sandwiches, and burgers with steak-cut french fries. Kountry fried chicken and chef's salads are also favorites.

Michelle's Cafe & Bakery

1384 Kuhio Hwy. ☎ **808/823-6006.** Reservations not accepted. Main courses $8.95–$12.95. No credit cards. Breakfast and lunch Mon–Fri 7:30am–5pm, Sat 7:30am–3pm, dinner Fri–Sat 6–9:30pm. MEDITERRANEAN/VEGETARIAN/SOUTHWESTERN.

Michelle O'Hearn, a talented California chef who apprenticed in Bay Area restaurants, moved to Kauai a few years back and, along with husband Nicholas Andersson, opened this nifty little place, small and cozy. Michelle is in the kitchen early in the morning, baking wonderful European breads (pumpkin seed, olive and basil, herb and cheese are a few specialties) and pastries that bring folks in early to shop and have a light breakfast: freshly squeezed juices, espresso, burritos ($3.95), and croissants with scrambled eggs and cheese ($2.95), sandwiches on homemade breads and focaccia are made fresh every morning. She does different lunch specials every day—usually vegetarian dishes like pesto fettuccine, polenta lasagne, calzones, perhaps a peanut-based West African stew—as well as chicken, turkey, and fish dishes; most are priced between $3.75 and $6.95. The ahi burger at $6.75 is very popular. Friday and Saturday evenings, magic happens at dinnertime, too, when Michelle whips up dishes like pasta primavera, New Orleans gumbo Sante Fe style, ahi with papaya salsa, and more, accompanied by tapenades, salads, and homemade desserts.

Norberto's El Cafe

1375 Kuhio Hwy. ☎ **808/822-3362.** Reservations not required. Main courses $2.95–$10.95 à la carte, $11.50–$14.95 complete dinners. AE, MC, V. Dinner Mon–Sat 5:30–9pm. MEXICAN/VEGETARIAN.

Norberto's has been a local favorite since 1977. The attractive, two-level dining room is decorated in Mexican style, and the food is as tasty as ever. Norberto's always cooks with fresh ingredients, does not use lard or any other animal fats (so vegetarians can feel comfortable here), and offers excellent value. Don't worry about breaking the budget, as complete dinners are reasonably priced and include soup, vegetables, refried beans, and Spanish rice; there's plenty of chips and hot salsa on the table to go with your margaritas or beer. The steak or chicken fajitas are just about our favorites, but olés, too, for the rellenos Tampico and the nifty Mex-Mix Plate: That's a chicken chimichanga, a chicken taquito, and an enchilada with Spanish rice and beans, all for $12.95. All dishes can be served vegetarian style if you ask. Be sure to try their Hawaiian taro-leaf enchiladas! If you have any room left, top your meal off with a piece of rum cake or chocolate-cream pie, both homemade and delicious. A good family choice.

Ono Family Restaurant

4-1292 Kuhio Hwy. ☎ **808/822-1710.** Reservations not required. Main courses $3.65–$13. AE, MC, V. Breakfast and lunch daily 7am–2pm; dinner 5:30–9pm daily. AMERICAN.

Ono means "delicious" in Hawaiian, and this restaurant in old Kapaa town lives up to its name. Pewter plates and fancy cookware hang on the wood-paneled walls, and European and Early American antiques and paintings add to the charm. This is a family-owned operation, and it shows in the care and attention that the owners lavish on their guests, especially senior citizens and children; many come back year after year because of that warm welcome. Omelets are featured at breakfast, and so are Canterbury eggs (grilled English muffins topped with turkey, ham, veggies, eggs, and cheese), at $6.25, and quite a way to start the day. Their $4.95 fish sandwich, with vegetables, sprouts, and Cheddar cheese on grilled Branola bread, is a meal in itself; super burgers cost $3.95 to $7.25; and for the health conscious, there is a variety of buffalo burgers, which have 70% less fat and 50% less cholesterol) than beef and taste just fine—they're $5.50 to $6.75. Be sure to try their Portuguese bean soup; it's an island classic. A variety of fresh fish meals are served daily, along with chicken and beef dishes. The price of a main course includes Portuguese bean soup or tossed salad, rice pilaf or fries, fresh sautéed vegetables, and Branola whole-wheat bread. There's a special menu for children.

Panda Garden

4-831 Kuhio Hwy., in Kauai Village, near Safeway. ☎ **808/822-0092.** Reservations not necessary. Main courses $6.95–$18. MC, V. Lunch daily 11am–2pm; dinner daily 4:30–9pm. CANTONESE/SZECHUAN.

It's delightful to dine in this beautiful and very upscale Chinese dining room, with its pink tablecloths and napkins, black lacquer furniture, lace curtains, and delicate watercolors on the walls. Mirrors all around the room reflect this elegance, and a huge, ornate gold *maneki neko* (welcoming cat) greets you at the door. The solicitous waiters glide about unobtrusively, but are happy to make suggestions for a memorable meal. You can't go wrong with their Peking duck, or one of the sizzling platters like shrimp or scallops with black bean sauce, or the cashew chicken, or the delicious (but spicy!) Kung Pau dishes—beef, shrimp, scallops, or chicken. There's a daily lunch-plate special at $5.95.

Papaya's Cafe

4-831 Kuhio Hwy., in Kauai Village, near Safeway. ☎ **808/823-0190.** Reservations not required. Main courses $5–$9. MC, V. Daily 8am–10pm. NATURAL FOODS.

Lovers of natural foods need seek no further. They can find everything they need at this cafe adjacent to the huge Papaya's Natural Foods store. The food is absolutely delicious. At lunch you could have something from the burger bar (nutty burger, tempeh burger, grilled chicken teriyaki burger, or grilled fish burger, $4.75 to $5.95), or go with a simple soup and salad meal for $3.75, a combination plate (a choice of any three salads at $6.75), or a grilled fish plate at $8.50. From 4pm on, they offer three made-to-order dinner specials—a fish dish, a chicken dish, and a pasta—all cooked with northern Italian flavors, and served with vegetarian Caesar salad and freshly baked garlic bread. Organically grown fruits and vegetables, mostly from local farms, are used whenever possible. Save room for some good desserts and for favorites from the espresso bar: cappuccino, lattes, mochas, and iced coffees. Call to find out if they're serving Sunday brunch: that's a special treat, offering strawberry-stuffed French toast and Belgian blue-corn waffles, just to mention a few possibilities. There's outdoor seating under umbrellaed tables, and more seats inside. They'll happily pack a picnic lunch to go.

Paradise Take 'n Bake Pizza

In Kauai Village, behind Safeway. ☎ **808/823-8253.** $9.95 small–$18.95 large pizzas. No credit cards. Daily 3–8pm. PIZZA.

This take-out place is much beloved by our friends who live in the area. If you have access to a kitchen, call ahead and they will have your pizza ready to go. They do some interesting combinations: pesto and shrimp, clam and bacon, pesto chicken, and kim chee pies to name a few, but the most unique is their breakfast pizza—yes, breakfast—with bacon, ham or sausage, and eggs or Denver style (small $7.95, medium $10.95, large $13.95). Take it home at night, bake it the next morning, and voila!—a bellisimo breakfast.

✪ Restaurant Kintaro

4-370 Kuhio Hwy., between Coco Palms and the Coconut Plantation. ☎ **808/822-3341.** Reservations recommended. Dinner $10.95–$26.95. AE, DC, JCB, MC, V. Dinner only, Mon–Sat 5:30–9:30pm. JAPANESE.

Exquisite is the word for the dining experience at this sparkling bright restaurant. The rather bland exterior does not even suggest the harmonious Japanese scene inside: kites and kimonos on the walls, blond woods, shoji screens, a long sushi bar from which the chefs turn out tender marvels. Several complete dinners run $12.50 to $14.95 and include a variety of delicious small dishes. First you are served chilled buckwheat noodles in a flavorful sauce, presented on a *zora*, a wooden box with bamboo top. Next, also served on traditional wooden platters, are miso soup, rice, Japanese pickled vegetables, and your main course—it could be the delicious chicken yakitori (boneless broiled chicken, onion, bell pepper, and teriyaki sauce and salad) or salmon yaki. Or it could be a tasty tempura combination. Kintaro is justifiably proud of its teppan cuisine, including steak, lobster, and fresh island fish with scallops, for $13.95 to $26.95. Be sure to have the green-tea ice cream for dessert. There are various sushi and sashimi combinations for appetizers or for those who wish to eat at the sushi bar.

Wailua Marina Restaurant

In Wailua River State Park. ☎ **808/822-4311.** Reservations recommended. Main courses $9.75–$26. AE, MC, V. Breakfast daily 9–11am; lunch daily 11am–2pm; dinner daily 5–9pm. SEAFOOD/STEAK.

Good food, good prices, and a very special setting have long made this place a favorite. You can dine riverside and catch the breezes on the open lanai, or indoors in the huge dining room with its slanted ceilings and murals, stuffed fish, and turtle shells on the wall. Although we wouldn't call the food gourmet, it is still a good deal for the price, especially since all dinners come with a tossed garden salad, vegetable of the day, a choice of starch, plus coffee or tea. "Special selections"—oxtail soup with ginger and parsley, baked stuffed pork chops, prime rib—are the most reasonable from $9 to $17.75. Charbroiled specials range from $13.95 up to around $25. Our favorite luncheon choices here are the sandwiches—including a Monte Cristo with ham and turkey, mahimahi on a bun, and pastrami on rye—all from $5.75 to $8.50. There's a special menu for children ages 3 to 9.

Worth a Splurge

✪ A Pacific Café

In Kauai Village, Kuhio Hwy. ☎ **808/822-0013.** Reservations recommended. Main courses $15.95–$23.95. AE, DC, MC, V. Dinner Tues–Sun 5:30–9pm. HAWAIIAN REGIONAL.

For a splurge meal worth every cent, indulge yourself with dinner at this restaurant, which has created a stir in island food circles. A Pacific Café is the creation of executive chef/owner Jean-Marie Josselin, who's garnered awards for creative cooking in Paris, on the mainland, and here in Hawaii, where he was formerly executive chef at the Coco Palms Resort. Josselin has created a stylish restaurant that boasts Asian art and decor, native Hawaiian woods and plants, and an open kitchen with rôtisserie and a wood-burning grill and wok, so guests can watch the chefs create their magic. And magic it is—Josselin creates extraordinarily good ethnic dishes of the Pacific Rim, using a blend of Asian, Hawaiian, and European culinary techniques.

All of Chef Josselin's salad greens, vegetables, and fresh herbs are grown on his own certified organic farm. Since the menu changes constantly to take advantage of the freshest local fish, game, and produce, there's no telling what you may encounter on a specific night, but here are some of his signature dishes: Appetizers include smoked shrimp lumpia with a curry lime dip, Peking duck and shrimp tacos with papaya-ginger salsa, or potato skins with smoked marlin and sour cream. For salads and soups, $5.50 to $8.75, how about a Caesar salad with spicy ahi, or baked potato soup with smoked marlin, sour cream, and chives. It's easy to make a meal on two or three of the appetizers, soups, and salads. From the wood-burning grill come such main dishes as wok-seared mahimahi with garlic sesame crust, grilled rack of lamb with a plum-tamarind sauce, or grilled fish skewer with angel hair pasta and Chinese pesto. All main courses are served with vegetables and rice. Save room for dessert, preferably the platter of assorted miniature pastries baked fresh every day or the trio of crème brûlées.

COCONUT PLANTATION MARKETPLACE

Coconut Marketplace has a variety of eating establishments, including that island standby particularly well known for its great breakfasts, **Jolly Roger,** for quick meals, **Aunt Sophie's Grill,** specializing in burgers, **Big Mel's Deli, Fish Hut, Taco Dude,** and **Paradise Chicken-'n'-Ribs.** For a more leisurely meal, it's **Wild Palms Bistro,** serving lunch and dinner every day, with palm trees at each table. For relaxing drinks in a picturesque setting, it's **Tradewinds: A South Seas Bar.**

THE NORTH SHORE: PRINCEVILLE, KILAUEA, HANALEI

Meals for Less than $20

Chuck's Steak House

At Princeville Center. ☎ **808/826-6211.** Reservations recommended for dinner and for parties of six or more at lunch. Main courses $14.50–$21.50, to market price for fish and lobster. AE, CB, DC, MC, V. Lunch Mon–Fri 11:30am–2:30pm; dinner daily 6–10pm. SEAFOOD/STEAK/SALAD.

This is rightfully one of the most popular places at Princeville Center. An attractive porch, plants, ceiling fans, dark walls, secluded booths, and antiques set a cozy scene. Lunch is fun here, with daily specials for $5.75–$8.50 and an array of salads, burgers, and sandwiches. Dinner features steaks and prime rib, seafood, and fresh fish specials. All meals include salad bar, hot bread and butter, and steamed rice or rice pilaf; the salad bar is available on its own for $8.50. For dessert, hesitate not: The mud pie is wonderful. Chuck's is also known for great tropical drinks; cocktails are served Monday through Friday from 11:30am to 11pm and on Saturday and Sunday from 5 to 11pm.

✪ Hanalei Gourmet

Old Hanalei School, Hanalei Center, 5-5161 Kuhio Hwy. ☎ **808/826-2524.** Reservations not accepted. Sandwiches and salads $3.95–$9.25; dinner specials $10–$15.95. MC, V. Mon–Thurs 8am–10:30pm, Fri–Sat 8am–midnight, Sun 8am–9pm. AMERICAN/DELI.

Ever since it opened in the superbly restored Old Hanalei School, Hanalei Gourmet has been deservedly one of the most popular spots in Hanalei with both locals and tourists. Half the operation is a bakery, cheese shop, and take-out deli, with a splendid wine cellar. This is the place to get your picnic fixings if you're hiking the Na Pali coast or kayaking up a river. The other half of the operation is a cheery sit-down cafe that serves tropical drinks, breakfast, lunch, and dinner with a gourmet touch. Breakfast features their own muesli cereal, a croissant sandwich, bagel with lox and cream cheese, and a tangy huevos Santa Cruz, for $4.25 to $6.50. Lunch and dinner offer generous Italian sandwiches (the Oregon bay shrimp open-face, on Na Pali brown bread, with bay shrimp and melted Jack cheese, is one of the best, at $7.50); imaginative salads and antipasti; varied pupu plates of meats, cheeses, and smoked fish; and bountiful "Shrimp Boils"—that's unpeeled shrimp boiled in seasoned broth and served with melted garlic butter, from $7.50. Dinner specials on the chalkboard might include ahi fettuccine Alfredo or spinach lasagne. They do original Mexican fish tacos on Thursday nights and Thai/Vietnamese/Cambodian specials on Tuesday and Saturday nights. Desserts, fresh from the bakery, are delicious and on the decadent side. There's live entertainment in the evenings, Tuesday through Saturday, when local performers join ranks, on occasion, with jazz stars from Honolulu and the mainland. Sunday, from 4 to 8pm, there's a light Hawaiian jam session. A lively spot.

Kilauea Bakery & Pau Hana Pizza

In the historic Kong Lung Center. ☎ **808/828-2020.** Reservations not accepted. Pizzas $7–$16; specialty pizzas $11–$25. No credit cards. Mon–Sat 6:30am–9pm. Pizza, 11am–9pm only. GOURMET PIZZA.

This tiny little cafe is much beloved by folks who live on Kauai's North Shore and by tourists heading for the Kilauea Lighthouse and the Princeville/Hanalei area. And with good reason. Tom and Katie Pickett, a young couple who live just around the corner, specialize in fabulous breads (chewy French sourdough, guava sourdough, Gorgonzola and olives, garlic and black pepper, and pumpkin walnut sweet bread, to mention just a few) and in fabulous pizzas, available by the slice or by the piece. You can build your pie to order with such ingredients as goat cheese, chipotle peppers, Kalamata olives, fresh pineapple, and smoked mahimahi (the latter most likely caught by Tom himself on one of his diving expeditions). Every day they do a few specialty pizzas like the Great Gonzo (roasted eggplant, red onion, goat cheese, and roasted garlic). Trust us, they're terrific. So are the cookies, the bagels, and the coffee, made from organically grown, fresh-ground and dark-roasted beans, drip brewed with filtered water in unbleached filter paper. Once you know about this place, driving north without a stop here is virtually impossible.

Taco Bobo's of Hanalei

Ching Young Village, 2nd floor. ☎ **808/826-9436.** Reservations not necessary. Pupus and antojitos $2.95–$6.95; main courses $6.95–$11.95. AE, MC, V. Daily 11:30am–9pm. MEXICAN/HAWAIIAN.

This is a cheerful, noisy place decorated wall-to-wall with serapes—on the walls, on the tables (covered with glass), hanging over the lattice room dividers. There are big, comfy rattan chairs and lots of potted palms. It's fun to sit by a window and look down on the passing parade. If you don't mind the very loud music, you can enjoy their terrific Mexican food. Pupus and antojitos, served until 10pm, include peel-and-dip boiled shrimp, chicken nachos and—a bow to the fact that this is Hawaii—sweet-and-sour meatballs served with pineapple and shoyu, local style teriyaki sticks, broiled luau kabobs of ham, pineapple, and papaya. Among the specialties of the house, we like the baked chimichanga, the kalua verde, the tacos luau style and camarone Yucatan—large shrimp, broiled in the manner of the Yucatan with chiles and spices, and served in a corn tortilla basket. The cantina serves up very good margaritas, plenty of beers by the bottle, California wines, and a few nonalcoholic drinks as well.

Zelo's Grill & Bar

At Princeville Center. ☎ **808/826-9700.** Reservations not accepted. Main courses $7.95–$13.95. MC, V. Daily 9:30am–9pm. AMERICAN.

Where can you find a goodly percentage of the employees of the Princeville Center come lunch or snack time? One of two places: either in Zelo's Grill, a pretty tile-and-woody spot with a counter and tables out on a small lanai—or in their offices enjoying Zelo's take-out goodies. We're not surprised: Zelo's serves tasty food at modest prices. At both lunch and dinner, for example, you can have dishes like their super spinach lasagne at $9.95, or Cajun chicken pasta for $10.95, or a yummy fish taco salad for $8.95. A variety of burgers (including cheddar chicken, grilled fish, Cajun, and veggie), plus full-meal salads (the grilled-chicken Caesar is excellent) are served up at both meals. Delicious pastas and fresh fish (market priced) as well as several specials, are offered at dinner each night.

Ching Young Village Shopping Center

There are several budget eateries at this shopping center. The **Village Snack and Bakery Shop** has plate lunches, such as fried chicken and teriyaki beef, for $5.95, and is also a popular spot for breakfast, which runs $2.95 to $4.95. The best treats here are the home-baked pies: guava, lilikoi chiffon, lemon-cream cheese, at $1.50 a slice. Box lunches are $5.75, with a salad and drink.

Or you can get your pizzas on a homemade whole-wheat crust with sesame seeds at **Pizza Hanalei,** which really works at making a good pie; they use fresh vegetable toppings and herbs picked from their own garden. Pies can be made with tofu instead of cheese. It's $2.35–$2.75 for a slice, $9.45 for a small pie, or try their unusual pizzaritto: That's cheese, vegetables, meats, and spices rolled up into a pizza shell and eaten like a burrito, $4.95.

Also at Hanalei, Tuesday through Sunday from 11am to 3pm, you'll find Roger Kennedy's ☻ **Tropical Taco**—a green truck next to the Hanalei River in the parking lot of the Dolphin Restaurant, where he dishes up gourmet-quality, all-organic burritos, tacos, and the like, all including beans, meat, lettuce, salsa, cheese, and sour cream (vegetarian combos, too), a complete lunch for around $3 to $5. The menu is on a surfboard hooked to the front of the "Taco Wagon." Take your food to the shady riverbank nearby and enjoy your picnic Mexicana.

THE SOUTHERN & WESTERN ROUTES
OLD KOLOA TOWN
Meals for Less than $10

Koloa Broiler

Koloa Rd. ☎ **808/742-9122**. Reservations not required. Main courses $7–$11.95. AE, CB, DC, DISC, JCB, MC, V. Daily 11am–10pm. AMERICAN.

If you don't like the way your food is done at this restaurant in the heart of Old Koloa Town, a few miles from Poipu Beach, you have no one but yourself to blame. This cute little place is one of those broil-it-yourself affairs—and that way, they really manage to keep the prices down. You can choose from top sirloin, marinated beef kebab, barbecued baby back ribs, mahimahi, barbecued chicken, and beef burger; fresh fish is usually available at market price. The price of all main courses includes salad bar, baked beans, rice, and sourdough bread. Lunch offers the same choices, but the burger is $6 rather than $7. The Koloa Broiler is a lively, fun kind of place, simply decorated (try to get a seat out on the lanai), with a bar, a list of exotic drinks, and lots of local people enjoying their meals.

Koloa Fish Market

5482 Koloa Rd. ☎ **808/742-6199**. Reservations not necessary. Main courses $4.95–$5.95. No credit cards. Mon–Sat 1–6pm. LOCAL.

The Koloa Fish Market really and truly is a market, specializing in freshly caught ahi and mahimahi, but it also has a lunch counter that dispenses great sandwiches and plate lunches at bargain-basement prices. You're sure to meet half the working population of tiny Koloa here at lunchtime; the ladies at the bank love it! It's in a little wooden building near the end of the main street in Koloa, across from the post office. There are no tables inside, but you can eat on the porch or take your goodies to the beach or the park. Plate lunches, such as laulau with kalua pig, long rice, and lomi salmon; fried chicken; roast pork; and fresh corned beef are served with rice and salad of the day; they're all $5.95. Sandwiches are $4.95.

Pancho & Lefty's Cantina & Restaurante

Koloa Rd., Old Koloa Town. ☎ **808/742-7377**. Reservations not required. Main courses $5.25–$20.95. AE, MC, V. Breakfast daily 8am–noon; lunch and dinner daily 11am–10pm. MEXICAN.

Everything about Pancho & Lefty's bespeaks sunny Mexico; parrots in the windows, a fountain of greenery, baskets, wooden tables, sombreros on the walls—even the salt-and-pepper shakers are in the shape of red peppers! The restaurant, which got started in Maui a few years ago, has been so successful that it's opened branches here and on the Big Island, and the food is the same—spicy, delicious, inexpensive. You can start the day with a Mexican breakfast—Lefty's Mexican omelet with chorizo and jalapeño, or huevos rancheros, or a breakfast burrito, $6.95 to $9.95, as well as the more usual American offerings. The menu is the same at lunch and dinner. You can't go wrong with the huge seafood salad in a taco shell ($9.95), the steak or chicken fajitas to which you add your own amounts of guacamole, salsa, and sour cream ($12.95 to $15.95), or with specialty items like the enchiladas rancheros or pechuga pollo relleno (chicken breast stuffed with Jack cheese and chiles, batter-fried and topped with enchilada sauce). Begin your meal with a tropical drink from the lively bar, end with an ice-cream pie for dessert, and top it all off with a Café Siesta—maybe a Mexican coffee (tequila and Kahlúa) or a non-Mexican, but altogether satisfying, Irish coffee.

POIPU BEACH

Meals for Less than $5

☻ Taqueria Nortenos

2827-A Poipu Rd., Koloa. ☎ **808/742-7222.** Reservations not required. $2.15–$5. Thurs–Tues 11am–11pm. Closed Weds. MEXICAN.

Next to the Kukuila Store in Koloa is a tiny taco bar that packs a mighty wallop. Owner Ed Sills, former chef at the prestigious Plantation Garden Restaurant, has been running his own place for several years now, turning out excellent food and keeping the prices low. You can get a meal here for under $5. Ed often does regional specialties, such as posole (pork-and-hominy stew) and enchiladas in the style of Sonora and Chalupa. Vegetarians can be accommodated nicely. When you want some good Mexican munchies, pop in for tacos, burritos, tostadas, or nachos. Pick up your food at the counter and eat in the tiny dining room or take it out. Call them in advance and they'll pack you a nice picnic for the beach.

Meals for Less than $15

La Griglia

Poipu Shopping Village, Poipu Rd. ☎ **808/742-2147.** Reservations not required. Main courses $9.95–$12.95. MC, V. Daily 11am–10pm. ITALIAN.

It could be a seaside cafe in Italy, but lots of folks who live in this area are grateful that this combination restaurant–latte bar–ice-cream parlor–paninoteca is right here on Kauai. La Griglia is small and pretty, with open windows, tile floors, koa wood tables, and lots of greenery; there's seating outdoors in good weather. A mural of an Italian seaside village by Kauai artist Ralph Adamson graces one wall. Thanks to the talents of Calabrese master chef Cathy Halter who created a five-star Italian restaurant in Portland and a chain of casual Italian eateries in Washington, La Griglia serves robust, flavorful Italian food that is healthful, delicious, and very reasonably priced. Cathy uses only the freshest of ingredients (local produce whenever possible), makes her own pastas, breads, rolls, and panini every day. As for those panini, they are "edible plates" covered with combinations of cheeses, veggies, and meats, made here on a special panini grill; at $6.95, they make a neat little meal along with an espresso or a latte. (We like the one with mozzarella, blackened chicken, lettuce, tomato, and Cajun dressing). Cathy also does a variety of sauces—marinara, puttanescae, a nice, light lemon chicken sauce, and a white cheese sauce—which can top burgers, pastas, lunch or dinner main dishes, or specials. Lunch pastas are $6.95; dinner pastas are $9.95. Some of Cathy's specials, which vary from day to day, could include pasta with vodka cream sauce, gnocchi verdi, chicken cacciatore, or seafood linguine, most are around $12.95. There's a rich tiramisu for dessert. Kids have their own menu (pasta and burgers, $2.95 to $3.25), so this is a good family choice. Bring your own wine and beer or pay through the nose at the nearby Whaler's Store.

Pizza Bella

Poipu Shopping Village, Poipu Rd. ☎ **808/742-9571.** Reservations not required. Main courses $5.25–$8.95. MC, V. Breakfast daily 7:30am–12 noon; lunch and dinner daily 12 noon–10pm. ITALIAN.

This is much more than your average pizza parlor. It has an attractive layout—black-and-white tile floors, white wicker chairs, greenery, ceiling fans, even a few outside tables. Nearby condo dwellers like to start the day here with an inexpensive breakfast. Eggs any style, blueberry pancakes, french toast, omelets, and the like are all $4.50 and under. The menu is the same the rest of the day: 10-inch, California-style gourmet pizzas—topped with homemade sauce and four cheeses; barbecued chicken and cilantro; a mélange of seafood, starting at $9.95. Less modern tastes might go for the old-fashioned pies, the hot and cold sandwiches, and several pastas, including a veggie lasagne. There's wine, beer, and a nice atmosphere. Keep Pizza Bella in mind for lunch or a light dinner if you're staying in the Poipu area. They also deliver.

Meals for About $15

Brennecke's Beach Broiler

2100 Hoone Rd., Poipu Beach. ☎ **808/742-7588.** Reservations only for dinner parties of 6 or more. Main courses $5.95–$28.95. DC, DISC, MC, V. Lunch daily 11am–4pm; dinner daily 4–10pm. AMERICAN.

Located on the second floor balcony directly across from Poipu Beach Park, Brennecke's likes to proclaim that it's "Right on the beach, right on the price." True. Cheerfully decorated with window boxes blossoming with bright flowers and an assortment of family photos and memorabilia, this popular restaurant is a lively place—day and night.

The menu offers plenty of possibilities, starting with a beautiful salad bar that's offered with most lunch and dinner main courses. Sandwiches and burgers are available at both lunch and dinner. On the low side of the dinner menu, try the creamy clam chowder, with sourdough bread and salad bar for $12.95; or the pasta primavera or Oriental chicken stir-fry, both with salad bar, for $14.95. Brennecke's is famous for its kiawe-broiled fresh-fish selections, which vary daily depending on what's biting; all are complete meals at $20.95. There's a keiki menu, too, from $3.95 to $6.95. Burgers and spaghetti are 99¢ when purchased with an adult meal.

During the Sunshine Happy Hour, 11am to 5pm, most drinks are reduced in price, and mai tais are $3. Lunch pupus are available. Browse in their Mini Deli for takeout sandwiches and snacks that you might want to take back to your apartment; it's open daily for coffee and pastry from 8am to 9pm.

Worth a Splurge

✪ Roy's Poipu Bar & Grill

Poipu Shopping Village, 2360 Kiahuna Plantation Drive. ☎ **808/742-5000.** Reservations strongly recommended, several days in advance for weekends. Main courses $14.95–$17.95. AE, CB, DC, DISC, MC, V. Dinner nightly 5:30–9pm. HAWAIIAN REGIONAL.

Roy Yamaguchi, perhaps Hawaii's most highly praised and award-winning chef for his innovative marriage of Asian-Pacific flavors and classic European techniques, has done it again. Already winning kudos for his restaurants on Oahu, Maui, Guam, and Tokyo, Roy has opened a new place on Kauai, and his Poipu Bar & Grill is another big winner. The lanai and the dining room are equally artful; we like to sit indoors and watch the chefs (all trained by Roy) at work in the glassed-in kitchen. The furniture is rattan with print upholstery, and all the art on the walls is for sale; ask your server if something interests you. The serving staff is exceptional—another Roy trademark. Since executive chef Mark "Mako" Segawa's menu varies from night to night—some two dozen items are featured on the "nightly special" sheet—you could go back several times and have something different and delicious each time. And the tab is very reasonable for food of this caliber. The night we were there on our last trip, our group feasted on appetizers of island-style potstickers with a lobster miso sauce, lemon grass crusted fish satay with a Thai peanut sauce, and an unusual escargot cassoulet with blanched garlic, ham, and mushrooms in a cabernet sauce. We couldn't pass up a couple of individual pizzas—mesquite-grilled chicken with feta cheese and a Puna goat cheese and shiitake pie ($6.95 and $7.50). (A pizza and a salad could be a complete meal for a light eater.) For our main courses, we went with pasta with shrimp and chicken, northern Chinese roast duck, and a crisp Thai stuffed chicken with almonds, green beans, and sticky rice. We skipped dessert, but we could have had mascarpone cheesecake or macadamia-nut tart, among others. The wine list is well chosen and not overpriced. We can't wait to go back.

HANAPEPE

Ⓢ Green Garden

Hwy. 50. ☎ **808/335-5422.** Reservations recommended for dinner. Main courses $6.50–$26.95. AE, MC, V. Breakfast and lunch Mon, Wed–Fri 9am–2:15pm. Sat 8am–2:15pm. Sun 7:30am–2:15pm; dinner Wed–Mon 5–9pm. AMERICAN.

The Green Garden is a Kauai tradition, a more than 40-year-old restaurant run by Sue Hamabata and her family. You'll feel as if you're sitting in the middle of a greenhouse, with orchids on the tables, plants everywhere, an entire screened wall facing a garden, bamboo chairs, and white walls.

For a real treat, do as the locals do: Call them at least half an hour in advance and order a family-style meal, with a variety of Chinese and local dishes. Or you can make a lunch on one of their sandwich specials, like the fresh fish on toast, for about $5.95 and under. Lunch selections for $5.50 to $7.35, include sweet-and-sour spareribs, a seafood special, and Korean-style boneless barbecued chicken. Dinner is a complete meal, featuring similar main courses, all accompanied by homemade soup or fruit cup, tossed salad, a starch, vegetables and rolls, and beverage. Kiawe broiler specials, such as filet mignon at $14.80, are also well priced. Be sure to save room for Sue's homemade pies—macadamia nut, lilikoi, chocolate cream—absolute marvels, and only $2. Note that if a tour bus happens to disgorge its hungry passengers here, things can get a bit hectic; better to come on the late side of the lunch hour.

The Espresso Bar

In the Hanapepe Book Store, 3830 Hanapepe Rd. ☎ **808/335-5011.** Reservations not necessary. Main courses $14.95–$16.95. No credit cards. Wed–Sun breakfast 8am–3pm, lunch 11am–2pm; Thurs–Sun dinner 6–9pm. NOUVELLE/DESSERT.

This charming place wears three hats: it's an espresso bar serving some of the best espresso and desserts on Kauai; it's a dinner restaurant three nights a week offering Italian vegetarian dishes using locally grown organic vegetables; and it's a book-and-gift shop, too (See Chapter 16). Folks rave about their breakfast treats: Baked frittata with homefries and healthnut toast; homefries with bellpeppers; multigrain waffles; or pancakes with bananas, applesauce, or fresh macadamia nuts ($3.75–$7.75). Come lunchtime, you can get a variety of garden burgers (the pesto garden burger is our favorite), pastas, soups, and salads ($2.75–$7). Now for those dinners: The menu changes nightly, but you can usually count on such appetizers as a vegetarian pâté or tomato-basil and garlic brushetta; a traditional minestrone, and a salad of locally grown baby greens. Two or three main courses are served each night—perhaps pasta primavera with portabello mushrooms, spinach and quatro fromage gnocchi, or the house marinara with fresh and sundried tomatoes. Desserts ($5.75) change nightly, too; we hope you get to try the tiramisu. No liquor license, so BYOB (corkage fee).

✪ Sinaloa

1-3259 Kaumualii Hwy. (Hwy. 50). ☎ **808/335-0006.** Reservations advised. Main courses $9.95–$13.95 (includes soup, chips, and salsa); lunch $2.45–$5.95. Mon–Tues and Thur 11am–3pm and 5–8:30pm; Fri–Sun 11am–3pm and 5–9pm; closed Wed. MEXICAN.

This festive taqueria and cantina just might serve the best Mexican food this side of the Americas. Don't let the rather imposing aquamarine facade deter you; the friendly staff and comfortable ambience will make you feel right at home once you cross the threshold. Sinaloa's airy, intimate dining room and bar are filled with the bright colors and whimsical folk art of Mexico, and—in true Mexican fashion—renowned artist Steve Leal (cousin of restaurateur Veronica Maccies) has created beautiful wall murals. The food, as well as the setting, will make you feel as if you've suddenly been transplanted. Dishes are based on Veronica's family recipes, and everything is prepared—including the homemade corn tortillas—exactly as you would expect it to be south of the border. Peruse the extensive, well-priced menu over a Mexican beer or a frothy margarita and a basket of fresh chips, (always accompanied by Sinaloa's delicious tangy green salsa). We were thrilled with the fish tacos (made with fresh local mahimahi), cheesy enchiladas, generously stuffed burritos, and hearty tortilla soup. Even if you're staying on the eastern or north shores, take some time to get a bite here—it's a great lunch or dinner stop on your way to or from Kokee State Park or Waimea Canyon.

Note: At press time, Sinaloa was considering opening at 3pm every day and phasing out their lunch menu entirely, in favor of a taco menu in the early hours. Please check before you go.

KALAHEO

Brick Oven Pizza

2-2555 Kaumualii Hwy. ☎ **808/332-8561.** Reservations not accepted. Main courses $2.50–$11.85. MC, V. Tues–Sat 11am–10pm, Sun 3–10pm. PIZZA/SANDWICHES.

On the main road in Kalaheo is this family-run, family-style restaurant that's been making delicious "pizza with the homemade touch" for many years now. It's a cozy restaurant with red-and-white gingham tablecloths in true pizzeria fashion. Children are treated especially nicely here. Hearth-baked pies with delicious crust, either whole wheat or white brushed with garlic butter, start at $7.95 for a 10-inch plain cheese pie, and go all the way up to $23.95 for a 15-inch pizza with almost everything. In addition to pizza, there are hot sandwiches, including a vegetarian one, and a yummy seafood-style pizza bread. Green salads are available, and so are wine and beer. Call ahead for pizza to go.

Kalaheo Coffee Co. & Cafe

2-2436 Kaumualii Highway, # A-2, at the light in Kalaheo. ☎ **808/332-5858.** Breakfast items $1.75–$7.50; sandwiches $4.25–$5.95; main dishes $6.50 and $6.98. No credit cards. Breakfast Tues–Sat 6–11am, Sun 7–11am; lunch Tues–Sat 10:30am–5pm, Sun 10:30am–2pm. COFFEES/DELI.

If you're getting an early start visiting Waimea Canyon or other points west, do yourself a favor and have breakfast at this cheery little spot, which only has six tables and a counter. We love their banana pancakes, the smoked salmon omelette, and their toasted bagel "Bennys"—like eggs Benedict, but on bagels, either with ham and cheese or veggies, topped with poached egg and Hollandaise sauce ($3.95 each). Have a latte, cappuccino, or mocha to go with your meal, and if you *really* need a jolt of energy, try their Morning Madness, with no less than four shots of espresso and steamed half-and-half. They'll fix a box lunch for your picnic, too.

"Lunch and beyond" dishes feature deli sandwiches, a grilled fresh veggie sandwich, and a nice salad of assorted field greens with marinated vegetables and pasta. The Coffee Cabinet offers coffees (by the pound, half-, and quarter-pound) from all over the world, including a good selection grown on Molokai and the Big Island.

Pomodoro Ristorante Italiano

In the Rainbow Shopping Plaza, Kalaheo. ☎ **808/332-5945.** Reservations recommended on weekends. Pasta specialties $8.95–$13.95; main courses $14.95–$18.95. MC, V. Dinner nightly 5:30–10pm. ITALIAN.

Pomodoro was brand new when we last visited Kauai and already the word was out. This charming little dining room, on the second floor of the Rainbow Plaza, was filled with diners happily lapping up the delicioso Italian kaukau. There's an attractive bar area just inside the door. The owner, Gerri, circulates around the attractive room, chatting with her guests and making sure everyone is happy, while her husband and his brother do the honors in the kitchen. There's nothing unusual or trendy about this food; it's all traditional, and all good. Start your meal with a steaming bowl of minestrone, or maybe the Caesar salad or the prosciutto and melon (or whatever fruit is in season). If you're choosing a pasta, then make it the house specialty, the lasagne, or the baked penne. Among the regular main courses, the chicken saltimbocca, the veal scaloppini alla marsala, and the calamari alla parmigiana are all very popular. They're all accompanied by pasta with vegetables and homemade garlic bread, which you can dip in balsamic vinegar or olive oil.

KOKEE

Kokee Lodge

In Kokee State Park. ☎ **808/335-6061.** Reservations not accepted. Salads, sandwiches, snacks, $2.95–$8.95. DC, DISC, MC, V. Daily 9am–4pm. AMERICAN.

If you're going to Waimea Canyon—and, of course, you should—it's nice to know that you can have breakfast or lunch at Kokee Lodge in Kokee State Park. The kitchen is presided over by Sherrie Orr, who adds her unique natural-foods touch to the menu. The rustic dining room affords views of both mountain and meadow. Two quiches—ham and Swiss or spinach and Swiss—are very popular at both breakfast and lunch. At lunch you can also get a variety of salads; sandwiches served on 12-grain bread and very "green" with green leaf lettuce and tomatoes; Portuguese bean soup (the local soul food); or chili. Any time of the day, try their delicious homemade hot cornbread, served with Kauai honey. Desserts—like lilikoi chiffon and Alakai Swamp pie—are always delicious. They serve Lappert's coffee (the best), a variety of teas, and cocktails, beer and wine, as well. Their "mug special" is very popular: A Kokee Lodge souvenir mug with a coffee drink, your choice of liquor, and tons of whipped cream—$7.99.

WAIMEA

The Grove Dining Room

At Waimea Plantation Cottages, 9400 Kaumualii Hwy. ☎ **808/338-2300.** Reservations recommended for dinner and Sunday Brunch. Main courses $9.95–$18.95; Sunday brunch $16.95 adults, $14.95 seniors, $8.95 children. CB, DC, MC, V. Lunch Tues–Fri 11:30am–2pm; dinner Tues–Thurs 5:30–9pm, Fri–Sat 5:30–10pm; brunch Sun 10am–2pm. AMERICAN.

Good restaurants are scarce in this part of the island, so it's nice to know about The Grove Dining Room; you could schedule a meal here before or after a trip to Waimea Canyon. The Grove is located in the faithfully restored main house (you may have seen it in "The Thorn Birds") of the old Waimea Plantation. The big, comfortable dining room is decorated with artifacts from the original plantation house, and the atmosphere is reminiscent of Old Hawaii; the ambience is peaceful and relaxing. The temptation to linger is very strong: Go ahead—no one will rush you. Our favorite times to come here are on a Friday or Saturday night or for Sunday Brunch—that's when the Kahelalani Serenaders, a talented group from the "Forbidden Island" of Niihau (their first language is Hawaiian), entertain. And Friday night also features a Hawaiian dinner of traditional foods for $19.95. On the regular dinner menu (also available on Friday nights), you could start with such appetizers as summer vegetable rolls with a spicy sweet-and-sour tamarind sauce or the Asian-style crab cake with plum and chili sauce. Then on to the likes of a Hawaiian seafood stir-fry on a bed of linguini, prime rib with horseradish sauce, Korean kalbi ribs, vegetarian lasagna, or fresh catch of the day. Lunch features special plates at $8.25 to $8.95, plus a variety of salads (including a pineapple fruit boat with watermelon sherbet) and sandwiches. Plantation Iced Tea (with pineapple spears!) makes a nice ending to the meal, along with their Kikiaola Sand Pie—a variation of the island favorite, mud pie. Beer, wine, and tropical drinks are all available; there's a Happy Hour, too, from 4 to 6pm.

16

What to See & Do on Kauai

Beautiful Kauai offers more than enough opportunities for hiking, beachgoing, camping, fishing, golf, water sports, and more—including just plain relaxing—to keep even the most ardent visitor busy for weeks. Even if you only have a few days, you can still experience much of the majesty and adventure that the Valley Isle has to offer.

1 Beaches

By Jeanette Foster

This is the island for extraordinary beaches, all kinds of beaches: From beaches that bark(!) to beaches from famous movie scenes, Kauai is known for its miles and miles of perfect white-sand beaches. These are the beaches of your dreams, the kind that would line the coasts of paradise.

POLIHALE STATE PARK

This is Kauai's longest white-sand beach, a 15-mile stretch that starts at Waimea and ends at Polihale. To get there, take Hi. 50 past Barking Sands Missile Range and follow the signs through the sugarcane fields to Polihale. The state park is 140 acres and has facilities for camping as well as restrooms, showers, picnic tables, and pavilions. Polihale's miles of white sand are bordered on one side by the sea cliffs that begin the Na Pali Coast; from the shore, you can see the forbidden island of Niihau rising in the distance. Swimming here can be treacherous, especially in the winter months when high surf generates dangerous water conditions, including powerful rip currents. Board surfers, however, welcome the winter surf. The safest swimming area is in a small protected inlet called Queen's Pond. This shallow sand-bottomed inlet is protected from normal waves and alongshore currents.

In addition to swimming and surfing, Polihale State Park is known for its Barking Sands Beach. Believe it or not, when the sand is rubbed (or walked on) the sound produced mimics that of a barking dog. The reason, according to scientists, is that the grains of sand are perforated with small holes that open to cave-like cavities. When the grains are rubbed together, they create vibrations resulting in the barking sound. This is a wonderful place to get away from it

Frommer's Favorite Kauai Experiences

Swimming and Snorkeling at Poipu Beach. Spend your day in the calm waters and among the reefs of this beautiful beach, one of the islands' best. When you've had enough of the water, relax on the fine white sand and take in the sights—this is one of the best people-watching beaches around.

Seeing Awe-Inspiring Waimea Canyon. Visit the "Grand Canyon of the Pacific" for one of the most spectacular views in all of Hawaii. Before your drive back down to sea level, enjoy a bowl of the Kokee Lodge's Portuguese bean soup and a piece of their lilikoi pie in the bracing mountain air.

Exploring the Na Pali Coast with Captain Zodiac. Have the time of your life riding the waves in a high-tech, inflatable rubber boat—there's no better (or more exciting) way to get up-close-and-personal with Kauai's spectacular, secluded coast.

A Visit to Spouting Horn Park. Watch the geysers shoot up through holes in the lava as the sea pounds relentlessly against the black rocks of the southern coast.

Driving the Northern Route, Hi. 56. Travel all the way to Hanalei—through verdant landscapes, over charming single-lane bridges, and past the spectacular Sleeping Giant—to catch one of Hawaii's most spectacular sunsets.

all, with two notes of caution: The midday sands heat up, so wear slippers; and the remoteness of the area has attracted thieves. Automobile break-ins are common; be sure not to leave anything valuable in your car.

SALT POND BEACH PARK

The only salt ponds still in production in Hawaii are located at Salt Pond Beach, just outside Hanapepe. For years local residents have come here in the summer to swim, fish, and collect salt; in fact, the people who dry and collect the salt have been doing so for generations. Salt Pond Beach Park lies between two rock points. The curved beach features a protected reef, tidal pools, and gently lapping waters. During periods of calm, swimming (even for children and water-resistant adults), scuba diving, and spear fishing are popular. The prevailing winds attract windsurfers offshore. During the winter, surfers ride the waves that funnel in. A lifeguard is on duty. Facilities include showers, restrooms, camping area, picnic area, pavilion, and parking lot. To get there, take Hi. 50 past Hanapepe, and turn on Lokokai Road.

POIPU BEACH PARK

On the south shore—where the sun always shines—is a beach park that offers all sorts of activities: excellent swimming from a white-sand beach, great reefs for snorkeling and diving, good fishing, nice waves for surfers, steady wind for windsurfers, small tidal pools for exploring, a grassy area for picnics, and hordes of people for people watching. Yes, Poipu is usually packed with visitors and local residents, but it's worth dealing with the crowds. There are bathrooms, showers, picnic facilities, and parking. To get to Poipu, turn on Poipu Beach Road, then right at Ho'owili Road.

BRENNECKE'S BEACH

Further east on Ho'owili Road is the site of what used to be one of the best bodysurfing sites in the state. Two hurricanes in a decade, however, have rearranged the beach somewhat. The sandbar, which at one time created near-perfect shorebreak waves in the summer, was wiped out by the last hurricane; boulders were deposited in its place. Expert bodysurfers still surf at high tide, but it certainly "ain't like it used to be." Board surfing still takes place outside the reef. No facilities.

DONKEY BEACH

For a secluded beach off the beaten path, take Hi. 56 past Kealia; look for the 11-mile marker and park your car on the road. You can't see the beach from the Kuhio Highway—walk a quarter-mile down the sugar cane road to get to it. You'll find a crescent-shaped white-sand beach at the base of a rocky, sloping pasture filled with ironwood trees, *hau, ilima,* and *naupaka,* and lined with heliotrope. Not many visitors come to this hidden spot. The surfing off shore is excellent. Swimming can be dangerous in the winter months, when the surf is up. Donkey Beach gets its name from the large herd of donkeys and mules that Lihue Plantation company once kept in the pasture behind the beach at Paliku. When Kealia was a sugar cane-plantation town, many of the donkeys and mules grazed along the shoreline pastures. Today only a few mules remain. There are no facilities.

HANALEI BAY

Hanalei means "lei-shaped," an apt description of this almost perfect semicircular bay, the largest on Kauai. Hanalei encompasses the area from Puu Poa in the east to Makahoa Point in the west; the location for the filming of *South Pacific,* this is some 2 miles of exquisite beach. With the dramatic Waialeale Mountain as a backdrop, the turquoise waters of the bay are great for swimming, bodyboarding, surfing, fishing, windsurfing, canoe paddling, kayaking, and boating (there is a boat ramp on the west bank of the Hanalei River). Facilities include a pavilion, restrooms, picnic tables, and parking. This place is always packed with both local residents and visitors, but you can usually find your very own stretch with a stroll down the beach. Weekdays are less crowded than weekends, but with a place this beautiful, everyone wants to enjoy it. To get there, make a right turn onto Aku Road after Ching Young Village in Hanalei, then another right on Weke Road.

HAENA BEACH PARK

For the active beachgoer, this one offers swimming in the summer—on the west end behind the reef is best—and surfing in the winter. Fishing for *papio* and *ulua* is great anytime of the year; in fact, fishermen used to call this beach Maniniholo ("traveling *manini* fish"), because it was the site of *hukilaus* (net fishing) in the summer. Maniniholo is also the name of the dry cave across the street from the park. The cave, really a lava tube that stretches several hundred feet inland, was once a sea cave (when the level of the ocean was much higher than it now is); waves have pounded the cave entrance to its current size. For the less animated vacationer, the beach park is also an excellent place to vegetate. Facilities include picnic tables, restrooms, showers, and campgrounds. To get to Haena Beach Park, take Hi. 56; the park is right off the road, about 5 miles past Haena.

2 Water Sports & Recreation

By Jeanette Foster

BOATING

Kauai has many areas accessible only by boat: the Fern Grotto, Wailua State Park, Huleia and Hanalei National Wildlife Refuges, Menehune Fish Pond, and numerous waterfalls. **Paradise River Boat Rentals,** at the Kilohana Plantation (☎ 808/245-9580), rents boats ranging from a Porta-Bote (for three people) for $95 a day to a Boston Whaler (six-person capacity) for $245 a day. Included are all the amenities, such as safety equipment, coolers, dry bags (for cameras, wallets, towels, etc.), and a comprehensive orientation on where to go. They also rent a range of ocean toys, from snorkel equipment to boogie boards.

For an "up-close-and-personal" tour of the Na Pali Coast, book with Captain Zodiac, P.O. Box 456, Hanalei (☎ 808/826-9371). Clancy Greff, known as "Captain Zodiac," was the first person to initiate the now-famous sea tours of the Na Pali coastline. The tours take place on 23-foot inflatable boats (known as Zodiacs), which allow passengers to get close to the incredible shoreline because they have a very shallow draft. The quick-moving boats are just inches from the water, giving the rider a feeling of intimacy with the marine world below. The tours, always dependent on the weather and sea conditions, consist of a $3^{1}/_{2}$- to 4-hour morning snorkeling and guided tour, a 3-hour afternoon tour (no snorkeling), and a 5-hour tour that includes landing on the normally inaccessible Nualolo Kai Beach, snorkeling, hiking, and lunch. Costs range from $65 for the afternoon cruise to $105 for the 5-hour cruise.

The best time of the year to take a Captain Zodiac cruise is during the summer months, when the ocean is calmer and Captain Zodiac can maneuver the boat into caves and up to hidden waterfalls. From October to March, the weather can be rough and trips may be canceled. On the other hand, if the weather is good these winter months are a good time to see whales. The water is usually calmer and the wind is usually diminished during the morning. But the downside is that more sightseeing boats are out in the morning. If you're on the trip that features snorkeling, bring your own gear if you have it; your gear will fit you better than gear provided by the boat. Nothing is worse than a leaky mask when you are snorkeling. Definitely bring your camera; they'll provide a sealing plastic bag to protect it from salt spray and water.

Once on board, sit on the starboard side (that's the right side as you face the front of the boat). Most of the sightseeing is on the way out; you'll have a perfect view. If you sit on the left, you will constantly have to turn your head to view the spectacular scenery.

A Word of Caution: An inflatable boat is very bouncy (sort of like riding on jello); Captain Zodiac recommends that pregnant women skip this trip, and warns that small children may not be comfortable in a shadeless, bouncing boat.

BODYBOARDING (BOOGIE BOARDING) & BODYSURFING

Bodyboarding consists of riding the waves on a small maneuverable board (often a boogie board) that supports the upper half of your body. Bodysurfing is surfing without a board; your body alone is the vehicle that rides the wave. Both bodyboarding and bodysurfing can be enjoyed at the same beaches. Fun in almost any size surf, the only equipment necessary is open heel fins and, in the case of bodyboarding, a board (also called a boogie board, belly board, or paipo board). The best beaches for bodysurfing and boogie boarding are Kalapaki Beach, next to Nawiliwili Bay, and Poipu Beach.

Boogie boards and fins can be rented for as little as $29 a week from **Snorkel Bob's Kauai Inc.,** 4480 Ahukini Rd., Lihue (☎ 808/245-9433), or on Poipu Road, just south of Poipu Shopping Village, in Poipu (☎ 808/742-8322). In Kapaa, boogie boards are available at **Kauai Water Ski & Surf Co.,** Kinipopo Shopping Village, 4-356 Kuhio Hwy., Kapaa (☎ 808/822-3574).

OCEAN KAYAKING

Kauai was made for kayaking. You can take the Huleia River into the Federal Wildlife Sanctuary—it's the only way the natural wildlife refuge can be explored. Or, take a leisure trip around Hanalei Bay. For the more adventurous, there's the Na Pali coast, featuring majestic cliffs and virgin beaches (not to mention open ocean conditions and steamroller waves). Equipment rental for a two-person kayak is around $50 a day. Kayak lessons and tours (some including snacks) range from $39 to $125. **Kayak Kauai Outfitters** (☎ 808/826-9844) has a range of tours, from the serene to the serious, and a plethora of information on where to go and what to see for more independent types.

SAILING

Kauai offers a range of sailing opportunities: Picture yourself cruising the rugged Na Pali coastline in a 42-foot ketch-rigged yacht under full sail, watching the sun set as you enjoy a tropical libation, or speeding through the aquamarine water in a 40-foot trimaran as porpoises play off the bow. Prices vary from $75 for a sail-snorkel cruise to $45 for a sunset cruise. Call **Bluewater Sailing,** in Hanalei (☎ 808/882-0525).

SCUBA DIVING

Diving on Kauai is dictated by the weather. During the winter, when heavy swells and high winds hit the island, diving is generally limited to the more protected south shore. In the summer, though, when the north Pacific storms subside, the magnificent north shore opens up.

Probably the best-known site along the south shore is Sheraton Caverns. Located off the Poipu Beach resort area, this dive site consists of a series of lava tubes interconnected by a chain of archways. A constant parade of fish stream by (even shy lion fish can be spotted in the crevices), brilliantly colored Hawaiian lobsters hide in the lava's tiny holes, and occasionally turtles meander by.

If you're lucky enough to be on Kauai during the summer (and if the weather gods are good to you), don't miss the north shore. One of the best dives is Oceanarium, located northwest of Hanalei Bay. A kaleidoscopic marine world can be found in this horseshoe-shaped cove. From the rare (long-handed spiny lobsters) to the more common (*ta'ape,* conger eels, and nudibranchs), the resident population is one of the more diverse on the island. The topography (pinnacles, ridges, and archways) is covered with cup coral, black coral trees, and enough nooks and crannies that it would take you a dozen dives to explore them all.

If you're not a certified scuba diver, take classes before you come to Kauai so you don't have to "waste" your vacation time learning the ropes and can dive right in. If you're unsure if scuba diving is for you, take an introductory dive; most

Beaches & Outdoor Activities on Kauai

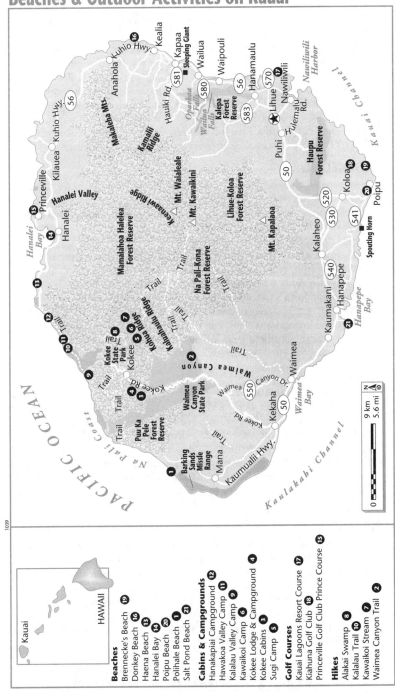

PACIFIC OCEAN

Kauai Channel

Nawiliwili Harbor

Hanalei Bay

Hanapepe Bay

Waimea Bay

Kaulakahi Channel

Kuhio Hwy. 56

Kealia
Kapaa
Sleeping Giant
Wailua
Waipouli
Hanamaulu

Anahola
Makaleha Mts.
Kamalii Ridge
Hauiki Rd.
581
Opaekaa Falls
Wailua Falls
580
Kalepa Forest Reserve
56
Lihue
Nawiliwili
570
Hulemalu Rd.
583
Puhi
Haupu Forest Reserve
Koloa
Poipu
Spouting Horn

Princeville
Kilauea
Hanalei
Hanalei Valley
Mamalahoa Halelea Forest Reserve
Keenawi Ridge
Mt. Waialeale
Mt. Kawaikini
Na Pali-Kona Forest Reserve
Lihue-Koloa Forest Reserve
Mt. Kapalaoa
Kalaheo
Kaumakani
Hanapepe
Kahihaunui Ridge
Kokee State Park
Kokee
Kokee Rd.
Waimea Canyon State Park
Waimea Canyon
Waimea Canyon Dr.
550
Kokee Rd.
Waimea Rd.
Waimea
Kekaha
50

Na Pali Coast
Trail
Puu Ka Pele Forest Reserve
Trail
Trail
Trail
Trail
Barking Sands Missle Range
Mana
Kaumualii Hwy.

50
520
530
541
540

Beaches
- 19 Brennecke's Beach
- 16 Donkey Beach
- 13 Haena Beach
- 14 Hanalei Bay
- 20 Poipu Beach
- 21 Polihale Beach
- 21 Salt Pond Beach

Cabins & Campgrounds
- 12 Hanakapiai Campground
- 11 Hawakoa Valley Camp
- 9 Kalalau Valley Camp
- 6 Kawaikoi Camp
- 4 Kokee Lodge & Campground
- 3 Kokee Cabins
- 5 Sugi Camp

Golf Courses
- 17 Kauai Lagoons Resort Course
- 18 Kiahuna Golf Club
- 15 Princeville Golf Club Prince Course

Hikes
- 8 Alakai Swamp
- 10 Kalalau Trail
- 7 Kawaikoi Stream
- 2 Waimea Canyon Trail

HAWAII

Kauai

N

9 km
5.6 mi

1089

dive operators offer these no-experience-necessary dives, which range from $40 to $95.

Since the best dives on Kauai are offshore, we suggest that you book with an operator for a two-tank dive off a dive boat for the most fulfilling experience. **Bubbles Below Scuba Charters,** 6251 Hauaala Rd., Kapaa (☎ 808/822-3483) offers two-tank boat dives for $75 and night dives for $60. They also feature a dive to the "Forbidden Island" of Niihau once a month. This three-tank dive is an all day affair—the boat leaves at 5am and doesn't come back until sunset. On the south side, call **Fathom Five Adventures,** 3450 Poipu Rd., Koloa (☎ 808/742-6991), which specializes in dives on the southern end of Kauai.

SNORKELING

Not everyone wants to dive deep, and that's fine—a large percentage of Kauai's inshore reefs can be seen while floating on top of the water, snorkeling. All you need is a mask, fins, and snorkel, which can be rented at **Snorkel Bob's Kauai Inc.,** 4480 Ahukini Rd., Lihue (☎ 808/245-9433) or in Poipu (☎ 808/742-8322) for $15 a week.

There are a range of sail-snorkeling cruises that not only teach you snorkeling and provide equipment, but also feed you lunch and cost about $65 to $75; check out **Captain Andy's Sailing Adventures,** in Koloa (☎ 808/822-7833), or **Captain Sundown's Catamaran Sailing,** in Hanalei (☎ 808/245-6117).

For snorkelers venturing out on their own, try Ke'e Beach, at the northern end of the island in the Haena State Park; Papaa Bay, north of Anahola; Ninini Beach, located near the northern point of Nawiliwili Bay; Poipu Beach Park; Loloa Landing; and Salt Pond Beach Park.

SNUBA

Snuba, a cross between scuba and snorkeling, has also come to Kauai. You can explore the underwater world without the experience and bulky equipment required by scuba. While Snuba diving, you have a mask and an air hose connected to the tank, which rides in a floating sled on the surface. The disadvantage of Snuba is that you are limited to a depth of 20 to 25 feet (as far as the air hose will reach). No experience is necessary; all required instruction is given the day you dive. **Snuba Tours of Kauai,** 5795 Lauloa Pl., Kapaa (☎ 808/823-8912) offers snuba to anyone over the age of eight. The 1 $1/2$-half hour guided tours are $49.

SURFING

Kauai's beaches offer all that a surfer—from the beginner to the expert—could want. The winter surf rolling into Hanalei is the most popular on the island; however, it's for experts only. The rest of us have to content ourselves with watching the seasoned wavecatchers carve up the waves. Beginners can head for Poipu's year-round surf (you'll find the best waves there in the summer). Another place for year-round surf is "Pinetrees" at Waioloi. The only problem with this site is that you have to paddle out a long way. Check with the local surf shops or phone **KUAI Surfline** (☎ 808/335-3611) to find out where the surf is up and to learn more about conditions.

Surfing lessons are available at $50 an hour (which includes all day equipment rental) from **Windsurf Kauai,** in Hanalei (☎ 808/828-6838). Poipu is also the site of numerous surfing schools that are happy to teach beginners how to ride the waves. There usually are a couple of surf instructors set up on Poipu Beach, if not, check with **Poipu Surf and Sport,** Poipu Shopping Village (☎ 808/742-1132), **Progressive Expressions,** 5425 Koloa Rd. (☎ 808/747-6041). Other shops for equipment rental (ranging from $12 a day to $65 a week) are **Hanalei Surf Co.,** 5-5161 Kuhio Hwy., Hanalei (☎ 808/826-9000), and **Pedal & Paddle,** Ching Young Village Shopping Center, Hanalei (☎ 808/826-9069).

WINDSURFING

If surfing isn't enough for you and sailing doesn't quite cut it, try windsurfing, a combination of the two sports. Lessons and equipment rental can be found at **Windsurf Kauai** in Hanalei (☎ 808/828-6838). They conduct their lessons on Anini Beach, one of the safest beaches for beginners to learn windsurfing. Classes are $75 (which includes equipment) for a three-hour lesson. Rentals are $50 a day. The more advanced windsurfers can try Kalapaki Beach if the winds are right.

WHALE WATCHING

When the giant humpback whales make their annual visit to Hawaii from Alaska, from December to March, they swim right past Kauai. A few seem to linger, and can be seen regularly during their winter stay. The best way to see whales is with **Liko Kauai Cruises,** in Waimea (☎ 808/338-0333). This is not your typical whale-watching cruise; it's a combination Na Pali coast tour-deep sea fishing-Hawaiian historical lecture-whale-watching extravaganza, with lunch. Liko offers a comfortable ride on a 37-foot cabin cruiser; he could squeeze in 32 passengers but, as he puts it, "whew, too many people for see the whales." So he limits the daily tours to 20 people. Cost is $85 for adults and $55 for children.

3 Hiking, Golf & Other Outdoor Activities

By Jeanette Foster

HIKING

The tropical beauty of Kauai is almost surreal, which is one reason so many memorable movies have been filmed here—there's simply no place like it. *South Pacific* was partly filmed on exquisite Lumahai Beach. Elvis Presley starred in *Blue Hawaii* and John Wayne appeared in *Donovan's Reef,* both filmed on Kauai. The South American scenes in *Raiders of the Lost Ark* were on Kauai, and so were scenes from *Jurassic Park, Uncommon Valor* and *The Thorn Birds,* among others.

Much of the beauty of Kauai is in its wild, untamed wilderness, much of which is accessible only by hiking into remote areas. For more information on hiking trails on Kauai, contact: **State Division of Parks,** P.O. Box 1671, Lihue, HI 96766 (☎ 808/241-3446), **State Division of Forestry and Wildlife,** P.O. Box 1671, Lihue, HI 96766 (☎ 808/245-4444), **Kauai County Parks and Recreation,** 4193 Hardy St., Lihue, HI 96766 (☎ 808/241-6660 or 808/245-1881), and **Kokee Lodge Manager,** P.O. Box 819, Waimea, HI 96796 (☎ 808/335-6061).

The **Hawaii Geographic Society,** 49 S. Hotel St., Suite 218, Honolulu, 96813 (☎ 808/538-3952), offers an excellent information packet for $7. The **Sierra Club Hawaii Chapter,** 1111 Bishop St., Suite 511, Honolulu 96813 (☎ 808/538-6616), schedules hikes throughout the year that are open to the public.

Another great resource is Craig Chisolm's *Kauai Hiking Trails,* available for $15 in local bookstores or from **Hawaii Geographic Maps & Books,** P.O. Box 1698, Honolulu, HI 96806.

For information on guided hiking-camping tours, see "Adventure Tours," below. Or, you can strike out on your own on the following excellent hiking trails:

WAIMEA CANYON TRIAL

The Waimea Canyon, otherwise known as the "Grand Canyon of the Pacific," is a mile wide, 10 miles long, and 3,000 feet deep. The best view of this carved expanse is from the Canyon Trail, which skirts the Waimea Canyon's north rim, passing an 800-foot waterfall and pool along the way.

This moderate hike is about 5 miles round trip, takes about four hours, and climbs from 3,000 feet to 3,600 feet. To get there, take Hi. 550 past the Waimea Canyon State Park. Just before the Kokee State Park sign, turn right down Halemau Road. If the road is wet, it will be impassible; park the car and start walking the mile to the trailhead. The trailhead is at the parking area, just off Halemau Road. The Canyon Trail descends down steep switchbacks through the ghost-like remains of a *koa* forest (toppled by Hurricane Iwa in 1982). Further down, the trail traverses a grass-covered hillside that opens onto a panoramic vista of the high cliffs of Waimea Canyon.

As you continue on the trail, the sounds of the Kokee Stream's Waipoo Falls are clearly heard. A short side trail on the left takes you to the falls and a large pool surrounded by ginger, *koa, ohia, lilikoi, kukui,* and *hala.* After a stop at the pool, continue on. Notice the war that native plants are waging with introduced species such as blackberry, lantana, oak trees, and Australian eucalyptus—the natives are not winning.

About a 1¹/₂-mile into the trail is a broad ridge overlooking both Waimea and Poomau Canyons. Go early in the morning for the best views and the best tropical birdwatching; they seem to prefer the early hours. The trail continues another mile, leveling out, and ends at the Kumuwela Lookout. From there, retrace your steps to return to your car.

KAWAIKOI STREAM

This easy, scenic one-hour hike is perfect for people who don't have a lot of time to explore Kokee State Park. The 2¹/₂-mile hike follows the banks of the remote Kawaikoi Stream, one of the waterways that drains the Alakai Swamp. The tannin from the lush vegetation along the stream stains the stream water the color of iced tea. There are two times during the year when this hike is not recommended: during the rainy season, when the road and trails are just too muddy, and during the trout-fishing season in August and September, when the crowds are just too overwhelming.

To get to the trailhead, take Hi. 550 from the Kokee State Park Headquarters to Kumuwela Road. Turn right. Continue for about 1.3 miles to a fork in the road. Take the left fork, Mohihi (Camp 10) Road, and continue to Kawaikoi Camp and Picnic Area. The trailhead is 100 yards to the left, across from the Sugi Grove Camp. The trail starts in a dense grove of Japanese sugi (cedar) and redwoods that were planted in the 1930s; it wanders along one side of the stream then loops over and wanders back. *Photographer's note:* This is an excellent area to photograph the rare waterfowl that live in the swamp. Bring a telephoto lens and approach quietly.

There are numerous camping sites close to this hike: Sugi Grove, Kawaiko Camp, and Kokee State Park. For further information, see "Camping and Wilderness Lodges" in Chapter 15.

ALAKAI SWAMP

This hike is not for everyone. First of all it is a strenuous, 7-mile hike that takes five hours. Second, it's through a bog with mud up to your knees. Third, it will probably rain the entire time. However, this hike does offer a glimpse into another world: the high mountain scrub rain forest of Alakai Swamp—Hawaii's largest swamp, covering 10 square miles in the center of Kauai—home to rare endemic birds and plants, protected by massive cliffs and rugged terrain.

The Alakai Swamp Trail allows a glimpse of the Alakai Wilderness Preserve. Come prepared for rain, mud, and bog. Hiking boots that will not be sucked off by mud that is up to your knees are a must. Photographers should carry several lens filters, as the mist and humid air at 4,000 feet will wreak havoc on your lens. The only silver lining is that there are no mosquitoes above 3,000 feet. Of course, it would be best to go during the dry season; the only problem is that this exceedingly wet, cloud-covered, rainy area averages 460 inches of rain a year— dry periods are very rare.

The trailhead is just off Mohihi (Camp 10) Road, just beyond the Forest Reserve entrance sign and the Alakai Shelter picnic area. From the parking lot the trail follows an old four-wheel drive road used during World War II to place telephone poles. The route is flat, with rain and mist blowing in and out. Carry a compass and stick to the trail; the Division of Forestry has brown and white trail markers with mileage indicators along the way (they are also in the process of building a boardwalk on the trail). The reward is at the end of the 3 1/2-mile trail: If you're lucky and the clouds have parted at the Kilohana Lookout, you'll have a view of the Wainiha Valley below and the beaches of Hanalei.

KALALAU TRAIL

Without a doubt, this is one of the most beautiful, most scenic hiking trails in all of Hawaii. The 6,500-acre Na Pali Coast State Park offers the most awe-inspiring views you'll find anywhere. The scenery is straight out of a Hollywood director's tropical dream—lush rain forests, verdant, stream-filled valleys, and steep, chiseled cliffs. Na Pali means "cliffs," and this is the place to view spectacular ones with sheer, 2,000-foot drops into a turbulent sea. Light pours through fruit-filled trees and breeze-rattled leaves, and the sounds of bird calls fill the air. There are no roads into this area; access is only by a single trail, or by boat, much as it was in ancient Hawaii.

The 11-mile (one way) hike along the Na Pali Coast is somewhat arduous; you should allow at least two days for the walk in if you plan to complete the entire round trip. For camping information, see "Camping and Wilderness Lodges" in Chapter 15. The Kalalau Trail passes through three camping sites and several valleys, and descends down to sea level once before reaching the "Garden of Eden" at Kalalau Beach. Although the trail is in good condition, people who suffer from a fear of heights may not enjoy the narrow ledges hanging over crashing surf a thousand feet below. During the rainy season, the trail becomes slippery, and there's always a danger of flash floods in the mountain valley streams. (In November 1990, a German tourist hiking along the trail was swept away and killed when he tried to cross a rain-swollen stream along the trial.) Also, be prepared for mosquitoes and plan to treat the water en route.

The trailhead is at the end of Hi. 56, near Ke'e Beach. The first 2 miles to Hanakapiai, the first valley, can be crowded with day hikers. A side trip up the valley to the Hanakapiai Falls is worth the trip to see the 120-foot-high mountain stream tumble down into a deep, clear pool. Anyone hiking or camping beyond Hanakapiai must get a permit from the State Division of Parks, 3060 Eiwa St., Lihue, HI 96766 (☎ 808/241-3444).

The trail gets rougher, the foliage thicker, and the climb steeper as you make your way to Hanakoa Valley. There is no beach here. The valley ends in a cliff that drops precipitously down to the ocean below. You know you have arrived in Hanakoa by the deteriorated shack on the trail. Five miles later you arrive at Kalalau Valley, a destination worth every step of the walk getting there. A clear stream bubbles through the lush valley, eventually crossing a 300-foot-wide white-sand beach before flowing into the ocean.

GOLF

Neither wind, nor rain, nor even hurricanes have stopped golfers from pursuing their sport on Kauai. Two hurricanes in a decade did little to deter ardent golfers from practicing their game on some of Hawaii's most challenging courses. Kauai's golf courses offer something for every golfer, from high handicapper to pro.

Carts are required at Kauai's golf courses; the cost is included in the greens fees.

KIAHUNA GOLF CLUB

Located in Koloa, this resort golf course is adjacent to the Poipu Beach Resort. This par-70, 6,353-yard course (designed by Robert Trent Jones Jr.) plays around four large archeological sites, ranging from an ancient Hawaiian temple to the remains of a Portuguese home and crypt built in the early 1800s. The Scottish-style-links course has rolling terrain, undulating greens, 70 sand bunkers, and near-constant winds. The third-hole, par-3, 185-yard goes over Waikomo Stream. At any given time, just about half the players on the course are Kauai residents; the other half, visitors. With greens fees at $45, this is probably the best choice for the budget-conscious golfer. Facilities include driving range, practice greens, snack bar, and twilight rates. Call 808/742-9595.

KAUAI LAGOONS RESORT

Choose from the Lagoons Course (which, despite its name, has only one water hazard) with 18 holes for the recreational golfer, or the Kauai Kiele Championship Course for the low-handicapper. The Lagoons Course is a links-style course with a bunker that's a little less severe than at Kiele. The emphasis on this 6,942-yard, par-72 course is the shore game. Both courses were designed by Jack Nicklaus. The Kiele is a mixture of tournament-quality challenge and high-traffic playability. The Kiele Course winds up with one of Hawaii's most difficult finishing holes, a 431-yard, par-4 played straight-away to an island greens. Amenities include airport transportation (jet in from a neighbor island for the day), practice facility, and spa. Greens fees are $100 at the Lagoon Course and $145 at the Kiele Course. Contact 808/241-6000.

PRINCEVILLE GOLF CLUB–PRINCE COURSE

This is a devil of a course. Designed by Robert Trent Jones Jr., it sits on 390 acres that have been molded to create ocean views from every hole. Some holes have a waterfall backdrop to the greens, others shoot into the hillside, and the famous par-4, 12th hole has a long tee shot off a cliff to a narrow, jungle-lined fairway, 100 feet below. Clearly the most challenging course on Kauai, accuracy is the magic word here. Being off the fairway here means your ball is in the ocean. Even Jones admits this is a tough, tough course: "The average vacation golfer may find the Prince Course intimidating, but they don't mind, because it's so beautiful," Jones says. "It becomes a great nature ride. You get the grandeur, the majesty of Kauai." Amen. Facilities include restaurant, health club/spa, locker, clubhouse, golf shop, and driving range. Greens fees are $140. Tees are constantly booked—everyone wants a crack at this course, so call way in advance. Contact 808/826-5000.

OTHER OUTDOOR ACTIVITIES

Kauai is a destination well suited to the active traveler. The local tennis courts are filled on weekends, canoe paddling is taken seriously, and even polo draws a crowd. You can find almost any sport here, from off-road bicycling to horseback riding along mountain trails to private waterfalls.

BICYCLING

Kauai Downhill, in Lihue (☎ 808/245-1774), offers a 12-mile sunrise bike tour (all downhill) of Waimea Canyon, complete with equipment, continental breakfast, and hotel pick up service, all for $60. To rent a bike on your own, contact **Kayak Kauai Outfitters,** 4-1340 Kuhio Hwy., Kapaa (☎ 808/822-9179); they not only rent 21-speed Raleigh mountain bikes for $20 a day, but also have maps of the best places to ride a bike.

Planning Your Time on Kauai: Let Chris "The Fun Lady" Do It For You

Chris "The Fun Lady," who can be found 365 days a year in her little office/shop at 4-746 Kuhio Highway in the Waipouli area of Kapaa (☎ 808/822-7447), is a good lady to know. Chris Gayagas and her husband, Doug, are like travel agents, only instead of booking travel, they book fun activities at no charge to you for their services. Chris hopes that her clients will come to see her the first or second day of their visit so she can help them plan all the fun things they might want to do. Often, she can get a better price for you than you might get dealing directly with the company providing the service. She can send you kayaking, deep-sea fishing, horseback riding, snorkeling, or scuba diving, or on a catamaran or zodiac adventure. She can book a trip to the Fern Grotto or Smith's luau (and even go with you—she always has a table reserved there). Just tell her what you want to do and when you want to do it, and Chris will brainstorm a way for you to do it at the best possible price. She also rents kayaks, Pro-Line snorkel gear, and boogie boards, and can book your trips to the other islands. Chris's office is part souvenir shop, with cute clothes for adults and kids, cookies, jams and jellies, jewelry, paperweights, knickknacks, and wooden postal cards (which we saw nowhere else).

—Faye Hammel

HORSEBACK RIDING

Pooku Stables in Hanelei (☎ 808/826-6777 or 826-7473) has a four-hour ride up to waterfalls, where you can stop and swim, finishing up with a picnic lunch for $70. **CJM Country Stables,** 1731 Kelaukia St., Koloa (☎ 808/742-6096), has a variety of different rides; one of the best is the Secret Beach Breakfast Ride, a three-hour ride that includes breakfast for $65.

SPECTATOR SPORTS

Two of the most popular spectator sports on Kauai are outrigger canoe racing and polo. Every weekend from Memorial Day to Labor Day canoe races are held on Kauai. Hundreds of residents, from children to grandparents, participate in the island-wide races held at different harbors or bays every week. For information on the canoe racing schedule, check the local papers.

Polo season begins in April and continues though the summer at Anini Beach Park on the north shore. For information call 808/245-3971.

TENNIS

The **Kauai County Parks and Recreation Department,** 4193 Hardy, Lihue, HI 96766 (☎ 808/241-6670), has a list of county tennis courts across the island, all of which are free and open to the public. The **Princeville Tennis Club,** Princeville Resort (☎ 808/826-9823), has courts available for rent ($9 per person per hour for resort guests); however, book early, as these are always in demand.

4 Adventure Tours

Sometimes, the best way to get to know a place and experience all its wonders is to see it with an experienced guide. Someone who is intimate with a place—such as Waimea Canyon or the Na Pali Coast—and its history can help you to discover it more completely and satisfyingly than you might have ever been able to on your own. They can also help you explore Kauai through a means—like ocean kayak, mountain bike, or a backpacking trip—that wouldn't otherwise have occurred to you, or that you're not quite familiar enough with in order to strike out on your own. While some outfitters are geared toward hardcore adventure travelers, most are happy to personalize their tours to suit most age, fitness, and experience levels.

Below are a number of outfitters and tour companies that can offer you a unique look at the natural wonders of the Valley Isle:

With **Kauai Mountain Tours,** P.O. Box 3069, Lihue, HI 96766 (☎ 808/ 245-7224), a knowledgeable guide will take you on a one-of-a-kind trip into the Na Pali Kona Forest Reserve in an air-conditioned four-wheel-drive vehicle that traverses the winding mountain roads around the back of Waimea Canyon. A seven-hour tour, including lunch, is $78 for adults, $55 for children 12 or younger. A five-hour tour without lunch is $55 for adults, $38 for children.

Crane Tours, c/o Bill Crane, 15101 Magnolia Blvd., H10, Sherman Oaks, CA 91403 (☎ 800/653-2545 or 818/784-2213, or Joan Weaver at 818/784-2213), offers both kayaking trips and moderately strenuous trips for experienced back-packers to the Na Pali Coast and Waimea Canyon. The cost is approximately $795 to $995. This company is known for excellent values, terrific meals, and thoughtful service. They also offer a variety of excursions to the Big Island.

Kauai—Nowhere in the entire national park system is there scenic beauty like this.
—Stewart Udall, 1963

Rick Haviland and his excellent crew at **Outfitters Kauai,** Poipu Plaza, 2827-A Poipu Rd. (P.O. Box 1149), Poipu Beach, Koloa, HI 96756 (☎ 808/742-9667), are known for a variety of enjoyable and well-run trips, via kayak or bicycle. In addition to simple half-day kayaking trips for beginners ($48) and one-day sea-kayaking adventures along Kauai's southeast coast in the shadow of 2,000-foot cliffs ($125 for a full-day excursion), this outfit also offers an escorted Kayak Experience along the Na Pali cliffs, either as a one-day trip from Haena to Polihale, or a two-day (or more) expedition featuring camping at Kalalau and Milolii—some of the most breathtakingly beautiful spots in the islands. Two-person kayaks may also be rented for self-guided tours to jungle rivers. Each boat comes with racks/straps to secure it to your car, maps, and information to help you select the ideal river. Cost is $30 or $45 for one- or two-person kayaks.

Outfitters Kauai also offers adventure for the cyclist. For personal tours, they rent mountain bikes of high quality, which are well maintained and well suited for off-road riding through Kauai's backcountry. They provide helmets, water bottles, spare tubes with pumps, and extensive trail information based on years of riding and exploring on Kauai. Car racks are available to carry bikes to other locations. Bikes rent for $20 a day, $60 for 4 days, $100 for a week.

New and very exciting are Outfitters Kauai's Kokee Mountain Bike Tours. Participants ride the cool, high forest backroads above Waimea Canyon in an ecosystem that supports plants, trees, and birds, many of which are found only here. A skilled guide discusses the legends and natural history of Kokee. The cost is $78. Outfitters Kauai also operates guided mountain-bike tours in the state parks of Hawaii.

Kayak Kauai Outbound, 1340 Kuhio Hwy., Kapaa (☎ 808/822-9179), or on main street in Hanalei (P.O. Box 508), Hanalei, HI 96714 (☎ 808/826-9844 or 800/437-3507; fax 808/822-0577), offers summer (May to September) sea-kayak voyages along 15 miles of Kauai's dramatic Na Pali coastline that involve some of the most challenging wilderness paddling to be found in Hawaii. Fully catered, six-day packages cost $1,050 per person. The company offers guided one-day sea kayak trips along the Na Pali coast, including lunch on an isolated beach ($125) and a three-hour soft adventure Hanalei Wildlife Refuge and Bay Snorkel tour ($45). Their private canoe/kayak rentals, beginning at $48 for two persons, are very popular with families. During winter—from October to April—you can sea kayak Kipu Kai, the "little Na Pali" on Kauai's south shore; lunch, snorkeling, and whale watching are included ($100). Fully catered, six-day sea-kayaking trips along the south shore from Lihue to Waimea, with hiking in the highlands of Kokee, are $1,050. Six-day backpacking tours along the Na Pali coast are $900. One-day guided hiking tours are available all over Kauai; there's also a guided Fern Grotto paddle and hike to a waterfall, lunch included, for $75. Mountain bike rentals ($20) and three-hour bike tours in Hanalei and Kapaa ($45) are new additions to the programs. Surfboarding lessons are $25 per hour.

5 Exploring Lihue

Once a sleepy plantation village, Lihue is beginning to look startlingly modern, with shopping centers, supermarkets, mega-resorts, and the like.

Grove Farm Homestead

P.O. Box 1631, Lihue, Kauai, HI 96766, ☎ **808/245-3202.** Admission $5. Two-hour tours given Mon and Wed–Thurs at 10am and 1pm. Call at least a week in advance, or write (reservations are accepted up to three months in advance).

A visit here takes a little advance planning, either by mail or by calling for reservations. But it's worth the effort, as this is a trip backward in time to the days of the old Hawaiian sugar plantations. Grove Farm Homestead has been lovingly preserved and still has a lived-in look. The plantation was founded by George N. Wilcox, the son of teachers who arrived with the fifth company of the American Board of Missions sent to Hawaii in the 1830s. (Part of Wilcox's original sugar plantation is now the site of Kukui Grove Center; see below). His niece, Miss Mabel Wilcox, who was born and lived at the homestead all her life, left her estate as a living museum. The homestead tour is leisurely and informative. The old homes are lovely, furnished with antiques, Oriental rugs, and handsome koa-wood furniture; there is an abundance of books, and sheet music is open on the piano. You'll visit the very different servants' quarters, too.

Kilohana Plantation

Hi. 50, ☎ **808/245-5608.** Daily from 9:30am. Directions: The Kilohana Plantation is located on Hi. 50, two miles southwest of Lihue, headed toward Poipu. It's on the other side of the road and very close to the Kukui Grove Shopping Center.

Gaylord Parke Wilcox, the nephew of the founder of Grove Farm Plantation, built his dream house back in 1935 and called it Kilohana, which, in Hawaiian, means "not to be surpassed." The Wilcox family lived at the estate for 35 years, during which time it was the setting for much of the cultural and social life of upper-class Kauai. Restored to look just as it did in the 1930s, with many of its actual furnishings and artifacts, it's now a combination historical house-museum and shopping bazaar, with boutiques taking over the old children's nursery, the family bedrooms, the library, the cloakrooms, and the restored guest cottages on the estate grounds. None of the shops are inexpensive, but all offer quality in accordance with Kilohana's standard of excellence.

Before you begin your shopping, stop in to have a look at the foyer of the main house, where you'll see two enormous monkeypod calabashes—reputedly the largest in the state of Hawaii. In the olden days, Hawaiian kings stored their feather quilts in such calabashes: Later, missionary women used them as "trunks" for patchwork quilts. These, however, are replicas, made for the movie *Hawaii.* Be sure to visit **Stones at Kilohana,** which specializes in arts and crafts from all over the Pacific, including Tonga, Samoa, New Guinea, and Fiji. You'll see traditional handwork, wood bowls, hand-screened aloha shirts, ritual and ceremonial items, Hawaiian photographs by such artists as Boone Morrison, Pegge Hopper prints, jewelry, pottery, and sculpture. **Kilohana Galleries** is noted for its collection of work by Hawaiian artists. Check out its Artisan's Room, too, for fine crafts—and its Hawaiian Collection Room for rare Niihau shell leis, wood carvings, and a good sampling of scrimshaw. **Sea Reflections** is the place for rare and unusual shells, shell sculptures, and a handsome selection of gold, black, and bamboo coral, as well as fresh water pearls. Handcrafted collectibles and imaginative gifts abound at **The**

Lihue

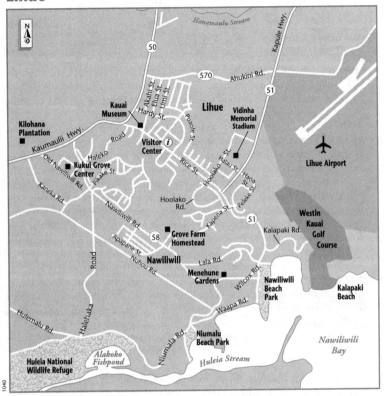

Library, a shop located in the original library of the home. **Kahn Galleries** showcases works by top Hawaiian artists. Hawaiian food products, crafts, and goods can be found at **The Country Store;** you can even order pineapple here to ship home.

In addition to browsing and shopping at Kilohana, you can take a 20-minute, horse-drawn carriage ride, an hour's ride through sugar cane fields, a guided tour, or a walk through the extensive manicured lawns and gardens. There's a full schedule of cultural events: hula performances, craft demonstrations, and the like. When you get hungry, you can have an excellent meal at the charming courtyard restaurant, **Gaylord's** (see "Where to Eat" in Chapter 15).

Kauai Museum

4428 Rice St. ☎ **808/245-6931.** Admission $5, adults; free for children under 17 accompanied by an adult. Mon–Fri 9am–4:30 pm, Sat 9am–1pm.

A visit to this museum is well worth your while. Stop in first at the Wilcox Building to examine the changing art, heritage, and cultural exhibits of both Asia and Hawaii. The Museum Shop here is one of our favorites, with its fine collections of South Pacific handcrafts, tapas, baskets, rare Niihau shell leis, Hawaiian books, prints, and koa calabashes. The Rice Building, entered through a covered paved walkway and courtyard, contains the permanent exhibit, "The Story of Kauai," an ecological and geological history complete with photographs, dioramas, and an exciting video. Be sure to see the Plantation Gallery, a permanent showcase for a collection of splendid Hawaiian quilts, koa furniture, china, etc.

SHOPPING

Kukui Grove Center

Hi. 50. ☎ **808/245-7784.**

Pint-sized Lihue now has the largest of all neighbor-island shopping malls, the $25-million Kukui Grove Center. Since it's just 4 miles from the airport on Hi. 50 (headed toward Poipu), it makes a logical first stop in town to stock up on food and vacation needs.

The outstanding shops, the ones that make Kukui Grove worth a special trip, are **Kauai Products** and **Indo-Pacific Trading Company.** Everything at Kauai Products is made on the island by local artisans, including the tapa print handbags and woven lauhala hats, tiles with Hawaiian quilt and ukelele designs, woven rugs (we loved the one with the humpback whale and leaping dolphins), and a large collection of watercolors, acrylics, and oils. The jewelry is special, too; we liked the dreamcatcher earrings embellished with precious stones. So are the distinctive muumuus by Stephanie, which feature prints of Hawaiian flowers, and the nifty aloha shirts by Jacqueline on Kauai. Help yourself to Kauai fresh-roasted coffee while you browse.

Indo-Pacific Trading Company is crammed full with goods from Java and Bali, from striking dresses, pareus, accessories, and jewelry for women, up front, to furniture, textiles, and quilts, in back. In between: carvings, museum-quality tapa cloth, ceremonial masks from Papua, New Guinea, original paintings, antique gongs, and much more.

Indonesian music plays in the background, and everything they play is for sale. There's a wonderful espresso bar here, which serves a variety of coffees, cakes, and pastries, as well as delicious vegetarian specials, including vegetable potpie, homemade soup, and *Gado-Gado,* from $5.50 to $6.50. All in all, a very difficult place to tear oneself away from.

Free entertainment is often presented on the mall stage; check the local papers for details. The Kukui Grove Center is open Monday through Wednesday and on Saturday from 9:30am to 5:30pm, on Thursday and Friday from 9:30am to 9pm, and on Sunday from 10am to 4pm.

Hilo Hattie's Fashion Center

3252 Kuhio Hwy. ☎ **808/245-3404.**

This is always a good budget stop for resort fashions. Call ahead and they'll take you to their factory outlet, where you can buy men's aloha shirts and women's short muumuus from $16, plus souvenirs, and macadamia-nut candies. There are always great specials here.

LIHUE AFTER DARK

Watch the papers for news of free shows put on at the **Kukui Grove Center**—these shows by local entertainers are sometimes every bit as good as those at the high-priced clubs. The shows often take place on Friday nights or Saturday mornings, right in the mall.

Kauai Comedy Club

In the Outrigger Kauai Beach Hotel, 4331 Kauai Beach Dr. ☎ **808/245-1955.** Cover $12.

If it's Thursday, you can catch local and mainland comics doing their acts here. Show time is at 8:30pm.

Hap's Hideaway
2975 Ewalu St. ☎ **808/245-3473.** No cover.

Looking for the cheapest drinks on Kauai? Hap's claims to have them, starting with 12-ounce draft beer for $1.75. Hap's shows live sports events via satellite on four color monitors. They also have more than 1,000 songs on the jukebox including Top-40 and country-and-western music, a happy hour that stretches from 11am to 2am, a Montana accent, and not even a trace of Polynesian atmosphere. A very friendly spot.

Si Cisco's Cantina
At the Kukui Grove Center. ☎ **808/245-8561.** No cover.

This is a popular bar and lounge where you can admire the western paintings on the walls, listen to local entertainers, and take your choice of the largest collection of tequilas on Kauai. They also serve up a great margarita in a 16-ounce mason jar.

6 Touring the Eastern & Northern Shores

Now you're ready for one of the big trips, an excursion by automobile along the glorious eastern and northern shores of Kauai. Hi. 56, which starts at Kuhio Highway in Lihue town, takes you the entire length of the tour. The distance is about 40 miles each way, and it will take you a full day.

KAPAIA & HANAMAULU

A few miles out of town on Kuhio Highway (Hi. 56), look for a quaint store called **The Kapaia Stitchery** (☎ 808/245-2281), which avid sewers and quilters seek out because it has the largest selection of fabrics on the island (Hawaiian-print fabrics start at about $6 per yard for cotton). It also has many handmade items, including the dresses, muumuus, pareus, and aloha shirts made by owner Julie Yukimura, which she sells at low prices. Julie also asks local craftspeople, especially senior citizens, to make things up for her. Most exciting of these are the patchwork coverlets made of Hawaiian fabrics by four local grandmothers: Prices are about $85 to $95 and would be at least twice as much anywhere else. Much-sought-after traditional Hawaiian quilts ($2,000 to $4,000) are also in good supply. Hawaiian quilting cushions can be made to order: $90 for an excellent piece of work. And do-it-yourselfers can find Hawaiian quilt pillow kits, hand-painted needlepoint, and original counted cross-stitch designs of local flowers and themes. There's always something new and interesting here; it's worth a stop.

Back on the road, look to your left for the turnoff to Wailua Falls. About 4 miles after the turnoff, watch for the white fence on the right of the road and listen for the sound of rushing water; soon you'll see the HVB marker. After you've seen the falls, don't be tempted to drive farther; turn around here and drive back.

WAILUA

Continuing on Hi. 56, you'll soon come to the mouth of the **Wailua River** and one of the most historic areas in Hawaii. Here, where the Polynesians first landed, were once seven *heiaus,* or temple sites, by the sacred (*wailua*) waters. Just before you get there, you'll come to **Lydgate Park** on the right, a grassy picnic area directly on the water, in which are the remains of an ancient "City of Refuge." You'll get a better idea of what a City of Refuge actually looked like when you see the restored one in Kona on the Big Island. But the concept here was precisely the same. In the days when the Hawaiians still carried on their polytheistic nature worship, life was bound by a rigid system of *kapus,* or taboos, violations that were punishable by death. But if an offender, or a prisoner of war, could run or swim to a City of Refuge, he could be purified and was then allowed to go free. Not too much of the City of Refuge remains, but if you wade out into the river you may discover some ancient carvings on the rocks, once part of the heiau. More practically, **Lydgate Park Beach** is one of the best beaches on Kauai for children. Two natural "pools," created by rocks, make it safe for them to swim and play in the ocean. The snorkeling is lovely, there are stripies and butterfly fish feeding on the rock, the water is clean and clear, and the sand is white. There are restrooms, showers, and barbecue pits near the beach. Recently, alas, there have been reports of vandalism here.

The Wailua, one of the two navigable rivers in Hawaii, is also the place where you can rent a tour boat for an idyllic 3-mile trip to the fantastically beautiful **Fern Grotto**—an enormous fern-fronted cave under a gentle cascade of water, unapproachable any other way. Personally, we'd love to take this trip in our own private craft and, instead of being "entertained," spend the time contemplating the rare tropical trees and flowers that line the bank and pondering about the old Kauai alii whose bones still lie undiscovered in the secret burial caves of the cliffs above. But the tour boats are well run, the captains are entertaining, and the musicians' singing the "Hawaiian Wedding Song" in the natural amphitheater of the Fern Grotto is a unique experience. The cost of the 1^{1}/$_{2}$-hour boat trip is $10 ($5 for children 3 to 12), and both **Waialeale Boat Tours** (☎ 808/822-4908) and **Smith Motor Boat Service** (☎ 808/822-3467) make the cruises. You should call in advance to make a reservation.

You may want to take a little excursion to visit **Smith's Tropical Paradise,** a 22^{1}/$_{2}$-acre botanical garden that features a Japanese garden, a replica of Easter Island, huge tiki heads, a tropical fruit garden, and a small Polynesian village. Adults pay $5; children, $2.50. Open 8:30am to 4pm. This is also the site of an excellent luau and Polynesian show on Mondays, Wednesdays, and Fridays; you can see the show alone for $10.50, or enjoy the whole shebang for about $45. For reservations, call 808/822-4654 or 808/822-9599.

At this point on Hi. 56, a side road called the **King's Highway** (named after the kings who had to be carried uphill in a litter lest their sacred feet touch the ground) leads to the restored heiau, **Holo-Holo-Ku.** It's so serene here now that it's hard to imagine that this was once a site for human sacrifice to calm the ancient gods.

Now you move on from Hawaiiana to observe some of the history of the Japanese settlers in Hawaii, recorded in a quaint cemetery just up the wooden stairs to the right of the heiau. If you continue driving along the King's Highway, you'll pass a rice field and soon, **Poliahu Heiau,** now a park that affords you a splendid view of the Wailua River. Next is **Opaekaa Falls,** plunging down from a high cliff (the name, quaintly, means rolling shrimp).

COCONUT MARKET PLACE   Back on the highway now, continue toward the Coconut Plantation hotels and there you'll find Coconut Marketplace. It's a handsome setup, with planked walkways, country decor, flowers and shrubs everywhere, and enough diverting shops (more than 70 at last count) to keep you busy for an hour or two.

Kauai's Eastern Shore: The Coconut Coast

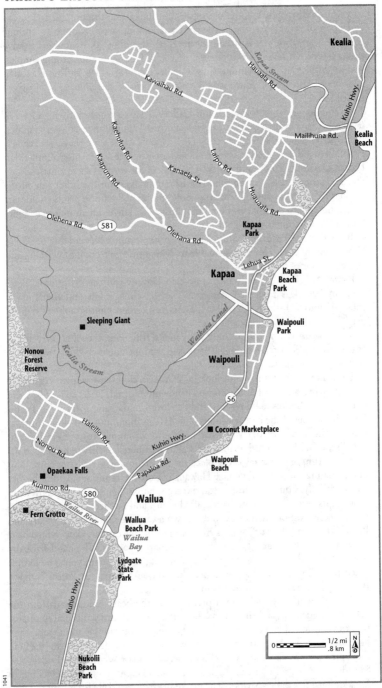

Kealia

Kapaa Stream

Hauaala Rd.

Kawaihau Rd.

Kuhio Hwy.

Mailihuna Rd.

Kealia Beach

Kaehulua Rd.

Laipo Rd.

Kaapuni Rd.

Kanaela St.

Hauaala Rd.

Olehena Rd.

581

Olehana Rd.

Kapaa Park

Lehua St.

Kapaa

Kapaa Beach Park

Waikaea Canal

■ **Sleeping Giant**

Waipouli Park

Nonou Forest Reserve

Kealia Stream

Waipouli

56

Haleilio Rd.

■ Coconut Marketplace

Nonou Rd.

Kuhio Hwy.

Waipouli Beach

Papaloa Rd.

■ **Opaekaa Falls**

Kuamoo Rd.

580

Wailua

Wailua River

■ **Fern Grotto**

Wailua Beach Park

Wailua Bay

Lydgate State Park

Kuhio Hwy.

0   1/2 mi
    .8 km

N

Nukolii Beach Park

1041

Ye Olde Ship Store is the place for maritime art, antiques, and a fabulous collection of scrimshaw, the largest on Kauai. All the work is done on antique fossilized ivory, which is becoming rarer all the time, and some distinctive pieces have high investment potential. If you're looking for something simpler, you might pick up some antique brass ship keys (ca. 1875–1925) from Hawaiian and other Pacific ships, which would make inexpensive and unusual little gifts— under $5.

Be sure to visit the exquisite **Kahn Gallery,** where a consistently high level of taste is evident in the selection of original artwork and limited-edition graphics. Note the lyrical glasslike sculptures by Donjo (you'd never guess they were acrylic). Featured island and international artists include Roy Tabora, George Sumner, Jan Parker, David Lee, and Randy Puckett. Posters of the work of these artists, among those of other artists, can be found at **Island Images,** on the other side of the marketplace. Small paintings to carry home and limited-edition prints could start low, although most are in the several-hundred-dollar range. There are several more Kahn galleries around the island.

Indo-Pacific Trading Company, which has a much bigger store at Kukui Grove (see above) is also represented here, with a nice collection of clothing and home accessories from Bali and Java.

Kauai Magic is the only magic shop in Hawaii and the proprietor, Peter Anthony Badua, is a talented magician. They have magic kits, individual magic tricks, Houdini T-shirts, as well as posters and signed photographs of famous magicians. The kids will like this one.

Kyle Vision Kites will not only sell you a terrific kite, they'll also teach you how to fly it. Prices range from $1.95 to $40, and include everything from Lotus Blossom windsocks to dinosaur kites.

The **Dragon Fly** has a unique look for Hawaiian clothing—women's casuals in beautiful pastel shades of 100% cotton, hand-embroidered. Prices start at $25 and styles include sundresses, jumpsuits, and baby wear in the same soft colors. **Tropic Casuals** has one of the best selections of children's muumuus and aloha shirts, as well as the usual resort wear for men and women. Note their Bird of Paradise, Coral Reef, and Banana Leaf scalloped umbrellas; they're original, $30.

Parrot Jungle of Kauai is the place for the environmentally conscious. This unique natural-history and vintage Hawaiiana store offers antique natural-history art, beautifully mounted butterflies and insects, books, figurines, original Matson Line Prints, educational toys, handcrafted items, and kitchenware with rain forest and conservation themes. A store or two away, the same owners, Mary and Patrick Dunn, run **Parrot Jungle's Bird Shop:** here one can buy captive-bred baby macaws, cockatoos, conures, eclectus, and Amazon parrots. The hand-fed baby parrots can be shipped or actually taken home on the plane with you! The Dunns breed these birds, as well as antelope, pheasant, and llamas, at Parrot Jungle's Breeding Center, in the nearby Wailua Homesteads.

The kids will get a kick out of playing with the heavy equipment from the defunct **Kilauea Sugar Mill** that has been transformed into sculptural fountains they can control. When they tire of that, they may enjoy running to the top of the high wooden tower to see the beautiful view. And they'll be delighted with the hula show presented by the local hula schools every Monday, Wednesday, Friday, and Saturday at 4:30pm. Be sure to check the calendar of events posted at each entrance for additional free daily activities. The marketplace is open daily from 9am to 9pm, with free entertainment every day.

KAPAA & KEALIA

From Hi. 56, back on the northern drive, you'll soon see a remarkable formation on the left as you enter Kapaa, the **Sleeping Giant**—the subject of another Menehune tall tale. The old fellow, so the story goes, was a kind of Gulliver whom the South Sea Lilliputians inadvertently killed.

On the opposite side of the road, opposite Foodland, look for a little store shaped like a Samoan house called **Marta's Boat,** 770 Kuhio Hwy. (☎ 808/822-3926). Marta Curry, who has five young children of her own, understands the needs of mothers and children and has a stock of items both pretty and practical, much of it handmade. Her specialty is 100% cotton (or silk or rayon; she does not carry blends) aloha clothing for children. She also has a good selection of educational toys, and her handmade 100% cotton baby quilts are especially lovely. Next door is an old Kauai favorite, a natural-foods store run by her husband, Ambrose Curry, where you might pick up a cooling bottled fruit drink or a snack, or stock up on supplies.

KAUAI VILLAGE SHOPPING CENTER   A stop at the Kauai Village Shopping Center, 4-831 Kuhio Hwy. (☎ 808/822-4904) on the mountain side of the road, is well worth your time. There are historical displays, a garden courtyard with waterfall, and over 30 shops and restaurants (with some of our favorites like A Pacific Cafe, Ginger's Grille, and Panda Garden: see preceding chapter), including the largest natural-foods store on the island and one of the famous Wyland Galleries.

If you're into health foods, then a stop at **Papaya's Natural Foods,** in Kauai Village (☎ 808/823-0190), is a must. This is the largest health-food store on Kauai, and one of the nicest in the islands. Their stock is extensive; they carry the best products (doctors send their patients here for vitamins and supplements), and they have a good selection of organic, locally grown produce. They also have a great deli counter and a wonderful little cafe (see "Where to Eat" in Chapter 15) where you can have everything from a soup-and-salad lunch for under $4, to a full meal. Be sure to check the interesting gift items made on Kauai.

Wyland, the artist whose studies of marine life are seen all over Hawaii, has a gallery here at Kauai Village (☎ 808/822-9855). Always worth a look.

KAPAA TRADE CENTER   There's something of a renaissance going on in downtown Kapaa; unusual gift shops and restaurants are blossoming, and it's easy to park the car, get out, and browse. Three shops of interest are virtually side by side at the Kapaa Trade Center on the ocean side of the road. First, there's **Far Fetched,** 1392 Kuhio Hwy. (☎ 808/823-8235)—the artistic wares in this shop have been fetched from far and wide. All are in exquisite taste and cover a wide price range. Plateware from Italy, glass from Mexico, rainsticks from South America, ikat woven cloths from Indonesia, begin to suggest the possibilities. There's a good selection of native Hawaiian crafts: wooden bowls, baskets, decorative *ipu* gourds, hand-painted Hawaiian figures by well-known island artists—and, for good measure, Tiffany-type lamps, handblown glass, and handsome papier-mâché plates. A must stop.

Beku Maru, at 1388 Kuhio Hwy. (☎ 808/822-1766), is a treasure trove of exotic women's clothing, much of it from Bali. Lots of adventurous looks can be put together here. They also have men's shirts and shorts. **Earth Beads,** 1392-A Kuhio Hwy. (☎ 808/822-0766), is stocked with semiprecious stones, trade beads, fimo beads, findings . . . everything one needs to create unusual jewelry. Finished pieces include handsome necklaces, bracelets, and earrings of semiprecious stones, crystals, coins, clays, glass, and more. Great fun.

MORE KAPAA SHOPPING   **Old Kapaa Town Antiques,** 1380 Kuhio Hwy. (☎ 808/823-6919), has a huge collection of old bottles and other vintage glassware as well as tons of funny old china and pottery. Be sure to check out their vintage aloha shirts, including the highly prized "silkies." They're open every day.

MOVING NORTH   Continuing on now, turn half a mile up the hill just before the bridge over Kealia Stream and you'll come to **St. Catherine's Catholic Church,** which boasts murals by leading Hawaiian artists: Jean Charlot, Juliette May Fraser, and Tseng Yu Ho.

Beyond Kealia, watch for the turnoff to **Anahola Beach** for a glimpse of one of those golden, jewel-like beaches that ring the island.

EAST KAUAI AFTER DARK

Jolly Roger
Coconut Plantation. ☎ **808/822-3451.** No cover.

Probably the longest happy hour—let's call it a "happy day"—takes place here daily from 11am to 7pm. Standard drinks are available at special prices. Karaoke begins every night at 8pm.

Outrigger Kauai Beach Hotel
4331 Kauia Beach Dr. ☎ **808/245-1855.**

Every Wednesday at 5pm, there's Polynesian entertainment at the hotel's Poolside Stage. You're expected to have a drink or two, but otherwise, there's no charge for this entertaining music-and-dance show.

KILAUEA

The first church you'll see as you drive into Kilauea town, **Christ Memorial Episcopal Church,** has only-in-Hawaii architecture, made of lava rock, with windows, executed in England, of the finest design and construction. Virtually kitty-corner from the church you'll find the **Hawaiian Art Museum,** 2488 Kolo Rd., which is a special project of Aloha International, a nonprofit group founded by Dr. Serge Kahili King, dedicated to "Peace Through Aloha." The museum/store is a major part of the fund-raising program for a world peace center being built on Kauai. Sunday morning meetings by the leaders of Aloha International are held here, as are classes and workshops on Hawaiian culture. The museum and its minitheater, showing videos, are free to the public. The gift shop is a delight, with many made-in-Hawaii arts and crafts, especially native-wood products; volcanic glass, native olivine, and kukui-nut jewelry; books on Hawaiian shamanism and Hawaiiana; Hawaiian music, videos, and maps; fine art cards, prints, and posters; potted native trees and plants; and novel gift items. Children's Hawaiian story and activity books, toys, and games are also featured as part of the attempt to preserve and pass on the essence of Hawaiian culture. Prices are reasonable, and all profits go to foster these worthy goals. (If you would like more information on Aloha International, write to them at P.O. Box 665, Kilauea, HI 96754 or phone 808/828-1253.)

Now follow the road for 2 more miles to **Kilauea Lighthouse** (turn right into Kilauea to Lighthouse Road, which becomes **Kilauea Point National Wildlife**

Refuge. Kilauea Lighthouse, high on a bluff that drops sharply to the sea on three sides, affords a magnificent view of the northern coastline of the island. Birds drift effortlessly in the wind like paper kites; below, the turquoise sea smashes against the black lava cliffs. The historic lighthouse was built in 1913, has an 8-foot-high clam-shaped lens, but is no longer operative (a small light, 30 feet north of the old structure, is the present Kilauea light). The old U.S. Coast Guard Lighthouse Station has been taken over by the U.S. Fish and Wildlife Service. Bird lovers will have a field day here, as the area is frequented by such exotic Pacific sea birds as the red-footed booby, the wedge-tailed shearwater, the white-tailed and red-tailed tropic bird, and the Laysan albatross. Whales, spinner dolphins, and Pacific sea-green turtles are also seen in the area. Docents at the visitor center next door to the lighthouse can answer questions and point out current wildlife activity. Check out the bookstore with its books on Hawaiian natural history. The Kilauea Point Refuge is open weekdays from 10am to 4pm.

On the way to Kilauea Lighthouse, the **Kong Lung Center** makes a good stop for shopping, stretching, and having a snack. The buildings are turn-of-the-century plantation, and the atmosphere is charming. The Kong Lung Company (☎ 808/ 828-1822) is Kauai's oldest plantation general store (1892) and it's very special, stocked with designer clothing, beautiful antiques, tasteful craft items (we spotted handsome African baskets and made-on-Kauai ceramics on our last visit), home accessories, and imaginative gift items.

Be sure to make a stop at **Kilauea Bakery & Pau Hana Pizza** in the Kong Lung Center to have pastry and coffee, or a wonderful slice of gourmet pizza and to pick up some specialty breads to take back home with you (see "Where to Eat," in Chapter 15).

Continue past **Kalihiwai Bay,** whose sleepy little village was twice destroyed by tidal waves, in 1946 and 1957, a reminder that the much-celebrated mildness of Hawaii is a sometime thing.

HANALEI
ATTRACTIONS

The glorious views continue. Keep watching for the lookout at **Hanalei Valley,** where you'll be treated to one of the special sights of the islands. The floor of Hanalei Valley, which you see below, is almost Asian, with neatly terraced taro patches and the silvery Hanalei River snaking through the dark greens of the mountains. (A sunset visit here is spectacular.) You may want to drive through the luxury resort development of **Princeville at Hanalei** and perhaps have lunch here at **Chuck's Steak House** or **Zelo's Café.**

Back on the road, you'll soon come to **Hanalei Beach,** one of the most imposing beaches in the islands, but swimming is safe only in summer months and only at the old boat pier at the river mouth. In winter, beware of high surf and undertow. To get to the beach, turn right at St. William's Catholic Church (another Jean Charlot mural is inside). There's a public pavilion, dressing rooms, and picnic facilities; your fellow bathers will include many local families.

In Hanalei Valley itself, history buffs will want to note the old **Waioli Mission.** The original church, built in 1841, is now used as a community center. More interesting, we think, is the old **Mission House,** restored in 1921 and full of fascinating furniture, books, and mementos of 19th-century Hawaii. On Tuesday, Thursday, and Saturday between 9am and 3pm, you can take a guided tour here, for which there is no admission charge, although donations are welcomed. Plan on 30 to 40 minutes for this excellent tour. For groups of 10 or more people, however, advance reservations are required and can be made by calling Barnes Riznik (☎ 808/245-3202) or writing to P.O. Box 1631, Lihue, Kauai, HI 96766.

SHOPPING

If you're a collector—of frogs or owls or horses or pigs—then the first shopping stop in this area should be **Silver Lining** at Princeville Center (☎ 808/826-7993). Paula, the proprietor, groups everything according to species, and the prices range from a few dollars to many, depending on whether the critter you crave is tiny and of wood or larger and of jade or silver. The last time we were there, Paula was displaying her personal collection of pigs—3,000 of them in a case that covered the entire back wall of the shop, ranging from tiny china porkers to immense papier-mâché and ceramic ones.

We loved the funky old Ching Young General Store that had sat in the middle of Hanalei town forever, so we looked upon its demise and the construction of the **Ching Young Village Shopping Center** with mixed emotions. The old-time aura is gone, certainly, but this is a pleasant and practical place with a few shops that are worth your time. Shops come and go, but you can count on **Spinning Dolphin** (☎ 808/826-7641) to be there. The people here create custom T-shirts, sweatshirts, and dresses, silk-screened while you watch, and claim to be the only shop in the entire state that does so. They have more than 75 exclusive designs. They also have an extensive selection of children's and infants' wear.

If you need some fresh organic produce, vitamins, or natural sandwiches, stop in at **Halalei Health & Natural Foods** (☎ 808/826-6990). **Hanalei Florist** can provide you with fresh flowers. Other practical resources at Ching Young Village include a **Big Save Market** and several fast-food operations.

Now visit one of Hanalei's newer attractions: the **Old Hanalei School** (☎ 808/826-7677). Built in 1926, this actually was an old school; it's on the National Register of Historic Places as architecturally significant, and its design became a standard throughout Hawaii for school buildings. Carol and Gaylord Wilcox, of the prominent Kauai family who also restored Kilohana Plantation, saved the old building, moved it four blocks from its original site, and have lovingly restored it, keeping its significant architectural details intact throughout.

Among the several shops here, **Tropical Tantrum** (☎ 808/822-7301) is one of the most popular, featuring hand-painted women's clothing by Lauri Johns and Parker Price, a brother-and-sister team from Texas. They also show works by other island artisans; prices start at around $60. There's a branch of **Kahn Gallery** (☎ 808/826-6677) here, with outstanding selections of original and limited-edition graphics by top artists. **Hanalei Surf** (☎ 808/826-9000) is for the big-waves set or just the casual beachgoer. They carry a full line of beach rentals and claim to have the lowest rental prices on the North Shore. Visitors are invited to stop in to see the owner's private collection of historic surfboards, including a 13-foot surfboard brought to Kauai, by Duke Kahanamoku in 1927.

Stop in at **The Hanalei Gourmet** (☎ 808/826-2524) here to pick up some cheese, wines, delicious deli and bakery items, or to get a picnic basket. You can also have a tasty meal here (see "Where to Eat" in Chapter 15) and join the local crowd for evenings of live music Tuesday through Saturday or for a jam session on Sunday from 5 to 8pm. You could have a nifty burger at **Bubba's** (which claims that it "cheats tourists, drunks, and attorneys," but don't believe it), or maybe some

Princeville & Hanalei

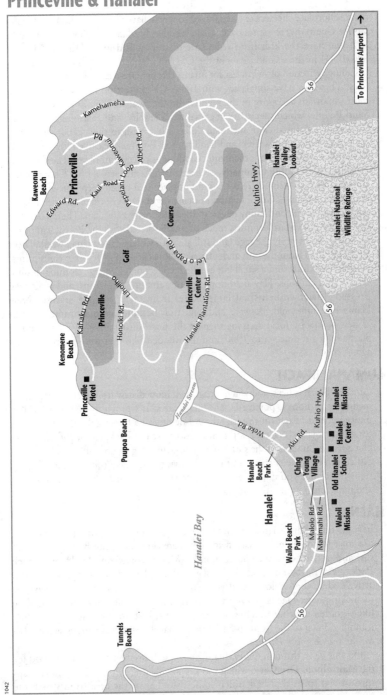

To Princeville Airport →

56

Kamehameha

Kaweonui Beach

Princeville

Kaweonui Rd.

Albert Rd.

Edward Rd.

Kaui Road

Pepelani Loop

Course

Golf

Lei o Papa Rd.

Kahaku Rd.

Honoiki Rd.

Liholiho

Kuhio Hwy.

Hanalei Valley Lookout

Princeville

Hanalei National Wildlife Refuge

Kenomene Beach

Princeville Center

Hanalei Plantation Rd.

56

Princeville Hotel

Puupoa Beach

Hanalei Stream

Weke Rd.

Aku Rd.

Kuhio Hwy.

Hanalei Mission

Hanalei Center

Old Hanalei School

Ching Young Village

Hanalei Beach Park

Hanalei

Malolo Rd.

Mahimahi Rd.

Waioli Mission

Waioli Beach Park

Hanalei Bay

56

Tunnels Beach

1042

divine chocolate cheesecake (guaranteed to wreak havoc with any diet) at **Hanalei Coffee Company,** an espresso cafe that also offers breakfast, lunch, and light meals.

If you have the kids in tow, be sure to stop at **Rainbow Ducks** (☎ 808/826-4741) in the second phase of the Old Hanalei School. This delightful shop has a huge selection of swimwear for infants through pre-teens and sandals for little ones. They also have sunglasses with 100% UV protection in children's sizes, a most important accessory in the islands. Another worthy shop in this complex is **Sand People,** which specializes in casual wear, jewelry, and charming, must-have baubles, like painted cloth mermaid dolls with starfish in their hands. We loved the great cotton knit sweaters and handpainted T-shirts, the carved toy boats, and the handpainted wooden ornaments. Clothing is pricey, but of good quality.

Yellowfish Trading Company, at the Hanalei Center across from Ching Young Village, (☎ 808/826-1227) is the kind of place that could keep one entertained for hours. Margaret "Gritt" Benton's fascinating shop is chockablock with objects quaint, wonderful, and funny, many of them distinctly Hawaiian. There's old (but well-preserved) rattan furniture, much of it upholstered with the Polynesian prints that used to be simply the rage (and still are with vintage Hawaiiana lovers). There are aloha shirts from the '40s and '50s, old silk neckties in awful marvelous prints, vintage bark cloth, and a small but excellent collection of vintage clothing in silks, velvets, and chiffons. Hawaiian flower prints, amazing old lamps, and some new pressed-flower embellished lampshades from Gritt's home state of New Hampshire, funky old glassware, and some truly beautiful antique furniture as well as new works by local artisans suggest the possibilities here. We even found plastic hula girl dolls, circa 1940, and the wooden tikis that were prized 40 years ago. A trip.

LUMAHAI BEACH

Lumahai Beach is next, and you'll recognize it immediately from pictures appearing in dozens of books, postcards, and magazines. It's probably the most widely photographed beach on the island, and deserves its fame: golden sand, a long tongue of black-lava rock stretching to the sea, a background of unearthly blue-green mountain. If the surf is not high, swimming will be safe here. It's a little difficult to find the entrance to the trail down to the beach (not indicated by any signs), but once you do, it's easy to get down. If the surf is up, admire the view and move on.

HAENA

beyond Lumahai Beach stretches the Haena region, where the shoreline gets dreamier by the mile. You can swim anywhere along here, but be very careful of surf and undertow in the winter months. Many people consider **Haena Beach Park** one of the best beaches on the island (although we personally prefer to swim at Ke'e, described below), and you won't go wrong swimming, camping, or picnicking here. Haena is what you always imagined the South Seas would be like—golden curving beaches, coconut palms, lush foliage, and jagged cliffs tumbling down to the sea. Is it any surprise that this spot was chosen as Bali Ha'i for the movie *South Pacific?*

On this drive through the Haena region, watch on the left side of the road for the **Maniniholo Dry Cave,** which was supposedly dug by the Menehunes to capture an evil spirit that had stolen some fish. This is the area from which the

Menehunes were also said to have left Hawaii. A short distance from here, up a small rise, is the first of two **Wet Caves,** the **Waikapalae;** about 200 yards farther is the second, the **Waikanaloa.** For once, the Menehunes were not responsible—the caves were reputedly dug by Pele in a search for fire. Finding fresh water instead, she left in disgust. It's reported that you can swim in these pools (the old Hawaiians used to jump off the ledges into them), but we think you'll do better to wait for the end of the road a few hundred yards ahead and an out-of-this-world beach, ❂ **Ke'e.** This is one of those gentle, perfect beaches that's almost impossible to tear yourself away from. As you loll on the sand under the towering mountains, listening to the Pacific, which has quieted down to a ripple beside you, it's not hard to picture this spot when it was the site of a most sacred temple of Laka, the goddess of the hula. Nearby are the remains of a heiau that guarded the sacred hula halau, to which novitiates came from all over the islands to study the dances, meles, and religious traditions of their people. From the cliffs above, specially trained men would throw burning torches into the sea (possibly in connection with temple rites). To your left are the cliffs of the **Na Pali Coast** (see below) and the end of your auto trip.

PRINCEVILLE/HANALEI AFTER DARK

Although most clubs levy no cover charge, that may change if there is a featured artist. And be sure to check local papers and/or call for information before you attend any of these: Performers and times change frequently.

Hanalei Gourmet
In the old Hanalei School Building, Hanalei Center. ☎ **808/826-2524.** No cover.

This casual cafe is always jumping! There's live music Tuesday through Saturday, a jam session Sunday from 5 to 8pm.

Happy Talk Lounge
In the Hanalei Bay Resort at Princeville. ☎ **808/826-6522.** No cover.

There's Hawaiian music Friday and Saturday nights from 6 to 10pm at this lovely open-air lounge. A jazz jam session takes place on Sundays from 3 to 7pm, with the public invited to sit in.

Princeville Hotel
At Princeville Resort. ☎ **808/826-9644.**

The Living Room at this glamorous resort is the scene for late afternoon tea and cocktails and one of the best sunset views on Kauai. Check with the hotel for information on a variety of entertainment events.

Tahiti Nui
Hi. 56, Hanalei. ☎ **808/826-6277.** Admission, luau $38 adults, $15 children 6–11, free for children under 5.

Tahiti Nui has been the place for local color for many years. Done up with pareu fabric, Tahitian wood carvings on the walls, bamboo, and a thatched ceiling, it's a super friendly place. There's Hawaiian and contemporary music in the lounge most nights and jazz after the Friday night luau. But the best entertainment here is impromptu; local entertainers often come in to sing, and owner Auntie Louise Marston, a bubbly Tahitian, can usually be persuaded to sing herself and do the hula. The Friday night luau is a local tradition; be sure you reserve in advance.

7 Seeing the Na Pali Coast

If you'd like to see the spectacularly beautiful Na Pali Coast, southwest of Haena, you have to see it one of three ways: by foot, by boat, or by helicopter. For information on the first, see "Hiking" earlier in this chapter.

Of the many boat trips offered, one is quite special: **Captain Zodiac Raft Expeditions,** P.O. Box 456, Hanalei, Kauai, HI 96714 (☎ 808/826-9371, or 800/422-7824), takes small groups out in boats similar to those used for shooting the rapids on the Colorado River. The trip is usually smooth and gentle, but can be as wet and wild as the Colorado River on occasion; a licensed Coast Guard captain is in command. For details, see "Boating" in "Water Sports & Recreation," above.

Helicopter trips are perhaps the most exciting way of all to see Kauai and to experience the grandeur of its remote and isolated areas. These are not inexpensive (figure roughly $2 a minute), with prices starting around $100 and going up to $200 per person for trips over Waimea Canyon and the Na Pali Coast and into the wilderness areas of Kauai. Early-morning and sunset flights can be the most beautiful of all. A number are now offering tours, and competition can be fierce. **Will Squyres** (☎ 808/245-7541) is a veteran helicopter-tour operator with thousands of flying miles under his belt; his tours are highly thought of. **Jack Harter** (☎ 808/245-3774) was the first of the Kauai helicopter pilots and still rates very highly. **Papillon Helicopters** (☎ 808/826-6591) is the largest in the state; **Island Helicopters Kauai** (☎ 808/245-8588) and **South Seas Helicopters** (☎ 808/245-7781) are both highly reputable. **Ohana Helicopters** (☎ 808/245-3996), one of the newer companies, is doing a nice job, as are **Pacific Island Helicopters** (☎ 808/335-3115) and **Safari Helicopters** (☎ 808/246-0136), which give each passenger a lot of personal attention and offers flights from $99. **Air Kauai** (☎ 808/246-4666), **Birds of Paradise** (☎ 808/335-3115), and **Na Pali** (☎ 808/245-6959) are all reputable. **Niihau Helicopters** (☎ 808/335-3500) is the only one with a license to fly over Niihau, the "forbidden island;" its inflight narration concerns that island's history. Photographers are advised to bring plenty of film and a wide-angle lens, if possible.

You should know, that there is controversy over helicopter flights which environmentalists fear damage the fragile ecosystems of the islands, and which have less-than-perfect safety records. But in 1994, the Federal Aeronautics Administration (FAA) instituted more stringent minimum-altitude and safety regulations in order to address these concerns. Unfortunately, because of the new allowable altitude minimums, your helicopter pilot might not be able to swoop down canyon walls or bring you as close to the pali as in times past. Check with the tour operators to see what their current parameters are, and to make sure that they can meet your expectations before you spend your money.

8 Touring the Southern & Western Shores

This tour is about as long as the eastern and northern one and requires another full day. Since the high point is Waimea Canyon, you might check with the forest ranger on duty before leaving (☎ 808/335-5871) to find out if there's fog over the canyon; if so, it might be preferable to save this trip for another day, if you have one. You may want a sweater, for the slightly cooler (but still pleasant) 4,000-foot altitude of the Kokee region. Most of this drive is along Hi. 50.

Starting from Lihue, you'll pass through the town of Puhi and then you'll see a mountain formation called Queen Victoria's Profile on your left. Continue driving until you see Hi. 52 on your left, which leads you through a spectacular arch of towering eucalyptus trees (popularly called the Tree Tunnel) and into the little town of Koloa.

KOLOA

Hawaii's first sugar-plantation town, Koloa was established in 1835 and continued through most of the 19th century as a busy seaport and home to a thriving sugar mill. The old plantation town has been restored, and now **Old Koloa Town** is an attractive collection of shops and restaurants, plus a few historic sites, such as the **Koloa Hotel,** a five-room inn built in 1898 for traveling salesmen from Honolulu, and its authentically restored *ofuro,* or Japanese bathhouse. Note the huge monkeypod tree planted in 1925; it stretches halfway across the road.

Some of the most enjoyable shopping on Kauai takes place here in Koloa, at the Koloa Ball Park, every Monday at noon—and other days at other island locales. It's called the **Sunshine Market,** similar to the greenmarkets and farmer's markets in other states and cities. Local vegetables and fruit growers truck in their produce fresh from their farms, and so do local flower growers and other vendors: The result is a shopping bonanza for anybody who likes to eat! Come early, because everything is snatched up in about an hour, as prices are incredibly low. Island papayas, bananas, lettuce, tomatoes, sprouts, you-name-it, are sold at a fraction of supermarket prices. There are usually a few trucks selling coconuts; the vendors will husk and crack them for you right there; you can drink the milk and take the rest of the coconut home, or eat it all.

In addition to the Monday at noon market at Koloa Ball Park, there's one on Tuesday at 3:30pm at Kalaheo Neighborhood Center; Wednesday at 3:30pm at Kapaa New Town Park; Thurs at 4:30pm at Kilauea Neighborhood Center; Friday at 3pm at Vidinha Stadium parking lot in Lihue; and 9am Saturday at Kekaha Neighborhood Center. These schedules may change, so for current updates, phone 808/241-6390.

POIPU

With its glorious dry climate, golden sandy beaches, and breathtakingly beautiful surf, Poipu is one of the choice areas of Kauai. From Koloa, Poipu Road leads you right into the heart of the area.

ATTRACTIONS

Poipu Beach is one of the best swimming beaches on the island. Since the hurricane, it has more sand than ever. Youngsters can swim in a shallow little pool; there's rolling surf farther out, and a picnic area and pavilion here, too. But please be warned: It's very, very easy to cut your feet on the rocks and coral here; we've seen it happen innumerable times. Please wear foot coverings to be safe. Another word of advice: Don't spend the *entire* day here, as there's plenty to see coming up ahead.

POIPU AFTER DARK

There have been many changes since the hurricane so, again, check local sources for latest information.

Brennecke's Beach Broiler
2100 Hoone Rd. ☎ **808/742-7588.** No cover.

Visitors are welcome to join the lively bunch of regulars clustered around the satellite-dish video receiver watching their favorite sports events.

Hyatt Regency Kauai
1571 Poipu Rd. ☎ **808/742-1234.** Wed, Thurs, Fri and Sat only.

There are various possibilities for nighttime entertainment at this enchanting resort. Stevenson's Library, an elegant library bar with game tables, TVs, and a book collection, is open every night; the Captain's Bar at poolside serves snacks and tropical drinks until early evening; Tidepools Lounge offers drinks in a spectacular setting overlooking a freshwater lagoon. There's live entertainment nightly at the Seaview Terrace and at Kuhio's, which offers high-tech entertainment and late-night dancing in an art-nouveau setting (until 2am). Disc jockey, dress code. Cover charge varies at Kuhio's; others charge no admission.

SAMPAN HARBOR, LAWAI, & KALAHEO

Trace your way back now to the fork in the road and this time take the other branch, the one on the right. Continuing past Kuhio Park (on the site of the birthplace of Prince Kuhio), you come to Kukuiula Small Boat Harbor, more familiarly known as **Sampan Harbor.** Be sure to walk out on the wharf for an absolutely gorgeous view; about a mile ahead to the right is **Spouting Horn,** where the water spurts up through several holes in the lava rock, and to your left the blue-green Pacific crashes upon the black rocks. When you can tear yourself away, have a look at the vendors selling jewelry outside the parking lot; quality is high and the prices are consistently among the lowest in the islands. A great place to take care of a lot of gift shopping.

Which eelskin wholesale house is the most wholesale? Hard to say, because such outfits abound in the islands (especially in Honolulu). Certainly, one of the biggest and best is **Lee Sands' Wholesale Eelskin Warehouse** at the Hawaiian Trading Post, which you can find right outside Lawai, on Koloa Road, where Hi. 50 meets Hi. 530. Sands, who claims to be the original importer of eelskin from Asia, sells to major eelskin distributors throughout the country and to such prestigious stores as Bloomingdale's in New York, where you can be certain the prices are much higher than what you find here. We saw lovely handbags from about $60. They have a large collection of Niihau-shell leis. Novelty items like wooden postcards and jewelry are also sold here.

Just outside Lee Sands' is a cute little hut called **Mustard's Last Stand,** where you're free to add not only mustard but also guacamole, sauerkraut, salsa, chili, fresh mushrooms, and three kinds of cheese to any hot dogs, sausages, or hamburgers you buy there. They also have Lappert's ice cream. If you've got the kids in tow, they may want to take time out from touring for a game of miniature of golf at **Geckoland,** a course with a Kauai theme. Open daily from 9am to 5:30pm.

You'll have to make reservations and pay $25 (subject to change) to tour the National Tropical Botanical Garden's two garden sites in Lawai, but nature lovers and photographers will find it eminently worthwhile. The 186-acre **Lawai Garden,** a research garden containing many rare and endangered Hawaiian species, adjoins the 100-acre **Allerton Garden,** formerly a private estate. For current tour and reservation information, call 808/332-7361.

Just outside Kalaheo, watch for enchanting **Kukui-O-Lono Park.** The entrance is through a majestic stone gate, just south of Kalaheo. The name means light of the god Lono; at one time kukui-oil torches here provided a beacon for fishermen at sea. Now the place is a public nine-hole golf course (greens fees are very reasonable) and a small park, where you can see a Stone Age Hawaiian exhibit and a charming Japanese garden. There are birds everywhere.

HANAPEPE

Another of the wondrous scenic views of Hawaii awaits you as you approach the town of Hanapepe. Stop at the overlook for a glorious vista of **Hanapepe Valley** below, where rice shoots, guava trees, and taro patches cover the fertile floor. Waimea Canyon is off in the distance to the left.

Hanapepe is quaint, with old wooden, balconied, tin-roofed buildings and an air not unlike that of an Old West town. A small artistic renaissance is happening here, as artists, attracted by the sun-drenched landscapes and the splendid light, move in. **James Hoyle Gallery,** 3900 Hanapepe Rd., is a must stop: Hoyle, who has been called a modern-day van Gogh, applies his brilliant brushstroke impressionist techniques to many Kauai scenes. While his hand-painted serigraphs are beyond our budget, posters start at $100. The **Lele Aka Gallery,** 3876 Hanapepe Rd., shows striking mystical paintings by Ralph Adam, and his selection of beautifully handcrafted Hawaiian-style drums. Have a look, too, at the **Andy Lopez Gallery,** 3878 Hanapepe Rd., and browse through the antique maps and prints and Hawaiian artifacts at **Kauai Fine Arts,** 3848 Hanapepe Rd. More galleries are opening here all the time.

Now, treat yourself to a lovely lunch at the **Green Garden** (see "Where to Eat" in Chapter 15), then drive a few miles farther on to the factory outlet store for **Lappert's Ice Cream,** that incredibly rich, incredibly delicious ice cream that uses fresh local ingredients: passion fruit, mango, and coconut–macadamia nut fudge are a few of the flavor possibilities. There are two reasons for getting your ice cream here: One, they have the best selection of flavors on the island; and two, since this is the factory outlet, they always have a scoop-of-the-day special for just 75¢ (as opposed to their regular price of $1.95 for a single scoop, $2.95 for a double). Even those who normally don't care much about ice cream become converts after the first swallow.

Readers Recommend

Olu Pua Gardens. "We stopped to visit the very beautiful Olu Pua Gardens, a botanical showplace in Kalaheo. But there's more than just magnificent plants, trees, and flowers: The guesthouse served as a stopping-off place for U.S. presidents and dignitaries en route to and from the Far Pacific. The drafts for the peace treaty ending the war with Japan were crafted there before being carried to Tokyo. The charming guide told us that Olu Pua is now up for sale, and they are hoping someone interested in preserving the grounds as is will buy it. Up to now it's not on any historical preservation list, but it certainly should be." —Helen Schwarz Robbins, Little Rock, Ark. [*Authors' Note:* Olu Pua is open Monday through Friday, for guided tours only, at 9:30 and 11:30am and 1:30 pm. It's located just past the town of Kalaheo, en route to Waimea Canyon.]

Art gallery, bookshop, coffee shop and restaurant, gift shop—the **Hanapepe Bookstore and Espresso Bar,** at 3830 Hanapepe Rd., is all these, as well as one of the most imaginative shops on Kauai. It started life long ago as a drugstore, and the counter from that store is now the centerpiece of a small dining area that serves gourmet vegetarian breakfasts, lunches, and dinners several days a week using locally grown organic vegetables and a variety of fresh Italian herbs and cheeses (see preceding chapter for details). The bookstore offers a fine collection of Hawaiian reading material for such a small shop: plenty of Kristin Zambucka and Herb Kane, Hawaiian stories for children, and many books on Hawaiian crafts and language. Locally made gift items include Hawaiian potpourri, carved wooden candelabra, silver and wooden jewelry, and pillow covers and bib aprons made in the patterns of Hawaiian quilts. There's also a super selection of greeting cards, including most of the magnificent Kim Taylor Reece photographic cards. Hawaiian background music sets the mood for browsing.

Just past Hanapepe, turn left at the sign that says HANAPEPE REFUSE TRANSFER STATION. Go three-tenths of a mile and turn right at the HVB marker, and you'll find yourself at **Salt Pond.** It looks like a marsh dotted with strange, covered walls, and it's here that salt is mined and dried (some of the drying beds in operation date back to the 17th century) as the Hawaiians have been doing it for centuries. You may be lucky and arrive while they are working; members of a local *hui* collect the crystals during the summer months. Then you can head for **Salt Pond Pavilion,** a great swimming and picnicking beach, with safe, calm water. This beach is a good place to recoup your strength for the next big series of sensations coming up at Waimea Canyon.

WAIMEA

But first you arrive at the town of Waimea, which, like Wailua, is steeped in history. A favorite deep-water harbor in the olden days, it was the center of government before the coming of Europeans and Americans, and the place where Captain Cook decided to come ashore in 1778. Whalers and trading ships put in here for provisions on their long voyages in the Pacific. It was also here that the first missionaries landed on Kauai, in 1820. And it was on this site that an employee of the Russian Fur Company, Dr. Anton Scheffer, built a fort and equipped himself with a Hawaiian retinue, promising Chief Kaumuali help in defeating Kamehameha. The latter got wind of the scheme and gave Kaumuali orders to get his foreign ally out of Hawaii—which he did, pronto. But the **ruins of the old fort,** a stone wall mostly hidden by weeds, are still here; an HVB marker points the way on your left, before you come to the Waimea River. The fort may one day be restored—already restrooms and parking facilities have been built, and some of the old stonework is now visible. Until then, however, there's not much else to see here; the interest is mostly historical.

After you've passed the **Captain Cook Monument** and just before the police station, look for the turnoff to the **Menehune Ditch.** Follow the river about 1¼ miles, past some Japanese shops, a Buddhist temple, taro patches, rice paddies, and tiny houses; when you come to a narrow bridge swinging across the river, stop and look for a stone wall protruding above the road for a few feet on the left side. This is all that remains visible of the Menehune Ditch, a remarkable engineering accomplishment that brought water to the neighboring fields several miles down from the mountain. The curious stonecutting here has convinced anthropologists that some pre-Polynesian race created the aqueduct. Who else but the Menehunes? It is said that they did the whole thing in one night and were rewarded by the pleased citizens of Waimea with a fantastic feast of shrimp, their favorite food. They later made so much noise celebrating that they woke the birds on Oahu, 100 miles away. While you're busy creating some legends of your own, you might see some Hawaiian Huck Finns, placidly floating down the river on rafts made of logs tied together, little bothered by either Menehunes or tourists.

The main highway now continues beyond **Kekaha** to the arid countryside around **Mana,** and beyond that to some enormous sand dunes known as the **Barking Sands.** The Kauaians swear that people say "woof" when they slide down the dunes. The U.S. Navy has now closed the area, so take the shorter drive to the canyon; you turn off the highway just past Waimea to Hi. 550.

WAIMEA CANYON

Now the road starts going up, through forests of eucalyptus, silver oak, and koa; soon you'll see the white ohia trees with their red blossoms of lehua (you'll see lehua again when you visit Volcanoes National Park in Hawaii). On you go to the first lookout, Waimea Canyon Lookout. Park your car and prepare yourself for one of the most spectacular views in all Hawaii. You're standing now at the top of a 3,657-foot gorge, about a mile wide and 10 miles long. Millions of years ago this was the scene of a tremendous geologic fault, a great crack in the dome of the island; erosion, streams, and ocean waves cut the cliffs into jagged shapes whose colors change with the sun and the clouds—blue and green in the morning, melting into vermilion, copper, and gold as the sun moves across it and finally sets. The gorge is comparable to, though smaller than, the Grand Canyon, and sometimes outdoes it in colorfulness.

Now the road continues another 8 miles, and you're at **Kokee State Park,** very different from anything else you've seen on Kauai. You're in the midst of bracing mountain country now, with wonderful hiking trails, freshwater streams for trout fishing (rainbow-trout season is each August and September) and swimming, wild fruit to pick in season, and wild pigs and goats to hunt. The forest ranger here will give you details on trails. You can relax for a few minutes at the **Kokee Museum,** right next to the **Kokee Lodge Restaurant** and **Kokee Cabins** (see Chapter 15), where you could spend a long, blissful holiday.

From here, it's just 4 miles to a spectacular climax for this trip, the view from the **Kalalau Lookout.** Driving the winding road for these last few miles, you will pass the Kokee tracking station, now world famous for its part in the success of the *Apollo II* mission to the moon. It was from this site that a laser beam was flashed to reflectors that Neil Armstrong had set up on the lunar surface. Beyond, at Kalalau, the thick tropical forest suddenly drops 4,000 feet down to the breathtakingly blue sea. Below, on the knifelike ridges, are the remnants of irrigation ditches, tar patches, and signs of careful cultivation that have been long since abandoned to the elements. Read Jack London's story, "Koolau the Leper" (in *A Hawaiian Reader*), for a fictional rendering of the indomitable Koolau, who hid in the ridges here and single-handedly held off the Hawaii National Guard in its attempt to get him to the leper colony at Molokai. His heroic wife crossed the dizzyingly narrow ridges hundreds of times in five years to bring food to her husband and son until they both died of the fearful disease and left her to return to her people alone.

Index

Surfing (*cont.*)
  Kauai, 524, 525, 526, 530–31, 537
  Lanai, 377, 378
  Maui, 299, 302, 304, 309
  Molokai, 360
  Oahu, 71, 111, 160, 162, 168, 164,
    231
  as spectator sport, 45, 48, 175

Taxes, 61, 67
Taxis
  Big Island, 388
  Kauai, 488, 489
  Maui, 242
  Molokai, 350
  Oahu, 78
Tedeschi Vineyards (Maui), 328
Telephones, telex and fax, 67–68, 81
Tennis
  Big Island, 450
  Kauai, 536
  Lanai, 382
  Maui, 316
  Molokai, 362
  Oahu, 71, 176
  as spectator sport, 316
Time, 61, 68–69
Tipping, 69
Toilets, 69
Tourist information, 43
Tours, organized
  adventure tours, 450–51, 536–37
  Big Island, 450–51, 464–65
  for disabled travelers, 192
  Kauai, 536–37, 542, 552
  Maui, 315, 329
  Molokai, 350
  Oahu, 191–92
Transportation
  money-saving tips, 4
Traveler's checks, 63
Triathlons, 50, 450
Trolleys. *See* Bus travel

University of Hawaii (Oahu), 74, 143–46,
  155, 184

USS *Arizona* Memorial (Oahu), 5, 14, 42,
  185–86, 187

Volcano Arts Center & Volcano House (Big
  Island), 460–62

Wahiawa (Oahu), 235–38
Waialae-Kahala (Oahu), 146–48
Waianapanapa State Park (Maui), 270, 302, 312,
  332
Waikiki, (Oahu), 74, 177
  accommodations, 82, 83–89, 93–101, 107
  beach, 70, 71, 160–61, 168, 178, 187
  restaurants, 111–22, 155, 157–58
  shopping, 193–97
Wailea (Maui), 245–51, 280–84, 321–24
Wailua (Kauai), 509–14, 541–44, 556
Wailuku (Maui), 240, 244, 274–76, 318–19
Waimea (Big Island), 386, 434, 470–72
Waimea (Kauai), 486, 522–23, 556–57
Waimea Canyon (Kauai), 6, 24, 42, 487, 525,
  532, 536, 552, 555, 557–58
Waimea Falls Park (Oahu), 42, 52, 222, 231–32
Waimea Valley (Oahu), 222, 231–32
Waipio Valley (Big Island), 434, 439, 467, 469
Whaler's Village (Maui), 294–95, 342–44, 241
Whale watching
  Big Island, 32, 437, 439, 444
  Kauai, 527, 531, 547
  Lanai, 383
  Maui, 166, 241, 304, 309
  Molokai, 360
  Oahu, 166
What things cost in Hawaii, 44
Windsurfing
  Big Island, 436, 439, 444
  Kauai, 525, 526, 531
  Maui, 241, 300, 302, 304, 309, 330
  Molokai, 347, 348
  Oahu, 162, 168
  as spectator sport, 49–50, 316

Zoos and aquariums
  Big Island, 454
  Molokai, 348, 368
  Oahu, 187, 188, 189, 219, 221–22, 224

Coupon good for 20% off the retail price of a dinner or cocktail show. Good for up to six people on a space available basis. Reservations required. No cash value. Not combinable with any other offers. Expires December 31, 1996.

MAGIC OF POLYNESIA®

Buy one adult cocktail show ticket at the regular price and save 50% on the second ticket with this coupon on Thursdays only. Discount good for up to six people on a space available basis. Reservations required. No cash value. Not valid with any other offer or on New Year's Eve. Expires December 30, 1996.

POLYNESIAN PALACE
Outrigger Reef Towers • 227 Lewers Street
Reservations: 923-SHOW

Coupon good for 10% off the regular price of an Oahu Coastal Cruise ticket. Reservations required. One coupon per person. Present coupon at time of purchase. No cash value. Not combinable with other offers. Expires December 31, 1996.

PARADISE CRUISE, LTD.
593-2493

10% DISCOUNT

on **"Maui's Best Adventure"** when you book direct
and mention **Frommer's Guides** at the time of booking

(no other discounts apply)

Call 800 654 7717

or e-mail

crusrbob@maui.net

Save $10

on any
Atlantis Submarines Adventure

*Voyage into Hawaii's underwater paradise in
the comfort and safety of a high-tech submarine.
Explore up-close the diverse and exotic
species that inhabit Hawaii's waters.
Every tour is a new adventure!*

Atlantis is the pioneer in passenger submarines.

For reservations and information,
please call
(800) 548-6262

Coupon good for 20% off the retail price, and is good
for up to four people on a space available basis.
Reservations required Not combinable with any other offer.
Valid through December 31, 1996.

This offer cannot be combined with any
other promotions and discounts.
Reservations must be made directly
with Papillon Hawaiian Helicopters.

Offer expires 12/31/96

SAVE $3.00

Present this coupon at the park ticket booth
and receive $3.00 off the regular adult admission.

VALID UNTIL 12/31/96

Limit two adults.
Cannot be combined with any other offer.

FRO 8/95

SAVE $3.00

Present this coupon at the park ticket booth
and receive $3.00 off the regular adult admission.

VALID UNTIL 12/31/96

Limit two adults.
Cannot be combined with any other offer.

FRO 8/95

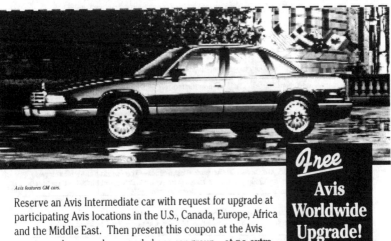

$15 Off A Weekly Rental Worldwide

Terms and Conditions: Coupon valid for $15 off Standard and SuperValue weekly rates at participating Avis locations in the U.S., Canada, Europe, Latin America and the Caribbean. For legal reasons, this offer does not apply in Germany. In the U.S. and Canada, this offer is valid on an Intermediate (Group C) through a Full Size 4-door (Group E) car for a minimum 5-day rental. Elsewhere, valid on Group B through Group E on Standard or SuperValue rates. May not be used in conjunction with any other coupon, promotion or offer. Offer not available during holiday and other blackout periods. Offer may not be available on all rates at all times. Coupon is nontransferable and nonrefundable. Coupon must be surrendered at time of rental; one per rental. Cars subject to availability at time of rental. **An advance reservation is required.** Taxes, local government surcharges and optional items, such as LDW, additional driver fee and refueling, are extra. Renter must meet Avis age, driver and credit requirements. Minimum age is 25 but may vary by location. Offer expires 12/14/96. Offer valid for $15 USD or equivalent in local currency at current Avis exchange rate at time of rental.

Rental Sales Agent Instructions

Automated Locations In The U.S., Canada, Latin America And The Caribbean. *At Checkout:* • In CPN, enter **MULA036**.
• Complete this information: RA #_____Rental Location _____
• Attach to COUPON tape.

Manual Locations In Canada, Latin America And The Caribbean. *At Checkout:* • Enter **MULA036** in box 15.
• Complete this information: RA #_____ Rental Location _____
• At car return, enter amount to be deducted in box 36. Subtract this amount from the totals of boxes 30 through 35.
• Submit COUPON to Marketing Department CHQ.

Automated Locations In Europe. *At Checkout:* • In AWD, enter **NO43007**.
• Enter M, followed by monetary value of the coupon in local currency, in the ADJUSTMT field.
• Submit Certificate with copy 1 of RA to country HQ.

Manual Locations In Europe. *At Checkout:* • In AWD, enter **NO43007**.
• Enter M, followed by monetary value of the coupon in local currency, in the ADJUSTMT box (42).
• Submit Certificate with copy 1 of RA to country HQ.

Country HQ Handling Instructions
• Renting country must absorb the cost of this promotion. Chargebacks not allowed.

© 1995 Wizard Co., Inc. 5/95 DTPS

FREE Worldwide Upgrade

Terms and Conditions: Coupon valid for a one-time, one-car-group upgrade at participating Avis locations in the U.S., Canada, Europe, Africa and the Middle East. For legal reasons, this offer does not apply in Germany. In the U.S. and Canada, this offer is valid on an Intermediate (Group C) through a Full Size 4-door (Group E) car. Maximum upgrade to Premium (Group G). Elsewhere, valid on Group A through Group E. Maximum upgrade to Group F. **Offer valid on daily, weekend and weekly rates** only in the U.S. and Canada, and Standard, SuperValue or Discover Europe rates elsewhere. Offer not available during holiday and other blackout periods. If reservation is for a car with automatic transmission, upgrade car will be an automatic. If reservation is for a car with manual transmission, upgrade car will be a manual. Coupon is nontransferable and nonrefundable. Coupon must be surrendered at time of rental; one per rental. Cars and upgrades are subject to availability at time of rental. **An advance reservation with request for upgrade is required.** Renter must meet Avis age, driver and credit requirements. Minimum age is 25 but may vary by location. Offer expires 12/14/96.

Rental Sales Agent Instructions

Automated Locations In The U.S. And Canada. *At Checkout:* • Assign customer a car one group higher than car group reserved. Upgrade to no higher than Group G. Charge for car group reserved. • In CPN, enter **UULA008**. • Complete this information: RA #_____ Rental Location _____
• Attach to COUPON tape.

Manual Locations In Canada. *At Checkout:* • Assign customer a car one group higher than car group reserved. Upgrade to no higher than Group G. Charge for car group reserved. • Enter **UULA008** in box 15. • Complete this information:
RA #_____Rental Location _____
• Submit COUPON to Marketing Department CHQ.

Automated And Manual Locations In Europe, Africa And The Middle East.
• Assign customer a car one group higher than car group reserved. Upgrade to no higher than Group F. Charge for car group reserved. • In AWD, enter **NO43003**. • Check in normally.

Country HQ Handling Instructions
• Submit COUPON to country Marketing Department. • Renting country must absorb cost of promotion. Chargebacks not allowed. • Complete this information: Rental Location_____
Rental Length _____ Days_____
• Car Group Reserved_____ Date_____

© 1995 Wizard Co., Inc. 5/95 DTPS

For your Information:

Offer available at participating airports in Hawaii and Florida. Leisure Weekly rentals require a 5 day minimum keep, including a Saturday night. Advance reservations required, standard rental conditions and blackout periods apply. Car must be returned to rental location or offer does not apply. This coupon must be surrendered at time of rental and may not be combined with any other discount, offer, coupon or promotion. Minimum rental age is 25.

Hertz rents Fords and other fine cars.

The following Frommer's guides are available from your favorite bookstore, or you can use the order form on the preceding page to request them as part of your membership in Frommer's Travel Book Club.

FROMMER'S COMPLETE TRAVEL GUIDES

(Comprehensive guides to sightseeing, dining and accommodations, with selections in all price ranges—from deluxe to budget)

FROMMER'S $-A-DAY GUIDES

(Dream Vacations at Down-to-Earth Prices)

FROMMER'S COMPLETE CITY GUIDES

(Comprehensive guides to sightseeing, dining, and accommodations in all price ranges)

Amsterdam, 8th Ed.	S176	Minneapolis/St. Paul, 4th Ed.	S159
Athens, 10th Ed.	S174	Montréal/Québec City '95	S166
Atlanta & the Summer Olympic		Nashville/Memphis, 1st Ed.	S141
Games '96 (avail. 11/95)	S181	New Orleans '96 (avail. 10/95)	S182
Atlantic City/Cape May, 5th Ed.	S130	New York City '96 (avail. 11/95)	S183
Bangkok, 2nd Ed.	S147	Paris '96 (avail. 9/95)	S180
Barcelona '93-'94	S115	Philadelphia, 8th Ed.	S167
Berlin, 3rd Ed.	S162	Prague, 1st Ed.	S143
Boston '95	S160	Rome, 10th Ed.	S168
Budapest, 1st Ed.	S139	St. Louis/Kansas City, 2nd Ed.	S127
Chicago '95	S169	San Antonio/Austin, 1st Ed.	S177
Denver/Boulder/Colorado Springs,		San Diego '95	S158
3rd Ed.	S154	San Francisco '96 (avail. 10/95)	S184
Disney World/Orlando '96 (avail. 9/95)	S178	Santa Fe/Taos/Albuquerque '95	S172
Dublin, 2nd Ed.	S157	Seattle/Portland '94-'95	S137
Hong Kong '94-'95	S140	Sydney, 4th Ed.	S171
Las Vegas '95	S163	Tampa/St. Petersburg, 3rd Ed.	S146
London '96 (avail. 9/95)	S179	Tokyo '94-'95	S144
Los Angeles '95	S164	Toronto, 3rd Ed.	S173
Madrid/Costa del Sol, 2nd Ed.	S165	Vancouver/Victoria '94-'95	S142
Mexico City, 1st Ed.	S175	Washington, D.C. '95	S153
Miami '95-'96	S149		

FROMMER'S FAMILY GUIDES

(Guides to family-friendly hotels, restaurants, activities, and attractions)

California with Kids	F105	San Francisco with Kids	F104
Los Angeles with Kids	F103	Washington, D.C. with Kids	F102
New York City with Kids	F101		

FROMMER'S WALKING TOURS

(Memorable strolls through colorful and historic neighborhoods, accompanied by detailed directions and maps)

Berlin	W100	Paris, 2nd Ed.	W112
Chicago	W107	San Francisco, 2nd Ed.	W115
England's Favorite Cities	W108	Spain's Favorite Cities (avail. 9/95)	W116
London, 2nd Ed.	W111	Tokyo	W109
Montréal/Québec City	W106	Venice	W110
New York, 2nd Ed.	W113	Washington, D.C., 2nd Ed.	W114

FROMMER'S AMERICA ON WHEELS

(Guides for travelers who are exploring the U.S.A. by car, featuring a brand-new rating system for accommodations and full-color road maps)

Arizona/New Mexico	A100	Florida	A102
California/Nevada	A101	Mid-Atlantic	A103

FROMMER'S SPECIAL-INTEREST TITLES

Arthur Frommer's Branson!	P107	Frommer's Where to Stay U.S.A., 11th Ed.	P102
Arthur Frommer's New World of Travel (avail. 11/95)	P112	National Park Guide, 29th Ed.	P106
Frommer's Caribbean Hideaways (avail. 9/95)	P110	USA Today Golf Tournament Guide	P113
Frommer's America's 100 Best-Loved State Parks	P109	USA Today Minor League Baseball Book	P111

FROMMER'S BEST BEACH VACATIONS

*(The top places to sun, stroll, shop, stay, play, party, and swim—with each
beach rated for beauty, swimming, sand, and amenities)*

California (avail. 10/95)	G100	Hawaii (avail. 10/95)	G102
Florida (avail. 10/95)	G101		

FROMMER'S BED & BREAKFAST GUIDES

*(Selective guides with four-color photos and full descriptions of
the best inns in each region)*

California	B100	Hawaii	B105
Caribbean	B101	Pacific Northwest	B106
East Coast	B102	Rockies	B107
Eastern United States	B103	Southwest	B108
Great American Cities	B104		

FROMMER'S IRREVERENT GUIDES

*(Wickedly honest guides for sophisticated travelers
and those who want to be)*

Chicago (avail. 11/95)	I100	New Orleans (avail. 11/95)	I103
London (avail. 11/95)	I101	San Francisco (avail. 11/95)	I104
Manhattan (avail. 11/95)	I102	Virgin Islands (avail. 11/95)	I105

FROMMER'S DRIVING TOURS

*(Four-color photos and detailed maps outlining
spectacular scenic driving routes)*

Australia	Y100	Italy	Y108
Austria	Y101	Mexico	Y109
Britain	Y102	Scandinavia	Y110
Canada	Y103	Scotland	Y111
Florida	Y104	Spain	Y112
France	Y105	Switzerland	Y113
Germany	Y106	U.S.A.	Y114
Ireland	Y107		

FROMMER'S BORN TO SHOP

*(The ultimate travel guides for discriminating
shoppers—from cut-rate to couture)*

Hong Kong (avail. 11/95)	Z100	London (avail. 11/95)	Z101